★ 1995 ★
PEOPLE
ENTERTAINMENT ALMANAC

★ 1995 ★

PEOPLE

ENTERTAINMENT ALMANAC

Created and Produced by
CADER BOOKS

LITTLE, BROWN AND COMPANY

Boston • New York • Toronto • London

First Edition

ISBN: 0-316-69885-7

10 9 8 7 6 5 4 3 2 1

Published simultaneously in Canada by Little, Brown & Company (Canada) Limited

Printed in the United States of America

CONTENTS

TUBE 167

SONG 219

STAFF

Editor-in-Chief
Michael Cader

Consulting Editor
Seth Godin

Senior Editor
Constance Herndon

Designer
Charles Kreloff

Layout Designer
Kris Tobiassen

Research
Chris Angelilli, Steve Arenholz, Steve Baumgartner, Eryn Brown, Meredith Cristano, Don Devich, Lisa DiMona, Geoffrey Klein, Kendall LaMontagne, Barbara Lewis, Carol Markowitz, Nanette Maxim, Megan O'Connor, Shira Solomon, Cara Sullivan, Amy Winger, Karen Watts

Photo Research
Meg Handler

PEOPLE Contributors
Richard Burgheim (Supervising Editor), Sarah Brennan, Steven Dougherty, Cutler Durkee, Nancy Eils, Dick Friedman, David Grogan, Jeremy Helligar, David Hiltbrand, Holly Holden, Eric Levin, Michael A. Lipton, Denise Lynch, Mary Carroll Marsden, Ralph Novak, James Oberman, J. D. Reed, Matt Semble, Elizabeth Sporkin, Randall Vest

Landon Y. Jones Jr., Managing Editor; Ann S. Moore, President; Robert D. Jurgrau, Business Manager

ACKNOWLEDGMENTS

Many people and organizations have generously lent their time, resources, and expertise to help make this project possible. Special thanks go to: Karen Aarons, Miss America Organization; Academy of Recording Arts and Sciences; Paula Allen, Barnes and Noble; Frank Alkyer, *Downbeat* magazine; American Film Institute; Susan Arnold, Waldenbooks; Bridget Aschenberg, ICM; Alan Axelrod; Bantam, Doubleday, Dell; Arnold Becker, CBS; Phil Berk, Los Angeles Film Critics Association; Michelle Beta; Richard Betz, MTV; *Billboard* magazine; Gugliemo Biraghi, Venice International Film Festival; Helen Blake, National Infomercial Marketing Association; Gary Bongiovanni, Pollstar; Sandy Bresler, Bresler, Kelly and Kipperman; Brad Cafarelli; Fr. John Catoir, Christophers; Center for the Book, Library of Congress; Center for Media and Public Affairs; Bob Christie, Academy of TV Arts and Sciences; Robert C. Christopher, The Pulitzer Prizes, Columbia University Graduate School of Journalism; Steve Clar; Sam Cohn; Ace Collins; Barbara Contardi, Association of Comedy Artists; Don Corathers, *Dramatics* magazine; Angela Corio, Recording Industry Association of America; Catherine Craig, American Zoetrope; Lisa Croke, Nielsen Media Research; Dan Cryer, National Book Critics Circle; Gary DaSilva; Doreen Dean, British Academy of Film and Television; Dramatists Guild; Marilyn Ducksworth, Putnam Publishing Group; Steve Dworman, *Infomercial Marketing Report*; Sarah Erickson, Carnegie Hall; Tom Evered, Blue Note Records; Kenneth Ewing; Harry Forbes, PBS; Jeremy Gerard, *Variety*; Heather Gifford, National Academy of Recording Artists; Debbie Gilwood; Deborah Hanauer, Entertainment Data, Inc.; Harcourt Brace; Susan Harley, League of American Theatres and Producers; Ted Hearne, John D. and Catherine T. MacArthur Foundation; Shanan Hein, Country Music Association; Leonard Hirschan, William Morris Agency; Patricia Hodges, Time Warner; Kay Hoffman, Berlin International Film Festival; Hollywood Chamber of Commerce; Hollywood Foreign Press Association; Fred Horton, WYNY; Dawn Hudson, Independent Feature Project West; Gary Ink, *Publishers Weekly*; M. Jackson, AUDELCO; Barbara Janowitz, Theater Communications Group; Dotty Jeffries, Amblin' Entertainment; Cindy Johnson, Mann Theatres; Jennifer Jones, Academy of Motion Picture Arts and Sciences; Steve Jukes, Judy Daish Associates; Pat Kingsley; Leonard Klady, *Variety*; Alfred A. Knopf, Inc.; John Krier, Exhibitor Relations; Judy Krug, American Library Association; Michael Kurchwara, New York Drama Critics Circle; Steve Leggett, National Film Registry, Library of Congress; Dottie McCarthy, John F. Kennedy Center for the Performing Arts; Robin MacDonald, World Film Festival of Toronto; Ken Mandlebaum, *Theater Week*; Howard Marcantel, National Academy of Cable Programming; Valerie Marcus, Tommy Boy Records; Donato Mednolia, Venice International Film Festival; Lisa Meredith, National Cable Forum; Jessica Morell; Jamie Morris, *Soap Opera Digest*; Art Murphy; Christine Murray, *The Village Voice*; Gary Necessary, George Schlatter Productions; Karen Kriendler Nelson, Richard Tucker Foundation; Jim O'Quinn, *American Theatre*; Paramount Communications; Charlotte Parker; Gilbert Parker; Ronnie Pugh, Country Music Hall of Fame; Quigley Publishing Company; Kelly Rebiero, 40 Acres and a Mule Film Productions; Joe Regal, Russell & Volkening; Andrew Rhodes, American Society of Magazine Editors; Sandy Rice; Rock and Roll Hall of Fame; Richard Rodzinski, Van Cliburn Competition; Bradley J. Rogers, Pollstar; Susan Roman, American Library Association; Ami Roosevelt; Howard Rosenstone, Rosenstone/Wender; Rebecca Saltman, Theater Communications Group; Shelley Sanderson, HarperCollins; Bill Schelble; Christie Shaw, Book Trust; John Sheehan, Center for Media and Public Affairs; Paul Shefrin, The Shefrin Company; Barry Sherman, University of Georgia; Alex Siegel, Random House; Gina Smith, Country Music Association; Smithsonian Institution, Division of Community Life; Barbara Spindel, People for the American Way; Robert Stein, United Talent Agency; Carol Stone, PMK; Gundar Strads, Before Columbus Foundation; Jack Tantleff, Tantleff Agency; Prof. Mark Tucker, Columbia University; Sylvester Vanetti, *Variety*; Viking Penguin; George Wachtel, League of American Theaters and Producers; Marc Weidenbaum, *Pulse*; Liz Weiss, National Society of Film Critics; Murray Weissman, Weissman Angellotti; *Whitaker's Almanack*; Wiley, Aitken & Stone, Inc.; Patricia Willis, Beinecke Library, Yale University; Marcia Winter, Yale School of Drama; Maria Zimmann, Nielsen Media Research; Marc Zubatkin, *Billboard* magazine.

PHOTO CREDITS

YEAR IN REVIEW
p. 2 Doug Beghtel/The Oregonian/Sygma; p. 4 Jeff Markowitz/Sygma;Ted Soqui/Sygma(2); p. 5 Christian Simonpietri/Sygma; p. 6 AP Photo/Bluey Thomson; Lisa Rose/Globe Photo; p. 7 Tribune Media Services; Courtesy of the Birmingham Barons; p. 8 Wide World Photos; p. 9 AP Photo/John Gaps; AP Photo/Doug Mills; p. 11 Richmond Newspapers; p. 12 Steve Granitz/Retna Ltd.; p. 13 AP Photo/Ed Baily; CBS Photo; p. 14 John Barrett/Globe Photo; p. 15 Joan Marcus/Marc Bryan-Brown/Walt Disney Theatrical Productions; p. 16 Peter Macdiarmid/Camera Press/Retna Ltd.; p. 17 Larry Downing/Sygma; p. 19 DR/Stills/Retna; Steve Granitz/Retna Ltd.; p. 20 Courtesy of Butterfield & Butterfield; p. 21 *Today* show publicity; p. 23 All Action/Stills Press; p. 26 Sandra Robinson/Retna Ltd.; p. 28 Charlie Hoselton/Retna Ltd.; p. 32 JFK Library/Sygma; p. 34 Ira Wyman/Sygma; p. 38 Dupin/Retna Ltd.; p. 40 Nancy Barr/Retna Ltd.; p. 47 AP Photo/Paul Sancya

TIMELINE
p. 51 Culver Pictures; AP/Wide World (2); Globe Photos; p. 52 Culver Pictures; AP/Wide World; p. 53 Frank Driggs Collection; p. 54 Culver Pictures; Kobal Collection; p. 55 Culver Pictures; p. 56 Culver Pictures; Kobal Collection; p. 59 AP/Wide World Photos; p. 60 AP/Wide World; Culver Pictures; p. 62 AP/Wide World; Courtesy of The Campbell's Soup Co.; p. 63 AP/Wide World(2); p. 64 AP/Wide World; Courtesy of Mattel, Inc.; p. 65 AP/Wide World; p. 66 Globe Photos; p. 68 Globe Photo; p. 69 Tunick/Retna Ltd.; p. 72 Globe Photos; Courtesy of Sony; p. 73 AP/Wide World; p. 74 Ralph Dominguez/Globe Photo; J.P. Laffont/Sygma; p. 76 AP/Wide World; p. 77 John Barrett/Globe Photos; p. 78 AP/Wide World

ROYALTY
p. 83 Alpha/Globe; p. 84 Andrew Murray/Sygma; p. 88 Sygma; p. 89 David Hartley/Rex Features; p. 91 Rex Features; p. 92 Steve Daniels/Alpha/Globe Photos; p. 93 Dennis Stone/Rex Features; p. 94 David Chancellor/Alpha/Globe Photos; SUN/Rex Features

SCREEN
p. 121 Ira Wyman/Sygma; Doc Pele/Stills/Retna Ltd.; PAT/Stills/Retna Ltd.; PAT/Garcia/Stills/Retna Ltd.; Alpha/Globe; Globe/Rangefinders; p. 135 Michael Ferguson/Globe Photo(2); p. 136 Michael Ferguson/Globe Photo; Steve Granitz/Retna Ltd.

TUBE
p. 184 Lisa Rose/Globe Photos; William Karel/Sygma; Globe/Rangefinders; Bruno Gaget/Retna Ltd.; Andrea Renault/Globe Photos

SONG
p. 241 Retna Ltd.; King Collection/Retna; A.J. Barrett/Retna Ltd.; p. 242 A.P.L./Retna Ltd.; Luciano Viti/Retna Ltd.; p. 245 Eddie Malluk/Retna Ltd.; Robert Matheu/Retna Ltd.; Gary Gershoff/ Retna Ltd.; Retna Ltd.; Beth Gwinn/Retna Ltd.; Redfern/Retna Ltd.

PEOPLE EXTRAS
p. 371 Lawerence Schwartzwald/Sygma

★ 1995 ★

PEOPLE

ENTERTAINMENT ALMANAC

Celebs frolic in Aspen • Motherhood after 60 • TV's Jerry Springer
People weekly
TERROR ON ICE
THE BIZARRE PLOT AGAINST NANCY KERRIGAN
EXCLUSIVE At home with the injured skater as she renews her quest for Olympic gold
Reports linked rival Tonya Harding's bodyguard Shawn Eckardt to the attack on Kerrigan
People weekly
REMEMBERING JACKIE
1929-1994
John Kennedy Jr. and Caroline Kennedy Schlossberg attended their mother's funeral in New York City; above, Caroline placed flowers on the casket at the service in Arlington National Cemetery
THE YEAR IN REVIEW
Special delivery for 90210's Gabrielle Carteris
People weekly
THE O.J. NOBODY KNEW
All his life he worked hard to be loved. But behind the smile and the charm was a dangerous temper and a desperate need to get what he wanted
Insets: As a college hotshot in 1967 and with ex-wife Nicole in 1993
People weekly
Lisa Marie & Michael
THE HONEYMOONERS!
Married—with (her) children, $350 million and baffling questions

JANUARY

Barbra Streisand opens the 5,005-room MGM Grand Hotel in Las Vegas with shows on New Year's Eve and New Year's Day—her first paid concerts in twenty-two years. The event produces the hoopla of an inauguration, a coronation, and Oscar night rolled into one. Among those shrugging off the show's $50 to $1,000 ticket price are Michael Jackson, Mel Gibson, Michael Douglas, Steven Spielberg, Frank and Kathie Lee Gifford, Donna Karan, Jay Leno, and First Mother Virginia Kelley (in her last public appearance before her death). In all, not counting the sales of $85 Barbra T-shirts, $45 silk boxer shorts, $25 programs, and other mementos, Streisand herself is expected to earn $6 to $7 million, before expenses, from the performances. From the opening song, "Everything's As If We Never Said Goodbye," from *Sunset Boulevard*, to the final, "For All We Know," a nervous Barbra holds the glittery audience in the palm of her well-manicured hand. At show's end she departs from her scripted, autobiographical, between-song patter to squeal: "I did it! I did it! I did it!" Spurred by the demand for more, she will go on to a thirteen-city tour through London and the U.S., drawing packed—and high-ticket—audiences at every stop of the way.

★

Remember **Heidi**? In an interview with *Vanity Fair* writer Lynn Hirschberg, the Hollywood Madam actually names names—or does she? The article claims Fleiss said her customers included Charlie Sheen, Shannen Doherty, and Jon Peters. "Charlie was a gentleman," Fleiss is quoted as saying. She indicates that he would pay for all of his friends, and was particularly fond of women dressed up as cheerleaders. For the record, Hirschberg also notes that Heidi's famous black book is neither black nor a single book, but rather a collection of red loose-leaf Gucci notebooks. But Fleiss denies Hirschberg's account, and her lawyer calls for a retraction. At this point it's hard to believe that anyone cared—but Heidi has to start facing the consequences. She goes to trial on August 22 on charges of pandering and cocaine possession; at the end of July she is indicted on fourteen separate counts that include tax evasion and money laundering.

★

It was a combination of stunning implausiblilities, mixing brutality, bravery, and, ultimately, the bizarre. The saga begins on the 6th when figure skater **Nancy Kerrigan** is viciously attacked by a club-wielding assailant. She suffers a severely bruised knee and quadriceps tendon and must watch as longtime rival **Tonya Harding** finishes first at the women's U.S. national championship in Detroit.

Down but undaunted, Kerrigan is nonetheless named to the 1994 U.S. Olympic team by the U.S. Figure Skating Association—displacing second-place finisher Michelle Kwan, 13. As the story unfolds, however, it becomes clear that Harding is the one who should have—and would have—been made to stay at home.

Figure skater Tonya Harding.

Within two weeks of the incident, authorities arrest Jeff Gillooly, Tonya Harding's former husband, Shane Stant, the unemployed carpenter who actually struck Kerrigan with a metal baton, and Stant's uncle, Derrick Brian Smith, who drove the getaway car. Stant and Smith are now serving eighteen-month sentences; Gillooly is fined $100,000, and will serve a maximum jail term of two years, in exchange for telling in full his version of what happened. In his testimony, Gillooly indicates that Harding knew about and approved the plan ahead of time, and made phone calls to obtain Kerrigan's practice schedule to aid in the attack.

In March, Harding strikes a plea bargain, pleading guilty to a felony count of conspiring to hinder a prosecution. A circuit court judge sentences her to three years of supervised probation and orders her to pay a $100,000 fine and resign from the U.S. Figure Skating Association. Harding must also create a $50,000 fund for the Special Olympics, reimburse the District Attorney's office $10,000 for expenses, serve 500 hours of community service, and undergo psychiatric evaluation and treatment. Asked if she had anything to say, Harding replies, "I'm really sorry that I interfered . . . "

Later the same month, a grand jury report concludes what many have come to believe on their own—Harding did help to plan the attack on Nancy Kerrigan, and would have been charged in the case if not for her plea agreement. The U.S. Figure Skating Association eventually concurs, and in June they ban Harding for life from the organization and strip her of her national championship, the first time they have ever taken such action.

Kerrigan battles back from her injury and produces two marvelous performances in the Winter Olympics in Lillehammer, only to lose by the slimmest of margins to Oksana Baiul of Ukraine. Harding, finishes a disappointing eighth.

But America's sweetheart quickly loses her luster. After her skating silver, Kerrigan really does go to Disney World, just as promised. Unfortunately, she brings a second-place attitude with her. Camera microphones record her saying to Mickey Mouse on a float: "This is so corny. This is so dumb. I hate it. This is the most corniest thing I've ever done." Her agent and a spokesman for Disney claim that she was remarking about displaying her medal while she and Mickey promenaded, but the Kerrigan smile will never look the same again.

But don't feel too bad for Nancy. Her package deal with Disney remains in place, providing $500,000 for the TV rights to her story, a second network skating special, a children's book, a video, and commercials for and continuing appearances at Disney World and Disneyland. And her appearance as host of *Saturday Night Live* draws some of the show's highest ratings in years.

Of course Tonya has her own acting deal, albeit on a more modest scale. She'll debut in the low-budget Hollywood feature *Breakaway*, playing "a waitress who inadvertently makes off with a cache of money," according to the press release. Other opportunities include an invitation to compete on *American Gladiators*, and she has sold the TV rights to her life story for $50,000 (she'll get another $450,000 if a movie is made).

★

There's been plenty of sex on television for decades, and now there's a little bit of protection on the side as **condoms** are allowed on as well. The networks begin airing public service ads that promote condom use.

★

Airlines celebrate the King's fifty-ninth birthday on January 8 by offering special fares on flights to Memphis. More than 3,000 fans fill the planes, many dressed as **Elvis** in order to save an extra $20. What can be in store for the sixtieth?

★

Michael Jackson gets a welcome bit of good news on January 12: a Los Angeles jury clears him of charges that he stole parts of other songs and integrated them into his hits *We Are the World*, *Thriller*, and *The Girl is Mine*.

Lorena Bobbitt on the stand in a Manassas, Virginia courtroom.

Lorena Bobbitt goes on trial January 10 in Manassas, Virginia, on charges of malicious wounding. Eleven days later the twenty-four-year-old manicurist is acquitted of all criminal charges, the jury concluding that she was temporarily insane when she cut her husband's penis off with a kitchen knife last June.

★

We'll never know who pulled the plug, but after weeks of rumors it becomes clear that **Shannen Doherty** is leaving *Beverly Hills, 90210*. Doherty tells *TV Guide*, "It was a mutual decision between Aaron Spelling and me. We backed each other against the wall. I feel no sadness." Spelling's only comment is "Shannen knows why she won't be on the show next year. I have no wish to hurt her and that will be my final comment."

Published reports indicated that Doherty caused problems with lateness on the set. But Shannen notes, "If he fired me because I was late, then he'd have to fire his daughter Tori. And he'd have to fire Luke and Jason and some of the others."

The judge declares a mistrial on the 13th in the murder trial of **Erik Menendez**, 23, after the jury is hopelessly deadlocked. On the 28th, a second jury in the separate murder trial of **Lyle Menendez**, 26, is also unable to reach a verdict. Prosecutors swiftly announce their plans to retry both for the August 1989 shooting of their parents.

Eric Menendez.

Lyle Menendez.

One battle of the bands from the '70s is settled: In a charity boxing match, former Partridge Family member Danny Bonaduce triumphs easily over Donny Osmond at Chicago's China Club.

★

Tragedy leads to commerce, as celebrity earthquake wreckage is offered for sale.

Hollywood shakes, and it has nothing to do with an action picture. **The Quake** hits Los Angeles at 4:31 A.M. on the 18th. Starting from the epicenter in Northridge in the San Fernando Valley, it rolls to 6.6 on the Richter scale. At least twenty-nine people die and major freeways are heavily damaged, including the Santa Monica Freeway, I 5, and Highway 14.

The tremors hit rich and poor alike, and many celebrities are left temporarily homeless. Warren Beatty, Jack Nicholson, and Walter Matthau all experience severe damage to their homes, with Matthau putting his total loss, including art works, sculpture, and a swimming pool that slid down a hillside, at $6 million.

Others affected included Jerry Van Dyke, who is lucky to escape after the roof caves in in his bedroom while he and his wife are asleep. Barbra Streisand loses a substantial number of antiques in her Beverly Hills home. Also experiencing severe damage to their homes, according to various accounts, are Denzel Washington, Wayne Gretzky, Jeff Bridges, Arsenio Hall, Kirstie Alley, Liza Minelli, David Caruso, Nick Turturro, Harry Hamlin, Elizabeth Ashley, Debbie Reynolds, and Shari Belafonte (whose Yorkshire terrier is crushed to death in the kitchen). As Tom Arnold sums it up, "We had too much stuff, and God let us know real quick."

★

In the end, it seemed, both sides wanted it both ways. There, on January 25, in front of the Santa Monica courthouse, stood attorneys for **Michael Jackson** and the fourteen-year-old boy who six months before had accused the pop superstar of sexually molesting him. Although his client was not backing off his story, said Larry Feldman, the boy's lawyer, he was now willing to drop the charges. In return, according to inside sources, the teenager would be paid between $15 and $20 million. "This," said Feldman, "will allow the parties to get on with their lives."

Then came Michael's lawyer, Johnnie Cochran Jr., who claimed his client wasn't backing off either. The settlement, said Cochran, was no admission of guilt. "Michael is an innocent man," he said. "The time has come for Michael Jackson . . . to get on with his life."

Ultimately, it may not have been so much a conclusion as a change of venue—from Santa Monica to the court of public opinion. The settlement is likely to remove the possibility of criminal charges being brought against Jackson, since California law does not compel minors to testify in sex crime cases. But California officials refuse to close the case, and continue to investigate.

★

Before he begins a speech in Sydney, Australia, on the 26th, **Prince Charles** is pushed toward safety by a security agent after an assailant allegedly fires two blank shots from a starter's pistol. Police arrest

Prince Charles, being whisked to safety at a speech in Sydney, Australia.

David Kang, 23, who is protesting the plight of Cambodian refugees in Australia, and the unruffled Prince goes ahead with his speech. Charles has another brush with a minor weapon later in his tour when an antimonarchist in New Zealand lunges at him with a can of air freshener, saying he wanted to "remove the stink of royalty."

★

Leona Helmsley was never one to shy away from a party, especially her own. So when the seventy-three-year-old onetime hotel queen gathers thirty-five loyal subjects on the 27th to celebrate the end of her twenty-one-month confinement for tax evasion, it seems, however briefly, like old times. Certainly no one is predicting Leona will mellow into gentle retirement at her $6 million home in Scottsdale, Arizona, where she begins the 750 hours of community service she must complete over the next three years. "She will see Harry. She will sun. She needs to heal," says gossip columnist and self-proclaimed friend Cindy Adams. "[But] there are a lot of people Leona's not happy with . . . the media, some lawyers. She's going to get back at them"

MTV Networks announces plans to begin shopping programming on its three channels, MTV, VH-1, and Nick at Nite, later in the year. Products will include recorded music and music-related merchandise. If the test is successful, plans are to expand the offerings to a new channel.

★

Oprah and fiancé Stedman Graham on their way to her fortieth birthday party.

Oprah turns 40 and throws herself a memorable bash at L'Orangerie in Los Angeles, followed by a slumber party with female friends in a $975-a-night bungalow at Hotel Bel-Air.

★

After a weak second half, the Buffalo Bills fall to the Dallas Cowboys, 30–13. The victory makes it ten in a row for NFC teams, and Buffalo's fourth straight defeat elevates them to record-holding losers. The game ranks as the tenth most popular **Super Bowl** ever, and the most watched championship in seven years. But the real news is that former Vice President **Dan Quayle** appears in a halftime ad for Wavy Lays potato(e) chips.

After seven months of resounding incriminations and flying fur, **Burt Reynolds**, 57, and **Loni Anderson**, 48, reach a surprisingly amicable divorce at month's end, on the eve of their scheduled appearance in a Stuart, Florida, court. Bottom line: Anderson gets $1.9 million toward purchasing a house, plus their $500,000 summer house in Highlands, N.C. And they will likely share custody of their adopted son, Quinton, 5. He'll live with his mother in Los Angeles, but Burt is expected to retain full visitation rights.

FEBRUARY

In what is becoming an all-too-common occurence, Dick Tracy learns of his impending divorce via a surprise delivery.

On the 7th the world learns that **Dick Tracy** and his wife of forty-five years, **Tess Trueheart**, are calling it quits as Dick is served with divorce papers. Apparently Tess has had enough of Dick's long hours and complete devotion to his job. The couple has three children, Bonnie Braids, Joe, and the adopted Junior. According to Michael Kilian, who currently creates the strip, the big news is meant "to bring Dick Tracy into contemporary times."

★

No Bull, **Michael Jordan** takes a swing at baseball. Jordan, who retired from pro basketball last fall, signs a contract with the Chicago White Sox. "Playing baseball is a dream I've had ever since I was a kid." He hasn't played since high school: "That's where I started, and that's how I envision myself finishing."

Michael Jordan, suited up for his newest team, the Birmingham Barons.

As it turns out, Mike doesn't make the big leagues, but is instead assigned to the Birmingham Barons, a Class AA team, which he joins on April 8. His salary is $850 a month, but that doesn't stop Jordan from buying the team a new bus to travel in for $250,000. "It's going to be one fun summer," Jordan said.

★

Soprano **Kathleen Battle**, 44, is fired by the Metropolitan Opera Company on the 7th for what general manager Joseph Volpe called "unprofessional actions during rehearsal." Among other things, Battle had reportedly missed numerous rehearsals, ordered other singers to leave while she rehearsed, and insisted that her entrances and exits be close to her dressing room. In response to her firing, the soprano issues a statement saying she is perplexed and claims, "We were working out all the artistic problems." Known almost as much for her temper as for her voice, Battle was supposed to star in the Met's revival of Donizetti's *Fille du Regiment*, beginning February 14.

Jack Nicholson plays golf. The only problem is he's on the streets of Los Angeles. Accused of smashing Robert Blank's windshield with a brisk nine-iron, he is charged with misdemeanor assault and vandalism. But in March, Blank drops the civil charges, after settling with Nicholson for an undisclosed sum, and a judge subsequently drops the criminal charges in May as a result of the settlement. "Now, I would never leave the car. I would go play golf like I was supposed to do," comments a chastened Nicholson.

★

On the 11th news first reaches the public of **Jacqueline Kennedy Onassis's** illness. According to her friend and spokeswoman Nancy Tuckerman, the former First Lady visited a doctor in January complaining of flu-like symptoms that were diagnosed as non-Hodgkin's lymphoma. "There is an excellent prognosis," reports Tuckerman. "The doctors are very, very optimistic."

★

One of the world's best-known paintings, ***The Scream***, by Norwegian Expressionist Edvard Munch (1863–1944) is stolen from the National Gallery in Oslo. A security video camera tapes two men entering the museum through a window. Fifty seconds later they fled with the multimillion-dollar painting, leaving a note: "Thanks for the poor security." On May 7, the painting is recovered in southern Norway, removed from its frame but otherwise unharmed.

★

Once again the world is abuzz with rumors of a reunion of the remaining **Beatles**. But Paul McCartney maintains, "There's as much chance of a Beatles reunion as reheating a souffle. When John was alive, there was a possibility. But without John, it will never happen." George Harrison adds, "There will never be a Beatles reunion as long as John Lennon remains dead." But the summer will bring other music reunions, including the Eagles and some of the original Woodstock crew.

After considering a host of other offers, including one from NBC to host a four-night-a-week news magazine, **Diane Sawyer** decides to stay at ABC—for a reported price

The seven-million-dollar woman, Diane Sawyer.

of approximately $7 million a year. Experts believe that Sawyer is now the second-highest-paid newswoman, after Barbara Walters, but Walters will later claim that Sawyer has surpassed her—and given her ammunition for her own contract negotiations.

★

Glenn Close is named to star in the $12-million production of Andrew Lloyd Webber's *Sunset Boulevard* when it comes to Broadway on November 17. Close is picked over Patti Lupone, who originated the role in London and was originally scheduled to star in New York. Retooled for its launch in Los Angeles featuring Close, the new version of the show performs so successfully that the London edition is then changed as well.

But Close's ascent proves to be Los Angeles's loss. In June, intended replacement **Faye Dunaway**, 53, is fired and Lloyd Webber shuts down the rest of the projected six-month L.A. run. He claims that despite three months of training, the Oscar-winning actress could not meet "the

OLYMPICS NEWS

The **U.S. alpine team** puts on a surprising display of strength at the Lillehammer games. **Tommy Moe Jr.** claims a gold as he wins the downhill event by a mere four one-hundreths of a second, and also captures a silver medal in the Super-G. American **Diann Roffe-Steinrotter** wins the women's super-giant slalom, and teammate **Liz McIntyre** takes the silver medal in the moguls competition. And **Picabo Street** continues the surprising run of the American alpine team, taking the silver medal in the women's downhill.

Dan Jensen celebrates sweet victory with his son.

★

Dan Jensen finds disappointment for a third time, as a slip on the ice in the 500-meter speed-skating race costs him a medal yet again. Later in the games he finally triumphs, winning the 1,000 meter in world record time.

★

Bonnie Blair wins both the 500-meter sprint and the 1,000-meter speed skating race, making her America's most successful female Olympian ever. With a record five gold medals and six medals overall, she also passes Eric Heiden as America's leading Winter Olympics athlete.

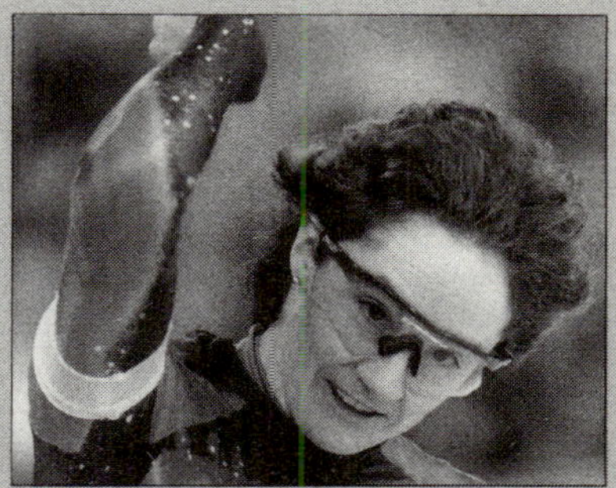

Bonnie Blair skates into the record books.

★

Cathy Turner, 31, takes a rough-and-tumble approach to the short-track 500-meter contest and is rewarded with a gold medal. But silver medalist Zhang Yanmei of China storms off the medal stand in protest and Turner will subsequently be disqualified in the longer 1,000-meter short track race.

★

After fevered weeks of anticipation the women's figure skating competition begins, and the telecast of the first round on the 24th, in which **Nancy Kerrigan** takes the lead, becomes the third-highest rated televised sports event, behind Super Bowl XVI and Super Bowl XVII. The drama of the competition is heightened after **Oksana Baiul** of Ukraine, in second place after the first round, collides with Tanja Szewczenko of Germany while skating backwards during a practice session. But in the final round Baiul edges out Kerrigan by the slimmest of margins for the gold medal.

musical demands of the role." Dunaway, who has never appeared in a stage musical, says that Andrew Lloyd Webber "severely damaged" her reputation. The two will meet in court.

★

The Jackson Family Honors plays to a less-than-packed, and less-than-thrilled house at the MGM Grand Hotel in Las Vegas. While Michael appears, he doesn't perform solo—in fact, he sings only four lines of "If You Only Believe" in the family finale. Sister Janet, on the other hand, skips the finale, but does perform "All Right," while LaToya does not show at all. The Jacksons are joined by such guests as honorees Elizabeth Taylor and Berry Gordy and performers Smokey Robinson, Gladys Knight, and Bruce Hornsby.

On April 1, amid reports of unpaid bills, co-producer of *The Jackson Family Honors* show Gary Smith announces that he is suing the family for $2.2 million owed to Smith-Hemion Productions.

★

Martin Lawrence performs such a raunchy monologue while hosting *Saturday Night Live* that parts of it are edited out of the delayed West Coast broadcast of the show. Callers complain that certain jokes about oral sex are too lewd. As part of the fallout, Lawrence is later banned by NBC from appearing on *The Tonight Show*.

★

For the first time since its founding in 1925, the annual anniversary issue cover of *The New Yorker*, published on the 21st, does not bear the image of urbane **Eustace Tilley**. Instead, the cover boasts R. Crumb's rendering of a '90s teen. "He's an anarchic character by the look of him—a rebel. He's Eustace's grandson—he's Elvis Tilley," says Tina Brown, editor of the magazine. She promises that Eustace will be back next year for his seventieth birthday.

★

Garrett Morris, 57, currently starring in *Martin*, is shot in a robbery attempt in Los Angeles on the 27th. Morris will comments later, "If the guy had just said clearly in English, 'Give me your money!' I would have given him my money."

★

On the 28th, **Greg Kinnear** debuts as the new host of NBC's *Later*—at the time, a much-anticipated development in the continuing realignment of late-night talk shows. His premiere guest is Julia Louis-Dreyfus.

MARCH

Roseanne features a controversial kiss between Roseanne Arnold and a lesbian character played by Mariel Hemingway. At one point, ABC indicated that the episode would not be shown.

★

Producer David Foster leads the **Grammys** with five awards and Whitney Houston takes home three trophies, while the soundtrack from *Aladdin* is also a big winner. But the most memorable moment comes when the cameras cut away while Frank Sinatra is rambling through his acceptance speech for a Grammy Legend Award. His publicist later claims that Frank didn't mind the interruption, but telecast host Garry Shandling apologizes on the air immediately afterwards.

★

Kurt Cobain, 27, the iconoclastic lead singer of grunge band Nirvana, takes a combination of the prescription drug Rohypnol, a Valium-like tranquilizer available in Europe, and chlorylhydrate, a prescription anesthetic—as well as a rare indulgence of champagne—on the 3rd. By the time his wife, Courtney Love, rises the next morning at 5:30, Cobain is lying on the floor in a coma. After a few days in the hospital he turns out to be fine—for the moment—but the incident becomes a haunting warning of what is to come.

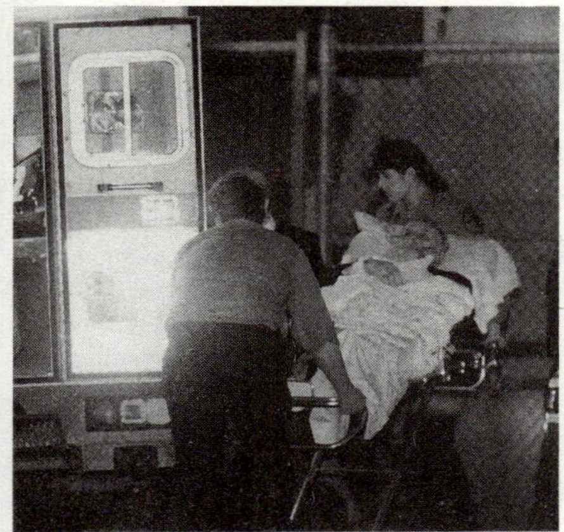

Frank Sinatra is rushed to a hospital after collapsing at a performance in Richmond, Virginia.

Frank Sinatra, 78, remains in the news as he suffers from a number of troubles during a performance in Richmond, Virginia. Despite having a TelePrompTer in front of him, he flubs lyrics to some of his standard songs. At one point in the program he remarks, "It's hot in here," and later on, while perched on a stool crooning "My Way," he suddenly asks for a chair and then falls face down to the floor. Unconscious for about a minute, Sinatra is later diagnosed as having suffered from dehydration, but rumors about his condition persist. Sinatra's friends acknowledge that the singer experiences occasional memory lapses but say he is not suffering from Alzheimer's.

★

In a year notable for high-profile, off-again-on-again separations, **Melanie Griffith**, 36, and **Don Johnson**, 44, get the bandwagon going. Griffith begins by filing for divorce on the 11th in Los Angeles County Superior Court, citing irreconcilable differences. Yet as the papers are being processed, their publicist announces that the divorce action has been withdrawn and calls it "an impulsive act that occurred during a moment of frustration and anger." The next night Griffith tells an interviewer, "I have terrible PMS and I just went a little crazy." Married for five years (this time around), the troubles will not blow over so easily.

Johnson was clearly battling substance abuse problems, as later developments show. In June, the redoubt of domestic bliss comes tumbling down when Don—after a binge of boozing, brawling, and partying—checks into the Betty Ford Center outside Palm Springs to undergo treatment for alcoholism and abuse of prescription drugs. A terse statement from his publicist says only that he "is expected to remain there for a period of four weeks." The message between the lines, however, is clear—an admitted alcoholic who sobered up in 1983, Johnson was again out of control, and his marriage was no longer on the rocks but probably in ruins. Griffith resettled near the couple's sprawling home in Colorado with children Alexander, 8, and Dakota, 4 (Jesse, 11, stayed with his father), and plans on relocating to the couple's Los Angeles home in the fall.

★

Turns out that the **Loch Ness "monster"** was a child's windup submarine fitted with a foot-long plastic neck. Two Nessie researchers, Alastair Boyd and David Martin, say the famous black-and-white snapshot that started the sensation when it was published in London's *Daily Mail* on April 21, 1934, was a hoax. Their revelation is based on information from the creator of this "Nessie," modelmaking enthusiast Christian Spurling, who confessed shortly before his death last November.

★

This month brings the revelation that if you watch ***Who Framed Roger Rabbit*** frame by frame on laser disc at home, you can see otherwise undetectable frontally nude shots of its cartoon star, Jessica Rabbit, not to mention sexually explicit sequences involving other characters. According to one reported Disney source, the company has known about the altered frames since the 1988 film was released on laser disc.

Actress **Zsa Zsa Gabor** files for Chapter 11 bankruptcy protection in Los Angeles. Last December, Gabor, who already had a long list of creditors, was ordered by a judge to pay Elke Sommer $1.25 million for unflattering remarks made about the actress in a German magazine. Gabor is appealing the judgment.

★

Virtually all the traditional romantic components are conspicuously absent in a shadowy back alley near Hollywood Boulevard when nineteen-year-old **Drew Barrymore**, acting on an impulse, informs her boyfriend of six weeks, Welsh-born Jeremy Thomas, 31, a Los Angeles bar owner, that she wants to pledge her celebrated, thrill-packed, and occasionally troubled life to him—forever. And so it is, at shortly after 5 a.m. on the 20th, that the couple is married in a ceremony that looks not at all like something from *Father of the Bride* but very much like a sweetly wacky outtake from *Reality Bites*. Unfortunately, the union lasts about as long as the latter ran in theaters—within five weeks they are separated, and within eight weeks they are officially divorced.

★

Actress **Whoopi Goldberg** hosts the Academy Awards ceremony, establishing a number of firsts: She's both the first African-American star and the first woman to host the show solo, as well as only the second Oscar winner to host by herself (Jack Lemmon is the other, hosting in 1963). As Whoopi says before the show, "To go from watching to winning to hosting in one lifetime is major." **Steven Spielberg** finally comes through with the big honors, as well as many others: *Schindler's List* wins seven awards, including Best Picture and Best Director, and his *Jurassic Park* wins another three.

Steven Spielberg basks in the end of his Oscar jinx with his mother and his wife, Kate Capshaw.

★

The **NFL** announces its most sweeping scoring changes ever: New rules include allowing a two-point conversion after touchdowns, moving kick-offs back to the thirty-yard-line, and using one-inch kicking tees.

★

Magic Johnson returns to the Los Angeles Lakers—this time as head coach, replacing Randy Pfund, whose losing record over two seasons was caused, in part, by Magic's departure.

★

The author of *Private Parts* goes public as **Howard Stern** announces his campaign for the Libertarian party nomination for governor of New York. With the slogan "A volt for every vote!," Stern supports reinstating the death penalty, promises nighttime construction crews to fix the roads, and advocates more toll-takers to move motorists along.

As he puts it in his popular but not necessarily politic way: "I am not perfect. I masturbate. I am 40 years old and maybe I talk about sex too much. But I am honest to a fault. Who else would reveal that the size of his genitals is under two inches. And I know the problems of New York because I come to work every day." Stern drops out of the campaign in the summer, after losing a battle over the requirement that he disclose his income.

Joey Buttafuoco, 38, is released from New York's Nassau County Correctional Facility after serving four months and nine days for statutory rape.

★

Joey Buttafuoco signals to the crowd that awaits his release from prison.

Elizabeth Taylor, 62, undergoes four hours of hip-replacement surgery in Los Angeles. The Oscar-winning actress, who suffers from osteoarthritis in her left hip, will require a walker or crutches for an eight-week period but is expected to make a complete recovery within a year.

★

Jimmy Johnson, 50, the Dallas Cowboys coach who led the team through five seasons and two consecutive Super Bowl victories, resigns after a long-standing personal feud with owner Jerry Jones, 51. Johnson, who has five more years left on his $1 million-a-year contract, has reportedly been given a pay-off and the right to work elsewhere by Jones, his onetime University of Arkansas football teammate. Barry Switzer, a former University of Oklahoma coach, is named as Johnson's replacement.

Madonna fouls out. In an appearance on the *Late Show with David Letterman*, Madonna spews fourteen obscenities—all deleted from the audio portion of the show. Dave tries repeatedly to usher her offstage, but she doesn't budge. The audience sides with Dave and the show draws high ratings, though word has it that Dave is offended by Madonna's language and attitude. But Madonna comments later: "All that was completely set up. Not every word, but he knew I was going to come on and say the word f— a lot. I was doing it as a protest against censorship."

★

Madonna enjoys her guest appearance on *Late Show with David Letterman*, but the fallout was considerable.

An unidentified seventeen-year-old Minneapolis high school senior files a civil suit accusing actor **Timothy Busfield**, 36, of sexual assault. Busfield denies the charges and promptly files his own suit against the woman's lawyers, charging them with extortion and with coercing her into making false charges. Known to the court as R.W., the woman alleges that while on the Minnesota set of *Little Big League*, Busfield invited the young extra into his trailer, fondled her, and asked her—in vain—to have sex with him.

When she complained to the production company, she charges, she was fired from her $50-a-day job.

Busfield vehemently denies all of R.W.'s allegations (she did not report the alleged incident to the police). Later, in June, actress Elizabeth Roberts, the thirty-nine-year-old wife of actor Eric Roberts and the sister-in-law of Julia Roberts, also claims that Busfield made inappropriate sexual overtures to her.

APRIL

In a Good Friday miracle, **Christie Brinkley**, 40, narrowly survives a helicopter crash on a peak south of Telluride, Colorado. Brinkley and her friends in the chopper—Ricky Taubman, 45, a Los Angeles real estate developer; Sandra Will Carradine, the founder of Telluride's Sheridan Arts Foundation, who is in her mid-40s and currently separated from actor Keith Carradine; Carradine's 11-year-old-son, Cade, who lives with her; pilot Tom Sharp, 35; and ski guide Mike Friedman, 37—survive an almost literal cliffhanger 12,800 feet up with few injuries. The danger is tragically underscored only two days later, when Walt Disney Company president Frank G. Wells, 62, and two companions are killed in a similar accident while skiing in Nevada.

But it remains a rocky month for Christie. On the 13th she and her husband of nine years, **Billy Joel**, 44, announce they "have agreed to an amicable separation." Their joint statement also says, "Although we have been separated since Thanksgiving, we felt it was best to keep the situation private, while we were resolving the details. This was out of enormous love and concern for our daughter [Alexa Ray, 8] and our desire to protect our friendship, which is one of great affection and respect. We have been there to support each other during critical times and expect to be there for each other in the future."

Christie Brinkley and Billy Joel in happier times.

What, then, is wrong with this picture? One person who has watched Brinkley closely suggests that Christie was tiring of the Mrs. Piano Man phase of her life. "She was happy to be in his world," says the source, "but I get a feeling she's just going to go for it. She's still got a great body, great looks, great confidence."

★

The creator of *Calvin and Hobbes*, **Bill Watterson**, begins a sabbatical from the strip that will last until the end of the year.

★

Charles Kuralt, 59, the veteran TV newsman and essayist, retires from CBS after thirty-seven years with the network with his final appearance on *Sunday Morning*. He turns over the reigns to Charles Osgood. Kuralt, who won eleven Emmy Awards during his career, says that though it is hard to leave CBS, he wants more time to work on a book about his twelve favorite locations in America.

Disney opens its first Broadway musical, ***Beauty and the Beast.*** Despite less-than-stellar reviews, the show sets a series of sales records, culminating in June on the day after the Tony awards are presented. The show claims only one statuette, but still sets the record for highest single-day ticket sales by a whopping margin. Including group sales, the one-day total stands at $1,296,722.50, far ahead of the record set by *The Phantom of the Opera* on November 23, 1987, of $920,271. The success of the musical augurs well for Disney's grander plans for Broadway. The company is currently renovating the New Amsterdam Theater, which will be reopened in 1996 and will be the home of a regular program of planned Disney musical productions.

Terrence Mann (Beast) and Susan Egan (Belle), stars of Disney's Broadway hit, *Beauty and the Beast.*

★

On the 8th **Kurt Cobain** joins a long and sad list of fellow rock stars: Janis Joplin, Jimi Hendrix, Jim Morrison—all dead at 27. Cobain takes his own life, shooting himself with a shotgun in his Seattle-area lakeside home. Suffering for seven years from chronic stomach pain, diagnosed as irritable bowel syndrome, Cobain had recently said in a *Rolling Stone* interview, "I wanted to kill myself every day. I came very close many times."

Wife Courtney Love reads aloud portions of Cobain's suicide note to thousands of fans gathered at a vigil, in which he thanks everyone "from the pit of my burning, nauseous stomach." The *Seattle Post-Intelligence* later reveals that Cobain had heroin in his system when he committed suicide, and he lay dead in his house for three days before being discovered.

The day before Cobain's death, Love had been charged in Los Angeles with possession of a controlled substance and drug paraphernalia. The substance, thought to be heroin, is actually a Hindu good-luck charm, and she is cleared. Love is further shaken in June by the overdose death of Hole bandmate Kristen Pfaff.

★

Ted Turner launches the **Turner Classic Movies** channel with a never-before-broadcast, uncut version of *Gone with the Wind.* The channel will draw on the 4,300 films from MGM, early Warners Brothers, and RKO that Turner owns. But who will be watching? With very few slots available on cable systems, the channel launches with one million subscribers—a far cry from the seventeen million that launched Turner's earlier movie channel, TNT.

★

In the second see-saw separation of the year, **Roseanne Arnold** files for divorce from husband **Tom** in Los Angeles Superior Court after a reported argument on the set of *Roseanne*, on grounds of irreconcilable differences. She also petitions for a restraining order, claiming, "I am now extremely afraid of him and am extremely afraid for my physical safety. . . . My life would be ruined if I continue in this abusive relationship."

The first round of the war is front-page news, as is their quick reconciliation three days later. But when it all starts up again on May 13, the public has moved on to newer and juicier feuds. By the time Roseanne files her formal divorce action on July 13, her and complaints have grown to 250 pages and it reads more like a trashy novel than a legal document. At issue, according to the court papers, are some $25 million worth of assets—and liabilities of almost equal value.

Tom's eponymous show is eventually dropped by CBS; swearing off television, he seeks support from Roseanne instead—to the tune of $100,000 a month, to subsidize the "extremely rich, opulent lifestyle" to which he had become accustomed. In July Roseanne legally truncates her name to what the world has called her for years—simply "Roseanne."

★

The **Year of Barbra** gets its second installment as she begins her first tour in twenty-seven years at Wembly Arena in London on the 20th. Backed by Marvin Hamlisch and a sixty-four-piece orchestra, the tour will go on to include 12 American appearances. Her first stop in the U.S. is Washington, D.C., and audience members include the President and the First Lady. Her New York engagement in July at Madison Square Garden officially smashes the record for the highest total concert gross at one venue: she rakes in $16.6 million, topping her own $13.7 million haul in Las Vegas and the Rolling Stones' $11.6 million take at Shea Stadium in 1989. But Barbra throws in a gift for the Big Apple; part of her last concert is carried live on the Jumbotron in Times Square.

Barbra Streisand at her concert at Wembly Arena in London.

★

This month brings a new equal-opportunity contest to beauty competitions, with the **Mr. Romance Model** pageant, held in Nashville, Tennessee. The hunks compete wearing jeans, evening wear, and costumes (including those of aristocrats, frontiersman, knights, and pirates).

★

A Los Angeles jury finds tressed-out singer **Michael Bolton**, 41, guilty of copyright infringement for making his 1991 hit "Love Is a Wonderful Thing" substantively similar to the Isley Brothers 1966 hit of the same name. Bolton's updated "Love," credited only to him and a cowriter, helped sell more than ten million copies of Bolton's album *Time, Love & Tenderness*. Bolton strongly reasserts his innocence, and files an appeal.

★

The legendary **Fillmore Auditorium** in San Francisco reopens on the 27th after being closed for almost five years due to earthquake damage. Carlos Santana notes, "The Fillmore was what Jimi Hendrix would call an electric church."

★

Prince Charles's beloved dog **Pooh**, 5, a Jack Russell terrier, disappears in the vicinity of Balmoral Castle. Newspapers offer rewards and subjects scour the countryside in hopes of finding the dog, son of the Prince's Tigger. Some even distribute meat scraps to lure Pooh home, but to no avail.

★

Former president **Richard Nixon** dies of a stroke at age 81. One-time foe George McGovern comments, "I think he became a more authentic, open, liberated person after he left politics. As a person, he was more humane, a better man the day he died than when he was in the White House."

MAY

Richard Gere and **Cindy Crawford** take out a full-page ad, at a cost of $30,000, in the *Times* of London to declare, "We are heterosexual and monogamous and take our commitment to each other very seriously. . . .We both look forward to having a family." In London, the surprising statement is scrutinized as closely as sheep entrails in ancient Rome. "A word suggests itself for this kind of extraordinary personal announcement," pronounced the *Daily Telegraph*. "It is the opposite of 'outing,' by which [closet] homosexuals are exposed by militant gays. This is the first such recorded 'inning' of the modern age."

★

The charge is as graphic as its implications are sleazy. **Paula Jones**, 27, files a federal civil rights lawsuit accusing **Bill Clinton** of making sexual advances to her in a Little Rock hotel room three years ago, when he was governor of Arkansas and she was an administrative assistant for the state's industrial development commission. She had agreed to meet Clinton, she said in a lurid twenty-page complaint, "because she thought it might lead to an enhanced employment opportunity with the state."

The Clintons ponder a difficult year.

She said the man who would be elected president of the United States eighteen months later dropped his pants and asked her for oral sex. She refused, she said, and left the suite. Afterward, Jones now claims, she "was treated in a hostile and rude manner" at her job and was denied raises. Now, three years later, Jones is asking $700,000 in damages for "intentional infliction of emotional distress."

Legal experts are divided as to whether Jones—who missed a legal deadline to file federal sexual harassment charges and has instead invoked a federal civil rights statute—can keep her unique case in court. An examination of her employment record indicates that after May 8, 1991, when the hotel-room encounter allegedly took place, she received several salary increases before voluntarily leaving her job in February 1993. As with most previous Clinton firestorms, the action quickly fades into the background as the White House seeks to have the action postponed until after the president's term of office is completed.

★

Police in Coral Gables, Florida, following a phone tip, call on tennis star **Jennifer Capriati**, 18, at the Gables Inn Motel and she permits a search: they find a small bag of marijuana in a gym duffel bag. As the story unfolds, it becomes evident that for Capriati this was not just a casual fling but part of a deeper descent into the world of drugs. Two days after the arrest, she enters the Addiction Treatment Center of Mount Sinai Medical Center in Miami Beach for a twenty-three-day stay. Upon departure, she enters a year-long drug counseling program in Miami. If she completes it successfully, her record will be expunged.

★

It was no joke when comedian **Bobcat Goldthwait**, 32, was charged with two misdemeanor counts for setting a chair on fire during his May 6 appearance on *The Tonight Show* in Burbank, California. Goldthwait faces a maximum $1,000 fine and a six-month jail sentence.

★

The Best Little Whorehouse Goes Public doesn't really interest the public at all—the $8 million Broadway show closes after only fifteen performances.

★

Just two years and eleven days after singer **Paula Abdul** and actor **Emilio Estevez** said, "I do," lawyers for the pair were filing papers making it clear that they don't. Why they couldn't remains a mystery. Although Abdul cited "irreconcilable differences" in the divorce papers, some published reports linked the *Mighty Ducks* star with such ex-girlfriends as former New York model Marla Hanson, 32, and Los Angeles actress Karen Maslich, 29. Both women deny a current romance with the actor, but Maslich says Abdul may have believed the rumors.

★

Star Trek: The Next Generation airs the final installment of its television mission on the 23rd, and cast and ship prepare for their journey into movieland. "All Good Things" is the last episode, in which a supernatural race is set to judge humanity's fitness to exist in the universe, and Capt. Jean-Luc Picard attempts to influence the outcome.

★

Apparently the price wasn't right, as **Dian Parkinson**, a model who worked with game-show host **Bob Barker** for eighteen years, seeks $8 million to settle out of court claims that she had sex with him only because she feared losing her job, which she quit in 1993. Barker angrily challenges Parkinson at a press conference, declaring, "She is not telling the truth. I think it's an injustice to the women who really are suffering when a woman files a cynical lawsuit for personal gain." Former colleagues of Parkinson allege that she appeared to be the aggressive one in the relationship.

His numbers in steady decline, **Arsenio Hall** closes up the dog pound as his last original show airs on the 27th. The key to Arsenio's initial success was startlingly simple: He took advantage of the fact that many young adults keep vampire's hours. And he offered this large pool of disenfranchised viewers-in-waiting a selection of younger, hipper guests—and they tuned in, despite Hall's anemic monologues and unctuous interview style. But once the mantle of hipness had passed from Arsenio to Letterman, Hall's nights were numbered. Now they are history.

But syndicator Paramount plans a new late-night tack for the new season in September with *The Jon Stewart Show*, featuring the hot former MTV talk-show host.

★

Nobel laureate **Aleksandr Solzhenitsyn,** 75, the Russian author expelled from the Soviet Union in 1974, returns to his homeland. Solzhenitsyn, the author of several books including *The Gulag Archipelago*, an account of life in Stalin-era concentration camps, has lived for the past eighteen years with his second wife, Natalia, and their sons, Yermolai, 23, Ignat, 21, and Stephan, 20, in Cavendish, Vermont.

★

The **Eagles** begin their sellout, thirty-seven-city "Hell Freezes Over" tour—in Irvine, California, on the 27th. The tour is expected to gross at least $175 million worldwide. The group features guitarist Glenn Frey, drummer Don Henley, guitarists Joe Walsh and Don Felder, and bassist Timothy B. Schmit (all are 46, except Frey, who is 45). Randy Meisner and Bernie Leadon are not included in the reunited group. The tour is sparked in part by the recent album *Common Thread: The Songs of the Eagles*, on which country stars sing the group's songs; the album is reported to have sold over three million copies.

JUNE

Fox launches its new cable channel, **fX**, on the 1st, claiming the largest cable introduction ever, with eighteen million homes (TNT was the previous leader, launched in 1988 with seventeen million homes.) Fox pulls off such a large introduction because cable operators agreed to provide space for the channel in exchange for the right to carry the Fox Network. Programmers say they are planning hip shows for the general-interest channel, geared to the 18- to 49-year old audience.

★

Pierce Brosnan, 42, is stirred but not shaken by the official announcement that he will be the next actor to portray James

The new 007, Pierce Brosnan.

Bond. He'll be the fifth actor to play 007 since Sean Connery donned a dinner jacket for *Dr. No* in 1962. *Goldeneye*, a saga involving an arms deal with Russia, begins shooting this fall and calls for the return of top spy M, gadget wizard Q, and Miss Moneypenny. Brosnan tells a press conference, "I'll probably show a bit of chest hair, but keep my clothes on. [Bond] will probably have condoms on the bedside table that glow in the dark."

Near midnight on the 12th, police responding to a 911 call find two bodies alongside the blood-washed walkway in front of a $600,000 condo in the Brentwood section of Los Angeles. One is a statuesque blonde woman, her beautiful face bruised and abraded. A young man is found lying in the bushes. The victims: Nicole Brown Simpson, 35, ex-wife of O. J. Simpson, and Ronald Goldman, 25, a waiter and part-time model.

Then comes the almost incomprehensible news that Simpson himself is to be arrested. Here is the strikingly handsome **Orenthal James Simpson**, who had risen from the housing projects of San Francisco's Portrero Hill to become a Heisman Trophy winner and National Football League superstar, then a successful NBC sportscaster and sometime movie actor, handcuffed in front of his $5-million Brentwood mansion. During three hours of questioning, Simpson, 46, protests his innocence, citing a brief business trip to Chicago the night of the murders, but on the 20th he is officially arraigned.

The infamous mug shot of O. J. Simpson.

The note he had left behind on June 17—declaring his love for Nicole and saying that their problems were within the normal ups and downs of any long-term relationship—has been described by at least one expert as a textbook example of a spouse abuser's denial. The day the letter is released Simpson disappears briefly before surfacing on an eerie slow-speed chase up L.A.'s 405 freeway. His last drive before surrendering to police, the spectacle keeps ninety-five millions viewers glued to their television sets. As the legal battle unfolds, viewers stay tuned in large numbers for every installment.

★

While her contemporaries are hitting the glass ceiling, **Princess Anne**, 43, is moving up—sort of. The Queen dubs her daughter a Lady Companion of the Most Noble Order of the Garter, making Anne only the second princess since the Middle Ages—her mother was the first, in 1947—to be so honored.

★

Butterfield & Butterfield auctions off the second-largest collection of **Elvis Presley** memorabilia (only Graceland has more) at the Las Vegas Hilton, featuring the entire contents of Jimmy Velvet's Elvis Presley Museum. The King's jumpsuit studded with faux turquoise stones goes for $101,500. One of his plastic combs fetched $1,092.50 And *Northern Exposure*'s John Corbett pays $68,500 for Elvis's birth certificate and $41,400 for the singer's American Express card. All in all, the auction tallies a whopping $2,365,837 from the sale of 617 objects. One thing Velvet wasn't willing to part with: "I have some of his pill bottles," he says, "but I won't put them on display."

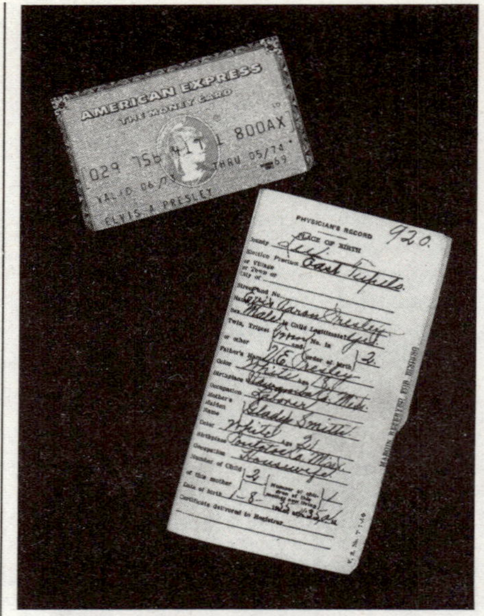

Part of the legacy offered at an auction of Elvis Presley memorabilia: the King's American Express card and his birth certificate.

★

Oprah Winfrey, the Incredible Shrinking Woman, invites 2,000 of her fans to the Grand Ballroom in the Hyatt Regency Chicago for a benefit sale of 900 dresses and other items from her wardrobe—a silk-and-satin history of her waistline from size eight to size twenty-two. The four hours of demi-delirium raise more than $150,000 for Chicago's Hull House, a community outreach organization, and Families First, a Sacramento group that provides food, shelter, and education for abused children.

★

NBC takes the street-level, glass-enclosed studio idea back to the future as the ***Today*** show hits the streets of New York: the corner of West 49th Street and Rockefeller Plaza to be exact. Hundreds of spectators gather for the inaugural show on the 20th, including a few protesters objecting to the

the on-air cooking of a live lobster the previous week. Guests include President Clinton, Barbara Walters, Aaron Neville, and Bill Cosby. The new studio harkens back to the show's original setting, from 1952 to 1958, when Dave Garroway hosted.

Today's new glass-enclosed studio.

★

Singer **George Michael** loses a restraint-of-trade lawsuit against Sony Music. The High Court in London dismisses Michael's claim that his current contract, which requires him to make six more albums with the record company, is unreasonable and unfair. Michael appeals the verdict, but the future of his career is left unclear, since he had vowed never to record for Sony again.

★

Princess Diana, 33, reaches an out-of-court settlement with London's L.A. Fitness club, where she was secretly photographed pumping iron last November. She gets an apology from the gym and an undisclosed payment from them to cover her legal fees. Her lawsuits against the photographer, Bryce Taylor, and Mirror Group Newspapers, which published the snapshots, are still pending.

Prince Charles sends Fleet Street into a frenzy by admitting to adultery in a televised documentary that nearly thirteen million people watch. The special had been intended by his handlers as part of a "charm offensive" to win support for the diffident Charles. Instead it allows viewers a glimpse of a complex man plagued by self-doubt—an introspective altruist who often dislikes his job but who does his best to find meaning in a role that, to outsiders, often seems absurd. But most notably, when asked if he had been faithful to the most glamorous woman in Britain, he answers, "Yes," then adds, "until it became clear that the marriage had irretrievably broken down."

★

CBS and **QVC** announce their plans to combine the two companies in a multimedia merger. A mere two weeks later the grand design falls apart when Comcast Corporation, the country's third-largest cable television company, makes a $2.1 billion offer to purchase QVC.

★

Pearl Jam members **Jeff Ament** and **Stone Gossard** appear before Congress on the 30th to lobby against **Ticketmaster**'s role in the business of providing concert tickets, following up on their complaint lodged with the Justice Department last month. "Ticketmaster is a nationwide ticket distribution service that has a virtual monopoly on the distribution of tickets to concerts," guitarist Gossard testifies. Pearl Jam had previously canceled their planned tour as a result of a dispute with Ticketmaster over the final ticket price, once their service charge was added on. The band wanted to keep the tab under $20 so that it would be affordable for their young following.

The following month Ticketmaster strikes back, filing a $306.8 million defamation lawsuit against three attorneys who have brought actions against the company.

JULY

Michael Keaton takes a pass on wearing the cape for a third time and Val Kilmer is named as the next Batman. The movie, *Batman Forever*, is slated for release in theaters next summer and will film in the fall. A source says that Keaton, who was paid an estimated $5 million for *Batman* and $10 million for *Batman Returns*, "was demanding" $15 million to reprise his role as the Caped Crusader, along with an additional "financial consideration" if production went past a certain date. But Harry Columby, Keaton's manager, says it was his client who "walked away" and that "money was never a factor." Columby claims Keaton left because of creative differences with the film's director, Joel Schumacher.

★

When the Pope picks up the pen, publishers bow their heads in grateful prayer. **Pope John Paul II** will publish a book of essays this fall called *Crossing the Threshold of Hope*. American rights are reportedly bought for $9 million by publisher Alfred A. Knopf. The book was purchased through agent Morton L. Janklow from Mondadori, the Pope's Italian publisher.

★

America has a new Osmond to admire, as **Amy Osmond**, 17, oldest child of Wayne Osmond of the six singing Osmond Brothers (and niece of Uncle Donny and Aunt Marie) is crowned Junior Miss. Amy's mother, Kathleen, 41, was a former Junior Miss runner-up who later gave up her Miss Utah crown to marry Wayne, now 42, in 1971.

Amy made her debut in 1982 as a young Marie in the TV movie *Side by Side*, the story of the Osmond family. A lasting memory from that experience, she says, was "throwing up in the backseat of the car on the way" to the studio. Little wonder, then, that she decided early on to be an obstetrician rather than go into showbiz. The top-ranked student in her high school class and a National Merit Scholar, Amy will use the $33,000 in cash and prizes towards expenses at Brigham Young University, which she will attend in the fall.

★

NYPD Blue makes television history by receiving a record twenty-six Emmy nominations, including a sweep of all five writing nominations and four out of five nominations for directing. *Star Trek: The Next Generation*, which was often overlooked during its now-complete seven-year run, finally garners a best drama nomination.

★

Hollywood is shaken for the second time this year, only this time it's not the ground that's moving. Walt Disney Co. chairman **Michael Eisner**, 52, undergoes quadruple coronary bypass surgery. Subsequently, Disney film chief Jeffrey Katzenberg, overseer of the studio's animation triumphs and of hits like *Pretty Woman*, resigns when he is not made second in command.

★

As a finale of the first World Cup soccer tournament held in the United States, the **Three Tenors**—Luciano Pavarotti, Placido Domingo, and José Carreras—reconvene for an encore concert on the 16th in Los Angeles at Dodger Stadium. The recording of the original Three Tenors concert ranks as the bestselling classical album ever, with reported sales of over 2.5 million copies in the U.S.

★

Call it dumpimony. Talk-show host **Larry King**, 60, files suit against ex-ladyfriend Rama Fox, 53, claiming that the woman he once lovingly called Pony slandered him with her depiction of their relationship's denouement, acting out of "malice, hatred, and ill will." Her true crime? She merely said in the July issue of *Washingtonian* magazine that she had dumped King. What the world needs to understand, says King's attorney, Mark A. Barondess, is that "Larry terminated the relationship."

For the generation raised singing themes from *The Brady Bunch* and *Gilligan's Island* with gusto, the news is not good. **ABC** progamming head Ted Harbert asks the network's producers to leave out opening themes and jump straight into the program, à la *Murphy Brown*.

AUGUST

Neverland meets Graceland as **Michael Jackson** and **Lisa Marie Presley** admit to getting hitched. On the 1st, Lisa Marie, 26, Elvis Presley's only child, issues a statement confirming the whispers that had been swirling for weeks: She had indeed wed the thirty-five-year-old pop genius. "My married name is Mrs. Lisa Marie Presley-Jackson," said the announcement, issued three weeks after a Dominican Republic judge produced a marriage license for all to see, dated May 26 and bearing the couple's signatures. "My marriage to Michael Jackson took place in a private ceremony outside the United States weeks ago," Presley-Jackson's statement continued. "I am very much in love with Michael, I dedicate my life to being his wife. I understand and suport him. We both look forward to raising a family."

Of course, Presley-Jackson already brings to the marriage two children. Danielle, 5, and Benjamin, 22 months, are respectively, her daughter and son by her first husband, rock bassist Danny Keough, 29, whom she married in 1988.

Admittedly, as a couple Michael and Lisa *are* kind of hard to reconcile. On the one hand, you have the 5' 3" Graceland heiress, who has her father's sensuous mouth, a $150 million estate that likely will be completely hers at age thirty, and an unswerving faith in the controversial Church of Scientology. On the other hand, there is the 5'10" but perpetually waiflike, notoriously germphobic, curio-at-large Jackson. The singer, who seems never to have had a serious romantic relationship, is still under investigation by L.A. and Santa Barbara authorities for allegedly molesting a now fourteen-year-old boy. And later in the month the boy's stepfather and sister file additional civil charges, seeking further damages.

But this much seems certain: The two definitely get along and enjoy hanging around together. When they stayed a week at Trump's Mar-a-Lago estate in Palm Beach, Fla., last winter, they spent each evening, says Trump, "holding hands and talking until the wee hours"—even if they did always adjourn to separate bedrooms. The *New York Post* reports that the newlyweds have spent many summer nights in the small but lavishly landscaped park atop New York City's Trump Tower. When the World's Most Famous Newlyweds go to Budapest to shoot a video for Jackson's new album, they are always seen side by side, holding hands (hers with wedding band, his without) and whispering private jokes. Of course, Jackson is also frequently seen carrying the diminutive Michu,

Michael Jackson and Lisa Marie Presley-Jackson in Hungary.

his longtime friend and frequent traveling companion, on his shoulder.

How long has this been going on? One employee of Jackson's who prefers to remain anonymous says that Lisa Marie "has known Michael almost all of her life. Elvis brought her around to meet the Jackson Five when she was a little kid, and they stayed in touch." Attorney John Coale, a friend of Lisa Marie, says her adult friendship with Jackson began in November 1992 in L.A. This past April, Lisa Marie announced that she was breaking up with Keough—who it now turns out, obtained a quickie, uncontested divorce in Santo Domingo on May 6 (they will share custody of the children). A mere eighteen days later, Jackson and his intended jetted to the deluxe spa Casa de Campo in the Dominican province of La Romana. From there it was viva La Vega, as the lovebirds proceeded to a town of that name for the May 26 nuptials, conducted by civil judge Hugo Francisco Alvarez Pérez.

Jackson is reportedly writing three songs for Lisa Marie and adding them to his next album, *History*, a greatest-hits collection due in the fall. And though criminal charges could still be brought against him, Jackson is once again the sweetly smiling pop idol who can draw adoring fans to a steamy New York City street corner on the chance that they may catch a glimpse of him and his new bride.

★

The Rolling Stones kick off their forty-city U.S. tour at Robert F. Kennedy Stadium in Washington. Joining the group for the first time is bassist Darryl Jones, 32, who has replaced the retired Bill Wyman. But the surviving Stones don't appear anywhere near retirement as they play twenty-seven songs in a concert that begins with "Not Fade Away" and lasts for two and a half hours. Keith Richards, 50, comments, "We're still a damn good band. So screw the press and their slagging about the Geritol Tour. Wait until you get our age and see how you run." The band's new album, *Voodoo Lounge*, debuts at No. 2 on the *Billboard* charts, behind the soundtrack for *The Lion King*.

★

CBS and David Letterman officially announce that **Tom Snyder** will join the network's late-night roster in the fall, hosting the *Late Late Show with Tom Snyder*, to be produced by Letterman's company, Worldwide Pants. Comments Snyder, "This is truly incredible. A year ago, this was no more in my mind that it would be to jump off the Empire State Building." It was Letterman who took over Snyder's time slot at NBC in 1982 after the network dropped the *Tomorrow* show.

★

After a number of conflicting reports, it becomes clear that **David Caruso** will leave *NYPD Blue* after the coming season's first four episodes to pursue his movie career. **Jimmy Smits** (*L.A. Law*) will join the cast in the fifth episode, playing a new character.

★

An onstage attack ends the singing tour of soap stud cum pop singer **Michael Damian**. Out promoting his new album, *Time of the Season*, Damian, 31, who plays Mr. Nice Guy Danny Romalotti on the CBS daytime serial *The Young and the Restless*, was attacked less than a minute into his first number during a concert outside of Boise, Idaho. The assailant, Mark Pina, 23, rushed the stage, shouting obscenities. It took four men and two sprays of Mace to pry Pina off Damian, who suffered bruised ribs, a cut knee, and whiplash. Though he canceled the remaining thirteen stops on the tour, Damian was healthy enough to fill in for Donny Osmond as the hero of *Joseph and the Amazing Technicolor Dreamcoat*. Pina's only comment: "It was something I needed to do."

★

Naomi Judd, 48, and her daughter **Wynonna**, 30, file suit in Nashville against their business partner, Steve Pritchard, 51, accusing him of fraud, breach of contract, and unjust enrichment. They seek unspecified damages, claiming he failed to turn over some of the money they earned as the Judds.

★

First it was called Greedstock for the $135 ticket prices, then Woodstockade for the chain-link fences, metal detectors, and Peace Patrol security squads on hand to keep order. Because of the rules forbidding alcohol and drugs, **Woodstock '94**—the twenty-fifth anniversary sequel to the mythic bacchanal—was dismissed as Woodstock Lite, the festival that wouldn't inhale.

But this year's Woodstock, like its legendary predecessor, turns out to have a life of its own. Security fences are toppled and the scent of weed indeed floats over the crowd of 350,000—of which little more than half are paying customers—long before the hard rains on Saturday afternoon turn the grassy pasture at the 840-acre Winston Farm outside Saugerties, N.Y., into a theater of mud.

Generation X-ers and their juniors and seniors mingle in peace, grooving to acts old (the Allman Brothers Band, Bob Dylan) and new (Green Day, Nine Inch Nails). Not to say there aren't culture clashes: some survivors of '69 are bewildered by the slam dancers and crowd surfers writhing ecstatically in the mosh pits. Still, grousing breeds solidarity, and there is plenty to grouse about—the 2,800 overflowing Port-O-Sans, overpriced food ($11 for a small pizza; $21 for breakfast rolls and beverages for three), and mile-long lines for shuttle buses to remote parking areas. But in the end the festival many assumed could never match the original leaves an identical legacy—of liter and mellow feelings. Said Eagles guitarist and festival guest Joe Walsh: "I'll remember this—forever."

REMEMBRANCES

JOHN CANDY

John Candy

Rarely before had he called his costars after hours—not because he was unfriendly, but because John Candy, who seemed to pop up in nearly every other movie during the past ten years, was at bottom a shy and self-conscious man. Still, just after midnight on March 4, he couldn't help himself, and he reached for the phone. Hours earlier, he had finished shooting his final scene in *Wagons East.* People who had witnessed the take felt that he had turned in the performance of his career.

So elated was the genial actor that he put in calls to costars Richard Lewis and Robert Picardo, and for a few minutes the actors reveled in their own and each other's accomplishments. "He was like a little kid who had had a great day at camp," says Picardo. "He wanted to thank us." With that, Candy hung up, soon turned out the light, and went to sleep. He never woke up.

Before he died, he looked cherubic, rosy-cheeked, hardly a day older than he did in 1984's *Splash*—but he did not look healthy. Carrying some 330 lbs. on his 6'3" frame—and often smoking a pack of cigarettes a day—Candy, 42, was tempting fate. His father, Sidney, a Toronto car salesman, had died of heart disease at the age of thirty-five, leaving his wife, Evangeline, to raise four-year-old John and his older brother, Jim, on her own. Gnawing at Candy was the knowledge that each pound he gained—and each cigarette he smoked—put him in further peril of leaving his own wife, Rosemary, 44, a potter, and their two children, Jennifer, 14, and Christopher, 9, in the same tragic situation.

Candy's obesity, of course, was not without its benefits. It set him apart as an actor in a career that spanned two decades and nearly forty feature films; in recent years, he was making upwards of $4 million per picture. The excess heft heightened the humorous effect, whether he was playing polka enthusiast Yosh Shmenge on the Emmy Award–winning *SCTV* series or Irv Blitzer, the coach of the Jamaican bobsled team in *Cool Runnings.*

Still, behind the self-deprecating jokes, Candy harbored considerable pain. "I'm the one who has to look in the mirror," he told PEOPLE in 1981, "and after a while it begins to eat at you."

Back in 1969, Candy had

enrolled in Toronto's Centennial Community College to study journalism and acting. Between classes he honed his craft in the local underground theater. In 1971, he met fellow Canadian Dan Aykroyd, who urged Candy to audition for the famed Second City comedy troupe, home to future *Saturday Night Live* stars John Belushi, Gilda Radner, and Bill Murray. "The next thing I knew," Candy told PEOPLE, "I was in Chicago, where I learned how to drink, stay up real late, and spell 'd-r-u-g-s.' "

In 1974, he left the fast life behind and returned to Toronto, where, along with Harold Ramis, Rick Moranis, fellow Shmenge brother Eugene Levy, and others, he starred in the hit television series *SCTV*, for which he eventually won two Emmys. In 1980, Candy made his movie mark as cop Burton Mercer in *The Blues Brothers*, and his career went into fast-forward after he appeared with Bill Murray in *Stripes*. Said Candy: "I went from macaroni and cheese to macaroni and lobster."

In the end, of course, no one can say for certain whether diet and self-denial would have prolonged Candy's life a single day. Only one thing is sure: Already Candy is missed.

KURT COBAIN

"Why?"

It was a mantra much repeated as fans, in shock, outrage, and sorrow, tried to understand why Kurt Cobain, the gifted yet chronically unhappy rocker, had gone alone to a small room above his garage in Seattle's quiet Madrona neighborhood and ended his life with a single shotgun blast.

Cobain's last nightmarish act was born of the same explosive anguish that fired the music of his band, Nirvana, and made it world famous. In the end, the humor that tempered the fury of Cobain's art, and the newfound happiness brought by the birth of the baby he adored, somehow deserted him. Pain, it seemed, was all that remained.

News of Cobain's death spread quickly on the morning of April 8 after Gary Smith, an electrician contracted to install a burglar alarm, discovered his body sprawled on the bare floor of the garage apartment. "Now he's gone and joined that stupid club," said Cobain's mother, Wendy O'Connor, alluding to the pantheon of rockers who died in their prime—among them Janis Joplin, Jim Morrison, and Jimi Hendrix, whose grave is fifteen miles south of Cobain's home. All had died, like Cobain, at 27.

Though widely believed to be winning his long struggle with heroin addiction, Cobain had backslid into old drug habits in the four weeks since his return from Rome, where on March 4 he had sunk into a coma after overdosing on a mixture of tranquilizers and champagne. Haunted by that incident, his wife, Courtney Love feared a suicide attempt and called police March 18 when Cobain locked himself in a room during a domestic quarrel. Police, who had responded to a similar call from Love last June, confiscated three handguns, a semiautomatic rifle, and twenty-five boxes of ammunition for safekeeping. Afterward, Courtney agreed to a so-called tough-love intervention and, with several friends, confronted Cobain on March 25 about his drug use. "I told him," she said, "You've got to be a good daddy. We've got to be good parents."

But the intervention backfired when Cobain bolted thirty-six hours after checking in on March 28 to the Exodus Recovery Center, a drug-treatment facility in Marina Del Rey, Calif. His mother reported him missing after four days, but Seattle police, informed that Cobain had purchased a shotgun, were unable to locate him. Nor could a private investigator hired by Love.

On the afternoon or evening of Tuesday, April 5, police believe, Cobain locked himself in the room above his garage and composed a note to his wife, friends, and fans. Writing in a tight, left-handed scrawl with a red ballpoint pen, Cobain alluded to the chronic, undiagnosed pains in his "burning, nauseous" stomach that had haunted him for years and had often made him consider suicide before. Heroin, he told Michael Azerrad, author of 1993's *Come as You Are: The Story of Nirvana,* was the only drug that quenched the fire in his gut. (Heroin and valium were reportedly found in Cobain's blood after his death.) Cobain agonized, too, about his music. "I don't have the passion anymore," he wrote.

In an April 9 phone interview with MTV's Kurt Loder, Love quoted Cobain's final missive: "It's not fun for me anymore. I can't live this life." So fearsome was the blast he fired to his head that authorities had to use fingerprints to identify the body. The next day, Love said, she clipped a lock of Cobain's blond hair. Later that night, she washed it, remembering how he hated to shampoo. She even wore some of Cobain's clothes in order, she hoped, to come to terms with the fact that she and Frances would never see him again. Suicide, she added, was the "Cobain curse."

Yet the pain that led Cobain to kill himself was not evident in early childhood. Born in 1967 in Aberdeen, a depressed logging town on the Washington coast 108 miles southwest of Seattle, he was the first of two children of homemaker Wendy Fradenburg and auto mechanic Donald Cobain. A precocious, energetic child who loved to draw and to sing Beatles tunes, Cobain was diagnosed as a hyperactive pre-schooler. Doctors prescribed Ritalin, an amphetamine-based drug that often kept him awake until 4 a.m. To counter the drug's side effects, he was also given sedatives. Yet Kurt remembered those days as "blissful times. . . I was constantly screaming and singing."

His world collapsed in 1975 when his parents divorced. They later conceded that their children, especially eight-year-old Kurt, had been seriously wounded by the legal and emotional battles that followed.

By his freshman year in high school, Cobain was smoking marijuana on an almost daily basis. Alienated from most of his classmates, especially jock types, whom he would taunt and spit at—and sometimes get beaten up by—Kurt grew his hair long and dyed it wild colors.

Meanwhile, Cobain had begun playing the guitar. After turning on to the Sex Pistols and other punk groups, he began to meld Zeppelin's heavy-metal power chords with the Pis-

Kurt Cobain

tols' punk iconoclasm. The result would, within a few years, help Nirvana become the avatar of Seattle's neo-punk grunge sound.

In 1987, Cobain, along with a high school friend, bassist Krist Novoselic, now 28, and a succession of drummers—Dave Grohl, 25, signed on in 1990—began performing his songs around Aberdeen and, later, in Olympia and Seattle. Taking the name Nirvana in 1987, the group released *Bleach*, which cost only $606.17 to record in 1989. Geffen Records signed the group two years later, and Cobain never fully recovered from the shock when Nirvana's next album, *Nevermind*, sold more than ten million copies worldwide and gave his generation an anthem, "Smells Like Teen Spirit." The song, full of verbal twists ("I feel stupid and contagious/Here we are now, entertain us"), startling guitar passages, and Cobain's primal screams, made him a superstar overnight.

As poster boy for today's lost generation, Kurt turned his torn jeans and grungy T-shirts into an anti-fashion statement of punk alienation. His hacked blond hair, sometimes bleached or dyed pink, hung over his eyes, obscuring surprisingly sensitive good looks.

Cobain could laugh at his own ambivalence—"Teenage angst has paid off well," he sang in the opening cut of Nirvana's last album, *In Utero*. But for all his onstage bravado he felt isolated and misunderstood.

During an outdoor candlelight vigil held in Seattle five days after Cobain's death, thousands of fans listened as organizers played a tape recording of Courtney's angry reading of her husband's suicide note. One depressed twenty-eight-year-old fan in the crowd went home afterward and, like the rock idol he had gone to mourn, killed himself with a shotgun.

For Cobain's widow, despair turned to rage. Breaking down on the tape-recorded message, Courtney interrupted her reading and cursed herself for submitting Cobain to the "tough-love bulls—t." Toward the end of the reading, she asked the assembled fans to chant. "Say 'You're a f—ker.' And then say you love him."

WILLIAM CONRAD

By the time William Conrad died of cardiac arrest in February at age 73, he'd lost seventy pounds due to ill health. But his appeal was shrink-proof. "People accepted him as the gruff, rough curmudgeon. Underneath, he was just a nice man," says TV executive Fred Silverman, who cast Conrad in two top-rated CBS series, *Cannon* (1971–76) and *Jake and the Fatman* (1987–92). But heft was only half his presence: His resonant, booming voice proved perfect for narrating *The Fugitive* and *Bullwinkle* cartoons. "When he did the narration for *Bullwinkle*, he turned comedic," says June Foray, the voice of Rocky the squirrel. "He lost all of his great profound voice, and it became hysterical."

It was, in fact, that voice that launched the Louisville, Ky., native into show business in the '40s; by his own reckoning, his resume included 7,500 radio jobs, including Marshal Matt Dillon on the original *Gunsmoke*. Later, when he finally found TV stardom, Conrad still loved mouthing off. "*Cannon* was crap," he groused after the show's run. "I was delighted to see it canceled."

His bulldog snarling was far worse than his bite. He lived quietly in Los Angeles with wife Tippy, widow of NBC newsman Chet Huntley. (He had a son, Christopher, 37, by first wife Susie, who died in 1979.) "Bill loved music, he loved travel, he loved food. He had many appetites," recalls Dean Hargrove, a *Fatman* producer. Says Tippy Conrad: "You get a guy like Bill, he simply wasn't concerned about whether he was successful or not. He just had a strong notion about what he wanted, and went ahead and did it."

BETTY FURNESS

Popular novels teem with vivacious young heroines who find glamour and romance in Hollywood, then struggle to find greater fulfillment. Few of these tales turn out as well as the story of Betty Furness.

That story began in New York City in 1930, when the fourteen-year-old daughter of a Union Carbide executive became a fashion model. Two years later she took a Hollywood screen test and was soon appearing with Robert Taylor (*Magnificent Obsession*) and Fred Astaire (*Swing Time*).

In the '50s the former starlet became one of TV's first, and most believable, pitchwomen—the face that launched a thousand refrigerators with the promise, "You can be *sure* if it's Westinghouse." Two decades later she again broke ground as one of the medium's first—and toughest—consumer reporters.

But Furness's odyssey was anything but smooth. When she died in April at 78 after a battle with stomach cancer, she had spent much of her career fighting discrimination, which she perceived as being based first on her sex, then on her age. In 1964, when she sought work as a news-interview host, Furness was rebuffed. "The networks," she said, "don't want women."

But Lyndon Johnson did want her as his special assistant for consumer affairs. She went on to head the consumer-affairs agencies of New York State and New York City, and in 1976 she became consumer reporter for *Today*. "She was my role model," says veteran anchor Jane Pauley. "There isn't anybody in television I admire more."

Near the end, Furness, an avid needlepointer, lived quietly in Hartsdale, N.Y., with her husband of twenty-six years, Leslie Midgley, a former executive producer with CBS News. "I once asked Betty what she would like people to think about her," recalls her longtime friend and producer Rita Satz, "and she replied, 'That I'm a pro.' She really was."

HENRY MANCINI

When choosing a title for his 1989 autobiography, Henry Mancini picked the question a movie songwriter might ask about the audience: *Did They Mention the Music?* In Mancini's case, people always did—often while announcing his latest Academy Award nomination. Mancini earned eighteen of those during his forty-year career, winning a Best Song Oscar for "Moon River" from *Breakfast at Tiffany's* (1961) and a Best Score Oscar for 1982's *Victor/Victoria*. Still busy at 70, Mancini was writing new songs for a stage version of *Victor/Victoria* in February when he learned that he was suffering from inoperable cancer of the liver and pancreas. He died in June at his home in Bel Air, Calif.

The son of an Italian immigrant steelworker, Mancini came to music by way of Aliquippa, Pa., where his father taught him flute and piano. After World War II service in the Air Force and the infantry, he joined the Glenn Miller Orchestra in 1946 and fell in love with its singer, Ginny O'Connor.

Over the next few decades—often in collaboration with lyricists Johnny Mercer and Leslie Bricusse—Mancini churned out theme music for more than a dozen TV shows (*Peter Gunn* and *Remington Steele* among them), scored more than eighty films and collected twenty Grammys. "He was the greatest songwriter since Irving Berlin," says Andy Williams, whose "Moon River" recording sold millions of copies and became a signature theme, "and he was the nicest man I ever knew."

MELINA MERCOURI

When the news reached Athens that the beloved symbol of Greek passion had died at age 68 of lung cancer on Sunday, March 6, at Memorial Sloan-Kettering Cancer Center in New York City, flags dropped to half-mast, theaters shut down, and radio and TV stations turned the airwaves over to

Mercouri and her husky-throated cabaret songs and clips from her signature 1960 film, *Never on Sunday.* The cause of her death might be considered a modern form of Greek tragedy. She often said that smoking was her "challenge against fear."

The daughter of a minister of the interior, she defied her parents at seventeen by marrying a wealthy Greek merchant much older than she (they divorced in 1962) and enrolling in the National Theatre of Greece. After triumphing onstage in Athens and Paris, she became an international star as a fiercely independent Piraeus prostitute in *Never on Sunday,* appearing opposite her then-lover, Jules Dassin, whom she married in 1966. (He was at her side when she died.)

But Mercouri chose to devote most of her ardor to Greek politics. When she spoke out against the military dictatorship that ruled Greece from 1967 to '74, she was stripped of her citizenship. She returned to Greece from Paris in 1974 after the election of the New Democracy Party. She served as a member of parliament from Piraeus from 1977 to '89, as culture minister from 1981 to '89 and helped found the Panhellenic Socialist Movement. "I thought she was the happiest she'd ever been, while in politics," said her friend of thirty years, costume designer Theoni Aldredge. "Melina was beautiful and flamboyant, and everything she did was to the utmost."

JACQUELINE BOUVIER KENNEDY ONASSIS

When was the last time one woman so affected the world? In the tiny French town of Pont-Saint-Esprit, where a century ago her great-grandfather earned his keep as a cabinetmaker, the flags at City Hall flew at half-staff. On the front steps of the Kennedy family estate in Palm Beach, a single red hibiscus left by a stranger fluttered in the warm breeze. And in New York City, a woman on a mountain bike rode up to the elegant entrance of 1040 Fifth Avenue and placed a bouquet of red roses on the ground. "She was part of the landscape," said Eileen Stukane before pedaling away. "I will miss her."

When Jacqueline Bouvier Kennedy Onassis died of cancer at age 64 on May 19, millions mourned across the country and across the world. No doubt much of what the nation felt was sorrow for itself. *Jac-leen,* as she liked to be called, had seemed inseparable from our personal histories: the American princess in the pillbox hat; the cosmopolitan First Lady flirting in fluent French with Charles de Gaulle; the stoic widow showing the country how to grieve with dignity; the celebrity mother insistent upon giving her children a sane upbringing; the surprisingly willing trophy wife of Greek shipping tycoon Aristotle Onassis; the dedicated book editor; the still-glamorous grandmother. Imagine living a life that full—and dying *young.* To those who had never heard the tiny voice that belied her larger-than-life stature, who never saw the nails bitten ragged beneath the ladylike gloves, it was easy to believe that the woman—like the legend—would never die.

On the morning of May 20, John Jr. descended from the apartment where he and Caroline had been raised, stood on the sidewalk where hundreds of reporters, cameramen, and well-wishers had gathered and issued a brief statement. "Last night, at around 10:15, my mother passed on," John said. "She was surrounded by her friends and family and her books and the people and the things that she loved. And she did it in her own way, and we all feel lucky for that, and now she's in God's hands."

John faced the press with the same calm that his 34-year old mother had displayed three decades earlier, when she stood on Air Force One in her blood-spattered pink Chanel suit as Lyndon B. Johnson was sworn in as president. She had seemed so young then but, as it turned out, her life was

Onassis (Cont.)

already more than half over. Now it was John's turn to be strong. He stayed at his mother's side constantly at New York Hospital–Cornell Medical Center and during her last day at home. He, like Caroline, had the chance to talk and reminisce virtually until the end.

"Three things came to mind," said John of the process of putting together a suitable service. "They were her love of words, the bonds of home and family, and her spirit of adventure." Left unstated was a fourth theme: Jackie's passion for privacy. On the morning of Monday, May 23, outside St. Ignatius Loyola, the Roman Catholic church where Jackie was baptized as an infant and confirmed as a twelve-year-old, police kept thousands of onlookers at a distance while guests—including members of the Kennedy clan (with the most notable exception of 103-year-old matriarch, Rose, who watched the procession on TV from her home in Hyannis Port), Hillary Rodham Clinton, former First Lady Lady Bird Johnson, New York City mayor Rudolph Guiliani, Yoko Ono, Carly Simon, Diane Sawyer, Mike Nichols, and Jackie's sister, Lee—filed inside.

Her body was transported on a chartered 737 Boeing jet from New York City to Washington, where a motorcade of motorcycles, buses, and limousines escorted Jackie through the black iron gate of Arlington National Cemetery. There, in front of a private gathering of fewer than 100 people that included the President and Mrs. Clinton, Jackie, in a mahogany casket covered with ferns and a cross of white lilies-of-the-valley, was laid to rest between her husband Jack and her stillborn daughter. Her son Patrick, who died two days after his birth in 1963, lies on the former president's other side. "God gave her very great gifts and imposed upon her great burdens," said President Clinton during the eleven-minute ceremony. "She bore them all with dignity and grace and uncommon common sense."

As Jackie's friends and family knelt to touch the coffin one last time, filing past the eternal flame that she herself first lit three decades ago, sixty-four bells rang out from the Washington National Cathedral across the Potomac River, one for each year of her extraordinary life. Then the black limousine drove out the gates, and the crowds began slowly to scatter. "We thought it was important to be here," said Marnie Abramson, a twenty-one-year-old student at Washington's American University. "We weren't even born then. She was a mystery. But this is the end of what happened

Jacqueline Bouvier Kennedy

to them. This is the closing of an era."

JFK once observed that his socially sheltered wife "had a little too much status and not quite enough quo." How could it have been otherwise? Jacqueline Lee Bouvier was born on July 28, 1929, into solid wealth and social prominence. She had everything a girl could want: clothes and horses and huge expanses of Long Island countryside—everything but peace at home. Her hard-drinking, raven-haired stockbroker father, John "Black Jack" Bouvier III, whose fortunes wobbled on his way to being wiped out by alcohol and paramours, shamelessly indulged his daughters' every whim. Jackie's perfectionist, class-conscious mother, Janet Lee Bouvier, suffered through her sham of a marriage, not always in silence, until 1940. Then she divorced Black Jack, ending one agony but sending her two daughters (Lee was born in 1933) into a state of shock. Years later friends would remember the young Jackie wandering around a Long Island riding club in a kind of daze.

In 1942 her mother married an even richer financier, Hugh D. Auchincloss, and "Uncle Hughdie," as Jackie and Lee called their stepfather, proved to be a stern but generous stepparent. Jackie attended Miss Porter's, an exclusive Connecticut girls' school, where she excelled both socially and academically and kept her own horse. Still, she remained deeply loyal to her father and resented her mother's continual disparagement of him. Jackie could be soft one moment and sharp the next, a younger version of the woman who would charm poets and presidents, then turn on glacial heel at a gala and leave the room. "There's always been in her a kind of loneliness or sadness," said Doris Kearns Goodwin, a longtime friend and author of *The Fitzgeralds and the Kennedys.*

Jackie made the dean's list at Vassar College and, after a year of study in Paris, went on to earn a degree in French literature from George Washington University. After graduation she took a $42.50-a-week job as the Inquiring Camera Girl of the *Washington Times-Herald* and set her sights on the peripatetic congressman from Massachusetts, thirty-four-year-old Jack Kennedy. Wealthy, handsome, and going places, JFK qualified as the catch of the decade. Jackie met him at a dinner party and was immediately smitten. She courted Kennedy through her column, inviting him to be interviewed and then asking the question, "Can you give any reason why a contented bachelor would want to get married?" The answer was that Jackie was Roman Catholic, which he knew would sit well with his religious family. (As for Jackie's family, Janet, a staunch Republican snob, was uneasy with the striving Kennedy clan.)

Jack took Jackie home to Hyannis Port. Imagine a single piece of China in a shop full of bulls. Jackie was, for the most part, appalled by the boisterous and competitive Kennedys, who seemed to argue and play their not-yet-famous touch-football games nonstop. She once joked to a friend, "I don't know if I'll live long enough to marry him." But she survived the hazing. Although she never got on well with pious Rose Kennedy, she became a favorite of peppery old patriarch Joe, whose fortune came in part from liquor distribution and who liked her because he perceived her as having "class."

From the start their life together was that mix of triumph and tragedy that the Kennedys would eventually raise to a national saga. JFK won election to the Senate in 1952; two years later he underwent life-threatening spinal surgery for a chronic back condition and was bedridden for months. Jackie had suffered a miscarriage before she became pregnant again in 1956. And again tragedy struck: a daughter was stillborn after Jackie had an emergency cesarean in the seventh month. In 1957, Caroline—JFK's adored "Buttons"—was born.

Onassis (Cont.)

Jacqueline Bouvier Kennedy Onassis

By then, though, Jack had little time for his family. He was obsessed with attaining the White House—and, reportedly, with bedding a long list of women. Did Jackie know what was going on? Maxine Cheshire, who then covered the White House for the *Washington Post*, claims that she did. Recalling a British embassy party at which a European woman who was rumored to be having an affair with JFK was also a guest, Cheshire says, "Jackie was physically nervous and obviously miserable. She had her hair up, and her hairpins kept falling out. [Her Secret Service agent] Clint Hill kept picking them up." Still, notes Jackie's Washington socialite friend and author Susan Alsop, wife of the late political columnist Joseph Alsop, Jack was at heart a family man. "There was so much talk about his girls. But in a dire situation, it was Jacqueline he wanted."

Always reluctant to campaign, Jackie happily forsook stumping for Jack's successful 1960 presidential bid because she was pregnant with John Jr., who was born that November. By January, however, she was ready for a new challenge. Restoring the dowdy residence-cum-museum to a state of grace and elegance became, along with raising her children, a top priority for the century's youngest First Lady, who was a mere 31 when she moved in. Much to her husband's consternation, she spent an estimated $2 million (raised from sales of a guidebook and from donations) redoing everything from having the Blue Room painted white to replacing the china and stemware.

America, and much of the world, could never get enough of Jackie. Her look became an international obsession, starting with the famous little beige coat with the sable collar and the pillbox hat she wore to JFK's January 1961 Inauguration.

Jackie's wicked sense of humor rarely failed her. It certainly delighted JFK, even when she mocked his own Boston-Irish accent ("Foah moah yeeahs"). Old friend Ben Bradlee, later executive editor of the *Washington Post*, once said of the First Couple, "They both so rarely show any emotion, except by laughter. They are the most remote and independent people I know."

That changed dramatically in August 1963. More than seven months into yet another pregnancy, Jackie gave birth to a son, Patrick, who suffered respiratory distress syndrome, a lung complication that afflicts some premature babies. He died two days later, and when the tearful President broke the news to Jackie, she reportedly hugged him and said that the only thing that she could not bear would be to lose him too.

Of course, she did lose him, and she did bear what happened on Nov. 22, 1963. A few days later, Jackie stood on the steps of the White House, waiting to lead a funeral procession that included more than forty world leaders. A world caught up in a nerve-racking Cold War was now focused entirely on the black-clad widow and her two small children. In those hours of confusion and grief, her rectitude never wavered. Said Charles de Gaulle, who marched behind the coffin: "She gave an example to the whole world of how to behave."

She moved in September 1964 to New York City, buying, for $200,000, a fifteen-room Fifth Avenue co-op. It was just a dozen blocks from the spacious apartment the Bouviers had kept during her childhood years, and it was here that she would live out the rest of her days. "The world is pouring terrible adoration at the feet of my children," she'd once confided to her decorator Billy Baldwin, "and I fear for them, for this awful exposure. How can I bring them up normally?" To that end, she attended the children's plays and recitals, phoned the mothers of Caroline's classmates when she learned that, intimidated by the youngster's fame, they weren't inviting her to their parties, and took John and Caroline—as she would her grandchildren some thirty years later—for carousel rides in Central Park.

By 1968, Jackie's most serious suitor would turn out to be among the least likely: the short, paunchy, often rumpled Aristotle Onassis. Jackie's romance with the Greek shipping tycoon, twenty-three years her senior, appalled the Kennedy clan. Bobby, who was running for president, begged her to end the romance, and Jackie agreed to put off talk of marriage until after the election.

Any lingering doubts she might have had about marrying Onassis vanished when Bobby was assassinated on June 5, 1968, just moments after he had won the California Democratic primary. "I despise America," a distraught Jackie told a friend. "If they are killing Kennedys, my children are No. 1 targets. I want to get out of this country." She did, on Oct. 20, when, in a small private ceremony, she wed Ari on the Greek isle of Skorpios. She was 39; he was 62.

Among Jackie's few defenders was Elizabeth Taylor. "I find Ari charming, kind, and considerate," she said. "I think that Jackie made an excellent choice." Certainly, it was a well-considered one; Ted Kennedy had negotiated with Onassis a prenuptial agreement that gave Jackie $3 million in cash *before* the two wed, plus $1 million for each of her children. Still, insists her longtime friend Joan Braden, "Jackie did not marry Ari for his money. He was fun and different and felt safe, and she was always looking for protection." If anyone took the marriage lightly, it was Onassis, says Braden: "To him, she was just another bauble, whereas to us she was a great heroine."

Yet though he had a fortune estimated at $500 million to $1 billion, Onassis was enraged by Jackie's prodigious shopping. The couple's arguments over money escalated, their differences grew more apparent, and the two spent less time together.

By 1973 the two were barely speaking, and after his son Alexander died in a plane crash, the devastated Onassis sought comfort not from his wife but from opera diva Maria Callas, with whom he had already resumed his longtime affair. A year later, driven in part by his daughter Christina's hatred of Jackie, he consulted lawyer Roy Cohn about a divorce.

Death intervened, however, when on March 15, 1975, Onassis died of bronchial pneumonia at a hospital in Paris. Twice widowed by the age of 45, Jacqueline was never to marry again. "I have always lived through men," she confided to a friend after Onassis's death. "Now I realize I can't do that anymore." Instead, during her final

Onassis (Cont.)

decades, she lived for things that truly mattered to her: her work and her loved ones.

In 1975 she took a job as a book editor, first at Viking and then, in 1978, at Doubleday. Until just a few weeks before her death, she went into her small, book-crammed New York City office three days a week. Though her colleagues were initially awed by the former First Lady in their midst, she charmed them by doling out Tootsie Rolls, sitting cross-legged on her office floor to go over manuscripts, and munching on raw carrots and cucumber sandwiches at her desk. She also had a mischievous streak. "If she had someone into her office who was haughty and arrogant," says Doubleday deputy publisher Bill Barry, "Jackie was capable of doing a pretty fair imitation after the meeting."

The dozen books a year that she edited reflected her eclectic tastes—works on dance, French and Russian history, art, as well as children's books by her friend Carly Simon and bestsellers by Michael Jackson and Bill Moyers. "I learned never to second-guess what she'd be interested in," says Doubleday editor Bruce Tracy, "because she was interested in just about everything."

When Jacqueline ventured out into society in recent years, it was because *she* wanted to, attending book parties for her authors and battling to preserve New York City landmarks on behalf of the Municipal Arts Society, including the successful 1978 fight to save Grand Central Station from destruction.

More often, though, she pursued her own hobbies—yoga, jogging around the Central Park reservoir, and waterskiing, sailing, and reading during the summers at her 464-acre Martha's Vineyard estate. An accomplished equestrian, she went riding near her Bernardsville, N.J., home or in the Middleburg, Va., hunt country where she rented a cottage. She also kept John, Caroline, and Caroline's three children foremost in her thoughts, talking about them, said a friend, "with gleams in her eyes."

It was with Maurice Tempelsman that Jacqueline found her safest haven. An erudite diamond merchant whom she first met in the 1950s, Tempelsman, 64, has been steadily at her side for the past decade or so (though he is separated but not divorced from his wife, Lily), advising her on her children, on the menus for dinner parties, and on her finances, reportedly quadrupling her $26 million settlement from the Onassis estate. "It's probably the happiest relationship she's ever had in her life," a former colleague once said. "She looks to him for support and companionship. She looks to him to make decisions."

She looked to her grandchildren to add light and joy to her later years and loved to baby-sit once a week for Rose, Tatiana, and Jack. On the day she died, she and friends looked at last year's snapshots from Jackie's Labor Day picnic on Martha's Vineyard and reminisced about teaching little Jack to sing "Itsy Bitsy Spider."

In his eulogy, Ted Kennedy spoke of seeing yet another member of his family transformed into a mythic figure. "Jackie would have preferred to be just herself," he said, "but the world insisted that she be a legend too." Yet her most extraordinary accomplishment is that she managed, in the face of endless curiosity and adulation, to fashion a life of privacy and dignity for herself and her children. She looked forward to moving gracefully into old age with some good books to read and a growing brood of grandchildren to play with. The greatest sorrow, finally, is that this was denied her.

GEORGE PEPPARD

His slightly raffish good looks gave the impression of smoothness, but his resume did not. A promising movie actor in the '60s (*Breakfast at Tiffany's, The Carpetbaggers*), he had gone on to be a major TV star in the '70s and '80s (*Banacek, The A-*

Team). But George Peppard was also a hard drinker, until he gave up booze in 1978, and a hard case as a husband, taking six wives—two of them Elizabeth Ashley. "Mine isn't a string of victories," he told his friend *New York Post* columnist Cindy Adams. "It's no golden past. I'm no George Peppard fan."

Yet many others were before Peppard's forty-year career ended with his death at 65 from pneumonia at Los Angeles Medical Center. A native of Detroit, Peppard at first intended to follow his father into building construction. Instead he joined the Marines out of prep school and wound up majoring in fine arts at Carnegie-Mellon University in Pittsburgh. He eventually gravitated to Lee Strasberg's famed Actor's Studio in New York City. "He had a wonderful, ironic sense of humor," recalls fellow alumnus Rip Torn. But George Hamilton, who made two films with Peppard (1959's *Home from the Hill* and 1963's *The Victors*), remembers him as "weighted down by a sort of inner sadness I could never really fathom."

Ashley, whom he met when they were filming 1964's *The Carpetbaggers*, said in her 1978 autobiography that Peppard once attacked her with a frying pan. Peppard denied it but later admitted that when he drank, "I turned into my own worst enemy." He made others, such as when he quit his role as the Boston investigator *Banacek* after three seasons.

Peppard, by then paying alimony to three ex-wives, was rescued from ruin in 1983 when he won the role of Col. Hannibal Smith in NBC's *The A-Team*, which enjoyed a five-year run.

For all the trouble his drinking caused, Peppard sober inspired affection and trust in his friends. "If George said he would stand by you, you knew he would, no matter what," says actor Pat Hingle. "There aren't many in Hollywood you can say that about."

CESAR ROMERO

In the '40s and '50s, he was one of Hollywood's most classically handsome leading men. Yet in the role he may be best remembered for—the Joker, Batman's maniacal archenemy in the campy '60s TV series—Romero's still-fabulous face was hidden beneath a thick layer of clownish greasepaint.

Romero, who died on New Year's Day at 86 of a blood clot, didn't mind forsaking his looks for a juicy, career-reviving part. But he balked when the producers asked him to shave off his proudest feature: his mustache. Recalls *Batman* star Adam West: "It was as if he'd be losing all those wonderful movies he made [*The Gay Caballero, Captain from Castile*] when he was the dashing Latin Romeo. So the producers said, 'Okay, just dab some white makeup over it.' But if you look closely, you can see the mustache through the greasepaint."

In his heyday you could always glimpse the suave, debonair Romero (a self-described "Latin from Manhattan" whose parents were formerly-wealthy Cuban émigrés) escorting the likes of Joan Crawford, Marlene Dietrich, and Ann Sheridan. Romance, however, was never in the Joker's cards. "I have no regrets," he once said of his un-altared status.

"He was elegant and eloquent," says one old friend, actress Anne Jeffreys. "His manners, his dress were impeccable. He was," she reflects, "the last of an era."

DICK SARGENT

Few gay personalities ever emerged from the closet quite as dramatically as Dick Sargent. From 1969 to 1972, the trimly handsome actor had established himself as "the second Darrin" after replacing Dick York as Elizabeth Montgomery's husband on the ABC sitcom *Bewitched.* Realizing that revealing his homosexuality could wreck his career, he posed with buxom actresses for magazine spreads and even added a phony failed marriage to his publicity bio.

But three years ago, Sargent, who died of prostate

cancer at 64 on July 8, grew tired of pretending. Incensed by Gov. Pete Wilson's decision to veto California's gay-rights bill, Sargent declared his sexuality before a sizable Hollywood gathering on National Coming Out Day. "It was such a relief," he said afterward. "It was like a healing. Now," he joked, "I'm a retroactive role model."

Born Richard Cox in Carmel, Calif. (his mother was a former silent-film actress; his father, a World War I hero and a Hollywood publicist), Sargent made, he later admitted, "a couple of good college tries at suicide" at Stanford. He drifted into movies, then got his break in *Bewitched*, which left him financially independent.

When he learned he had cancer in 1989, Sargent stayed involved in gay-rights issues. Five days before his death, Sargent threw his annual Fourth of July bash at his house atop the Hollywood Hills. Throughout his illness, Elizabeth Montgomery was a constant visitor. "He was a great friend," she said. "I will miss his love, his sense of humor, and his courage."

Telly Savalas

TELLY SAVALAS

Telly Savalas, TV's Kojak, "took all of life's detours," says his brother Teddy. "He packed so much in, he lived more like 210 years." In fact, he died of bladder cancer on Jan. 22, one day after his seventy-second birthday.

A lollipop seemed lodged permanently in one corner of his mouth. A welter of ex-wives and children always knew where they could reach him. And, oh, yeah, he greeted everyone with a husky, "Who loves ya, baby?" But some inexplicable combination of telegenetics and testosterone made Telly Savalas a star and an improbable sex symbol. He was already 51 in 1973 when he took on the role of dapper, street-smart police detective Theo Kojak—and metamorphosed from character actor to pop-cultural icon.

"Life was so great, everything was positive with him," recalls producer Howard W. Koch, with whom Savalas owned the racehorse Telly's Pop, which won about $350,000 in purse money in the mid-'70s. Savalas's idea of a balanced life was to mix a moderate amount of wine, quite a few women (he left behind six children, ages 7 to 42, by three wives and a long-term lover), and a little song (his album *Telly* was released in 1974, followed by *Who Loves Ya, Baby?* in 1976). He was also a gambler. In 1985, playing in the World Series of Poker in Las Vegas, Telly lost $10,000 in 30 minutes—but never his composure.

Aristotle "Telly" Savalas was teaching adult-education classes in Garden City in 1959 when an agent asked if he knew an actor who could speak with a European accent. He tried out himself—and landed a part on TV's *Armstrong Circle Theater.* Soon after, Burt Lancaster saw Savalas on the CBS series *The Witness* and gave him a role in his 1961 movie *The Young Savages.* The next year, he again played opposite Lancaster in *Birdman of Alcatraz,* winning an Oscar nomination for his role as a convict who comes to share Birdman's obsession. Savalas would go on to appear in numerous other films, including *The Dirty Dozen.* Still, *Kojak* notwithstanding, the pivotal role of his career may have been Pontius Pilate in 1965's *The Greatest Story Ever Told.* Director George Stevens ordered Savalas to shave his head, thus changing the actor's destiny.

Not that he had ever had difficulty attracting women. In addition to his marriages, Savalas, starting in 1969, had a long-term relationship with British actress Sally Adams, mother of Nicollette Sheridan. Although Savalas would call Adams his wife, and the two had a son together (Nicholas, now 20 and the boyfriend of actress Tori Spelling), the lovers never wed. In 1980, Adams filed a $5 million palimony suit against Savalas, eventually settling for a reported $1 million. Four years later, Savalas wed his third and last wife, Julie Hovland, a former Minnesota travel agent.

"The challenge," he once said, "is to live long enough to raise my children." At times, other family relationships troubled him as well. Nicollette Sheridan had taken Savalas's name when the actor lived with her mother. But later she expressed bitterness toward him. "He left my life very abruptly," she said of Savalas in 1985, "and as far as I am concerned, he's out of my life for good."

Still, at his funeral, held as St. Sophia's Greek Orthodox Cathedral in L.A., Savalas was remembered as a man who had exited life on a note of high-pitched harmony. Nicollette and Nick were in attendance, as were Sally Adams and the actor's current and former wives. All things considered, Telly was, as Christina says, "a wonderful papa." But he was also, in a very real sense, Kojak, the Who-Loves-Ya-Baby man. "Telly loved people," said Father Kenzios. "He had an image to uphold, and he didn't want to let anybody down."

RICHARD SCARRY

"I love to fill my books with details that can entertain and amuse a child for a long time," Richard Scarry once said. "The more Scotch tape to hold the pages of a book together, the greater its success."

By the Scotch-tape standard, or any other, Scarry's books were hugely successful. When he died April 30 of a heart attack at 74 at a hospital near his home in Gstaad, Switzerland, more than 250 of his titles, including *What Do People Do All Day?, Best Storybook Ever,* and *Best Mother Goose Ever,* were in print in 30 languages. Seven of the 50 top-selling juvenile books of all time were his creations, and earlier this year Showtime launched an animated series called *The Busy World of Richard Scarry.*

A Boston native, Scarry was one of five children born to Barbara and John, a dry-goods store owner. Scarry studied at the Boston Museum School of Fine Arts and, after serving in World War II, began creating children's books in 1946. His breakthrough came in 1963 with the *Best Word Book Ever.*

Scarry's last books, a pop-up series, were published in 1992. "It is a precious thing to be communicating to children, helping them discover the gift of language and thought," Scarry said. "I'm happy to be doing it." His only son, Richard Jr., 40, carries on the family mission under the nom de plume of Huck Scarry.

DINAH SHORE

When Frances Rose Shore began to sing, you could almost smell the chicken fryin' in an ancient iron skillet and hear the crickets hummin' in the soft southern

Dinah Shore

night. Where did that marvelous sound come from? Well, she was a Nashville girl with a Jewish cantor for a granduncle and a black nanny who took her to gospel services on Sunday nights. Blessed with that eclectic heritage, Frances Rose grew up to be Dinah Shore, one of the most popular female vocalists of the big-band era. But it was her Emmy-winning TV career (beginning with *The Dinah Shore Show* in 1951 and followed by a half dozen more talk and variety shows during the next forty years) that indelibly displayed the beguiling homespun charm that became Shore's trademark.

When she died at her Beverly Hills home on Feb. 24, at 76, her ex-husband, actor George Montgomery, 77, their daughter Melissa Ann Hime, 46, and their adopted son, John David Montgomery, 40, were at her bedside.

Shore's spirit was lyrical. "I know I'm gushy," she once said. "I guess it's a carryover from my cheerleader days." One of two daughters of Samuel Aaron Shore, a Nashville department store owner, and his wife, Anna (who died when Frances Rose was a teenager and Bessie, her other daughter, was in her 20s), she had been a cheerleader at Hume-Fogg High School and later at Vanderbilt University. But Frances could also warble. So she headed for New York City and sang "Dinah" in her audition at a local radio station, WNEW. That got her a new name and a job singing for $5 a week with a promising young crooner, Frank Sinatra, then 22, who dubbed Shore "The Dixie Flyer" and began a lifelong friendship with her.

Shore's bluesy style quickly lifted her into the ranks of the popular singers of the day—Helen O'Connell, Margaret Whiting, Jo Stafford. In 1940 she recorded her first hit, "Yes, My Darling Daughter," and her 1942 recording of "Blues in the Night" sold a million copies.

By her own estimate, though, Shore was "not photogenic" enough for the big screen. But she was just perfect for the television, which played to her girl-next-door vitality. General Motors capitalized on Shore, and her *Dinah Shore Chevy Show* spawned the theme song heard round the land, "See the USA in Your Chevrolet."

Shore's interests widened. She took up golf because Colgate wanted her to sponsor a tournament—and the Dinah Shore Classic became a fixture on the LPGA tour. Her marriage to Montgomery, however, was not so enduring. In 1962 the couple divorced. Another marriage, to contractor Maurice Smith in 1963, lasted less than a year.

Shore never wed again—but she certainly loved once more. In the '70s, she fell hard for Burt Reynolds, nineteen years her junior, after he appeared on her show. "He was the love of her life," says her old friend Lee Minnelli, widow of director Vincente Minnelli. "When he left her for a younger woman, Sally Field [in 1976], she was devastated. But you'd never know it from her demeanor."

Putting heartbreak aside, Shore threw herself into her talk show career. She stayed fit playing tennis and golf. Then, about a year ago, according to Barbara Sinatra, Shore began complaining of stomach pains. "Even after she told us about her illness," says close friend Angie Dickinson, "she felt she would get well."

On March 1, some of Shore's inner circle held a private wake for her at their favorite eatery, Jimmy's, in Beverly Hills—on what would have been Dinah's 77th birthday. "We had a birthday cake with one candle," Dickinson recalls, "and we never blew it out. We kept her place open at the table."

★

Character actor **Claude Akins**, 67, best remembered as Sheriff Lobo on the NBC comedy-adventure series *B.J. and the Bear* and its spinoff, *Lobo* (1979-81), of stomach cancer at his Altadena, Calif., home.

Actor **Herbert Anderson**, 77, better known as owlish father Henry Mitchell on the CBS sitcom *Dennis the Menace* (1959–1963), in his sleep at his Palm Springs, Calif., home. Anderson, who began his career in 1939, also appeared in Broadway shows such as *The Caine Mutiny Court Martial* (1953) and films including *The Male Animal* (1942).

Paul Anderson, 61, once recognized as the "world's strongest man," of complications stemming from kidney failure in Vidalia, Ga.

Ezra Taft Benson, 94, the thirteenth head of the Mormon Church, of congestive heart failure. During his presidency the church grew by 2.8 million. He was secretary of agriculture under Eisenhower and a strong supporter of the John Birch Society.

Dr. Stuart Berger, 40, author of *Dr. Berger's Immune Power Diet*, from a heart attack brought on by obesity and cocaine in his Manhattan apartment.

Baron Marcel Bich, 79, who created the Bic ballpoint pen, in Paris.

Merwyn Bogue, 86, better known as Ish Kabibble, a member of the Kay Kyser band between 1931 and 1951 and a regular on 1949's *Kay Kyser's Kollege of Musical Knowledge*, of pulmonary disease at his home in Joshua Tree, Calif. During his years with the band, Bogue, who wore his hair combed forward, was introduced as "the guy with the low-cut bangs and the high-kicking cornet."

Actor **Sorrell Booke**, 64, best remembered as blustery Mayor Jefferson Davis "Boss" Hogg on *The Dukes of Hazzard*, of cancer.

Former pro golfer **Julius Boros**, 74, winner of the U.S. Open in 1952 and 1963, of a heart attack while sitting in a golf cart at his favorite spot near the 16th hole at the Coral Ridge Country Club in Fort Lauderdale, Fla.

John Bradley, 70, the last survivor among the six American service men who raised the U.S. flag on Iwo Jima in the 1945 Pulitzer Prize–winning photo, of a stroke at an Antigo, Wis., hospital. Bradley was the only Navy man in the group; the other five were Marines.

Author **Charles Bukowski**, 73, poet, novelist, screenwriter (*Barfly*) who chronicled his life as an alcoholic amid Los Angeles's underclass, of leukemia.

Actor **Pat Buttram**, 78, who played Mr. Haney on *Green Acres*, of kidney failure.

Pulitzer Prize-winning photographer **Kevin Carter**, 33, of apparent suicide in Johannesburg. Carter won this year's Pulitzer for feature photography for his haunting photo of a starving Sudanese child stalked by a vulture.

Singer **Dorothy Collins**, 67, of a heart attack at her home in Watervliet, N.Y. Collins was a star for eight years of the 1950s hit television show *Your Hit Parade.* She also appeared on *Candid Camera* between 1961 and 1963. In 1971 she was nominated for a Tony Award for her performance in Stephen Sondheim's *Follies* on Broadway.

Estimable actor **Joseph Cotten**, 88, who made his screen debut in *Citizen Kane*, of pneumonia.

Electric violinist **"Papa" John Creach**, 76, a classically trained musician who got his nickname when he performed with the '70s rock group Jefferson Airplane, of heart and respiratory complications. He also performed with the group Hot Tuna.

British actor **Peter Cushing**, 81, best known for his roles in at least twenty horror movies, including Baron Frankenstein in *The Curse of Frankenstein* (1957), of cancer, in Caterbury, England.

Gaunt character actor **Royal Dano**, 71, who often played cowboys and villains but is most remembered for playing Abe Lincoln on the CBS-TV classic *Omnibus*, of lung disease.

French photographer **Robert Doisneau**, 81, best remembered for his images of Parisian street life, in Paris after complications during heart surgery.

Anne Scripps Douglas, 47, great-great-granddaughter of James E. Scripps, founder of the *Detroit News*, of blows to the head, in her Bronxville, N.Y., home. Police believe Douglas was beaten to death by her husband Scott. His car was abandoned, with the motor running, on the Tappan Zee Bridge and his body was recovered later.

Psychoanalyst **Erik Erikson**, 91, best known for his personality-development theory, which divides life into eight stages, and coiner of the term "identity crisis," of an infection in a Harwich, Mass., nursing home.

Colombian soccer star, **Andrés Escobar**, 27, in Medellín of six gunshot wounds fired in apparent retaliation for his inadvertently scoring a goal for the United States in Colombia's June 22 World Cup match.

After fourteen years of appeals, convicted serial killer **John Wayne Gacy**, 52, was put to death by lethal injection at Stateville penitentiary in Joliet, Ill. Gacy was convicted of murdering thirty-three young men and boys during the 1970s.

Albert Goldman, 66, a former *Life* music columnist who later wrote biting, unauthorized bios of Lenny Bruce, Elvis Presley, and John Lennon, of a heart attack. He had been working on a Jim Morrison biography.

Former big-league pitcher **Harvey Haddix**, 68, of emphysema at a Springfield, Ohio, hospital. In 1959, Haddix pitched twelve innings of perfect baseball for the Pittsburgh Pirates, only to suffer a heartbreaking loss in the thirteenth when the Milwaukee Braves' Joe Adcock hit the ball out of the park.

William A. Henry III, 44, *Time* magazine's drama critic, of a heart attack while in Maidenhead, England. Henry, who won two Pulitzer Prizes as a reporter at the *Boston Globe,* joined the newsweekly in 1981. He was also the author of several books, including *The Great One*, a 1992 biography of Jackie Gleason, and *In Defense of Elitism*. Henry was a frequent contributor to PEOPLE.

Romanian-born French playwright **Eugène Ionesco**, 84, who used farce to explore themes of alienation and conformity, of an undisclosed illness at his home in Paris. Between 1950 and 1980, Ionesco wrote twenty-eight surrealistic plays, most notably *The Bald Soprano* (1950), *The Chairs* (1952), and *Rhinoceros* (1959).

Derek Jarman, 52, the British filmmaker best known for his homosexually themed movies such as *Edward II* and *Blue*, of AIDS at a London hospital.

Irving B. Kahn, 76, the cable-TV pioneer who created the TelePrompTer, of a heart attack.

Good Morning America veterinarian **Stephen Kritsick**, 42, who regularly dispensed on-air pet care advice from 1986 to 1993, of AIDS-related lymphoma, at his parent's home in Lexington, Mass.

Angela Lakeberg, 11 months, the Siamese twin who was surgically separated from her sister Amy last August, of cardio-respiratory complications at a Philadelphia hospital. Amy died during the operation.

British actor **David Langton**, 82, best known to Americans as Lord Bellamy in the *Masterpiece Theatre* series on PBS, *Upstairs, Downstairs*, of a heart attack at his home in England.

Walter Lantz, 94, creator of Woody Woodpecker, of heart disease in Los Angeles.

Christopher Lasch, 61, author of *The Culture of Narcissism*, of cancer.

William Levitt, 86, whose more than 17,000 tract houses on Long Island, N.Y., set the pattern for affordable suburban housing after World War II, of kidney failure, at a Manhasset, N.Y., hospital.

Italian actress **Giulietta Masina**, 73, the wife of Federico Fellini, of lung cancer, in Rome. Best known for playing Gelsomina in *La Strada*.

Morty, 6, the moose who appears at the opening of *Northern Exposure*, of an illness linked with cobalt and copper mineral deficiencies.

Composer and singer **Harry Nilsson**, 52, best known for "Everybody's Talking," his Grammy Award–winning theme for 1969's *Midnight Cowboy*, of a heart attack at his Agoura Hills, Calif., home.

Actor **Cameron Mitchell**, 75, who played hard-drinking Buck Cannon on the NBC series *The High Chaparral* (1967–71), of lung cancer at his Pacific Palisades, Calif., home. During his forty-year career, Mitchell appeared in more than ninety films, including *The Oxbow Incident* (1943), as well as several theater productions. In 1949 he won praise from critics for his performance as Happy in the original Broadway staging of *Death of a Salesman.* Mitchell reprised his role in the 1951 film version.

Sardonic humorist **Henry Morgan**, 79, whose barbed humor—often directed at his own sponsors—endeared him to radio audiences in the '40s and made him a popular panelist on TV's *I've Got A Secret* in the '50s and '60s, of lung cancer at his home in New York City. Though Morgan was blacklisted in the '50s, his acerbic humor continued to find an audience, and he went on to appear as a regular on NBC's *That Was the Week That Was* (1964) and *My World and Welcome to It* (1969–70).

Voluptuous **Anita Morris**, 50, who tantalized Broadway audiences in a see-through lace bodysuit in the musical *Nine* (1982), of cancer at her L.A. home.

Kentucky Rep. **William Natcher**, 84, whose 18,401 consecutive congressional votes earned him a place in the *Guinness Book of World Records*, of a heart and lung ailments in a Maryland hospital.

Allan G. Odell, 90, who created the celebrated Burma-Shave roadside signs that once dotted most of the country, of natural causes.

Thomas P. "Tip" O'Neill Jr., five-time speaker of the House and the cheerfully rumpled embodiment of old-fashioned Democratic politics, in Boston of a heart attack at the age of 81. Elected to Congress in 1952, O'Neill gained national attention in 1967 when he broke with Lyndon Johnson over Vietnam and later relished battling with Ronald Reagan. O'Neill made famous the phrase, "All politics is local."

Scientist and humanist **Linus Pauling**, 93, of prostate cancer at his home in Big Sur, Calif. Known as the champion of vitamin C, he was the only person to receive two unshared Nobel Prizes.

Teflon creator **Roy Plunkett**, 83, who helped spawn a multi-billion-dollar plastic industry when he inadvertently invented the nonstick substance more than fifty years ago, of cancer at a Corpus Christi nursing home.

British author **Dennis Potter**, 59, best known for his TV dramas *The Singing Detective* (1986) and *Pennies from Heaven* (1978), of pancreatic cancer at his home in Ross-on-Wye, England.

Dixy Lee Ray, 79, former chairwoman of the U.S. Atomic Energy Commission and governor of Washington state, of a bronchial condition.

Actor **Fernando Rey**, 76, best remembered as the smooth-talking narcotics merchant Charnier in the *The French Connection*, of cancer.

Emmy-winning filmmaker **Marlon Riggs**, 37, whose publicly funded 1989 documentary about gay black men, *Tongues Untied*, was condemned as pornography by conservative Pat Buchanan during the 1992 presidential primaries, of AIDS, in Oakland, Calif.

Actor **Gilbert Roland**, 88, best remembered for his eleven-role stint as the Cisco Kid, of prostate cancer.

Lubavitcher leader Rabbi **Menachem Mendel Schneerson**, 92, head of one of the world's largest Hasidic Jewish communities, of stroke-related complications at a New York City hospital. Schneerson, who had an estimated 250,000 followers worldwide, left no designated successor.

Top Formula One racer **Ayrton Senna**, 34, in Italy of head injuries after his race car, going 185 mph, hit a concrete wall during the San Marino Grand Prix in Imola, Italy. Qualifying for the same race the day before, **Roland Ratzenberger**, 31, died of head injuries when his car hit a concrete barrier.

Journalist and author **Randy Shilts**, 42, whose 1987 best-seller *And The Band Played On* was a scathing study of the dilatory official response to the AIDS epidemic, of complications from the disease at his Sonoma, Calif., home.

Character actor **Hal Smith**, 77, best remembered as Otis Campbell, the town drunk on *The Andy Griffith Show*, in his sleep.

Actor **Ezra Stone**, 76, remembered best for his Broadway and radio role as Henry Aldrich, in an auto accident.

Earl Strom, 66, a flamboyant, fearless referee who worked in the NBA for thirty-three years before his retirement in 1990, of a cancerous brain tumor at his Pottstown, Pa., home. Said Red Auerbach, president of the Boston Celtics: "He was the best there ever was."

Character actor **Barry Sullivan**, 81, of a respiratory ailment at his home in Sherman Oaks, Calif. His long career included roles in the original version of *The Great Gatsby* (1949), *Jeopardy* (1953), and *Tell Them Willie Boy Is Here* (1969), as well as in Steven Spielberg's TV movie *Night Gallery* (1969).

British actor **Bill Travers**, 72, best known for his role as George Adamson, the lion-loving game warden in the movie *Born Free*, in his sleep at his home in England.

Actress and performance artist **Danitra Vance**, 35, of breast cancer in Markham, Ill. In 1985, Vance became the first black woman in the cast of *Saturday Night Live*.

Pioneer gospel singer **Marion Williams**, 66, known for her swooping vocal style, of vascular complications from diabetes at a Philadelphia hospital. Williams, who had recorded ten albums, was awarded a so-called genius fellowship worth $374,000 from the MacArthur Foundation last year. She was the first singer to be so honored.

Former University of Oklahoma football coach **Bud Wilkinson**, 77, of congestive heart failure.

MARRIAGES

It was, by all accounts, a spectacularly un-Deadlike affair. For this Valentine's Day trip down the aisle with filmmaker Deborah Koons, 44, the gray-bearded guitarist **Jerry Garcia** shunned his usual T-shirt and jeans. Instead, Garcia, 51, sported a sober suit as the couple said their vows at Christ Episcopal Church in Sausalito, Calif., before about fifty friends and family members, including his five bandmates and three grown daughters from his two previous marriages.

The erstwhile hippie did go to the altar tieless (eschewing even his own line of Jerry Garcia neckware), but he reportedly bowed to Koons's wish for a traditional ceremony. "It was very Episcopal," says Garcia's friend, musician David Grisman. "It wasn't New Age at all."

For many outsiders, there was nearly as much curiosity about the bride as the wedding itself. A former educational filmmaker who just completed her first feature—a comedy titled *Poco Loco*—Koons met Garcia at a Dead show in the early '70s. After a brief fling, they reportedly separated. Their romance heated up again last year, as Garcia recovered from an illness brought on by obesity-related diabetes, the disease that caused him to lapse into a near-fatal coma in 1986. Friends say Koons, who encouraged him to diet and exercise, helped Garcia regain his health. Judging from the good vibes on Valentine's Day, she brought him some happiness as well.

★

The man who once said he had little time for *amore* because "I'm too much in love with myself" married a woman he met through his e-mail. The wedding, at the Fairfax County, Va., home of Supreme Court Justice Clarence Thomas, was a closely guarded secret. According to a press release, Justice Thomas married **Rush Limbaugh**, 43, and Marta Fitzgerald, 35, in "well under the groom's imposed time limit of fifteen minutes." Afterward the ten guests repaired to a sit-down dinner followed by "cigars and adult beverages on the deck."

According to the bride's second husband, Tom Fitzgerald of Memphis, Marta sent Limbaugh (current mailbox: 70277.2502@compuserve.com) an electronic message in 1990 asking how to stand up to a Reagan-bashing history professor at the University of North Florida, where she was a student. Limbaugh never replied. In a February newspaper interview, Fitzgerald said his former wife later wrote Limbaugh a scathing letter, calling him pompous. And evidently that was enough for the Most Dangerous Man in America, as Limbaugh has been known to call himself. He and Marta soon began exchanging e-mail messages through Compuserve, a computer network. Later he reportedly escorted Marta, who was divorced from Fitzgerald in 1992, to the '94 Super Bowl, Israel, and New Orleans. This spring, Marta moved to New York City, where Limbaugh lives in an Upper West Side Manhattan apartment.

★

Welcome folks, to the **Wayne Newton** nuptials. Precisely on cue, blindingly blond Cleveland attorney Kathleen McCrone, 30, arrived at the singer's antibellum Las Vegas mansion in a white horse-drawn carriage for the traditional ceremony. The lavishness of the event—which featured a forest of nine-foot tulip-draped topiaries and a pink-and-blue helicopter that shuttled the newlyweds to their reception at a nearby country club—made it far and away the best show in town. "When we started planning the wedding, I envisioned Kat as a reincarnation of Grace Kelly." said Newton, 52.

Newton's marital enthusiasm marks a turnaround from his glum demeanor in the wake of the dissolution of his seventeen-year marriage to flight attendant Elaine Okamura in 1985 and subsequent severe business setbacks, which led him to file for reorganization under a Chapter 11 bankruptcy in 1992. Through it all, Newton says his greatest source of support has been McCrone, a federal judge's daughter whom he met when she visited him backstage after a Vegas show in 1990.

★

Until the very last, their spokespeople swore it wasn't happening. And for a few tense minutes on the blessed day itself, it seemed, at least, as if it might not happen as planned. The bride's mother, Vanessa Redgrave, didn't show up (filming in Italy, she sent a note instead). Two minibuses full of guests got lost and arrived late—as did several individual stragglers. Actor Aidan Quinn didn't pull his gleaming black Toyota Camry up to the clapboard farmhouse in rural Millbrook, N.Y., ninety miles north of New York City, until nearly 5:30 p.m.—half an hour *after* the black-tie event was to begin. But by six, the remaining seventy-plus guests—including Mia Farrow, Lauren Bacall, and *Schindler's List* Oscar nominee Ralph Fiennes—were seated beneath the huge white tent not far from the 180-year-old barn. And a few moments later, in a forty-minute ceremony during which a priest conducted mass, a choir sang, "Morning Has Broken," and a herd of cows chewed their cud in the nearby pasture, **Natasha Richardson**, 31, of Britain's prolific Redgrave acting dynasty, and **Liam Neeson**, 42, working-class Irish kid turned Hollywood hunk and *Schindler's* star, exchanged wedding vows.

★

The bride wore cleavage. The 89-year-old groom, speaking from his wheelchair, assured the eleven people in attendance that he sure did adore his new 26-year-old wife, for whom he already had purchased $1 million worth of jewelry. Thus was **Anna Nicole Smith**, big-boned Guess jeans model, *Playboy* Playmate of the Year (1993) and actress *(Naked Gun 33⅓)*, joined in holy matrimony with fellow Texan J. Howard Marshall II, a Houston oilman believed to be worth more than $500 million.

The culmination of a courtship that began several years ago, it was the second wedding for Smith, who had married in haste back home in Mexia, Tex., when she was only seventenn. That short-lived marriage, to sixteen-year-old Billy Smith, who worked with her at Jim's Krispy Fried Chicken, produced now eight-year-old Daniel, a ring bearer at his mom's latest nuptials. This was the third time up the aisle for Marshall, who was previously married in 1931 and 1961—well before his present wife was even born. (His second wife, Bettye Bohannon, died in 1991.)

★

Actress **Rosanna Arquette**, 34, and L.A. restaurateur Jon Sidel, 32, in an outdoor wedding ceremony in Hollywood.

Actress **Drew Barrymore**, 19, and Welsh-born Los Angeles bar owner, Jeremy Thomas, 31, in a 5 a.m. ceremony at Thomas' bar after becoming engaged at 2 a.m. that same morning. The marriage lasted twenty-nine days.

Actress **Teresa Blake**, 30, who plays Gloria Chandler on the ABC soap *All My Children*, and **Mike McGuire**, 35, drummer for the country band Shenandoah.

The President's brother, **Roger Clinton**, 37, and Molly Martin, 25, eight-months-pregnant at the time, in Dallas.

After a two-year engagement, crooner **Harry Connick Jr.**, 26, and former Victoria's Secret model **Jill Goodacre**, 30, at the St. Louis Cathedral in New Orleans.

Screenwriter **Joe Eszterhas**, 49, who wrote *Sliver*, and Naomi Baka, 35, an artist. The couple have a four-month-old son, Joseph.

Beverly Hills, 90210's **Jenny Garth**, 22, and musician Dan Clark, 25, in Beverly Hills. The couple met two years ago when Garth saw

Clark perform in a Los Angeles coffeehouse.

Lightning Jack star **Cuba Gooding Jr.**, 26, and his girlfriend of seven years, Sara Kapfer, 24, a teacher's aide, in a sunset ceremony.

Grammy-winning record producer **Jim "Jam" Harris**, 35, and fashion stylist Lisa Padilla, 25, in Beverly Hills. The couple met in 1990 while filming a music video.

Singer **Johnny Hallyday**, 50, often touted as France's answer to Elvis (le Roi), remarried his third wife, Adeline Blondiau, 23, in Las Vegas, two years after their divorce.

The Wonder Years actor **Jason Hervey**, 22, and socialite Kelley O'Neill, 27, accompanied by 300 guests, twenty-three cakes, and Clarence Clemons on sax.

Pop genius **Michael Jackson**, 35, and Elvis's daughter, **Lisa Marie Presley**, 26, in La Vega, Santo Domingo.

Robert F. Kennedy Jr., 40, an environmental lawyer, and designer Mary Richardson, 34.

Actress and TV talk show host **Ricki Lake**, 25 and artist Rob Sussman, 27, in Las Vegas.

Rep. **Susan Molinari**, 36, of Staten Island, N.Y., and fellow Republican Rep. **Bill Paxon**, 40, of Amherst, N.Y., in Doylestown, Pa. It's the second marriage for Molinari, the first for Paxon.

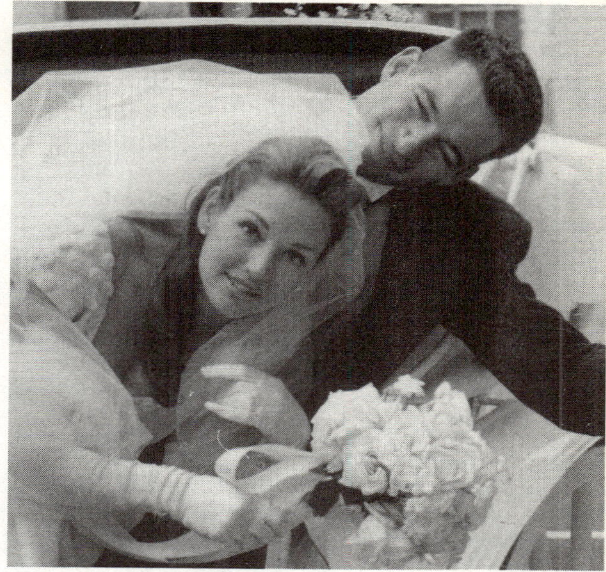

Harry Connick Jr. and Jill Goodacre.

Actor **Edward James Olmos**, 46, and actress **Lorraine Bracco** (*Medicine Man*), 39, in a private ceremony in Manhattan. It is the second marriage for both. Bracco's former husband is actor Harvey Keitel.

Dolores O'Riordan, 22, lead singer of the pop group the Cranberries, and Don Burton, 32, assistant tour manager for Duran Duran.

Actor **Lou Diamond Phillips**, 32, and New Jersey model Kelly Preston, 26, at his home in Hollywood.

Former model **Donna Rice**, 36, whose 1987 involvement with Colorado senator Gary Hart cost him his bid for the presidency, and governmental consultant Jack Hughes, 42, in Natchez, Miss.

"I dos," echoed in the White House rose garden for the first time since the 1971 nuptials of Tricia Nixon. President and Mrs. Clinton hosted the wedding of Mrs. Clinton's brother, **Tony Rodham**, 39, and Nicole Boxer, 26, daughter of California Senator Barbara Boxer.

Supermodel **Niki Taylor**, 19, and Matt Martinez, 24, a former linebacker for Arena football's Miami Hooters.

Country music's **Trisha Yearwood**, 29, and Maverick's bassist **Robert Reynolds**, 32.

PARTINGS

Singer **Paula Abdul**, 31, and actor **Emilio Estevez**, 32, after two years.

Roseanne Arnold, 41, and her second husband, **Tom Arnold**, 38, citing "irreconcilable differences," after three years.

Drew Barrymore, 19, and her husband of twenty-nine days, Jeremy Thomas, 31, an L.A. bar owner.

Not feelin' good—about his marriage, that is—the Godfather of Soul, **James Brown**, 61, and his fourth wife, Adrienne, 43.

Phil Collins, 43, and his second wife, Jill, 36, a former schoolteacher, after ten years of marriage.

Shannen Doherty, 23, and part-time rock musician Ashley Hamilton, 19, after five months of marriage.

Two-time Oscar-winning actress **Sally Field**, 47, and her second husband, Alan Greisman, 46, head of Savoy Pictures. The couple were married nine years and have one child, Samuel, 6.

Musician/composer **Billy Joel**, 44, and supermodel **Christie Brinkley**, 40, after nine years of marriage.

Don Johnson, 44, and **Melanie Griffith**, 36, after Johnson checked into the Betty Ford Center to undergo treatment for alcoholism and abuse of prescription drugs.

Robert F. Kennedy Jr., 40, an environmental lawyer, and his wife of twelve years Emily Black, 37, also an attorney.

Actor **Lorenzo Lamas**, 36, and his third wife, actress **Kathleen Kinmont**, 28, costars of the syndicated action series *Renegade.*

Actress **Diane Lane**, 29, and actor **Christopher Lambert**, 36. The couple, who married in 1988, have a daughter, Eleanor, 10 months.

Tonight Show band leader **Branford Marsalis**, 33, and his wife Teresa, a singer, married for nearly nine years.

Actor **Nick Nolte**, 53, and Rebecca Linger, 35, his third wife.

Elvis's daughter **Lisa Marie Presley**, 26, and musician Danny Keough, 30.

Burt Reynolds, 57, and **Loni Anderson**, 48, reached a surprisingly amicable divorce agreement after months of resounding recriminations.

Matthew Sorum, 33, drummer for the rock band Guns N' Roses and his wife, Kai, 25, an actress. In May, Sorum was charged with spousal battery for allegedly beating his bride of one year at their Malibu home.

Actor **William Shatner**, 62, and his wife of twenty years, actress Marcy Lafferty, 47.

BIRTHS

Model **Kim Alexis**, 34, and her husband, former National Hockey League star **Ron Duguay**, 36; their first child together, Noah Fernand.

Actress **Kirstie Alley**, 39, and husband **Parker Stevenson**, 42, adopted a baby girl, Lillie Price, their second child.

Skid Row lead singer **Sebastian Bach**, 25, and his wife, Maria, 30; their second son, London Siddhartha Halford.

Singer **Anita Baker**, 35, and her husband, real estate developer Walter Bridgeforth, 36; their second child, Edward Carlton.

Mikhail Baryshnikov, 46, and ex-ballerina Lisa Rinehart, 34; their third child together, Sofia-Luisa.

Tennis champ **Boris Becker**, 26, and his wife, model-actress Barbara Feltus, 27; their first child, a boy.

Actress **Annette Bening**, 36, and her husband, actor **Warren Beatty**, 57, their second child, a son (not named at press time).

Country singer **Garth Brooks**, 32, and wife Sandy, 28; their second child, August Anna.

Soap actress **Kimberly Brown**, 32, who played Sheila Forrester on CBS's *The Bold and the Beautiful*, and her husband Gary Pelzer, 40, manager of a boat rental company; their first baby, Alexes Marie.

Actor **LeVar Burton**, 37, and his wife Stephanie, 40, a makeup artist; their first child, Michaela Jean.

Beverly Hills, 90210 star **Gabrielle Carteris**, 32, and her husband, stockbroker Charles Isaacs, 34; their first child, daughter Kelsey Rose.

First Brother **Roger Clinton**, 37, and his bride of two months, Molly, 26, a former computer saleswoman; their first child, Tyler Cassidy.

Billy Ray Cyrus, 32, and his wife, Leticia, 27; their first son, Braison Chance.

Jan DeBoer, 41, and his wife, **Roberta**, 36, the Michigan couple who last year lost custody of their adopted daughter, whom they called Jessica, to her biological parents, Cara and Dan Schmidt, brought home an adopted newborn baby boy, Casey Mitchell.

Retired tennis champ **Chris Evert**, 39, and her husband, **Andy Mill**, 41, a former Olympic skier; their second child, Nicholas Joseph.

Actor **Judd Hirsch**, 59, and his wife, Bonni, 35, a fashion designer; their first child, Montana Eve.

Robert F. Kennedy Jr., 40, and his wife Mary Richardson, 34, an architectural designer; their first child, a son, Conor.

Donna Harris Lewis, 29, widow of Boston Celtics captain Reggie Lewis, 27; her second child, daughter Regiena Sarah. Ironically, Lewis and her husband learned of her pregnancy on July 27, the same day he died of cardiac arrest while shooting baskets in a college gym.

Actress **Virginia Madsen**, 32, and **Antonio Sabato Jr.**, 22, who played the hunky Jagger on ABC's *General Hospital;* their first child, Jack Antonio.

Rocker **John Mellencamp**, 42, and his wife, model **Elaine Irwin**, 24; their first child together, son Hud.

Michelle Pfeiffer, 36, and TV producer **David Kelley**, 38; their second child, John Henry.

Onetime *Dukes of Hazzard* star **John Schneider**, 40, and his wife, Elly, 28, a former dancer; their first baby together, a girl, Karis Lynn.

Married With Children's **Katey Sagal**, 38, and her husband, drummer **Jack White**; their first child, Sarah Grace.

Mötley Crüe bass player **Nikki Sixx**, 35, and his wife Brandi, 25; daughter Storm Brieann.

Bruce Springsteen, 44, and his wife, singer **Patti Scialfa**, 37; their third child, a son.

Princess Stephanie, 28, and boyfriend Daniel Ducruet, 28; daughter Pauline, the second out-of-wedlock child for the rambunctious princess and her former bodyguard.

While his CD *Sax by the Fire* played during the delivery, *Entertainment Tonight* cohost and musician **John Tesh**, 41, and his wife, actress **Connie Sellecca**, 38; their first child together, Prima Sellecchia (Sellecca's name was originally Sellecchia).

Wheel of Fortune's **Vanna White**, 37, and her husband, **George Santopietro**, 47, a Los Angeles restaurateur; their first child, Nicholas.

Bruce Willis, 38, and **Demi Moore**, 31; their third daughter, Tallulah Belle.

THE PEOPLE TIMELINE

A POP CULTURE TIMELINE

Here is a selective chronicle of the events and inventions, milestones and hallmarks, people and productions that have entertained us and changed life in our century.

Sarah Bernhardt in 1896.

1900

THE BROWNIE BOX CAMERA, the first consumer-oriented camera, is introduced by Eastman Kodak. It sells for $1.

PHILOSOPHER Friedrich Nietzsche dies after eleven years of madness.

THE HOT DANCE around the nation is the cake walk, invented by African Americans in the late 18th century.

STAGE ACTRESS SARAH BERNHARDT, 56, makes her film debut in *Hamlet's Duel*. She plays Hamlet.

THE GERMAN COUNT Ferdinand von Zeppelin's famous airship makes its first flight on July 20.

1901

VICTORIA, Queen of England and Ireland, and Empress of India, dies on January 22 at age 82, marking the end of the Victorian Era.

THE VICTOR Talking Machine Company is formed by Emile Berliner and Eldridge Johnson. "His Master's Voice" is the registered trademark for their gramophones, called Victrolas.

1902

BEATRIX POTTER creates the first of her legendary Peter Rabbit children's stories.

1903

THE GREAT TRAIN ROBBERY, starring Max Anderson, is released, marking the debut of the first male movie star.

THE WORLD SERIES is launched, pitting the winners of the National and the American Leagues against each other: this year, the Boston Red Stockings triumph over the Pittsburgh Pirates.

ORVILLE AND WILBUR WRIGHT fly the first powered, heavier-than-air airplane at Kitty Hawk, N.C., on December 17.

Orville Wright with his 1908 model plane.

1904

HELEN KELLER graduates with honors from Radcliffe, thanks to the years of devoted assistance of Anne Sullivan, who will go down in history as the Miracle Worker.

FREUD introduces the idea of neuroses in *The Psychopathology of Everyday Life*, his first major work of psychoanalysis.

THE TEDDY BEAR, created by the German

Richard Sterb, and inspired by President Theodore Roosevelt, who refused to kill a bear cub on a hunting trip, makes its debut.

1905

THE WORLD'S FIRST all-motion-picture theater opens in Pittsburgh. The cost is 10¢ for a showing of *Poor But Honest.*

ESSENTIAL for the development of the TV camera, Albert Einstein's theory of the photoelectric effect is published.

1906

FERDINAND "JELLY ROLL" MORTON, jazz's first great composer, writes "The King Porter Stomp."

Jelly Roll Morton, circa 1923.

THE SAN FRANCISCO EARTHQUAKE kills hundreds on April 18 and causes hundreds of millions of dollars in damage throughout the Bay Area as the city crashes and burns.

UPTON SINCLAIR publishes his meat-packing exposé, *The Jungle*, which prompts Congress to pass labor reform laws in addition to the Pure Food & Drug Act and the Meat Packing Act of 1906.

1907

FLORENZ ZIEGFELD offers his first version of the *Ziegfeld Follies*, an extravaganza that will continue for 24 years.

HENRY ADAMS'S masterful autobiography, *The Education of Henry Adams*, is published privately; the Nobel Prize for Biography will be awarded to Adams posthumously in 1919.

THE BROTHERS Auguste and Louis Lumière announce the development of a practical method of color photography.

THE FIRST MOTION PICTURE with both sound and color is shown in Cleveland.

THE RINGLING BROTHERS buy out their circus archrivals, Barnum and Bailey, although the two circuses will be operated separately until 1919.

1908

A L'ECU D'OR becomes the earliest dated pornographic film.

THE FIRST MODEL T, know as the Tin Lizzy, is produced on October 1 at Ford's Detroit plant.

G. A. SMITH'S *A Visit to the Seaside* (Britain) becomes the first commercial color film to be released.

1909

ROLLER COASTERS become increasingly popular in amusement parks all over the country.

VITAGRAPH'S *Les Misérables* becomes the first feature film produced in the U.S.

THE FIRST ANIMATED CARTOON, *Gertie the Dinosaur*, is released.

ROBERT EDWIN PEARY becomes the first person ever to reach the North Pole.

1910

AUTHOR MARK TWAIN (Samuel Longhorne Clemens) dies at 74.

THOMAS EDISON demonstrates his "kinetophone," which successfully displays talking motion pictures.

1911

JEAN, Larry Trimble's pet collie, becomes the first canine star on the big screen. Hired by Vitagraph, she earns $10 more per week than Trimble earns as an actor-writer.

1912

SEIZING ON A CRAZE that has millions of Americans doing the tango, the turkey trot, the hesitation waltz, and the one-step, Victor releases a series of recordings intended for dancing.

THE TITANIC sinks after hitting an iceberg on April 14, drowning 1,595 people.

ZANE GREY publishes his most famous Western, *Riders of the Purple Sage*.

THE FIRST BLUES SONG is published by W. C. Handy. Originally called "Memphis Blues," it becomes a hit as "Mr. Crump."

PERHAPS THE BEST all-around athlete in history, Native American track and field star Jim Thorpe dominates the Olympics, winning gold medals for both the pentathlon and the decathlon. But his medals are taken away from him when it is discovered that he played semipro baseball two years before.

Jim Thorpe in peak form.

STUNT FLYING becomes a staple across the country, taking a terrible toll of pioneering aviators.

1913

DUKE ELLINGTON writes his first song, "Soda Fountain Rag," at the age of fourteen.

BILLBOARD magazine publishes its first song-popularity chart by listing leading songs in vaudeville as well as bestselling sheet music.

1914

CHARLIE CHAPLIN creates the legendary Little Tramp in his second film, *Kid's Auto Races*.

Charlie Chaplin while filming *Kid's Auto Races.*

THE TARZAN SAGA begins with the publication of *Tarzan of the Apes* by Edgar Rice Burrroughs.

ASCAP—the American Society of Composers, Authors, and Publishers—is formed to empower artists to collect fees for the performance and use of their work.

THE PANAMA CANAL opens on May 18.

WORLD WAR I breaks out on July 28. One of the many consequences is that movie production outside of the United States will be suspended, allowing American filmmakers to dominate the industry.

1915

ALBERT EINSTEIN proposes the General Theory of Relativity.

AUDREY MUNSON reveals all as she becomes the first leading lady to appear on the screen nude in *Inspiration.*

MARGARET SANGER is jailed for writing about birth control in her book *Family Limitation*.

THE MOST FAMOUS MOVIE of the silent era, D. W. Griffith's *The Birth of a Nation* opens in New York to great success, but is bitterly criticized for its racism.

AFTER COUNTLESS "farewell" tours, the divine Sarah Bernhardt finally faces the end of her stage career when her leg is amputated at the age of 71; the next year, however, she stages what proves at last to be her final one-for-the-road, this time playing Portia in *The Merchant of Venice* with an artificial leg.

THE PROVINCETOWN PLAYERS are organized in Massachusetts and become the first to present the works of playwright Eugene O'Neill. The next year the group moves its already highly influential theater to New York where it begins the off-Broadway theater movement.

USING VACUUM tubes, AT&T introduces long-distance service between New York and San Francisco.

THE MOVIE BUSINESS moves to Hollywood, California, in search of good weather and cheap labor. By 1915, half of all American films are made there.

1916

NOTORIOUS SIBERIAN MONK Gregory Rasputin is murdered. Rasputin was a confidant and advisor to the Czarina after using his hypnotic powers to "cure" the Empress's heir, Alexis, of hemophilia.

1917

THE FIRST PULITZER PRIZES are awarded, in the categories of biography, history, and journalism. The award for drama is added the following year.

1918

PRESIDENT WOODROW WILSON proclaims his Fourteen Points for world peace; World War I comes to an end on January 18.

DAYLIGHT-SAVING TIME is introduced in America.

1919

JACK DEMPSEY, known as the Manassa Mauler, wins the world heavyweight boxing championship.

1920

MAMIE SMITH becomes the first black singer to record a vocal blues performance with "Crazy Blues."

THE NATION'S FIRST RADIO stations—KDKA, Pittsburgh and WWJ, Detroit—hit the airwaves.

1921

THE FIRST MISS AMERICA pageant is held on September 9, won by Margaret Gorman, Miss Washington, D.C.

Margaret Gorman, the first Miss America.

READER'S DIGEST begins publication.

1922

THE FIRST 3-D feature film is released when Nat Deverich creates *Power of Love*.

NANOOK OF THE NORTH by Robert J. Flaherty is released and comes to be regarded as one of the greatest documentaries ever filmed.

THE TECHNICOLOR film process makes its initial successful run.

JAMES JOYCE'S *Ulysses* is published in Paris by the expatriate American Sylvia Beach; though one of the greatest novels of the century, it remains banned in the U.S. until December 6, 1933, when a judge rules that the book does not contain "the leer of a sensualist."

1923

LEE DEFOREST devises a method of recording sound directly on film. Producers utilize the technology to create vaudeville shorts.

THE FIRST of the great Western epics, *The Covered Wagon*, is released to huge success.

TIME magazine begins publication, providing the news in an elegant, succint format.

1924

STAGE LEGENDS Alfred Lunt and Lynn Fontanne first appear together as a team in a play called *The Guardsman*.

1925

THE FIRST national spelling bee is held.

THE AGE OF THE CHARLESTON bounces into dancehalls across America.

THE NEW YORKER is founded on February 21, edited by Harold Ross. The first issue bears the image of Eustace Tilley, who will come to serve as the magazine's unofficial symbol and patriarch.

THE CLASSIC NOVEL of the Jazz Age appears with *The Great Gatsby* by F. Scott Fitzgerald.

1926

TELEVISION is invented in Scotland by John Logie Baird, but the Depression and World War II stifle development of the industry until the 1950s.

NBC RADIO is founded.

NEW YORK TALKS to London in the first successful transatlantic radiotelephone conversation.

MAE WEST writes and stars in a play called *Sex*, the performance that launches her career as the greatest sex symbol of the era and that also inspires the police to close the show and sentence West to ten days in a workhouse.

Janet Gaynor in *Seventh Heaven*, one of the films that won her the first Best Actress Academy Award.

THE BOOK-OF-THE-MONTH-CLUB is founded, the first of the mail-order book programs. The first offering is Sylvia Townsend Warner's novel, *Lolly Willowes*.

MINIATURE GOLF is introduced in Lookout Mountain, Tennessee, and from there it expands to over 40,000 courses within three years.

THE SUN ALSO RISES, the classic novel of disillusionment in the postwar years, is written by Ernest Hemingway.

1927

THE FIRST ACADEMY AWARDS are presented at the Hollywood Roosevelt Hotel in Los Angeles, May 16. Douglas Fairbanks Sr. presents all of the awards in five minutes. The first winner for Best Picture is the now-forgotten Clara Bow vehicle, *Wings*.

THE AGE OF THE TALKIES arrives with the Warner Bros. release of the wildly successful film *The Jazz Singer*, starring Al Jolson.

THE FIRST CAR RADIOS are introduced.

CHARLES LINDBERGH makes the first nonstop solo flight across the Atlantic, from New York to Paris.

1928

TELEVISION comes to a home in Schenectady, N.Y., and begins receiving regularly scheduled broadcasts, three afternoons a week, on its 1½-inch-square screen.

WOMEN COMPETE in the Olympics (in Amsterdam) for the first time.

AMELIA EARHART becomes the first woman to fly across the Atlantic Ocean when she lands in London.

MICKEY MOUSE debuts in Walt Disney's first cartoon, *Plane Crazy*. The public however, meets him first in *Steamboat Willie*, which is released before its progenitor.

Mickey Mouse in *Steamboat Willie.*

1929

THE STOCK MARKET crashes on October 24, Black Thursday, abruptly beginning the transition from the Roaring Twenties to the Great Depression.

KODAK introduces 16mm color movie film.

1930

SINCLAIR LEWIS becomes the first American to win the Nobel Prize for Literature.

THE FIRST SUPERMARKET opens in Queens, N.Y., offering low prices, huge selection, and achieving tremendous success overnight.

THE HAYS OFFICE creates a production code to enforce self-censorship in the film business.

GARBO TALKS, in Eugene O'Neill's *Anna Christie*, her first speaking role.

1931

THE WORLD'S TALLEST building, the Empire State Building, is opened to the public. RCA and NBC install a TV transmitter atop the building.

AL "SCARFACE" CAPONE, all-time great American gangster, goes to jail for tax evasion.

SCRABBLE is invented by New York architect Alfred Butts, but the game is turned down by every game manufacturer; not until 1948 is the game widely distributed, and not until 1952 does word of mouth turn it into a bonanza.

1932

THE LINDBERGH BABY is kidnapped on May 1, only to be discovered dead twelve days later, after the parents pay a $50,000 ransom.

OF THEE I SING, a musical comedy written by George and Ira Gershwin with book by George S. Kaufman and Morrie Ryskind, becomes the first musical to win a Pulitzer Prize.

BIG TIME VAUDEVILLE begins its final fade-out as the last two-a-day show opens at the Palace on Broadway.

1933

ECSTASY, in which Hedy Lamarr appears nude, becomes the first film in which a sexual experience is depicted.

FRANCES PERKINS becomes the first woman to hold a Cabinet post when she is appointed as secretary of labor by Franklin Delano Roosevelt.

THE FIRST DRIVE-IN cinema is built in Camden, N.J., accommodating 400 cars, and opens with *Wife Beware*.

PRESIDENT ROOSEVELT holds the first Fireside Chat on March 12, a radio address to the entire nation.

PROHIBITION is repealed with the ratification of the Twenty-First Amendment on December 5. The watering holes that soon cover the country—bars, saloons, cocktail lounges—have a new feature, the jukebox.

THE FIRST NATIONAL FOOTBALL LEAGUE championship playoff pits the Chicago Bears against the New York Giants on December 17. The Bears win, 23–21.

1934

JOHN DILLINGER, Public Enemy No. 1, is gunned down in Chicago by FBI agents.

1935

IN AN ATTEMPT to assist an ailing theater community hit badly by the Depression, the Federal Theatre Project is instituted by Congress as part of the Works Progress Administration. It is disbanded in 1939.

BECKY SHARP, the first full-length color feature film, opens.

THE FIRST NIGHT baseball game in the major leagues is played between the Cincinnati Reds and the Philadelphia Phillies. Cincinnati wins, 2–1.

GEORGE AND DOROTHY GERSHWIN'S opera *Porgy and Bess* opens.

1936

MARGARET MITCHELL'S *Gone with the Wind* is published, selling a million copies in six months and winning the Pulitzer Prize in 1937. It will be her only book.

FDR is reelected president in the greatest Democratic landslide ever, carrying 48 states.

EUGENE O'NEILL, the great American dramatist, is awarded the Nobel Prize for Literature.

1937

VENTRILOQUIST EDGAR BERGEN and Charlie McCarthy premiere on NBC. They will remain hugely popular with audiences when the show makes the move from radio to TV.

JOHN STEINBECK'S *Of Mice and Men* is published.

THE FIRST worldwide radio broadcast to be received in the U.S. brings us the coronation of King George VI of England on May 12.

1938

WALT DISNEY'S *Snow White and the Seven Dwarfs* tops the movie charts, making Disney internationally famous, and goes on to become an all-time classic.

OUR TOWN, by Thornton Wilder, is produced (and not in a high school theater). It wins a Pulitzer.

THE DIRIGIBLE *Hindenburg* bursts into flames as it lands in New Jersey May 6, marking the virtual end of lighter-than-air transportation. Simultaneously, the first coast-to-coast radio broadcast is conducted by Herbert Morrison, who reports on the disaster.

THE RADIO PLAY *War of the Worlds* (based on the novel by H.G. Wells) is broadcast on October 30 by Orson Welles, causing widespread panic among listeners who believe its story of an invasion from Mars.

1939

THE FIRST GOLDFISH is swallowed by a Harvard undergrad, beginning a fad that quickly sweeps across the nation and sets off such variations on the theme as eating light bulbs and biting snakes' heads off.

THE GOLDEN GATE Exposition in San Francisco and the World's Fair in New York open, respectively, on February 18 and April 30.

LOU NOVA squares off against Max Baer in the first televised prizefight, direct from Yankee Stadium. Nova wins in eleven rounds.

RHETT BUTLER'S infamous observation in the film version of *Gone with the Wind*, "Frankly, my dear, I don't give a damn," breaks the taboo against cursing in the movies.

AT THE NEW YORK WORLD'S FAIR thousands ogle RCA TV sets featuring a 12-inch screen reflected in a cabinet-lid mirror.

1940

RICHARD WRIGHT'S masterpiece, *Native Son*, is published to wide acclaim; it is later adapted for a successful Broadway run.

A WORKABLE COLOR TV is announced by Peter Goldmark, chief television engineer at CBS.

CONGRESS passes the Selective Service Act, the first U.S. peacetime draft law ever.

1941

THE FIRST TV AD comes on the air, marking the advent of commercial television; the spot, for Bulova watches, lasts ten seconds and costs the company $9.

A DATE that will live in infamy: Japan bombs Pearl Harbor on December 7, bringing the U.S. into World War II.

1942

RODGERS AND HAMMERSTEIN tranform the musical comedy with their production of *Oklahoma!*

BING CROSBY releases "White Christmas," from the film *Holiday Inn*, and it becomes the biggest-selling song from a movie in history.

1943

GEORGE WASHINGTON CARVER, 81, dies in Tuskegee Alabama. Born into slavery, he developed inventive uses for peanuts, soybeans, and other traditional Southern crops, which proved to be a boon to agriculture in the region.

1944

PAPER SHORTAGES during World War II force the publishing business to experiment with softcover bindings for its books, with stunning success.

1945

SMELL-O-VISION is created by Swiss inventor Hans E. Laube, who develops a "smell pack" that is stimulated by TV waves to produce an odor to accompany what is being shown on the screen.

WORLD WAR II comes to an end. Germany surrenders on May 8 (V-E Day). The first atomic bombs ever to be used in war are dropped by the U.S. on Hiroshima on August 6 and Nagasaki three days later, leading to the surrender of Japan on August 15 (V-J Day).

1946

WINSTON CHURCHILL coins the term "iron curtain" in a speech at Westminster College in Missouri.

THE U.S. detonates a nuclear bomb on Bikini Atoll on July 5 in the South Pacific. Five days later, designer Louis Reard commemorates the blast at a fashion show in Paris, where a certain itsy-bitsy, teeny-weeny two-piece bathing suit makes its first appearance.

THE CANNES FILM FESTIVAL premieres in September.

THE FIRST TV SOAP OPERA, *Faraway Hill*, debuts on the DuMont network.

CONSUMERS RUSH to buy the new 10-inch RCA TV set for $375. This "Model T of television" ushers in the TV age.

1947

THE POLAROID Land camera is patented by Dr. Edwin Land, providing prints that develop inside the camera within a minute. It enters the market the following year, selling for $90.

JACKIE ROBINSON becomes the first African American to sign with a major league baseball team. His first game with the Brooklyn Dodgers is an exhibition game against the New York Yankees.

Jackie Robinson, six weeks before his first game as a Brooklyn Dodger.

NBC'S *KRAFT TELEVISION* *Theatre* introduces serious drama. Overnight, cheese sales soar and Madison Avenue melts.

ACCORDING TO one source, the first flying saucer sighting is reported on June 25.

APPROXIMATELY four million baseball fans catch the World Series on TV for the first time as the New York Yankees and the Brooklyn Dodgers battle it out. The Yanks go on to win the series.

THE FIRST ANTOINETTE PERRY (TONY) Awards for excellence in the theater are handed out. No best play award is included, but José Ferrer wins as best actor, and best actress awards go to Ingrid Bergman and Helen Hayes.

THE TRANSISTOR is invented by Bell Telephone Laboratories; it becomes one of the most significant advances in the history of consumer electronics, paving the way for the miniaturization of TV sets, radios, and gear like CD players that haven't yet been invented.

1948

TED MACK'S ORIGINAL AMATEUR HOUR premieres in January. By year's end, the first "ratings sweep" declares it the most popular show on TV.

COMPANIES try to corner the phonograph recording market with improvements on the old 78 rpm disks. Columbia introduces the first long-playing commercial record, the 33⅓ rpm disk, and RCA releases the 45.

LEE STRASBERG takes over the Actor's Studio, introducing the Method acting techniques that will profoundly influence such students as Marlon Brando, Paul Newman, James Dean, and Marilyn Monroe.

THE MOTORCYCLE CLAN Hell's Angels is formed.

THE ED SULLIVAN SHOW premieres to an initially poor viewer response. The influential variety program will stay on the air until 1971.

THE TERM "COLD WAR" is popularized by a speech before the Senate War Investigation Committee.

TV SET SALES skyrocket with an estimated 250,000 sets installed every month.

NORMAN MAILER'S first novel, *The Naked and the Dead*, comes out. It remains one of the most important fictional works about World War II.

1949

CHIC YOUNG'S "Blondie" is the most popular comic strip in the world.

THE FIRST CABLE television systems go into homes.

ARTHUR MILLER'S play *Death of a Salesman*, the first dramatic tragedy to feature a common man as a protagonist, wins a Pulitzer Prize.

UNERRING CRUSADER RABBIT debuts as the first made-for-TV animated cartoon.

Ed Sullivan (center), with guest Jackie Gleason and co-producer Marlo Lewis in 1949.

1950

MCCARTHYISM begins in February when the obscure U.S. Senator Joseph McCarthy alleges that the federal goverment is infested with Communists.

Joseph McCarthy in 1954.

GOOD 'OL CHARLIE BROWN enters American culture as Charles Schulz creates the legendary comic strip "Peanuts."

TELEVISION takes its first late-night variety plunge with *Broadway Open House*, and "dumb blonde" Dagmar (Jennie Lewis) becomes the first boob-tube sex symbol.

THE FIRST AMERICAN TROOPS land in Korea on July 1 after soldiers from North Korea invade South Korea. Although the move is described as a United Nations' action, American soldiers comprise the vast majority of foreign troops. With news footage being aired on American TVs, it is also the first living-room war.

HOLLYWOOD'S first million-dollar property deal: Columbia acquires the rights to the successful Broadway play *Born Yesterday* from the writer Garson Kanin.

A. C. NIELSEN begins gathering ratings data for TV, employing electronic viewing records along with written logs to determine the popularity of shows.

BELL LABORATORIES and Western Electric create the first telephone answering machine.

THE SITCOM laugh track is introduced on *The Hank McCune Show*, a program that also has the added distinction of being canceled midseason.

THE FIRST CREDIT CARD is introduced through the Diners Club.

THE CISCO KID, starring Duncan Renaldo and Leo Carillo, is the first TV series filmed in color. At the time, there are fewer than 100 experimental color sets in the U.S.

THE 1949 NOBEL PRIZE for Literature is retroactively awarded to William Faulkner. No prize was awarded the previous year because none of the candidates had won a majority of the votes.

1951

PAY-PER-VIEW dies a premature death after Zenith begins testing its "Phonevision" in Chicago. Viewers can dial a phone number and watch a recent feature film for $1. But skittish movie studios decide not to make first-run films available, fearing the consequences.

SENATE HEARINGS on organized crime rivet the nation. Mobster Frank Costello allows only his hands to be shown.

UNIVAC I, the first commercially built computer, goes into operation at the Census Bureau in Philadelphia.

CBS broadcasts the first commercial color telecast on June 25 with a one hour special from New York to four other cities.

NBC begins the first network coast-to-coast programming.

AMOS 'N' ANDY bows with TV's first all-black cast. Though canceled in 1953, reruns air until 1966, when protests about racial stereotyping force withdrawal of the show from syndication.

I LOVE LUCY debuts to tremendous success, creating the mold for TV sitcoms.

CLEVELAND DJ Alan Freed, the first to introduce black R&B to a white audience on station WJW, coins the term "rock 'n' roll."

CBS debuts its "unblinking eye," which evolves into TV's most famous logo.

GIAN CARLO MENOTTI'S *Amahl and the Night Visitors* becomes the first made-for-TV opera on Christmas Eve. It becomes a perennial seasonal favorite.

1952

THE REVISED STANDARD edition of the Old Testament, only the third authorized Protestant revision in 341 years, becomes a No. 1 bestseller on February 15 and sets records by selling 1.6 million copies in eight weeks; the old record was held by *Gone with the Wind*, which sold 1 million books in six months.

THE MOUSETRAP, originally a play created by Agatha Christie for the eightieth birthday of Britain's Queen Mary, premieres in London. It will become the single longest-running theatrical work of all time.

***MAD* MAGAZINE** and the *National Enquirer* make their debuts.

AMERICAN BANDSTAND comes to ABC.

UNIDENTIFIED FLYING OBJECTS capture the imagination of Americans. No longer looked on as simply science fiction, the national fascination with U.F.O.s even prompted the U.S. Air Force to publish possible photographs of the phenomena.

THE FIRST HYDROGEN BOMB is detonated on November 1, and Americans' fear of complete annihilation intensifies.

IN AN ATTEMPT to combat the appeal of "free" TV, Hollywood introduces 3-D film in the form of *Bwana Devil*. While not a new development, 3-D gains great popularity for several years in the early 1950s.

PANTY RAIDS occur in epic proportions at college sororities across the nation.

TWO OF TELEVISION'S biggest all-time hits—the *Today* show, hosted by Dave Garoway, and *Guiding Light*—begin broadcasting on NBC and CBS, respectively; both programs are still going strong today.

THE MARILYN MONROE image crystallizes with four film releases, helping movie theaters draw Americans away from their TV sets.

ART LINKLETTER tosses a *House Party* on September 1, and the bash lasts longer (seventeen years) than any daytime variety show. People *are* funny.

VEEP HOPEFUL Richard Nixon makes a politician's first direct TV appeal on September 23, citing his dog, Checkers, in his successful quest to beat fund-misuse charges and save his career.

CHRISTINE JORGENSON returns from Denmark where she had undergone the first publicized sex-change operation.

1953

I LOVE LUCY features the birth of Little Ricky on January 19 as the real Lucille Ball gives birth to Desi Arnaz Jr. The landmark show draws a record ninety-two percent share of TV sets in use, or forty-four million viewers—a record to date. Turns out the "dual birth" was no happy accident, since Desi junior was born by a scheduled caesarean section. The event received more media attention than Dwight Eisenhower's inauguration, which took place the following day. Eisenhower and Nixon form the first Republican administration in twenty-four years.

DESI JR. scores again when the first issue of *TV Guide* is published, featuring him on the cover.

AT AGE 27, Queen Elizabeth II is crowned as England's monarch.

JULIUS AND ETHEL ROSENBERG are executed, the only American civilians ever to receive such a penalty for espionage.

THE DISC JOCKEY Top forty radio format is established on KOWH, an Omaha station, featuring a limited number of records played over and over, hourly news breaks, and sporadic chatter from the announcer.

CINEMASCOPE premieres with *The Robe* and its widescreen format becomes a huge hit with filmgoers.

***PLAYBOY* MAGAZINE** is founded by twenty-seven-year-old Hugh Hefner with a first issue featuring the nude Marilyn Monroe on its cover.

THE FIRST ROCK AND ROLL song hits the Billboard charts: Bill Haley and His Comets' "Crazy, Man, Crazy."

THE RCA compatible color television is approved by the FCC and becomes the industry standard.

HOUSTON'S KUHT debuts as the country's first noncommercial educational TV station; within ten years there will be seventy-five other such stations.

Marilyn Monroe and Joe DiMaggio on their wedding day.

1954

MARILYN MONROE marries former New York Yankees star Joe DiMaggio, a second marriage for both. Alas, the match is not meant to be—Marilyn files for divorce nine months later.

TELEVISION JOURNALIST Edward R. Murrow launches the first major attack on Joseph McCarthy's witch-hunt tactics on CBS's *See It Now*, inspiring a groundswell of support for the senator's critics and ultimately precipitating his downfall.

SEGREGATION in schools is declared unconstitutional on May 14 in the landmark case *Brown vs. Board of Education.*

ELVIS PRESLEY cuts his first record, the double-sided 45 "That's All Right (Mama)"/"Blue Moon of Kentucky."

THE FIRST COLOR TV sets and the first transistor radios are marketed.

***TONIGHT!*,** later known as *The Tonight Show*, premieres with Steve Allen as host.

SWANSON brings out the very first TV dinners—ominously, turkey—for sixty-nine cents.

The original Swanson turkey TV dinner.

1955

CONTRALTO MARIAN ANDERSON becomes the first African American to sing a major role at the Metropolitan Opera, appearing as Ulrica in Verdi's *Masked Ball.*

A NEW ERA in domestic politics is launched with the first filmed presidential press conference. Both TV and motion picture newsreel photographers cover the event.

WALT DISNEY'S TV show, *Disneyland*, first appears on ABC and quickly becomes one of the most successful programs on the tube. One segment, "Davey Crockett, Indian Fighter," instigates a full-blooded Davey Crockett mania, which sweeps the country. Over 3,000 Crockett-related items sell in crazy numbers, from coonskin caps to Bill Hayes's song "Ballad of Davey Crockett," which rises to the top of the charts.

ANN LANDERS launches her advice column in the *Chicago Sun-Times.*

BILL HALEY and His Comets' "Rock Around the Clock" goes to No. 1 on *Billboard*'s charts on June 6, marking the undisputable ascent of rock 'n' roll.

DISNEYLAND, the first theme amusement park, opens south of Los Angeles in Anaheim.

JAMES DEAN stars in *Rebel Without a Cause*, his second and penultimate starring role before crashing his Porsche later in the year, and dying at age 26. His death gives rise to his enduring status as a cult hero, embodying the spirit of rebelliousness so sought after by America's younger generation.

BOB KEESHAN debuts as the Captain on *Captain Kangaroo*, which goes on to become the longest-running kids' show. *The Mickey Mouse Club* begins as well.

IN ONE OF THE greatest record deals of all time, RCA buys Elvis's contract—for an unprecedented $40,000—from Sam Phillips's Sun Records.

COMIC BOOK popularity reaches unprecedented heights, with sales soaring beyond a billion. Concern over their violent content increases in due measure, prompting New York State to ban the sale of certain graphic comics to minors.

"Uncle Walt" surveys Disneyland's progress.

1956

ACTRESS GRACE KELLY retires from Hollywood and marries Prince Rainier III of Monaco, a member of the thousand-year-old Grimaldi dynasty, in one of the most publicized marriages of the century.

Grace Kelly marrying Prince Rainier.

BEAT POET ALAN GINSBERG'S *"Howl" and Other Poems* is released and its publisher is promptly brought up on obscenity charges that are later successfully defended in court.

MARILYN MONROE weds husband No. 3, Pulitzer- and Tony award–winning playwright Arthur Miller (it's his second marriage). The two are divorced in 1961.

DEAN MARTIN and Jerry Lewis are a team no more. They divorce on July 25, exactly ten years after they first appeared together in Atlantic City.

NBC'S Huntley and Brinkley are TV's first co-anchors: "Goodnight, Chet." "Goodnight, David."

IN HIS FIRST YEAR of stardom, Elvis releases "Don't Be Cruel"/"Hound Dog," a double-sided 45 that still stands as the biggest hit of all time on *Billboard*'s charts. His appearance on Ed Sullivan's *Toast of the Town* on September 9, shot discreetly above the pelvis, earns the highest rating for any regularly scheduled program, drawing an estimated audience of 50 million people. He also appears in his first movie this year, *Love Me Tender*.

1957

LEONARD BERNSTEIN is named the first American musical director of the New York Philharmonic.

BOBBY FISCHER, 14, wins the U.S. chess championship.

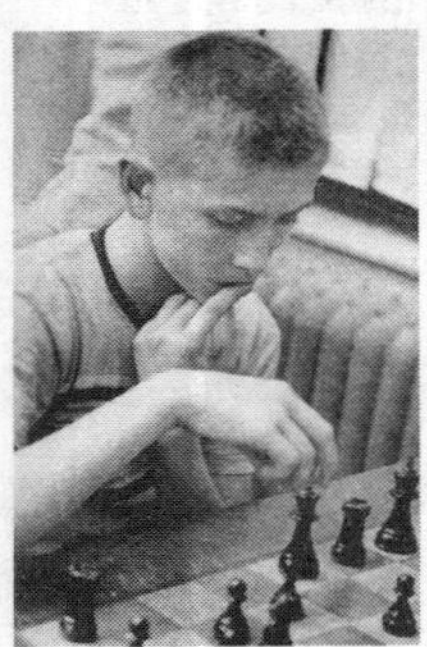

Bobby Fischer.

THE HULA HOOP is introduced and takes America by storm, selling over 45 million by 1958.

DICK CLARK'S *American Bandstand* moves from a local Philadelphia station to its national debut. It becomes the longest-running variety show in TV history.

THE SOVIET UNION launches *Sputnik*, setting off the space race.

LEAVE IT TO BEAVER debuts on CBS, presenting the audience with the most typically American family to date.

THE *NAT "KING" COLE SHOW*, the first major series with an African-American host, is canceled after a year, for lack of a national sponsor.

1958

VLADIMIR NABOKOV'S sensational novel *Lolita* is published by Putnam after being rejected as too obscene by four other American publishers.

DJS AT ST. LOUIS'S KWK radio station complete their "Record Breaking Week" when, at the insistence of the management, "undesirable" records are given a final play on the airwaves and then ceremoniously destroyed. Most of the sacrificed recordings are of rock 'n' roll music.

SCIENTISTS at the ESSO Gas Research Center—now EXXON—announce on July 28 that they have found that drivers waste gas when they listen to rock 'n' roll because they tend to jiggle the pedals in time with the beat.

VAN CLIBURN becomes the first American to win a gold medal at the Tchaikovsky International Piano Festival. His subsequent recording of the composer's *Piano Concerto No. 1* is the first classical record to go gold.

THE BROOKLYN DODGERS and the New York Giants move to California, bringing Major League Baseball to the West Coast.

THE GRAMMY AWARDS are launched. Ignoring the rising predominance of rock 'n' roll, the organizers present best album of the year to Henry Mancini and name "Volare" by Domenico Modugno as best song.

QUIZ SHOW scandals erupt with an initial investigation of answer-feeding on a program called *Dotto* prompted by a complaint by contestant Eddie Hilgemeier. By the end of the year most quiz shows are pulled off the air.

1959

BARBIE is introduced to the toy world, created by Ruth and Elliot Handler, who founded Mattel in 1945. The doll's proportions, if copied on a human scale, would be 33-18-28.

The original Barbie doll.

Barbie was named for the Handlers' daughter, Barbara, just as their son, Ken, was later honored when his parents created a male companion doll.

ISLAND IN THE SUN, starring James Mason, Dorothy Dandridge, Harry Belafonte, and Joan Fontaine, becomes the first film to portray interracial romance.

THE U.S. POSTMASTER GENERAL bans *Lady Chatterly's Lover* by D. H. Lawrence, but sales skyrocket after courts hold that the book is not obscene.

AMERICANS SEE THE WORLD from a new perspective as Explorer VI sends down the first photograph of Earth taken from outer space.

THE TELEPHONE BOOTH-JAMMING fad hits this year and fades almost as quickly. The fad first catches hold on the West Coast and moves quickly across the country, the record being set with thirty-two squashed students at Modesto Junior College in California.

MOTOWN RECORDS is founded in Detroit by songwriter Berry Gordy Jr.

IS TELEVISION KING? In December, for the first time, TV rings up more in commercial sales ($1.24 billion) than Hollywood cashes in box-office receipts ($1.235 billion).

1960

ELVIS PRESLEY'S army career, which began in March of 1958, comes to a close.

A CONGRESSIONAL investigation into payola determines that radio DJs have been receiving payments from record companies to play their disks. Dick Clark and Alan Freed are the particular focus of allegations, and Freed eventually loses his job.

THE FIRST feature "smellie," Michael Todd Jr.'s *A Scent of Mystery,* made with Smell-O-Vision, is released to general indifference.

SHOT IN about a month, Alfred Hitchcock's *Psycho* sets new movie attendance records and earns a mint as one of the most frightening films ever made.

THE TWIST is introduced by nineteen-year-old Chubby Checker.

BEN-HUR collects a record eleven Oscars out of twelve nominations.

Chubby Checker, doing the twist in 1961.

THE FANTASTICKS debuts May 3. It will become the longest-running off-Broadway show ever, hitting its 14,000th performance on March 2, 1994—and still going strong at the Sullivan Street Playhouse in Greenwich Village. Since its beginning, notable performers have included Kevin Kline, Richard Chamberlain, and Jerry Orbach.

THE FLINTSTONES debuts as prime time's first animated sitcom.

THE FDA sanctions the widespread use of birth control pills as it approves the public sale of Enovid at $10 to $11 for a month's supply.

1961

THE FIRST FRENCH KISS on the Hollywood big screen takes place between Natalie Wood and Warren Beatty in *Splendor in the Grass.*

BOB DYLAN gives his first solo performance, opening for blues musician John Lee Hooker in New York City's Gerde's Folk City.

ABC'S WIDE WORLD OF SPORTS with Jim McKay is introduced and runs on Saturday afternoons, showing us "the thrill of victory and the agony of defeat."

ALAN B. SHEPARD JR. becomes the first American astronaut to go into space on May 5.

SATURDAY NIGHT AT THE MOVIES debuts as the first regular TV showcase for major motion pictures.

1962

JACQUELINE KENNEDY takes the country on a televised tour of the White House.

THE FIRST USE OF NUDITY in advertising appears in *Harper's Bazaar* in a bare-breasted photo by Richard Avedon.

THE FIRST JAMES BOND movie, *Dr. No*, is released starring Sean Connery, 32.

DIRECT-DIAL long-distance telephone service begins in the U.S.

MARILYN MONROE dies of a barbituate overdose at age 36 on August 5.

LEE J. COBB is a frontier judge in *The Virginian*, the first ninety-minute TV series. In a nine-year run, its cast includes Lee Majors and David Hartman.

JOHNNY CARSON takes over *The Tonight Show* where he will reign as King of Television until he retires in 1992.

1963

WEIGHT WATCHERS enters the market, turning dieting into big business.

BETTY FRIEDAN publishes her landmark feminist tract, *The Feminine Mystique*.

FOLKSY, unflappable Julia Child bubbles up on *The French Chef* and becomes public TV's first star; she'll keep TV cooking for the next ten years.

THE BEATLES release their first single in the U.S., "Please Please Me," in February along with their LP *Introducing the Beatles*.

CLEOPATRA, with Elizabeth Taylor and Richard Burton, scores as both the top money-maker of the year and one of the biggest flops in all movie history as its vast costs far overrun its huge budget; Taylor alone receives $1,750,000 for her participation.

PEBBLES FLINTSTONE is born to parents Wilma and Fred on February 22 at the Bedrock Rockapedia Hospital.

TROLLS are introduced. Billed as good luck charms, their ugliness is a charm indeed, producing sales in the millions.

THE FUGITIVE debuts September 17; David Janssen runs. He'll catch the one-armed man—and a then-record prime-time audience—in the '67 finale. That episode still ranks as the third most-watched episode of a television series ever.

PRESIDENT JOHN F. KENNEDY, 46, is assassinated in Dallas on November 22. The immediacy of television's coverage of the surrounding events transforms TV into a witness to history and binds together a nation in mourning.

1964

FIVE THOUSAND SCREAMING FANS greet the Beatles at Kennedy Airport in New York on February 7, when the band arrives for its first American tour. Two days later the Fab Four appear on *The Ed Sullivan Show*. They draw an estimated seventy-five percent of all TV viewers, making it the most-watched hour of television to date. Songs include "All My Loving," "She Loves You," and "I Want To Hold Your Hand."

THE MOOG, the first commercial music synthesizer, is developed.

ELIZABETH TAYLOR finally meets her match, again, as she marries husband No. 5, Richard Burton, just ten days after getting a divorce from Eddie Fisher. The two had met on the set of *Cleopatra*.

THE FIRST home video recorder is invented in Japan by the Sony Corporation.

IN HIS BOOK *Understanding Media*, Marshall McLuhan declares that the

The Beatles begin their first American tour.

"medium is the message." Nobody gets it, but everybody talks about it.

LYNDON B. JOHNSON'S "daisy" campaign spot airs once on September 7, suggesting that Republican opponent Barry Goldwater is nuke-happy. Fallout: LBJ wins in a landslide.

PEYTON PLACE airs September 15 as the first prime-time soap and becomes a smash hit.

G.I. JOE is introduced by Hasbro and sells for $4.

MARTIN LUTHER KING JR. receives the Nobel Peace Prize. Jean-Paul Sartre is awarded the Nobel Prize for Literature and becomes the first person to reject the honor.

1965

SOUPY SALES asks his loyal young viewers to send him "those little green pieces of paper" from dad's wallet, "and I'll send *you* a postcard from Puerto Rico." The January 1 stunt draws a big enough response to get Sales suspended by the station, but viewers protest and he is reinstated.

BELLBOTTOMS grace the nation's hips, and lava lamps make a splash, selling 2.5 million units this year alone.

THE FIRST AMERICAN COMBAT TROOPS not deployed in an advisory capacity land in South Vietnam, turning a local conflict into an undeclared large-scale international war.

THE NATIONAL ENDOWMENT for the Arts and Humanities is established by Congress.

"(I CAN'T GET NO) SATISFACTION," the classic Rolling Stones tune, becomes a number one hit in the U.S., sealing the British invasion as one of the dominant musical developments of the decade.

THE BEATLES play before 55,000 fans at New York's Shea Stadium August 15 to open their third U.S. tour.

THE SOUND OF MUSIC is released, eventually overtaking *Gone with the Wind* to rank for a time as the top box-office earner ever.

GO-GO DANCING and its accompanying little white boots quickly wax and then wane in popularity among disco goers.

CINEMA'S thirty-four-year rule against nudity is broken when a scene in *The Pawnbroker* is approved by the ratings board as essential to the plot.

CBS AND NBC adopt virtually all-color formats starting with the fall season.

BILL COSBY becomes the first African-American TV star in *I Spy*.

SONY introduces the first commercial home video tape recorder. The size of an overnight bag, it costs $995.

1966

"YESTERDAY," the most recorded song in the history of popular music, is released by Paul McCartney in the first solo by a Beatle. The record label, however, still reads "Beatles."

THE CINEMA'S blue language ban finally falls with *Who's Afraid of Virginia Woolf?*

JOHN LENNON makes his most infamous remark on August 5 by saying that he and his Beatle bandmates are "more popular than Jesus." Subsequently radio stations across the country take Beatle songs off the air.

LSD is pulled off the market by its manufacturer, Sandoz Pharmaceuticals, after being banned by the government in response to controversy over the hallucinogen's recreational uses.

STAR TREK is launched September 8, literally, and will remain on the air until 1969. It will become one of the few series to be more popular in syndication than in its network run.

FOR ADHERENTS to the "Paul is dead" theory, November 9 marks the date of the Beatle's supposed decapitation.

STEREO CASSETTE TAPE RECORDERS are introduced, a breakthrough for tape cartridges.

1967

THE FIRST SUPER BOWL is held on January 15, broadcast in color on both CBS and NBC; setting a model for future contests, the Green Bay Packers defeat the Kansas City Chiefs in a lopsided game, 35–10.

Priscilla and Elvis Presley.

THE BLACK PANTHER PARTY is founded in Oakland by Huey Newton and Bobby Seale.

ELVIS PRESLEY weds Priscilla Beaulieu on May 1 at the Aladdin Hotel in Las Vegas.

THE MONTEREY INTERNATIONAL POP FESTIVAL in California features such performers as Janis Joplin, Jimi Hendrix, the Mamas and the Papas, and the Grateful Dead.

RIOTING breaks out in Detroit as racial tension builds; over 17,000 people are arrested in what proves to be the worst U.S. riot of the century.

FOLKSINGER PETE SEEGER is finally allowed to appear on TV (on *The Smothers Brothers Comedy Hour*) after having been blacklisted for seventeen years for his leftist politics.

HAIR has its off-Broadway premiere at the Public Theatre in New York.

ROLLING STONE magazine begins publication under the direction of twenty-one-year-old Jann Wenner.

PRESIDENT LYNDON B. JOHNSON signs a law insuring federal support for public TV, and the Corporation for Public Broadcasting is created.

THE FIRST SO-CALLED SPAGHETTI WESTERN, Sergio Leone's *A Fistful of Dollars*, is released in the U.S. Filmed in 1964, it stars Clint Eastwood.

INTERRACIAL ROMANCE unfolds on TV as Mia and Paul fall for each other on *Love Is a Many Splendored Thing*.

BOXER MUHAMMAD ALI is stripped of his heavyweight title after refusing to serve in the army during the Vietnam War.

THE FIRST HUMAN HEART transplant is performed by Dr. Christiaan Barnard in South Africa on Louis Washkansky, who lives for eighteen days.

MAO TSE-TUNG'S QUOTATIONS, better known as the Red Book, is the biggest-selling read in the world this year.

1968

CARDIGAN-CARRYING MISTER ROGERS opens his Neighborhood February 19, beginning a twenty-six-year run that will establish a PBS record.

ARTHUR CLARKE and Stanley Kubrick's *2001: A Space Odyssey* is released, introducing the evil computer, Hal, an antihero that becomes a cultural icon.

THE EARLIEST-KNOWN HEIDI scandal: With fifty seconds left and the New York Jets leading the Oakland Raiders, NBC cuts from the game to the movie *Heidi*. The Raiders go on to win by scoring two touchdowns in nine seconds.

CIVIL RIGHTS LEADER Martin Luther King Jr. is assassinated April 4 at age 39 on the balcony outside of his motel room in Memphis, Tennessee. Days later, many American cities erupt in riots.

ROBERT F. KENNEDY, 42, is assassinated June 5 by Sirhan Sirhan in a Los Angeles hotel after winning the California Democratic presidential primary. As a response, David Crosby writes "A Long Time Coming."

AT THE SUMMER OLYMPIC GAMES in Mexico City, American runners Tommy Smith and John Carlos give the black power salute as they receive their gold and bronze medals, resulting in their suspension from competition.

PRESIDENTIAL CANDIDATE Richard Nixon appears on *Laugh-In* and says, "Sock it to me!"

JULIA, premiering September 17, is the first TV series to star a black woman in a non-menial role as Diahann Carroll plays a nurse who is also a single parent.

MIKE WALLACE and Harry Reasoner start grilling as *60 Minutes* starts ticking September 24; the news program will eventually top the ratings for all other shows.

1969

THE BEATLES stage their last public performance January 30 from a rooftop in London.

JIM MORRISON, lead singer for the Doors, is arrested for lewd and lascivious behavior after exposing himself at a concert in Miami.

JOHN LENNON and Yoko Ono tie the knot on Gibraltar March 20.

THE FIRST FULL-FRONTAL male nudity appears in film with Alan Bates and Oliver Reed in Ken Russell's *Women in Love*.

CAST MEMBERS of the play *Oh! Calcutta!* are arrested for indecent exposure in Los Angeles.

THE SUPREME COURT rules that laws prohibiting the private possession of obscene material by adults are unconstitutional.

PRINCE CHARLES is officially crowned Prince of Wales.

UPON WALKING ON THE MOON on July 20, Neil Armstrong proclaims, "That's one small step for a man, one giant leap for mankind."

ACTRESS SHARON TATE, wife of director Roman Polanski, is found murdered along with four others—the victims of Charles Manson's cult, known as The Family. Although not present at the house that night, would-be rock musician and psychopath Manson is convicted of the grisly killings and imprisoned.

Woodstock patrons, cleaning off the mud no doubt.

THE WOODSTOCK Music and Art Festival is held August 15–17 in Upstate New York. Playing before an audience of around 400,000, featured performers include the Who, the Grateful Dead, Janis Joplin, Joe Cocker, Santana, Jimi Hendrix, Jefferson Airplane, and Crosby, Stills & Nash.

SESAME STREET debuts, starring Big Bird, Oscar, Bert, Ernie, Cookie Monster, Grover, and Kermit, and marking a radical departure for children's TV programming.

TINY TIM marries Miss Vickie before forty-five million witnesses on *The Tonight Show*.

1970

RECORDING TOGETHER for the last time, the Beatles cut "I Me Mine" January 3. The historic breakup happens on April 10, when Paul McCartney announces that he will not record with John Lennon again. By the end of the year, John, Paul, George, and Ringo have all released albums of their own.

EVERYTHING *You Ever Wanted to Know About Sex, but Were Afraid to Ask* by Dr. David Reuben becomes a No. 1 bestseller.

JIMI HENDRIX and Janis Joplin both die drug-related deaths this year at age 27.

THE FILM VERSION of *M*A*S*H*, with Elliott Gould and Donald Sutherland, is officially banned from military installations for "reducing the conventions and paraphernalia of war to total idiocy."

MASTERPIECE THEATRE is introduced on National Educational Television, hosted by Alistair Cooke and featuring BBC dramas.

TV'S PARTRIDGE FAMILY records "I Think I Love You," which becomes a smash hit first in the show's story line and then in real life, and makes David Cassidy a teen idol.

WATERBEDS hit the market, and although technical problems often produce flooding, sales skyrocket.

MONDAY NIGHT FOOTBALL takes its bow September 21 (with the New York Jets vs. the Cleveland Browns) and strains U.S. marriages, but

Don Meredith, Howard Cosell, and Frank Gifford will boost ABC's ratings.

1971

TV NETWORKS lose $200 million in annual advertising when cigarette ads are banned January 2.

CBS'S controversial *All in the Family* is introduced, featuring the bigoted Archie Bunker, whose offensive diatribes and hilarious family members drive the show's great popularity.

EXCERPTS FROM THE PENTAGON PAPERS, leaked by Daniel Ellsberg, are published in the *New York Times*, showing that presidential administrations had indeed recognized the futility of the Vietnam War but had escalated involvement anyway and lied about it. The Nixon administration attempts to block publication but the Supreme Court rules in favor of the newspaper on First Amendment grounds.

BILL GRAHAM closes down Fillmore East and Fillmore West in New York City and San Francisco, unable to pay the increasing prices charged by the musicians he has showcased for so long.

MUHAMMAD ALI'S conviction for draft evasion is overturned by the Supreme Court, which rules that the boxer's pacifist religious convictions were sincere.

JIM MORRISON, 27, dies in a Paris bathtub on July 3.

HOSTED BY GEORGE HARRISON, the Concert for Bangladesh initiates the rise of the celebrity fundraiser. The concert features Ringo Starr, Eric Clapton, and Bob Dylan, but while its success is great, only a small fraction of its proceeds make it to the starving people of Bangladesh.

LEGENDARY ALLMAN BROTHERS' Band member Duane Allman is killed October 29 in a motorcycle accident near Macon, Georgia.

1972

MS., edited by Gloria Steinem, publishes its premiere issue in January.

RECLUSIVE MULTIMILLIONAIRE Howard Hughes exposes as a hoax an upcoming "autobiography" supposedly written with, but actually forged by, author Clifford Irving.

PONG, the first commercial computer game, is created by Atari.

BURT REYNOLDS poses nude for the centerfold of *Cosmopolitan*.

AT THE SUMMER OLYMPICS in Munich, eleven Israeli Olympians are killed by Arab terrorists and the games are suspended for the first time in history.

THE SAPPY, inspirational *Jonathan Livingston Seagull* establishes itself as the bestselling book since *Gone with the Wind*.

DEEP THROAT becomes one of the most successful porn films ever made; produced on a budget of $40,000, it goes on to gross around $40 million.

THE SUBSCRIPTION-BASED Home Box Office cable channel goes on the air in Wilkes-Barre, Pennsylvania, with 365 subscribers. The first offering is a Paul Newman movie, *Sometimes a Great Notion.*

1973

ROE V. WADE is upheld by the Supreme Court, legalizing unrestricted abortion in the first trimester of pregnancy.

A CEASE-FIRE agreement is signed on January 27 that essentially ends the Vietnam War.

SACHEEN LITTLEFEATHER refuses Marlon Brando's Oscar for Best Actor on his behalf to protest the treatment of Native Americans. (He was nominated for *The Godfather.)*

PBS'S *Steambath* takes on a taboo as Valerie Perrine becomes the first woman to bare her breasts in a dramatic TV program.

AT THE AGE OF 38, Seiji Ozawa becomes the youngest permanant conductor of the Boston Symphony.

A BREAK-IN at Democratic party headquarters at the Watergate Hotel is discovered, eventually leading to the only resignation of a sitting president in American history when Richard Nixon is forced to leave office on August 9 of the following year.

PUNK/NEW WAVE club CBGB and OMFUG (which stands for Country, Bluegrass, Blues and Other Music for Uplifting Gourmandizers) opens its doors on Manhattan's divey Bowery, becoming home to such performers as Blondie, Talking Heads, Patti Smith, the Ramones, the Police, Joan Jett, and Sid Vicious. As Joey Ramone put it twenty years later, "It's a birthplace. It's like a big womb there. It's very primitive, very primal."

BILLIE JEAN KING trounces male chauvinist pig Bobby Riggs in tennis's ballyhooed "Battle of the Sexes."

IN A REVERSAL of its traditional position, the American Psychiatric Association declares that homosexuality is not a mental illness.

1974

THE AUTOBIOGRAPHY OF MISS JANE PITTMAN, starring Cicely Tyson, becomes one of TV's most highly praised and successful special programs, going on to win nine Emmys.

HEIRESS PATRICIA HEARST is kidnapped by the Simbionese Liberation Army, which she later joins and with which she commits a robbery. Nineteen months after her kidnapping, Hearst is captured and convicted.

AFTER TEN YEARS OF MARRIAGE, Cher files for divorce from her husband and performing partner Sonny Bono. She marries Gregg Allman of the Allman Brothers band only four days after the divorce is finalized.

PEOPLE magazine is launched by Time, Inc., in February.

The first cover of PEOPLE.

EVEL KNIEVEL fails his attempt to jump the Snake River Canyon on his motorcycle, but survives.

ONE THOUSAND FANS at a David Cassidy concert in London are injured during a frenzy following the teen idol's appearance. One concertgoer dies.

FLORIDA TV commentator Chris Chubbuck announces her own suicide at the end of the news broadcast, and proceeds to shoot herself in the head on the air.

ALEKSANDR SOLZHENITSYN is expelled from Russia for his dissident writings; this year *The Gulag Archipelago* is also published in the West.

STREAKING becomes a momentary fad, primarily on college campuses, although the madness eventually extends to telecasts of the Academy Awards and *The Tonight Show*.

RUSSIAN DANCER EXTRAORDINAIRE Mikhail Barishnikov defects to the West, quickly electrifying the American dance scene.

KAREN SILKWOOD is killed in a suspicious car crash on November 13. A laboratory worker at the Kerr-McGee plutonium plant, she was on her way to meet with a reporter to discuss safety hazards at her workplace.

1975

THE VIETNAM WAR officially comes to an end.

JOHN LENNON wins a four-year-long battle against American immigration authorities when they drop his case for humanitarian reasons due to the pregnancy of Yoko Ono.

SATURDAY NIGHT LIVE hits the airwaves from New York City, with guest host George Carlin.

RICHARD BURTON and Elizabeth Taylor marry for the second time, only a year after their first divorce.

THE VIDEOCASSETTE recorder/player is introduced by Sony.

MOOD RINGS are introduced and reach their peak in only a few months, selling more than twenty million before passing from popular fancy. Maintenance-free pet rocks also hit the short-term big time in 1975.

1976

THE MINISERIES comes to commercial TV, as *Rich Man, Poor Man* airs, starring Peter Strauss, Susan Blakely, and Nick Nolte.

BRITAIN'S PRINCESS MARGARET scandalizes the world with an illicit liaison on the island of Mustique with brewery heir Roddy Llewellyn. She and her husband, Lord Snowden, separate later this year.

GONE WITH THE WIND is telecast over two evenings on NBC, earning the highest ratings to date.

1977

ALEX HALEY'S novel *Roots*, a story of his quest for his ancestors in Africa and America, is made into the most successful miniseries in history. It mesmerizes the country for over a week, drawing approximately 130 million people to watch at least one of its eight episodes.

Karen Lynn Gorney and John Travolta spread *Saturday Night Fever.*

STUDIO 54 opens its doors in New York, becoming the quintessential glamorous nightclub until owners Steve Rubell and Ian Shrager are arrested for tax evasion.

GEORGE LUCAS releases *Star Wars*, which goes on to become the third-highest-grossing movie of all time.

THE KING IS DEAD: Elvis Presley passes on at Graceland, his palatial estate in Memphis, Tennessee, on August 16.

SOAP introduces prime time's first gay character—Billy Crystal as Jodie Dallas.

RONALD ZAMORA, 15, confesses to murder and claims TV made him do it; he will be convicted in the first televised trial.

SATURDAY NIGHT FEVER premieres in New York on December 14, launching the disco era.

1978

FORMER FIRST LADY Betty Ford breaks the stigma of addiction by entering a rehabilitation clinic on April 21.

THE WORLD'S FIRST test-tube baby, Louise Brown, is born July 25 in England.

AT 25 HOURS and $25 million, the dramatization of James Michener's *Centennial* is the most outsized program yet produced for TV.

JIM JONES leads his followers to a mass death in Jonestown, Guyana, on November 18. Nine hundred fourteen members of his cult commit suicide or kill each other.

SONY invents the revolutionary Walkman, the first portable cassette player.

The first Walkman from Sony.

1979

RAP MUSIC is ushered into the commercial age when the Sugarhill Gang releases "Rapper's Delight." Earlier in the year a Brooklyn group called the Fatback Band had produced "King Tim III (Personality Jock)," a disk widely regarded as the first rap record.

WHILE THE WOMEN on TV's *Charlie's Angels* changed outfits on average eight times per show, a guest appearance this year by Farrah Fawcett (who left the show in 1977) easily breaks the record: in one hour-long program she changes clothes twelve times.

1980

THE U.S. HOCKEY TEAM beats the Soviet Union during the winter Olympics at Lake Placid, on their way to winning their first gold medal since 1960—and only their second gold since the Olympics began.

POST-IT NOTES enter the market, revolutionizing the office and the refrigerator.

TED KOPPEL'S *Nightline*, begun as an ABC series following the status of U.S. hostages in Iran, brings hard news in the wee hours.

TV'S FIRST ALL-NEWS SERVICE begins with Ted Turner's Cable News Network on June 1. Broadcasting twenty-four hours a day, the network loses $16 million in a year, but grabs seven million viewers.

COMEDIAN RICHARD PRYOR is badly burned when a flammable drug mixture used to make "freebase," a cocaine derivative, explodes in his face.

WITH SUCH BLOCKBUSTER musicals as *A Chorus Line*, *Oh! Calcutta!*, and *Evita* on the boards, Broadway box offices collect almost $200 million, a dramatic increase over a five-year period. Road shows during this period experience an even greater success.

HALF THE NATION'S VIEWERS tune in on November 21 to find out "Who Shot J.R.?," more viewers than for any other single TV show in history, to date.

MARK DAVID CHAPMAN shoots and kills John Lennon on December 8 outside the singer's apartment in New York City.

Charles and Diana's Wedding.

1981

A WAVE OF PNEUMONIA and cancer that is killing homosexual men across the country is traced to a mysterious breakdown in the body's disease fighting system, to be referred to later as Acquired Immune Deficiency Syndrome, or AIDS.

HILL STREET BLUES premieres.

TICKETS TO BROADWAY'S *The Life and Adventures of Nicholas Nickleby* go on sale at the Plymouth Theatre for a record-setting $100 each.

PRESIDENT RONALD REAGAN is shot in an assassination attempt on March 30 that leaves his press secretary, James Brady, paralyzed for life. John Hinckley apparently undertakes the assassination in an attempt to impress Jodie Foster.

THE VIDEO GAME PAC-MAN devours the market as young people everywhere are seized with acute Pac-mania.

CHARLES, PRINCE OF WALES, and Lady Diana Spencer are married July 29 at Saint Paul's Cathedral in London.

MTV unveils music for your eyes on August 1. The channel's opener: "Video Killed the Radio Star," by the Buggles.

SANDRA DAY O'CONNOR becomes the first woman Supreme Court Justice in U.S. history.

PRIVATE SATELLITE DISHES sprout after the FCC gives them the okay. By the end of the 1980s, there will be 2 million nationwide.

1982

OZZY OSBOURNE bites the head off a live bat thrown at him during a performance on January 20, a moment that is immortalized in heavy metal chronicles.

THE REVEREND SUN MYUNG MOON performs a mass ceremony at Madison Square Garden, marrying some 4,150 of his followers, the "Moonies."

MICHAEL JACKSON'S *Thriller* is released. Selling over 20 million copies in 1983 and 1984 alone, it becomes the biggest-selling album in history.

Michael Jackson.

ACTOR AND COMEDIAN John Belushi dies March 5 of an overdose of cocaine and heroin in a Hollywood hotel room.

CHARLES AND DI produce their first offspring, Prince William, on June 21, the latest heir to the British throne.

PRINCESS GRACE dies on September 14 after an automobile accident.

THE WATCHMAN, Sony's portable microtelevision, is invented.

THE FIRST ARTIFICIAL HEART is transplanted into Barney C. Clark, age 61, in Utah. He lives for 112 days.

1983

CABLE TV subscribers reach the thirty million mark.

SINGER KAREN CARPENTER dies of anorexia nervosa on February 4.

M*A*S*H ends its eleven-year, fourteen-Emmy run with the largest audience ever to watch a single TV show.

ASTRONAUT SALLY RIDE becomes the first American woman in space as she blasts off June 18 with four colleagues aboard the space shuttle *Challenger*.

VANESSA WILLIAMS becomes the first African American to win the Miss America pageant. The singer relinquishes her title two months before her term ends in 1984, when it is discovered that she posed nude and that the revealing photos are going to be published in *Penthouse*.

THE CHILLING TV DRAMA *The Day After,* with Jason Robards, explores the aftermath of nuclear war, hardening both pro- and anti-freeze positions.

CABBAGE PATCH DOLLS, introduced by Coleco Industries, become the holy grail of the 1983 holiday season.

1984

HOME TAPING OF TV programming is held not to be in violation of copyright law by the Supreme Court, which throws out a suit brought against Sony by MCA and Walt Disney.

THE FIRST successful case of surrogate conception is reported in California.

GERALDINE FERRARO becomes the first woman to run for vice president as presidential candidate Walter Mondale names the Queens congresswoman as his running mate; the pair lose the election to President Reagan and Vice President George Bush in a landslide.

Adoptable Cabbage Patch Kids.

GYMNAST MARY LOU RETTON wins two gold, two silver, and two bronze Olympic medals for the U.S.

SIDNEY BIDDLE BARROWS is arrested. Known as the Mayflower Madam, she included numerous famous and powerful people among her clients.

THE COSBY SHOW premieres.

THE FIRST ALL-RAP RADIO format is introduced by KDAY in Los Angeles.

RUN-DMC becomes the first rap group to have an album—*Run-DMC*—certified gold.

BOB GELDOF and Band Aid's "Do They Know It's Christmas" raises money to help feed the starving people of Africa.

1985

"WE ARE THE WORLD" is recorded by forty-five pop music superstars under the auspices of USA for Africa.

CRACK COCAINE hits the streets, further devastating already blighted urban areas.

PIANO MAN BILLY JOEL and supermodel Christie Brinkley tie the knot.

MADONNA begins her road debut, "The Virgin Tour," on April 10.

THE MUSIC INDUSTRY'S benefit for African famine relief, Live Aid, is staged in London and Philadelphia and beamed all over the world.

ROCK HUDSON becomes the first major public figure to die of AIDS, at 59, on October 2.

1986

THE SPACE SHUTTLE *CHALLENGER* explodes January 28 shortly after launching, killing everyone on board including schoolteacher Christa McAuliffe, the first private citizen to go into space.

FILIPINO FIRST LADY Imelda Marcos is revealed to possess 2,700 pairs of shoes in March.

ARNOLD SCHWARZENEGGER and Maria Shriver are married.

JOHNNY CARSON stops talking to Joan Rivers when she accepts an offer to host a late night show on the Fox network.

CAROLINE KENNEDY marries artist-designer Edwin Schlossberg.

PRINCE ANDREW marries Sarah Ferguson in London on July 23.

ORIGINALLY A LOCAL PROGRAM called *A.M. Chicago*, *The Oprah Winfrey Show* goes national on September 8 and establishes its host as one of the most successful personalities in show business.

DIRECTORS, stars, and movie buffs see red as Turner Broadcasting colorizes black-and-white classics. First to run: Jimmy Cagney's *Yankee Doodle Dandy*.

1987

JESSICA HAHN is implicated in a scandal with TV evangelist Jim Bakker.

VAN GOGH'S *Irises* is auctioned at $53,900,000, the highest price ever paid for a painting at the time.

PRINCE CHARLES and Diana begin leading separate lives in March as their marriage starts to deteriorate.

PRESIDENTIAL CANDIDATE Gary Hart's connection with model Donna Rice destroys his political aspirations and he is forced to withdraw from the race.

GARRISON KEILLOR broadcasts his last radio show, "A Prairie Home Companion," from Lake Wobegon on June 13 and moves to New York City.

PORN QUEEN CICCIOLINA wins a seat in Italian Parliament on June 16.

BRUCE WILLIS and Demi Moore are married November 21 in Las Vegas.

1988

TV PREACHER JIMMY SWAGGART admits his involvement with pornography and prostitutes. His February 21 statement, "I have sinned," deals a serious setback to electronic evangelism.

SONNY BONO is elected mayor of Palm Springs, California.

THE VERY LAST Playboy Club in America closes July 30 in Lansing, Michigan.

ACTRESS ROBIN GIVENS files for divorce on October 7 from world heavyweight champion Mike Tyson, claiming that the fighter is violent.

TALK SHOW HOST PHIL DONAHUE wears a dress on November 18 to boost his ratings.

BENAZIR BHUTTO of Pakistan becomes the first woman to lead an Islamic nation.

PAN AM FLIGHT 103 explodes over Lockerbie, Scotland, killing all 259 passengers.

THE ERA of the personal video arrives when Sony introduces the Video Walkman, an ultra-compact VCR with a three-inch color screen.

1989

LATE-NIGHT TV gets its first regular African-American host on January 3 with comedian Arsenio Hall.

VIRTUAL REALITY, the term as well as the equipment to achieve it, is invented by Jaron Lanier.

NOVELIST SALMAN RUSHDIE is forced into hiding after a death threat is issued by Islamic militants angry over what they see as sacrilege in his book *The Satanic Verses*.

Salman Rushdie.

KIM BASINGER steps in to rescue near-bankrupt Braselton, Georgia by buying the town for a reported $20 million.

LUCILLE BALL, perhaps the most beloved television star in history, dies on April 26.

ACTOR ROB LOWE is identified by Fulton County, Georgia officials in a soft-porn video with an under-aged girl.

***PLAYBOY* FOUNDER** Hugh Hefner marries former *Playboy* Playmate Kimberley Conrad.

JOSE MENENDEZ and his wife, Kitty, are found murdered August 20 in their $4 million Beverly Hills mansion. Their sons, Lyle and Erik, will later be accused of murdering their parents for money, though at their trials the brothers claim that years of sexual and psychological abuse by their parents drove them to kill in self-defense.

PETE ROSE, Cincinnati Reds manager and one of the greatest baseball players in history, is banned from the game for life for gambling.

TV GUIDE boasts a picture on the cover of the newly slim Oprah Winfrey, but the image turns out to be a composite of Oprah's head and Ann-Margret's body.

PRINCESS ANNE issues a palace statement on August 31 that she is officially separating from her husband, Mark Phillips.

THE BERLIN WALL falls on November 9.

SAN FRANCISCO GIANTS pitcher Dave Dravecky retires after an aborted comeback attempt from cancer in his pitching arm.

1990

THE SIMPSONS spins off *The Tracey Ullman Show* and makes the fledgling Fox network a real contender as a fourth network.

NELSON MANDELA is released from prison after twenty-seven years of incarceration for leading a campaign against the South African government.

SONY creates the first portable compact disc player, the Discman.

M. C. HAMMER releases *Please Hammer Don't Hurt 'Em*, which becomes the biggest selling rap record in history.

DONALD AND IVANA TRUMP divorce.

MILLI VANILLI is accused of fraud for using voices other than its own on its Grammy-winning album, *Girl You Know It's True*. The group is forced to surrender the award.

IN THE FIRST such ruling against a music group in the U.S., a Florida judge declares 2 Live Crew's album *As Nasty As They Wanna Be* obscene and bans all sales of the rap recording to minors. The move ignites a campaign against censorship in the music business.

TWIN PEAKS debuts on ABC as a two-hour movie with limited commercial interruption.

SEINFELD, a show about "nothing," quietly debuts on May 31.

AMERICA RELIVES the war between the states with Ken Burns's indelible PBS documentary *The Civil War*.

IN AN EFFORT to raise money for AIDS research, the *Red Hot & Blue* album is released on October 30, featuring such stars as U2, David Byrne, and the Neville Brothers performing Cole Porter songs.

1991

OPERATION DESERT SHIELD turns into Desert Storm on January 16 as the Allied forces attack Iraq to liberate Kuwait. CNN's Bernard Shaw, Peter Arnett, and John Holliman cover the events for the world, broadcasting from downtown Baghdad.

THE GODFATHER OF SOUL, James Brown, is released from a Georgia prison after serving two years of a six-year sentence for aggravated assault, not stopping for police, and carrying a gun.

RODNEY KING'S beating by Los Angeles police is recorded by an observer with a home video camera on March 3.

DR. JACK KEVORKIAN'S attempts to help people commit suicide first come to light.

WILLIAM KENNEDY SMITH, nephew of Teddy Kennedy, is accused of rape by a Florida woman; after a harrowing trial, he is exonerated.

PAUL RUBENS, creator of the much-admired *Pee Wee's Playhouse* and the character Pee Wee Herman, is busted in Florida for indecent exposure.

LIZ TAYLOR marries husband number seven, thirty-nine-year-old Larry Fortensky, a carpenter she met at the Betty Ford Center where they were both being treated for alcohol and drug dependency. The wedding, held on Michael Jackson's estate, draws such guests as Nancy Reagan.

THE TELEVISED Anita Hill/Clarence Thomas hearings galvanize the nation with charges of sexual harassment against a Supreme Count nominee; Thomas is narrowly approved for the post.

MAGIC JOHNSON announces his retirement from professional basketball because he has tested positive for the HIV virus.

MEDIA MOGUL TED TURNER and actress-cum-fitness-guru Jane Fonda are married.

1992

ARTHUR ASHE, tennis star and beloved public figure, dies of AIDS.

MIKE TYSON is convicted of raping beauty contestant Desiree Washington.

TAMMY FAYE BAKKER files for divorce from husband, Jim, who's still in prison on a fraud conviction and not eligible for parole for another three years.

FERGIE AND ANDY separate after six years of marriage.

A *MURPHY BROWN* segment in which the unmarried Murphy gives birth spurs the wrath of Vice President Dan Quayle and instigates a nationwide debate over family values.

LONG ISLAND TEENAGER Amy Fisher shoots Mary Joe Buttafucco.

JOHNNY CARSON ends his reign over late-night talk shows on May 22 with his last appearance on *The Tonight Show*.

CANDIDATE BILL CLINTON appears on *The Arsenio Hall Show*, complete with dark shades and saxophone, to perform

Newlyweds Elizabeth Taylor and Larry Fortensky.

Heartbreak Hotel with the show's "posse."

WOODY ALLEN and Mia Farrow begin a bitter custody battle over their son Satchel, 4, and two children they adopted together, Moses, 14, and daughter Dylan, 7. The dispute is fueled by Allen's affair with Farrow's adopted daughter Soon Yi.

Woody Allen, after doctors cleared him of child abuse allegations, in 1993.

THE TORONTO BLUE JAYS become the first non-American team to win that most American of sports championship, the World Series, with a 4–2 series win over Ted Turner's Atlanta Braves.

PRINCE CHARLES and Lady Diana are formally separated.

1993

THE U.S. POSTAL SERVICE releases its commemorative Elvis stamp, featuring the youthful Elvis, the overwhelming selection of the voting public.

BILL WYMAN leaves the Rolling Stones in January. He is 56.

DR. DRE'S album *The Chronic* (named after a very potent form of marijuana) reaches No. 1 on the *Billboard* charts and becomes the most successful hard-core rap album to date.

AS PART OF A BURST of public appearances, Michael Jackson is interviewed by Oprah Winfrey live from his Neverland Valley Ranch. Jackson claims that his lightened skin color is due to a rare skin disease, and says that he is in love with Brooke Shields. Over ninety million viewers tune in, making it one of the most widely watched programs in history. Jackson drew a comparable number of viewers for his halftime performance during the Super Bowl earlier this year.

AFTER YEARS OF PROMISE, the Rock and Roll Hall of Fame, designed by I. M. Pei, finally breaks ground in June in Cleveland. Pete Townshend, on hand to help dig the ceremonial dirt, notes "Let's hope it doesn't become a monolith to a bunch of dinosaurs."

PRINCE, born Prince Rogers Nelson, turns 35 on June 7 and, in a most confusing commemoration, changes his name to a symbol that no one knows how to pronounce.

JULIA ROBERTS and Lyle Lovett wed.

SATANIC VERSES author Salman Rushdie appears onstage in August with U2's Bono at a British concert in Wembley Stadium, and then vanishes, as always, into the night.

THE GROUP 10,000 MANIACS goes 10,000 separate ways as lead vocalist Natalie Merchant leaves for a solo career.

MICHAEL JACKSON is accused of fondling a thirteen-year-old Los Angeles boy at the singer's home earlier in the year. The reclusive Jackson has long been noted for his strong attachments to kids, but this story shocks disbelieving fans worldwide. Jackson strongly denies the charge from his *Dangerous* tour in Thailand, his associates claiming that the boy's father is attempting to extort $20 million from the musician.

PALESA JACQUI MOFOKENG becomes the first black woman ever crowned Miss South Africa.

SNOOP DOGGY DOGG is charged with murder, along with two other men, in the August shooting of Phillip Woldemariam. Snoop, whose November release, *Doggy Style*, will become one of the biggest hits of the year, claims the shooting was in self-defense.

THE MISS AMERICA PAGEANT, falling in popularity, shakes up the competition by requiring that contestants do their own hair and makeup in September.

PEARL JAM releases their second wildly successful album, *Vs.*, which sets a first-week record as the fastest-selling album ever—1.2 million copies in five days.

RECYCLING THE LEFTOVERS, '70s rocker Meatloaf releases *Bat out of Hell II*, a follow-up to his 1977 epic and one of the year's biggest and most surprising hits.

ACTOR RIVER PHOENIX dies outside of a chic L.A. nightclub, the Viper Room, owned in part by Johnny Depp, on October 31. The young actor had a reputation for clean living and a strict vegetarian diet, but coroners find high levels of cocaine and morphine as well as Valium and marijuana in Phoenix's system, and his death is attributed to "acute multiple-drug intoxication."

EVANDER HOLYFIELD regains the heavyweight crown from Riddick Bowe in a majority decision, but not until after the fight is interrupted in round seven by a parachutist dropping into the open-air ring at Caesar's Palace.

IN MEXICO CITY, Michael Jackson cancels the remainder of his Dangerous tour, announcing that sexual abuse charges have deeply traumatized him and left him addicted to painkillers. His decade-long relationship with Pepsi is terminated even as he enters a clinic for detox treatment. Meanwhile, *Dangerous* sales worldwide surpass twenty million.

RAPPER TUPAC SHAKUR is arrested in October for allegedly shooting two off-duty police officers.

HOLIDAY TELEVISION viewers breathe a sigh of relief in December as Republic Pictures announces that it will severely limit broadcasts of the 1946 seasonal classic, *It's a Wonderful Life.* The following month, Republic sells broadcasts exclusively to NBC, which plans to show the film in its original black-and-white version.

Denzel Washington and the real MALCOLM X

People weekly

IT'S OVER

For two decades Charles has sought comfort and companionship with a married woman. Now his bond with Camilla Parker Bowles could cost him the throne.

Oprah's passionate TV blitz against child abuse

People weekly

FERGIE'S FINAL FOLLY?

The Palace ponders dumping the Duchess after she's photographed topless, necking with her American "financial adviser," in front of Princesses Bea, 4, and Eugenie, 2

The Duchess of York and Texas businessman John Bryan

THE MERRY MEN AND WOMEN OF WINDSOR

"I want to be as famous," the ambitious young Andy Warhol proclaimed back in the 1950s, "as the queen of England." He might as well have said that he wanted to be as famous as the Atlantic Ocean. The British royal family has something that vast and immemorial about it. In the three centuries of its reign in the public eye, other crowned families of Europe have been executed or packed off. But the Windsors still occupy the throne, as implacable and enduring as the planet Jupiter.

It hasn't been easy. The Windsors are expected to behave like the Cleavers even when they're feeling like the Simpsons. Being famous is more than their fate; in a sense it's their job. As the real decision-making power of the monarchy has dwindled, the public symbolism has become more important. On more than one occasion in the past, however, Britons have seemed ready to rid themselves of a dynasty that could look costly, shiftless, and Teutonic. The lessons of the past are not lost on the Windsors, who take their family history not just as a source of pride but also as a series of warnings to the present. Like her father, George VI, Elizabeth II has been a model of dignity and decorum. But a stroll among her ancestors in the National Portrait Gallery is enough to remind her of any number of hot-blooded blue bloods in her line.

Where does the Windsor saga begin? Actually, with the German Hanoverian kings. The royals like to consider Queen Victoria their matriarch because, while she was from the House of Hanover herself, her marriage to Prince Albert of Saxe-Coburg-Gotha established the present branch of the family tree. So emphasizing Albert's line allows the Windsors to distance themselves from Victoria's Hanoverian predecessors. Starting with **George I**, who was imported to England from Germany in 1714, the five increasingly preposterous rulers had made the British people rue almost the very idea of royalty.

After monarchs who alternated between extravagant skirt-chasing and outright incompetence, **Victoria** acceded to the crown in 1837, the niece of the last Hanoverian king, William IV. Immediately she made it her business to undo their legacy. She brought the monarchy a bit of wholesome romance through a devoted marriage to her German husband, **Prince Albert**. Indeed the transformation of the royal reputation may be Albert's achievement even more than Victoria's. With the middle classes taking power from the spoiled and lazy aristocrats, Albert gave them a royal family that the common man could both look up to and identify with: wreathed in pomp and ceremony but frugal, sober, dutiful, and monogamous.

Though Victoria's name has come to stand for prudishness, it was as much Albert who brought the moralizing strain to their marriage. As a young woman, the Queen didn't blush to size him up bluntly in her diary. ("Such a pretty mouth," she noted. "A beautiful figure, broad in the shoulders, and a fine waist.") But Albert worried that their children would take after his wayward parents, who had divorced in a tangle of adulteries. Above all he vowed that Edward, heir to the throne, would be raised in an atmosphere of hard schooling and abstinence. Naturally, Edward grew up to be dim, jolly, and goatish.

Upon Albert's death in 1861, Victoria, just 42 years old, plunged down a black hole of widowhood. Albert's bedroom was kept as it was on the day of his death, even to the extent of having fresh bedclothes laid out every night. She eventually roused herself sufficiently to regain the public's affection, and lived long enough to see her nine children and forty grandchildren married into most of the royal families of Europe. On her deathbed she was supported by her grandson Kaiser Wilhelm of Germany, who thirteen years later would lead his nation into war against hers.

When Victoria died in 1901, after the longest reign in her nation's history, her reputation for rectitude had become so stultifying that her womanizing heir, son **Edward VII**, found himself lionized for the same habits that had caused so much trouble for so many Hanoverian kings. Throughout his life the insatiable Edward conducted a series of lengthy affairs with some of the most celebrated beauties of the day, including the actresses Lillie Langtry and Sarah Bernhardt. With prosperity at home and vast empire abroad, the public was willing to overlook the moral lapses of a robust and even randy monarch. After nine popular years on the throne he was followed by **George V**, prim, exacting, and a stickler for impeccable dress. George led the country through World War I when he changed the family name from the Germanic Saxe-Coburg-Gotha to Windsor. He also encouraged closer ties between the royals and the people by allowing the Windsors to marry British nobles and commoners. Indeed among the first to benefit from this new trend was the present Queen Mother, a noblewoman who married George's son Albert, the future George VI.

George VI became the monarch, however, only after his elder brother abdicated. Crowned **Edward VIII** in 1936, the young man was already intent upon marriage to Wallis Warfield Simpson, a divorced American married to a British businessman. But the government would hear nothing of it and presented Edward with a choice—the lady or the land—hoping that he would choose the former and in the process remove a king who showed signs of Nazi sympathies. After a reign of almost a year, he resigned and, bearing the newly invented title of Duke of Windsor, he left England for the Continent and Wallis Simpson. They would return home only for rare visits—and, decades later, to be buried.

England was shaken—indeed on the night of Edward's abdication the sentries around Buckingham Palace were issued live ammunition for the first time in modern history. The public's reaction may have been overestimated, but when Edward's younger brother, Albert, now **George VI**, came to the throne in December 1936, all of Britain was poised for the worst.

For that matter, so was Albert. He had never expected to be king (formal speaking engagements left him shaken and depressed), and when he learned he was suddenly to take the throne, he went to his mother, Queen Mary, and wept for an hour. No wonder it was rumored that George VI was too frail to survive the coronation ceremony.

But his very narrowness and humility turned out to be qualities that were once again in favor among the British people. George VI and his wife, the current **Queen Mother**, Elizabeth, provided Britain with a center of gravity during the grim days of World War II, remaining in Buckingham Palace even when London was being fractured by German bombs and refusing to send Princesses Elizabeth and Margaret out of the country. No wonder Adolf Hitler called her "the most dangerous woman in Europe." King George's family represented what the English wanted during these terrible years: a conscientious and principled king, a winning queen, and two likable young princesses, Elizabeth and Margaret.

The Queen Mother.

Still thriving at 94, the Queen Mother has become a beloved national institution. Adored for her approachability and cheerful mien, the QM was described by photographer Cecil Beaton as "the great mother figure and nanny of us all." A red-hot number in the '20s, she still likes "drinky-poos" (gin and tonic) before dinner, but she has never forgiven President Jimmy Carter for his shameful breach of etiquette: he

Queen Elizabeth and Prince Philip at the July wedding of Sarah Armstrong-Jones.

FOLLOW THE ROYAL LINE

The Windsors are but the latest of many families to rule the kingdom. Here is the complete lineage for Britain's crown according to *Whitaker's Almanac*, listed by year of accession.

Saxons and Danes	
Egbert	827
Ethelwulf	839
Ethelbald	858
Ethelbert	858
Ethelred	866
Alfred the Great	871
Edward the Elder	899
Athelstan	925
Edmund	940
Edred	946
Edwy	955
Edgar	959
Edward the Martyr	975
Ethelred II	978
Edmund Ironside	1016
Canute the Dane	1017
Harold I	1035
Hardicanute	1040
Edward the Confessor	1042
Harold II	1066
The House of Normandy	
William I	1066
William II	1087
Henry I	1100
Stephen	1135
The House of Plantagenet	
Henry II	1154
Richard I	1189
John	1199
Henry III	1216
Edward I	1272
Edward II	1307
Edward III	1327
Richard II	1377
The House of Lancaster	
Henry IV	1399
Henry V	1413
Henry VI	1422
The House of York	
Edward IV	1461
Edward V	1483
Richard II	1483
The House of Tudor	
Henry VII	1485
Henry VIII	1509
Edward VI	1547
Jane	1553
Mary I	1553
Elizabeth I	1558
The House of Stuart	
James I (VI of Scotland)	1603
Charles I	1625
[Commonwealth declared, 1649]	
The House of Stuart (restored)	
Charles II	1660
James II (VII of Scotland)	1685
William II and Mary II	1689
Anne	1702
The House of Hanover	
George I	1714
George II	1727
George III	1760
George IV	1820
William IV	1830
Victoria	1837
The House of Saxe-Coburg	
Edward VII	1901
The House of Windsor	
George V	1910
Edward VIII	1936
George VI	1936
Elizabeth II	1952

kissed her on the lips.

London merchants quake when they see her coming. It's not her taste in tulle, it's that she reportedly rarely pays her accounts. And she's still keen as a tack. Says one old friend of her wicked wit: "She doesn't take prisoners."

Born Lady Elizabeth Bowes-Lyon, the serenely beautiful young woman was the Di of her day. But fearing life in the royal fishbowl, she twice rejected marriage proposals from the painfully shy, stammering Prince Albert, who called her "the most wonderful person in the world."

It is amazing that this five-foot-tall aristocrat, the last Empress of India and the honorary colonel of eighteen regiments, who has probably never cooked a meal or made a bed, is considered "everybody's mum." But the festivities surrounding her ninetieth birthday in 1990 confirmed the devotion she has long inspired.

When King George, a heavy smoker, died of lung cancer in 1952 at the age of 57, his daughter **Elizabeth II** took up the scepter knowing that her main job would be to preserve the gains her parents had made. Admittedly, Elizabeth is a figurehead, a constitutional monarch who reigns but does not rule. Yet no one trifles with the 68-year-old woman known at Buckingham Palace as The Boss. Part of her power is ex officio: It is bad form to contradict Her Most Excellent Majesty, Elizabeth the Second, by the Grace of God, of the United Kingdom of Great Britain and Northern Ireland and of Her other Realms and Territories, Queen, Head of the Commonwealth, Defender of the Faith. It is also hard to disagree with someone whom *Fortune* reckons as the world's richest woman.

But much of Elizabeth's authority arises from the immovable force of her character. This is the monarch who at 27 overrode the objections of advisers and ordered her coronation to be televised because, she said, "I have to be seen to be believed." Who continued to appear in public and ride in open cars after her husband's favorite uncle, Lord

PALACE PATOIS: A GLOSSARY

The royals not only live differently from us common folk, they also speak differently. In addition to talking a British version of Yuppie-speak that one argot arbiter calls haute Sloane, the Queen and her kin have coined or cultivated a few colorful terms all their own.

Fish Face
A nickname Diana used for Charles.

Sausage
Philip's affectionate nickname for the Queen.

Buck House or **B.P.**
Buckingham Palace.

K.P.
Kensington Palace, where Charles and Di lived together in better days

Dorgi
The result of an accidental mating between one of the Queen's corgis and Margaret's dachshund.

Husky
Not a dog, but a padded jacket worn for pheasant shooting.

Unhelpful
Queen Mother's term for troublesome people she dislikes.

Chinless Day
The Queen with a Sense of Humor Failure (S.O.H.F.). "I'm in one of my chinless days," she'll say, chin down. Happy days are "chin days."

How Amusing
What the Queen says, seconds before walking off, when she is not amused.

Mountbatten, was assassinated by an IRA bomb in 1979. And who in 1982 coolly kept a disturbed intruder talking on the edge of her bed until she could summon help.

She grew up during the London blitz and matured in the ensuing period of austerity. The world's wealthiest woman still wanders around Buckingham Palace turning off lights. The heat is kept low and there are no objections; there never are. And when one of her favorite dogs killed a hare, the Queen carefully picked it up and presented it to the kitchen staff. "We can eat this," she announced.

When Elizabeth II rings, a staff of 300 jumps. When the queen is in London, the PM calls on her every Tuesday to brief her on government business. Though not a quick study, Elizabeth is assiduous, has a phenomenal memory, and frequently embarrasses ministers by knowing more about the issues than they do.

Elizabeth's hold on her subjects begins with her family. When as a thirteen-year-old she met a dashing cadet, she instantly decided that he was Midshipman Right. Five years later she had not changed her mind, and so in 1947 she married **Prince Philip** of Greece, a great-great-grandchild of Queen Victoria. Britain's sceptered marriage has survived for almost fifty years.

Although Elizabeth has inevitably dominated her husband in the public realm, in the world of the Windsor family the duke of Edinburgh has had authority over educating the children: first Prince Charles and Princess Anne, later Princes Andrew and Edward. But Elizabeth's will is what holds the family and the royal public image together.

Her own image is not universally admired, at least from a fashion point of view. Dressing in a style that can be characterized as pseudo-frumpy, the queen stays out of the tabloids and gets her work done. While her hair is done every Monday at four p.m. by Charles Martyn, her hairdresser for the last two decades, she reads state papers and seldom glances in the mirror. Not everyone is happy about her diffidence. "I sometimes wish she had been a bit more of a clothes person," wistfully admits her couturier of four decades, Sir Hard Amies. "She doesn't care, basically. She listens to our advice, then goes off and wears shabby shoes because they're comfortable." But in fact Elizabeth does care about her appearance. Her outfits—the boxy, brightly colored clothes, clunky handbags, unfashionable reading glasses—are chosen with great deliberation to be unthreatening to women, unobtrusive to men, and easily seen by the crowds that line her path. If she were chic, she would be French, but this queen is British to her bones. That means a love of silver service and afternoon tea, bland food, sweetish wine, jigsaw puzzles, Dick Francis mysteries, and, most of all, tramps in the country amid her Thoroughbreds and her dogs. The queen feeds her six corgis and two dorgis (a dachshund-corgi mix) herself, cutting up their meat and mixing it with biscuits in their separate bowls set out every afternoon by a footman.

No one takes better care of business than Her Majesty, who has long since realized that her maritally unstable offspring have created a throne-threatening PR problem for the House of Windsor. At the close of 1992, in a now-famous speech she noted, "It has turned out to be an *annus horribilis*." If not the language of the common man, it was certainly a sentiment commonly understood. And things got even more horrible a few days after that speech. On the Queen's forty-fifth wedding anniversary, a fire gutted a corner of Windsor Castle, causing damages of up to $60 million. As a debate brewed over who should bear the cost of repairs, Elizabeth, with her unerring sense for image damage control, proclaimed that she would give up a centuries-old royal perk by commencing to pay income tax on her private fortune, as well as pony up $8.5 million toward refurbishing the Castle. And perhaps most tellingly, the Queen announced that she was removing from the Civil List the Princes Andrew and Edward and the Princesses Anne and Margaret. That meant that she was switching from the public to her personal dole the annual upkeep of this spoiled quartet, not to mention their spendthrift spouses, present or future. And in 1993 she went one step further, conceding that marketing the mystique of the monarchy was in order. On August 7, she opened nineteen state rooms in Buckingham Palace to public tours (leaving 631 rooms still off-limits) while she and the family were taking their annual summer retreat to Balmoral.

Ultimately, when verbal snipers zero in on every other royal soul, Elizabeth has risen above criticism. Her popularity continues unabated despite the scandals whirling around almost all of her children, chief among them Charles, Prince of Wales, and his wife, Princess Diana.

THE VULGAR SUBJECT

Loaded as they are, money is something the Windsors prefer not to tarnish themselves with. They never carry cash, not a penny. And it's not because they carry American Express instead. Elizabeth's famous pockectbook is a stage prop. It sometimes contains only mints for her horses. Otherwise, the Windsors come in contact with currency the way other people encounter God—mostly on Sundays. Before church, Charles is reportedly provided with a £5 note for the collection plate; he likes to have it sprayed and ironed by his valet, then neatly creased and left for him beneath his clove box. You know, the box that holds your before-dinner clove. You probably have one around somewhere.

The Windsor wealth is complicated. A considerable portion is their own, acquired by them or their ancestors with personal funds. That would include Sandringham and Balmoral, two of the royal country estates, which they own the way the Cartwrights owned the Ponderosa. Both were purchased during Queen Victoria's reign. But the greater part of the wealth that surrounds them is held in trust for the nation. That means the Windsors can wear it, sit on it, eat off it and go lightheartedly skipping down its glinting corridors. They just can't sew any name tags on it or cart it off to Christie's for auction.

If Britain should ever decide to get rid of the royal family, though, it would be a messy divorce. There's some confusion about which of their property belongs to the state and which is their own. In particular, who rightly possesses the lavish gifts from foreign potentates? Like the 2,000-year-old necklace from Egypt's former King Farouk?

By anyone's count, though, the total number is a whopper. In 1993 *Fortune* calculated that the Queen was the ninth richest person in the world. *Fortune* put Elizabeth's worth at $7.8 billion, but other appraisers believe it be much higher, given such personal assets as her racehorses, stamp collection, and art acquisitions. Charles, meanwhile, was believed to be worth about $400 million as of 1991, which would still place him among Britain's 40 wealthiest people. To paraphrase Mel Brooks: It is good to be Queen.

THE NEXT—AND PROBLEM—WINDSORS

Pity **Charles, the Prince of Wales.** Not only must he spend his life waiting to become king of England, he isn't even left in peace in the meantime. The windsurfing-parachuting-scuba-diving Action Prince of the '70s and the oratorical Philosopher Prince of the '80s has become in the public mind the Selfish Prince of the '90s. Whatever exquisite pleasures he pursues, he stands accused of conduct unbefitting a Man with Royal Responsibilities.

Charles has tried to please. Until he was thirty-two years old he lived at home with his parents. Then he found a lovely bride and promptly fulfilled his duty to begat heirs. Now all he can do is try not to go bonkers with boredom waiting for his hardy mum to pass him the scepter. Elizabeth is ticking away better than Big Ben, and Charles could end up like his great-great-grandfather, King Edward VII, who held the title of Prince of Wales for almost sixty years before his mother, Queen Victoria, passed away.

Prince Charles in a characteristic moment in a year of reflection, admission, and transition.

But in the meantime, Charles has been a relatively energetic prince of Wales. He has eschewed some preferred hobbies of heirs apparent—falconing, gambling, and conspicuous wenching (although lately that seems to be slipping)—and contributed eloquently and provocatively to the public discourse on the preservation of architecture, the environment, and the language. True enough, he has become a tad eccentric. He awakens to farming programs on the radio. He eats odd vegetable dishes like nettle soup and sells organic bread stone-ground from whole meal grown on his own farm. He believes in homeopathic medicine, frets about disappearing peat bogs, and collects antique lavatory seats. Yet all of these activities are at worst harmless, at best valuable, for an extraordinarily wealthy, inordinately spoiled gentleman patiently biding his time. As heir apparent he gets no income from the Civil List, but he does receive ample income from several estates—plus claim, by law and ancient tradition, to any whales that wash ashore.

There had been a fatal flaw in Charles's childhood: he didn't have one. Unlike prior generations of royal children, who were educated by palace tutors, he was sent to boarding schools—notably Gordonstoun, in harsh northeastern Scotland, a boot camp with books. In the '60s, when the youth of the world were exploding with passion, Charles was attending Trinity College, Cambridge, playing the cello in his tweeds. His mother, the titular head of the diminished British Commonwealth, had precious little time for him. She mostly wanted him to behave, and he did. While his upbringing didn't prepare him to be a regular guy, it certainly taught him how to be a king. But that hasn't been enough to keep together his marriage with **Lady Diana Spencer**. Despite having two adored sons, **Prince William** and **Prince Harry**, in December 1992 the Prince and Princess of Wales announced an official separation that finally ended the long charade of their once idealized, now desperately unhappy, marriage.

And 1993 saw the last hope of a happy ending fail. January brought the worldwide publication of a racy taped phone chat between Prince Charles and his confidante, Camilla Parker Bowles, wife of a brigadeer in the Royal Army Veterinary Corps who bears the title of Silver Stick in Waiting to the Queen. Charles revealed, among other steamy things, his surprising desire to live inside her "trousers or something." He purportedly declared his love for her and gushed, "In the next life, I should like to come back as your knickers."

Then in March came new revelations of a sexually charged phone conversation in which Diana discussed with *her* confidant, James Gilbey, her fear of getting pregnant. By November, Di was snapping to photographers, breaking into tears at charity events and complaining that she felt isolated and persecuted. So on December 3, when the tearful princess announced that she was greatly curtailing her public life, it appeared that the Palace had finally succeeded in reining her in. "The dream is over. The people's darling will never become queen," proclaimed columnist John Casey in the *Evening Standard*, urging Brits to dump Diana and rally round the "slightly absurd" Charles.

The Palace hoped that 1994, marking the twenty-fifth anniversary of his investiture as prince of Wales, would be the Year of Charles—a year in which he would repair an image tarnished by his disastrous marriage. The prince is clearly fighting an uphill battle for the hearts of his countryment. While he earned high marks for his solo performance on a seventeen-day January-February trip to New Zealand and Australia, where he displayed admirable sangfroid when a protester brandished a starter's pistol at him, he lost ground with a May speech in which he attacked political correctness. And his trip to Russia, also in January, was overshadowed by a bungled public relations offensive: After his friends told the tabloids that Princess Diana had lavished $240,000 on personal expenses in a single year, her camp revealed that, in the same period, he spent $650,000 for must-haves, including manicures and polo ponies.

Still, the headlines from ITV's *Charles, the Private Man, the Public Role,* hardly seemed to help his cause. When host Jonathan Dim-

Diana enjoys a light moment with sons William (left) and Harry on a ski trip in Lech, Austria.

bleby (a New Age devotee approved by Charles) asked the prince whether he had tried to be faithful to the most glamorous woman in Britain, he answered, "Yes," then added, "until it became clear that the marriage had irretrievable broken down." (Dimbleby did not press him, and Charles gave no specifics about when he deemed it dead.)

Aside from admitting that he had broken his marriage vows, Charles gave the impression that he was temperamentally unsuited to inherit his mother's job. Describing himself as "a private person" who "isn't very good at being a performing monkey," he complained about the intrusions of the media and the pain of having to follow a schedule set out months in advance. "I can't describe the horror of it," he said. And he confessed that he would prefer to be seen as a "defender of faith" rather than the Defender of the Faith—supporting the notion that he hopes that by the time he is king, the monarch will no longer head the Church of England.

In any case, Charles and his wife have reached a kind of détente. Despite her attempts to upstage him in public, their private relationship is slightly more civil than it once was. On June 11, when they met at Ludgrove for their sons' sports day, Di greeted him with a well-documented peck on the cheek.

While some have speculated that the Camilla scandal will inspire the Queen to pass over him and make William her heir, Charles himself has no doubt that he will be the next monarch.

If you're heartbroken that Diana might not be queen and hasn't had the romance of the century, don't dab your eyes—there are no tears in her teacup. "Most people think that of the two—Charles and Diana—Diana is the one with steel," asserts Brian Hoey, author of *The New Court*. "She's her own woman, and she knows exactly what she wants to do, in the same way the Queen Mother did and does. She's a very tough lady. She's had to be."

For Diana is first and foremost a Spencer. That means she is more English than half the royal family, according to a recent genealogical study. Way down yonder in the twenty-first century, when her son Prince William accedes to the throne, he will have more English blood in him than any monarch since James I, who, though mostly Scottish, was twenty-five percent English.

Indeed Di was never cowed by the royal family. She first took aim at Charles when she was sweet sixteen during a pheasant shoot. And she pursued the heir as only a Sloaney English seductress would—disguised in tartans, tweeds, twin-sets, and pearls, a cross between Mary Poppins and Mata Hari. And the world knows, she got her man.

Immediately and single-handedly she lent fresh glamour and force to a fairly dowdy dynasty. As princess of Wales she put her life and soul into the most wrenching social issues without ever flinching. "Against the advice of friends," adds author Hoey, "she was the first royal to shake hands without a glove with an AIDS patient. She knew that that photograph would help allay fears. It was a very brave thing to do."

Diana began with one overriding duty—to produce an heir, preferably male—and she was fortunate enough within two years of her marriage to produce two towheads, known as the heir and the spare. And now the boys must ricochet among very different worlds, something to which Wills and Harry are still adjusting. By all accounts, William, who lives with the burden of being Charles's heir, has felt the pain most acutely. Once an extrovert, he has become noticeably quieter. And when the Waleses were still under the same roof, it often fell to William to comfort his mother when she was distraught. He reportedly told one friend that he wanted to be a policeman, in order to "look after my mother."

By contrast, second son Harry is "a mischievous imp," as Diana's brother, Earl Spencer put it, who shows fewer signs of distress. Bold on the ski slopes and a terror on the go-cart track, he loves plants and animals (as does Dad) and worships his older brother. Both are boarders at Ludgrove School in Berkshire, where newspapers are scarce and TV viewing is strictly limited. While they receive no special treatment in the classroom, the two are attended by a rotating crew of Royal Protection Squad bodyguards, one of whom sleeps next to Wills's spartan dorm room. So close is the bond between the brothers and their minders that Charles sometimes tries to enforce a bit of distance.

On school breaks, the boys alternate between their parents, who share custody. Diana kits them out in jeans and baseball caps, lavishes hugs and kisses, and takes them to McDonald's. Charles, raised among the Windsors, who lavish affection on dogs and horses rather than children, rarely touches his sons in public; weekends with Dad usually mean dressing in suits or landed-gentry tweed jackets.

Although Diana remains affectionate with her boys, for much of the year she has seemed to Windsor watchers like a woman adrift. With William and Harry at school, Di's role as a mother is hardly enough, and after giving up her much-loved charity work, she seems to be at a loss. Sources close to Diana say that she has seemed mercurial: Although it was her idea to dismiss her detectives, she finds it hard to handle the press without them.

The alliance that has raised eyebrows—and provoked envy—on Fleet Street is her friendship with the *Daily Mail*'s Richard Kay. The thirty-eight-year-old bachelor befriended Di during her trip to Zimbabwe in July 1993. "He has become a sort of self-appointed press secretary," says a veteran Palace watcher. "He gives her unqualified support, and she gives him inside information." Even observers sympathetic to Diana believe that her alliance with Kay has pointed up her vulnerability and lack of judgment. They note that she encouraged friends to speak to Andrew Morton—whose *Diana: Her True Story* helped alienate the Windsors forever—and that unburdening herself to Kay could lead to a similar embarrassment.

If there is a cure for Diana's presumed malaise, royal watchers believe it may involve returning to public life—at least part-time. Di herself has hinted that she may not be in retirement forever. In April, she made a surprise appearance at a lunch for the charity

The Princess doesn't step out as much as previously, but when she does her glamour remains unrivaled.

Help the Hospices. When newsmen asked whether they would be seeing more of her, she said coyly, "You may be." And her Red Cross role of part-time roving ambassador has taken her to Geneva and will include trips to observe relief efforts, though her workload remains light. Her missions are expected to claim no more than a few days a year, and the Palace reportedly wants to "keep the lid on her Swiss role so she can't upstage Charles again," according to a story in *Today*.

Of course Diana and Charles are not the only royals having trouble making peace with the idea of a loveless marriage. Hitched for sixteen years, Charles's younger sister, **Princess Anne,** and Captain Mark Phillips were initially drawn together by their passion for horses (both are extraordinary equestrians). But Anne's interests were much broader—she is president of Save the Children Fund and was even nominated for the Nobel Peace Prize a few years back. Says Anne of her work, "You have to decide at the end of the day if you can live with yourself." You also have to decide if you can live with your husband, and the affirmative answer increasingly came into doubt. Finally the couple separated in 1989, and after divorcing, Anne married long-time love Timothy Laurence, five years her junior, in December 1992. As close to her mother as any of her siblings, Anne staged her second wedding as an intimate family affair, attended by only a handful of relatives including her two children with Phillips, **Peter** and **Zara**.

Anne's second brother, rowdy **Prince Andrew, Duke of York**, has had his share—perhaps the lion's share—of marital bad luck as well. After a plucky performance in the Falklands conflict, helicopter pilot Andy seemed interested mainly in oat-sewing and club-crawling with a string of steamy ladies, culminating in former soft-porn star Koo Stark. What well-bred English girl would marry Andrew and put up with him?

And so when the prince's roving eye fell upon Sarah Ferguson in 1985, the nation breathed a collective sigh of relief. A strapping, worldly wench who loved a good time, Fergie seemed perfectly suited to her happy-go-lucky hubby. But while **Sarah, Duchess of York**, produced two lovely daughters, **Princesses Beatrice** and **Eugenie**, she also committed gaffe after gaffe. If the Yorks often struck the public as a pair of heedless hedonists, at least they originally seemed besotted with each other—a touching assumption not applicable to all Windsor marriages. But Fergie's erratic behavior quickly brought that into doubt as well. After a series of romantic trysts and crass missteps on her part, the Duchess was formally separated from the Duke in 1992. Later that year London tabs were abrim with graphic photos of Fergie on the Riviera cavorting topless with her American-born "financial advisor," John Bryan, who was shown smooching the bare instep of her foot while her two young daughters looked on.

Prince Andrew and Queen Elizabeth, at the Windsor horse show.

This August she confessed that the publication of those photos had been her "most humiliating experience." Fergie admitted that, "During the first years of my marriage I probably had an excessive ego. The St. Tropez photos forced me to change and care more about others than myself." But what is she thinking of Andrew these days? Although the two exchanged kisses at a summer charity golf game, chums say a rematch is unlikely. "They are very good friends, and that is how they wish to remain," a pal told the London *Daily Express*.

The youngest of Elizabeth's four children, **Prince Edward** seems like a dinghy in the wake of bigger boats, bobbing and bailing as his three older siblings surge ahead with their lives, however troubled. More underestimated than underdeveloped, however, Edward has blazed a difficult path that has brought him both criticism and success. Brits, and his queenly mother, are ambivalent about him for quitting the Royal Marines in 1987, a move that earned him the label "Wimp of Windsor" and that fueled speculation about his sexual preference. But Edward's independence of mind may make him the most interesting member of the royal family yet. He has become, for instance, the first child of a reigning monarch to—gulp—take a real job, initially as a gofer with Andrew Lloyd Webber's Really Useful Theatre Company. After becoming overseas manager of *Cats* and *Starlight Express*, Edward left Webber's company and now is joint managing director of a television production company, Ardent Productions. His business cards read simply, "Edward Windsor."

Fergie on an outing with Beatrice (left) and Eugenie.

Loyal to his dreams as well as the British ideal of monarchy, the queen's youngest child is, ran one editorial, "on the way to becoming the first really modern royal." He also appears on his way to becoming the next married royal. Dating London public relations rep Sophie Rhys-Jones—a Di look-alike who is distantly related to the princess—since last winter, Edward has been trying to take things slowly.

In a public letter at the end of last year, asking the media to allow the "friendship" to progress in peace, he wrote, "Other members of my immediate family have

A ROYAL CALENDAR

A listing of birthdays and other special royal milestones. (Source: *Whitaker's Almanac*)

Prince Andrew	February 19, 1960	Princess Beatrice	August 8, 1988
Prince Edward	March 10, 1964	Princess Anne	August 15, 1950
Princess Eugenie	March 23, 1990	Princess Margaret	August 21, 1930
Queen Elizabeth	April 21, 1926	Prince Henry	September, 15, 1984
The Queen's coronation	June 2, 1953	Duchess of York (Sarah)	October 15, 1959
Prince Philip	June 10, 1921	Prince Charles	November 14, 1948
Prince William	June 21, 1982	The Queen's wedding	November 20, 1947
Princess Diana	July 1, 1961	Princess Alexandra	December 25, 1936
Queen Mother	August 4, 1900		

been subjected to similar attention and it has not been at all beneficial to their relationships." Finally, on May 2, at Balmoral, Edward watchers got what they'd been waiting for when the prince gave Sophie a kiss in full view of photographers.

Edward's fascination with the theater is hardly unusual among the Windsors. Indeed if the family reigned in Beverly Hills instead of Westminster, the queen's younger sister, **Princess Margaret**, would be the family's Elizabeth Taylor. She has been onstage since age six, when she had a walk-on part in her father's coronation. With her theatrical props—a tortoiseshell cigarette holder, a tumbler of Famous Grouse whisky, and a circle of intimates in the arts—the Princess has played varied roles: tragic lover, wife, mother, divorcée, and regal grand dame. She emanates star quality, complete with romantic intrigues, erratic public behavior, mysterious health problems, and Sunset Boulevard brass. "I can't imagine anything more wonderful," she once said, "than being who I am."

Precocious and irrepressible as a child, the violet-eyed and theatrical Margaret wrapped George VI around her finger. Other men proved harder to keep. As a teenager she fell hard for a dashing fighter pilot named Peter Townsend, sixteen years her senior, but finally passed him up at twenty-two when her union with the divorced Townsend was declared acceptable only if she gave up her claim to the throne and her royal income and if she would live abroad for five years.

Several years later Margaret walked the aisle with photographer Antony Armstrong-Jones (who became **Lord Snowdon** after the wedding). She produced two children with the artistic commoner: David (**Viscount Linley)** and **Lady Sarah Armstrong-Jones**. But their eighteen-year marriage was not a picture-book affair. Initially rejecting separation as too scandalous, both partners discreetly sizzled with old and new flames until the tabs ran pictures of Margaret and her lover Roddy Llewellyn, a gardener and wanna-be pop singer seventeen years her junior. An uncontested divorce was granted in 1978.

But Margaret's son, David, did his part to show the happy side of royal life—his marriage in 1993 to Serena Stanhope, a blue blood with cover-girl looks, was a windfall for the monarchy, and their lavish nuptials at St. Margaret's Church were billed as the Wedding of the Year, drawing 650 guests.

As dazzling as the lives of the Windsors seem, ultimately being royal carries with it an incalculable personal price tag. Family members live with the nozzles of public fascination open full against them. And it's an irony of their station that even though they live their whole lives in public, they can barely speak their minds there. But the true value of the royal family lies in the realm of moist eyes and lumps in the throat. They give Britain a symbol of nationhood, something as sumptuous and venerable as a work of art—a source of incalculable pride and pleasure. Most British will tell you the Windsors are worth every penny of their keep.

Sophie Rhys-Jones, a distant relative of Diana's, may be the next bright hope of the Windsors.

Edward and Sophie Rhys-Jones out for a stroll.

SUCCESSION: THE BUCK HOUSE BULLPEN

Under rules codified in the eighteenth century, rightful candidates to the British crown move up inexorably except for two disqualifiers: they cannot be Catholic (or marry into that faith) or be born out of wedlock. Unlike some European monarchies, which abide by the centuries-old Salic law—the exclusion of women from succession—the Court of St. James owes its vitality in great part to females. Victoria and the current queen, for instance, are two of history's longest-reigning sovereigns. This is not to say that Britain's accession rules are not sexist; a monarch is succeeded by his or her eldest son, then by that son's sons in descending order of age, and only then by that son's daughters. The line starts again with the monarch's next youngest son, and so on, ending with the sovereign's daughters and their children. After the offspring are accounted for, the sovereign's brothers come next, followed finally by sisters. From there the line marches through uncles, aunts, and full courts of cousins, including, currently at No. 32, James Lascelles, 41, a onetime Albuquerque, N.M., deejay.

Herewith, the top twenty-five in the royal bullpen:

1. HRH The Prince of Wales (Prince Charles), 45

2. HRH Prince William of Wales, 12 (son of Prince Charles)

3. HRH Prince Henry of Wales, 10 (second son of Prince Charles)

4. HRH The Duke of York (Prince Andrew), 34 (second son of Queen Elizabeth)

5. HRH Princess Beatrice of York, 6 (daughter of Prince Andrew)

6. HRH Princess Eugenie of York, 4 (second daughter of Prince Andrew)

7. HRH Prince Edward, 30 (third son of Queen Elizabeth)

8. HRH The Princess Royal (Princess Anne), 44 (daughter of Queen Elizabeth—for now, the highest ranking divorced royal)

9. Peter Phillips, 18 (the highest ranking commoner, son of Princess Anne)

10. Zara Phillips, 13 (daughter of Princess Anne)

11. HRH Princess Margaret, 64 (sister of Queen Elizabeth)

12. Viscount Linley (David), 32 (son of Princess Margaret)

13. Lady Sarah Armstrong-Jones, 30 (daughter of Princess Margaret)

14. HRH The Duke of Gloucester, 50 (grandson of King George V, Queen Elizabeth's cousin)

15. The Earl of Ulster (Alexander), 20 (son of the duke of Gloucester)

16. Lady Davina Windsor, 17 (daughter of the duke of Gloucester)

17. Lady Rose Windsor, 14 (second daughter of the duke of Gloucester)

18. HRH The Duke of Kent (Edward), 59 (cousin to both Queen Elizabeth and Prince Philip and son of George, duke of Kent, younger brother of Kings Edward VII and George VI)

19. Lord Downpatrick, 6 (son of the duke of Kent's eldest son, the earl of St. Andrews, who was dropped from the line when he married a Catholic)

20. Lord Nicholas Windsor, 24 (second son of the duke of Kent)

21. Lady Helen "Melons" Windsor, 30 (daughter of the duke of Kent)

22. Lord Frederick Windsor, 15 (son of Prince Michael of Kent, who was dropped from the line for marrying a Catholic; Queen Elizabeth's cousin Prince Michael is the younger brother of the duke of Kent)

23. Lady Gabriella Windsor, 13 (daughter of Prince Michael)

24. HRH Princess Alexandra, 58 (Queen Elizabeth's cousin, granddaughter of King George V)

25. James Ogilvy, 30 (son of Princess Alexandra)

ROYAL HOUSES AROUND THE WORLD

Most of them have little or no actual political power, but hereditary monarchies are clinging to their traditional thrones in several countries. Herewith an international round-up of places where the crown still glitters.

BELGIUM

Current monarch: King Albert II (crowned 1993)

King Albert II, prince of Liège, was born on June 6, 1934. He is the son of King Leopold III and Queen Astrid, princess of Sweden, and the brother of the late King Baudouin of Belgium.

The Royal Family:

King Albert II was married to Paola Ruffo di Calabria, the daughter of a princely Italian family, in 1959. The king and queen have three children: Prince Philippe (b. 1960), Princess Astrid (b. 1962), who is now married to the Archduke Lorenz of East Austria, and Prince Laurent (b. 1963). The royal palace is in Brussels.

DENMARK

Current monarch: Queen Margarethe II (crowned 1972)

Margarethe Alexandrine Torhilder Ingrid, the eldest daughter of King Frederik IX and Queen Ingrid of Denmark, was born on April 16, 1940.

The Royal Family:

Margarethe married French diplomat Henri-Marie-Jean-André, count de Laborde de Monpezat, in 1967 (he changed his name to Prince Henrik upon marriage). The queen and consort have two sons, Prince Frederik (b. 1963) and Prince Joachim (b. 1969). Crown Prince Frederik, as the official heir to the Danish throne, will eventually become King Frederik X. Besides the official residence in Copenhagen, the family also has a small mansion in southern France at Cahors, the home district of Prince Henrik.

JAPAN

Current monarch: Emperor Akihito (crowned 1989)

Born on December 23, 1933, Emperor Akihito is the eldest son of the late Emperor Hirohito (posthumously known as Emperor Showa) and Empress Nagako.

The Royal Family:

Emperor Akihito married Michiko Shoda in 1959. She is the eldest daughter of the Shoda family, a prominent name in Japanese industrial and academic circles. The emperor and empress live in the imperial palace in Tokyo, and they have three children: Crown Prince Naruhito (b. 1960; married in 1993 to Crown Princess Masako amid much public attention), Prince Akishino (b. 1965; married in 1990 to Princess Akishino), and Princess Sayako (b. 1969).

LIECHTENSTEIN

Current monarch: Prince Hans Adam II (crowned 1989)

His Serene Highness Prince Hans Adam II is the eldest son of the late Prince Franz Josef II of Liechtenstein and Countess Gina von Wilczek. He was born on February 14, 1945.

The Royal Family:

Hans Adam II married Countess Marie Kinsky von Wchinitz and Tettau of Prague in 1967. The couple has four children: Crown Prince Alois (b. 1968; married to Duchess Sophie of Bavaria in 1993), Prince Maximilian (b. 1969), Prince Constantin (b. 1972), and Princess Tatjana (b. 1973). The royal family resides in the Vaduz Castle.

LUXEMBOURG

Current monarch: Grand Duke Jean (crowned 1964)

Grand Duke Jean was born on January 5, 1921. He is the eldest son of the late Grand Duchess Charlotte and Prince Felix of Luxembourg, prince of Bourbon Parma. He is the direct descendant of French kings Henri IV, Louis XIII, and Louis XIV.

The Royal Family:

Grand Duke Jean was married to Princess Joséphine-Charlotte of Belgium in 1953. She is the daughter of Prince Leopold of Belgium and Princess Astrid of Sweden, and the sister of the late King Baudouin of Belgium. The royal couple resides in the Castle of Colmar-Berg in Luxembourg, and they have five children: Princess Marie-Astrid (b. 1954), Prince Henri (b. 1955; the hereditary grand duke of Luxembourg), Prince Jean and his twin sister Princess Margaretha (b. 1957), and Prince Guillaume (b. 1963).

MONACO

Current monarch: Prince Rainier III (crowned 1949)

The Sovereign Prince of Monaco and head of the House of Grimaldi, Prince Rainier III, was born on May 31, 1923. He is the grandson of the late Prince Louis II of Monaco and the son of Princess Charlotte and Prince Pierre, count of Polignac.

The Royal Family:

Prince Rainier III married American actress Grace Kelly (1928–1982) in 1956. She was the daughter of John B. and Margaret Kelly of Philadelphia. The couple had three children: Princess Caroline (b. 1957), Crown Prince Albert (b. 1958), and Princess Stephanie (b. 1965). The royal palace is in Monte Carlo, and the family owns a private residence in Paris.

THE NETHERLANDS

Current monarch: Queen Beatrix (crowned 1980)

Beatrix Wilhemina Armgard was born on January 31, 1938, the first child of Queen Juliana and Prince Bernhard of the Netherlands.

The Royal Family:

Queen Beatrix was married to a German diplomat, Claus von Amsberg, in 1966, and the royal couple now resides in the Huis ten Bosch Palace in the Hague. The queen and prince have three sons: Prince Willem-Alexander Claus Georg Ferdinand (b. 1967), Prince Johan Friso Bernhard Christiaan David (b. 1968), and Prince Constantijn Christof Frederik Aschwin (b. 1969).

NORWAY

Current monarch: King Harald (crowned 1991)

Born on February 21, 1937, King Harald is the firstborn son of the late King Olav V and Princess Märtha.

The Royal Family

The announcement that King Harald was to marry commoner Sonja Haraldsen in 1968 triggered much debate about the future of the Norwegian monarchy. Since their marriage, however, Queen Sonja has been accepted by the public. The king and queen, who reside in the royal palace in Oslo, have a daughter, Princess Märtha Louise (b. 1971), and a son, Crown Prince Haakon (b. 1973).

SPAIN

Current monarch: King Juan Carlos (crowned 1975)

Juan Carlos Víctor María de Borbón y Borbón was born on January 5, 1938. He is the first son of Don Juan de Borbón y Battenberg and Doña María de las Mercedes de Borbón y Orléans, and the grandson of King Alfonso XIII and Queen Victoria Eugenia, who was herself the granddaughter of Queen Victoria of England.

The Royal Family:

King Juan Carlos married Princess Sofía, the daughter of King Paul I and Queen Fredericka of Greece, in 1961. The king and queen have three children: Princess Elena (b. 1963), Princess Cristina (b. 1964), and Crown Prince Felipe (b. 1968). The Palacio de La Zarzuela, their official residence, is situated five kilometers outside of Madrid. The royal family's summer residence, the Palace of Marivent, is in the city of Las Palmas on the island of Mallorca.

SWEDEN

Current monarch: Carl XVI Gustaf (crowned 1973)

Carl XVI Gustaf was born on April 30, 1946, the youngest child and only son of Prince Gustaf Adolf of Sweden and Princess Sibylla of Sachsen-Coburg-Gotha.

The Royal Family

Carl XVI Gustaf married commoner Silvia Renate Sommerlath, daughter of Walther and Alice Sommerlath of the Federal Republic of Germany, in 1976. The king and queen have three children: Princess Victoria (b. 1977), Prince Carl Philip (b. 1979), and Princess Madeleine (b. 1982). In 1980 the Swedish act of succession was changed to allow females the same rights of succession as males; the crown passes to the eldest child regardless of sex. Thus, eldest daughter Victoria has been named the crown princess and successor to Karl XVI Gustaf. The family lived in the royal palace in Stockholm until 1981, when they moved to Drottningholm Palace on the outskirts of the city.

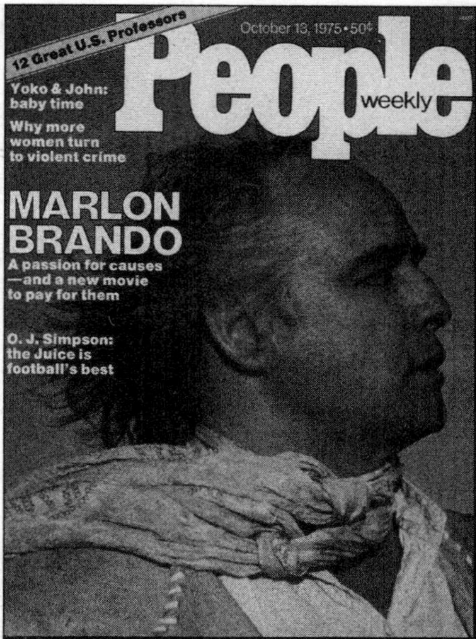

12 Great U.S. Professors
October 13, 1975 • 50¢
People weekly
Yoko & John: baby time
Why more women turn to violent crime
MARLON BRANDO
A passion for causes —and a new movie to pay for them
O. J. Simpson: the Juice is football's best
People weekly
EXCLUSIVE PHOTOS
JULIA'S WEDDING ALBUM!
The inside story of her whirlwind romance and surprise marriage to LYLE LOVETT
Newlyweds Julia Roberts and Lyle Lovett in Marion, Ind.

SCREEN

May 16, 1977 • 60¢
People weekly
Bonnie Franklin: TV's top Mom turns hoofer
Don King: on the ropes?
Erica Jong's happy landing
JANE FONDA
America loves her again—but ex-husband Vadim recalls her years of fear & rebellion
Aretha • Ringo's grandchild • Claus von Bulow
Heather Thomas kicks cocaine
People weekly
Maria Shriver's man
ARNOLD
Why JFK's niece loves the savviest, silliest strong man in showbiz

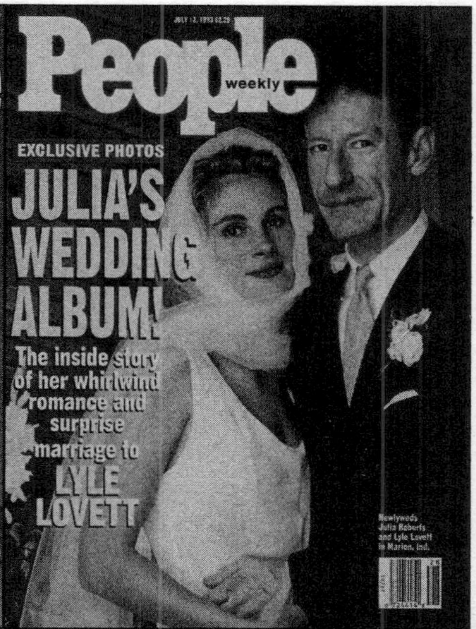

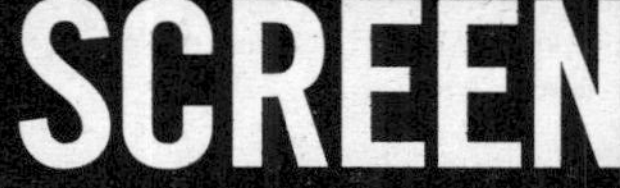

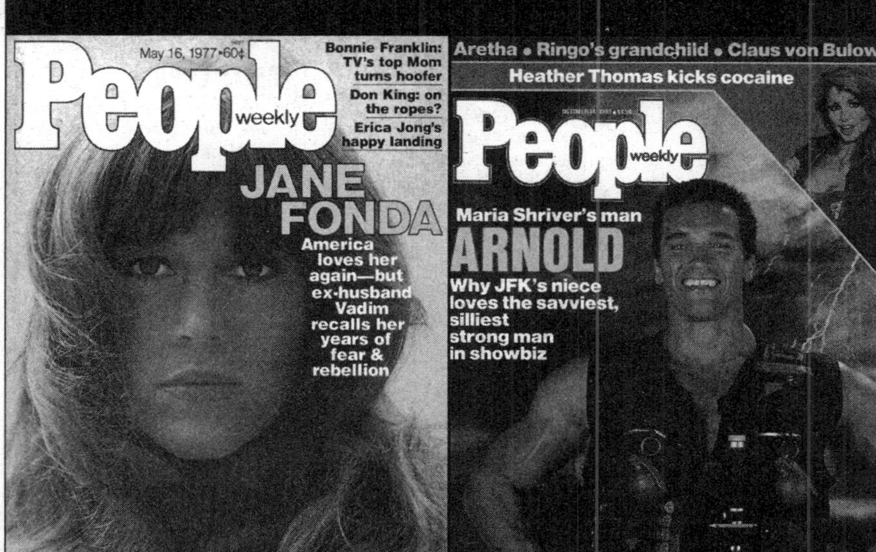

ACE VENTURA: PET DETECTIVE

Jim Carrey, Courteney Cox, Sean Young

On the eve of the Super Bowl, Snowflake, the Miami Dolphins' mascot, is kidnapped; in utter desperation, the team's director of marketing (Cox) turns to Carrey, a Robin Williams type run badly amok, to solve the mystery of the missing mammal. And then—holy halftime!—the Dolphins' star quarterback (Dan Marino as himself) also makes an unscheduled disappearance. Once again, Carrey is on the case despite the disapproval of the local police lieutenant (Young), who may not be quite what she seems. Replete with rude noises, pathetic table manners, and bathroom jokes that would discredit a second grader, *Ace Ventura* is an endeavor that all concerned should omit from their resumes. (PG-13)

BACKBEAT

Stephen Dorff, Sheryl Lee

Stu Sutcliffe (Dorff), an art-school friend of John Lennon's, played bass with the Beatles in the early days but quickly decided he would be happier being a painter and settling down with his lover, Astrid Kirchherr (Lee). He died of a brain hemorrhage at age 21 in 1962. As far as one can tell from *Backbeat*, his chief influence on the Fab Four would seem to have been the mop top, a variation on a haircut Astrid gave him. In other words, *Backbeat* fails to make any sense of this pop-musical footnote. Lennon, at least, is well played by Ian Hart—who, oddly, had the same part in *The Hours and Times*, a smaller, quieter, and altogether superior 1992 film that speculated about Lennon's relationship with manager Brian Epstein. (R)

BAD GIRLS

Madeleine Stowe, Mary Stuart Masterson, Andie MacDowell, Drew Barrymore, James LeGros

An oater about four prostitutes running from the law, *Bad Girls* simply has too much yappin' and too much plot. Despite this, and actually almost because of its excesses, the movie has a certain loopy, lurid appeal. Stowe, Masterson, MacDowell, and Barrymore stomp around in breeches as if auditioning for the *I Love Lucy* grape-mashing scene. As one of them says in one of the movie's hoot-worthier lines, "We sold our bodies. Why can't we sell wood?" (R)

BARCELONA

Taylor Nichols, Chris Eigeman, Tushka Bergen

Nichols is a sales rep for a Chicago-based corporation, doing a tour of duty in Barcelona. Confused about work and confused about love, he confides to his shiftless, feckless, and aggravating cousin (Eigeman), a Navy lieutenant on shore leave, his plan to go out with only "plain or even rather homely women." All lofty intentions are off when he meets Bergen, a beauteous translator who shares his love for disco music. The romance is played out against a rising tide of political tension and violence, and a rising tide of tension between the cousins. Nichols and Eigeman play off each other with great verve. Together, they're the strongest part of *Barcelona*, which, however fetching and witty, seems less a narrative than a series of blackout sketches. (PG-13)

BEING HUMAN

Robin Williams

There's a certain haziness of meaning and purpose that hangs over all of *Being Human*, making this ambitious comedy-drama about man's search for family and sense of belonging across the centuries a movie that probably requires more patience and forbearance than the average filmgoer is willing to give. In a series of five vignettes, Williams plays a man named Hector who, whether a caveman, a slave in the Roman Empire, a medieval Crusader, a sixteenth-century Portugese nobleman or a '90s slumlord, needs to make peace with himself and with the ties binding him to those he loves. *Human* is not without its affecting moments, but in the end, it's notable more for the movie it's trying to be than for the one it actually is. (PG-13)

BELLE EPOQUE

Fernando Fernan Gomez, Jorge Sanz, Maribel Verdu, Ariadna Gil, Miriam Diaz-Aroca, Penelope Cruz

The Academy Award winner as the year's best foreign-language film, this Spanish production is an amusingly sexy romp about a young man who sleeps with all four sisters in a family while managing to stay in the good graces of not only the women but their father too. Not since *Cousin, Cousine*, the 1975 French hit, has there been a European film with as cheery an attitude toward promiscuity. (R)

BEVERLY HILLS COP III

Eddie Murphy, Timothy Carhart, John Saxon, Judge Reinhold, Hector Elizondo, Theresa Randle

The latest and least in the movie series about the righteous Detroit cop (Murphy) who keeps chasing cases all the way to Beverly Hills, *Cop III* is one big yawn and no yucks. The *Baretta*-on-a-bad-day script is populated with cardboard villains and boys-and-their-toys car chases and gunfights. Other than the sight early on of two fatso mechanics lip-synching and boogying to Diana Ross and the Supremes' "Come See About Me" and Bronson Pinchot reprising his Serge role from *Cop I*, there is not an honest laugh to be had. (R)

BLINK

Madeleine Stowe, Aidan Quinn

Stowe, a professional violinist who has been blind since childhood, regains partial sight after a cornea transplant. Soon afterward she glimpses a serial murderer fleeing his crime, then becomes romantically involved with Quinn, the police detective who's trying to solve the case. The story may sound like standard issue disabled-woman-in-distress, but *Blink* succeeds because it offers flinty characters we haven't seen before, surprising plot twists, credible suspense, and gritty dialogue. Although it never quite transcends its genre limitations, *Blink* is a sleeper that deserves to be seen. (R)

BLUE CHIPS

Nick Nolte, Mary McDonnell, Shaquille O'Neal

Nolte is basketball coach at a Los Angeles university; he has won two national titles but now has a losing team. Will he compromise his principles to let rich alumni pay off the high-school stars he needs to recruit? Little restraint is shown by anyone, and none by Nolte, who seems to think he is doing Hamlet at Inchon as he shows anguish by willing instant furrows into his brow. As for O'Neal, who plays Nolte's prime prospect, he is a terrible actor and renders most of his lines incomprehensible with mush-mouthed diction. (PG-13)

BODY SNATCHERS

Gabrielle Anwar, Terry Kinney, Meg Tilly, Billy Wirth

Even beyond the context of the political paranoia of its 1950s origins, this tale about aliens who take over the bodies of humans remains scarily absorbing and difficult to shrug off. This is the third film to be based on Jack Finney's 1954 novel *The Body Snatchers*, this time directed by New York cult favorite Abel Ferrara, who enhances the mounting suspense with lots of murky lighting and ominous music. The seedpod aliens that metamor-

TOP MOVIES OF 1994

Week by week, here are the movies that have ranked No. 1 at the box office so far in 1994. (Source: *Variety*)

Film	Week (end of)	Film	Week (end of)
Mrs. Doubtfire	January 6	Bad Girls	April 28
Mrs. Doubtfire	January 13	No Escape	May 5
Philadelphia	January 20	Four Weddings and a Funeral	May 12
Philadelphia	January 27	The Crow	May 19
Mrs. Doubtfire	February 3	Maverick	May 26
Ace Ventura: Pet Detective	February 10	The Flintstones	June 2
Ace Ventura: Pet Detective	February 17	The Flintstones	June 9
On Deadly Ground	February 24	Speed	June 16
On Deadly Ground	March 3	Wolf	June 23
Ace Ventura: Pet Detective	March 10	The Lion King	July 1
Guarding Tess	March 17	Forrest Gump	July 8
Naked Gun 33-1/3: The Final Insult	March 24	Forrest Gump	July 15
D2: The Mighty Ducks	March 31	Forrest Gump	July 21
D2: The Mighty Ducks	April 7	Forrest Gump	July 28
D2: The Mighty Ducks	April 14	The Mask	August 4
Four Weddings and a Funeral	April 21	Clear and Present Danger	August 11
		Clear and Present Danger	August 18

phose into their sleeping targets now resemble brussels sprouts on megadoses of minoxidil, and the formerly subtle transformation process has been heavily grossed up. But Ferrara has kept the suspense of the conclusion, when Anwar and her boyfriend, Wirth, fleeing the aliens, have to pretend they've been transformed. (R)

CITY SLICKERS II: THE LEGEND OF CURLY'S GOLD

Billy Crystal, Daniel Stern, Jack Palance, Jon Lovitz, Patricia Wettig

Billy Crystal looks a whole lot better with his shirt off than you ever would have thought. And that is the biggest surprise in store for viewers of this amiable but excessively hardworking sequel to 1991's *City Slickers*. Palance is back, as the evil twin brother of the crusty old character he played so craftily in the original. You keep wishing, as the plot plods along, that the movie would relax, be a little wackier, and do more with such assets as Lovitz—who is at his stentorian, self-pitying best as Crystal's do-nothing brother with a passion for reciting scenes from *The Godfather*. (PG-13)

THE CLIENT

Susan Sarandon, Tommy Lee Jones

The Client is a surefooted piece of commercial moviemaking with a premise that can't be beat. Just before he kills himself, a Mafia lawyer tells an eleven-year-old boy (played with touching bravado by Brad Renfro) the whereabouts of the body of a U.S. senator slain by the attorney's client, a Mob hit man. Out to make him talk is a politically ambitious federal prosecutor (Jones); out to shut him up for good is the Mafia assassin (Anthony LaPaglia). The only one with the kid's interests at heart is his lawyer (Sarandon). It's a joy to watch Sarandon and Jones duel with each other. No one can do high dudgeon ("What wanton hubris is this?") as well as Jones, and no one can do sexy-but-that's-not-what's-at-issue-here like Sarandon. For Grisham fans this is the real thing; for non-Grisham fans, the hell with the book, just see the movie. (PG-13)

CROOKLYN

Alfre Woodard, Delroy Lindo, Zelda Harris

Both slight and affecting, *Crooklyn*, the saga of a black family struggling to make ends meet and make sense of things in '70s Brooklyn, is Spike Lee's most conventional, most affectionate work. Woodard is a schoolteacher and mother of five, a woman with a gimlet eye and a terrible swift sword. But her wrath is essentially turned away by her winsome, scapegrace, petty-thief only daughter (Harris), through whose eyes *Crooklyn*, a small, slice-of-life story, unfolds. While this movie seems to want to explore the relationship between a mother and daughter and is about a young girl's coming of age, little happens on-screen or even subtextually to support such themes. But Woodard does her usual fine, fine work, and Harris is a real find. (PG-13)

THE CROW

Brandon Lee, Ernie Hudson, Rochelle Davis, Michael Wincott, Sofia Shinas

Buried somewhere within this chaotically directed mess may be an exciting fantasy adventure film. While filming *The Crow* last year, Brandon Lee was accidentally killed in an on-set shooting mishap during one of the movie's countless bad fight scenes. That accident is no excuse for the seemingly purposeful lack of focus in the camera work. The unimaginative script concerns an aspiring rock musician who is killed in an incomprehensible—and frenetically staged—attack by a drug gang led by Wincott. A mysterious, mystical raven, visiting Lee's grave, helps him come back to life (with intermittent superpowers) so he can hunt down Wincott. Lee, supported by a little girl admirer, the precocious Davis, and cop Hudson, then sets off for the film's clunkily arranged showdown. (R)

8 SECONDS

Luke Perry, Stephen Baldwin

Perry is convincing as the late real-life rodeo star Lane Frost, an aw-heck redneck who loves his mom and pop, drinks Coca-Cola (not booze), and breaks up barroom brawls when he can. Cynthia Geary is a bit too perky as his long-suffering wife. But Perry's cornball charisma is well balanced by Baldwin, who as his crude cowboy pal has a wicked smile, a wily tongue, and a love of soiled socks that only a real rodeo man could muster. Unfortunately, the appealing acting can't make up for the lack of dramatic tension; the events are so ploddingly played out no one cares and *8 Seconds* is more like 6,240 seconds of ho-hum moviegoing. (PG-13)

EVEN COWGIRLS GET THE BLUES

Uma Thurman, Lorraine Bracco, Rain Phoenix, Angie Dickinson

Director Gus Van Sant has done such interesting, grungily offbeat stuff in the past (*Drugstore Cowboy, My Own Pri-*

vate Idaho) that you may be inclined to forgive him this sophomoric bit of '70s countercultural whimsy based on Tom Robbins's famous cult novel. It's meant to be dreamlike, but it's closer to a nap, what with its twinkly feel-goodedness, its karmic, bubbleheaded cuteness, and its long line of stars—Keanu Reeves, John Hurt, Crispin Glover, Sean Young, Noriyuki "Pat" Morita—who float by like dandelion puffs. (R)

FAREWELL MY CONCUBINE

Gong Li

This two and a half-hour epic about the travails of two singers in the Peking Opera is a lot more fun than it has any right to be, possibly because it's ultimately not so much about China's bloody twentieth-century history as it is about show business. This may sound morally imbecilic, given that *Concubine* covers, in often ugly detail, such nightmares as the Communist revolution, the Japanese occupation during World War II, and the Cultural Revolution of the '60s. Still, this is a sumptuous, campy, backstage melodrama—the sort of story in which a little boy, watching an opera, can stand up, tears streaming down his face, and shout, "What does it take to become a star!" And then there is Li. You could stage a scene with thousands of extras, a blizzard, cannon fire, and galloping horses, and the camera would still single out the extraordinary face of this woman: a movie star of the first magnitude. (R)

THE FLINTSTONES

John Goodman, Rick Moranis, Elizabeth Perkins, Rosie O'Donnell

Anyone who grew up with the classic prime-time cartoon will quickly get caught up (and bogged down) in point-by-point comparisons. 1. Does Goodman capture the spirit of the prehistoric, two-dimensional Fred? (Yes; far better than Moranis does Barney Rubble.) 2. Rosie O'Donnell has Betty Rubble's snigger down pat—and makes a better Betty than Perkins does a Wilma Flintstone. 3. Dino, the family pet, is still a cartoon, albeit a computer-animated one. (Shouldn't they have found a real dinosaur for the part, some sort of large, domesticated lizard?) 4. Kyle MacLachlan, as Fred's suavely villainous boss, looks strikingly like Rock Quarry, the TV version's parody of Rock Hudson. Ultimately, *The Flintstones* leaves you fidgety and dissatisfied, as if you had just spent ninety-two minutes taking apart a pile of pebbles, stone by stone, and then built another identical one two feet away. (PG)

FORREST GUMP

Tom Hanks, Sally Field, Robin Wright, Gary Sinise

America's loss of innocence as filtered through the eyes of an innocent—that's the theme of this plodding, heavy-handed parable. Hanks plays a child of the early-'50s South who wears leg braces because of a back that a doctor describes as "crooked as a politician" and has an IQ of seventy-five. He also has a determined mother (Sally Field), who's full of such stitch-it-on-a-sampler wisdom as "stupid is as stupid does." From early on, Hanks's only friend is the local drunk's abused daughter (Wright). Still, he commands attention. Chased one day by bullies, Hanks flees, his braces inexplicably disintegrate, and he finds his gift: He can run like the wind. That talent wins him kudos from President John F. Kennedy when he makes the all-American squad. Later, as a member of the U.S. ping-pong

1994'S TOP GROSSERS

This list is by no means final—it was compiled while most of these hits were still playing widely, and more blockbusters are likely to arrive with the year-end holidays—but as of August 18, these were the year's most popular films:

1. *The Lion King*
2. *Forrest Gump*
3. *The Flintstones*
4. *True Lies*
5. *Speed*
6. *Maverick*
7. *The Mask*
8. *Ace Ventura: Pet Detective*
9. *The Client*
10. *Wolf*

team that opens China, he will meet President Nixon, in the process inadvertently blowing the whistle on the Watergate burglars. Despite all that happens, he can't forget Wright, who represents depredation (she takes drugs and contemplates suicide) as surely as Hanks represents triumph. But triumph is not a word to associate with *Forrest Gump*, which unfolds awkwardly and has an uncertainty of tone and bathos enough to float an ark. (PG-13)

FOUR WEDDINGS AND A FUNERAL

Andie MacDowell, Hugh Grant

This confection of a movie is set in houses of worship around the British Isles. Grant is a man who keeps his heart under house arrest until, in the course of his irresponsibilities as a best man (he forgets the rings), he meets a beautiful, witty, and elusive American magazine editor (MacDowell). With a striking lack of success, Grant tries not to pursue MacDowell or to fall in love with her, even as he keeps running into her—at a funeral and three more weddings, one of them hers, one of them his. There are plenty of sly moments to savor here: Grant's cadre of unmarried friends providing salty commentary at each wedding, all the while desperately seeking mates; celebrated English comic Rowan Atkinson, clumsily officiating at one union and coming up with "awful wedded wife" and "johned in holy matrimony"; and a literate script with references to cultural icons as disparate as Oscar Wilde, W. H. Auden, and David Cassidy. (R)

GO FISH

V. S. Brodie, Guinevere Turner

Max has a simple goal: "I just want to find a girlfriend," she says. How she finds one, and how her friends conspire to make sure that the two fall in love, is at the heart of this funny, fresh romantic comedy. Made on a shoestring budget, *Go Fish* does for young urban lesbians what Spike Lee did for black urban professionals in *She's Gotta Have It*: It opens a door on which big studio filmmakers never even bother to knock. The find in the movie is Turner, who plays Max as a slouchily adorable, wisecracking mass of longing. (NR)

GUARDING TESS

Shirley MacLaine, Nicolas Cage

Tess concentrates on exploring the changing relationship between Cage, a by-the-book Secret Service agent assigned to guard a tyrannical former First Lady (MacLaine), and the more mercurial MacLaine, who regards agents as her personal waiters and golf caddies. The two start off as antagonists but come to respect and even love each other, albeit platonically. MacLaine, playing less broadly here than she has in some recent appearances, is a tart treat, and Cage, all hard-fought restraint and slow burn, matches her. (PG-13)

THE HOUSE OF THE SPIRITS

Meryl Streep, Jeremy Irons, Glenn Close, Winona Ryder, Antonio Banderas

This adaptation of Isabel Allende's epic of love, loss, redemption, and spiritualism has removed all the juice from the best-selling 1985 novel, leaving a hacienda-high pile of pulp. Those who have not read the fanciful, ironic *The House of the Spirits* will be baffled by the movie, which frequently leaves relationships and motivations unexplained. Those who have read the novel will probably be annoyed by the liberties the screenwriters have taken. (R)

THE HUDSUCKER PROXY

Tim Robbins, Jennifer Jason Leigh, Paul Newman

This latest offering from the gifted Coen brothers (director Joel and producer Ethan) has no heart. Instead it is a methodical dissection of the populist comedies made by Frank Capra and Preston Sturges in the '30s and '40s. The setting is an Oz-like New York City in 1958, where a midwestern galoot (Robbins) arrives hoping to make it big with his invention, the hula hoop. He is plucked almost immediately from the mailroom of the giant Hudsucker Industries and named president, the dupe in a stock manipulation scheme cooked up by greedy board members. The goings-on matter not a whit, since the Coens so patently don't care about their characters. (PG)

I LOVE TROUBLE

Nick Nolte, Julia Roberts

You know a movie has the blahs when you can't decide which of the following you care about less: whether the couple on-screen will solve the mystery or get into bed with each other. Straight out of the *His Girl Friday* school of newspaper romances, *Trouble* is anemically formulaic and completely uninspired. Nolte and Roberts play rival Chicago reporters working on the same story. He's a famous columnist who hasn't done any real legwork in years. She's the tyro with drive and instincts. Nolte, working at half speed and seemingly bored, sports a preternatural tan that keeps threatening to turn orange. Roberts, all fierce rectitude and legs, confuses feistiness with smarts. (PG)

I'LL DO ANYTHING

Nick Nolte, Tracey Ullman, Whittni Wright, Joely Richardson, Albert Brooks, Julie Kavner

Watching the stiff, sluggish Nolte try to do light comedy in this Hollywood satire evokes memories of hippo ballerinas in *Fantasia*. But Nolte is hardly the only one responsible for broadening and flattening this story of a hapless actor who reluctantly takes custody of his young daughter. Albert Brooks is a caricature of a crass film executive; Ullman is loud and abrasive as Nolte's Southerner ex-wife, overdrawling as she does what sounds like an imitation of Delta Burke; and little Wright is altogether too convincing as an insufferable, caterwauling brat. And the relationship between Brooks (no relation to director James) and Kavner, an amorous spinster who is Albert's audience research expert, is staged transparently as a battle of neuroses—it's like Richard Lewis dating himself. Small favors dept.: James Brooks originally filmed this movie as a musical, then pulled the songs after adverse audience reaction in previews. This could have been a lot worse with Nolte trying to sing. (PG-13)

IN THE NAME OF THE FATHER

Daniel Day-Lewis, Pete Postlethwaite

This movie tries tendentiously to make a case for those who argue that Britain misrules Northern Ireland, violates Irish civil rights, and knowingly compromises its own legal system. The story, though, is adapted from the self-serving memoir of Irishman Gerry Conlon, a petty thief from Belfast who served fifteen years in a British prison after he was convicted of involvement in the terror bombing of a suburban London pub in 1974. Conlon insisted that he was innocent and that his confession had been extorted through physical and psychological brutality. Sheridan buys Conlon's story uncritically. Every Englishman here is a corrupt anti-Irish bigot, except Emma Thompson, who plays a sympathetic lawyer who pleads Conlon's appeal and gets the case retried. (R)

THE INKWELL

Larenz Tate, Joe Morton, Suzzanne Douglas, Glynn Turman

This movie means well, and that's its problem. A black *Summer of '42* crossed with *The Jeffersons* and *Good Times*, it keeps hitting all the wrong notes while striving earnestly to hit the right ones. Set in 1976, *The Inkwell* tells how an introverted sixteen-year-old (Tate) blossoms socially and learns some hard truths about life over the course of a summer vacation on Martha's Vineyard. Although the movie is determinedly heartwarming and its message about finding one's self and respecting differing points of view is commendable, twenty-two-year-old Matty Rich has directed this way too broadly, like a TV situation comedy on overdrive. (R)

INTERSECTION

Richard Gere, Sharon Stone, Lolita Davidovich

Gere plays an architect torn between his estranged wife (Stone) and his girlfriend (Davidovich). The movie quickly telegraphs just how clichéd it will be: Stone, the ice queen, is blond, and the passionate Davidovich is, you guessed it, a redhead. Stone, Davidovich. Davidovich, Stone. Who's it going to be? Any decision would be better than indecision, but Gere just can't get into gear. Neither does the movie. Gere's acting here consists mostly of raking fingers through his hair; Davidovich overdoes the girlishness by half; and Stone, cast against type as the wronged wife, displays a remarkably anemic presence. (R)

IT COULD HAPPEN TO YOU

Nicolas Cage, Rosie Perez, Bridget Fonda

This urban fairy tale, with its echoes of old Capra and Sturges pictures, is about a good-guy cop (Cage) who, finding himself unable to pay the tip one day, promises a sweet but harassed waitress (Fonda) that if his lottery ticket hits, he will split the proceeds with her. It does and he does, much to the consternation of his money-worshipping hairdresser wife (Perez). But the movie runs out of comic oomph. Cage again proves that he has become an appealingly loopy leading man. There's nothing subtle, as usual, about Perez as she flashes her manicure and screeches her lines, but that doesn't keep her from stealing scenes. Fonda is the disappointment, never achieving a magical effervescence in her syrupy part. (PG)

THE LION KING

Voices of Jeremy Irons, Whoopi Goldberg

What gives this latest Disney cartoon a real excitement is its story, a swift, sometimes brutal tale of dynastic trouble in the animal kingdom. *The Lion King* isn't exactly Disney's answer to *I, Claudius* (or, a suggestion that has been floated elsewhere, *Hamlet)*, but it's a nice, even welcome change of pace after such fairy tales as *Beauty and the Beast* and *Aladdin*. As usual, the animators have come up with splendid villains. Uncle Scar, mangy-coated and bony-shouldered, is a flawless realization of Irons' special talent, which is to suggest wickedness born of neurotic suffering. And his hench-hyena, Shenzi, has Whoopi Goldberg's sarcastic merriment and shrewd, appraising eyes. The music, by Elton John with lyrics by Tim Rice, is heavy on Broadway-style belting and AM-radio pop ballads. *The Lion King* is big, bold, and roaringly loud. But it's somehow saddening to think that Bambi, with his light-stepping hooves and simple heart, wouldn't last ten seconds here. (G)

LITTLE BUDDHA

Keanu Reeves, Alex Wiesendanger, Ying Ruocheng

Little Buddha is supposed to be all about enlightenment—a Tibetan Buddhist monk (Ruocheng) zeroes in on a little American boy (Wiesendanger) as the possible reincarnation of a beloved teacher—but it feels more like a guided tour of corporate headquarters. Every detail is polished to a uniform shine, displayed in its proper place and accorded its due, hushed respect. Director Bernardo Bertolucci intertwines the modern tale with the ancient story of Prince Siddhartha (Reeves, in a variety of togas, hairstyles, and jewelry) and his search for spiritual meaning. Trying to whip things up near the end, the director unexpectedly tosses in a few Cecil B. De Mille storm effects, and Reeves, finally achieving nirvana, is surrounded by a butter-colored nimbus that makes him look like a divine piece of toast. (PG)

MAVERICK

James Garner, Mel Gibson, Jodie Foster, James Coburn, Alfred Molina

Let's all tip our Stetsons in salute to the return of good, clean fun. This large-scale western is as playful and consistently ingratiating as the 1957–62 ABC-TV series that inspired it. Gibson plays Garner's old role, Bret Maverick, while Garner is a retired sheriff shepherding Gibson and conwoman Foster toward a big poker game on a riverboat out of St. Louis. Screenwriter William Goldman evokes his *Butch Cassidy and the Sundance Kid* with a literate script full of amusing twists and marred only slightly by obscenities. If the conclusion is a bit enigmatic, almost never has the prospect of a sequel been so welcome. (PG)

NAKED

David Thewlis

That wonderful British writer-director Mike Leigh (*High Hopes, Life Is Sweet*) continues down his brave, lonely road, making movies about believable people living and suffering under painfully believable circumstances. Thewlis, the near-homeless man at the center of this bleak movie, is a brilliant, borderline-disturbed twenty-seven-year-old misanthrope, newly arrived in London who bums around working-class and slum areas. He batters and baffles everyone with his sarcasm, his preposterously overdeveloped vocabulary (a bird tattoo becomes an "ornithological mutation"), and his numbing meditations on the Meaninglessness of It All. The movie is a kind of scummy picaresque, much of it nightmarishly memorable. (NR)

NAKED GUN 33⅓: THE FINAL INSULT

Leslie Nielsen, Priscilla Presley, O. J. Simpson, George Kennedy, Fred Ward

This chucklefest continues the misadventures of Lt. Frank Drebin (Nielsen) of TV's lamented *Police Squad*. Nielsen has retired and become a househusband, watching soap operas and baking cupcakes while his wife, Presley, works as a prosecuting attorney. He returns to the force to help his old sidekicks Kennedy and Simpson hunt terrorist-for-hire Ward, who is out to wreak havoc at the Academy Awards. The plot, of course, is just a superstructure on which to hang sight gags and throwaway lines, this time at the expense of, among others, Spike Lee, Tonya Harding, women who hyphenate their last names, and chronically addicted baseball player Steve Howe. This movie is harmless fun defined. (PG-13)

NAKED IN NEW YORK

Eric Stoltz, Mary-Louise Parker, Kathleen Turner, Tony Curtis, Jill Clayburgh

With Martin Scorsese serving as executive producer, this first full-length film by director Dan Algrant can at least boast an eccentric cast and some odd cameo appearances, including Whoopi Goldberg as a stone-carved face in a frieze outside a Manhattan theater. Much of *Naked* is about a young, urban, jokily intense kind of guy (Stoltz) and his collapsing relationship with a WASPy, spacey photographer (Parker) while he pursues a playwriting career. What is oddest about this odd little coming-of-age movie is that it should feel so awfully dated. (R)

THE PAPER

Michael Keaton, Glenn Close, Robert Duvall, Marisa Tomei

The newspaper market continues to shrink and the age of smart-mouthed, ink-stained movies like *The Front Page* and *Sweet Smell of Success* is long over. Which makes *The Paper*, about a day in the life of a struggling New York tabloid, almost an exercise in nostalgia. Ron Howard has directed this comedy-drama with a confident smoothness. But after building to an energetic high, *The Paper* loses its punch. The plot is reduced to telegraphic, almost hysterical headline-ese: medical emergencies, a crazed gunman, and a bloody-nosed fight between Keaton and Close in the newsroom that plays like a badly staged parody of *Fatal Attraction*. (R)

REALITY BITES

Winona Ryder, Ethan Hawke, Ben Stiller

This slick comedy-drama seems to have been cloned from genetic material developed in the labs at MTV. Should Ryder give her heart to world-weary slacker Hawke, or to Stiller, a rising executive with an MTV-style network? Any intelligent adult would pick Stiller. He's moderately sensitive, he drives a nice car, and he knows as much *One Day at a Time* trivia as Ryder's smugly pop-cultivated friends. Hawke, however, uses the word "ontological" on his answering-machine message, and sings about being and nothingness. Jack Kerouac would have tossed him from a speeding vehicle. There have been plenty of movies in the past year that dealt more authentically with coming-of-age issues: *Dazed and Confused, Ruby in Paradise, Naked, Menace II Society*. Even the unjustly despised *Cabin Boy*. (PG-13)

RENAISSANCE MAN

Danny DeVito, Gregory Hines

A sort of cross between *Private Benjamin* and *Dead Poets Society*, this comedy-drama tells the story of a fired advertising executive (DeVito) who takes a temporary job with the Army teaching remedial English to a group of soldiers known as the Double D squad, for "dumber than dogs—t." How DeVito and his gang discover a sense of self-worth and purpose while studying Shakespeare makes for a somewhat predictable but ultimately entertaining film. Drected by Penny Marshall (*A League of Their Own*), *Renaissance Man* has its minor lapses and excesses of sentiment, but any movie clever enough to turn Hamlet into a military marching chant ("Hamlet's mom, she is the queen/She buys it in the final scene") is worth a look. (PG-13)

SERIAL MOM

Kathleen Turner

Turner confirms here what 1989's *The War of the Roses* first suggested: her great talent is for ruthless rage. Combine that with writer-director John Waters' perverse genius for tongue-in-cheek, B-grade melodrama and you have a movie that is genuinely funny and deeply unsettling. Take that as a recommendation. Turner, a suburban housewife with psychopathic tendencies, furiously murders neighbors, high school teachers, and local teenagers, bop bop bop. She has it in for those who fail to rewind videotapes, sort out trash for recycling, or observe the time-honored fashion rule about not wearing white shoes after Labor Day. It's hard to explain how frightening, yet exhilarating, it is to see Turner racing down a sunny, tree-lined street waving a large kitchen knife or heaving a lethal air conditioner out a window, but Waters has included an old movie clip that perhaps helps: it's of Joan Crawford wielding an ax in *Strait-Jacket*, one of her '60s cheapo slashers. The difference is that Crawford, trying to be terrifying, is camp, while Turner, starring in a movie that is essentially camp, is terrifying. (R)

THE SHADOW

Alec Baldwin, Penelope Ann Miller, John Lone, Peter Boyle, Ian McKellen

As penumbral superhero action films go, *The Shadow* beats the feathers off *The Crow*; it's faster, wittier, and clearer of plot, and it takes its supernatural mumbo jumbo less seriously. This is a comic book brought neatly to life, and nobody is pretending it's anything more. Writer David Koepp shows some principles (there are no "Oh, Expletive!" lines) and a modest sense of humor: When Baldwin meets his main foe, Lone, a diabolical

Genghis Khan descendant who comes back to life, he says, "So, what are you doing in the Big Apple?" Director Russell Mulcahy wastes the Baldwin-Lone showdown, using it before the movie's climactic scene. The conclusion puts an unsatisfying end to an otherwise enjoyable experience. (PG-13)

SHADOWLANDS

Anthony Hopkins, Debra Winger

This three-hankie weeper, set in the 1950s, tells the embellished but basically true story of C. S. Lewis, the renowned British scholar and author of the classic children's series *The Chronicles of Narnia*, and his relationship with American writer Joy Gresham. Lewis's (Hopkins) tidy bachelor existence takes a hairpin turn when he meets Gresham (Winger), a forthright American fan with whom he has had a long correspondence and who has made the trip abroad with her young son (the very good Joseph Mazzello) to escape a troubled marriage. What begins as a union of convenience becomes one of deep abiding love, hideously cut short by developments best not divulged here. There's a built-in poignancy to this saga, but ultimately the encounters between Hopkins and Winger are too similar and simply too brief. Still, it is Hopkins who steals *Shadowlands*. The shy, sweet smile that flits across his face when he unexpectedly spies Winger at one of his lectures could give you hope any time. (PG)

SIRENS

Hugh Grant, Sam Neill, Elle Macpherson

Grant's gentle, diffident appeal can be seen to much better effect in the British romantic comedy *Four Weddings and a Funeral*, but anyone interested in a showcase for supermodel Macpherson's statuesque form need look no further. A cleric just arrived at his new post in 1930s Sydney, Grant is dispatched by his bishop to persuade a notorious local painter (Neill) to remove a profane drawing from an upcoming exhibit. Grant and his sexually repressed wife (pale, pretty Tara Fitzgerald) spend several days with Neill, his family, and his three models, who are unabashedly bohemian. Director-writer John Duigan seems to mean for this to be a sort of leafy paradise of the libido, and *Sirens* does have its lulling, sensual moments. But just as often it crosses the line into something like bare-breasted kitsch. (R)

SPEED

Keanu Reeves, Dennis Hopper, Jeff Daniels, Sandra Bullock

In this gripping if by-the-book action thriller, a madman (Hopper) plants a bomb on a Los Angeles city bus. Let the bus's pace fall below fifty miles an hour and it will explode. When the bus driver is shot by a hysterical passenger, Reeves, a cop on the L.A.P.D. swat team, turns the wheel over to a regular passenger (Bullock, in a bright performance), who has been taking the bus since her driver's license was revoked for speeding. *Speed* taps into every cliché of the genre and the acting of Reeves is almost as wooden as the dialogue. Still, the very fact that much of the story unfolds on a speeding bus and later on a speeding subway provides an intrinsic, inexorable sense of momentum.(R)

TRUE LIES

Arnold Schwarzenegger, Jamie Lee Curtis, Tia Carrere, Eliza Dushku, Tom Arnold, Art Malik, Bill Paxton

Like a simultaneous Bond film and Mel Brooks Bond parody, this action comedy is fast, flashy, furious, and funny. Schwarzenegger plays an ace field operative for an antiterrorist U.S. intelligence agency. His wife, Curtis, thinks he is just a salesman who travels a lot. When Arnold suspects Curtis of having an affair with Paxton, Schwarzenegger starts following her, using his agency friends and techniques. That gets everybody involved in a plot by a group of H-bomb-packing Arab terrorists led by Malik and supplied by Carrere. Schwarzenegger insinuates himself smoothly into the often ironic script by his old *Terminator* collaborator, director James Cameron. Curtis too sells the film's vacillation between farce and fracas, seeming athletic enough to cold-cock Arnold and sexy enough to turn him on with a seductive dance. Cameron's script is often ingenious and always original. The stunt work is dazzling. Terrific film. (R)

WHAT'S EATING GILBERT GRAPE

Johnny Depp, Juliette Lewis, Leonardo DiCaprio

This precious movie follows the American-gothic-gone-rancid adventures of the dysfunctional Grape clan. Its members include Gilbert (Depp, his hair dyed a preternatural red), a grocery clerk who's the family provider; his 500-pound mother

(Darlene Cates), who hasn't left the house since her husband killed himself seven years ago; and Gilbert's retarded young brother (DiCaprio). Enter the free-spirited Lewis, who stirs up feelings in Depp, including a profound longing to hightail it out of his one-horse Iowa hamlet. A little too studiously grotesque, it all goes on for too long. (PG-13)

WHEN A MAN LOVES A WOMAN

Meg Ryan, Andy Garcia

Ryan is a school guidance counselor, the mother of two young girls, and an alcoholic; Garcia is her second husband, an airline pilot and an enabler in this pallid, mawkish drama of a family in crisis. After almost drowning in a drinking-related accident, Ryan vows to cut down, quickly falls off the wagon, and ends up in a treatment center. Yet when she comes out sober, edgy, and accusatory, Garcia doesn't know how to handle this new wife. It's a compelling situation. Unfortunately, it's unclear just which story the filmmakers want to tell. This movie is a little bit the saga of an alcoholic, a little bit about a man trying to cope with an alcoholic wife, and a little bit the story of an alcoholic wife trying to cope with a husband who's trying to cope. But it's never enough of any one thing. (R)

WOLF

Jack Nicholson, Michelle Pfeiffer, Kate Nelligan, Christopher Plummer, James Spader

This original, upscale werewolf movie is five percent scary but ninety-five percent entertaining. Nicholson plays a Manhattan book editor who hits a wolf while driving in Vermont and is bitten by the animal while trying to help it. On returning to New York City, he turns into a murderous werewolf whenever the moon is full; loses his job in a takeover by rapacious business tycoon Plummer; and realizes his wife of sixteen years, Nelligan, is having an affair with his professional rival, Spader. But he also meets the unattached Pfeiffer, Plummer's daughter. George Waggner's moody, thoughtful 1941 horror classic *The Wolf Man* remains the best werewolf movie. This film is less well cast and surprisingly less sexy, but it's more colorful (mostly more bloody), brighter, more playful, and faster, with an appealingly twisty ending. (R)

WYATT EARP

Kevin Costner, Gene Hackman, Dennis Quaid, Michael Madsen, Linden Ashby, Catherine O'Hara, Mare Winningham, Isabella Rossellini, JoBeth Williams

The achievement of this western epic is that it remains involving even though it is three hours and fifteen minutes long, convoluted, bloody, heavy-handed and so given to idle psychoanalysis that it is a lot closer to Freud (Sigmund) than to Ford (John). In this incarnation, Earp is an anxiety-riven character who can't make a career choice between being a lawman and trying out the crackpot get-rich-quick schemes he keeps coming up with. All the angst makes the part more amenable to Costner, whose low-key acting style is ill-suited to all-out action. Director and cowriter Lawrence Kasdan does provide a possible explanation for Costner's conflicted identity in the person of Hackman as the Earp boys' obtrusive, sanctimonious father. Hackman wanders the landscape, rattling off specious platitudes and butting into his sons' lives—until he is suddenly written out in the middle of the movie. Intermittently wussy, constantly tortured, and full of Hamletian indecisiveness, this Wyatt Earp isn't your father's western hero, but he's nevertheless a fascinating fellow. (PG-13)

YOU SO CRAZY

Martin Lawrence

This concert film continues where Lawrence left off on his album *Talkin' S*——. Lawrence peppers his routine with advice—everything from avoiding crack to using condoms—which does not, however, hide his contradictory philosophies. Nowhere is this more apparent then in his routine on the evils of racism. While repeating a "gotta get over this racism" mantra, Lawrence suggests that Mexican-Americans made out best from the L.A.-riot looting. He also inserts an all-purpose "white guy" whenever someone stupid is needed for a particular anecdote. In another section, Lawrence discusses tolerating gays before hastily pointing out that he is in fact "for the ladies." Offensive in some areas and boring in many others, Lawrence is at his best dissecting the ups and inevitable downs of relationships, whipping the audience into a frenzy with his dead-on portrayal of lovers on the brink. (R)

THE MYTH GREW, THE HOLLY WOULDN'T

An irreverent history of the once-respectable town that gave us Sam Goldwyn, Sylvester Stallone, a Technicolor Tara, Star Wars, and—a long time ago—oranges.

Over a hundred years ago, before Sensurround or Steadicam, before the Lubitsch touch or the Hays Office, before real butterlike flavoring or Dish Night, before key grips, key lights, or Keye Luke, before *Scream, Blacula, Scream!*, before Hayley or Tuesday or Pia or Pee-wee, there was Hollywood. In February of 1887 the Kansas Prohibitionist Harvey Wilcox registered a map of his 120-acre citrus ranch, which he hoped to subdivide, with the L.A. County Recorder's office. He called his slice of paradise Hollywood, after the country home of a woman his wife had met on a train. (Wilcox tried growing holly on his property. It died.) For a few years, Hollywood remained as he had intended: a quiet, respectable, booze-free suburb, dotted with fig and orange trees. It was a lovely place, and doomed.

Doomed because, back East, the movie business was being born. Thomas Edison had invented the Kinetoscope, a moving picture peep-show machine for a single viewer. Realizing that projected movies were the coming thing, however, he acquired Thomas Armat's invention, a combination camera/projector called the Vitascope, and began fine-tuning the process.

By 1905 nickelodeon theaters were the rage, screening one-reel silents to packed houses. Edison, seeing firsthand that a combination of artificial light and fake cowboys could produce real money, helped to form a patent trust with eight major film companies, hoping to stop competitors from making movies without paying royalties. It worked, but for less than ten years: A group of producers on the run from Edison's patent agents in the East swarmed to Southern California, where some of them banded together to upend Edison's monopoly in court. Still others later set up the first Hollywood studio in an old roadhouse that was failing because, under a local ordinance, it couldn't serve drinks.

The town flourished. Along with the emergence of sophisticated camera movement and editing *(The Birth of a Nation, The Wind)* the first stars were born. Among them were Lillian Gish, Charlie Chaplin, Mary Pickford, and the exotic Theda Bara, whose name, it was pointed out, was an anagram for "Arab death." Movies were still silent, but the venues were not. In addition to organists, people were often hired to stand behind the screen to provide such sound effects as horses' hooves or gunshots.

Then in October of 1927 came the premiere of Warner Brothers' *The Jazz Singer*, which featured several sound sequences. Audiences were amazed as the sound of Al Jolson pretending to be a cantor's son pretending to be black pretended to come right off the screen. The picture was a sensation. The talkies weren't good for everybody, however. The careers of actors with high or squeaky voices ended abruptly, and even stars who were successful hated the crude early recording process. "They made me sound as if I'd been castrated," complained the ever-ironic Tallulah Bankhead. On the other hand, talkies were great for stage-trained and literary talent from the East, and writers, directors, dialogue coaches, and actors spilled off the Santa Fe Chief upon its every arrival in L.A.

Movies became a national pastime, then a mania. Marlene Dietrich was photographed wearing slacks in 1930, and women everywhere mimicked her leggy look. Clark Gable appeared without an undershirt in *It Happened One Night* and caused a crisis in the underwear business. Americans went to the movies at least once a week and then glued themselves to *Photoplay* or

Modern Screen for the dish on their favorite stars. Gossip's grand dames and arch-rivals—Hedda Hopper and Louella Parsons, who enjoyed a combined daily readership of seventy-five million—were possibly Hollywood's most powerful women. Parsons' outlook was perhaps excessively movie-centric. In 1939, a few days after the Nazi invasion of Albania, she wrote, "The deadly dullness of the last week was lifted today when Darryl Zanuck admitted he had bought all rights to Maurice Maeterlinck's *The Bluebird*." But then, it was a movie-centric age, a time when Americans believed Hollywood to be a charmed place whose genial, witty, drunk citizens were forever inviting each other over to start sex scandals and drug fads.

Like every other industry, movies had been hit hard by the Depression. Attendance, ticket prices, and box office revenues all dropped, and theaters used gimmicks such as dish giveaways and bingo games to lure audiences. At the same time, the industry was stung by edicts from the Motion Picture Producers and Distributors Association of America, a self-regulating body set up in 1922 to oversee movie morality, with Will H. Hays as its head; later came the tough Production Code of 1930, a dos-and-don'ts guide to screen behavior. (Among the dictums: "Pointed profanity—this includes the words God, Lord, Jesus, Christ, unless used reverently, hell, s.o.b., damn, Gawd—or every other profane or vulgar expression, however used, is forbidden.")

Occasionally, movies dealt with hard times (*The Grapes of Wrath* with Henry Fonda) or politics (*Mr. Smith Goes to Washington* with James Stewart), but mostly they provided glorious escapes: Hitchcock's thrillers, Cagney's gangster shoot-em-ups, Cary Grant's screwball comedies, Busby Berkeley's dance extravaganzas, and *Gone with the Wind*. With the arrival in 1935 of *Becky Sharp*, the first full-length color feature, the studios began churning out color movies as fast as they could.

As the country's attention shifted from its economic woes to World War II, Hollywood became flush with patriotic films; gung-ho war epics were the big draws. When people weren't going to those, they flocked to any marquee that had Humphrey Bogart's name on it. Above all, there was 1941's *Citizen Kane*, Orson Welles's tour de force of cinematic technique

This Golden Age of cinema was an era of supreme power for the studios and the legendary tyrant-moguls who ran them. Louis B. Mayer, Harry Cohn, Jack Warner, Samuel Goldwyn, David O. Selznick, and Irving Thalberg often generated more ink than their movies, much of it the apocryphal concoction of hyperactive press agents. It's doubtful that Goldwyn really manufactured these oft-repeated sparklers: "Gentlemen, include me out!" or "I had a good idea this morning, but I didn't like it" or "In two words, im possible!" and probably untrue that when told that Lillian Hellman's *The Children's Hour* was about lesbians, he responded, "Don't worry about it, we'll make them Americans." But it is true that Columbia chief Harry Cohn hit the ceiling after reading the script for the biblical epic *Joseph and His Brethren*, in which characters said, "Yes, sire" and "No, sire." Fumed Cohn: "I may not be a college man, but I know goddamn well that in biblical times people did not go around saying, 'Yes-siree' and 'No-siree.' "

The moguls controlled their talented employees' slightest moves. Names were changed ("I think the 'e' made the whole f...... difference," Carole Lombard observed), along with, in some cases, teeth, noses, hairlines, and hair color. For 1927's *King of Kings*, Cecil B. DeMille's two stars, H.B. Warner (Jesus Christ) and Dorothy Cummings (Mary), had to sign agreements not to appear for five years in roles that might compromise their holy images. DeMille also ordered them not to be seen swimming, playing cards, riding in convertibles, going to clubs or ball games, or engaging in other un-biblical activities during shooting.

The end to the moguls'

omnipotence came in several crippling waves. In 1948, the studios were financially weakened when the U.S. Supreme Court upheld a lower court ruling that ordered eight major studios to divest themselves of the theaters they owned. Then came television—from 1948 to 1953, annual U.S. movie attendance dropped from around four billion to less than two billion.

The worst drain on Hollywood's morale, however, came during the Red Scare of the late '40s and early '50s, when the studios' practice was to blacklist anyone thought to have Communist leanings. It was Hollywood's lowest moment. Careers were destroyed by innuendo, people informed on their friends, and writers and directors went to jail for refusing to testify before the House Un-American Activities Committee.

The industry soldiered bravely into the '50s, with the studios searching frantically for ways to give people in movies what they couldn't get on TV. As it turned out, 3-D was unsuccessful (too many headaches), but producers had better luck with wider screen shapes such as Cinemascope, which made the movies look as long and as low as the finned Cadillacs of the era. Americans developed a passion for foreign films, and French New Wave film critics such as François Truffaut and Jean-Luc Godard became the New Wave filmmakers, after writing articles that hailed many U.S.-made Westerns and gritty gangster pictures as the symbolic masterpieces of visionary *auteurs*. Later, the French would determine that Jerry Lewis was a genius.

As the studio system waned and filmmakers and stars became pricey free agents, audiences began turning fickle. In the '60s and '70s, big names no longer guaranteed a bonanza at the box office. *Cleopatra* had Elizabeth Taylor (which was more than Eddie Fisher could say when filming was over) but no luck. *The Great Gatsby* had Robert Redford but no punch. Meanwhile, youth-quake entries from left field—*Easy Rider, American Graffiti,* and *Animal House*, for example—became huge hits.

The business had never been known for its serenity, but such unpredictability gave Hollywood worse jitters than usual. Even today, the town is in the midst of a somewhat bumpy transition. A new wave of merger fever is sweeping the business. Conglomerates have bought up once-independent studios and foreign corporations have bought up once-American conglomerates. The old-guard moguls have been replaced by the more cheerful but less powerful "baby moguls." Bottom-line mentality dominates decision making, and the fate of studio executives can hang on the success of a single big-budget gamble. (Remember *Heaven's Gate*gate?) Getting movies made at all today requires a miraculous collusion of factors: the availability of stars who will speak to each other, the coordination of everybody's schedule, and getting everything started before the studio changes its management, its owners, or its mind.

Yet the Hollywood of the '90s is in better health than most people expected it to be. A *Schindler's List* shows that even the gravest subject matter can make a great picture and a box-office success, while a *Jurassic Park* suggests that recipes as classic as We're-in-the-house-with-the-monster are still kicking. (That both pictures are by the same director is typical of a business, and an audience, blessed with wide-ranging appetites.) Neither TV, cable, videocassettes, pay-per-view, nor the lethal fat content now ascribed to snack-bar popcorn has killed off the practice of going to the movies. Those who go still lose themselves there, and replay the scenes for days on the little screens behind their eyes—screens that, in many cases, are larger than those at the shopping mall multiplex.

Author Charlie Haas, the president and sole employee of Prose King ("Screenwriting at its Least Stupid"), has writing credits on Over the Edge, Tex, Gremlins 2, *and* Matinee. *He lives in Oakland, California, slightly out of the fray.*

THE TOP 100 FILMS OF ALL-TIME

The following lists the largest money-making movies of all time based on domestic (U.S. and Canada) box-office grosses. Figures are accurate through August 18, 1994; summer blockbusters (such as *The Lion King* and *Forrest Gump*) are still earning. (Source: *Variety*)

Rank	Film (year of release)	B.O. Gross
1.	*E.T., the Extra-Terrestrial* (1982)	$399,804,539
2.	*Jurassic Park* (1993)	346,250,210
3.	*Star Wars* (1977)	322,000,000
4.	*Home Alone* (1990)	285,761,243
5.	*Return of the Jedi* (1983)	263,000,000
6.	*Jaws* (1975)	260,000,000
7.	*Batman* (1989)	251,188,924
8.	*The Lion King* (1994)	247,028,386
9.	*Raiders of the Lost Ark* (1981)	242,374,454
10.	*Beverly Hills Cop* (1984)	234,760,478
11.	*The Empire Strikes Back* (1980)	223,000,000
12.	*Ghostbusters* (1984)	220,855,498
13.	*Mrs. Doubtfire* (1993)	219,131,586
14.	*Ghost* (1990)	217,631,306
15.	*Aladdin* (1992)	217,350,219
16.	*Back to the Future* (1985)	208,242,016
17.	*Terminator 2: Judgment Day* (1991)	204,843,345
18.	*Indiana Jones and the Last Crusade* (1989)	197,171,806
19.	*Forrest Gump* (1994)	195,464,921
20.	*Gone With the Wind* (1939)	191,749,436
21.	*Dances with Wolves* (1990)	184,208,848
22.	*The Fugitive* (1993)	183,875,760
23.	*Indiana Jones and the Temple of Doom* (1984)	179,870,271
24.	*Pretty Woman* (1990)	178,406,268
25.	*Tootsie* (1982)	177,200,000
26.	*Top Gun* (1986)	176,781,728
27.	*Snow White and the Seven Dwarfs* (1937)	175,263,233
28.	*"Crocodile" Dundee* (1986)	174,634,806
29.	*Rain Man* (1988)	172,825,435
30.	*Home Alone 2: Lost in New York* (1992)	172,704,311
31.	*Three Men and a Baby* (1987)	167,780,960
32.	*Robin Hood: Prince of Thieves* (1991)	165,493,908
33.	*The Exorcist* (1973)	165,000,000
34.	*Batman Returns* (1992)	162,831,698
35.	*The Sound of Music* (1965)	160,476,331
36.	*The Firm* (1993)	158,340,292
37.	*Fatal Attraction* (1987)	156,645,693
38.	*The Sting* (1973)	156,000,000
39.	*Who Framed Roger Rabbit* (1988)	154,112,492
40.	*Beverly Hills Cop II* (1987)	153,665,036
41.	*Grease* (1978)	153,112,492
42.	*Rambo: First Blood Part II* (1985)	150,415,432
43.	*Gremlins* (1984)	148,168,459
44.	*Lethal Weapon 2* (1989)	147,253,986
45.	*Beauty and the Beast* (1991)	145,863,363
46.	*Lethal Weapon 3* (1992)	144,731,527
47.	*101 Dalmatians* (1961)	143,992,148
48.	*National Lampoon's Animal House* (1978)	141,600,000
49.	*A Few Good Men* (1992)	141,340,178
50.	*Look Who's Talking* (1989)	140,088,813
51.	*Sister Act* (1992)	139,605,150
52.	*Platoon* (1986)	137,963,328
53.	*Teenage Mutant Ninja Turtles* (1990)	135,265,915
54.	*Superman* (1978)	134,218,018
55.	*The Godfather* (1972)	133,698,921
56.	*The Rocky Horror Picture Show* (1975)	132,846,189
57.	*The Silence of the Lambs* (1991)	130,726,716
58.	*Honey, I Shrunk the Kids* (1989)	130,724,172
59.	*An Officer and a Gentleman* (1982)	129,795,549
60.	*The Jungle Book* (1967)	128,647,178
61.	*Close Encounters of the Third Kind* (1977)	128,290,347
62.	*Coming to America* (1988)	128,152,301
63.	*Rocky IV* (1985)	127,873,414
64.	*Smokey and the Bandit* (1977)	126,737,428
65.	*Sleepless in Seattle* (1993)	126,551,583
66.	*The Flintstones* (1994)	126,173,140
67.	*Good Morning Vietnam* (1987)	123,922,370
68.	*City Slickers* (1991)	123,829,734
69.	*Rocky III* (1982)	122,823,192
70.	*The Bodyguard* (1992)	121,823,192
71.	*Wayne's World* (1992)	121,697,323
72.	*The Hunt for Red October* (1990)	120,709,868
73.	*Hook* (1991)	119,654,823
74.	*Blazing Saddles* (1974)	119,500,000
75.	*Total Recall* (1990)	119,394,839
76.	*On Golden Pond* (1981)	118,710,777
77.	*Back to the Future Part II* (1989)	118,450,002
78.	*Basic Instinct* (1992)	117,727,224
79.	*Die Hard 2* (1990)	117,323,878
80.	*Rocky* (1976)	117,235,247
81.	*The Towering Inferno* (1974)	116,000,000
82.	*True Lies* (1994)	115,733,737
83.	*The Karate Kid Part II* (1986)	115,103,979
84.	*American Graffiti* (1973)	115,000,000
85.	*Big* (1988)	114,968,774
86.	*The Addams Family* (1991)	113,502,246
87.	*Ghostbusters II* (1984)	112,494,738
88.	*One Flew Over the Cuckoo's Nest* (1975)	112,000,000
89.	*Twins* (1988)	111,936,388
90.	*Doctor Zhivago* (1965)	111,721,913
91.	*Speed* (1994)	111,116,005
92.	*Star Trek IV: The Voyage Home* (1986)	109,713,132
93.	*"Crocodile" Dundee II* (1988)	109,306,210
94.	*Terms of Endearment* (1983)	108,423,489
95.	*Superman II* (1980)	108,185,706
96.	*A League of Their Own* (1992)	107,404,544
97.	*Indecent Proposal* (1993)	106,614,059
98.	*Driving Miss Daisy* (1989)	106,593,296
99.	*Love Story* (1970)	106,397,186
100.	*Kramer vs. Kramer* (1979)	106,260,500

THE TOP 100 FILMS OF 1993

These are the movies that captured our hearts—and wallets—last year. Films are ranked according to their North American box-office grosses. (Starred films were released in 1992 but earned much of their income in 1993; grosses include 1993 only.)
(Source: *Variety*)

Rank	Film	B.O. Gross
1.	*Jurassic Park*	$338,929,640
2.	*The Fugitive*	179,290,645
3.	*The Firm*	158,348,367
4.	*Sleepless in Seattle*	126,533,006
5.	*Aladdin**	118,899,051
6.	*Mrs. Doubtfire*	111,764,830
7.	*Indecent Proposal*	106,614,059
8.	*In the Line of Fire*	102,314,283
9.	*Cliffhanger*	84,049,211
10.	*A Few Good Men**	78,211,341
11.	*Free Willy*	77,698,625
12.	*Groundhog Day*	70,906,973
13.	*Dave*	63,270,710
14.	*Rising Sun*	63,095,271
15.	*Scent of a Woman**	63,095,253
16.	*Cool Runnings*	61,092,737
17.	*The Crying Game**	59,343,181
18.	*Demolition Man*	56,453,846
19.	*Rookie of the Year*	53,579,269
20.	*The Pelican Brief*	51,985,379
21.	*Dennis the Menace*	51,270,765
22.	*Sommersby*	50,081,992
23.	*Last Action Hero*	50,016,394
24.	*The Nightmare Before Christmas*	48,888,327
25.	*The Three Musketeers*	47,965,452
26.	*The Bodyguard**	46,889,287
27.	*Malice*	45,089,764
28.	*Made in America*	44,942,695
29.	*The Good Son*	44,383,848
30.	*Addams Family Values*	44,370,629
31.	*Teenage Mutant Ninja Turtles III*	42,273,609
32.	*Homeward Bound*	41,833,324
33.	*Snow White and the Seven Dwarfs*	41,634,471
34.	*The Beverly Hillbillies*	41,617,157
35.	*Falling Down*	40,903,593
36.	*Hocus Pocus*	39,514,713
37.	*What's Love Got To Do with It?*	39,100,956
38.	*Hot Shots! Part Deux*	38,911,970
39.	*Home Alone 2: Lost in New York*	37,607,487
40.	*Wayne's World II*	37,180,404
41.	*Alive*	36,733,909
42.	*Son-in-Law*	36,448,400
43.	*Sliver*	36,300,000
44.	*Robin Hood: Men in Tights*	35,699,287
45.	*Sister Act 2: Back in the Habit*	35,638,977
46.	*Dragon: The Bruce Lee Story*	35,112,679
47.	*Carlito's Way*	34,144,807
48.	*Hard Target*	32,533,954
49.	*The Sandlot*	32,416,586
50.	*Cop and a Half*	31,888,714
51.	*The Age of Innocence*	31,421,099
52.	*The Joy Luck Club*	31,348,664
53.	*The Secret Garden*	31,181,347
54.	*Forever Young**	31,162,196
55.	*Point of No Return*	30,038,362
56.	*A Perfect World*	28,311,872
57.	*Loaded Weapon I*	27,979,399
58.	*Menace II Society*	27,899,866
59.	*Poetic Justice*	27,515,786
60.	*Beethoven's 2nd*	27,015,950
61.	*Unforgiven**	26,697,447
62.	*My Life*	25,727,307
63.	*The Man Without a Face*	24,760,338
64.	*The Adventures of Huck Finn*	24,103,594
65.	*Striking Distance*	23,798,623
66.	*Benny and Joon*	23,202,734
67.	*The Program*	23,004,026
68.	*Guilty as Sin*	22,866,222
69.	*Much Ado About Nothing*	22,550,957
70.	*Nowhere to Run*	22,189,039
71.	*Rudy*	21,610,531
72.	*Coneheads*	21,274,717
73.	*Super Mario Brothers*	20,915,465
74.	*Another Stakeout*	20,208,496
75.	*Fire in the Sky*	20,100,000
76.	*Like Water For Chocolate*	19,535,913
77.	*Sniper*	18,994,653
78.	*Untamed Heart*	18,899,204
79.	*Posse*	18,289,763
80.	*Born Yesterday*	17,952,857
81.	*CB4*	17,953,778
82.	*Used People**	17,312,701
83.	*A Bronx Tale*	17,266,971
84.	*Sidekicks*	17,239,856
85.	*Tombstone*	16,856,353
86.	*Heart and Souls*	16,581,714
87.	*Remains of the Day*	16,192,243
88.	*Jason Goes to Hell: The Final Friday*	15,935,068
89.	*The Piano*	15,480,971
90.	*Needful Things*	15,185,672
91.	*Grumpy Old Men*	15,041,488
92.	*Indian Summer*	14,904,910
93.	*The Vanishing*	14,543,394
94.	*Hoffa**	13,927,466
95.	*Geronimo: An American Legend*	13,736,475
96.	*The Crush*	13,609,396
97.	*Body of Evidence*	13,275,426
98.	*A Far Off Place*	12,890,752
99.	*The Distinguished Gentleman*	12,771,848
100.	*Weekend at Bernie's II*	12,741,891

THE TOP 50 FOREIGN-LANGUAGE FILMS

The rankings of top-grossing foreign-language films were long dominated by two 1960s imports—the Swedish soft-porn flick, *I Am Curious (Yellow)*, and the Italian classic, *La Dolce Vita*—until the sudden emergence in 1993 of *Like Water for Chocolate*. This Mexican charmer passed the $20 million mark in early 1994 and is still going strong. (Source: *Variety*)

Rank	Film (year of U.S. release, director, country of origin)
1.	*Like Water for Chocolate* (1993, Arau, Mexico)
2.	*I Am Curious (Yellow)* (1969, Sjoman, Sweden)
3.	*La Dolce Vita* (1960, Fellini, Italy)
4.	*La Cage aux folles* (1979, Molinaro, France/Italy)
5.	*Z* (1969, Costa-Gavras, France)
6.	*A Man and a Woman* (1966, Lelouch, France)
7.	*Cinema Paradiso* (1990, Tornatore, Italy/France)
8.	*Emmanuelle* (1975, Jaeckin, France)
9.	*Das Boot* (1982, Peterson, Germany)
10.	*Story of O* (1975, Jaeckin, France)
11.	*8½* (1963, Fellini, Italy)
12.	*Yesterday, Today and Tomorrow* (1964, de Sica, Italy)
13.	*Marriage Italian Style* (1964, de Sica, Italy)
14.	*Elvira Madigan* (1967, Widerberg, Sweden)
15.	*Dear John* (1964, Lindgren, Sweden)
16.	*Cousin, Cousine* (1976, Tacchella, France)
17.	*My Life as a Dog* (1987, Hallström, Sweden)
18.	*Fanny and Alexander* (1983, Bergman, Sweden)
19.	*Women on the Verge of a Nervous Breakdown* (1988, Almodóvar, Spain)
20.	*Ran* (1985, Kurosawa, Japan)
21.	*Two Women* (1961, de Sica, Italy)
22.	*Without a Stitch* (1970, Meineche, Denmark)
23.	*The Wedding Banquet* (1993, Lee, Taiwan)
24.	*Diva* (1982, Beineix, France)
25.	*Swept Away* (1975, Wertmüller, Italy)

Rank	Film (year of U.S.release, director, country of origin)
26.	*La Cage aux folles II* (1981, Molinaro, France)
27.	*Belle Epoque* (1993, Trueba, Spain)
28.	*Cyrano de Bergerac* (1990, Rappeneau, France)
29.	*Indochine* (1992, Wargnier, France)
30.	*Europa, Europa* (1991, Holland, France/Germany)
31.	*Jean de Florette* (1987, Berri, France)
32.	*King of Hearts* (1967, de Broca, France/England)
33.	*Au revoir, les enfants* (1988, Malle, France)
34.	*Madame Rosa* (1978, Mizrahi, France)
35.	*Babette's Feast* (1988, Axel, Denmark)
36.	*Farewell My Concubine* (1993, Chen, Hong Kong)
37.	*The Garden of the Finzi-Continis* (1971, de Sica, Italy)
38.	*Manon of the Spring* (1987, Berri, France)
39.	*La Femme Nikita* (1990, Besson, France/Italy)
40.	*Seven Beauties* (1976, Wertmüller, Italy)
41.	*Bread and Chocolate* (1978, Brusati, Italy)
42.	*Amarcord* (1974, Fellini, Italy)
43.	*Mediterraneo* (1991, Salvatores, Italy)
44.	*The Emigrants* (1972, Troell, Sweden)
45.	*Get Out Your Handkerchiefs* (1979, Blier, France)
46.	*Entre nous* (1983, Kurys, France)
47.	*Tie Me Up, Tie Me Down* (1990, Almodóvar, Spain)
48.	*The Return of Martin Guerre* (1982, Vigne, France)
49.	*Mephisto* (1982, Szabó, Hungary)
50.	*La Traviata* (1982, Zeffirelli, Italy)

THROUGH A DIFFERENT LENS

The top-grossing domestic movies of all time are nearly all recently released films, thanks to ever-increasing ticket prices. But what if the playing field is leveled? Exhibitor Relations has compiled the following inflation-adjusted list of the highest-grossing films of all time. Figures are as of August, 1994.

Rank	Title	Opening Date	Adjusted Gross
1.	*Gone with the Wind*	1939	$821,790,000
2.	*Star Wars*	1977	597,793,722
3.	*The Ten Commandments*	1958	542,340,000
4.	*The Sound of Music*	1965	531,497,608
5.	*Jaws*	1975	530,246,305
6.	*E.T., the Extra-Terrestrial*	1982	526,457,394
7.	*Doctor Zhivago*	1965	513,920,786
8.	*Jungle Book*	1967	459,728,526
9.	*Snow White*	1937	451,260,000
10.	*101 Dalmations*	1961	411,122,409

THE BIGGEST HITS, YEAR BY YEAR

The following are the top five movies of the year based on data from *Variety*, beginning with 1939, when a Hollywood legend, *Gone with the Wind*, hit the theaters. Dollar figures listed are rentals (the amount of money collected by the studio), rather than box-office grosses, a relatively new method of tracking a film's box-office strength. (Figures for 1941 films, with the exception of *Sergeant York*, are rough estimates.)

1939

1. Gone with the Wind	$77,641,106
2. The Wizard of Oz	4,544,851
3. The Hunchback of Notre Dame (tie)	1,500,000
3. Jesse James (tie)	1,500,000
3. Mr. Smith Goes to Washington (tie)	1,500,000

1940

1. Fantasia	$41,660,000
2. Pinocchio	40,442,000
3. Boom Town	4,586,415
4. Rebecca (tie)	1,500,000
4. Santa Fe Trail (tie)	1,500,000

1941

1. Sergeant York	$6,135,707
2. Dive Bomber (tie)	1,500,000
2. Honky Tonk (tie)	1,500,000
2. The Philadelphia Story (tie)	1,500,000
2. A Yank in the R.A.F. (tie)	1,500,000

1942

1. Bambi	$47,265,000
2. Mrs. Miniver	5,390,009
3. Yankee Doodle Dandy	4,719,681
4. Random Harvest	4,665,501
5. Casablanca	4,145,178

1943

1. This Is the Army	$8,301,000
2. For Whom the Bell Tolls	7,100,000
3. The Outlaw	5,075,000
4. The Song of Bernadette	5,000,000
5. Stage Door Canteen	4,339,532

1944

1. Going My Way	$6,500.000
2. Meet Me in St. Louis	5,132,202
3. Since You Went Away	4,924,756
4. 30 Seconds over Tokyo	4,471,080
5. White Cliffs of Dover	4,045,250

1945

1. The Bells of St. Mary's	$8,000,000
2. Leave Her to Heaven	5,500,000
3. Spellbound	4,970,583
4. Anchors Away	4,778,679
5. The Valley of Decision	4,566,374

1946

1. Song of the South	$29,228,717
2. The Best Years of Our Lives (tie)	11,300,000
2. Duel in the Sun (tie)	11,300,000
4. The Jolson Story	7,600,000
5. Blue Skies	5,700,000

1947

1. Welcome Stranger	$6,100,000
2. The Egg and I	5,500,000
3. Unconquered	5,250,000
4. Life with Father	5,057,000
5. Forever Amber	5,000,000

1948

1. The Red Shoes	$5,000,000
2. Red River	4,506,825
3. The Paleface	4,500,000
4. The Three Musketeers	4,306,876
5. Johnny Belinda	4,266,000

1949

1. Samson and Delilah	$11,500,000
2. Battleground	5,051,143
3. Jolson Sings Again (tie)	5,000,000
3. The Sands of Iwo Jima (tie)	5,000,000
5. I Was a Male War Bride	4,100,000

1950

1. Cinderella	$41,087,000
2. King Solomon's Mines	5,586,000
3. Annie Get Your Gun	4,919,394
4. Cheaper by the Dozen	4,425,000
5. Father of the Bride	4,054,405

1951

1. Quo Vadis?	$11,901,662
2. Alice in Wonderland	7,196,000
3. Show Boat	5,533,000
4. David and Bathsheba	4,720,000
5. The Great Caruso	4,531,000

1952

1. This is Cinerama	$15,400,000
2. The Greatest Show on Earth	14,000,000
3. The Snows of Kilimanjaro	6,500,000
4. Ivanhoe	6,258,000
5. Hans Christian Andersen	6,000,000

1953

1. Peter Pan	$37,584,000
2. The Robe	17,500,000
3. From Here to Eternity	12,200,000
4. Shane	9,000,000
5. How To Marry a Millionaire	7,300,000

1954

1. White Christmas	$12,000,000
2. 20,000 Leagues Under the Sea	11,267,000
3. Rear Window	9,812,271
4. The Caine Mutiny	8,700,000
5. The Glenn Miller Story	7,590,994

1955

1. Lady and the Tramp	$40,249,000
2. Cinerama Holiday	12,000,000
3. Mister Roberts	8,500,000
4. Battle Cry	8,100,000
5. Oklahoma!	7,100,000

1956

1. The Ten Commandments	$43,000,000
2. Around the World in 80 Days	23,120,000
3. Giant	14,000,000
4. Seven Wonders of the World	12,500,000
5. The King and I	8,500,000

1957

1. The Bridge on the River Kwai	$17,195,000
2. Peyton Place	11,500,000
3. Sayonara	10,500,000
4. Old Yeller	10,050,000
5. Raintree County	5,962,839

1958

1. South Pacific	$17,500,000
2. Auntie Mame	9,300,000
3. Cat on a Hot Tin Roof	8,785,162
4. No Time for Sergeants	7,500,000
5. Gigi	7,321.423

1959

1. Ben-Hur	$36,992,088
2. Sleeping Beauty	21,998,000
3. The Shaggy Dog	12,317,000
4. Operation Petticoat	9,321,555
5. Darby O'Gill and the Little People	8,336,000

1960

1. Swiss Family Robinson	$20,178,000
2. Psycho	11,200,000
3. Spartacus	10,300,454
4. Exodus	8,331,582
5. The Alamo	7,918,776

1961

1. 101 Dalmatians	$68,648,000
2. West Side Story	19,645,570
3. Guns of Navarone	13,000,000
4. El Cid	12,000,000
5. The Absent-Minded Professor	11,426,000

1962

1. How the West Was Won	$20,932,883
2. Lawrence of Arabia	20,310,000
3. The Longest Day	17,600,000
4. In Search of the Castaways	9,975,000
5. The Music Man	8,100,000

1963

1. Cleopatra	$26,000,000
2. It's a Mad Mad Mad Mad World	20,849,786
3. Tom Jones	16,925,988
4. Irma La Douce	11,921,784
5. The Sword in the Stone	10,475,000

1964

1. Mary Poppins	$45,000,000
2. Goldfinger	22,997,706
3. The Carpetbaggers	15,500,000
4. My Fair Lady	12,000,000
5. From Russia with Love	9,924,279

1965

1. The Sound of Music	$79,748,000
2. Doctor Zhivago	47,116,811
3. Thunderball	28,621,434
4. Those Magnificent Men in Their Flying Machines	14,000,000
5. That Darn Cat	12,628,000

1966

1. Hawaii	$15,553,018
2. The Bible	15,000,000
3. Who's Afraid of Virginia Woolf?	14,500,000
4. A Man for All Seasons	12,750,000
5. Lt. Robin Crusoe, USN	10,164,000

1967

1. The Jungle Book	$60,964,000
2. The Graduate	44,090,729
3. Guess Who's Coming to Dinner	25,500,000
4. Bonnie and Clyde	22,800,000
5. The Dirty Dozen	20,403,826

1968

1. Funny Girl	$26,325,000
2. 2001: A Space Odyssey	25,521,917
3. The Odd Couple	20,000,000
4. Bullitt	19,000,000
5. Romeo and Juliet	17,473,000

1969

1. Butch Cassidy and the Sundance Kid	$46,039,000
2. The Love Bug	23,150,000
3. Midnight Cowboy	20,499,282
4. Easy Rider	19,100,000
5. Hello, Dolly!	15,200,000

1970

1. Love Story	$50,000,000
2. Airport	45,220,118
3. M*A*S*H	36,720,000
4. Patton	28,100,000
5. The Aristocats	26,462,000

1971

1. Fiddler on the Roof	$38,251,196
2. Billy Jack	32,500,000
3. The French Connection	26,315,000
4. Summer of '42	20,500,000
5. Diamonds Are Forever	19,726,829

1972

1. The Godfather	$86,275,000
2. The Poseidon Adventure	42,000,000
3. What's Up Doc?	28,000,000
4. Deliverance	22,600,000
5. Jeremiah Johnson	21,900,000

1973

1. The Exorcist	$89,000,000
2. The Sting	78,212,000
3. American Graffiti	55,128,175
4. Papillon	22,500,000
5. The Way We Were	22,457,000

1974

1. The Towering Inferno	$52,000,000
2. Blazing Saddles	47,800,000
3. Young Frankenstein	38,823,000
4. Earthquake	35,849,994
5. The Trial of Billy Jack	31,100,000

1975

1. Jaws	$129,549,325
2. One Flew Over the Cuckoo's Nest	59,939,701
3. The Rocky Horror Picture Show	40,020,000
4. Shampoo	23,822,000
5. Dog Day Afternoon	22,500,000

1976

1. Rocky	$56,524,972
2. A Star Is Born	37,100,000
3. King Kong	36,915,000
4. Silver Streak	30,018,000
5. All the President's Men	30,000,000

1977

1. Star Wars	$193,500,000
2. Close Encounters of the Third Kind	82,750,000
3. Saturday Night Fever	74,100,000
4. Smokey and the Bandit	58,949,939
5. The Goodbye Girl	41,839,170

1978

1. Grease	$96,300,000
2. Superman	82,800,000
3. National Lampoon's Animal House	70,826,000
4. Every Which Way but Loose	51,900,000
5. Jaws 2	50,431,964

1979

1. Kramer vs. Kramer	$59,986,335
2. Star Trek: The Motion Picture	56,000,000
3. The Jerk	42,989,656
4. Rocky II	42,169,387
5. Alien	40,300,000

1980

1. The Empire Strikes Back	$141,600,000
2. 9 to 5	59,100,000
3. Stir Crazy	58,364,420
4. Airplane!	40,610,000
5. Any Which Way You Can	40,500,000

1981

1. Raiders of the Lost Ark	$115,598,000
2. Superman II	65,100,000
3. On Golden Pond	61,174,744
4. Arthur	42,000,000
5. Stripes	40,886,589

1982

1. E.T., the Extra-Terrestrial	$228,618,939
2. Tootsie	96,292,736
3. Rocky III	66,262,796
4. An Officer and a Gentleman	55,223,000
5. Porky's	54,000,000

1983

1. Return of the Jedi	$168,002,414
2. Terms of Endearment	50,250,000
3. Trading Places	40,600,000
4. WarGames	38,519,833
5. Superman III	37,200,000

1984

1. Ghostbusters	$130,211,324
2. Indiana Jones and the Temple of Doom	109,000,000
3. Beverly Hills Cop	108,000,000
4. Gremlins	79,500,000
5. The Karate Kid	43,432,881

1985

1. Back to the Future	$104,408,738
2. Rambo: First Blood Part II	78,919,250
3. Rocky IV	76,023,246
4. The Color Purple	47,900,000
5. Out of Africa	43,103,469

1986

1. Top Gun	$79,400,000
2. "Crocodile" Dundee	70,227,000
3. Platoon	69,742,143
4. The Karate Kid, Part II	58,362,026
5. Star Trek IV: The Voyage Home	56,820,071

1987

1. Three Men and a Baby	$81,313,000
2. Beverly Hills Cop II	80,857,776
3. Fatal Attraction	70,000,000
4. Good Morning, Vietnam	58,103,000
5. The Untouchables	36,866,530

1988

1. Rain Man	$86,813,000
2. Who Framed Roger Rabbit	81,244,000
3. Coming To America	65,000,000
4. "Crocodile" Dundee II	57,300,000
5. Twins	57,715,127

1989

1. Batman	$150,500,000
2. Indiana Jones and the Last Crusade	115,500,000
3. Lethal Weapon 2	79,500,000
4. Back to the Future Part II	72,319,630
5. Honey, I Shrunk the Kids	72,007,000

1990

1. Home Alone	$140,099,000
2. Ghost	98,200,000
3. Pretty Woman	81,905,530
4. Dances with Wolves	81,537,971
5. Teenage Mutant Ninja Turtles	67,650,000

1991

1. Terminator 2: Judgment Day	$112,500,000
2. Robin Hood: Prince of Thieves	86,000,000
3. Beauty and the Beast	69,415,000
4. Hook	65,000,000
5. City Slickers	60,750,000

1992

1. Home Alone 2: Lost in New York	$103,377,614
2. Batman Returns	100,100,000
3. Aladdin	82,539,083
4. Lethal Weapon 3	80,000,000
5. A Few Good Men	71,000,000

1993

1. Jurassic Park	$208,000,000
2. Mrs. Doubtfire	109,761,240
3. The Fugitive	92,600,000
4. The Firm	77,047,044
5. Sleepless in Seattle	64,930,137

THE GREATEST FLICKS? THE ENVELOPE, PLEASE . . .

They are the celluloid touchstones of our inner life, the enduring echos of various generations and the most bittersweet of social commentary played out ten yards high. Not to be confused with an artsy *Cahiers de Cinema* list, these are PEOPLE's Top 50 Flicks.

The African Queen
All About Eve
Batman
Ben-Hur
The Big Chill
Butch Cassidy and the Sundance Kid
Casablanca
Citizen Kane
City Lights
Dances with Wolves
Doctor Zhivago
Double Indemnity
E.T., the Extra-Terrestrial
Exodus
The Exorcist
Fantasia
Father of the Bride (the original)
Ghost
Giant
The Godfather
Gone With the Wind
The Graduate
High Noon
Indiana Jones and the Temple of Doom
It's A Wonderful Life
Jaws
Lawrence of Arabia
Mary Poppins
Mildred Pierce
Miracle on 34th Street
Mr. Smith Goes to Washington
National Lampoon's Animal House
A Night at the Opera
Psycho
Rebel Without a Cause
A Room With a View
The Searchers
Some Like It Hot
The Silence of the Lambs
Singin' in the Rain
The Sound of Music
Star Wars
Thelma and Louise
The Thin Man
The Third Man
Tootsie
2001: A Space Odyssey
Unforgiven
The Wizard of Oz
Wuthering Heights

ALL-TIME INTERNATIONAL BOX- OFFICE CHAMPS

At home *E.T.* is still the king of the grosses, but once you factor in international revenues, *Jurassic Park* rules. These are the biggest films worldwide, and the results are surprisingly different from the list of North American favorites. (Sources: *Variety*, *The Hollywood Reporter*, and *The New York Times*)

Rank	Film, Year of Release	B.O. Gross (millions)	Rank	Film, Year of Release	B.O. Gross (millions)
1.	*Jurassic Park*, 1993 (est.)	$900.0	11.	*Pretty Woman*, 1990	454.4
2.	*E.T., the Extra-Terrestrial*, 1982	701.1	12.	*Mrs. Doubtfire*, 1993	420.0
3.	*Ghost*, 1990	517.6	13.	*Batman*, 1989	411.2
4.	*Star Wars*, 1977	513.0	14.	*Rain Man*, 1988	405.8
5.	*The Bodyguard*, 1992	507.6	15.	*The Empire Strikes Back*, 1980	405.0
6.	*Indiana Jones and the Last Crusade*, 1989	494.8	16.	*Dances with Wolves*, 1990	394.2
7.	*Aladdin*, 1992	490.0	17.	*Robin Hood: Prince of Thieves*, 1991	390.5
8.	*Terminator 2: Judgment Day*, 1991	490.0	18.	*Return of the Jedi*, 1983	381.0
9.	*Home Alone*, 1990	474.7	19.	*The Fugitive*, 1993	369.1
10.	*Jaws*, 1975	458.0	20.	*Back to the Future*, 1985	364.1

PEOPLE'S HOLLYWOOD COSMOLOGY

Whether they charmed or challenged us, these all-time movie greats always left us wanting more. Emulated but never equalled, they are the grandest stars in the galaxy of the dark: twenty-five men, twenty-five women, and seven ensembles. As you can see right off, we're judging charisma or creativity, not character.

MEN

Woody Allen
Humphrey Bogart
Marlon Brando
Charlie Chaplin
Sean Connery

Tom Cruise
James Dean

Clint Eastwood
Errol Flynn
Henry Fonda
Harrison Ford
Clark Gable
Cary Grant
Eddie Murphy
Paul Newman
Jack Nicholson
Lawrence Olivier
Gregory Peck
Robert Redford
Roy Rogers
Arnold Schwarzenegger
Jimmy Stewart
Spencer Tracy
Rudolph Valentino
John Wayne

WOMEN

Julie Andrews
Ingrid Bergman
Joan Crawford
Bette Davis
Doris Day
Marlene Dietrich

Jodie Foster
Greta Garbo
Ava Gardner
Judy Garland
Lillian Gish

Whoopi Goldberg
Rita Hayworth
Audrey Hepburn
Katharine Hepburn
Grace Kelly
Deborah Kerr
Vivien Leigh
Sophia Loren
Marilyn Monroe

Julia Roberts
Elizabeth Taylor
Shirley Temple
Lana Turner
Mae West

ENSEMBLES

Abbott & Costello
Crosby & Hope
Laurel & Hardy
Martin & Lewis
The Marx Brothers

Our Gang
Sarandon & Davis

FOOTPRINTS OF THE STARS

The first footprints at Grauman's Chinese Theater, as it was originally called, were made by Norma Talmadge in 1927 when, legend holds, she accidentally stepped in wet concrete outside the building. Since then over 180 stars have been immortalized, along with their hands, feet—and sometimes noses (Jimmy Durante), fists (John Wayne), and legs (Betty Grable). Following the most recent inductions of Harrison Ford and Michael Keaton in 1994, the Forecourt of the Stars at Mann's includes:

Abbott & Costello
Don Ameche
Julie Andrews
Edward Arnold
Fred Astaire
Gene Autry
John Barrymore
Freddie Bartholomew
Anne Baxter
Wallace Beery
Jack Benny
Edgar Bergen
Joan Blondell
Humphrey Bogart
Charles Boyer
Joe E. Brown
Yul Brynner
George Burns
Cantinflas
Eddie Cantor
Maurice Chevalier
Gary Cooper
Jackie Cooper
Jeanne Crain
Joan Crawford
Bing Crosby
Tom Cruise
Bebe Daniels
Linda Darnell
Marion Davies
Bette Davis
Doris Day
Olivia DeHavilland
Cecil B. DeMille
Kirk Douglas
Marie Dressler
Donald Duck
Irene Dunne
Jimmie Durante
Deanna Durbin
Clint Eastwood
Nelson Eddy
Douglas Fairbanks
Alice Faye
Rhonda Fleming
Henry Fonda
Joan Fontaine
Harrison Ford
Clark Gable
Ava Gardner
Judy Garland
Greer Garson
Janet Gaynor
Mel Gibson
Betty Grable
Cary Grant
Rosa Grauman (founder Sid Grauman's mother)
Sid Grauman
Ann Harding
Jean Harlow
Rex Harrison
William S. Hart
Susan Hayward
Rita Hayworth
Van Heflin
Sonja Henie
Jean Hersholt
Charlton Heston
Bob Hope
Rock Hudson
George Jessel
Van Johnson
Al Jolson
Danny Kaye
Michael Keaton
Gene Kelly
Deborah Kerr
Alan Ladd
Dorothy Lamour
Charles Laughton
Jack Lemmon
Mervyn LeRoy
Harold Lloyd
Sophia Loren
Myrna Loy
George Lucas
William Lundigan
Jeanette MacDonald
Ali MacGraw
Shirley MacLaine
Victor McLaglen
Steve McQueen
Fredric March
Dean Martin
Tony Martin
The Marx Brothers
James Mason
Marcello Mastroianni
Lauritz Melchior
Ray Milland
Hayley Mills
Carmen Miranda
Tom Mix
Marilyn Monroe
Colleen Moore
Eddie Murphy
George Murphy
Hildegarde Neff
Pola Negri
Paul Newman
Jack Nicholson
Jack Oakie
Margaret O'Brien
Donald O'Connor
Louella Parsons
Gregory Peck
Mary Pickford
Ezio Pinza
Sidney Poitier
Dick Powell
Eleanor Powell
William Powell
Tyrone Power
Anthony Quinn
George Raft
Burt Reynolds
Debbie Reynolds
Ritz Brothers
Edward G. Robinson
May Robson
Ginger Rogers
Roy Rogers
Mickey Rooney
Jane Russell
Rosalind Russell
Peter Sellers
Norma Shearer
Jean Simmons
Frank Sinatra
Red Skelton
Steven Spielberg
Sylvester Stallone
Barbara Stanwyck
Star Trek crew (William Shatner, Leonard Nimoy, DeForest Kelley, James Doohan, Nichelle Nichols, George Takei, Walter Koenig)
Star Wars characters
George Stevens
Jimmy Stewart
Gloria Swanson
Constance Talmadge
Norma Talmadge
Elizabeth Taylor
Robert Taylor
Shirley Temple
Danny Thomas
Gene Tierney
John Travolta
Lana Turner
Rudy Vallee
Dick Van Dyke
W. S. Van Dyke
Raoul Walsh
John Wayne
Clifton Webb
Oskar Werner
Richard Widmark
Esther Williams
Jane Withers
Natalie Wood
Joanne Woodward
Monty Woolley
Jane Wyman
Diana Wynyard
Loretta Young
Adolph Zukor

THE BRIGHTEST STARS OF THE YEAR

In today's high-pressure movie business, the most valuable commodity is a star who shines so bright that he or she can "open" a movie—filling seats on the basis of pure popularity rather than on the allure of the film. Every year since 1933, Quigley Publishing has polled more than 500 moviehouse owners nationwide to determine which stars they regarded as the biggest box-office draw.

1933

1. Marie Dressler
2. Will Rogers
3. Janet Gaynor
4. Eddie Cantor
5. Wallace Beery
6. Jean Harlow
7. Clark Gable
8. Mae West
9. Norma Shearer
10. Joan Crawford

1934

1. Will Rogers
2. Clark Gable
3. Janet Gaynor
4. Wallace Beery
5. Mae West
6. Joan Crawford
7. Bing Crosby
8. Shirley Temple
9. Marie Dressler
10. Norma Shearer

1935

1. Shirley Temple
2. Will Rogers
3. Clark Gable
4. Fred Astaire and Ginger Rogers
5. Joan Crawford
6. Claudette Colbert
7. Dick Powell
8. Wallace Beery
9. Joe E. Brown
10. James Cagney

1936

1. Shirley Temple
2. Clark Gable
3. Fred Astaire and Ginger Rogers
4. Robert Taylor
5. Joe E. Brown
6. Dick Powell
7. Joan Crawford
8. Claudette Colbert
9. Jeanette MacDonald
10. Gary Cooper

1937

1. Shirley Temple
2. Clark Gable
3. Robert Taylor
4. Bing Crosby
5. William Powell
6. Jane Withers
7. Fred Astaire and Ginger Rogers
8. Sonja Henie
9. Gary Cooper
10. Myrna Loy

1938

1. Shirley Temple
2. Clark Gable
3. Sonja Henie
4. Mickey Rooney
5. Spencer Tracy
6. Robert Taylor
7. Myrna Loy
8. Jane Withers
9. Alice Faye
10. Tyrone Power

1939

1. Mickey Rooney
2. Tyrone Power
3. Spencer Tracy
4. Clark Gable
5. Shirley Temple
6. Bette Davis
7. Alice Faye
8. Errol Flynn
9. James Cagney
10. Sonja Henie

1940

1. Mickey Rooney
2. Spencer Tracy
3. Clark Gable
4. Gene Autry
5. Tyrone Power
6. James Cagney
7. Bing Crosby
8. Wallace Beery
9. Bette Davis
10. Judy Garland

1941

1. Mickey Rooney
2. Clark Gable
3. Abbott and Costello
4. Bob Hope
5. Spencer Tracy
6. Gene Autry
7. Gary Cooper
8. Bette Davis
9. James Cagney
10. Spencer Tracy

1942

1. Abbott and Costello
2. Clark Gable
3. Gary Cooper
4. Mickey Rooney
5. Bob Hope
6. James Cagney
7. Gene Autry
8. Betty Grable
9. Greer Garson
10. Spencer Tracy

1943

1. Betty Grable
2. Bob Hope
3. Abbott and Costello
4. Bing Crosby
5. Gary Cooper
6. Greer Garson
7. Humphrey Bogart
8. James Cagney
9. Mickey Rooney
10. Clark Gable

1944

1. Bing Crosby
2. Gary Cooper
3. Bob Hope
4. Betty Grable
5. Spencer Tracy
6. Greer Garson
7. Humphrey Bogart
8. Abbott and Costello
9. Cary Grant
10. Bette Davis

1945

1. Bing Crosby
2. Van Johnson
3. Greer Garson
4. Betty Grable
5. Spencer Tracy
6. Humphrey Bogart/ Gary Cooper
7. Bob Hope
8. Judy Garland
9. Margaret O'Brien
10. Roy Rogers

1946

1. Bing Crosby
2. Ingrid Bergman
3. Van Johnson
4. Gary Cooper
5. Bob Hope
6. Humphrey Bogart
7. Greer Garson
8. Margaret O'Brien
9. Betty Grable
10. Roy Rogers

1947

1. Bing Crosby
2. Betty Grable
3. Ingrid Bergman
4. Gary Cooper
5. Humphrey Bogart
6. Bob Hope
7. Clark Gable
8. Gregory Peck
9. Claudette Colbert
10. Alan Ladd

1948

1. Bing Crosby
2. Betty Grable
3. Abbott and Costello
4. Gary Cooper
5. Bob Hope
6. Humphrey Bogart
7. Clark Gable
8. Cary Grant
9. Spencer Tracy
10. Ingrid Bergman

1949

1. Bob Hope
2. Bing Crosby
3. Abbott and Costello
4. John Wayne
5. Gary Cooper
6. Cary Grant
7. Betty Grable
8. Esther Williams
9. Humphrey Bogart
10. Clark Gable

1950

1. John Wayne
2. Bob Hope
3. Bing Crosby
4. Betty Grable
5. James Stewart
6. Abbott and Costello
7. Clifton Webb
8. Esther Williams
9. Spencer Tracy
10. Randolph Scott

1951

1. John Wayne
2. Dean Martin and Jerry Lewis
3. Betty Grable
4. Abbott and Costello
5. Bing Crosby
6. Bob Hope
7. Randolph Scott
8. Gary Cooper
9. Doris Day
10. Spencer Tracy

1952

1. Dean Martin and Jerry Lewis
2. Gary Cooper
3. John Wayne
4. Bing Crosby
5. Bob Hope
6. James Stewart
7. Doris Day
8. Gregory Peck
9. Susan Hayward
10. Randolph Scott

1953

1. Gary Cooper
2. Dean Martin and Jerry Lewis
3. John Wayne
4. Alan Ladd
5. Bing Crosby
6. Marilyn Monroe
7. James Stewart
8. Bob Hope
9. Susan Hayward
10. Randolph Scott

1954

1. John Wayne
2. Dean Martin and Jerry Lewis
3. Gary Cooper
4. James Stewart
5. Marilyn Monroe
6. Alan Ladd
7. William Holden
8. Bing Crosby
9. Jane Wyman
10. Marlon Brando

1955

1. James Stewart
2. Grace Kelly
3. John Wayne
4. William Holden
5. Gary Cooper
6. Marlon Brando
7. Dean Martin and Jerry Lewis
8. Humphrey Bogart
9. June Allyson
10. Clark Gable

1956

1. William Holden
2. John Wayne
3. James Stewart
4. Burt Lancaster
5. Glenn Ford
6. Dean Martin and Jerry Lewis
7. Gary Cooper
8. Marilyn Monroe
9. Kim Novak
10. Frank Sinatra

1957

1. Rock Hudson
2. John Wayne
3. Pat Boone
4. Elvis Presley
5. Frank Sinatra
6. Gary Cooper
7. William Holden
8. James Stewart
9. Jerry Lewis
10. Yul Brynner

1958

1. Glenn Ford
2. Elizabeth Taylor
3. Jerry Lewis
4. Marlon Brando
5. Rock Hudson
6. William Holden
7. Brigitte Bardot
8. Yul Brynner
9. James Stewart
10. Frank Sinatra

1959

1. Rock Hudson
2. Cary Grant
3. James Stewart
4. Doris Day
5. Debbie Reynolds
6. Glenn Ford
7. Frank Sinatra
8. John Wayne
9. Jerry Lewis
10. Susan Hayward

1960

1. Doris Day
2. Rock Hudson
3. Cary Grant
4. Elizabeth Taylor
5. Debbie Reynolds
6. Tony Curtis
7. Sandra Dee
8. Frank Sinatra
9. Jack Lemmon
10. John Wayne

1961

1. Elizabeth Taylor
2. Rock Hudson
3. Doris Day
4. John Wayne
5. Cary Grant
6. Sandra Dee
7. Jerry Lewis
8. William Holden
9. Tony Curtis
10. Elvis Presley

1962

1. Doris Day
2. Rock Hudson
3. Cary Grant
4. John Wayne
5. Elvis Presley
6. Elizabeth Taylor
7. Jerry Lewis
8. Frank Sinatra
9. Sandra Dee
10. Burt Lancaster

1963

1. Doris Day
2. John Wayne
3. Rock Hudson
4. Jack Lemmon
5. Cary Grant
6. Elizabeth Taylor
7. Elvis Presley
8. Sandra Dee
9. Paul Newman
10. Jerry Lewis

1964

1. Doris Day
2. Jack Lemmon
3. Rock Hudson
4. John Wayne
5. Cary Grant
6. Elvis Presley
7. Shirley MacLaine
8. Ann-Margret
9. Paul Newman
10. Jerry Lewis

1965

1. Sean Connery
2. John Wayne
3. Doris Day
4. Julie Andrews
5. Jack Lemmon
6. Elvis Presley
7. Cary Grant
8. James Stewart
9. Elizabeth Taylor
10. Richard Burton

1966

1. Julie Andrews
2. Sean Connery
3. Elizabeth Taylor
4. Jack Lemmon
5. Richard Burton

6. Cary Grant
7. John Wayne
8. Doris Day
9. Paul Newman
10. Elvis Presley

1967

1. Julie Andrews
2. Lee Marvin
3. Paul Newman
4. Dean Martin
5. Sean Connery
6. Elizabeth Taylor
7. Sidney Poitier
8. John Wayne
9. Richard Burton
10. Steve McQueen

1968

1. Sidney Poitier
2. Paul Newman
3. Julie Andrews
4. John Wayne
5. Clint Eastwood
6. Dean Martin
7. Steve McQueen
8. Jack Lemmon
9. Lee Marvin
10. Elizabeth Taylor

1969

1. Paul Newman
2. John Wayne
3. Steve McQueen
4. Dustin Hoffman
5. Clint Eastwood
6. Sidney Poitier
7. Lee Marvin
8. Jack Lemmon
9. Katharine Hepburn
10. Barbra Streisand

1970

1. Paul Newman
2. Clint Eastwood
3. Steve McQueen
4. John Wayne
5. Elliott Gould
6. Dustin Hoffman
7. Lee Marvin
8. Jack Lemmon
9. Barbra Streisand
10. Walter Matthau

1971

1. John Wayne
2. Clint Eastwood
3. Paul Newman
4. Steve McQueen
5. George C. Scott
6. Dustin Hoffman
7. Walter Matthau
8. Ali MacGraw
9. Sean Connery
10. Lee Marvin

1972

1. Clint Eastwood
2. George C. Scott
3. Gene Hackman
4. John Wayne
5. Barbra Streisand
6. Marlon Brando
7. Paul Newman
8. Steve McQueen
9. Dustin Hoffman
10. Goldie Hawn

1973

1. Clint Eastwood
2. Ryan O'Neal
3. Steve McQueen
4. Burt Reynolds
5. Robert Redford
6. Barbra Streisand
7. Paul Newman
8. Charles Bronson
9. John Wayne
10. Marlon Brando

1974

1. Robert Redford
2. Clint Eastwood
3. Paul Newman
4. Barbra Streisand
5. Steve McQueen
6. Burt Reynolds
7. Charles Bronson
8. Jack Nicholson
9. Al Pacino
10. John Wayne

1975

1. Robert Redford
2. Barbra Streisand
3. Al Pacino
4. Charles Bronson
5. Paul Newman
6. Clint Eastwood
7. Burt Reynolds
8. Woody Allen
9. Steve McQueen
10. Gene Hackman

1976

1. Robert Redford
2. Jack Nicholson
3. Dustin Hoffman
4. Clint Eastwood
5. Mel Brooks
6. Burt Reynolds
7. Al Pacino
8. Tatum O'Neal
9. Woody Allen
10. Charles Bronson

1977

1. Sylvester Stallone
2. Barbra Streisand
3. Clint Eastwood
4. Burt Reynolds
5. Robert Redford
6. Woody Allen
7. Mel Brooks
8. Al Pacino
9. Diane Keaton
10. Robert De Niro

1978

1. Burt Reynolds
2. John Travolta
3. Richard Dreyfuss
4. Warren Beatty
5. Clint Eastwood
6. Woody Allen
7. Diane Keaton
8. Jane Fonda
9. Peter Sellers
10. Barbra Streisand

1979

1. Burt Reynolds
2. Clint Eastwood
3. Jane Fonda
4. Woody Allen
5. Barbra Streisand
6. Sylvester Stallone
7. John Travolta
8. Jill Clayburgh
9. Roger Moore
10. Mel Brooks

1980

1. Burt Reynolds
2. Robert Redford
3. Clint Eastwood
4. Jane Fonda
5. Dustin Hoffman
6. John Travolta
7. Sally Field
8. Sissy Spacek
9. Barbra Streisand
10. Steve Martin

1981

1. Burt Reynolds
2. Clint Eastwood
3. Dudley Moore
4. Dolly Parton
5. Jane Fonda
6. Harrison Ford
7. Alan Alda
8. Bo Derek
9. Goldie Hawn
10. Bill Murray

1982

1. Burt Reynolds
2. Clint Eastwood
3. Sylvester Stallone
4. Dudley Moore
5. Richard Pryor
6. Dolly Parton
7. Jane Fonda
8. Richard Gere
9. Paul Newman
10. Harrison Ford

1983

1. Clint Eastwood
2. Eddie Murphy
3. Sylvester Stallone
4. Burt Reynolds
5. John Travolta
6. Dustin Hoffman
7. Harrison Ford
8. Richard Gere
9. Chevy Chase
10. Tom Cruise

1984

1. Clint Eastwood
2. Bill Murray
3. Harrison Ford
4. Eddie Murphy
5. Sally Field
6. Burt Reynolds
7. Robert Redford
8. Prince
9. Dan Aykroyd
10. Meryl Streep

1985

1. Sylvester Stallone
2. Eddie Murphy
3. Clint Eastwood
4. Michael J. Fox
5. Chevy Chase
6. Arnold Schwarzenegger
7. Chuck Norris
8. Harrison Ford
9. Michael Douglas
10. Meryl Streep

1986

1. Tom Cruise
2. Eddie Murphy
3. Paul Hogan
4. Rodney Dangerfield
5. Bette Midler
6. Sylvester Stallone
7. Clint Eastwood
8. Whoopi Goldberg
9. Kathleen Turner
10. Paul Newman

1987

1. Eddie Murphy
2. Michael Douglas
3. Michael J. Fox
4. Arnold Schwarzenegger
5. Paul Hogan
6. Tom Cruise
7. Glenn Close
8. Sylvester Stallone
9. Cher
10. Mel Gibson

1988

1. Tom Cruise
2. Eddie Murphy
3. Tom Hanks
4. Arnold Schwarzenegger
5. Paul Hogan
6. Danny De Vito
7. Bette Midler
8. Robin Williams
9. Tom Selleck
10. Dustin Hoffman

1989

1. Jack Nicholson
2. Tom Cruise
3. Robin Williams
4. Michael Douglas
5. Tom Hanks
6. Michael J. Fox
7. Eddie Murphy
8. Mel Gibson
9. Sean Connery
10. Kathleen Turner

1990

1. Arnold Schwarzenegger
2. Julia Roberts
3. Bruce Willis
4. Tom Cruise
5. Mel Gibson
6. Kevin Costner
7. Patrick Swayze
8. Sean Connery
9. Harrison Ford
10. Richard Gere

1991

1. Kevin Costner
2. Arnold Schwarzenegger
3. Robin Williams
4. Julia Roberts
5. Macaulay Culkin
6. Jodie Foster
7. Billy Crystal
8. Dustin Hoffman
9. Robert De Niro
10. Mel Gibson

1992

1. Tom Cruise
2. Mel Gibson
3. Kevin Costner
4. Jack Nicholson
5. Macaulay Culkin
6. Whoopi Goldberg
7. Michael Douglas
8. Clint Eastwood
9. Steven Seagal
10. Robin Williams

1993

1. Clint Eastwood
2. Tom Cruise
3. Robin Williams
4. Kevin Costner
5. Harrison Ford
6. Julia Roberts
7. Tom Hanks
8. Mel Gibson
9. Whoopi Goldberg
10. Sylvester Stallone
11. Meg Ryan
12. Arnold Schwarzenegger
13. Demi Moore
14. Macaulay Culkin
15. Jack Nicholson
16. Al Pacino
17. Denzel Washington
18. Sean Connery
19. Michael Douglas
20. Tommy Lee Jones

STAR LIGHT, STAR BRIGHT

PEOPLE analyzed Quigley Publishing's list of the top ten stars of the years since 1933 to come up with an all-time list of the most popular actors ever. Here they are, along with their total scores. (We awarded points on a descending scale of 10, based on the year-by-year Quigley rankings.)

Rank	Actor	Score
1.	John Wayne	172
2.	Clint Eastwood	165
3.	Bing Crosby	111
4.	Gary Cooper	102
5.	Clark Gable	91
6.	Burt Reynolds	90
7.	Bob Hope	84
8.	Paul Newman	76
9.	Doris Day	72
10.	Rock Hudson	69
11.	Betty Grable	66
12.	Cary Grant	62
13.	Tom Cruise	61
14.	Eddie Murphy (tie)	57
14.	Abbott & Costello (tie)	57
16.	James Stewart	56
17.	Robert Redford	55
18.	Elizabeth Taylor	52
19.	Sylvester Stallone	50
20.	Shirley Temple	49
21.	Spencer Tracy (tie)	48
21.	Barbra Streisand (tie)	48
23.	Steve McQueen	47
24.	Mickey Rooney (tie)	46
24.	Dean Martin & Jerry Lewis (tie)	46
26.	Dustin Hoffman	42
27.	Jack Lemmon	40
28.	Arnold Schwarzenegger	38
29.	Julie Andrews	35
30.	Humphrey Bogart (tie)	34
30.	Gary Cooper (tie)	34
32.	William Holden	33
33.	Sean Connery	32
34.	Kevin Costner	30
35.	Elvis Presley (tie)	29
35.	Jack Nicholson (tie)	29
35.	Harrison Ford	29
38.	Will Rogers (tie)	28
38.	Jane Fonda (tie)	28
38.	Robin Williams	28
41.	John Travolta	24
42.	Mel Gibson	20
43.	Woody Allen (tie)	22
43.	Michael Douglas (tie)	22
43.	Jerry Lewis (tie)	22
46.	Michael J. Fox (tie)	20
46.	Paul Hogan (tie)	20
46.	Lee Marvin (tie)	20
46.	Robert Taylor (tie)	20
50.	Fred Astaire & Ginger Rogers (tie)	19
50.	Wallace Beery (tie)	19
50.	Marlon Brando (tie)	19
50.	Sidney Poitier (tie)	19

THE HOLLYWOOD BLACKLIST

The House Committee on Un-American Activities investigated the entertainment business for subversive activities—i.e., communist connections—starting in 1947. By the end of the hearings in 1958, roughly a hundred film, television, radio, theater, and music industry figures had been questioned. Approximately one-third of those people provided the committee with the names of others who were alleged sympathizers. The remainder, insisting that their political beliefs were a private matter, took either the First or the Fifth Amendment and refused to name names; some of these men and women were jailed, almost all were blackballed, and many had their careers ruined.

The following were some of the most well known of the informers who identified over 300 communist sympathizers:

Lee J. Cobb, actor (*On the Waterfront, Twelve Angry Men, Death of a Salesman, Exodus*, "The Virginian")

Sterling Hayden, actor (*The Asphalt Jungle, Johnny Guitar, Dr. Strangelove*)

Roy Huggins, writer/director/producer ("Cheyenne," "Maverick," "The Rockford Files")

Elia Kazan, director (*Gentleman's Agreement, On the Waterfront, A Streetcar Named Desire*)

Isobel Lennert, screenwriter (*East Side, West Side, Anchors Aweigh, Meet Me in Las Vegas*)

Clifford Odets, playwright (*Waiting for Lefty, Golden Boy*)

Jerome Robbins, dancer/choreographer/assoc. director, New York City Ballet (*Fancy Free, Interplay, Dances at a Gathering*)

Robert Rossen, director (*Body and Soul, All the King's Men*)

Budd Schulberg, screenwriter/novelist (*On the Waterfront*)

Leo Townsend, screenwriter (*Night and Day, Beach Blanket Bingo, Bikini Beach*)

The following, six of them Oscar winners at some point in their careers, refused to incriminate themselves or to inform on others, and as a result were either jailed, blacklisted, or forced to leave the country.

Herschel Bernardi, actor (*The Front*)

Howard Da Silva, actor (*Mommy Dearest*)

Carl Foreman, director/screenwriter (screenwriter, *High Noon*)

Dashiell Hammett, novelist (*The Thin Man, The Maltese Falcon*)

Lillian Hellman, playwright/screenwriter (*The Little Foxes, The Watch on the Rhine*)

Howard Koch, radio writer/screenwriter/playwright ("War of the Worlds," *Casablanca*)

Ring Lardner Jr., screenwriter (*Woman of the Year, Laura, M*A*S*H*)

Philip Loeb, actor ("The Goldbergs")

Joseph Losey, director (*The Concrete Jungle, The Damned, The Servant, Modesty Blaise, Boom!, The Go-Between*)

Albert Maltz, screenwriter/playwright (*This Gun for Hire, Destination Tokyo, The House I Live In, Pride of the Marines, The Robe*)

Arthur Miller, playwright/screenwriter (*Death of a Salesman, The Crucible, The Misfits*)

Zero Mostel, actor/comedian (*A Funny Thing Happened on the Way to the Forum, The Producers, Fiddler on the Roof*)

Dorothy Parker, short-story writer/screenwriter ("Laments for the Living," *A Star is Born*)

John Randolph, actor (*Come Back, Little Sheba, Serpico*)

Paul Robeson, actor/singer (*The Emperor Jones, Show Boat*)

Waldo Salt, screenwriter (*Midnight Cowboy, Serpico, Coming Home*)

Robert Adrian Scott, screenwriter/producer (producer, *Murder, My Sweet, Crossfire*)

Pete Seeger, musician (coauthor, "If I Had a Hammer")

Gale Sondergaard, actress (*Anthony Adverse, A Night to Remember, The Spider Woman*)

Dalton Trumbo, screenwriter (*Kitty Foyle, Thirty Seconds over Tokyo, The Brave One* [under the name of Robert Rich], *Exodus, Hawaii, Spartacus*)

Sam Wanamaker, actor (*The Spy Who Came in from the Cold, Private Benjamin*)

Nedrick Young, screenwriter (*The Defiant Ones, Inherit the Wind*)

CREDITS OF THE SUPERSTARS

Here are twenty-five filmographies for some of the most important, most popular, and most intriguing people in Hollywood today. The filmographies list only full-length feature films to which these actors and directors contributed significantly. Films are listed by their year of release, including some early films by now-famous figures that have been released directly onto video years after filming.

WOODY ALLEN

Director/screenwriter/actor

What's New, Pussycat? (screenwriter/actor, 1965)

What's Up, Tiger Lily? (director/screenwriter/actor, 1966)

Casino Royale (co-screenwriter/actor, 1967)

Take the Money and Run (director/co-screenwriter/actor, 1969)

Bananas (director/screenwriter/actor, 1971)

Play It Again, Sam (screenwriter/actor, 1972)

Everything You Always Wanted To Know About Sex (*but were afraid to ask)* (director/co-screenwriter/actor, 1972)

Sleeper (director/screenwriter/actor, 1973)

Love and Death (director/screenwriter/actor, 1975)

The Front (actor, 1976)

Annie Hall (director/co-screenwriter/actor, 1977; Academy Awards for best picture, best director, best original screenplay)

Interiors (director/screenwriter, 1978)

Manhattan (director/co-screenwriter/actor, 1979)

Stardust Memories (director/screenwriter/actor, 1980)

A Midsummer Night's Sex Comedy (director/screenwriter/actor, 1982)

Zelig (director/screenwriter/actor, 1983)

Broadway Danny Rose (director/screenwriter/actor, 1984)

The Purple Rose of Cairo (director/screenwriter, 1985)

Hannah and Her Sisters (director/screenwriter/actor, 1986; Academy Award for best original screenplay)

Radio Days (director/screenwriter/actor, 1987)

King Lear (actor, 1987)

September (director/screenwriter, 1987)

Another Woman (director/screenwriter, 1988)

"Oedipus Wrecks," in *New York Stories* (director/co-screenwriter/actor, 1989)

Crimes and Misdemeanors (director/screenwriter/actor, 1989)

Alice (director/screenwriter, 1990)

Scenes From a Mall (actor, 1991)

Shadows and Fog (director/screenwriter/actor, 1992)

Husbands and Wives (director/screenwriter/actor, 1992)

Manhattan Murder Mystery (director/screenwriter/actor, 1993)

Bullets Over Broadway (director, 1994)

GLENN CLOSE

Actor

The World According to Garp (1982)

The Big Chill (1983)

The Stone Boy (1984)

Greystoke: The Legend of Tarzan, Lord of the Apes (Voice, 1984)

The Natural (1984)

Jagged Edge (1985)

Maxie (1985)

Fatal Attraction (1987)

Dangerous Liaisons (1988)

Light Years (cartoon voice, 1988)

Immediate Family (1989)

Hamlet (1990)

Reversal of Fortune (1990)

Meeting Venus (1991)

The Paper (1994)

The House of the Spirits (1994)

SEAN CONNERY

Actor

No Road Back (1956)

Action of the Tiger (1957)

Another Time, Another Place (1958)

Hell Drivers (1957)

Time Lock (1957)

A Night to Remember (1958)

Tarzan's Greatest Adventure (1959)

Darby O'Gill and the Little People (1959)

On the Fiddle (1961)

The Frightened City (1961)

The Longest Day (1962)

Dr. No (1962)

From Russia with Love (1963)

Goldfinger (1964)

Woman of Straw (1964)

Marnie (1964)

Thunderball (1965)

The Hill (1965)

A Fine Madness (1966)

You Only Live Twice (1967)

Shalako (1968)

Bowler and Bonnet (1969, director)

The Molly Maguires (1970)

The Red Tent (1971)

The Anderson Tapes (1971)

Diamonds Are Forever (1971)

The Offence (or *Something like the Truth*, 1973)

Zardoz (1974)

Murder on the Orient Express (1974)

Ransom (1974)

The Wind and the Lion (1975)

The Man Who Would Be King (1975)

The Terrorists (1975)

Robin and Marian (1976)

The Next Man (1976)

A Bridge Too Far (1977)

The Great Train Robbery (1979)

Meteor (1979)

Cuba (1979)

Outland (1981)

Time Bandits (1981)

Wrong is Right (1981)

G'ole (1982)

Five Days One Summer (1982)

Never Say Never Again (1983)

Sword of the Valiant (1984)

Highlander (1985)

The Name of the Rose (1986)

The Untouchables (1987; Academy Award for best supporting actor)

The Presidio (1988)

Memories of Me (1988)

Indiana Jones and the Last Crusade (1989)

Family Business (1989)

The Hunt for Red October (1990)

The Russia House (1990)

Highlander II: The Quickening (1991)

Robin Hood: Prince of Thieves (1991)

Medicine Man (1992)

Rising Sun (1993)

A Good Man in Africa (1994)

FRANCIS FORD COPPOLA

Director/producer/screenwriter

Dementia 13 (director/screenwriter, 1963)

Is Paris Burning? (screenwriter, 1966)

This Property Is Condemned (screenwriter, 1966)

You're a Big Boy Now (director/screenwriter, 1966)

Finian's Rainbow (director, 1968)

The Rain People (director/screenwriter, 1969)

Patton (co-screenwriter, 1970; Academy Award for best screenplay)

The Godfather (director/co-screenwriter, 1972; Academy Award for best screenplay)

The Conversation (director/co-producer/screenwriter, 1974)

The Godfather, Part II (director/co-producer/coscreenwriter, 1974; Academy Awards for best director, best picture, best screenplay)

The Great Gatsby (screenwriter, 1974)

Apocalypse Now (director/producer/co-screenwriter/musical co-composer, 1979)

One from the Heart (director/co-screenwriter, 1982)

The Outsiders (director/producer, 1983)

Rumble Fish (director/co-screenwriter, 1983)

The Cotton Club (director/co-screenwriter, 1984)

Rip Van Winkle (for cable television) (director, 1985)

Captain EO (director, 1986)

Peggy Sue Got Married (director, 1986)

Gardens of Stone (director/co-producer, 1987)

Tucker: The Man and his Dream (director, 1988)

"Life Without Zoe," in *New York Stories* (director/co-screenwriter, 1989)

The Godfather, Part III (director/producer/co-screenwriter, 1990)

Bram Stoker's Dracula (director/producer, 1992)

Mary Shelley's Frankenstein (producer, 1994)

KEVIN COSTNER
Actor/director/producer

Shadows Run Black (actor, 1981)

Night Shift (actor, 1982)

Stacy's Knights (actor, 1982)

The Big Chill (played corpse, all other scenes edited out, 1983)

The Gunrunner (actor, 1983)

Table for Five (actor, 1983)

Testament (actor, 1983)

American Flyers (actor, 1985)

Fandango (actor, 1985)

Silverado (actor, 1985)

Sizzle Beach, U.S.A. (actor, 1986)

No Way Out (actor, 1987)

The Untouchables (actor, 1987)

Bull Durham (actor, 1988)

Chasing Dreams (actor, 1989)

Field of Dreams (actor, 1989)

Dances with Wolves (actor/director/producer, 1990; Academy Awards for best picture, best director)

Revenge (actor, 1990)

Robin Hood: Prince of Thieves (actor, 1991)

JFK (actor, 1991)

The Bodyguard (actor/producer, 1992)

A Perfect World (actor, 1993)

Wyatt Earp (actor/producer, 1994)

The War (actor, 1994)

TOM CRUISE
Actor

Endless Love (1981)

Taps (1981)

Losin' It (1983)

The Outsiders (1983)

Risky Business (1983)

All the Right Moves (1983)

Legend (1985)

Top Gun (1986)

The Color of Money (1986)

Cocktail (1988)

Rain Man (1988)

Born on the Fourth of July (1989)

Days of Thunder (1990)

Far and Away (1992)

A Few Good Men (1992)

The Firm (1993)

Interview with the Vampire (1994)

CLINT EASTWOOD
Actor/director/producer

Francis in the Navy (actor, 1955)

Lady Godiva (actor, 1955)

Never Say Goodbye (actor,1955)

Revenge of the Creature (actor, 1955)

Tarantula (actor, 1955)

The Traveling Saleslady (actor, 1956)

Star in the Dust (actor, 1956)

Escapade in Japan (actor, 1957)

Ambush at Cimarron Pass (actor, 1958)

Lafayette Escadrille (actor, 1958)

A Fistful of Dollars (actor, 1964)

For a Few Dollars More (actor, 1965)

The Good, the Bad, and the Ugly (actor, 1966)

Coogan's Bluff (actor, 1968)

Hang 'Em High (actor, 1968)

The Witches (actor, 1968)

Where Eagles Dare (actor, 1968)

Paint Your Wagon (actor, 1969)

Kelly's Heroes (actor, 1970)

Two Mules for Sister Sara (actor, 1970)

The Beguiled (actor, 1971)

Dirty Harry (actor, 1971)

Play Misty For Me (actor/director, 1971)

Joe Kidd (actor, 1972)

Breezy (actor, 1973)

High Plains Drifter (actor/director, 1973)

Magnum Force (actor, 1973)

Thunderbolt and Lightfoot (actor, 1974)

The Eiger Sanction (actor/director, 1974)

The Outlaw Josey Wales (actor/director, 1975)

The Enforcer (actor, 1976)

The Gauntlet (actor/director, 1977)

Every Which Way but Loose (actor, 1978)

Escape from Alcatraz (actor, 1979)

Any Which Way You Can (actor, 1980)

Bronco Billy (actor/director, 1980)

Firefox (actor/director/producer, 1982)

Honkytonk Man (actor/director/producer, 1982)

Sudden Impact (actor/director/producer, 1983)

City Heat (actor, 1984)

Tightrope (actor/producer, 1984)

Pale Rider (actor/director/producer, 1985)

Heartbreak Ridge (actor/director/producer, 1986)

Bird (director/producer, 1988)

The Dead Pool (actor/producer, 1988)

Pink Cadillac (actor, 1989)

The Rookie (actor/director, 1990)

White Hunter, Black Heart (actor/director/producer, 1990)

Unforgiven (actor/director/producer, 1992; Academy Awards for best director and best film)

In the Line of Fire (actor/producer, 1993)

A Perfect World (actor/director, 1993)

JODIE FOSTER
Actor/director

Napoleon and Samantha (1972)

Kansas City Bomber (1972)

Tom Sawyer (1973)

One Little Indian (1973)

Alice Doesn't Live Here Anymore (1974)

Echoes of a Summer (1976)

Bugsy Malone (1976)

Taxi Driver (1976)

Freaky Friday (1976)

The Little Girl Who Lives Down the Lane (1977)

Candleshoe (1977)

Moi, fleur bleue (1977)

Il Casotto (1977)

Carny (1980)

Foxes (1980)

O'Hara's Wife (1982)

Les Sang des autres (*The Blood of Others*) (1984)

Hotel New Hampshire (1984)

Mesmerized (actor/co-producer, 1986)

Siesta (1987)
Five Corners (1987)
The Accused (1988; Academy Award for best actress)
Stealing Home (1988)
Backtrack (1990)
The Silence of the Lambs (1991; Academy Award for best actress)
Little Man Tate (actor/director, 1991)
Shadows and Fog (1992)
Sommersby (1993)
Maverick (1994)
Nell (1994)

MEL GIBSON
Actor/director

Summer City (1977)
Tim (1979)
Mad Max (1979)
Attack Force Z (1981)
Gallipoli (1981)
The Road Warrior (1981)
The Year of Living Dangerously (1982)
The Bounty (1984)
Mrs. Soffel (1984)
The River (1984)
Mad Max Beyond Thunderdome (1985)
Lethal Weapon (1987)
Tequila Sunrise (1988)
Lethal Weapon 2 (1989)
Air America (1990)
Bird on a Wire (1990)
Hamlet (1990)
Forever Young (1992)
Lethal Weapon 3 (1992)
The Man Without a Face (actor/director, 1993)
Maverick (1994)

WHOOPI GOLDBERG
Actor

The Color Purple (1985)
Jumpin' Jack Flash (1986)
Burglar (1987)
Fatal Beauty (1987)
Clara's Heart (1988)
The Telephone (1988)
Beverly Hills Brats (1989)
Homer and Eddie (1989)
Ghost (1990; Academy Award for best supporting actress)
The Long Walk Home (1990)
Soapdish (1991)
The Player (1992)
Sarafina! (1992)
Sister Act (1992)
Made in America (1993)
Sister Act 2: Back in the Habit (1993)
Corrina, Corrina (1994)
The Lion King (cartoon voice, 1994)

ANTHONY HOPKINS
Actor

The Lion in Winter (1968)
Hamlet (1969)
The Looking Glass War (1970)
When Eight Bells Toll (1971)
Young Winston (1972)
A Doll's House (1973)
The Girl From Petrovka (1974)
Juggernaut (1974)
All Creatures Great and Small (1975)
Audrey Rose (1977)
A Bridge Too Far (1977)
International Velvet (1978)
Magic (1978)
A Change of Seasons (1980)
The Elephant Man (1980)
The Bounty (1984)
Blunt (1986)
The Good Father (1986)
84 Charing Cross Road (1987)
The Dawning (1988)
A Chorus of Disapproval (1987)
Desperate Hours (1990)
The Silence of the Lambs (1991; Academy Award for best actor)
The Remains of the Day (1993)
Shadowlands (1993)
The Trial (1993)
The Road to Wellville (1994)

SPIKE LEE
Director/producer/screenwriter/actor

She's Gotta Have It (director/producer/screenwriter/actor, 1986)
School Daze (director/producer/screenwriter/actor, 1988)
Do the Right Thing (director/producer/screenwriter/actor, 1989)
Mo' Better Blues (director/producer/screenwriter/actor, 1990)
Lonely in America, (actor, 1990)
Jungle Fever (director/producer/screenwriter/actor, 1991)
Malcolm X (director/producer/co-screenwriter/actor, 1992)
Crooklyn (director/producer/co-screenwriter/actor, 1994)

DEMI MOORE
Actor

Choices (1981)
Parasite (1982)
Young Doctors in Love (1982)
Blame it on Rio (1984)
No Small Affair (1984)
St. Elmo's Fire (1985)
About Last Night (1986)
One Crazy Summer (1986)
Wisdom (1986)
The Seventh Sign (1988)
We're No Angels (1989)
Ghost (1990)
Mortal Thoughts (actor/co-producer, 1991)
Nothing But Trouble (1991)
The Butcher's Wife (1991)
A Few Good Men (1992)
Indecent Proposal (1993)

JACK NICHOLSON
Actor/producer/screenwriter/director

Cry Baby Killer (1958)
Studs Lonigan (1960)
Too Soon To Love (1960)
The Wild Ride (1960)
Little Shop of Horrors (1961)
The Broken Land (1962)
The Raven (1963)
The Terror (1963)
Thunder Island (screenwriter, 1963)
Back Door to Hell (1964)
Flight to Fury (actor/screenwriter, 1966)
Ride in the Whirlwind (actor/producer/screenwriter, 1966)
Hell's Angels on Wheels (1966)
The Shooting (actor/producer, 1967)
The Trip (screenwriter, 1967)
Head (actor/producer/screenwriter, 1968)
Psych-Out (1968)
Easy Rider (1969)
Five Easy Pieces (1970)
On a Clear Day You Can See Forever (1970)
Rebel Rousers (1970)
Carnal Knowledge (1971)
Drive, He Said (director/producer/screenwriter, 1971)
A Safe Place (1971)
The King of Marvin Gardens (1972)
The Last Detail (1973)
Chinatown (1974)
The Fortune (1975)
One Flew Over the Cuckoo's Nest (1975; Academy Award for best actor)
The Passenger (1975)
Tommy (1975)
The Last Tycoon (1976)
The Missouri Breaks (1976)
Goin' South (actor/director, 1978)
The Shining (1980)
The Border (1981)
The Postman Always Rings Twice (1981)
Reds (1981)
Terms of Endearment (1983; Academy Award for best supporting actor)
Prizzi's Honor (1985)
Heartburn (1986)
Broadcast News (1987)
Ironweed (1987)
The Witches of Eastwick (1987)
Batman (1989)
The Two Jakes (actor/director, 1990)
Man Trouble (1992)
A Few Good Men (1992)
Hoffa (1992)
Wolf (1994)

MICHELLE PFEIFFER
Actor

The Hollywood Knights (1980)
Falling in Love Again (1980)
Charlie Chan and the Curse of the Dragon Queen (1981)
Grease 2 (1982)
Scarface (1983)
Into the Night (1985)
Ladyhawke (1985)
Sweet Liberty (1986)
Amazon Women on the Moon (1987)
The Witches of Eastwick (1987)
Dangerous Liaisons (1988)
Married to the Mob (1988)
Tequila Sunrise (1988)
The Fabulous Baker Boys (1989)
The Russia House (1990)
Frankie and Johnny (1991)
Batman Returns (1992)
Love Field (1992)
The Age of Innocence (1993)
Wolf (1994)

JULIA ROBERTS
Actor

Satisfaction (1988)
Mystic Pizza (1988)
Blood Red (1989)
Steel Magnolias (1989)
Pretty Woman (1990)
Flatliners (1990)
Sleeping With the Enemy (1991)
Dying Young (1991)
Hook (1991)
The Player (1992)
The Pelican Brief (1993)
I Love Trouble (1994)

MEG RYAN
Actor

Rich and Famous (1981)
Amityville 3-D (1983)
Armed and Dangerous (1986)
Top Gun (1986)
Innerspace (1987)
Promised Land (1987)
D.O.A. (1988)
The Presidio (1988)
When Harry Met Sally . . . (1989)
Joe Versus the Volcano (1990)
The Doors (1991)
Prelude to a Kiss (1992)
Sleepless in Seattle (1993)
Flesh and Bone (1993)
When a Man Loves a Woman (1994)

ARNOLD SCHWARZENEGGER
Actor

Hercules in New York (1974)
Stay Hungry (1976)
Pumping Iron (1977)
The Villain (1979)
Conan the Barbarian (1982)
Conan the Destroyer (1984)
The Terminator (1984)
Commando (1985)
Red Sonja (1985)
Raw Deal (1986)
Predator (1987)
The Running Man (1987)
Red Heat (1988)
Twins (1988)
Total Recall (1989)
Kindergarten Cop (1990)
Terminator 2: Judgment Day (1991)
Last Action Hero (1993)
True Lies (1994)
Junior (1994)

MARTIN SCORSESE
Director/producer/screenwriter

Who's That Knocking at My Door? (director/screenwriter/actor, 1967)
Street Scenes 1970 (director/actor, 1970)
Boxcar Bertha (director, 1972)
Mean Streets (director/screenwriter, 1973)
Alice Doesn't Live Here Anymore (director, 1974)
Taxi Driver (director, 1976)
New York, New York (director, 1977)
The Last Waltz (director/actor, 1978)
Raging Bull (director/actor, 1980)
The King of Comedy (director/actor, 1983)
After Hours (director, 1985)
The Color of Money (director, 1986)
The Last Temptation of Christ (director, 1988)
"Life Lessons," in *New York Stories* (director, 1989)
GoodFellas (director/co-screenwriter, 1990)
The Grifters (producer, 1990)
Cape Fear (director, 1991)
The Age of Innocence (director/co-screenwriter, 1993)

STEVEN SPIELBERG
Director/producer/screenwriter

Duel (director, 1971)
The Sugarland Express (director/co-screenwriter,1974)
Jaws (director, 1975)
Close Encounters of the Third Kind (director/screenwriter, 1977)
1941 (director, 1979)
Raiders of the Lost Ark (director, 1981)
E.T., the Extra-Terrestrial (director/co-producer, 1982)
Poltergeist (co-producer/co-screenwriter, 1982)
"Kick the Can" in *Twilight Zone—The Movie* (director/co-producer, 1983)
Indiana Jones and the Temple of Doom (director, 1984)
The Color Purple (director/co-producer, 1985)
Special Academy Award presented in 1986, the Irving G. Thalberg Award, for consistently high quality of filmmaking
Empire of the Sun (director/co-producer, 1987)
Always (director/co-producer, 1989)
Indiana Jones and the Last Crusade (director, 1989)
Hook (director, 1991)
An American Tail II: Fievel Goes West (co-producer, 1991)
Jurassic Park (director, 1993)
Schindler's List (director/producer, 1993; Academy Awards for best director, best picture)

SYLVESTER STALLONE
Actor/director/screenwriter

A Party at Kitty and Stud's (reissued as *The Italian Stallion)* (actor, 1970)
Bananas (actor, 1971)
The Lords of Flatbush (actor/co-screenwriter, 1974)
Capone (actor, 1975)
Death Race 2000 (actor, 1975)
Farewell, My Lovely (actor, 1975)
No Place to Hide (actor, 1975)
The Prisoner of Second Avenue (actor, 1975)
Cannonball (actor, 1976)
Rocky (actor/screenwriter/fight choreographer, 1976)
F.I.S.T. (actor/co-screenwriter, 1978)
Paradise Alley (actor/director/screenwriter, 1978)
Rocky II (actor/director/screenwriter/fight choreographer, 1979)
Victory (actor, 1981)
Nighthawks (actor, 1981)
First Blood (actor/co-screenwriter, 1982)
Rocky III (actor/director/screenwriter/fight choreographer, 1982)
Staying Alive (director/co-producer/co-screenwriter, 1983)
Rhinestone (actor/co-screenwriter, 1984)
Rambo: First Blood, Part II (actor/co-screenwriter, 1985)
Rocky IV (actor/director/screenwriter, 1985)
Cobra (actor/screenwriter, 1986)
Over the Top (actor/co-screenwriter, 1987)
Rambo III (actor/co-screenwriter, 1988)
Lock Up (actor, 1989)
Tango and Cash (actor, 1989)
Rocky V (actor/screenwriter, 1990)
Oscar (actor, 1991)
Stop! or My Mom Will Shoot (actor, 1992)
Cliffhanger (actor/co-screenwriter, 1993)
Demolition Man (actor, 1993)
The Specialist (actor, 1994)

SHARON STONE
Actor

Stardust Memories (1980)
Deadly Blessing (1981)
Bolero (France) (1981)
Irreconcilable Differences (1984)
King Solomon's Mines (1985)
Allan Quartermain and the Lost City of Gold (1987)
Action Jackson (1988)
Above the Law (1988)
Personal Choice (Beyond the Stars) (1989)
Blood and Sand (1989)
Total Recall (1990
He Said, She Said (1991)
Scissors (1991)
Year of the Gun (1991)
Basic Instinct (1992)
Where Sleeping Dogs Lie (1992)
Diary of a Hitman (1992)
Sliver (1993)
Intersection (1994)
The Specialist (1994)

MERYL STREEP
Actor

Julia (1977)
The Deer Hunter (1978)
Manhattan (1979)
The Seduction of Joe Tynan (1979)
Kramer vs. Kramer (1979; Academy Award for best supporting actress)
The French Lieutenant's Woman (1981)
Sophie's Choice (1982; Academy Award for best actress)
Still of the Night (1982)
Silkwood (1983)
Falling in Love (1984)
Plenty (1985)
Out of Africa (1985)
Heartburn (1986)
Ironweed (1987)
A Cry in The Dark (1988)
She-Devil (1989)
Postcards from the Edge (1990)
Defending Your Life (1991)
The House of the Spirits (1994)
The River Wild (1994)

EMMA THOMPSON
Actor

Henry V (1989)
The Tall Guy (1989)
Impromptu (1990)
Dead Again (1991)
Howard's End (1992)
Peter's Friends (1992)
Much Ado About Nothing (1993)
The Remains of the Day (1993)
In the Name of the Father (1993)
Junior (1994)

DENZEL WASHINGTON
Actor

Carbon Copy (1981)
A Soldier's Story (1984)
Power (1986)
Cry Freedom (1987)
Glory (1989; Academy Award for best supporting actor)
For Queen and Country (1989)
Reunion (1989)
The Mighty Quinn (1989)
Mo' Better Blues (1990)
Heart Condition (1990)
Ricochet (1991)
Mississippi Masala (1991)
Malcolm X (1992)
Much Ado About Nothing (1993)
The Pelican Brief (1993)
Philadelphia (1993)

SEX FIRSTS ON THE SILVER SCREEN

- The first kiss appeared in *The Widow Jones* (1896).
- The first French kiss took place between Natalie Wood and Warren Beatty in *Splendor in the Grass* (1961).
- The first homosexual kiss occurred in the orgy scene in Cecil B. DeMille's *Manslaughter* (1922).
- The first leading lady to kiss another was Marlene Dietrich in Josef von Sternberg's *Morocco* (1930).
- The first kiss in a Japanese film was finally allowed in *Twenty-Year-Old Youth* (1946).
- The longest single kiss on record took place between Regis Toomey and Jane Wyman in *You're in the Army Now* (1940); the smooch lasted three minutes and five seconds. (Naomi Levine spent fifty minutes being kissed in Andy Warhol's fifty-minute film *Kiss*, but she had three partners.)
- The first leading lady to appear nude was Audrey Munson in *Inspiration* (1915).
- The first full male nudity featured Alan Bates and Oliver Reed in Ken Russell's *Women in Love* (1969).
- The first time sex was depicted was in *Ecstasy* with Hedy Lamarr (Czechoslovakia, 1932).
- The earliest known pornographic film was *A l'ecu d'or* (France, 1908).
- The first hard-core pornographic feature shown in American cinemas was *Deep Throat* (1972).
- The first film about homosexuality was Richard Oswald's *Anders als die Andern* (Germany, 1919).
- The first American film about homosexuality was Joseph Mankiewicz's *Suddenly Last Summer* (1959).

THE TOP VIDEOS, YEAR-BY-YEAR

Billboard magazine has been tracking bestselling videos since 1980 and started ranking video rentals in 1982. Sales lists are now dominated by children's videos and exercise tapes with a growing smattering of soft porn, while rentals are led by a combination of certified hits and films that viewers passed up at the box office.

1980

Sales
1. *The Godfather*
2. *Saturday Night Fever*
3. *Superman*
4. *M*A*S*H*
5. *The Godfather, Part II*
6. *Blazing Saddles*
7. *10*
8. *Grease*
9. *The Sound of Music*
10. *Halloween*

1981

Sales
1. *Airplane*
2. *Caddyshack*
3. *9 to 5*
4. *Superman*
5. *Alien*
6. *Star Trek*
7. *Fame*
8. *Ordinary People*
9. *Elephant Man*
10. *Popeye*

1982

Sales
1. *Clash of the Titans*
2. *An American Werewolf in London*
3. *Atlantic City*
4. *Stir Crazy*
5. *The Jazz Singer*
6. *Blue Lagoon*
7. *Kramer vs. Kramer*
8. *Casablanca*
9. *Raging Bull*
10. *Jane Fonda's Workout*

Rentals
1. *Clash of the Titans*
2. *An American Werewolf in London*
3. *Arthur*
4. *Star Wars*
5. *Fort Apache, the Bronx*
6. *For Your Eyes Only*
7. *On Golden Pond*
8. *Stripes*
9. *The Cannonball Run*
10. *Superman II*

1983

Sales
1. *Jane Fonda's Workout*
2. *Star Trek II: The Wrath of Khan*
3. *An Officer and a Gentleman*
4. *The Compleat Beatles*
5. *Rocky III*
6. *Playboy Vol. I*
7. *Poltergeist*
8. *Star Wars*
9. *Blade Runner*
10. *Road Warrior*

Rentals
1. *An Officer and a Gentleman*
2. *Star Trek II: The Wrath of Khan*
3. *The Road Warrior*
4. *Rocky III*
5. *Poltergeist*
6. *First Blood*
7. *Das Boot*
8. *Night Shift*
9. *Blade Runner*
10. *Sophie's Choice*

1984

Sales
1. *Jane Fonda's Workout*
2. *Raiders of the Lost Ark*
3. *Making Michael Jackson's "Thriller"*
4. *Flashdance*
5. *Duran Duran*
6. *Risky Business*
7. *48 Hrs.*
8. *Do It Debbie's Way*
9. *Trading Places*
10. *The Jane Fonda Workout Challenge*

Rentals
1. *Raiders of the Lost Ark*
2. *Risky Business*
3. *Flashdance*
4. *48 Hrs.*
5. *Tootsie*
6. *Mr. Mom*
7. *Sudden Impact*
8. *Trading Places*
9. *Blue Thunder*
10. *Making Michael Jackson's "Thriller"*

1985

Sales
1. *Jane Fonda's Workout*
2. *Prime Time*
3. *Making Michael Jackson's "Thriller"*
4. *Purple Rain*
5. *Gone with the Wind*
6. *The Jane Fonda Workout Challenge*
7. *Raiders of the Lost Ark*
8. *Raquel, Total Beauty and Fitness*
9. *We Are the World—The Video Event*
10. *Wham! The Video*

Rentals
1. *The Karate Kid*
2. *The Terminator*
3. *Police Academy*
4. *Romancing the Stone*
5. *Revenge of the Nerds*
6. *The Natural*
7. *Starman*
8. *The Empire Strikes Back*
9. *Bachelor Party*
10. *Splash*

1986

Sales
1. *Jane Fonda's New Workout*
2. *Jane Fonda's Workout*
3. *Pinocchio*
4. *Beverly Hills Cop*
5. *The Sound of Music*
6. *Jane Fonda's Prime Time Workout*
7. *Casablanca*
8. *Gone with the Wind*
9. *The Wizard of Oz*
10. *The Best of John Belushi*

Rentals
1. *Back to the Future*
2. *Beverly Hills Cop*
3. *Prizzi's Honor*
4. *Witness*
5. *Ghostbusters*
6. *Rambo: First Blood, Part II*
7. *Return of the Jedi*
8. *Cocoon*
9. *Mask*
10. *Gremlins*

1987

Sales
1. *Jane Fonda's Low Impact Aerobic Workout*
2. *Jane Fonda's New Workout*
3. *Sleeping Beauty*
4. *Top Gun*
5. *Callanetics*
6. *The Sound of Music*
7. *Kathy Smith's Body Basics*
8. *Indiana Jones and the Temple of Doom*
9. *Star Trek III: The Search for Spock*
10. *Star Trek II: The Wrath of Khan*

Rentals
1. *Short Circuit*
2. *Top Gun*
3. *Back to School*
4. *Indiana Jones and the Temple of Doom*
5. *Down and Out in Beverly Hills*
6. *The Color of Money*
7. *Ferris Bueller's Day Off*
8. *Stand By Me*
9. *Ruthless People*
10. *Aliens*

1988

Sales
1. *Lady and the Tramp*
2. *Callanetics*
3. *Jane Fonda's Low Impact Aerobic Workout*
4. *Star Trek IV: The Voyage Home*
5. *Start Up With Jane Fonda*
6. *An American Tale*
7. *Jane Fonda's New Workout*
8. *Pink Floyd: The Wall*
9. *Dirty Dancing*
10. *Sleeping Beauty*

Rentals
1. *Dirty Dancing*
2. *Lethal Weapon*
3. *Fatal Attraction*
4. *The Untouchables*
5. *The Witches of Eastwick*
6. *No Way Out*
7. *Outrageous Fortune*

8. *Robocop*
9. *Stakeout*
10. *Tin Men*

1989

Sales

1. *Cinderella*
2. *E.T., the Extra-Terrestrial*
3. *Jane Fonda's Complete Workout*
4. *Moonwalker*
5. *Callanetics*
6. *Dirty Dancing*
7. *The Wizard of Oz: The Fiftieth Anniversary Edition*
8. *Lethal Weapon*
9. *U2 Rattle and Hum*
10. *Pink Floyd: The Delicate Sound of Thunder*

Rentals

1. *Big*
2. *Die Hard*
3. *A Fish Called Wanda*
4. *Three Men and a Baby*
5. *Beetlejuice*
6. *Coming to America*
7. *Cocktail*
8. *Twins*
9. *Bull Durham*
10. *"Crocodile" Dundee II*

1990

Sales

1. *Bambi*
2. *New Kids on the Block: Hangin' Tough Live*
3. *The Little Mermaid*
4. *Lethal Weapon 2*
5. *The Wizard of Oz: The Fiftieth Anniversary Edition*
6. *Batman*
7. *Honey, I Shrunk The Kids*
8. *The Land Before Time*
9. *Who Framed Roger Rabbit*
10. *Teenage Mutant Ninja Turtles: Cowabunga, Shredhead*

Rentals

1. *Look Who's Talking*
2. *When Harry Met Sally*
3. *Parenthood*
4. *K-9*
5. *Dead Poets Society*
6. *Steel Magnolias*
7. *Sea of Love*
8. *Turner & Hooch*
9. *Black Rain*
10. *Internal Affairs*

1991

Sales

1. *Pretty Woman*
2. *The Little Mermaid*
3. *Peter Pan*
4. *The Jungle Book*
5. *Three Tenors in Concert*
6. *Richard Simmons: Sweatin' to the Oldies*
7. *Teenage Mutant Ninja Turtles: The Movie*
8. *The Terminator*
9. *Ducktales: The Movie*
10. *Total Recall*

Rentals

1. *Ghost*
2. *Pretty Woman*
3. *GoodFellas*
4. *Bird on a Wire*
5. *Flatliners*
6. *The Hunt for Red October*
7. *Kindergarten Cop*
8. *Total Recall*
9. *Sleeping with the Enemy*
10. *Another 48 Hrs.*

1992

Sales

1. *Fantasia*
2. *101 Dalmations*
3. *The Jungle Book*
4. *Robin Hood: Prince of Thieves*
5. *Cherfitness: A New Attitude*
6. *Fievel Goes West*
7. *1992 Playboy Video Playmate Calendar*
8. *Home Alone*
9. *The Rescuers Down Under*
10. *Playboy: Sexy Lingerie IV*

Rentals

1. *Thelma and Louise*
2. *The Silence of the Lambs*
3. *The Fisher King*
4. *City Slickers*
5. *Backdraft*
6. *Cape Fear*
7. *The Hand That Rocks the Cradle*
8. *Father of the Bride*
9. *Deceived*
10. *What About Bob?*

1993

Sales

1. *Beauty and the Beast*
2. *Pinocchio*
3. *101 Dalmations*
4. *Playboy Celebrity Centerfold: Jessica Hahn*
5. *Sister Act*
6. *Playboy Playmate of the Year 1993: Anna Nicole Smith*
7. *Cindy Crawford/Shape Your Body Workout*
8. *Home Alone 2: Lost in New York*
9. *Disney's Sing Along Songs: Friend Like Me*
10. *Beethoven*
11. *Homeward Bound: The Incredible Journey*
12. *Batman Returns*
13. *Dances with Wolves*
14. *Casablanca* (fiftieth anniversary)
15. *Little Nemo: Adventures in Slumberland*
16. *Teenage Mutant Ninja Turtles III*
17. *Star Trek VI: The Undiscovered Country*
18. *McClintock!*
19. *Playboy: Wet and Wild V*
20. *Barney's Magical Musical Adventure*
21. *Beyond the Mind's Eye*
22. *Barney in Concert*
23. *The Rescuers*
24. *Barney's Best Manners*
25. *Country Line Dancing*

Rentals

1. *Sister Act*
2. *Patriot Games*
3. *Under Siege*
4. *A League of Their Own*
5. *A Few Good Men*
6. *Scent of a Woman*
7. *Unforgiven*
8. *Sneakers*
9. *Passenger 57*
10. *The Bodyguard*
11. *Housesitter*
12. *My Cousin Vinny*
13. *The Last of the Mohicans*
14. *Basic Instinct* (director's cut)
15. *Falling Down*
16. *Lethal Weapon 3*
17. *The Distinguished Gentleman*
18. *Single White Female*
19. *Far and Away*
20. *Consenting Adults*
21. *Forever Young*
22. *Boomerang*
23. *The Mighty Ducks*
24. *Groundhog Day*
25. *A River Runs Through It*

THE GOOD, THE BAD, AND (YES) THE ELEGANT

This was the year Hollywood got all dressed up to go somewhere—the sixty-sixth annual Academy Awards—and, for a change, decided to go in style. Now, if only they gave out Oscars for costumes not in the movies.

Call it the age of gravitas. Gone were the purples and greens of Whoopi's yesteryear, the extraterrestrial Geena Davis, ready for lift-off, the single-sleeved Kim Basinger, the kookily corn-rowed Juliette Lewis. Missing altogether was Cher. Instead the stars came out,

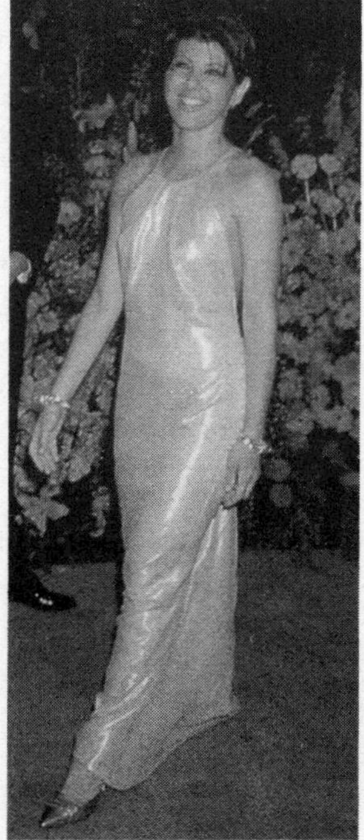

Bare Essentials: "The dress was meant to invoke a '30s mood," says Vera Wang, who did a champagne gown for Marisa Tomei. "She didn't want black or any kind of beading."

as if by mutual agreement, styled with a subdued elegance appropriate to *Schindler's* year and exuding a good old-fashioned Hollywood glamour that did Oscar (and Oskar) proud. Viewers of the sixty-sixth annual Academy Awards were treated to a shimmering parade of whites, creams, and eggshells; silks, satins, and velvets; slips, sheaths, shawl collars, and significant black dresses. Sequins were scarce and faux pas were few. The one indulgence? Some $4 million worth of Harry Winston's borrowed jewels glittered around the necks and wrists of Dolly Parton, Rosie O'Donnell, and Goldie Hawn, among others.

Awards-night host Whoopi Goldberg set the tone—in a sober, cognac-colored velvet gown that she had requested from Oscar-telecast costumer Ray Aghayan just five days before the show. Apart from a few glancing verbal jabs (at Bob Dole and the Grammys) during the presentations, her most outrageous act of the evening was to don a fussy Armani tux and liberate her hair halfway through the show. As for Marisa Tomei and Best Actress Holly Hunter (in

Little Girl Blue: Anna Paquin, 11, was a surprise winner for Best Supporting Actress—and her beaded snood was Most Surprising Headgear.

Vera Wang confections), Goldie Hawn and Madeleine Stowe (in Calvin Klein), Nicole Kidman in a columnar black velvet Valentino, Glenn Close in a severe silver Armani, and Whitney Houston and Janet Jackson in swanky white pantsuits, all created not waves but ripples of satisfaction.

The evening's award for

Squandered Opportunity to Make a Statement goes to usually daring, always statuesque Geena Davis, whose Ruth Meyers draped white dress with plunging neck- and backline was less than it might have been. "She's a screen goddess," cries minimalist designer Michael Kors. "She should look like one." Thank heavens, Kors says, for Sharon Stone's sartorial instincts. Clad in a clingy black Valentino slit up the front as far as legal limits permit, her hair marcelled in '30s waves, the femme fatale oozed fabulousness. "There may not be great talent there," says Kors, "but she looks like a movie star."

Reality Beads: "It's old, it's from the 1940s," said Best Supporting Actress nominee Winona Ryder of her stunning studded gown, not her strapping escort Kevin Haley.

Also looking like movie stars, for a change, were the men, who played variations on the tuxedo theme to wonderful effect. Most of Generation U (for under forty-five) went tieless, white shirt optional (Christian Slater, Jeff Bridges, Antonio Banderas), while those who hauled out the old tux-and-tie combo—like Paul Newman, Jeremy Irons, Clint Eastwood, Alec Baldwin, Tom Hanks and Harrison Ford—proved that classic is classy.

Of course all that seamless taste and good behavior do not necessarily come naturally. Observed Best Screenplay winner (for *The Piano*) Jane Campion, in black-and-white-striped pants and an oversize white shirt with a tux jacket: "It's so hard to make an effort to look glamorous. I'm just relieved this evening is over." And *Fearless* Rosie Perez—with her father Ismael Serrano as a date—knew she'd better not look as "outgoing as I usually do." She settled for a snug black-velvet Armani with a train, and she spoke, no doubt, for many of her fellow stars when she moaned at the end of the evening, "I'm dying to get out of this dress."

Bruce Springsteen brought some casual music-world elegance to the ceremonies, and collected his first Oscar.

OSCAR—DECADE BY DECADE

Sixty-six, an age for savoring life's achievements—even though one's joints might creak. "He rattles," says Olivia de Havilland, holding her 1949 Oscar to the phone receiver and shaking him to illustrate. Ernest Borgnine, a 1955 winner, complains that his Oscar "flakes." Jack Lemmon, who took his *Mr. Roberts* Oscar home in 1956, says the statue rusted: "I had to send him back to the Academy to be redipped." But, ah, how nice to have the old guy around.

Sure, like any sixty-six-year-old, Oscar has taken his lumps. He's been called "a cruel joke" (Marion Davies), "a heartbreaker" (Orson Welles), and "something to be feared" (George C. Scott). But don't count him out. Oscar's imprimatur can add $25 million or more to a winning film's gross, double an actor's salary, and at least triple the size of his ego.

What a shock, then, to learn that Oscar started life as a patsy. In 1927, MGM kingpin Louis B. Mayer and thirty-five cronies decided to form an Academy of Motion Picture Arts and Sciences. Forget the high-toned blather of the first charter seeking "the improvement and advancement of the . . . profession." What Mayer really wanted was to stop the advance of film unions. An Academy would keep labor disputes in the hands of the studios. As a carrot to actors, writers, directors, and technicians, Mayer formed a committee to find "some little way" of rewarding merit in film.

While Mayer finagled, MGM art director Cedric Gibbons doodled a sketch of a naked man with a sword, standing on a reel of film. Today Oscar is a thirteen-and-a-half inch, eight-and-a-half pound trophy cast in a metal alloy, then plated in turn with copper, nickel, silver, and finally gold. At Oscar's debut in 1929, some laughed. Screenwriter Frances (*The Champ*) Marion believed Hollywood had found its ideal symbol, "an athletic body . . . with half his head, that part which held his brains, completely sliced off."

But, hey, Oscar didn't need brains. The studio bosses controlled the nominations and virtually hand-picked the winners. It took years for Oscar to clean house—the Academy did not even start using sealed envelopes until 1941. Since then the Academy, which has grown from a scant thirty-six members in 1927 to the 4,523 voting members of today, has tried to discourage actions, especially expensive ad campaigns, to influence voting. It hasn't succeeded, of course. But Oscar, by dint of sheer perseverance, has become, in the words of 1957 winner Alec (*The Bridge on the River Kwai*) Guinness, "the most highly prized [award] of all." At this point, the grandstanding and costumes have become as much a reason for tuning in the Oscars as finding out the winners. "Well, hell—let's face it," says Katharine Hepburn, recipient of a record four Oscars for acting, "It's our track meet. It's painful but it's thrilling."

THE FIRST DECADE 1927-1936

Oscar threw his first party in 1929. The press stayed away. A black-tie crowd clapped politely as all twelve awards were distributed in under five minutes. The three Best Actor nominees didn't bother to show up. Janet Gaynor, first Best Actress winner, gamely tried to act thrilled. "Had I known what it would come to mean in the next few years," she said later, "I'm sure I'd have been overwhelmed." It was the first and last Oscar bust. The Depression and the sound era soon made movies into the ideal escapism, and Oscar's touch came to mean box office gold. Some aspired to win. Others conspired. As ever in Hollywood, greed, jealousy and raw ambition added up to a helluva show.

The first Best Actor winner, Emil Jannings, had scooted home to Germany before collecting his Oscar scroll. His later Nazi propaganda films—done, he said, under duress—made him a favorite with Hitler. Marlene Dietrich disputed the Fuhrer on the talents of her *Blue Angel* costar: "He was a terrrible ham."

★

First ceremony: Hollywood's elite jammed the Roosevelt Hotel to hear Al Jolson put down the Oscar as a "paperweight." Jolie's film, *The Jazz Singer*—an early talkie—had been disqualified; only silent films were eligible. The Academy was suspicious of new trends. Some things never change.

★

The WW I air extravaganza *Wings*, starring Buddy Rogers, Clara Bow, and Richard Arlen, was the first Best Picture winner. With tinted color in the battle scenes and noise machines in the theaters to simulate plane crashes, here was a primitive *Top Gun* that showed the Academy's early fondness for spectacle.

★

In 1930, Norma Shearer, winner for *The Divorcée*, posed for a photograph with Oscar two days *before* the ceremony. "She sleeps with the boss," sniped Joan Crawford. Rumor had it that MGM's Irving Thalberg pressured employees to vote for his wife.

Oscar's first tie: Fredric March (Dr. Jekyll and Mr. Hyde) and Wallace Beery (The Champ) shared the 1931 gold. Both had recently adopted children. "Odd," said March, "that Wally and I were given awards for best male performance."

★

Clark Gable and Claudette Colbert both took Oscars for Frank Capra's 1934 comedy, *It Happened One Night*, as did Capra and the film—the only clean sweep in Academy history until *One Flew over the Cuckoo's Nest* duplicated the feat in 1975. No one expected it. Everybody still thinks Gable won for *Gone with the Wind*.

★

The Academy invents a new category, Best Song, prompted by Fred Astaire and Ginger Rogers's dancing and singing of "The Continental" in 1934's *The Gay Divorcee*.

★

Bette Davis collects an award for 1935's *Dangerous*, and gives the statue its name. Reflecting that the trophy "resembled the backside" of her first husband, bandleader Harmon Oscar Nelson Jr., she dubbed her prize Oscar. The moniker stuck.

THE SECOND DECADE 1937–1946

The Oscar ceremony was establishment now, broadcast on radio. In 1939 Gone with the Wind *became the most popular and profitable film ever. But this was also a time of war, as reflected in movies from* Mrs. Miniver *to* The Best Years of Our Lives. *Winston Churchill hailed Miniver as "propaganda worth a hundred battleships." As a wartime cost-cutting measure, the Academy ended its elaborate banquets and took the show inside a theater, where food and drink could no longer detract from the ego battles.*

Walt Disney is given a special honorary award for 1938's *Snow White and the Seven Dwarfs*, featuring one large Oscar and seven tiny ones.

★

Gone with the Wind, then the costliest movie in history ($3,957,000) wins eight Oscars, a record not broken until 1958's *Gigi*. Leigh was the triumphant victor, Gable the disgruntled loser. "This was my last chance," he groaned. He was right.

Hattie McDaniel, Miss Scarlett's maid, was the first black actor to win an Oscar. Hattie sobbed on accepting her plaque (supporting players didn't receive full statues until 1943).

★

Playing George M. Cohan in 1942, James Cagney—America's favorite tough guy—became the first actor to win an Oscar for a musical. "Don't forget," said Jimmy in his acceptance speech, "it was a pretty good part."

Bogie told Ingrid Bergman in *Casablanca* that their wartime love story "didn't amount to a hill of beans in this crazy world." Except for winning the Best Picture Oscar of 1943 and the hearts of all romantics.

★

Barry Fitzgerald's role as a twinkly old priest in 1944's *Going My Way* made him a popular winner. But at home a few days later, he forgot that wartime Oscars were made of plaster instead of bronze and decapitated his prize with a golf club.

★

The Lost Weekend, the Best Picture of 1945, offered an unsparing portrait of an alcoholic, by Ray Milland. "I gave it everything I had," said the actor. He must have. Accepting the Oscar, a speechless Milland simply bowed and departed.

THE THIRD DECADE
1947–1956

No sooner had the war ended over there than the Academy embarked on its own war at home. The enemy? Television. The little black box was emptying movie theaters at an alarming rate. The studios retaliated at first with sex, violence, and Cinemascope, then gave in. So did Oscar. The Academy Awards were telecast for the first time in 1953. Variety's *headline heralded a new era: "1ST MAJOR PIX-TV WEDDING BIG CLICK."*

Many years prior, actor Walter Huston said he asked his son, John, "If you ever become a writer or director, please find a good part for your old man." John complied with *Treasure of the Sierra Madre* and won 1948 Oscars for both of them.

★

Joseph Mankiewicz's crackerjack 1950 comedy *All About Eve* still holds the record—14 nominations. Though *Eve* won six Oscars, including Best Picture, costars Bette Davis and Anne Baxter both lost to *Born Yesterday*'s Judy Holliday.

★

Vivien Leigh copped her second Best Actress Oscar in 1951 for *A Streetcar Named Desire*. When the award was announced in Hollywood, Leigh was in New York starring in *Antony and Cleopatra* with then-husband Laurence Olivier.

★

In Hollywood, Donald O'Connor watched Shirley Booth's reaction in New York on being named 1952's Best Actress for *Come Back, Little Sheba*. Meanwhile, the largest single audience (about 80 million) in TV's five-year history saw the first Oscarcast.

★

Having fought to play Maggio in 1953's *From Here to Eternity*, Frank Sinatra triumphed. Said the Best Supporting Actor, "I ducked the party and took a walk. Just me and Oscar." The salty version of James Jones's Army-barracks novel won a whopping eight Oscars, including Best Picture. And Deborah Kerr's sexy roll on the sand with Burt Lancaster cracked her saintly image.

★

A year before her royal wedding in 1956, *The Country Girl*'s Grace Kelly scored an upset victory over Judy Garland in *A Star is Born*. The Kelly girl confided: "I wanted to win so badly, I was afraid that I would stand up no matter which name was read out."

★

First-time film producer Michael Todd caught the 1956 Best Picture Oscar with his star-studded *Around the World in 80 Days*. "Imagine this—and being married to Liz, too," he enthused.

THE FOURTH DECADE
1957–1966

The times they were a-changing. Drugs, hippies, the youth movement, civil rights demonstrations, the Kennedy assassination: Many films dealt with these social and political upheavals. But you couldn't tell by Oscar. Relevant was out; big was in. The Academy awarded either historical epics (Ben-Hur, The Bridge on the River Kwai, Lawrence of Arabia, A Man for All Seasons) *or blockbuster musicals* (Gigi, West Side Story, My Fair Lady, The Sound of Music). *The most controversial move on the Academy's part was to issue a formal slap to those who tried to "buy" Oscar nominations by purchasing self-congratulatory ads in the trade papers. Few paid heed.*

Joanne Woodward, the new Mrs. Paul Newman, collected her 1957 Oscar for *The Three Faces of Eve* in a $100 dress she made herself. Joan Crawford claimed Hollywood glamour "had been set back twenty years." When Paul finally won his Oscar, twenty-nine years later, clothes weren't a problem. He didn't show up at all.

★

In 1959 Best Picture *Ben-Hur* took a record eleven Oscars, including Best Actor for Charlton Heston, who got the part after Burt Lancaster dropped out. "It was hard work," said Chuck, who drove a mean chariot. But some questioned his talents. "That Heston," said actor Aldo Ray, "what a hamola."

★

Denounced in Congress in 1950 for her adulterous affair with Roberto Rossellini, Ingrid Bergman ended her decade-long Hollywood exile by presenting a 1959 Best Picture Oscar to *Gigi* producer Arthur Freed. She said her recipe for happiness was "good health and a poor memory."

★

Sporting a tracheotomy scar from a near-fatal bout of pneumonia, Liz Taylor scored a sympathy Oscar for 1960's *Butterfield 8*. In 1966 Liz won Oscar No. 2 for *Who's Afraid of Virginia Woolf?*, but railed at the Academy when fifth husband Richard Burton failed to win too.

★

"I'd like to think it will help," said Sidney Poitier after Anne Bancroft opened the envelope and, for 1963's *Lilies of the Field*, he became the first black Best Actor winner. "But I don't believe my Oscar will be a magic wand that will wipe away the restrictions on job opportunities for Negro actors."

★

Sisters and Best Actress nominees Lynn and Vanessa Redgrave, cited respectively for 1966's *Georgy Girl* and *Morgan!*, were only the second sister nominees in Oscar history. And they came from a notable British acting family to boot. Maybe so. But Liz Taylor still whopped them both.

THE FIFTH DECADE 1967–1976

Oscar neared its half-century mark in a reactionary mood. Breakthrough films such as Bonnie and Clyde, The Graduate, *and* Easy Rider *ended up losers. In 1968, the year of* 2001: A Space Odyssey, Oliver! *won the Best Picture prize. Yikes. No wonder a streaker felt the need to defame one of the decade's Academy telecasts. Then, a rebel cry was heard in filmland. Newcomers Dustin Hoffman and Jon Voight dared to duke it out with the Duke, John Wayne, for the statue. They failed, but their X-rated* Midnight Cowboy *took the Best Picture prize in 1969. Jane Fonda raised hackles with her Vietnam views and won anyway. The warring factions of the Academy were creating sparks.*

For the second time in Oscar history, a tie was declared. *Funny Girl*'s Barbra Streisand and *The Lion in Winter*'s Katharine Hepburn received the same number of votes from the 1968 Academy's 3,030 members. Designer Edith Head was "shocked," not by the tie but by Streisand's tacky peekaboo pantsuit.

★

John Wayne had to let it all hang out in 1969 as bloated, one-eyed Rooster Cogburn to finally collect his first Oscar at 62 after 250 movies. "Wow," drawled the Duke, "if I had known, I would have put that eye patch on thirty-five years earlier."

★

Deriding the Oscars as a "meat parade," George C. Scott declined his nomination as 1970's Best Actor. "My God!" exclaimed Goldie Hawn as she opened the envelope and read the winner's name, "It's George C. Scott."

★

When Marlon Brando was voted 1972's Best Actor, he sent Apache Sacheen Littlefeather to reject the Oscar for all the Native Americans Hollywood had demeaned. "Childish," scowled Charlton Heston. "Wonderful," gushed Jane Fonda.

★

Would-be comic Robert Opel snuck backstage at the 1974 Oscars ceremony, flustering emcee David Niven as the cameras cut away to spare home viewers the streaker's shortcomings. The hit of a dull show, Opel was found murdered five years later in his San Francisco sex shop.

★

Struggling actor Sylvester Stallone took half a week to write a script for himself about an underdog fighter. He lost the Best Actor Oscar, but the sleeper film won the title as Best Picture of 1976. "*Rocky* will be remembered," said Sly with typical modesty. As time would tell, the real issue is if Rocky will ever go away.

THE SIXTH DECADE

1977–1986

Oscar had a goal now. Ignoring the films of George Lucas and Steven Spielberg became a full-time job. The Hardy Boys of the zap-happy set combined their youthful fantasies with dazzling special effects to create eight of the top ten box office hits of all time (E.T., Star Wars, Return of the Jedi, The Empire Strikes Back, Jaws, Raiders of the Lost Ark, Indiana Jones, *and* Back to the Future). *Not a Best Picture winner in the bunch. The Academy, doing penance for scorning Vietnam in the previous decade, annointed politically themed films from* The Deer Hunter *to* Platoon. *A vote for* Gandhi, *the movie, was a vote for Gandhi, the man. Oscar, typically late, began sporting a social conscience.*

Accepting her Best Supporting Actress Oscar for 1976's *Julia*, Vanessa Redgrave dismissed as "Zionist hoodlums" those who showed up to protest her politics. The audience booed, Vanessa had to dine later with her two bodyguards, and a confused Jack Nicholson commented, "What are these Zionists? I've been skiing."

★

"It's simply terrific. This is something," sputtered Diane Keaton after accepting the 1977 Best Actress prize for *Annie Hall* from first winner Janet Gaynor. Her co-star and former boyfriend Woody Allen stayed home and shrugged off the Academy as meaningless: "I just don't think they know what they're doing."

★

Robert Redford and Warren Beatty have never won Oscars for their acting. That might make sense. Instead, each (Redford for 1980's *Ordinary People* and Beatty for 1981's *Reds*) took the prize as Best Director—a pinnacle Hitchcock, Bergman, Fellini, and Orson Welles never reached. Go figure.

★

Jane Fonda rushed from the 1982 Academy Awards show to present her ailing father and *On Golden Pond* costar, Henry, with the long-overdue first Oscar of his 47-year career. "Hell, if I hadn't won, I wouldn't be able to walk with my head up anymore," Fonda said to his wife, Shirlee. He died five months later.

★

Gidget gets respect: For 1984's *Places in the Heart*, Sally Field won a second Oscar and spoke the words that will haunt her forever: "You like me! You like me!"

★

Perennial also-ran Paul Newman won for reprising his 1961 *Hustler* role in 1986's *The Color of Money*. "After losing six times, I felt it cruel and unusual punishment to attend," said the no-show.

★

Writer-director Oliver Stone took the 1986 Best Picture Oscar for *Platoon*, based on his wartime experiences in Vietnam—a film almost no studio wanted to make.

★

In 1987 Marlee Matlin of *Children of a Lesser God* became the first hearing-impaired Best Actress winner. "After I'm alone I'm going to scream," she said.

THE SEVENTH DECADE

1987-1994 and counting

Oscar continues his old traditions by heaping awards on elder statesmen — from Clint Eastwood, Paul Newman, and Sean Connery to Jack Palance and Jessica Tandy—who should have been recognized long ago. Best Director continued to be a fickle category—many films, such as The Prince of Tides, *were honored with numerous nominations for everyone but the director. But the drought finally ended for traditional punching bag Steven Spielberg. Of course it took the culturally significant* Schindler's List *to get the Oscar monkey off of Spielberg's back (after three previous Best Director nominations), rather than his second-highest grossing movie of all time,* Jurassic Park*—making it clear that he was chosen as best director, not most successful.*

In 1987, a barely dressed, slightly tattooed Cher wins Best Actress and announces, "I don't think that this means I am somebody, but I guess I'm on my way."

★

The telecast hits new lows in production values in 1988, with the dreadful Snow White musical opening giving Oscar a black eye.

★

Whoopi Goldberg becomes only the second African-American woman to claim an acting award, as Best Supporting Actress for her role in 1990's *Ghost.*

★

Jack Palance shows he's no old-timer by performing one-handed push-ups by way of accepting his Best Supporting Actor statuette for *City Slickers*. And he provides Oscar host Billy Crystal with a year's worth of material.

★

Anna Paquin, 11, is the youngest winner since 1973, taking Best Supporting Actress for her role in 1993's *The Piano.*

THE OLDEST PROFESSIONS IN THE CELLULOID WORLD

How deep does the fantasy world depicted in the movies run? No one expects to come home to Tom Cruise or Julia Roberts at night, but do the movies reflect how we live our lives? Analyzing the lead roles in 2,305 films from 1920 to 1990, *The Guinness Book of Movie Facts and Feats* compiled a fascinating chronicle of what actors and actresses pretend they do for a living.

The Ten Most Common Professions, From 1920–90

Men	Percentage	Women	Percentage
Policemen/sheriff/federal agent	12.7	Singer/dancer	21.5
Doctor/psychiatrist	5.7	Actress	10.0
Armed services officer	5.0	Office worker	8.0
Lawyer	5.0	Nurse	4.6
Noncommissioned armed services	3.9	Journalist	3.9
Journalist	3.9	Prostitute/madam	3.6
Businessman	3.6	Hotel/restaurant/bar worker	3.3
Sportsman	3.4	Student	3.3
Musician/songwriter	3.1	Secret agent	3.1
Farmer/rancher	3.1	Teacher	3.1

THE ACADEMY AWARDS

	1927–28	1928–29	1929–30
Picture	*Wings*	*Broadway Melody*	*All Quiet on the Western Front*
Actor	Emil Jannings, *The Last Command; The Way of All Flesh*	Warner Baxter, *In Old Arizona*	George Arliss, *Disraeli*
Actress	Janet Gaynor, *Seventh Heaven; Street Angel; Sunrise*	Mary Pickford, *Coquette*	Norma Shearer, *The Divorcée*
Director	Frank Borzage, *Seventh Heaven*; Lewis Milestone, *Two Arabian Knights*	Frank Lloyd, *The Divine Lady; Weary River; Drag*	Lewis Milestone, *All Quiet on the Western Front*
Adapted Screenplay	Benjamin Glazer, *Seventh Heaven*	—	—
Original Story	Ben Hecht, *Underworld*	Hans Kraly, *The Patriot*	Frances Marion, *The Big House*
Cinematography	*Sunrise*	*White Shadows in the South Seas*	*With Byrd at the South Pole*
Interior Decoration	*The Dove* and *The Tempest*	*The Bridge of San Luis Rey*	*King of Jazz*
Sound	—	—	*The Big House*

OSCAR RECORDS

Most awards in any category: Walt Disney, twenty-six regular and six special

Most awards to a single film: *Ben-Hur* in 1959, with eleven

Most nominated films to receive no awards: *The Turning Point* and *The Color Purple,* with eleven each

Most Best Actor awards: Spencer Tracy, Fredric March, Gary Cooper, Marlon Brando, and Dustin Hoffman, with two each

Most Best Director awards: John Ford with four, for *The Informer, The Grapes of Wrath, How Green Was My Valley,* and *The Quiet Man*

Most Best Actress awards: Katharine Hepburn with four, for *Morning Glory, Guess Who's Coming to Dinner, The Lion in Winter,* and *On Golden Pond*

Best Actress awards for debut performances: Shirley Booth for *Come Back, Little Sheba*, Barbra Streisand for *Funny Girl*, and Marlee Matlin for *Children of a Lesser God*

First African-American Oscar winner: Hattie McDaniel, Best Supporting Actress, in *Gone with the Wind*

	1930–31	1931–32	1932–33
Picture	*Cimarron*	*Grand Hotel*	*Cavalcade*
Actor	Lionel Barrymore, *A Free Soul*	Wallace Beery, *The Champ*; Fredric March, *Dr. Jekyll and Mr. Hyde*	Charles Laughton, *The Private Life of Henry VIII*
Actress	Marie Dressler, *Min and Bill*	Helen Hayes, *The Sin of Madelon Claudet*	Katharine Hepburn, *Morning Glory*
Supporting Actor	—	—	—
Supporting Actress	—	—	—
Director	Norman Taurog, *Skippy*	Frank Borzage, *Bad Girl*	Frank Lloyd, *Cavalcade*
Adapted Screenplay/ Screenplay	Howard Estabrook, *Cimarron*	Edwin Burke, *Bad Girl*	Victor Heerman and Sarah Y. Mason, *Little Women*
Original Story	John Monk Saunders, *The Dawn Patrol*	Francis Marion, *The Champ*	Robert Lord, *One Way Passage*
Song	—	—	—
Score	—	—	—
Cinematography	*Tabu*	*Shanghai Express*	*A Farewell to Arms*
Interior Decoration	*Cimarron*	*Transatlantic*	*Cavalcade*
Film Editing	—	—	—
Sound	Paramount Studio Sound Department	Paramount Studio Sound Department	*A Farewell to Arms*
Short Films	—	*Flower and Trees* (Cartoons); *The Music Box* (Comedy); *Wrestling Swordfish* (Novelty)	*The Three Little Pigs* (Cartoons); *So This Is Harris* (Comedy); *Krakatoa* (Novelty)

1934	1935	1936	1937
It Happened One Night	*Mutiny on the Bounty*	*The Great Ziegfeld*	*The Life of Emile Zola*
Clark Gable, *It Happened One Night*	Victor McLaglen, *The Informer*	Paul Muni, *The Story of Louis Pasteur*	Spencer Tracy, *Captains Courageous*
Claudette Colbert, *It Happened One Night*	Bette Davis, *Dangerous*	Luise Rainer, *The Great Ziegfeld*	Luise Rainer, *The Good Earth*
—	—	Walter Brennan, *Come and Get It*	Joseph Schildkraut, *The Life of Emile Zola*
—	—	Gale Sondergaard, *Anthony Adverse*	Alice Brady, *In Old Chicago*
Frank Capra, *It Happened One Night*	John Ford, *The Informer*	Frank Capra, *Mr. Deeds Goes to Town*	Leo McCarey, *The Awful Truth*
Robert Riskin, *It Happened One Night*	Dudley Nichols, *The Informer*	Pierre Collings and Sheridan Gibney, *The Story of Louis Pasteur* (Screenplay)	Heinz Herald, Geza Herczeg, and Norman Reilly Raine, *The Life of Emile Zola* (Screenplay)
Arthur Caesar, *Manhattan Melodrama*	Ben Hecht and Charles MacArthur, *The Scoundrel*	Pierre Collings and Sheridan Gibney, *The Story of Louis Pasteur* (Story)	William A. Wellman and Robert Carson, *A Star is Born* (Story)
"The Continental" *(The Gay Divorcée)*	"Lullaby of Broadway" *(Gold Diggers of 1935)*	"The Way You Look Tonight" *(Swing Time)*	"Sweet Leilani" *(Waikiki Wedding)*
One Night of Love	*The Informer*	*Anthony Adverse*	*100 Men and a Girl*
Cleopatra	*A Midsummer Night's Dream*	*Anthony Adverse*	*The Good Earth*
The Merry Widow	*The Dark Angel*	*Dodsworth*	*Lost Horizon*
Eskimo	*A Midsummer Night's Dream*	*Anthony Adverse*	*Lost Horizon*
One Night of Love	*Naughty Marietta*	*San Francisco*	*The Hurricane*
The Tortoise and the Hare (Cartoons); *La Cucaracha* (Comedy); *City of Wax* (Novelty)	*Three Orphan Kittens* (Cartoons); *How To Sleep* (Comedy); *Wings over Mt. Everest* (Novelty)	*Country Cousin* (Cartoons); *Bored of Education* (One-Reel); *The Public Pays* (Two-Reel); *Give Me Liberty* (Color)	*The Old Mill* (Cartoons); *Private Life of the Gannetts* (One-Reel); *Torture Money* (Two-Reel); *Penny Wisdom* (Color)

	1938	1939	1940
Picture	*You Can't Take It with You*	*Gone with the Wind*	*Rebecca*
Actor	Spencer Tracy, *Boys Town*	Robert Donat, *Goodbye, Mr. Chips*	James Stewart, *The Philadelphia Story*
Actress	Bette Davis, *Jezebel*	Vivien Leigh, *Gone with the Wind*	Ginger Rogers, *Kitty Foyle*
Supporting Actor	Walter Brennan, *Kentucky*	Thomas Mitchell, *Stagecoach*	Walter Brennan, *The Westerner*
Supporting Actress	Fay Bainter, *Jezebel*	Hattie McDaniel, *Gone with the Wind*	Jane Darwell, *The Grapes of Wrath*
Director	Frank Capra, *You Can't Take It with You*	Victor Fleming, *Gone with the Wind*	John Ford, *The Grapes of Wrath*
Screenplay	Ian Dalrymple, Cecil Lewis, and W. P. Lipscomb, *Pygmalion*	Sidney Howard, *Gone with the Wind*	Donald Ogden Stewart, *The Philadelphia Story*
Original Screenplay/ Original Story	Eleanore Griffin and Dore Schary, *Boys Town*	Lewis R. Foster, *Mr. Smith Goes to Washington*	Preston Sturges, *The Great McGinty;* Benjamin Glazer and John S. Toldy, *Arise, My Love*
Song	"Thanks for the Memory" *(Big Broadcast of 1938)*	"Over the Rainbow" *(The Wizard of Oz)*	"When You Wish upon a Star" *(Pinocchio)*
Score/Original Score	*Alexander's Ragtime Band; Adventures of Robin Hood*	*Stagecoach; The Wizard of Oz*	*Tin Pan Alley; Pinocchio*
Cinematography	*The Great Waltz*	*Wuthering Heights* (B&W); *Gone with the Wind* (Color)	*Rebecca* (B&W); *The Thief of Bagdad* (Color)
Interior Decoration	*Adventures of Robin Hood*	*Gone with the Wind*	*Pride and Prejudice* (B&W); *The Thief of Bagdad* (Color)
Film Editing	*Adventures of Robin Hood*	*Gone with the Wind*	*North West Mounted Police*
Sound	*The Cowboy and the Lady*	*When Tomorrow Comes*	*Strike Up the Band*
Special Effects	—	*The Rains Came*	*The Thief of Bagdad*
Short Films	*Ferdinand the Bull* (Cartoons); *That Mothers Might Live* (One-Reel); *Declaration of Independence* (Two-Reel)	*The Ugly Duckling* (Cartoons); *Busy Little Bears* (One-Reel); *Sons of Liberty* (Two-Reel)	*Milky Way* (Cartoons); *Quicker 'N a Wink* (One-Reel); *Teddy, the Rough Rider* (Two-Reel)
Documentaries	—	—	—

1941	1942	1943	1944
How Green Was My Valley	*Mrs. Miniver*	*Casablanca*	*Going My Way*
Gary Cooper, *Sergeant York*	James Cagney, *Yankee Doodle Dandy*	Paul Lukas, *Watch on the Rhine*	Bing Crosby, *Going My Way*
Joan Fontaine, *Suspicion*	Greer Garson, *Mrs. Miniver*	Jennifer Jones, *The Song of Bernadette*	Ingrid Bergman, *Gaslight*
Donald Crisp, *How Green Was My Valley*	Van Heflin, *Johnny Eager*	Charles Coburn, *The More the Merrier*	Barry Fitzgerald, *Going My Way*
Mary Astor, *The Great Lie*	Teresa Wright, *Mrs. Miniver*	Katina Paxinou, *For Whom the Bell Tolls*	Ethel Barrymore, *None but the Lonely Heart*
John Ford, *How Green Was My Valley*	William Wyler, *Mrs. Miniver*	Michael Curtiz, *Casablanca*	Leo McCarey, *Going My Way*
Sidney Buchman and Seton I. Miller, *Here Comes Mr. Jordan*	George Froeschel, James Hilton, Claudine West, and Arthur Wimperis, *Mrs. Miniver*	Julius J. Epstein, Philip G. Epstein, and Howard Koch, *Casablanca*	Frank Butler and Frank Cavett, *Going My Way*
Harry Segall, *Here Comes Mr. Jordan*; Herman J. Mankiewicz and Orson Welles, *Citizen Kane*	Michael Kanin and Ring Lardner Jr., *Woman of the Year*; Emeric Pressburger, *The Invaders*	Norman Krasna, *Princess O'Rourke;* William Saroyan, *The Human Comedy*	Lamar Trotti, *Wilson;* Leo McCarey, *Going My Way*
"The Last Time I Saw Paris" *(Lady Be Good)*	"White Christmas" *(Holiday Inn)*	"You'll Never Know" *(Hello, Frisco, Hello)*	"Swinging on a Star" *(Going My Way)*
All That Money Can Buy (Dramatic); *Dumbo* (Musical)	*Now, Voyager* (Dramatic or Comedy); *Yankee Doodle Dandy* (Musical)	*The Song of Bernadette* (Dramatic or Comedy); *This Is the Army* (Musical)	*Since You Went Away* (Dramatic or Comedy); *Cover Girl* (Musical)
How Green Was My Valley (B&W); *Blood and Sand* (Color)	*Mrs. Miniver* (B&W); *The Black Swan* (Color)	*The Song of Bernadette* (B&W); *The Phantom of the Opera* (Color)	*Laura* (B&W); *Wilson* (Color)
How Green Was My Valley (B&W) *Blossoms in the Dust* (Color)	*This Above All* (B&W); *My Gal Sal* (Color)	*The Song of Bernadette* (B&W); *The Phantom of the Opera* (Color)	*Gaslight* (B&W); *Wilson* (Color)
Sergeant York	*The Pride of the Yankees*	*Air Force*	*Wilson*
That Hamilton Woman	*Yankee Doodle Dandy*	*This Land Is Mine*	*Wilson*
I Wanted Wings	*Reap the Wild Wind*	*Crash Dive*	*Thirty Seconds over Tokyo*
Lend a Paw (Cartoons); *Of Pups and Puzzles* (One-Reel); *Main Street on the March* (Two-Reel)	*Der Fuehrer's Face* (Cartoons); *Speaking of Animals and Their Families* (One-Reel); *Beyond the Line of Duty* (Two-Reel)	*Yankee Doodle Mouse* (Cartoons); *Amphibious Fighters* (One-Reel); *Heavenly Music* (Two-Reel)	*Mouse Trouble* (Cartoons); *Who's Who in Animal Land* (One-Reel); *I Won't Play* (Two-Reel)
Churchill's Island	*Battle of Midway; Kokoda Front Line; Moscow Strikes Back; Prelude to War*	*December 7th* (Shorts); *Desert Victory* (Features)	*With the Marines at Tarawa* (Shorts); *The Fighting Lady* (Features)

	1945	1946	1947
Picture	*The Lost Weekend*	*The Best Years of Our Lives*	*Gentleman's Agreement*
Actor	Ray Milland, *The Lost Weekend*	Fredric March, *The Best Years of Our Lives*	Ronald Colman, *A Double Life*
Actress	Joan Crawford, *Mildred Pierce*	Olivia de Havilland, *To Each His Own*	Loretta Young, *The Farmer's Daughter*
Supporting Actor	James Dunn, *A Tree Grows in Brooklyn*	Harold Russell, *The Best Years of Our Lives*	Edmund Gwenn, *Miracle on 34th Street*
Supporting Actress	Anne Revere, *National Velvet*	Anne Baxter, *The Razor's Edge*	Celeste Holm, *Gentleman's Agreement*
Director	Billy Wilder, *The Lost Weekend*	William Wyler, *The Best Years of Our Lives*	Elia Kazan, *Gentleman's Agreement*
Screenplay	Charles Brackett and Billy Wilder, *The Lost Weekend*	Robert E. Sherwood, *The Best Years of Our Lives*	George Seaton, *Miracle on 34th Street*
Original Screenplay/ Original Story	Richard Schweizer, *Marie-Louise*; Charles G. Booth, *The House on 92nd Street*	Muriel and Sydney Box, *The Seventh Veil;* Clemence Dane, *Vacation from Marriage*	Sidney Sheldon, *The Bachelor and the Bobby-Soxer*; Valentine Davies, *Miracle on 34th Street*
Song	"It Might As Well Be Spring" *(State Fair)*	"On the Atchison, Topeka and Santa Fe" *(The Harvey Girls)*	"Zip-A-Dee-Doo-Dah" *(Song of the South)*
Score—Dramatic or Comedy/ Musical	*Spellbound*; *Anchors Aweigh*	*The Best Years of Our Lives; The Jolson Story*	*A Double Life; Mother Wore Tights*
Cinematography	*The Picture of Dorian Gray* (B&W); *Leave Her to Heaven* (Color)	*Anna and the King of Siam* (B&W); *The Yearling* (Color)	*Great Expectations* (B&W); *Black Narcissus* (Color)
Costume Design	—	—	—
Interior Decoration, through 1946; Art Direction—Set Decoration, from 1947	*Blood on the Sun* (B&W); *Frenchman's Creek* (Color)	*Anna and the King of Siam* (B&W); *The Yearling* (Color)	*Great Expectations* (B&W); *Black Narcissus* (Color)
Film Editing	*National Velvet*	*The Best Years of Our Lives*	*Body and Soul*
Sound	*The Bells of St. Mary's*	*The Jolson Story*	*The Bishop's Wife*
Special Effects	*Wonder Man*	*Blithe Spirit*	*Green Dolphin Street*
Short Films	*Quiet Please* (Cartoons); *Stairway to Light* (One-Reel); *Star in the Night* (Two-Reel)	*The Cat Concerto* (Cartoons); *Facing Your Danger* (One-Reel); *A Boy and His Dog* (Two-Reel)	*Tweetie Pie* (Cartoons); *Goodbye Miss Turlock* (One-Reel); *Climbing the Matterhorn* (Two-Reel)
Documentaries	*Hitler Lives?* (Shorts); *The True Glory* (Features)	*Seeds of Destiny* (Shorts)	*First Steps* (Shorts); *Design for Death* (Features)

1948	1949	1950	1951
Hamlet	*All the King's Men*	*All About Eve*	*An American in Paris*
Laurence Olivier, *Hamlet*	Broderick Crawford, *All the King's Men*	José Ferrer, *Cyrano de Bergerac*	Humphrey Bogart, *The African Queen*
Jane Wyman, *Johnny Belinda*	Olivia de Havilland, *The Heiress*	Judy Holliday, *Born Yesterday*	Vivien Leigh, *A Streetcar Named Desire*
Walter Huston, *Treasure of Sierra Madre*	Dean Jagger, *Twelve O'Clock High*	George Sanders, *All About Eve*	Karl Malden, *A Streetcar Named Desire*
Claire Trevor, *Key Largo*	Mercedes McCambridge, *All the King's Men*	Josephine Hull, *Harvey*	Kim Hunter, *A Streetcar Named Desire*
John Huston, *Treasure of Sierra Madre*	Joseph L. Mankiewicz, *A Letter to Three Wives*	Joseph L. Mankiewicz, *All About Eve*	George Stevens, *A Place in the Sun*
John Huston, *Treasure of Sierra Madre*	Joseph L. Mankiewicz, *A Letter to Three Wives*	Joseph L. Mankiewicz, *All About Eve*	Michael Wilson and Harry Brown, *A Place in the Sun*
Richard Schweizer and David Wechsler, *The Search*	Douglas Morrow, *The Stratton Story*; Robert Pirosh, *Battleground* (Story and Screenplay)	Edna and Edward Anhalt, *Panic in the Streets*; Charles Brackett, Billy Wilder, and D.M. Marshman Jr., *Sunset Boulevard* (Story and Screenplay)	Paul Dehn and James Bernard, *Seven Days to Noon*; Alan Jay Lerner, *An American in Paris* (Story and Screenplay)
"Buttons and Bows" *(The Paleface)*	"Baby, It's Cold Outside" *(Neptune's Daughter)*	"Mona Lisa" *(Captain Carey, USA)*	"In the Cool, Cool, Cool of the Evening" *(Here Comes the Groom)*
The Red Shoes; *Easter Parade*	*The Heiress*; *On the Town*	*Sunset Boulevard*; *Annie Get Your Gun*	*A Place in the Sun*; *An American in Paris*
The Naked City (B&W); *Joan of Arc* (Color)	*Battleground* (B&W); *She Wore a Yellow Ribbon* (Color)	*The Third Man* (B&W); *King Solomon's Mines* (Color)	*A Place in the Sun* (B&W); *An American in Paris* (Color)
Hamlet (B&W); *Joan of Arc* (Color)	*The Heiress* (B&W); *Adventures of Don Juan* (Color)	*All About Eve* (B&W); *Samson and Delilah* (Color)	*A Place in the Sun* (B&W); *An American in Paris* (Color)
Hamlet (B&W); *The Red Shoes* (Color)	*The Heiress* (B&W); *Little Women* (Color)	*Sunset Boulevard* (B&W); *Samson and Delilah* (Color)	*A Streetcar Named Desire* (B&W); *An American in Paris* (Color)
The Naked City	*Champion*	*King Solomon's Mines*	*A Place in the Sun*
The Snake Pit	*Twelve O'Clock High*	*All About Eve*	*The Great Caruso*
Portrait of Jennie	*Mighty Joe Young*	*Destination Moon*	*When Worlds Collide*
The Little Orphan (Cartoons); *Symphony of a City* (One-Reel); *Seal Island* (Two-Reel)	*For Scent-imental Reasons* (Cartoons); *Aquatic House Party* (One-Reel); *Van Gogh* (Two-Reel)	*Gerald McBoing-Boing* (Cartoons); *Grandad of Races* (One-Reel); *In Beaver Valley* (Two-Reel)	*Two Mouseketeers* (Cartoons); *World of Kids* (One-Reel); *Nature's Half Acre* (Two-Reel)
Toward Independence (Shorts); *The Secret Land* (Features)	*A Chance To Live* and *So Much for So Little* (Shorts); *Daybreak in Udi* (Features)	*Why Korea?* (Shorts); *The Titan: Story of Michelangelo* (Features)	*Benjy* (Shorts); *Kon-Tiki* (Features)

	1952	1953	1954
Picture	*The Greatest Show on Earth*	*From Here to Eternity*	*On the Waterfront*
Actor	Gary Cooper, *High Noon*	William Holden, *Stalag 17*	Marlon Brando, *On the Waterfront*
Actress	Shirley Booth, *Come Back, Little Sheba*	Audrey Hepburn, *Roman Holiday*	Grace Kelly, *The Country Girl*
Supporting Actor	Anthony Quinn, *Viva Zapata!*	Frank Sinatra, *From Here to Eternity*	Edmond O'Brien, *The Barefoot Contessa*
Supporting Actress	Gloria Grahame, *The Bad and the Beautiful*	Donna Reed, *From Here to Eternity*	Eva Marie Saint, *On the Waterfront*
Director	John Ford, *The Quiet Man*	Fred Zinnemann, *From Here to Eternity*	Elia Kazan, *On the Waterfront*
Screenplay	Charles Schnee, *The Bad and the Beautiful*	Daniel Taradash, *From Here to Eternity*	George Seaton, *The Country Girl*
Story/Story and Screenplay	Frederic M. Frank, Theodore St. John, and Frank Cavett, *The Greatest Show on Earth*; T.E.B. Clarke, *The Lavender Hill Mob*	Ian McLellan Hunter, *Roman Holiday*; Charles Brackett, Walter Reisch, and Richard Breen, *Titanic*	Philip Yordan, *Broken Lance*; Budd Schulberg, *On the Waterfront*
Song	"High Noon (Do Not Forsake Me, Oh My Darlin')" *(High Noon)*	"Secret Love" *(Calamity Jane)*	"Three Coins in the Fountain" *(Three Coins in the Fountain)*
Score—Dramatic or Comedy/Musical	*High Noon; With a Song in My Heart*	*Lili; Call Me Madam*	*The High and the Mighty*; *Seven Brides for Seven Brothers*
Cinematography	*The Bad and the Beautiful* (B&W); *The Quiet Man* (Color)	*From Here to Eternity* (B&W); *Shane* (Color)	*On the Waterfront* (B&W); *Three Coins in the Fountain* (Color)
Costume Design	*The Bad and the Beautiful* (B&W); *Moulin Rouge* (Color)	*Roman Holiday* (B&W); *The Robe* (Color)	*Sabrina* (B&W); *Gate of Hell* (Color)
Art Direction—Set Decoration	*The Bad and the Beautiful* (B&W); *Moulin Rouge* (Color)	*Julius Caesar* (B&W); *The Robe* (Color)	*On the Waterfront* (B&W); *20,000 Leagues Under the Sea* (Color)
Film Editing	*High Noon*	*From Here to Eternity*	*On the Waterfront*
Foreign Language Film	—	—	—
Sound	*Breaking the Sound Barrier*	*From Here to Eternity*	*The Glenn Miller Story*
Special Effects	*Plymouth Adventure*	*The War of the Worlds*	*20,000 Leagues Under the Sea*
Short Films	*Johann Mouse* (Cartoons); *Light in the Window* (One-Reel); *Water Birds* (Two-Reel)	*Toot, Whistle, Plunk and Boom* (Cartoons); *The Merry Wives of Windsor Overture* (One-Reel); *Bear Country* (Two-Reel)	*When Magoo Flew* (Cartoons); *This Mechanical Age* (One-Reel); *A Time Out of War* (Two-Reel)
Documentaries	*Neighbours* (Shorts); *The Sea Around Us* (Features)	*The Alaskan Eskimo* (Shorts); *The Living Desert* (Features)	*Thursday's Children* (Shorts); *The Vanishing Prairie* (Features)

1955	1956	1957	1958
Marty	*Around the World in 80 Days*	*The Bridge on the River Kwai*	*Gigi*
Ernest Borgnine, *Marty*	Yul Brynner, *The King and I*	Alec Guinness, *The Bridge on the River Kwai*	David Niven, *Separate Tables*
Anna Magnani, *The Rose Tattoo*	Ingrid Bergman, *Anastasia*	Joanne Woodward, *The Three Faces of Eve*	Susan Hayward, *I Want to Live!*
Jack Lemmon, *Mister Roberts*	Anthony Quinn, *Lust for Life*	Red Buttons, *Sayonara*	Burl Ives, *The Big Country*
Jo Van Fleet, *East of Eden*	Dorothy Malone, *Written on the Wind*	Miyoshi Umeki, *Sayonara*	Wendy Hiller, *Separate Tables*
Delbert Mann, *Marty*	George Stevens, *Giant*	David Lean, *The Bridge on the River Kwai*	Vincente Minnelli, *Gigi*
Paddy Chayefsky, *Marty*	James Poe, John Farrow, and S.J. Perelman, *Around the World in 80 Days* (Adapted)	Pierre Boulle, *The Bridge on the River Kwai* (Adapted)	Alan Jay Lerner, *Gigi* (Adapted)
Daniel Fuchs, *Love Me or Leave Me*; William Ludwig and Sonya Levien, *Interrupted Melody*	Dalton Trumbo (aka Robert Rich), *The Brave One*; Albert Lamorisse, *The Red Balloon*	George Wells, *Designing Woman*	Nathan E. Douglas and Harold Jacob Smith, *The Defiant Ones*
"Love is a Many-Splendored Thing" *(Love Is a Many-Splendored Thing)*	"Whatever Will Be, Will Be (Que Será, Será)" *(The Man Who Knew Too Much)*	"All the Way" *(The Joker Is Wild)*	"Gigi" *(Gigi)*
Love is a Many-Splendored Thing; *Oklahoma!*	*Around the World in 80 Days*; *The King and I*	*The Bridge on the River Kwai*	*The Old Man and the Sea*; *Gigi*
The Rose Tattoo (B&W); *To Catch a Thief* (Color)	*Somebody Up There Likes Me* (B&W); *Around the World in 80 Days* (Color)	*The Bridge on the River Kwai*	*The Defiant Ones* (B&W); *Gigi* (Color)
I'll Cry Tomorrow (B&W); *Love Is a Many-Splendored Thing* (Color)	*The Solid Gold Cadillac* (B&W); *The King and I* (Color)	*Les Girls*	*Gigi*
The Rose Tattoo (B&W); *Picnic* (Color)	*Somebody Up There Likes Me* (B&W); *The King and I* (Color)	*Sayonara*	*Gigi*
Picnic	*Around the World in 80 Days*	*The Bridge on the River Kwai*	*Gigi*
—	*La Strada* (Italy)	*The Nights of Cabiria* (Italy)	*My Uncle* (France)
Oklahoma!	*The King and I*	*Sayonara*	*South Pacific*
The Bridges at Toko-Ri	*The Ten Commandments*	*The Enemy Below*	*tom thumb*
Speedy Gonzales (Cartoon); *Survival City* (One-Reel); *The Face of Lincoln* (Two-Reel)	*Mister Magoo's Puddle Jumper* (Cartoons); *Crashing the Water Barrier* (One-Reel); *The Bespoke Overcoat* (Two-Reel)	*Birds Anonymous* (Cartoons); *The Wetback Hound* (Live Action)	*Knighty Knight Bugs* (Cartoons); *Grand Canyon* (Live Action)
Men Against the Arctic (Shorts); *Helen Keller in Her Story* (Features)	*The True Story of the Civil War* (Shorts); *The Silent World* (Features)	*Albert Schweitzer* (Features)	*AMA Girls* (Shorts); *White Wilderness* (Features)

	1959	1960	1961
Picture	*Ben-Hur*	*The Apartment*	*West Side Story*
Actor	Charlton Heston, *Ben-Hur*	Burt Lancaster, *Elmer Gantry*	Maximilian Schell, *Judgment at Nuremburg*
Actress	Simone Signoret, *Room at the Top*	Elizabeth Taylor, *Butterfield 8*	Sophia Loren, *Two Women*
Supporting Actor	Hugh Griffith, *Ben-Hur*	Peter Ustinov, *Spartacus*	George Chakiris, *West Side Story*
Supporting Actress	Shelley Winters, *The Diary of Anne Frank*	Shirley Jones, *Elmer Gantry*	Rita Moreno, *West Side Story*
Director	William Wyler, *Ben-Hur*	Billy Wilder, *The Apartment*	Robert Wise and Jerome Robbins, *West Side Story*
Adapted Screenplay	Neil Paterson, *Room at the Top*	Richard Brooks, *Elmer Gantry*	Abby Mann, *Judgment at Nuremberg*
Story and Screenplay	Russell Rouse and Clarence Greene, story; Stanley Shapiro and Maurice Richlin, screenplay, *Pillow Talk*	Billy Wilder and I.A.L. Diamond, *The Apartment*	William Inge, *Splendor in the Grass*
Song	"High Hopes" *(A Hole in the Head)*	"Never on Sunday" *(Never on Sunday)*	"Moon River" *(Breakfast at Tiffany's)*
Score	*Ben-Hur* (Dramatic or Comedy); *Porgy and Bess* (Musical)	*Exodus* (Dramatic or Comedy); *Song Without End (The Story of Franz Liszt)* (Musical)	*Breakfast at Tiffany's* (Dramatic or Comedy); *West Side Story* (Musical)
Cinematography	*The Diary of Anne Frank* (B&W); *Ben-Hur* (Color)	*Sons and Lovers* (B&W); *Spartacus* (Color)	*The Hustler* (B&W); *West Side Story* (Color)
Costume Design	*Some Like It Hot* (B&W); *Ben-Hur* (Color)	*The Facts of Life* (B&W); *Spartacus* (Color)	*La Dolce Vita* (B&W); *West Side Story* (Color)
Art Direction—Set Decoration	*The Diary of Anne Frank* (B&W); *Ben-Hur* (Color)	*The Apartment* (B&W); *Spartacus* (Color)	*The Hustler* (B&W); *West Side Story* (Color)
Film Editing	*Ben-Hur*	*The Apartment*	*West Side Story*
Foreign Language Film	*Black Orpheus* (France)	*The Virgin Spring* (Sweden)	*Through a Glass Darkly* (Sweden)
Sound	*Ben-Hur*	*The Alamo*	*West Side Story*
Sound Effects (Editing)	—	—	—
Visual Effects	—	—	—
Special Effects	*Ben-Hur*	*The Time Machine*	*The Guns of Navarone*
Short Films	*Moonbird* (Cartoons); *The Golden Fish* (Live Action)	*Munro* (Cartoons); *Day of the Painter* (Live Action)	*Ersatz (The Substitute)* (Cartoons); *Seawards the Great Ships* (Live Action)
Documentaries	*Glass* (Shorts); *Serengeti Shall Not Die* (Features)	*Giuseppina* (Shorts); *The Horse with the Flying Tail* (Features)	*Project Hope* (Shorts); *Le Ciel et la boue (Sky Above and Mud Beneath)* (Features)

1962	1963	1964	1965
Lawrence of Arabia	*Tom Jones*	*My Fair Lady*	*The Sound of Music*
Gregory Peck, *To Kill a Mockingbird*	Sidney Poitier, *Lilies of the Field*	Rex Harrison, *My Fair Lady*	Lee Marvin, *Cat Ballou*
Anne Bancroft, *The Miracle Worker*	Patricia Neal, *Hud*	Julie Andrews, *Mary Poppins*	Julie Christie, *Darling*
Ed Begley, *Sweet Bird of Youth*	Melvyn Douglas, *Hud*	Peter Ustinov, *Topkapi*	Martin Balsam, *A Thousand Clowns*
Patty Duke, *The Miracle Worker*	Margaret Rutherford, *The V.I.P.s*	Lila Kedrova, *Zorba the Greek*	Shelley Winters, *A Patch of Blue*
David Lean, *Lawrence of Arabia*	Tony Richardson, *Tom Jones*	George Cukor, *My Fair Lady*	Robert Wise, *The Sound of Music*
Horton Foote, *To Kill a Mockingbird*	John Osborne, *Tom Jones*	Edward Anhalt, *Becket*	Robert Bolt, *Doctor Zhivago*
Ennio de Concini, Alfredo Giannetti, and Pietro Germi, *Divorce—Italian Style*	James R. Webb, *How the West Was Won*	S. H. Barnett, story; Peter Stone and Frank Tarloff, screenplay, *Father Goose*	Frederic Raphael, *Darling*
"Days of Wine and Roses" *(Days of Wine and Roses)*	"Call Me Irresponsible" *(Papa's Delicate Condition)*	"Chim Chim Cher-ee" *(Mary Poppins)*	"The Shadow of Your Smile" *(The Sandpiper)*
Lawrence of Arabia (Original); *The Music Man* (Adaptation)	*Tom Jones* (Original); *Irma La Douce* (Adaptation)	*Mary Poppins* (Original); *My Fair Lady* (Adaptation)	*Doctor Zhivago* (Original); *The Sound of Music* (Adaptation)
The Longest Day (B&W); *Lawrence of Arabia* (Color)	*Hud* (B&W); *Cleopatra* (Color)	*Zorba the Greek* (B&W); *My Fair Lady* (Color)	*Ship of Fools* (B&W); *Doctor Zhivago* (Color)
Whatever Happened to Baby Jane? (B&W); *The Wonderful World of the Brothers Grimm* (Color)	*8½* (B&W); *Cleopatra* (Color)	*The Night of the Iguana* (B&W); *My Fair Lady* (Color)	*Darling* (B&W); *Doctor Zhivago* (Color)
To Kill a Mockingbird (B&W); *Lawrence of Arabia* (Color)	*America America* (B&W); *Cleopatra* (Color)	*Zorba the Greek* (B&W); *My Fair Lady* (Color)	*Ship of Fools* (B&W); *Doctor Zhivago* (Color)
Lawrence of Arabia	*How the West Was Won*	*Mary Poppins*	*The Sound of Music*
Sundays and Cybèle (France)	*8½* (Italy)	*Yesterday, Today and Tomorrow* (Italy)	*The Shop on Main Street* (Czechoslovakia)
Lawrence of Arabia	*How the West Was Won*	*My Fair Lady*	*The Sound of Music*
—	*It's a Mad, Mad, Mad, Mad World*	*Goldfinger*	*The Great Race*
—	*Cleopatra*	*Mary Poppins*	*Thunderball*
The Longest Day	—	—	—
The Hole (Cartoons); *Heureux anniversaire* (Live Action)	*The Critic* (Cartoons); *An Occurrence at Owl Creek Bridge* (Live Action)	*The Pink Phink* (Cartoons); *Casals Conducts: 1964* (Live Action)	*The Dot and the Line* (Cartoons); *The Chicken* (*Le Poulet*) (Live Action)
Dylan Thomas (Shorts); *Black Fox* (Features)	*Chagall* (Shorts); *Robert Frost: A Lover's Quarrel with the World* (Features)	*Nine from Little Rock* (Shorts); *Jacques-Yves Cousteau's World Without Sun* (Features)	*To Be Alive!* (Shorts); *The Eleanor Roosevelt Story* (Features)

	1966	1967	1968
Picture	*A Man for All Seasons*	*In the Heat of the Night*	*Oliver!*
Actor	Paul Scofield, *A Man for All Seasons*	Rod Steiger, *In the Heat of the Night*	Cliff Robertson, *Charly*
Actress	Elizabeth Taylor, *Who's Afraid of Virginia Woolf?*	Katharine Hepburn, *Guess Who's Coming to Dinner*	Katharine Hepburn, *The Lion in Winter;* Barbra Streisand, *Funny Girl*
Supporting Actor	Walter Matthau, *The Fortune Cookie*	George Kennedy, *Cool Hand Luke*	Jack Albertson, *The Subject Was Roses*
Supporting Actress	Sandy Dennis, *Who's Afraid of Virginia Woolf?*	Estelle Parsons, *Bonnie and Clyde*	Ruth Gordon, *Rosemary's Baby*
Director	Fred Zinnemann, *A Man for All Seasons*	Mike Nichols, *The Graduate*	Carol Reed, *Oliver!*
Adapted Screenplay	Robert Bolt, *A Man for All Seasons*	Stirling Silliphant, *In the Heat of the Night*	James Goldman, *The Lion in Winter*
Story and Screenplay	Claude Lelouch, story; Pierre Uytterhoeven and Claude Lelouch, screenplay, *A Man and a Woman*	William Rose, *Guess Who's Coming to Dinner?*	Mel Brooks, *The Producers*
Song	"Born Free" *(Born Free)*	"Talk to the Animals" *(Doctor Dolittle)*	"The Windmills of Your Mind" *(The Thomas Crown Affair)*
Score	*Born Free* (Original); *A Funny Thing Happened on the Way to the Forum* (Adaptation)	*Thoroughly Modern Millie* (Original); *Camelot* (Adaptation)	*The Lion in Winter* (Nonmusical); *Oliver!* (Musical)
Cinematography	*Who's Afraid of Virginia Woolf?* (B&W); *A Man For All Seasons*	*Bonnie and Clyde*	*Romeo and Juliet*
Costume Design	*Who's Afraid of Virginia Woolf?* (B&W); *A Man for All Seasons* (Color)	*Camelot*	*Romeo and Juliet*
Art Direction—Set Decoration	*Who's Afraid of Virginia Woolf?* (B&W); *Fantastic Voyage* (Color)	*Camelot*	*Oliver!*
Film Editing	*Grand Prix*	*In the Heat of the Night*	*Bullitt*
Foreign Language Film	*A Man and a Woman* (France)	*Closely Watched Trains* (Czechoslovakia)	*War and Peace* (U.S.S.R.)
Sound	*Grand Prix*	*In the Heat of the Night*	*Oliver!*
Sound Effects (Editing)	*Grand Prix*	*The Dirty Dozen*	—
Visual Effects	*Fantastic Voyage*	*Doctor Dolittle*	*2001: A Space Odyssey*
Short Films	*Herb Alpert and the Tijuana Brass Double Feature* (Cartoons); *Wild Wings* (Live Action)	*The Box* (Cartoons); *A Place to Stand* (Live Action)	*Winnie the Pooh and the Blustery Day* (Cartoons); *Robert Kennedy Remembered* (Live Action)
Documentaries	*A Year Toward Tomorrow* (Shorts); *The War Game* (Features)	*The Redwoods* (Shorts); *The Anderson Platoon* (Features)	*Why Man Creates* (Shorts); *Journey into Self* (Features)

1969	1970	1971	1972
Midnight Cowboy	*Patton*	*The French Connection*	*The Godfather*
John Wayne, *True Grit*	George C. Scott, *Patton*	Gene Hackman, *The French Connection*	Marlon Brando, *The Godfather*
Maggie Smith, *The Prime of Miss Jean Brodie*	Glenda Jackson, *Women in Love*	Jane Fonda, *Klute*	Liza Minnelli, *Cabaret*
Gig Young, *They Shoot Horses, Don't They?*	John Mills, *Ryan's Daughter*	Ben Johnson, *The Last Picture Show*	Joel Grey, *Cabaret*
Goldie Hawn, *Cactus Flower*	Helen Hayes, *Airport*	Cloris Leachman, *The Last Picture Show*	Eileen Heckart, *Butterflies Are Free*
John Schlesinger, *Midnight Cowboy*	Franklin J. Schaffner, *Patton*	William Friedkin, *The French Connection*	Bob Fosse, *Cabaret*
Waldo Salt, *Midnight Cowboy*	Ring Lardner Jr., *M*A*S*H*	Ernest Tidyman, *The French Connection*	Mario Puzo and Francis Ford Coppola, *The Godfather*
William Goldman, *Butch Cassidy and the Sundance Kid*	Francis Ford Coppola and Edmund H. North, *Patton*	Paddy Chayefsky, *The Hospital*	Jeremy Larner, *The Candidate*
"Raindrops Keep Fallin' on My Head" *(Butch Cassidy and the Sundance Kid)*	"For All We Know" *(Lovers and Other Strangers)*	"Theme from *Shaft*" *(Shaft)*	"The Morning After" *(The Poseidon Adventure)*
Butch Cassidy and the Sundance Kid (Nonmusical); *Hello Dolly!* (Musical)	*Love Story* (Original Score); *Let It Be* (Original Song Score)	*Summer of '42* (Dramatic); *Fiddler on the Roof* (Adapted)	*Limelight* (Dramatic); *Cabaret* (Adapted)
Butch Cassidy and the Sundance Kid	*Ryan's Daughter*	*Fiddler on the Roof*	*Cabaret*
Anne of the Thousand Days	*Cromwell*	*Nicholas and Alexandra*	*Travels with My Aunt*
Hello Dolly!	*Patton*	*Nicholas and Alexandra*	*Cabaret*
Z	*Patton*	*The French Connection*	*Cabaret*
Z (Algeria)	*Investigation of a Citizen Above Suspicion* (Italy)	*The Garden of the Finzi-Continis* (Italy)	*The Discreet Charm of the Bourgeoisie* (France)
Hello Dolly!	*Patton*	*Fiddler on the Roof*	*Cabaret*
—	—	—	—
Marooned	*Tora! Tora! Tora!*	*Bedknobs and Broomsticks*	—
It's Tough to Be a Bird (Cartoons); *The Magic Machines* (Live Action)	*Is It Always Right To Be Right?* (Cartoons); *The Resurrection of Broncho Billy* (Live Action)	*The Crunch Bird* (Animated); *Sentinels of Silence* (Live Action)	*A Christmas Carol* (Animated); *Norman Rockwell's World . . . An American Dream* (Live Action)
Czechoslovakia 1968 (Shorts); *Arthur Rubinstein—The Love of Life* (Features)	*Interviews with My Lai Veterans* (Shorts); *Woodstock* (Features)	*Sentinels of Silence* (Shorts); *The Hellstrom Chronicle* (Features)	*This Tiny World* (Shorts); *Marjoe* (Features)

	1973	1974	1975
Picture	*The Sting*	*The Godfather Part II*	*One Flew over the Cuckoo's Nest*
Actor	Jack Lemmon, *Save the Tiger*	Art Carney, *Harry and Tonto*	Jack Nicholson, *One Flew over the Cuckoo's Nest*
Actress	Glenda Jackson, *A Touch of Class*	Ellen Burstyn, *Alice Doesn't Live Here Anymore*	Louise Fletcher, *One Flew over the Cuckoo's Nest*
Supporting Actor	John Houseman, *The Paper Chase*	Robert De Niro, *The Godfather Part II*	George Burns, *The Sunshine Boys*
Supporting Actress	Tatum O'Neal, *Paper Moon*	Ingrid Bergman, *Murder on the Orient Express*	Lee Grant, *Shampoo*
Director	George Roy Hill, *The Sting*	Francis Ford Coppola, *The Godfather Part II*	Milos Forman, *One Flew over the Cuckoo's Nest*
Adapted Screenplay	William Peter Blatty, *The Exorcist*	Francis Ford Coppola and Mario Puzo, *The Godfather Part II*	Lawrence Hauben and Bo Goldman, *One Flew over the Cuckoo's Nest*
Original Screenplay	David S. Ward, *The Sting*	Robert Towne, *Chinatown*	Frank Pierson, *Dog Day Afternoon*
Song	"The Way We Were" *(The Way We Were)*	"We May Never Love Like This Again" *(The Towering Inferno)*	"I'm Easy" *(Nashville)*
Score	*The Way We Were* (Original); *The Sting* (Adaptation)	*The Godfather Part II* (Original); *The Great Gatsby* (Adaptation)	*Jaws* (Original); *Barry Lyndon* (Adaptation)
Cinematography	*Cries and Whispers*	*The Towering Inferno*	*Barry Lyndon*
Costume Design	*The Sting*	*The Great Gatsby*	*Barry Lyndon*
Art Direction—Set Decoration	*The Sting*	*The Godfather Part II*	*Barry Lyndon*
Film Editing	*The Sting*	*The Towering Inferno*	*Jaws*
Foreign Language Film	*Day for Night* (France)	*Amarcord* (Italy)	*Dersu Uzala* (U.S.S.R.)
Sound	*The Exorcist*	*Earthquake*	*Jaws*
Visual Effects	—	—	—
Short Films	*Frank Film* (Animated); *The Bolero* (Live Action)	*Closed Mondays* (Animated); *One-Eyed Men Are Kings* (Live Action)	*Great* (Animated); *Angel and Big Joe* (Live Action)
Documentaries	*Princeton: A Search for Answers* (Shorts); *The Great American Cowboy* (Features)	*Don't* (Shorts); *Hearts and Minds* (Features)	*The End of the Game* (Shorts); *The Man Who Skied down Everest* (Features)

1976	1977	1978	1979
Rocky	*Annie Hall*	*The Deer Hunter*	*Kramer vs. Kramer*
Peter Finch, *Network*	Richard Dreyfuss, *The Goodbye Girl*	Jon Voight, *Coming Home*	Dustin Hoffman, *Kramer vs. Kramer*
Faye Dunaway, *Network*	Diane Keaton, *Annie Hall*	Jane Fonda, *Coming Home*	Sally Field, *Norma Rae*
Jason Robards, *All the President's Men*	Jason Robards, *Julia*	Christopher Walken, *The Deer Hunter*	Melvyn Douglas, *Being There*
Beatrice Straight, *Network*	Vanessa Redgrave, *Julia*	Maggie Smith, *California Suite*	Meryl Streep, *Kramer vs. Kramer*
John G. Avildsen, *Rocky*	Woody Allen, *Annie Hall*	Michael Cimino, *The Deer Hunter*	Robert Benton, *Kramer vs. Kramer*
William Goldman, *All the President's Men*	Alvin Sargent, *Julia*	Oliver Stone, *Midnight Express*	Robert Benton, *Kramer vs. Kramer*
Paddy Chayefsky, *Network*	Woody Allen and Marshall Brickman, *Annie Hall*	Nancy Dowd, story; Waldo Salt and Robert C. Jones, screenplay, *Coming Home*	Steve Tesich, *Breaking Away*
"Evergreen" *(A Star Is Born)*	"You Light Up My Life" *(You Light Up My Life)*	"Last Dance" *(Thank God It's Friday)*	"It Goes Like It Goes" *(Norma Rae)*
The Omen (Original); *Bound for Glory* (Adaptation)	*Star Wars* (Original); *A Little Night Music* (Adaptation)	*Midnight Express* (Original); *The Buddy Holly Story* (Adaptation)	*A Little Romance* (Original); *All That Jazz* (Adaptation)
Bound for Glory	*Close Encounters of the Third Kind*	*Days of Heaven*	*Apocalypse Now*
Fellini's Casanova	*Star Wars*	*Death on the Nile*	*All That Jazz*
All the President's Men	*Star Wars*	*Heaven Can Wait*	*All That Jazz*
Rocky	*Star Wars*	*The Deer Hunter*	*All That Jazz*
Black and White in Color (Ivory Coast)	*Madame Rosa* (France)	*Get Out Your Handkerchiefs* (France)	*The Tin Drum* (Federal Republic of Germany)
All the President's Men	*Star Wars*	*The Deer Hunter*	*Apocalypse Now*
—	*Star Wars*	—	*Alien*
Leisure (Animated); *In the Region of Ice* (Live Action)	*Sand Castle* (Animated); *I'll Find a Way* (Live Action)	*Special Delivery* (Animated); *Teenage Father* (Live Action)	*Every Child* (Animated); *Board and Care* (Live Action)
Number Our Days (Shorts); *Harlan County, U.S.A.* (Features)	*Gravity Is My Enemy* (Shorts); *Who Are the DeBolts? And Where Did They Get Nineteen Kids?* (Features)	*The Flight of the Gossamer Condor* (Shorts); *Scared Straight!* (Features)	*Paul Robeson: Tribute to an Artist* (Shorts); *Best Boy* (Features)

	1980	1981	1982
Picture	*Ordinary People*	*Chariots of Fire*	*Gandhi*
Actor	Robert De Niro, *Raging Bull*	Henry Fonda, *On Golden Pond*	Ben Kingsley, *Gandhi*
Actress	Sissy Spacek, *Coal Miner's Daughter*	Katharine Hepburn, *On Golden Pond*	Meryl Streep, *Sophie's Choice*
Supporting Actor	Timothy Hutton, *Ordinary People*	John Gielgud, *Arthur*	Louis Gossett Jr., *An Officer and a Gentleman*
Supporting Actress	Mary Steenburgen, *Melvin and Howard*	Maureen Stapleton, *Reds*	Jessica Lange, *Tootsie*
Director	Robert Redford, *Ordinary People*	Warren Beatty, *Reds*	Richard Attenborough, *Gandhi*
Adapted Screenplay	Alvin Sargent, *Ordinary People*	Ernest Thompson, *On Golden Pond*	Costa-Gavras and Donald Stewart, *Missing*
Original Screenplay	Bo Goldman, *Melvin and Howard*	Colin Welland, *Chariots of Fire*	John Briley, *Gandhi*
Song	"Fame" *(Fame)*	"Arthur's Theme (Best That You Can Do)" *(Arthur)*	"Up Where We Belong" *(An Officer and a Gentleman)*
Original Score	*Fame*	*Chariots of Fire*	*E.T., the Extra-Terrestrial; Victor/Victoria* (Song Score/Adaptation)
Cinematography	*Tess*	*Reds*	*Gandhi*
Costume Design	*Tess*	*Chariots of Fire*	*Gandhi*
Art Direction—Set Decoration	*Tess*	*Raiders of the Lost Ark*	*Gandhi*
Film Editing	*Raging Bull*	*Raiders of the Lost Ark*	*Gandhi*
Foreign Language Film	*Moscow Does Not Believe in Tears* (U.S.S.R.)	*Mephisto* (Hungary)	*Volver A Empezar (To Begin Again)* (Spain)
Sound	*The Empire Strikes Back*	*Raiders of the Lost Ark*	*Gandhi*
Sound Effects (Editing)	—	—	*E.T., the Extra-Terrestrial*
Makeup	—	*An American Werewolf in London*	*Quest for Fire*
Visual Effects	—	*Raiders of the Lost Ark*	*E.T., the Extra-Terrestrial*
Short Films	*The Fly* (Animated); *The Dollar Bottom* (Live Action)	*Crac* (Animated); *Violet* (Live Action)	*Tango* (Animated); *A Shocking Accident* (Live Action)
Documentaries	*Karl Hess: Toward Liberty* (Shorts); *From Mao to Mozart: Isaac Stern in China* (Features)	*Genocide* (Shorts); *Close Harmony* (Features)	*If You Love This Planet* (Shorts); *Just Another Missing Kid* (Features)

1983	1984	1985	1986
Terms of Endearment	*Amadeus*	*Out of Africa*	*Platoon*
Robert Duvall, *Tender Mercies*	F. Murray Abraham, *Amadeus*	William Hurt, *Kiss of the Spider Woman*	Paul Newman, *The Color of Money*
Shirley MacLaine, *Terms of Endearment*	Sally Field, *Places in the Heart*	Geraldine Page, *The Trip To Bountiful*	Marlee Matlin, *Children of a Lesser God*
Jack Nicholson, *Terms of Endearment*	Haing S. Ngor, *The Killing Fields*	Don Ameche, *Cocoon*	Michael Caine, *Hannah and Her Sisters*
Linda Hunt, *The Year of Living Dangerously*	Peggy Ashcroft, *A Passage to India*	Anjelica Huston, *Prizzi's Honor*	Dianne Wiest, *Hannah and Her Sisters*
James L. Brooks, *Terms of Endearment*	Milos Forman, *Amadeus*	Sydney Pollack, *Out of Africa*	Oliver Stone, *Platoon*
James L. Brooks, *Terms of Endearment*	Peter Shaffer, *Amadeus*	Kurt Luedtke, *Out of Africa*	Ruth Prawer Jhabvala, *A Room with a View*
Horton Foote, *Tender Mercies*	Robert Benton, *Places in the Heart*	William Kelley, Pamela Wallace, and Earl W. Wallace, *Witness*	Woody Allen, *Hannah and Her Sisters*
"Flashdance . . . What a Feeling" *(Flashdance)*	"I Just Called To Say I Love You" *(The Woman in Red)*	"Say You, Say Me" *(White Nights)*	"Take My Breath Away" *(Top Gun)*
The Right Stuff; Yentl (Song Score/Adaptation)	*A Passage to India*; *Purple Rain* (Song Score)	*Out of Africa*	*'Round Midnight*
Fanny & Alexander	*The Killing Fields*	*Out of Africa*	*The Mission*
Fanny & Alexander	*Amadeus*	*Ran*	*A Room with a View*
Fanny & Alexander	*Amadeus*	*Out of Africa*	*A Room with a View*
The Right Stuff	*The Killing Fields*	*Witness*	*Platoon*
Fanny & Alexander (Sweden)	*Dangerous Moves* (Switzerland)	*The Official Story* (Argentina)	*The Assault* (The Netherlands)
The Right Stuff	*Amadeus*	*Out of Africa*	*Platoon*
The Right Stuff	—	*Back to the Future*	*Aliens*
—	*Amadeus*	*Mask*	*The Fly*
Return of the Jedi	*Indiana Jones and the Temple of Doom*	*Cocoon*	*Aliens*
Sundae in New York (Animated); *Boys and Girls* (Live Action)	*Charade* (Animated); *Up* (Live Action)	*Anna & Bella* (Animated); *Molly's Pilgrim* (Live Action)	*A Greek Tragedy* (Animated); *Precious Images* (Live Action)
Flamenco at 5:15 (Shorts); *He Makes Me Feel Like Dancin'* (Features)	*The Stone Carvers* (Shorts); *The Times of Harvey Milk* (Features)	*Witness to War: Dr. Charlie Clements* (Shorts); *Broken Rainbow* (Features)	*Women—For America, for the World* (Shorts); *Artie Shaw: Time Is All You've Got* and *Down and Out in America* (Features)

	1987	1988	1989
Picture	*The Last Emperor*	*Rain Man*	*Driving Miss Daisy*
Actor	Michael Douglas, *Wall Street*	Dustin Hoffman, *Rain Man*	Daniel Day-Lewis, *My Left Foot*
Actress	Cher, *Moonstruck*	Jodie Foster, *The Accused*	Jessica Tandy, *Driving Miss Daisy*
Supporting Actor	Sean Connery, *The Untouchables*	Kevin Kline, *A Fish Called Wanda*	Denzel Washington, *Glory*
Supporting Actress	Olympia Dukakis, *Moonstruck*	Geena Davis, *The Accidental Tourist*	Brenda Fricker, *My Left Foot*
Director	Bernardo Bertolucci, *The Last Emperor*	Barry Levinson, *Rain Man*	Oliver Stone, *Born on the Fourth of July*
Adapted Screenplay	Mark Peploe and Bernardo Bertolucci, *The Last Emperor*	Christopher Hampton, *Dangerous Liaisons*	Tom Schulman, *Dead Poets Society*
Original Screenplay	John Patrick Shanley, *Moonstruck*	Ronald Bass and Barry Morrow, *Rain Man*	Alfred Uhry, *Driving Miss Daisy*
Song	"(I've Had) The Time of My Life" *(Dirty Dancing)*	"Let the River Run" *(Working Girl)*	"Under the Sea" *(The Little Mermaid)*
Original Score	*The Last Emperor*	*The Milagro Beanfield War*	*The Little Mermaid*
Cinematography	*The Last Emperor*	*Mississippi Burning*	*Glory*
Costume Design	*The Last Emperor*	*Dangerous Liaisons*	*Henry V*
Art Direction—Set Decoration	*The Last Emperor*	*Dangerous Liaisons*	*Batman*
Film Editing	*The Last Emperor*	*Who Framed Roger Rabbit*	*Born on the Fourth of July*
Foreign Language Film	*Babette's Feast* (Denmark)	*Pelle the Conqueror* (Denmark)	*Cinema Paradiso* (Italy)
Sound	*The Last Emperor*	*Bird*	*Glory*
Sound Effects (Editing)	—	*Who Framed Roger Rabbit*	*Indiana Jones and the Last Crusade*
Makeup	*Harry and the Hendersons*	*Beetlejuice*	*Driving Miss Daisy*
Visual Effects	*Innerspace*	*Who Framed Roger Rabbit*	*The Abyss*
Short Films	*The Man Who Planted Trees* (Animated); *Ray's Male Heterosexual Dance Hall* (Live Action)	*Tin Toy* (Animated); *The Appointments of Dennis Jennings* (Live Action)	*Balance* (Animated); *Work Experience* (Live Action)
Documentaries	*Young at Heart* (Shorts); *The Ten-Year Lunch: The Wit and the Legend of the Algonquin Round Table* (Features)	*You Don't Have to Die* (Shorts); *Hotel Terminus: The Life and Times of Klaus Barbie* (Features)	*The Johnstown Flood* (Shorts); *Common Threads: Stories from the Quilt* (Features)

1990	1991	1992	1993
Dances with Wolves	*The Silence of the Lambs*	*Unforgiven*	*Schindler's List*
Jeremy Irons, *Reversal of Fortune*	Anthony Hopkins, *The Silence of the Lambs*	Al Pacino, *Scent of a Woman*	Tom Hanks, *Philadelphia*
Kathy Bates, *Misery*	Jodie Foster, *The Silence of the Lambs*	Emma Thompson, *Howards End*	Holly Hunter, *The Piano*
Joe Pesci, *GoodFellas*	Jack Palance, *City Slickers*	Gene Hackman, *Unforgiven*	Tommy Lee Jones, *The Fugitive*
Whoopi Goldberg, *Ghost*	Mercedes Ruehl, *The Fisher King*	Marisa Tomei, *My Cousin Vinny*	Anna Paquin, *The Piano*
Kevin Costner, *Dances with Wolves*	Jonathan Demme, *The Silence of the Lambs*	Clint Eastwood, *Unforgiven*	Steven Spielberg, *Schindler's List*
Michael Blake, *Dances with Wolves*	Ted Tally, *The Silence of the Lambs*	Ruth Prawer Jhabvala, *Howards End*	Steven Zaillian, *Schindler's List*
Bruce Joel Rubin, *Ghost*	Callie Khouri, *Thelma & Louise*	Neil Jordan, *The Crying Game*	Jane Campion, *The Piano*
"Sooner or Later (I Always Get My Man)" *(Dick Tracy)*	"Beauty and the Beast" *(Beauty and the Beast)*	"A Whole New World" *(Aladdin)*	"Streets of Philadelphia" (*Philadelphia*)
Dances with Wolves	*Beauty and the Beast*	*Aladdin*	*Schindler's List*
Dances with Wolves	*JFK*	*A River Runs Through It*	*Schindler's List*
Cyrano de Bergerac	*Bugsy*	*Bram Stoker's Dracula*	*The Age of Innocence*
Dick Tracy	*Bugsy*	*Howards End*	*Schindler's List*
Dances with Wolves	*JFK*	*Unforgiven*	*Schindler's List*
Journey of Hope (Switzerland)	*Mediterraneo* (Italy)	*Indochine* (France)	*Belle Epoque* (Spain)
Dances with Wolves	*Terminator 2: Judgment Day*	*The Last of the Mohicans*	*Jurassic Park*
The Hunt for Red October	*Terminator 2: Judgment Day*	*Bram Stoker's Dracula*	*Jurassic Park*
Dick Tracy	*Terminator 2: Judgment Day*	*Bram Stoker's Dracula*	*Mrs. Doubtfire*
Total Recall	*Terminator 2: Judgment Day*	*Death Becomes Her*	*Jurassic Park*
Creature Comforts (Animated); *The Lunch Date* (Live Action)	*Manipulation* (Animated); *Session Man* (Live Action)	*Mona Lisa Descending a Staircase* (Animated); *Omnibus* (Live Action)	*The Wrong Trousers* (Animated); *Black Rider* (Live Action)
Days of Waiting (Shorts); *American Dream* (Features)	*Deadly Deception: General Electric, Nuclear Weapons and Our Environment* (Shorts); *In the Shadow of the Stars* (Features)	*Educating Peter* (Shorts); *The Panama Deception* (Features)	*Defending Our Lives* (Shorts) *Am a Promise: The Children of Stanton Elementary School* (Features)

FILM AWARDS

NATIONAL SOCIETY OF FILM CRITICS

Annual Awards for Best Film

1966 Blow-Up
1967 Persona
1968 Shame
1969 Z
1970 M*A*S*H
1971 Claire's Knee
1972 The Discreet Charm of the Bourgeoisie
1973 Day for Night
1974 Scenes from a Marriage
1975 Nashville
1976 All The President's Men
1977 Annie Hall
1978 Get Out Your Handkerchiefs
1979 Breaking Away
1980 Melvin and Howard
1981 Atlantic City
1982 Tootsie
1983 Night of the Shooting Stars
1984 Stranger Than Paradise
1985 Ran
1986 Blue Velvet
1987 The Dead
1988 The Unbearable Lightness of Being
1989 Drugstore Cowboy
1990 GoodFellas
1991 Life Is Sweet
1992 Unforgiven
1993 Schindler's List

SUNDANCE FILM FESTIVAL

GRAND JURY PRIZE

1978 Girlfriends
1979 Spirit in the Wind
1981 Heartland
Gal Young Un

Dramatic

1982 Street Music
1983 Purple Haze
1984 Old Enough
1985 Blood Simple
1986 Smooth Talk
1987 Waiting for the Moon
Trouble with Dick
1988 Heat and Sunlight
1989 True Love
1990 Chameleon Street
1991 Poison
1992 In the Soup
1993 Ruby in Paradise
Public Access
1994 What Happened Was . . .

FILMMAKERS TROPHY

Dramatic

1989 Powwow Highway
1990 House Party
1991 Privilege
1992 Zebrahead
1993 Fly By Night
1994 Clerks

AUDIENCE AWARD

Dramatic

1989 sex, lies, and videotape
1990 Longtime Companion
1991 One Cup of Coffee
1992 The Waterdance
1993 El Mariachi
1994 Spanking the Monkey

CANNES FILM FESTIVAL

Palme d'Or for Best Film

1946 La Bataille du rail (France)
1947 Antoine et Antoinette (France)
1948 No festival
1949 The Third Man (G.B.)
1950 No festival
1951 Miracle in Milan (Italy)
Miss Julie (Sweden)
1952 Othello (Morocco)
Two Cents Worth of Hope (Italy)
1953 Wages of Fear (France)
1954 Gate of Hell (Japan)
1955 Marty (U.S.)
1956 World of Silence (France)
1957 Friendly Persuasion (U.S.)
1958 The Cranes are Flying (U.S.S.R.)
1959 Black Orpheus (France)
1960 La Dolce Vita (Italy)
1961 Viridiana (Spain)
Une Aussi longue absence (France)
1962 The Given Word (Brazil)
1963 The Leopard (Italy)
1964 The Umbrellas of Cherbourg (France)
1965 The Knack (G.B.)
1966 A Man and a Woman (France)
Signore e Signori (Italy)
1967 Blow-Up (G.B.)
1968 Festival disrupted; no awards given
1969 If . . . (G.B.)
1970 M*A*S*H (U.S.)
1971 The Go-Between (G.B.)
1972 The Working Class Goes to Paradise (Italy)
The Mattei Affair (Italy)
1973 Scarecrow (U.S.)
The Hireling (G.B.)
1974 The Conversation (U.S.)
1975 Chronicle of the Burning Years (Algeria)
1976 Taxi Driver (U.S.)
1977 Padre Padrone (Italy)
1978 L'Albero Degli Zoccoli (Italy)
1979 The Tin Drum (Germany)
Apocalypse Now (U.S.)
1980 All That Jazz (U.S.)
Kagemusha (Japan)
1981 Man of Iron (Poland)
1982 Missing (U.S.)
Yol (Turkey)
1983 The Ballad of Narayama (Japan)
1984 Paris, Texas (Germany)
1985 When Father Was Away On Business (Yugoslavia)
1986 The Mission (G.B.)
1987 Under the Sun of Satan (France)
1988 Pelle the Conqueror (Denmark)
1989 sex, lies, and videotape (U.S.)
1990 Wild at Heart (U.S.)
1991 Barton Fink (U.S.)
1992 The Best Intentions (Denmark)
1993 The Piano (New Zealand)
Farewell My Concubine (Hong Kong)
1994 Pulp Fiction (U.S.)

VENICE FILM FESTIVAL

Golden Lion [for Best Film or Best Foreign Film]

1932 No official award
1933 No festival
1934 Man of Aran (G.B.)
1935 Anna Karenina (U.S.)
1936 Der Kaiser von Kalifornien (Germany)
1937 Un Carnet debal (France)
1938 Olympia (Germany)
1939 No award given
1940 Der Postmeister (Germany)
1941 Ohm Kruger (Germany)
1942 Der grosse König (Germany)
1943 No festival
1944 No festival
1945 No festival
1946 The Southerner (U.S.)

1947 Sirena (Czechoslovakia)
1948 Hamlet (G.B.)
1949 Manon (France)
1950 Justice is Done (France)
1951 Rashomon (Japan)
1952 Forbidden Games (France)
1953 No award given
1954 Romeo and Juliet (Italy/G.B.)
1955 Ordet (Denmark)
1956 No award given
1957 Aparajito (India)
1958 Muhomatsu no Issho (Japan)
1959 Il Generale della Rovere (Italy)
1960 Le Passage du Rhin (France)
1961 Last Year at Marienbad (France)
1962 Childhood of Ivan (U.S.S.R.)
1963 Le Mani sulla città (Italy)
1964 Red Desert (Italy)
1965 Of a Thousand Delights (Italy)
1966 Battle of Algiers (Italy)
1967 Belle de jour (France)
1968 Die Aristen in der Zirkuskuppel (Germany)

Jury and award system discontinued 1969–79

1980 Gloria (U.S.)
Atlantic City (France/Canada)
1981 Die Bleierne Zeit (Germany)
1982 The State of Things (Germany)
1983 Prénom Carmen (France/Switzerland)
1984 Year of the Quiet Sun (Poland)
1985 Sans toit ni loi (Vagabonde) (France)
1986 Le Rayon vert (France)
1987 Au revoir, les enfants (France)
1988 The Legend of the Holy Drinker (Italy)
1989 A City of Sadness (Taiwan)
1990 Rosencrantz and Guildenstern Are Dead (G.B.)
1991 Urga (U.S.S.R./France)
1992 Qiu Ju (China)
1993 Blue (France)
Short Cuts (U.S.)

BERLIN FILM FESTIVAL AWARD

Golden Bear Award for Best Film

1953 The Wages of Fear (France)
1954 Hobson's Choice (G.B.)
1955 The Rats (Germany)
1956 Invitation to the Dance (G.B.)
1957 Twelve Angry Men (U.S.)
1958 The End of the Day (Sweden)
1959 The Cousins (France)
1960 Lazarillo de Tormes (Spain)
1961 La Notte (Italy)
1962 A Kind of Loving (G.B.)
1963 Oath of Obedience (Germany)
The Devil (Italy)
1964 Dry Summer (Turkey)
1965 Alphaville (France)
1966 Cul-de-Sac (G.B.)
1967 Le Depart (Belgium)
1968 Ole Dole Duff (Sweden)
1969 Early Years (Yugoslavia)
1970 No award
1971 The Garden of the Finzi-Continis (Italy)
1972 The Canterbury Tales (Italy)
1973 Distant Thunder (India)
1974 The Apprenticeship of Duddy Kravitz (Canada)
1975 Orkobefogadas (Hungary)
1976 Buffalo Bill and the Indians (U.S.) [award declined]
1977 The Ascent (U.S.S.R.)
1978 The Trouts (Spain)
The Words of Max (Spain)
1979 David (Germany)
1980 Heartland (U.S.)
Palermo Oder Wolfsburg (Germany)
1981 Di Presa Di Presa (Spain)
1982 Die Sehnsucht der Veronica Voss (Germany)
1983 Ascendancy (G.B.)
The Beehive (Spain)
1984 Love Streams (U.S.)
1985 Wetherby (G.B.)
Die Frau und der Fremde (Germany)
1986 Stammhein (Germany)
1987 The Theme (U.S.S.R.)
1988 Red Sorghum (China)
1989 Rain Man (U.S.)
1990 Music Box (U.S.)
Larks on a String (Czechoslovakia)
1991 House of Smiles (Italy)
1992 Grand Canyon (U.S.)
1993 The Woman from the Lake of Scented Souls (China)
The Wedding Banquet (Taiwan/U.S.)
1994 In the Name of the Father (UK/Ireland)

INDEPENDENT SPIRIT AWARDS

These prizes are considered the Oscars of the independent film world.

Best Feature

1986 After Hours
1987 Platoon
1988 River's Edge
1989 Stand and Deliver
1990 sex, lies, and videotape
1991 The Grifters
1992 Rambling Rose
1993 The Player
1994 Short Cuts

Best First Feature

1987 Spike Lee, director
She's Gotta Have It
1988 Emile Ardolino, director
Dirty Dancing
1989 Donald Petrie, director
Mystic Pizza
1990 Michael Lehmann, director
Heathers
1991 Whit Stillman, producer/director
Metropolitan
1992 Matty Rich, director
Straight Out of Brooklyn
1993 Neal Jimenez and Michael Steinberg, directors
The Waterdance
1994 Robert Rodriquez, director
El Mariachi

Best Director

1986 Martin Scorsese
After Hours
1987 Oliver Stone
Platoon
1988 John Huston
The Dead
1989 Ramon Menendez
Stand and Deliver
1990 Steven Soderbergh
sex, lies, and videotape
1991 Charles Burnett
To Sleep with Anger
1992 Martha Coolidge
Rambling Rose
1993 Carl Franklin
One False Move
1994 Robert Altman
Short Cuts

Best Screenplay

1986 Horton Foote
The Trip to Bountiful
1987 Oliver Stone
Platoon
1988 Neal Jimenez
River's Edge
1989 Ramon Menendez and Tom Musca
Stand and Deliver
1990 Gus Van Sant Jr. and Daniel Yost
Drugstore Cowboy
1991 Charles Burnett
To Sleep with Anger
1992 Gus Van Sant Jr.
My Own Private Idaho
1993 Neal Jimenez
The Waterdance

1994 Robert Altman and Frank Barhydt
Short Cuts

Best Cinematographer

1986 Toyomichi Kurita
Trouble In Mind
1987 Bob Richardson
Platoon
1988 Haskell Wexler
Matewan
1989 Sven Nykvist
The Unbearable Lightness of Being
1990 Robert Yeoman
Drugstore Cowboy
1991 Fred Elmes
Wild at Heart
1992 Walt Lloyd
Kafka
1993 Frederick Elmes
Night on Earth
1994 Lisa Rinzler
Menace II Society

Best Actor

1986 M. Emmet Walsh
Blood Simple
1987 James Woods
Salvador
1988 Dennis Quaid
The Big Easy
1989 Edward James Olmos
Stand and Deliver
1990 Matt Dillon
Drugstore Cowboy
1991 Danny Glover
To Sleep with Anger
1992 River Phoenix
My Own Private Idaho
1993 Harvey Keitel
Bad Lieutenant
1994 Jeff Bridges
American Heart

Best Actress

1986 Geraldine Page
The Trip to Bountiful
1987 Isabella Rossellini
Blue Velvet
1988 Sally Kirkland
Anna
1989 Jodie Foster
Five Corners
1990 Andie MacDowell
sex, lies, and videotape
1991 Anjelica Huston
The Grifters
1992 Judy Davis
Impromptu
1993 Fairuza Balk
Gas, Food, Lodging
1994 Ashley Judd
Ruby in Paradise

Best Supporting Actor

1988 Morgan Freeman
Street Smart
1989 Lou Diamond Phillips
Stand and Deliver
1990 Max Perlich
Drugstore Cowboy
1991 Bruce Davison
Longtime Companion
1992 David Strathairn
City of Hope
1993 Steve Buscemi
Reservoir Dogs
1994 Christopher Lloyd
Twenty Bucks

Best Supporting Actress

1988 Anjelica Huston
The Dead
1989 Rosanna De Soto
Stand and Deliver
1990 Laura San Giacomo
sex, lies, and videotape
1991 Sheryl Lee Ralph
To Sleep with Anger
1992 Diane Ladd
Rambling Rose
1993 Alfre Woodard
Passion Fish
1994 Lili Taylor
Household Saints

Best Foreign Film

1986 Kiss of the Spider Woman
1987 A Room with a View
1988 My Life as a Dog
1989 Wings of Desire
1990 My Left Foot
1991 Sweetie
1992 An Angel at My Table
1993 The Crying Game
1994 The Piano

MTV MOVIE AWARDS

Best Movie

1992 Terminator 2: Judgment Day
1993 A Few Good Men
1994 Menace II Society

Best Male Performance

1992 Arnold Schwarzenegger
Terminator 2: Judgment Day
1993 Denzel Washington
Malcolm X
1994 Tom Hanks
Philadelphia

Best Female Performance

1992 Linda Hamilton
Terminator 2: Judgment Day
1993 Sharon Stone
Basic Instinct
1994 Janet Jackson
Poetic Justice

Breakthrough Performance

1992 Edward Furlong
Terminator 2: Judgment Day
1993 Marisa Tomei
My Cousin Vinny
1994 Alicia Silverstone
The Crush

Most Desirable Male

1992 Keanu Reeves
Point Break
1993 Chistian Slater
Untamed Heart
1994 William Baldwin
Sliver

Most Desirable Female

1992 Linda Hamilton
Terminator 2: Judgment Day
1993 Sharon Stone
Basic Instinct
1994 Janet Jackson
Poetic Justice

Best On-Screen Duo

1992 Mike Myers and Dana Carvey
Wayne's World
1993 Mel Gibson and Danny Glover
Lethal Weapon 3
1994 Harrison Ford and Tommy Lee Jones
The Fugitive

Best Villain

1992 Rebecca DeMornay
The Hand That Rocks the Cradle
1993 Jennifer Jason Leigh
Single White Female
1994 Alicia Silverstone
The Crush

Best Comedic Performance

1992 Billy Crystal
City Slickers
1993 Robin Williams
Aladdin

1994 Robin Williams
Mrs. Doubtfire

Best Song
1992 Bryan Adams
"(Everything I Do) I Do It For You" (*Robin Hood: Prince of Thieves*)
1993 Whitney Houston
"I Will Always Love You" (*The Bodyguard*)
1994 Michael Jackson
"Will You Be There" (*Free Willy)*

Best Kiss
1992 Macaulay Culkin and Anna Chlumsky
My Girl
1993 Marisa Tomei and Christian Slater
Untamed Heart
1994 Woody Harrelson and Demi Moore
Indecent Proposal

Best Action Sequence
1992 Terminator 2: Judgment Day
1993 Lethal Weapon 3
1994 The Fugitive

Best New Filmmaker Award
1992 John Singleton
Boyz N the Hood
1993 Carl Franklin
One False Move
1994 Steven Zaillian
Searching for Bobby Fischer

Lifetime Achievement Award
1992 Jason Voorhees
Friday the 13th
1993 The Three Stooges
1994 Richard Roundree
Shaft film series

DIRECTOR'S GUILD AWARDS

For Theatrical Direction

Year	Film	Director
1948–49	A Letter To Three Wives	Joseph Mankiewicz
1949–50	All The King's Men	Robert Rossen
1950–51	All About Eve	Joseph Mankiewicz
1951	A Place in the Sun	George Stevens
1952	The Quiet Man	John Ford
1953	From Here to Eternity	Fred Zinnemann
1954	On the Waterfront	Elia Kazan
1955	Marty	Delbert Mann
1956	Giant	George Stevens
1957	Bridge on the River Kwai	David Lean
1958	Gigi	Vincente Minnelli
1959	Ben-Hur	William Wyler
1960	The Apartment	Billy Wilder
1961	West Side Story	Robert Wise and Jerome Robbins
1962	Lawrence of Arabia	David Lean
1963	Tom Jones	Tony Richardson
1964	My Fair Lady	George Cukor
1965	The Sound of Music	Robert Wise
1966	A Man for All Seasons	Fred Zinnemann
1967	The Graduate	Mike Nichols
1968	The Lion In Winter	Anthony Harvey
1969	Midnight Cowboy	John Schlesinger
1970	Patton	Franklin J. Schaffner
1971	The French Connection	William Friedkin
1972	The Godfather	Francis Ford Coppola
1973	The Sting	George Roy Hill
1974	The Godfather, Part II	Francis Ford Coppola
1975	One Flew over the Cuckoo's Nest	Milos Forman
1976	Rocky	John G. Avildsen
1977	Annie Hall	Woody Allen
1978	The Deer Hunter	Michael Cimino
1979	Kramer vs. Kramer	Robert Benton
1980	Ordinary People	Robert Redford
1981	Reds	Warren Beatty
1982	Gandhi	Richard Attenborough
1983	Terms of Endearment	James L. Brooks
1984	Amadeus	Milos Forman
1985	The Color Purple	Steven Spielberg
1986	Platoon	Oliver Stone
1987	The Last Emperor	Bernardo Bertolucci
1988	Rain Man	Barry Levinson
1989	Born on the Fourth of July	Oliver Stone
1990	Dances with Wolves	Kevin Costner
1991	The Silence of the Lambs	Jonathan Demme
1992	Unforgiven	Clint Eastwood
1993	Schindler's List	Steven Spielberg

Hey, joggers: let's run the 100 (miles, that is)
JULY 14, 1980 • 75¢
People weekly
Custody-fight kidnapping
C&W throb Eddie Rabbitt
WHO SHOT J.R.?
Five Dallas insiders know, some famous Texans guess—and you can too (your ballot is on page 89)
December 6, 1976•50¢
People weekly
Bardot, the new name in labels
Bill Bradley, cerebral jock
Picasso's widow ends mourning a multimillionaire
Charlie's Angels
How three sweet Southern girls became TV's hit team
TUBE
NAUGHTY NASTASSIA KINSKI
CAT'S MEOW
People weekly
A Miss America conquers a stroke
The ultimate health spa
Black stars vs. Hollywood
General Hospital's
TONY GEARY
Looking for life after Luke, he breaks in a raunchy casino act and admits his 'affair' with Liz was a phony
Hollywood bows to Neil Simon
How to fix dinner for 140—White House style
Will Bobby Orr ever skate again?
March 27, 1978•60¢
People weekly
Farewell to The Family
We'll miss them and they'll miss each other

BABYLON 5

Syndicated

Spun off from a middling sci-fi movie last spring, this project about a twenty-third-century space station hasn't made many changes in its transition to a series. The visual aspects are excellent, but the stories falter and the scripts are feeblest when they ape the philosophical tenor of the current *Star Trek* franchises. Babble on, space dudes. It doesn't help the show to have such a wooden presence at the helm. As Commander Sinclair, lead actor Michael O'Hare is like Lorne Greene under hypnosis. Grade: C+

BAKERSFIELD P.D.

Fox

This cop comedy was by far the funniest program of the new season last fall. And it was the lowest-rated one—but the network generously revived the program for a summer run. Bakersfield is *Hill Street Blues* meets *Mayberry R.F.D.*—with an attitude. Giancarlo Esposito stars as an African-American cop who ends up working with a collection of the strangest yokels this side of Floyd the Barber. The jokes are subtle, the show laughtrackless, and there are even attempts to fold in a moral or two without getting pedantic about it. This series is as funny as TV gets. Grade: A

BIRDLAND

ABC

Brian Dennehy is a big guy with a big talent. In his third TV series in three decades (after *Big Shamus, Little Shamus* and *Star of the Family*), he finally gets a role commensurate with his stature. Dennehy plays the head of a hospital psychiatric unit first in New York, then in Oakland. He gives the hospital administrators fits with his disdain for budgets and procedure. And the good doctor's personal life is something of a mess. But he's also a healer with an uncommonly common touch. The show deftly balances the serious and the comic. Grade: B+

THE BYRDS OF PARADISE

ABC

Aloha. Timothy Busfield (*thirtysomething*) plays a Yale professor and widower with three children who decides to make a fresh start in Hawaii as a prep-school headmaster. The show is simply (and simpily) a Polynesian version of *Going to Extremes*, last year's series about medical-school students in the Caribbean. It runs aground on the same shoals: a slavishly metronomic seriocomic rhythm, an attitude toward the native population that vacillates between glorification and condescension, overwritten scripts, and a parade of tortuously idiosyncratic minor characters. Grade: C

CHRISTY

CBS

Based on Catherine Marshall's novel, this series stars Kellie Martin (*Life Goes On*) as an inquisitive young woman of some refinement who takes a job at a mission school deep in the Great Smoky Mountains of Tennessee in 1912. In a curious bit of casting, Tyne Daly (*Cagney & Lacey*) plays her Quaker mentor. It takes some adjustment for Martin to understand these rough-hewn mountain people and their superstitions, blood feuds, and stubborn pride. Filmed on location in the mist-shrouded Smokies, this wholesome show is much like *The Waltons* and *Dr. Quinn*, but rendered with a more literate sensibility and more conviction. The acting, however, isn't particularly distinguished. Grade: B

THE CRITIC

ABC

Jay Sherman is a plump, balding, divorced New Yorker. But this nebbish pursues a noble profession: critic. He's the host of TV's *Coming Attractions*, on which he dismissively rates movies on the "Shermometer." Oh, by the way, Sherman is a cartoon (voice by Jon Lovitz). This animated series is slyly amusing when sticking it to showbiz, taking sarcastic swipes at everyone from Steven Seagal to Gene Shalit. At its best, it's still several strides behind the savage, protean wit of *The Simpsons*, and the humor sputters when the focus is personal—detailing Sherman's dating woes or his relationship with his son. Grade: B

DEAD AT 21

MTV

Jack Noseworthy, who looks like a grunge-era Opie, plays a twenty-year-old who discovers he is part of a secret bioengineering experiment that will make his brain flame out before he's completely legal—unless a ruthless government agent (Whip Hubley) kills him first. Hmm, doesn't leave the dude much time to find the twisted genius who messed with his head. So Noseworthy takes it on the lam with a jaded Gen-X demoiselle (Lisa Dean Ryan). MTV's first foray into an adventure series marries the chase premise of *The Fugitive* with the generational paranoid tone of *Wild Palms*. Too bad the writing and production values are so lame. Grade: C+

DUCKMAN
USA

The hero of this grown-up cartoon is a bumbling private detective and ineffectual paterfamilias. He's hapless, hectored, henpecked, and trying to quit smoking. No wonder Duckman is one cranky drake. In temperament, the crudely drawn Duckman (voice provided by *Seinfeld*'s Jason Alexander) is like his relative Daffy, constantly blowing gaskets over life's frustrations. Inventive and daft, this cartoon is just plain ducky. Grade: B+

THE GEORGE CARLIN SHOW
Fox

Carlin plays George O'Grady, a New York City neighborhood guy and an aging iconoclast—not a big stretch. O'Grady's main haunt is a musty working-class bar, more like Moe's Tavern on *The Simpsons* than *Cheers*. The class act of the place is a shifty bookie (Alex Rocco). The sitcom's flavor is somewhat bland, with just a whiff of desperation about it. But the mix of characters is likable, and how many Fox shows can you say that about? Grade: B

MIDDLEMARCH
PBS

Masterpiece Theatre takes on another daunting task: dramatizing George Eliot's labyrinthine 1871 novel. The sumptuous re-creation of life in a provincial British town in early Victorian times dines on social injustice, self-seeking, dashed idealism, poor judgment, and outright folly. There are numerous plots and myriad characters. The miniseries is beautifully acted and Eliot's ingenious plot is ultimately involving. But there is no gainsaying that this is demanding and ponderous fare. *Middlemarch* is a thick, rather bland pudding served out formally over six Sabbaths. Grade: B

MODELS INC.
Fox

Sure this eagerly anticipated *Melrose Place* spinoff is about fashion models, but all is not vanity in Fox's latest drama of the depraved. It's part underwear ad, part catfight, part *Lifestyles of the Rich and Famous* and part psycho ward. So far it's also pretty stiff and strident. The only old pro in the cast is *Dallas* vet Linda Gray, executing an over-the-top Lucrezia Borgia imitation here. But there's no one to root for except the questionable innocent played by Cassidy Rae. Even so, this is passable prime-time fare. Grade: B-

MONTY
Fox

Henry Winkler plays Monty Richardson, a comically castigative, conservative TV personality on a small Long Island station. Of course, it's coincidental that his sidekick (played by Tom McGowan) is a dead ringer for Rush Limbaugh. From his TV pulpit, Monty can bully the world, baiting environmentalists, chiding liberals and deriding Democrats. At home, however, Monty finds it considerably harder to play the demagogue of the breakfast table. Monty's principal antagonist is his prospective daughter-in-law (China Kantner), a free spirit with a sharp tongue. This is essentially a contrived and scattered update of *All in the Family*. Grade: B

PRIME SUSPECT 3
PBS

Our favorite British bulldog, Detective Chief Inspector Jane Tennison, is back and working the seedier side of London. In this brawny sequel, Tennison (Helen Mirren) has transferred to the vice squad in Soho, an underworld of transvestite clubs and young homeless runaways. In this tantalizing *Mystery!* feast, Mirren is once again marvelous as a determined professional swimming against a tide of intrigue. In *Prime Suspect 2* she gave up smoking; this time she gives up something considerably more precious. David Thewlis is memorable as a dissolute and dangerous chicken hawk. Grade: A

THE REAL WORLD
MTV

It's the third go-round for MTV's melting-pot concept, which throws together a group of young strangers into a communal setting and films the results. So we get seven new faces in a new city (San Francisco). It's clear by now that the one thing the creators of this show demand of their subjects is sparks—preferably romantic, but failing that, antagonistic. This crowd may not be so accommodating. Sure, the gloves start coming off over the hygiene habits of Puck, the rowdy, anarchic bike messenger, but when this septet has a problem they sit down and talk about it. BOR-ING!!! Grade: B-

ROBOCOP
Syndicated

It's 2005, and Motor City is a shambles. The forces of evil run rampant. Fortunately for us, a supremely efficient law-enforcement machine patrols the streets of Detroit. Yes, as you probably guessed from the title, the B-movie cyber-action series is now a TV cyber-action series. Richard Eden plays the former cop killed in the line of duty, then reanimated and mechanized. The formula translates well to the small screen in part because the original source material was pretty cheesy to begin with and in part because the RoboDude is one potent multimedia icon. Grade: B

704 HAUSER
CBS

Norman Lear, the creator of *All in the Family*, puts a twist on his old hit. The setting is the same: the Bunkers' modest tract house in Queens, N.Y. But the outspoken head of the household is now Ernest Cumberbatch (John Amos), a grumpy African-American, having heated polemical arguments with his ultraconservative son (T. E. Russell). Yes, it's role reversal time. But the politics grow more fuzzy with each episode (we're repeatedly told Amos is a liberal, but there's no evidence that this is the case). The result is a show that's talky, stale, and rarely funny. Grade: C

THESE FRIENDS OF MINE
ABC

An irresistible treat, this japery combines the bent appeal of *Seinfeld*, *Mad About You* and the best parts of *Anything but Love*. Like those shows, it's built around the silly antics of a tight-knit group of adults who bond to each other in a very adolescent way. *These Friends* (now called *Ellen*) has something those series don't: stand-up comedian Ellen DeGeneres as the star. With her pop-eyed innocence, her self-aware goofiness, she's a sitcom natural. Grade: A-

THUNDER ALLEY
ABC

TV perennial Ed Asner (Lou Grant, et al.) is a former stock car driver who now runs an Indiana garage. Then his divorced daughter (Diane Venora) and her three noisy young kids move in with him above the shop. The show is supposed to contrast generational child-rearing techniques: the traditional authoritarian method vs. the more nurturing '90s approach. In fact, it's not much more than a half hour of kiddie giddiness and senior stridency. Grade: C-

THUNDER IN PARADISE
Syndicated

This unapologetically gaudy flamer stars retired wrestler Hulk Hogan (who henceforth wants to be referred to as Terry Hogan) and Chris Lemmon. Together they own and operate a high-tech armed-to-the-gunwales cigarette boat. Hogan is the muscle. Lemmon is the brains. The beauty is provided by Carol Alt as a beachfront bartendress. Only one aspect of the series remains Rabelaisian: in order to give the Hulkster a decent workout, the villains have to be gargantuan. Except for the bad guys, however, everything about the show seems to be shrinking a little already. Grade: C+

TO PLAY THE KING
PBS

As if Bob Packwood hadn't done enough to tarnish the reputation of politicians, Francis Urquhart is back. In this scintillating sequel to *House of Cards*, Urquhart (played once again with brilliant sangfroid by Ian Richardson) is firmly entrenched as Britain's prime minister. But he's rankled by the new monarch, the slightly eccentric but outspoken king (Michael Kitchen) who has recently ascended to the throne. Urquhart sets about schooling the new king in how brutal political hardball can be. Grade: A

VIPER
NBC

The creators of this show must have had an easy time pitching it to the network: "It's *Knight Rider* meets *Robocop*." 'Nuf said, dudes! In this futuristic adventure fantasy, Dorian Harewood plays a wheelchair-bound scientist who designs a sleek, high-tech crime-fighting automobile (actually it's a customized Dodge Viper). James McCaffrey plays a career criminal who gets a personality and memory transplant and is installed as the car's driver. But McCaffrey's unsavory past keeps reaching out for him. Visually and vehicularly, the show is definitely cool. But the plots and characters land firmly on the hackneyed side of the street. Grade: C+

WHAT'S ON CABLE TONIGHT?

As systems upgrade to accommodate the much-vaunted 500-channel promised land, the answer to this question will soon be, "Everything." But for now, a guide is helpful. The following is a complete list of all national cable television networks, according to the 1994 National Cable Television Association listing.

Action Pay Per View—action, adventure, thriller movies

Adam and Eve Channel—adult movies

American Movie Classics (AMC)—Hollywood's greatest films

Americana Television Network—American music, people, and pastimes

America's Disability Channel—programming dedicated to the interests of the disabled

America's Talking—all talk

Arts & Entertainment Network—comedy, drama, documentaries, performing arts

Black Entertainment Television (BET)—sports, drama, sitcoms, specials

The Box—viewer-programmed music videos of all types

Bravo—cultural offerings including films, arts specials, interviews

Cable Health Club—aerobics, fitness, health

Cable Video Store—movies and special events

Caribbean Satellite Network—music and information from the Caribbean

The Cartoon Network—cartoons

Cinemax—films

Country Music Television (CMT)—country videos

CNBC—business, personal finance, and talk programming

Cable News Network (CNN)—news, weather, sports

Comedy Central—all-comedy programming

Courtroom Television Network—live and taped trial coverage and legal features

The Crime Channel—crime-related programming, including series, news, features

C-SPAN (Cable Satellite Public Affairs Network)—straight national and international news

C-SPAN 2—live coverage of the U.S. Senate and public affairs programming

Deep Dish TV—educational programming

The Discovery Channel—nature, history, technology, and adventure

The Disney Channel—family entertainment

E! Entertainment Television—celebrity interviews, news, features

The Employment Channel—job listings, employment news, and training

Encore—films of the '60s–'80s

Encore Thematic Multiplex—movies, with "mood on demand" viewing options

ESPN—broad appeal and narrow interest sports programming

ESPN2—sports programming targeting light to moderate sports viewers 18- to 34- years old.

EWTN: The Catholic Cable Network—religious programming

Faith & Values Channel—interfaith religious programming

The Family Channel—variable programming for children and families

Flix—movies from the '60s–'90s

FoxNet—regular Fox network programs via cable

fX—entertainment and lifestyle programming and cable rebroadcasts for ages 18–49

Galavisión—Spanish-language movies, sports, news

GEMS Television—Spanish-language women's programming

Home Box Office (HBO)—films, specials, sports

Headline News—half-hour newscasts, from CNN

Home Shopping Network I—discount shopping at home

Home Shopping Network II—more shopping at home

The International Channel—foreign-language news and entertainment from around the world

Jewish Television Network—news, public affairs, entertainment

Jones Computer Network—computer instruction, news, commentary, courses

KTLA/UV—Los Angeles station with movies, specials, local news and sports

KTVT/UV—Dallas/Fort Worth station with movies, news, local sports

The Learning Channel—educational programming

Lifetime Television—programming aimed at women, including fitness, parenting, feature shows

Mind Extension University: The Educational Network—educational programming

MOR Music TV—music video hits from the '50s–'90s.

The Movie Channel (TMC)—movies, from blockbusters to classics

MTV: Music Television —music videos and pop culture programming

NASA Select Television—space program coverage and other educational material

The Nashville Network (TNN)—country music entertainment

National Empowerment Television—public affairs programming

The New Inspirational Network—multidenominational religious programming

Nickelodeon/Nick at Nite—kids' programming during the day; TV classics after hours

The 90s Channel—social and political documentaries

Nostalgia Television—entertainment, lifestyle, and information for active older people

Playboy TV—adult entertainment

Prime Sports Channel Networks—national sports

Q2—fashion resources during the week; part lifestyle magazine and part specialty store on weekends

QVC—home-shopping service

Request Television—pay-per-view movies and events

Sci-Fi Channel—fantasy, horror, and sci-fi series, movies, originals

Scola—international TV news, broadcast to schools

Sega Channel—video games on demand

Showtime—movies, series, specials, boxing, other entertainment

Spice—adult movies

Spice 2—more adult movies

TBS—Atlanta superstation specializing in movies, sports, comedies, kids' shows

Telemundo—Spanish-language programming with movies, game shows, news, sports

Television Food Network (TVFN)—food, fitness, health

TheatreVisioN—pay-per-view movies and special events

Trinity Broadcasting Network—religious programming

Turner Classic Movies—vintage films from the Turner archives, including the MGM library

Turner Network Television (TNT)—vintage and original films, sports, kids' shows, specials

The Travel Channel—travel news, entertainment, information

TV-Japan—news, sports, drama, education, from Japan

U Network—student-produced programming in all genres

Univision—Spanish-speaking programs, with movies, sports, international newscasts

USA Network—all-entertainment network

ValueVision—home shopping

Video Hits One (VH1)—music videos targeted to the 25-to-35-year-old audience

Viewer's Choice—films, sports, musical events

Viewer's Choice: Continuous Hits 1, 2, 3—three channels offering recent movies

Viewer's Choice: Hot Choice—action-adventure and R-rated adult-appeal movies and specials

Viva Television Network, Inc.—Spanish-language entertainment, culture, educational programs

The Weather Channel—local, national and international forecasts

WGN/UV—Chicago station featuring specials, news, movies, local sports

Worship—Christian music set to scenic videos

WPIX/UV—New York station with specials, news, movies, local sports

WSBK—Boston station offering movies, specials, and local sports

WWOR—New York station with movies, kids' shows, local sports

Z Music—Christian music and specials

CABLE'S TOP 20 NETWORKS

Ranked by the number of subscribers' homes in which they are available, these are cable's leading networks. (Source: National Cable Television Association)

1. ESPN
2. Cable News Network (CNN)
3. The Discovery Channel
4. USA Network
5. The Nashville Network (TNN)
6. The Family Channel
7. TBS
8. C-SPAN
9. Arts & Entertainment Network
10. Nickelodeon/Nick at Nite
11. Turner Network Television (TNT)
12. MTV
13. Lifetime Television
14. The Weather Channel
15. Headline News
16. CNBC
17. VH1 (Video Hits One)
18. QVC
19. American Movie Classics (AMC)
20. WGN/UVI

THE MOST POPULAR SHOWS ON TV

The following chart shows the most watched programs on TV every year beginning in 1949. (Sources: *Variety* [1949–50, month of October] and *Nielsen Media Research*, 1994)

1949–50

	Show	Network
1.	The Texaco Star Theater	NBC
2.	Toast of the Town (Ed Sullivan)	CBS
3.	Arthur Godfrey's Talent Scouts	CBS
4.	Fireball Fun for All	NBC
5.	Philco Television Playhouse	NBC
6.	Fireside Theatre	NBC
7.	The Goldbergs	CBS
8.	Suspense	CBS
9.	The Ford Television Theater	CBS
10.	Cavalcade of Stars	DUMONT

1950–51

	Show	Network
1.	The Texaco Star Theater	NBC
2.	Fireside Theatre	NBC
3.	Your Show of Shows	NBC
4.	Philco Television Playhouse	NBC
5.	The Colgate Comedy Hour	NBC
6.	Gillette Cavalcade of Sports	NBC
7.	Arthur Godfrey's Talent Scouts	CBS
8.	Mama	CBS
9.	Robert Montgomery Presents	NBC
10.	Martin Kane, Private Eye	NBC
11.	Man Against Crime	CBS
12.	Somerset Maugham Theatre	NBC
13.	Kraft Television Theatre	NBC
14.	Toast of the Town (Ed Sullivan)	CBS
15.	The Aldrich Family	NBC
16.	You Bet Your Life	NBC
17.	Armstrong Circle Theater (tie)	NBC
17.	Big Town (tie)	CBS
17.	Lights Out (tie)	NBC
20.	The Alan Young Show	CBS

1951–52

	Show	Network
1.	Arthur Godfrey's Talent Scouts	CBS
2.	The Texaco Star Theater	NBC
3.	I Love Lucy	CBS
4.	The Red Skelton Show	NBC
5.	The Colgate Comedy Hour	NBC
6.	Fireside Theatre	NBC
7.	The Jack Benny Program	CBS
8.	Your Show of Shows	NBC
9.	You Bet Your Life	NBC
10.	Arthur Godfrey and His Friends	CBS
11.	Mama	CBS
12.	Philco Television Playhouse	NBC
13.	Amos 'n' Andy	CBS
14.	Big Town	CBS
15.	Pabst Blue Ribbon Bouts	CBS
16.	Gillette Cavalcade of Sports	NBC
17.	The Alan Young Show	CBS
18.	All-Star Revue (tie)	NBC
18.	Dragnet (tie)	NBC
20.	Kraft Television Theatre	NBC

1952–53

	Show	Network
1.	I Love Lucy	CBS
2.	Arthur Godfrey's Talent Scouts	CBS
3.	Arthur Godfrey and His Friends	CBS
4.	Dragnet	NBC
5.	The Texaco Star Theater	NBC
6.	The Buick Circus Hour	NBC
7.	The Colgate Comedy Hour	NBC
8.	Gangbusters	NBC
9.	You Bet Your Life	NBC
10.	Fireside Theatre	NBC
11.	The Red Buttons Show	CBS
12.	The Jack Benny Program	CBS
13.	Life with Luigi	CBS
14.	Pabst Blue Ribbon Bouts	CBS
15.	Goodyear Television Playhouse	NBC
16.	The Life of Riley	NBC
17.	Mama	CBS
18.	Your Show of Shows	NBC
19.	What's My Line?	CBS
20.	Strike It Rich	CBS

1953–54

	Show	Network
1.	I Love Lucy	CBS
2.	Dragnet	NBC
3.	Arthur Godfrey's Talent Scouts (tie)	CBS
3.	You Bet Your Life (tie)	NBC
5.	The Bob Hope Show	NBC
6.	The Buick-Berle Show	NBC
7.	Arthur Godfrey and His Friends	CBS
8.	The Ford Television Theater	NBC
9.	The Jackie Gleason Show	CBS
10.	Fireside Theatre	NBC
11.	The Colgate Comedy Hour (tie)	NBC
11.	This Is Your Life (tie)	NBC
13.	The Red Buttons Show	CBS
14.	The Life of Riley	NBC
15.	Our Miss Brooks	CBS
16.	Treasury Men in Action	NBC
17.	All-Star Revue (Martha Raye)	NBC
18.	The Jack Benny Program	CBS
19.	Gillette Cavalcade of Sports	NBC
20.	Philco Television Playhouse	NBC

1954–55

	Show	Network
1.	I Love Lucy	CBS
2.	The Jackie Gleason Show	CBS
3.	Dragnet	NBC
4.	You Bet Your Life	NBC
5.	Toast of the Town (Ed Sullivan)	CBS
6.	Disneyland	ABC
7.	The Bob Hope Show	NBC
8.	The Jack Benny Program	CBS
9.	The Martha Raye Show	NBC
10.	The George Gobel Show	NBC
11.	The Ford Television Theater	NBC
12.	December Bride	CBS
13.	The Buick-Berle Show	NBC
14.	This Is Your Life	NBC
15.	I've Got a Secret	CBS
16.	Two for the Money	CBS
17.	Your Hit Parade	NBC
18.	The Millionaire	CBS
19.	General Electric Theater	CBS
20.	Arthur Godfrey's Talent Scouts	CBS

1955–56

1.	The $64,000 Question	CBS
2.	I Love Lucy	CBS
3.	The Ed Sullivan Show	CBS
4.	Disneyland	ABC
5.	The Jack Benny Program	CBS
6.	December Bride	CBS
7.	You Bet Your Life	NBC
8.	Dragnet	NBC
9.	I've Got a Secret	CBS
10.	General Electric Theater	CBS
11.	Private Secretary (tie)	CBS
11.	The Ford Television Theater (tie)	NBC
13.	The Red Skelton Show	CBS
14.	The George Gobel Show	NBC
15.	The $64,000 Challenge	CBS
16.	Arthur Godfrey's Talent Scouts	CBS
17.	The Lineup	CBS
18.	Shower of Stars	CBS
19.	The Perry Como Show	NBC
20.	The Honeymooners	CBS

1956–57

1.	I Love Lucy	CBS
2.	The Ed Sullivan Show	CBS
3.	General Electric Theater	CBS
4.	The $64,000 Question	CBS
5.	December Bride	CBS
6.	Alfred Hitchcock Presents	CBS
7.	I've Got a Secret (tie)	CBS
7.	Gunsmoke (tie)	CBS
9.	The Perry Como Show	NBC
10.	The Jack Benny Program	CBS
11.	Dragnet	NBC
12.	Arthur Godfrey's Talent Scouts	CBS
13.	The Millionaire (tie)	CBS
13.	Disneyland (tie)	ABC
15.	Shower of Stars	CBS
16.	The Lineup	CBS
17.	The Red Skelton Show	CBS
18.	You Bet Your Life	NBC
19.	The Life and Legend of Wyatt Earp	ABC
20.	Private Secretary	CBS

1957–58

1.	Gunsmoke	CBS
2.	The Danny Thomas Show	CBS
3.	Tales of Wells Fargo	NBC
4.	Have Gun, Will Travel	CBS
5.	I've Got a Secret	CBS
6.	The Life and Legend of Wyatt Earp	ABC
7.	General Electric Theater	CBS
8.	The Restless Gun	NBC
9.	December Bride	CBS
10.	You Bet Your Life	NBC
11.	Alfred Hitchcock Presents (tie)	CBS
11.	Cheyenne (tie)	ABC
13.	The Tennessee Ernie Ford Show	NBC
14.	The Red Skelton Show	CBS
15.	Wagon Train (tie)	NBC
15.	Sugarfoot (tie)	ABC
15.	Father Knows Best (tie)	CBS
18.	Twenty-One	NBC
19.	The Ed Sullivan Show	CBS
20.	The Jack Benny Program	CBS

1958–59

1.	Gunsmoke	CBS
2.	Wagon Train	NBC
3.	Have Gun, Will Travel	CBS
4.	The Rifleman	ABC
5.	The Danny Thomas Show	CBS
6.	Maverick	ABC
7.	Tales of Wells Fargo	NBC
8.	The Real McCoys	ABC
9.	I've Got a Secret	CBS
10.	Wyatt Earp	ABC
11.	The Price Is Right	NBC
12.	The Red Skelton Show	CBS
13.	Zane Grey Theater (tie)	CBS
13.	Father Knows Best (tie)	CBS
15.	The Texan	CBS
16.	Wanted: Dead or Alive (tie)	CBS
16.	Peter Gunn (tie)	NBC
18.	Cheyenne	ABC
19.	Perry Mason	CBS
20.	The Tennessee Ernie Ford Show	NBC

1959–60

1.	Gunsmoke	CBS
2.	Wagon Train	NBC
3.	Have Gun, Will Travel	CBS
4.	The Danny Thomas Show	CBS
5.	The Red Skelton Show	CBS
6.	Father Knows Best (tie)	CBS
6.	Sunset Strip (tie)	ABC
8.	The Price Is Right	NBC
9.	Wanted: Dead or Alive	CBS
10.	Perry Mason	CBS
11.	The Real McCoys	ABC
12.	The Ed Sullivan Show	CBS
13.	The Bing Crosby Show	ABC
14.	The Rifleman	ABC
15.	The Tennessee Ernie Ford Show	NBC
16.	The Lawman	ABC
17.	Dennis the Menace	CBS
18.	Cheyenne	ABC
19.	Rawhide	CBS
20.	Maverick	ABC

1960–61

1.	Gunsmoke	CBS
2.	Wagon Train	NBC
3.	Have Gun, Will Travel	CBS
4.	The Andy Griffith Show	CBS
5.	The Real McCoys	ABC
6.	Rawhide	CBS
7.	Candid Camera	CBS
8.	The Untouchables (tie)	ABC
8.	The Price Is Right (tie)	NBC
10.	The Jack Benny Program	CBS
11.	Dennis the Menace	CBS
12.	The Danny Thomas Show	CBS
13.	My Three Sons (tie)	ABC
13.	77 Sunset Strip (tie)	ABC
15.	The Ed Sullivan Show	CBS
16.	Perry Mason	CBS
17.	Bonanza	NBC
18.	The Flintstones	ABC
19.	The Red Skelton Show	CBS
20.	Alfred Hitchcock Presents	NBC

1961–62

1. Wagon Train NBC
2. Bonanza NBC
3. Gunsmoke CBS
4. Hazel NBC
5. Perry Mason CBS
6. The Red Skelton Show CBS
7. The Andy Griffith Show CBS
8. The Danny Thomas Show CBS
9. Dr. Kildare NBC
10. Candid Camera CBS
11. My Three Sons ABC
12. The Garry Moore Show CBS
13. Rawhide CBS
14. The Real McCoys ABC
15. Lassie CBS
16. Sing Along with Mitch NBC
17. Dennis the Menace (tie) CBS
17. Marshal Dillon (tie) (Gunsmoke reruns) CBS
19. Ben Casey ABC
20. The Ed Sullivan Show CBS

1962–63

1. The Beverly Hillbillies CBS
2. Candid Camera (tie) CBS
2. The Red Skelton Show (tie) CBS
4. Bonanza (tie) NBC
4. The Lucy Show (tie) CBS
6. The Andy Griffith Show CBS
7. Ben Casey (tie) ABC
7. The Danny Thomas Show (tie) CBS
9. The Dick Van Dyke Show CBS
10. Gunsmoke CBS
11. Dr. Kildare (tie) NBC
11. The Jack Benny Program (tie) CBS
13. What's My Line? CBS
14. The Ed Sullivan Show CBS
15. Hazel NBC
16. I've Got a Secret CBS
17. The Jackie Gleason Show CBS
18. The Defenders CBS
19. The Garry Moore Show (tie) CBS
19. To Tell the Truth (tie) CBS

1963–64

1. The Beverly Hillbillies CBS
2. Bonanza NBC
3. The Dick Van Dyke Show CBS
4. Petticoat Junction CBS
5. The Andy Griffith Show CBS
6. The Lucy Show CBS
7. Candid Camera CBS
8. The Ed Sullivan Show CBS
9. The Danny Thomas Show CBS
10. My Favorite Martian CBS
11. The Red Skelton Show CBS
12. I've Got a Secret (tie) CBS
12. Lassie (tie) CBS
12. The Jack Benny Program (tie) CBS
15. The Jackie Gleason Show CBS
16. The Donna Reed Show ABC
17. The Virginian NBC
18. The Patty Duke Show ABC
19. Dr. Kildare NBC
20. Gunsmoke CBS

1964–65

1. Bonanza NBC
2. Bewitched ABC
3. Gomer Pyle, U.S.M.C. CBS
4. The Andy Griffith Show CBS
5. The Fugitive ABC
6. The Red Skelton Hour CBS
7. The Dick Van Dyke Show CBS
8. The Lucy Show CBS
9. Peyton Place (II) ABC
10. Combat ABC
11. Walt Disney's Wonderful World of Color NBC
12. The Beverly Hillbillies CBS
13. My Three Sons ABC
14. Branded NBC
15. Petticoat Junction (tie) CBS
15. The Ed Sullivan Show (tie) CBS
17. Lassie CBS
18. The Munsters (tie) CBS
18. Gilligan's Island (tie) CBS
20. Peyton Place (V) ABC

1965–66

1. Bonanza NBC
2. Gomer Pyle, U.S.M.C. CBS
3. The Lucy Show CBS
4. The Red Skelton Hour CBS
5. Batman (II) ABC
6. The Andy Griffith Show CBS
7. Bewitched (tie) ABC
7. The Beverly Hillbillies (tie) CBS
9. Hogan's Heroes CBS
10. Batman (I) ABC
11. Green Acres CBS
12. Get Smart NBC
13. The Man from U.N.C.L.E. NBC
14. Daktari CBS
15. My Three Sons CBS
16. The Dick Van Dyke Show CBS
17. Walt Disney's Wonderful World of Color (tie) NBC
17. The Ed Sullivan Show (tie) CBS
19. The Lawrence Welk Show (tie) ABC
19. I've Got a Secret (tie) CBS

1966–67

1. Bonanza NBC
2. The Red Skelton Hour CBS
3. The Andy Griffith Show CBS
4. The Lucy Show CBS
5. The Jackie Gleason Show CBS
6. Green Acres CBS
7. Daktari (tie) CBS
7. Bewitched (tie) ABC
7. The Beverly Hillbillies (tie) CBS
10. Gomer Pyle, U.S.M.C. (tie) CBS
10. The Virginian (tie) NBC
10. The Lawrence Welk Show (tie) ABC
10. The Ed Sullivan Show (tie) CBS
14. The Dean Martin Show (tie) CBS
14. Family Affair (tie) CBS
16. Smothers Brothers Comedy Hour CBS
17. The CBS Friday Night Movie (tie) CBS
17. Hogan's Heroes (tie) CBS
19. Walt Disney's Wonderful World of Color NBC
20. Saturday Night at the Movies NBC

1967–68

1. The Andy Griffith Show CBS
2. The Lucy Show CBS
3. Gomer Pyle, U.S.M.C. CBS
4. Gunsmoke (tie) CBS
4. Family Affair (tie) CBS
4. Bonanza (tie) NBC
7. The Red Skelton Hour CBS
8. The Dean Martin Show NBC
9. The Jackie Gleason Show CBS
10. Saturday Night at the Movies NBC
11. Bewitched ABC
12. The Beverly Hillbillies CBS
13. The Ed Sullivan Show CBS
14. The Virginian NBC
15. The CBS Friday Night Movie (tie) CBS
15. Green Acres (tie) CBS
17. The Lawrence Welk Show ABC
18. Smothers Brothers Comedy Hour CBS
19. Gentle Ben CBS
20. Tuesday Night at the Movies NBC

1968–69

1. Rowan and Martin's Laugh-In NBC
2. Gomer Pyle, U.S.M.C. CBS
3. Bonanza NBC
4. Mayberry R.F.D. CBS
5. Family Affair CBS
6. Gunsmoke CBS
7. Julia NBC
8. The Dean Martin Show NBC
9. Here's Lucy CBS
10. The Beverly Hillbillies CBS
11. Mission: Impossible (tie) CBS
11. Bewitched (tie) ABC
11. The Red Skelton Hour (tie) CBS
14. My Three Sons CBS
15. The Glen Campbell Goodtime Hour CBS
16. Ironside NBC
17. The Virginian NBC
18. The F.B.I. ABC
19. Green Acres CBS
20. Dragnet NBC

1969–70

1. Rowan and Martin's Laugh-In NBC
2. Gunsmoke CBS
3. Bonanza NBC
4. Mayberry R.F.D. CBS
5. Family Affair CBS
6. Here's Lucy CBS
7. The Red Skelton Hour CBS
8. Marcus Welby, M.D. ABC
9. The Wonderful World of Disney NBC
10. The Doris Day Show CBS
11. The Bill Cosby Show NBC
12. The Jim Nabors Hour CBS
13. The Carol Burnett Show CBS
14. The Dean Martin Show NBC
15. My Three Sons (tie) CBS
15. Ironside (tie) NBC
15. The Johnny Cash Show (tie) ABC
18. The Beverly Hillbillies CBS
19. Hawaii Five-O CBS
20. Glen Campbell Goodtime Hour CBS

1970–71

1. Marcus Welby, M.D. ABC
2. The Flip Wilson Show NBC
3. Here's Lucy CBS
4. Ironside NBC
5. Gunsmoke CBS
6. The ABC Movie of the Week ABC
7. Hawaii Five-O CBS
8. Medical Center CBS
9. Bonanza NBC
10. The F.B.I. ABC
11. The Mod Squad ABC
12. Adam-12 NBC
13. Rowan and Martin's Laugh-In (tie) NBC
13. The Wonderful World of Disney (tie) NBC
15. Mayberry R.F.D. CBS
16. Hee Haw CBS
17. Mannix CBS
18. The Men from Shiloh NBC
19. My Three Sons CBS
20. The Doris Day Show CBS

1971–72

1. All in the Family CBS
2. The Flip Wilson Show NBC
3. Marcus Welby, M.D. ABC
4. Gunsmoke CBS
5. The ABC Movie of the Week ABC
6. Sanford and Son NBC
7. Mannix CBS
8. Funny Face (tie) CBS
8. Adam-12 (tie) NBC
10. The Mary Tyler Moore Show CBS
11. Here's Lucy CBS
12. Hawaii Five-O CBS
13. Medical Center CBS
14. The NBC Mystery Movie NBC
15. Ironside NBC
16. The Partridge Family ABC
17. The F.B.I. ABC
18. The New Dick Van Dyke Show CBS
19. The Wonderful World of Disney NBC
20. Bonanza NBC

1972–73

1. All in the Family CBS
2. Sanford and Son NBC
3. Hawaii Five-O CBS
4. Maude CBS
5. Bridget Loves Bernie (tie) CBS
5. The NBC Sunday Mystery Movie (tie) NBC
7. The Mary Tyler Moore Show (tie) CBS
7. Gunsmoke (tie) CBS
9. The Wonderful World of Disney NBC
10. Ironside NBC
11. Adam-12 NBC
12. The Flip Wilson Show NBC
13. Marcus Welby, M.D. ABC
14. Cannon CBS
15. Here's Lucy CBS
16. The Bob Newhart Show CBS
17. ABC Tuesday Movie of the Week ABC
18. NFL Monday Night Football ABC
19. The Partridge Family (tie) ABC
19. The Waltons (tie) CBS

1973–74

1.	All in the Family	CBS
2.	The Waltons	CBS
3.	Sanford and Son	NBC
4.	M*A*S*H	CBS
5.	Hawaii Five-O	CBS
6.	Maude	CBS
7.	Kojak (tie)	CBS
7.	The Sonny and Cher Comedy Hour (tie)	CBS
9.	The Mary Tyler Moore Show (tie)	CBS
9.	Cannon (tie)	CBS
11.	The Six Million Dollar Man	ABC
12.	The Bob Newhart Show (tie)	CBS
12.	The Wonderful World of Disney (tie)	NBC
14.	The NBC Sunday Mystery Movie	NBC
15.	Gunsmoke	CBS
16.	Happy Days	ABC
17.	Good Times (tie)	CBS
17.	Barnaby Jones (tie)	CBS
19.	NFL Monday Night Football (tie)	ABC
19.	The CBS Friday Night Movie (tie)	CBS

1974–75

1.	All in the Family	CBS
2.	Sanford and Son	NBC
3.	Chico and the Man	NBC
4.	The Jeffersons	CBS
5.	M*A*S*H	CBS
6.	Rhoda	CBS
7.	Good Times	CBS
8.	The Waltons	CBS
9.	Maude	CBS
10.	Hawaii Five-O	CBS
11.	The Mary Tyler Moore Show	CBS
12.	The Rockford Files	NBC
13.	Little House on the Prairie	NBC
14.	Kojak	CBS
15.	Police Woman	NBC
16.	S.W.A.T.	ABC
17.	The Bob Newhart Show	CBS
18.	The Wonderful World of Disney (tie)	NBC
18.	The Rookies (tie)	ABC
20.	Mannix	CBS

1975–76

1.	All in the Family	CBS
2.	Rich Man, Poor Man	ABC
3.	Laverne and Shirley	ABC
4.	Maude	CBS
5.	The Bionic Woman	ABC
6.	Phyllis	CBS
7.	Sanford and Son (tie)	NBC
7.	Rhoda (tie)	CBS
9.	The Six Million Dollar Man	ABC
10.	The ABC Monday Night Movie	ABC
11.	Happy Days	ABC
12.	One Day at a Time	CBS
13.	The ABC Sunday Night Movie	ABC
14.	The Waltons (tie)	CBS
14.	M*A*S*H (tie)	CBS
16.	Starsky and Hutch (tie)	ABC
16.	Good Heavens (tie)	ABC
18.	Welcome Back, Kotter	ABC
19.	The Mary Tyler Moore Show	CBS
20.	Kojak	CBS

1976–77

1.	Happy Days	ABC
2.	Laverne and Shirley	ABC
3.	The ABC Monday Night Movie	ABC
4.	M*A*S*H	CBS
5.	Charlie's Angels	ABC
6.	The Big Event	NBC
7.	The Six Million Dollar Man	ABC
8.	The ABC Sunday Night Movie (tie)	ABC
8.	Baretta (tie)	ABC
8.	One Day at a Time (tie)	CBS
11.	Three's Company	ABC
12.	All in the Family	CBS
13.	Welcome Back, Kotter	ABC
14.	The Bionic Woman	ABC
15.	The Waltons (tie)	CBS
15.	Little House on the Prairie (tie)	NBC
17.	Barney Miller	ABC
18.	60 Minutes (tie)	CBS
18.	Hawaii Five-O (tie)	CBS
20.	NBC Monday Night at the Movies	NBC

1977–78

1.	Laverne and Shirley	ABC
2.	Happy Days	ABC
3.	Three's Company	ABC
4.	Charlie's Angels (tie)	ABC
4.	All in the Family (tie)	CBS
4.	60 Minutes (tie)	CBS
7.	Little House on the Prairie	NBC
8.	M*A*S*H (tie)	CBS
8.	Alice (tie)	CBS
10.	One Day at a Time	CBS
11.	How the West Was Won	ABC
12.	Eight Is Enough	ABC
13.	Soap	ABC
14.	The Love Boat	ABC
15.	NBC Monday Night Movie	NBC
16.	NFL Monday Night Football	ABC
17.	Barney Miller (tie)	ABC
17.	Fantasy Island (tie)	ABC
19.	The Amazing Spider-Man (tie)	CBS
19.	Project U.F.O. (tie)	NBC

1978–79

1.	Laverne and Shirley	ABC
2.	Three's Company	ABC
3.	Mork & Mindy	ABC
4.	Happy Days (tie)	ABC
4.	The Ropers (tie)	ABC
6.	What's Happening!! (tie)	ABC
6.	Alice (8:30) (tie)	CBS
8.	M*A*S*H	CBS
9.	One Day at a Time (Monday)	CBS
10.	Taxi	ABC
11.	60 Minutes (tie)	CBS
11.	Charlie's Angels (tie)	ABC
13.	Angie	ABC
14.	Alice (9:30)	CBS
15.	All in the Family	CBS
16.	WKRP in Cincinnati (tie)	CBS
16.	Soap (tie)	ABC
18.	Eight Is Enough	ABC
19.	All in the Family	CBS
20.	Barney Miller (tie)	ABC
20.	CBS Sunday Night Movie (tie)	CBS

1979–80

1.	60 Minutes	CBS
2.	Three's Company	ABC
3.	That's Incredible	ABC
4.	M*A*S*H	CBS
5.	Alice	CBS
6.	Dallas	CBS
7.	Flo	CBS
8.	The Jeffersons	CBS
9.	The Dukes of Hazzard	CBS
10.	One Day at a Time	CBS
11.	WKRP in Cincinnati	CBS
12.	Goodtime Girls	ABC
13.	Archie Bunker's Place	CBS
14.	Taxi	ABC
15.	Eight Is Enough	ABC
16.	Little House on the Prairie	NBC
17.	House Calls	CBS
18.	Real People	NBC
19.	CHiPs	NBC
20.	Happy Days	ABC

1980–81

1.	Dallas	CBS
2.	60 Minutes	CBS
3.	The Dukes of Hazzard	CBS
4.	Private Benjamin	CBS
5.	M*A*S*H	CBS
6.	The Love Boat	ABC
7.	The NBC Tuesday Night Movie	NBC
8.	House Calls	CBS
9.	The Jeffersons (tie)	CBS
9.	Little House on the Prairie (tie)	NBC
11.	The Two of Us	CBS
12.	Alice	CBS
13.	Real People (tie)	NBC
13.	Three's Company (tie)	ABC
15.	The NBC Movie of the Week (tie)	NBC
15.	One Day at a Time (tie)	CBS
17.	Too Close for Comfort (tie)	ABC
17.	Magnum, P.I. (tie)	CBS
19.	Diff'rent Strokes (tie)	NBC
19.	NFL Monday Night Football (tie)	ABC

1981–82

1.	Dallas (9:00)	CBS
2.	Dallas (10:00)	CBS
3.	60 Minutes	CBS
4.	Three's Company (tie)	ABC
4.	CBS NFL Football Post 2 (tie)	CBS
6.	The Jeffersons	CBS
7.	Joanie Loves Chachi	ABC
8.	The Dukes of Hazzard (9:00)	CBS
9.	Alice (tie)	CBS
9.	The Dukes of Hazzard (8:00) (tie)	CBS
11.	The ABC Monday Night Movie (tie)	ABC
11.	Too Close for Comfort (tie)	ABC
13.	M*A*S*H	CBS
14.	One Day at a Time	CBS
15.	NFL Monday Night Football	ABC
16.	Falcon Crest	CBS
17.	Archie Bunker's Place (tie)	CBS
17.	The Love Boat (tie)	ABC
19.	Hart to Hart	ABC
20.	Trapper John, M.D.	CBS

1982–83

1.	60 Minutes	CBS
2.	Dallas	CBS
3.	M*A*S*H (tie)	CBS
3.	Magnum, P.I. (tie)	CBS
5.	Dynasty	ABC
6.	Three's Company	ABC
7.	Simon & Simon	CBS
8.	Falcon Crest	CBS
9.	NFL Monday Night Football	ABC
10.	The Love Boat	ABC
11.	One Day at a Time (Sunday)	CBS
12.	Newhart (Monday)	CBS
13.	The Jeffersons (tie)	CBS
13.	The A Team (tie)	NBC
15.	The Fall Guy (9:00)	ABC
16.	Newhart (Sunday, 9:30)	CBS
17.	The Mississippi	CBS
18.	9 to 5	ABC
19.	The Fall Guy	ABC
20.	The ABC Monday Night Movie	ABC

1983–84

1.	Dallas	CBS
2.	Dynasty	ABC
3.	The A Team	NBC
4.	60 Minutes	CBS
5.	Simon & Simon	CBS
6.	Magnum, P.I.	CBS
7.	Falcon Crest	CBS
8.	Kate & Allie	CBS
9.	Hotel	ABC
10.	Cagney & Lacey	CBS
11.	Knots Landing	CBS
12.	The ABC Sunday Night Movie (tie)	ABC
12.	The ABC Monday Night Movie (tie)	ABC
14.	TV's Bloopers & Practical Jokes	NBC
15.	AfterMASH	CBS
16.	The Fall Guy	ABC
17.	The Four Seasons	CBS
18.	The Love Boat	ABC
19.	Riptide	NBC
20.	The Jeffersons	CBS

1984–85

1.	Dynasty	ABC
2.	Dallas	CBS
3.	The Cosby Show	NBC
4.	60 Minutes	CBS
5.	Family Ties	NBC
6.	The A Team (tie)	NBC
6.	Simon & Simon (tie)	CBS
8.	Knots Landing	CBS
9.	Murder, She Wrote	CBS
10.	Falcon Crest (tie)	CBS
10.	Crazy Like a Fox (tie)	CBS
12.	Hotel	ABC
13.	Cheers	NBC
14.	Riptide (tie)	NBC
14.	Who's the Boss? (tie)	ABC
16.	Magnum, P.I.	CBS
17.	Hail to the Chief	ABC
18.	Newhart	CBS
19.	Kate & Allie	CBS
20.	The NBC Monday Night Movie	NBC

1985–86

1. The Cosby Show NBC
2. Family Ties NBC
3. Murder, She Wrote CBS
4. 60 Minutes CBS
5. Cheers NBC
6. Dallas (tie) CBS
6. Dynasty (tie) ABC
6. The Golden Girls (tie) NBC
9. Miami Vice NBC
10. Who's the Boss? ABC
11. Perfect Strangers ABC
12. Night Court NBC
13. The CBS Sunday Night Movie CBS
14. Highway to Heaven (tie) NBC
14. Kate & Allie (tie) CBS
16. NFL Monday Night Football ABC
17. Newhart CBS
18. Knots Landing (tie) CBS
18. Growing Pains (tie) ABC
20. 227 NBC

1986–87

1. The Cosby Show NBC
2. Family Ties NBC
3. Cheers NBC
4. Murder, She Wrote CBS
5. Night Court NBC
6. The Golden Girls NBC
7. 60 Minutes CBS
8. Growing Pains ABC
9. Moonlighting ABC
10. Who's the Boss? ABC
11. Dallas CBS
12. Nothing in Common NBC
13. Newhart CBS
14. Amen NBC
15. 227 NBC
16. Matlock (tie) NBC
16. CBS Sunday Night Movie (tie) CBS
16. NBC Monday Night Movie (tie) NBC
19. NFL Monday Night Football (tie) ABC
19. Kate & Allie (tie) CBS

1987–88

1. The Cosby Show NBC
2. A Different World NBC
3. Cheers NBC
4. Growing Pains (Tuesday) ABC
5. Night Court NBC
6. The Golden Girls NBC
7. Who's the Boss? ABC
8. 60 Minutes CBS
9. Murder, She Wrote CBS
10. The Wonder Years ABC
11. Alf NBC
12. Moonlighting (tie) ABC
12. L.A. Law (tie) NBC
14. NFL Monday Night Football ABC
15. Matlock (tie) NBC
15. Growing Pains (Wednesday) (tie) ABC
17. Amen NBC
18. Family Ties NBC
19. Hunter NBC
20. The CBS Sunday Night Movie CBS

1988–89

1. Roseanne (9:00) (tie) ABC
1. The Cosby Show (tie) NBC
3. Roseanne (8:30) (tie) ABC
3. A Different World (tie) NBC
5. Cheers NBC
6. 60 Minutes CBS
7. The Golden Girls NBC
8. Who's the Boss? ABC
9. The Wonder Years ABC
10. Murder, She Wrote CBS
11. Empty Nest NBC
12. Anything but Love ABC
13. Dear John NBC
14. Growing Pains ABC
15. Alf (tie) NBC
15. L.A. Law (tie) NBC
17. Matlock NBC
18. Unsolved Mysteries (tie) NBC
18. Hunter (tie) NBC
20. In the Heat of the Night NBC

1989–90

1. Roseanne ABC
2. The Cosby Show NBC
3. Cheers NBC
4. A Different World NBC
5. America's Funniest Home Videos ABC
6. The Golden Girls NBC
7. 60 Minutes CBS
8. The Wonder Years ABC
9. Empty Nest NBC
10. Chicken Soup ABC
11. NFL Monday Night Football ABC
12. Unsolved Mysteries NBC
13. Who's the Boss? ABC
14. L.A. Law (tie) NBC
14. Murder, She Wrote (tie) CBS
16. Grand NBC
17. In the Heat of the Night NBC
18. Dear John NBC
19. Coach ABC
20. Matlock NBC

1990–91

1. Cheers NBC
2. 60 Minutes CBS
3. Roseanne ABC
4. A Different World NBC
5. The Cosby Show NBC
6. NFL Monday Night Football ABC
7. America's Funniest Home Videos ABC
8. Murphy Brown CBS
9. America's Funniest People (tie) ABC
9. Designing Women (tie) CBS
9. Empty Nest (tie) NBC
12. Golden Girls NBC
13. Murder, She Wrote CBS
14. Unsolved Mysteries NBC
15. Full House ABC
16. Family Matters ABC
17. Coach (tie) ABC
17. Matlock (tie) NBC
19. In the Heat of the Night NBC
20. Major Dad CBS

1991–92

	Show	Network
1.	60 Minutes	CBS
2.	Roseanne	ABC
3.	Murphy Brown	CBS
4.	Cheers	NBC
5.	Home Improvement	ABC
6.	Designing Women	CBS
7.	Coach	ABC
8.	Full House	ABC
9.	Murder, She Wrote (tie)	CBS
9.	Unsolved Mysteries (tie)	NBC
11.	Major Dad (tie)	CBS
11.	NFL Monday Night Football (tie)	ABC
13.	Room For Two	ABC
14.	The CBS Sunday Night Movie	CBS
15.	Evening Shade	CBS
16.	Northern Exposure	CBS
17.	A Different World	NBC
18.	The Cosby Show	NBC
19.	Wings	NBC
20.	America's Funniest Home Videos (tie)	ABC
20.	Fresh Prince of Bel Air (tie)	NBC

1992–93

	Show	Network
1.	60 Minutes	CBS
2.	Roseanne	ABC
3.	Home Improvement	ABC
4.	Murphy Brown	CBS
5.	Murder, She Wrote	CBS
6.	Coach	ABC
7.	NFL Monday Night Football	ABC
8.	The CBS Sunday Night Movie (tie)	CBS
8.	Cheers (tie)	NBC
10.	Full House	ABC
11.	Northern Exposure	CBS
12.	Rescue: 911	CBS
13.	20/20	ABC
14.	The CBS Tuesday Night Movie (tie)	CBS
14.	Love & War (tie)	CBS
16.	Fresh Prince of Bel Air (tie)	NBC
16.	Hangin' With Mr. Cooper (tie)	ABC
16.	The Jackie Thomas Show (tie)	ABC
19.	Evening Shade	CBS
20.	Hearts Afire (tie)	CBS
20.	Unsolved Mysteries (tie)	NBC

1993–94

	Show	Network
1.	Home Improvement	ABC
2.	60 Minutes	CBS
3.	Seinfeld	NBC
4.	Roseanne	ABC
5.	Grace Under Fire	ABC
6.	These Friends of Mine	ABC
7.	Frasier	NBC
8.	Coach (tie)	ABC
8.	NFL Monday Night Football (tie)	ABC
10.	Murder, She Wrote	CBS
11.	Murphy Brown	CBS
12.	Thunder Alley	ABC
13.	The CBS Sunday Night Movie	CBS
14.	20/20	ABC
15.	Love & War	CBS
16.	Primetime Live (tie)	ABC
16.	Wings (tie)	NBC
18.	NYPD Blue	ABC
19.	Homicide	NBC
20.	Northern Exposure	CBS

HOSTS WITH THE MOST FUTURE

Monty Hall, Bob Barker, and Pat Sajak are well-known game-show masters, but an unexpected host of TV legends have apprenticed as quiz masters. Here are just a few:

Host	Show(s)
Johnny Carson	*Who Do You Trust?* and *Earn Your Vacation*
Walter Cronkite	*It's News to Me*
Buddy Hackett	*You Bet Your Life*
Moss Hart	*Answer Yes or No*
Ernie Kovacs	*Time Will Tell* and *Take a Good Look*
Oscar Levant	*G.E. Guest House*
Jack Paar	*Bank on the Stars*
Carl Reiner	*The Celebrity Game*
Rod Serling	*Liar's Club*
Dick Van Dyke	*Laugh Line* and *Mother's Day*
Mike Wallace	*Guess Again, Who's the Boss?, The Big Surprise,* and *Who Pays*

1993–94 SPECIAL RATINGS

The following are Nielsen ratings for a variety of special categories for the most recent season.

QUIZ AND GAME SHOWS

1.	Wheel of Fortune	Kingsworld/ Camelot
2.	Jeopardy	Kingsworld/ Camelot
3.	Wheel of Fortune (Weekend)	Kingsworld/ Camelot
4.	The Price is Right 2	CBS
5.	The Price is Right 1	CBS
6.	Family Feud	All American TV
7.	Classic Concentration	NBC
8.	Caesar's Challenge	NBC

SATURDAY MORNING CHILDREN'S PROGRAMS

1.	X-Men	FOX
2.	Terrible Thunderlizards	FOX
3.	Power Rangers-SAT	FOX
4.	Garfield & Friends II (tie)	CBS
4.	Taz-Mania (tie)	FOX
4.	Tiny Toons (tie)	FOX
7.	Carmen Sandiego	FOX
8.	Bobby's World (tie)	FOX
8.	Eek the Cat (tie)	FOX
8.	Eek/Thunderlizards (tie)	FOX

SOAPS

1.	The Young and the Restless	CBS
2.	All My Children	ABC
3.	General Hospital	ABC
4.	The Bold and the Beautiful	CBS
5.	As the World Turns	CBS
6.	Days of Our Lives (tie)	NBC
6.	One Life to Live (tie)	ABC
8.	Guiding Light	CBS
9.	Another World	NBC
10.	Loving	ABC

SYNDICATED TALK SHOWS

1.	The Oprah Winfrey Show	Kingwood/ Camelot
2.	Sally Jessy Raphael	Multimedia
3.	Donahue	Multimedia
4.	Live—Regis & Kathie Lee	Buena Vista TV
5.	The Maury Povich Show	Paramount/ Premier
6.	Geraldo	Tribune Entertainment
7.	Rush Limbaugh	Multimedia
8.	The Montel Williams Show	Viacom
9.	The Arsenio Hall Show	Paramount/ Premier
10.	Vicki!	Group W Productions

THE TOP TEN TV INFOMERCIALS

This unique form of advertising in the guise of programming was first seen on American television in 1984 when advertising was deregulated, and the affliction has metastasized since. The following list presents the top-grossing infomercials, based on the total dollars grossed during each ad's most profitable year. (Source: *Steve Dworman's Infomercial Marketing Report*)

1. Soloflex (minigym)
2. NordicTrack (cross-country ski machine)
3. Psychic Friends Network (1-900 psychic line)
4. Juiceman (juice extractor)
5. Jane Fonda's Treadmill
6. Victoria Jackson Cosmetics
7. ProForm Crosswalk (treadmill)
8. BluBlocker Sunglasses (sun block sunglasses)
9. Lori Davis Haircare
10. Victoria Principal's Principal Secret (skin care products)
10. Susan Powter: Stop the Insanity (weight loss program)
10. Mike Levey: Avri Car Wax

THE "BEST" INFOMERCIALS

The National Infomercial Marketing Association has given out awards for the best of this strange breed beginning in 1992.

	Infomercial of the Year	*Best Female Presenter*	*Best Male Presenter*
1992	"Personal Power," Tony Robbins	Victoria Jackson	Mike Levey
1993	"Stop the Insanity!" Susan Powter	Susan Powter	Jake Steinfeld

TV'S MOST VIOLENT SHOWS

Public pressure over the content of television programming is usually directed squarely at the major networks, but recent studies indicate that a significant majority of TV violence occurs on syndicated shows. Indeed a handful of independently distributed offerings contains more serious violence than the combined prime-time schedules of the four major networks.

The following list of the most violent series from the beginning of the 1993–94 season is ranked according to the prevalence of serious violence—acts likely to cause significant harm, including armed and unarmed assault, sexual assault, gunplay, and suicide. The number of violent scenes listed here is based on a count taken from the premiere episode of each of these shows. (Source: Center for Media and Public Affairs)

Rank	Program	Scenes of serious violence	Total violence
1.	Highlander (syndicated)	31	52
2.	Acapulco H.E.A.T. (syndicated)	25	31
3.	Renegade (syndicated)	24	42
4.	The Adventures of Brisco County, Jr. (Fox)	21	64
5.	Star Trek: The Next Generation (syndicated)	17	29
6.	The Untouchables (syndicated)	13	25
7.	SeaQuest DSV (NBC)	10	12
8.	Star Trek: Deep Space Nine (syndicated)	9	11
9.	Walker, Texas Ranger (CBS)	8	43
10.	South of Sunset (CBS)	7	17

PBS'S MOST POPULAR PROGRAMS

Viewers often associate PBS with cultural programming and British imports, but for the most part it's wild animals that draw the viewers.

1. *National Geographic Special:* "The Incredible Machine" (1975)
2. *National Geographic Special:* "The Sharks" (1982)
3. *National Geographic Special:* "Land of the Tigers" (1985)
4. *National Geographic Special:* "The Grizzlies" (1987)
5. *National Geographic Special:* "Polar Bear Alert" (1982)
6. *National Geographic Special:* "Rain Forest" (1983)
7. *National Geographic Special:* "In the Shadow of Vesuvius" (1987)
8. *National Geographic Special:* "In the Realm of the Alligator" (1986)
8. *National Geographic Special:* "Save the Panda" (1983)
10. *National Geographic Special:* "Lions of the African Night" (1987)
11. *National Geographic Special:* "Among Wild Chimpanzees" (1984)
12. *The Civil War:* "Most Hallowed Ground" (1990)
13. *National Geographic Special:* "Living Sands of Namib" (1978)
13. *National Geographic Special:* "Etosha" (1981)
13. *Death of a Princess (1980)*

THE TOP 50 TELEVISION SHOWS

These single broadcasts drew the largest audiences in TV history. (Source: Nielsen Media Research, 1994)

Rank	Program	Date
1.	M*A*S*H	February 28, 1983
2.	Dallas (Who Shot J.R.?)	November 21, 1980
3.	Roots, Part 8 (conclusion)	January 30, 1977
4.	Super Bowl XVI	January 24, 1982
5.	Super Bowl XVII	January 30, 1983
6.	Winter Olympics	February 23, 1994
7.	Super Bowl XX	January 26, 1986
8.	Gone with the Wind, Part 1	November 7, 1976
9.	Gone with the Wind, Part 2	November 8, 1976
10.	Super Bowl XII	January 15, 1978
11.	Super Bowl XIII	January 21, 1979
12.	Bob Hope Christmas Show	January 15, 1970
13.	Super Bowl XVIII (tie)	January 22, 1984
13.	Super Bowl XIX (tie)	January 20, 1985
15.	Super Bowl XIV	January 20, 1980
16.	The Day After	November 20, 1983
17.	Roots, Part 6 (tie)	January 28, 1977
17.	The Fugitive (tie)	August 29, 1967
19.	Super Bowl XXI	January 25, 1987
20.	Roots, Part 5	January 27, 1977
21.	Super Bowl XXVIII (tie)	January 29, 1994
21.	Cheers (tie)	May 20, 1993
23.	The Ed Sullivan Show (TV debut of the Beatles)	February 9, 1964
24.	Super Bowl XXVII	January 31, 1993
25.	Bob Hope Christmas Show	January 14, 1971
26.	Roots, Part 3	January 25, 1977
27.	Super Bowl XI (tie)	Janaury 9, 1977
27.	Super Bowl XV (tie)	January 25, 1981
29.	Super Bowl VI	January 16, 1972
30.	Roots, Part 2	January 24, 1977
31.	The Beverly Hillbillies	January 8, 1964
32.	Roots, Part 4 (tie)	January 26, 1977
32.	The Ed Sullivan Show (with the Beatles) (tie)	February 16, 1964
34.	Super Bowl XXIII	January 22, 1989
35.	The 43rd Academy Awards	April 7, 1970
36.	The Thorn Birds, Part 3	March 29, 1983
37.	The Thorn Birds, Part 4	March 30, 1983
38.	NFC championship game	January 10, 1982
39.	The Beverly Hillbillies	January 15, 1964
40.	Super Bowl VII	January 14, 1973
41.	Thorn Birds, Part 2	March 28, 1983
42.	Super Bowl IX (tie)	January 12, 1975
42.	The Beverly Hillbillies (tie)	February 26, 1964
44.	Super Bowl X (tie)	January 18, 1976
44.	Airport (tie)	November 11, 1973
44.	Love Story (tie)	October 1, 1972
44.	Cinderella (tie)	February 22, 1965
44.	Roots, Part 7 (tie)	January 29, 1977
49.	The Beverly Hillbillies	March 25, 1964
50.	The Beverly Hillbillies	February 6, 1964

MOST WATCHED MOVIES ON TELEVISION

This list includes network prime-time feature films, both those made specifically for TV (*) and those made for theatrical release. Although *The Wizard of Oz* only appears twice in this list, it has earned high ratings for five different broadcasts, making it overall the most popular movie ever shown on TV. (Source: Nielsen Media Research, 1993)

Rank	Movie	Air Date
1.	Gone with the Wind, Part 1	November 7, 1976
2.	Gone with the Wind, Part 2	November 8, 1976
3.	The Day After*	November 20, 1983
4.	The Thorn Birds, Part 3*	March 29, 1983
5.	The Thorn Birds, Part 4*	March 30, 1983
6.	The Thorn Birds, Part 2*	March 28, 1983
7.	Love Story (tie)	October 1, 1972
7.	Airport (tie)	November 11, 1973
9.	The Thorn Birds, Part 1*	March 27, 1983
10.	The Godfather, Part 2	November 18, 1974
11.	Jaws	November 4, 1979
12.	The Poseidon Adventure	October 27, 1974
13.	True Grit (tie)	November 12, 1972
13.	The Birds (tie)	January 16, 1968
15.	Patton	November 19, 1972
16.	The Bridge on the River Kwai	September 25, 1966
17.	Jeremiah Johnson (tie)	January 18, 1976
17.	Helter Skelter, Part 2 (tie)*	April 2, 1976
19.	Rocky (tie)	February 4, 1979
19.	Ben-Hur (tie)	February 14, 1971
21.	The Godfather, Part 1	November 16, 1974
22.	Little Ladies of the Night (tie)*	January 16, 1977
22.	Shogun, Part 3 (tie)*	September 17, 1980
24.	The Wizard of Oz	December 13, 1959
25.	The Burning Bed*	October 8, 1984
26.	The Wizard of Oz	January 26, 1964
27.	Shogun, Part 4*	September 18, 1980
28.	Planet of the Apes (tie)	September 14, 1973
28.	Helter Skelter, Part 1 (tie)*	April 1, 1976
30.	Holocaust, Part 4*	April 19, 1978

50 TV STARS WHO MADE A DIFFERENCE

Designating TV's immortals is like wearing a Michigan sweatshirt to a Notre Dame pep rally: You're just asking for an argument. After long debate, PEOPLE's editors enshrined these diverse talents into our cathode-ray Cooperstown.

James Arness
Lucille Ball
Roseanne Arnold
Milton Berle
David Brinkley
Carol Burnett
Raymond Burr
Johnny Carson

David Caruso
Sid Caesar
Richard Chamberlain
Dick Clark
Howard Cosell
Walter Cronkite
Walt Disney
Phil Donahue
Patty Duke
Peter Falk

Farrah Fawcett

Fred Flintstone
Michael J. Fox
Monty Hall
James Garner
Jackie Gleason
Kelsey Grammer
Bryant Gumbel
Larry Hagman
Alfred Hitchcock
David Janssen
Kermit
Ted Koppel
Ernie Kovacs
Michael Landon
David Letterman

Susan Lucci
Ricky Nelson
Bob Newhart
Fess Parker
Martha Quinn
Carroll O'Connor
The Original Not Ready for Prime Time Players
Donna Reed
Fred Rogers
Phil Silvers
Ed Sullivan
Dick Van Dyke
Mike Wallace
Barbara Walters

Oprah Winfrey
Robert Young

THE VIDEO VALHALLA: 50 FORMATIVE SHOWS

The mark of all great television shows is their profound, or at least pervasive, impact on the pop culture. No sooner are they on the air than it's impossible to remember how we got along without them. Herewith, PEOPLE's shows of shows:

All in the Family	1971-79
All My Children	1970-present
The Andy Griffith Show	1960-68
Barney Miller	1975-82
The Beverly Hillbillies	1962-71
Bonanza	1959-73
The Brady Bunch	1969-74
The Bullwinkle Show	1961-73
Charlie's Angels	1976-81
Cheers	1982-93
The Cosby Show	1984-92
Dallas	1978-91
The Dick Van Dyke Show	1961-66
Dragnet	1952-59
(Series remake)	1967-70
Dynasty	1981-89
Family Ties	1982-89
Father Knows Best	1954-63
Gunsmoke	1955-75
Hill Street Blues	1981-87
Home Improvement	1991-present
The Honeymooners	1955-56
Jeopardy	1964-75
(Series remake)	1978-79
(Syndication)	1984-present
L.A. Law	1986-94
The Larry Sanders Show	1992-present
Leave It to Beaver	1957-63
The Mary Tyler Moore Show	1970-77
M*A*S*H	1972-83
Miami Vice	1984-89
Mission: Impossible	1966-73
Moonlighting	1985-89
Murphy Brown	1988-present
Nightline	1980-present
Northern Exposure	1990-present
N.Y.P.D. Blue	1993-present
The Odd Couple	1970-75
Roots	1977
Roseanne	1988-present
Rowan and Martin's Laugh-In	1968-73
Seinfeld	1990-present
Sesame Street	1969-present
The Simpsons	1990-present
60 Minutes	1968-present
Star Trek	1966-69
thirtysomething	1987-91
Today	1952-present
The Tonight Show	1954-present
The Twilight Zone	1959-64
(Series remake)	1985-88
The Waltons	1972-81
The Young and the Restless	1973-present
Your Show of Shows	1950-54

WHAT'S IN A NAME?

Is a favorite show any less sweet by a different name? The creators often thought so. And so many of the most popular shows of all time began with names other than those that became familiar to millions. A sampling follows (when a show had multiple names, they are listed in sequence).

Original Name	Final Name
The Alley Cats	Charlie's Angels
45 Minutes from Harlem	Diff'rent Strokes
Country Cousins/ The Eddie Albert Show	Green Acres
Cyborg	The Six Million Dollar Man
Danny Doyle	I Spy
Eye-Opener	CBS Morning Show
Family Business	The Partridge Family
The Flagstones	The Flintstones
McHale's Men	McHale's Navy
Mr. Solo/Solo	The Man From U.N.C.L.E.
New Family in Town	Happy Days
Occupation Unknown	What's My Line?
Oil	Dynasty
Ozark Widow/Dern Tootin'/ Whistle Stop	Petticoat Junction
The Rise and Shine Revue	Today
Spencer's Mountain	The Waltons
Sunset 77	77 Sunset Strip
Those Were the Days	All in the Family

NICK AT NITE'S CLASSIC TV COUNTDOWN

Beginning in 1989, Nick at Nite has celebrated the New Year with a countdown hosted by Casey Kasem in which their selections of the year's twenty-five best episodes are aired. The criteria include viewer requests, ratings, and critical commentary, as well as the guest star quotient (celebrities before they hit big), historical importance (first episodes, TV Land marriages and births), and moments that are just plain quintessential or bizarre (Oliver out in the *Green Acres* fields setting Lisa's "hotzcakes" on fire to keep his tomato plants safe from frost).

1993 SELECTIONS

1. *The Bob Newhart Show,* "Death Be My Destiny"

The elevators behind Carol's reception area were often used as comic props, opening to reveal surprises and closing to end conversations abruptly, but in this episode they took center stage. Bob steps into the open elevator shaft, and his close call with "Mr. Death" creates a phobia that he can't beat. It's a case of "psychologist, analyze thyself."

2. *The Mary Tyler Moore Show,* "Chuckles Bites the Dust"

Chuckles the Clown is the host of a kiddy show on WJM. In a terrible accident, while dressed as a Peanut, Chuckles is shucked—and killed—by a rogue elephant. Mary can't believe how quickly people begin making sick jokes about the tragedy . . . until the classic funeral scene.

3. *The Dick Van Dyke Show,* "Coast to Coast Big Mouth"

Laura Petrie is chosen from the audience to be in a game show. During the on-air interview, she is tricked into revealing that Alan Brady is bald. Carl Reiner, as Alan Brady, rants hilariously in the classic scene where he tells his toupees they're out of work.

4. *Dragnet,* "The LSD Story"

This episode is more popularly known as "Blue Boy" after its antagonist, a teenage boy who has painted his face blue and yellow and buried his head in the ground on an acid trip. Blue Boy's lunatic ravings and Joe Friday's moralizing have made this episode one of Nick at Nite's all-time most requested. It was also the very first episode in Jack Webb's "comeback" tour with the show. *Dragnet* had been off the air since 1959, but motivated in part by America's growing drug problem, producer-writer-director-star Webb decided in 1967 to revive the show.

5. *The Bob Newhart Show,* "Over the River and Through the Woods"

With Emily out of town, Dr. Bob Hartley spends Thanksgiving watching football with Howard, Jerry, and Mr. Carlin. Thanks to an old William and Mary football tradition and a jug of vodka and cider they get plowed and send out for fifteen orders of "moo goo gai pan," among other things.

6. *The Partridge Family,* "Soul Club"

Thanks to a crazy booking mix-up, Shirley drives the bus into downtown Detroit to play a club owned by guest stars Richard Pryor and Lou Gossett Jr. If they can't attract an audience, the club will go under. The gang goes to work, Reuben hustles, Keith writes a song that's "kind of an afro thing," and Danny recruits a group of militant African-American martial arts students to join the cause. Very seventies, and very cool.

7. *The Dick Van Dyke Show,* "The Curious Thing about Women"

Laura opens a piece of Rob's mail, causing a minor spat. But then Rob turns the event into a sketch on *The Alan Brady Show* and the spat becomes a full-fledged fight, until Rob can demonstrate to Laura that " 'twas curiosity killed the cat."

8. *Get Smart,* "And Baby Makes Four, Part II"

The historic episode in which Max and 99's twins are born, this was the conclusion of a two-part misadventure that featured Simon the Likable, a Kaos agent whose prime weapon was that no one could resist liking him. In the end it is Max's mother-in-law who foils the forces of badness.

9. *The Lucy Show,* "Lucy Goes to Marineland"

One of the episodes most often requested by viewers, this show features guest-starring appearances by then Los Angeles Angels baseball star Jimmy Piersall, Harvey Korman,

Lucille Ball's real-life kids, Lucie and Desi Arnaz, and all the creatures of Marineland, as Lucy ends up in the tank with a passel of seals and dolphins.

10. *The Mary Tyler Moore Show,* "Better Late . . . That's a Pun . . . Than Never."

Sweet, naive, innocent, upstanding Mary Richards getting fired? A night of silly joking around backfires when a ludicrous obituary Mary has written accidentally goes on the air. Those who loved Wee Willy Williams may never forgive Mary, but Lou finally does.

The following are the highest-ranking episodes of other classic TV series shown on Nick at Nite.

Dobie Gillis, "The Best Dressed Man"

A definitive chapter in Dobie's endless quest for the heart of money-grubbing but beautiful Thalia Menninger. Guest stars Warren Beatty as Dobie's arch-rival Milton Armitage, Tuesday Weld as Thalia, and Mel Blanc as the manager of the clothing store that spurs Dobie to compete with Milton's sartorial verve.

Bewitched, "Divided, He Falls"

Darrin is split into two Darrins—the fun side and the serious side—by Endora, of course. The "fun" Dick York is unreal: "Sam, why don't you 'whap' us up some champagne."

Mork and Mindy, "Mork Goes Erk"

Morgan Fairchild, as Susan Taylor, invites Mork, Mindy, and Mr. Bickley to join her EST-like encounter group. Ellsworth, the cynical, mean-spirited, invective-hurling leader of the ERK (Ellsworth Revitalization Konditioning) group is played by none other than David Letterman. Letterman has seldom been seen out of the friendly confines of his own show since.

Mr. Ed, "Clint Eastwood Meets Mr. Ed"

Guest starring, naturally, Clint Eastwood, who was then better known as Rowdy Yates of *Rawhide* than as a movie star. The story is Mr. Ed's romancing of a filly who happens to be Eastwood's. Naturally, Wilbur is the one who gets in trouble and Clint plays the heavy.

F-Troop, "Bye Bye Balloon"

Harvey Korman guest stars in the role of Colonel Heinrich Von Zeppel, a Prussian balloonist who arrives at Fort Courage to whip the men into shape. The episode also features the classic moment when the hot air balloon floats over the Hekawi camp and Chief Wild Eagle calls out memorably: "It . . . is . . . balloon!"

The Patty Duke Show, "The Cousins"

It wasn't until this, the thirty-sixth episode of the show, that the makers of "The Patty Duke Show" went back and told the origin of the story, returning to the fateful day that the worldly and intellectual Cathy Lane arrived in Brooklyn Heights. But have no fear, psychopathologists have now firmly established that you cannot "lose your mind when cousins are two of a kind."

Green Acres, "Don't Trust Little Old Ladies"

Though many lump the story of Lisa and Oliver Douglas's dislocation to Hooterville in with all the other rural comedies of that era—*Beverly Hillbillies, Petticoat Junction,* et al.—in fact, *Green Acres* was a strange and wonderful show like none other. It combined surrealism and nonsense that Salvador Dali and Lewis Carroll would have admired, and never more so than in this episode, where a little old lady's weather predictions lead Oliver to dream that he and Lisa are mechanical characters in a Bavarian clock. The final scene is Oliver and Lisa at night out in the field among tomato plants that are being warmed by flaming pancakes.

My Three Sons, "Coincidence"

Though it settled in to more standard family comedy adventures in its later years, in its black-and-white years this long-running show often tried unusual stories and plot devices. "Coincidence" is a prime example, and could well have been an episode of *The Twilight Zone.* Steve is fed up with the chaos of his house, but then, shortly after an encounter with a leprechaun-like gentleman (played by Billy Barty), he arrives at a parallel female version of his own household, meeting a woman and her three daughters: Mike, Bobby, and Kip.

Car 54, Where Are You?, "How Smart Can You Be?"

This is the classic episode in which Gunther Toody poses the questions: "Could Leonard Bernstein subsist on termites? Is he nocturnal? Does he have strong blunt claws?" It's all a part of Toody's effort to become as smart as his partner, Francis Muldoon. His system is to read the encyclopedia, but he has only gotten as far as "aardvark." The episode also includes Toody's classic monologue on nonchalance and its impact on major league ballplayers, and whether Yogi Berra or Mickey Mantle is more nonchalant, or even too nonchalant.

JOIN THE LIVE STUDIO AUDIENCE

Say what you want about television, but at least it's free (more or less). Not only that, but you can also obtain free tickets to see a wide variety of talk shows, game shows, and situation comedies, most of which tape in either New York or Los Angeles. Here's how.

TALK SHOWS AND LATE-NIGHT SHOWS

Donahue
Send a postcard indicating the number of tickets desired to NBC Tickets, 30 Rockefeller Plaza, New York, NY 10112. Tickets are available to those sixteen or over; please allow two to four weeks for delivery. For an updated New York taping schedule call (212) 664-3056.

Geraldo
Call (212) 265-1283 for recorded information about tickets and the New York taping schedule, or send a self-addressed stamped envelope with ticket requests to Geraldo Tickets, CBS Television, 524 W. 57th Street, New York, NY 10019.

The Jane Whitney Show
Call (212) 957-1340 and speak with an audience representative for information about the New York taping schedule and requests for free tickets. You must be eighteen or older, and there is a four-ticket limit per request.

Leeza
Free tickets are available on a first-come–first-serve basis from the Paramount Studios Visitor Center on 860 North Gower Street in Hollywood up to five days prior to taping. For recorded ticket and taping information call the Paramount Studio guest relations line at (213) 956-5575. Production schedules vary from week to week, so the most precise information is available by speaking with a representative from the Paramount business office at (213) 956-1777 from 9:00 to 5:00, Monday through Friday.

Late Night with Conan O'Brien
Mail one postcard per show (no letters) with name, address, and number of tickets desired to NBC Tickets, 30 Rockefeller Plaza, New York, NY 10112. No specific dates can be requested and tickets are only available to those sixteen or over. Standby tickets (one per person, no guarantee of admission) are available Monday through Friday at 9:00 a.m. at the page desk in the downstairs main NBC lobby (same address as above). For more information call (212) 664-3055, or (212) 664-3056 for an updated schedule of shows.

Late Show with David Letterman
Send a postcard with name and address to Tickets, Ed Sullivan Theater, 1697 Broadway, New York, NY 10010. Available to those sixteen and older, the tickets are usually mailed within three months; if no response is received, another card should be sent. Only two tickets are issued per request, and specific dates cannot generally be accommodated. There are, however, a number of standby tickets available every day at the theater; numbers are issued each day at noon (though a waiting line forms much earlier) and distributed at 5:00. It is recommended that the studio audience dress warmly since the studio is kept cold during taping.

Live with Regis and Kathie Lee
For ticket and New York taping information call (212) 456-3537. To request tickets by mail, send a postcard with your name, address, phone number, and the number of tickets desired (limit of four per request) to Live Tickets, Ansonia Station, P.O. Box 777, New York, NY 10023. Audience members must be 18 or over to attend the taping. On the morning of each show, a limited number of standby tickets are issued at the ticket office on W. 67th Street and Columbus Avenue at 8:00 a.m., but these tickets do not guarantee admission to the taping.

Maury Povich
For ticket information and New York taping schedules call the ticket hotline, (212) 989-3622, and leave a message indicating your name, address, phone number, and the number of tickets and dates desired; a representative will mail the tickets and information to you.

The Montel Williams Show
Call the ticket line at (212) 840-1700 for tickets and for the New York taping schedule. To request tickets by mail, send a postcard with your name, address, phone number, and the number of tickets desired to Montel Williams Tickets, 1500 Broadway–Suite 700, New York, NY 10036.

Oprah
Tickets are not available by mail, but show information can be obtained and reservations to appear in the studio audience in Chicago can be made

by calling (312) 591-9222. These lines are often busy, so try calling early in the day.

The Ricki Lake Show
To request tickets by mail, send a postcard with your address and number of tickets desired to The Ricki Lake Show, Ticket Office, 401 Fifth Avenue, 7th Floor, New York, NY 10016. There is a limit of four tickets per request, and you must be at least eighteen years old to attend the New York taping. For further information and schedules of topics, speak with a representative at (212) 889-6767.

Rush Limbaugh: The Television Show
For free tickets call (212) 397-7367, Monday through Thursday, 10 a.m.–1 p.m. For further New York taping schedules and information call (212) 397-4675.

Sally Jessy Raphael
Call (212) 582-1722 for ticket and New York taping information between 8:30 a.m. and 10:30 p.m. Monday through Friday, or send a postcard with your address and the number of tickets desired to Sally Jessy Raphael Tickets, P.O. Box 1400, Radio City Station, New York, NY 10101.

Saturday Night Live
To obtain tickets for next season, send *one* postcard (no letters) with name, address, and number of *SNL* tickets desired to NBC Tickets, 30 Rockefeller Plaza, New York, NY 10112. A ticket lottery is drawn in August to fill audience requests for the entire season. It is not possible to request specific dates, but standby tickets are available (fifty for the dress rehearsal and fifty for the live taping). These are distributed on the day of the show's taping at 9:15 a.m. at the side entrance of the GE Building on W. 49th Street, opposite the Rockefeller Center Garage. One standby ticket per person is available, for either the rehearsal or the live show. Standby tickets do not guarantee admission, and one must be sixteen or over to attend. For more information call (212) 664-3055, or to speak with a ticket representative call (212) 664-3056.

The Tonight Show with Jay Leno
Send a self-addressed stamped envelope with the number of tickets desired to NBC Tickets, 3000 W. Alameda Ave., Burbank, CA 91523. Tickets are also available at the Burbank ticket counter on the day of the taping, starting at 5:30 p.m. (line begins forming one hour prior). For recorded ticket distribution information, taping schedules, group bookings, and directions to the Burbank, California studios, call NBC Studios at (818) 840-3537.

LOS ANGELES-AREA SITCOMS

Audiences Unlimited distributes limited numbers of tickets for most of the situation comedies shot before live audiences in the Los Angeles area. They have tickets for the favorites—such as *Roseanne*, *Murphy Brown* and *Home Improvement*—as well as newer sitcoms, a few game shows, and talk shows. For a recorded message giving a weekly list of tickets available, the times and locations of taping, call (818) 506-0067. A one-month advance show taping-filming schedule is available by sending a self-addressed stamped envelope to Audiences Unlimited, 100 Universal City Plaza, Building 153, Universal City, CA 91608. Tickets are available by mail from the same address. Tickets are mailed ten days to two weeks prior to show date and are limited for all shows, so include alternate choices.

Tickets are also available from Audiences Unlimited's three box offices starting on Wednesdays for shows scheduled for the following week:

1. Fox Television Center, 5746 Sunset Boulevard, Hollywood; tickets are available 8:30 a.m.–6:00 p.m. Monday through Friday and 12:00–6:00 p.m. on weekends.
2. Panorama Mall, Van Nuys and Roscoe Blvds., Panorama City; tickets are distributed at the information/security desk 12:00–8:00 p.m. Monday through Friday and 12:00–6:00 p.m. on weekends.
3. The Glendale Galleria, Central and Broadway, Glendale; tickets are available daily at the information desk during mall hours.

All tickets are available on a first-come–first-serve basis and occasionally on the day of the show, but earlier arrival is suggested for the best selection. Some of the more popular shows such as *Home Improvement* and *Roseanne* tend to go first or have tickets available only by mail, so it is best to call or write ahead for tickets.

WIN FABULOUS PRIZES AND BECOME A STAR

We all play along with the game shows when we watch at home, but only a few of us make it onto the air to play the games for real. Here are the wheres and hows on becoming a contestant on the leading shows.

American Gladiators
The show holds open tryouts for its competitors once a year (usually in April or May). Details on the locations, times, and requirements for the tryouts are not readily available until early spring. For further information, call the *American Gladiators* hotline in Calif. at (310) 284-9181.

Family Feud
While *Family Feud* usually tapes in Los Angeles, contestant searches take place on a regular basis in New York City and San Diego as well as in L.A. Four family members (related by blood or marriage) must appear together for a preliminary audition/interview; if they pass this stage they are invited for a second audition. Those families chosen are flown to Los Angeles to appear as contestants on the show. For further information and to schedule auditions, call the *Family Feud* contestant lines, in New York at (212) 755-3383, in San Diego at (619) 223-2101, and in Los Angeles at (213) 965-6700. Tickets for the studio audience are available from the CBS ticket window, Television City, 7800 Beverly Boulevard, Los Angeles, on the day of the taping. The show is taped sporadically (generally every six to eight weeks) and sometimes goes on the road, so it is best to check with a CBS ticket representative at (213) 852-2458 for the most current ticket and audience information.

Jeopardy!
To be a contestant on *Jeopardy!* you must pass a fifty-question test. Los Angeles test dates are available from the *Jeopardy!* contestant line, (213) 466-3931, Monday through Friday from 10:00 to 4:30. The test dates are scheduled erratically throughout the year, so call two to three weeks prior to being in the Los Angeles area to schedule an appointment. For information about out-of-town contestant searches call the number above. Successful test-takers are then invited to play a mock version of the game, and if that goes well they will be called once there is an opening (which could be as soon as two weeks or never at all). To inquire about general taping information and schedules, and to request tickets for the Los Angeles studio audience, call (213) 466-4487.

MTV: *The Grind*, etc.
MTV airs several shows with audience participants and dancers, among them *The Grind* and the annual spring break specials. Many of these shows require auditions and/or advance reservations. Call MTV's Viewer Services Hotline at (212) 258-8700 for the latest schedules of shows requiring live audiences and information on their procedures to follow to become a participant, from 8:30 to 5:30, Monday through Friday.

Nickelodeon: *Guts*, *Legends of the Hidden Temple*, and others
Nickelodeon produces several kids' shows that require audience participation, such as *Guts* and *Legends of the Hidden Temple*. These shows are filmed on erratic schedules at Universal Studios Theme Park in Orlando, Fla.. Call Nickelodeon's Viewer Services in New York (212) 258-7579 or in Fla. (407) 363-8500 at least two weeks in advance of being in Orlando to find out taping schedules. Free tickets are distributed at the theme park on a first-come–first-serve basis on the day of the taping. To gain access to the theme park, you have to purchase the regular-price admission pass. (Call (407) 363-8500 for general theme park information.) Tickets do not guarantee admission to the tapings, and there are different age limits for kids who wish to participate as contestants.

The Price Is Right
Since all of the contestants on *The Price is Right* are randomly selected from the audience, call CBS Tickets in Los Angeles at (213) 852-2458 for the most up-to-date taping schedule and ticket information. *The Price Is Right* is usually taped twice daily on Mondays, Tuesdays, and Wednesdays at 1:15 and 4:45. Tickets can be obtained by mail (allow four to six weeks for delivery) from the CBS ticket window, Television City, 7800 Beverly Boulevard, Los Angeles, CA 90036. Tickets are also distributed at this location for the 1:15 show starting at 8 a.m., and for the 4:45 show starting at 11:00 a.m. (However, the lines begin forming at least two hours prior to distribution times.)

Wheel of Fortune
Contestant auditions are held sporadically throughout the year, both in Los Angeles and during contestant searches around the U.S. The most up-to-date information on audition schedules is available by calling (818) 972-8088.

STARS WITH SOAPY ROOTS

Many of the most familiar faces in the entertainment world first appeared on the small screen of daytime TV. Test your soap-opera memory against our list.

Actor	Character	Soap
Armand Assante	Dr. Mike Powers	The Doctors
Phylicia Rashad	Courtney Wright	One Life to Live
Kevin Bacon	T.J.	The Guiding Light
Alec Baldwin	Billy Allison Aldrich	The Doctors
Bonnie Bedelia	Sandy Porter	Love of Life
Robby Benson	Bruce Carson	Search for Tomorrow
Tom Berenger	Timmy Siegel	One Life to Live
Corbin Bernsen	Kenny Graham	Ryan's Hope
Ellen Burstyn	Dr. Kate Bartok	The Doctors
Tia Carrere	Jade Soong	General Hospital
Dixie Carter	Olivia Brandeis "Brandy" Henderson	The Edge of Night
Nell Carter	Ethel Green	Ryan's Hope
Jill Clayburgh	Grace Bolton	Search for Tomorrow
Ted Danson	Tom Conway	Somerset
Olympia Dukakis	Barbara Moreno	Search for Tomorrow
Morgan Fairchild	Jennifer Phillips	Search for Tomorrow
Laurence Fishburne	Joshua West	One Life to Live
Richard Grieco	Rick Gardner	One Life to Live
Larry Hagman	Ed Gibson	The Edge of Night
Mark Hamill	Kent Murray	General Hospital
David Hasselhoff	Bill "Snapper" Foster	The Young and the Restless
Hal Holbrook	Grayling Dennis	The Brighter Day
Kate Jackson	Daphne Harridge	Dark Shadows
Tommy Lee Jones	Dr. Mark Toland	One Life to Live
James Earl Jones	Dr. Jim Frazier	The Guiding Light
Kevin Kline	Woody Reed	Search for Tomorrow
Don Knotts	Wilbur Peabody	Search for Tomorrow
Diane Ladd	Kitty Styles	The Secret Storm
Judith Light	Karen Martin	One Life to Live
Hal Linden	Larry Carter	Search for Tomorrow
Ray Liotta	Joey Perini	Another World
Garry Marshall	Bert Atwater	Days of Our Lives
Demi Moore	Jackie Templeton	General Hospital
Luke Perry	Ned Bates	Loving
Christopher Reeve	Benno ("Beanie" or "Ben") Harper	Love of Life
Eric Roberts	Ted Bancroft	Another World

Actor	Character	Soap
Meg Ryan	Betsy Stewart	As the World Turns
Susan Sarandon	Sarah	Search for Tomorrow
Kyra Sedgwick	Julia Shearer	Another World
Tom Selleck	Jed Andrews	The Young and the Restless
Grant Show	Rick Hyde	Ryan's Hope
Christian Slater	D. J. LaSalle	Ryan's Hope
Rick Springfield	Dr. Noah Drake	General Hospital
John Stamos	Blackie Parrish	General Hospital
Janine Turner	Laura Templeton	General Hospital
Kathleen Turner	Nola Dancy Aldrich	The Doctors
Blair Underwood	Bobby Blue	One Life to Live
Joan Van Ark	Janene Whitney	Days of Our Lives
Christopher Walken	Michael Bauer	The Guiding Light
Sigourney Weaver	Avis Ryan	Somerset
Billy Dee Williams	Dr. Jim Frazier	The Guiding Light
JoBeth Williams	Brandy Sheloo	The Guiding Light

ONE LONG LIFE TO LIVE

Soap operas have been one of the enduring success stories of television programming. The grandaddy, *The Guiding Light*, was transplanted directly from radio in 1952. Other longtime survivors: (Source: *Soap Opera Digest*)

The Guiding Light	1952*–present
As the World Turns	1956–present
Search for Tomorrow	1951*–86
General Hospital	1963–present
Another World	1964–present
Love of Life	1951*–80
The Edge of Night	1956–84
Days of Our Lives	1965–present
All My Children	1970–present
The Young and the Restless	1973–present
The Secret Storm	1954*–74

* *These shows began as fifteen-minute programs.*

PRIME TIME'S TOP 40

There's something infectious about television theme songs. Here are the ones that hit highest on the *Billboard* charts. (The list excludes songs that were hits prior to their adoption as television anthems.)

Song	Show	Performer	Chart Position/Year
S.W.A.T.	S.W.A.T.	Rhythm Heritage	1/1975
Welcome Back	Welcome Back, Kotter	John Sebastian	1/1976
Miami Vice	Miami Vice	Jan Hammer	1/1985
Believe It or Not	The Greatest American Hero	Joey Scarbury	2/1981
Dragnet	Dragnet	Ray Anthony Orchestra	3/1953
Secret Agent Man	Secret Agent Man	Johnny Rivers	3/1966
Hawaii Five-O	Hawaii Five-O	The Ventures	4/1969
Happy Days	Happy Days	Pratt and McClain	5/1976
Makin' It	Makin' It	David Naughton	5/1979
Peter Gunn	Peter Gunn	Ray Anthony Orchestra	8/1959
Three Stars Will Shine Tonight	Dr. Kildare	Richard Chamberlain	10/1962
The Rockford Files	The Rockford Files	Mike Post	10/1975
Hill Street Blues	Hill Street Blues	Mike Post and Larry Carlton	10/1981
Zorro	Zorro	The Chordettes	17/1958
Batman	Batman	The Marketts	17/1966
Different Worlds	Angie	Maureen McGovern	18/1979
Bonanza	Bonanza	Al Caiola	19/1961
Keep Your Eye on the Sparrow	Baretta	Rhythm Heritage	20/1976
Mr. Lucky	Mr. Lucky	Henry Mancini Orchestra	21/1960
The Dukes of Hazzard	The Dukes of Hazzard	Waylon Jennings	21/1980
Moonlighting	Moonlighting	Al Jarreau	23/1987
Making Our Dreams Come True	Laverne & Shirley	Cyndi Grecco	25/1976
Magnum, P.I.	Magnum, P.I.	Mike Post	25/1982
Ben Casey	Ben Casey	Valjean	28/1962
Blue Star	Medic	Felicia Sanders	29/1955
Route 66	Route 66	Nelson Riddle Orchestra	30/1962
Ballad of Paladin	Have Gun Will Travel	Duane Eddy	33/1962
Seattle	Here Come the Brides	Perry Como	38/1969
The Men	The Men	Isaac Hayes	38/1972
Mission: Impossible	Mission: Impossible	Lalo Schifrin	41/1968
Those Were the Days	All in the Family	Carroll O'Connor and Jean Stapleton	43/1971
The Ballad of Jed Clampett	Beverly Hillbillies	Lester Flatt and Earl Scruggs	44/1962
Charlie's Angels	Charlie's Angels	Henry Mancini	45/1977
Dynasty	Dynasty	Bill Conti	52/1982
My Three Sons	My Three Sons	Lawrence Welk Orchestra	55/1961

YES, BUT IS IT ART?

It's no accident that the Smithsonian is known as the nation's attic. Tucked away at the Museum of American History at the Smithsonian Institution is one of the most extensive collections of television memorabilia in the country. Although most of it is kept in storage, the starred objects below are displayed publicly. A partial catalogue of the choicest:

All in the Family
Archie and Edith Bunker's chairs*
Wooden end table with lace doily and ashtray*
Beer cans*

American Bandstand
Podium used on 1950s edition

Barney Miller
Assignment board
Jail door
Barney Miller's police badge*
Nick Yemana's coffee cup*

Bozo the Clown
Costume worn by Larry Hagman

The Camel News Caravan
John Cameron Swayze's desk plaque

The Carol Burnett Show
Charwoman costume worn by Carol Burnett*

Dallas
J. R. Ewing's hat

The Edge of Night
Gold pocket watch that exposed Sky Whitney's impostor
Miniature carousel

Gunsmoke
Matt Dillon's hat

Happy Days
Fonzie's leather jacket*

Howdy Doody
The "Howdy Doody" puppet*
Seltzer bottle used by Clarabell the Clown

Lassie
Timmy's costume

Magnum, P.I.
Detroit Tigers baseball cap
Hawaiian shirt

The Mary Tyler Moore Show
Ted Knight's blue blazer*

M*A*S*H
Alcohol brewing still and martini glasses
Hawkeye Pierce's Hawaiian shirt
Directional signpost
Door to the "Swamp"
Klinger's gold lamé dress, Cleopatra-style headdress, and pink wool coat
Script from final episode
Toledo Mudhens pennant* and uniform

Mister Rogers' Neighborhood
Sweater worn by Fred Rogers

Mutual of Omaha's Wild Kingdom
Map of Himalayan countries used when Sir Edmund Hillary cohosted
Pith helmet and safari jacket worn by Marlin Perkins

Romper Room
The Do Bee's costume*

Search for Tomorrow
Scissors used to stab Stephanie Wyatt's third husband

Sesame Street
Ernie's rubber duckie
Susan's, Bob's, and Mr. Hooper's costumes
Sesame Street sign
The Kermit puppet
Oscar the Grouch with his trash can*

Star Trek
Hand phaser

The Waltons
Radio set

STAR TREK: THE ORIGINAL VOYAGE

As wildly popular as *Star Trek* has become in syndication, the original program only aired for three years, beginning with the 1966–67 season. Created by Gene Roddenberry, the show was set aboard the starship *Enterprise* in the twenty-third century and featured Captain Kirk, Science Officer Spock, and a multicultural range of fellow spaceniks adventuring around the universe. While many of the *Star Trek* spin-offs have become successful in their own right, for the true Trekkie nothing will ever rival the original episodes of the first three years (now aired in nearly fifty countries), which are listed below in order of presentation.

1966–67

Man Trap	September 8, 1966
Charlie X	September 15, 1966
Where No Man Has Gone Before	September 22, 1966
The Naked Time	September 29, 1966
The Enemy Within	October 10, 1966
Mudd's Women	October 13, 1966
What Are Little Girls Made Of?	October 20, 1966
Miri	October 27, 1966
Dagger of the Mind	November 3, 1966
Corbomite Maneuver	November 10, 1966
The Menagerie I	November 17, 1966
The Menagerie II	November 24, 1966
Conscience of the King	December 8, 1966
Balance of Terror	December 15, 1966
Shore Leave	December 29, 1966
The Galileo Seven	January 5, 1967
Squire of Gothos	January 12, 1967
Arena	January 19, 1967
Tomorrow Is Yesterday	January 26, 1967
Court-Martial	February 2, 1967
Return of the Archons	February 9, 1967
Space Seed	February 16, 1967
Taste of Armageddon	February 23, 1967
This Side of Paradise	March 2, 1967
Devil in the Dark	March 9, 1967
Errand of Mercy	March 23, 1967
Alternative Factor	March 30, 1967
The City on the Edge of Forever	April 6, 1967
Operation Annihilate!	April 13, 1967

1967–68

Amok Time	September 15, 1967
Who Mourns for Adonais?	September 22, 1967
Changeling	September 29, 1967
Mirror, Mirror	October 6, 1967
The Apple	October 13, 1967
Doomsday Machine	October 20, 1967
Catspaw	October 27, 1967
I, Mudd	November 3, 1967
Metamorphosis	November 10, 1967
Journey to Babel	November 17, 1967
The Deadly Years	December 8, 1967
Obsession	December 15, 1967
Wolf in the Fold	December 22, 1967
The Trouble with Tribbles	December 29, 1967
Gamesters of Triskelion	January 5, 1968
A Piece of the Action	January 12, 1968
Immunity Syndrome	January 19, 1968
A Private Little War	February 2, 1968
Return to Tomorrow	February 9, 1968
Patterns of Force	Feburary 16, 1968
By Any Other Name	February 23, 1968
Omega Glory	March 1, 1968
The Ultimate Computer	March 8, 1968
Bread and Circuses	March 15, 1968
Friday's Child	March 22, 1968
Assignment Earth	March 29, 1968

1968–69

Spock's Brain	September 20, 1968
Enterprise Incident	September 27, 1968
Paradise Syndrome	October 4, 1968
And the Children Shall Lead Them	October 11, 1968
Is There in Truth No Beauty?	October 18, 1968
Spectre of the Gun	October 25, 1968
Day of the Dove	November 1, 1968
For the World Is Hollow and I Have Touched the Sky	November 8, 1968
The Tholian Web	November 15, 1968
Plato's Children	November 22, 1968
Wink of an Eye	November 29, 1968
The Empath	December 6, 1968
Whom Gods Destroy	December 13, 1968
Elaan of Trois	December 20, 1968
Let That Be Your Last Battlefield	January 10, 1969
Mark of Gideon	January 17, 1969
That Which Survives	Janruary 24, 1969
The Lights of Zetar	January 31, 1969
Requiem For Methuselah	February 14, 1969
The Way to Eden	February 21, 1969
The Cloud Minders	February 28, 1969
Savage Curtain	March 7, 1969
All Our Yesterdays	March 14, 1969
Turnabout Intruder	April 4, 1969

THE MANY LIVES OF *STAR TREK*

Watching the original TV version of *Star Trek* transformed into perhaps the most successful rerun on the air, producer Gene Roddenberry agreed to launch the story again—and again. The following list chronicles the multiform life of the *Star Trek* vision throughout the years.

1. *Star Trek*, NBC prime time, 1966–69
2. *Star Trek*, NBC cartoon, 1973–75
3. *Star Trek: The Motion Picture*, Paramount Pictures, 1979
3. *Star Trek II: The Wrath of Khan*, Paramount Pictures, 1982
4. *Star Trek III: The Search for Spock*, Paramount Pictures, 1984
5. *Star Trek IV: The Voyage Home*, Paramount Pictures, 1986
6. *Star Trek: The Next Generation*, syndicated prime time, 1987–94
7. *Star Trek V: The Final Frontier*, Paramount Pictures, 1989
8. *Star Trek VI: The Undiscovered Country*, Paramount Pictures, 1991
9. *Star Trek: Deep Space Nine*, syndicated prime time, 1993–
10. *Star Trek: Generations*, Paramount Pictures, 1994
11. *Star Trek: Voyager*, syndicated prime time, 1995 (projected)

THE EMMY AWARDS

As the television industry has grown, so has the business of television awards. So much so that the Emmys are now presented in two separate ceremonies to accommodate the wealth of categories. The following presents a wide selection of winners in major areas through the years.

	1949	1950
Actor	—	Alan Young
Actress	—	Gertrude Berg
Drama	—	*Pulitzer Prize Playhouse*, ABC
Variety Program	—	*The Alan Young Show*, CBS
Game Show	—	*Truth or Consequences*, CBS
Children's Show	*Time for Beany*, KTLA	*Time for Beany*, KTLA

	1951	1952	1953
Actor	Sid Caesar	Thomas Mitchell	Donald O'Connor, *Colgate Comedy Hour*, NBC
Actress	Imogene Coca	Helen Hayes	Eve Arden, *Our Miss Brooks*, CBS
Drama	*Studio One*, CBS	*Robert Montgomery Presents*, NBC	*U.S. Steel Hour*, ABC
Mystery, Action, or Adventure	—	*Dragnet*, NBC	*Dragnet*, NBC
Comedy	*Red Skelton Show*, NBC	*I Love Lucy*, CBS	*I Love Lucy*, CBS
Comedian	Red Skelton, NBC	Lucille Ball, CBS; Jimmy Durante, NBC	—
Variety Program	*Your Show of Shows*, NBC	*Your Show of Shows*, NBC	*Omnibus*, CBS
Game Show	—	*What's My Line?*, CBS	*This is Your Life*, NBC; *What's My Line?*, CBS
Children's Program	—	*Time for Beany*, KTLA	*Kukla, Fran & Ollie*, NBC

	1954	1955	1956
Actor	Danny Thomas, *Make Room for Daddy*, ABC	Phil Silvers, *The Phil Silvers Show*, CBS	Robert Moss, *Father Knows Best*, NBC
Actress	Loretta Young, *The Loretta Young Show*, NBC	Lucille Ball, *I Love Lucy*, CBS	Loretta Young, *The Loretta Young Show*, NBC
Drama	*U.S. Steel Hour*, ABC	*Producers' Showcase*, NBC	*Playhouse 90*, CBS
Mystery, Action, or Adventure	*Dragnet*, NBC	*Disneyland*, ABC	—
Comedy	*Make Room for Daddy*, ABC	*The Phil Silvers Show*, CBS	—
Comedian	—	Phil Silvers, CBS; Nanette Fabray, NBC	Sid Caesar, *Caesar's Hour*, NBC; Nanette Fabray, *Caesar's Hour*, NBC
Variety Series	*Disneyland*, ABC	*The Ed Sullivan Show*, CBS	—
Game Show	*This Is Your Life*, NBC	*The $64,000 Question*, CBS	—
Children's Program	*Lassie*, CBS	*Lassie*, CBS	—

	1957	1958–59	1959–60
Drama	*Gunsmoke*, CBS	*The Alcoa Hour/Goodyear Playhouse*, NBC; *Playhouse 90*, CBS	*Playhouse 90*, CBS
Actor—Series	—	Raymond Burr, *Perry Mason*, CBS (Drama)	Robert Stack, *The Untouchables*, ABC
Actress—Series	—	Loretta Young, *The Loretta Young Show*, NBC (Drama)	Jane Wyatt, *Father Knows Best*, CBS
Supporting Actor—Series	—	Dennis Weaver, *Gunsmoke*, CBS	—
Supporting Actress—Drama Series	—	Barbara Hale, *Perry Mason*, CBS	—
Director—Drama	—	George Schaefer, *Little Moon of Aloban*, NBC; Jack Smight, *Eddie*, NBC	Robert Mulligan, *The Moon and Sixpence*, NBC
Writer—Drama	—	James Costigan, *Little Moon of Alban*, NBC; Alfred Brenner, and Ken Hughes, *Eddie*, NBC	Rod Serling, *The Twilight Zone*, CBS
Comedy	*The Phil Silvers Show*, CBS	*The Jack Benny Show*, CBS	*Art Carney Special*, NBC
Actor—Comedy Series	Robert Young, *Father Knows Best*, NBC	Jack Benny, *The Jack Benny Show*, CBS	Dick Van Dyke, *The Dick Van Dyke Show*, CBS
Actress—Comedy Series	Jane Wyatt, *Father Knows Best*, NBC	Jane Wyatt, *Father Knows Best*, CBS & NBC	Jane Wyatt, *Father Knows Best*, CBS
Supporting Actor—Comedy Series	Carl Reiner, *Caesar's Hour*, NBC	Tom Poston, *The Steve Allen Show*, NBC	—
Supporting Actress—Comedy Series	Ann B. Davis, *The Bob Cummings Show*, CBS and NBC	Ann B. Davis, *The Bob Cummings Show*, NBC	—
Director—Comedy/Comedy Series	—	Peter Tewksbury, *Father Knows Best*, CBS	Ralph Levy and Bud Yorkin, *The Jack Benny Hour Specials*, CBS
Writer—Comedy/Comedy Series	Nat Hiken, Billy Friedberg, Phil Sharp, Terry Ryan, Coleman Jacoby, Arnold Rosen, Sidney Zelinko, A.J. Russell, and Tony Webster, *The Phil Silvers Show*, CBS	Sam Perrin, George Balzer, Hal Goldman, and Al Gordon, *The Jack Benny Show*, CBS	Sam Perrin, George Balzer, Hal Goldman, and Al Gordon, *The Jack Benny Show*, CBS
Variety Program	*The Dinah Shore Chevy Show*, NBC	*The Dinah Shore Chevy Show*, NBC	*The Fabulous Fifties*, CBS
Game Show	—	*What's My Line?* CBS	—
Children's Program	—	—	*Huckleberry Hound*, SYN

	1960–61	1961–62	1962–63
Actor	Raymond Burr, *Perry Mason,* CBS	E.G. Marshall, *The Defenders,* CBS	E.G. Marshall, *The Defenders,* CBS
Actress	Barbara Stanwyck, *The Barbara Stanwyck Show,* NBC	Shirley Booth, *Hazel,* NBC	Shirley Booth, *Hazel,* NBCc
Drama	*Macbeth,* NBC	*The Defenders,* CBS	*The Defenders,* CBS
Director—Drama	George Schaefer, *Macbeth,* NBC	Franklin Schaffner, *The Defenders,* CBS	Stuart Rosenberg, *The Defenders,* CBS
Writer—Drama	Rod Serling, *The Twilight Zone,* CBS	Reginald Rose, *The Defenders,* CBS	Robert Thorn, Reginald Rose, *The Defenders,* CBS
Comedy	*The Jack Benny Show,* CBS	*The Bob Newhart Show,* NBC	*The Dick Van Dyke Show,* CBS
Director—Comedy	Sheldon Leonard, *The Danny Thomas Show,* CBS	Nat Hiken, *Car 54, Where Are You?,* NBC	John Rich, *The Dick Van Dyke Show,* CBS
Writer—Comedy	Sherwood Schwartz, Dave O'Brien, Al Schwartz, Martin Ragaway, and Red Skelton, *The Red Skelton Show,* CBS	Carl Reiner, *The Dick Van Dyke Show,* CBS	Carl Reiner, *The Dick Van Dyke Show,* CBS
Variety Program	*Astaire Time,* NBC	*The Garry Moore Show,* CBS	*The Andy Williams Show,* NBC
Individual Performance—Variety or Music Program/Series	Fred Astaire, *Astaire Time,* NBC	Carol Burnett, *The Garry Moore Show,* CBS	Carol Burnett,*Julie and Carol at Carnegie Hall,* CBS; *Carol and Company,* CBS
Panel, Quiz or Audience Participation	—	—	*College Bowl,* CBS
Children's Program	*Young People's Concert: Aaron* Copland's Birthday Party, CBS	*New York Philharmonic Young People's Concerts with Leonard Bernstein,* CBS	*Walt Disney's Wonderful World of Color,* NBC

	1963–64	1964–65	1965–66
Drama	*The Defenders*, CBS	In 1964–65 the entire award system was changed for one year, and there were no awards given in individual categories that in any way match the categories from other years.	*The Fugitive*, ABC
Actor—Drama Series	Jack Klugman, *The Defenders*, CBS		Bill Cosby, *I Spy*, NBC
Actress—Drama Series	Shelley Winters, *Two Is The Number*, NBC		Barbara Stanwyck, *The Big Valley*, ABC
Supporting Actor—Drama Series	Albert Parker, *One Day In The Life of Ivan Denisovich*, NBC	—	James Daly, *Eagle in a Cage*, NBC
Supporting Actress—Drama Series	Ruth White, *Little Moon of Alban*, NBC	—	Lee Grant, *Peyton Place*, ABC
Writer—Drama	Ernest Kinay, *The Defenders*, CBS	—	Sidney Pollack, *The Game*, NBC
Director—Drama	Tom Gries, *East Side/West Side*, CBS	—	Millard Lampell, *Eagle in a Cage*, NBC
Comedy	*The Dick Van Dyke Show*, CBS	—	*The Dick Van Dyke Show*, CBS
Actor—Comedy Series	Dick Van Dyke, *The Dick Van Dyke Show*, CBS	—	Dick Van Dyke, *The Dick Van Dyke Show*, CBS
Actress—Comedy Series	Mary Tyler Moore, *The Dick Van Dyke Show*, CBS	—	Mary Tyler Moore, *The Dick Van Dyke Show*, CBS
Supporting Actor—Comedy Series	—	—	Don Knotts, *The Andy Griffith Show*, CBS
Supp. Actress—Comedy Series	—	—	Alice Pearce, *Bewitched*, ABC
Director—Comedy	Jerry Paris, *The Dick Van Dyke Show*, CBS	—	William Asher, *Bewitched*, ABC
Writer—Comedy	Carl Reiner, Sam Denoff, and Bill Penky, *The Dick Van Dyke Show*, CBS	—	Bill Persky, Sam Denoff, *The Dick Van Dyke Show*, CBS
Variety Program	*The Danny Kaye Show*, CBS	—	*The Andy Williams Show*, NBC
Director—Variety or Music	Robert Scheerer, *The Danny Kaye Show*, CBS	—	Alan Handley, *The Julie Andrews Show*, NBC
Writer—Variety	—	—	Al Gordon, Hal Goldman, and Sheldon Keller, *An Evening with Carol Channing*, CBS
Children's Program	*Discovery '63-'64*, ABC	—	*A Charlie Brown Christmas*, CBS

	1966–67	1967–68	1968–69
Drama Series	*Mission: Impossible*, CBS	*Mission: Impossible*, CBS	*NET Playhouse*, NET
Actor—Drama Series	Bill Cosby, *I Spy*, NBC	Bill Cosby, *I Spy*, NBC	Carl Betz, *Judd, for the Defense*, ABC
Actress—Drama Series	Barbara Bain, *Mission: Impossible*, CBS	Barbara Bain, *Mission: Impossible*, CBS	Barbara Bain, *Mission: Impossible*, CBS
Supporting Actor—Drama	Eli Wallach, *The Poppy Is Also a Flower*, ABC	Milburn Stone, *Gunsmoke*, CBS	—
Supporting Actress—Drama	Agnes Moorehead, *The Wild, Wild West*, CBS	Barbara Anderson, *Ironside*, NBC	Susan Saint James, *The Name of the Game*, NBC
Director—Drama	Alex Segal, *Death of a Salesman*, CBS	Paul Bogart, *Dear Friends*, CBS	David Green, *The People Next Door*, CBS
Writer—Drama	Bruce Geller, *Mission: Impossible*, CBS	Loring Mandel, *Do Not Go Gentle into That Good Night*, CBS	J.P. Miller, *The People Next Door*, CBS
Comedy	*The Monkees*, NBC	*Get Smart*, NBC	*Get Smart*, NBC
Actor—Comedy Series	Don Adams, *Get Smart*, NBC	Don Adams, *Get Smart*, NBC	Don Adams, *Get Smart*, NBC
Actress—Comedy Series	Lucille Ball, *The Lucy Show*, CBS	Lucille Ball, *The Lucy Show*, CBS	Hope Lange, *The Ghost and Mrs. Muir*, NBC
Supporting Actor—Comedy Series	Don Knotts, *The Andy Griffith Show*, CBS	Werner Klemperer, *Hogan's Heroes*, CBS	Werner Klemperer, *Hogan's Heroes*, CBS
Supporting Actress—Comedy Series	Frances Bavier, *The Andy Griffith Show*, CBS	Marion Lorne, *Bewitched*, ABC	—
Director—Comedy/Comedy Series	James Frawley, *The Monkees*, NBC	Bruce Bilson, *Get Smart*, NBC	—
Writer—Comedy/Comedy Series	Buck Henry and Leonard Stern, *Get Smart*, NBC	Allan Burns and Chris Hayward, *He and She*, CBS	Alan Blye, Bob Einstein, Murray Roman, Carl Gottlieb, Jerry Music, Steve Martin, Cecil Tuck, Paul Wayne, Cy Howard, and Mason Williams, *The Smothers Brothers Comedy Hour*, CBS
Variety Program	*The Andy Williams Show*, NBC	*Rowan and Martin's Laugh-In*, NBC	*Rowan and Martin's Laugh-In*, NBC
Director—Variety or Music	Fielder Cook, *Brigadoon*, ABC	Jack Haley, Jr., *Movin' with Nancy*, NBC	—
Writer—Variety or Music	Mel Brooks, Sam Denoff, Bill Persky, Carl Reiner, and Mel Tolkin, *The Sid Caesar, Imogene Coca, Carl Reiner, Howard Morris Special*, CBS	Chris Beard, Phil Hahn, Jack Hanrahan, Coslough Johnson, Paul Keyes, Marc London, Allan Manings, David Panich, Hugh Wedlock, and Digby Wolfe, *Rowan and Martin's Laugh-In*, NBC	—
Children's Program	*Jack and the Beanstalk*, NBC	—	—

	1969–70	1970–71	1971–72
Drama	*Marcus Welby, M.D.*, ABC	*The Bold Ones: The Senator,* NBC	*Elizabeth R*, PBS
Actor—Drama Series	Robert Young, *Marcus Welby, M.D.*, ABC	Hal Holbrook, *The Bold Ones: The Senator*, NBC	Peter Falk, *Columbo*, NBC
Actress—Drama Series	Susan Hampshire, *The Forsyte Saga*, NET	Susan Hampshire, *The First Churchills*, PBS	Glenda Jackson, *Elizabeth R.*, PBS
Supporting Actor—Drama Series	James Brolin, *Marcus Welby, M.D.*, ABC	David Burns, *The Price*, NBC	Jack Warden, *Brian's Song*, ABC
Supporting Actress—Drama Series	Gail Fisher, *Mannix*, CBS	Margaret Leighton, *Hamlet*, NBC	Jenny Agutter, *The Snow Goose*, NBC
Director—Drama Series	—	Daryl Duke, *The Bold Ones: The Senator*, NBC	Alexander Singer, *The Bold Ones: The Lawyers*, NBC
Writer—Drama	Richard Levinson and William Link, *My Sweet Charlie*, NBC	Joel Oliansky, *The Bold Ones: The Senator*, NBC	Richard L. Levinson and William Link, *Columbo*, NBC
Comedy	*My World and Welcome to It*, NBC	*All in the Family*, CBS	*All in the Family*, CBS
Actor—Comedy Series	William Windom, *My World and Welcome to It*, NBC	Jack Klugman, *The Odd Couple*, ABC	Carroll O'Connor, *All in the Family*, CBS
Actress—Comedy Series	Hope Lange, *The Ghost and Mrs. Muir*, ABC	Jean Stapleton, *All in the Family*, CBS	Jean Stapleton, *All in the Family*, CBS
Supporting Actor—Comedy Series	Michael Constantine, *Room 222*, ABC	Edward Asner, *The Mary Tyler Moore Show*, CBS	Edward Asner, *The Mary Tyler Moore Show*, CBS
Supporting Actress—Comedy Series	Karen Valentine, *Room 222*, ABC	Valerie Harper, *The Mary Tyler Moore Show*, CBS	Valerie Harper, *The Mary Tyler Moore Show*, CBS; Sally Struthers, *All in the Family, CBS*
Director—Comedy Series	—	Jay Sandrich, *The Mary Tyler Moore Show*, CBS	John Rich, *All in the Family*, CBS
Writer—Comedy Series	—	James L. Brooks and Allan Burns, *The Mary Tyler Moore Show*, CBS	Burt Styler, *All in the Family*, CBS
Drama/Comedy Special	—	—	*Brian's Song*, ABC
Variety or Music Series	*The David Frost Show*, SYN	*The David Frost Show, SYN (Talk); The Flip Wilson Show*, NBC (Music)	*The Dick Cavett Show, ABC (Talk), The Carol Burnett Show*, CBS (Music)
Director—Variety or Music	—	Mark Warren, *Rowan and Martin's Laugh-In*, NBC	Art Fisher, *The Sonny & Cher Comedy Hour*, CBS
Writer—Variety or Music	—	Herbert Baker, Hal Goodman, Larry Klein, Bob Weiskopf, Bob Schiller, Norman Steinberg, and Flip Wilson, *The Flip Wilson Show*, NBC	Don Hinkley, Stan Hart, Larry Siegel, Woody Kling, Roger Beatty, Art Baer, Ben Joelson, Stan Burns, Mike Marmer, and Arnie Rosen, *The Carol Burnett Show*, CBS
Daytime Drama Series	—	—	*The Doctors*, NBC
Children's Program	*Sesame Street*, NET	*Sesame Street*, PBS	*Sesame Street*, PBS

	1972–73	1973–74	1974–75
Drama	*The Waltons*, CBS	*Upstairs, Downstairs*, PBS	*Upstairs, Downstairs*, PBS
Actor—Drama Series	Richard Thomas, *The Waltons*, CBS	Telly Savalas, *Kojak*, CBS	Robert Blake, *Baretta*, ABC
Actress—Drama Series	Michael Learned, *The Waltons*, CBS	Michael Learned, *The Waltons*, CBS	Jean Marsh, *Upstairs, Downstairs*, PBS
Supporting Actor—Drama/Drama Series	Scott Jacoby, *That Certain Summer*, ABC	Michael Moriarty, *The Glass Menagerie*, ABC	Will Geer, *The Waltons*, CBS
Supporting Actress—Drama/Drama Series	Ellen Corby, *The Waltons*, CBS	Joanna Miles, *The Glass Menagerie*, ABC	Ellen Corby, *The Waltons*, CBS
Director—Drama	Joseph Sargent, *The Marcus Nelson Murders*, CBS	John Korty, *The Autobiography of Miss Jane Pittman*, CBS	George Cukor, *Love Among the Ruins*, ABC
Director—Drama Series	Jerry Thorpe, *Kung Fu*, ABC	Robert Butler, *The Blue Knight*, NBC	Bill Bain, *Upstairs, Downstairs*, PBS
Writer—Drama Series	John McGreevey, *The Waltons*, CBS	Joanna Lee, *The Waltons*, CBS	Howard Fast, *Benjamin Franklin*, CBS
Comedy	*All in the Family*, CBS	*M*A*S*H*, CBS	*The Mary Tyler Moore Show*, CBS
Actor—Comedy Series	Jack Klugman, *The Odd Couple*, ABC	Alan Alda, *M*A*S*H*, CBS	Tony Randall, *The Odd Couple*, ABC
Actress—Comedy Series	Mary Tyler Moore, *The Mary Tyler Moore Show*, CBS	Mary Tyler Moore, *The Mary Tyler Moore Show*, CBS	Valerie Harper, *Rhoda*, CBS
Supporting Actor—Comedy Series	Ted Knight, *The Mary Tyler Moore Show*, CBS	Rob Reiner, *All in the Family*, CBS	Ed Asner, *The Mary Tyler Moore Show*, CBS
Supporting Actress—Comedy Series	Valerie Harper, *The Mary Tyler Moore Show*, CBS	Cloris Leachman, *The Mary Tyler Moore Show*, CBS	Betty White, *The Mary Tyler Moore Show*, CBS
Director—Comedy Series	Jay Sandrich, *The Mary Tyler Moore Show*, CBS	Jackie Cooper, *M*A*S*H*, CBS	Gene Reynolds, *M*A*S*H*, CBS
Writer—Comedy Series	Michael Ross, Bernie West, and Lee Kalcheim, *All in the Family*, CBS	Treva Silverman, *The Mary Tyler Moore Show*, CBS	Ed. Weinberger and Stan Daniels, *The Mary Tyler Moore Show*, CBS
Drama/Comedy Special	*A War of Children*, CBS	*The Autobiography of Miss Jane Pittman*, CBS	*The Law*, NBC
Variety Series	*The Julie Andrews Hour*, ABC	*The Carol Burnett Show*, CBS	*The Carol Burnett Show*, CBS
Director—Variety or Music	Bill Davis, *The Julie Andrews Hour*, ABC	Dave Powers, *The Carol Burnett Show*, CBS	Dave Powers, *The Carol Burnett Show*, CBS

	1972–73	1973–74	1974–75
Writer—Variety or Music Series	Stan Hart, Larry Siegel, Gail Parent, Woody Kling, Roger Beatty, Tom Patchett, Jay Tarses, Robert Hilliard, Arnie Kogen, Bill Angelos, and Buz Kohan, *The Carol Burnett Show*, CBS	Ed Simmons, Gary Belkin, Roger Beatty, Arnie Kogen, Bill Richmond, Gene Perret, Rudy De Luca, Barry Levinson, Dick Clair, Jenna McMahon, and Barry Harman, *The Carol Burnett Show*, CBS	Ed Simmons, Gary Belkin, Roger Beatty, Arnie Kogen, Bill Richmond, Gene Perret, Rudy De Luca, Barry Levinson, Dick Clair, and Jenna McMahon, *The Carol Burnett Show*, CBS
Variety, Music, or Comedy Special	*Singer Presents Liza with a "Z"*, CBS	*Lilly Tomlin*, CBS	*An Evening with John Denver*, ABC
Miniseries/Limited Series	*Tom Brown's Schooldays*, PBS	*Columbo*, NBC	*Benjamin Franklin*, CBS
Actor—Miniseries/ Limited Series	Anthony Murphy, *Tom Brown's Schooldays*, PBS	William Holden, *The Blue Knight*, NBC	Peter Falk, *Columbo*, NBC
Actress—Miniseries/ Limited Series	Susan Hampshire, *Vanity Fair*, PBS	Mildred Natwick, *The Snoop Sisters*, NBC	Jessica Walter, *Amy Prentiss*, NBC
Daytime Drama Series	*The Edge of Night*, CBS	*The Doctors*, NBC	*The Young and the Restless*, CBS
Actor—Daytime Drama Series	—	Macdonald Carey, *Days of Our Lives*, NBC	Macdonald Carey, *Days of Our Lives*, NBC
Actress—Daytime Drama Series	—	Elizabeth Hubbard, *The Doctors*, NBC	Susan Flannery, *Days of Our Lives*, NBC
Host—Game Show	—	Peter Marshall, *The Hollywood Squares*, NBC	Peter Marshall, *The Hollywood Squares*, NBC
Host—Talk or Service	—	Dinah Shore, *Dinah's Place*, NBC	Barbara Walters, *Today*, NBC
Game Show	—	*Password*, ABC	*Hollywood Squares*, NBC
Talk, Service or Variety Series	—	*The Merv Griffin Show*, SYN	*Dinah!* SYN
Children's Special	—	*Marlo Thomas and Friends in Free To Be . . . You and Me*, ABC	*Yes, Virginia, There Is a Santa Claus*, ABC
Children's Entertainment Series	—	*Zoom, PBS*	Star Trek, NBC

	1975–76	1976–77	1977–78
Drama	*Police Story*, NBC	*Upstairs, Downstairs*, PBS	*The Rockford Files*, NBC
Actor—Drama Series	Peter Falk, *Columbo*, NBC	James Garner, *The Rockford Files*, NBC	Edward Asner, *Lou Grant*, CBS
Actress—Drama Series	Michael Learned, *The Waltons*, CBS	Lindsay Wagner, *The Bionic Woman*, ABC	Sada Thompson, *Family*, ABC
Supporting Actor—Drama Series	Anthony Zerbe, *Harry-O*, ABC	Gary Frank, *Family*, ABC	Robert Vaughn, *Washington: Behind Closed Doors*, ABC
Supp. Actress—Drama Series	Ellen Corby, *The Waltons*, CBS	Kristy McNichol, *Family*, ABC	Nancy Marchand, *Lou Grant*, CBS
Director—Drama Series	David Greene, *Rich Man, Poor Man*, ABC	David Greene, *Roots*, ABC	Marvin J. Chomsky, *Holocaust*, NBC
Writer—Drama Series	Sherman Yellen, *The Adams Chronicles*, PBS	Ernest Kinoy, and William Blinn, *Roots*, ABC	Gerald Green, *Holocaust*, NBC
Comedy	*The Mary Tyler Moore Show*, CBS	*The Mary Tyler Moore Show*, CBS	*All in the Family*, CBS
Actor—Comedy Series	Jack Albertson, *Chico and the Man*, NBC	Carroll O'Connor, *All in the Family*, CBS	Carroll O'Connor, *All in the Family*, CBS
Actress—Comedy Series	Mary Tyler Moore, *The Mary Tyler Moore Show*, CBS	Beatrice Arthur, *Maude*, CBS	Jean Stapleton, *All in the Family*, CBS

	1975–76	1976–77	1977–78
Supporting Actor—Comedy Series	Ted Knight, *The Mary Tyler Moore Show*, CBS	Gary Burghoff, *M*A*S*H*, CBS	Rob Reiner, *All in the Family*, CBS
Supporting Actress—Comedy Series	Betty White, *The Mary Tyler Moore Show*, CBS	Mary Kay Place, *Mary Hartman, Mary Hartman*, SYN	Julie Kavner, *Rhoda*, CBS
Director—Comedy/Comedy Series	Gene Reynolds, *M*A*S*H*, CBS	Alan Alda, *M*A*S*H*, CBS	Paul Bogart, *All in the Family*, CBS
Writer—Comedy Series	David Lloyd, *The Mary Tyler Moore Show*, CBS	Allan Burns, James L. Brooks, Ed. Weinberger, Stan Daniels, David Lloyd, and Bob Ellison, *The Mary Tyler Moore Show*, CBS	Bob Weiskopf and Bob Schiller (Teleplay); Barry Harman, and Harve Brosten (Story), *All in the Family*, CBS
Drama/Comedy Special	*Eleanor and Franklin*, ABC	*Eleanor and Franklin: The White House Years*, ABC	*The Gathering*, ABC
Variety Series	*NBC's Saturday Night*, NBC	*Van Dyke and Company*, NBC	*The Muppet Show*, SYN
Limited Series	*Upstairs, Downstairs*, PBS	*Roots*, ABC	*Holocaust*, NBC
Actor—Limited Series	Hal Holbrook, *Sandburg's Lincoln*, NBC	Christopher Plummer, *The Moneychangers*, NBC	Michael Moriarty, *Holocaust*, NBC
Actress—Limited Series	Rosemary Harris, *Notorious Women*, PBS	Patty Duke Astin, *Captains and the Kings*, NBC	Meryl Streep, *Holocaust*, NBC
Daytime Drama Series	*Another World*, NBC	*Ryan's Hope*, ABC	*Days of Our Lives*, NBC
Actor—Daytime Drama Series	Larry Haines, *Search for Tomorrow*, CBS	Val Dufour, *Search for Tomorrow*, CBS	James Pritchett, *The Doctors*, NBC
Actress—Daytime Drama Series	Helen Gallagher, *Ryan's Hope*, ABC	Helen Gallagher, *Ryan's Hope*, ABC	Laurie Heineman, *Another World*, NBC
Host—Game Show	Allen Ludden, *Password*, ABC	Bert Convy, *Tattletales*, CBS	Richard Dawson, *Family Feud*, ABC
Host—Talk or Service Series	Dinah Shore, *Dinah!*, SYN	Phil Donahue, *Donahue*, SYN	Phil Donahue, *Donahue*, SYN
Game Show	*The $20,000 Pyramid*, ABC	*Family Feud*, ABC	*The Hollywood Squares*, NBC
Talk, Service or Variety Series	*Dinah!*, SYN	*The Merv Griffin Show*, SYN	*Donahue*, SYN
Children's Entertainment Series	*Big Blue Marble*, SYN	*Zoom!*, PBS	*Captain Kangaroo*, CBS

	1978–79	1979–80	1980–81
Drama	*Lou Grant*, CBS	*Lou Grant*, CBS	*Hill Street Blues*, NBC
Actor—Drama Series	Ron Leibman, *Kaz*, CBS	Ed Asner, *Lou Grant*, CBS	Daniel J. Travanti, *Hill Street Blues*, NBC
Actress—Drama Series	Mariette Hartley, *The Incredible Hulk*, CBS	Barbara Bel Geddes, *Dallas*, CBS	Barbara Babcock, *Hill Street Blues*, NBC
Supporting Actor—Drama Series	Stuart Margolin, *The Rockford Files*, NBC	Stuart Margolin, *The Rockford Files*, NBC	Michael Conrad, *Hill Street Blues*, NBC
Supporting Actress—Drama Series	Kristy McNichol, *Family*, ABC	Nancy Marchand, *Lou Grant*, CBS	Nancy Marchand, *Lou Grant*, CBS
Director—Drama Series	Jackie Cooper, *The White Shadow*, CBS	Roger Young, *Lou Grant*, CBS	Robert Butler, *Hill Street Blues*, NBC
Writer—Drama Series	Michele Gallery, *Lou Grant*, CBS	Seth Freeman, *Lou Grant*, CBS	Michael Kozoll and Steven Bochco, *Hill Street Blues*, NBC
Comedy	*Taxi*, ABC	*Taxi*, ABC	*Taxi*, ABC
Actor—Comedy Series	Carroll O'Connor, *All in the Family*, CBS	Richard Mulligan, *Soap*, ABC	Judd Hirsch, *Taxi*, ABC
Actress—Comedy Series	Ruth Gordon, *Taxi*, ABC	Cathryn Damon, *Soap*, ABC	Isabel Sanford, *The Jeffersons*, CBS
Supporting Actor—Comedy Series	Robert Guillaume, *Soap*, ABC	Harry Morgan, M*A*S*H, CBS	Danny De Vito, *Taxi*, ABC
Supporting Actress—Comedy Series	Sally Struthers, *All in the Family*, CBS	Loretta Swit, *M*A*S*H*, CBS	Eileen Brennan, *Private Benjamin*, CBS
Director—Comedy Series	Noam Pitlik, *Barney Miller*, ABC	James Burrows, *Taxi*, ABC	James Burrows, *Taxi*, ABC
Writer—Comedy Series	Alan Alda, *M*A*S*H*, CBS	Bob Colleary, *Barney Miller*, ABC	Michael Leeson, *Taxi*, ABC
Drama/Comedy Special	*Friendly Fire*, ABC	*The Miracle Worker*, NBC	*Playing for Time*, CBS
Variety Program	*Steve & Eydie Celebrate Irving Berlin*, NBC	*Baryshnikov on Broadway*, ABC	*Lily: Sold Out*, CBS
Director—Variety or Music	—	Dwight Hemion, *Baryshnikov on Broadway*, ABC	Don Mischer, *The Kennedy Center Honors: A National Celebration of the Performing Arts*, CBS

	1978–79	1979–80	1980–81
Writer—Variety or Music	—	Buz Kohan, *Shirley MacLaine. . . Every Little Movement*, CBS	Jerry Juhl, David Odell, Chris Langham, *The Muppet Show*, SYN
Limited Series	*Roots: The Next Generations*, ABC	*Edward & Mrs. Simpson*, SYN	*Shogun*, NBC
Actor—Limited Series	Peter Strauss, *The Jericho Mile*, ABC	Powers Boothe, *Guyana Tragedy: The Story of Jim Jones*, CBS	Anthony Hopkins, *The Bunker*, CBS
Actress—Limited Series	Bette Davis, *Strangers: The Story of a Mother and Daughter*, CBS	Patty Duke Astin, *The Miracle Worker*, NBC	Vanessa Redgrave, *Playing for Time*, CBS
Supporting Actor—Limited Series or Special	Marlon Brando, *Roots: The Next Generations*, ABC	George Grizzard, *The Oldest Living Graduate*, NBC	David Warner, *Masada*, ABC
Supporting Actress—Limited Series or Special	Esther Rolle, *Summer of My German Soldier*, NBC	Mare Winningham, *Amber Waves*, ABC	Jane Alexander, *Playing for Time*, CBS
Director—Limited Series or Special	David Greene, *Friendly Fire*, ABC	Marvin J. Chomsky, *Attica*, ABC	James Goldstone, *Kent State*, NBC
Writer—Limited Series or Special	Patrick Nolan and Michael Mann, *The Jericho Mile*, ABC	David Chase, *Off the Minnesota Strip*, ABC	Arthur Miller, *Playing for Time*, CBS
Daytime Drama Series	*Ryan's Hope*, ABC	*Guiding Light*, CBS	*General Hospital*, ABC
Actor—Daytime Drama Series	Al Freeman, Jr., *One Life to Live*, ABC	Douglass Watson, *Another World*, NBC	Douglass Watson, *Another World*, NBC
Actress—Daytime Drama Series	Irene Dailey, *Another World*, NBC	Judith Light, *One Life to Live*, ABC	Judith Light, *One Life to Live*, ABC
Supporting Actor—Daytime Drama Series	Peter Hansen, *General Hospital*, ABC	Warren Burton, *All My Children*, ABC	Larry Haines, *Search for Tomorrow*, CBS
Supporting Actress—Daytime Drama Series	Suzanne Rogers, *Days of Our Lives*, NBC	Francesca James, *All My Children*, ABC	Jane Elliot, *General Hospital*, ABC
Host—Game Show	Dick Clark, *The $20,000 Pyramid*, ABC	Peter Marshall, *The Hollywood Squares*, NBC	Peter Marshall, *The Hollywood Squares*, NBC
Host—Talk or Service	Phil Donahue, *Donahue*, SYN	Phil Donahue, *Donahue*, SYN	Hugh Downs, *Over Easy*, PBS
Game Show	*The Hollywood Squares*, NBC	*The Hollywood Squares*, NBC; *The $20,000 Pyramid*, ABC	*The $20,000 Pyramid*, ABC
Talk, Service or Variety Series	*Donahue*, SYN	*Donahue*, SYN	*Donahue*, SYN
Children's Program	*Christmas Eve on Sesame Street*, PBS	—	*Donahue and Kids*, NBC
Children's Entertainment Series	*Kids Are People Too*, ABC	*Hot Hero Sandwich*, NBC	*Captain Kangaroo*, CBS

EMMY AWARDS

	1981–82	1982–83	1983–84
Drama	*Hill Street Blues*, NBC	*Hill Street Blues*, NBC	*Hill Street Blues*, NBC
Actor—Drama Series	Daniel J. Travanti, *Hill Street Blues*, NBC	Ed Flanders, *St. Elsewhere*, NBC	Tom Selleck, *Magnum, P.I.*, CBS
Actress—Drama Series	Michael Learned, *Nurse*, CBS	Tyne Daly, *Cagney & Lacey*, CBS	Tyne Daly, *Cagney & Lacey*, CBS
Supporting Actor—Drama Series	Michael Conrad, *Hill Street Blues*, NBC	James Coco, *St. Elsewhere*, NBC	Bruce Weitz, *Hill Street Blues*, NBC
Supporting Actress—Drama Series	Nancy Marchand, *Lou Grant*, CBS	Doris Roberts, *St. Elsewhere*, NBC	Alfre Woodard, *Hill Street Blues*, NBC
Director—Drama Series	Harry Harris, *Fame*, NBC	Jeff Bleckner, *Hill Street Blues*, NBC	Corey Allen, *Hill Street Blues*, NBC
Writer—Drama Series	Steven Bochco, Anthony Yerkovich, Jeffrey Lewis, and Michael Wagner (Teleplay); Michael Kozoll and Steven Bochco (Story), *Hill Street Blues*, NBC	David Milch, *Hill Street Blues*, NBC	John Ford Noonan (Teleplay); John Masius, and Tom Fontana (Story), *St. Elsewhere*, NBC
Comedy	*Barney Miller*, ABC	*Cheers*, NBC	*Cheers*, NBC
Actor—Comedy Series	*Alan Alda*, M*A*S*H, CBS	Judd Hirsch, *Taxi*, NBC	John Ritter, *Three's Company*, ABC
Actress—Comedy Series	Carol Kane, *Taxi*, ABC	Shelley Long, *Cheers*, NBC	Jane Curtin, *Kate & Allie*, CBS
Supporting Actor—Comedy Series	Christopher Lloyd, *Taxi*, ABC	Christopher Lloyd, *Taxi*, NBC	Pat Harrington, Jr., *One Day at a Time*, CBS
Supp. Actress—Comedy Series	Loretta Swit, *M*A*S*H*, CBS	Carol Kane, *Taxi*, NBC	Rhea Perlman, *Cheers*, NBC
Director—Comedy Series	Alan Rafkin, *One Day at a Time*, CBS	James Burrows, *Cheers*, NBC	Bill Persky, *Kate & Allie*, CBS
Writer—Comedy Series	Ken Estin, *Taxi*, ABC	Glen Charles, Les Charles, *Cheers*, NBC	David Angel, *Cheers*, NBC
Drama/Comedy Special	*A Woman Called Golda*, SYN	*Special Bulletin*, NBC	*Something About Amelia*, ABC
Variety, Music, or Comedy Program	*Night of 100 Stars*, ABC	*Motown 25: Yesterday, Today, Forever*, NBC	*The 6th Annual Kennedy Center Honors: A Celebration of the Performing Arts*, CBS
Individual Performance—Variety or Music Program	—	Leontyne Price, *Live From Lincoln Center: Leontyne Price, Zubin Mehta, and the New York Philharmonic*, PBS	Cloris Leachman, *Screen Actors Guild 50th Anniversary Celebration*, CBS
Director—Variety or Music	Dwight Hemion, *Goldie and Kids Listen to Us*, ABC	Dwight Hemion, *Sheena Easton Act I*, NBC	Dwight Hemion, *Here's Television Entertainment*, NBC
Writer—Variety or Music	John Candy, Joe Flaherty, Eugene Levy, Andrea Martin, Rick Moranis, Catherine O'Hara, Dave Thomas, Dick Blasucci, Paul Flaherty, Bob Dolman, John McAndrew, Doug Steckler, M. Bert Rich, Jeffrey Barron, Michael Short, Chris Cluess, Stuart Kreisman, and Brian McConnachie, *SCTV Comedy Network*, NBC	John Candy, Joe Flaherty, Eugene Levy, Andrea Martin, Martin Short, Dick Blasucci, Paul Flaherty, John McAndrew, Doug Steckler, Bob Dolman, Michael Short, and Mary Charlotte Wilcox, *SCTV Network*, NBC	Steve O'Donnell, Gerard Mulligan, Sanford Frank, Joseph E. Toplyn, Christopher Elliott, Matt Wickline, Jeff Martin, Ted Greenberg, David Yazbek, Merrill Markoe, and David Letterman, *Late Night with David Letterman*, NBC

	1981–82	1982–83	1983–84
Limited Series	*Marco Polo*, NBC	*Nicholas Nickleby*, SYN	*Concealed Enemies*, PBS
Actor—Limited Series or Special	Mickey Rooney, *Bill*, CBS	Tommy Lee Jones, *The Executioner's Song*, NBC	Laurence Olivier, *King Lear*, SYN
Actress—Limited Series or Special	Ingrid Bergman, *A Woman Called Golda*, SYN	Barbara Stanwyck, *The Thorn Birds*, ABC	Jane Fonda, *The Dollmaker*, ABC
Supporting Actor—Limited Series or Special	Laurence Olivier, *Brideshead Revisited*, PBS	Richard Kiley, *The Thorn Birds*, ABC	Art Carney, *Terrible Joe Moran*, CBS
Supporting Actress—Limited Series or Special	Penny Fuller, *Elephant Man*, ABC	Jean Simmons, *The Thorn Birds*, ABC	Roxana Zal, *Something About Amelia*, ABC
Director—Limited Series or Special	Marvin J. Chomsky, *Inside the Third Reich*, ABC	John Erman, *Who Will Love My Children?* ABC	Jeff Bleckner, *Concealed Enemies*, PBS
Writer—Limited Series or Special	Corey Blechman (Teleplay); Barry Morrow (Story), *Bill*, CBS	Marshall Herskovitz (Teleplay); Edward Zwick, Marshall Herskovitz (Story), *Special Bulletin*, NBC	William Hanley, *Something About Amelia*, ABC
Daytime Drama Series	*The Guiding Light*, CBS	*The Young & The Restless*, CBS	*General Hospital*, ABC
Actor—Daytime Drama Series	Anthony Geary, *General Hospital*, ABC	Robert Woods, *One Life to Live*, ABC	Larry Bryggman, *As the World Turns*, CBS
Actress—Daytime Drama Series	Robin Strasser, *One Life To Live*, ABC	Dorothy Lyman, *All My Children*, ABC	Erika Slezak, *One Life To Live*, ABC
Supporting Actor—Daytime Drama Series	David Lewis, *General Hospital*, ABC	Darnell Williams, *All My Children*, ABC	Justin Deas, *As the World Turns*, CBS
Supporting Actress—Daytime Drama Series	Dorothy Lyman, *All My Children*, ABC	Louise Shaffer, *Ryan's Hope*, ABC	Judi Evans, *The Guiding Light*, CBS
Host—Game Show	Bob Barker, *The Price Is Right*, CBS	Betty White, *Just Men!*, NBC	Bob Barker, *The Price Is Right*, CBS
Host—Talk or Service	Phil Donahue, *Donahue*, SYN	Phil Donahue, *Donahue*, SYN	Gary Collins, *Hour Magazine*, SYN
Game Show	*Password Plus*, NBC	*The New $25,000 Pyramid*, CBS	*The $25,000 Pyramid*, CBS
Talk or Service Series	*The Richard Simmons Show*, SYN	*This Old House*, PBS	*Woman to Woman*, SYN
Children's Program	*The Wave*, ABC	*Big Bird in China*, NBC	*He Makes Me Feel Like Dancin'*, NBC
Children's Series	*Captain Kangaroo*, CBS	*Smurfs*, NBC	*Captain Kangaroo*, CBS

	1984–85	1985–86	1986–87
Drama	*Cagney and Lacey,* CBS	*Cagney & Lacey,* CBS	*L. A. Law,* NBC
Actor—Drama Series	William Daniels, *St. Elsewhere,* NBC	William Daniels, *St. Elsewhere,* NBC	Bruce Willis, *Moonlighting,* ABC
Actress—Drama Series	Tyne Daly, *Cagney & Lacey,* CBS	Sharon Gless, *Cagney & Lacey,* CBS	Sharon Gless, *Cagney & Lacey,* CBS
Supporting Actor—Drama Series	Edward James Olmos, *Miami Vice,* NBC	John Karlen, *Cagney & Lacey,* CBS	John Hillerman, *Magnum, P.I.,* CBS
Supporting Actress—Drama Series	Betty Thomas, *Hill Street Blues,* NBC	Bonnie Bartlett, *St. Elsewhere,* NBC	Bonnie Bartlett, *St. Elsewhere,* NBC
Director—Drama Series	Karen Arthur, *Cagney & Lacey,* CBS	Georg Stanford Brown, *Cagney & Lacey,* CBS	Gregory Hoblit, *L.A. Law,* NBC
Writer—Drama Series	Patricia M. Green, *Cagney & Lacey,* CBS	Tom Fontana, John Tinker, and John Masius, *St. Elsewhere,* NBC	Steven Bochco, Terry Louise Fisher, *L.A. Law,* NBC
Comedy	*The Cosby Show,* NBC	*The Golden Girls,* NBC	*The Golden Girls,* NBC
Actor—Comedy Series	Robert Guillaume, *Benson,* ABC	Michael J. Fox, *Family Ties,* NBC	Michael J. Fox, *Family Ties,* NBC
Actress—Comedy Series	Jane Curtin, *Kate & Allie,* CBS	Betty White, *The Golden Girls,* NBC	Rue McClanahan, *The Golden Girls,* NBC
Supporting Actor—Comedy Series	John Larroquette, *Night Court,* NBC	John Larroquette, *Night Court,* NBC	John Larroquette, *Night Court,* NBC
Supporting Actress—Comedy Series	Rhea Perlman, *Cheers,* NBC	Rhea Perlman, *Cheers,* NBC	Jackée Harry, *227,* NBC
Director—Comedy Series	Jay Sandrich, *The Cosby Show,* NBC	Jay Sandrich, *The Cosby Show,* NBC	Terry Hughes, *The Golden Girls,* NBC
Writer—Comedy Series	Ed. Weinberger, Michael Leeson, *The Cosby Show,* NBC	Barry Fanaro and Mort Nathan, *The Golden Girls,* NBC	Gary David Goldberg, Alan Uger, *Family Ties,* NBC
Drama/Comedy Special	*Do You Remember Love,* CBS	*Love Is Never Silent,* NBC	*Promise,* CBS
Variety, Music, or Comedy Program	*Motown Returns to the Apollo,* NBC	*The Kennedy Center Honors: A Celebration of the Performing Arts,* CBS	*The 1987 Tony Awards,* CBS
Individual Performance—Variety or Music Program	George Hearn, *Sweeney Todd,* PBS	Whitney Houston, *The 28th Annual Grammy Awards,* CBS	Robin Williams, *A Carol Burnett Special: Carol, Carl, Whoopi & Robin,* ABC
Director—Variety or Music	Terry Hughes, *Sweeney Todd,* PBS	Waris Hussein, *Copacabana,* CBS	Don Mischer, *The Kennedy Center Honors: A Celebration of the Performing Arts,* CBS
Writer—Variety or Music	Gerard Mulligan, Sandy Frank, Joe Toplyn, Chris Elliott, Matt Wickline, Jeff Martin, Eddie Gorodetsky, Randy Cohen, Larry Jacobson, Kevin Curran, Fred Graver, Merrill Markoe, and David Letterman, *Late Night with David Letterman,* NBC	David Letterman, Steve O'Donnell, Sandy Frank, Joe Toplyn, Chris Elliott, Matt Wickline, Jeff Martin, Gerard Mulligan, Randy Cohen, Larry Jacobson, Kevin Curran, Fred Graver, and Merrill Markoe, *Late Night with David Letterman,* NBC	Steve O'Donnell, Sandy Frank, Joe Toplyn, Chris Elliott, Matt Wickline, Jeff Martin, Gerard Mulligan, Randy Cohen, Larry Jacobson, Kevin Curran, Fred Graver, Adam Resnick, and David Letterman, *Late Night with David Letterman,* NBC

	1984–85	1985–86	1986–87
Miniseries	*The Jewel in the Crown*, PBS	*Peter the Great*, NBC	*A Year in the Life*, NBC
Actor—Miniseries	Richard Crenna, *The Rape of Richard Beck*, ABC	Dustin Hoffman, *Death of a Salesman*, CBS	James Woods, *Promise*, CBS
Actress—Miniseries	Joanne Woodward, *Do You Remember Love*, CBS	Marlo Thomas, *Nobody's Child*, CBS	Gena Rowlands, *The Betty Ford Story*, ABC
Supporting Actor—Miniseries or Special	Karl Malden, *Fatal Vision*, NBC	John Malkovich, *Death of a Salesman*, CBS	Dabney Coleman, *Sworn to Silence*, ABC
Supporting Actress—Miniseries/ Limited Series or Special	Kim Stanley, *Cat on a Hot Tin Roof*, PBS	Colleen Dewhurst, *Between Two Women*, ABC	Piper Laurie, *Promise*, CBS
Director—Miniseries or Special	Lamont Johnson, *Wallenberg: A Hero's Story*, NBC	Joseph Sargent, *Love Is Never Silent*, NBC	Glenn Jordan, *Promise*, CBS
Writer—Miniseries or Special	Vickie Patik, *Do You Remember Love*, CBS	Ron Cowen and Daniel Lipman (Teleplay); Sherman Yellen (Story), *An Early Frost*, NBC	Richard Friedenberg (Teleplay); Kenneth Blackwell, Tennyson Flowers, and Richard Friedenberg (Story), *Promise*, CBS
Daytime Drama Series	*The Young and the Restless*, CBS	*The Young and the Restless*, CBS	*As the World Turns*, CBS
Actor—Daytime Drama Series	Darnell Williams, *All My Children*, ABC	David Canary, *All My Children*, ABC	Larry Bryggman, *As the World Turns*, CBS
Actress—Daytime Drama Series	Kim Zimmer, *Guiding Light*, CBS	Erika Slezak, *One Life To Live*, ABC	Kim Zimmer, *Guiding Light*, CBS
Supporting Actor—Daytime Drama Series	Larry Gates, *Guiding Light*, CBS	John Wesley Shipp, *As the World Turns*, CBS	Gregg Marx, *As the World Turns*, CBS
Supporting Actress—Daytime Drama Series	Beth Maitland, *The Young and the Restless*, CBS	Leann Hunley, *Days of Our Lives*, NBC	Kathleen Noone, *All My Children*, ABC
Ingenue—Daytime Drama Series	Tracey E. Bregman, *The Young and the Restless*, CBS	Ellen Wheeler, *Another World*, NBC	Martha Byrne, *As the World Turns*, CBS
Younger Leading Man—Daytime Drama Series	Brian Bloom, *As the World Turns*, CBS	Michael E. Knight, *All My Children*, ABC	Michael E. Knight, *All My Children*, ABC
Host—Game Show	Dick Clark, *The $25,000 Pyramid*, CBS	Dick Clark, *The $25,000 Pyramid*, CBS	Bob Barker, *The Price Is Right*, CBS
Host—Talk or Service	Phil Donahue, *Donahue*, SYN	Phil Donahue, *Donahue*, SYN	Oprah Winfrey, *The Oprah Winfrey Show*, SYN
Game Show	*The $25,000 Pyramid*, CBS	*The $25,000 Pyramid*, CBS	*The $25,000 Pyramid*, CBS
Talk, Service or Variety Series	*Donahue*, SYN	*Donahue*, SYN	*The Oprah Winfrey Show*, SYN
Children's Program	*Displaced Person*, PBS	*Anne of Green Gables*, PBS	*Jim Henson's The Storyteller: Hans My Hedgehog*, NBC
Children's Series	*Sesame Street*, PBS	*Sesame Street*, PBS	*Sesame Street*, PBS

	1987–88	1988–89	1989–90
Drama	*thirtysomething*, ABC	*L.A. Law*, NBC	*L.A. Law*, NBC
Actor—Drama Series	Richard Kiley, *A Year in the Life*, NBC	Carroll O'Connor, *In the Heat of the Night*, NBC	Peter Falk, *Columbo*, ABC
Actress—Drama Series	Tyne Daly, *Cagney & Lacey*, CBS	Dana Delany, *China Beach*, ABC	Patricia Wettig, *thirtysomething*, ABC
Supporting Actor—Drama Series	Larry Drake, *L.A. Law*, NBC	Larry Drake, *L.A. Law*, NBC	Jimmy Smits, *L.A. Law*, NBC
Supporting Actress—Drama Series	Patricia Wettig, *thirtysomething*, ABC	Melanie Mayron, *thirtysomething*, ABC	Marg Helgenberger, *China Beach*, ABC
Director—Drama Series	Mark Tinker, *St. Elsewhere*, NBC	Robert Altman, *Tanner '88*, HBO	Thomas Carter, *Equal Justice*, ABC; Scott Winant, *thirtysomething*, ABC
Writer—Drama Series	Paul Haggis, Marshall Herskovitz, *thirtysomething*, ABC	Joseph Dougherty, *thirtysomething*, ABC	David E. Kelley, *L.A. Law*, NBC
Comedy	*The Wonder Years*, ABC	*Cheers*, NBC	*Murphy Brown*, CBS
Actor—Comedy Series	Michael J. Fox, *Family Ties*, NBC	Richard Mulligan, *Empty Nest*, NBC	Ted Danson, *Cheers*, NBC
Actress—Comedy Series	Beatrice Arthur, *The Golden Girls*, NBC	Candice Bergen, *Murphy Brown*, CBS	Candice Bergen, *Murphy Brown*, CBS
Supporting Actor—Comedy Series	John Larroquette, *Night Court*, NBC	Woody Harrelson, *Cheers*, NBC	Alex Rocco, *The Famous Teddy Z*, CBS
Supporting Actress—Comedy Series	Estelle Getty, *The Golden Girls*, NBC	Rhea Perlman, *Cheers*, NBC	Bebe Neuwirth, *Cheers*, NBC
Director—Comedy Series	Gregory Hoblit, *Hooperman*, ABC	Peter Baldwin, *The Wonder Years*, ABC	Michael Dinner, *The Wonder Years*, ABC
Writer—Comedy Series	Hugh Wilson, *Frank's Place*, CBS	Diane English, *Murphy Brown*, CBS	Bob Brush, *The Wonder Years*, ABC
Drama/Comedy Special	*Inherit the Wind*, NBC	*Day One*, CBS	*Caroline?* CBS; *The Incident*, CBS
Variety, Music, or Comedy Program	*Irving Berlin's 100th Birthday Celebration*, CBS	*The Tracey Ullman Show*, FOX	*In Living Color*, FOX
Individual Performance—Variety or Music Program	Robin Williams, *ABC Presents a Royal Gala*, ABC	Linda Ronstadt, *Canciones de Mi Padre*, PBS	Tracey Ullman, *The Best of the Tracey Ullman Show*, FOX
Director—Variety or Music	Patricia Birch and Humphrey Burton, *Celebrating Gershwin* , PBS	Jim Henson, *The Jim Henson Hour*, NBC	Dwight Hemion, *The Kennedy Center Honors: A Celebration of the Performing Arts*, CBS

	1987–88	1988–89	1989–90
Writer—Variety or Music	Jackie Mason, *Jackie Mason on Broadway*, HBO	James Downey, head writer; John Bowman, A. Whitney Brown, Gregory Daniels, Tom Davis, Al Franken, Shannon Gaughan, Jack Handey, Phil Hartman, Lorne Michaels, Mike Myers, Conan O'Brien, Bob Odenkirk, Herb Sargent, Tom Schiller, Robert Smigel, Bonnie Turner, Terry Turner, and Christine Zander, writers; George Meyer, additional sketches, *Saturday Night Live*, NBC	Billy Crystal, *Billy Crystal: Midnight Train to Moscow*, HBO; James L. Brooks, Heide Perlman, Sam Simon, Jerry Belson, Marc Flanagan, Dinah Kirgo, Jay Kogen, Wallace Wolodarsky, Ian Praiser, Marilyn Suzanne Miller, Tracey Ullman, *The Tracey Ullman Show*, FOX
Miniseries	*The Murder of Mary Phagan*, NBC	*War and Remembrance*, ABC	*Drug Wars: The Camarena Story*, NBC
Actor—Miniseries or Special	Jason Robards, *Inherit the Wind*, NBC	James Woods, *My Name is Bill W.*, ABC	Hume Cronyn, *Age-Old Friends*, HBO
Actress—Miniseries or Special	Jessica Tandy, *Foxfire*, CBS	Holly Hunter, *Roe vs. Wade*, NBC	Barbara Hershey, *A Killing in a Small Town*, CBS
Supporting Actor—Miniseries or Special	John Shea, *Baby M*, ABC	Derek Jacobi, *The Tenth Man*, CBS	Vincent Gardenia, *Age-Old Friends*, HBO
Supporting Actress—Miniseries or Special	Jane Seymour, *Onassis: The Richest Man in the World*, ABC	Colleen Dewhurst, *Those She Left Behind*, NBC	Eva Marie Saint, *People Like Us*, NBC
Director—Miniseries or Special	Lamont Johnson, *Gore Vidal's Lincoln*, NBC	Simon Wincer, *Lonesome Dove*, CBS	Joseph Sargent, *Caroline?* CBS
Writer—Miniseries or Special	William Hanley, *The Attic: The Hiding of Anne Frank*, CBS	Abby Mann, Robin Vote, and Ron Hutchison, *Murderers Among Us: The Simon Wiesenthal Story*, HBO	Terrence McNally, *Andre's Mother*, PBS
Daytime Drama Series	*Santa Barbara*, NBC	*Santa Barbara*, NBC	*Santa Barbara*, NBC
Actor—Daytime Drama Series	David Canary, *All My Children*, ABC	David Canary, *All My Children*, ABC	A. Martinez, *Santa Barbara*, NBC
Actress—Daytime Drama Series	Helen Gallagher, *Ryan's Hope*, ABC	Marcy Walker, *Santa Barbara*, NBC	Kim Zimmer, *Guiding Light*, CBS
Supp. Actor—Daytime Drama	Justin Deas, *Santa Barbara*, NBC	Justin Deas, *Santa Barbara*, NBC	Henry Darrow, *Santa Barbara*, NBC
Supporting Actress—Daytime Drama Series	Ellen Wheeler, *All My Children*, ABC	Debbi Morgan, *All My Children*, ABC; Nancy Lee Grahn, *Santa Barbara*, NBC	Julia Barr, *All My Children*, ABC
Ingenue—Daytime Drama Series	Julianne Moore, *As the World Turns*, CBS	Kimberly McCullough, *General Hospital*, ABC	Cady McClain, *All My Children*, ABC
Younger Leading Man—Daytime Drama Series	Billy Warlock, *Days of Our Lives*, NBC	Justin Gocke, *Santa Barbara*, NBC	Andrew Kavovit, *As the World Turns*, CBS
Host—Game Show	Bob Barker, *The Price Is Right*, CBS	Alex Trebek, *Jeopardy!*, SYN	Alex Trebek, *Jeopardy!*, SYN; Bob Barker, *The Price Is Right*, CBS
Host—Talk or Service Show	Phil Donahue, *Donahue*, SYN	Sally Jessy Raphael, *Sally Jessy Raphael*, SYN	Joan Rivers, *The Joan Rivers Show*, SYN
Game Show	*The Price Is Right*, CBS	*The $25,000 Pyramid*, CBS	*Jeopardy!*, SYN
Talk, Service, or Variety Series	*The Oprah Winfrey Show*, SYN	*The Oprah Winfrey Show*, SYN	*Sally Jessy Raphael*, SYN
Children's Program	*The Secret Garden*, CBS	*Free To Be . . . A Family*, ABC	*A Mother's Courage: The Mary Thomas Story*, NBC
Children's Series	*Sesame Street*, PBS	*Newton's Apple*, PBS	*Reading Rainbow*, PBS

	1990–91	1991–92	1992–93
Drama	*L.A. Law*, NBC	*Northern Exposure*, CBS	*Picket Fences*, CBS
Actor—Drama Series	James Earl Jones, *Gabriel's Fire*, ABC	Christopher Lloyd, *Avonlea*, DIS	Tom Skerritt, *Picket Fences*, CBS
Actress—Drama Series	Patricia Wettig, *thirtysomething*, ABC	Dana Delany, *China Beach*, ABC	Kathy Baker, *Picket Fences*, CBS
Supporting Actor—Drama Series	Timothy Busfield, *thirtysomething*, ABC	Richard Dysart, *L.A. Law*, NBC	Chad Lowe, *Life Goes On*, ABC
Supporting Actress—Drama Series	Madge Sinclair, *Gabriel's Fire*, ABC	Valerie Mahaffey, *Northern Exposure*, CBS	Mary Alice, *I'll Fly Away*, NBC
Director—Drama Series	Thomas Carter, *Equal Justice*, ABC	Eric Laneuville, *I'll Fly Away*, NBC	Barry Levinson, *Homicide—Life on the Street*, NBC
Writer—Drama Series	David E. Kelley, *L.A. Law*, NBC	Andrew Schneider and Diane Frolov, *Northern Exposure*, CBS	Tom Fontana, *Homicide—Life on the Street*, NBC
Comedy	*Cheers*, NBC	*Murphy Brown*, CBS	*Seinfeld*, NBC
Actor—Comedy Series	Burt Reynolds, *Evening Shade*, CBS	Craig T. Nelson, *Coach*, ABC	Ted Danson, *Cheers*, NBC
Actress—Comedy Series	Kirstie Alley, *Cheers*, NBC	Candice Bergen, *Murphy Brown*, CBS	Roseanne Arnold, *Roseanne*, ABC
Supporting Actor—Comedy Series	Jonathan Winters, *Davis Rules*, ABC	Michael Jeter, *Evening Shade*, CBS	Michael Richards, *Seinfeld*, NBC
Supp. Actress—Comedy Series	Bebe Neuwirth, *Cheers*, NBC	Laurie Metcalf, *Roseanne*, ABC	Laurie Metcalf, *Roseanne*, ABC
Director—Comedy Series	James Burrows, *Cheers*, NBC	Barnet Kellman, *Murphy Brown*, CBS	Betty Thomas, *Dream On*, HBO
Writer—Comedy Series	Gary Dontzig and Steven Peterman, *Murphy Brown*, CBS	Elaine Pope and Larry Charles, *Seinfeld*, NBC	Larry David, *Seinfeld*, NBC
Variety, Music, or Comedy Program	*The 63rd Annual Academy Awards*, ABC	*The Tonight Show Starring Johnny Carson*, NBC	*Saturday Night Live*, NBC
Individual Performance—Variety or Music Program	Billy Crystal, *The 63rd Annual Academy Awards*, ABC	Bette Midler, *The Tonight Show Starring Johnny Carson*, NBC	Dana Carvey, *Saturday Night Live*, NBC
Director—Variety or Music	Hal Gurnee, *Late Night with David Letterman*, NBC	Patricia Birch, *Unforgettable with Love: Natalie Cole Sings the Songs of Nat King Cole*, PBS	Walter C. Miller, *The 1992 Tony Awards*, CBS
Writer—Variety or Music	Hal Kanter and Buz Kohan, writers; Billy Crystal, David Steinberg, Bruce Vilanch, and Robert Wuhl (Special Material), *The 63rd Annual Academy Awards*, ABC	Hal Kanter and Buz Kohan, writers); Billy Crystal, Marc Shaiman, David Steinberg, Robert Wuhl, and Bruce Vilanch, special material, *The 64rd Annual Academy Awards*, ABC	Judd Apatow, Robert Cohen, David Cross, Brent Forrester, Jeff Kahn, Bruce Kirschbaum, Bob Odenkirk, Sultan Pepper, Dino Stamatopoulos, Ben Stiller, *The Ben Stiller Show*, FOX
Made for Television Movie	—	*Miss Rose White Hallmark Hall of Fame*, NBC	*Barbarians at the Gate*, HBO; *Stalin*, HBO
Miniseries	*Separate but Equal*, ABC	*A Woman Named Jackie*, NBC	*Prime Suspect 2*, PBS

	1990–91	1991–92	1992–93
Actor—Miniseries or Special	John Gielgud, *Summer's Lease*, PBS	Beau Bridges, *Without Warning: The James Brady Story*, HBO	Robert Morse, *Tru*, PBS
Actress—Miniseries or Special	Lynn Whitfield, *The Josephine Baker Story*, HBO	Gena Rowlands, *Face of a Stranger*, CBS	Holly Hunter, *The Positively True Adventures of the Alleged Texas Cheerleader-Murdering Mom*, HBO
Supporting Actor—Miniseries or Special	James Earl Jones, *Heat Wave*, TNT	Hume Cronyn, *Neil Simon's Broadway Bound*, ABC	Beau Bridges, *The Positively True Adventures of the Alleged Texas Cheerleader-Murdering Mom*, HBO
Supporting Actress—Miniseries or Special	Ruby Dee, *Decoration Day*, NBC	Amanda Plummer, *Miss Rose White*, NBC	Mary Tyler Moore, *Stolen Babies*, LIF
Director—Miniseries or Special	Brian Gibson, *The Josephine Baker Story*, HBO	Daniel Petrie, *Mark Twain and Me*, DIS	James Sadwith, *Sinatra*, CBS
Writer—Miniseries or Special	Andrew Davies, *House of Cards*, PBS	John Falsey and Joshua Brand, *I'll Fly Away*, NBC	Jane Anderson, *The Positively True Adventures of the Alleged Texas Cheerleader-Murdering Mom*, HBO
Daytime Drama Series	*As the World Turns*, CBS	*All My Children*, ABC	*All My Children*, ABC
Actor—Daytime Drama Series	Peter Bergman, *The Young and the Restless*, CBS	Peter Bergman, *The Young and the Restless*, CBS	Michael Zaslow, *Guiding Light*, CBS
Actress—Daytime Drama Series	Finola Hughes, *General Hospital*, ABC	Erika Slezak, *One Life to Live*, ABC	Hillary B. Smith, *One Life to Live*, ABC
Supporting Actor—Daytime Drama Series	Bernie Barrow, *Loving*, ABC	Thom Christopher, *One Life to Live*, ABC	Justin Deas, *Guiding Light*, CBS
Supporting Actress—Daytime Drama Series	Jess Walton, *The Young and the Restless*, CBS	Maeve Kinkead, *Guiding Light*, CBS	Susan Haskell, *One Life to Live*, ABC
Younger Actress—Daytime Drama Series	Anne Heche, *Another World*, NBC	Tricia Cast, *The Young and the Restless*, CBS	Melissa Hayden, *Guiding Light*, CBS
Younger Leading Man—Daytime Drama Series	Rick Hearst, *Guiding Light*, CBS	Kristoff St. John, *The Young and the Restless*, CBS	Roger Howarth, *One Life to Live*, ABC
Host—Game Show	Bob Barker, *The Price Is Right*, CBS	Bob Barker, *The Price Is Right*, CBS	Bob Barker, *The Price Is Right*, CBS
Host—Talk or Service Show	Oprah Winfrey, *The Oprah Winfrey Show*, SYN	Oprah Winfrey, *The Oprah Winfrey Show*, SYN	Oprah Winfrey, *The Oprah Winfrey Show*, SYN
Game Show	*Jeopardy!*, SYN	*Jeopardy!*, SYN	*Jeopardy!*, SYN
Talk, Service, or Variety Series	*The Oprah Winfrey Show*, SYN	*The Oprah Winfrey Show*, SYN	*The Oprah Winfrey Show*, SYN
Children's Program	*You Can't Grow Home Again: A 3-2-1 Contact Extra*, PBS	*Mark Twain and Me*, DIS	*Rugrats*, NICK
Children's Series	*Sesame Street*, PBS	*Sesame Street*, PBS	*Sesame Street*, PBS

1993-94

Drama	*Picket Fences*, CBS
Actor—Drama Series	Dennis Franz, *NYPD Blue*, ABC
Actress—Drama Series	Sela Ward, *Sisters*, NBC
Supporting Actor—Drama Series	Fyvush Finkel, *Picket Fences*, CBS
Supporting Actress—Drama Series	Leigh Taylor-Young, *Picket Fences*, CBS
Director—Drama Series	Daniel Sackheim, *NYPD Blue*, ABC
Writer—Drama Series	*NYPD Blue*, ABC
Comedy	*Frasier*, NBC
Actor—Comedy Series	Kelsey Grammer, *Frasier*, NBC
Actress—Comedy Series	Candice Bergen, *Murphy Brown*, CBS
Supporting Actor—Comedy Series	Michael Richards, *Seinfeld*, NBC
Supp. Actress—Comedy Series	Laurie Metcalf, *Roseanne*, ABC
Director—Comedy Series	James Burrows, *Frasier*, NBC
Writer—Comedy Series	*Frasier*, NBC
Variety, Music, or Comedy Series	*Late Show With David Letterman*, CBS
Variety, Music, or Comedy Special	*The Kennedy Center Honors*, CBS
Individual Performance—Variety or Music Program	Tracey Ullman, *Tracey Ullman Takes On New York*, HBO
Director—Variety or Music	Walter C. Miller, *The Tony Awards*, CBS
Writer—Variety or Music	*Dennis Miller Live*, HBO

1993-94

Made for Television Movie	*And the Band Played On,* HBO
Miniseries	*Mystery: Prime Suspect 3,* PBS
Actor—Miniseries or Special	Hume Cronyn, *Hallmark Hall of Fame: To Dance With the White Dog,* CBS
Actress—Miniseries or Special	Kirstie Alley, *David's Mother,* CBS
Supporting Actor—Miniseries or Special	Michael Goorjian, *David's Mother,* CBS
Supporting Actress—Miniseries or Special	Cicely Tyson, *Oldest Living Confederate Widow Tells All,* CBS
Director—Miniseries or Special	John Frankenheimer, *Against the Wall,* HBO
Writer—Miniseries or Special	*David's Mother,* CBS

In this issue

Friends of Jack Benny say goodbye

Expert's warning on the pitfalls of buying gold

Lynn the G-rated Redgrave stars as 'The Happy Hooker'

Craig Claiborne is (and has) the last word on food

ELVIS IS 40!

A heroin scandal hits Boy George

Winger & Redford's matchmaker

People weekly

On a blind date with PRINCE

Would you trust this man with your daughter?

Prince Rogers Nelson, 28, creator, director and star of *Under the Cherry Moon*

SONG

Repackaged Liz . . . and what a bundle!

People weekly

What nightmares can tell you

Sen. Jake Garn's space odyssey

The Pritikin suicide

MADONNA

THE ORDEAL OF OUR HOSTAGE HEROES

An insider's poignant story of the fight to free them and a look at their challenge now: making new lives

People weekly

FRANK SINATRA inaugurates a cleaned-up act

Anthony Hopkins is as hot as his tub scene with Bo Derek

Nancy Reagan's cosmetics guru

THE SIGN
Ace of Base

Even after Ace of Base top-tenned with their first U.S. single, "All That She Wants," detractors dismissed the four photogenic Swedes as a sugar-pop sequel to fellow Scandinavians ABBA. But the quartet's debut album, *The Sign*, is a clear signal that more hits are on the way. Instead of reheating moldy white-bread pop, the group blends reggae syncopation, strobe light grooves, and a jejune point of view, cooking up forty-five minutes of delirious fun.

UNDER THE PINK
Tori Amos

This incomparable songwriter, with her deft piano playing and compelling voice, performs songs that make you feel. Following 1992's impressive debut album, *Little Earthquakes*, Amos plunges fearlessly into such weighty topics as sexual guilt, anger, and religious confusion—territory from which she seems to emerge healed and healthy. Throughout, her lush melodies and elaborate arrangements grow stronger with each listening.

ZINGALAMADUNI
Arrested Development

In life, political correctness can be boring; in rap, it's refreshing. And compared with gangsta rap's brutal amorality and casual sexism, Arrested Development's good-natured Afrocentric positivism seems downright rebellious. On this second album, the Georgia-based collective continues to purvey its spiritually based brand of political awareness and racial pride, wrapping its messages in jazzy free-flowing beats. There is anger, but more commonly forgiveness and tolerance.

ILL COMMUNICATION
The Beastie Boys

If ever a group screamed novelty act, it was the Beastie Boys in 1986 when they crashed the hip-hop party with *Licensed to Ill.* Three groundbreaking albums later, they have established themselves as auteurs of a sort, finessing their sonic mayhem by juxtaposing comic, often profane rhymes with rich, textured soundscapes. The brilliant *Ill Communication* can verge on the experimental, and it succeeds mightily. The Beasties are one of the few bands capable of being both ridiculous and awe inspiring in the same breath.

MTV UNPLUGGED
Tony Bennett

There's no disputing Generation X's current infatuation with the sixty-seven-year-old Bennett. As this splendid CD shows, Bennett is a multigenerational crowd pleaser who can still wrap those husky pipes around a tune with style and panache. Guest appearances include duets with k.d. lang and Elvis Costello. Hearing the prototypical angry rocker and the aging, happy-go-lucky balladeer sounding like old pals makes you realize how this disc could narrow the generation gap.

THE ONE THING
Michael Bolton

Bolton cowrote all but two of the songs for this, his seventh album. On the opening cut, the surprisingly graceful "Said I Loved You . . . But I Lied," his tar paper voice finds nuance and true, quiet passion. From then on, however, the album suffocates under the weight of its overstuffed production and the sentimental schmaltz that Bolton and his songwriting collaborators can't seem to get enough of.

FRUITCAKES
Jimmy Buffett

On his first studio album in five years, Jimmy Buffett turns his tequila-addled wit to such diverse topics as boat people, space aliens, state lotteries, earthquakes, TV evangelists, reggae music, and Junior Mints. And that's just the two opening tracks. Buffet's rabid fans, addicted to his party-hearty trop-rock, will find plenty to satisfy. Buffett has cleverly slipped some sober sides into the mix, but his forte remains survival as a middle-aged crazy, good-naturedly preparing for the ultimate decline and fall of Western civilization.

DAVID BYRNE
David Byrne

The wildly unpredictable (and uneven) solo career of the former Talking Heads front man has forced loyalists to become either politely indulgent or maddeningly frustrated. Byrne has explored everything from Brazilian pop to an off-kilter interpretation of Dixieland jazz, yet his solo forays have never eclipsed what he created with the now-disbanded Heads. Until now. Playing with a noisy stripped-down rock quartet, Byrne has returned to the quirky, nervous energy of his early days.

AMERICAN RECORDINGS
Johnny Cash

Guns, murder, blunts, and booze: Move over Tupac, there's a new OG in town. Actually, make that an old Original Gangsta, 'cause Cash was singing about shooting men in Reno just to watch 'em die back when gangsta rappers were mere pups. This album straddles a fine line between artful exploitation of the Man in Black legend and lame parody. Fortunately, Cash's humanity prevails. The album is an acoustic, close-to-the-bone collection that zeros in on the singer's deep, rich voice—a voice as mysterious as it is familiar, as dignified as it is raw and emotional.

COHEN LIVE
Leonard Cohen

Cohen delivers his hits with such overwhelming weariness that he seems destined to expire with the next note. His toneless, sludgy voice, backed by an equally limp band, makes Tom Waits sound like Pavarotti. Since the thirteen tracks here were culled from more than 200 shows during recent tours, presumably he considers these renditions to be particularly flattering. Scary thought.

SHE
Harry Connick Jr.

Those who think that Harry Connick Jr. is little more than a piano-plunking Frank Sinatra manqué had better listen again: His latest album is closer in spirit and sound to a rollicking Louisiana Saturday night than an evening of Cole Porter's upscale pop. Jazz and easy-listening purists who reveled in Connick's *When Harry Met Sally* . . . soundtrack need not fret, however. Connick is still VH-1 material—just funky, hyperkinetic, and Cajun-spiced as well.

BRUTAL YOUTH
Elvis Costello

Though Costello's solo efforts have been mostly satisfying since splitting with the Attractions in 1986, there's something reassuring about the music he makes with his band. *Brutal Youth* has the spunk of an old New Wave disc, although there's a jazzier groove on some cuts that lend a stylish sophistication few other rock bands can match. Costello remains the wise guy, tossing off barbed lines to an unfaithful love or anyone else who gets in the way. Sarcasm. Anger. A touch of nastiness. Just like the good old days.

GOD SHUFFLED HIS FEET
Crash Test Dummies

So what have we here . . . another neo-folkie, pseudo-hippie, sort of Celtic, dryly humorous, exceptionally literate pop band? Yup, and there may be more; if this Canadian quintet continues turning out quality discs like this, there will surely be imitators. This second CD from the Dummies features a dozen tunes that sound like nothing you've heard before yet are completely hummable from the very first listen.

THE COLOUR OF MY LOVE
Celine Dion

It's getting tough to tell today's pop ingenues apart. The third U.S. release from French-Canadian songbird Dion could be the latest from Mariah Carey. Same power pipes, same song selection. But while vocal somersaults bog down Carey's work, Dion quietly makes mushy blather sound like gospel. She still needs to find her niche, and taking any musical risk would be welcome, but she perfects her romantic pitch with *The Colour of My Love.*

WHEN LOVE FINDS YOU
Vince Gill

Vince Gill's formula—mournful understated ballads about heartbreak, sung in a pure, quavering tenor—is hard to beat. Not since Smoky Robinson's Motown heyday has an artist created such gorgeous rhapsodies of remorse; "Whenever You Come Around," the second track here, shimmers with aching passion. Such is Gill's way with romantic ruin that even when he shakes off the blues to whoop it up, he seems to be biding his time, just waiting for the girl to leave so he can start hurting again.

THE FUNKY HEADHUNTER
Hammer

After a three-year break, Hammer is back with a hard, mean-street edge and the calculated scowl to go with it. His "people" may label his new roughneck persona as artistic growth, but it smells like desperation. The real drag is that *The Funky Headhunter* is dull. "It's All Good" pulsates with intensity, but most of the album is lifeless. In hindsight, all the abuse Hammer got in the past seems unfair. *U Can't Touch This* wasn't a sellout. This is.

TAKE ME AS I AM
Faith Hill

Lithe-voiced and lively, Hill is a Mississippian who learned to sing belting hymns in a Baptist church. A blues singer Hill isn't: she sounds most comfortable on more formally arranged tunes. Yet despite those limitations and the fact that she generally avoids the traditional woman-as-victim stance of female country singers, she is most entertaining on this album's rougher-sounding upbeat tracks. This is as enjoyable and promising a debut as anything since Patty Loveless's 1988 *If My Heart Had Windows.*

SWAMP OPHELIA
Indigo Girls

The mood Indigo is increasingly bold and assertive. The sixth album from this Atlanta duo evinces little of the gentleness and passivity we have come to associate with folk music. But then Emily Saliers and Amy Ray have always had a distinctive knack for investing prettiness with passion. This time even their acoustic guitar strumming is emphatic.

WHO I AM

Alan Jackson

Blessed with an offhand, effortless style and a no-nonsense batch of mostly self-penned songs, country crooner Alan Jackson charms as a regular Joe who could be the guy next door. Classic, pop-free country is still the name of the game Jackson's fourth time out, and nowhere is his approach more effective than on "Gone Country." In lesser hands the tune would teeter into yee-haw territory. But skillful navigation and a clear, honest voice inject it with a reflective mournfulness that elevates the predictable into the pleasurable.

DIARY OF A MAD BAND

Jodeci

The last few years have seen an avalanche of sharp-dressed, smooth-talking, hip-hop-flavored R&B acts, and the kings of the heap are Jodeci. All of which makes this one of the more anticipated R&B records in a long time. Jodeci's soaring harmonies here find a rock-solid foundation of bass lines. But despite the band's lush ballads, a few of their ballistic, up-tempo tracks are laced with a lyric swagger that presents women as objects of ridicule or simply prey. When you have Jodeci's skill, it seems dumb to squander it on theme music for the Spur Posse.

HIGH-TECH REDNECK

George Jones

In which we find the ol' Possum in better voice than we've heard him in years, which means we actually get about a half-dozen voices, from a taut tenor twang through clenched-teeth expressions of agony to (the sure goose bump raiser) a hushed, compassionate whisper. *High-Tech Redneck* has two centerpieces: the title track and "The Visit." Those are the attention getters, but what makes this a good album is the supporting tunes' generally high quality.

PRETTY CLOSE TO THE TRUTH

Jim Lauderdale

Pretty Close to the Truth is the best country album in the past two years. Actually "country" is a misnomer. "Roots-pop" comes closer. The last time ballads as achingly melodic as "Why Do I Love You?" were around, Lennon and McCartney were writing them. Nor is Lauderdale afraid to holler and bawl his guts out; on "When the Devil Starts Crying," is it Satan, or just another guy his woman's falling for? It hardly matters—the singer wails as if he can see the flames of Hades.

IN THIS HOUSE, ON THIS MORNING

The Wynton Marsalis Septet

It's time to abandon the notion that Wynton Marsalis's music is cerebral and bloodless. This record has got as much fire and down-home fervor as any jazz album since . . . well, since who knows when. Marsalis built *In This House* on the structure of an African-American church service. If this music doesn't get you moving, check your pulse—you may be dead.

WALKING AWAY A WINNER

Kathy Mattea

Kathy Mattea has one of Nashville's strongest set of pipes; thanks to them she can kick some very ho-hum tunes into high gear. And therein lies the problem with this album: Mattea's no-nonsense mezzo-soprano is wasted on the slightly cornpone fare here. The Grammy winner is best at solid, gutsy I-will-survive numbers, like the title track. The rest of the album is an assortment of wishy-washy pop that merely maintains Mattea's status as a great talent who doesn't always choose the best material.

WHAT A CRYING SHAME

The Mavericks

The Mavericks represent an endangered species in '90s Nashville: taut, hard-edged country rock that draws on the '50s and '60s honky-tonk traditions. The comparisons that come to mind are with Dwight Yoakam, Los Lobos, and Roy Orbison. On this, the group's second album, the songs are strong and crafty touches abound. The tour de force is "I Should Have Been True," which swells and builds, riding a quavering vocal to a shamelessly over-the-top climax.

PROSE COMBAT

MC Solaar

The brightest light in the hip-hop galaxy is Claude M'Barali, a.k.a. MC Solaar. The rapper was born in Senegal and raised in France, where he is the biggest thing since Mickey Rourke. Solaar's flow is jazzy, fluid, playful, witty, free of misogyny, race baiting, and violent imagery. And, oh yes, it's also in French. But Solaar's rich, sexy voice is so evocative, you feel what he's expressing even if you can't understand what he's saying.

MOONLIGHT BECOMES YOU
Willie Nelson

Billed as the follow-up to 1978's *Stardust*, this is, in fact, the fourth album of pre-rock standards that Nelson has cut since *Stardust*. Problem is, Willie may be runnin' out of chestnuts—these tunes are mostly second-tier standards. But Willie, as usual, throws us a curve. The best thing here isn't from Tin Pan Alley, it's a new version of his own haunting "December Day," which simply underscores the fact that Nelson's best songs are fully on a par with the classics he loves.

LIVE ON THE PLANET EARTH
The Neville Brothers

This first live album in a decade, culled from various stops on their recent global tour, finds the four New Orleans siblings living up to their reputation as a devastatingly good live act, navigating the warm waters of funk, pop, jazz, and gospel with grace and passion. To listeners weaned on the computer-driven sterility of much of today's black pop, the Neville Brothers' organic approach and peace-brothers-and-sisters rhetoric may seem passé. But timeless songs and Aaron Neville's honey-voiced singing go a long way toward explaining why these soul men continue to attract new fans.

FAR BEYOND DRIVEN
Pantera

Pantera's third album makes one wonder how Judas Priest was ever considered dissonant. Guitarist Dimebag Darrell sets an abrasive chug over which a rabid Phil Anselmo spews profane lyrics about sex and religion. (Singing is heard exactly once.) Pantera's speed metal is not particularly fast, it's just brutal. But *Driven* sold 186,000 copies its first week, debuting at No. 1 on the *Billboard* chart. For a band viable for its lack of viability, this may be a problem.

THE DIVISION BELL
Pink Floyd

Rock's dark shamans have always been fond of the big gesture. But the band's talent and vision have always stayed a few steps ahead of their pretensions. Until now. Their strategy remains the same, but the band's arch, dynamic style is undone here by vacuous melodies. Too much of the pale clockwork pop on *The Division Bell* sounds like bad Genesis. Only a few tracks retain the haunting quality that is the group's signature. So Pink Floyd strikes out, but at least they go down swinging.

LAST OF THE INDEPENDENTS
Pretenders

Chrissie Hynde's no-nonsense sexual bravado and impeccable pop smarts have been influencing how women rock since the 1979 debut of her band, the Pretenders. On this, the Pretenders' best album in a decade, Hynde continues to tackle her favorite subject, love, in a way that may frustrate longtime fans. Her female protagonists constantly give, rarely get, waste a ton of time waiting for "him" to return, and accept physical abuse with charity. Fictional or not, it's a shockingly regressive stance. Fortunately, such is her emotional force that Hynde manages to transform even iffy sexual politics into powerful rock.

MUSE SICK–N–HOUR MESS AGE
Public Enemy

With its first album in nearly three years, Public Enemy is out to prove that it's still hip-hop's No. 1. Though far from a failure, the result is hampered by its numbing length, less than forceful production, and predictable racial rants. Yet Public Enemy shows lively signs of its former self, especially on the finger popping "Give It Up" and the ominous "So Whatcha Gone Do Now?" The latter, which criticizes gangsta rap and its emphasis on violence, may be the most challenging cut this group has recorded, reminding you of what made them so important in the first place.

LONGING IN THEIR HEARTS
Bonnie Raitt

Bluesy Bonnie's music can help you rattle the saloon walls till closing time, then soothe your jangled nerves in the harsh morning light. Again, Raitt's versatility is on exhibit in this collection, which ranges from the tightly coiled, funky stomp of "Love Sneakin' Up on You" to such disarming ballads as "You." She is blessed with an innate soulfulness and an unmistakable, smokey, single-malt voice. And when she's in top form, she can deliver the wild and the mellow more nimbly than anyone in pop music.

VOODOO LOUNGE
The Rolling Stones

Even by the lax standards of a band that has been coasting on its reputation for years, *Voodoo Lounge* is nothing more than a rubber-stamp effort. Its rockers rely heavily on formula and the fifty-year-old Jagger's increasingly less believable me-so-horny lyrics. The album's gutsiest tracks come from Keith Richards, whose gravelly, sage stylings are better suited to a rock-and-roll artist firmly entrenched in middle age. Die-hard Stones fans may be willing to accept another predictable album, but the more discerning will wish that the band had tried to produce an innovative album, not one that preaches to the converted.

VERY NECESSARY
Salt-N-Pepa

Today's female MCs are getting harder and rougher, so it should be no shock that Salt-N-Pepa's fourth album is raunchy, rowdy, and fully befitting the girls whose hits include "Let's Talk About Sex." Yet Salt-N-Pepa never allow themselves to be exploited. Okay, there's the somewhat regressive line about wanting to have some guy's baby (on "Whatta Man"), but missteps like that are easily forgotten on an album that includes a poignant call for AIDS education.

HEART, SOUL & A VOICE
Jon Secada

Something happened to Jon Secada on his way to the bank: he found soul. While the string of hits from his 1992 self-titled debut was mindless pop at its infectious best, the Grammy-winning Secada is now ready to give R&B's smoothest operators a run for their romantic constituency. His second effort offers more sweet hooks and several pleasant surprises. While his R&B mode can sometimes seem too nostalgic or derivative, it can also sound as authentic as its inspiration: that sinuous groove on "Good Feelings," which could stir the ghost of Marvin Gaye, is about as good as soul music gets.

CHIEF BOOT KNOCKA
Sir Mix-A-Lot

Sir Mix-A-Lot's salacious shout-out to the glories of the female posterior, "Baby Got Back," sold more than 2.5 million copies and won him a Grammy in 1992. So it's not surprising that he still has behinds on his mind. Mix-A-Lot specializes in bass-driven hip hop that's low on content and high on innuendo. But unlike some less clever rappers, he has a sly if sexist wit and embellishes his fantasies with an oily charm that can only be called cheeky.

EXPERIMENTAL JET SET, TRASH AND NO STAR
Sonic Youth

Sonic Youth has perfected the art of cool. That disarming sangfroid is on display on this ninth album, which abandons the political ranting of 1992's *Dirty* for the more esoteric point of view of Youth's earlier work. That said, *Jet* doesn't look like the album that will push these perennial toasts of the underground to the top of the charts.

SUPERUNKNOWN
Soundgarden

Though they started grinding out the Seattle sound years before flannel became a fashion statement, Soundgarden has ventured beyond Grungeville's city limits into the Superunknown. The music is still loud, the lyrics are still heavy, and the lead singer still works his way into a primal frenzy. But this time, for every full-throttle face-melter like "Spoonman," there's a slow, moody change of pace such as the elegant "Black Hole Sun." This diverse disc is the best from a band that was already at the top of its form.

TURN IT UPSIDE DOWN
Spin Doctors

The peculiar charm of the Spin Doctors' 1991 triple-Platinum debut, *Pocket Full of Kryptonite*, was the band's complete lack of guile and apparent disinterest in making a hit album. There was nothing commercial about it; in fact, they seemed to be making it up as they went along. Nothing much has changed with this cheerful and long-awaited follow-up. From freely associating lyrics to jam-loving instrumentals, the hippie-dippy, blues-based Docs are as unpredictable as ever.

PURPLE
Stone Temple Pilots

Stone Temple Pilots sprang up out of nowhere in 1992 and vaulted to the top of the charts with a debut album that was chock full of a faceless metallic grunge occasionally leavened by self-pitying acoustic interludes. This album mostly sticks to that formula. STP have been accused of modeling themselves after (if not outright ripping off) Pearl Jam and Alice in Chains. Ultimately, though, *Purple* is the punk equivalent of purple prose: overwrought, ham-handed hard rock tainted by the unmistakable odor of hackwork.

LOVE AND LUCK
Marty Stuart

Despite a handful of solid hits—not to mention his taste for rooster hair and rhinestone jackets—Stuart has never seemed to stand out in the Nashville crowd. His seventh album, *Love and Luck*, should finally change that. Now his fans are treated to a rolling ride through blues, rock, gospel, and traditional country. With his warm voice hugging every turn, Stuart's brand of souped-up country takes listeners for a flat-out spin that may leave them a bit dizzy but thoroughly enthralled.

FORCE OF NATURE
Koko Taylor

More than four decades after she was rescued from her day job as a cleaning woman and put onto a Chess Records roster that included Muddy Waters and Howlin' Wolf, the reigning Queen of Chicago Blues is still belting out blues in a gravel voice with ferocious intensity. The best blues have an earthy grit, and Taylor is not one to smooth out any edges. The result here is foot-stomping music that's rough, raw, and wonderfully upbeat from a veteran, no-frills vocalist who doesn't do it any other way.

MIRROR BLUE
Richard Thompson

There is no denying Thompson's guitar artistry. He and his group, Fairport Convention, were central to Britain's folk-rock movement of the '60s, and he later refined his style with his now–ex-wife, Linda. Thompson's latest effort is more raw and stripped down than usual. He is a master storyteller, and the centerpiece on *Mirror Blue* is the brutally truthful "The Way It Shows," a mournful song of misdirected passions on which his guitar seems to cry with cathartic clarity. A guitarist-songwriter this captivating still needs compelling songs to drive. Thankfully, Thompson has plenty.

THIS IS ME
Randy Travis

Back in the mid-'80s he was part of country music's vanguard, his back-to-basics balladry an antidote to the treacly country pop then clogging airwaves. Less than a decade later, Randy Travis is suddenly a conservative—a star who banks on a classy voice, not big-budget videos or flashy stagecraft. With *This Is Me*, he also emerges as rightful heir to such higher-grade mainstream stars of the '50s and '60s as George Jones and Buck Owens. Every song here is good, all of them guaranteed to appeal to Travis's stronghold.

TEN FEET TALL AND BULLETPROOF
Travis Tritt

Given the current crop of sensitive New Age cowboys, it's refreshing to hear unrepentant good ol' boy Travis Tritt still raucously strutting his stuff on his latest album. Whether singing about getting into T-R-O-U-B-L-E in the bedroom or the barroom, Tritt's hard-driving swagger seems to just plain be in his blood. Then again, anyone who has duetted in the past year with Patti LaBelle and David Lee Roth, as Tritt has, is likely to do anything, politically correct or otherwise—bless his ornery little hide.

WHO DO WE THINK WE ARE?
Turtle Island String Quartet

The Kronos Quartet may have been the first, but it's not the only string quartet to toss its tuxedos and infiltrate the frontiers of jazz, bluegrass, world music, and even Jimi Hendrix tunes. The difference is that while Kronos visits these territories, Turtle Island dwells in them. The group's interplay in cuts like Charlie Parker's bebop classic "Moose the Mooche" is ripe and irrepressible, but the most haunting cut is the jazz standard "You've Changed."

BLUE LIGHT 'TIL DAWN
Cassandra Wilson

Hailed as one of the best of jazz's new breed, singer Cassandra Wilson has delivered a mesmerizing album that gracefully blurs the lines between jazz, blues, R&B, and pop. Wilson's rich, whispery alto and achingly understated delivery are pure seduction. *Blue Light 'til Dawn* is complex, challenging, and vividly communicative soul music by a singer who deserves widespread attention.

ANGELA WINBUSH
Angela Winbush

This songbird isn't just another pretty voice looking to the guys for direction. Writing, producing, and playing most of her own material, Stevie Wonder's former background vocalist has already hooked the R&B world with a string of hits. Now Winbush wants the rest of pop's universe to sing along to her third solo release. But they'll probably have trouble keeping up. Whether climbing to a siren wail or slithering down to a husky growl, Angela sounds so relaxed she could have sent these Valentines from the Jacuzzi.

ROCK AND ROLL HALL OF FAME

The Rock and Roll Hall of Fame and its museum are expected to open in mid-1995 in Cleveland. Presenting exhibitions and housing an extensive music archive, the Hall will also continue to select the greatest rock and roll musicians for induction every January. In order to be eligible, a nominee must have released a record at least twenty-five years prior to induction; the early influences list honors the formative figures of rock music.

1986

Chuck Berry
James Brown
Ray Charles
Sam Cooke
Fats Domino
The Everly Brothers
Buddy Holly
Jerry Lee Lewis
Elvis Presley
Little Richard

Early Influences

Robert Johnson
Jimmie Rodgers
Jimmy Yancey

Nonperformers

Alan Freed
Sam Phillips

Lifetime Achievement Award

John Hammond

1987

The Coasters
Eddie Cochran
Bo Diddley
Aretha Franklin
Marvin Gaye
Bill Haley
B. B. King
Clyde McPhatter
Ricky Nelson
Roy Orbison
Carl Perkins
Smokey Robinson
Big Joe Turner
Muddy Waters
Jackie Wilson

Early Influences

Louis Jordan
T-Bone Walker
Hank Williams

Nonperformers

Leonard Chess
Ahmet Ertegun
Jerry Leiber and Mike Stoller
Jerry Wexler

1988

The Beach Boys
The Beatles
The Drifters
Bob Dylan
The Supremes

Early Influences

Woodie Guthrie
Leadbelly
Les Paul

Nonperformers

Berry Gordy Jr.

1989

Dion
Otis Redding
The Rolling Stones
The Temptations
Stevie Wonder

Early Influences

The Ink Spots
Bessie Smith
The Soul Stirrers

Nonperformers

Phil Spector

1990

Hank Ballard
Bobby Darin
The Four Seasons
The Four Tops
The Kinks
The Platters
Simon & Garfunkel
The Who

Early Influences

Louis Armstrong
Charlie Christian
Ma Rainey

Nonperformers

Lamont Dozier
Gerry Goffin and Carole King
Brian Holland and Eddie Holland

1991

LaVern Baker
The Byrds
John Lee Hooker
The Impressions
Wilson Pickett
Jimmy Reed
Ike and Tina Turner

Early Influences

Howlin' Wolf

Nonperformers

Dave Bartholomew
Ralph Bass

Lifetime Achievement Award

Nesuhi Ertegun

1992

Bobby "Blue" Bland
Booker T. & The MGs
Johnny Cash
Jimi Hendrix Experience
The Isley Brothers
Sam and Dave
The Yardbirds

Early Influences

Elmore James
Professor Longhair

Nonperformers

Leo Fender
Doc Pomus
Bill Graham

1993

Ruth Brown
Cream
Creedence Clearwater Revival
The Doors
Etta James
Frankie Lymon & The Teenagers
Van Morrison
Sly & The Family Stone

Early Influences

Dinah Washington

Nonperformers

Dick Clark
Milt Gabler

1994

The Animals
The Band
Duane Eddy
The Grateful Dead
Elton John
John Lennon
Bob Marley
Rod Stewart

Early Influences

Willie Dixon

Nonperformers

Johnny Otis

COUNTRY MUSIC HALL OF FAME

Located in Nashville along with everything else in country music, the Country Music Hall of Fame inducts its honorees each autumn. The enshrined elite:

1962 Roy Acuff
1963 (elections held but no one candidate received enough votes)
1964 Tex Ritter
1965 Ernest Tubb
1966 James R. Denny, George D. Hay, Uncle Dave Macon, Eddy Arnold
1967 Red Foley, J. L. Frank, Jim Reeves, Stephen H. Sholes
1968 Bob Wills
1969 Gene Autry
1970 Original Carter Family (A. P. Carter, Maybelle Carter, Sara Carter), Bill Monroe
1971 Arthur Edward Satherley
1972 Jimmie Davis
1973 Patsy Cline, Chet Atkins
1974 Owen Bradley, Frank "Pee Wee" King
1975 Minnie Pearl
1976 Paul Cohen, Kitty Wells
1977 Merle Travis
1978 Grandpa Jones
1979 Hubert Long, Hank Snow
1980 Connie B. Gay, Original Sons of the Pioneers, Johnny Cash
1981 Vernon Dalhart, Grant Turner
1982 Lefty Frizzell, Marty Robbins, Roy Horton
1983 Little Jimmy Dickens
1984 Ralph Peer, Floyd Tillman
1985 Lester Flatt and Earl Scruggs
1986 Wesley Rose, The Duke of Paducah
1987 Rod Brasfield
1988 Roy Rogers, Loretta Lynn
1989 Jack Stapp, Hank Thompson, Cliffie Stone
1990 Tennessee Ernie Ford
1991 Boudleaux and Felice Bryant
1992 George Jones, Frances Preston
1993 Willie Nelson

JAZZ HALL OF FAME

Downbeat magazine, the country's leading jazz publication, has conducted an annual poll of both readers and critics to determine the greatest luminaries of the jazz world. The honorees:

	Readers' poll	Critics' poll
1952	Louis Armstrong	—
1953	Glenn Miller	—
1954	Stan Kenton	—
1955	Charlie Parker	—
1956	Duke Ellington	—
1957	Benny Goodman	—
1958	Count Basie	—
1959	Lester Young	—
1960	Dizzy Gillespie	—
1961	Billie Holiday	Coleman Hawkins
1962	Miles Davis	Bix Beiderbecke
1963	Thelonious Monk	Jelly Roll Morton
1964	Eric Dolphy	Art Tatum
1965	John Coltrane	Earl Hines
1966	Bud Powell	Charlie Christian
1967	Billy Strayhorn	Bessie Smith
1968	Wes Montgomery	Sidney Bechet, Fats Waller
1969	Ornette Coleman	Pee Wee Russell, Jack Teagarden
1970	Jimi Hendrix	Johnny Hodges
1971	Charles Mingus	Roy Eldridge, Django Reinhardt
1972	Gene Krupa	Clifford Brown
1973	Sonny Rollins	Fletcher Henderson
1974	Buddy Rich	Ben Webster
1975	Cannonball Adderley	Cecil Taylor
1976	Woody Herman	King Oliver
1977	Paul Desmond	Benny Carter
1978	Joe Venuti	Rahsaan Roland Kirk
1979	Ella Fitzgerald	Lennie Tristano
1980	Dexter Gordon	Max Roach
1981	Art Blakey	Bill Evans
1982	Art Pepper	Fats Navarro
1983	Stephane Grappelli	Albert Ayler
1984	Oscar Peterson	Sun Ra
1985	Sarah Vaughan	Zoot Sims
1986	Stan Getz	Gil Evans
1987	Lionel Hampton	Johnny Dodds, Thad Jones, Teddy Wilson
1988	Jaco Pastorius	Kenny Clarke
1989	Woody Shaw	Chet Baker
1990	Red Rodney	Mary Lou Williams
1991	Lee Morgan	John Carter
1992	Maynard Ferguson	James P. Johnson
1993	Gerry Mulligan	Edward Blackwell
1994	Frank Zappa	(to be named January 1995)

Lifetime Achievement Award

(given to nonmusicians for meritorious service to the jazz community)

1981 John Hammond
1982 George Wein
1983 Leonard Feather
1984 Dr. Billy Taylor
1985 Dr. Lawrence Berk
1986 Orrin Keepnews
1987 David Baker
1988 John Conyers Jr.*
1989 Norman Granz
1990 Rudy Van Gelder
1991 Bill Cosby
1992 Rich Matteson
1993 Gunther Schuller

*Special Achievement Award

TOP CONCERT APPEARANCES

The following survey lists the most successful individual concert appearances, based on box-office grosses, for 1993 and for all time. A concert appearance is defined here as all performances in a visit to a single town. (Source: Pollstar)

1993

1. Bette Midler	New York City
2. Paul Simon/Simon & Garfunkel	New York City
3. Garth Brooks	Irving, Texas
4. Billy Joel	New York City
5. Grateful Dead	Las Vegas
6. Grateful Dead	East Rutherford, New Jersey
7. Grateful Dead	Washington, D.C.
8. Billy Joel	Philadelphia
9. Grateful Dead	Chicago
10. Grateful Dead	New York City
11. Rod Stewart	New York City
12. Neil Diamond	Inglewood, California
13. Grateful Dead	Boston
14. Grateful Dead	Eugene, Oregon
15. Grateful Dead	Uniondale, New York
16. Jimmy Buffett	Cincinnati
17. Madonna	New York City
18. Luther Vandross	New York City
19. Rod Stewart	Los Angeles
20. Billy Joel	Syracuse, New York

ALL TIME

1. Barbra Streisand	New York City, 1994
2. Barbra Streisand	Las Vegas, 1993
3. The Rolling Stones	New York City, 1989
4. Bette Midler	New York City, 1993
5.The Rolling Stones	East Rutherford, New Jersey, 1994
6. The Rolling Stones	Los Angeles, 1989
7. Paul Simon/Simon & Garfunkel	New York City, 1993
8. Barbra Streisand	Auburn Hills, Michigan, 1994
9. Billy Joel/Elton John	Philadelphia, 1994
10. Bruce Springsteen & The E Street Band	East Rutherford, New Jersey, 1985
11. Bruce Springsteen & The E Street Band	East Rutherford New Jersey, 1992
12. Bruce Springsteen & The E Street Band	Los Angeles, 1985
13. The Rolling Stones	Atlantic City, New Jersey, 1989
14. Pink Floyd	Montreal, 1994
15. Pink Floyd	Oakland, California, 1994
16. The Who	East Rutherford, New Jersey, 1989
17. Pink Floyd	Philadelphia, 1994
18. The Eagles	Irvine, California, 1994
19. Pink Floyd	Foxboro, Massachusetts, 1994
20. The Eagles	Mountain View, California, 1994

TOP CONCERT TOURS

These are the most successful North American tours of all time, along with year-by-year leaders since 1985, when Pollstar first began tracking the concert industry. The rankings are based on grosses rather than attendance. (Source: Pollstar)

ALL TIME

Rank	Artist	Year of tour
1.	Pink Floyd	1994
2.	Rolling Stones	1989
3.	New Kids on the Block	1990
4.	U2	1992
5.	Barbra Streisand	1994
6.	Grateful Dead	1993
7.	Billy Joel	1990
8.	The Who	1989
9.	The Jacksons	1988
10.	Bruce Springsteen & The E Street Band	1985
11.	Paul McCartney	1990
12.	Bon Jovi	1989
13.	U2	1987
14.	Grateful Dead	1991
15.	Grateful Dead	1992
16.	Guns N' Roses/Metallica	1992
17.	Rod Stewart	1993
18.	Neil Diamond	1993
19.	Grateful Dead	1990
20.	Grateful Dead	1989

1985

Rank	Artist	Cities played
1.	Bruce Springsteen & The E Street Band	21
2.	Tina Turner	90
3.	Bryan Adams	129
4.	Kenny Rogers	80
5.	Prince & The Revolution	22
6.	Foreigner	105
7.	Willie Nelson and Family	97
8.	Ratt	139
9.	The Grateful Dead	40
10.	REO Speedwagon	94
11.	Mötley Crüe	91
12.	Iron Maiden	81
13.	Daryl Hall and John Oates	51
14.	Phil Collins	28
15.	Dio, featuring Ronnie James Dio	92
16.	AC/DC	57
17.	Chicago	48
18.	U2	30
19.	Triumph	74
20.	Dire Straits	41

1986

Rank	Artist	Cities/Shows
1.	ZZ Top	91/132
2.	Van Halen	77/109
3.	Neil Diamond	22/64
4.	Alabama	127/127
5.	Kenny Rogers	116/143
6.	Journey	52/69
7.	The Monkees	174/211
8.	Bob Dylan and Tom Petty	31/41
9.	Lionel Richie	40/60
10.	Bill Cosby	23/46
11.	Bob Seger & The Silver Bullet Band	40/60
12.	Billy Joel	32/42
13.	David Lee Roth	74/78
14.	Aerosmith	80/81
15.	Stevie Wonder	49/53
16.	Loverboy	118/118
17.	Run–D.M.C.	82/82
18.	Grateful Dead	16/39
19.	Julio Iglesias	51/71
20.	Beach Boys	90/97

1987

Rank	Artist	Cities/Shows
1.	U2	50/79
2.	Bon Jovi	104/130
3.	Pink Floyd	28/60
4.	Grateful Dead	37/84
5.	David Bowie	31/45
6.	Mötley Crüe	92/100
7.	Whitney Houston	77/89
8.	Huey Lewis & The News	89/101
9.	Boston	37/69
10.	Alabama	117/127
11.	Genesis	18/30
12.	Heart	82/88
13.	Madonna	19/22
14.	Billy Joel	42/57
15.	Kenny Rogers	78/99
16.	Luther Vandross	51/65
17.	Tina Turner	71/78
18.	Bryan Adams	81/84
19.	Def Leppard	58/59
20.	Fleetwood Mac	45/48

1988

Rank	Artist	Cities/Shows
1.	Pink Floyd	23/35
2.	Van Halen's "Monsters of Rock"	23/26
3.	Def Leppard	94/112
4.	Grateful Dead	33/80
5.	Aerosmith	96/105
6.	Michael Jackson	19/54
7.	AC/DC	105/110
8.	Rod Stewart	82/88
9.	"Rat Pack/Ultimate Event"	23/41
10.	George Michael	32/46
11.	Whitesnake	83/84
12.	Bruce Springsteen & The E Street Band	21/43
13.	Robert Plant	88/92
14.	Luther Vandross/Anita Baker	26/42
15.	INXS	75/81
16.	John Cougar Mellencamp	45/54
17.	Kenny Rogers	88/167
18.	New Edition	67/70
19.	Randy Travis	98/119
20.	Sting	75/79

1989

Rank	Artist	Cities/Shows
1.	The Rolling Stones	33/60
2.	The Who	27/39
3.	Bon Jovi	129/143
4.	Grateful Dead	33/73
5.	New Kids on the Block	112/143
6.	Neil Diamond	29/69
7.	Metallica	134/140
8.	Elton John	32/47
9.	Rod Stewart	61/71
10.	Beach Boys/Chicago	57/59
11.	Poison	82/83
12.	R.E.M.	84/87
13.	Cinderella	135/136
14.	Barry Manilow	44/123
15.	George Strait	90/104
16.	New Edition	48/49
17.	Kenny Rogers	85/115
18.	Alabama	77/79
19.	Reba McEntire	111/126
20.	Randy Travis	88/105

1990

Rank	Artist	Cities/Shows
1.	New Kids on the Block	122/152
2.	Billy Joel	53/95
3.	Paul McCartney	21/32
4.	Grateful Dead	27/63
5.	Janet Jackson	62/89
6.	Aerosmith	92/101
7.	M. C. Hammer	132/138
8.	Mötley Crüe	103/108
9.	Phil Collins	27/56
10.	Eric Clapton	48/57
11.	David Bowie	41/51
12.	Madonna	12/32
13.	KISS	121/121
14.	Rush	56/63
15.	Depeche Mode	32/33
16.	Randy Travis	98/125
17.	Whitesnake	99/101
18.	Fleetwood Mac	54/62
19.	Kenny Rogers	66/105
20.	Alabama	102/103

1991

Rank	Artist	Cities/Shows
1.	Grateful Dead	27/76
2.	ZZ Top	85/106
3.	The Judds	116/126
4.	Rod Stewart	47/59
5.	Paul Simon	72/76
6.	Guns N' Roses	30/43
7.	Bell Biv Devoe/Johnny Gill/Keith Sweat	66/72
8.	Michael Bolton	70/103
9.	Garth Brooks	94/111
10.	Clint Black	92/100
11.	AC/DC	57/60
12.	Sting	64/81
13.	Luther Vandross	50/60
14.	Scorpions	90/93
15.	Van Halen	42/46
16.	Frank Sinatra	30/53
17.	Randy Travis	93/107
18.	Jimmy Buffett	37/51
19.	Jane's Addiction (includes "Lollapalooza")	56/66
20.	Yes	55/57

1992

Rank	Artist	Cities/Shows
1.	U2	61/73
2.	Grateful Dead	23/55
3.	Guns N' Roses/Metallica	25/25
4.	Neil Diamond	26/69
5.	Bruce Springsteen	36/59
6.	Genesis	24/28
7.	Elton John	32/49
8.	Metallica	87/102
9.	Eric Clapton	30/37
10.	Hammer	123/130
11.	Bryan Adams	92/94
12.	Jimmy Buffett	43/64
13.	"Lollapalooza II"	29/35
14.	Garth Brooks	78/79
15.	Reba McEntire	102/111
16.	Ozzy Osbourne	80/88
17.	John Mellencamp	44/55
18.	Harry Connick Jr.	43/87
19.	Def Leppard	72/77
20.	Rush	52/55

1993

Rank	Artist	Cities/Shows
1.	Grateful Dead	29/81
2.	Rod Stewart	54/68
3.	Neil Diamond	43/75
4.	Paul McCartney	23/23
5.	Bette Midler	29/71
6.	Billy Joel	22/39
7.	Garth Brooks	29/54
8.	Jimmy Buffett	32/52
9.	Reba McEntire	97/105
10.	Kenny G	82/97
11.	"Lollapalooza III"	29/34
12.	Aerosmith	61/66
13.	Clint Black/Wynonna	70/73
14.	Van Halen	32/40
15.	Alan Jackson	98/105
16.	Luther Vandross	42/49
17.	Peter Gabriel	31/38
18.	Def Leppard	90/91
19.	Depeche Mode	40/49
20.	Elton John	27/34

BILLBOARD'S TOP 10 SINGLES

It must have been a different era indeed if a bestselling single was titled "Smoke, Smoke, Smoke (That Cigarette)" (check out 1947). Other chart-toppers of the past half-century:

1946

1. "Prisoner of Love," Perry Como
2. "To Each His Own," Eddy Howard
3. "The Gypsy," Ink Spots
4. "Five Minutes More," Frank Sinatra
5. "Rumors Are Flying," Frankie Carle
6. "Oh! What It Seemed To Be," Frankie Carle
7. "Personality," Johnny Mercer & The Pied Pipers
8. "South America, Take It Away," Bing Crosby & The Andrews Sisters
9. "The Gypsy," Dinah Shore
10. "Oh! What It Seemed To Be," Frank Sinatra

1947

1. "Near You," Francis Craig
2. "Peg O' My Heart," Harmonicats
3. "Heartaches," Ted Weems
4. "Linda," Ray Noble Orchestra & Buddy Clark (tie)
4. "Smoke, Smoke, Smoke (That Cigarette)," Tex Williams (tie)
6. "I Wish I Didn't Love You So," Vaughn Monroe
7. "Peg O' My Heart," Three Suns
8. "Anniversary Song," Al Jolson
9. "Near You," Larry Green Orchestra
10. "That's My Desire," Sammy Kaye

1948

1. "Twelfth Street Rag," Pee Wee Hunt
2. "Manana," Peggy Lee
3. "Now Is the Hour," Bing Crosby
4. "A Tree in the Meadow," Margaret Whiting
5. "My Happiness," Jon & Sandra Steele
6. "You Can't Be True, Dear," Ken Griffin & Jerry Wayne
7. "Little White Lies," Dick Haymes
8. "You Call Everybody Darlin'," Al Trace
9. "My Happiness," Pied Pipers
10. "I'm Looking Over a Four Leaf Clover," Art Mooney

1949

1. "Riders in the Sky," Vaughn Monroe Orchestra
2. "That Lucky Old Sun," Frankie Laine
3. "You're Breaking My Heart," Vic Damone
4. "Some Enchanted Evening," Perry Como
5. "Slipping Around," Jimmy Wakely & Margaret Whiting
6. "I Can Dream, Can't I?" Andrews Sisters & Gordon Jenkins
7. "Cruising Down the River," Russ Morgan Orchestra
8. "A Little Bird Told Me," Evelyn Knight & The Stardusters
9. "Mule Train," Frankie Laine
10. "Jealous Heart," Al Morgan

1950

1. "Goodnight Irene," Gordon Jenkins & The Weavers
2. "Mona Lisa," Nat King Cole
3. "Third Man Theme," Anton Karas
4. "Sam's Song," Gary & Bing Crosby
5. "Simple Melody," Gary & Bing Crosby
6. "Music, Music, Music," Teresa Brewer
7. "Third Man Theme," Guy Lombardo
8. "Chattanoogie Shoe Shine Boy," Red Foley
9. "Harbor Lights," Sammy Kaye
10. "It Isn't Fair," Sammy Kaye & Don Cornell

1951

1. "Too Young," Nat King Cole
2. "Because of You," Tony Bennett
3. "How High the Moon," Les Paul & Mary Ford
4. "Come on-a My House," Rosemary Clooney
5. "Be My Love," Mario Lanza
6. "On Top of Old Smoky," Weavers
7. "Cold, Cold Heart," Tony Bennett
8. "If," Perry Como
9. "Loveliest Night of the Year," Mario Lanza
10. "Tennessee Waltz," Patti Page

1952

1. "Blue Tango," Leroy Anderson
2. "Wheel of Fortune," Kay Starr
3. "Cry," Johnnie Ray
4. "You Belong to Me," Jo Stafford
5. "Auf Wiederseh'n, Sweetheart," Vera Lynn
6. "I Went to Your Wedding," Patti Page
7. "Half as Much," Rosemary Clooney
8. "Wish You Were Here," Eddie Fisher & Hugo Winterhalter
9. "Here in My Heart," Al Martino
10. "Delicado," Percy Faith

1953

1. "Song From Moulin Rouge," Percy Faith
2. "Vaya con Dios," Les Paul & Mary Ford
3. "Doggie in the Window," Patti Page
4. "I'm Walking Behind You," Eddie Fisher
5. "You, You, You," Ames Brothers
6. "Till I Waltz Again with You," Teresa Brewer
7. "April in Portugal," Les Baxter
8. "No Other Love," Perry Como
9. "Don't Let the Stars Get in Your Eyes," Perry Como
10. "I Believe," Frankie Laine

1954

1. "Little Things Mean a Lot," Kitty Kallen
2. "Wanted," Perry Como
3. "Hey, There," Rosemary Clooney
4. "Sh-Boom," Crew Cuts
5. "Make Love to Me," Jo Stafford
6. "Oh! My Pa-Pa," Eddie Fisher
7. "I Get So Lonely," Four Knights
8. "Three Coins in the Fountain," Four Aces
9. "Secret Love," Doris Day
10. "Hernando's Highway," Archie Bleyer

1955

1. "Cherry Pink and Apple Blossom White," Perez Prado
2. "Rock Around the Clock," Bill Haley & His Comets

3. "The Yellow Rose of Texas," Mitch Miller
4. "Autumn Leaves," Roger Williams
5. "Unchained Melody," Les Baxter
6. "The Ballad of Davy Crockett," Bill Hayes
7. "Love Is a Many-Splendored Thing," Four Aces
8. "Sincerely," McGuire Sisters
9. "Ain't That a Shame," Pat Boone
10. "Dance with Me Henry," Georgia Gibbs

1956

1. "Heartbreak Hotel," Elvis Presley
2. "Don't Be Cruel," Elvis Presley
3. "Lisbon Antigua," Nelson Riddle
4. "My Prayer," Platters
5. "The Wayward Wind," Gogi Grant
6. "Hound Dog," Elvis Presley
7. "The Poor People of Paris," Les Baxter
8. "Whatever Will Be Will Be (Que Sera Sera)," Doris Day
9. "Memories Are Made of This," Dean Martin
10. "Rock and Roll Waltz," Kay Starr

1957

1. "All Shook Up," Elvis Presley
2. "Love Letters in the Sand," Pat Boone
3. "Little Darlin'," Diamonds
4. "Young Love," Tab Hunter
5. "So Rare," Jimmy Dorsey
6. "Don't Forbid Me," Pat Boone
7. "Singing the Blues," Guy Mitchell
8. "Young Love," Sonny James
9. "Too Much," Elvis Presley
10. "Round and Round," Perry Como

1958

1. "Volare (Nel Blu Dipinto Di Blu)," Domenico Modugno
2. "All I Have To Do Is Dream/ Claudette," Everly Brothers
3. "Don't/I Beg of You," Elvis Presley
4. "Witch Doctor," David Seville
5. "Patricia," Perez Prado
6. "Sail Along Silvery Moon/Raunchy," Billy Vaughn
7. "Catch a Falling Star/Magic Moments," Perry Como
8. "Tequila," Champs
9. "It's All in the Game," Tommy Edwards
10. "Return to Me," Dean Martin

1959

1. "The Battle of New Orleans," Johnny Horton
2. "Mack the Knife," Bobby Darin
3. "Personality," Lloyd Price
4. "Venus," Frankie Avalon
5. "Lonely Boy," Paul Anka
6. "Dream Lover," Bobby Darin
7. "The Three Bells," Browns
8. "Come Softly to Me," Fleetwoods
9. "Kansas City," Wilbert Harrison
10. "Mr. Blue," Fleetwoods

1960

1. "Theme from *A Summer Place*," Percy Faith
2. "He'll Have To Go," Jim Reeves
3. "Cathy's Clown," Everly Brothers
4. "Running Bear," Johnny Preston
5. "Teen Angel," Mark Dinning
6. "It's Now or Never," Elvis Presley
7. "Handy Man," Jimmy Jones
8. "I'm Sorry," Brenda Lee
9. "Stuck on You," Elvis Presley
10. "The Twist," Chubby Checker

1961

1. "Tossin' and Turnin'," Bobby Lewis
2. "I Fall to Pieces," Patsy Cline
3. "Michael," Highwaymen
4. "Cryin'," Roy Orbison
5. "Runaway," Del Shannon
6. "My True Story," Jive Five
7. "Pony Time," Chubby Checker
8. "Wheels," String-a-Longs
9. "Raindrops," Dee Clark
10. "Wooden Heart (Muss I Denn)," Joe Dowell

1962

1. "Stranger on the Shore," Mr. Acker Bilk
2. "I Can't Stop Loving You," Ray Charles
3. "Mashed Potato Time," Dee Dee Sharp
4. "Roses Are Red," Bobby Vinton
5. "The Stripper," David Rose
6. "Johnny Angel," Shelley Fabares
7. "Loco-motion," Little Eva
8. "Let Me In," Sensations
9. "The Twist," Chubby Checker
10. "Soldier Boy," Shirelles

1963

1. "Sugar Shack," Jimmy Gilmer & The Fireballs
2. "Surfin' USA," Beach Boys
3. "The End of the World," Skeeter Davis
4. "Rhythm of the Rain," Cascades
5. "He's So Fine," Chiffons
6. "Blue Velvet," Bobby Vinton
7. "Hey Paula," Paul & Paula
8. "Fingertips II," Little Stevie Wonder
9. "Washington Square," Village Stompers
10. "It's All Right," Impressions

1964

1. "I Want To Hold Your Hand," Beatles
2. "She Loves You," Beatles
3. "Hello, Dolly!" Louis Armstrong
4. "Oh, Pretty Woman," Roy Orbison
5. "I Get Around," Beach Boys
6. "Everybody Loves Somebody," Dean Martin
7. "My Guy," Mary Wells
8. "We'll Sing in the Sunshine," Gale Garnett
9. "Last Kiss," J. Frank Wilson & The Cavaliers
10. "Where Did Our Love Go," Supremes

1965

1. "Wooly Bully," Sam the Sham & The Pharaohs
2. "I Can't Help Myself," Four Tops
3. "(I Can't Get No) Satisfaction," Rolling Stones
4. "You Were on My Mind," We Five
5. "You've Lost That Lovin' Feelin'," Righteous Brothers
6. "Downtown," Petula Clark
7. "Help!," Beatles
8. "Can't You Hear My Heartbeat," Herman's Hermits
9. "Crying in the Chapel," Elvis Presley
10. "My Girl," Temptations

1966

1. "The Ballad of the Green Berets," S/Sgt. Barry Sadler
2. "Cherish," Association
3. "(You're My) Soul and Inspiration," Righteous Brothers
4. "Reach Out I'll Be There," Four Tops
5. "96 Tears," ? & the Mysterians
6. "Last Train to Clarksville," Monkees
7. "Monday, Monday," Mamas & the Papas
8. "You Can't Hurry Love," Supremes
9. "Poor Side of Town," Johnny Rivers
10. "California Dreamin'," Mamas & the Papas

1967

1. "To Sir with Love," Lulu
2. "The Letter," Box Tops
3. "Ode to Billie Joe," Bobby Gentry
4. "Windy," Association
5. "I'm a Believer," Monkees
6. "Light My Fire," Doors
7. "Somethin' Stupid," Nancy Sinatra & Frank Sinatra
8. "Happy Together," Turtles
9. "Groovin'," Young Rascals
10. "Can't Take My Eyes Off You," Frankie Valli

1968

1. "Hey Jude," Beatles
2. "Love Is Blue (L'Amour Est Blue)," Paul Mauriat
3. "Honey," Bobby Goldsboro
4. "(Sittin' on) The Dock of the Bay," Otis Redding
5. "People Got To Be Free," Rascals
6. "Sunshine of Your Love," Cream
7. "This Guy's in Love with You," Herb Alpert
8. "The Good, the Bad and the Ugly," Hugo Montenegro
9. "Mrs. Robinson," Simon & Garfunkel
10. "Tighten Up," Archie Bell & The Drells

1969

1. "Sugar, Sugar," Archies
2. "Aquarius/Let the Sunshine In," Fifth Dimension
3. "I Can't Get Next to You," Temptations
4. "Honky Tonk Women," Rolling Stones
5. "Everyday People," Sly & The Family Stone
6. "Dizzy," Tommy Roe
7. "Hot Fun in the Summertime," Sly & The Family Stone
8. "I'll Never Fall in Love Again," Tom Jones
9. "Build Me Up Buttercup," Foundations
10. "Crimson and Clover," Tommy James & The Shondells

1970

1. "Bridge over Troubled Water," Simon & Garfunkel
2. "(They Long To Be) Close to You," Carpenters
3. "American Woman/No Sugar Tonight," Guess Who
4. "Raindrops Keep Fallin' on My Head," B. J. Thomas
5. "War," Edwin Starr
6. "Ain't No Mountain High Enough," Diana Ross
7. "I'll Be There," Jackson 5
8. "Get Ready," Rare Earth
9. "Let It Be," Beatles
10. "Band of Gold," Freda Payne

1971

1. "Joy to the World," Three Dog Night
2. "Maggie May/Reason To Believe," Rod Stewart
3. "It's Too Late/I Feel the Earth Move," Carole King
4. "One Bad Apple," Osmonds
5. "How Can You Mend a Broken Heart," Bee Gees
6. "Indian Reservation," Raiders
7. "Go Away Little Girl," Donny Osmond
8. "Take Me Home, Country Roads," John Denver with Fat City
9. "Just My Imagination (Running Away with Me)," Temptations
10. "Knock Three Times," Dawn

1972

1. "The First Time Ever I Saw Your Face," Roberta Flack
2. "Alone Again (Naturally)," Gilbert O'Sullivan
3. "American Pie," Don McLean
4. "Without You," Nilsson
5. "Candy Man," Sammy Davis Jr.
6. "I Gotcha," Joe Tex
7. "Lean on Me," Bill Withers
8. "Baby Don't Get Hooked on Me," Mac Davis
9. "Brand New Key," Melanie
10. "Daddy Don't You Walk So Fast," Wayne Newton

1973

1. "Tie a Yellow Ribbon 'Round the Ole Oak Tree," Tony Orlando & Dawn
2. "Bad, Bad Leroy Brown," Jim Croce
3. "Killing Me Softly with His Song," Roberta Flack
4. "Let's Get It On," Marvin Gaye
5. "My Love," Paul McCartney & Wings
6. "Why Me," Kris Kristofferson
7. "Crocodile Rock," Elton John
8. "Will It Go Round in Circles," Billy Preston
9. "You're So Vain," Carly Simon
10. "Touch Me in the Morning," Diana Ross

1974

1. "The Way We Were," Barbra Streisand
2. "Seasons in the Sun," Terry Jacks
3. "Love's Theme," Love Unlimited Orchestra
4. "Come and Get Your Love," Redbone
5. "Dancing Machine," Jackson 5
6. "The Loco-motion," Grand Funk Railroad
7. "TSOP," MFSB
8. "The Streak," Ray Stevens
9. "Bennie and the Jets," Elton John
10. "One Hell of a Woman," Mac Davis

1975

1. "Love Will Keep Us Together," Captain & Tennille
2. "Rhinestone Cowboy," Glen Campbell
3. "Philadelphia Freedom," Elton John
4. "Before the Next Teardrop Falls," Freddy Fender
5. "My Eyes Adored You," Frankie Valli
6. "Shining Star," Earth, Wind & Fire
7. "Fame," David Bowie
8. "Laughter in the Rain," Neil Sedaka
9. "One of These Nights," Eagles
10. "Thank God I'm a Country Boy," John Denver

1976

1. "Silly Love Songs," Wings
2. "Don't Go Breaking My Heart," Elton John & Kiki Dee
3. "Disco Lady," Johnnie Taylor
4. "December, 1963 (Oh, What a Night)," Four Seasons
5. "Play That Funky Music," Wild Cherry
6. "Kiss and Say Goodbye," Manhattans
7. "Love Machine, Pt. 1," Miracles
8. "50 Ways To Leave Your Lover," Paul Simon
9. "Love Is Alive," Gary Wright
10. "A Fifth of Beethoven," Walter Murphy & The Big Apple Band

1977

1. "Tonight's the Night (Gonna Be Alright)," Rod Stewart
2. "I Just Want To Be Your Everything," Andy Gibb
3. "Best of My Love," Emotions
4. "Love Theme from *A Star Is Born*," Barbra Streisand
5. "Angel in Your Arms," Hot
6. "I Like Dreamin'," Kenny Nolan

7. "Don't Leave Me This Way," Thelma Houston
8. "(Your Love Has Lifted Me) Higher and Higher," Rita Coolidge
9. "Undercover Angel," Alan O'Day
10. "Torn Between Two Lovers," Mary MacGregor

1978

1. "Shadow Dancing," Andy Gibb
2. "Night Fever," Bee Gees
3. "You Light Up My Life," Debby Boone
4. "Stayin' Alive," Bee Gees
5. "Kiss You All Over," Exile
6. "How Deep Is Your Love," Bee Gees
7. "Baby Come Back," Player
8. "Love Is Thicker Than Water," Andy Gibb
9. "Boogie Oogie Oogie," A Taste of Honey
10. "Three Times a Lady," Commodores

1979

1. "My Sharona," Knack
2. "Bad Girls," Donna Summer
3. "Le Freak," Chic
4. "Da Ya Think I'm Sexy," Rod Stewart
5. "Reunited," Peaches & Herb
6. "I Will Survive," Gloria Gaynor
7. "Hot Stuff," Donna Summer
8. "Y.M.C.A.," Village People
9. "Ring My Bell," Anita Ward
10. "Sad Eyes," Robert John

1980

1. "Call Me," Blondie
2. "Another Brick in the Wall," Pink Floyd
3. "Magic," Olivia Newton-John
4. "Rock with You," Michael Jackson
5. "Do That to Me One More Time," Captain & Tennille
6. "Crazy Little Thing Called Love," Queen
7. "Coming Up," Paul McCartney
8. "Funkytown," Lipps, Inc.
9. "It's Still Rock and Roll to Me," Billy Joel
10. "The Rose," Bette Midler

1981

1. "Bette Davis Eyes," Kim Carnes
2. "Endless Love," Diana Ross & Lionel Richie
3. "Lady," Kenny Rogers
4. "(Just Like) Starting Over," John Lennon
5. "Jessie's Girl," Rick Springfield
6. "Celebration," Kool & The Gang
7. "Kiss on My List," Daryl Hall & John Oates
8. "I Love a Rainy Night," Eddie Rabbitt
9. "9 to 5," Dolly Parton
10. "Keep On Loving You," REO Speedwagon

1982

1. "Physical," Olivia Newton-John
2. "Eye of the Tiger," Survivor
3. "I Love Rock 'n' Roll," Joan Jett & The Blackhearts
4. "Ebony and Ivory," Paul McCartney & Stevie Wonder
5. "Centerfold," J. Geils Band
6. "Don't You Want Me," Human League
7. "Jack and Diane," John Cougar
8. "Hurts So Good," John Cougar
9. "Abracadabra," Steve Miller Band
10. "Hard To Say I'm Sorry," Chicago

1983

1. "Every Breath You Take," Police
2. "Billie Jean," Michael Jackson
3. "Flashdance . . . What a Feeling," Irene Cara
4. "Down Under," Men at Work
5. "Beat It," Michael Jackson
6. "Total Eclipse of the Heart," Bonnie Tyler
7. "Maneater," Daryl Hall & John Oates
8. "Baby Come to Me," Patti Austin with James Ingram
9. "Maniac," Michael Sembello
10. "Sweet Dreams (Are Made of This)," Eurythmics

1984

1. "When Doves Cry," Prince
2. "What's Love Got To Do with It," Tina Turner
3. "Say Say Say," Paul McCartney & Michael Jackson
4. "Footloose," Kenny Loggins
5. "Against All Odds (Take a Look at Me Now)," Phil Collins
6. "Jump," Van Halen
7. "Hello," Lionel Richie
8. "Owner of a Lonely Heart," Yes
9. "Ghostbusters," Ray Parker Jr.
10. "Karma Chameleon," Culture Club

1985

1. "Careless Whisper," Wham! featuring George Michael
2. "Like a Virgin," Madonna
3. "Wake Me Up Before You Go-Go," Wham!
4. "I Want To Know What Love Is," Foreigner
5. "I Feel for You," Chaka Khan
6. "Out of Touch," Daryl Hall & John Oates
7. "Everybody Wants To Rule the World," Tears for Fears
8. "Money for Nothing," Dire Straits
9. "Crazy for You," Madonna
10. "Take on Me," a-ha

1986

1. "That's What Friends Are For," Dionne & Friends
2. "Say You, Say Me," Lionel Richie
3. "I Miss You," Klymaxx
4. "On My Own," Patti LaBelle & Michael McDonald
5. "Broken Wings," Mr. Mister
6. "How Will I Know," Whitney Houston
7. "Party All the Time," Eddie Murphy
8. "Burning Heart," Survivor
9. "Kyrie," Mr. Mister
10. "Addicted to Love," Robert Palmer

1987

1. "Walk Like an Egyptian," Bangles
2. "Alone," Heart
3. "Shake You Down," Gregory Abbott
4. "I Wanna Dance with Somebody (Who Loves Me)," Whitney Houston
5. "Nothing's Gonna Stop Us Now," Starship
6. "C'est La Vie," Robbie Nevil
7. "Here I Go Again," Whitesnake
8. "The Way It Is," Bruce Hornsby & The Range
9. "Shakedown," Bob Seger
10. "Livin' On a Prayer," Bon Jovi

1988

1. "Faith," George Michael
2. "Need You Tonight," INXS
3. "Got My Mind Set on You," George Harrison
4. "Never Gonna Give You Up," Rick Astley
5. "Sweet Child o' Mine," Guns N' Roses
6. "So Emotional," Whitney Houston
7. "Heaven Is a Place on Earth," Belinda Carlisle
8. "Could've Been," Tiffany
9 "Hands to Heaven," Breathe
10. "Roll with It," Steve Winwood

1989

1. "Look Away," Chicago
2. "My Prerogative," Bobby Brown
3. "Every Rose Has Its Thorn," Poison
4. "Straight Up," Paula Abdul
5. "Miss You Much," Janet Jackson
6. "Cold Hearted," Paula Abdul
7. "Wind Beneath My Wings," Bette Midler
8. "Girl You Know It's True," Milli Vanilli
9. "Baby, I Love Your Way/Firebird Medley," Will to Power
10. "Giving You the Best That I Got," Anita Baker

1990

1. "Hold On," Wilson Phillips
2. "It Must Have Been Love," Roxette
3. "Nothing Compares 2 U," Sinead O'Connor
4. "Poison," Bell Biv Devoe
5. "Vogue," Madonna
6. "Vision of Love," Mariah Carey
7. "Another Day in Paradise," Phil Collins
8. "Hold On," En Vogue
9. "Cradle of Love," Billy Idol
10. "Blaze of Glory," Jon Bon Jovi

1991

1. "(Everything I Do) I Do It for You," Bryan Adams
2. "I Wanna Sex You Up," Color Me Badd
3. "Gonna Make You Sweat," C+C Music Factory
4. "Rush Rush," Paula Abdul
5. "One More Try," Timmy T.
6. "Unbelievable," EMF
7. "More Than Words," Extreme
8. "I Like the Way (The Kissing Game)," Hi-Five
9. "The First Time," Surface
10. "Baby Baby," Amy Grant

1992

1. "End of the Road," Boyz II Men
2. "Baby Got Back," Sir Mix-A-Lot
3. "Jump," Kris Kross
4. "Save the Best for Last," Vanessa Williams
5. "Baby-Baby-Baby," TLC
6. "Tears in Heaven," Eric Clapton
7. "My Lovin' (You're Never Gonna Get It)," En Vogue
8. "Under the Bridge," Red Hot Chili Peppers
9. "All 4 Love," Color Me Badd
10. "Just Another Day," Jon Secada

1993

1. "I Will Always Love You," Whitney Houston
2. "Whoomp! (There It Is)," Tag Team
3. "Can't Help Falling in Love," UB40
4. "That's the Way Love Goes," Janet Jackson
5. "Freak Me," Silk
6. "Weak," SWV
7. "If I Ever Fall in Love," Shai
8. "Dreamlover," Mariah Carey
9. "Rump Shaker," Wreckx-N-Effect
10. "Informer," Snow

RAP WRAPPED UP

While rap got its footing in the African-American community among both musicians and fans, you don't have to be black to dig the rhythm and the rhymes. Still daunted by the genre? Then here's a best-of guide for newcomers to the rap party, a baker's dozen of albums by eleven artists.

Arrested Development	*3 Years, 5 Months and 2 Days in the Life of . . .*
A Tribe Called Quest	*Midnight Marauders*
Beastie Boys	*Licensed to Ill*
Beastie Boys	*Paul's Boutique*
De La Soul	*3 Feet High & Rising*
Dr. Dre	*The Chronic*
Grandmaster Flash & The Furious Five	*Greatest Messages*
L.L. Cool J	*Mama Said Knock You Out*
Public Enemy	*It Takes a Nation of Millions to Hold Us Back*
Run-D.M.C.	*Run-D.M.C.*
Run-D.M.C.	*King of Rock*
Salt-N-Pepa	*Blacks' Magic*
Yo-Yo	*You better ask somebody*

BILLBOARD'S TOP 10 ALBUMS

The times certainly have been a changin' to judge from *Billboard*'s list of top-selling albums since tabulation began almost forty years ago.

1956

1. *Calypso*, Harry Belafonte
2. *My Fair Lady*, original cast
3. *The King and I*, soundtrack
4. *The Eddy Duchin Story*, soundtrack
5. *Elvis Presley*, Elvis Presley
6. *High Society*, soundtrack
7. *Songs for Swingin' Lovers*, Frank Sinatra
8. *Belafonte*, Harry Belafonte
9. *The Platters*, Platters
10. *Oklahoma!*, soundtrack

1957

1. *My Fair Lady*, original cast
2. *Hymns*, Tennessee Ernie Ford
3. *Oklahoma!*, soundtrack
4. *Around the World in 80 Days*, soundtrack
5. *The King and I*, soundtrack
6. *Calypso*, Harry Belafonte
7. *Love Is the Thing*, Nat King Cole
8. *The Eddy Duchin Story*, soundtrack
9. *Songs of the Fabulous Fifties*, Roger Williams
10. *Film Encores*, Mantovani

1958

1. *My Fair Lady*, original cast
2. *The Music Man*, original cast
3. *Johnny's Greatest Hits*, Johnny Mathis
4. *South Pacific*, soundtrack
5. *Come Fly with Me*, Frank Sinatra
6. *Around the World in 80 Days*, soundtrack
7. *Warm*, Johnny Mathis
8. *South Pacific*, original cast
9. *Ricky*, Ricky Nelson
10. *The King and I*, soundtrack

1959

1. *Music from "Peter Gunn,"* Henry Mancini
2. *Gigi*, soundtrack
3. *South Pacific*, soundtrack
4. *From the Hungry i*, Kingston Trio
5. *The Kingston Trio at Large*, Kingston Trio
6. *Sing Along with Mitch*, Mitch Miller
7. *Inside Shelley Berman*, Shelley Berman
8. *Exotica, Vol. 1*, Martin Denny
9. *My Fair Lady*, original cast
10. *Flower Drum Song*, original cast

1960

1. *The Sound of Music*, original cast
2. *Inside Shelley Berman*, Shelley Berman
3. *The Button-Down Mind of Bob Newhart*, Bob Newhart
4. *Sixty Years of Music America Loves Best, Vol. I*, various artists
5. *Here We Go Again*, Kingston Trio
6. *Sold Out*, Kingston Trio
7. *Heavenly*, Johnny Mathis
8. *South Pacific*, soundtrack
9. *Faithfully*, Johnny Mathis
10. *Outside Shelley Berman*, Shelley Berman

1961

1. *Camelot*, original cast
2. *Great Motion Picture Themes*, various artists
3. *Never on Sunday*, soundtrack
4. *The Sound of Music*, original cast
5. *Exodus*, soundtrack
6. *Knockers Up*, Rusty Warren
7. *G.I. Blues*, Elvis Presley/soundtrack
8. *Sing Along with Mitch*, Mitch Miller
9. *Calcutta*, Lawrence Welk
10. *Tonight in Person*, Limeliters

1962

1. *West Side Story*, soundtrack
2. *Breakfast at Tiffany's*, Henry Mancini
3. *Blue Hawaii*, Elvis Presley/soundtrack
4. *West Side Story*, original cast
5. *The Sound of Music*, original cast
6. *Time Out*, Dave Brubeck
7. *Camelot*, original cast
8. *Your Twist Party*, Chubby Checker
9. *Knockers Up*, Rusty Warren
10. *Judy at Carnegie Hall*, Judy Garland

1963

1. *West Side Story*, soundtrack
2. *Peter, Paul and Mary*, Peter, Paul & Mary
3. *Moving*, Peter, Paul & Mary
4. *Joan Baez in Concert*, Joan Baez
5. *I Left My Heart in San Francisco*, Tony Bennett
6. *Moon River and Other Great Movie Themes*, Andy Williams
7. *Lawrence of Arabia*, soundtrack
8. *Days of Wine and Roses*, Andy Williams
9. *Oliver*, original cast
10. *Modern Sounds in Country and Western Music, Vol. 2*, Ray Charles

1964

1. *Hello, Dolly!*, original cast
2. *In the Wind*, Peter, Paul & Mary
3. *Honey in the Horn*, Al Hirt
4. *The Barbra Streisand Album*, Barbra Streisand
5. *West Side Story*, soundtrack
6. *Peter, Paul and Mary*, Peter, Paul & Mary
7. *The Second Barbra Streisand Album*, Barbra Streisand
8. *Meet the Beatles*, Beatles
9. *The Third Barbra Streisand Album*, Barbra Streisand
10. *Moon River and Other Great Movie Themes*, Andy Williams

1965

1. *Mary Poppins*, soundtrack
2. *Beatles '65*, Beatles
3. *The Sound of Music*, soundtrack
4. *My Fair Lady*, soundtrack
5. *Fiddler on the Roof*, original cast
6. *Goldfinger*, soundtrack
7. *Hello, Dolly!*, original cast
8. *Dear Heart*, Andy Williams
9. *Introducing Herman's Hermits*, Herman's Hermits
10. *Beatles VI*, Beatles

1966

1. *Whipped Cream and Other Delights*, Herb Alpert & The Tijuana Brass
2. *The Sound of Music*, soundtrack
3. *Going Places*, Herb Alpert & The Tijuana Brass
4. *Rubber Soul*, Beatles
5. *What Now My Love*, Herb Alpert & The Tijuana Brass
6. *If You Can Believe Your Eyes and Ears*, Mamas & the Papas
7. *Dr. Zhivago*, soundtrack
8. *Revolver*, Beatles

9. *Color Me Barbra*, Barbra Streisand
10. *Ballad of the Green Berets*, S/Sgt. Barry Sadler

1967

1. *More of the Monkees*, Monkees
2. *The Monkees*, Monkees
3. *Dr. Zhivago*, soundtrack
4. *The Sound of Music*, soundtrack
5. *The Temptations' Greatest Hits*, Temptations
6. *A Man and a Woman*, soundtrack
7. *S.R.O.*, Herb Alpert & The Tijuana Brass
8. *Whipped Cream and Other Delights*, Herb Alpert & The Tijuana Brass
9. *Going Places*, Herb Alpert & The Tijuana Brass
10. *Sgt. Pepper's Lonely Hearts Club Band*, Beatles

1968

1. *Are You Experienced?*, Jimi Hendrix Experience
2. *The Graduate*, Simon & Garfunkel/soundtrack
3. *Disraeli Gears*, Cream
4. *Magical Mystery Tour*, Beatles/soundtrack
5. *Diana Ross and the Supremes' Greatest Hits*, Diana Ross & The Supremes
6. *Sgt. Pepper's Lonely Hearts Club Band*, Beatles
7. *Doors*, Doors
8. *Parsley, Sage, Rosemary and Thyme*, Simon & Garfunkel
9. *Vanilla Fudge*, Vanilla Fudge
10. *Blooming Hits*, Paul Mauriat & His Orchestra

1969

1. *In-a-Gadda-Da-Vida*, Iron Butterfly
2. *Hair*, original cast
3. *Blood, Sweat and Tears*, Blood, Sweat & Tears
4. *Bayou Country*, Creedence Clearwater Revival
5. *Led Zeppelin*, Led Zeppelin
6. *Johnny Cash at Folsom Prison*, Johnny Cash
7. *Funny Girl*, soundtrack
8. *The Beatles (The White Album)*, Beatles
9. *Donovan's Greatest Hits*, Donovan
10. *The Association's Greatest Hits*, Association

1970

1. *Bridge over Troubled Water*, Simon & Garfunkel
2. *Led Zeppelin II*, Led Zeppelin
3. *Chicago*, Chicago
4. *Abbey Road*, Beatles
5. *Santana*, Santana
6. *Get Ready*, Rare Earth
7. *Easy Rider*, soundtrack
8. *Butch Cassidy and the Sundance Kid*, soundtrack
9. *Joe Cocker!*, Joe Cocker
10. *Three Dog Night Was Captured Live at the Forum*, Three Dog Night

1971

1. *Jesus Christ Superstar*, various artists
2. *Tapestry*, Carole King
3. *Close to You*, Carpenters
4. *Pearl*, Janis Joplin
5. *Abraxas*, Santana
6. *The Partridge Family Album*, Partridge Family
7. *Sweet Baby James*, James Taylor
8. *Tea for the Tillerman*, Cat Stevens
9. *Greatest Hits*, Sly & The Family Stone
10. *Chicago III*, Chicago

1972

1. *Harvest*, Neil Young
2. *Tapestry*, Carole King
3. *American Pie*, Don McLean
4. *Teaser and the Firecat*, Cat Stevens
5. *Hot Rocks, 1964–71*, Rolling Stones
6. *Killer*, Alice Cooper
7. *First Take*, Roberta Flack
8. *America*, America
9. *Music*, Carole King
10. *Madman Across the Water*, Elton John

1973

1. *The World Is a Ghetto*, War
2. *Summer Breeze*, Seals & Crofts
3. *Talking Book*, Stevie Wonder
4. *No Secrets*, Carly Simon
5. *Lady Sings the Blues*, Diana Ross
6. *They Only Come Out at Night*, Edgar Winter Group
7. *I Am Woman*, Helen Reddy
8. *Don't Shoot Me, I'm Only the Piano Player*, Elton John
9. *I'm Still in Love with You*, Al Green
10. *Seventh Sojourn*, Moody Blues

1974

1. *Goodbye Yellow Brick Road*, Elton John
2. *John Denver's Greatest Hits*, John Denver
3. *Band on the Run*, Paul McCartney & Wings
4. *Innervisions*, Stevie Wonder
5. *You Don't Mess Around with Jim*, Jim Croce
6. *American Graffiti*, soundtrack
7. *Imagination*, Gladys Knight & The Pips
8. *Behind Closed Doors*, Charlie Rich
9. *The Sting*, soundtrack
10. *Tres Hombres*, ZZ Top

1975

1. *Elton John—Greatest Hits*, Elton John
2. *John Denver's Greatest Hits*, John Denver
3. *That's the Way of the World*, Earth, Wind & Fire
4. *Back Home Again*, John Denver
5. *Phoebe Snow*, Phoebe Snow
6. *Heart Like a Wheel*, Linda Ronstadt
7. *Captain Fantastic and the Brown Dirt Cowboy*, Elton John
8. *An Evening with John Denver*, John Denver
9. *AWB*, Average White Band
10. *On the Border*, Eagles

1976

1. *Frampton Comes Alive*, Peter Frampton
2. *Fleetwood Mac*, Fleetwood Mac
3. *Wings at the Speed of Sound*, Wings
4. *Greatest Hits, 1971–1975*, Eagles
5. *Chicago IX—Chicago's Greatest Hits*, Chicago
6. *The Dream Weaver*, Gary Wright
7. *Desire*, Bob Dylan
8. *A Night at the Opera*, Queen
9. *History—America's Greatest Hits*, America
10. *Gratitude*, Earth, Wind & Fire

1977

1. *Rumours*, Fleetwood Mac
2. *Songs in the Key of Life*, Stevie Wonder
3. *A Star Is Born*, Barbra Streisand/Kris Kristofferson/soundtrack
4. *Hotel California*, Eagles
5. *Boston*, Boston
6. *A New World Record*, Electric Light Orchestra

7. *Part 3*, K.C. & The Sunshine Band
8. *Silk Degrees*, Boz Scaggs
9. *Night Moves*, Bob Seger & The Silver Bullet Band
10. *Fleetwood Mac*, Fleetwood Mac

1978

1. *Saturday Night Fever*, Bee Gees/various artists/soundtrack
2. *Grease*, John Travolta/Olivia Newton-John/soundtrack
3. *Rumours*, Fleetwood Mac
4. *The Stranger*, Billy Joel
5. *AJA*, Steely Dan
6. *Feels So Good*, Chuck Mangione
7. *The Grand Illusion*, Styx
8. *Simple Dreams*, Linda Ronstadt
9. *Point of Know Return*, Kansas
10. *Slowhand*, Eric Clapton

1979

1. *52nd Street*, Billy Joel
2. *Spirits Having Flown*, Bee Gees
3. *Minute by Minute*, Doobie Brothers
4. *Cars*, Cars
5. *Breakfast in America*, Supertramp
6. *Live and More*, Donna Summer
7. *Pieces of Eight*, Styx
8. *Bad Girls*, Donna Summer
9. *Parallel Lines*, Blondie
10. *Blondes Have More Fun*, Rod Stewart

1980

1. *The Wall*, Pink Floyd
2. *The Long Run*, Eagles
3. *Off the Wall*, Michael Jackson
4. *Glass Houses*, Billy Joel
5. *Damn the Torpedoes*, Tom Petty & The Heartbreakers
6. *Against the Wind*, Bob Seger & The Silver Bullet Band
7. *In the Heat of the Night*, Pat Benatar
8. *Eat to the Beat*, Blondie
9. *In Through the Out Door*, Led Zeppelin
10. *Kenny*, Kenny Rogers

1981

1. *Hi Infidelity*, REO Speedwagon
2. *Double Fantasy*, John Lennon & Yoko Ono
3. *Greatest Hits*, Kenny Rogers
4. *Christopher Cross*, Christopher Cross
5. *Crimes of Passion*, Pat Benatar
6. *Paradise Theatre*, Styx
7. *Back in Black*, AC/DC
8. *Voices*, Daryl Hall & John Oates
9. *Zenyatta Mondatta*, Police
10. *The River*, Bruce Springsteen

1982

1. *Asia*, Asia
2. *Beauty and the Beat*, Go-Go's
3. *4*, Foreigner
4. *American Fool*, John Cougar
5. *Freeze-Frame*, J. Geils Band
6. *Escape*, Journey
7. *Get Lucky*, Loverboy
8. *Bella Donna*, Stevie Nicks
9. *Chariots of Fire*, Vangelis/soundtrack
10. *Ghost in the Machine*, Police

1983

1. *Thriller*, Michael Jackson
2. *Business as Usual*, Men at Work
3. *Synchronicity*, Police
4. *H2O*, Daryl Hall & John Oates
5. *1999*, Prince
6. *Lionel Richie*, Lionel Richie
7. *Jane Fonda's Workout Record*, Jane Fonda
8. *Pyromania*, Def Leppard
9. *Kissing To Be Clever*, Culture Club
10. *Olivia's Greatest Hits, Vol. 2*, Olivia Newton-John

1984

1. *Thriller*, Michael Jackson
2. *Sports*, Huey Lewis & The News
3. *Can't Slow Down*, Lionel Richie
4. *An Innocent Man*, Billy Joel
5. *Colour by Numbers*, Culture Club
6. *1984*, Van Halen
7. *Eliminator*, ZZ Top
8. *Sychronicity*, Police
9. *Footloose*, soundtrack
10. *Seven and the Ragged Tiger*, Duran Duran

1985

1. *Born in the U.S.A.*, Bruce Springsteen
2. *Reckless*, Bryan Adams
3. *Like a Virgin*, Madonna
4. *Make It Big*, Wham!
5. *Private Dancer*, Tina Turner
6. *No Jacket Required*, Phil Collins
7. *Beverly Hills Cop*, various artists/soundtrack
8. *Suddenly*, Billy Ocean
9. *Purple Rain*, Prince & The Revolution
10. *Songs from the Big Chair*, Tears for Fears

1986

1. *Whitney Houston*, Whitney Houston
2. *Heart*, Heart
3. *Scarecrow*, John Cougar Mellencamp
4. *Afterburner*, ZZ Top
5. *Brothers in Arms*, Dire Straits
6. *Control*, Janet Jackson
7. *Welcome to the Real World*, Mr. Mister
8. *Promise*, Sade
9. *No Jacket Required*, Phil Collins
10. *Primitive Love*, Miami Sound Machine

1987

1. *Slippery When Wet*, Bon Jovi
2. *Graceland*, Paul Simon
3. *Licensed To Ill*, Beastie Boys
4. *The Way It Is*, Bruce Hornsby & The Range
5. *Control*, Janet Jackson
6. *The Joshua Tree*, U2
7. *Fore!*, Huey Lewis & The News
8. *Night Songs*, Cinderella
9. *Rapture*, Anita Baker
10. *Invisible Touch*, Genesis

1988

1. *Faith*, George Michael
2. *Dirty Dancing*, soundtrack
3. *Hysteria*, Def Leppard
4. *Kick*, INXS
5. *Bad*, Michael Jackson
6. *Appetite for Destruction*, Guns N' Roses
7. *Out of the Blue*, Debbie Gibson
8. *Richard Marx*, Richard Marx
9. *Tiffany*, Tiffany
10. *Permanent Vacation*, Aerosmith

1989

1. *Don't Be Cruel*, Bobby Brown
2. *Hangin' Tough*, New Kids on the Block
3. *Forever Your Girl*, Paula Abdul
4. *New Jersey*, Bon Jovi
5. *Appetite for Destruction*, Guns N' Roses
6. *The Raw & the Cooked*, Fine Young Cannibals
7. *GNR Lies*, Guns N' Roses
8. *Traveling Wilburys*, Traveling Wilburys
9. *Hysteria*, Def Leppard
10. *Girl You Know It's True*, Milli Vanilli

1990

1. *Janet Jackson's Rhythm Nation 1814*, Janet Jackson
2. *. . . But Seriously*, Phil Collins
3. *Soul Provider*, Michael Bolton
4. *Pump*, Aerosmith
5. *Please Hammer Don't Hurt 'Em*, M.C. Hammer
6. *Forever Your Girl*, Paula Abdul

7. *Dr. Feelgood,* Mötley Crüe
8. *The End of Innocence,* Don Henley
9. *Cosmic Thing,* B-52's
10. *Storm Front,* Billy Joel

1991

1. *Mariah Carey,* Mariah Carey
2. *No Fences,* Garth Brooks
3. *Shake Your Money Maker,* The Black Crowes
4. *Gonna Make You Sweat,* C&C Music Factory
5. *Wilson Phillips,* Wilson Phillips
6. *To the Extreme,* Vanilla Ice
7. *Please Hammer Don't Hurt 'Em,* M.C. Hammer
8. *The Immaculate Collection,* Madonna
9. *Empire,* Queensryche
10. *I'm Your Baby Tonight,* Whitney Houston

1992

1. *Ropin' the Wind,* Garth Brooks
2. *Dangerous,* Michael Jackson
3. *Nevermind,* Nirvana
4. *Some Gave All,* Billy Ray Cyrus
5. *Achtung Baby,* U2
6. *No Fences,* Garth Brooks
7. *Metallica,* Metallica
8. *Time, Love and Tenderness,* Michael Bolton
9. *Too Legit to Quit,* Hammer
10. *Totally Crossed Out,* Kris Kross

1993

1. *The Bodyguard,* soundtrack
2. *Breathless,* Kenny G
3. *Unplugged,* Eric Clapton
4. *Janet,* Janet Jackson
5. *Some Gave All,* Billy Ray Cyrus
6. *The Chronic,* Dr. Dre
7. *Pocket Full of Kryptonite,* Spin Doctors
8. *Ten,* Pearl Jam
9. *The Chase,* Garth Brooks
10. *Core,* Stone Temple Pilots

BILLBOARD NUMBER ONES FOR 1994

Week-by-week, here are the most popular songs and albums so far in 1994. (Source: *Billboard.*)

Music Box, Mariah Carey — January 8
"Hero," Mariah Carey

Doggy Style, Snoop Doggy Dogg — January 15
"Hero," Mariah Carey

Music Box, Mariah Carey — January 22
"All for Love," Bryan Adams/Rod Stewart/Sting

Music Box, Mariah Carey — January 29
"All for Love," Bryan Adams/Rod Stewart/Sting

Music Box, Mariah Carey — February 5
"All for Love," Bryan Adams/Rod Stewart/Sting

Jar of Flies, Alice in Chains — February 12
"The Power of Love," Celine Dion

Kickin' It Up, John Michael Montgomery — February 19
"The Power of Love," Celine Dion

Toni Braxton, Toni Braxton — February 26
"The Power of Love," Celine Dion

Music Box, Mariah Carey — March 5
"The Power of Love," Celine Dion

Music Box, Mariah Carey — March 12
"The Sign," Ace of Base

Toni Braxton, Toni Braxton — March 19
"The Sign," Ace of Base

Superunknown, Soundgarden — March 26
"The Sign," Ace of Base

The Sign, Ace of Base — April 2
"The Sign," Ace of Base

Far Beyond Driven, Pantera — April 9
"Bump N' Grind," R. Kelly

Longing in Their Hearts, Bonnie Raitt — April 16
"Bump N' Grind," R. Kelly

The Division Bell, Pink Floyd — April 23
"Bump N' Grind," R. Kelly

The Division Bell, Pink Floyd — April 30
"Bump N' Grind," R. Kelly

The Division Bell, Pink Floyd — May 7
"The Sign," Ace of Base

The Division Bell, Pink Floyd — May 14
"The Sign," Ace of Base

Not a Moment Too Soon, Tim McGraw — May 21
"I Swear," All-4-One

Not a Moment Too Soon, Tim McGraw — May 28
"I Swear," All-4-One

The Crow soundtrack — June 4
"I Swear," All-4-One

The Sign, Ace of Base — June 11
"I Swear," All-4-One

Ill Communication, Beastie Boys — June 18
"I Swear," All-4-One

Purple, Stone Temple Pilots — June 25
"I Swear," All-4-One

Purple, Stone Temple Pilots — July 2
"I Swear," All-4-One

Purple, Stone Temple Pilots — July 9
"I Swear," All-4-One

The Lion King soundtrack — July 16
"I Swear," All-4-One

The Lion King soundtrack — July 23
"I Swear," All-4-One

The Lion King soundtrack — July 30
"I Swear," All-4-One

The Lion King soundtrack — August 6
"Stay (I Missed You)," Lisa Loeb & Nine Stories

The Lion King soundtrack — August 13
"Stay (I Missed You)," Lisa Loeb & Nine Stories

The Lion King soundtrack — August 20
"Stay (I Missed You)," Lisa Loeb & Nine Stories

THE ROCK OF AGES: *PEOPLE'S* FAVORITE 50

Say you're sentenced to life in the Biosphere. Or you're about to retire hip in Telluride. What rock and roll albums would you absolutely, positively, have to have? PEOPLE's record rack holds fifty, chosen to meet the single criteria set forth in the sacred Presley Dialogues: "Have you heard the news? There's good rockin' tonight."

The Band	*Music from Big Pink* (1968)
The Beatles	*A Hard Days Night* (British version) (1964)
The Beatles	*Rubber Soul* (1965)
The Beatles	*Sgt. Pepper's Lonely Hearts Club Band* (1967)
Chuck Berry	*Chuck Berry's Golden Hits* (1967)

David Bowie	*The Rise and Fall of Ziggy Stardust and the Spiders from Mars* (1972)
James Brown	*20 All-Time Greatest Hits* (1991)
Buffalo Springfield	*Buffalo Springfield 1958-77* (1976)
The Byrds	*20 Essential Tracks from the Boxed Set, 1965–1990* (1992)
The Clash	*London Calling* (1979)
Elvis Costello	*My Aim Is True* (1977)
Derek and the Dominos	*Layla and Other Assorted Love Songs* (1970)
Bob Dylan	*Bringing It All Back Home* (1965)
Bob Dylan	*Highway 61 Revisited* (1965)

Bob Dylan	*John Wesley Harding* (1968)
Aretha Franklin	*I Never Loved A Man (The Way I Love You)* (1967)
Marvin Gaye	*What's Goin' On* (1971)
Jimi Hendrix Experience	*Are You Experienced?* (1967)
Janis Joplin	*Cheap Thrills* (1967)
Jefferson Airplane	*Volunteers* (1969)
The Kinks	*Lola Versus Powerman and the Moneygoround* (1970)
Led Zeppelin	*Led Zeppelin* (1969)
Jerry Lee Lewis	*Original Golden Hits*, Vols. 1 and 2 (1969)
Little Richard	*Grooviest 17 Original Hits* (1959)
Joni Mitchell	*Court and Spark* (1974)
Moby Grape	*Moby Grape* (1967)
Van Morrison	*The Best of Van Morrison* (1990)

Nirvana	*Nevermind* (1991)

Parliament Funkadelic	*Tear the Roof Off* (1993).
Wilson Pickett	*Wilson Pickett's Greatest Hits* (1973)
Elvis Presley	*The Sun Sessions* (1987)

Prince	*1999* (1982)
Public Enemy	*It Takes a Nation of Millions To Hold Us Back* (1988)
R.E.M.	*Murmur* (1983)
Otis Redding	*History of Otis Redding* (1968)
The Replacements	*Tim* (1985)
The Rolling Stones	*Out of Our Heads* (1965)
The Rolling Stones	*Beggars' Banquet* (1968)
The Rolling Stones	*Exile on Main Street* (1972)
Leon Russell	*Leon Russell and the Shelter People* (1971)
Sly & The Family Stone	*Anthology* (1981)
Phil Spector	*Back To Mono* (1991)

Bruce Springsteen	*Born To Run* (1975)
Rod Stewart	*Storyteller* (boxed set) (1992)
The Supremes, The Four Tops, Smokey Robinson & The Miracles, The Jackson 5, The Temptations, Mary Wells, et al.	*Hitsville USA:The Motown Singles Collection* (1992)
Matthew Sweet	*Girlfriend* (1991)
Talking Heads	*Talking Heads 77* (1977)
U2	*Achtung, Baby* (1991)
The Who	*Meaty Beaty Big and Bouncey* (1971)

MTV'S TOP 100 VIDEOS OF ALL TIME

Monitoring the ever-quickening pulse of music video production, MTV's staff periodically selects an all-time best list. Their criteria: MTV air play, "lasting relevance," audience research, and album sales.

1. Nirvana, *Smells Like Teen Spirit*
2. Aerosmith, *Cryin'*
3. Red Hot Chili Peppers, *Under the Bridge*
4. Michael Jackson, *Thriller*
5. Pearl Jam, *Jeremy*
6. Guns N' Roses, *November Rain*
7. Dr. Dre, *Nuthin' But a "G" Thing*
8. Metallica, *Enter Sandman*
9. Stone Temple Pilots, *Plush*
10. Van Halen, *Right Now*
11. Boyz II Men, *End of the Road*
12. Aerosmith, *Amazing*
13. Madonna, *Vogue*
14. Guns N' Roses, *Sweet Child o' Mine*
15. Salt-N-Pepa (with En Vogue) *Whatta Man*
16. R.E.M., *Losing My Religion*
17. Nirvana, *Heart-Shaped Box*
18. Whitney Houston, *I Will Always Love You*
19. Pearl Jam, *Even Flow*
20. U2, *With or Without You*
21. Snoop Doggy Dogg, *Gin and Juice*
22. Blind Melon, *No Rain*
23. Janet Jackson, *If*
24. Red Hot Chili Peppers, *Give It Away*
25. Eric Clapton, *Tears in Heaven*
26. Nirvana, *Come as You Are*
27. Madonna, *Express Yourself*
28. Metallica, *The Unforgiven*
29. House of Pain, *Jump Around*
30. Stone Temple Pilots, *Creep*
31. Michael Jackson, *Billie Jean*
32. Aerosmith, *Janie's Got a Gun*
33. Salt-N-Pepa, *Shoop*
34. Peter Gabriel, *Sledgehammer*
35. Guns N' Roses, *Don't Cry*
36. Lenny Kravitz, *Are You Gonna Go My Way*
37. Janet Jackson, *Again*
38. Beastie Boys, *(You Gotta) Fight for Your Right to Party*
39. Nirvana, *All Apologies*
40. U2, *One*
41. Dr. Dre, *Dre Day*
42. Tom Petty, *Free Fallin'*
43. Run-D.M.C. (with Aerosmith), *Walk This Way*
44. Aerosmith, *Crazy*
45. En Vogue, *My Lovin' (You're Never Gonna Get It)*
46. Pearl Jam, *Alive*
47. Black Crowes, *Hard To Handle*
48. Boyz II Men, *It's So Hard To Say Goodbye to Yesterday*
49. Guns N' Roses, *Paradise City*
50. Snoop Doggy Dogg, *What's My Name?*
51. Soul Asylum, *Runaway Train*
52. Madonna, *Like a Prayer*
53. Nirvana, *In Bloom*
54. The Police, *Every Breath You Take*
55. Janet Jackson, *That's the Way Love Goes*
56. Metallica, *One*
57. Tom Petty, *Mary Jane's Last Dance*
58. Michael Jackson, *Beat It*
59. Aerosmith, *Livin' On the Edge*
60. Onyx, *Slam*
61. Guns N' Roses, *Welcome to the Jungle*
62. Red Hot Chili Peppers, *Soul to Squeeze*
63. Mariah Carey, *Dreamlover*
64. Nirvana, *Lithium*
65. Van Halen, *Jump*
66. Cypress Hill, *Insane in the Brain*
67. Counting Crows, *Mr. Jones*
68. Aerosmith, *Sweet Emotion*
69. Janet Jackson, *Love Will Never Do Without You*
70. Smashing Pumpkins, *Disarm*
71. Bryan Adams, *Everything I Do (I Do It for You)*
72. Warren G & Nate Dogg, *Regulate*
73. Temple of the Dog, *Hunger Strike*
74. Bon Jovi, *Wanted Dead or Alive*
75. Naughty by Nature, *Hip Hop Hooray*
76. U2, *I Still Haven't Found What I'm Looking For*
77. Us3, *Cantaloop*
78. Dire Straits, *Money for Nothing*
79. Guns N' Roses, *Patience*
80. En Vogue, *Free Your Mind*
81. Aerosmith, *Dude Looks Like a Lady*
82. Ice Cube, *It Was a Good Day*
83. Metallica, *Nothing Else Matters*
84. Duran Duran, *Hungry Like the Wolf*
85. Salt-N-Pepa, *Let's Talk About Sex*
86. Faith No More, *Epic*
87. Tom Petty, *Into the Great Wide Open*
88. Smashing Pumpkins, *Today*
89. Young MC, *Bust a Move*
90. Aerosmith, *What It Takes*
91. INXS, *Need You Tonight/Mediate*
92. Guns N' Roses, *U Could Be Mine*
93. 4 Non Blondes, *What's Up*
94. AC/DC, *You Shook Me All Night Long*
95. Madonna, *Into the Groove*
96. Queen, *Bohemian Rhapsody*
97. Janet Jackson, *Rhythm Nation*
98. Beck, *Loser*
99. Phil Collins, *In the Air Tonight*
100. Aerosmith, *Love in an Elevator*

THE 25 BEST COUNTRY ALBUMS

Here's a PEOPLE starter set of country albums for folks looking to familiarize themselves with the essence of Nashville—or just have a great listen:

Clint Black	*Killin' Time* (1989)
Suzy Bogguss	*Somewhere Between* (1989)
Byrds	*Sweetheart of the Rodeo* (1968)
Johnny Cash	*Johnny Cash in Folsom Prison* (1968)
Rosanne Cash	*Seven-Year Ache* (1981)
Patsy Cline	*Patsy Cline* (1957; 1988)
Davis Daniel	*Fighting Fire with Fire* (1991)
Vince Gill	*When I Call Your Name* (1989)
Merle Haggard	*Songs I'll Always Sing* (1976)
Emmylou Harris	*Blue Kentucky Girl* (1979)
Emmylou Harris, Dolly Parton, Linda Ronstadt	*Trio* (1987)
Waylon Jennings, Willie Nelson, Jessi Colter, Tompall Glaser	*Wanted: The Outlaws* (1976)
George Jones	*Wine-Colored Roses* (1986)
The Judds	*Love Can Build A Bridge* (1990)
Lyle Lovett	*Pontiac* (1988)
Willie Nelson	*Red-Headed Stranger* (1975)
Nitty Gritty Dirt Band	*Will the Circle Be Unbroken* (1972)
K. T. Oslin	*'80s Ladies* (1987)
Webb Pierce	*In the Jailhouse Now* (1955)
Elvis Presley	*Elvis in Nashville* (1988)
Ricky Skaggs	*Don't Cheat in Our Hometown* (1983)
Jo-el Sonnier	*Come on Joe* (1988)
Tanya Tucker	*What Do I Do with Me* (1991)
Hank Williams	*Wait for the Light To Shine* (1963)
Dwight Yoakam	*Guitars, Cadillacs, and Hillbilly Music* (1986)

THE 50 GREATEST COUNTRY STARS WORKING TODAY

There are guys with bigger hats, gals with bigger hair, and groups with bigger bank accounts, but there are no country acts more distinctive and entertaining, in the view of the PEOPLE editors, than the following fifty:

Asleep at the Wheel
Chet Atkins

Clint Black
Suzy Bogguss
Garth Brooks
Carlene Carter

Johnny Cash
Rosanne Cash

Mary-Chapin Carpenter

Davis Daniel
Lacy J. Dalton
Vince Gill
Nanci Griffith
Merle Haggard
Emmylou Harris
Alan Jackson
Waylon Jennings
George Jones
Kris Kristofferson
Patty Loveless

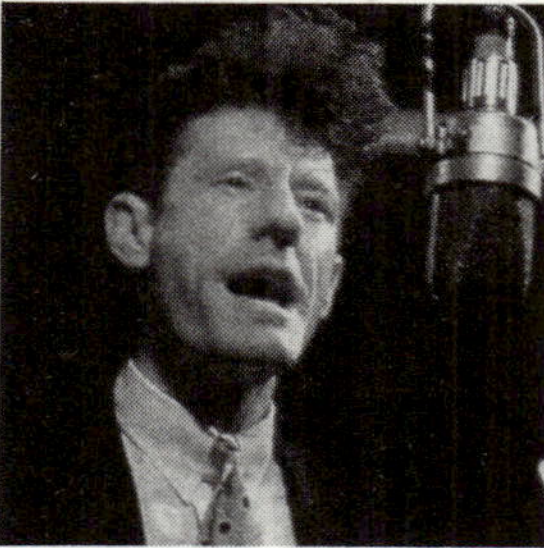

Lyle Lovett
Loretta Lynn
Kathy Mattea
Reba McEntire
Ronnie Milsap
John Michael Montgomery
Lorrie Morgan
Anne Murray
Willie Nelson
The Nitty Gritty Dirt Band
K. T. Oslin
Buck Owens

Dolly Parton
Collin Raye
Kenny Rogers
Linda Ronstadt
Earl Scruggs
Ricky Skaggs
Jo-el Sonnier
Ray Stevens
George Strait
Sweethearts of the Rodeo
Randy Travis
Travis Tritt
Tanya Tucker
Kelly Willis
Tammy Wynette
Wynonna

Trisha Yearwood
Dwight Yoakam

GREAT TITLES TO COUNTRY SONGS

A case could be made that the aptest aphorists of pop culture are country songwriters. Herewith, some of C & W's quirkier titles:

"Divorce Me C.O.D.," Merle Travis

"Don't You Think This Outlaw Bit's Done Got Out of Hand," Waylon Jennings

"Heaven's Just a Sin Away," The Kendells

"I Cheated Me Right Out of You," Moe Bandy

"If I Said You Have a Beautiful Body Would You Hold It Against Me?," Bellamy Brothers

"I Forgot More Than You'll Ever Know," Davis Sisters

"I'll Never Get Out of This World Alive," Hank Williams Sr.

"I'm Gonna Hire a Wino to Decorate Our Home," David Frizzell

"I'm the Only Hell (Mama Ever Raised)," Johnny Paycheck

"It's Not Love (But It's Not Bad)," Merle Haggard

"I've Enjoyed About as Much of This as I Can Stand," Porter Wagoner

"The Lord Knows I'm Drinkin'," Cal Smith

"Mama's in the Graveyard, Papa's in the Pen (Papa Loved Mama and Mama Loved Men)," Garth Brooks

"Marriage Has Ruined More Good Love Affairs," Jan Howard

"Maximum Security to Minimum Wage," Don King

"Now I Lay Me Down To Cheat," David Allan Coe

"She's Actin' Single (I'm Drinkin' Doubles)," Gary Stewart

"She Got the Goldmine (I Got the Shaft)," Jerry Reed

"Sleeping Single (in a Double Bed)," Barbara Mandrell

"Take an Old Cold Tater and Wait," Little Jimmy Dickens

"Take This Job and Shove It," Johnny Paycheck

"Yonder Comes a Sucker," Jim Reeves

"You Just Hurt My Last Feeling," Sammi Smith

"You're Gonna Ruin My Bad Reputation," Ronnie McDowell

"You're Out Doing What I'm Here Doing Without," Gene Watson

"You're the Reason Our Kids Are Ugly," Loretta Lynn

"Waitin' in Your Welfare Line," Buck Owens

"What's Made Milwaukee Famous (Has Made a Loser Out of Me)," Jerry Lee Lewis

"When It's Springtime in Alaska (It's Forty Below)," Johnny Horton

PEOPLE'S 20 TRAILBLAZERS OF C & W MUSIC

Many of these legendary divas and dudes of the Grand Ole Opry are now dead, but their music and influence live forever—from Nashville to Austin to Bakersfield, wherever country artists are at work.

Roy Acuff
Eddy Arnold
Gene Autry
Boudleaux Bryant
The Carter Family
Patsy Cline
Spade Cooley
Tennessee Ernie Ford
Lefty Frizzell
Bill Monroe
Minnie Pearl
Tex Ritter
Marty Robbins
Jimmie Rodgers
Roy Rogers
Hank Snow
Ernest Tubb
Kitty Wells
Hank Williams Sr.
Bob Wills

JAZZ: ESSENTIAL LISTENING

Not encyclopedic or definitive, this is simply a list of fifty marvelous jazz albums. The recordings here date from the '20s to the '90s and they cover a range of styles. Any jazz purist, or for that matter, impurist, will find sins of omission and commission on this list. All we, the jazz jury at PEOPLE, can say is that these albums have enriched our lives immeasurably and given us an almost embarassing amount of pleasure. To us, these recordings are the easiest sort of listening, full of wit, passion, invention, and beauty.

Louis Armstrong	*Hot Fives and Sevens,* Vol. 2 or 3 (1926–27)
Chet Baker	*My Funny Valentine* (1954)
Count Basie	*The Original American Decca Recordings* (1937–39)
Bix and Tram Beiderbecke	*The Bix Beiderbecke Story,* Vol. 2 (1927–28)
Art Blakey & The Jazz Messengers	*Buhaina's Delight* (1961)
Clifford Brown and Max Roach	*Clifford Brown and Max Roach* (1954–55)
Betty Carter	*Betty Carter* (1966)
Ornette Coleman	*The Shape of Jazz To Come* (1959–60)
Ornette Coleman	*Free Jazz* (1960)
John Coltrane	*Coltrane* (1957)
John Coltrane	*Meditations* (1965)
Miles Davis	*Kind of Blue* (1959)
Miles Davis and Gil Evans	*Porgy and Bess* (1958)
Paul Desmond and Gerry Mulligan	*Two of a Mind* (1962)
Eric Dolphy	*Out To Lunch* (1964)
Duke Ellington	*The Blanton-Webster Band* (1940-42)
Duke Ellington & The Jungle Band	*Rockin' in Rhythm,* Vol. 3 (1929–31)
Bill Evans	*The Village Vanguard Sessions* (1961)
Art Farmer	*Something To Live For* (1987)
Ella Fitzgerald	*The Gershwin Songbook* (1959)
Ella Fitzgerald	*The Intimate Ella* (1960)
Stan Getz	*The Roost Quartets 1950-51* (1950–51)
Benny Goodman	*Carnegie Hall Concert* (1938)
Charlie Haden & Quartet	*Haunted Heart* (1990)
Lionel Hampton	*The Complete Lionel Hampton* (1937–41)
Herbie Hancock	*Maiden Voyage* (1965)
Coleman Hawkins	*Body and Soul: The Complete Coleman Hawkins,* Vol. 1 (1929–40)
Coleman Hawkins	*The Complete Coleman Hawkins* (1944)
Fletcher Henderson and Don Redman	*Developing an American Orchestra, 1923–1937* (1923–37)
Billie Holiday	*The Quintessential Billie Holiday,* Vol. 3, 4, or 5 (1938–38)
James P. Johnson	*Snowy Morning Blues* (1930, 1944)
Abbey Lincoln	*The World Is Falling Down* (1990)
Charles Mingus	*New Tijuana Moods* (1957)
Thelonious Monk	*The Unique Thelonious Monk* (1956)
Thelonious Monk	*Alone in San Francisco* (1959)
Thelonious Monk	*Monk's Dream* (1962)
Gerry Mulligan	*What Is There to Say?* (1958–59)
Oliver Nelson	*Blues and the Abstract Truth* (1961)

King Oliver	*King Oliver's Jazz Band 1923* (1923)
Charlie Parker	*The Charlie Parker Story* (1945)
Charlie Parker (with Dizzy Gillespie, Max Roach, Bud Powell, and Charles Mingus)	*The Greatest Jazz Concert Ever* (1953)
Bud Powell	*The Amazing Bud Powell,* Vol. 1 (1949–51)
Bud Powell	*The Genius of Bud Powell* (1951)
Sonny Rollins	*A Night at the Village Vanguard,* Vols. 1 and 2 (1957)
John Scofield	*Time on My Hands* (1989)
Art Tatum	*The Tatum Solo Masterpieces,* Vol. 3 (1953–55)
Cecil Taylor	*Unit Structures* (1966)
Sarah Vaughan and Clifford Brown	*Sarah Vaughan With Clifford Brown* (1954)
Fats Waller	*The Joint Is Jumpin'* (1929–43)
Lester Young	*The Complete Lester Young* (1943–44)

JAZZ: TODAY'S GREATS

The cutting edge of jazz is honed on the whetstone of tradition, the grit of the blues, and the rich oil of swing. Only today there are more ways than ever to voice the blues and percolate rhythm, to reassess tradition and carry it on. Here are twenty-five contemporary greats and eight younger stars who are pursuing that quest in a personal and significant way:

The Masters

Benny Carter, alto sax (b. 1907)
Betty Carter, vocals (b. 1930)
Ron Carter, bass (b. 1937)
Ornette Coleman, alto and tenor sax/violin/trumpet (b. 1930)
Chick Corea, piano (b. 1941)
Ella Fitzgerald, vocals (b. 1918)
Tommy Flanagan, piano (b. 1930)
Herbie Hancock, piano (b. 1940)
Joe Henderson, tenor sax (b. 1937)
Milt Jackson, vibes (b. 1923)
Illinois Jacquet, tenor sax (b. 1921)
Keith Jarrett, piano (b. 1945)
J. J. Johnson, slide trombone (b. 1924)
Hank Jones, piano (b. 1918)
John Lewis, piano (b. 1920)
Wynton Marsalis, trumpet (b. 1961)
Gerry Mulligan, baritone sax (b. 1927)
Oscar Peterson, piano (b. 1925)
Max Roach, drums (b. 1925)
Sonny Rollins, tenor sax (b. 1929)
John Scofield, guitar (b. 1951)
Wayne Shorter, tenor sax (b. 1933)
Clark Terry, trumpet (b. 1920)
McCoy Tyner, piano (b. 1938)
Tony Williams, drums (b. 1945)

On the Rise

Bill Frisell, guitar (b. 1951)
Christian McBride, bass (1971)
Nicholas Payton, trumpet (1974)
Danilo Perez, piano (b. 1966)
Joshua Redman, tenor sax (b. 1969)
David Sanchez, tenor sax (b. 1968)
Jackie Terrason, piano (b. 1963)
Cassandra Wilson, vocals (b. 1955)

50 GREAT CLASSICAL RECORDINGS

We can't really presume to pick a classical library for all tastes, but PEOPLE's editors will hazard this tendentious consensus of outstanding recordings:

Johann Sebastian Bach	*Brandenburg Concertos*, Munich Bach Orchestra/Karl Richter
Johann Sebastian Bach	*The Well-Tempered Clavier*, BWV 846-893, Davitt Moroney
Samuel Barber	*Adagio for Strings*, Saint Louis Symphony Orchestra/Leonard Slatkin
Béla Bartók	*String Quartets Nos. 1–6*, Emerson Quartet
Ludwig van Beethoven	*Symphonies Nos. 1–9, Complete Cycles*, Berlin Philharmonic/Herbert von Karajan
Ludwig van Beethoven	*Piano Sonata in C Minor, Op. 13, "Pathétique,"* Wilhelm Kempff
Ludwig van Beethoven	*Piano Sonata in C Sharp Minor, Op. 27, No. 2, "Moonlight,"* Wilhelm Kempff
Hector Berlioz	*Symphonie fantastique*, French National Radio Orchestra/Sir Thomas Beecham
Leonard Bernstein	*Chichester Psalms*, John Paul Bogart; Camerata Singers, New York Philharmonic/Leonard Bernstein
Georges Bizet	*Carmen*, Agnes Baltsa, José Carreras; Chorus of the Paris Opéra, Berlin Philharmonic/Herbert von Karajan
Johannes Brahms	*Violin Concerto in D, Op. 77*, Itzhak Perlman; Chicago Symphony Orchestra/Carlo Maria Giulini
Benjamin Britten	*War Requiem, Op. 66*, Lorna Haywood, Anthony Rolfe Johnson, Benjamin Luxon; Atlanta Boy Choir, Atlanta Symphony Orchestra & Chorus/Robert Shaw
Frédéric Chopin	*26 Preludes*, Dmitri Alexeev
Aaron Copland	*Appalachian Spring*, New York Philharmonic/Leonard Bernstein
Claude Debussy	*Images*, Claudio Arrau
Antonín Dvorák	*Symphony No. 9 in E Minor, Op. 95, "From the New World,"* London Symphony Orchestra/István Kertész
César Franck	*Symphony in D Minor*, Berlin Radio Symphony Orchestra/Vladimir Ashkenazy
George Gershwin	*Rhapsody in Blue*, Columbia Symphony Orchestra, New York Philharmonic/Leonard Bernstein
George Gershwin	*Porgy and Bess*, Willard White, Leona Mitchell; Cleveland Orchestra & Chorus/Lorin Maazel
George Frideric Handel	*Messiah*, Heather Harper, Helen Watts, John Wakefield, John Shirley-Quirk; London Symphony Orchestra & Choir/Sir Colin Davis
Joseph Haydn	*Symphonies Nos. 93-104, "London,"* Royal Concertgebouw Orchestra/Sir Colin Davis
Joseph Haydn	*String Quartets, Op. 76, "Erdödy,"* Takács Quartet
Charles Ives	*Three Places in New England*, Boston Symphony Orchestra/Michael Tilson Thomas
Franz Liszt	*Les Préludes*, Philadelphia Orchestra/Riccardo Muti
Gustav Mahler	*Symphony No. 9 in D*, Vienna Philharmonic/Bruno Walter
Felix Mendelssohn	*Violin Concerto in E Minor, Op. 64*, Kyung Wha Chung; Montreal Symphony Orchestra/Charles Dutoit

Wolfgang Amadeus Mozart	*Symphony No. 41 in C, K. 551, "Jupiter,"* Columbia Symphony Orchestra/Bruno Walter
Wolfgang Amadeus Mozart	*A Little Night Music, K. 525*, Prague Chamber Orchestra/Sir Charles Mackerras
Wolfgang Amadeus Mozart	*The Marriage of Figaro*, Samuel Ramey, Lucia Popp; London Opera Chorus, London Philharmonic Orchestra/Sir George Solti
Wolfgang Amadeus Mozart	*Don Giovanni*, Eberhard Wächter, Joan Sutherland, Elisabeth Schwarzkopf; Philharmonia Orchestra & Chorus/Carlo Maria Giulini
Modest Mussorgsky	*Pictures at an Exhibition*, Montreal Symphony Orchestra/Charles Dutoit
Giacomo Puccini	*La Bohème*, Mirella Freni, Luciano Pavarotti; Chorus of the Deutsche Oper Berlin, Berlin Philharmonic/Herbert von Karajan
Sergei Prokofiev	*Symphony No. 1 in D, Op. 25, "Classical,"* Berlin Philharmonic/Herbert von Karajan
Sergei Rachmaninoff	*Piano Concerto No. 2 in C Minor, Op. 18*, Vladimir Ashkenazy; London Symphony Orchestra/André Previn
Nikolai Rimsky-Korsakov	*Scheherazade, Op. 35*, Royal Concertgebouw Orchestra/Kirill Kondrashin
Gioacchino Rossini	*The Barber of Seville*, Leo Nucci, William Matteuzzi, Cecilia Bartoli; Chorus & Orchestra of the Teatro Comunale di Bologna/Giuseppe Patanè
Camille Saint-Saëns	*The Carnival of the Animals*, Montreal Symphony Orchestra, London Sinfonietta/Charles Dutoit
Domenico Scarlatti	*Keyboard Sonatas*, Vladimir Horowitz
Arnold Schoenberg	*Verklärte Nacht (Transfigured Night), Op. 4*, Jiri Najnar, Vaclav Bernasek; Talich Quartet
Franz Schubert	*Die Schöne Müllerin, D. 795; Winterreise, D. 911*, Dietrich Fischer-Dieskau, Gerald Moore
Robert Schumann	*Op. 19, "Carnaval: Pretty Scenes on Four Notes,"* Artur Rubinstein
Dmitri Shostakovich	*Symphony No. 5 in D Minor, Op. 47*, Royal Concertgebouw Orchestra/Bernard Haitink
Jean Sibelius	*Symphony No. 5 in E Flat, Op. 82*, Boston Symphony Orchestra/Sir Colin Davis
Igor Stravinsky	*The Rite of Spring*, New York Philharmonic, Cleveland Orchestra/Pierre Boulez
Piotr Ilyich Tchaikovsky	*Symphony No. 6 in B Minor, Op. 74, "Pathétique,"* Leningrad Philharmonic/Evgeny Mravinsky
Piotr Ilyich Tchaikovsky	*Piano Concerto No. 1 in B Flat Minor, Op. 23*, Van Cliburn; RCA Symphony Orchestra/Kirill Kondrashin
Giuseppe Verdi	*Requiem*, Elisabeth Schwarzkopf, Christa Ludwig, Nicolai Gedda, Nicolai Ghiaurov; Philharmonia Orchestra & Chorus/Carlo Maria Giulini
Giuseppe Verdi	*La Traviata*, Joan Sutherland, Luciano Pavarotti; London Opera Chorus, National Philharmonic Orchestra/Richard Bonynge
Antonio Vivaldi	*Concertos for Violin, Strings, and Continuo, Op. 8, Nos. 1–4, "The Four Seasons,"* Alan Loveday; Academy of St. Martin-in-the-Fields/Sir Neville Marriner
Richard Wagner	*The Ring of the Nibelung*, Birgit Nilsson, Wolfgang Windgassen; Chorus & Orchestra of the Bayreuth Festival/Karl Böhm

THE 25 LEADING CLASSICAL PERFORMERS

While the music they play was generally composed long before we were born, today's greatest musicians infuse the past with a fresh vigor that lends the classics a dazzling new life. The following artists, all still actively performing and recording, represent the finest today's concert halls have to offer.

Vladimir Ashkenazy, pianist (b. 1937)
Emanuel Ax, pianist (b. 1949)
Cecilia Bartoli , mezzo-soprano (b. 1967)
Kathleen Battle, soprano (b. 1948)
Van Cliburn, pianist (b. 1934)
Plácido Domingo, tenor (b. 1941)
Marilyn Horne, mezzo-soprano (b. 1934)
Yevgeny Kissin, piano (b. 1971)
Katia and Marielle Labèque, pianists (b. 1950, 1952)
Yo-Yo Ma, cellist (b. 1955)
Midori, violin (b. 1971)
Anne-Sophie Mutter, violin (b. 1963)
Jessye Norman, soprano (b. 1948)
Christopher Parkening, guitar (b. 1947)
Luciano Pavarotti, tenor (b. 1935)
Murray Perahia, pianist (b. 1947)
Itzhak Perlman, violinist (b.1945)
Jean-Pierre Rampal, flutist (b. 1922)
Mstislav Rostropovich, cellist (b. 1927)
Isaac Stern, violinist (b. 1920)
Kiri Te Kanawa, soprano (b. 1944)
Dawn Upshaw, soprano (b. 1960)
Frederica von Stade, mezzo-soprano (b. 1945)
André Watts, pianist (b. 1946)
Pinchas Zukerman, violinist (b. 1948)

VICTORIA'S SECRET

Four of the ten biggest selling classical recordings have been released by Victoria's Secret, the lingerie store that ordinarily specializes in bustiers and silk nightgowns. The recordings are a compilation of what Victoria's Secret calls "classical songs" performed by the London Symphony Orchestra—catchy little numbers by Bach, Handel, Tchaikovsky, and Mozart. Begun as a spinoff of the music that plays in the company's stores, the Classics by Request series "combines delicate lingerie images with unparalleled performances," say the firm's publicists. "Now Victoria's Secret touches the heart of a woman with song as well as silk and satin."

THE 50 GREATEST CLASSICAL COMPOSERS

They're all dead white men, but they sure could write a tune. Here are the classics of the classical composers as selected by PEOPLE:

Johann Sebastian Bach (German, 1685–1750)
Samuel Barber (American, 1910–81)
Béla Bartók (Hungarian, 1881–1945)
Ludwig van Beethoven (German, 1770–1827)
Hector Berlioz (French, 1803–69)
Leonard Bernstein (American, 1918–90)
Georges Bizet (French, 1838–75)
Johannes Brahms (German, 1833–97)
Benjamin Britten (British, 1913–76)
John Cage (American, 1912–92)
Elliott Carter (American, b. 1908)
Frédéric Chopin (Polish, 1810–49)
Aaron Copland (American, 1900–90)
François Couperin (French, 1668–1733)
Claude Debussy (French, 1862–1918)
Antonín Dvorák (Czech, 1841–1904)
Gabriel Fauré (French, 1845–1924)
César Franck (Belgian/French, 1822–90)
George Gershwin (American, 1898–1937)
George Frideric Handel (German/British, 1685–1759)
Franz Joseph Haydn (Austrian, 1732–1809)
Paul Hindemith (German, 1895–1963)
Charles Ives (American, 1874–1954)
Leos Janácek (Czech, 1854–1928)
Franz Liszt (Hungarian, 1811–86)
Gustav Mahler (Bohemian/Austrian, 1860–1911)
Felix Mendelssohn (German, 1809–47)
Claudio Monteverdi (Italian, 1567–1643)
Wolfgang Amadeus Mozart (Austrian, 1756–91)
Giovanni da Palestrina (Italian, c. 1525–94)
Sergei Prokofiev (Russian, 1891–1953)
Giacomo Puccini (Italian, 1858–1924)
Sergei Rachmaninoff (Russian, 1873–1943)
Jean-Philippe Rameau (French, 1683–1764)
Maurice Ravel (French, 1875–1937)
Camille Saint-Saëns (French, 1835–1921)
Domenico Scarlatti (Italian, 1685–1757)
Arnold Schoenberg (Austrian, 1874–1951)
Franz Schubert (Austrian, 1797–1828)
Dmitri Shostakovich (Russian, 1906–75)
Jean Sibelius (Finnish, 1865–1957)
Johann Strauss (Austrian, 1825–99)
Richard Strauss (German, 1864–1949)
Igor Stravinsky (Russian, 1882–1971)
Piotr Ilyitch Tchaikovsky (Russian, 1840–93)
Georg Philipp Telemann (German, 1681–1767)
Ralph Vaughan Williams (British, 1872–1958)
Guiseppe Verdi (Italian, 1813–1901)
Antonio Vivaldi (Italian, 1678–1741)
Richard Wagner (German, 1813–83)

MUSICAL PERIODS

As it turns out, classical music isn't all so classical. In an effort to sort out baroque quartets and romantic symphonies from classical sonatas and modern operas, here's the chronological breakdown of musical periods:

Period	*Dates*
Renaissance	1450–1600
Baroque	1600–1750
Classical	1750–1825
Romantic	1825–1910
Modern	1910–present

MAJOR AMERICAN SYMPHONY ORCHESTRAS

From Miami to Seattle, American cities are supporting some of the finest symphonies in the world. The following orchestras, twenty-five of the most important in the U.S., are listed with their conductors or music directors.

Atlanta Symphony Orchestra	Yoel Levi	Atlanta, GA
Baltimore Symphony Orchestra	David Zinman	Baltimore, MD
Boston Symphony Orchestra	Seiji Ozawa	Boston, MA
Buffalo Philharmonic Orchestra	Maximiano Valdes	Buffalo, NY
Chicago Symphony Orchestra	Daniel Barenboim	Chicago, IL
Cincinnati Symphony Orchestra	Jesus Lopez-Cobos	Cincinnati, OH
Cleveland Orchestra	Christoph von Dohnanyi	Cleveland, OH
Detroit Symphony Orchestra	Neeme Jarvi	Detroit, MI
Houston Symphony	Christopher Eschenbach	Houston, TX
Los Angeles Chamber Orchestra	Christof Perick	Los Angeles, CA
Los Angeles Philharmonic	Esa-Pekka Salonen	Los Angeles, CA
Louisville Orchestra	Lawrence Leighton Smith	Louisville, KY
Minnesota Orchestra	Edo de Waart	Minneapolis, MN
National Symphony Orchestra	Mstislav Rostropovich	Washington, DC
New Jersey Symphony Orchestra	Zdenek Macal	Newark, NJ
New World Symphony	Michael Tilson Thomas	Miami Beach, FL
New York Philharmonic	Kurt Masur	New York, NY
Philadelphia Orchestra	Wolfgang Sawallisch	Philadelphia, PA
Pittsburgh Symphony Orchestra	Lorin Maazel	Pittsburgh, PA
Rochester Philharmonic Orchestra	Mark Elder	Rochester, NY
St. Louis Symphony Orchestra	Leonard Slatkin	St. Louis, MO
St. Paul Chamber Orchestra	Hugh Wolff	St. Paul, MN
San Francisco Symphony	Herbert Blomstedt	San Francisco, CA
Seattle Symphony Orchestra	Gerard Schwarz	Seattle, WA
Utah Symphony Orchestra	Joseph Silverstein	Salt Lake City, UT

MTV VIDEO MUSIC AWARDS

BEST VIDEO OF THE YEAR

1984	Cars	*You Might Think*
1985	Don Henley	*The Boys of Summer*
1986	Dire Straits	*Money for Nothing*
1987	Peter Gabriel	*Sledgehammer*
1988	INXS	*Need You Tonight/Mediate*
1989	Neil Young	*This Note's for You*
1990	Sinead O'Connor	*Nothing Compares 2 U*
1991	R.E.M.	*Losing My Religion*
1992	Van Halen	*Right Now*
1993	Pearl Jam	*Jeremy*

BEST MALE VIDEO

1984	David Bowie	*China Girl*
1985	Bruce Springsteen	*I'm on Fire*
1986	Robert Palmer	*Addicted to Love*
1987	Peter Gabriel	*Sledgehammer*
1988	Prince	*U Got the Look*
1989	Elvis Costello	*Veronica*
1990	Don Henley	*The End of the Innocence*
1991	Chris Isaak	*Wicked Game* (Concept)
1992	Eric Clapton	*Tears in Heaven* (Performance)
1993	Lenny Kravitz	*Are You Gonna Go My Way*

BEST FEMALE VIDEO

1984	Cyndi Lauper	*Girls Just Want To Have Fun*
1985	Tina Turner	*What's Love Got To Do with It*
1986	Whitney Houston	*How Will I Know*
1987	Madonna	*Papa Don't Preach*
1988	Suzanne Vega	*Luka*
1989	Paula Abdul	*Straight Up*
1990	Sinead O'Connor	*Nothing Compares 2 U*
1991	Janet Jackson	*Love Will Never Do Without You*
1992	Annie Lennox	*Why*
1993	k.d. lang	*Constant Craving*

BEST CONCEPT VIDEO

1984	Herbie Hancock	*Rockit*
1985	Glenn Frey	*Smuggler's Blues*
1986	a-ha	*Take On Me*
1987	Peter Gabriel/ Stephen Johnson	*Sledgehammer*
1988	Pink Floyd	*Learning To Fly*

BEST GROUP VIDEO

1984	ZZ Top	*Legs*
1985	USA for Africa	*We Are the World*
1986	Dire Straits	*Money for Nothing*
1987	Talking Heads	*Wild Wild Life*
1988	INXS	*Need You Tonight/Mediate*
1989	Living Colour	*Cult of Personality*
1990	B-52s	*Love Shack*
1991	R.E.M.	*Losing My Religion*
1992	U2	*Even Better Than the Real Thing*
1993	Pearl Jam	*Jeremy*

BEST STAGE PERFORMANCE IN A VIDEO

1984	Van Halen	*Jump*
1985	Bruce Springsteen	*Dancing in the Dark*
1986	Bryan Adams/ Tina Turner	*It's Only Love*
1987	Bon Jovi	*Livin' On a Prayer*
1988	Prince	*U Got the Look*
1989	Living Colour	*Cult of Personality*

BEST NEW ARTIST IN A VIDEO

1984	Eurythmics	*Sweet Dreams (Are Made of This)*
1985	til' tuesday	*Voices Carry*
1986	a-ha	*Take On Me*
1987	Crowded House	*Don't Dream It's Over*
1988	Guns N' Roses	*Welcome to the Jungle*
1989	Living Colour	*Cult of Personality*
1990	Michael Penn	*No Myth*
1991	Jesus Jones	*Right Here, Right Now*
1992	Nirvana	*Smells Like Teen Spirit*
1993	Stone Temple Pilots	*Plush*

BEST RAP VIDEO

1989	D.J. Jazzy Jeff & The Fresh Prince	*Parents Just Don't Understand*
1990	M.C. Hammer	*U Can't Touch This*
1991	L.L. Cool J	*Mama Said Knock You Out*
1992	Arrested Development	*Tennessee*
1993	Arrested Development	*People Everyday*

BEST DANCE VIDEO

1989	Paula Abdul	*Straight Up*
1990	M.C. Hammer	*U Can't Touch This*
1991	C + C Music Factory	*Gonna Make You Sweat (Everybody Dance Now)*
1992	Prince & The New Power Generation	*Cream*
1993	En Vogue	*Free Your Mind*

BEST METAL/HARD ROCK VIDEO

1989	Guns N' Roses	*Sweet Child o' Mine*
1990	Aerosmith	*Janie's Got a Gun*
1991	Aerosmith	*The Other Side*
1992	Metallica	*Enter Sandman*
1993	Pearl Jam	*Jeremy*

BEST R&B VIDEO

1993	En Vogue	*Free Your Mind*

BEST VIDEO FROM A FILM

1987	Talking Heads	*Wild Wild Life*
1988	Los Lobos	*La Bamba*
1989	U2 with B.B. King	*When Love Comes to Town*
1990	Billy Idol	*Cradle of Love [Ford Fairlaine]*

1991	Chris Isaak	*Wicked Game [Wild at Heart]*
1992	Queen	*Bohemian Rhapsody [Wayne's World]*
1993	Alice in Chains	*Would? [Singles]*

BEST OVERALL PERFORMANCE IN A VIDEO

1984	Michael Jackson	*Thriller*
1985	Philip Bailey/ Phil Collins	*Easy Lover*
1986	David Bowie and Mick Jagger	*Dancing in the Streets*
1987	Peter Gabriel	*Sledgehammer*

MOST EXPERIMENTAL VIDEO

1984	Herbie Hancock	*Rockit*
1985	Art of Noise; Zbigniew Rybczynski	*Close (to the Edit)*
1986	a-ha; Steven Barron	*Take On Me*
1987	Peter Gabriel; Stephen Johnson, Peter Gabriel	*Sledgehammer*

BEST POST MODERN VIDEO

1989	R.E.M.	*Orange Crush*
1990	Sinead O'Connor	*Nothing Compares 2 U*

BEST ALTERNATIVE VIDEO

1991	Jane's Addiction	*Been Caught Stealing*
1992	Nirvana	*Smells Like Teen Spirit*
1993	Nirvana	*In Bloom* (Version 1—Dresses)

BEST SPECIAL EFFECTS IN A VIDEO

1984	Herbie Hancock	*Rockit*
1985	Tom Petty & The Heartbreakers; Tony Mitchell, Kathy Dougherty, Peter Cohen	*Don't Come Around Here No More*
1986	a-ha; Michael Patterson	*Take On Me*
1987	Peter Gabriel; Stephen Johnson, Peter Lord	*Sledgehammer*
1988	Squeeze; Jim Francis, Dave Barton	*Hourglass*
1989	Michael Jackson; Jim Blashfield	*Leave Me Alone*
1990	Tears For Fears; Jim Blashfield	*Sowing the Seeds of Love*
1991	Faith No More; David Faithful, Ralph Ziman	*Falling to Pieces*
1992	U2; Simon Taylor	*Even Better Than the Real Thing*
1993	Peter Gabriel; Real World Productions/ Colossal Pictures	*Steam*

BEST DIRECTION IN A VIDEO

1984	ZZ Top; Tim Newman	*Sharp Dressed Man*
1985	Don Henley; John Baptiste Mondino	*The Boys of Summer*
1986	a-ha; Steven Barron	*Take On Me*
1987	Peter Gabriel; Stephen Johnson	*Sledgehammer*
1988	George Michael; Andy Morahan, George Michael	*Father Figure*
1989	Madonna; David Fincher	*Express Yourself*
1990	Madonna; David Fincher	*Vogue*
1991	R.E.M.; Tarsem	*Losing My Religion*
1992	Van Halen; Mark Fenske	*Right Now*
1993	Pearl Jam; Mark Pellington	*Jeremy*

BREAKTHROUGH VIDEO

1988	INXS	*Need You Tonight/Mediate*
1989	Art of Noise, featuring Tom Jones	*Kiss*
1990	Tears for Fears; Jim Blashfield	*Sowing the Seeds of Love*
1991	R.E.M.; Tarsem	*Losing My Religion*
1992	Red Hot Chili Peppers; Stephane Sednaoui	*Give It Away*
1993	Los Lobos; Ondrej Rudavsky, Axel Erickson	*Kiko & The Lavender Moon*

VIDEO VANGUARD AWARDS

1984 The Beatles, David Bowie, Richard Lester
1985 David Byrne, Kevin Godley and Lol Creme, Russell Mulcahy
1986 Madonna and Zbigniew Rybeznski
1987 Julien Temple and Peter Gabriel
1988 Michael Jackson
1989 George Michael
1990 Janet Jackson

MICHAEL JACKSON VIDEO VANGUARD AWARD

1991 Bon Jovi, Wayne Isham
1992 Guns N' Roses

VIEWER'S CHOICE AWARD

1984	Michael Jackson	*Thriller*
1985	USA for Africa	*We Are the World*
1986	a-ha	*Take On Me*
1987	U2	*With or Without You*
1988	INXS	*Need You Tonight/Mediate*
1989	Madonna	*Like a Prayer*
1990	Aerosmith	*Janie's Got a Gun*

THE GRAMMY AWARDS

Even more so than most award-giving bodies, the National Academy of Recording Arts and Sciences has switched, added, deleted, and renamed its various award categories on a regular basis. The following chart gathers the majority of continuing categories that honor mainstream musical achievement. That means you won't find the awards for polka or jacket liner notes, but you will find years of musical greats (and electorate gaffes) in an easy-to-follow format.

	1958	1959	1960
Record of the Year	Domenico Modugno, "Nel Blu Dipinto Di Blu (Volare)"	Bobby Darin, "Mack the Knife"	Percy Faith, "Theme from A Summer Place"
Album of the Year	Henry Mancini, *The Music from Peter Gunn*	Frank Sinatra, *Come Dance with Me*	Bob Newhart, *Button Down Mind*
Song of the Year	Domenico Modugno, "Nel Blu Dipinto Di Blu (Volare)"	Jimmy Driftwood, "The Battle of New Orleans"	Ernest Gold, "Theme from *Exodus*"
Pop Vocal, Female	Ella Fitzgerald, *Ella Fitzgerald Sings the Irving Berlin Song Book*	Ella Fitzgerald, "But Not for Me"	Ella Fitzgerald, *Mack the Knife, Ella in Berlin*
Pop Vocal, Male	Perry Como, "Catch a Falling Star"	Frank Sinatra, *Come Dance with Me*	Ray Charles, *Genius of Ray Charles*
New Artist	—	Bobby Darin	Bob Newhart
Pop Vocal, Duo or Group with Vocal	Louis Prima and Keely Smith, "That Old Black Magic"	Mormon Tabernacle Choir, "Battle Hymn of the Republic"	Eydie Gormé and Steve Lawrence, "We Got Us"
Rhythm and Blues Song	Champs, "Tequila"	Dinah Washington, "What a Diff'rence a Day Makes"	Ray Charles, "Let the Good Times Roll"
Jazz, Soloist	—	Ella Fitzgerald, *Ella Swings Lightly*	—
Jazz, Group	Count Basie, *Basie*	Jonah Jones, *I Dig Chicks*	André Previn, *West Side Story*
Jazz, Big Band/ Large Ensemble Performance	—	—	Henry Mancini, *The Blues and the Beat*
Folk Recording	—	Kingston Trio, *The Kingston Trio at Large*	Harry Belafonte, *Swing Dat Hammer*
Cast Show Album	*The Music Man*	*Porgy and Bess*	*The Sound of Music*
Comedy Recording (Spoken Word/Musical)	David Seville, "The Chipmunk Song"	Shelley Berman, *Inside Shelley Berman;* Homer & Jethro, *The Battle of Kookamonga*	Bob Newhart, *Button Down Mind Strikes Back;* Paul Weston and Jo Stafford, *Jonathan and Darlene Edwards in Paris*
Classical Orchestral Performance	Felix Slatkin, Hollywood Bowl Symphony, *Gaîeté Parisienne*	Charles Munch, conductor, Boston Symphony, *Debussy: Images for Orchestra*	Fritz Reiner, conductor, Chicago Symphony, *Bartók: Music for Strings, Percussion and Celeste*
Opera Recording	Roger Wagner Chorale, *Virtuoso*	Erich Leinsdorf, conductor, Vienna Philharmonic, *Mozart: The Marriage of Figaro*	Erich Leinsdorf, conductor, Rome Opera House Chorus and Orchestra, *Puccini: Turandot* (Solos: Tebaldi, Nilsson, Bjoerling, Tozzi)
Chamber Music Performance	Hollywood String Quartet, *Beethoven: Quartet 130*	Artur Rubinstein, *Beethoven: Sonata No. 21 in C, Op. 53; "Waldstein" Sonata No. 18 in E Flat, Op. 53, No. 3*	Laurindo Almeida, *Conversations with the Guitar*

	1961	1962	1963
Record of the Year	Henry Mancini, "Moon River"	Tony Bennett, "I Left My Heart in San Francisco"	Henry Mancini, "The Days of Wine and Roses"
Album of the Year	Judy Garland, *Judy at Carnegie Hall*	Vaughn Meader, *The First Family*	Barbra Streisand, *The Barbra Streisand Album*
Song of the Year	Henry Mancini and Johnny Mercer, "Moon River"	Leslie Bricusse and Anthony Newley, "What Kind of Fool Am I"	Johnny Mercer and Henry Mancini, "The Days of Wine and Roses"
(Pop) Vocal, Female	Judy Garland, *Judy at Carnegie Hall*	Ella Fitzgerald, *Ella Swings Brightly with Nelson Riddle*	Barbra Streisand, *The Barbra Streisand Album*
(Pop) Vocal, Male	Jack Jones, "Lollipops and Roses"	Tony Bennett, "I Left My Heart in San Francisco"	Jack Jones, "Wives and Lovers"
New Artist	Peter Nero	Robert Goulet	Swingle Singers
Pop Vocal, Duo or Group with Vocal	Lambert, Hendricks & Ross, *High Flying*	Peter, Paul & Mary, "If I Had a Hammer"	Peter, Paul & Mary, "Blowin' in the Wind"
Rhythm and Blues Song	Ray Charles, "Hit the Road, Jack"	Ray Charles, "I Can't Stop Loving You"	Ray Charles, "Busted"
Jazz, Soloist/Small Group	André Previn, *André Previn Plays Harold Arlen*	Stan Getz, *Desafinado*	Bill Evans, *Conversations with Myself*
Jazz, Big Band/Large Ensemble Performance	Stan Kenton, *West Side Story*	Stan Kenton, *Adventures in Jazz*	Woody Herman Band, *Encore: Woody Herman, 1963*
Contemporary Folk	Belafonte Folk Singers, *Belafonte Folk Singers at Home and Abroad*	Peter, Paul & Mary, "If I Had a Hammer"	Peter, Paul & Mary, "Blowin' in the Wind"
Cast Show Album	*How To Succeed in Business Without Really Trying*	*No Strings*	*She Loves Me*
Comedy Recording	Mike Nichols and Elaine May, *An Evening with Mike Nichols and Elaine May*	Vaughn Meader, *The First Family*	Allen Sherman, *Hello Mudduh, Hello Faddah*
Classical Album	Igor Stravinsky, conductor, Columbia Symphony, *Stravinsky Conducts, 1960: Le Sacre du Printemps; Petruchka*	Vladimir Horowitz, *Columbia Records Presents Vladimir Horowitz*	Benjamin Britten, conductor, London Symphony Orchestra and Chorus, *Britten: War Requiem*
Classical Orchestral Performance	Charles Munch, conductor, Boston Symphony, *Ravel: Daphnis et Chloe*	Igor Stravinsky, conductor, Columbia Symphony, *Stravinsky: The Firebird Ballet*	Erich Leinsdorf, conductor, Boston Symphony, *Bartók: Concerto for Orchestra*
Opera Recording	Gabriele Santini, conductor, Rome Opera Chorus and Orchestra *Puccini: Madama Butterfly*	Georg Solti, conductor, Rome Opera House Orchestra and Chorus (Solos: Price, Vickers, Gorr, Merrill, Tozzi), *Verdi: Aïda*	Erich Leinsdorf, conductor, RCA Italiana Orchestra and Chorus (Solos: Price, Tucker, Elias), *Puccini: Madama Butterfly*
Chamber Music Performance	Jascha Heifetz, Gregor Piatigorsky, William Primrose, *Beethoven: Serenade, Op. 8; Kodaly: Duo for Violin & Cello, Op. 7*	Jascha Heifetz, Gregor Piatigorsky, William Primrose, *The Heifetz-Piatigorsky Concerts with Primrose, Pennario and Guests*	Julian Bream Consort, *An Evening of Elizabethan Music*

GRAMMY AWARDS

	1964	1965	1966
Record of the Year	Stan Getz and Astrud Gilberto, "The Girl from Ipanema"	Herb Alpert & The Tijuana Brass, "A Taste of Honey"	Frank Sinatra, "Strangers in the Night"
Album of the Year	Stan Getz and Joao Gilberto, *Getz/Gilberto*	Frank Sinatra, *September of My Years*	Frank Sinatra, *Sinatra: A Man & His Music*
Song of the Year	Jerry Herman, "Hello, Dolly!"	Paul Francis Webster and Johnny Mandel, "The Shadow of Your Smile (Love Theme from *The Sandpiper*)"	John Lennon and Paul McCartney, "Michelle"
Pop Vocal, Female	Barbra Streisand, "People"	Barbra Streisand, *My Name Is Barbra*	Eydie Gorme, "If He Walked into My Life"
Pop Vocal, Male	Louis Armstrong, "Hello, Dolly!"	Frank Sinatra, "It Was a Very Good Year"	Frank Sinatra, "Strangers in the Night"
Rock Vocal Female, Male	Petula Clark, "Downtown"	Petula Clark, "I Know a Place"; Roger Miller, "King of the Road"	Paul McCartney, "Eleanor Rigby"
New Artist	The Beatles	Tom Jones	—
Pop Vocal, Duo or Group	The Beatles, *A Hard Day's Night*	Anita Kerr Quartet, *We Dig Mancini*	Anita Kerr Quartet, "A Man and a Woman"
Rock Performance, Duo or Group with Vocal	—	Statler Brothers, "Flowers on the Wall"	The Mamas & The Papas, "Monday, Monday"
Rhythm and Blues Song	Nancy Wilson, "How Glad I Am"	James Brown, "Papa's Got a Brand New Bag"	Ray Charles, "Crying Time"
R&B Vocal	—	—	Ray Charles, "Crying Time"
R&B Duo or Group with Vocal	—	—	Ramsey Lewis, "Hold It Right There"
Country Song	Roger Miller, "Dang Me"	Roger Miller, "King of the Road"	Bill Sherrill and Glenn Sutton, "Almost Persuaded"
Country Vocal, Female	Dottie West, "Here Comes My Baby"	Jody Miller, "Queen of the House"	Jeannie Seely, "Don't Touch Me"
Country Vocal, Male	Roger Miller, "Dang Me"	Roger Miller, "King of the Road"	David Houston, "Almost Persuaded"
Jazz, Group	Stan Getz, *Getz/Gilberto*	Ramsey Lewis Trio, *The "In" Crowd*	Wes Montgomery, *Goin' Out of My Head*
Jazz, Big Band/ Large Ensemble Performance	Laurindo Almeida, *Guitar from Ipanema*	Duke Ellington Orchestra, *Ellington '66*	—
Gospel Performance, Duo, Group, Choir or Chorus	—	George Beverly Shea and Anita Ker Quartet, *Southland Favorites*	Porter Wagoner & the Blackwood Bros., *Grand Old Gospel*
Folk Recording	Gale Garnett, *We'll Sing in the Sunshine*	Harry Belafonte, Miriam Makeba, *An Evening with Belafonte/Makeba*	Cortelia Clark, *Blues in the Street*
Cast Show Album	*Funny Girl*	*On a Clear Day You Can See Forever*	*Mame*
Comedy Recording	Bill Cosby, *I Started Out as a Child*	Bill Cosby, *Why Is There Air?*	Bill Cosby, *Wonderfulness*

	1964	1965	1966
Classical Album	Leonard Bernstein, conductor, New York Philharmonic, *Bernstein: Symphony No. 3*	Vladimir Horowitz, *Horowitz at Carnegie Hall: An Historic Return*	Morton Gould conductor, Chicago Symphony, *Ives: Symphony No. 1 in D Minor*
Classical Orchestral Performance	Erich Leinsdorf, conductor, Boston Symphony, *Mahler: Symphony No. 5 in C Sharp Minor;* Berg: *Wozzeck Excerpts*	Leopold Stokowski, conductor, American Symphony, *Ives: Symphony No. 4*	Erich Leinsdorf, conductor, Boston Symphony, *Mahler: Symphony No. 6 in A Minor*
Opera Recording	Herbert von Karajan, conductor, Vienna Philharmonic and Chorus (Solos: Price, Corelli, Merrill, Freni), *Bizet: Carmen*	Karl Bohm, conductor, Orchestra of German Opera, Berlin, (Solos: Fischer-Dieskau, Lear, Wunderlich), *Berg: Wozzeck*	Georg Solti, conductor, Vienna Philharmonic (Solos: Nilsson, Crespin, Ludwig, King, Hotter), *Wagner: Die Walküre*
Chamber Music Performance	Jascha Heifetz, Gregor Piatigorsky (Jacob Lateiner, piano), *Beethoven: Trio No. 1 in E Flat, Op. 1, No. 1*	Juilliard String Quartet, *Bartók: The Six String Quartets*	Boston Symphony Chamber Players, *Boston Symphony Chamber Players*

	1967	1968	1969
Record of the Year	5th Dimension, "Up, Up and Away"	Simon & Garfunkel, "Mrs. Robinson"	5th Dimension, "Aquarius/Let the Sunshine In"
Album of the Year	The Beatles, *Sgt. Pepper's Lonely Hearts Club Band*	Glen Campbell, *By the Time I Get to Phoenix*	Blood, Sweat & Tears, *Blood, Sweat & Tears*
Song of the Year	Jim Webb, "Up, Up and Away"	Bobby Russell, "Little Green Apples"	Joe South, "Games People Play"
Pop Vocal, Female	Bobbie Gentry, "Ode to Billie Joe"	Dionne Warwick, "Do You Know the Way To San Jose"	Peggy Lee, "Is That All There Is"
Pop Vocal, Male	Glen Campbell, "By the Time I Get to Phoenix"	José Feliciano, "Light My Fire"	Harry Nilsson, "Everybody's Talkin"
New Artist	Bobbie Gentry	José Feliciano	Crosby, Stills & Nash
Pop Vocal	5th Dimension, "Up, Up and Away"	Simon & Garfunkel, "Mrs. Robinson"	5th Dimension, "Aquarius/Let the Sunshine In"
Rock Performance, Duo or Group	5th Dimension, "Up, Up and Away"	—	—
Rhythm and Blues Song	Aretha Franklin, "Respect"	Otis Redding and Steve Cropper, "(Sittin' On) the Dock of the Bay"	Richard Spencer, "Color Him Father"
R&B Vocal, Female	Aretha Franklin, "Respect"	Aretha Franklin, "Chain of Fools"	Aretha Franklin, "Share Your Love With Me"
R&B Vocal, Male	Lou Rawls, "Dead End Street"	Otis Redding, "(Sittin' On) the Dock of the Bay"	Joe Simon, "The Chokin' Kind"

	1967	1968	1969
R&B Duo or Group with Vocal	Sam & Dave, "Soul Man"	The Temptations, "Cloud Nine"	The Isley Brothers, "It's Your Thing"
Country Song	John Hartford, "Gentle on My Mind"	Bobby Russell, "Little Green Apples"	Shel Silverstein, "A Boy Named Sue"
Country Vocal, Female	Tammy Wynette, "I Don't Wanna Play House"	Jeannie C. Riley, "Harper Valley P.T.A."	Tammy Wynette, "Stand By Your Man"
Country Vocal, Male	Glen Campbell, "Gentle on My Mind"	Johnny Cash, "Folsom Prison Blues"	Johnny Cash, "A Boy Named Sue"
Country Performance, Duo or Group with Vocal	Johnny Cash and June Carter, "Jackson"	Flatt & Scruggs, "Foggy Mountain Breakdown"	Waylon Jennings & The Kimberlys, "MacArthur Park"
Jazz, Group	Cannonball Adderley Quintet, *Mercy, Mercy, Mercy*	Bill Evans Trio, *Bill Evans at the Montreux Jazz Festival*	Wes Montgomery, *Willow Weep For Me*
Jazz, Big Band/ Large Ensemble Performance	Duke Ellington, *Far East Suite*	Duke Ellington, *And His Mother Called Him Bill*	Quincy Jones, "Walking in Space"
Gospel Performance, Duo, Group, Choir or Chorus	Porter Wagoner & The Blackwood Bros. Quartet, *More Grand Old Gospel*	Happy Goodman Family, *The Happy Gospel of the Happy Goodmans*	Porter Wagoner & the Blackwood Bros., *In Gospel Country*
Folk Recording	John Hartford, "Gentle on My Mind"	Judy Collins, "Both Sides Now"	Joni Mitchell, *Clouds*
Cast Show Album	*Cabaret*	*Hair*	*Promises, Promises*
Comedy Recording	Bill Cosby, *Revenge*	Bill Cosby, *To Russell, My Brother, Whom I Slept With*	Bill Cosby, *The Best of Bill Cosby*
Classical Album	Pierre Boulez, conductor, Orchestra and Chorus of Paris National Opera (Solos: Berry, Strauss, Uhl, Doench), *Berg: Wozzeck;* Leonard Berstein, conductor, London Symphony, *Mahler: Symphony No. 8 in E Flat Major ("Symphony of a Thousand")*	—	Walter Carlos, *Switched-On Bach*
Classical Orchestral Performance	Igor Stravinsky, conductor, Columbia Symphony, *Stravinsky: Firebird & Petrouchka Suites*	Pierre Boulez, conductor, New Philharmonic Orchestra, *Boulez Conducts Debussy*	Pierre Boulez, conductor, Cleveland Orchestra, *Boulez Conducts Debussy, Vol. 2: "Images Pour Orchestre"*
Opera Recording	Pierre Boulez, conductor, Orchestra and Chorus of Paris National Opera (Solos: Berry, Strauss, Uhl, Doench), *Berg: Wozzeck*	Erich Leinsdorf, conductor, New Philharmonic Orchestra and Ambrosian Opera Chorus (Soloists: Price, Troyanos, Raskin, Milnes, Shirley, Flagello), *Mozart: Cosi fan tutte*	Herbert von Karajan, conductor, Berlin Philharmonic (Soloists: Thomas, Stewart, Stolze, Dernesch, Keleman, Dominguez, Gayer, Ridderbusch), *Wagner: Siegfried*
Chamber Music Performance	Ravi Shankar and Yehudi Menuhin, *West Meets East*	E. Power Biggs with Edward Tarr Brass Ensemble and Gabrieli Consort, Vittorio Negri, conductor, *Gabrieli: Canzoni for Brass, Winds, Strings & Organ*	The Philadelphia, Cleveland, and Chicago Brass Ensembles, *Gabrieli: Antiphonal Music of Gabrieli (Canzoni for Brass Choirs)*

	1970	1971	1972
Record of the Year	Simon & Garfunkel, "Bridge Over Troubled Water"	Carole King, "It's Too Late"	Roberta Flack, "The First Time Ever I Saw Your Face"
Album of the Year	Simon & Garfunkel, *Bridge Over Troubled Water*	Carole King, *Tapestry*	George Harrison and Friends (Ravi Shankar, Bob Dylan, Leon Russell, Ringo Starr, Billy Preston, Eric Clapton, Klaus Voorman, others), *The Concert for Bangla Desh*
Song of the Year	Paul Simon, "Bridge Over Troubled Water"	Carole King, "You've Got a Friend"	Ewan MacColl, "The First Time Ever I Saw Your Face"
Pop Vocal, Female	Dionne Warwick, "I'll Never Fall In Love Again"	Carole King, "Tapestry"	Helen Reddy, "I Am Woman"
Pop Vocal, Male	Ray Stevens, "Everything Is Beautiful"	James Taylor, "You've Got a Friend"	Nilsson, "Without You"
New Artist	The Carpenters	Carly Simon	America
Pop Vocal, Duo or Group with Vocal	Carpenters, "Close to You"	Carpenters, *Carpenters*	Roberta Flack and Donny Hathaway, "Where Is the Love"
Rhythm and Blues Song	Ronald Dunbar, General Johnson, "Patches"	Bill Withers, "Ain't No Sunshine"	Barrett Strong and Norman Whitfield, "Papa Was a Rolling Stone"
R&B Vocal, Female	Aretha Franklin, "Don't Play That Song"	Aretha Franklin, "Bridge Over Troubled Water"	Aretha Franklin, "Young, Gifted & Black"
R&B Vocal, Male	B.B. King, "The Thrill Is Gone"	Lou Rawls, "A Natural Man"	Billy Paul, "Me and Mrs. Jones"
R&B Duo or Group with Vocal	The Delfonics, "Didn't I (Blow Your Mind This Time)"	Ike and Tina Turner, "Proud Mary"	The Temptations, "Papa Was a Rolling Stone"
Country Song	Marty Robbins, "My Woman, My Woman, My Wife"	Kris Kristofferson, "Help Me Make It Through the Night"	Ben Peters, "Kiss an Angel Good Mornin'"
Country Vocal, Female	Lynn Anderson, "Rose Garden"	Sammi Smith, "Help Me Make It Through the Night"	Donna Fargo, "Happiest Girl in the Whole U.S.A."
Country Vocal, Male	Ray Price, "For the Good Times"	Jerry Reed, "When You're Hot, You're Hot"	Charley Pride, *Charley Pride Sings Heart Songs*
Country Performance, Duo or Group with Vocal	Johnny Cash and June Carpenter, "If I Were a Carpenter"	Conway Twitty and Loretta Lynn, "After the Fire Is Gone"	The Statler Brothers, "Class of '57"
Traditional Blues Recording	T-Bone Walker, "Good Feelin'"	Muddy Waters, *They Call Me Muddy Waters*	Muddy Waters, *The London Muddy Waters Session*
Jazz, Soloist	—	Bill Evans, *The Bill Evans Album*	Gary Burton, *Alone at Last*
Jazz, Group	Bill Evans, *Alone*	Bill Evans Trio, *The Bill Evans Album*	Freddie Hubbard, *First Light*
Jazz, Big Band/ Large Ensemble Performance	Miles Davis, *Bitches Brew*	Duke Ellington, *New Orleans Suite*	Duke Ellington, *Togo Brava Suite*
Gospel Performance, Duo, Group, Choir or Chorus	Oak Ridge Boys, "Talk About the Good Times"	Charley Pride, "Let Me Live"	Blackwood Brothers, *L-O-V-E*
Cast Show Album	*Company*	*Godspell*	*Don't Bother Me I Can't Cope*
Comedy Recording	Flip Wilson, *The Devil Made Me Buy This Dress*	Lily Tomlin, *This Is a Recording*	George Carlin, *FM & AM*

	1970	1971	1972
Classical Album	Colin Davis, conductor, Royal Opera House Orchestra and Chorus (Solos: Vickers, Veasey Lindholm), *Berlioz: Les Troyens*, Philips	Vladimir Horowitz, *Horowitz Plays Rachmaninoff*	Georg Solti, conductor, Chicago Symphony, Vienna Boys Choir, Vienna State Opera Chorus, Vienna Singverein Chorus and soloists, *Mahler: Symphony No. 8 in E Flat Major (Symphony of a Thousand)*
Classical Orchestral Performance	Pierre Boulez, conductor, Cleveland Orchestra, *Stravinsky: Le Sacre du printemps*	Carlo Maria Giulini, conductor, Chicago Symphony, *Mahler: Symphony No. 1 in D Major*	Georg Solti, conductor, Chicago Symphony, *Mahler: Symphony No. 7 in E Minor*
Opera Recording	Colin Davis, conductor, Royal Opera House Orchestra and Chorus (Solos: Vickers, Veasey, Lindholm), *Berlioz: Les Troyens*	Erich Leinsdorf, conductor, London Symphony and John Alldis Choir (Solos: Price, Domingo, Milnes, Bumbry, Raimondi), *Verdi: Aïda*	Colin Davis, conductor, BBC Symphony/Chorus of Covent Garden (Solos: Gedda, Eda-Pierre, Soyer, Berbie), *Berlioz: Benvenuto Cellini*
Chamber Music Performance	Eugene Istomin, Isaac Stern, Leonard Rose, *Beethoven: The Complete Piano Trios*	Juilliard Quartet, *Debussy: Quartet in G Minor/Ravel: Quartet in F Major*	Julian Bream and John Williams, *Julian & John*

	1973	1974	1975
Record of the Year	Roberta Flack, "Killing Me Softly with His Song"	Olivia Newton-John, "I Honestly Love You"	Captain & Tennille, "Love Will Keep Us Together"
Album of the Year	Stevie Wonder, *Innervisions*	Stevie Wonder, *Fulfillingness' First Finale*	Paul Simon, *Still Crazy After All These Years*
Song of the Year	Norman Gimbel and Charles Fox, "Killing Me Softly with His Song"	Marilyn and Alan Bergman, Marvin Hamlisch, "The Way We Were"	Stephen Sondheim, "Send In the Clowns"
Pop Vocal, Female	Roberta Flack, "Killing Me Softly with His Song"	Olivia Newton-John, "I Honestly Love You"	Janis Ian, "At Seventeen"
Pop Vocal, Male	Stevie Wonder, "You Are the Sunshine of My Life"	Stevie Wonder, *Fulfillingness' First Finale*	Paul Simon, *Still Crazy After All These Years*
New Artist	Bette Midler	Marvin Hamlisch	Natalie Cole
Pop Vocal, Duo or Group with Vocal	Gladys Knight & The Pips, "Neither One of Us (Wants To Be the First To Say Goodbye)"	Paul McCartney & Wings, "Band on the Run"	Eagles, "Lyin' Eyes"
Rhythm and Blues Song	Stevie Wonder, "Superstition"	Stevie Wonder, "Living for the City"	H. W. Casey, Richard Finch, Willie Clarke, and Betty Wright, "Where Is the Love"
R&B Vocal, Female	Aretha Franklin, "Master of Eyes"	Aretha Franklin, "Ain't Nothing Like the Real Thing"	Natalie Cole, "This Will Be"
R&B Vocal, Male	Stevie Wonder, "Superstition"	Stevie Wonder, "Boogie On Reggae Woman"	Ray Charles, "Living for the City"

	1973	1974	1975
R&B Duo or Group with Vocal	Gladys Knight & The Pips, "Midnight Train to Georgia"	Rufus, "Tell Me Something Good"	Earth, Wind & Fire, "Shining Star"
Country Song	Kenny O'Dell, "Behind Closed Doors"	Norris Wilson and Bill Sherrill, "A Very Special Love Song"	Chips Moman and Larry Butler, "(Hey Won't You Play) Another Somebody Done Somebody Wrong Song"
Country Vocal, Female	Olivia Newton-John, "Let Me Be There"	Anne Murray, "Love Song"	Linda Ronstadt, "I Can't Help It (If I'm Still in Love with You)"
Country Vocal, Male	Charlie Rich, "Behind Closed Doors"	Ronnie Milsap, "Please Don't Tell Me How the Story Ends"	Willie Nelson, "Blue Eyes Crying in the Rain"
Country Performance, Duo or Group with Vocal	Kris Kristofferson and Rita Coolidge, "From the Bottle to the Bottom"	The Pointer Sisters, "Fairytale"	Kris Kristofferson and Rita Coolidge, "Lover Please"
Traditional Blues Recording	Doc Watson, *Then and Now*	Doc and Merle Watson, *Two Days in November*	Muddy Waters, *The Muddy Waters Woodstock Album*
Jazz, Soloist	Art Tatum, *God Is in the House*	Charlie Parker, *First Recordings!*	Dizzy Gillespie, *Oscar Peterson and Dizzy Gillespie*
Jazz, Group	Supersax, *Supersax Plays Bird*	Oscar Peterson, Joe Pass, and Niels Pedersen, *The Trio*	Return to Forever featuring Chick Corea, *No Mystery*
Jazz, Big Band/ Large Ensemble Performance	Woody Herman, *Giant Steps*	Woody Herman, *Thundering Herd*	Phil Woods with Michel Legrand & His Orchestra, *Images*
Cast Show Album	*A Little Night Music*	*Raisin*	*The Wiz*
Comedy Recording	Cheech & Chong, *Los Cochinos*	Richard Pryor, *That Nigger's Crazy*	Richard Pryor, *Is It Something I Said?*
Classical Album	Pierre Boulez, conductor, New York Philharmonic, *Bartók: Concerto for Orchestra*	Georg Solti, conductor, Chicago Symphony, *Berlioz: Symphonie Fantastique*	Georg Solti, conductor, Chicago Symphony, *Beethoven: Symphonies (9) Complete*
Classical Orchestral Performance	Pierre Boulez, conductor, New York Philharmonic, *Bartók: Concerto for Orchestra*	Georg Solti, conductor, Chicago Symphony, *Berlioz: Symphonie Fantastique*	Pierre Boulez, conductor, New York Philharmonic, *Ravel: Daphnis et Chloë*
Opera Recording	Leonard Bernstein, conductor, Metropolitan Opera Orchestra and Manhattan Opera Chorus (Solos: Horne, McCracken, Maliponte, Krause), *Bizet: Carmen*	Georg Solti, conductor, London Philharmonic (Soloists: Caballé, Domingo, Milnes, Blegen, Raimondi), *Puccini: La Bohème*	Colin Davis, conductor, Royal Opera House, Covent Garden (Solos: Caballé, Baker, Gedda, Ganzarolli, Van Allen, Cotrubas), *Mozart: Cosi fan tutte*
Chamber Music Performance	Gunther Schuller and New England Ragtime Ensemble, *Joplin: The Red Back Book*	Artur Rubinstein, Henryk Szeryng, and Pierre Fournier, *Brahms: Trios (complete)/Schumann: Trio No. 1 in D Minor*	Artur Rubinstein, Henryk Szeryng, and Pierre Fournier, *Shubert: Trios Nos. 1 in B Flat Major Op. 99 & 2 in E Flat Major Op. 100*

	1976	1977	1978
Record of the Year	George Benson, "This Masquerade"	Eagles, "Hotel California"	Billy Joel, "Just the Way You Are"
Album of the Year	Stevie Wonder, *Songs in the Key of Life*	Fleetwood Mac, *Rumours*	The Bee Gees and others, *Saturday Night Fever*
Song of the Year	Bruce Johnston, "I Write the Songs"	Joe Brooks, "You Light Up My Life"; Barbra Streisand, "Love Theme from *A Star Is Born* (Evergreen)"	Billy Joel, "Just the Way You Are"
(Pop) Vocal, Female	Linda Ronstadt, *Hasten Down the Wind*	Barbra Streisand, "Love Theme from *A Star Is Born* (Evergreen)"	Anne Murray, "You Needed Me"
(Pop) Vocal, Male	Stevie Wonder, *Songs in the Key of Life*	James Taylor, "Handy Man"	Barry Manilow, "Copacabana (At the Copa)"
New Artist	Starland Vocal Band	Debby Boone	A Taste of Honey
Pop Vocal, Duo or Group with Vocal	Chicago, "If You Leave Me Now"	The Bee Gees, "How Deep Is Your Love"	The Bee Gees, *Saturday Night Fever*
Rhythm and Blues Song	Boz Scaggs and David Paich, "Lowdown"	Leo Sayer and Vini Poncia, "You Make Me Feel Like Dancing"	Paul Jabara, "Last Dance"
R&B Vocal, Female	Natalie Cole, "Sophisticated Lady (She's a Different Lady)"	Thelma Houston, "Don't Leave Me This Way"	Donna Summer, "Last Dance"
R&B Vocal, Male	Stevie Wonder, "I Wish"	Lou Rawls, *Unmistakably Lou*	George Benson, "On Broadway"
R&B Duo or Group with Vocal	Marilyn McCoo and Billy Davis, Jr., "You Don't Have To Be a Star (To Be in My Show)"	Emotions, "Best of My Love"	Earth, Wind & Fire, "All 'n All"
Country Song	Larry Gatlin, "Broken Lady"	Richard Leigh, "Don't It Make My Brown Eyes Blue"	Don Schlitz, "The Gambler"
Country Vocal, Female	Emmylou Harris, *Elite Hotel*	Crystal Gayle, "Don't It Make My Brown Eyes Blue"	Dolly Parton, *Here You Come Again*
Country Vocal, Male	Ronnie Milsap, "(I'm a) Stand by My Woman Man"	Kenny Rogers, "Lucille"	Willie Nelson, "Georgia on My Mind"
Country Performance, Duo or Group with Vocal	Amazing Rhythm Aces, "The End Is Not in Sight (The Cowboy Tune)"	The Kendalls, "Heaven's Just a Sin Away"	Waylon Jennings and Willie Nelson, "Mamas Don't Let Your Babies Grow Up To Be Cowboys"
Ethnic or Traditional Recording	John Hartford, *Mark Twang*	Muddy Waters, *Hard Again*	Muddy Waters, *I'm Ready*
Jazz, Soloist	Count Basie, *Basie & Zoot*	Oscar Peterson, *The Giants*	Oscar Peterson, *Montreux '77, Oscar Peterson Jam*
Jazz, Group	Chick Corea, *The Leprechaun*	Phil Woods, *The Phil Woods Six—Live from the Showboat*	Chick Corea, *Friends*
Jazz, Big Band/ Large Ensemble Performance	Duke Ellington, *The Ellington Suites*	Count Basie & His Orchestra, *Prime Time*	Thad Jones and Mel Lewis, *Live in Munich*
Cast Show Album	*Bubbling Brown Sugar*	*Annie*	*Ain't Misbehavin'*
Comedy Recording	Richard Pryor, *Bicentennial Nigger*	Steve Martin, *Let's Get Small*	Steve Martin, *A Wild and Crazy Guy*
Classical Album	Artur Rubinstein with Daniel Barenboim, conductor, London Philharmonic, *Beethoven: The Five Piano Concertos*	Leonard Bernstein, Vladimir Horowitz, Isaac Stern, Mstislav Rostropovich, Dietrich Fischer-Dieskau, Yehudi Menuhin, Lyndon Woodside, *Concert of the Century* (recorded live at Carnegie Hall May 18, 1976)	Itzhak Perlman with Carlo Maria Giulini, conductor, Chicago Symphony, *Brahms: Concerto for Violin in D Major*

	1976	1977	1978
Classical Orchestral Performance	Georg Solti, conductor, Chicago Symphony, *Strauss: Also Sprach Zarathustra*	Carlo Maria Giulini, conductor, Chicago Symphony, *Mahler: Symphony No. 9 in D Major*	Herbert von Karajan, conductor, Berlin Philharmonic, *Beethoven: Symphonies (9) Complete*
Opera Recording	Lorin Maazel conductor, Cleveland Orchestra and Chorus (Solos: Mitchell, White), *Gershwin: Porgy & Bess*	John De Main, conductor, Houston Grand Opera Production (Solos: Albert, Dale, Smith, Shakesnider, Lane, Brice, Smalls), *Gershwin: Porgy & Bess*	Julius Rudel, conductor, New York City Opera Orchestra and Chorus (Solos: Sills, Titus), *Lehar: The Merry Widow*
Chamber Music Performance	David Munrow, conductor, The Early Music Consort of London, *The Art of Courtly Love*	Juilliard Quartet, *Schöenberg: Quartets for Strings*	Itzhak Perlman and Vladimir Ashkenazy, *Beethoven: Sonatas for Violin and Piano*

	1979	1980	1981
Record of the Year	The Doobie Brothers, "What a Fool Believes"	Christopher Cross, "Sailing"	Kim Carnes, "Bette Davis Eyes"
Album of the Year	Billy Joel, *52nd Street*	Christopher Cross, *Christopher Cross*	John Lennon and Yoko Ono, *Double Fantasy*
Song of the Year	Kenny Loggins and Michael McDonald, "What a Fool Believes"	Christopher Cross, "Sailing"	Donna Weiss and Jackie DeShannon, "Bette Davis Eyes"
Pop Vocal, Female	Dionne Warwick, "I'll Never Love This Way Again"	Bette Midler, "The Rose"	Lena Horne, *Lena Horne: The Lady and Her Music Live on Broadway*
Pop Vocal, Male	Billy Joel, *52nd Street*	Kenny Loggins, "This Is It"	Al Jarreau, *Breakin' Away*
Rock Vocal, Female	Donna Summer, "Hot Stuff"	Pat Benatar, *Crimes of Passion*	Pat Benatar, "Fire and Ice"
Rock Vocal, Male	Bob Dylan, "Gotta Serve Somebody"	Billy Joel, *Glass Houses*	Rick Springfield, "Jessie's Girl"
New Artist	Rickie Lee Jones	Christopher Cross	Sheena Easton
Pop Vocal, Duo or Group with Vocal	The Doobie Brothers, *Minute by Minute*	Barbra Streisand and Barry Gibb, "Guilty"	The Manhattan Transfer, "Boy from New York City"
Rock Performance, Duo or Group with Vocal	The Eagles, "Heartache Tonight"	Bob Seger & The Silver Bullet Band, *Against the Wind*	The Police, "Don't Stand So Close to Me"
Rhythm and Blues Song	David Foster, Jay Graydon, and Bill Champlin, "After the Love Has Gone"	Reggie Lucas and James Mtume, "Never Knew Love Like This Before"	Bill Withers, William Salter, and Ralph MacDonald, "Just the Two of Us"
R&B Vocal, Female	Dionne Warwick, "Déjà Vu"	Stephanie Mills, "Never Knew Love Like This Before"	Aretha Franklin, "Hold on, I'm Comin'"
R&B Vocal, Male	Michael Jackson, "Don't Stop 'Till You Get Enough"	George Benson, *Give Me the Night*	James Ingram, "One Hundred Ways"
R&B Duo or Group with Vocal	Earth, Wind & Fire, "After the Love Has Gone"	Manhattans, "Shining Star"	Quincy Jones, *The Dude*
Country Song	Bob Morrison and Debbie Hupp, "You Decorated My Life"	Willie Nelson, "On the Road Again"	Dolly Parton, "9 to 5"
Country Vocal, Female	Emmylou Harris, *Blue Kentucky Girl*	Anne Murray, "Could I Have This Dance"	Dolly Parton, "9 to 5"
Country Vocal, Male	Kenny Rogers, "The Gambler"	George Jones, "He Stopped Loving Her Today"	Ronnie Milsap, "(There's) No Gettin' Over Me"
Country Performance, Duo or Group with Vocal	Charlie Daniels Band, "The Devil Went Down to Georgia"	Roy Orbison and Emmylou Harris, "That Lovin' You Feelin' Again"	Oak Ridge Boys, "Elvira"
Ethnic or Traditional Recording	Muddy Waters, *Muddy "Mississippi" Waters Live*	Dr. Isaiah Ross, Maxwell Street Jimmy, Big Joe William, Son House, Rev. Robert Wilkins, Little Brother Montgomery, and Sunnyland Slim, *Rare Blues*	B. B. King, *There Must Be a Better World Somewhere*
Jazz Vocal, Female	Ella Fitzgerald, *Fine and Mellow*	Ella Fitzgerald, *A Perfect Match/Ella & Basie*	Ella Fitzgerald, *Digital III at Montreux*
Jazz Vocal, Male	—	George Benson, "Moody's Mood"	Al Jarreau, "Blue Rondo à la Turk"
Jazz, Soloist	Oscar Peterson, *Jousts*	Bill Evans, *I Will Say Goodbye*	John Coltrane, *Bye, Bye Blackbird*

	1979	1980	1981
Jazz, Group	Gary Burton and Chick Corea, *Duet*	Bill Evans, *We Will Meet Again*	Chick Corea and Gary Burton, *Chick Corea and Gary Burton in Concert, Zurich, October 28, 1979*
Jazz, Big Band/ Large Ensemble Performance	Duke Ellington, *At Fargo, 1940 Live*	Count Basie and Orchestra, *On the Road*	Gerry Mulligan & His Orchestra, *Walk on the Water*
Jazz Fusion Performance, Vocal or Instrumental	Weather Report, *8:30*	Manhattan Transfer, "Birdland"	Grover Washington Jr., *Winelight*
Cast Show Album	*Sweeney Todd*	*Evita*	*Lena Horne: The Lady and Her Music Live on Broadway*
Comedy Recording	Robin Williams, *Reality . . . What a Concept*	Rodney Dangerfield, *No Respect*	Richard Pryor, *Rev. Du Rite*
Classical Album	Georg Solti, conductor, Chicago Symphony Orchestra, *Brahms: Symphonies (4) Complete*	Pierre Boulez, conductor, Orchestre d l'Opera de Paris (Solos: Stratas, Minton, Mazura, Toni Blankenheim), *Berg: Lulu*	Georg Solti, conductor, Chicago Symphony Orchestra and Chorus (Solos: Buchanan, Zakai), *Mahler: Symphony No. 2 in C Minor*
Classical Orchestral Performance	Georg Solti, conductor, Chicago Symphony, *Brahms: Symphonies (4) Complete*	Georg Solti, conductor, Chicago Symphony, *Bruckner: Symphony No. 6 in A Major*	Georg Solti, conductor, Chicago Symphony, *Mahler: Symphony No. 2 in C Minor*
Opera Recording	Colin Davis, conductor, Orchestra and Chorus of the Royal Opera House, Covent Garden (Solos: Vickers, Harper, Summers), *Britten: Peter Grimes*	Pierre Boulez, conductor, Orchestre d l'Opera de Paris (Solos: Stratas, Minton, Mazura, Blankenheim), *Berg: Lulu*	Charles Mackerras, conductor, Vienna Philharmonic (Solos: Zahradnicek, Zitek, Zidek), *Janacek: From the House of the Dead*
Chamber Music Performance	Dennis Russel Davies, conductor, St. Paul Chamber Orchestra, *Copland: Appalachian Spring*	Itzhak Perlman and Pinchas Zukerman, *Music for Two Violins (Moszkowski: Suite for Two Violins/Shostakovich: Duets/ Prokofiev: Sonata for Two Violins)*	Itzhak Perlman, Lynn Harrell, and Vladimir Ashkenazy, *Tchaikovsky: Piano Trio in A Minor*

GRAMMY AWARDS

	1982	1983	1984
Record of the Year	Toto, "Rosanna"	Michael Jackson, "Beat It"	Tina Turner, "What's Love Got To Do with It"
Album of the Year	Toto, *Toto IV*	Michael Jackson, *Thriller*	Lionel Richie, *Can't Slow Down*
Song of the Year	Johnny Christopher, Mark James, and Wayne Thompson, "Always on My Mind"	Sting, "Every Breath You Take"	Graham Lyle and Terry Britten, "What's Love Got To Do with It"
Pop Vocal, Female	Melissa Manchester, "You Should Hear How She Talks About You"	Irene Cara, "Flashdance . . . What a Feeling"	Tina Turner, "What's Love got To Do with It"
Pop Vocal, Male	Lionel Richie, "Truly"	Michael Jackson, *Thriller*	Phil Collins, "Against All Odds (Take a Look at Me Now)"
Rock Vocal, Female	Pat Benatar, "Shadows of the Night"	Pat Benatar, "Love Is a Battlefield"	Tina Turner, "Better Be Good to Me"
Rock Vocal, Male	John Cougar, "Hurts So Good"	Michael Jackson, "Beat It"	Bruce Springsteen, "Dancing in the Dark"
New Artist	Men at Work	Culture Club	Cyndi Lauper
Pop Vocal, Duo or Group with Vocal	Joe Cocker and Jennifer Warnes, "Up Where We Belong"	The Police, "Every Breath You Take"	Pointer Sisters, "Jump (For My Love)"
Rock Performance, Duo or Group with Vocal	Survivor, "Eye of the Tiger"	The Police, *Synchronicity*	Prince and the Revolution, *Purple Rain*
Rhythm and Blues Song	Jay Graydon, Steve Lukather, and Bill Champlin, "Turn Your Love Around"	Michael Jackson, "Billie Jean"	Prince, "I Feel for You"
R&B Vocal, Female	Jennifer Holliday, "And I Am Telling You I'm Not Going"	Chaka Khan, *Chaka Khan*	Chaka Khan, "I Feel for You"
R&B Vocal, Male	Marvin Gaye, "Sexual Healing"	Michael Jackson, "Billie Jean"	Billy Ocean, "Caribbean Queen (No More Love on the Run)"
R&B Duo or Group with Vocal	Dazz Band,"Let It Whip"; Earth, Wind & Fire, "Wanna Be With You"	Rufus & Chaka Khan, "Ain't Nobody"	James Ingram and Michael McDonald, "Yah Mo B There"
Country Song	Johnny Christopher, Wayne Thompson, and Mark James, "Always on My Mind"	Mike Reed, "Stranger in My House"	Steve Goodman, "City of New Orleans"
Country Vocal, Female	Juice Newton, "Break It To Me Gently"	Anne Murray, "A Little Good News"	Emmylou Harris, "In My Dreams"
Country Vocal, Male	Willie Nelson, "Always on My Mind"	Lee Greenwood, "I.O.U."	Merle Haggard, "That's the Way Love Goes"
Country Performance, Group	Alabama, *Mountain Music*	Alabama, *The Closer You Get*	The Judds, "Mama He's Crazy"
Traditional Blues Recording	Clarence "Gatemouth" Brown, *Alright Again*	B. B. King, *Blues 'n' Jazz*	John Hammond, Stevie Ray Vaughan & Double Trouble, Sugar Blue, Koko Taylor & The Blues Machine, Luther "Guitar Junior" Johnson, and J. B. Hutto & The New Hawks, *Blues Explosion*
Reggae Recording	—	—	Black Uhuru, *Anthem*
Jazz Vocal, Female	Sarah Vaughan, *Gershwin Live!*	Ella Fitzgerald, *The Best Is Yet to Come*	—
Jazz Vocal, Male	Mel Torme, *An Evening with George Shearing and Mel Torme*	Mel Torme, *Top Drawer*	Joe Williams, *Nothin' but the Blues*
Jazz, Soloist	Miles Davis, *We Want Miles*	Wynton Marsalis, *Think of One*	Wynton Marsalis, *Hot House Flowers*

	1982	1983	1984
Jazz, Group	Phil Woods Quartet, *"More" Live*	The Phil Woods Quartet, *At the Vanguard*	Art Blakey & The Jazz Messengers, *New York Scene*
Jazz, Big Band/ Large Ensemble Performance	Count Basie & His Orchestra, *Warm Breeze*	Rob McConnell and The Boss Brass, *All in Good Time*	Count Basie & His Orchestra, *88 Basie Street*
Jazz Fusion Performance	Pat Metheny Group, *Offramp*	Pat Metheny Group, *Travels*	Pat Metheny Group, *First Circle*
Gospel Performance, Female	—	Amy Grant, "Ageless Medley"	Amy Grant, "Angels"
Gospel Performance, Male	—	Russ Taff, *Walls of Glass*	Michael W. Smith, *Michael W. Smith 2*
Gospel Performance, Duo, Group, Choir or Chorus	—	Sandi Patti and Larnelle Harris, "More Than Wonderful"	Debby Boone and Phil Driscoll, "Keep the Flame Burning"
Ethnic or Traditional Folk Recording	Queen Ida, *Queen Ida and the Bon Temps Zydeco Band on Tour*	Clifton Chenier & His Red Hot Louisiana Band, *I'm Here*	Elizabeth Cotten, *Elizabeth Cotten Live!*
Cast Show Album	*Dreamgirls*	*Cats (Complete Original Broadway Cast Recording)*	*Sunday in the Park with George*
Comedy Recording	Richard Pryor, *Live on the Sunset Strip*	Eddie Murphy, *Eddie Murphy: Comedian*	"Weird Al" Yankovic, "Eat It"
Classical Album	Glenn Gould, *Bach: The Goldberg Variations*	Georg Solti, conductor, Chicago Symphony, *Mahler: Symphony No. 9 in D Major*	Neville Marriner, conductor, Academy of St. Martin-in-the-Fields/Ambrosian Opera Chorus/Choristers of Westminster Abbey, *Amadeus (Original Soundtrack)*
Classical Orchestral Performance	James Levine, conductor, Chicago Symphony, *Mahler: Symphony No. 7 in E Minor (Song of the Night)*	Georg Solti, conductor, Chicago Symphony, *Mahler: Symphony No. 9 in D Major*	Leonard Slatkin, conductor, St. Louis Symphony, *Prokofiev: Symphony No. 5 in B Flat, Op. 100*
Opera Recording	Pierre Boulez, conductor, Bayreuth Festival Orchestra (Solos: Jones, Altmeyer, Wenkel, Hofmann, Jung, Jerusalem, Zednik, McIntyre, Salminen, Becht), *Wagner: Der Ring des Nibelungen*	James Levine, conductor, The Metropolitan Opera Orchestra and Chorus (Solos: Stratas, Domingo, MacNeill), *Verdi: La Traviata*	Lorin Maazel, conductor, Orchestre National de France/Choeurs et Maitrise de Radio France (Solos: Johnson, Esham, Domingo, Raimondi), *Bizet: Carmen*
Chamber Music Performance	Richard Stoltzman and Richard Goode, *Brahms: The Sonatas for Clarinet & Piano, Op. 120*	Mstislav Rostropovich and Rudolph Serkin, *Brahms: Sonata for Cello & Piano in E Minor, Op. 38 & Sonata in F Major, Op. 99*	Juilliard String Quartet, *Beethoven: The Late String Quartets*

	1985	1986	1987
Record of the Year	USA for Africa, "We Are the World"	Steve Winwood, "Higher Love"	Paul Simon, "Graceland"
Album of the Year	Phil Collins, *No Jacket Required*	Paul Simon, *Graceland*	U2, *The Joshua Tree*
Song of the Year	Michael Jackson and Lionel Richie, "We Are the World"	Burt Bacharach and Carole Bayer Sager, "That's What Friends Are For"	James Horner, Barry Mann, and Cynthia Weil, "Somewhere Out There"
Pop Vocal, Female	Whitney Houston, "Saving All My Love for You"	Barbra Streisand, *The Broadway Album*	Whitney Houston, "I Wanna Dance with Somebody (Who Loves Me)"
Pop Vocal, Male	Phil Collins, *No Jacket Required*	Steve Winwood, "Higher Love"	Sting, *Bring on the Night*
Rock Vocal, Female	Tina Turner, "One of the Living"	Tina Turner, "Back Where You Started"	—
Rock Vocal, Male	Don Henley, "The Boys of Summer"	Robert Palmer, "Addicted to Love"	Bruce Springsteen, *Tunnel of Love*
New Artist	Sade	Bruce Hornsby and the Range	Jody Watley
Pop Vocal, Duo or Group with Vocal	USA for Africa, "We Are the World"	Dionne Warwick & Friends featuring Elton John, Gladys Knight and Stevie Wonder, "That's What Friends Are For"	Bill Medley and Jennifer Warnes, "(I've Had) The Time of My Life"
Rock Performance, Group	Dire Straits, "Money for Nothing"	Eurythmics, "Missionary Man"	U2, *The Joshua Tree*
New Age Recording	—	Andreas Vollenweider, *Down to the Moon*	Yusef Lateef, *Yusef Lateef's Little Symphony*
Rhythm and Blues Song	Narada Michael Walden and Jeffrey Cohen, "Freeway of Love"	Anita Baker, Louis A. Johnson, Gary Bias, "Sweet Love"	Bill Withers, "Lean on Me"
R&B Vocal, Female	Aretha Franklin, "Freeway of Love"	Anita Baker, *Rapture*	Aretha Franklin, *Aretha*
R&B Vocal, Male	Stevie Wonder, *In Square Circle*	James Brown, "Living in America"	Smokey Robinson, "Just To See Her"
R&B Duo or Group with Vocal	Commodores, "Nightshift"	Prince & The Revolution, "Kiss"	Aretha Franklin and George Michael, "I Knew You Were Waiting (For Me)"
Country Song	Jimmy L. Webb, "Highwayman"	Jamie O'Hara, "Grandpa (Tell Me 'Bout the Good Old Days)"	Paul Overstreet and Don Schlitz, *Forever and Ever, Amen*
Country Vocal, Female	Rosanne Cash, "I Don't Know Why You Don't Want Me"	Reba McEntire, "Whoever's in New England"	K. T. Oslin, "80's Ladies"
Country Vocal, Male	Ronnie Milsap, "Lost in the Fifties Tonight (In the Still of the Night)"	Ronnie Milsap, *Lost in the Fifties Tonight*	Randy Travis, *Always & Forever*
Country Performance, Duo or Group with Vocal	The Judds, *Why Not Me*	The Judds, "Grandpa (Tell Me 'Bout the Good Old Days)"	Dolly Parton, Linda Ronstadt, and Emmylou Harris, *Trio*
Country Vocal, Collaboration	—	—	Ronnie Milsap and Kenny Rogers, "Make No Mistake, She's Mine"
Traditional Blues Recording	B. B. King, "My Guitar Sings the Blues"	Albert Collins, Robert Cray, and Johnny Copeland, *Showdown*	Professor Longhair, *Houseparty New Orleans Style*
Contemporary Blues	—	—	Robert Cray Band, *Strong Persuader*

	1985	1986	1987
Reggae Recording	Jimmy Cliff, *Cliff Hanger*	Steel Pulse, *Babylon the Bandit*	Peter Tosh, *No Nuclear War*
Jazz Vocal, Female	Cleo Laine, *Cleo at Carnegie, the 10th Anniversary Concert*	Diane Schuur, *Timeless*	Diane Schuur, *Diane Schuur & The Count Basie Orchestra*
Jazz Vocal, Male	Jon Hendricks and Bobby McFerrin, "Another Night in Tunisia"	Bobby McFerrin, " 'Round Midnight"	Bobby McFerrin, "What Is This Thing Called Love"
Jazz, Soloist	Wynton Marsalis, *Black Codes from the Underground*	Miles Davis, *Tutu*	Dexter Gordon, *The Other Side of 'Round Midnight*
Jazz, Group	Wynton Marsalis Group, *Black Codes from the Underground*	Wynton Marsalis, *J Mood*	Wynton Marsalis, *Marsalis Standard Time, Volume I*
Jazz, Big Band/ Large Ensemble Performance	John Barry and Bob Wilber, *The Cotton Club*	The Tonight Show Band with Doc Severinsen, *The Tonight Show Band with Doc Severinsen*	The Duke Ellington Orchestra, conducted by Mercer Ellington, *Digital Duke*
Jazz Fusion Performance, Vocal or Instrumental	David Sanborn, *Straight to the Heart*	Bob James and David Sanborn, *Double Vision*	Pat Metheny Group, *Still Life (Talking)*
Gospel Performance, Female	Amy Grant, *Unguarded*	Sandi Patti, *Morning Like This*	Deniece Williams, "I Believe in You"
Gospel Performance, Male	Larnelle Harris, "How Excellent Is Thy Name"	Philip Bailey, *Triumph*	Larnelle Harris, *The Father Hath Provided*
Gospel Performance, Duo, Group, Choir or Chorus	Larnelle Harris and Sandi Patti, "I've Just Seen Jesus"	Sandi Patti & Deniece Williams, "They Say"	Mylon LeFevre & Broken Heart, *Crack the Sky*
Traditional Folk Recording	Rockin' Sidney, "My Toot Toot"	Doc Watson, *Riding the Midnight Train*	Ladysmith Black Mambazo, *Shaka Zulu*
Contemporary Folk Recording	—	Arlo Guthrie, John Hartford, Richie Havens, Bonnie Koloc, Nitty Gritty Dirt Band, John Prine and others, *Tribute to Steve Goodman*	Steve Goodman, *Unfinished Business*
Cast Show Album	*West Side Story*	*Follies in Concert*	*Les Misérables*
Comedy Recording	Whoopi Goldberg, *Whoopi Goldberg*	Bill Cosby, *Those of You With or Without Children, You'll Understand*	Robin Williams, *A Night at the Met*
Classical Album	Robert Shaw, conductor, Atlanta Symphony Orchestra and Chorus, (Solo: Aler) *Berlioz: Requiem*	Vladimir Horowitz, *Horowitz: The Studio Recordings, New York 1985*	Vladimir Horowitz, *Horowitz in Moscow*
Classical Orchestral Performance	Robert Shaw, conductor, Atlanta Symphony Orchestra, *Fauré: Pelléas et Mélisande*	Georg Solti, conductor, Chicago Symphony Orchestra, *Liszt: A Faust Symphony*	Georg Solti, conductor, Chicago Symphony Orchestra, *Beethoven: Symphony No. 9 in D Minor*
Opera Recording	Georg Solti, conductor, Chicago Symphony Orchestra and Chorus (Solos: Mazura, Langridge), *Schoenberg: Moses und Aaron*	John Mauceri, conductor, New York City Opera Chorus and Orchestra (Solos: Mills, Clement, Eisler, Lankston, Castle, Reeve, Harrold, Billings), *Bernstein: Candide*	James Levine, conductor, Vienna Philharmonic (Solos: Tomowa-Sintow, Battle, Baltsa, Lakes, Prey), *R. Strauss: Ariadne auf Naxos*
Chamber Music Performance	Emanuel Ax and Yo-Yo Ma, *Brahms: Cello and Piano Sonatas in E Major & F Major*	Yo-Yo Ma and Emanuel Ax, *Beethoven: Cello & Piano Sonata No. 4 in C and Variations*	Itzhak Perlman, Lynn Harrell, and Vladimir Ashkenazy, *Beethoven: The Complete Piano Trios*

	1988	1989	1990
Record of the Year	Bobby McFerrin, "Don't Worry, Be Happy"	Bette Midler, "Wind Beneath My Wings"	Phil Collins, "Another Day in Paradise"
Album of the Year	George Michael, *Faith*	Bonnie Raitt, *Nick of Time*	Quincy Jones, *Back on the Block*
Song of the Year	Bobby McFerrin, "Don't Worry, Be Happy"	Larry Henley and Jeff Silbar, "Wind Beneath My Wings"	Julie Gold, "From a Distance"
Pop Vocal, Female	Tracy Chapman, "Fast Car"	Bonnie Raitt, "Nick of Time"	Mariah Carey, "Vision of Love"
Pop Vocal, Male	Bobby McFerrin, "Don't Worry, Be Happy"	Michael Bolton, "How Am I Supposed to Live Without You"	Roy Orbison, "Oh Pretty Woman"
Rock Vocal, Female	Tina Turner, *Tina Live in Europe*	Bonnie Raitt, *Nick of Time*	Alannah Myles, "Black Velvet"
Rock Vocal, Male	Robert Palmer, "Simply Irresistible"	Don Henley, *The End of the Innocence*	Eric Clapton, "Bad Love"
New Artist	Tracy Chapman	No award (Milli Vanilli)	Mariah Carey
Pop Vocal, Duo or Group with Vocal	The Manhattan Transfer, *Brasil*	Linda Ronstadt and Aaron Neville, "Don't Know Much"	Linda Ronstadt with Aaron Neville, "All My Life"
Rock Performance, Duo or Group with Vocal	U2, "Desire"	Traveling Wilburys, *Traveling Wilburys, Volume I*	Aerosmith, "Janie's Got a Gun"
New Age Recording	Shadowfax, *Folksongs for a Nuclear Village*	Peter Gabriel, *Passion (Music from The Last Temptation of Christ)*	Mark Isham, *Mark Isham*
Hard Rock	Jethro Tull, *Crest of a Knave*	Living Colour, "Cult of Personality"	Living Colour, *Time's Up*
Metal	—	Metallica, "One"	Metallica, "Stone Cold Crazy"
Alternative	—	—	Sinéad O'Connor, *I Do Not Want What I Haven't Got*
Rap Performance, Solo	D.J. Jazzy Jeff & The Fresh Prince, "Parents Just Don't Understand"	Young MC, "Bust a Move"	M.C. Hammer, "U Can't Touch This"
Rap Performance by a Duo or Group	—	—	Ice-T, Melle Mel, Big Daddy Kane, Kool Moe Dee, and Quincy Jones III, "Back on the Block"
Rhythm and Blues Song	Anita Baker, Skip Scarborough, and Randy Holland, "Giving You the Best That I Got"	Kenny Gamble and Leon Huff, "If You Don't Know Me By Now"	Rick James, Alonzo Mille, and M.C. Hammer, "U Can't Touch This"
R&B Vocal, Female	Anita Baker, "Giving You the Best That I Got"	Anita Baker, *Giving You the Best That I Got*	Anita Baker, *Compositions*
R&B Vocal, Male	Terence Trent D'Arby, *Introducing the Hardline According to Terence Trent D'Arby*	Bobby Brown, "Every Little Step"	Luther Vandross, "Here and Now"
R&B Duo or Group with Vocal	Gladys Knight & The Pips, "Love Overboard"	Soul II Soul featuring Caron Wheeler, "Back to Life"	Ray Charles and Chaka Khan, "I'll Be Good to You"
Country Song	K. T. Oslin, "Hold Me"	Rodney Crowell, "After All This Time"	Jon Vezner and Don Henry, "Where've You Been"

	1988	1989	1990
Country Vocal, Female	K. T. Oslin, "Hold Me"	k.d. lang, *Absolute Torch and Twang*	Kathy Mattea, "Where've You Been"
Country Vocal, Male	Randy Travis, *Old 8 x 10*	Lyle Lovett, *Lyle Lovett and His Large Band*	Vince Gill, "When I Call Your Name"
Country Performance, Duo or Group with Vocal	The Judds, "Give a Little Love"	The Nitty Gritty Dirt Band, *Will the Circle Be Unbroken, Volume 2*	The Kentucky Headhunters, *Pickin' on Nashville*
Country Vocal, Collaboration	Roy Orbison and k.d. lang, "Crying"	Hank Williams Jr. and Hank Williams Sr., "There's a Tear in My Beer"	Chet Atkins and Mark Knopfler, "Poor Boy Blues"
Traditional Blues Recording	Willie Dixon, *Hidden Charms*	John Lee Hooker and Bonnie Raitt, "I'm in the Mood"	B.B. King, *Live at San Quentin*
Contemporary Blues	The Robert Cray Band, "Don't Be Afraid of the Dark"	Stevie Ray Vaughan & Double Trouble, *In Step*	The Vaughan Brothers, *Family Style*
Reggae Recording	Ziggy Marley & The Melody Makers, *Conscious Party*	Ziggy Marley & The Melody Makers, *One Bright Day*	Bunny Wailer, *Time Will Tell—A Tribute to Bob Marley*
Jazz Vocal, Female	Betty Carter, *Look What I Got!*	Ruth Brown, *Blues on Broadway*	Ella Fitzgerald, *All That Jazz*
Jazz Vocal, Male	Bobby McFerrin, "Brothers"	Harry Connick Jr., *When Harry Met Sally . . .*	Harry Connick Jr., *We Are in Love*
Jazz, Soloist	Michael Brecker, *Don't Try This at Home*	Miles Davis, *Aura*	Oscar Peterson, *The Legendary Oscar Peterson Trio Live at the Blue Note*
Jazz, Group	McCoy Tyner, Pharaoh Sanders, David Murray, Cecil McBee, and Roy Haynes, *Blues for Coltrane: A Tribute to John Coltrane*	Chick Corea Akoustic Band, *Chick Corea Akoustic Band*	Oscar Peterson Trio, *The Legendary Oscar Peterson Trio Live at the Blue Note*
Jazz, Big Band/ Large Ensemble Performance	Gil Evans & The Monday Night Orchestra, *Bud & Bird*	Miles Davis, *Aura*	George Benson featuring the Count Basie Orchestra; Frank Foster, conductor, "Basie's Bag"
Jazz Fusion Performance, Vocal or Instrumental	Yellowjackets, *Politics*	Pat Metheny Group, *Letter from Home*	Quincy Jones, "Birdland"
Gospel Performance, Female	Amy Grant, *Lead Me On*	CeCe Winans, "Don't Cry"	—
Gospel Performance, Male	Larnelle Harris, *Christmas*	BeBe Winans, "Meantime"	—
Gospel Performance, Duo, Group, Choir or Chorus	The Winans, *The Winans Live at Carnegie Hall*	Take 6, "The Savior Is Waiting"	Rev. James Cleveland, *Having Church*
Traditional Folk Recording	Various artists, *Folkways: A Vision Shared—A Tribute to Woody Guthrie and Leadbelly*	Bulgarian State Female Vocal Choir, *Le Mystère des voix bulgares, Vol. II*	Doc Watson, *On Praying Ground*
Contemporary Folk Recording	Tracy Chapman, *Tracy Chapman*	Indigo Girls, *Indigo Girls*	Shawn Colvin, *Steady On*
Cast Show Album	*Into the Woods*	*Jerome Robbins' Broadway*	*Les Misérables, The Complete Symphonic Recording*

	1988	1989	1990
Comedy Recording	Robin Williams, *Good Morning, Vietnam*	"Professor" Peter Schickele, *P.D.Q. Bach: 1712 Overture and Other Musical Assaults*	"Professor" Peter Schickele, *P.D.Q. Bach: Oedipus Tex & Other Choral Calamities*
Classical Album	Robert Shaw, conductor, Atlanta Symphony Orchestra and Chorus, *Verdi: Requiem and Operatic Choruses*	Emerson String Quartet, *Bartók: 6 String Quartets*	Leonard Bernstein, conductor, New York Philharmonic, *Ives: Symphony No. 2 (and Three Short Works)*
Classical Orchestral Performance	Robert Shaw, conductor, Atlanta Symphony Orchestra, *Rorem: String Symphony;* Louis Lane, conductor, Atlanta Symphony Orchestra, *Sunday Morning* and *Eagles*	Leonard Bernstein, conductor, New York Philharmonic, *Mahler: Sym. No. 3 in D Min.*	Leonard Bernstein, conductor, Chicago Symphony, *Shostakovich: Symphonies No. 1, Op. 10, and No. 7, Op. 60*
Opera Recording	Georg Solti, conductor, Vienna State Opera Choir & Vienna Philharmonic (Solos: Domingo, Norman, Randova, Nimsgern, Sotin, Fischer-Dieskau), *Wagner: Lohengrin*	James Levine, conductor, Metropolitan Opera Orchestra (Solos: Lakes, Moll, Morris, Norman, Behrens, Ludwig), *Wagner: Die Walküre*	James Levine, conductor, Metropolitan Opera Orchestra (Solos: Morris, Ludwig, Jerusalem, Wlaschiha, Moll, Zednik, Rootering), *Wagner: Das Rheingold*
Chamber Music Performance	Murray Perahia and Sir Georg Solti, pianos, with David Corkhill and Evelyn Glennie, percussion, *Bartók: Sonata for Two Pianos and Percussion; Brahms: Variations on a Theme by Joseph Haydn for Two Pianos*	Emerson String Quartet, *Bartók: 6 String Quartets*	Itzhak Perlman, violin; Daniel Barenboim, piano, *Brahms: The Three Violin Sonatas*

	1991	1992	1993
Record of the Year	Natalie Cole (with Nat "King" Cole), "Unforgettable"	Eric Clapton, "Tears in Heaven"	Whitney Houston, "I Will Always Love You"
Album of the Year	Natalie Cole, *Unforgettable*	Eric Clapton, *Unplugged*	Whitney Houston and others, *The Bodyguard—Original Soundtrack*
Song of the Year	Irving Gordon, "Unforgettable"	Eric Clapton and Will Jennings, "Tears in Heaven"	Alan Menken and Tim Rice, "A Whole New World"
Pop Vocal, Female	Bonnie Raitt, "Something to Talk About"	k.d. lang, "Constant Craving"	Whitney Houston, "I Will Always Love You"
Pop Vocal, Male	Michael Bolton, "When a Man Loves a Woman"	Eric Clapton, "Tears in Heaven"	Sting, "If I Ever Lose My Faith In You"
Rock Vocal, Female	Bonnie Raitt, *Luck of the Draw*	Melissa Etheridge, "Ain't It Heavy"	—
Rock Vocal, Male	—	Eric Clapton, *Tears in Heaven*	—
Rock Song/ Rock Vocal Performance, Solo	Sting, "Soul Cages"	Eric Clapton and Jim Gordon, *Layla*	Meat Loaf, "I'd Do Anything for Love (But I Won't Do That)"
New Artist	Mark Cohn	Arrested Development	Toni Braxton
Pop Vocal, Duo or Group with Vocal	R.E.M., "Losing My Religion"	Celine Dion and Peabo Bryson, "Beauty and the Beast"	Peabo Bryson and Regina Belle, "A Whole New World"
Rock Performance, Duo or Group with Vocal	Bonnie Raitt and Delbert McClinton, "Good Man, Good Woman"	U2, *Achtung Baby*	Aerosmith, "Living on the Edge"
New Age Recording	Mannheim Steamroller, *Fresh Aire 7*	Enya, *Sheperd Moons*	Paul Winter Consort, *Spanish Angel*
Hard Rock	Van Halen, *For Unlawful Carnal Knowledge*	Red Hot Chili Peppers, "Give It Away"	Stone Temple Pilots, "Plush"
Metal	Metallica, *Metallica*	Nine Inch Nails, "Wish"	Ozzy Ozbourne, "I Don't Want To Change the World"
Alternative	R.E.M., *Out of Time*	Tom Waits, *Bone Machine*	U2, *Zooropa*
Rap Performance, Solo	L.L. Cool J, "Mama Said Knock You Out"	Sir Mix-A-Lot, "Baby Got Back"	Dr. Dre, "Let Me Ride"
Rap Performance by a Duo or Group	D.J. Jazzy Jeff & The Fresh Prince, "Summertime"	Arrested Development, "Tennessee"	Digable Planets, "Rebirth of Slick (Cool Like Dat)"
Rhythm and Blues Song	Luther Vandross, Marcus Miller, and Teddy Vann, "Power of Love/Love Power"	L.A. Reid, Babyface, and Daryl Simmons, "End of the Road"	Janet Jackson, James Harris III, and Terry Lewis, "That's the Way Love Goes"
R&B Vocal, Female	Patti LaBelle, *Burnin'*; Lisa Fischer; "How Can I Ease the Pain"	Chaka Khan, *The Woman I Am*	Toni Braxton, "Another Sad Love Song"
R&B Vocal, Male	Luther Vandross, *Power of Love*	Al Jarreau, *Heaven and Earth*	Ray Charles, "A Song For You"
R&B Duo or Group with Vocal	Boyz II Men, *Cooleyhigh harmony*	Boyz II Men, "End of the Road"	Sade, "No Ordinary Love"
Country Song	Naomi Judd, John Jarvis, and Paul Overstreet, "Love Can Build a Bridge"	Vince Gill and John Barlow Jarvis, "I Still Believe in You"	Lucinda Williams, "Passionate Kisses"
Country Vocal, Female	Mary-Chapin Carpenter, "Down at the Twist and Shout"	Mary-Chapin Carpenter, "I Feel Lucky"	Mary-Chapin Carpenter, "Passionate Kisses"
Country Vocal, Male	Garth Brooks, *Ropin' the Wind*	Vince Gill, *I Still Believe in You*	Dwight Yoakam, "Ain't That Lonely Yet"

	1991	1992	1993
Country Performance, Duo or Group with Vocal	The Judds, "Love Can Build a Bridge"	Emmylou Harris & The Nash Ramblers, *Emmylou Harris & The Nash Ramblers at the Ryman*	Brooks & Dunn, "Hard Workin' Man"
Country Vocal, Collaboration	Steve Wariner, Ricky Skaggs, and Vince Gill, "Restless"	Travis Tritt and Marty Stuart, "The Whiskey Ain't Workin' "	Reba McEntire and Linda Davis, "Does He Love You"
Traditional Blues Recording	B. B. King, *Live at the Apollo*	Dr. John, *Goin' Back to New Orleans*	B.B. King, *Blues Summit*
Contemporary Blues	Buddy Guy, *Damn Right, I've Got the Blues*	Stevie Ray Vaughan & Double Trouble, *The Sky Is Crying*	Buddy Guy, *Feels Like Rain*
Reggae Recording	Shabba Ranks, *As Raw as Ever*	Shabba Ranks, *X-tra Naked*	Inner Circle, *Bad Boys*
Jazz, Soloist	Stan Getz, "I Remember You"	Joe Henderson, "Lush Life"	Joe Henderson, "Miles Ahead"
Jazz, Group	Oscar Peterson Trio, *Saturday Night at the Blue Note*	Branford Marsalis, *I Heard You Twice the First Time*	Joe Henderson, *So Near, So Far (Musings for Miles)*
Jazz, Big Band/ Large Ensemble Performance	Dizzy Gillespie & The United Nation Orchestra, *Live at the Royal Festival Hall*	McCoy Tyner Big Band, *The Turning Point*	Miles Davis and Quincy Jones, *Miles and Quincy Live at Montreaux*
Jazz Fusion Performance	—	Pat Metheny, *Secret Story*	—
Gospel Performance, Duo, Group, Choir or Chorus	Sounds of Blackness, *The Evolution of Gospel*	Music & Arts Seminar Mass Choir; Edwin Hawkins, choir director, *Edwin Hawkins Music & Arts Seminar Mass Choir: Recorded Live in Los Angeles*	Brooklyn Tabernacle Choir; Carol Cymbala, choir director, *Live . . . We Come Rejoicing*
Traditional Folk Recording	Ken Burns and John Colby, *The Civil War*	The Chieftains, *Another Country*	The Chieftains, *The Celtic Harp*
Contemporary Folk Recording	John Prine, *The Missing Years*	The Chieftains, *An Irish Evening Live at the Grand Opera House, Belfast*	Nanci Griffith, *Other Voices/Other Rooms*
Cast Show Album	*The Will Rogers Follies*	*Guys and Dolls*	*The Who's Tommy*
Comedy Recording	"Professor" Peter Schickele, *P.D.Q. Bach: WTWP Classical Talkity-Talk Radio*	"Professor" Peter Schickele, *P.D.Q. Bach: Music for an Awful Lot of Winds & Percussion*	George Carlin, *Jammin' in New York*
Classical Album	Leonard Bernstein, conductor, London Symphony Orchestra (Solos: Hadley, Anderson, Ludwig, Green, Gedda, Jones), *Bernstein: Candide*	Leonard Bernstein, conductor, Berlin Philharmonic Orchestra, *Mahler: Symphony No. 9*	Pierre Boulez, conductor, Chicago Symphony Orchestra and Chorus; John Alen John Tomlinson, baritone, *Bartók: The Wooden Prince & C*
Classical Orchestral Performance	Daniel Barenboim, conductor, Chicago Symphony Orchestra, *Corigliano: Symphony No. 1*	Leonard Bernstein, conductor, Berlin Philharmonic Orchestra, *Mahler: Symphony No. 9*	Pierre Boulez, conductor, Chicago Symphony, *Bartók: The Wooden Prince*
Opera Recording	James Levine, conductor, Metropolitan Opera Orchestra and Chorus (Solos: Behrens, Studer, Schwarz, Goldberg, Weikl, Wlaschiha, Salminen), *Wagner: Götterdämmerung*	Georg Solti conductor, Vienna Philharmonic (Solos: Domingo, Varady, Van Dam, Behrens, Runkel, Jo), *R. Strauss: Die Frau Ohne Schatten*	John Nelson, conductor, English Chamber Orchestra and Ambrosian Opera Chorus (Solos: Battle, Horne, Ramey, Aler, McNair, Chance, Mackie, Doss); *Handel: Semele*
Chamber Music Performance	Isaac Stern and Jamie Laredo, violins; Yo-Yo Ma, cello; Emanuel Ax, piano, *Brahms: Piano Quartets*	Yo-Yo Ma, cello; Emanuel Ax, piano, *Brahms: Sonatas for Cello & Piano*	Anne-Sophie Mutter, violin, and James Levine, conductor, Chicago Symphony, *Berg: Violoin Concerto/Rihm: Time Chant*

THE COUNTRY MUSIC ASSOCIATION AWARDS

	1967	1968	1969
Entertainer	Eddy Arnold	Glen Campbell	Johnny Cash
Song	Dallas Frazier, "There Goes My Everything"	Bobby Russell, "Honey"	Bob Ferguson, "Carroll County Accident"
Female Vocalist	Loretta Lynn	Tammy Wynette	Tammy Wynette
Male Vocalist	Jack Greene	Glen Campbell	Johnny Cash
Album	Jack Greene, *There Goes My Everything*	Johnny Cash, *Johnny Cash at Folsom Prison*	Johnny Cash, *Johnny Cash at San Quentin Prison*
Single	Jack Greene, "There Goes My Everything"	Jeannie C. Riley, "Harper Valley P.T.A."	Johnny Cash, "A Boy Named Sue"
Vocal Group	The Stoneman Family	Porter Wagoner and Dolly Parton	Johnny Cash and June Carter
Musician	Chet Atkins	Chet Atkins	Chet Atkins

	1970	1971	1972
Entertainer	Merle Haggard	Charley Pride	Loretta Lynn
Song	Kris Kristofferson, "Sunday Morning Coming Down"	Freddie Hart, "Easy Loving"	Freddie Hart, "Easy Loving"
Female Vocalist	Tammy Wynette	Lynn Anderson	Loretta Lynn
Male Vocalist	Merle Haggard	Charley Pride	Charley Pride
Album	Merle Haggard, *Okie from Muskogee*	Ray Price, *I Won't Mention It Again*	Merle Haggard, *Let Me Tell You About a Song*
Single	Merle Haggard, "Okie From Muskogee"	Sammi Smith, "Help Me Make It Through the Night"	Donna Fargo, "The Happiest Girl in the Whole U.S.A."
Vocal Group	The Glaser Brother	The Osborne Brothers	The Statler Brothers
Vocal Duo	Porter Wagoner and Dolly Parton	Porter Wagoner and Dolly Parton	Conway Twitty and Loretta Lynn
Musician	Jerry Reed	Jerry Reed	Charlie McCoy

	1973	1974	1975
Entertainer	Roy Clark	Charlie Rich	John Denver
Song	Kenny O'Dell, "Behind Closed Doors"	Don Wayne, "Country Bumpkin"	John Denver, "Back Home Again"
Female Vocalist	Loretta Lynn	Olivia Newton-John	Dolly Parton
Male Vocalist	Charlie Rich	Ronnie Milsap	Waylon Jennings
Album	Charlie Rich, *Behind Closed Doors*	Charlie Rich, *A Very Special Love Song*	Ronnie Milsap, *A Legend in My Time*
Single	Charlie Rich, "Behind Closed Doors"	Cal Smith, "Country Bumpkin"	Freddy Fender, "Before the Next Teardrop Falls"
Vocal Group	The Statler Brothers	The Statler Brothers	The Statler Brothers
Vocal Duo	Conway Twitty and Loretta Lynn	Conway Twitty and Loretta Lynn	Conway Twitty and Loretta Lynn
Musician	Charlie McCoy	Don Rich	Johnny Gimble

	1976	1977	1978
Entertainer	Mel Tillis	Ronnie Milsap	Dolly Parton
Song	Larry Weiss, "Rhinestone Cowboy"	Roger Bowling & Hal Bynum, "Lucille"	Richard Leigh, "Don't It Make My Brown Eyes Blue"
Female Vocalist	Dolly Parton	Crystal Gayle	Crystal Gayle
Male Vocalist	Ronnie Milsap	Ronnie Milsap	Don Williams
Album	Waylon Jennings, Willie Nelson, Tompall Glaser, Jessi Colter, *Wanted—The Outlaws*	Ronnie Milsap, *Ronnie Milsap Live*	Ronnie Milsap, *It Was Almost Like a Song*
Single	Waylon Jennings & Willie Nelson, "Good Hearted Woman"	Kenny Rogers, "Lucille"	The Kendalls, "Heaven's Just a Sin Away"
Vocal Group	The Statler Brothers	The Statler Brothers	The Oak Ridge Boys
Vocal Duo	Waylon Jennings & Willie Nelson	Jim Ed Brown & Helen Cornelius	Kenny Rogers and Dottie West
Musician	Hargus "Pig" Robbins	Roy Clark	Roy Clark

	1979	1980	1981
Entertainer	Willie Nelson	Barbara Mandrell	Barbara Mandrell
Song	Don Schlitz, "The Gambler"	Bobby Braddock & Curly Putman, "He Stopped Loving Her Today"	Bobby Braddock & Curly Putman, "He Stopped Loving Her Today"
Female Vocalist	Barbara Mandrell	Emmylou Harris	Barbara Mandrell
Male Vocalist	Kenny Rogers	George Jones	George Jones
Album	Kenny Rogers, *The Gambler*	Original Motion Picture Sound-track, *Coal Miner's Daughter*	Don Williams, *I Believe in You*
Single	Charlie Daniels Band, "The Devil Went Down to Georgia"	George Jones, "He Stopped Lov-ing Her Today"	Oak Ridge Boys, "Elvira"
Vocal Group	The Statler Brothers	The Statler Brothers	Alabama
Horizon Award	—	—	Terri Gibbs
Vocal Duo	Kenny Rogers and Dottie West	Moe Bandy and Joe Stampley	David Frizzell and Shelly West
Musician	Charlie Daniels	Roy Clark	Chet Atkins

	1982	1983	1984
Entertainer	Alabama	Alabama	Alabama
Song	Johnny Christopher, Wayne Car-son, Mark James, "Always On My Mind"	Johnny Christopher, Wayne Car-son, Mark James, "Always On My Mind"	Larry Henley, Jeff Silbar, "Wind Beneath My Wings"
Female Vocalist	Janie Fricke	Janie Fricke	Reba McEntire
Male Vocalist	Ricky Skaggs	Lee Greenwood	Lee Greenwood
Album	Willie Nelson, *Always on My Mind*	Alabama, *The Closer You Get*	Anne Murray, *A Little Good News*
Single	Willie Nelson, "Always on My Mind"	John Anderson, "Swingin' "	Anne Murray, "A Little Good News"
Vocal Group	Alabama	Alabama	The Statler Brothers
Horizon Award	Ricky Skaggs	John Anderson	The Judds
Vocal Duo	David Frizzell and Shelly West	Merle Haggard and Willie Nelson	Willie Nelson & Julio Iglesias
Musician	Chet Atkins	Chet Atkins	Chet Atkins

	1985	1986	1987
Entertainer	Ricky Skaggs	Reba McEntire	Hank Williams Jr.
Song	Lee Greenwood, "God Bless the USA"	Paul Overstreet, Don Schlitz, "On the Other Hand"	Paul Overstreet, Don Schlitz, "Forever and Ever, Amen"
Female Vocalist	Reba McEntire	Reba McEntire	Reba McEntire
Male Vocalist	George Strait	George Strait	Randy Travis
Album	George Strait, *Does Fort Worth Ever Cross Your Mind*	Ronnie Milsap, *Lost in the Fifties Tonight*	Randy Travis, *Always and Forever*
Single	The Judds, "Why Not Me"	Dan Seals, "Bop"	Randy Travis, "Forever and Ever, Amen"
Vocal Group	The Judds	The Judds	The Judds
Horizon Award	Sawyer Brown	Randy Travis	Holly Dunn
Vocal Duo	Anne Murray and Dave Loggins	Dan Seals and Marie Osmond	Ricky Skaggs and Sharon White
Musician	Chet Atkins	Johnny Gimble	Johnny Gimble
Music Video	Hank Williams Jr., *All My Rowdy Friends Are Comin' Over Tonight*	George Jones, *Who's Gonna Fill Their Shoes*	Hank Williams Jr., *My Name Is Bocephus*

	1988	1989	1990
Entertainer	Hank Williams Jr.	George Strait	George Strait
Song	K.T. Oslin, "80's Ladies"	Max D. Barnes, Vern Gosdin, "Chiseled in Stone"	Jon Vezner, Don Henry, "Where've You Been"
Female Vocalist	K.T. Oslin	Kathy Mattea	Kathy Mattea
Male Vocalist	Randy Travis	Ricky Van Shelton	Clint Black
Album	Hank Williams Jr., *Born to Boogie*	Nitty Gritty Dirt Band, *Will the Circle Be Unbroken, Vol. II*	Kentucky HeadHunters, *Pickin' on Nashville*
Single	Kathy Mattea, "Eighteen Wheels and a Dozen Roses"	Keith Whitley, "I'm No Stranger to the Rain"	Vince Gill, "When I Call Your Name"
Vocal Group	Highway 101	Highway 101	Kentucky HeadHunters
Vocal Event	Dolly Parton, Emmylou Harris, Linda Ronstadt, *Trio*	Hank Williams Jr., Hank Williams Sr.	Lorrie Morgan, Keith Whitley
Horizon Award	Ricky Van Shelton	Clint Black	Garth Brooks
Vocal Duo	The Judds	The Judds	The Judds
Musician	Chet Atkins	Johnny Gimble	Johnny Gimble
Music Video	—	Hank Williams Jr., Hank Williams Sr., *There's a Tear in My Beer*	Garth Brooks, *The Dance*

	1991	1992	1993
Entertainer of the Year	Garth Brooks	Garth Brooks	Vince Gill
Song of the Year	Vince Gill, Tim DuBois, "When I Call Your Name"	Vince Gill, Max D. Barnes, "Look at Us"	Vince Gill, John Barlow Jarvis, "I Still Believe in You"
Female Vocalist of the Year	Tanya Tucker	Mary-Chapin Carpenter	Mary-Chapin Carpenter
Male Vocalist of the Year	Vince Gill	Vince Gill	Vince Gill
Album of the Year	Garth Brooks, *No Fences*	Garth Brooks, *Ropin' the Wind*	Vince Gill, *I Still Believe in You*
Single of the Year	Garth Brooks, "Friends in Low Places"	Billy Ray Cyrus, "Achy Breaky Heart"	Alan Jackson, "Chattahoochee"
Vocal Group of the Year	Kentucky HeadHunters	Diamond Rio	Diamond Rio
Vocal Event of the Year	Mark O'Connor & The New Nashville Cats (featuring Vince Gill, Ricky Skaggs, and Steve Wariner)	Marty Stuart, Travis Tritt	George Jones with Vince Gill, Mark Chesnutt, Garth Brooks, Travis Tritt, Joe Diffie, Alan Jackson, Pam Tillis, T. Graham Brown, Patty Loveless, Clint Black, *I Don't Need Your Rockin' Chair*
Horizon Award	Travis Tritt	Suzy Bogguss	Mark Chesnutt
Vocal Duo of the Year	The Judds	Brooks & Dunn	Brooks & Dunn
Musician of the Year	Mark O'Connor	Mark O'Connor	Mark O'Connor
Music Video of the Year	Garth Brooks, *The Thunder Rolls*	Alan Jackson, *Midnight in Montgomery*	Alan Jackson, *Chattahoochee*

May 10, 1976 • 50¢
People weekly
TRUMAN CAPOTE
His wicked gossip makes him 'The Tiny Terror'
Business—or funny business? Julia Roberts' night out
People weekly
Julia Roberts and Ethan Hawke
OPRAH'S DIET GURU
Chef Rosie Daley helped TV's weight-loss champ shed 72 lbs. eating low-fat fries and guilt-free desserts (recipes inside!). Says Oprah: 'Rosie changed my life'
Daley's recipe collection is the fastest-selling cookbook ever
Beach-bumming with model Christie Brinkley
People weekly
The Eagles fly solo
...and so does Bruce Jenner
Garfield
America's No. 1 pussonality—a literary lion with six best-sellers at once—launches his TV career
The Fonz on 42nd St.
An expert calls incest the new 'epidemic'
Jimmy Carter's Girl Friday
May 9, 1977 • 60¢
People weekly
ROOTS
Back to Africa with an embattled ALEX HALEY

PAGES

THE HALDEMAN DIARIES

Edited by Stephen Ambrose

What they lack in sensational revelations—there are none—these journals of Nixon White House chief of staff H. R. "Bob" Haldeman make up for in fascinating details of the day-to-day workings of the American political system and the large- and small-minded people who run it. In the diaries Haldeman never tried to lionize his boss, although he never really criticized the president either. Most intriguing are his tales of bickering among Nixon insiders. And Nixon himself comes across as much more compassionate than his public image. Haldeman's meticulous detailing of the array of crises Nixon faced can also only generate sympathy for Nixon—or anyone who occupies the White House.

VISITING MRS. NABOKOV AND OTHER EXCURSIONS

Martin Amis

This first-rate collection of thirty-three essays, travelogues, and interviews has the effect of revealing Amis in a warmer, more humane light than his novels do. The subjects range from Nabokov's late widow to Salman Rushdie (who grants him a poignant interview) and the looking-glass maze of corridors at the Pentagon, where Amis stalks the wizards of nuclear science. But his literary boyhood, his adult life, and his sense of outrage at the buildup of the world's weaponry, all haunt the peripheries, as if this were not a bundle of essays but a stealth autobiography.

MY LIVES

Roseanne Arnold

Roseanne may indeed have twenty separate personalities, as she claims in this, her second autobiography. But only one of them—the vindictive Roseanne—showed up to write it. Packed with more pop psychology than Oprah during sweeps week, *My Lives* reads like the transcript of a hellish therapy session, excoriating everyone whom the star feels turned her into a diva of dysfunction. The biggest bogeyman is her father, whose alleged molestation of young Roseanne is recounted as a recovered memory. Which would be fine if *My Lives* were nearly as funny and moving as Roseanne's highly rated TV show.

COME AS YOU ARE: THE STORY OF NIRVANA

Michael Azerrad

In one of their first meetings, Kurt Cobain and future wife Courtney Love—the most infamous punk couple since Sid and Nancy—expressed their mutual attraction in a unique way. They duked it out. "It was a mating ritual for dysfunctional people," Courtney explained. Azerrad includes that and other great moments in grunge history in this all-warts bio, a fascinating study of Cobain. He dominates the story as he did his band and all who fell into his orbit—save Courtney. With its chronicle of Cobain's struggles to overcome heroin addiction—he began shooting it to relieve chronic stomach pains—the book stands as something of an obituary.

MIDNIGHT IN THE GARDEN OF GOOD AND EVIL

John Berendt

The author became a part-time resident of Savannah in the early '80s and a participant in its complicated and eccentric society. The characters he introduces in this nonfiction work are as colorful as any created in novels. But the heart of the book is the sensational trial involving Savannah's premier citizen, antiques dealer Jim Williams, who is charged with killing his companion/handyman, Danny Hansford, "a walking streak of sex." Berendt has a keen and sympathetic eye, and while the book sometimes drags, his intimate portrait of Savannah is impossible to resist.

WITHOUT A HERO AND OTHER STORIES

T. Coraghessan Boyle

Still smoking from the success of his last novel, *The Road to Wellville,* Boyle once again takes on American culture and excess in this collection of wickedly comical stories. His strange mix of characters includes a would-be astronomer who hires a professional organizer to dispose of his wife's 120 potholders and 600 doilies, and a man who falls for an animal-rights activist and finds himself spray-painting "Meat Is Death" across shrink-wrapped supermarket specials. In Boyle's world anything can happen and usually does. It's worth a visit.

CHARADE

Sandra Brown

Cat Delaney is a soap star whose own life has the dramatic elements of a TV movie of the week. As Brown's suspense tale opens, Cat is awakened in the intensive care unit at a Los Angeles hospital where she has been waiting for a heart transplant. Cat's change of heart is more than literal. She leaves Hollywood, becomes a do-good talk show host, and gets involved with an attractive man. There is only one nuisance: patients who received donor hearts on the day of Cat's own successful surgery are having fatal "accidents." It seems a stalker wants a certain donor's heart stopped, and Cat fears she may be next on his list. And so it goes in this typical Brown page-turner. There are lots of glamorous parties, beautiful people, and steamy sex. Brown has once again hit her mark and created a compelling heroine who is feisty yet feminine.

THANK YOU FOR SMOKING

Christopher Buckley

With near-daily reports of tobacco company cover-ups, Buckley's novel couldn't be more timely. His protagonist, Nick Naylor, chief spokesman for the industry-sponsored Academy of Tobacco Studies, is a master of media manipulation, the sort of job that earns him a death threat—and a bizarre kidnapping. But when Nick escapes, he becomes something of a hero. Buckley's plot is silly and slender; it's his irresistible characters who keep the action rolling. Among them: Naylor's closest friends, Bobby Jay Bliss and Polly Bailey, who pick up their paychecks as flaks for guns and alcohol, respectively. *Bonfire of the Vanities?* Not quite. But almost as good as a smoke.

DIXIE CITY JAM

James Lee Burke

Detective Dave Robicheaux of the New Iberia sheriff's office was a student diving in the waters off Baton Rouge when he saw his first Nazi submarine, a wreck left over from World War II. Nearly fifty years later he's back at sea, hunting for a long-sunken sub and buried treasure; he's also caught in an old-fashioned mob war, squaring off with a crazed neo-Nazi named Will Buchalter. The resulting jambalaya boils out to be the best book in the Robicheaux series. Steeped in passion and intrigue, this book also boasts an ending that will resonate after the last wave of summer rolls to the shore.

THE PALACE THIEF

Ethan Canin

Moral failure is the central territory of Canin's rich new collection of novellas. These are stories of ordinary citizens who stumble into extraordinary circumstances and are unable to rise to the occasion. But Canin shows abundant compassion for his characters—a trait he has honed as a resident at San Francisco General Hospital. Canin's characters stare their failures down. Like parachutists who jump out of planes using faulty chutes, they have time to contemplate the consequences of their actions. Readers of *The Palace Thief* will want to catch these falling characters before they hit the ground.

THE LATE SHIFT

Bill Carter

Comedy may not be pretty, but the campaign waged by Jay Leno and David Letterman for Johnny Carson's *Tonight Show* throne should at least be good for a few yuks. Yet rather than explore how these professional pals dealt with their game of high-stakes musical chairs, Carter concentrates on executive-suite machinations. Though well reported, this is pretty soporific stuff, not helped by the author's tin ear for prose. Worse, Carter portrays Leno as an unreflective Rain Man of one-liners and Letterman as a churlish lone wolf in need of constant petting. Warts-and-all journalism has its place, but surely these guys can't be all warts.

REMEMBER ME

Mary Higgins Clark

A casual observer would conclude that Menley Nichols has a charmed life: a devoted husband, a healthy infant daughter, a career as the author—and now, she has Remember House, an oceanfront Cape Cod haven. But Menley is only beginning to deal with the death of her two-year-old son in a car accident for which she was responsible. The birth of a new baby has left her vulnerable, disoriented, and, her husband suspects, dangerous to their child. A doozy of a ghost story with a contemporary edge, *Remember Me* is filled with the long-ago pain of the house's first mistress, a sea captain's wife who was wrenched from her newborn after being falsely accused of adultery. As the pressure mounts to separate Menley from her baby, she struggles to find the true villain in this parallel, 18th-century betrayal. The book pulls off the gothic mystery brilliantly, harkening back to the best of Daphne du Maurier.

LIFE AFTER GOD

Douglas Coupland

This collection of eight short stories is the third book by Coupland, whose 1991 novel, *Generation X,* christened the age group born between 1961 and 1981. These bare-bones tales catch Xers in varying states of misery. A couple of the book's lost-at-the-strip-mall characters are compelling. But most are cardboard creations whose sole distinguishing quality is self-pity. Fans will hope he ditches the self-indulgent wailings and regains his hip, funny point of view. Growing up, even in the '90s, doesn't have to be this humorless.

DISCLOSURE

Michael Crichton

Tom Sanders is reeling from the unexpected punch of a sexual harassment suit. It's the usual: An office sexual encounter has turned bitter, leading to furious accusations and countercharges. The big difference here is that it's Tom who is claiming harassment. Crichton places his ninth novel in the cauldron of contemporary sexual politics, and the result is bound to ruffle more than a few feathers. But by turning the issue upside down, Crichton offers a fresh and provocative story. The plot is fun, but many readers will yearn for more sociological and psychological probing.

THE WATERWORKS

E.L. Doctorow

The year is 1871. Martin Pemberton, a struggling freelance reporter in New York, has just seen his father passing by in a horse-drawn omnibus. Problem is, Martin's father is dead—or at least, he was until now. Thus begins Doctorow's dark and compelling new novel. The author takes readers into a gothic city whose frightening underworld brings orphans and wealthy old men together in an evil doctor's brilliant but grotesque experiments. Doctorow fans won't be disappointed by the historical richness and modern sensibility of this mysterious tale.

PADDY CLARKE HA HA HA

Roddy Doyle

This 100-yard dash of a novel set in Dublin is told entirely in the voice of a ten-year-old hellion. Paddy Clarke and his mates run wild through the working-class suburb of Barrytown. But while our hero may regard the real world as a boring place, it's apparent that a disturbing drama is unfolding at home. His parents are heading for a split, and anxiety begins to nudge Paddy's carefree daily routine. Readers of Doyle's best-selling "Barrytown Trilogy" *(The Commitments, The Snapper,* and *The Van)* know that the author has a genius for quick-witted, detailed storytelling. *Paddy Clarke,* which won Britain's coveted Booker Prize last fall, is a bittersweet, respectful, and vivid chronicle of youth, which deserves a wide audience.

THE BINGO PALACE

Louise Erdrich

With her complex portrait of life on the Chippewa Reservation in North Dakota, Erdrich has created one of the most compelling accounts of people and place in American fiction today. This, her fourth volume in a series that began with *Love Medicine,* opens with the return to the reservation of Lipsha Morrissey, incurable dreamer and roustabout. His uncle, Lyman Lamartine, gives Lipsha a job sweeping out the bingo hall, a routine brightened by his quest for Shawnee Ray Toose, a dancer who steals his heart. That Shawnee might be Lyman's love, and is in fact the mother of his child, is of no real concern to Lipsha. Erdrich's poetic style graces the darkest moment, bringing a strange beauty to the most passionate and decisive scenes.

DELUSIONS OF GRANDMA

Carrie Fisher

The actress-turned-author is back with another smart, edgy novel in which the angst is spiced with pungent wit. In this offering, the quirky, unpredictable Cora Sharpe, a screenwriter and veteran of numerous star-crossed love affairs, is drawn to a man who is so different from the narcissists and control freaks she usually falls for that she's utterly perplexed. Theirs is an odd, poignant match, especially when she becomes pregnant. Against the backdrop of Ray's steadiness and capacity for settling down—which, alas, turns out not to be contagious—Cora must find her true self so that she can create a real home for her unborn child. Her feistiness and intelligence are endearing, but sometimes she's too smart for her own good. Still, by the time the baby comes, she's shifted into a new gear and the examined life starts being lived more fully.

SLEEP WITH THE ANGELS: A MOTHER CHALLENGES AIDS

Mary Fisher

Fisher captured Americans' hearts, and broke many of them, too, at the Republican National Convention in 1992, when she announced: "I represent [the] AIDS community. . . . Though I am female, and contracted this disease in marriage, I am one with the lonely gay man sheltering a flickering candle from the cold wind of his family's rejection." Fisher, 45, learned that she was HIV positive in 1991 but remains asymptomatic. She could have spent the rest of her life in anonymity, but instead she has taken her gospel on the road, pleading for compassion for the afflicted and sounding the alarm to those still untouched. This collection of excerpts from twenty four of her speeches is both poetic and poignant. Even without Fisher's elegiac delivery, her words have the power to galvanize.

THE FIST OF GOD

Frederick Forsyth

This gripping fictional "inside story" of the Gulf War combines derring-do entertainment with a political message. Forsyth apparently believes the U.S. and its allies were very lucky not to have faced biological, chemical, or nuclear warfare, and he blames them for letting a tin-pot dictator buy access to the technology of mass destruction. But mostly this is a propulsive narrative. Forsyth's lone ranger is British major Mike Martin, dark enough and fluent enough in Arabic to infiltrate occupied Kuwait and wartime Iraq. The author doesn't squander a lot of time on Hollywood-style romance. This is a boy book: action and danger are the kicks.

DECIDER

Dick Francis

Francis makes only minor adjustments to his winning formula in his thirty-second novel. In a nod to the '90s, thirty-five-year-old Lee Morris is married and the caring father of six sons. An architect, Morris happens to hold a few shares in a racetrack that is largely owned by the belligerent Stratton clan. As Morris is drawn into the family infighting over the track's future, he places himself and eventually his children in grave danger. *Decider* doesn't exactly burst out of the starting gate. But champion jockey that he was and canny author that he is, Francis knows just the right moment to smartly apply the crop and punch his story into high gear. A hint of romance, a startling revelation, and a fiery finish leave the reader eager for the next Francis fix.

A FROLIC OF HIS OWN

William Gaddis

Anyone who dreams of their day in court might wisely heed the plight of Oscar Crease, the hero of this book. Plaintiff, defendant, and lay expert in countless suits, Oscar's current obsession is his plagiarism case against the producers of a Hollywood movie that bears a striking resemblance to a play he once wrote. As the legalities start to consume him, the novel becomes less about litigation than about finding a reward for life's misfortunes. Harry, Oscar's brother-in-law, realizes how futile this is. "Justice?" he asks. "You get justice in the next world; in this world you have the law." Oscar, his family, and friends—all of whom are seeking their own reparations—ignore him. Constantly pleading their cases, they listen to each other only when they get interrupted. Gaddis is an inventive, sophisticated writer, and the argument he has prepared for and against Oscar is a dizzy romp of a novel—important, original, and intelligent.

OBSESSION: THE LIVES AND TIMES OF CALVIN KLEIN

Steven Gaines and Sharon Churcher

It's easy to see why Calvin Klein reportedly tried to kill this book. Vividly told and packed with intimate revelations, *Obsession* dynamites the designer's refined image. The fashion giant and his closest friends refused to cooperate, but the authors did their best to let nothing come between them and their Calvin. The book is particularly unflinching when it deals with Klein's personal life. And yet, for all its frankness in depicting Klein's bisexuality, vanity, and drug use, *Obsession* is best when providing a behind-the-scenes look at the fashion world, where power plays, questionable deals, and his own manic perfectionism helped Klein revolutionize the clothing industry. Ultimately, Klein comes across as a singularly gifted man given to indulging his enormous appetite for more.

COLORED PEOPLE

Henry Louis Gates Jr.

The overarching theme of this funny and absorbing memoir of a West Virginia childhood spanning the civil rights years is change from a segregated society to an integrated one. This is a social shift Gates views with gratitude for his own expanded opportunities, yet with deep lament for the loss of separate and, in their way, equal institutions. Gates has been a professor of literature at Yale, Cornell, Duke, and now Harvard, and is one of America's premier intellectuals. Yet he continues to feel the tug of Piedmont, W. Va. The reader can see, hear, and even smell the rickety houses, the muddy streets, the jukebox bars. Better, the reader can see them with Gates's loving eyes and hear them with his keen ear for the distant music of so recent and so utterly vanished a time.

K IS FOR KILLER

Sue Grafton

A distraught mother is convinced that her daughter's death was at the hands of a murderer still on the loose. An incriminating videotape shows the victim to be more than a random target. A weary detective looks at a body and a life that offer little in the way of clues. All these faces and facts come to the attention of P.I. Kinsey Millhone, who is, as always, working on too much coffee and too little sleep. Millhone soon finds herself knee-deep in vice and violence. The eleventh book in this series (*J Is for Judgment, I Is for Innocent*) is by far the eeriest. Grafton exhibits a sharp ear for dialogue, a quarter-horse pace, and her characters are as real as any this side of Elmore Leonard. This mystery series gains strength with each passing letter.

THE CHAMBER

John Grisham

Set on Mississippi's death row, this is a dark and thoughtful tale pulsing with moral uncertainties. When Adam Hall, a young lawyer, fights to take on the pro bono case of Sam Cayhall, 69, it is for purely personal reasons. Cayhall, convicted in a KKK bombing that killed a Mississippi lawyer and his sons, is Adam's grandfather. Arrogant and angry, Hall sets out to save Sam from the gas chamber and to make sense of the Cayhalls' legacy of hatred. But he uncovers more than he wants and softens as he does so. The action of *The Chamber* is in the last-minute legal battle, but the story is in its struggling, tormented, too-human characters.

A MAP OF THE WORLD

Jane Hamilton

Alice Goodwin has always thought that one huge mistake "or else an unfortunate accident" is what it takes for a life to cave in. Her thinking on that score, in this extraordinary story of a family's disintegration, is confirmed one summer day when it is her turn to baby-sit the two daughters of her best friend, Theresa. When the frazzled Alice steals a few minutes to be alone, Theresa's two-year-old wanders off and drowns in the Goodwin's pond. Subsequently, Alice, a nurse at a local elementary school, becomes a target when a deeply troubled child accuses her of sexual abuse. The book tells a haunting story of the loss of innocence, and of shame, guilt, and betrayal. While Hamilton does have a tendency to overwrite, the details observed are astonishingly vivid and moving, making an impressive achievement.

CRIMINAL CONVERSATION

Evan Hunter

Michael Welles, a headline-hungry district attorney, is determined to bring down New York City's powerful crime boss, but the mobster is slick, sinister, and not as vulnerable as he appears. Between the two stands a beautiful woman, married to one man and mistress to the other. This is Hunter's best book since 1974's *Streets of Gold*. During that span he wrote some twenty books under his pen name, Ed McBain, establishing himself as squad leader of the mystery field. *Criminal Conversation* has the same violent intensity as any McBain book and comes equipped with the expected doses of precision plotting, sharp dialogue, and well-defined characters. Plus lots of sex. It is positive proof that under whichever name he writes, Hunter/McBain delivers the goods.

LOVE CAN BUILD A BRIDGE

Naomi Judd, with Bud Schaetzle

Judd's autobiography is full of the dogged optimism and irrepressible cuteness that marked her years as half of one of the most successful duos in country-music history. But to her credit, Naomi isn't afraid to bare the more discordant moments in the struggle that took her from rural Kentucky to country music's Mount Olympus. Naomi says she's telling the family's story to offer readers "living proof that it pays to believe in miracles." Hokey? Definitely. But with her words, as with her music, Naomi has a way of making you believe.

LEADING WITH MY HEART

Virginia Kelley with James Morgan

The family members of presidents often seem to exist for no loftier purpose than to embarrass their relatives. President Clinton's mother, Virginia, who died in January 1994 of breast cancer, would seem to have had enormous faux pas potential. She'd been married five times, was hooked on horse racing, favored boldly colored clothes, and never shrank from speaking her mind. But what emerges here is the portrait of a strong, fun-loving woman who never lost the capacity to learn from her mistakes, and who had dignity, heart, and determination to spare. This posthumously published autobiography is a frank accounting—often funny, often poignant—of Kelley's life.

LOVERS

Judith Krantz

In Judith *(Scruples)* Krantz's eighth novel we meet Gigi Orsini, bright beautiful daughter of film producer Vito Orsini. Gigi is living with director Zach Nevsky, who not only works for Vito but is the brother of her best friend, Sasha, who is soon to marry Vito and become . . . get this: Gigi's stepmother. Will Gigi resolve any of the multiple dysfunctional subplots that characterize this book? Oh, what an obvious plot we weave. But then, who reads Krantz for the story? We read her instead for her delicious name dropping and her unapologetic rich-lady sensibility. Even this mediocre Krantz work has enough of those elements to keep us reading.

PRINCE CHARMING

Wendy Leigh

Leigh can be faulted for not having chosen a more worthy subject than John F. Kennedy Jr., who at 33 is hardly the world's richest subject for a biography. But the author does her best to wring substance out of his life by repeating what a nice and sexy guy Kennedy is in this uncritical recapitulation of his life. Still, Leigh has little fresh to offer. Kennedy family groupies may find the book a handy fantasy feeder. But it is more along the lines of a letter from a loving aunt than a historical document.

W.E.B. DU BOIS: BIOGRAPHY OF A RACE (1868–1919)

David Levering Lewis

W.E.B. Du Bois knew the pain of being black in America at the turn of the century. As a sociologist in the 1890s, he studied African-American life and saw firsthand the results of the Jim Crow laws. Yet as historian Lewis shows in his fine portrait of Du Bois's first fifty years, he never lost faith in democracy. A radical in his time, Du Bois derided the notion of gradual integration and demanded total equality now. He also argued, forcefully, that it was the responsibility of successful blacks to help those less fortunate. Moving from academia to activism, Du Bois eventually cofounded the NAACP. Lewis's scholarly biography shows how moral and creative energies can spring from alienation and repression. It was a lesson that Du Bois taught throughout his life and one that makes his story heroic and compelling.

THE SILENT WOMAN

Janet Malcolm

The silent woman at the center of Malcolm's meditation on the problem of biography is Sylvia Plath, the poet who committed suicide in 1963. Who is the Plath who emerges from the voluminous biographies, essays, and articles written about her? Malcolm implies that no one has got it right. And you wouldn't want to be on Malcolm's bad side. The controversial journalist (*In the Freud Archives, The Journalist and Murderer*) performs character assassination with surgical precision, and often her victims seem to get exactly what they deserve. Only poet Ted Hughes, Plath's husband, escapes in this brilliant exploration of talent, early death, and the carnivorous world of journalism.

UNDUE INFLUENCE

Steve Martini

Martini isn't as fluent as John Grisham, and his grammar and syntax are shaky, but he knows how to grip a reader. The hook here is a hotshot lawyer honoring his dead wife by defending her wayward sister, charged with murdering her ex's new spouse. The author, a former trial attorney, is fascinating on legal strategy. The ending sputters, but even then the obligatory shoot-out and twisty revelations do not seem as silly as they might.

THE CROSSING

Cormac McCarthy

McCarthy is back with his vision of a stark and perilous world, his prose still spare and brilliantly exact. Again his protagonist is a teenage boy, Billy Parham, whose moorings to home and family have been severed. Billy ventures on horseback from his New Mexico border town into pre-World War II Mexico, where he discovers a world that is by turns mystical, comforting, and unspeakably cruel. McCarthy's books are filled with intense observations, but what distinguishes this are the fables within the narrative. In stories told by ancient priests, gypsies, and a blind man, McCarthy takes Aquinian forays into the nature of God and reality. It's hard going, but the effort is rewarded with language that is honest to the bone.

BLACK BETTY
Walter Mosley

This latest caper with Ezekiel "Easy" Rawlins showcases Mosley's reluctant sleuth at his edgy best. The year is 1961 when a white private eye turns up at Easy's door in L.A. with an old photograph of a missing black beauty. So begins the search for "Black Betty," whom Easy knew from Houston. When last seen, Betty had been working as a maid for a powerful Beverly Hills family, but she disappeared after a mysterious death in her employer's family. As always, Mosley's grip on character is compelling, and his plot churns along. It is, however, Easy's somber exhaustion in an era of supposed change that gives this book its special chill.

NOW YOU SEE HER
Whitney Otto

As Kiki Shaw approaches forty, she finds herself disappearing. Strange things are happening: she sometimes sees no reflection in the mirror; a coworker rifles through her office desk as if she were invisible. All of which prompts Kiki to evaluate her life and conclude that "it seems to consist primarily of Other Lives." The relationships of her own mother and friends inspire Kiki's musings as she traces her life back to her childhood. Otto, author of the best-selling *How to Make an American Quilt,* scores again with these stories of engaging women who are struggling for identity in a society that doesn't really "see" them.

WALKING SHADOW
Robert B. Parker

One of the saddest recent experiences for mystery fans has been to watch the steady decline of Robert B. Parker, creator of the ultimate meat-neck detective Spenser. All the old quirks remain—the jokey brooding about machismo and feminism, the stunted sentences, the labored puns—but the poetry has gone out of the storytelling and the kinetic thrill has gone out of the scenes of violence. In Parker's twenty-sixth novel, a stage director is being stalked, then an actor is murdered onstage during a performance. But Parker doesn't get nearly enough mileage out of this setup, and the plot feels convoluted and arbitrary. Better to buy a paperback copy of *Looking for Rachel Wallace* or *The Judas Goat* and remember what Parker used to be.

CROSSING THE RIVER
Caryl Phillips

Sometimes history can be as simple as a voice and a voyage. At least that's the conceit guiding this sensitive novel about the African diaspora, which describes the lives of three siblings—Nash, Martha, and Travis—who are brought to the New World as slaves. Theirs are bittersweet stories, defying the logic of time, which explore how black life evolved beyond slavery. Nash's odyssey, set in the 1820s, unfolds through his letters to his former master. Martha's fate leaves her destitute in the West, an old runaway cut off from her only daughter. Travis becomes an American GI in World War II England. Phillips brilliantly evokes the different historical settings and explores themes of remorse, abandonment, and self-reliance with complexity and understatement.

THE LONGINGS OF WOMEN
Marge Piercy

It's hard to imagine what these three have in common. There's Leila Landsman, a middle-aged writer who finally divorces her philandering husband; Mary Burke, Leila's secretly homeless cleaning lady; and Becky Burgess, a housewife who convinces her teen lover to murder her husband. But in this absorbing novel, Piercy connects these disparate lives, finding that their needs and desires are remarkably similar. The connections are precarious. But Piercy's sense of time and place are extraordinary. Mary, Becky, and Leila are powerful examples of how women fight for their dignity in the most unspeakable circumstances. To repeat that point while keeping the reader eagerly turning pages is Piercy's most notable achievement.

SECRETS OF A SPARROW

Diana Ross

Secrets of a Sparrow is self-serving, self-indulgent nonsense. It's tempting to add "humorless" to the list, but that's not quite accurate. After all, Ross does have a hilarious propensity for drawing parallels between world events and her life. Of course, to hear Ross tell it, every incident in her life has mythic importance. And while no one can argue about the good intentions that propelled her free Central Park concert ten years ago—she wanted to gather corporate funding for a children's playground—she writes about the event as though it were the dismantling of the Berlin Wall.

BRAZIL

John Updike

Much of *Brazil* takes place deep in the Brazilian jungle, with a plot involving characters who magically switch races. Tristao is a black teenager from the slums when he meets fair Isabel on a Rio beach. Soon after their initial coupling, Isabel's rich uncle separates them: in race-conscious Brazil, such mingling of blood and class is unacceptable. But even after the two run off to the jungle, they are forever bound to each other. That their desperate efforts fail to save the lovers will come as no surprise to readers familiar with the legend of the doomed Tristan and Isolde. But then, *Brazil* merely uses the story as a vehicle to explore some typical Updikian themes: the social politics of love, the connection between sex and violence, and the inevitable failure of most social contracts.

FINNEGAN'S WEEK

Joseph Wambaugh

Finbar Finnegan is a San Diego detective who would rather be an actor. Bobbie Ann "Bad Dog" is a Navy command investigator intent on finding 2,000 pairs of stolen boots. Nell Salter is an environmental-crimes cop who wants to put an abusive marriage behind her and a child killer in her gunsights. The three have nothing in common until their respective trails lead to the front door of a disposal company and a drum filled with a supertoxic chemical. The language here is rough and the plot tight, with three lead characters who jump off the page and a secondary crew both frightening and funny. *Finnegan's Week* is all the proof necessary that the former L.A.P.D. police sergeant is still a top cop.

THE HOPE

Herman Wouk

As historical events go, the creation and evolution of the state of Israel seems an exciting candidate for dramatization. Unfortunately, Wouk, a gifted storyteller, has not mixed those ingredients into a successful novel. His fictional characters' interactions with one another and with real historical figures are often clumsy; his military maneuvers are sometimes confusing and frequently opaque. Still, in this work, Wouk has invented plenty of behind-the-scenes machinations that make for frequent page turning—as well as educational reading. To those interested in this sort of Peyton Place of Palestine, this lengthy novel is intermittently edifying and entertaining. For others, *The Hope* is simply hard Wouk.

FICTION AND NONFICTION BESTSELLERS

Publishers Weekly began charting the nation's top-selling hardcover fiction in 1895. The first nonfiction lists were published regularly beginning in 1917, and during World War I the trade magazine even tracked the most popular war books. (The Winston Churchill on the fiction lists, by the way, is an American novelist who died in 1947. His British statesman namesake was, of course, a bestselling and Nobel Prize-winning writer of nonfiction.) These rankings are not based on net sales figures but rather on publishers' reports of copies shipped and billed.

1900

Fiction

1. *To Have and To Hold*, Mary Johnston
2. *Red Pottage*, Mary Cholmondeley
3. *Unleavened Bread*, Robert Grant
4. *The Reign of Law*, James Lane Allen
5. *Eben Holden*, Irving Bacheller
6. *Janice Meredith*, Paul Leicester Ford
7. *The Redemption of David Corson*, Charles Frederic Goss
8. *Richard Carvel*, Winston Churchill
9. *When Knighthood Was in Flower*, Charles Major
10. *Alice of Old Vincennes*, Maurice Thompson

1901

Fiction

1. *The Crisis*, Winston Churchill
2. *Alice of Old Vincennes*, Maurice Thompson
3. *The Helmet of Navarre*, Bertha Runkle
4. *The Right of Way*, Gilbert Parker
5. *Eben Holden*, Irving Bacheller
6. *The Visits of Elizabeth*, Elinor Glyn
7. *The Puppet Crown*, Harold MacGrath
8. *Richard Yea-and-Nay*, Maurice Hewlett
9. *Graustark*, George Barr McCutcheon
10. *D'ri and I*, Irving Bacheller

1902

Fiction

1. *The Virginian*, Owen Wister
2. *Mrs. Wiggs of the Cabbage Patch*, Alice Caldwell Hegan
3. *Dorothy Vernon of Haddon Hall*, Charles Major
4. *The Mississippi Bubble*, Emerson Hough
5. *Audrey*, Mary Johnston
6. *The Right of Way*, Gilbert Parker
7. *The Hound of the Baskervilles*, A. Conan Doyle
8. *The Two Vanrevels*, Booth Tarkington
9. *The Blue Flower*, Henry van Dyke
10. *Sir Richard Calmady*, Lucas Malet

1903

Fiction

1. *Lady Rose's Daughter*, Mary Augusta Ward
2. *Gordon Keith*, Thomas Nelson Page
3. *The Pit*, Frank Norris
4. *Lovey Mary*, Alice Hegan Rice
5. *The Virginian*, Owen Wister
6. *Mrs. Wiggs of the Cabbage Patch*, Alice Hegan Rice
7. *The Mettle of the Pasture*, James Lane Allen
8. *Letters of a Self-Made Merchant to His Son*, George Horace Lorimer
9. *The One Woman*, Thomas Dixon Jr.
10. *The Little Shepherd of Kingdom Come*, John Fox Jr.

1904

Fiction

1. *The Crossing*, Winston Churchill
2. *The Deliverance*, Ellen Glasgow
3. *The Masquerader*, anonymous (Katherine Cecil Thurston)
4. *In the Bishop's Carriage*, Miriam Michelson
5. *Sir Mortimer*, Mary Johnston
6. *Beverly of Graustark*, George Barr McCutcheon
7. *The Little Shepherd of Kingdom Come*, John Fox Jr.
8. *Rebecca of Sunnybrook Farm*, Kate Douglas Wiggin
9. *My Friend Prospero*, Henry Harland
10. *The Silent Places*, Stewart Edward White

1905

Fiction

1. *The Marriage of William Ashe*, Mary Augusta Ward
2. *Sandy*, Alice Hegan Rice
3. *The Garden of Allah*, Robert Hichens
4. *The Clansman*, Thomas Dixon Jr.
5. *Nedra*, George Barr McCutcheon
6. *The Gambler*, Katherine Cecil Thurston
7. *The Masquerader*, anonymous (Katherine Cecil Thurston)
8. *The House of Mirth*, Edith Wharton
9. *The Princess Passes*, C. N. and A. M. Williamson
10. *Rose o' the River*, Kate Douglas Wiggin

1906

Fiction

1. *Coniston*, Winston Churchill
2. *Lady Baltimore*, Owen Wister
3. *The Fighting Chance*, Robert W. Chambers
4. *The House of a Thousand Candles*, Meredith Nicholson
5. *Jane Cable*, George Barr McCutcheon
6. *The Jungle*, Upton Sinclair
7. *The Awakening of Helena Ritchie*, Margaret Deland
8. *The Spoilers*, Rex Beach
9. *The House of Mirth*, Edith Wharton
10. *The Wheel of Life*, Ellen Glasgow

1907

Fiction

1. *The Lady of the Decoration*, Frances Little
2. *The Weavers*, Gilbert Parker
3. *The Port of Missing Men*, Meredith Nicholson
4. *The Shuttle*, Frances Hodgson Burnett
5. *The Brass Bowl*, Louis J. Vance
6. *Satan Sanderson*, Hallie Erminie Rives
7. *The Daughter of Anderson Crow*, George Barr McCutcheon
8. *The Younger Set*, Robert W. Chambers
9. *The Doctor*, Ralph Connor
10. *Half a Rogue*, Harold MacGrath

1908

Fiction

1. *Mr. Crewe's Career*, Winston Churchill
2. *The Barrier*, Rex Beach
3. *The Trail of the Lonesome Pine*, John Fox Jr.

4. *The Lure of the Mask*, Harold MacGrath
5. *The Shuttle*, Frances Hodgson Burnett
6. *Peter*, F. Hopkinson Smith
7. *Lewis Rand*, Mary Johnston
8. *The Black Bag*, Louis J. Vance
9. *The Man from Brodney's*, George Barr McCutcheon
10. *The Weavers*, Gilbert Parker

1909

Fiction

1. *The Inner Shrine*, anonymous (Basil King)
2. *Katrine*, Elinor Macartney Lane
3. *The Silver Horde*, Rex Beach
4. *The Man in Lower Ten*, Mary Roberts Rinehart
5. *The Trail of the Lonesome Pine*, John Fox Jr.
6. *Truxton King*, George Barr McCutcheon
7. *54-40 or Fight*, Emerson Hough
8. *The Goose Girl*, Harold MacGrath
9. *Peter*, F. Hopkinson Smith
10. *Septimus*, William J. Locke

1910

Fiction

1. *The Rosary*, Florence Barclay
2. *A Modern Chronicle*, Winston Churchill
3. *The Wild Olive*, anonymous (Basil King)
4. *Max*, Katherine Cecil Thurston
5. *The Kingdom of Slender Swords*, Hallie Erminie Rives
6. *Simon the Jester*, William J. Locke
7. *Lord Loveland Discovers America*, C. N. and A. M. Williamson
8. *The Window at the White Cat*, Mary Roberts Rinehart
9. *Molly Make-Believe*, Eleanor Abbott
10. *When a Man Marries*, Mary Roberts Rinehart

1911

Fiction

1. *The Broad Highway*, Jeffrey Farnol
2. *The Prodigal Judge*, Vaughan Kester
3. *The Winning of Barbara Worth*, Harold Bell Wright
4. *Queed*, Henry Sydnor Harrison
5. *The Harvester*, Gene Stratton Porter
6. *The Iron Woman*, Margaret Deland
7. *The Long Roll*, Mary Johnston
8. *Molly Make-Believe*, Eleanor Abbott
9. *The Rosary*, Florence Barclay
10. *The Common Law*, Robert W. Chambers

1912

Fiction

1. *The Harvester*, Gene Stratton Porter
2. *The Street Called Straight*, Basil King
3. *Their Yesterdays*, Harold Bell Wright
4. *The Melting of Molly*, Maria Thompson Daviess
5. *A Hoosier Chronicle*, Meredith Nicholson
6. *The Winning of Barbara Worth*, Harold Bell Wright
7. *The Just and the Unjust*, Vaughan Kester
8. *The Net*, Rex Beach
9. *Tante*, Anne Douglas Sedgwick
10. *Fran*, J. Breckenridge Ellis

Nonfiction

1. *The Promised Land*, Mary Antin
2. *The Montessori Method*, Maria Montessori
3. *South America*, James Bryce
4. *A New Conscience and an Ancient Evil*, Jane Addams
5. *Three Plays*, Eugène Brieux
6. *Your United States*, Arnold Bennett
7. *Creative Evolution*, Henri Bergson
8. *How to Live on Twenty-Four Hours a Day*, Arnold Bennett
9. *Woman and Labor*, Olive Schreiner
10. *Mark Twain*, Albert Bigelow Paine

BANNED BESTSELLERS

Books enrich our lives, but to a certain vocal part of the population they can enrage as well. While every year brings what some see as a new threat to the moral fabric of our nation, such as last year's *Daddy's Roommate*, certain classics, from *The Adventures of Huckleberry Finn* to *Catcher in the Rye*, can be counted upon to rouse the ire of someone year after year. The most challenged books in school libraries and curriculums, in the last year and over the last decade, according to People for the American Way:

1982–94

1. *Of Mice and Men*, John Steinbeck
2. *The Catcher in the Rye*, J. D. Salinger
3. *The Chocolate War*, Robert Cormier
4. *Scary Stories To Tell in the Dark*, Alvin Schwartz
5. *The Adventures of Huckleberry Finn*, Mark Twain
6. *Go Ask Alice*, anonymous
7. *I Know Why the Caged Bird Sings*, Maya Angelou
8. *The Witches*, Roald Dahl
9. *The Bridge to Terabithia*, Katherine Paterson
10. *A Light in the Attic*, Shel Silverstein

1993–94

1. *Annie on My Mind*, Nancy Garden
2. *Scary Stories To Tell in the Dark*, Alvin Schwartz
3. *I Know Why the Caged Bird Sings*, Maya Angelou
4. *The Chocolate War*, Robert Cormier
5. *The Adventures of Huckleberry Finn*, Mark Twain
6. *Of Mice and Men*, John Steinbeck
7. *Go Ask Alice*, anonymous
8. *More Scary Stories To Tell in the Dark*, Alvin Schwartz
9. *Scary Stories 3: More Tales to Chill Your Bones*, Alvin Schwartz

1913

Fiction

1. *The Inside of the Cup*, Winston Churchill
2. *V. V.'s Eyes*, Henry Sydnor Harrison
3. *Laddie*, Gene Stratton Porter
4. *The Judgment House*, Sir Gilbert Parker
5. *Heart of the Hills*, John Fox Jr.
6. *The Amateur Gentleman*, Jeffrey Farnol
7. *The Woman Thou Gavest Me*, Hall Caine
8. *Pollyanna*, Eleanor H. Porter
9. *The Valiants of Virginia*, Hallie Erminie Rives
10. *T. Tembarom*, Frances Hodgson Burnett

Nonfiction

1. *Crowds*, Gerald Stanley Lee
2. *Germany and the Germans*, Price Collier
3. *Zone Policeman 88*, Harry A. Franck
4. *The New Freedom*, Woodrow Wilson
5. *South America*, James Bryce
6. *Your United States*, Arnold Bennett
7. *The Promised Land*, Mary Antin
8. *Auction Bridge To-Day*, Milton C. Work
9. *Three Plays*, Eugène Brieux
10. *Psychology and Industrial Efficiency*, Hugo Munsterberg

1914

Fiction

1. *The Eyes of the World*, Harold Bell Wright
2. *Pollyanna*, Eleanor H. Porter
3. *The Inside of the Cup*, Winston Churchill
4. *The Salamander*, Owen Johnson
5. *The Fortunate Youth*, William J. Locke
6. *T. Tembarom*, Frances Hodgson Burnett
7. *Penrod*, Booth Tarkington
8. *Diane of the Green Van*, Leona Dalrymple
9. *The Devil's Garden*, W. B. Maxwell
10. *The Prince of Graustark*, George Barr McCutcheon

1915

Fiction

1. *The Turmoil*, Booth Tarkington
2. *A Far Country*, Winston Churchill
3. *Michael O'Halloran*, Gene Stratton Porter
4. *Pollyanna Grows Up*, Eleanor H. Porter
5. *K*, Mary Roberts Rinehart
6. *Jaffery*, William J. Locke
7. *Felix O'Day*, F. Hopkinson Smith
8. *The Harbor*, Ernest Poole
9. *The Lone Star Ranger*, Zane Grey
10. *Angela's Business*, Henry Sydnor Harrison

1916

Fiction

1. *Seventeen*, Booth Tarkington
2. *When a Man's a Man*, Harold Bell Wright
3. *Just David*, Eleanor H. Porter
4. *Mr. Britling Sees It Through*, H. G. Wells
5. *Life and Gabriella*, Ellen Glasgow
6. *The Real Adventure*, Henry Kitchell Webster
7. *Bars of Iron*, Ethel M. Dell
8. *Nan of Music Mountain*, Frank H. Spearman
9. *Dear Enemy*, Jean Webster
10. *The Heart of Rachael*, Kathleen Norris

1917

Fiction

1. *Mr. Britling Sees It Through*, H. G. Wells
2. *The Light in the Clearing*, Irving Bacheller
3. *The Red Planet*, William J. Locke
4. *The Road to Understanding*, Eleanor H. Porter
5. *Wildfire*, Zane Grey
6. *Christine*, Alice Cholmondeley
7. *In the Wilderness*, Robert S. Hichens
8. *His Family*, Ernest Poole
9. *The Definite Object*, Jeffrey Farnol
10. *The Hundredth Chance*, Ethel M. Dell

General Nonfiction

1. *Rhymes of a Red Cross Man*, Robert W. Service
2. *The Plattsburg Manual*, O. O. Ellis and E. B. Garey
3. *Raymond*, Sir Oliver Lodge
4. *Poems of Alan Seeger*, Alan Seeger
5. *God the Invisible King*, H. G. Wells
6. *Laugh and Live*, Douglas Fairbanks
7. *Better Meals for Less Money*, Mary Green

War Books

1. *The First Hundred Thousand*, Ian Hay
2. *My Home in the Field of Honor*, Frances W. Huard
3. *A Student in Arms*, Donald Hankey
4. *Over the Top*, Arthur Guy Empey
5. *Carry On*, Coningsby Dawson
6. *Getting Together*, Ian Hay
7. *My Second Year of the War*, Frederick Palmer
8. *The Land of Deepening Shadow*, D. Thomas Curtin
9. *Italy, France and Britain at War*, H. G. Wells
10. *The Worn Doorstep*, Margaret Sherwood

1918

Fiction

1. *The U. P. Trail*, Zane Grey
2. *The Tree of Heaven*, May Sinclair
3. *The Amazing Interlude*, Mary Roberts Rinehart
4. *Dere Mable*, Edward Streeter
5. *Oh, Money! Money!*, Eleanor H. Porter
6. *Greatheart*, Ethel M. Dell
7. *The Major*, Ralph Connor
8. *The Pawns Count*, E. Phillips Oppenheim
9. *A Daughter of the Land*, Gene Stratton Porter
10. *Sonia*, Stephen McKenna

General Nonfiction

1. *Rhymes of a Red Cross Man*, Robert W. Service
2. *Treasury of War Poetry*, G. H. Clark
3. *With the Colors*, Everard J. Appleton
4. *Recollections*, Viscount Morley
5. *Laugh and Live*, Douglas Fairbanks
6. *Mark Twain's Letters*, Albert Bigelow Paine, editor
7. *Adventures and Letters of Richard Harding Davis*, Richard Harding Davis
8. *Over Here*, Edgar Guest
9. *Diplomatic Days*, Edith O'Shaughnessy
10. *Poems of Alan Seeger*, Alan Seeger

War Books

1. *My Four Years in Germany*, James W. Gerard
2. *The Glory of the Trenches*, Coningsby Dawson
3. *Over the Top*, Arthur Guy Empey
4. *A Minstrel in France*, Harry Lauder
5. *Private Peat*, Harold R. Peat
6. *Outwitting the Hun*, Lieut. Pat O'Brien
7. *Face to Face with Kaiserism*, James W. Gerard
8. *Carry On*, Coningsby Dawson
9. *Out to Win*, Coningsby Dawson
10. *Under Fire*, Henri Barbusse

1919

Fiction

1. *The Four Horsemen of the Apocalypse*, V. Blasco Ibañez
2. *The Arrow of Gold*, Joseph Conrad
3. *The Desert of Wheat*, Zane Grey
4. *Dangerous Days*, Mary Roberts Rinehart
5. *The Sky Pilot in No Man's Land*, Ralph Connor
6. *The Re-Creation of Brian Kent*, Harold Bell Wright
7. *Dawn*, Gene Stratton Porter
8. *The Tin Soldier*, Temple Bailey
9. *Christopher and Columbus*, "Elizabeth"
10. *In Secret*, Robert W. Chambers

Nonfiction

1. *The Education of Henry Adams*, Henry Adams
2. *The Years Between*, Rudyard Kipling
3. *Belgium*, Brand Whitlock
4. *The Seven Purposes*, Margaret Cameron
5. *In Flanders Fields*, John McCrae
6. *Bolshevism*, John Spargo

1920

Fiction

1. *The Man of the Forest*, Zane Grey
2. *Kindred of the Dust*, Peter B. Kyne
3. *The Re-Creation of Brian Kent*, Harold Bell Wright
4. *The River's End*, James Oliver Curwood
5. *A Man for the Ages*, Irving Bacheller
6. *Mary-Marie*, Eleanor H. Porter
7. *The Portygee*, Joseph C. Lincoln
8. *The Great Impersonation*, E. Phillips Oppenheim
9. *The Lamp in the Desert*, Ethel M. Dell
10. *Harriet and the Piper*, Kathleen Norris

Nonfiction

1. *Now It Can Be Told*, Philip Gibbs
2. *The Economic Consequences of the Peace*, John M. Keynes
3. *Roosevelt's Letters to His Children*, Joseph B. Bishop, editor
4. *Theodore Roosevelt*, William Roscoe Thayer
5. *White Shadows in the South Seas*, Frederick O'Brien
6. *An American Idyll*, Cornelia Stratton Parker

1921

Fiction

1. *Main Street*, Sinclair Lewis
2. *The Brimming Cup*, Dorothy Canfield
3. *The Mysterious Rider*, Zane Grey
4. *The Age of Innocence*, Edith Wharton
5. *The Valley of Silent Men*, James Oliver Curwood
6. *The Sheik*, Edith M. Hull
7. *A Poor Wise Man*, Mary Roberts Rinehart
8. *Her Father's Daughter*, Gene Stratton Porter
9. *The Sisters-in-Law*, Gertrude Atherton
10. *The Kingdom Round the Corner*, Coningsby Dawson

Nonfiction

1. *The Outline of History*, H. G. Wells
2. *White Shadows in the South Seas*, Frederick O'Brien
3. *The Mirrors of Downing Street*, A Gentleman with a Duster (pseudonym for Harold Begbie)
4. *The Autobiography of Margot Asquith*, Margot Asquith
6. *Peace Negotiations*, Robert Lansing

1922

Fiction

1. *If Winter Comes*, A.S.M. Hutchinson
2. *The Sheik*, Edith M. Hull
3. *Gentle Julia*, Booth Tarkington
4. *The Head of the House of Coombe*, Frances Hodgson Burnett
5. *Simon Called Peter*, Robert Keable
6. *The Breaking Point*, Mary Roberts Rinehart
7. *This Freedom*, A.S.M. Hutchinson
8. *Maria Chapdelaine*, Louis Hémon
9. *To the Last Man*, Zane Grey
10. *Babbitt*, Sinclair Lewis (tie)
10. *Helen of the Old House*, Harold Bell Wright (tie)

Nonfiction

1. *The Outline of History*, H. G. Wells
2. *The Story of Mankind*, Hendrik Willem Van Loon
3. *The Americanization of Edward Bok*, Edward Bok
4. *Diet and Health*, Lulu Hunt Peters
5. *The Mind in the Making*, James Harvey Robinson
6. *The Outline of Science*, J. Arthur Thomson
7. *Outwitting Our Nerves*, Josephine A. Jackson and Helen M. Salisbury
8. *Queen Victoria*, Lytton Strachey
9. *Mirrors of Washington*, anonymous (Clinton W. Gilbert)
10. *Painted Windows*, A Gentleman with a Duster (pseudonym for Harold Begbie)

1923

Fiction

1. *Black Oxen*, Gertrude Atherton
2. *His Children's Children*, Arthur Train
3. *The Enchanted April*, "Elizabeth"
4. *Babbitt*, Sinclair Lewis
5. *The Dim Lantern*, Temple Bailey
6. *This Freedom*, A.S.M. Hutchinson
7. *The Mine with the Iron Door*, Harold Bell Wright
8. *The Wanderer of the Wasteland*, Zane Grey
9. *The Sea-Hawk*, Rafael Sabatini
10. *The Breaking Point*, Mary Roberts Rinehart

Nonfiction

1. *Etiquette*, Emily Post
2. *The Life of Christ*, Giovanni Papini
3. *The Life and Letters of Walter H. Page*, Burton J. Hendrick, editor
4. *The Mind in the Making*, James Harvey Robinson
5. *The Outline of History*, H. G. Wells
6. *Diet and Health*, Lulu Hunt Peters
7. *Self-Mastery Through Conscious Auto-Suggestion*, Emile Coué
8. *The Americanization of Edward Bok*, Edward Bok
9. *The Story of Mankind*, Hendrik Willem Van Loon
10. *A Man from Maine*, Edward Bok

1924

Fiction

1. *So Big*, Edna Ferber
2. *The Plastic Age*, Percy Marks
3. *The Little French Girl*, Anne Douglas Sedgwick
4. *The Heirs Apparent*, Philip Gibbs
5. *A Gentleman of Courage*, James Oliver Curwood
6. *The Call of the Canyon*, Zane Grey
7. *The Midlander*, Booth Tarkington
8. *The Coast of Folly*, Coningsby Dawson
9. *Mistress Wilding*, Rafael Sabatini
10. *The Homemaker*, Dorothy Canfield Fisher

Nonfiction

1. *Diet and Health*, Lulu Hunt Peters
2. *The Life of Christ*, Giovanni Papini
3. *The Boston Cooking School Cook Book*, Fannie Farmer, editor
4. *Etiquette*, Emily Post

5. *Ariel*, André Maurois
6. *The Cross Word Puzzle Books*, Prosper Buranelli, et al.
7. *Mark Twain's Autobiography,* Mark Twain
8. *Saint Joan*, Bernard Shaw
9. *The New Decalogue of Science*, Albert E. Wiggam
10. *The Americanization of Edward Bok*, Edward Bok

1925

Fiction

1. *Soundings*, A. Hamilton Gibbs
2. *The Constant Nymph*, Margaret Kennedy
3. *The Keeper of the Bees*, Gene Stratton Porter
4. *Glorious Apollo*, E. Barrington
5. *The Green Hat*, Michael Arlen
6. *The Little French Girl*, Anne Douglas Sedgwick
7. *Arrowsmith*, Sinclair Lewis
8. *The Perennial Bachelor*, Anne Parrish
9. *The Carolinian*, Rafael Sabatini
10. *One Increasing Purpose*, A.S.M. Hutchinson

Nonfiction

1. *Diet and Health*, Lulu Hunt Peters
2. *The Boston Cooking School Cook Book*, rev. ed., Fannie Farmer, editor
3. *When We Were Very Young*, A. A. Milne
4. *The Man Nobody Knows*, Bruce Barton
5. *The Life of Christ,* Giovanni Papini
6. *Ariel*, André Maurois
7. *Twice Thirty*, Edward Bok
8. *Twenty-Five Years*, Lord Grey
9. *Anatole France Himself*, J. J. Brousson
10. *The Cross Word Puzzle Books*, Prosper Buranelli, et al.

1926

Fiction

1. *The Private Life of Helen of Troy*, John Erskine
2. *Gentlemen Prefer Blondes*, Anita Loos
3. *Sorrell and Son*, Warwick Deeping
4. *The Hounds of Spring*, Sylvia Thompson
5. *Beau Sabreur*, P. C. Wren
6. *The Silver Spoon*, John Galsworthy
7. *Beau Geste*, P. C. Wren
8. *Show Boat*, Edna Ferber
9. *After Noon*, Susan Ertz
10. *The Blue Window*, Temple Bailey

Nonfiction

1. *The Man Nobody Knows*, Bruce Barton
2. *Why We Behave Like Human Beings*, George A. Dorsey
3. *Diet and Health*, Lulu Hunt Peters
4. *Our Times*, Vol. I, Mark Sullivan
5. *The Boston Cooking School Cook Book*, rev. ed., Fannie Farmer, editor
6. *Auction Bridge Complete*, Milton C. Work
7. *The Book Nobody Knows*, Bruce Barton
8. *The Story of Philosophy*, Will Durant
9. *The Light of Faith*, Edgar A. Guest
10. *Jefferson and Hamilton*, Claude G. Bowers

1927

Fiction

1. *Elmer Gantry*, Sinclair Lewis
2. *The Plutocrat*, Booth Tarkington
3. *Doomsday*, Warwick Deeping
4. *Sorrell and Son*, Warwick Deeping
5. *Jalna*, Mazo de la Roche
6. *Lost Ecstasy*, Mary Roberts Rinehart
7. *Twilight Sleep*, Edith Wharton
8. *Tomorrow Morning*, Anne Parrish
9. *The Old Countess*, Anne Douglas Sedgwick
10. *A Good Woman*, Louis Bromfield

Nonfiction

1. *The Story of Philosophy*, Will Durant
2. *Napoleon*, Emil Ludwig
3. *Revolt in the Desert*, T. E. Lawrence
4. *Trader Horn*, Vol. I, Alfred Aloysius Horn and Ethelreda Lewis
5. *We*, Charles A. Lindbergh
6. *Ask Me Another*, Julian Spafford and Lucien Esty
7. *The Royal Road to Romance*, Richard Halliburton
8. *The Glorious Adventure*, Richard Halliburton
9. *Why We Behave Like Human Beings*, George A. Dorsey
10. *Mother India*, Katherine Mayo

1928

Fiction

1. *The Bridge of San Luis Rey*, Thornton Wilder
2. *Wintersmoon*, Hugh Walpole
3. *Swan Song*, John Galsworthy
4. *The Greene Murder Case*, S. S. Van Dine
5. *Bad Girl*, Viña Delmar
6. *Claire Ambler*, Booth Tarkington
7. *Old Pybus*, Warwick Deeping
8. *All Kneeling*, Anne Parrish
9. *Jalna*, Mazo de la Roche
10. *The Strange Case of Miss Annie Spragg*, Louis Bromfield

Nonfiction

1. *Disraeli*, André Maurois
2. *Mother India*, Katherine Mayo
3. *Trader Horn*, Vol. I, Alfred Aloysius Horn and Ethelreda Lewis
4. *Napoleon*, Emil Ludwig
5. *Strange Interlude*, Eugene O'Neill
6. *We*, Charles A. Lindbergh
7. *Count Luckner, the Sea Devil*, Lowell Thomas
8. *Goethe*, Emil Ludwig
9. *Skyward*, Richard E. Byrd
10. *The Intelligent Woman's Guide to Socialism and Capitalism*, George Bernard Shaw

1929

Fiction

1. *All Quiet on the Western Front*, Erich Maria Remarque
2. *Dodsworth*, Sinclair Lewis
3. *Dark Hester*, Anne Douglas Sedgwick
4. *The Bishop Murder Case*, S. S. Van Dine
5. *Roper's Row*, Warwick Deeping
6. *Peder Victorious*, O. E. Rölvaag
7. *Mamba's Daughters*, DuBose Heyward
8. *The Galaxy*, Susan Ertz
9. *Scarlet Sister Mary*, Julia Peterkin
10. *Joseph and His Brethren*, H. W. Freeman

Nonfiction

1. *The Art of Thinking*, Ernest Dimnet
2. *Henry the Eighth*, Francis Hackett
3. *The Cradle of the Deep*, Joan Lowell
4. *Elizabeth and Essex*, Lytton Strachey
5. *The Specialist,* Chic Sale
6. *A Preface to Morals*, Walter Lippmann
7. *Believe It or Not*, Robert L. Ripley
8. *John Brown's Body*, Stephen Vincent Benét
9. *The Tragic Era*, Claude G. Bowers
10. *The Mansions of Philosophy*, Will Durant

1930

Fiction

1. *Cimarron*, Edna Ferber
2. *Exile*, Warwick Deeping
3. *The Woman of Andros*, Thornton Wilder
4. *Years of Grace*, Margaret Ayer Barnes
5. *Angel Pavement*, J. B. Priestley
6. *The Door*, Mary Roberts Rinehart
7. *Rogue Herries*, Hugh Walpole
8. *Chances*, A. Hamilton Gibbs
9. *Young Man of Manhattan*, Katharine Brush
10. *Twenty-Four Hours*, Louis Bromfield

Nonfiction

1. *The Story of San Michele*, Axel Munthe
2. *The Strange Death of President Harding*, Gaston B. Means and May Dixon Thacker
3. *Byron*, André Maurois
4. *The Adams Family*, James Truslow Adams
5. *Lone Cowboy*, Will James
6. *Lincoln*, Emil Ludwig
7. *The Story of Philosophy*, Will Durant
8. *The Outline of History*, H. G. Wells
9. *The Art of Thinking*, Ernest Dimnet
10. *The Rise of American Civilization*, Charles and Mary Beard

1931

Fiction

1. *The Good Earth*, Pearl S. Buck
2. *Shadows on the Rock*, Willa Cather
3. *A White Bird Flying*, Bess Streeter Aldrich
4. *Grand Hotel*, Vicki Baum
5. *Years of Grace*, Margaret Ayer Barnes
6. *The Road Back*, Erich Maria Remarque
7. *The Bridge of Desire*, Warwick Deeping
8. *Back Street*, Fannie Hurst
9. *Finch's Fortune*, Mazo de la Roche
10. *Maid in Waiting*, John Galsworthy

Nonfiction

1. *Education of a Princess*, Grand Duchess Marie
2. *The Story of San Michele*, Axel Munthe
3. *Washington Merry-Go-Round*, anonymous (Drew Pearson and Robert S. Allen)
4. *Boners: Being a Collection of Schoolboy Wisdom, or Knowledge as It Is Sometimes Written*,compiled by Alexander Abingdon; illustrated by Dr. Seuss
5. *Culbertson's Summary*, Ely Culbertson
6. *Contract Bridge Blue Book*, Ely Culbertson
7. *Fatal Interview*, Edna St. Vincent Millay
8. *The Epic of America*, James Truslow Adams
9. *Mexico*, Stuart Chase
10. *New Russia's Primer*, Mikhail Ilin

1932

Fiction

1. *The Good Earth*, Pearl S. Buck
2. *The Fountain*, Charles Morgan
3. *Sons*, Pearl S. Buck
4. *Magnolia Street*, Louis Golding
5. *The Sheltered Life*, Ellen Glasgow
6. *Old Wine and New*, Warwick Deeping
7. *Mary's Neck*, Booth Tarkington
8. *Magnificent Obsession*, Lloyd C. Douglas
9. *Inheritance*, Phyllis Bentley
10. *Three Loves*, A. J. Cronin

Nonfiction

1. *The Epic of America*, James Truslow Adams
2. *Only Yesterday*, Frederick Lewis Allen
3. *A Fortune to Share*, Vash Young
4. *Culbertson's Summary*, Ely Culbertson
5. *Van Loon's Geography*, Hendrik Willem Van Loon
6. *What We Live By*, Ernest Dimnet
7. *The March of Democracy*, James Truslow Adams
8. *Washington Merry-Go-Round*, anonymous (Drew Pearson and Robert S. Allen)
9. *The Story of My Life*, Clarence Darrow
10. *More Merry-Go-Round*, anonymous (Drew Pearson and Robert S. Allen)

1933

Fiction

1. *Anthony Adverse*, Hervey Allen
2. *As the Earth Turns*, Gladys Hasty Carroll
3. *Ann Vickers*, Sinclair Lewis
4. *Magnificent Obsession*, Lloyd C. Douglas
5. *One More River*, John Galsworthy
6. *Forgive Us Our Trespasses*, Lloyd C. Douglas
7. *The Master of Jalna*, Mazo de la Roche
8. *Miss Bishop*, Bess Streeter Aldrich
9. *The Farm*, Louis Bromfield
10. *Little Man, What Now?*, Hans Fallada

Nonfiction

1. *Life Begins at Forty*, Walter B. Pitkin
2. *Marie Antoinette*, Stefan Zweig
3. *British Agent*, R. H. Bruce Lockhart
4. *100,000,000 Guinea Pigs*, Arthur Kallet and F. J. Schlink
5. *The House of Exile*, Nora Waln
6. *Van Loon's Geography*, Hendrik Willem Van Loon
7. *Looking Forward*, Franklin D. Roosevelt
8. *Contract Bridge Blue Book of 1933*, Ely Culbertson
9. *The Arches of the Years*, Halliday Sutherland
10. *The March of Democracy*, Vol. II, James Truslow Adams

1934

Fiction

1. *Anthony Adverse*, Hervey Allen
2. *Lamb in His Bosom*, Caroline Miller
3. *So Red the Rose*, Stark Young
4. *Good-Bye, Mr. Chips*, James Hilton
5. *Within This Present*, Margaret Ayer Barnes
6. *Work of Art*, Sinclair Lewis
7. *Private Worlds*, Phyllis Bottome
8. *Mary Peters*, Mary Ellen Chase
9. *Oil for the Lamps of China*, Alice Tisdale Hobart
10. *Seven Gothic Tales*, Isak Dinesen

Nonfiction

1. *While Rome Burns*, Alexander Woollcott
2. *Life Begins at Forty*, Walter B. Pitkin
3. *Nijinsky*, Romola Nijinsky
4. *100,000,000 Guinea Pigs*, Arthur Kallet and F. J. Schlink
5. *The Native's Return*, Louis Adamic
6. *Stars Fell on Alabama*, Carl Carmer
7. *Brazilian Adventure*, Peter Fleming
8. *Forty-two Years in the White House*, Ike Hoover
9. *You Must Relax*, Edmund Jacobson
10. *The Life of Our Lord*, Charles Dickens

1935

Fiction

1. *Green Light*, Lloyd C. Douglas
2. *Vein of Iron*, Ellen Glasgow
3. *Of Time and the River*, Thomas Wolfe
4. *Time Out of Mind*, Rachel Field
5. *Good-Bye, Mr. Chips*, James Hilton
6. *The Forty Days of Musa Dagh*, Franz Werfel
7. *Heaven's My Destination*, Thornton Wilder
8. *Lost Horizon*, James Hilton
9. *Come and Get It*, Edna Ferber
10. *Europa*, Robert Briffault

Nonfiction

1. *North to the Orient*, Anne Morrow Lindbergh
2. *While Rome Burns*, Alexander Woollcott

3. *Life with Father*, Clarence Day
4. *Personal History*, Vincent Sheean
5. *Seven Pillars of Wisdom*, T. E. Lawrence
6. *Francis the First*, Francis Hackett
7. *Mary Queen of Scotland and the Isles*, Stefan Zweig
8. *Rats, Lice and History*, Hans Zinsser
9. *R. E. Lee*, Douglas Southall Freeman
10. *Skin Deep*, M. C. Phillips

1936

Fiction

1. *Gone with the Wind*, Margaret Mitchell
2. *The Last Puritan*, George Santayana
3. *Sparkenbroke*, Charles Morgan
4. *Drums Along the Mohawk*, Walter D. Edmonds
5. *It Can't Happen Here*, Sinclair Lewis
6. *White Banners*, Lloyd C. Douglas
7. *The Hurricane*, Charles Nordhoff and James Norman Hall
8. *The Thinking Reed*, Rebecca West
9. *The Doctor*, Mary Roberts Rinehart
10. *Eyeless in Gaza*, Aldous Huxley

Nonfiction

1. *Man the Unknown*, Alexis Carrel
2. *Wake Up and Live!*, Dorothea Brande
3. *The Way of a Transgressor*, Negley Farson
4. *Around the World in Eleven Years*, Patience, Richard, and Johnny Abbe
5. *North to the Orient*, Anne Morrow Lindbergh
6. *An American Doctor's Odyssey*, Victor Heiser
7. *Inside Europe*, John Gunther
8. *Live Alone and Like It*, Marjorie Hillis
9. *Life with Father*, Clarence Day
10. *I Write As I Please*, Walter Duranty

1937

Fiction

1. *Gone with the Wind*, Margaret Mitchell
2. *Northwest Passage*, Kenneth Roberts
3. *The Citadel*, A. J. Cronin
4. *And So—Victoria*, Vaughan Wilkins
5. *Drums Along the Mohawk*, Walter D. Edmonds
6. *The Years*, Virginia Woolf
7. *Theatre*, W. Somerset Maugham
8. *Of Mice and Men*, John Steinbeck
9. *The Rains Came*, Louis Bromfield
10. *We Are Not Alone*, James Hilton

Nonfiction

1. *How To Win Friends and Influence People*, Dale Carnegie
2. *An American Doctor's Odyssey*, Victor Heiser
3. *The Return to Religion*, Henry C. Link
4. *The Arts*, Hendrik Willem Van Loon
5. *Orchids on Your Budget*, Marjorie Hillis
6. *Present Indicative*, Noel Coward
7. *Mathematics for the Million*, Lancelot Hogben
8. *Life with Mother*, Clarence Day
9. *The Nile*, Emil Ludwig
10. *The Flowering of New England*, Van Wyck Brooks

1938

Fiction

1. *The Yearling*, Marjorie Kinnan Rawlings
2. *The Citadel*, A. J. Cronin
3. *My Son, My Son!*, Howard Spring
4. *Rebecca*, Daphne du Maurier
5. *Northwest Passage*, Kenneth Roberts
6. *All This, and Heaven Too*, Rachel Field
7. *The Rains Came*, Louis Bromfield
8. *And Tell of Time*, Laura Krey
9. *The Mortal Storm*, Phyllis Bottome
10. *Action at Aquila*, Hervey Allen

Nonfiction

1. *The Importance of Living*, Lin Yutang
2. *With Malice Toward Some*, Margaret Halsey
3. *Madame Curie*, Eve Curie
4. *Listen! The Wind*, Anne Morrow Lindbergh
5. *The Horse and Buggy Doctor*, Arthur E. Hertzler
6. *How To Win Friends and Influence People*, Dale Carnegie
7. *Benjamin Franklin*, Carl Van Doren
8. *I'm a Stranger Here Myself*, Ogden Nash
9. *Alone*, Richard E. Byrd
10. *Fanny Kemble*, Margaret Armstrong

1939

Fiction

1. *The Grapes of Wrath*, John Steinbeck
2. *All This, and Heaven Too*, Rachel Field
3. *Rebecca*, Daphne du Maurier
4. *Wickford Point*, John P. Marquand
5. *Escape*, Ethel Vance
6. *Disputed Passage*, Lloyd C. Douglas
7. *The Yearling*, Marjorie Kinnan Rawlings
8. *The Tree of Liberty*, Elizabeth Page
9. *The Nazarene*, Sholem Asch
10. *Kitty Foyle*, Christopher Morley

Nonfiction

1. *Days of Our Years*, Pierre van Paassen
2. *Reaching for the Stars*, Nora Waln
3. *Inside Asia*, John Gunther
4. *Autobiography with Letters*, William Lyon Phelps
5. *Country Lawyer*, Bellamy Partridge
6. *Wind, Sand and Stars*, Antoine de St. Exupéry
7. *Mein Kampf*, Adolf Hitler
8. *A Peculiar Treasure*, Edna Ferber
9. *Not Peace but a Sword*, Vincent Sheean
10. *Listen! The Wind*, Anne Morrow Lindbergh

1940

Fiction

1. *How Green Was My Valley*, Richard Llewellyn
2. *Kitty Foyle*, Christopher Morley
3. *Mrs. Miniver*, Jan Struther
4. *For Whom the Bell Tolls*, Ernest Hemingway
5. *The Nazarene*, Sholem Asch
6. *Stars on the Sea*, F. van Wyck Mason
7. *Oliver Wiswell*, Kenneth Roberts
8. *The Grapes of Wrath*, John Steinbeck
9. *Night in Bombay*, Louis Bromfield
10. *The Family*, Nina Fedorova

Nonfiction

1. *I Married Adventure*, Osa Johnson
2. *How to Read a Book*, Mortimer Adler
3. *A Smattering of Ignorance*, Oscar Levant
4. *Country Squire in the White House*, John T. Flynn
5. *Land Below the Wind*, Agnes Newton Keith
6. *American White Paper*, Joseph W. Alsop Jr. and Robert Kintnor
7. *New England: Indian Summer*, Van Wyck Brooks
8. *As I Remember Him*, Hans Zinsser
9. *Days of Our Years*, Pierre van Paassen
10. *Bet It's a Boy*, Betty B. Blunt

1941

Fiction

1. *The Keys of the Kingdom*, A. J. Cronin
2. *Random Harvest*, James Hilton
3. *This Above All*, Eric Knight
4. *The Sun Is My Undoing*, Marguerite Steen

5. *For Whom the Bell Tolls*, Ernest Hemingway
6. *Oliver Wiswell*, Kenneth Roberts
7. *H. M. Pulham, Esquire*, John P. Marquand
8. *Mr. and Mrs. Cugat*, Isabel Scott Rorick
9. *Saratoga Trunk*, Edna Ferber
10. *Windswept*, Mary Ellen Chase

Nonfiction

1. *Berlin Diary*, William L. Shirer
2. *The White Cliffs*, Alice Duer Miller
3. *Out of the Night*, Jan Valtin
4. *Inside Latin America*, John Gunther
5. *Blood, Sweat and Tears*, Winston S. Churchill
6. *You Can't Do Business with Hitler*, Douglas Miller
7. *Reading I've Liked*, Clifton Fadiman, editor
8. *Reveille in Washington*, Margaret Leech
9. *Exit Laughing*, Irvin S. Cobb
10. *My Sister and I*, Dirk van der Heide

1942

Fiction

1. *The Song of Bernadette*, Franz Werfel
2. *The Moon Is Down*, John Steinbeck
3. *Dragon Seed*, Pearl S. Buck
4. *And Now Tomorrow*, Rachel Field
5. *Drivin' Woman*, Elizabeth Pickett
6. *Windswept*, Mary Ellen Chase
7. *The Robe*, Lloyd C. Douglas
8. *The Sun Is My Undoing*, Marguerite Steen
9. *Kings Row*, Henry Bellamann
10. *The Keys of the Kingdom*, A. J. Cronin

Nonfiction

1. *See Here, Private Hargrove*, Marion Hargrove
2. *Mission to Moscow*, Joseph E. Davies
3. *The Last Time I Saw Paris*, Elliot Paul
4. *Cross Creek*, Marjorie Kinnan Rawlings
5. *Victory Through Air Power*, Major Alexander P. de Seversky
6. *Past Imperfect*, Ilka Chase
7. *They Were Expendable*, W. L. White
8. *Flight to Arras*, Antoine de St. Exupéry
9. *Washington Is Like That*, W. M. Kiplinger
10. *Inside Latin America*, John Gunther

1943

Fiction

1. *The Robe*, Lloyd C. Douglas
2. *The Valley of Decision*, Marcia Davenport
3. *So Little Time*, John P. Marquand
4. *A Tree Grows in Brooklyn*, Betty Smith
5. *The Human Comedy*, William Saroyan
6. *Mrs. Parkington*, Louis Bromfield
7. *The Apostle*, Sholem Asch
8. *Hungry Hill*, Daphne du Maurier
9. *The Forest and the Fort*, Hervey Allen
10. *The Song of Bernadette*, Franz Werfel

Nonfiction

1. *Under Cover*, John Roy Carlson
2. *One World*, Wendell L. Willkie
3. *Journey Among Warriors*, Eve Curie
4. *On Being a Real Person*, Harry Emerson Fosdick
5. *Guadalcanal Diary*, Richard Tregaskis
6. *Burma Surgeon*, Lt. Col. Gordon Seagrave
7. *Our Hearts Were Young and Gay*, Cornelia Otis Skinner and Emily Kimbrough
8. *U. S. Foreign Policy*, Walter Lippmann
9. *Here Is Your War*, Ernie Pyle
10. *See Here, Private Hargrove*, Marion Hargrove

1944

Fiction

1. *Strange Fruit*, Lillian Smith
2. *The Robe*, Lloyd C. Douglas
3. *A Tree Grows in Brooklyn*, Betty Smith
4. *Forever Amber*, Kathleen Winsor
5. *The Razor's Edge*, W. Somerset Maugham
6. *The Green Years*, A. J. Cronin
7. *Leave Her to Heaven*, Ben Ames Williams
8. *Green Dolphin Street*, Elizabeth Goudge
9. *A Bell for Adano*, John Hersey
10. *The Apostle*, Sholem Asch

Nonfiction

1. *I Never Left Home*, Bob Hope
2. *Brave Men*, Ernie Pyle
3. *Good Night, Sweet Prince*, Gene Fowler
4. *Under Cover*, John Roy Carlson
5. *Yankee from Olympus*, Catherine Drinker Bowen
6. *The Time for Decision*, Sumner Welles
7. *Here Is Your War*, Ernie Pyle
8. *Anna and the King of Siam*, Margaret Landon
9. *The Curtain Rises*, Quentin Reynolds
10. *Ten Years in Japan*, Joseph C. Grew

1945

Fiction

1. *Forever Amber*, Kathleen Winsor
2. *The Robe*, Lloyd C. Douglas
3. *The Black Rose*, Thomas B. Costain
4. *The White Tower*, James Ramsey Ullman
5. *Cass Timberlane*, Sinclair Lewis
6. *A Lion Is In the Streets*, Adria Locke Langley
7. *So Well Remembered*, James Hilton
8. *Captain from Castile*, Samuel Shellabarger
9. *Earth and High Heaven*, Gwethalyn Graham
10. *Immortal Wife*, Irving Stone

Nonfiction

1. *Brave Men*, Ernie Pyle
2. *Dear Sir*, Juliet Lowell
3. *Up Front*, Bill Mauldin
4. *Black Boy*, Richard Wright
5. *Try and Stop Me*, Bennett Cerf
6. *Anything Can Happen*, George and Helen Papashvily
7. *General Marshall's Report*, U.S. War Department General Staff
8. *The Egg and I*, Betty MacDonald
9. *The Thurber Carnival*, James Thurber
10. *Pleasant Valley*, Louis Bromfield

1946

Fiction

1. *The King's General*, Daphne du Maurier
2. *This Side of Innocence*, Taylor Caldwell
3. *The River Road*, Frances Parkinson Keyes
4. *The Miracle of the Bells*, Russell Janney
5. *The Hucksters*, Frederic Wakeman
6. *The Foxes of Harrow*, Frank Yerby
7. *Arch of Triumph*, Erich Maria Remarque
8. *The Black Rose*, Thomas B. Costain
9. *B. F.'s Daughter*, John P. Marquand
10. *The Snake Pit*, Mary Jane Ward

Nonfiction

1. *The Egg and I*, Betty MacDonald
2. *Peace of Mind*, Joshua L. Liebman
3. *As He Saw It*, Elliott Roosevelt
4. *The Roosevelt I Knew*, Frances Perkins
5. *Last Chapter*, Ernie Pyle
6. *Starling of the White House*, Thomas Sugrue and Col. Edmund Starling
7. *I Chose Freedom*, Victor Kravchenko
8. *The Anatomy of Peace*, Emery Reves
9. *Top Secret*, Ralph Ingersoll
10. *A Solo in Tom-Toms*, Gene Fowler

1947

Fiction

1. *The Miracle of the Bells*, Russell Janney

2. *The Moneyman*, Thomas B. Costain
3. *Gentleman's Agreement*, Laura Z. Hobson
4. *Lydia Bailey*, Kenneth Roberts
5. *The Vixens*, Frank Yerby
6. *The Wayward Bus*, John Steinbeck
7. *House Divided*, Ben Ames Williams
8. *Kingsblood Royal*, Sinclair Lewis
9. *East Side, West Side*, Marcia Davenport
10. *Prince of Foxes*, Samuel Shellabarger

Nonfiction

1. *Peace of Mind*, Joshua L. Liebman
2. *Information Please Almanac, 1947*, John Kieran, editor
3. *Inside U.S.A.*, John Gunther
4. *A Study of History*, Arnold J. Toynbee
5. *Speaking Frankly*, James F. Byrnes
6. *Human Destiny*, Pierre Lecomte du Noüy
7. *The Egg and I*, Betty MacDonald
8. *The American Past*, Roger Butterfield
9. *The Fireside Book of Folk Songs*, Margaret B. Boni, editor
10. *Together*, Katharine T. Marshall

1948

Fiction

1. *The Big Fisherman*, Lloyd C. Douglas
2. *The Naked and the Dead*, Norman Mailer
3. *Dinner at Antoine's*, Frances Parkinson Keyes
4. *The Bishop's Mantle*, Agnes Sligh Turnbull
5. *Tomorrow Will Be Better*, Betty Smith
6. *The Golden Hawk*, Frank Yerby
7. *Raintree County*, Ross Lockridge Jr.
8. *Shannon's Way*, A. J. Cronin
9. *Pilgrim's Inn*, Elizabeth Goudge
10. *The Young Lions*, Irwin Shaw

Nonfiction

1. *Crusade in Europe*, Dwight D. Eisenhower
2. *How to Stop Worrying and Start Living*, Dale Carnegie
3. *Peace of Mind*, Joshua L. Liebman
4. *Sexual Behavior in the Human Male*, A. C. Kinsey, et al.
5. *Wine, Women and Words*, Billy Rose
6. *The Life and Times of the Shmoo*, Al Capp
7. *The Gathering Storm*, Winston Churchill
8. *Roosevelt and Hopkins*, Robert E. Sherwood
9. *A Guide to Confident Living*, Norman Vincent Peale
10. *The Plague and I*, Betty MacDonald

1949

Fiction

1. *The Egyptian*, Mika Waltari
2. *The Big Fisherman*, Lloyd C. Douglas
3. *Mary*, Sholem Asch
4. *A Rage to Live*, John O'Hara
5. *Point of No Return*, John P. Marquand
6. *Dinner at Antoine's*, Frances Parkinson Keyes
7. *High Towers*, Thomas B. Costain
8. *Cutlass Empire*, Van Wyck Mason
9. *Pride's Castle*, Frank Yerby
10. *Father of the Bride*, Edward Streeter

Nonfiction

1. *White Collar Zoo*, Clare Barnes Jr.
2. *How to Win at Canasta*, Oswald Jacoby
3. *The Seven Storey Mountain*, Thomas Merton
4. *Home Sweet Zoo*, Clare Barnes Jr.
5. *Cheaper by the Dozen*, Frank B. Gilbreth Jr. and Ernestine Gilbreth Carey
6. *The Greatest Story Ever Told*, Fulton Oursler
7. *Canasta, the Argentine Rummy Game*, Ottilie H. Reilly
8. *Canasta*, Josephine Artayeta de Viel and Ralph Michael
9. *Peace of Soul*, Fulton J. Sheen
10. *A Guide to Confident Living*, Norman Vincent Peale

1950

Fiction

1. *The Cardinal*, Henry Morton Robinson
2. *Joy Street*, Frances Parkinson Keyes
3. *Across the River and into the Trees*, Ernest Hemingway
4. *The Wall*, John Hersey
5. *Star Money*, Kathleen Winsor
6. *The Parasites*, Daphne du Maurier
7. *Floodtide*, Frank Yerby
8. *Jubilee Trail*, Gwen Bristow
9. *The Adventurer*, Mika Waltari
10. *The Disenchanted*, Budd Schulberg

Nonfiction

1. *Betty Crocker's Picture Cook Book*
2. *The Baby*
3. *Look Younger, Live Longer*, Gayelord Hauser
4. *How I Raised Myself from Failure to Success in Selling*, Frank Bettger

THE 30 MOST WIDELY TRANSLATED AUTHORS

Each year UNESCO publishes an index of international translations, which is summarized in a list of those authors whose works have been translated most widely. The most current list is based on data from 1987, because of the length of time it takes the office to compile and process the information. (Source: UNESCO, *Statistical Yearbook*, 1993)

1. Agatha Christie (Britain)
2. Walt Disney/Disney Productions (U.S.A.)
3. Vladimir I. Lenin (Russia)
4. Jules Verne (France)
5. Mikhail Gorbachev (Russia)
6. Enid Blyton (Britain)
7. Barbara Cartland (Britain)
8. Isaac Asimov (U.S.A.)
9. Alistair MacLean (Britain)
10. René de Goscinny (Asterix comics, France)
11. Georges Simenon (Belgium)
12. Stephen King (U.S.A.)
13. Hans Christian Andersen (Denmark)
14. Arthur Conan Doyle (Britain)
15. Victoria Holt (Britain)
16. Jack London (U.S.A.)
17. Mark Twain (U.S.A.)
18. Willy Vandersteen (Belgium)
19. William Shakespeare (Britain)
20. Karl Marx (Germany)
21. Fyodor Dostoevsky (Russia)
22. Leo Tolstoy (Russia)
23. Ernest Hemingway (U.S.A.)
24. Pope John Paul II (Holy See)
25. Frederick Engels (Germany)
26. Aleksandr Pushkin (Russia)
27. Wilhelm Grimm (Germany)
28. Danielle Steel (U.S.A.)
29. Jakob Grimm (Germany)
30. Harold Robbins (U.S.A.)

5. *Kon-Tiki*, Thor Heyerdahl
6. *Mr. Jones, Meet the Master*, Peter Marshall
7. *Your Dream Home*, Hubbard Cobb
8. *The Mature Mind*, H. A. Overstreet
9. *Campus Zoo*, Clare Barnes Jr.
10. *Belles on Their Toes*, Frank Gilbreth Jr. and Ernestine Gilbreth Carey

1951

Fiction

1. *From Here to Eternity*, James Jones
2. *The Caine Mutiny*, Herman Wouk
3. *Moses*, Sholem Asch
4. *The Cardinal*, Henry Morton Robinson
5. *A Woman Called Fancy*, Frank Yerby
6. *The Cruel Sea*, Nicholas Monsarrat
7. *Melville Goodwin, U.S.A.*, John P. Marquand
8. *Return to Paradise*, James A. Michener
9. *The Foundling*, Cardinal Spellman
10. *The Wanderer*, Mika Waltari

Nonfiction

1. *Look Younger, Live Longer*, Gayelord Hauser
2. *Betty Crocker's Picture Cook Book*
3. *Washington Confidential*, Jack Lait and Lee Mortimer
4. *Better Homes and Gardens Garden Book*
5. *Better Homes and Gardens Handyman's Book*
6. *The Sea Around Us*, Rachel L. Carson
7. *Thorndike-Barnhart Comprehensive Desk Dictionary*, Clarence L. Barnhart, editor
8. *Pogo*, Walt Kelly
9. *Kon-Tiki*, Thor Heyerdahl
10. *The New Yorker Twenty-Fifth Anniversary Album*

1952

Fiction

1. *The Silver Chalice*, Thomas B. Costain
2. *The Caine Mutiny*, Herman Wouk
3. *East of Eden*, John Steinbeck
4. *My Cousin Rachel*, Daphne du Maurier
5. *Steamboat Gothic*, Frances Parkinson Keyes
6. *Giant*, Edna Ferber
7. *The Old Man and the Sea*, Ernest Hemingway
8. *The Gown of Glory*, Agnes Sligh Turnbull
9. *The Saracen Blade*, Frank Yerby
10. *The Houses in Between*, Howard Spring

Nonfiction

1. *The Holy Bible: Revised Standard Version*
2. *A Man Called Peter*, Catherine Marshall
3. *U.S.A. Confidential*, Jack Lait and Lee Mortimer
4. *The Sea Around Us*, Rachel L. Carson
5. *Tallulah*, Tallulah Bankhead
6. *The Power of Positive Thinking*, Norman Vincent Peale
7. *This I Believe*, Edward P. Morgan, editor; Edward R. Murrow, foreword
8. *This Is Ike*, Wilson Hicks, editor
9. *Witness*, Whittaker Chambers
10. *Mr. President*, William Hillman

1953

Fiction

1. *The Robe*, Lloyd C. Douglas
2. *The Silver Chalice*, Thomas B. Costain
3. *Désirée*, Annemarie Selinko
4. *Battle Cry*, Leon M. Uris
5. *From Here to Eternity*, James Jones
6. *The High and the Mighty*, Ernest K. Gann
7. *Beyond This Place*, A. J. Cronin
8. *Time and Time Again*, James Hilton
9. *Lord Vanity*, Samuel Shellabarger
10. *The Unconquered*, Ben Ames Williams

Nonfiction

1. *The Holy Bible: Revised Standard Version*
2. *The Power of Positive Thinking*, Norman Vincent Peale
3. *Sexual Behavior in the Human Female*, Alfred C. Kinsey, et al.
4. *Angel Unaware*, Dale Evans Rogers
5. *Life Is Worth Living*, Fulton J. Sheen
6. *A Man Called Peter*, Catherine Marshall
7. *This I Believe*, Edward P. Morgan, editor; Edward R. Murrow, foreword
8. *The Greatest Faith Ever Known*, Fulton Oursler and G.A.O. Armstrong
9. *How to Play Your Best Golf*, Tommy Armour
10. *A House Is Not a Home*, Polly Adler

1954

Fiction

1. *Not as a Stranger*, Morton Thompson
2. *Mary Anne*, Daphne du Maurier
3. *Love Is Eternal*, Irving Stone
4. *The Royal Box*, Frances Parkinson Keyes
5. *The Egyptian*, Mika Waltari
6. *No Time for Sergeants*, Mac Hyman
7. *Sweet Thursday*, John Steinbeck
8. *The View from Pompey's Head*, Hamilton Basso
9. *Never Victorious, Never Defeated*, Taylor Caldwell
10. *Benton's Row*, Frank Yerby

Nonfiction

1. *The Holy Bible: Revised Standard Version*
2. *The Power of Positive Thinking*, Norman Vincent Peale
3. *Better Homes and Gardens New Cook Book*
4. *Betty Crocker's Good and Easy Cook Book*
5. *The Tumult and the Shouting*, Grantland Rice
6. *I'll Cry Tomorrow*, Lillian Roth, Gerold Frank and Mike Connolly
7. *The Prayers of Peter Marshall*, Catherine Marshall, editor
8. *This I Believe, 2*, Raymond Swing, editor
9. *But We Were Born Free*, Elmer Davis
10. *The Saturday Evening Post Treasury*, Roger Butterfield, editor

1955

Fiction

1. *Marjorie Morningstar*, Herman Wouk
2. *Auntie Mame*, Patrick Dennis
3. *Andersonville*, MacKinlay Kantor
4. *Bonjour Tristesse*, Françoise Sagan
5. *The Man in the Gray Flannel Suit*, Sloan Wilson
6. *Something of Value*, Robert Ruark
7. *Not As a Stranger*, Morton Thompson
8. *No Time for Sergeants*, Mac Hyman
9. *The Tontine*, Thomas B. Costain
10. *Ten North Frederick*, John O'Hara

Nonfiction

1. *Gift from the Sea*, Anne Morrow Lindbergh
2. *The Power of Positive Thinking*, Norman Vincent Peale
3. *The Family of Man*, Edward Steichen
4. *A Man Called Peter*, Catherine Marshall
5. *How to Live 365 Days a Year*, John A. Schindler
6. *Better Homes and Gardens Diet Book*
7. *The Secret of Happiness*, Billy Graham
8. *Why Johnny Can't Read*, Rudolf Flesch
9. *Inside Africa*, John Gunther
10. *Year of Decisions*, Harry S Truman

1956

Fiction

1. *Don't Go Near the Water*, William Brinkley
2. *The Last Hurrah*, Edwin O'Connor
3. *Peyton Place*, Grace Metalious
4. *Auntie Mame*, Patrick Dennis
5. *Eloise*, Kay Thompson
6. *Andersonville*, MacKinlay Kantor
7. *A Certain Smile*, Françoise Sagan
8. *The Tribe That Lost Its Head*, Nicholas Monsarrat
9. *The Mandarins*, Simone de Beauvoir
10. *Boon Island*, Kenneth Roberts

Nonfiction

1. *Arthritis and Common Sense*, rev. ed., Dan Dale Alexander
2. *Webster's New World Dictionary of the American Language*, concise ed., David B. Guralnik
3. *Betty Crocker's Picture Cook Book*, 2nd. ed.
4. *Etiquette*, Frances Benton
5. *Better Homes and Gardens Barbecue Book*
6. *The Search for Bridey Murphy*, Morey Bernstein
7. *Love or Perish*, Smiley Blanton, M.D.
8. *Better Homes and Gardens Decorating Book*
9. *How To Live 365 Days a Year*, John A. Schindler
10. *The Nun's Story*, Kathryn Hulme

1957

Fiction

1. *By Love Possessed*, James Gould Cozzens
2. *Peyton Place*, Grace Metalious
3. *Compulsion*, Meyer Levin
4. *Rally Round the Flag, Boys!*, Max Shulman
5. *Blue Camellia*, Frances Parkinson Keyes
6. *Eloise in Paris*, Kay Thompson
7. *The Scapegoat*, Daphne du Maurier
8. *On the Beach*, Nevil Shute
9. *Below the Salt*, Thomas B. Costain
10. *Atlas Shrugged*, Ayn Rand

Nonfiction

1. *Kids Say the Darndest Things!*, Art Linkletter
2. *The FBI Story*, Don Whitehead
3. *Stay Alive All Your Life*, Norman Vincent Peale
4. *To Live Again*, Catherine Marshall
5. *Better Homes and Gardens Flower Arranging*
6. *Where Did You Go? Out. What Did You Do? Nothing*, Robert Paul Smith
7. *Baruch: My Own Story*, Bernard M. Baruch
8. *Please Don't Eat the Daisies*, Jean Kerr
9. *The American Heritage Book of Great Historic Places*
10. *The Day Christ Died*, Jim Bishop

1958

Fiction

1. *Doctor Zhivago*, Boris Pasternak
2. *Anatomy of a Murder*, Robert Traver
3. *Lolita*, Vladimir Nabokov
4. *Around the World with Auntie Mame*, Patrick Dennis
5. *From the Terrace*, John O'Hara
6. *Eloise at Christmastime*, Kay Thompson
7. *Ice Palace*, Edna Ferber
8. *The Winthrop Woman*, Anya Seton
9. *The Enemy Camp*, Jerome Weidman
10. *Victorine*, Frances Parkinson Keyes

Nonfiction

1. *Kids Say the Darndest Things!*, Art Linkletter
2. *'Twixt Twelve and Twenty*, Pat Boone
3. *Only in America*, Harry Golden
4. *Masters of Deceit*, Edgar Hoover
5. *Please Don't Eat the Daisies*, Jean Kerr
6. *Better Homes and Gardens Salad Book*
7. *The New Testament in Modern English*, J. P. Phillips, trans.
8. *Aku-Aku*, Thor Heyerdahl
9. *Dear Abby*, Abigail Van Buren
10. *Inside Russia Today*, John Gunther

1959

Fiction

1. *Exodus*, Leon Uris
2. *Doctor Zhivago*, Boris Pasternak
3. *Hawaii*, James Michener
4. *Advise and Consent*, Allen Drury
5. *Lady Chatterley's Lover*, D. H. Lawrence
6. *The Ugly American*, William J. Lederer and Eugene L. Burdick
7. *Dear and Glorious Physician*, Taylor Caldwell
8. *Lolita*, Vladimir Nabokov
9. *Mrs. 'Arris Goes to Paris*, Paul Gallico
10. *Poor No More*, Robert Ruark

Nonfiction

1. *'Twixt Twelve and Twenty*, Pat Boone
2. *Folk Medicine*, D. C. Jarvis
3. *For 2¢ Plain*, Harry Golden
4. *The Status Seekers*, Vance Packard
5. *Act One*, Moss Hart
6. *Charley Weaver's Letters from Mamma*, Cliff Arquette
7. *The Elements of Style*, William Strunk Jr. and E. B. White
8. *The General Foods Kitchens Cookbook*
9. *Only in America*, Harry Golden
10. *Mine Enemy Grows Older*, Alexander King

1960

Fiction

1. *Advise and Consent*, Allen Drury
2. *Hawaii*, James A. Michener
3. *The Leopard*, Giuseppe di Lampedusa
4. *The Chapman Report*, Irving Wallace
5. *Ourselves To Know*, John O'Hara
6. *The Constant Image*, Marcia Davenport
7. *The Lovely Ambition*, Mary Ellen Chase
8. *The Listener*, Taylor Caldwell
9. *Trustee from the Toolroom*, Nevil Shute
10. *Sermons and Soda-Water*, John O'Hara

Nonfiction

1. *Folk Medicine*, D. C. Jarvis
2. *Better Homes and Gardens First Aid for Your Family*
3. *The General Foods Kitchens Cookbook*
4. *May This House Be Safe from Tigers*, Alexander King
5. *Better Homes and Gardens Dessert Book*
6. *Better Homes and Gardens Decorating Ideas*
7. *The Rise and Fall of the Third Reich*, William L. Shirer
8. *The Conscience of a Conservative*, Barry Goldwater
9. *I Kid You Not*, Jack Paar
10. *Between You, Me and the Gatepost*, Pat Boone

1961

Fiction

1. *The Agony and the Ecstasy*, Irving Stone
2. *Franny and Zooey*, J. D. Salinger
3. *To Kill a Mockingbird*, Harper Lee
4. *Mila 18*, Leon Uris
5. *The Carpetbaggers*, Harold Robbins
6. *Tropic of Cancer*, Henry Miller

7. *Winnie Ille Pu*, Alexander Lenard, trans.
8. *Daughter of Silence*, Morris West
9. *The Edge of Sadness*, Edwin O'Connor
10. *The Winter of Our Discontent*, John Steinbeck

Nonfiction

1. *The New English Bible: The New Testament*
2. *The Rise and Fall of the Third Reich*, William Shirer
3. *Better Homes and Gardens Sewing Book*
4. *Casserole Cook Book*
5. *A Nation of Sheep*, William Lederer
6. *Better Homes and Gardens Nutrition for Your Family*
7. *The Making of the President, 1960*, Theodore H. White
8. *Calories Don't Count*, Dr. Herman Taller
9. *Betty Crocker's New Picture Cook Book: New Edition*
10. *Ring of Bright Water*, Gavin Maxwell

1962

Fiction

1. *Ship of Fools*, Katherine Anne Porter
2. *Dearly Beloved*, Anne Morrow Lindbergh
3. *A Shade of Difference*, Allen Drury
4. *Youngblood Hawke*, Herman Wouk
5. *Franny and Zooey*, J. D. Salinger
6. *Fail-Safe*, Eugene Burdick and Harvey Wheeler
7. *Seven Days in May*, Fletcher Knebel and Charles W. Bailey II
8. *The Prize*, Irving Wallace
9. *The Agony and the Ecstasy*, Irving Stone
10. *The Reivers*, William Faulkner

Nonfiction

1. *Calories Don't Count*, Dr. Herman Taller
2. *The New English Bible: The New Testament*
3. *Better Homes and Gardens Cook Book: New Edition*
4. *O Ye Jigs & Juleps!*, Virginia Cary Hudson
5. *Happiness Is a Warm Puppy*, Charles M. Schulz
6. *The Joy of Cooking: New Edition*, Irma S. Rombauer and Marion Rombauer Becker
7. *My Life in Court*, Louis Nizer
8. *The Rothschilds*, Frederic Morton
9. *Sex and the Single Girl*, Helen Gurley Brown
10. *Travels with Charley*, John Steinbeck

1963

Fiction

1. *The Shoes of the Fisherman*, Morris L. West
2. *The Group*, Mary McCarthy
3. *Raise High the Roof Beam, Carpenters, and Seymour—An Introduction*, J. D. Salinger
4. *Caravans*, James A. Michener
5. *Elizabeth Appleton*, John O'Hara
6. *Grandmother and the Priests*, Taylor Caldwell
7. *City of Night*, John Rechy
8. *The Glass-Blowers*, Daphne du Maurier
9. *The Sand Pebbles*, Richard McKenna
10. *The Battle of the Villa Fiorita*, Rumer Godden

Nonfiction

1. *Happiness Is a Warm Puppy*, Charles M. Schulz
2. *Security Is a Thumb and a Blanket*, Charles M. Schulz
3. *J.F.K.: The Man and the Myth*, Victor Lasky
4. *Profiles in Courage: Inaugural Edition*, John F. Kennedy
5. *O Ye Jigs & Juleps!*, Virginia Cary Hudson
6. *Better Homes and Gardens Bread Cook Book*
7. *The Pillsbury Family Cookbook*
8. *I Owe Russia $1200*, Bob Hope
9. *Heloise's Housekeeping Hints*
10. *Better Homes and Gardens Baby Book*

MOST INFLUENTIAL BOOKS

The Bible has overwhelmingly had the greatest impact on American readers' lives, according to a survey conducted by the Library of Congress and the Book-of-the-Month Club in 1991. The full list:

1. The Bible
2. *Atlas Shrugged*, Ayn Rand
3. *The Road Less Traveled*, M. Scott Peck
4. *To Kill a Mockingbird*, Harper Lee
5. *The Lord of the Rings*, J.R.R. Tolkein
6. *Gone with the Wind*, Margaret Mitchell
7. *How To Win Friends and Influence People*, Dale Carnegie
8. *The Book of Mormon*
9. *The Feminine Mystique*, Betty Friedan (tie)
9. *A Gift from the Sea*, Anne Morrow Lindbergh (tie)
9. *Man's Search for Meaning*, Victor Frankl (tie)
9. *Passages*, Gail Sheehy (tie)
9. *When Bad Things Happen to Good People*, Harold S. Kushner (tie)

1964

Fiction

1. *The Spy Who Came in From the Cold*, John Le Carré
2. *Candy*, Terry Southern and Mason Hoffenberg
3. *Herzog*, Saul Bellow
4. *Armageddon*, Leon Uris
5. *The Man*, Irving Wallace
6. *The Rector of Justin*, Louis Auchincloss
7. *The Martyred*, Richard E. Kim
8. *You Only Live Twice*, Ian Fleming
9. *This Rough Magic*, Mary Stewart
10. *Convention*, Fletcher Knebel and Charles W. Bailey, II

Nonfiction

1. *Four Days*, American Heritage and United Press Internanational
2. *I Need All the Friends I Can Get*, Charles M. Schulz
3. *Profiles in Courage: Memorial Edition*, John F. Kennedy
4. *In His Own Write*, John Lennon
5. *Christmas Is Together-Time*, Charles M. Schulz
6. *A Day in the Life of President Kennedy*, Jim Bishop
7. *The Kennedy Wit*, compiled by Bill Adler
8. *A Moveable Feast*, Ernest Hemingway
9. *Reminiscences*, General Douglas MacArthur
10. *The John F. Kennedys*, Mark Shaw

1965

Fiction

1. *The Source*, James A. Michener
2. *Up the Down Staircase*, Bel Kaufman
3. *Herzog*, Saul Bellow
4. *The Looking Glass War*, John Le Carré
5. *The Green Berets*, Robin Moore
6. *Those Who Love*, Irving Stone
7. *The Man with the Golden Gun*, Ian Fleming
8. *Hotel*, Arthur Hailey
9. *The Ambassador*, Morris West
10. *Don't Stop the Carnival*, Herman Wouk

Nonfiction

1. *How To Be a Jewish Mother*, Dan Greenburg
2. *A Gift of Prophecy*, Ruth Montgomery
3. *Games People Play*, Eric Berne, M.D.
4. *World Aflame*, Billy Graham
5. *Happiness Is a Dry Martini*, Johnny Carson
6. *Markings*, Dag Hammarskjöld
7. *A Thousand Days*, Arthur Schlesinger Jr.
8. *My Shadow Ran Fast*, Bill Sands
9. *Kennedy*, Theodore C. Sorensen
10. *The Making of the President, 1964*, Theodore H. White

1966

Fiction

1. *Valley of the Dolls*, Jacqueline Susann
2. *The Adventurers*, Harold Robbins
3. *The Secret of Santa Vittoria*, Robert Crichton
4. *Capable of Honor*, Allen Drury
5. *The Double Image*, Helen MacInnes
6. *The Fixer*, Bernard Malamud
7. *Tell No Man*, Adela Rogers St. Johns
8. *Tai-Pan*, James Clavell
9. *The Embezzler*, Louis Auchincloss
10. *All in the Family*, Edwin O'Connor

Nonfiction

1. *How to Avoid Probate*, Norman F. Dacey
2. *Human Sexual Response*, William Howard Masters and Virginia E. Johnston
3. *In Cold Blood*, Truman Capote
4. *Games People Play*, Eric Berne, M.D.
5. *A Thousand Days*, Arthur M. Schlesinger Jr.
6. *Everything but Money*, Sam Levenson
7. *The Random House Dictionary of the English Language*
8. *Rush to Judgment*, Mark Lane
9. *The Last Battle*, Cornelius Ryan
10. *Phyllis Diller's Housekeeping Hints*, Phyllis Diller

1967

Fiction

1. *The Arrangement*, Elia Kazan
2. *The Confessions of Nat Turner*, William Styron (tie)
2. *The Chosen*, Chaim Potok (tie)
4. *Topaz*, Leon Uris
5. *Christy*, Catherine Marshall
6. *The Eighth Day*, Thornton Wilder
7. *Rosemary's Baby*, Ira Levin
8. *The Plot*, Irving Wallace
9. *The Gabriel Hounds*, Mary Stewart
10. *The Exhibitionist*, Henry Sutton

Nonfiction

1. *Death of a President*, William Manchester
2. *Misery Is a Blind Date*, Johnny Carson
3. *Games People Play*, Eric Berne, M.D.
4. *Stanyan Street & Other Sorrows*, Rod McKuen
5. *A Modern Priest Looks at His Outdated Church*, Father James Kavanaugh
6. *Everything but Money*, Sam Levenson
7. *Our Crowd*, Stephen Birmingham
8. *Edgar Cayce—The Sleeping Prophet*, Jess Stearn (tie)
8. *Better Homes and Gardens Favorite Ways with Chicken* (tie)
8. *Phyllis Diller's Marriage Manual*, Phyllis Diller (tie)

1968

Fiction

1. *Airport*, Arthur Hailey
2. *Couples*, John Updike
3. *The Salzburg Connection*, Helen MacInnes
4. *A Small Town in Germany*, John Le Carré
5. *Testimony of Two Men*, Taylor Caldwell
6. *Preserve and Protect*, Allen Drury
7. *Myra Breckinridge*, Gore Vidal
8. *Vanished*, Fletcher Knebel
9. *Christy*, Catherine Marshall
10. *The Tower of Babel*, Morris L. West

Nonfiction

1. *Better Homes and Gardens New Cook Book*
2. *The Random House Dictionary of the English Language: College Edition*, Laurence Urdang, editor
3. *Listen to the Warm*, Rod McKuen
4. *Between Parent and Child*, Haim G. Ginott
5. *Lonesome Cities*, Rod McKuen
6. *The Doctor's Quick Weight Loss Diet*, Erwin M. Stillman and Samm Sinclair Baker
7. *The Money Game*, Adam Smith
8. *Stanyan Street & Other Sorrows*, Rod McKuen
9. *The Weight Watcher's Cook Book*, Jean Nidetch
10. *Better Homes and Gardens Eat and Stay Slim*

1969

Fiction

1. *Portnoy's Complaint*, Philip Roth
2. *The Godfather*, Mario Puzo
3. *The Love Machine*, Jacqueline Susann
4. *The Inheritors*, Harold Robbins
5. *The Andromeda Strain*, Michael Crichton
6. *The Seven Minutes*, Irving Wallace
7. *Naked Came the Stranger*, Penelope Ashe
8. *The Promise*, Chaim Potok

9. *The Pretenders*, Gwen Davis
10. *The House on the Strand*, Daphne du Maurier

Nonfiction

1. *American Heritage Dictionary of the English Language*, William Morris, editor
2. *In Someone's Shadow*, Rod McKuen
3. *The Peter Principle*, Laurence J. Peter and Raymond Hull
4. *Between Parent and Teenager*, Dr. Haim G. Ginott
5. *The Graham Kerr Cookbook*, the Galloping Gourmet
6. *The Selling of the President 1968*, Joe McGinniss
7. *Miss Craig's 21-Day Shape-Up Program for Men and Women*, Marjorie Craig
8. *My Life and Prophecies*, Jeane Dixon with René Noorbergen
9. *Linda Goodman's Sun Signs*, Linda Goodman
10. *Twelve Years of Christmas*, Rod McKuen

1970

Fiction

1. *Love Story*, Erich Segal
2. *The French Lieutenant's Woman*, John Fowles
3. *Islands in the Stream*, Ernest Hemingway
4. *The Crystal Cave*, Mary Stewart
5. *Great Lion of God*, Taylor Caldwell
6. *QB VII*, Leon Uris
7. *The Gang That Couldn't Shoot Straight*, Jimmy Breslin
8. *The Secret Woman*, Victoria Holt
9. *Travels with My Aunt*, Graham Greene
10. *Rich Man, Poor Man*, Irwin Shaw

Nonfiction

1. *Everything You Wanted To Know About Sex but Were Afraid To Ask*, David Reuben, M.D.
2. *The New English Bible*
3. *The Sensuous Woman*, "J"
4. *Better Homes and Gardens Fondue and Tabletop Cooking*
5. *Up the Organization*, Robert Townsend
6. *Ball Four*, Jim Bouton
7. *American Heritage Dictionary of the English Language*, William Morris
8. *Body Language*, Julius Fast
9. *In Someone's Shadow*, Rod McKuen
10. *Caught in the Quiet*, Rod McKuen

1971

Fiction

1. *Wheels*, Arthur Hailey
2. *The Exorcist*, William P. Blatty
3. *The Passions of the Mind*, Irving Stone
4. *The Day of the Jackal*, Frederick Forsyth
5. *The Betsy*, Harold Robbins
6. *Message from Malaga*, Helen MacInnes
7. *The Winds of War*, Herman Wouk
8. *The Drifters*, James A. Michener
9. *The Other*, Thomas Tryon
10. *Rabbit Redux*, John Updike

Nonfiction

1. *The Sensous Man*, "M"
2. *Bury My Heart at Wounded Knee*, Dee Brown
3. *Better Homes and Gardens Blender Cook Book*
4. *I'm O.K., You're O.K.*, Thomas Harris
5. *Any Woman Can!*, David Reuben, M.D.
6. *Inside the Third Reich*, Albert Speer
7. *Eleanor and Franklin*, Joseph P. Lash
8. *Wunnerful, Wunnerful!*, Lawrence Welk
9. *Honor Thy Father*, Gay Talese
10. *Fields of Wonder*, Rod McKuen

1972

Fiction

1. *Jonathan Livingston Seagull*, Richard Bach
2. *August, 1914*, Alexander Solzhenitsyn
3. *The Odessa File*, Frederick Forsyth
4. *The Day of the Jackal*, Frederick Forsyth
5. *The Word*, Irving Wallace
6. *The Winds of War*, Herman Wouk
7. *Captains and the Kings*, Taylor Caldwell
8. *Two from Galilee*, Marjorie Holmes
9. *My Name Is Asher Lev*, Chaim Potok
10. *Semi-Tough*, Dan Jenkins

Nonfiction

1. *The Living Bible*, Kenneth Taylor
2. *I'm O.K., You're O.K.*, Thomas Harris
3. *Open Marriage*, Nena and George O'Neill
4. *Harry S. Truman*, Margaret Truman
5. *Dr. Atkins' Diet Revolution*, Robert C. Atkins
6. *Better Homes and Gardens Menu Cook Book*
7. *The Peter Prescription*, Laurence J. Peter
8. *A World Beyond*, Ruth Montgomery
9. *Journey to Ixtlan*, Carlos Castaneda
10. *Better Homes and Gardens Low-Calorie Desserts*

1973

Fiction

1. *Jonathan Livingston Seagull*, Richard Bach
2. *Once Is Not Enough*, Jacqueline Susann
3. *Breakfast of Champions*, Kurt Vonnegut
4. *The Odessa File*, Frederick Forsyth
5. *Burr*, Gore Vidal
6. *The Hollow Hills*, Mary Stewart
7. *Evening in Byzantium*, Irwin Shaw
8. *The Matlock Paper*, Robert Ludlum
9. *The Billion Dollar Sure Thing*, Paul E. Erdman
10. *The Honorary Consul*, Graham Greene

Nonfiction

1. *The Living Bible*, Kenneth Taylor
2. *Dr. Atkins' Diet Revolution*, Robert C. Atkins
3. *I'm O.K., You're O.K.*, Thomas Harris
4. *The Joy of Sex*, Alex Comfort
5. *Weight Watchers Program Cookbook*, Jean Nidetch
6. *How To Be Your Own Best Friend*, Mildred Newman, et al.
7. *The Art of Walt Disney*, Christopher Finch
8. *Better Homes and Gardens Home Canning Cookbook*
9. *Alistair Cooke's America*, Alistair Cooke
10. *Sybil*, Flora R. Schreiber

1974

Fiction

1. *Centennial*, James A. Michener
2. *Watership Down*, Richard Adams
3. *Jaws*, Peter Benchley
4. *Tinker, Tailor, Soldier, Spy*, John Le Carré
5. *Something Happened*, Joseph Heller
6. *The Dogs of War*, Frederick Forsyth
7. *The Pirate*, Harold J. Robbins
8. *I Heard the Owl Call My Name*, Margaret Craven
9. *The Seven-Per-Cent Solution*, John H. Watson, M.D., Nicholas Meyer, editor
10. *The Fan Club*, Irving Wallace

Nonfiction

1. *The Total Woman*, Marabel Morgan
2. *All the President's Men*, Carl Bernstein and Bob Woodward
3. *Plain Speaking: An Oral Biography of Harry S. Truman*, Merle Miller
4. *More Joy: A Lovemaking Companion to The Joy of Sex*, Alex Comfort
5. *Alistair Cooke's America*, Alistair Cooke
6. *Tales of Power*, Carlos A. Castaneda
7. *You Can Profit from a Monetary Crisis*, Harry Browne
8. *All Things Bright and Beautiful*, James Herriot
9. *The Bermuda Triangle*, Charles Berlitz with J. Manson Valentine
10. *The Memory Book*, Harry Lorayne and Jerry Lucas

1975

Fiction

1. *Ragtime*, E. L. Doctorow
2. *The Moneychangers*, Arthur Hailey
3. *Curtain*, Agatha Christie
4. *Looking for Mister Goodbar*, Judith Rossner
5. *The Choirboys*, Joseph Wambaugh
6. *The Eagle Has Landed*, Jack Higgins
7. *The Greek Treasure: A Biographical Novel of Henry and Sophia Schliemann*, Irving Stone
8. *The Great Train Robbery*, Michael Crichton
9. *Shogun*, James Clavell
10. *Humboldt's Gift*, Saul Bellow

Nonfiction

1. *Angels: God's Secret Agents*, Billy Graham
2. *Winning Through Intimidation*, Robert Ringer
3. *TM: Discovering Energy and Overcoming Stress*, Harold H. Bloomfield
4. *The Ascent of Man*, Jacob Bronowski
5. *Sylvia Porter's Money Book*, Sylvia Porter
6. *Total Fitness in 30 Minutes a Week*, Laurence E. Morehouse and Leonard Gross
7. *The Bermuda Triangle*, Charles Berlitz with J. Manson Valentine
8. *The Save-Your-Life Diet*, David Reuben
9. *Bring on the Empty Horses*, David Niven
10. *Breach of Faith: The Fall of Richard Nixon*, Theodore H. White

1976

Fiction

1. *Trinity*, Leon Uris
2. *Sleeping Murder*, Agatha Christie
3. *Dolores*, Jacqueline Susann
4. *Storm Warning*, Jack Higgins
5. *The Deep*, Peter Benchley
6. *1876*, Gore Vidal
7. *Slapstick: or, Lonesome No More!*, Kurt Vonnegut
8. *The Lonely Lady*, Harold Robbins
9. *Touch Not the Cat*, Mary Stewart
10. *A Stranger in the Mirror*, Sidney Sheldon

Nonfiction

1. *The Final Days*, Bob Woodward and Carl Bernstein
2. *Roots*, Alex Haley
3. *Your Erroneous Zones*, Dr. Wayne W. Dyer
4. *Passages: The Predictable Crises of Adult Life*, Gail Sheehy
5. *Born Again*, Charles W. Colson
6. *The Grass Is Always Greener Over the Septic Tank*, Erma Bombeck
7. *Angels: God's Secret Agents*, Billy Graham
8. *Blind Ambition: The White House Years*, John Dean
9. *The Hite Report: A Nationwide Study of Female Sexuality*, Shere Hite
10. *The Right and the Power: The Prosecution of Watergate*, Leon Jaworski

1977

Fiction

1. *The Silmarillion*, J.R.R. Tolkien; Christopher Tolkien
2. *The Thorn Birds*, Colleen McCullough
3. *Illusions: The Adventures of a Reluctant Messiah*, Richard Bach
4. *The Honourable Schoolboy*, John Le Carré
5. *Oliver's Story*, Erich Segal
6. *Dreams Die First*, Harold Robbins
7. *Beggarman, Thief*, Irwin Shaw
8. *How To Save Your Own Life*, Erica Jong
9. *Delta of Venus: Erotica*, Anaïs Nin
10. *Daniel Martin*, John Fowles

Nonfiction

1. *Roots*, Alex Haley
2. *Looking Out for #1*, Robert Ringer
3. *All Things Wise and Wonderful*, James Herriot
4. *Your Erroneous Zones*, Dr. Wayne W. Dyer
5. *The Book of Lists*, David Wallechinsky, Irving Wallace, and Amy Wallace
6. *The Possible Dream: A Candid Look at Amway*, Charles Paul Conn
7. *The Dragons of Eden: Speculations on the Evolution of Human Intelligence*, Carl Sagan
8. *The Second Ring of Power*, Carlos Castaneda
9. *The Grass Is Always Greener over the Septic Tank*, Erma Bombeck
10. *The Amityville Horror*, Jay Anson

1978

Fiction

1. *Chesapeake*, James A. Michener
2. *War and Remembrance*, Herman Wouk
3. *Fools Die*, Mario Puzo
4. *Bloodlines*, Sidney Sheldon
5. *Scruples*, Judith Krantz
6. *Evergreen*, Belva Plain
7. *Illusions: The Adventures of a Reluctant Messiah*, Richard Bach
8. *The Holcroft Covenant*, Robert Ludlum
9. *Second Generation*, Howard Fast
10. *Eye of the Needle*, Ken Follett

Nonfiction

1. *If Life Is a Bowl of Cherries—What Am I Doing in the Pits?*, Erma Bombeck
2. *Gnomes*, Wil Huygen and Rien Poortvliet
3. *The Complete Book of Running*, James Fixx

AMERICA'S POETS LAUREATE

To honor America's greatest poets, the Librarian of Congress names a poet laureate. The annointed:

Robert Penn Warren	1986–87
Richard Wilbur	1987–88
Howard Nemerov	1988–90
Mark Strand	1990–91
Joseph Brodsky	1991–92
Mona Van Duyn	1992–93
Rita Dove	1993–95

4. *Mommie Dearest*, Christina Crawford
5. *Pulling Your Own Strings*, Dr. Wayne W. Dyer
8. *RN: The Memoirs of Richard Nixon*, Richard Nixon
7. *A Distant Mirror: The Calamitous Fourteenth Century*, Tuchman
8. *Faeries*, Brian Froud and Alan Lee
9. *In Search of History: A Personal Adventure*, Theodore H. White
10. *The Muppet Show Book*, the Muppet People

1979

Fiction

1. *The Matarese Circle*, Robert Ludlum
2. *Sophie's Choice*, William Styron
3. *Overload*, Arthur Hailey
4. *Memories of Another Day*, Harold Robbins
5. *Jailbird*, Kurt Vonnegut
6. *The Dead Zone*, Stephen King
7. *The Last Enchantment*, Mary Stewart
8. *The Establishment*, Howard Fast
9. *The Third World War: August 1985*, Gen. Sir John Hackett, et al.
10. *Smiley's People*, John Le Carré

Nonfiction

1. *Aunt Erma's Cope Book*, Erma Bombeck
2. *The Complete Scarsdale Medical Diet*, Herman Tarnower, M.D., and Samm Sinclair Baker
3. *How to Prosper During the Coming Bad Years*, Howard J. Ruff
4. *Cruel Shoes*, Steve Martin
5. *The Pritikin Program for Diet and Exercise*, Nathan Pritikin and Patrick McGrady Jr.
6. *White House Years*, Henry Kissinger
7. *Lauren Bacall By Myself*, Lauren Bacall
8. *The Brethren: Inside the Supreme Court*, Bob Woodward and Scott Armstrong
9. *Restoring the American Dream*, Robert J. Ringer
10. *The Winner's Circle*, Charles Paul Conn

1980

Fiction

1. *The Covenant*, James A. Michener
2. *The Bourne Identity*, Robert Ludlum
3. *Rage of Angels*, Sidney Sheldon
4. *Princess Daisy*, Judith Krantz
5. *Firestarter*, Stephen King
6. *The Key to Rebecca*, Ken Follett
7. *Random Winds*, Belva Plain
8. *The Devil's Alternative*, Frederick Forsyth
9. *The Fifth Horseman*, Larry Collins and Dominique Lapierre
10. *The Spike*, Arnaud de Borchgrave and Robert Moss

Nonfiction

1. *Crisis Investing: Opportunities and Profits in the Coming Great Depression*, Douglas R. Casey
2. *Cosmos*, Carl Sagan
3. *Free to Choose: A Personal Statement*, Milton and Rose Friedman
4. *Anatomy of an Illness as Perceived by the Patient*, Norman Cousins
5. *Thy Neighbor's Wife*, Gay Talese
6. *The Sky's the Limit*, Dr. Wayne W. Dyer
7. *The Third Wave*, Alvin Toffler
8. *Craig Claiborne's Gourmet Diet*, Craig Claiborne with Pierre Franey
9. *Nothing Down*, Robert Allen
10. *Shelley: Also Known as Shirley*, Shelley Winters

1981

Fiction

1. *Noble House*, James Clavell
2. *The Hotel New Hampshire*, John Irving
3. *Cujo*, Stephen King
4. *An Indecent Obsession*, Colleen McCullough
5. *Gorky Park*, Martin Cruz Smith
6. *Masquerade*, Kit Williams
7. *Goodbye, Janette*, Harold Robbins
8. *The Third Deadly Sin*, Lawrence Sanders
9. *The Glitter Dome*, Joseph Wambaugh
10. *No Time for Tears*, Cynthia Freeman

Nonfiction

1. *The Beverly Hills Diet*, Judy Mazel
2. *The Lord God Made Them All*, James Herriot
3. *Richard Simmons' Never-Say-Diet Book*, Richard Simmons
4. *A Light in the Attic*, Shel Silverstein
5. *Cosmos*, Carl Sagan
6. *Better Homes & Gardens New Cook Book*
7. *Miss Piggy's Guide to Life*, Miss Piggy as told to Henry Beard
8. *Weight Watchers 365-Day Menu Cookbook*
9. *You Can Negotiate Anything*, Herb Cohen
10. *A Few Minutes with Andy Rooney*, Andrew A. Rooney

1982

Fiction

1. *E.T., the Extra-Terrestrial Storybook*, William Kotzwinkle
2. *Space*, James A. Michener
3. *The Parsifal Mosaic*, Robert Ludlum
4. *Master of the Game*, Sidney Sheldon
5. *Mistral's Daughter*, Judith Krantz
6. *The Valley of Horses*, Jean M. Auel
7. *Different Seasons*, Stephen King
8. *North and South*, John Jakes
9. *2010: Odyssey Two*, Arthur C. Clarke
10. *The Man from St. Petersburg*, Ken Follett

Nonfiction

1. *Jane Fonda's Workout Book*, Jane Fonda
2. *Living, Loving and Learning*, Leo Buscaglia
3. *And More by Andy Rooney*, Andrew A. Rooney
4. *Better Homes & Gardens New Cookbook*
5. *Life Extension: Adding Years to Your Life And Life to Your Years—A Practical Scientific Approach*, Durk Pearson and Sandy Shaw
6. *When Bad Things Happen to Good People*, Harold S. Kushner
7. *A Few Minutes with Andy Rooney*, Andrew A. Rooney
8. *The Weight Watchers Food Plan Diet Cookbook*, Jean Nidetch
9. *Richard Simmons' Never-Say-Diet Cookbook*, Richard Simmons
10. *No Bad Dogs: The Woodhouse Way*, Barbara Woodhouse

1983

Fiction

1. *Return of the Jedi Storybook*, Joan D. Vinge, adapt.
2. *Poland*, James A. Michener
3. *Pet Sematary*, Stephen King
4. *The Little Drummer Girl*, John Le Carré
5. *Christine*, Stephen King
6. *Changes*, Danielle Steel
7. *The Name of the Rose*, Umberto Eco
8. *White Gold Wielder: Book Three of The Second Chronicles of Thomas Covenant*, Stephen R. Donaldson
9. *Hollywood Wives*, Jackie Collins
10. *The Lonesome Gods*, Louis L'Amour

Nonfiction

1. *In Search of Excellence: Lessons from America's Best-Run Companies*, Thomas J. Peters and Robert H. Waterman Jr.

2. *Megatrends: Ten New Directions Transforming Our Lives*, John Naisbitt
3. *Motherhood: The Second Oldest Profession*, Erma Bombeck
4. *The One Minute Manager*, Kenneth Blanchard and Spencer Johnson
5. *Jane Fonda's Workout Book*, Jane Fonda
6. *The Best of James Herriot*, James Herriot
7. *The Mary Kay Guide to Beauty: Discovering Your Special Look*
8. *On Wings of Eagles*, Ken Follett
9. *Creating Wealth*, Robert G. Allen
10. *The Body Principal: The Exercise Program for Life*, Victoria Principal

1984

Fiction

1. *The Talisman*, Stephen King and Peter Straub
2. *The Aquitaine Progression*, Robert Ludlum
3. *The Sicilian*, Mario Puzo
4. *Love and War*, John Jakes
5. *The Butter Battle Book*, Dr. Seuss
6. *". . . And Ladies of the Club,"* Helen Hooven Santmyer
7. *The Fourth Protocol*, Frederick Forsyth
8. *Full Circle*, Danielle Steel
9. *The Life and Hard Times of Heidi Abromowitz*, Joan Rivers
10. *Lincoln: A Novel*, Gore Vidal

Nonfiction

1. *Iacocca: An Autobiography*, Lee Iacocca with William Novak
2. *Loving Each Other*, Leo Buscaglia
3. *Eat to Win: The Sports Nutrition Bible*, Robert Haas, M.D.
4. *Pieces of My Mind*, Andrew A. Rooney
5. *Weight Watchers Fast and Fabulous Cookbook*
6. *What They Don't Teach You at Harvard Business School: Notes from a Street-Smart Executive*, Mark H. McCormack
7. *Women Coming of Age*, Jane Fonda with Mignon McCarthy
8. *Moses the Kitten*, James Herriot
9. *The One Minute Salesperson*, Spencer Johnson, M.D., and Larry Wilson
10. *Weight Watchers Quick Start Program Cookbook*, Jean Nidetch

1985

Fiction

1. *The Mammoth Hunters*, Jean M. Auel
2. *Texas*, James A. Michener
3. *Lake Wobegon Days*, Garrison Keillor
4. *If Tomorrow Comes*, Sidney Sheldon
5. *Skeleton Crew*, Stephen King
6. *Secrets*, Danielle Steel
7. *Contact*, Carl Sagan
8. *Lucky*, Jackie Collins
9. *Family Album*, Danielle Steel
10. *Jubal Sackett*, Louis L'Amour

Nonfiction

1. *Iacocca: An Autobiography*, Lee Iacocca with William Novak
2. *Yeager: An Autobiography*, Gen. Chuck Yeager and Leo Janos
3. *Elvis and Me*, Priscilla Beaulieu Presley with Sandra Harmon
4. *Fit for Life*, Harvey and Marilyn Diamond
5. *The Be-Happy Attitudes*, Robert Schuller
6. *Dancing in the Light*, Shirley MacLaine
7. *A Passion for Excellence: The Leadership Difference*, Thomas J. Peters and Nancy K. Austin
8. *The Frugal Gourmet*, Jeff Smith
9. *I Never Played the Game*, Howard Cosell with Peter Bonventre
10. *Dr. Berger's Immune Power Diet*, Stuart M. Berger, M.D.

1986

Fiction

1. *It*, Stephen King
2. *Red Storm Rising*, Tom Clancy
3. *Whirlwind*, James Clavell
4. *The Bourne Supremacy*, Robert Ludlum
5. *Hollywood Husbands*, Jackie Collins
6. *Wanderlust*, Danielle Steel
7. *I'll Take Manhattan*, Judith Krantz
8. *Last of the Breed*, Louis L'Amour
9. *The Prince of Tides*, Pat Conroy
10. *A Perfect Spy*, John Le Carré

Nonfiction

1. *Fatherhood*, Bill Cosby
2. *Fit for Life*, Harvey and Marilyn Diamond
3. *His Way: The Unauthorized Biography of Frank Sinatra*, Kitty Kelley
4. *The Rotation Diet*, Martin Katahn
5. *You're Only Old Once*, Dr. Seuss
6. *Callanetics: Ten Years Younger in Ten Hours*, Callan Pinckney
7. *The Frugal Gourmet Cooks with Wine*, Jeff Smith
8. *Be Happy—You Are Loved!*, Robert H. Schuller
9. *Word for Word*, Andrew A. Rooney
10. *James Herriot's Dog Stories*, James Herriot

1987

Fiction

1. *The Tommyknockers*, Stephen King
2. *Patriot Games*, Tom Clancy
3. *Kaleidoscope*, Danielle Steel
4. *Misery*, Stephen King
5. *Leaving Home: A Collection of Lake Wobegon Stories*, Garrison Keillor
6. *Windmills of the Gods*, Sidney Sheldon
7. *Presumed Innocent*, Scott Turow
8. *Fine Things*, Danielle Steel
9. *Heaven and Hell*, John Jakes
10. *The Eyes of the Dragon*, Stephen King

Nonfiction

1. *Time Flies*, Bill Cosby
2. *Spycatcher: The Candid Autobiography of a Senior Intelligence Officer*, Peter Wright with Paul Greengrass
3. *Family: The Ties That Bind . . . and Gag!*, Erma Bombeck
4. *Veil: The Secret Wars of the CIA, 1981–1987*, Bob Woodward
5. *A Day in the Life of America*, Rick Smolan and David Cohen
6. *The Great Depression of 1990*, Ravi Batra
7. *It's All in the Playing*, Shirley MacLaine
8. *Man of the House: The Life and Political Memoirs of Speaker Tip O'Neill*, Thomas P. O'Neill Jr. with William Novak
9. *The Frugal Gourmet Cooks American*, Jeff Smith
10. *The Closing of the American Mind*, Allan Bloom

1988

Fiction

1. *The Cardinal of the Kremlin*, Tom Clancy
2. *The Sands of Time*, Sidney Sheldon
3. *Zoya*, Danielle Steel
4. *The Icarus Agenda*, Robert Ludlum
5. *Alaska*, James A. Michener
6. *Till We Meet Again*, Judith Krantz
7. *The Queen of the Damned*, Anne Rice
8. *To Be the Best*, Barbara Taylor Bradford
9. *One: A Novel*, Richard Bach
10. *Mitla Pass*, Leon Uris

Nonfiction

1. *The 8-Week Cholesterol Cure*, Robert E. Kowalski
2. *Talking Straight*, Lee Iacocca with Sonny Kleinfield

3. *A Brief History of Time: From the Big Bang to Black Holes*, Steven W. Hawking
4. *Trump: The Art of the Deal*, Donald J. Trump with Tony Schwartz
5. *Gracie: A Love Story*, George Burns
6. *Elizabeth Takes Off*, Elizabeth Taylor
7. *Swim with the Sharks without Being Eaten Alive*, Harvey MacKay
8. *Christmas in America*, David Cohen, editor
9. *Weight Watchers Quick Success Program Book*, Jean Nidetch
10. *Moonwalk*, Michael Jackson

1989

Fiction

1. *Clear and Present Danger*, Tom Clancy
2. *The Dark Half*, Stephen King
3. *Daddy*, Danielle Steel
4. *Star*, Danielle Steel
5. *Caribbean*, James A. Michener
6. *The Satanic Verses*, Salman Rushdie
7. *The Russia House*, John Le Carré
8. *The Pillars of the Earth*, Ken Follet
9. *California Gold*, John Jakes
10. *While My Pretty One Sleeps*, Mary Higgins Clark

Nonfiction

1. *All I Really Need To Know I Learned in Kindergarten: Uncommon Thoughts on Common Things*, Robert Fulghum
2. *Wealth Without Risk: How To Develop a Personal Fortune Without Going Out on a Limb*, Charles J. Givens
3. *A Woman Named Jackie*, C. David Heymann
4. *It Was on Fire When I Lay Down on It*, Robert Fulghum
5. *Better Homes and Gardens New Cook Book*
6. *The Way Things Work*, David Macaulay
7. *It's Always Something*, Gilda Radner
8. *Roseanne: My Life as a Woman*, Roseanne Barr
9. *The Frugal Gourmet Cooks Three Ancient Cuisines: China, Greece, and Rome*, Jeff Smith
10. *My Turn: The Memoirs of Nancy Reagan*, Nancy Reagan with William Novak

1990

Fiction

1. *The Plains of Passage*, Jean M. Auel
2. *Four Past Midnight*, Stephen King
3. *The Burden of Proof*, Scott Turow
4. *Memories of Midnight*, Sidney Sheldon
5. *Message from Nam*, Danielle Steel
6. *The Bourne Ultimatum*, Robert Ludlum
7. *The Stand: The Complete and Uncut Edition*, Stephen King
8. *Lady Boss*, Jackie Collins
9. *The Witching Hour*, Anne Rice
10. *September*, Rosamunde Pilcher

Nonfiction

1. *A Life on the Road*, Charles Kuralt
2. *The Civil War*, Geoffrey C. Ward with Ric Burns and Ken Burns
3. *The Frugal Gourmet on Our Immigrant Heritage: Recipes You Should Have Gotten from Your Grandmother*, Jeff Smith
4. *Better Homes and Gardens New Cook Book*
5. *Financial Self-Defense: How To Win the Fight for Financial Freedom*, Charles J. Givens
6. *Homecoming: Reclaiming and Championing Your Inner Child*, John Bradshaw
7. *Wealth Without Risk: How To Develop a Personal Fortune Without Going Out on a Limb*, Charles J. Givens
8. *Bo Knows Bo*, Bo Jackson and Dick Schaap
9. *An American Life: An Autobiography*, Ronald Reagan
10. *Megatrends 2000: Ten New Directions for the 1990s*, John Naisbitt and Patricia Aburdene

1991

Fiction

1. *Scarlett: The Sequel to Margaret Mitchell's "Gone with the Wind,"* Alexandra Ripley
2. *The Sum of All Fears*, Tom Clancy
3. *Needful Things*, Stephen King
4. *No Greater Love*, Danielle Steel
5. *Heartbeat*, Danielle Steel
6. *The Doomsday Conspiracy*, Sidney Sheldon
7. *The Firm*, John Grisham
8. *Night Over Water*, Ken Follet
9. *Remember*, Barbara Taylor Bradford
10. *Loves Music, Loves to Dance*, Mary Higgins Clark

Nonfiction

1. *Me: Stories of My Life*, Katharine Hepburn
2. *Nancy Reagan: The Unauthorized Biography*, Kitty Kelley
3. *Uh-Oh: Some Observations from Both Sides of the Refrigerator Door*, Robert Fulghum
4. *Under Fire: An American Story*, Oliver North with William Novak
5. *Final Exit: The Practicalities of Self-Deliverance and Assisted Suicide for the Dying*, Derek Humphry
6. *When You Look Like Your Passport Photo, It's Time to Go Home*, Erma Bombeck
7. *More Wealth Without Risk*, Charles J. Givens
8. *Den of Thieves*, James B. Stewart
9. *Childhood*, Bill Cosby
10. *Financial Self-Defense*, Charles J. Givens

1992

Fiction

1. *Dolores Claiborne*, Stephen King
2. *The Pelican Brief*, John Grisham
3. *Gerald's Game*, Stephen King
4. *Mixed Blessings*, Danielle Steel
5. *Jewels*, Danielle Steel
6. *The Stars Shine Down*, Sidney Sheldon
7. *Tale of the Body Thief*, Anne Rice
8. *Mexico*, James A. Michener
9. *Waiting to Exhale*, Terry McMillan
10. *All Around the Town*, Mary Higgins Clark

Nonfiction

1. *The Way Things Ought To Be*, Rush Limbaugh
2. *It Doesn't Take a Hero: The Autobiography*, Gen. H. Norman Schwarzkopf
3. *How to Satisfy a Woman Every Time*, Naura Hayden
4. *Every Living Thing*, James Herriot
5. *A Return to Love*, Marianne Williamson
6. *Sam Walton: Made in America*, Sam Walton
7. *Diana: Her True Story*, Andrew Morton
8. *Truman*, David McCullough
9. *Silent Passage*, Gail Sheehy
10. *Sex*, Madonna

1993

Fiction

1. *The Bridges of Madison County*, Robert James Waller
2. *The Client*, John Grisham
3. *Slow Waltz at Cedar Bend*, Robert James Waller
4. *Without Remorse*, Tom Clancy
5. *Nightmares and Dreamscapes*, Stephen King
6. *Vanished*, Danielle Steel
7. *Lasher*, Anne Rice
8. *Pleading Guilty*, Scott Turow
9. *Like Water for Chocolate*, Laura Esquivel

10. *The Scorpio Illusion,* Robert Ludlum
11. *The Golden Mean,* Nick Bantock
12. *I'll Be Seeing You,* Mary Higgins Clark
13. *A Dangerous Fortune,* Ken Follett
14. *Mr. Murder,* Dean Koontz
15. *Gai-Jin,* James Clavell
16. *The Hope,* Herman Wouk
17. *Streets of Laredo,* Larry McMurtry
18. *Griffin & Sabine,* Nick Bantock
19. *Star Wars #4: The Truce at Bankura,* Kathy Tyers
20. *Sacred Clowns,* Tony Hillerman
21. *Star Wars #3: The Last Command,* Timothy Zahn
22. *The Night Manager,* John Le Carré
23. *Homeland,* John Jakes
24. *Decider,* Dick Francis
25. *November of the Heart,* LaVyrle Spencer

Nonfiction

1. *See I Told You So,* Rush Limbaugh
2. *Private Parts,* Howard Stern
3. *Seinlanguage,* Jerry Seinfeld
4. *Embraced by the Light,* Betty J. Eadie with Curtis Taylor
5. *Ageless Body, Timeless Mind,* Deepak Chopra
6. *Stop the Insanity,* Susan Powter
7. *Women Who Run with the Wolves,* Clarissa Pinkola Estes
8. *Men Are from Mars, Women Are from Venus,* John Gray
9. *The Hidden Life of Dogs,* Elizabeth Marshall Thomas
10. *And If You Play Golf, You're My Friend,* Harvey Penick with Bud Shrake
11. *The Way Things Ought To Be,* Rush Limbaugh
12. *Beating the Street,* Peter Lynch with John Rothchild
13. *Harvey Penick's Little Red Book,* Harvey Penick with Bud Shrake
14. *Wouldn't Take Nothing for My Journey Now,* Maya Angelou
15. *Further Along the Road Less Traveled,* M. Scott Peck, M.D.
16. *Maybe (Maybe Not),* Robert Fulghum
17. *Eat More, Weigh Less,* Dean Ornish, M.D.
18. *A Marriage Made in Heaven . . . or Too Tired for an Affair,* Erma Bombeck
19. *Reengineering the Corporation,* Michael Hammer and James Champy
20. *Healing and the Mind,* Bill Moyers
21. *Love Can Build a Bridge,* Naomi Judd with Budd Schaetzle
22. *Star Trek Memories,* William Shatner with Chris Kreski
23. *A Woman's Worth,* Marianne Williamson
24. *The Downing Street Years,* Margaret Thatcher
25. *The Winner Within,* Pat Riley

LITERATURE GOES TO THE MOVIES

It's no secret that many movies, both good and bad, are based on books. This list presents a small sampling of unusual, delightful, and suprising books by leading writers that were turned into well-known movies. (The dates after the titles indicate the year of the film version's release.)

Altered States (1981), Paddy Chayefsky
The Birds (1963), Daphne du Maurier
The Blue Angel (1930, 1959), Heinrich Mann
The Body Snatcher (1945), Robert Louis Stevenson
Breakfast at Tiffany's (1961), Truman Capote
The Chant of Jimmie Blacksmith (1979), Thomas Keneally
Chitty, Chitty, Bang, Bang (1968), Ian Fleming
The Death and Life of Dith Pran (released as *The Killing Fields,* 1984), Sidney Schanberg
Deliverance (1972), James Dickey
Do Androids Dream of Electric Sheep? (released as *Blade Runner,* 1982), Philip K. Dick
Don't Look Now (1971), Daphne du Maurier
The Executioners (released as *Cape Fear,* 1962, 1991), J. D. MacDonald
The Godfather (1972), Mario Puzo
The Hamlet (originally *The Long, Hot Summer,* 1957) William Faulkner
The Last Picture Show (1971), Larry McMurtry
Lolita (1962), Vladimir Nabokov
The Magnificent Ambersons (1942), Booth Tarkington
The Maltese Falcon (1941; also released as *Satan Met a Lady,* 1937), Dashiell Hammett
Mildred Pierce (1945), James M. Cain
The Natural (1984), Bernard Malamud
The Postman Always Rings Twice (1946, 1981), James M. Cain
Re-Animator (1985), H. P. Lovecraft and Herbert West
The Seven Pillars of Wisdom (released as *Lawrence of Arabia,* 1962), T. E. Lawrence
Tales from the South Pacific (produced as the musical *South Pacific* and later released as a film, 1958), James Michener
The Turn of the Screw (released as *The Innocents,* 1961), Henry James
Two Hours to Doom (released as *Dr. Strangelove,* 1964), Peter George

BESTSELLING CHILDREN'S BOOKS

Publishers Weekly started breaking out a separate children's bestseller list recently; here are the past three year's results.

1991

1. *The Jolly Christmas Postman*, Janet and Allan Ahlberg
2. *Carl's Afternoon in the Park*, Alexandra Day
3. *Where's Waldo? The Magnificent Poster Book*, Martin Handford
4. *Disney's Beauty and the Beast*, A. L. Singer, illustrated by Ron Dias and Rick Gonzales
5. *Six by Seuss*, Dr. Seuss
6. *If You Give a Moose a Muffin*, Laura Joffe Numeroff, illustrated by Felicia Bond
7. *Disney's Little Mermaid Pop-Up*, illustrated by Kerry Martin
8. *Children's Letters to God: The New Collection*, compiled by Stuart Hample and Eric Marshall; illustrated by Tom Bloom
9. *The Random House Children's Encyclopedia*
10. *Brother Eagle, Sister Sky*, Chief Seattle, illustrated by Susan Jeffers

1992

1. *Disney's Aladdin*, adapted by Karen Kreider, illustrated by Darrell Baker
2. *Aladdin*, Walt Disney Staff
3. *The Sign of the Seahorse*, Graeme Base
4. *Walt Disney's The Little Mermaid*, adapted by Betty Birney, illustrated by Kerry Martin and Fred Marvin
5. *Walt Disney's Pinocchio*, adapted by Diane Muldrow, illustrated by Fred Marvin
6. *Walt Disney's Bambi*, adapted by Denise Lewis Patrick, illustrated by Mones
7. *Walt Disney's Snow White*, adapted by Denise Lewis Patrick, illustrated by Mones
8. *Walt Disney's Dumbo*, adapted by Rita Balducci, illustrated by Phil Ortiz and Diana Wakeman
9. *Walt Disney's Cinderella*, adapted by Rita Balducci, illustrated by Mones
10. *Brown Bear, Brown Bear, What Do You See?* (25th anniversary edition), Bill Martin Jr., illustrated by Eric Carle

1993

1. *Barney's Farm Animals*, Kimberly Kearns and Marie O'Brien, illustrated by Karen Malzeke-McDonald
2. *Barney's Favorite Mother Goose Rhymes*, Stephen White, illustrated by Mary Grace Eubank
3. *Baby Bop's Toys*, Kimberly Kearns and Marie O'Brien
4. *Barney's Color Surprise*, Mary Ann Dudko and Margie Larsen
5. *Baby Bop's Counting Book*, Mary Ann Dudko and Margie Larsen
6. *Where's Waldo? In Hollywood*, Martin Handford
7. *Aladdin (Disney Classic)*
8. *Baby Bop Discovers Shapes*, Stephen White, illustrated by Larry Daste
9. *Poky Puppy's First Christmas*, Justine Korman, illustrated by Jean Chandler
10. *Beauty and the Beast: Teapot's Tale*, Justine Korman, illustrated by Peter Emslie

LITERARY LISTENING—BESTSELLING BOOKS ON TAPE, 1993

Americans have been doing a lot of reading behind the wheel, and as this list of bestselling books on tape reveals, our tastes are pretty broad. Based on 1993's most successful audio books, as sold by Waldenbooks and Barnes & Noble, this list is not a true ranking of bestsellers, but since the two giant chains sell a significant number of the nation's audio books, it does give us a good gauge of the year's most popular listening.

1. *See I Told You So*, Rush Limbaugh
2. *The Client*, John Grisham
3. *The Way Things Ought To Be*, Rush Limbaugh
4. *Seven Habits of Highly Effective People*, Steven Covey
5. *The Pelican Brief*, John Grisham
6. *Jurassic Park*, Michael Crichton
7. *Without Remorse*, Tom Clancy
8. *The Bridges of Madison County*, Robert James Waller
9. *The Firm*, John Grisham
10. *Awaken the Giant Within*, Anthony Robbins
11. *Ageless Body, Timeless Mind*, Deepak Chopra
12. *A Christmas Carol*, Charles Dickens
13. *Star Wars #3:—The Last Command*, Timothy Zahn
14. *Star Wars Original Radio Drama*, Lucas Films
15. *Lake Wobegon USA*, Garrison Keillor

THE *PEOPLE* BOOKSHELF

PEOPLE hasn't been reviewing books long enough to tell you the best of the century, but here are the books we loved the most over the past seventeen years.

FICTION

The Accidental Tourist, Anne Tyler
All the Pretty Horses, Cormac McCarthy
An Indecent Obsession, Colleen McCollough
Anagrams, Lorrie Moore
Anton the Dove Fancier, Bernard Gotfryd
August, Judith Rossner
Before and After, Rosellen Brown
Beloved, Toni Morrison
Birdy, William Wharton
The Blooding, Joseph Wambaugh
Body and Soul, Frank Conroy
The Bonfire of the Vanities, Tom Wolfe
Breathing Lessons, Anne Tyler
Cat's Eye, Margaret Atwood
Clockers, Richard Price
Collaborators, Janet Kauffman
The Collected Stories, Isaac Bashevis Singer
The Color Purple, Alice Walker
A Confederacy of Dunces, John Kennedy Toole
Dinner at the Homesick Restaurant, Anne Tyler
The Dragons of Eden, Carl Sagan
Dutch Shea Jr., John Gregory Dunne
East is East, T. Coraghessan Boyle
Ellis Island, Mark Helprin
Enchantment, Daphne Merkin
Eye of the Needle, Ken Follett
Fanny, Erica Jong
Final Payments, Mary Gordon
The Firm, John Grisham
The First Man in Rome, Colleen McCullough
For Love, Sue Miller
Foreign Affairs, Alison Lurie
Get Shorty, Elmore Leonard
The Glass House, Laura Furman
The Good Mother, Sue Miller
Gorky Park, Martin Cruz Smith
Happy To Be There, Garrison Keillor
Her First American, Lore Segal
The Honourable Schoolboy, John Le Carré
The House of the Spirits, Isabel Allende
Illumination Night, Abbie Hoffman
Labrava, Elmore Leonard
Lake Wobegon Days, Garrison Keillor
Lancelot, Walker Percy
A Lesson Before Dying, Ernest J. Gaines
Libra, Don DeLillo
A Light in the Attic, Shel Silverstein
Life Its Ownself, Dan Jenkins
Love in the Time of Cholera, Gabriel García Márquez
Machine Dreams, Jayne Anne Phillips
The Mambo Kings Play Songs of Love, Oscar Hijuelos
Maus: A Survivor's Tale, II: And Here My Troubles Begin, Art Spiegelman
Me and My Baby View the Eclipse, Lee Smith
Memoirs of an Invisible Man, H. F. Saint
Monkeys, Susan Minot
Monsignor Quixote, Graham Greene
More Die of Heartbreak, Saul Bellow
Music for Chameleons, Truman Capote
The Natural Man, Ed McClanahan
Noble House, James Clavell
Owning Jolene, Shelby Hearon
Patrimony, Philip Roth
Perfume, Patrick Süskind
Poodle Springs, Raymond Chandler and Robert B. Parker
The Pope of Greenwich Village, Vincent Park
Presumed Innocent, Scott Turow
The Progress of Love, Alice Munro
Quinn's Book, William Kennedy
Rabbit at Rest, John Updike
The Robber Bride, Margaret Atwood
Roger's Version, John Updike
The Russia House, John Le Carré
Salvador, Joan Didion
The Secret History, Donna Tartt
Seventh Heaven, Alice Hoffman
She's Come Undone, Wally Lamb
The Sicilian, Mario Puzo
Smilla's Sense of Snow, Peter Hoeg
A Soldier of the Great War, Mark Helprin
Sophie's Choice, William Styron
Talking to the Dead, Sylvia Watanabe
Tracks, Louise Erdrich
The Tree of Life, Hugh Nissenson
True Confessions, John Gregory Dunne
The Twenty-Seventh City, Jonathan Franzen
Typical American, Gish Jen

Waiting to Exhale, Terry McMillan

The White Hotel, D. M. Thomas

Winter's Tale, Mark Helprin

World's Fair, E. L. Doctorow

The Yellow Wind, David Grossman

NONFICTION

American Caesar, William Manchester

American Prospects, Joel Sternfeld

Backlash, Susan Faludi

Best Intentions, Robert Sam Anson

The Best of Dear Abby, Abigail Van Buren

Blue Highways, William Least Heat Moon

The Bookmakers's Daughter, Shirley Abbott

Cameraworks, David Hockney

The Chimpanzees of Gombe, Jane Goodall

The Culture of Narcissism, Christopher Lasch

Dave Barry Slept Here, Dave Barry

Den of Thieves, James B. Stewart

The Devil's Candy, Julie Salamon

A Distant Mirror, Barbara Tuchman

The Duke of Deception, Geoffrey Wolff

Edie, Jean Stein, edited with George Plimpton

Edith Sitwell, Victoria Glendinning

The Fatal Shore, Robert Hughes

Fatal Vision, Joe McGinniss

Fatherhood, Bill Cosby

The Forbidden Experiment, Roger Shattuck

Fungus the Bogeyman, Raymond Briggs

The Girl I Left Behind, Jane O'Reilly

The Glass House, Laura Furman

Goldwyn: A Biography, A. Scott Berg

"The Good War," Studs Terkel

The Hidden Life of Dogs, Elizabeth Marshall

Home Before Dark, Susan Cheever

Hometown, Peter Davis

House, Tracy Kidder

I Dream A World, Brian Lanker

In and Out of the Garden, Sara Midda

Ingrid Bergman: My Story, Ingrid Bergman and Alan Burgess

January Sun, Richard Stengel

The Kennedys: An American Dream, Peter Collier and David Horowitz

Kissinger, Walter Isaacson

The Knife and Gun Club, Eugene Richards

The Last Lion, William Manchester

Laura Z., A Life, Laura Z. Hobson

Lauren Bacall By Myself, Lauren Bacall

Lenin's Tomb, David Remnick

A Life of Picasso, John Richardson

Little League Confidential, Bill Geist

The Lives of John Lennon, Albert Goldman

Loitering with Intent, Peter O'Toole

Maida Heatter's Book of Great Chocolate Desserts, Maida Heatter

The Man Who Mistook His Wife for a Hat, Oliver Sacks

Means of Ascent, Robert A. Caro

The Medusa and the Snail, Lewis Thomas

Midair, Frank Conroy

Miss Manners' Guide to Excruciatingly Correct Behavior, Judith Martin

Mister Rogers Talks With Parents, Fred Rogers and Barry Head

Moonshine, Alec Wilkinson

The Non-Runner's Book, Vic Ziegel and Lewis Grossberger

On Boxing, Joyce Carol Oates

On Photography, Susan Sontag

Pablo Picasso, A Retrospective, edited by William Rubin

Payback, Joe Klein

Photoportraits, Henri Cartier-Bresson

President Kennedy, Richard Reeves

The Ragman's Son, Kirk Douglas

The Rise of Theodore Roosevelt, Edmund Morris

A Rumor of War, Philip Caputo

Saul Steinberg, Harold Rosenberg

Serpentine, Thomas Thompson

Side Effects, Woody Allen

The Sketchbooks of Picasso, Pablo Picasso

The Snow Leopard, Peter Mathiessen

The Story of English, Robert McCrum, William Cran, and Robert MacNeil

Sylvia Plachy's Unguided Tour, Sylvia Plachy

The Teamsters, Steven Brill

The Years of Lyndon Johnson: The Path to Power, Robert A. Caro

Truman, David McCullough

Why Are They Weeping?, photographed by David C. Turnley and written by Alan Cowell

Workers, Sebastião Salgado

A Writer's Beginnings, Eudora Welty

THE *PEOPLE* TRASH HEAP

PEOPLE's reviewers read these books because they had to—it's their job. But you have a choice. The following is a selection of books "Picks & Pans" judged as the worst—or most over-rated—from the past seventeen years.

FICTION

A Bloodsmoor Romance, Joyce Carol Oates
A Matter of Honor, Jeffrey Archer
A Prayer for Owen Meany, John Irving
Alnilam, James Dickey
American Psycho, Bret Easton Ellis
Ancient Evenings, Norman Mailer
Answer as a Man, Taylor Caldwell
Any Woman's Blues, Erica Jong
Ascent Into Hell, Andrew M. Greeley
Beast, Peter Benchley
The Big Hype, Avery Corman
The Bourne Ultimatum, Robert Ludlum
Brain, Robin Cook
Children of Light, Robert Stone
The Children's Story, James Clavell
Christine, Stephen King
The Coup, John Updike
Daddy, Danielle Steel
The Devil's Alternative, Frederick Forsyth
Doctors, Erich Segal
Elvis, Albert Goldman
Empress, Sylvia Wallace
Fever, Robin Cook
Floating Dragon, Peter Straub
.44, Jimmy Breslin and Dick Schaap
Free to Love, Ivana Trump
Friends in High Places, John Weitz
The Girl of the Sea of Cortez, Peter Benchley
Godplayer, Robin Cook
Happy Endings, Sally Quinn
Heartburn, Nora Ephron
The Holcroft Covenant, Robert Ludlum
Home Front, Patti Davis with Maureen Strange Foster
The Hope, Herman Wouk
A House of Secrets, Patti Davis
I Dream a World, Brian Lanker
Illusions: The Adventures of a Reluctant Messiah, Richard Bach
In Praise of the Stepmother, Mario Vargas Llosa
Inside, Outside, Herman Wouk
The Island, Peter Benchley
Lace, Shirley Conran
Lasher, Anne Rice
The Last Days of America, Paul Erdman
Legion, William Peter Blatty
Lord of the Dance, Andrew M. Greeley
Love and War, John Jakes
Lucky, Jackie Collins
Lust, Susan Minot
The Mammoth Hunters, Jean M. Auel
Manhattan, Neal Travis
Maybe, Lillian Hellman
Megan's Book of Divorce, Erica Jong
Memories of Another Day, Harold Robbins
Men In Love, Nancy Friday
The Men's Club, Leonard Michaels
Message from Nam, Danielle Steel
Mindbend, Robin Cook
The Minstrel, Bernard Benson
Monímbo, Robert Moss and Arnaud de Borchgrave
The Mosquito Coast, Paul Theroux
The Mummy, Anne Rice
Murder in the White House, Margaret Truman
Nature's End, Whitley Streiber and James Kunetka
The Ninth Configuration, William Peter Blatty
Of Love and Shadows, Isabel Allende
The Old Neighborhood, Avery Corman
Oliver's Story, Erich Segal
The Origin, Irving Stone
Outbreak, Robin Cook
The Paper Men, William Golding
Parachutes and Kisses, Erica Jong
The Pigeon, Patrick Süskind
The Pillars of the Earth, Ken Follett
The Plagiarist, Benjamin Cheever
Pinball, Jerzy Kosinski
Prime Time, Joan Collins
Postcards from the Edge, Carrie Fisher
"Q" Clearance, Peter Benchley
Queen of the Damned, Anne Rice
Regrets Only, Sally Quinn
Rock Star, Jackie Collins
The Runaway Soul, Harold Brodkey
S., John Updike
Sailor Song, Ken Kesey
Savages, Shirley Conran
Scruples, Judith Krantz
See You Later, Alligator, William F. Buckley Jr.
Slaves of New York, Tama Janowitz
Slow Waltz at Cedar Bend, Robert James Waller

Smart Women, Judy Blume
Spellbinder, Harold Robbins
Sphinx, Robin Cook
Star, Danielle Steel
The Story of Henri Todd, William F. Buckley Jr.
Story of My Life, Jay McInerney
The Talisman, Stephen King and Peter Straub
The Temple of My Familiar, Alice Walker
Texas, James Michener
Tinsel, William Goldman
Vox, Nicholson Baker
The Walnut Door, John Hersey
Whirlwind, James Clavell
The Winners, Dominick Dunne
West of Sunset, Dirk Bogarde

NONFICTION

An Affair to Remember, Maureen Donaldson and William Royce
Among the Porcupines, Carol Matthau
Andrew Wyeth: The Helga Pictures, John Wilmerding
Bardot Deneuve Fonda, Roger Vadim
The Beverly Hills Diet, Judy Mazel
Beyond Reason, Margaret Trudeau
Blown Away, A. E. Hotchner
The Book of Lists, David Wallechinsky, Irving Wallace, and Amy Wallace
Brando for Breakfast, Anna Kashfi and E. P. Stein
Brother Billy, Ruth Carter Stapleton
Bus 9 to Paradise, Leo Buscaglia
Cary Grant: The Lonely Heart, Charles Higham and Roy Moseley
Character: America's Search for Leadership, Gail Sheehy
Cruel Shoes, Steve Martin
Dance with the Devil, Kirk Douglas
Dancing in the Light, Shirley MacLaine
Elizabeth Taylor, The Last Star, Kitty Kelley
Family—The Ties That Bind . . . and Gag!, Erma Bombeck
Feminine Force: Release the Power Within to Create the Life You Deserve, Georgette Mosbacher
Flight of the Avenger: George Bush at War and in Love, Joe Hyams
Garbo: Her Story, Antoni Gronowicz
Give War a Chance, P. J. O'Rourke
Glory Days: Bruce Springsteen in the 1980s, Dave Marsh
Good Guys, Bad Guys, Shere Hite and Kate Colleran
Having It All, Helen Gurley Brown
The Hite Report on Male Sexuality, Shere Hite
How to Take Charge of Your Life, Bernard Berkowitz and Mildred Newman
I Remember, Dan Rather
In the American West, Richard Avedon
It's All in the Playing, Shirley MacLaine
The Jackson Phenomenon, Elizabeth O. Colton
Just Enough Rope, Joan Braden
The Killing of the Unicorn, Peter Bogdanovich
The Last Brother, Joe McGinniss
Laurence Olivier: A Biography, Donald Spoto
Life's Little Instruction Book, H. Jackson Brown Jr.
The Linda Evans Beauty and Exercise Book, Linda Evans
The Lives of John Lennon, Albert Goldman
Metropolitan Life, Fran Lebowitz
More Memories, Ralph Emery
Not That You Asked, Andrew A. Rooney
Now You Know, Kitty Dukakis
Number One, Billy Martin and Peter Golenboch
On Your Own, Brooke Shields
The One Minute Father, Spencer Johnson, M.D.
The One Minute Mother, Spencer Johnson, M.D.
Out on a Limb, Shirley MacLaine
A Place at the Table, Bruce Bawer
The Power to Heal, edited by Rick Smolan, Phillip Moffitt, and Matthew Naythons, M.D.
Pulling Your Own Strings, Dr. Wayne Dyer
Restoring the American Dream, Robert Ringer
Revolution from Within, Gloria Steinem
RN: The Memoirs of Richard Nixon, Richard Nixon
Running and Being, Dr. George Sheehan
The Second Seduction, Frances Lear
Secrets of a Sparrow, Diana Ross
Sex, Madonna
Shelley: Also Known As Shirley, Shelley Winters
Social Studies, Fran Lebowitz
Tennessee: Cry of the Heart, Dotson Rader
Thy Neighbor's Wife, Gay Talese
Transformation, Whitley Streiber
Uh-Oh, Robert Fulghum
Wasted: The Preppie Murder, Linda Wolfe
Willie, Willie Nelson with Bud Shrake
Women and Love, Shere Hite
Women's Work, Anne Tolstoi Wallach
Woody Allen: A Biography, Eric Lax

BIBLIOGRAPHIES OF THE BIG AUTHORS

These are complete listings for a broad selection of the most popular, most admired, most criticized, and most eagerly devoured authors today. For each, all full-length works, poetry, and plays are listed, followed by the year of publication.

MARGARET ATWOOD

Fiction
The Edible Woman (1969)
Surfacing (1972)
Lady Oracle (1976)
Life Before Man (1979)
Bodily Harm (1981)
Murder in the Dark (1983)
Bluebeard's Egg (1983)
The Handmaid's Tale (1985)
Cat's Eye (1988)
The Robber Bride (1993)
Good Bones and Simple Murders (1994)

Poetry
The Animals in That Country (1968)
The Journals of Susanna Moodie (1970)
Procedures for Underground (1970)
Power Politics (1971)
You Are Happy (1974)
Two-Headed Poems (1978)
True Stories (1981)
Snake Poems (1983)
Interlunar (1984)

Children's books
Up in the Tree (1978)
Anna's Pet (1980)
For the Birds (1990)

Nonfiction
Survival: A Thematic Guide to Canadian Literature (1972)
Days of the Rebels, 1815–1840 (1977)

SAUL BELLOW

Fiction
Dangling Man (1944)
The Victim (1947)
The Adventures of Augie March (1953; National Book Award)
Seize the Day (1956)
Henderson the Rain King (1959)
Herzog (1964; National Book Award)
Mr. Sammler's Planet (1970; National Book Award)
Humbolt's Gift (1975; Pulitzer Prize)
The Dean's December (1982)
More Die of Heartbreak (1987)

Nonfiction
To Jerusalem and Back: A Personal Account (1976)
It All Adds Up (1994)

Play
The Last Analysis, a Play (produced in 1964)

Nobel Prize for Literature, 1976

TOM CLANCY

Fiction
The Hunt for Red October (1984)
Red Storm Rising (1986)
Patriot Games (1987)
The Cardinal of the Kremlin (1988)
Clear and Present Danger (1989)
The Sum of All Fears (1991)
Without Remorse (1993)
Debt of Honor (1994)

Nonfiction
Submarine: A Guided Tour Inside a Nuclear Warship (1993)

PAT CONROY

Fiction
The Boo (1970)
The Water Is Wide (1972)
The Great Santini (1976)
The Lords of Discipline (1980)
The Prince of Tides (1986)
Beach Music (1994)

MICHAEL CRICHTON

Fiction
The Andromeda Strain (1969)
Five Patients (1970)
The Terminal Man (1972)
Westworld (1974)
The Great Train Robbery (1975)
Eaters of the Dead (1976)
Congo (1980)
Sphere (1987)
Jurassic Park (1990)
Rising Sun (1992)
Disclosure (1994)

Fiction written as John Lange
Odds On (1960)
Scratch One (1967)
Easy Go (1968; re-published as *The Last Tomb*, 1974)
Zero Cool (1969)
The Venom Business (1969)
Drug of Choice (1970)
Grave Descend (1970)
Binary (1971)

Fiction written as Jeffrey Hudson
A Case of Need (1968)

Nonfiction
Five Patients: The Hospital Explained (1970)
Jasper Johns (1977)
Electronic Life: How To Think about Computers (1983)
Travels (autobiography, 1988)

ROBERTSON DAVIES

Fiction
The Diary of Samuel Marchbanks (1947)
The Table Talk of Samuel Marchbanks (1949)
Fortune, My Foe (1949)
At My Heart's Core (1950)
Tempest-Tost (1951)
A Masque of Aesop (1952)
Leaven of Malice (1954)
A Jig for the Gypsy (1954)
A Mixture of Frailties (1958)
A Voice from the Attic (1960)
A Masque of Mr. Punch (1963)
Samuel Marchbanks' Almanack (1967)
Stephen Leacock (1970)
Feast of Stephen (1970)
Fifth Business (1970)
The Manticore (1972)
Question Time (1975)
World of Wonders (1975)
One Half of Robertson Davies (1977)
The Rebel Angels (1981)
High Spirits (1982)
What's Bred in the Bone (1985)
The Papers of Samuel Marchbanks (1985)
The Lyre of Orpheus (1988)
Murther and Walking Spirits (1991)
The Cunning Man (1994)

Nonfiction
Shakespeare's Boy Actors (1939)
Shakespeare for Young Players: A Junior Course (1942)
The Heart of a Merry Christmas (1970)
Stephen Leacock (1970)
The Revels History of Drama in English, Vol. 6: 1750-1880 (coauthor, 1975)
One Half of Robertson Davies: Provocative Pronouncements on a Wide Rage of Topics (1977)
The Enthusiams of Robertson Davies (1979)
Robertson Davies: The Well-Tempered Critic: One Man's View of Theatre and Letters in Canada (1981)

Plays
A Play of Our Lord's Nativity (1946)
Fortune, My Foe (1948)
At My Heart's Core (1952)
A Masque of Aesop (1952)
A Jig for Gypsy (1954)
Love and Libel (based on *Leaven of Malice*, 1960)
A Masque of Mr. Punch (1962)
The Voice of the People (1968)
Brothers in the Black Art (1974)
Question Time (1975)
Pontiac and the Green Man (1977)

E. L. DOCTOROW

Fiction
Welcome to Hard Times (1960)
Big as Life (1966)
The Book of Daniel (1971)
Ragtime (1975; National Book Critics Circle Award)
Loon Lake (1980)
World's Fair (1985)
Billy Bathgate (1989; National Book Critics Circle Award)
The Waterworks (1994)

Nonfiction
Jack London, Hemingway, and the Constitution: Selected Writings, 1977–1992 (1993)

LOUISE ERDRICH

Fiction
Love Medicine (1984; National Book Critics Circle Award)
The Beet Queen (1986)
Tracks (1988)
The Crown of Columbus (coauthor, 1991)
The Bingo Palace (1994)

Poetry
Jacklight (1984)
Baptism of Desire (1989)

JOHN GRISHAM

Fiction
A Time to Kill (1989)
The Firm (1991)
The Pelican Brief (1992)
The Client (1993)
The Chamber (1994)

MARK HELPRIN

Fiction
Refiner's Fire (1977)
Winter's Tale (1983)
A Soldier of the Great War (1991)

Children's books
Swan Lake (1989)

STEPHEN KING

Fiction
Carrie (1975)
Salem's Lot (1976)
The Shining (1977)
The Stand (1978)
The Dead Zone (1979)
Firestarter (1980)
Cujo (1981)
The Dark Tower: The Gunslinger (1982)
Christine (1983)
Pet Sematary (1983)
The Talisman (coauthor, 1984)
Cycle of the Werewolf (1985)
It (1986)
The Eyes of the Dragon (1987)
Misery (1987)
The Tommyknockers (1987)
The Dark Half (1989)
The Dark Tower II: The Drawing of Three (1989)
The Dark Tower III: The Waste Lands (1991)
Needful Things (1991)
Gerald's Game (1992)
Dolores Claiborne (1992)
Insomnia (1994)

Fiction written as Richard Bachman
Rage (1977)
The Long Walk (1979)
The Running Man (1982)
Thinner (1984)
Roadwork: A Novel of the First Energy Crisis (1981)

Nonfiction
Danse Macabre (1981)

JOHN LE CARRÉ
(pseudonym of David Cornwell)

Fiction
Call for the Dead (1960)
A Murder of Quality (1962)
The Spy Who Came in from the Cold (1964)
The Incongruous Spy (1964)
The Looking Glass War (1965)
A Small Town in Germany (1968)
The Naive and Sentimental Lover (1971)
Tinker, Tailor, Soldier, Spy (1977)
Smiley's People (1980)
The Honourable Schoolboy (1982)
The Little Drummer Girl (1983)
A Perfect Spy (1986)
The Russia House (1989)
The Secret Pilgrim (1991)
The Night Manager (1993)

ROBERT LUDLUM

Fiction
The Scarlatti Inheritance (1971)
The Osterman Weekend (1972)
The Matlock Paper (1973)
The Gemini Contenders (1976)
The Chancellor Manuscript (1977)
The Holcroft Covenant (1978)
The Matarese Circle (1979)
The Bourne Identity (1980)
The Parsifal Mosaic (1982)
The Aquitane Progression (1984)
The Bourne Supremacy (1986)
The Icarus Agenda (1988)
The Bourne Ultimatum (1990)
The Road to Omaha (1992)
The Scorpio Illusion (1993)

Fiction written as Jonathan Ryder
Trevayne (1973)
The Cry of the Halidon (1974)

Fiction written as Michael Shepherd
The Road to Gandolfo (1975)

NORMAN MAILER

Fiction
The Naked and the Dead (1948)
Barbary Shore (1951)
The Deer Park (1955; screenplay, *Wild 90*, 1967)
An American Dream (1965)
Why Are We in Vietnam? (1967)
The Executioner's Song (1979; Pulitzer Prize; screenplay 1982)
Ancient Evenings (1983)
Tough Guys Don't Dance (1984; screenplay 1987)
Huckleberry Finn, Alive at One Hundred (1984)
Harlot's Ghost (1992)

Nonfiction
The Armies of the Night: History as a Novel, the Novel as History (1968; Pulitzer Prize; National Book Award)
Miami and the Siege of Chicago (1968; National Book Award)
Of a Fire on the Moon (1970)
King of the Hill: On the Fight of the Century (1971)
St. George and the Godfather (1971)
The Prisoner of Sex (1971)
Marilyn: A Biography (1973)
The Faith of Grafitti (1974)
The Fight (1975)
Of a Small and Modest Malignancy, Wicked and Bristling with Dots (1980)

JAMES A. MICHENER

Fiction
Tales of the South Pacific (1947; Pulitzer Prize)
The Fires of the Spring (1949)
The Bridges of Toko-Ri (1953)
Sayonara (1954)
Hawaii (1959)
Caravans (1963)
The Source (1965)
The Drifters (1971)
Centennial (1974)
Chesapeake (1978)

The Covenant (1980)
Space (1982)
Poland (1983)
Texas (1985)
Legacy (1987)
Alaska (1988)
Carribean (1989)
The Eagle and the Raven (1990)
The Novel (1991)
Mexico (1992)
Recessional (1994)

Children's book
South Pacific (1992)

Nonfiction
Voice of Asia (1951)
The Floating World (1954)
The Bridge at Andau (1957)
Facing East (1961)
Iberia: Spanish Travels and Reflections (1968)
America vs. America: The Revolution in Middle-Class Values (1969)
Presidential Lottery: The Reckless Gamble in Our Electoral System (1969)
A Study of the Art of Jack Levine (1970)
Kent State: What Happened and Why (1971)
Sports in America (1976)
The World Is My Home (memoirs, 1992)
Literary Reflections: Michener on Michener, Hemingway, Capote, and Others (1993)

TONI MORRISON

Fiction
The Bluest Eye (1969)
Sula (1973)
Song of Solomon (1977; National Book Critics Circle Award)
Tar Baby (1981)
Beloved (1987; Pulitzer Prize)
Jazz (1992)

Nonfiction
Playing in the Dark: Whiteness and the Literary Imagination (1992)

Play
Dreaming Emmett (1986)

Nobel Prize for Literature, 1993

THOMAS PYNCHON

Fiction
V (1963)
The Crying of Lot 49 (1965)
Gravity's Rainbow (1973)
Vineland (1990)

ANNE RICE

Fiction
Interview with the Vampire (1976)
The Feast of All Saints (1980)
Cry to Heaven (1982)
The Vampire Lestat (1985)
The Queen of the Damned (1988)
The Mummy or Ramses the Damned (1989)
The Witching Hour (1990)
Tale of the Body Thief (1992)
Lasher (1993)
Taltos (1994)

Fiction written as A. N. Roquelaure
The Claiming of Sleeping Beauty (1983)
Beauty's Punishment (1984)
Beauty's Release: The Continued Erotic Adventures of Sleeping Beauty (1985)

Fiction written as Anne Rampling
Exit to Eden (1985)
Belinda (1986)

PHILIP ROTH

Fiction
Goodbye, Columbus (1959; National Book Award)
Letting Go (1962)
When She Was Good (1967)
Portnoy's Complaint (1969)
Our Gang (1971)
The Breast (1972)
The Great American Novel (1973)
My Life as a Man (1974)
Reading Myself and Others (1975)
The Professor of Desire (1977)
The Ghost Writer (1979)
Zuckerman Unbound (1981)
The Anatomy Lesson (1983)
Zuckerman Bound (1985)
The Counterlife (1987)
Deception (1990)
Operation Shylock (1993)

Nonfiction
The Facts: A Novelist's Autobiography (1988)
Patrimony: A True Story (memoirs, 1991)

SALMAN RUSHDIE

Fiction
Grimus (1975)
Midnight's Children (1981)
Shame (1983)
The Satanic Verses (1989)
Haroun and the Sea of Stories (1991; Booker Prize)

Nonfiction
The Jaguar Smile: A Nicaraguan Journey (1987)

MAURICE SENDAK

Children's books
Kenny's Window (1956)
Very Far Away (1957)
The Sign on Rosie's Door (1960)
Chicken Soup with Rice (1962)
One Was Johnny (1962)
Alligators All Around (1962)
Pierre (1962)
Where the Wild Things Are (1963; Caldecott Medal)
Hector Protector [and] As I Went Over the Water (1965)
Higglety Pigglety Pop! or, There Must Be More to Life (1967)
In the Night Kitchen (1970)
Ten Little Rabbits: A Counting Book with Mino the Magician (1970)
Maurice Sendak's Really Rosie (1975)
Some Swell Pup; or Are You Sure You Want a Dog? (1976)
Seven Little Monsters (1977)
Outside Over There (1981)
We Are All in the Dumps with Jack and Guy (1993)

Hans Christian Anderson Award, 1970

DANIELLE STEEL

Fiction
Going Home (1973)
Passion's Promise (1977)
Now and Forever (1978)
The Promise (1978)
Season of Passion (1979)
Summer's End (1979)
To Love Again (1980)
The Ring (1980)
Loving (1980)
Remembrance (1981)
Palomino (1981)
Once in a Lifetime (1982)
Crossings (1982)
A Perfect Stranger (1982)
Thurston House (1983)
Changes (1983)
Full Circle (1984)
Family Album (1985)
Secrets (1985)
Wanderlust (1986)
Fine Things (1987)
Kaleidoscope (1987)
Zoya (1988)
Star (1989)
Daddy (1989)
Message from Nam (1990)
Heartbeat (1991)
No Greater Love (1991)
Jewels (1992)
Mixed Blessings (1992)
Vanished (1993)
Accident (1994)
The Gift (1994)
Wings (1994)

Children's books
Max and the Babysitter (1989)
Martha's Best Friend (1989)
Max's Daddy Goes to the Hospital (1989)
Martha's New Daddy (1989)
Max's New Baby (1989)
Martha's New School (1989)
Max Runs Away (1990)
Martha's New Puppy (1990)
Max and Grandma and Grandpa Winky (1991)
Martha and Hilary and the Stranger (1991)
Freddie's Trip (1992)

Freddie's First Night Away (1992)
Freddie and the Doctor (1992)
Freddie's Accident (1992)

Poetry
Love Poems by Danielle Steel (1981)

Nonfiction
Having a Baby (1984)

ANNE TYLER

Fiction
If Morning Ever Comes (1964)
The Tin Can Tree (1965)
A Slipping-Down Life (1970)
The Clock Winder (1972)
Celestial Navigation (1974)
Searching for Caleb (1976)
Earthly Possessions (1977)
Morgan's Passing (1980)
Dinner at the Homesick Restaurant (1982)
The Accidental Tourist (1985)
Breathing Lessons (1988; Pulitzer Prize)
Saint Maybe (1991)

Children's books
Tumble Tower (1993)

JOHN UPDIKE

Fiction
The Poorhouse Fair (1959)
Rabbit, Run (1960)
The Centaur (1963; National Book Award)
Of the Farm (1965)
Couples (1968)
Rabbit Redux (1971)
A Month of Sundays (1975)
Marry Me: A Romance (1976)
The Coup (1978)
Rabbit Is Rich (1981; Pulitzer Prize; American Book Award; National Book Critics Circle Award)
The Witches of Eastwick (1984)
Roger's Version (1986)
S. (1988)
Rabbit at Rest (1990)
Memoirs of the Ford Administration (1992)
Brazil (1994)

Nonfiction
Self Consciousness (memoirs, 1989)

Children's books
The Magic Flute (1962)
The Ring (1964)
A Child's Calendar (1965)
Bottom's Dream (1969)

ALICE WALKER

Fiction
The Third Life of Grange Copeland (1970)
Meridian (1976)
The Color Purple (1982; Pulitzer Prize)
The Temple of My Familiar (1989)
Possessing the Secret of Joy (1992)

Nonfiction
Warrior Marks (1993)

Poetry
Once (1976)
Revolutionary Petunias and Other Poems (1973)
Goodnight, Willie Lee, I'll See You in the Morning (1984)
Horses Make a Landscape Look More Beautiful (1984)

FROM GREAT BEGINNINGS, GREAT NOVELS GROW

Every great book has to start somehow—this is how selected authors began their tales.

"At a village of la Mancha, whose name I do not wish to remember, there lived a little while ago one of those gentlemen who are wont to keep a lance in the rack, an old buckler, a lean horse, and a swift greyhound."
— *The Adventures of Don Quixote de la Mancha*, Miguel de Cervantes

"Alice was beginning to get very tired of sitting by her sister on the bank and of having nothing to do: once or twice she had peeped into the book her sister was reading, but it had no pictures or conversations in it, 'and what is the use of a book,' thought Alice, 'without pictures or conversations?' "
— *Alice in Wonderland*, Lewis Carroll

"Happy families are all alike, but an unhappy family is unhappy in its own way."
— *Anna Karenina*, Leo Tolstoy

"It was a queer, sultry summer, the summer they electrocuted the Rosenbergs, and I didn't know what I was doing in New York."
— *The Bell Jar*, Sylvia Plath

"There are songs that come free from the blue-eyed grass, from the dust of a thousand country roads."
— *The Bridges of Madison County*, Robert James Waller

"Buck did not read the newspapers, or he would have known that trouble was brewing, not alone for himself, but for every tide-water dog, strong of muscle and with warm, long hair, from Puget Sound to San Diego."
— *The Call of the Wild*, Jack London

"On top of everything, the cancer wing was Number 13."
— *The Cancer Ward*, Alexander Solzhenitsyn

"Nobody was really surprised when it happened, not really, not at the subconscious level where savage things grow."
— *Carrie*, Stephen King

"It was love at first sight."
— *Catch-22*, Joseph Heller

"If you really want to hear about it, the first thing you'll probably want to know is where I was born, and what my lousy childhood was like, and how my parents were occupied and all before they had me, and all that David Copperfield kind of crap, but I don't feel like going into it, if you want to know the truth."
— *A Catcher in the Rye*, J. D. Salinger

" 'Where's Papa going with that ax?' said Fern to her mother as they were setting the table for breakfast."
— *Charlotte's Web*, E. B. White

"What's it going to be then, eh?"
— *A Clockwork Orange*, Anthony Burgess

"Whether I shall turn out to be the hero of my own life, or whether that station will be held by anybody else, these pages must show."
— *David Copperfield*, Charles Dickens

"I had the story, bit by bit, from various people, and, as generally happens in such cases, each time it was a different story."
— *Ethan Frome*, Edith Wharton

"There were 117 psychoanalysts on the Pan Am flight to Vienna and I'd been treated by at least six of them."
— *Fear of Flying*, Erica Jong

"riverrun, past Eve and Adam's, from swerve of shore to bend of bay, brings us by a commodius vicus of recirculation back to Howth Castle and Environs."
— *Finnegans Wake*, James Joyce

"Scarlett O'Hara was not beautiful, but men seldom realized it when caught by her charm as the Tarleton twins were."
— *Gone with the Wind*, Margaret Mitchell

"This is the saddest story I have ever heard."
— *The Good Soldier*, Ford Maddox Ford

"To the red country and part of the gray country of Oklahoma, the last rains came gently, and they did not cut the scarred earth."
— *The Grapes of Wrath*, John Steinbeck

Steinbeck

"In my younger and more vulnerable years my father gave me some advice that I've been turning over in my mind ever since."
— *The Great Gatsby*, F. Scott Fitzgerald

"It is three hundred forty-eight years, six months, and nineteen days ago today that the citizens of Paris were awakened by the pealing of all the bells in the triple precincts of the City, the University, and the Town."
— *The Hunchback of Notre-Dame*, Victor Hugo

"Many years later, as he faced the firing squad, Colonel Aureliano Buendía was to remember that distant afternoon when his father took him to discover ice."
— *A Hundred Years of Solitude*, Garbriel García Márquez

"Whenever my mother talks to me, she begins the conversation as if we were already in the middle of an argument."
— *The Kitchen God's Wife*, Amy Tan

" 'Christmas won't be Christmas without any presents,' grumbled Jo, lying on the rug."
— *Little Women*, Louisa May Alcott

"Lolita, light of my life, fire of my loins."
— *Lolita*, Vladimir Nabokov

"When Augustus came out on the porch the blue pigs were eating a rattlesnake—not a very big one."
— *Lonesome Dove*, Larry McMurtry

"What can you say about a twenty-five-year-old girl who died?"
— *Love Story*, Erich Segal

"When Gregor Samsa woke up one morning from unsettling dreams, he found himself changed in his bed into a monstrous vermin."
— *Metamorphosis*, Franz Kafka

"Call me Ishmael."
— *Moby Dick*, Herman Melville

"The sun shone, having no alternative, on the nothing new."
— *Murphy*, Samuel Beckett

"It was a bright cold day in April, and the clocks were striking thirteen."
— *1984*, George Orwell

"He was an old man who fished alone in a skiff in the Gulf Stream and he had gone eighty-four days now without taking a fish."
— *The Old Man and the Sea*, Ernest Hemingway

"Jinn and Phyllis were spending a wonderful holiday, in space, as far away as possible from the inhabited stars."
— *Planet of the Apes*, Pierre Boulle

"She was so deeply imbedded in my consciousness that for the first year of school I seem to have believed that each of my teachers was my mother in disguise."
— *Portnoy's Complaint*, Philip Roth

"Under certain circumstances there are few hours in life more agreeable than the hour dedicated to the ceremony known as afternoon tea."
— *The Portrait of a Lady*, Henry James

"Last night I dreamt I went to Manderley again."
— *Rebecca*, Daphne du Maurier

"For a long time I used to go to bed early."
— *Remembrance of Things Past* (Vol. I, *Swann's Way*), Marcel Proust

"In our family, there was no clear line between religion and fly fishing."
— *A River Runs Through It*, Norman MacLean

"It was the best of times, it was the worst of times, it was the age of wisdom, it was the age of foolishness, it was the epoch of belief, it was the epoch of incredulity, it was the season of Light, it was the season of Darkness, it was the spring of hope, it was the winter of despair, we had everything before us, we had nothing before us, we were all going direct to Heaven, we were all going direct the other way—in short, the period was so far like the present period, that some of its noisiest authorities insisted on its being received, for good or for evil, in the superlative degree of comparison only."
— *A Tale of Two Cities*, Charles Dickens

"True!—nervous—very, very dreadfully nervous I had been and am; but why will you say that I am mad?"
— *The Tell-Tale Heart*, Edgar Allan Poe

"Here is Edward Bear, coming downstairs now, bump, bump,

LITERARY AWARDS

NATIONAL BOOK CRITICS CIRCLE AWARDS

[Year listed is the year before award was given]

Fiction

1976 John Gardner
October Light
1977 Toni Morrison
Song of Solomon
1978 John Cheever
The Stories of John Cheever
1979 Thomas Flanagan
The Year of the French
1980 Shirley Hazzard
The Transit of Venus
1981 John Updike
Rabbit is Rich
1982 Stanley Elkin
George Mills
1983 William Kennedy
Ironweed
1984 Louise Erdrich
Love Medicine
1985 Anne Tyler
The Accidental Tourist
1986 Reynolds Price
Kate Vaiden
1987 Philip Roth
The Counterlife
1988 Bharati Mukherjee
The Middleman and Other Stories
1989 E.L. Doctorow
Billy Bathgate
1990 John Updike
Rabbit at Rest
1991 Jane Smiley
A Thousand Acres
1992 Cormac McCarthy
All the Pretty Horses
1993 Ernest Gaines
A Lesson in Dying

General Nonfiction

1976 Maxine Hong Kingston
The Woman Warrior: Memoirs of a Girlhood Among Ghosts
1977 Walter Jackson Bate
Samuel Johnson
1978 Maureen Howard
Facts of Life
1979 Telford Taylor
Munich: The Price of Peace
1980 Ronald Steel
Walter Lippmann and the American Century
1981 Stephen Jay Gould
The Mismeasure of Man
1982 Robert A. Caro
The Path of Power: The Years of Lyndon Johnson
1983 Seymour M. Hersh
The Price of Power: Kissinger in the Nixon White House
1984 Freeman Dyson
Weapons and Hope
1985 J. Anthony Lukas
Common Ground: A Turbulent Decade in the Lives of Three American Families
1986 John W. Dower
War Without Mercy: Race and Power in the Pacific War
1987 Richard Rhodes
The Making of the Atomic Bomb
1988 Taylor Branch
Parting the Waters: America in the King Years, 1954–63
1989 Michael Dorris
The Broken Cord
1990 Shelby Steele
The Content of Our Character: A New Vision of Race in America
1991 Susan Faludi
Backlash: The Undeclared War Against American Women
1992 Norman Maclean
Young Men and Fire
1993 Alan Lomax
The Land Where the Blues Began

Biography and Autobiography

1983 Joyce Johnson
Minor Characters
1984 Joseph Frank
Dostoevsky: The Years of Ordeal, 1850-1859
1985 Leon Edel
Henry James: A Life
1986 Theodore Rosengarten
Tombee: Portrait of a Cotton Planter
1987 Donald R. Howard
Chaucer: His Life, His Works, His World
1988 Richard Ellman
Oscar Wilde
1989 Geoffrey C. Ward
A First-Class Temperament: The Emergence of Franklin Roosevelt
1990 Robert A. Caro
Means of Ascent: The Years of Lyndon Johnson, Vol. II
1991 Philip Roth
Patrimony: A True Story
1992 Carol Brightman
Writing Dangerously: Mary McCarthy and Her World
1993 Edmund White
Genet

Poetry

1976 Elizabeth Bishop
Geography III
1977 Robert Lowell
Day by Day
1978 L.E. Sissman, edited by Peter Davison
Hello, Darkness: The Collected Poems of L.E. Sissman
1979 Philip Levine
Ashes and 7 Years from Somewhere
1980 Frederick Seidel
Sunrise
1981 A.R. Ammons
A Coast of Trees
1982 Katha Pollitt
Antarctic Traveler
1983 James Merrill
The Changing Light at Sandover
1984 Sharon Olds
The Dead and the Living
1985 Louise Gluck
The Triumph of Achilles
1986 Edward Hirsch
Wild Gratitude
1987 C.K. Williams
Flesh and Blood
1988 Donald Hall
The One Day
1989 Rodney Jones
Transparent Gestures
1990 Amy Gerstler
Bitter Angel
1991 Albert Goldbarth
Heaven and Earth: A Cosmology
1992 Hayden Carruth
Collected Shorter Poems, 1946-1991
1993 Mark Doty
My Alexandria

Criticism

1976 Bruno Bettelheim
The Uses of Enchantment: The Meaning and Importance of Fairy Tales
1977 Susan Sontag
On Photography
1978 Meyer Schapiro
Modern Art: 19th and 20th Centuries, Selected Papers
1979 Elaine Pagels
The Gnostic Gospels

1980 Helen Vendler
Part of Nature, Part of Us: Modern American Poets
1981 Virgil Thomson
A Virgil Thomson Reader
1982 Gore Vidal
The Second American Revolution and Other Essays, 1976-82
1983 John Updike
Hugging the Shore: Essays and Criticism
1984 Robert Hass
Twentieth Century Pleasures: Prose on Poetry
1985 William H. Gass
Habitations of the Word: Essays
1986 Joseph Brodsky
Less Than One: Selected Essays
1987 Edwin Denby, edited by Robert Cornfield and William MacKay
Dance Writings
1988 Clifford Geertz
Works and Lives: The Anthropologist as Author
1989 John Clive
Not by Fact Alone: Essays on the Writing and Reading of History
1990 Arthur C. Danto
Encounters and Reflections: Art in the Historical Present
1991 Lawrence L. Langer
Holocaust Testimonies: The Ruins of Memory
1992 Garry Wills
Lincoln at Gettysburg: The Words That Remade America
1993 John Dizikes
Opera in America: A Cultural History

NEWBERRY MEDAL BOOKS

For children's literature

1922 Henrik van Loon
The Story of Mankind
1923 Hugh Lofting
The Voyages of Doctor Dolittle
1924 Charles Hawes
The Dark Frigate
1925 Charles Finger
Tales from Silver Lands
1926 Arthur Chrisman
Shen of the Sea
1927 Will James
Smoky, the Cowhorse
1928 Dhan Mukerji
Gay Neck, the Story of a Pigeon
1929 Eric P. Kelly
The Trumpeter of Krakow
1930 Rachel Field
Hitty, Her First Hundred Years
1931 Elizabeth Coatsworth
The Cat Who Went to Heaven
1932 Laura Armer
Waterless Mountain
1933 Elizabeth Lewis
Young Fu of the Upper Yangtze
1934 Cornelia Meigs
Invincible Louisa
1935 Monica Shannon
Dobry
1936 Carol Brink
Caddie Woodlawn
1937 Ruth Sawyer
Roller Skates
1938 Kate Seredy
The White Stag
1939 Elizabeth Enright
Thimble Summer
1940 James Daugherty
Daniel Boone
1941 Armstrong Sperry
Call It Courage
1942 Walter Edmonds
The Matchlock Gun
1943 Elizabeth Gray
Adam of the Road
1944 Esther Forbes
Johnny Tremain
1945 Robert Lawson
Rabbit Hill
1946 Lois Lenski
Strawberry Girl
1947 Carolyn Bailey
Miss Hickory
1948 William Pène du Bois
The Twenty-One Balloons
1949 Marguerite Henry
King of the Wind
1950 Marguerite de Angeli
The Door in the Wall
1951 Elizabeth Yates
Amos Fortune, Free Man
1952 Eleanor Estes
Ginger Pye
1953 Ann Nolan Clark
Secret of the Andes
1954 Joseph Krumgold
...And Now Miguel
1955 Meindert DeJong
The Wheel on the School
1956 Jean Lee Latham
Carry On, Mr. Bowditch
1957 Virginia Sorenson
Miracles on Maple Hill
1958 Harold Keith
Rifles for Watie
1959 Elizabeth George Speare
The Witch of Blackbird Pond
1960 Joseph Krumgold
Onion John
1961 Scott O'Dell
Island of the Blue Dolphins
1962 Elizabeth George Speare
The Bronze Bow
1963 Madeleine L'Engle
A Wrinkle in Time
1964 Emily Neville
It's Like This, Cat
1965 Maia Wojciechowska
Shadow of a Bull
1966 Elizabeth Borton de Trevino
I, Juan de Pareja
1967 Irene Hunt
Up a Road Slowly
1968 E.L. Konigsburg
From the Mixed-Up Files of Mrs. Basil E. Frankweiler
1969 Lloyd Alexander
The High King
1970 William H. Armstrong
Sounder
1971 Betsy Byars
Summer of the Swans
1972 Robert C. O'Brien
Mrs. Frisby and the Rats of NIMH
1973 Jean Craighead George
Julie of the Wolves
1974 Paula Fox
The Slave Dancer
1975 Virginia Hamilton
M.C. Higgins, the Great
1976 Susan Cooper
The Grey King
1977 Mildred D. Taylor
Roll of Thunder, Hear My Cry
1978 Katherine Paterson
Bridge to Terabithia
1979 Ellen Raskin
The Westing Game
1980 Joan W. Blos
A Gathering of Days
1981 Katherine Paterson
Jacob Have I Loved
1982 Nancy Willard
A Visit to William Blake's Inn: Poems for Innocent and Experienced Travelers
1983 Cynthia Voight
Dicey's Song
1984 Beverly Cleary
Dear Mr. Henshaw
1985 Robin McKinley
The Hero and the Crown
1986 Patricia MacLachlan
Sarah, Plain and Tall
1987 Sid Fleischman
The Whipping Boy
1988 Russell Freedman
Lincoln: A Photobiography
1989 Paul Fleischman
Joyful Noise: Poems for Two Voices
1990 Lois Lowry
Number the Stars

1991 Jerry Spinelli
Maniac Magee
1992 Phyllis Reynolds Naylor
Shiloh
1993 Cynthia Rylant
Missing May
1994 Lois Lowry
The Giver

CALDECOTT MEDAL BOOKS

For children's picture books

1938 Helen Dean Fish, ill. by Dorothy P. Lathrop
Animals of the Bible
1939 Thomas Handforth
Mei Li
1940 Ingri and Edgar Parin d'Aulaire
Abraham Lincoln
1941 Robert Lawson
They Were Strong and Good
1942 Robert McCloskey
Make Way for Ducklings
1943 Virginia Lee Burton
The Little House
1944 James Thurber, ill. by Louis Slobodkin
Many Moons
1945 Rachel Field, ill. by Elizabeth Orton Jones
Prayer for a Child
1946 Maude and Mishka Petersham
The Rooster Crows
1947 Golden MacDonald, ill. by Leonard Weisgard
The Little Island
1948 Alvin Tresselt, ill. by Roger Duvoisin
White Snow, Bright Snow
1949 Berta and Elmer Hader
The Big Snow
1950 Leo Politi
Song of the Swallows
1951 Katherine Milhous
The Egg Tree
1952 Will Lipkind, ill. by Nicolas Mordvinoff
Finders Keepers
1953 Lynd Ward
The Biggest Bear
1954 Ludwig Bemelmans
Madeline's Rescue
1955 Marcia Brown
Cinderella
1956 John Langstaff, ill. by Feodor Rojankovsky
Frog Went A-Courtin'
1957 Janice Udry, ill. by Marc Simont
A Tree is Nice
1958 Robert McCloskey
Time of Wonder
1959 Barbara Cooney
Chanticleer and the Fox
1960 Marie Hall Ets and Aurora Labastida
Nine Days to Christmas
1961 Ruth Robbins, ill. by Nicolas Sidjakov
Baboushka and the Three Kings
1962 Marcia Brown
Once a Mouse
1963 Ezra Jack Keats
The Snowy Day
1964 Maurice Sendak
Where the Wild Things Are
1965 Beatrice Schenk de Regniers, ill. by Beni Montresor
May I Bring a Friend?
1966 Sorche Nic Leodhas, ill. by Nonny Hogrogian
Always Room for One More
1967 Evaline Ness
Sam, Bangs & Moonshine
1968 Barbara Emberley, ill. by Ed Emberly
Drummer Hoff
1969 Arthur Ransome, ill. by Uri Shulevitz
The Fool of the World and the Flying Ship
1970 William Steig
Sylvester and the Magic Pebble
1971 Gail E. Haley
A Story a Story
1972 Nonny Hogrogian
One Fine Day
1973 Lafcadio Hearn, retold by Arlene Mosel, ill. by Blair Lent
The Funny Little Woman
1974 Harve Zemach, picts. by Margot Zemach
Duffy and the Devil
1975 Gerald McDermott
Arrow to the Sun
1976 Verna Aardema, picts. by Leo and Diane Dillon
Why Mosquitoes Buzz in People's Ears
1977 Margaret Musgrove, picts. by Leo and Diane Dillon
Ashanti to Zulu
1978 Peter Spier
Noah's Ark
1979 Paul Goble
The Girl Who Loved Wild Horses
1980 Donald Hall, picts. by Barbara Cooney
Ox-Cart Man
1981 Arnold Lobel
Fables
1982 Chris Van Allsburg
Jumanji
1983 Blaise Cendrars, trans. and ill. by Marcia Brown
Shadow
1984 Alice and Martin Provensen
The Glorious Flight: Across the Channel with Louis Blériot
1985 Margaret Hodges, ill. by Trina Schart Hyman
Saint George and the Dragon
1986 Chris Van Allsburg
The Polar Express
1987 Arthur Yorinks, ill. by Richard Egielski
Hey, Al
1988 Jane Yolen, ill. by John Schoenherr
Owl Moon
1989 Karen Ackerman, ill. by Stephen Gammell
Song and Dance Man
1990 Ed Young
Lon Po Po
1991 David Macaulay
Black and White
1992 David Wiesner
Tuesday
1993 Emily Arnold McCully
Mirette on the High Wire
1994 Allen Say
Grandfather's Journey

BOLLINGEN PRIZE IN POETRY

1949 Wallace Stevens
1950 John Crowe Ransom
1951 Marianne Moore
1952 Archibald MacLeish
William Carlos Williams
1953 W.H. Auden
1954 Leonie Adams
Louise Bogan
1955 Conrad Aiken
1956 Allen Tate
1957 e.e. cummings
1958 Theodore Roethke
1959 Delmore Schwartz
1960 Yvor Winters
1961 Richard Eberhart
John Hall Wheelock
1962 Robert Frost
1965 Horace Gregory
1967 Robert Penn Warren
1969 John Berryman
Karl Shapiro
1971 Richard Wilbur
Mona Van Duyn
1973 James Merrill
1975 A.R. Ammons
1977 David Ignatov
1979 W.S. Merwin
1981 May Swenson
Howard Nemerov
1983 Anthony E. Hecht
John Hollander

1985 John Ashbery
Fred Chappell
1987 Stanley Kunitz
1989 Edgar Bowers
1991 Laura (Riding) Jackson
Donald Justice
1993 Mark Strand

BOOKER PRIZE

British award for fiction

1969 P.H. Newby
Something to Answer For
1970 Bernice Rubens
The Elected Member
1971 V.S. Naipaul
In a Free State
1972 John Berger
G
1973 J.G. Farrell
The Siege of Krishnapur
1974 Nadine Gordimer
The Conservationist
1975 Ruth Prawer Jhabvala
Heat and Dust
1976 David Storey
Saville
1977 Paul Scott
Staying On
1978 Iris Murdoch
The Sea, the Sea
1979 Penelope Fitzgerald
Offshore
1980 William Golding
Rites of Passage
1981 Salman Rushdie
Midnight's Children
1982 Thomas Keneally
Schindler's Ark
1983 J.M. Coetzee
Life & Times of Michael K
1984 Anita Brookner
Hotel du Lac
1985 Keri Hulme
The Bone People
1986 Kingsley Amis
The Old Devils
1987 Penelope Lively
Moon Tiger
1988 Peter Carey
Oscar and Lucinda
1989 Kazuo Ishiguro
The Remains of the Day
1990 A.S. Byatt
Possession
1991 Ben Okri
The Famished Road
1992 Michael Ondaatje
The English Patient
Barry Unsworth
Sacred Hunger
1993 Roddy Doyle
Paddy Clark Ha Ha Ha

NATIONAL MAGAZINE AWARDS

Public Service/Public Interest

1970 Life
1971 The Nation
1972 Philadelphia
1973 [not awarded]
1974 Scientific American
1975 Consumer Reports
1976 Business Week
1977 Philadelphia
1978 Mother Jones
1979 New West
1980 Texas Monthly
1981 Reader's Digest
1982 The Atlantic Monthly
1983 Foreign Affairs
1984 The New Yorker
1985 The Washingtonian
1986 Science 85
1987 Money
1988 The Atlantic Monthly
1989 California
1990 Southern Exposure
1991 Family Circle
1992 Glamour
1993 The Family Therapy Network
1994 Philadelphia Magazine

Specialized Journalism

1970 Philadelphia
1971 Rolling Stone
1972 Architectural Record
1973 Psychology Today
1974 Texas Monthly
1975 Medical Economics
1976 United Mine Workers Journal
1977 Architectural Record
1978 Scientific American
1979 National Journal
1980 IEEE Spectrum

Design/Visual Excellence

1970 Look
1971 Vogue
1972 Esquire
1973 Horizon
1974 Newsweek
1975 Country Journal
National Lampoon
1976 Horticulture
1977 Rolling Stone
1978 Architectural Digest
1979 Audubon
1980 GEO
1981 Attenzione
1982 Nautical Quarterly
1983 New York
1984 House & Garden
1985 Forbes
1986 Time
1987 Elle
1988 Life
1989 Rolling Stone
1990 Esquire
1991 Condé Nast Traveler
1992 Vanity Fair
1993 Harper's Bazaar
1994 Allure

Reporting (Excellence)/News Reporting

1970 The New Yorker
1971 The Atlantic Monthly
1972 The Atlantic Monthly
1973 New York
1974 The New Yorker
1975 The New Yorker
1976 Audubon
1977 Audubon
1978 The New Yorker
1979 Texas Monthly
1980 Mother Jones
1981 National Journal
1982 The Washingtonian
1983 Institutional Investor
1984 Vanity Fair
1985 Texas Monthly
1986 Rolling Stone
1987 Life
1988 Baltimore Magazine
The Washingtonian
1989 The New Yorker
1990 The New Yorker
1991 The New Yorker
1992 The New Republic
1993 IEEE Spectrum
1994 The New Yorker

General Excellence (Under 100,000 circulation)

1981 ARTnews
1982 Camera Arts
1983 Louisiana Life
1984 The American Lawyer
1985 Manhattan, inc.
1986 New England Monthly
1987 New England Monthly
1988 The Sciences
1989 The Sciences
1990 7 Days
1991 The New Republic
1992 The New Republic
1993 Lingua Franca
1994 Print

General Excellence (100,000–400,000)

1981 Audubon
1982 Rocky Mountain Magazine
1983 Harper's Magazine
1984 Outside
1985 American Heritage
1986 3-2-1 Contact
1987 Common Cause
1988 Hippocrates
1989 American Heritage

1990 Texas Monthly
1991 Interview
1992 Texas Monthly
1993 American Photo
1994 Wired

General Excellence (400,000–1,000,000)
1981 Business Week
1982 Science 81
1983 Science 82
1984 House & Garden
1985 American Health
1986 Discover
1987 Elle
1988 Fortune
1989 Vanity Fair
1990 Metropolitan Home
1991 Condé Nast Traveler
1992 Mirabella
1993 The Atlantic Monthly
1994 Health

General Excellence (over 1,000,000)
1981 Glamour
1982 Newsweek
1983 Life
1984 National Geographic
1985 Time
1986 Money
1987 People Weekly
1988 Parents
1989 Sports Illustrated
1990 Sports Illustrated
1991 Glamour
1992 National Geographic
1993 Newsweek
1994 Business Week

Essays and Criticism
1978 Esquire
1979 Life
1980 Natural History
1981 Time
1982 The Atlantic Monthly
1983 The American Lawyer
1984 The New Republic
1985 Boston
1986 The Sciences
1987 Outside
1988 Harper's Magazine
1989 Harper's Magazine
1990 Vanity Fair
1991 The Sciences
1992 The Nation
1993 The American Lawyer
1994 Harper's Magazine

Fiction
1978 The New Yorker
1979 The Atlantic Monthly
1980 Antaeus
1981 The North American Review
1982 The New Yorker
1983 The North American Review
1984 Seventeen
1985 Playboy
1986 The Georgia Review
1987 Esquire
1988 The Atlantic
1989 The New Yorker
1990 The New Yorker
1991 Esquire
1992 Story
1993 The New Yorker
1994 Harper's Magazine

Single Topic Issue
1979 Progressive Architecture
1980 Scientific American
1981 Business Week
1982 Newsweek
1983 IEEE Spectrum
1984 Esquire
1985 American Heritage
1986 IEEE Spectrum
1987 Bulletin of the Atomic Scientists
1988 Life
1989 Hippocrates
1990 National Geographic
1991 The American Lawyer
1992 Business Week
1993 Newsweek
1994 Health

Personal Service/Service to the Individual
1974 Sports Illustrated
1975 Esquire
1976 Modern Medicine
1977 Harper's Magazine
1978 Newsweek
1979 The American Journal of Nursing
1980 Saturday Review
1982 Philadelphia
1983 Sunset
1984 New York
1985 The Washingtonian
1986 Farm Journal
1987 Consumer Reports
1988 Money
1989 Good Housekeeping
1990 Consumer Reports
1991 New York
1992 Creative Classroom
1993 Good Housekeeping
1994 Fortune

Special Interests
1986 Popular Mechanics
1987 Sports Afield
1988 Condé Nast Traveler
1989 Condé Nast Traveler
1990 Arts & Antiques
1991 New York
1992 Sports Afield
1993 Philadelphia
1994 Outside

Photography
1985 Life
1986 Vogue
1987 National Geographic
1988 Rolling Stone
1989 National Geographic
1990 Texas Monthly
1991 National Geographic
1992 National Geographic
1993 Harper's Bazaar
1994 Martha Stewart Living

Feature Writing
1988 The Atlantic Monthly
1989 Esquire
1990 The Washingtonian
1991 U.S. News & World Report
1992 Sports Illustrated
1993 The New Yorker
1994 Harper's Magazine

Chris Evert • Prince Rainier • Ollie North • Chappaquiddick
People weekly
GOOD NIGHT, SWEET PRINCE
Laurence Olivier
1907-1989
Rosalynn: Jimmy Carter's 'secret weapon'
Patty's shrink: 'Anyone can be brainwashed'
March 15, 1976 • 50¢
People weekly
LIZ
Un-Burtoned again, she goes home to mother —and to Henry
STAGE
The man who dresses Cher in feathers
Sen. Church vs. Rocky on the CIA
June 30, 1975 • 40¢
People weekly
BETTE MIDLER
Tender, tacky and back on top
Princess Anne & Mark: inside a royal marriage
People weekly
In this issue
DUSTIN HOFFMAN
More like Lenny than The Graduate
Margaux Hemingway has the name and the face
Agnew's surprising partner
An expert tells why women drink
Singer Paul Williams: This is a teen idol?

BROADWAY SHOWS OF THE 1993–94 SEASON

The recent year on Broadway was marked by a surge in new plays, as well as a surge in ticket prices. This was due largely to expensive productions like *Angels in America* and *The Kentucky Cycle.* Most new plays failed to recoup their investments, as did most new musicals; fortunately, a number of revivals (including *Camelot* and *My Fair Lady*) were generally more successful—albeit some of these relied on the ever-burgeoning tour circuit to break into the black.

(M) stands for musical and (R) for revival.

New Productions

A Grand Night for Singing (M-R)
A Little More Magic
Abe Lincoln in Illinois (R)
An Inspector Calls (R)
Angels in America: Perestroika
Any Given Day
Beauty and the Beast (M)
The Best Little Whorehouse Goes Public (M)
Black Comedy/White Liars (R)
Broken Glass
Camelot (M-R)
Carousel (M-R)
Cyrano—The Musical (M)
Damn Yankees (M-R)
The Flowering Peach (R)
The Government Inspector (R)
Gray's Anatomy
Grease (M-R)
In the Summer House (R)
Jackie Mason: Politically Incorrect
Joseph and the Amazing Technicolor Dreamcoat (M-R)
The Kentucky Cycle
Laughter on the 23rd Floor
Medea (R)
Mixed Emotions
My Fair Lady (M-R)
No Man's Land (R)
Passion (M)
Picnic (R)
The Red Shoes (M)
The Rise and Fall of Little Voice
Sally Marr . . . and Her Escorts
She Loves Me (M-R)
Timon of Athens (R)
Twilight, Los Angeles: 1992
The Twilight of the Golds
Wonderful Tennessee

Holdovers from Previous Seasons

Angels in America: Millenium Approaches
Blood Brothers (M)
Cats (M)
Crazy for You (M)
Falsettos (M)
Fool Moon
Guys and Dolls (M-R)
Jelly's Last Jam (M)
Kiss of the Spider Woman (M)
Les Misérables (M)
Miss Saigon (M)
Shakespeare for My Father
Someone Who'll Watch over Me
The Goodbye Girl (M)
The Phantom of the Opera (M)
The Sisters Rosensweig
The Who's Tommy (M)
The Will Rogers Follies (M)

ON THE ROAD

The Great White Way draws most of the attention in the theater world, but it no longer generates the most bucks. Road shows have increased their take strongly over the last fifteen years, and their increases far outstrip those on Broadway, to the point that the road now pulls in almost twice as much revenue. Note that theater revenues in general jumped dramatically beginning in the late '70s, when the blockbuster British musicals began to establish a significant presence. (Source: *Variety*)

Season	Broadway box office/total shows during most profitable week	Road box office/total shows during most profitable week
1965–66	$53.8 million/29 shows	$32.2 million/16 shows
1970–71	$55.3 million/30 shows	$52.5 million/19 shows
1975–76	$70.8 million/29 shows	$52.6 million/19 shows
1980–81	$194.5 million/34 shows	$218.9 million/30 shows
1985–86	$190.6 million/23 shows	$235.6 million/23 shows
1990–91	$267.2 million/22 shows	$450.2 million/27 shows
1991–92	$292.4 million/28 shows	$502.7 million/25 shows
1992–93	$327.7 million/21 shows	$620.6 million/34 shows
1993–94	$356.0 million/21 shows	$687.7 million/30 shows

LONGEST-RUNNING SHOWS ON BROADWAY

The following is a list of the longest-running shows on Broadway (as of August 21, 1994) based on the number of performances over 1,000 (excluding previews).

(M) stands for musical and (R) for revival. (Source: *League of American Theatres and Producers*)

Show	Performances
A Chorus Line (M) (1975–90)	6,137
Oh! Calcutta! (M-R) (1976–89)	5,962
Cats (M) (1982–)	4,957
42nd Street (M) (1980–89)	3,485
Grease (M) (1972–80)	3,388
Fiddler on the Roof (M) (1964–72)	3,242
Life with Father (1939–47)	3,224
Tobacco Road (1933–41)	3,182
Les Misérables (M) (1987–)	3,045
Hello, Dolly! (M) (1964–70)	2,844
Phantom of the Opera (M) (1988–)	2,757
My Fair Lady (M) (1956–62)	2,717
Annie (M) (1977–83)	2,377
Man of La Mancha (M) (1965–71)	2,329
Abie's Irish Rose (1922–27)	2,327
Oklahoma! (M) (1943–48)	2,212
South Pacific (M) (1949–54)	1,925
Magic Show (M) (1974–78)	1,920
Pippin (M) (1972–77)	1,908
Gemini (1977–81)	1,819
Deathtrap (1978–82)	1,793
Harvey (1944–49)	1,775
Dancin' (M) (1978–82)	1,774
La Cage aux folles (M) (1983–87)	1,761
Hair (M) (1968–72)	1,742
The Wiz (M) (1975–79)	1,672
Born Yesterday (1946–49)	1,642
Ain't Misbehavin' (M) (1978–82)	1,604
Best Little Whorehouse in Texas (M) (1978–82)	1,584
Mary, Mary (1961–64)	1,572
Evita (M) (1979–83)	1,567
Voice of the Turtle (1943–48)	1,557
Barefoot in the Park (1963–64)	1,532
Dreamgirls (1981–85)	1,521
Mame (M) (1966–70)	1,503
Same Time, Next Year (1976–78)	1,453
Arsenic and Old Lace (1941–44)	1,444
The Sound of Music (M) (1959–63)	1,443
How To Succeed in Business Without Really Trying (M) (1961–65)	1,417
Hellzapoppin (M) (1938–41)	1,404
Miss Saigon (M) (1991–)	1,401
The Music Man (M) (1957–61)	1,375
Funny Girl (M) (1964–67)	1,348
Mummenschanz (M) (1977–80)	1,326
Oh! Calcutta! (M) (1969–72)	1,314
Brighton Beach Memoirs (1983–86)	1,299
Angel Street (M) (1941–44)	1,295
Lightnin' (1918–21)	1,291
Promises, Promises (M) (1968–72)	1,281
The King and I (M) (1951–54)	1,246
Cactus Flower (1965–68)	1,234
Torch Song Trilogy (1982–85)	1,222
Sleuth (1970–73)	1,222
1776 (M) (1969–72)	1,217
Equus (1974–77)	1,209
Sugar Babies (M) (1979–82)	1,208
Guys and Dolls (M) (1950–53)	1,200
Cabaret (M) (1966–69)	1,166
Amadeus (1980–83)	1,161
Mister Roberts (1948–51)	1,157
Annie Get Your Gun (M) (1946–49)	1,147
The Seven Year Itch (1952–55)	1,141
Butterflies Are Free (1969–72)	1,128
Pins and Needles (M) (1937–40)	1,108
Plaza Suite (1968–70)	1,097
They're Playing Our Song (M) (1979–81)	1,082
Kiss Me, Kate (M) (1948–51)	1,071
Don't Bother Me, I Can't Cope (M) (1972–74)	1,065
Pajama Game (M) (1954–56)	1,063
Shenandoah (M) (1975–77)	1,050
Crazy for You (1992–)	1,046
Teahouse of the August Moon (1953–56)	1,027
Damn Yankees (M) (1955–57)	1,019
Grand Hotel (M) (1989–92)	1,018
Never Too Late (1962–65)	1,007
Beatlemania (1977–79)	1,006

BROADWAY'S FAVORITES: PLACE THAT TUNE

Know the song but can't place the musical in which it originally appeared? Here is a checklist of some Great White Way melodies that linger on.

Song	Show
"Almost Like Being in Love"	*Brigadoon*
"Anything You Can Do"	*Annie Get Your Gun*
"Bali Ha'i"	*South Pacific*
"The Ballad of Mack the Knife"	*The Threepenny Opera*
"Bewitched, Bothered, and Bewildered"	*Pal Joey*
"A Bushel and a Peck"	*Guys and Dolls*
"Climb Ev'ry Mountain"	*The Sound of Music*
"Everything's Coming Up Roses"	*Gypsy*
"Getting to Know You"	*The King and I*
"I Cain't Say No"	*Oklahoma!*
"I Could Have Danced All Night"	*My Fair Lady*
"I Don't Know How To Love Him"	*Jesus Christ Superstar*
"I Get a Kick Out of You"	*Anything Goes*
"I Got Plenty o' Nothin' "	*Porgy and Bess*
"I Got Rhythm"	*Girl Crazy*
"I Got the Sun in the Morning"	*Annie Get Your Gun*
"I Feel Pretty"	*West Side Story*
"I Whistle a Happy Tune"	*The King and I*
"If Ever I Would Leave You"	*Camelot*
"It Ain't Necessarily So"	*Porgy and Bess*
"I've Grown Accustomed to Her Face"	*My Fair Lady*
"Let the Sunshine In"	*Hair*
"Lover, Come Back to Me"	*The New Moon*
"Luck Be a Lady"	*Guys and Dolls*
"Maria"	*West Side Story*
"Memory"	*Cats*
"My Favorite Things"	*The Sound of Music*
"Oh, What a Beautiful Mornin' "	*Oklahoma!*
"Ol' Man River"	*Show Boat*
"On the Street Where You Live"	*My Fair Lady*
"The Quest (The Impossible Dream)"	*Man of La Mancha*
"Seventy-Six Trombones"	*The Music Man*
"Shall We Dance?"	*The King and I*
"Smoke Gets in Your Eyes"	*Roberta*
"Some Enchanted Evening"	*South Pacific*
"The Sound of Music"	*The Sound of Music*
"Summertime"	*Porgy and Bess*
"Sunrise, Sunset"	*Fiddler on the Roof*
"Tea for Two"	*No, No, Nanette*
"Thank Heaven for Little Girls"	*Gigi*
"There Is Nothin' Like a Dame"	*South Pacific*
"There's No Business Like Show Business"	*Annie Get Your Gun*
"This Is the Army, Mr. Jones"	*This Is the Army*
"Till There Was You"	*The Music Man*
"Tonight"	*West Side Story*
"You'll Never Walk Alone"	*Carousel*
"You're the Top"	*Anything Goes*
"We Need a Little Christmas"	*Mame*

GREAT SOUNDTRACKS, PAST AND PRESENT

Broadway shows both famous and obscure have produced a remarkable number of our most beloved songs, as this list attests. Complete soundtracks are listed below, along with the composer and lyricist, respectively. (If one name is listed, the same person is both tunesmith and wordsmith.)

Annie
Charles Strouse and Martin Charnin
Maybe, It's the Hard-Knock Life, Tomorrow, We'd Like To Thank You, Herbert Hoover, Dumb Dog, Sandy, Little Girls, I Think I'm Gonna Like It Here, N.Y.C., Easy Street, You Won't Be an Orphan for Long, You're Never Fully Dressed Without a Smile, Something Was Missing, I Don't Need Anything but You, Annie, A New Deal for Christmas

Annie Get Your Gun
Irving Berlin
Colonel Buffalo Bill, Doin' What Comes Natur'lly, The Girl That I Marry, You Can't Get a Man with a Gun, I'm a Bad, Bad Man, There's No Business Like Show Business, They Say It's Wonderful, An Old Fashioned Wedding, My Defenses Are Down, I'm an Indian, Too, I Got Lost in His Arms, I Got the Sun in the Morning, Anything You Can Do

Anything Goes
Cole Porter
All Through the Night, I Get a Kick out of You, You're the Top, Anything Goes, Bon Voyage, It's Delovely, Friendship, Public Enemy Number One, Let's Step Out, Take Me Back to Manhattan, Blow, Gabriel, Blow, Be Like the Bluebird, The Gypsy in Me

Brigadoon
Frederick Loewe and Alan Jay Lerner
Brigadoon, Waitin' for My Dearie, The Love of My Life, Down on MacConnachy Square, I'll Go Home with Bonnie Jean, The Heather on the Hill, Come to Me, Bend to Me, Almost Like Being in Love, There but for You Go I, My Mother's Wedding Day, From This Day On

Bye Bye Birdie
Charles Strouse and Lee Adams
One Last Kiss, One Boy, An English Teacher, Baby, Talk to Me, A Lot of Livin' to Do, Rosie, Put on a Happy Face, Kids, The Telephone Hour, How Lovely to Be a Woman, Honestly Sincere, Hymn for a Sunday Evening, What Did I Ever See in Him?, Spanish Rose

Cabaret
John Kander and Fred Ebb
Willkommen, Don't Tell Mama, Perfectly Marvelous, It Couldn't Please Me More, Tomorrow Belongs to Me, Why Should I Wake Up?, Married, Meeskite, Cabaret, So What?, Telephone Song, Two Ladies, The Money Song, If You Could See Her, What Would You Do?

Camelot
Frederick Loewe and Alan Jay Lerner
Camelot, C'est Moi, The Lusty Month of May, If Ever I Would Leave You, What Do the Simple Folk Do?, I Loved You Once in Silence, Guenevere, Follow Me, How To Handle a Woman, I Wonder What the King Is Doing Tonight, The Simple Joys of Maidenhood, Follow Me, Then You May Take Me to the Fair, Before I Gaze at You Again, The Seven Deadly Virtues, Fie on Goodness

Cats
Andrew Lloyd Webber and T .S. Eliot
Jellicle Songs for Jellicle Cats, The Naming of Cats, Invitation to the Jellicle Ball, Old Gumbie Cat, Rum Tum Tugger, Grizabella the Glamour Cat, Bustopher Jones, Mungojerri and Rumpleteazer, Old Deuteronomy, The Awefull Battle of the Pekes and Pollicles, Marching Song of the Pollicle Dogs, Jellicle Ball, Memory, Moments of Happiness, Gus the Theatre Cat, Growltiger's Last Stand, Skimble Shanks, Macavity, Mr. Mistoffolees, Journey to the Heaviside Layer, The Ad-Dressing of Cats

A Chorus Line
Marvin Hamlisch and Edward Kleban
I Hope I Get It, I Can Do That, Joanne, And . . . , At the Ballet, Sing!, Hello Twelve, Hello Thirteen, Hello Love, Nothing, Dance: Ten, Looks: Three, The Music and the Mirror, One, The Tap Combination, What I Did for Love

Company
Stephen Sondheim
Company, The Little Things You Do Together, Sorry-Grateful, You Could Drive a Person Crazy, Someone Is Waiting, Another Hundred People, Getting Married Today, Side by Side by Side, What Would We Do Without You?, Barcelona, The Ladies Who Lunch, Being Alive, Poor Baby, Tick-tock

Damn Yankees
Richard Adler and Jerry Ross
Goodbye, Old Girl, Heart, A Little Brains, a Little Talent, A Man Doesn't Know, Whatever Lola Wants, Who's Got the Pain?, Near to You, Two Lost Souls, Six Months Out of Every Year, Shoeless Joe from Hannibal, Mo., Those Were the Good Old Days

Fiddler on the Roof
Jerry Bock and Sheldon Harnick
Tradition, Matchmaker, Matchmaker, If I Were a Rich Man, To Life, Far from the Home I Love, Sunrise, Sunset, Do You Love Me?, Miracle of Miracles, Anatevka

Finian's Rainbow
Burton Lane and E. Y. Harburg
This Time of the Year, How Are Things in Glocca Morra?, If This Isn't Love, Look to the Rainbow, Old Devil Moon, Something Sort of Grandish, Necessity, When the Idle Poor Become the Idle Rich, When I'm Not Near the Girl I Love, That Great Come-and-Get-It Day

Funny Girl
Jule Styne and Bob Merrill
I'm the Greatest Star, Cornet Man, People, If a Girl Isn't Pretty, Who Taught Her Everything, His Love Makes Me Beautiful, I Want to Be Seen with You Tonight, Henry Street, Find Yourself a Man, You Are Woman, Don't Rain on My Parade, Sadie, Sadie, Who Are You Now?, The Music That Makes Me Dance, Rat-tat-tat-tat

George M!
George M. Cohan songs in a new musical
Ring to the Name of Rose, Give My Regards to Broadway, Forty-Five Minutes from Broadway, So Long, Mary, Mary's a Grand Old Name, Yankee Doodle Dandy, Over There, You're a Grand Old Flag, Musical Moon, Oh, You Wonderful Boy, All Aboard for Broadway, Twentieth-Century Love, My Town, Billie, Push Me Along in My Pushcart, Popularity, Down by the Erie, Mary, All Our Friends, Nellie Kelly, I Love You, Harrigan, Over There

Gigi
Frederick Loewe and Alan Jay Lerner
Thank Heaven for Little Girls, It's a Bore, Paris Is Paris Again, She Is Not Thinking of Me, The Night They Invented Champagne, I Remember It Well, Gigi, I'm Glad I'm Not Young Anymore, The Earth and Other Minor Things, In This Wide, Wide World

Girl Crazy
George and Ira Gershwin
Bidin' My Time, Could You Use Me?, Sam and Delilah, Embraceable You, I Got Rhythm, But Not for Me, Treat Me Rough, Boy!, What Love Has Done to Me!, Cactus Time in Arizona, Barbary Coast

Grease
Jim Jacobs and Warren Casey
Alma Mater, Alma Mater, Summer Nights, Those Magic Changes, Freddy My Love, Greased Lightnin', Mooning, Look At Me I'm Sandra Dee, We Go Together, Shakin' at the High School Hop, It's Raining on Prom Night, Born to Hand-Jive, Beauty School Dropout, Alone at a Drive-In Movie, Rock 'n' Roll Party Queen, There Are Worse Things I Could Do, All Choked Up

Guys and Dolls
Frank Loesser
Fugue for Tinhorns, The Oldest Established, I'll Know, A Bushel and a Peck, Adelaide's Lament, Guys and Dolls, If I Were a Bell, My Time of Day, I've Never Been in Love Before, Take Back Your Mink, More I Cannot Wish You, Luck Be a Lady, Sue Me, Sit Down,You're Rockin' the Boat, Marry the Man Today, Follow the Fold

Gypsy
Jule Styne and Stephen Sondheim
Let Me Entertain You, Some People, Small World, Little Lamb, You'll Never Get Away from Me, All I Need Is the Girl, Everything's Coming Up Roses, Together, Wherever We Go, Mr. Goldstone, I Love You, Dainty June and Her Farmboys, If Mama Was Married, You Gotta Have a Gimmick, Rose's Turn

Hair
Galt MacDermott, Gerome Ragni, and James Rado
Aquarius, Ain't Got No, I Got Life, Air, Hair, Easy To Be Hard, Frank Mills, Hare Krishna, Where Do I Go?, Good Morning Starshine, Going Down, Dead End, Electric Blues, Manchester, White Boys, Black Boys, Walking in Space, Exanaplanetooch, The Climax

Hello, Dolly!
Jerry Herman
It Takes a Woman, Put on Your Sunday Clothes, Ribbons Down My Back, Before the Parade Passes By, Elegance, Dancing, Motherhood, Hello Dolly!, It Only Takes a Moment, So Long, Dearie, I Put My Hand In, Elegance

How To Succeed in Business Without Really Trying
Frank Loesser
The Company Way, A Secretary Is Not a Toy, Grand Old Ivy, Been a Long Day, Paris Original, Rosemary, I Believe in You, Brotherhood of Man, Happy to Keep His Dinner Warm, Coffee Break, Cinderella, Darling, Love from a Heart of Gold

The King and I
Richard Rodgers and Oscar Hammerstein II
I Whistle a Happy Tune, My Lord and Master, Hello, Young Lovers, March of the Siamese Children, A Puzzlement, Getting To Know You, We Kiss in a Shadow, Something Wonderful, I Have Dreamed, Shall We Dance?, Shall I Tell You What I Think of You?, Western People Funny, Song of the King

Man of La Mancha
Mitch Leigh and Joe Darion
Man of La Mancha (I, Don Quixote), It's All the Same, Dulcinea, I Really Like Him, Little Bird, Little Bird, To Each His Dulcinea, The Quest (The Impossible Dream), I'm Only Thinking of Him, What Do You Want of Me?, The Barber's Song, Golden Helmet, Aldonza, A Little Gossip

Les Misérables
Claude-Michel Schönberg, Herbert Krettzmer, and Alain Boublil
At the End of the Day, I Dreamed a Dream, Lovely Ladies, Who Am I?, Come to Me, Castle on a Cloud, Master of the House, Full of Love, One Day More, On My Own, A Little Fall of Rain, Drink with Me to Days Gone By, Bring Him Home, Dogs Eats Dog, Soliliquy, Turning, Empty Chairs at Empty Tables, Wedding Chorale, Beggars at the Feast

The Music Man
Meredith Willson
Rock Island, Trouble, Piano Lesson, Goodnight, My Someone, Seventy-Six Trombones, The Sadder-but-Wiser Girl, Marian the Librarian, My White Knight, Wells Fargo Wagon, Shi-poopi, Lida Rose, Will I Ever Tell You?, Gary, Indiana, Till There Was You

My Fair Lady
Frederick Loewe and Alan Jay Lerner
Why Can't the English?, Wouldn't It Be Loverly?, With a Little Bit of Luck, I'm an Ordinary Man, Just You Wait, The Rain in Spain, I Could Have Danced All Night, On the Street Where You Live, Show Me, Get Me to the Church on Time, A Hymn to Him, Without You, I've Grown Accustomed to Her Face, You Did It

The New Moon
Sigmund Romberg and Oscar Hammerstein II
Marianne, Softly, as in a Morning Sunrise, Wanting You, Lover, Come Back to Me, I Was a Stranger in Paris, One Kiss, Stouthearted Man

No, No, Nanette
Vincent Youmans, Otto Harbach, and Irving Caesar
No, No, Nanette, Too Many Rings Around Rosie, I Want to Be Happy, Tea for Two, You Can Dance with Any Girl at All, Where Has My Hubby Gone Blues, I've Confessed to the Breeze, Call of the Sea, Telephone Girlie, Waiting for You, Take a Little One-Step

Oklahoma!
Richard Rodgers and Oscar Hammerstein II
Oh, What a Beautiful Mornin', The Surrey with the Fringe on Top, Kansas City, I Cain't Say No, Many a New Day, People Will Say We're in Love, Pore Jud, Lonely Room, Out of My Dreams, All er Nothin', The Farmer and the Cowman, Oklahoma

Oliver!
Lionel Bart
Food Glorious Food, Oliver!, Boy for Sale, That's Your Funeral, Where Is Love?, Consider Yourself, You've Got to Pick a Pocket or Two, It's a Fine Life, I'd Do Anything, Be Back Soon, Oom-pah-pah, My Name, As Long As He Needs Me, Who Will Buy This Won-

derful Morning?, Reviewing the Situation, I Shall Scream

Pal Joey
Richard Rodgers and Lorenz Hart
You Mustn't Kick It Around, I Could Write a Book, That Terrific Rainbow, Happy Hunting Horn, Bewitched, Bothered, and Bewildered, The Flower Garden of My Heart, Zip, Den of Iniquity, Take Him, What Is a Man?, What Do I Care for a Dame, Plant You Now, Dig You Later, Do It the Hard Way

Phantom of the Opera
Andrew Lloyd Webber, Charles Hart, and Richard Stilgoe
Think of Me, Angel of Music, Little Lotte, The Mirror, The Phantom of the Opera, The Music of the Night, I Remember, Stranger Than You Dreamt It, Magical Lasso, Notes, Prima Donna, Poor Fool He Makes Me Laugh, Why Have You Brought Me Here?, Raoul I've Been There, All I Ask of You, Masquerade, Why So Silent?, Twisted Every Way, Wishing You Were Somehow Here Again, Wandering Child, Bravo Bravo, The Point of No Return, Down One More, Track Down This Murderer

Porgy and Bess
George Gershwin, DuBose Heyward, and Ira Gershwin
Summertime, A Woman Is a Sometime Thing, Gone, Gone, Gone, My Man's Gone Now, It Takes a Long Pull To Get There, I Got Plenty o' Nuttin', What You Want wid Bess?, Bess, You Is My Woman Now, Oh, I Cain't Sit Down, It Ain't Necessarily So, I Loves You Porgy, A Red-Headed Woman, There's a Boat Dat's Leavin' Soon for New York, Bess, Oh Where's My Bess?, I'm on My Way

Roberta
Jerome Kern and Otto Harbach
You're Devastating, Yesterdays, The Touch of Your Hand, Smoke Gets in Your Eyes, Let's Begin, I'll Be Hard to Handle, I Won't Dance, Lovely to Look At

Show Boat
Jerome Kern and Oscar Hammerstein II
Make Believe, Ol' Man River, Can't Help Lovin' Dat Man, Till Good Luck Comes My Way, I Might Fall Back on You, Life upon the Wicked Stage, You Are Love, Why Do I Love You?, Bill, Cotton Blossom, Where's the Mate for Me?, How'd You Like To Spoon with Me?, Nobody Else but Me, I Have the Room Above Her, After the Ball, Dance Away the Night

The Sound of Music
Richard Rodgers and Oscar Hammerstein II
The Sound of Music, Maria, My Favorite Things, Do-Re-Mi, Sixteen Going on Seventeen, The Lonely Goatherd, So Long, Farewell, No Way to Stop It, An Ordinary Couple, How Can Love Survive?, Climb Ev'ry Mountain, Edelweiss

South Pacific
Richard Rodgers and Oscar Hammerstein II
Dites-moi, A Cockeyed Optimist, Some Enchanted Evening, Bloody Mary, There Is Nothin' Like a Dame, Bali Ha'i, I'm Gonna Wash That Man Right Outa My Hair, A Wonderful Guy, Younger Than Springtime, Happy Talk, Honey Bun, You've Got To Be Carefully Taught, This Nearly Was Mine

This Is the Army
Irving Berlin
This Is the Army, Mr. Jones, I Left My Heart at the Stage Door Canteen, I'm Getting Tired So I Can Sleep, Mandy, American Eagles, With My Head in the Clouds, The Army's Made a Man out of Me, Oh, How I Hate to Get Up in the Morning, Poor Little Me, I'm on KP, Your Country and My Country, My Sweetie, We're on Our Way to France

The Threepenny Opera
Kurt Weill and Berthold Brecht
The Ballad of Mack the Knife, Wedding Song, Pirate Jenny, Army Song, Love Song, Ballad of the Easy Life, Barbara Song, Jealousy Duet, Useless Song, Solomon Song, Ballad of the Pimp, Song About the Inadequacy of Human Ambition

West Side Story
Leonard Bernstein and Stephen Sondheim
Jet Song, Something's Coming, Maria, Tonight, America, Cool, I Feel Pretty, Somewhere, Gee, Officer Krupke!, One Hand, One Heart, A Boy Like That, I Have a Love

THEATER'S LEADING LIGHTS

Selected for their prominent contributions to today's theater, the following artists are responsible for many of the most important plays currently being produced in the English language. Each list of works notes every play, screenplay, or teleplay created by the artist (aside from one-acts), as well as major awards won by the work and the year of its first production.

BETH HENLEY
playwright/screenwriter

Parade (1975)

Crimes of the Heart (1979, screenplay 1987; Pulitzer)

The Wake of Jamey Foster (1982)

The Moon Watch (screenplay, 1983)

The Miss Firecracker Contest (1984)

The Debutante Ball (1985)

The Lucky Spot (1986)

True Stories (coauthor, screenplay, 1986)

Nobody's Fool (screenplay, 1987)

Abundance (1989)

Signature (1990)

Control Freak (1992)

ANDREW LLOYD WEBBER
composer

Joseph and the Amazing Technicolor Dreamcoat (1968)

Jesus Christ Superstar (1971)

Jeeves (1974)

Evita (1976; Tony)

Cats (1982; Tony, Grammy)

Song and Dance (1982)

Starlight Express (1984)

Phantom of the Opera (1986)

Aspects of Love (1989)

Sunset Boulevard (1993)

DAVID MAMET
playwright/screenwriter

Lakeboat (1970)

The Duck Variations (1972)

Mackinac (children's play, 1974)

The Poet and the Rent (1974)

Squirrels (1974)

Sexual Perversity in Chicago (1974)

American Buffalo (1975)

Marranos (1975)

Reunion (1976)

Dark Pony (1977)

The Woods (1977)

The Revenge of the Space Pandas, or Binky Rudich and the Two-Speed Clock (1977)

The Water Engine: An American Fable (1977)

A Life in the Theatre (1977)

Lone Canoe or The Explorer (1979)

The Postman Always Rings Twice (screenplay, 1981)

The Verdict (screenplay, 1982)

Edmond (1982)

Glengarry Glen Ross (1983; Pulitzer)

Disappearance of the Jews (1983)

Red River (adaptor, 1983)

Vermont Sketches (1984)

The Frog Prince (1984)

Joseph Dintenfass (1984)

The Spanish Prisoner (1985)

The Cherry Orchard (adaptor, 1985)

The Shawl (1985)

Three Sisters (adaptor, 1985)

The Untouchables (screenplay, 1987)

House of Games (screenplay, 1987)

Things Change (coauthor screenplay, 1987)

Speed-the-Plow (1988)

We're No Angels (1989)

Bobby Gould in Hell (1989)

Homicide (screenplay, 1991)

Oleanna (1992)

Hoffa (screenplay, 1992)

The Village (novel, 1994)

ARTHUR MILLER
playwright/screenwriter

Honors at Dawn (1936)

No Villain (1936)

The Half-Bridge (written 1943, never produced)

The Pussycat and the Expert Plumber Who Was a Man (radio play, 1943)

William Ireland's Confession (radio play, 1942)

The Man Who Had All the Luck (1944)

That They May Win (1944)

The Story of G. I. Joe (screenplay, 1945)

Grandpa and the Statue (radio play, 1942)

The Story of Gus (radio play 1942)

All My Sons (1947)

Death of A Salesman (1948)

An Enemy of the People (adaptor, 1950)

The Crucible (1953; Tony)

A View from the Bridge (1955)

A Memory of Two Mondays (1955)

The Witches of Salem (screenplay, 1958)

The Misfits (screenplay, 1961)

After the Fall (1964)

Incident at Vichy (1964)

The Price (1968)

Fame (1971)

The Creation of the World and Other Business (1972; musical version, *Up From Paradise,* 1982)

The Archbishop's Ceiling (1977)

The American Clock (adaptor, 1979)

Playing for Time (adaptor, teleplay, 1981)

Two-Way Mirror (1982)

The Golden Years (radio play, 1987)

Everybody Wins (screenplay, 1990)

The Ride Down Mt. Morgan (1991)

The Last Yankee (1993)

Broken Glass (1994)

Gellburg (1994)

MARSHA NORMAN
playwright/screenwriter

Getting Out (1977)

It's the Willingness (teleplay, 1978)

Circus Valentine (1979)

Third and Oak (1978)

In Trouble at Fifteen (teleplay, 1980)

The Holdup (1980)

'Night, Mother (1983; Pulitzer; screenplay, 1984)

Traveler in the Dark (1984)

Sarah and Abraham (1987)

The Secret Garden (book and lyrics, 1989; Tony)

Face of a Stranger (teleplay, 1992)

Loving Daniel Boone (1992)

The Red Shoes (book and lyrics, 1993)

HAROLD PINTER
playwright/screenwriter

The Room (1957)

The Birthday Party (1958; screenplay, 1968; teleplay, 1987)

The Dumb Waiter (1959)

The Caretaker (1960)

A Night Out (radio play, 1960)

The Collection (teleplay, 1961)

The Servant (screenplay, 1963)

The Lover (1963)

The Pumpkin Eater (screenplay, 1964)

The Tea Party (1965)

The Homecoming (1965; screenplay, 1973)

The Quiller Memorandum (screenplay, 1966)

Accident (screenplay, 1967)

The Basement (1967)

Landscape (1968)

Silence (1969)

The Go-Between (screenplay, 1970)

The Last Tycoon (screenplay, 1971)

Old Times (1971)

The Proust Screenplay: A la recherche du temps perdu (screenplay, 1973)

No Man's Land (1975)

Players (radio play, 1975)

Betrayal (1978; screenplay, 1982)

Langrishe, Go Down (adaptor, screenplay, 1978)

The Hothouse (1980)

The French Lieutenant's Woman (screenplay, 1981)

Other Places (1982)

Turtle Diary (screenplay, 1985)

Reunion (screenplay, 1989)

The Comfort of Strangers (screenplay, 1990)

The Handmaid's Tale (adaptor, screenplay, 1993)

Moonlight (1993)

The Trial (screenplay, 1993)

SAM SHEPARD
playwright, screenwriter

Up to Thursday (1965)

Dog (1965)

Rocking Chair (1965)

4-H Club (1965)

La Turista (1967)

Forensic and the Navigators (1967)

Me and My Brother (coauthor, screenplay, 1967)

Operation Sidewinder (1969)

The Unseen Hand (1969)

Zabriskie Point (coauthor, screenplay, 1970)

Cowboy Mouth (coauthor, 1971)

Ringaleenio (screenplay, 1971)

The Tooth of Crime (1972)

Blue Bitch (1973)

Nightwalk (coauthor, 1973)

Little Ocean (1974)

Geography of a Horse Dreamer (1974)

The Sad Lament of Pecos Bill on the Eve of Killing His Wife (1976)

Suicide in B Flat (1976)

Angel City (1977)

Curse of the Starving Class (1977)

Inacoma (1977)

Buried Child (1978; Pulitzer)

Seduced (1978)

Jackson's Dance (coauthor, 1980)

True West (1980)

Black Bart and the Sacred Hills (1981)

Fool for Love (1983; screenplay, 1985)

Superstitions (1983)

Paris, Texas (coauthor, screenplay, 1984)

A Lie of the Mind (1985)

The War in Heaven: Angel's Monologue (teleplay, 1985)

States of Shock (1989)

Simpatico (1994)

NEIL SIMON
playwright, screenwriter

Adventures of Marco Polo: A Musical Fantasy (coauthor, book, 1959)

Heidi (coadaptor, 1959)

Come Blow Your Horn (coauthor, 1961)

Little Me (adaptor, 1962)

Barefoot in the Park (originally *Nobody Loves Me*, 1962; screenplay, 1967)

The Odd Couple (1965; Tony; screenplay, 1968; female version, 1985)

Sweet Charity (book, 1966)

The Star-Spangled Girl (1966)

Promises, Promises (book, 1968)

Plaza Suite (1968; screenplay, 1971)

The Last of the Red-Hot Lovers (1969)

The Gingerbread Lady (1970)

The Out-of-Towners (screenplay, 1970)

The Prisoner of Second Avenue (1971; screenplay, 1975)

The Heartbreak Kid (screenplay, 1972)

The Sunshine Boys (1972)

The Good Doctor (adaptor, 1973)

Seesaw (1973)

God's Favorite (1974)

California Suite (1976; screenplay 1978)

Murder by Death (screenplay, 1976)

The Goodbye Girl (screenplay, 1977; book, 1993)

Chapter Two (1977; screenplay, 1979)

The Cheap Detective (1978)

They're Playing Our Song (book, 1979)

I Ought To Be in Pictures (1980; screenplay, 1982)

Seems Like Old Times (1980)

Fools (1981)

Only When I Laugh (1982)

Max Dugan Returns (1983)

Actors and Actresses (1983)

Brighton Beach Memoirs (1982; Pulitzer; screenplay, 1986)

Biloxi Blues (1984)

The Slugger's Wife (1985)

Broadway Bound (1986)

Rumors (1988)

Lost in Yonkers (1991)

Jake's Women (1992)

Laughter on the 23rd Floor (1993).

A special Tony was awarded to Mr. Simon in 1975 for overall contribution to the theater.

STEPHEN SONDHEIM
composer/lyricist

West Side Story (lyrics, 1957)

Gypsy (lyrics, 1959)

A Funny Thing Happened on the Way to the Forum (music and lyrics, 1962)

Anyone Can Whistle (music and lyrics, 1964)

Do I Hear a Waltz? (lyrics, 1965)

The Mad Show (co-lyricist, 1966)

Company (music and lyrics, 1970; Tony)

Follies (music and lyrics, 1971; Tony)

A Little Night Music (music and lyrics, 1973; Tony)

The Frogs (music and lyrics, 1974)

Candide (revival, co-lyricist, 1973)

Pacific Overtures (music and lyrics, 1976)

Sweeney Todd (music and lyrics, 1979; Tony)

Merrily We Roll Along (1981)

Sunday in the Park with George (music and lyrics, 1984; Pulitzer)

Assassins (1991)

Passion (music and lyrics, 1994; Tony)

TOM STOPPARD
playwright

A Walk on the Water (1963)

The Dissolution of Dominic Boot (radio play, 1964)

"M" is for Moon Among Other Things (radio play, 1964)

The Gamblers (1965)

If You're Glad I'll Be Frank (radio play, 1966)

Rozencrantz and Guildenstern Are Dead (1966; Tony)

Tango (adaptor, 1966)

A Separate Peace (teleplay, 1966)

Albert's Bridge (radio play, 1967)

Teeth (teleplay, 1967)

Another Moon Called Earth (teleplay, 1967)

Neutral Ground (teleplay, 1968)

The Real Inspector Hound (1968)

After Magritte (1970)

Where Are They Now? (radio play, 1970)

Dogg's Our Pet (1971)

Jumpers (1972)

Artist Descending a Staircase (radio play, 1972; stage, 1988)

Travesties (1974; Tony)

Dirty Linen, and New-found-land (1976)

The Fifteen Minute Hamlet (1976)

Professional Foul (teleplay, 1977)

Every Good Boy Deserves Favour: A Play for Actors and Orchestra (1977)

Night and Day (1978)

Undiscovered Country (adaptor, 1979)

Dogg's Hamlet and Cahoot's MacBeth (1979)

On the Razzle (adaptor, 1981)

The Real Thing (1982; Tony)

The Dog It Was That Died (radio play, 1982)

The Love for Three Oranges (adaptor, 1983)

Rough Crossing (1984)

Squaring the Circle: Poland 1980–81 (TV docudrama, 1984)

Dalliance (adaptor, 1986)

Largo Desolato (adaptor, 1986)

In the Native State (radio play, 1991)

Arcadia (1993)

TOMMY TUNE

director, choreographer, performer

Seesaw (1973, actor; Tony)

The Club (director, 1976)

Sunset (director, 1977)

The Best Little Whorehouse in Texas (co-director and choreographer, 1978)

Double Feature (choreographer, 1979)

A Day in Hollywood/A Night in the Ukraine (director and choreographer, 1980; Tony for best choreographer)

Cloud 9 (director, 1981)

Nine (director and choreographer, 1982; Tony for best director)

My One and Only (co-director, co-choreographer, actor, 1983; Tonys for best choreographer and best actor)

Stepping Out (director, 1987)

Grand Hotel (1989; Tonys for best director and best choreographer)

The Will Rogers Follies (director, choreographer, 1991; Tonys for best director and best choreographer)

The Best Little Whorehouse Goes Public (co-director, 1994)

WENDY WASSERSTEIN

playwright /screenwriter

Any Woman Can't (1973)

When Dinah Shore Ruled the Earth (coauthor, 1977)

Uncommon Women and Others (teleplay, 1978)

The Sorrows of Gin (adaptor, teleplay, 1981)

Hard Sell (1980)

Isn't It Romantic? (1981)

Tender Offer (1983)

The Man in a Case (adaptor, 1985)

Miami (coauthor, book, 1985)

Drive, She Said (1988)

The Heidi Chronicles (1988; Pulitzer, Tony)

Kiss, Kiss Darling (1991)

The Sisters Rosenzweig (1993)

The Object of My Affection (1994).

AUGUST WILSON

Black Bart and the Sacred Hills (1981)

Jitney (1982)

Joe Turner's Come and Gone (1983)

Ma Rainey's Black Bottom (1984)

Fences (1985; Pulitzer, Tony)

The Piano Lesson (1987; Pulitzer)

Two Trains Running (1990)

SCHOOLS FOR STARS

The Yale School of Drama and the Juilliard School have produced a dazzling roster of leading talents, both within the realm of theater as well as in the acting world at large. This list notes just a few of the well-schooled familiar names in the entertainment world.

Yale School of Drama

Angela Bassett, actress
Robert Brustein, director/writer
Christopher Durang, playwright
Jill Eikenberry, actress
John Guare, playwright
A. R. Gurney, playwright
Julie Harris, actress
Ken Howard, actor
David Henry Hwang, playwright/screenwriter
Albert Innaurato, playwright
Tama Janowitz, writer
Elia Kazan, director
Stacy Keach, actor
Christopher Lehmann-Haupt, writer
Mark Linn-Baker, actor
Santo Loquasto, set designer
Paul Newman, actor
Carrie Nye, actress
Talia Shire, actress
Meryl Streep, actress/director
Ted Tally, playwright/screenwriter
John Turturro, actor/director
Joan Van Ark, actress
Wendy Wasserstein, playwright
Sigourney Weaver, actress
Edmund Wilson, writer
Henry Winkler, actor/director

Juilliard School Drama Division

Christine Baranski, actress
Andre Braugher, actor
Kelsey Grammer, actor
William Hurt, actor
Patti LuPone, actress/singer
Val Kilmer, actor
Perry King, actor
Linda Kozlowski, actress
Kevin Kline, actor/director
Kelly McGillis, actress
Elizabeth McGovern, actress
Gregory Mosher, director
Mandy Patinkin, actor
Christopher Reeve, actor
David Ogden Stiers, actor
Jeanne Tripplehorn, actress
Robin Williams, actor/comedian

MAJOR BRITISH IMPORTS ON BROADWAY

Some of the most significant shows on Broadway over the last twenty years have been imported from Britain. The following list outlines the major figures behind them and gives the year of their American premiere.

Amadeus, Peter Shaffer, director Peter Hall (1980)

Aspects of Love, Andrew Lloyd Webber, Don Black, and Charles Hart, director Trevor Nunn, producer Cameron Mackintosh (1989)

Betrayal, Harold Pinter, director Peter Hall (1980)

Cats, Andrew Lloyd Webber, Trevor Nunn, director Trevor Nunn, producer Cameron Mackintosh (1982)

Equus, Peter Shaffer, director John Dexter (1974)

Evita, Andrew Lloyd Webber and Tim Rice, director Harold Prince (1979)

Jesus Christ Superstar, Andrew Lloyd Webber and Tim Rice, director Tim O'Horgan (1971)

Joseph and the Amazing Technicolor Dreamcoat, Andrew Lloyd Webber and Tim Rice, director Tony Tanner (1982)

Les Liaisons Dangereuses, Christopher Hampton, Royal Shakespeare Company production, director Howard Davies (1987)

Les Misérables, by Claude-Michel Schönberg, Alain Boublil, Herbert Kretzmer, directors and adaptors Trevor Nunn and John Caird (1987)

Me and My Girl, L. Arthur Rose, Douglas Furber, Noel Gay, director Mike Ockrent (1986)

Miss Saigon, Claude-Michel Schönberg, Alain Boublil, Richard Maltby, director Nicholas Hytner (1991)

Nicholas Nickleby, David Edgar, directors Trevor Nunn and John Caird, producer Cameron Mackintosh (1986)

Noises Off, Michael Frayn, director Michael Blakemore (1983)

The Norman Conquests, Alan Ayckbourn, director Eric Thompson (1975

Oliver!, Lionel Bart, director Peter Coe, producer Cameron Mackintosh (1984)

The Phantom of the Opera, Andrew Lloyd Webber, Charles Hart, Richard Stilgoe, director Harold Prince (1988)

Plenty, David Hare, director David Hare (1983)

The Real Thing, Tom Stoppard, director Mike Nichols (1984)

Rocky Horror Show, Richard O'Brien, director Jim Sharman (1975)

Some Americans Abroad, Richard Nelson, director Roger Mitchell, Royal Shakespeare Company production (1990)

Starlight Express, Andrew Lloyd Webber and Richard Stilgoe, director Trevor Nunn (1987)

Sunset Boulevard, by Andrew Lloyd Webber, Don Black, and Christopher Hampton (1994)

MUSICAL THEATER HALL OF FAME

Rock 'n roll has one and so do most sports, so it seems fitting that musical theater—perhaps the most American of all inventions—should have one, too. The Musical Theater Hall of Fame, organized by a committee of theater experts and fans from New York University, announced its first set of inductees in November 1993.

Inductees:
Jerome Kern
George and Ira Gershwin
Richard Rodgers
Oscar Hammerstein II
Alan Jay Lerner
Frederick Loewe
Ethel Merman

Honorees:
Carol Channing
Jule Styne

MAJOR SHOWS THAT BEGAN IN REGIONAL THEATERS

Beginning in the '70s, the creative impetus in American drama began to shift away from the increasingly expensive Broadway venues and toward regional and nonprofit theaters. While most major playwrights once wrote directly for Broadway production, regional theaters have more commonly become the place of origination for America's most important plays. The following productions may have gone on to national and even international fame, but all began in regional theaters.

American Buffalo, by David Mamet, Goodman Theater, Chicago

Angels in America, by Tony Kushner, Eureka Theatre Company, San Francisco

Annie, by Thomas Meehan, Martin Charnin, and Charles Strouse, Goodspeed Opera House, East Haddam, Connecticut

Big River, adapted by William Hauptman from Mark Twain, La Jolla Playhouse, La Jolla, California

Buried Child, by Sam Shepard, Magic Theater, San Francisco

California Suite, by Neil Simon, Hartman Theatre, Stanford, Connecticut

Children of a Lesser God, by Mark Medoff, Mark Taper Forum, Los Angeles

The Colored Museum, by George C. Wolfe, Crossroads Theatre Company, New Brunswick, New Jersey

Conversations with my Father, by Herb Gardner, Seattle Repertory Theatre

Crimes of the Heart, by Beth Henley, Actors Theatre of Louisville

Eastern Standard, by Richard Greenberg, Seattle Repertory Theatre

Fences, by August Wilson, Yale Repertory Theatre, New Haven, Connecticut

The Gin Game, by D. L. Coburn, Long Wharf Theatre, New Haven, Connecticut

Glengarry Glen Ross, by David Mamet, Goodman Theatre, Chicago

The Heidi Chronicles, by Wendy Wasserstein, Seattle Repertory Theatre

I'm Not Rappaport, by Herb Gardner, Seattle Repertory Theatre

In the Belly of the Beast, adapted by Adrian Hall from Jack Henry Abbott, Trinity Repertory Company, Providence, Rhode Island

Into the Woods, by James Lapine and Stephen Sondheim, Old Globe Theatre, San Diego

Jelly's Last Jam, by George C. Wolff, Jelly Roll Morton, and Susan Birkenhead, Mark Taper Forum, Los Angeles

Joe Turner's Come and Gone, by August Wilson, Yale Repertory Theatre, New Haven, Connecticut

Love Letters, by A. R. Gurney, Long Wharf Theatre, New Haven, Connecticut

Ma Rainey's Black Bottom, by August Wilson,Yale Repertory Theatre, New Haven, Connecticut

Master Harold and the Boys, by Athol Fugard, Yale Repertory Theatre, New Haven, Connecticut

'Night, Mother, by Marsha Norman, American Repertory Theatre, Cambridge, Massachusetts

Prelude to a Kiss, by Craig Lucas, South Coast Repertory, Costa Mesa, California

Quilters, by Molly Newman and Barbara Damashek, Denver Center Theatre Company

Streamers, by David Rabe, Long Wharf Theatre, New Haven, Connecticut

True West, by Sam Shepard, Steppenwolf Theatre Company, Chicago

Two Trains Running, by August Wilson, Yale Repertory Theatre, New Haven, Connecticut

The Wake of Jamey Foster, by Beth Henley, Hartford Stage Company, Hartford, Connecticut

The Who's "Tommy," by Pete Townshend and Wayne Cilento, La Jolla Playhouse, La Jolla, California

MAJOR REGIONAL THEATERS AND THEIR DIRECTORS

Actors Theatre of Louisville, Louisville, Kentucky, Jon Jory, producing director
Alley Theatre, Houston, Gregory Boyd, artistic director
Alliance Theatre Company, Atlanta, Kenny Leon, artistic director
American Conservatory Theater, San Francisco, Carey Perloff, artistic director
American Repertory Theatre, Cambridge, Massachusetts, Robert Brustein, artistic director
Arena Stage, Washington, D.C., Douglas Wager, artistic director
Center Stage, Baltimore, Irene Lewis, artistic director
Dallas Theater Center, Dallas, Jeff West, managing director
Goodman Theatre, Chicago, Robert Falls, artistic director
Goodspeed Opera House, East Haddam, Connecticut, Michael P. Price, executive director
Guthrie Theater, Minneapolis, Garland Wright, artistic director
Hartford Stage Company, Hartford, Connecticut, Mark Lamos, artistic director
La Jolla Playhouse, La Jolla, California, Des McAnuff, artistic director
Long Wharf Theatre, New Haven, Connecticut, Arvin Brown, artistic director
Mark Taper Forum, Los Angeles, Gordon Davidson, artistic director
McCarter Theatre Center, Princeton, New Jersey, Emily Mann, artistic director
Milwaukee Repertory Theater, Milwaukee, Joseph Hanreddy, artistic director
Old Globe Theatre, San Diego, Jack O'Brien, artistic director
Oregon Shakespeare Festival, Ashland and Portland, Oregon, Henry Woronicz, artistic director
Seattle Repertory Theatre, Seattle, Daniel Sullivan, artistic director
Shakespeare Theatre, Washington, D.C., Michael Kahn, artistic director
South Coast Repertory, Costa Mesa, California, David Emmes, producing artistic director
Steppenwolf Theatre Company, Chicago, Randall Arney, artistic director
Trinity Repertory Company, Providence, Rhode Island, Richard Jenkins, artistic director
Yale Repertory Theatre, New Haven, Connecticut, Stan Wojewodski Jr., artistic director

WHAT'S HOT IN HIGH SCHOOL DRAMA

Here's a list of the most popular full-length shows for high-school performance in the United States, over the last year and over the entire post–World War II period through 1984. In the September 1985 issue of *Dramatics* magazine, one theater educator lamented the list's conservatism—its preponderance of musicals, oldies, and shows by American playwrights.

1993

1. *Oklahoma!*, Richard Rodgers and Oscar Hammerstein II
2. *The Crucible*, Arthur Miller (tie)
2. *A Midsummer's Night's Dream*, William Shakespeare (tie)
2. *Our Town*, Thornton Wilder (tie)
5. *Bye Bye Birdie*, Michael Stewart, Charles Strouse, and Lee Adams
6. *Grease*, Jim Jacobs and Warren Casey
7. *Steel Magnolias*, Robert Harling (tie)
7. *The Curious Savage*, John Patrick (tie)
9. *Once upon a Mattress*, Jay Thompson, Marshall Barer, Dean Fuller, and Mary Rodgers
10. *Arsenic and Old Lace*, Joseph Kesselring
11. *West Side Story*, Arthur Laurents, Leonard Bernstein, and Stephen Sondheim (tie)
11. *The Wizard of Oz*, various adaptations of the novel (tie)
13. *The Miracle Worker*, William Gibson
14. *Fiddler on the Roof*, Jerry Bock, Sheldon Harnick, and Joseph Stein (tie)
14. *Rumors*, Neil Simon (tie)
14. *The Music Man*, Meredith Wilson (tie)
14. *Meet Me in St. Louis*, Sally Benson, Hugh Martin, and Ralph Blane (tie)
18. *You Can't Take It with You*, Moss Hart and George S. Kaufman (tie)
18. *Annie*, Charles Strouse, Martin Charnin, and Thomas Meehan (tie)
18. *Guys and Dolls*, Frank Loesser, Jo Swerling, and Abe Burrows (tie)
18. *Love, Death, and the Prom*, Jon Jory (tie)
22. *A Christmas Carol*, various adaptations (tie)
22. *Harvey*, Mary Chase (tie)
24. *You're a Good Man, Charlie Brown*, John Gordon and Clark Gesner (tie)
24. *The Diary of Anne Frank*, Frances Goodrich and Albert Hackett (tie)
24. *Dracula*, various adaptations (tie)
24. *The Little Shop of Horrors*, Howard Ashman and Alan Menken (tie)
24. *The Nerd*, Larry Shue (tie)

1945–1984

1. *You Can't Take It with You*, Moss Hart and George S. Kaufman
2. *Our Town*, Thornton Wilder
3. *Arsenic and Old Lace*, Joseph Kesselring
4. *Harvey*, Mary Chase
5. *The Curious Savage*, John Patrick
6. *Oklahoma!*, Richard Rodgers and Oscar Hammerstein II
7. *The Miracle Worker*, William Gibson (tie)
7. *The Diary of Anne Frank*, Frances Goodrich and Albert Hackett (tie)
9. *The Music Man*, Meredith Wilson (tie)
9. *Our Hearts Were Young and Gay*, Jean Kerr (tie)
9. *The Night of January 16*, Ayn Rand (tie)
12. *Bye Bye Birdie*, Michael Stewart, Charles Strouse, and Lee Adams
13. *The Man Who Came to Dinner*, George S. Kaufman and Moss Hart
14. *Up the Down Staircase* Christopher Sergel (from the book by Bel Kaufman) (tie)
14. *You're a Good Man, Charlie Brown*, John Gordon and Clark Gesner (tie)
14. *The Sound of Music*, Richard Rodgers and Oscar Hammerstein II (tie)
17. *Guys and Dolls*, Frank Loesser, Jo Swerling, and Abe Burrows
18. *Godspell*, John Michael Tebelak and Stephen Schwartz
19. *Teahouse of the August Moon*, John Patrick
20. *The Crucible*, Arthur Miller

THE TONY AWARDS

	1947	1948	1949
Actor (Dramatic)	Fredric March, *Years Ago*; Jose Ferrer, *Cyrano de Bergerac*	Basil Rathbone, *The Heiress*; Henry Fonda, *Mister Roberts*; Paul Kelly, *Command Decision*	Rex Harrison, *Anne of the Thousand Days*
Actress (Dramatic)	Helen Hayes, *Happy Birthday*; Ingrid Bergman, *Joan of Lorraine*	Jessica Tandy, *A Streetcar Named Desire*; Judith Anderson, *Medea*; Katharine Cornell, *Antony and Cleopatra*	Martita Hunt, *The Madwoman of Chaillot*
Supporting Actor (Dramatic)	—	—	Arthur Kennedy, *Death of a Salesman*
Supporting Actress (Dramatic)	Patricia Neal, *Another Part of the Forest*	—	Shirley Booth, *Goodbye, My Fancy*
Play	—	*Mister Roberts*	*Death of a Salesman*
Actor (Musical)	—	Paul Hartman, *Angel in the Wings*	Ray Bolger, *Where's Charley?*
Actress (Musical)	—	Grace Hartman, *Angel in the Wings*	Nanette Fabray, *Love Life*
Supporting Actor (Musical)	David Wayne, *Finian's Rainbow*	—	—
Supporting Actress (Musical)	—	—	—
Musical	—	—	*Kiss Me Kate*
Director	Elia Kazan, *All My Sons*	—	Elia Kazan, *Death of a Salesman*
Score	—	—	Cole Porter, *Kiss Me Kate*
Author (Dramatic)	—	Thomas Heggen and Joshua Logan, *Mister Roberts*	Arthur Miller, *Death of a Salesman*
Author (Musical)	—		Bella and Samuel Spewack, *Kiss Me Kate*
Scenic Designer	—	Horace Armistead, *The Medium*	Jo Mielziner, *Sleepy Hollow; Summer and Smoke; Anne of the Thousand Days; Death of a Salesman; South Pacific*
Costume Designer	—	—	Lemuel Ayers, *Kiss Me Kate*
Choreographer	Agnes de Mille, *Brigadoon*; Michael Kidd, *Finian's Rainbow*	Jerome Robbins, *High Button Shoes*	Gower Champion, *Lend an Ear*
Producer (Dramatic)	—	Leland Hayward, *Mister Roberts*	Kermit Bloomgarden and Walter Fried, *Death of a Salesman*
Producer (Musical)	—	—	Saint-Subber and Lemuel Ayers, *Kiss Me Kate*
Conductor and Musical Director	—	—	Max Meth, *As the Girls Go*
Stage Technician	—	George Gebhardt; George Pierce	—

1950	1951	1952	1953
Sydney Blackmer, *Come Back, Little Sheba*	Claude Rains, *Darkness At Noon*	Jose Ferrer, *The Shrike*	Tom Ewell, *The Seven Year Itch*
Shirley Booth, *Come Back, Little Sheba*	Uta Hagen, *The Country Girl*	Julie Harris, *I Am a Camera*	Shirley Booth, *Time of the Cuckoo*
—	Eli Wallach, *The Rose Tattoo*	John Cromwell, *Point of No Return*	John Williams, *Dial M for Murder*
—	Maureen Stapleton, *The Rose Tattoo*	Marian Winters, *I Am a Camera*	Beatrice Straight, *The Crucible*
The Cocktail Party	*The Rose Tattoo*	*The Fourposter*	*The Crucible*
Ezio Pinza, *South Pacific*	Robert Alda, *Guys and Dolls*	Phil Silvers, *Top Banana*	Thomas Mitchell, *Hazel Flagg*
Mary Martin, *South Pacific*	Ethel Merman, *Call Me Madam*	Gertrude Lawrence, *The King & I*	Rosalind Russell, *Wonderful Town*
Myron McCormick, *South Pacific*	Russell Nype, *Call Me Madam*	Yul Brynner, *The King & I*	Hiram Sherman, *Two's Company*
Juanita Hall, *South Pacific*	Isabel Bigley, *Guys And Dolls*	Helen Gallagher, *Pal Joey*	Sheila Bond, *Wish You Were Here*
South Pacific	*Guys And Dolls*	*The King & I*	*Wonderful Town*
Joshua Logan, *South Pacific*	George S. Kaufman, *Guys and Dolls*	Jose Ferrer, *The Shrike; The Fourposter; Stalag 17*	Joshua Logan, *Picnic*
Richard Rodgers, *South Pacific*	Frank Loesser, *Guys and Dolls*	—	Leonard Bernstein, *Wonderful Town*
T.S. Eliot, *The Cocktail Party*	Tennessee Williams, *The Rose Tattoo*	—	Arthur Miller, *The Crucible*
Oscar Hammerstein II and Joshua Logan, *South Pacific*	Jo Swerling and Abe Burrows, *Guys and Dolls*	—	Joseph Fields and Jerome Chodorov, *Wonderful Town*
Jo Mielziner, *The Innocents*	Boris Aronson, *The Rose Tattoo; The Country Girl; Season in the Sun*	Jo Mielziner, *The King & I*	Raoul Pene du Bois, *Wonderful Town*
Aline Bernstein, *Regina*	Miles White, *Bless You All*	Irene Sharaff, *The King and I*	Miles White, *Hazel Flagg*
Helen Tamiris, *Touch and Go*	Michael Kidd, *Guys and Dolls*	Robert Alton, *Pal Joey*	Donald Saddler, *Wonderful Town*
Gilbert Miller, *The Cocktail Party*	Cheryl Crawford, *The Rose Tattoo*	—	Kermit Bloomgarden, *The Crucible*
Richard Rodgers, Oscar Hammerstein II, Leland Hayward, and Joshua Logan, *South Pacific*	Cy Feuer and Ernest H. Martin, *Guys and Dolls*	—	Robert Fryer, *Wonderful Town*
Maurice Abravanel, *Regina*	Lehman Engel, *The Consul*	Max Meth, *Pal Joey*	Lehman Engel, *Wonderful Town; Gilbert and Sullivan Season*
Joe Lynn, master propertyman, *Miss Liberty*	Richard Raven, *The Autumn Garden*	Peter Feller, master carpenter, *Call Me Madam*	Abe Kurnit, *Wish You Were Here*

	1954	1955	1956
Actor (Dramatic)	David Wayne, *The Teahouse of the August Moon*	Alfred Lunt, *Quadrille*	Paul Muni, *Inherit the Wind*
Actress (Dramatic)	Audrey Hepburn, *Ondine*	Nancy Kelly, *The Bad Seed*	Julie Harris, *The Lark*
Featured/Supporting Actor (Dramatic)	John Kerr, *Tea and Sympathy*	Francis L. Sullivan, *Witness for the Prosecution*	Ed Begley, *Inherit the Wind*
Featured/Supporting Actress (Dramatic)	Jo Van Fleet, *The Trip to Bountiful*	Patricia Jessel, *Witness for the Prosecution*	Una Merkel, *The Ponder Heart*
Play	*The Teahouse of the August Moon*	*The Desperate Hours*	*The Diary of Anne Frank*
Actor (Musical)	Alfred Drake, *Kismet*	Walter Slezak, *Fanny*	Ray Walston, *Damn Yankees*
Actress (Musical)	Dolores Gray, *Carnival In Flanders*	Mary Martin, *Peter Pan*	Gwen Verdon, *Damn Yankees*
Featured/Supporting Actor Role (Musical)	Harry Belafonte, *John Murray Anderson's Almanac*	Cyril Ritchard, *Peter Pan*	Russ Brown, *Damn Yankees*
Featured/Supporting Actress (Musical)	Gwen Verdon, *Can-Can*	Carol Haney, *The Pajama Game*	Lotte Lenya, *The Threepenny Opera*
Musical	*Kismet*	*The Pajama Game*	*Damn Yankees*
Director	Alfred Lunt, *Ondine*	Robert Montgomery, *The Desperate Hours*	Tyrone Guthrie, *The Matchmaker; Six Characters in Search of an Author; Tamburlaine the Great*
Director (Dramatic)	—	—	—
Director (Musical)	—	—	—
Score	Alexander Borodin, *Kismet*	Richard Adler and Jerry Ross, *The Pajama Game*	Richard Adler and Jerry Ross, *Damn Yankees*
Author (Dramatic)	John Patrick, *The Teahouse of the August Moon*	Joseph Hayes, *The Desperate Hours*	Frances Goodrich and Albert Hackett, *The Diary of Anne Frank*
Author (Musical)	Charles Lederer and Luther Davis, *Kismet*	George Abbott and Richard Bissell, *The Pajama Game*	George Abbott and Douglass Wallop, *Damn Yankees*
Scenic Designer	Peter Larkin, *Ondine; The Teahouse of the August Moon*	Oliver Messel, *House of Flowers*	Peter Larkin, *Inherit the Wind; No Time for Sergeants*
Costume Designer	Richard Whorf, *Ondine*	Cecil Beaton, *Quadrille*	Alvin Colt, *The Lark/Phoenix '55/ Pipe Dream*
Choreographer	Michael Kidd, *Can-Can*	Bob Fosse, *The Pajama Game*	Bob Fosse, *Damn Yankees*
Producer (Dramatic)	Maurice Evans and George Schaefer, *The Teahouse of the August Moon*	Howard Erskine and Joseph Hayes, *The Desperate Hours*	Kermit Bloomgarden, *The Diary of Anne Frank*
Producer (Musical)	Charles Lederer, *Kismet*	Frederick Brisson, Robert Griffith, and Harold S. Prince, *The Pajama Game*	Frederick Brisson, Robert Griffith, Harold S. Prince in association with Albert B. Taylor, *Damn Yankees*
Conductor and Musical Director	Louis Adrian, *Kismet*	Thomas Schippers, *The Saint of Bleecker Street*	Hal Hastings, *Damn Yankees*
Stage Technician	John Davis, *Picnic*	Richard Rodda, *Peter Pan*	Harry Green, electrician and sound man, *The Middle of the Night; Damn Yankees*

1957	1958	1959	1960
Fredric March, *Long Day's Journey into Night*	Ralph Bellamy, *Sunrise at Campobello*	Jason Robards Jr., *The Disenchanted*	Melvyn Douglas, *The Best Man*
Margaret Leighton, *Separate Tables*	Helen Hayes, *Time Remembered*	Gertrude Berg, *A Majority of One*	Anne Bancroft, *The Miracle Worker*
Frank Conroy, *The Potting Shed*	Henry Jones, *Sunrise at Campobello*	Charlie Ruggles, *The Pleasure of His Company*	Roddy McDowall, *The Fighting Cock*
Peggy Cass, *Auntie Mame*	Anne Bancroft, *Two for the Seesaw*	Julie Newmar, *The Marriage-Go-Round*	Anne Revere, *Toys In the Attic*
Long Day's Journey into Night	*Sunrise at Campobello*	*J.B.*	*The Miracle Worker*
Rex Harrison, *My Fair Lady*	Robert Preston, *The Music Man*	Richard Kiley, *Redhead*	Jackie Gleason, *Take Me Along*
Judy Holliday, *Bells Are Ringing*	Gwen Verdon, *New Girl In Town*; Thelma Ritter, *New Girl In Town*	Gwen Verdon, *Redhead*	Mary Martin, *The Sound of Music*
Sydney Chaplin, *Bells Are Ringing*	David Burns, *The Music Man*	Russell Nype, *Goldilocks;* cast of *La Plume de ma tante*	Tom Bosley, *Fiorello!*
Edith Adams, *Li'l Abner*	Barbara Cook, *The Music Man*	Pat Stanley, *Goldilocks;* cast of *La Plume de ma tante*	Patricia Neway, *The Sound of Music*
My Fair Lady	*The Music Man*	*Redhead*	*Fiorello!*
Moss Hart, *My Fair Lady*	—	Elia Kazan, *J.B.*	—
—	Vincent J. Donehue, *Sunrise at Campobello*	—	Arthur Penn, *The Miracle Worker*
—	—	—	George Abbott, *Fiorello!*
Frederick Loewe, *My Fair Lady*	Meredith Willson, *The Music Man*	Albert Hague, *Redhead*	Jerry Bock, *Fiorello!*; Richard Rodgers, *The Sound of Music*
Eugene O'Neill, *Long Day's Journey into Night*	Dore Schary, *Sunrise at Campobello*	Archibald MacLeish, *J.B.*	William Gibson, *The Miracle Worker*
Alan Jay Lerner, *My Fair Lady*	Meredith Willson and Franklin Lacey, *The Music Man*	Herbert and Dorothy Fields, Sidney Sheldon, and David Shaw, *Redhead*	Jerome Weidman and George Abbott, *Fiorello!;* Howard Lindsay and Russel Crouse, *The Sound of Music*
Oliver Smith, *A Clearing in the Woods; Candide; Auntie Mame; My Fair Lady; Eugenia; A Visit to a Small Planet*	Oliver Smith, *West Side Story*	Donald Oenslager, *A Majority of One*	Howard Bey, *Toys in the Attic* (Dramatic); Oliver Smith, *The Sound of Music* (Musical)
Cecil Beaton, *Little Glass Clock/ My Fair Lady*	Motley, *The First Gentleman*	Robert Ter-Arutunian, *Redhead*	Cecil Beaton, *Saratoga*
Michael Kidd, *Li'l Abner*	Jerome Robbins, *West Side Story*	Bob Fosse, *Redhead*	Michael Kidd, *Destry Rides Again*
Leigh Connell, Theodore Mann, and Jose Quintero, *Long Day's Journey into Night*	Lawrence Langner, Theresa Helburn, Armina Marshall, and Dore Schary, *Sunrise at Campobello*	Alfred de Liagre, Jr., *J.B.*	Fred Coe, *The Miracle Worker*
Herman Levin, *My Fair Lady*	Kermit Bloomgarden, Herbert Greene, Frank Productions, *The Music Man*	Robert Fryer and Lawrence Carr, *Redhead*	Robert Griffith and Harold Prince, *Fiorello!;* Leland Hayward and Richard Halliday, *The Sound of Music*
Franz Allers, *My Fair Lady*	Herbert Greene, *The Music Man*	Salvatore Dell'Isola, *Flower Drum Song*	Frederick Dvonch, *The Sound of Music*
Howard McDonald (posthumous), carpenter, *Major Barbara*	Harry Romar, *Time Remembered*	Sam Knapp, *The Music Man*	John Walters, chief carpenter, *The Miracle Worker*

	1961	1962	1963
Actor (Dramatic)	Zero Mostel, *Rhinoceros*	Paul Scofield, *A Man for All Seasons*	Arthur Hill, *Who's Afraid of Virginia Woolf?*
Actress (Dramatic)	Joan Plowright, *A Taste of Honey*	Margaret Leighton, *Night of the Iguana*	Uta Hagen, *Who's Afraid of Virginia Woolf?*
Featured/Supporting Actor (Dramatic)	Martin Gabel, *Big Fish, Little Fish*	Walter Matthau, *A Shot in the Dark*	Alan Arkin, *Enter Laughing*
Featured/Supporting Actress (Dramatic)	Colleen Dewhurst, *All the Way Home*	Elizabeth Ashley, *Take Her, She's Mine*	Sandy Dennis, *A Thousand Clowns*
Play	*Becket*	*A Man for All Seasons*	*Who's Afraid of Virginia Woolf?*
Actor (Musical)	Richard Burton, *Camelot*	Robert Morse, *How To Succeed in Business Without Really Trying*	Zero Mostel, *A Funny Thing Happened on the Way to the Forum*
Actress (Musical)	Elizabeth Seal, *Irma La Douce*	Anna Maria Alberghetti, *Carnival*	Vivien Leigh, *Tovarich*
Featured/Supporting Actor (Musical)	Dick Van Dyke, *Bye, Bye Birdie*	Charles Nelson Reilly, *How To Succeed in Business Without Really Trying*	David Burns, *A Funny Thing Happened on the Way to the Forum*
Featured/Supporting Actress (Musical)	Tammy Grimes, *The Unsinkable Molly Brown*	Phyllis Newman, *Subways Are for Sleeping*	Anna Quayle, *Stop the World—I Want To Get Off*
Musical	*Bye, Bye Birdie*	*How To Succeed in Business Without Really Trying*	*A Funny Thing Happened on the Way to the Forum*
Director (Dramatic)	John Gielgud, *Big Fish, Little Fish*	Noel Willman, *A Man for All Seasons*	Alan Schneider, *Who's Afraid of Virginia Woolf?*
Director (Musical)	Gower Champion, *Bye, Bye Birdie*	Abe Burrows, *How To Succeed in Business Without Really Trying*	George Abbott, *A Funny Thing Happened on the Way to the Forum*
Score	—	Richard Rodgers, *No Strings*	Lionel Bart, *Oliver!*
Author (Dramatic)	Jean Anouilh, *Becket*	Robert Bolt, *A Man for All Seasons*	—
Author (Musical)	Michael Stewart, *Bye, Bye Birdie*	Abe Burrows, Jack Weinstock, and Willie Gilbert, *How To Succeed in Business Without Really Trying*	Burt Shevelove and Larry Gelbart, *A Funny Thing Happened on the Way to the Forum*
Scenic Designer	Oliver Smith, *Becket* (Dramatic); Oliver Smith, *Camelot* (Musical)	Will Steven Armstrong, *Carnival*	Sean Kenny, *Oliver!*
Costume Designer	Motley, *Becket;* Adrian and Tony Duquette, *Camelot*	Lucinda Ballard, *The Gay Life*	Anthony Powell, *The School for Scandal*
Choreographer	Gower Champion, *Bye, Bye Birdie*	Agnes de Mille, *Kwamina;* Joe Layton, *No Strings*	Bob Fosse, *Little Me*
Producer (Dramatic)	David Merrick, *Becket*	Robert Whitehead and Roger L. Stevens, *A Man for All Seasons*	Richard Barr and Clinton Wilder, Theatre 1963, *Who's Afraid of Virginia Woolf?*
Producer (Musical)	Edward Padula, *Bye, Bye Birdie*	Cy Feuer and Ernest Martin, *How To Succeed in Business Without Really Trying*	Harold Prince, *A Funny Thing Happened on the Way to the Forum*
Conductor and Musical Director	Franz Allers, *Camelot*	Elliot Lawrence, *How To Succeed in Business Without Really Trying*	Donald Pippin, *Oliver!*
Stage Technician	Teddy Van Bemmel, *Becket*	Michael Burns, *A Man for All Seasons*	—

1964	1965	1966	1967
Alec Guinness, *Dylan*	Walter Matthau, *The Odd Couple*	Hal Holbrook, *Mark Twain Tonight!*	Paul Rogers, *The Homecoming*
Sandy Dennis, *Any Wednesday*	Irene Worth, *Tiny Alice*	Rosemary Harris, *The Lion in Winter*	Beryl Reid, *The Killing of Sister George*
Hume Cronyn, *Hamlet*	Jack Albertson, *The Subject Was Roses*	Patrick Magee, *Marat/Sade*	Ian Holm, *The Homecoming*
Barbara Loden, *After the Fall*	Alice Ghostley, *The Sign In Sidney Brustein's Window*	Zoe Caldwell, *Slapstick Tragedy*	Marian Seldes, *A Delicate Balance*
Luther	*The Subject Was Roses*	*Marat/Sade*	*The Homecoming*
Bert Lahr, *Foxy*	Zero Mostel, *Fiddler on the Roof*	Richard Kiley, *Man of La Mancha*	Robert Preston, *I Do! I Do!*
Carol Channing, *Hello, Dolly!*	Liza Minnelli, *Flora, the Red Menace*	Angela Lansbury, *Mame*	Barbara Harris, *The Apple Tree*
Jack Cassidy, *She Loves Me*	Victor Spinetti, *Oh, What a Lovely War!*	Frankie Michaels, *Mame*	Joel Grey, *Cabaret*
Tessie O'Shea, *The Girl Who Came to Supper*	Maria Karnilova, *Fiddler on the Roof*	Beatrice Arthur, *Mame*	Peg Murray, *Cabaret*
Hello, Dolly!	*Fiddler on the Roof*	*Man of La Mancha*	*Cabaret*
Mike Nichols, *Barefoot in the Park*	Mike Nichols, *Luv/The Odd Couple*	Peter Brook, *Marat/Sade*	Peter Hall, *The Homecoming*
Gower Champion, *Hello, Dolly!*	Jerome Robbins, *Fiddler on the Roof*	Albert Marre, *Man of La Mancha*	Harold Prince, *Cabaret*
Jerry Herman, *Hello, Dolly!*	Jerry Bock and Sheldon Harnick, *Fiddler on the Roof*	Mitch Leigh and Joe Darion, *Man of La Mancha*	John Kander and Fred Ebb, *Cabaret*
John Osborne, *Luther*	Neil Simon, *The Odd Couple*	—	—
Michael Stewart, *Hello, Dolly!*	Joseph Stein, *Fiddler on the Roof*	—	—
Oliver Smith, *Hello, Dolly!*	Oliver Smith, *Baker Street/Luv/The Odd Couple*	Howard Bay, *Man of La Mancha*	Boris Aronson, *Cabaret*
Freddy Wittop, *Hello, Dolly!*	Patricia Zipprodt, *Fiddler on the Roof*	Gunilla Palmstierna-Weiss, *Marat/Sade*	Patricia Zipprodt, *Cabaret*
Gower Champion, *Hello, Dolly!*	Jerome Robbins, *Fiddler on the Roof*	Bob Fosse, *Sweet Charity*	Ronald Field, *Cabaret*
Herman Shumlin, *The Deputy*	Claire Nichtern, *Luv*	—	—
David Merrick, *Hello, Dolly!*	Harold Prince, *Fiddler on the Roof*	—	—
Shepard Coleman, *Hello, Dolly!*	—	—	—
—	—	—	—

	1968	1969	1970
Actor (Dramatic)	Martin Balsam, *You Know I Can't Hear You When the Water's Running*	James Earl Jones, *The Great White Hope*	Fritz Weaver, *Child's Play*
Actress (Dramatic)	Zoe Caldwell, *The Prime of Miss Jean Brodie*	Julie Harris, *Forty Carats*	Tammy Grimes, *Private Lives*
Featured/Supporting Actor (Dramatic)	James Patterson, *The Birthday Party*	Al Pacino, *Does a Tiger Wear a Necktie?*	Ken Howard, *Child's Play*
Featured/Supporting Actress (Dramatic)	Zena Walker, *Joe Egg*	Jane Alexander, *The Great White Hope*	Blythe Danner, *Butterflies Are Free*
Play	*Rosencrantz and Guildenstern Are Dead*	*The Great White Hope*	*Borstal Boy*
Actor (Musical)	Robert Goulet, *The Happy Time*	Jerry Orbach, *Promises, Promises*	Cleavon Little, *Purlie*
Actress (Musical)	Leslie Uggams, *Hallelujah, Baby!*; Patricia Routledge, *Darling of the Day*	Angela Lansbury, *Dear World*	Lauren Bacall, *Applause*
Featured/Supporting Actor (Musical)	Hiram Sherman, *How Now, Dow Jones*	Ronald Holgate, *1776*	Rene Auberjonois, *Coco*
Featured/Supporting Actress (Musical)	Lillian Hayman, *Hallelujah, Baby!*	Marian Mercer, *Promises, Promises*	Melba Moore, *Purlie*
Musical	*Hallelujah, Baby!*	*1776*	*Applause*
Director (Dramatic)	Mike Nichols, *Plaza Suite*	Peter Dews, *Hadrian VII*	Joseph Hardy, *Child's Play*
Director (Musical)	Gower Champion, *The Happy Time*	Peter Hunt, *1776*	Ron Field, *Applause*
Book (Musical)	—	—	—
Score	Jule Styne, Betty Comden, and Adolph Green, *Hallelujah, Baby!*	—	—
Scenic Designer	Desmond Heeley, *Rosencrantz and Guildenstern Are Dead*	Boris Aronson, *Zorba*	Howard Bay, *Cry for Us All*; Jo Mielziner, *Child's Play*
Costume Designer	Desmond Heeley, *Rosencrantz and Guildenstern Are Dead*	Louden Sainthill, *Canterbury Tales*	Cecil Beaton, *Coco*
Lighting Designer	—	—	Jo Mielziner, *Child's Play*
Choreographer	Gower Champion, *The Happy Time*	Joe Layton, *George M!*	Ron Field, *Applause*
Producer (Dramatic)	The David Merrick Arts Foundation, *Rosencrantz and Guildenstern Are Dead*	—	—
Producer (Musical)	Albert Selden, Hal James, Jane C. Nusbaum, and Harry Rigby, *Hallelujah, Baby!*	—	—

1971	1972	1973	1974
Brian Bedford, *The School for Wives*	Cliff Gorman, *Lenny*	Alan Bates, *Butley*	Michael Moriarty, *Find Your Way Home*
Maureen Stapleton, *Gingerbread Lady*	Sada Thompson, *Twigs*	Julie Harris, *The Last of Mrs Lincoln*	Colleen Dewhurst, *A Moon for the Misbegotten* (Revival)
Paul Sand, *Story Theatre*	Vincent Gardenia, *The Prisoner of Second Avenue*	John Lithgow, *The Changing Room*	Ed Flanders, *A Moon for the Misbegotten* (Revival)
Rae Allen, *And Miss Reardon Drinks a Little*	Elizabeth Wilson, *Sticks and Bones*	Leora Dana, *The Last of Mrs Lincoln*	Frances Sternhagen, *The Good Doctor*
Sleuth	*Sticks and Bones*	*That Championship Season*	*The River Niger*
Hal Linden, *The Rothschilds*	Phil Silvers, *A Funny Thing Happened on the Way to the Forum* (Revival)	Ben Vereen, *Pippin*	Christopher Plummer, *Cyrano*
Helen Gallagher, *No, No, Nanette*	Alexis Smith, *Follies*	Glynis Johns, *A Little Night Music*	Virginia Capers, *Raisin*
Keene Curtis, *The Rothschilds*	Larry Blyden, *A Funny Thing Happened on the Way to the Forum* (Revival)	George S. Irving, *Irene*	Tommy Tune, *Seesaw*
Patsy Kelly, *No, No, Nanette*	Linda Hopkins, *Inner City*	Patricia Elliot, *A Little Night Music*	Janie Sell, *Over Here!*
Company	*Two Gentlemen of Verona*	*A Little Night Music*	*Raisin*
Peter Brook, *Midsummer Night's Dream*	Mike Nichols, *The Prisoner of Second Avenue*	A.J. Antoon, *That Championship Season*	Jose Quintero, *A Moon for the Misbegotten* (Revival)
Harold Prince, *Company*	Harold Prince and Michael Bennett, *Follies*	Bob Fosse, *Pippin*	Harold Prince, *Candide*
George Furth, *Company*	John Guare and Mel Shapiro, *Two Gentlemen of Verona*	Hugh Wheeler, *A Little Night Music*	Hugh Wheeler, *Candide*
Stephen Sondheim, *Company*	Stephen Sondheim, *Follies*	Stephen Sondheim, *A Little Night Music*	Frederick Loewe (Music); Alan Jay Lerner (Lyrics), *Gigi*
Boris Aronson, *Company*	Boris Aronson, *Follies*	Tony Walton, *Pippin*	Franne and Eugene Lee, *Candide*
Raoul Pene du Bois, *No, No, Nanette*	Florence Klotz, *Follies*	Florence Klotz, *A Little Night Music*	Franne Lee, *Candide*
H.R. Poindexter, *Story Theatre*	Tharon Musser, *Follies*	Jules Fisher, *Pippin*	Jules Fisher, *Ulysses in Nighttown*
Donald Saddler, *No, No, Nanette*	Michael Bennett, *Follies*	Bob Fosse, *Pippin*	Michael Bennett, *Seesaw*
Helen Bonfils, Morton Gottlieb, and Michael White, *Sleuth*	—	—	—
Harold Prince, *Company*	—	—	—

	1975	1976	1977
Actor (Dramatic)	John Kani and Winston Ntshona, *Sizwe Banzi Is Dead & The Island*	John Wood, *Travesties*	Al Pacino, *The Basic Training of Pavlo Hummel*
Actress (Dramatic)	Ellen Burstyn, *Same Time, Next Year*	Irene Worth, *Sweet Bird of Youth*	Julie Harris, *The Belle of Amherst*
Featured Actor (Dramatic)	Frank Langella, *Seascape*	Edward Herrmann, *Mrs. Warren's Profession*	Jonathan Pryce, *Comedians*
Featured Actress (Dramatic)	Rita Moreno, *The Ritz*	Shirley Knight, *Kennedy's Children*	Trazana Beverley, *For Colored Girls Who Have Considered Suicide/When the Rainbow Is Enuf*
Play	*Equus*	*Travesties*	*The Shadow Box*
Actor (Musical)	John Cullum, *Shenandoah*	George Rose, *My Fair Lady*	Barry Bostwick, *The Robber Bridegroom*
Actress (Musical)	Angela Lansbury, *Gypsy*	Donna McKechnie, *A Chorus Line*	Dorothy Loudon, *Annie*
Featured Actor (Musical)	Ted Ross, *The Wiz*	Sammy Williams, *A Chorus Line*	Lenny Baker, *I Love My Wife*
Featured Actress (Musical)	Dee Dee Bridgewater, *The Wiz*	Carole Bishop, *A Chorus Line*	Delores Hall, *Your Arms Too Short To Box with God*
Musical	*The Wiz*	*A Chorus Line*	*Annie*
Director (Dramatic)	John Dexter, *Equus*	Ellis Rabb, *The Royal Family*	Gordon Davidson, *The Shadow Box*
Director (Musical)	Geoffrey Holder, *The Wiz*	Michael Bennett, *A Chorus Line*	Gene Saks, *I Love My Wife*
Book (Musical)	James Lee Barrett, *Shenandoah*	James Kirkwood and Nicholas Dante, *A Chorus Line*	Thomas Meehan, *Annie*
Score	Charlie Smalls (Music & Lyrics), *The Wiz*	Marvin Hamlisch (Music); Edward Kleban (Lyrics), *A Chorus Line*	Charles Strouse (Music); Martin Charnin (Lyrics), *Annie*
Scenic Designer	Carl Toms, *Sherlock Holmes*	Boris Aronson, *Pacific Overtures*	David Mitchell, *Annie*
Costume Designer	Geoffrey Holder, *The Wiz*	Florence Klotz, *Pacific Overtures*	Theoni V. Aldredge, *Annie;* Santo Loquasto, *The Cherry Orchard*
Lighting Designer	Neil Patrick Jampolis, *Sherlock Holmes*	Tharon Musser, *A Chorus Line*	Jennifer Tipton, *The Cherry Orchard*
Choreographer	George Faison, *The Wiz*	Michael Bennett and Bob Avian, *A Chorus Line*	Peter Gennaro, *Annie*
Reproduction of a Play or Musical	—	—	*Porgy and Bess*

1978	1979	1980	1981
Barnard Hughes, *Da*	Tom Conti, *Whose Life Is It Anyway?*	John Rubinstein, *Children of a Lesser God*	Ian McKellen, *Amadeus*
Jessica Tandy, *The Gin Game*	Constance Cummings, *Wings;* Carole Shelley, *The Elephant Man*	Phyllis Frelich, *Children of a Lesser God*	Jane Lapotaire, *Piaf*
Lester Rawlins, *Da*	Michael Gough, *Bedroom Farce*	David Rounds, *Morning's at Seven*	Brian Backer, *The Floating Light Bulb*
Ann Wedgeworth, *Chapter Two*	Joan Hickson, *Bedroom Farce*	Dinah Manoff, *I Ought To Be in Pictures*	Swoosie Kurtz, *Fifth of July*
Da	*The Elephant Man*	*Children of a Lesser God*	*Amadeus*
John Cullum, *On the Twentieth Century*	Len Cariou, *Sweeney Todd*	Jim Dale, *Barnum*	Kevin Kline, *The Pirates of Penzance*
Liza Minnelli, *The Act*	Angela Lansbury, *Sweeney Todd*	Patti LuPone, *Evita*	Lauren Bacall, *Woman of the Year*
Kevin Kline, *On the Twentieth Century*	Henderson Forsythe, *The Best Little Whorehouse in Texas*	Mandy Patinkin, *Evita*	Hinton Battle, *Sophisticated Ladies*
Nell Carter, *Ain't Misbehavin'*	Carlin Glynn, *The Best Little Whorehouse in Texas*	Priscilla Lopez, *A Day in Hollywood, a Night in the Ukraine*	Marilyn Cooper, *Woman of the Year*
Ain't Misbehavin'	*Sweeney Todd*	*Evita*	*42nd Street*
Melvin Bernhardt, *Da*	Jack Hofsiss, *The Elephant Man*	Vivian Matalon, *Morning's at Seven*	Peter Hall, *Amadeus*
Richard Maltby Jr., *Ain't Misbehavin'*	Harold Prince, *Sweeney Todd*	Harold Prince, *Evita*	Wilford Leach, *The Pirates of Penzance*
Betty Comden and Adolph Green, *On the Twentieth Century*	Hugh Wheeler, *Sweeney Todd*	Tim Rice, *Evita*	Peter Stone, *Woman of the Year*
Cy Coleman (Music); Betty Comden and Adolph Green (Lyrics), *On the Twentieth Century*	Stephen Sondheim (Music & Lyrics), *Sweeney Todd*	Andrew Lloyd Webber (Music); Tim Rice (Lyrics), *Evita*	John Kander (Music); Fred Ebb (Lyrics), *Woman of the Year*
Robin Wagner, *On the Twentieth Century*	Eugene Lee, *Sweeney Todd*	John Lee Beatty, *Talley's Folly;* David Mitchell, *Barnum*	John Bury, *Amadeus*
Edward Gorey, *Dracula*	Franne Lee, *Sweeney Todd*	Theoni V. Aldredge, *Barnum*	Willa Kim, *Sophisticated Ladies*
Jules Fisher, *Dancin'*	Roger Morgan, *The Crucifer of Blood*	David Hersey, *Evita*	John Bury, *Amadeus*
Bob Fosse, *Dancin'*	Michael Bennett and Bob Avian, *Ballroom*	Tommy Tune and Thommie Walsh, *A Day in Hollywood, a Night in the Ukraine*	Gower Champion, *42nd Street*
Dracula	—	Elizabeth I. McCann, Nelle Nugent, Ray Larsen, producers, *Morning's at Seven*	Joseph Papp, producer, *The Pirates of Penzance*

	1982	1983	1984
Actor (Dramatic)	Roger Rees, *The Life and Adventures of Nicholas Nickleby*	Harvey Fierstein, *Torch Song Trilogy*	Jeremy Irons, *The Real Thing*
Actress (Dramatic)	Zoe Caldwell, *Medea*	Jessica Tandy, *Foxfire*	Glenn Close, *The Real Thing*
Featured Actor (Dramatic)	Zakes Mokae, *Master Harold . . . and the Boys*	Matthew Broderick, *Brighton Beach Memoirs*	Joe Mantegna, *Glengarry Glen Ross*
Featured Actress (Dramatic)	Amanda Plummer, *Agnes of God*	Judith Ivey, *Steaming*	Christine Baranski, *The Real Thing*
Play	*The Life and Adventures of Nicholas Nickleby*	*Torch Song Trilogy*	*The Real Thing*
Actor (Musical)	Ben Harney, *Dreamgirls*	Tommy Tune, *My One and Only*	George Hearn, *La Cage Aux Folles*
Actress (Musical)	Jennifer Holliday, *Dreamgirls*	Natalia Makarova, *On Your Toes*	Chita Rivera, *The Rink*
Featured Actor (Musical)	Cleavant Derricks, *Dreamgirls*	Charles "Honi" Coles, *My One and Only*	Hinton Battle, *The Tap Dance Kid*
Featured Actress (Musical)	Liliane Montevecchi, *"Nine"*	Betty Buckley, *Cats*	Lila Kedrova, *Zorba*
Musical	*"Nine"*	*Cats*	*La Cage aux folles*
Director (Dramatic)	Trevor Nunn and John Caird, *The Life and Adventures of Nicholas Nickleby*	Gene Saks, *Brighton Beach Memoirs*	Mike Nichols, *The Real Thing*
Director (Musical)	Tommy Tune, *"Nine"*	Trevor Nunn, *Cats*	Arthur Laurents, *La Cage aux folles*
Book (Musical)	Tom Eyen, *Dreamgirls*	T. S. Eliot, *Cats*	Harvey Fierstein, *La Cage aux folles*
Score	Maury Yeton (Music & Lyrics), *"Nine"*	Andrew Lloyd Webber (Music); T. S. Eliot (Lyrics), *Cats*	Jerry Herman (Music & Lyrics), *La Cage aux folles*
Scenic Designer	John Napier and Dermot Hayes, *The Life and Adventures of Nicholas Nickleby*	Ming Cho Lee, *K2*	Tony Straiges, *Sunday in the Park with George*
Costume Designer	William Ivey Long, *"Nine"*	John Napier, *Cats*	Theoni V. Aldredge, *La Cage aux folles*
Lighting Designer	Tharon Musser, *Dreamgirls*	David Hersey, *Cats*	Richard Nelson, *Sunday in the Park with George*
Choreographer	Michael Bennett and Michael Peters, *Dreamgirls*	Thommie Walsh and Tommy Tune, *My One and Only*	Danny Daniels, *The Tap Dance Kid*
Reproduction of a Play or Musical	Barry and Fran Weissler, CBS Video Enterprises, Don Gregory, producers, *Othello*	Alfred De Liagre Jr., Roger L. Stevens, John Mauceri, Donald R. Seawell, Andre Pastoria, producers, *On Your Toes*	Robert Whitehead, Roger L. Stevens, producers, *Death of a Salesman*

1985	1986	1987	1988
Derek Jacobi, *Much Ado About Nothing*	Judd Hirsch, *I'm Not Rappaport*	James Earl Jones, *Fences*	Ron Silver, *Speed-the-Plow*
Stockard Channing, *Joe Egg*	Lily Tomlin, *The Search for Signs of Intelligent Life in the Universe*	Linda Lavin, *Broadway Bound*	Joan Allen, *Burn This*
Barry Miller, *Biloxi Blues*	John Mahoney, *The House of Blue Leaves*	John Randolph, *Broadway Bound*	B. D. Wong, *M. Butterfly*
Judith Ivey, *Hurlyburly*	Swoosie Kurtz, *The House of Blue Leaves*	Mary Alice, *Fences*	L. Scott Caldwell, *Joe Turner's Come and Gone*
Biloxi Blues	*I'm Not Rappaport*	*Fences*	*M. Butterfly*
—	George Rose, *The Mystery of Edwin Drood*	Robert Lindsay, *Me and My Girl*	Michael Crawford, *The Phantom of the Opera*
—	Bernadette Peters, *Song & Dance*	Maryann Plunkett, *Me and My Girl*	Joanna Gleason, *Into the Woods*
Ron Richardson, *Big River*	Michael Rupert, *Sweet Charity*	Michael Maguire, *Les Misérables*	Bill McCutcheon, *Anything Goes*
Leilani Jones, *Grind*	Bebe Neuwirth, *Sweet Charity*	Frances Ruffelle, *Les Misérables*	Judy Kaye, *The Phantom of the Opera*
Big River	*The Mystery of Edwin Drood*	*Les Misérables*	*The Phantom of the Opera*
Gene Saks, *Biloxi Blues*	Jerry Zaks, *The House of Blue Leaves*	Lloyd Richards, *Fences*	John Dexter, *M. Butterfly*
Des McAnuff, *Big River*	Wilford Leach, *The Mystery of Edwin Drood*	Trevor Nunn and John Caird, *Les Misérables*	Harold Prince, *The Phantom of the Opera*
William Hauptman, *Big River*	Rupert Holmes, *The Mystery of Edwin Drood*	Alain Boublil and Claude-Michel Schönberg, *Les Misérables*	James Lapine, *Into the Woods*
Roger Miller (Music & Lyrics), *Big River*	Rupert Holmes (Music & Lyrics), *The Mystery of Edwin Drood*	Claude-Michel Schönberg (Music); Herbert Kretzmer, and Alain Boublil (Lyrics), *Les Misérables*	Stephen Sondheim (Music & Lyrics), *Into the Woods*
Heidi Landesman, *Big River*	Tony Walton, *The House of Blue Leaves*	John Napier, *Les Misérables*	Maria Bjornson, *The Phantom of the Opera*
Florence Klotz, *Grind*	Patricia Zipprodt, *Sweet Charity*	John Napier, *Starlight Express*	Maria Björnson, *The Phantom of the Opera*
Richard Riddell, *Big River*	Pat Collins, *I'm Not Rappaport*	David Hersey, *Starlight Express*	Andrew Bridge, *The Phantom of the Opera*
—	Bob Fosse, *Big Deal*	Gillian Gregory, *Me and My Girl*	Michael Smuin, *Anything Goes*
The Shubert Organization, Emanuel Azenberg, Roger Berlind, Ivan Bloch, MTM Enterprises, Inc., producers, *Joe Egg*	Jerome Minskoff, James M. Nederlander, Arthur Rubin, Joseph Harris, producers, *Sweet Charity*	Jay H. Fuchs, Steven Warnick, Charles Patsos, producers, *All My Sons*	Lincoln Center Theater, Gregory Mosher, Bernard Gersten, producers, *Anything Goes*

	1989	1990	1991
Actor (Dramatic)	Philip Bosco, *Lend Me a Tenor*	Robert Morse, *Tru*	Nigel Hawthorne, *Shadowlands*
Actress (Dramatic)	Pauline Collins, *Shirley Valentine*	Maggie Smith, *Lettice & Lovage*	Mercedes Ruehl, *Lost in Yonkers*
Featured Actor (Dramatic)	Boyd Gaines, *The Heidi Chronicles*	Charles Durning, *Cat on a Hot Tin Roof*	Kevin Spacey, *Lost in Yonkers*
Featured Actress (Dramatic)	Christine Baranski, *Rumors*	Margaret Tyzack, *Lettice & Lovage*	Irene Worth, *Lost in Yonkers*
Play	*The Heidi Chronicles*	*The Grapes of Wrath*	*Lost in Yonkers*
Actor (Musical)	Jason Alexander, *Jerome Robbins' Broadway*	James Naughton, *City of Angels*	Jonathan Pryce, *Miss Saigon*
Actress (Musical)	Ruth Brown, *Black and Blue*	Tyne Daly, *Gypsy*	Lea Salonga, *Miss Saigon*
Featured Actor (Musical)	Scott Wise, *Jerome Robbins' Broadway*	Michael Jeter, *Gypsy*	Hinton Battle, *Miss Saigon*
Featured Actress (Musical)	Debbie Shapiro, *Jerome Robbins' Broadway*	Randy Graff, *City of Angels*	Daisy Eagan, *The Secret Garden*
Musical	*Jerome Robbins' Broadway*	*City of Angels*	*The Will Rogers Follies*
Director (Dramatic)	Jerry Zaks, *Lend Me a Tenor*	Frank Galati, *The Grapes of Wrath*	Jerry Zaks, *Six Degrees of Separation*
Director (Musical)	Jerome Robbins, *Jerome Robbins' Broadway*	Tommy Tune, *Grand Hotel, the Musical*	Tommy Tune, *The Will Rogers Follies*
Book (Musical)	—	Larry Gelbart, *City of Angels*	Marsha Norman, *The Secret Garden*
Score	—	Cy Colman (Music); David Zippel (Lyrics), *City of Angels*	Cy Coleman (Music); Betty Comden and Adolph Green (Lyrics), *The Will Rogers Follies*
Scenic Designer	Santo Loquasto, *Cafe Crown*	Robin Wagner, *City of Angels*	Heidi Landesman, *The Secret Garden*
Costume Designer	Claudio Segovia, Hector Orezzoli, *Black and Blue*	Santo Loquasto, *Grand Hotel, the Musical*	Willa Kim, *The Will Rogers Follies*
Lighting Design	Jennifer Tipton, *Jerome Robbins' Broadway*	Jules Fisher, *Grand Hotel, the Musical*	Jules Fisher, *The Will Rogers Follies*
Choreographer	Cholly Atkins, Henry LeTang, Frankie Manning, Fayard Nicholas, *Black and Blue*	Tommy Tune, *Grand Hotel, the Musical*	Tommy Tune, *The Will Rogers Follies*
Reproduction of a Play or Musical	Lincoln Center Theater, Gregory Mosher, Bernard Gersten, producers, *Our Town*	Barry and Fran Weissler, Kathy Levin, Barry Brown, producers, *Gypsy*	Barry and Fran Weissler, Pace Theatrical Group, *Fiddler on the Roof*

1992	1993	1994
Judd Hirsch, *Conversations with My Father*	Ron Leibman, *Angels in America: Millennium Approaches*	Stephen Spinella, *Angels in America: Perestroika*
Glenn Close, *Death and the Maiden*	Madeline Kahn, *The Sisters Rosensweig*	Diana Rigg, *Medea*
Larry Fishburne, *Two Trains Running*	Stephen Spinella, *Angels in America: Millennium Approaches*	Jeffrey Wright, *Angels in America: Perestroika*
Brid Brennan, *Dancing at Lughnasa*	Debra Monk, *Redwood Curtain*	Jane Adams, *An Inspector Calls*
Dancing at Lughnasa	*Angels in America: Millennium Approaches*	*Angels in America: Perestroika*
Gregory Hines, *Jelly's Last Jam*	Brent Carver, *Kiss of the Spider Woman—The Musical*	Boyd Gaines, *She Loves Me*
Faith Prince, *Guys and Dolls*	Chita Rivera, *Kiss of the Spider Woman—The Musical*	Donna Murphy, *Passion*
Scott Waara, *The Most Happy Fella*	Anthony Crivello, *Kiss of the Spider Woman—The Musical*	Jarrod Emick, *Damn Yankees*
Tonya Pinkins, *Jelly's Last Jam*	Andrea Martin, *My Favorite Year*	Audra Ann McDonald, *Carousel*
Crazy for You	*Kiss of the Spider Woman—The Musical*	*Passion*
Patrick Mason, *Dancing at Lughnasa*	George C. Wolfe, *Angels in America: Millennium Approaches*	Stephen Baldry, *An Inspector Calls*
Jerry Zaks, *Guys and Dolls*	Des McAnuff, *The Who's Tommy*	Nicholas Hynter, *Carousel*
William Finn and James Lapine, *Falsettos*	Terrence McNally, *Kiss of the Spider Woman—The Musical*	James Lapine, *Passion*
William Finn, *Falsettos*	John Kander (Music); Fred Ebb (Lyrics), *Kiss of the Spider Woman—The Musical;* Pete Townshend (Music and Lyrics), *The Who's Tommy*	Stephen Sondheim, *Passion*
Tony Walton, *Guys and Dolls*	John Arnone, *The Who's Tommy*	Bob Crowley, *Carousel*
William Ivey Long, *Crazy for You*	Florence Klotz, *Kiss of the Spider Woman—The Musical*	Ann Hould-Ward, *Beauty and the Beast*
Jules Fisher, *Jelly's Last Jam*	Chris Parry, *The Who's Tommy*	Rick Fisher, *An Inspector Calls*
Susan Stroman, *Crazy for You*	Wayne Cilento, *The Who's Tommy*	Kenneth McMillan, *Carousel*
Dodger Productions, Roger Berlind, Jujamcyn Theaters/TV Asahi, Kardana Productions, John F. Kennedy Center for the Performing Arts, *Guys and Dolls*	Roundabout Theatre Company and Todd Haimes, *Anna Christie*	Noel Pearson, the Shubert Organization, Capital Cities/ABC, Joseph Harris, *An Inspector Calls* (Dramatic); Lincoln Center Theater, Andre Bishop, Bernard Gersten, the Royal National Theater, Cameron Mackintosh, the Rodgers & Hammerstein Organization, *Carousel* (Musical)

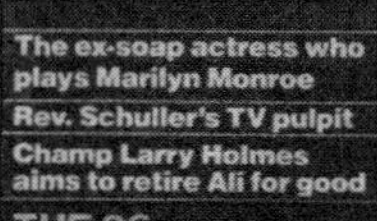

PEOPLE EXTRAS

Meredith Baxter Birney's family ties
A chat with the President
Gumby's back
The Far Side's Gary Larson
People weekly
MEL GIBSON THE SEXIEST MAN ALIVE

SPECIAL DOUBLE ISSUE
People weekly
December 30-January 6, 1975 • 40¢
THE 25 MOST INTRIGUING People OF 1974
&
SOME PREDICTIONS AND PERSONALITIES FOR 1975

TWO DECADES OF PEOPLE'S MOST INTRIGUING

Every December, in its Christmas double issue, the PEOPLE editors single out the twenty-five most intriguing people of the past year. We reprint the roll of honorees, with a brief description for each, to remind readers of their notability (or notoriety) and to relive twenty years of history.

1974

Gerald Ford—The president copes with an office he didn't seek
Patty Hearst—The kidnapped newspaper heiress turned terrorist might be another face in the crowd—but in disguise
Joe Hirshhorn—He heaps the land with beauty by donating 2,000 sculptures and 4,000 paintings to Smithsonian's new Hirshhorn Museum
Kay Graham—The publisher of the *Washington Post* emerges as the big winner of Watergate
Yasir Arafat—A tough soldier takes the point for Palestine and addresses the United Nations
Faye Dunaway—A panther of an actress springs back to the top in *Chinatown, Towering Inferno,* and *The Day of the Condor*
Alexander Solzhenitsyn—The Russian exile's Nobel honors are late but sweet
Nelson Rockefeller—The vice president-elect has his finances questioned by Congress; being rich turns out to be a problem
Leon Jaworski—The Watergate prosecutor knew Nixon was lying, but couldn't say it
Erica Jong—A hit author who is like her uninhibited heroine in *Fear of Flying*
Francis Ford Coppola—*Godfather II* confirms him as cinema's creative king
Muhammad Ali—The title wasn't enough for the world heavyweight champ—he wants another son
Pat Nixon—The last First Lady deals stoically with her husband's fall from grace
John Glenn—Could the Ohio senator and former astronaut be the Ike of the '70s?
Sherlock Holmes—He emerges from Victorian England as the most omnipresent literary figure of 1974
Carter Heyward—One of eleven women ordained as Episcopal priests (the ordinations were later declared invalid) defies her church to serve her God
Stevie Wonder—A blind artist brings soul to all his music
Alexander Calder—Now it seems every U.S. city must have one of his stabiles
Charlie Finley—The owner of the Oakland A's doesn't win friends, just the World Series
Ella Grasso—In the year of political women, hers is the biggest name of all
J. Kenneth Jamieson—Exxon's chief has big profits and big problems
Jimmy Connors—He catches fire; his romance catches cold
Gunnar Myrdal—Nobel Prize winner in economics is honored for his "pioneering work in the theory of money and economic fluctuations"
Valerie Harper—*Rhoda*'s a winner on her own, and so much for TV taboos
Mikhail Barishnikov—The former Kirov Ballet star defects to Toronto, and ballet is changed forever

1975

Betty Ford—The president's secret weapon is a refreshing First Lady high on being herself
Richard Zanuck—Son of Darryl F., he makes his own name coproducing Hollywood's most toothsome grosser ever (*Jaws*)
Frank E. Fitzsimmons—The boss of 2.2 million teamsters is Nixon's buddy and shows he is "not Hoffa's puppet"
Charles Manson—Although he is in prison, he may have influenced Squeaky Fromme in her failed assassination of President Ford
Daniel Patrick Moynihan—Fighting Irishman at the U.N. talks tough—and, many Americans feel, talks sense too
James Coleman—The University of Chicago professor blamed for busing says it backfired

Indira Ghandi—After six months of rule in India, her popularity soars
Cher Bono Allman—Move over Liz 'n' Dick, this ricochet bride is the new First Lady of splitsville
Andrei Sakharov—The Nobel Peace Prize winner is a man under siege in his own country
Teng Hsiao-Ping—After years of obscurity, a tough, blunt, outspoken man steps into the big shoes of Chinese leadership
Patty Hearst—Was she a volunteer terrorist or a victim of her captors?
Christina Onassis—The only daughter of the late shipping magnate Aristotle Onassis has the ships and the gold, and marries her father's rival
Leonard Matlovich—The ex–Air Force sergeant is discharged after admitting his homosexuality and sets up the Matlovich Foundation for Civil Rights
Dolly Parton—There's a brain under that beehive of Nashville's new queen-in-waiting
Fred Lynn—An all-American boy dazzles Boston and baseball in his miraculous rookie year
Frank Borman—An ex–astronaut takes the controls of a company in a financial tailspin and gets Eastern Airlines off the ground
Rosemary Rogers—The master of the erotic gothic takes her readers past the bedroom door
Werner Erhard—In the wake of TM and Zen, a former encyclopedia huckster is the smooth guru of est
Woody Allen—A winning klutz moves from snappy one-liners to triple creative threat—actor, director, and author with his latest, *Without Feathers*
Marabel Morgan—The Florida housewife behind *The Total Woman* cashes in on the antifeminist backlash
Jerry Brown—A young governor avoids the mansion, limos, and labels—and California loves him
Don King—A flashy ex-con turned promoter is the new lord of the rings
Hercule Poirot—Who kills the famed Belgian detective after fifty-five years? No, not the butler, but Dame Agatha Christie
Anwar Sadat—The president of Egypt opens the Suez Canal, closed since the Six Day War in 1967
Gelsey Kirkland—The prima ballerina of the American Ballet dances a triumphant *Giselle,* highlighting a great year in ballet

1976

Jimmy Carter—The president-elect wants to be the "citizen president"
Farrah Fawcett-Majors—The shape of things to come? The nation watches an "Angel" turn into a star
Andrew Wyeth—Is he America's most popular painter? The thought grieves some critics, who see him as "the rich man's Norman Rockwell"
Betty Williams—After seven bloody years, an anguished mother whose three children were killed starts her own movement and asks Ulster to give peace a chance
Andrew Young—The first black ambassador to the United Nations. When this former congressman speaks, Jimmy Carter listens
Juan Carlos I—The new Spanish king takes aim at Franco's fascist legacy and hands power to the people
Linda Ronstadt—A vagabond grows into country rock's First Lady
Reverend Sun Myung Moon—Troubles build up for the mysterious head of the Unification Church
Bert Jones—A cool, calm Colt is pro football's man with the golden arm
Julius Nyerere—Tanzania's superstar of black African diplomacy acts as a buffer between ruling white Ian Smith's government and the black nationalists of Rhodesia
Carl Sagan—The Viking I expedition on Mars provides vicarious adventure for a would-be space explorer
Fred Silverman—Since TV's superprogrammer switched channels, ABC enjoys Happy Days and Mashes CBS
Liz Ray—The woman whose affair with Representative Wayne Hays set off the steamiest Washington sex scandal in years brings out a book and gets religion
C. W. McCall—After "Convoy," the year's bestselling single, Rubberduck is king of the road
Shere Hite—That report on women's sexuality becomes a bestseller, and its author moves on to men
Donald Kendall—With the Soviets part of the Pepski Gen-

eration, Pepsico's chief is now waging war on Coke
Vivian Reed—The star of Broadway's *Bubbling Brown Sugar* proves that black is beautiful at the box office
Ron Kovic—Crippled Vietnam veteran–turned–antiwar activist and author of *Born on the Fourth of July* sells movie rights for $150, 000—and is a new breed of Yankee Doodle Dandy
Chevy Chase—He's hot and you're not: *Saturday Night*'s stumblebum says so much for tepid TV
Regine—The queen mother of the disco craze opens clubs all over the globe
Har Gobind Khorana—A shy genius gives the world its first man-made working gene
Nadia Comaneci—The Rumanian Olympic champion prepares for the 1980 games in Moscow. In Montreal she was just about perfect—now she wants even more.
Robert Redford—The actor turns producer with *All the President's Men* and shows he's not just a pretty face
Don Shomron—The Israeli general who led the Entebbe raid to save 105 hostages is a global hero and can't understand why
King Kong—Producer Dino De Laurentis sees and monkey does—$200 million, he hopes

1977

Jimmy Carter—The first year at 1600: he likes it, Rosalynn is chilly, and Amy's adjusting
Diane Keaton—Her gamble on *Looking for Mr. Goodbar* put Woody Allen's flaky foil in the Hollywood catbird seat
General Omar Torrijos—Ratify the canal treaties or bring in the marines, says Panama's strongman
Steven Ross—An impresario of all parlors (originally funeral), the founder-chairman of Warner Communications is the greatest showman on earth
Midge Costanza—A pushy little broad with a quick tongue is Carter's pipeline to the people as the assistant for public liaison
Anwar Sadat and Menachem Begin—Is it a possible secret weapon of peace that the president of Egypt and the prime minister of Israel are so much alike?
Ted Turner—After the Americas Cup the sea gets a little choppy for the cable entrepreneur and baseball team owner
Margaret Trudeau—The runaway wife of Canada's prime minister, Pierre Trudeau, says of her old life, "Politics is an ugly and thankless role. What I did was never really praised or appreciated."
Robert Byrd—A self-made fiddler calls the tunes in the world's most exclusive club
Susanne Albrecht—A brutal murder of an old friend makes her the dark queen of German terrorism.
Lily Tomlin—The actress/comedian won a Tony for her one-woman show *Appearing Nitely*. "Is this the country to whom I'm speaking?" Happily for America the answer is yes
Billy Carter—President Carter's baby brother and typical southern "sly ole boy" has an agent and a career as spokesmen for products such as "Billy's Beer." He may be a royal pain to some, but his brother is still amused
Anita Bryant—After a *très* ungay year, she is still praising the Lord and passing the orange juice
Shaun Cassidy—The star of *The Hardy Boys* moonlights as a pop star, and preadolescent America is swooning
Jacqueline Onassis—Quits her editor's job at Viking and gets $25 million from stepdaughter Christina Onassis
Jasper Johns—In the '70s the enigmatic master of pop art—known for depictions of the stars and stripes, targets, alphabets, and lightbulbs—stays on target
Toni Morrison—"O-o-o-ooh she done fly" into the literary top rank with *Song of Solomon*
Dr. Robert Linn—His liquid protein diet has him in fat city, but some unexplained deaths worry the FDA
Tracy Austin—Out of the cradle and onto the courts comes a new tennis wunderkind, at fourteen the youngest player ever to be invited to Wimbledon
Rosalyn Yalow—All this: winner of the 1977 Nobel Prize for medicine, first laureate educated only in the United States, sixth woman science winner, second woman medicine winner
Reggie Jackson—Once he was just a hot dog; now he's a candy bar and a millionaire Yankee hero
Stevie Nicks—A songwriting soprano with fragile vocal cords casts her sexy spell on rock
George Lucas—From the void he created the droid and a new "force" in film

Princess Caroline—Grace and Rainier's grown-up little girl will wed Junot in June . . . maybe

1978

Pope John Paul II—A tough Polish priest molds the papacy to his own ebullient personality
Queen Noor al-Hussein—The blue-jeaned American queen says of her king, "I'd be delighted to have his child"
G. William Miller—The chairman of the Federal Reserve says of inflation, in effect, "We have nothing to fear but fear itself"
Teng Hsiao-Ping—Tough, resilient, the vice-premier gives China less of Mao, and more of himself
Brooke Shields—Pretty baby at thirteen: One horse, three movies, beaucoup bucks, but no beau
Melvin Gottlieb—The dream this Princeton physicist pursues is limitless energy from nuclear fusion
Louise Brown—The first test-tube baby is doing just fine, thank you, but the fuss is far from over
Reverend Jim Jones—When this religious demagogue felt his encampment was threatened by Congress and newsmen, he offered a deadly communion to his followers
John Belushi—With the hit movie *Animal House*, TV's man of mugs is becoming a hard act to outgross—in every way
Jimmy Carter—Camp David buoyed him, Ted Kennedy and Jerry Brown aren't worrisome, and Amy is better on the violin
Jim Fixx—Author of *The Complete Book of Running*, a how-to book on the simplest sport in the world that becomes the year's runaway bestseller
Garry Marshall—TV writer and producer of the hits *Laverne and Shirley, Happy Days,* continues his successful career with *Mork and Mindy*
Arlene Blum—The University of California biochemist who led the first all-woman expedition up Annapurna, the tenth highest peak in the world, masters her mountain, but two fellow climbers are part of the price
Howard Jarvis—The crusader against high property taxes may have changed the future of U.S. politics following the endorsement of his Proposition 13 by California voters in June
Miss Piggy—The famed Muppet pig states, "I want children, my career, and the frog—not necessarily in that order"
Luciano Pavarotti—It's supertenor, opera's newest sex symbol
Cheryl Tiegs—This model's photos still bring out the beast, but her new goal is survival in the TV jungle
Meat Loaf—Rock's newest (and heftiest) hero takes a Texas-size bite into the music biz
Sir Freddie Laker—The founder of the Skytrain revolutionized air fares with cheap transatlantic flights and has a knighthood to prove his success
Nancy Lopez—The golfer has a fantastic year, finishing first in nine out of twenty-five tournaments and is named Rookie Player and Golfer of the Year
John Travolta—Stayin' Alive is the word for the solitary new superstar besieged by his fans
James Crosby—The man who brought big-time gambling to Atlantic City hopes for the city's economic rebirth
John Irving—His novel *The World According to Garp* is on the bestseller list, and the revenues allow the down-to-earth Vermonter to work full-time on his upcoming work, *The Hotel New Hampshire*
Donna Summer—The queen of disco is softening her act, but she'd still love to love you, baby.
Burt Reynolds—Life isn't always easy for a star working on a new image: sensitivity

1979

Rosalynn Carter—The former First Lady skirts the charge that she is too involved in government policy formation, and instead emphasizes the Carters as a family
Aleksandr Godunov—The Russian danseur defects to the United States "to dance more often," but his volatile personality may be the reason he has yet to perform
Marvin Mitchelson—The millionaire divorce lawyer makes "palimony" a household threat
Bo Derek—Shows the world that she's a 10 as costar to Dudley Moore, and is credited with bringing sex back to films
Lee Iacocca—Struggles valiantly to get Chrysler into gear under the threat of bankruptcy
Sly Stallone—Comes off the canvas for the biggest movie purse of the year, *Rocky II,* and is already thinking ahead to *Rocky III*
Megan Marshack—After a year of seclusion, former vice

president Nelson Rockefeller's secretary and companion on the night of his death is back in New York
Mani Said al-Otaiba—Leader of OPEC, he writes poetry and tames his Arab colleagues with cordial threats
Joan Kennedy—Sobers up to be at Ted's side for the campaign
Johnny Carson—Carson announces that he plans to give up his seventeen-year reign and $2.5-million contract at NBC and may entertain offers from ABC
Ayatollah Khomeini—The fate of the hostages is still unknown, but Iran's fanatic ruler leads his nation toward chaos with growing social and economic problems
Tom Wolfe—After six years of writer's block, his latest, *The Right Stuff,* is his biggest seller
Joan Baez—The brave anti-warrior raises her voice for the boat people and refugees of Cambodia and is accused of changing her tune on Vietnam
Sebastian Coe—After setting three world records, this British runner takes time out to prepare for the Olympics in Moscow, complete his postgraduate studies, and take a break from all the "razzmatazz"
Gloria Vanderbilt—Living up to her genes, the poor little rich girl brings new chic to a bottom line with her top-grossing designer jeans
Bruce Babbitt—The Arizona governor, a member of the presidential commission to investigate Three Mile Island, believes nuclear power is a necessary evil that must be better regulated
Meryl Streep—A big year for the most intelligent actress now at work, with *Manhattan, Kramer vs. Kramer,* and *The Deer Hunter*
Willie Stargell—Captain of the Pittsburgh Pirates, voted MVP this year, but didn't need an award to get the respect and love of his team
Pope John Paul II—Good receptions all over the world indicate a fine first year for the new pope, although his message is often a bitter pill to swallow.
Paul Volcker—The chairman of the Federal Reserve leads an exemplary frugal life, which he brings to the office
Jesse Jackson—Reverend Jackson jets around the world offering support and often inflammatory statements
Dan Aykroyd—*Saturday Night Live* loses the brilliant actor/writer, who is moving on to make more movies
Margaret Thatcher—The first female prime minister of England is not a promotion for feminist ideals, but advocates a nostalgic return "to economic Calvinism: hard work, self reliance, and upward mobility"
William Webster—America's top cop takes aim at a tough target: modernizing and de-Hooverizing the FBI
Deborah Harry—Gentlemen and record buyers prefer this platinum blondie: she switches disco to a new wavelength

1980

Ronald Reagan—America's new president settles into his new home and reflects on his health, his children, and his divorce
Goldie Hawn—*Private Benjamin* liberates a beloved ding-a-ling, promoting her to captain of her soul
Lech Walesa—An unemployed electrician becomes a working-class hero to Poland and the free world
Colonel Charlie Beckwith—The commander of the failed mission to rescue American hostages in Iran emerges as a quiet hero
Herbert Boyer—If nothing else, his forays into genetic engineering can turn this scientist into a multimillionaire
Mary Cunningham—Blond, beautiful, and no longer at Bendix, she's looking for room at the top
Fidel Castro—He grinned after solving 125,000 problems, but now he faces a new one: Reagan
Mel Weinberg—A king con artist sets up Abscam for the FBI and snares some unsuspecting politicians
Sugar Ray Leonard—Who is the greatest? A tough little man wins the boxing championship and the title
Robert Redford—First time behind the scenes, a superstar directs a fine film and says, "I'll phase out acting"
Jean Harris—Was the death of Scarsdale Diet's Dr. Tarnower's an accident or murder? Only the quiet headmistress knows
Stephen King—A mild down-easter discovers terror is the ticket
Grete Waitz—A swift Norwegian teacher gives the cold shoulder to the other women runners in the world
Baron St. Helens—An English diplomat's name lives on as a killer volcano

The Reverend Jerry Falwell—A TV preacher sells America on flag, family, and freedom, of sorts
Pat Benatar—Rock finds its missing lynx: she's doing time in the top ten for what she calls *Crimes of Passion*
Lee Rich—Like J. R. Ewing's assailant, the producer behind *Dallas* aims to please, and does
Sonia Johnson—In the battle for the Equal Rights Amendment, a Mormon feminist waits for the balloon to go up
Sam Shepard—Mr. Funk of off Broadway may be the Redford of the '80s—if he can play it his way
Richard Pryor—Having been through the fire, he's back with a new self and, he says, no bad habits
Eudora Welty—The critics bow before the small-town tales of a masterly Southern writer
Soichiro Honda—The Henry Ford of the Japanese auto industry is known as "Pop" to his workers
Beverly Sills—Bubbles from Brooklyn has stopped singing and begun bossing the company she once graced, the New York City Opera
Dan Rather—Asked if he could hold Walter Cronkite's audience, the new CBS Atlas shrugged
Brooke Shields—From *Blue Lagoon* to blue ads for blue jeans, nothing is coming between her and success

1981

Ronald Reagan—The president and his lady speak of fears, family, and the nation's future
Elizabeth Taylor—Old Violet Eyes is back and having a spectacular time—onstage and off
Lech Walesa—Poland's prayers for freedom rest in a man of faith—and bold deeds
Bradford Smith—The man whose Voyager project took us to the planets may face a permanent grounding from Reagan's budget axe
Bryant Gumbel—The new *Today* show host aims to be king of the mountain on morning TV
Crown Prince Fahd—The Saudi heir-apparent works to preserve the peace
Rabbit Angstrom—John Updike's fictional hero returns fat, rich, and ready for the '80s
Ted Turner—In his one-man air war, cable's Captain Courageous stares down the big guns of network TV
Princess Diana—A kindergarten teacher becomes a princess—she and Charles beguile the world and he begets an heir
Gloria Monty—As producer of ABC's *General Hospital*, she's behind the biggest bubble in showbiz: soap operas
David Stockman—Reagan's budget director is nearly done in by his own hand, the one that would tighten the nation's belt
Lena Horne—A glamorous grandmother wants audiences to wonder, "how does the old broad do it?"
John McEnroe—He's number one in tennis, but superbrat's score with the public is still love-hate
Edgar Bronfman—Seagram's liquor baron enlivens a year of corporate merger mania
Barbara Mandrell—Without hemming or hee-hawing, a new country queen takes on TV and wins
Thomas Sowell—A maverick social thinker attracts attention and decides he doesn't like it
Wolfgang Amadeus Mozart—After two centuries, Austria's child prodigy has become the world's favorite composer
Tom Selleck—More modest than macho, he's the hot-as-a-pistol heartthrob of *Magnum P.I.*
Mick Jagger—Mr. Rolling Stone finds sweet satisfaction with rock's richest tour ever
Richard Viguerie—A direct-mail genius is funding the sound effects for that thunder on the right wing
Nicholas Nickleby—At $100 a seat it could have been a bleak house on Broadway, but Dickens proved a smash
Sandra Day O'Connor—Up at 4 a.m. to read briefs, she learns that a woman justice's work is never done
Harrison Ford—He's the new breed of action star—little ego, medium fame, big bucks
Fernando Valenzuela—Baseball almost struck out, but a Mexican rookie conjures up a magical season
Elizabeth McGovern—A talented beauty soars from high school to stardom as a dippy sex kitten in *Ragtime*

1982

Ronald Reagan—Two years into his term, the president considers his "confinement" in the White House, riding, reading, and a peg-legged pig

Joan Jett—Rock's latest leading lady earns her stripes with a hard look and a hit song
Ariel Sharon—Stunned by backlash from the Beirut massacre, the defiant Israeli defense minister battles on
Princess Stephanie—Numbed by her mother's death, a sad teenager has lost her zest for life
Jessica Lange—A talented beauty gets a monkey off her back with two major films, *Tootsie* and *Frances*
Herschel Walker—Forget the Heisman—Georgia's got the trophy that counts: the best running back in football, bar none
Larry Gelbart—After ten years, *M*A*S*H* departs, but the man who wrote the show has a wacky new hit called *Tootsie*
Margaret Thatcher—With Churchill to inspire her, a dogged prime minister triumphs in a nasty little war in the Falkland Islands
Dr. William DeVries—A surgeon touches the soul with a new machine, the artificial heart
Princess Diana—She may have those newlywed blues, but she's still Britain's darling
Yuri Andropov—Emerging from the shadows of the Soviet KGB, a master spy takes over Brezhnev's Kremlin
George Wallace—Politically recast as a friend of blacks, he seeks their votes and forgiveness—and gets both
Paolo Rossi—A handsome soccer hero leads Italy to the World Cup and wins back the hearts of his countrymen
Randall Forsberg—A Massachusetts scholar sounds a nationwide call to (freeze) arms
Norma Kamali—Wowing Seventh Avenue has been no sweat for fashion's Greta Garbo
E.T.—Short on looks (but not fans), an alien finds his home in Hollywood
Richard Gere—*Officer* makes a star, if not quite a gentleman, out of a movie maverick
Sam Knox—An authority on the scourge of the sexes, herpes, offers some consoling facts to the legions of victims
Andrew Lloyd Webber—From the Bible to back alleys, Broadway's hottest composer strikes all the right notes
Evelyn Waugh—A curmudgeon's elegy for England's upper crust, *Brideshead Revisited* becomes the TV event of 1982
Barbra Streisand—At forty, the Brooklyn songbird returns to the Old World to conquer a new one—directing *Yentl*
Ted Koppel—A clear-eyed newshawk surveys war and peace and revolutionizes night-owl journalism on *Nightline*
Kiri Te Kanawa—New Zealand's diva hits the top in opera and wins a title by acting nothing like a dame
Reverend Sun Myung Moon—The Unification Church's controversial leader is convicted of tax evasion, but he still wins converts
Paul Newman—*The Verdict* is in: a risky role may win Blue Eyes that elusive Oscar gold
Bill Agee and Mary Cuningham—The Bendix takeover didn't take, but this famous couple makes one merger that works

1983

Ronald Reagan—The president finishes out a tough year with the bombing of Syrian antiaircraft nests in the mountains east of Beirut
Debra Winger—A Hollywood sexpot turns serious actress and scores on her own *Terms*
Fidel Castro—The aging lion of revolution in Latin America gets savvy—and pulls in his claws
The Cabbage Patch Kids—Glassy of eye and poker of face, this chubby, alien horde masks a plot to take over the planet
Jesse Jackson—An explosive orator's campaign breeds fusion and fission for the Democratic party
William Gates—Dropping out of Harvard pays off for a computer whiz kid who's making hard cash from Microsoft software
Sam Shepard—He has it all as a laureate of stage and screen—so now what does he want? Anonymity
Chun Byung In—The career of an "infallible" pilot ends in the debris of Korean Air Lines flight 007, shot down over Soviet airspace in August
Mr. T—The terror of the *A-Team* is indisputably the show-business manic of the year
Ben Lexcen—An impish Aussie designer and his magic keel haul the America's Cup Down Under after 132 years of U.S. ownership
Joan Rivers—Where's Johnny Carson? Home, watching a *Tonight Show* guest host skewer guests and boost his ratings
Robert Mastruzzi—A Bronx high school principal won't let his school be less than the best

Eddie Murphy—It's no joke—this movie star makes folks mad, but he's got it made
Matthew Broderick—Oh, to be young and hot in Hollywood; yet instead of acting up, the leader of the brat pack is buttoned-down
Barbara McClintock—After six decades of research, the shy discoverer of biology's "jumping genes" wins her Nobel prize
Harvey Fierstein—Brooklyn's funny boy takes Broadway on a gay mad whirl with *La Cage aux folles*
Philip Johnson—The grand old man of architecture comes full circle, designing the downfall of his own glass box
Vanessa Williams—A thorny crown goes with the job of being the first black Miss America
Richard Chamberlain—He gets no awards from his peers, but the public hails the king of miniseries
Michael Jackson—Thanks to a *Thriller* album, the former small fry of the Jacksons becomes the biggest star in pop
Rei Kawakubo—Japan's Stravinsky of fashion rocks the West with her atonal, asymmetric sad rags
Konrad Kujau—A Nazi-obsessed amateur forger fakes the Führer's diaries and nearly fools the world
Alice Walker—*The Color Purple*, her protagonist's letters to God, bring her a bestseller and a Pulitzer
Alfred Hitchcock—Five buried treasures from the master of suspense prove to be the movie event of 1983
Jennifer Beals—Dazzling looks and a ripped wardrobe turn a dancing Yalie into a flashy star

1984

Geraldine Ferraro—A tough, savvy, and zestful political pioneer loses the battle for vice president but wins a historic war for women
Bruce Springsteen—Placing himself beyond the presidential reach, the Boss transcends mere legend to become a symbol of all that once was right about America
Andrei Gromyko—For nearly half a century, this most durable diplomat has been the poker face of Soviet foreign policy
José Napoleón Duarte—On the broad shoulders of this gutsy president rest El Salvador's hopes of emerging from a nightmare civil war
Mary Lou Retton—L.A.'s golden girl Olympian marches to a new beat as Madison Avenue's million-dollar baby
Richard Gere—This elusive screen actor seems bent on preserving the silence that marks him as a Hollywood enigma
Peter Ueberroth—An organizational wizard turns the L.A. Olympic Games into a glowing personal triumph
Joe Kittinger—In the year's greatest adventure, a hard-nosed pilot transforms a POW fantasy into a dream come true with a solo flight across the Atlantic in a hot air balloon
Farrah Fawcett—With *The Burning Bed*, her career surges, and at thirty-seven she's a happy mother-to-be—proud papa Ryan O' Neal hopes they're altar-bound
Clint Eastwood—As *Tightrope*'s kinky cop he reveals new and darker dimensions that leave astonished critics cheering
Betty Ford—The former First Lady publicly tackles her problems with alcohol and painkillers—and helps cure a nation's ills
John Malkovich—A versatile young Chicago actor storms Broadway in *Death of a Salesman* and stakes a claim on Oscar in two of the year's best movies, *Places in the Heart* and *The Killing Fields*
Kathleen Turner—The star of *Romancing the Stone* mixes sex and sensitivity to become the hottest actress since Streep
Sparky Anderson—He managed the Detroit Tigers to victory in the World Series and also leads the league in rough-hewn rhetoric
Tina Turner—After eight years of deep rivers and high mountains, a self-professed "Soul Survivor" strides back into the rock 'n' roll promised land with her new album, *Private Dancer*
William Kennedy—At fifty-six, Albany's patient author watches the work of a lifetime pay off with a Pulitzer Prize, *Cotton Club*, movie deals and a $264,000 MacArthur "genius grant"
Lee Iaccoca—With his autobiography riding atop the bestseller list, Chrysler's blunt shirtsleeve philosopher offers a plan to fix the sputtering economy
Vanessa Williams—The first black Miss America's reign is distinguished by dignity, delight, and talent—until the discovery that she had posed nude forces her resignation

John Torrington—From his ice-shrouded tomb in the Canadian Arctic, a nineteenth-century explorer sheds new light on the chilling fate of Britain's ill-fated Franklin expedition
James Baker—President Ronald Reagan remains curiously ageless as his chief of staff grows older quickly—could there be a connection?
Kathleen Morris—A controversial Minnesota prosecutor vows to continue the legal fight against sexual abuse of children
John Henry—This equine geriatric marvel has traveled from coast to coast and convincingly proved that the race is not always to the youngest
Bill Murray—This ghostbuster is the comedy star of the year's biggest box-office hit ($220 million), but if you think it's gone to his head—get outta here
Baby Fae—A wondering world watches as a child with a transplanted baboon heart fights for life
Michael Jackson—*People* ran five covers, seventy-three photos, and 33,205 words on the singer during 1984—what more is there to say?

1985

Bob Geldof—Moved by scenes of mass starvation, this scruffy Irishman raises a cry with a song and rouses the world to save the hungry
Joe Kennedy—The best-known name in American politics surfaces again as Bobby's eldest son announces for the congressional seat once held by his Uncle Jack
Corazon Aquino—As the ghost of her assassinated husband haunts the rule of Philipine president Ferdinand Marcos, a housewife rides an emotional swell to political prominence
William Perry—He can block, run, do endorsements. At 308 pounds, The Refrigerator is the big surprise of the football season
Akira Kurosawa—Japan's feisty grand old man of the movies comes back from despair to film *Ran*, a feudal version of *King Lear* that may turn out to be his greatest triumph
Nelson Mandela—Banished behind prison walls since 1964, a legendary black leader may yet save South Africa from the horror of racial war
Steven Rosenberg—By energizing the body's natural defenses, a surgeon at the National Cancer Institute may have made the biggest step in thirty years toward a cancer cure
Rambo—His deeds are the stuff of cinema legend from here to Haiphong, but to the folks of one small western town, he's just a local boy with a preposterous set of pecs
Bernhard Goetz—New York's subway vigilante acted out our angriest fantasies, but a year later the questions remain—is he a hero or a villain, a victim or a criminal?
William Hurt—His risky transvestite role in *Kiss of the Spider Woman* makes him an Oscar favorite as Best Actor, but he'd rather hide from the world than try to be world-famous
Uli Derickson—TWA Flight 847's flight attendant becomes the heroine of a hijacking
The Springsteens—The storybook year of Beauty and the Boss ends on a harmonious note with Bruce and Julianne Phillips at ease at last in New Jersey
Cathleen Webb—The New Hampshire housewife says she faked a rape that sent a man to prison for years, and suddenly finds herself an unlikely celebrity
Rupert Murdoch—The empire-building publisher of the *New York Post* and freshly minted American citizen takes on television, Hollywood, and morality
Dwight Gooden—Vulnerable only to kryptonite, baseball's best pitcher is quiet but deadly, playing a game he hasn't learned how to lose
Don Johnson—Every woman wants his body, every man wants his clothes—that's why he's America's Friday night vice
Princess Diana—No matter where she is she embodies dreams and always looks just like a princess
Mel Fisher—In a season of shipwreck salvagings, Captain Audacious pulls thirty-four tons of Spanish silver from the drink
Michael J. Fox—The comedy star of the year's No. 1 movie, *Back to the Future*, and the No. 2 TV show, *Family Ties*, puts on the dog as the boy king of Hollywood
Mengele's Bones—Discovery of the moldering remains of the Nazis' infamous "Angel of Death" ends the most intense manhunt of the century
Whoopi Goldberg—She's been on welfare and on Broadway; now she's on-screen in *The Color Purple*

Hulk Hogan—The World Wrestling Federation's heavyweight champion talks about his biceps, his California home, and milk, his breakfast of champions
Rock Hudson—His name stood for Hollywood's golden age of wholesome heroics and lighthearted romance—until he becomes the most famous person to die of AIDS
Gracie Mansion—A hip gallery owner brings world fame to the brassy, flashy, sometimes trashy art that grows in Manhattan's revitalized East Village
Madonna—She's a big girl now—rich, famous, and married to actor Sean Penn—but once upon a time, the reigning queen of all things pop was just another wannabe

1986

Sarah, Duchess of York—Breaking out of the royal mold, a commoner marries her prince and wins a nation's heart without losing hold of an independent personality
Ivan Boesky—It isn't insight but inside tips that make this risk arbitrageur the demon of Wall Street
Dr. Seuss—*You're Only Old Once!* made us hoot, made us cheer / Seuss wrote it for oldsters, it came out this year
Bette Midler—No longer the wacked-out Divine Miss M, she becomes a mother and mainstream box-office draw in two hugely successful Disney films
Oliver North—After a series of bombshell disclosures, the question remains—was the President's marine a hero or a loose cannon?
Daniel Ortega—The forty-one-year-old president of Nicaragua wears baseball caps, wields his own AK-47, and bedevils the Reagan state department
Raymond Hunthausen—Seen by the Vatican as the shepherd who strayed, Seattle's progressive archbishop believes he's keeping the faith
Bob Hoskins—A pudgy, pint-size dynamo known as the Cockney Cagney shapes up as the actor of the year with appearances in *Sweet Liberty* and *Mona Lisa*
Terry Waite—An envoy from the Church of England inspires international trust and obtains freedom for hostages in Beirut
Howard the Duck—George Lucas's feathered friend turns out to be a turkey, as *Howard the Duck* loses $35 million
Greg LeMond—Becoming the first American to win the Tour de France is no easy feat for the twenty-five-year-old cyclist, who has to battle a mentor's betrayal
Run–D.M.C.—Rap's Kings of (Hollis) Queens persuade skeptical rock fans to "Walk This Way"
Paul Hogan—An Aussie smoothy makes *Crocodile Dundee* America's favorite easy-watching movie
Debi Thomas—The U.S. women's figure-skating champion finds the time to study microbiology at Stanford
Helga—A Pennsylvania housekeeper bewitches the art world, as it is revealed that she posed for hundreds of previously unknown Andrew Wyeth paintings
Tom Cruise—A fave rave of the teen scene grows up to be the box-office *Top Gun* of 1986
David Letterman—The *Late Night* host's askew humor finally finds a home in the heartland
Vanna White—The latest in the line of Lite Celebrities, the letter-turning bombshell of *Wheel of Fortune* rakes in endorsements, writes a book, and leaves some wondering why she's famous at all
Pat Robertson—A television preacher bids to move from God's House to the White House
Beth Henley—A Mississippi playwright goes Hollywood with a trio of quirky comedies: *True Stories*, *Nobody's Fool*, and *Crimes of the Heart*
Jerome P. Horwitz—AZT, the anticancer drug he developed twenty-two years ago, is now our best hope in the battle against AIDS
David Byrne—Letting down his avant-garde, the Talking Head celebrates a wondrous, wacky America in his movie *True Stories*
Max Headroom—With electrons for blood, computers for brains, and an ego as big as all TV, this nonhuman talk show host is Chairman of the Tube
William Rehnquist—In all matters large and small, the new chief justice of the Supreme Court goes his own way
Whitney Houston—Singer Cissy Houston's shy daughter emerges as pop's prettiest commercial monster

1987

Ronald Reagan—Entering his eighth year in office, the president remains vigorous and completes his term with a Hollywood finish
Mikhail Gorbachev—The Russian leader who put a

human face on communism takes the West by storm and ushers in an age of optimism
Baby Jessica McClure—Up and running after her fall down a Midland, Texas, well and her televised rescue, she gets on with a normal toddler's life
Gary Hart—Undaunted by negative press on his personal life, the Colorado senator reenters the 1988 presidential race
Oliver North—An all-American marine charms his way through the Iran-Contra hearings but will probably still pay for his involvement in the arms-for-hostages scandal
Princess Diana—Hints of discord follow the princess into her sixth year of marriage, as she and Charles spend more and more time apart and she begins to test the limits of acceptable royal behavior
Patient Zero—Randy Shilts's book *And the Band Played On* identifies French Canadian Gaetan Dugas as a major transmitter of the AIDS virus. Forty of the 248 homosexuals diagnosed with the disease in 1982 had either had sexual relations with the flight steward or with someone else who had
Cher—Sonny's onetime partner, who says she "refuses to accept other people's limitations," soars as her roles in *The Witches of Eastwick* and *Moonstruck* bring her power, happiness, and a wider audience
Christian Lacroix—A new designer's whimsical approach to his trade revolutionizes the high-fashion world and caters to the most chic of the stars
Dennis Quaid—His sure-footed sex appeal and engaging grin ignite the screen in *The Big Easy*
Vincent Van Gogh—Despite bouts with depression so severe they drove him to suicide, Vincent Van Gogh is emerging as the most marketable Postimpressionist of the twentieth century
Church Lady—*Saturday Night Live*'s most biting holy roller flourishes in a year of sex scandals, church scams, and other *special* sins
Michael Douglas—Playing a lech in *Fatal Attraction* and a slimy corporate raider in *Wall Street,* Kirk's son steps into the spotlight
Donna Fawn Hahn—Rice, Hall, and Jessica, the women who fell with Gary Hart, Ollie North, and Jim Bakker, are actually all the same person—the three faces of Eve
Magic Johnson—This talented point guard is leading the Los Angeles Lakers to the top of the NBA—and smiling all the way
Bono—Struggling with sainthood, this rock musician spray-paints a work of art in San Francisco and tries to chip away at his heroic status
Brigitte Nielsen—Newly divorced from Sylvester Stallone, she remains notorious for her leggy sexuality and questionable motives in love
Tracey Ullman—Host of her own show on Fox, this British comedian astonishes and delights her audience, always hoping to avoid the bland
Jerry Garcia—Despite more than just a touch of grey, the middle-aged hippie priest is still getting by—and is singing to a new generation of Grateful Dead fans
Oprah Winfrey—The leading voice among talk show hosts is using television to fight apartheid as well as racism at home
Donald Trump—Emerging as an icon for the '80s, this real estate mogul is pushing his way around in the media and in the marketplace
Glenn Close—A forty-year-old actress battles her earth-mother image and becomes a screen siren with fatal attraction
Garrison Keillor—The creator of National Public Radio's *A Prairie Home Companion* is happy with life in the aftermath of his show
William Casey—Dying before he is able to testify in the Iran-Contra hearings, Ronald Reagan's CIA director admitted using any means necessary to defend the free world as he saw it
Tammy Faye Bakker—Hurt by a drug addiction and her husband's dalliance with Jessica Hahn, America's most unusual makeup consumer stuns *Nightline* audiences and made herself a national joke

1988

George Bush—The president-elect is a gentleman of the old school and a family man who is not above a bare-knuckled brawl when it comes to politics
Roseanne Barr—Looking at her, it's difficult to distinguish art from life—Roseanne plays the larger-than-life housewife both on and off the small screen
Athina Roussel—Now only three, she will inherit over $1 billion when she turns eigh-

teen—but money won't buy the love she lost with the death of her mother, Christina Onassis
The Cyberpunk—The nerds rise again, as "misfit" hackers wreak havoc on America's information networks
Mike Tyson—The heavyweight champion's most formidable opponent proves to be his beautiful wife, Robin Givens
Lisa Marie Presley—The King's daughter lives down a princess image by marrying a sober fellow and settling down
Benazir Bhutto—A Radcliffe-and-Oxford-educated feminist becomes prime minister of Pakistan and discovers the challenges posed in being the first woman to lead an Islamic nation
Liz Taylor—In another roller-coaster year, Liz writes an upbeat autobiography, raises millions to fight AIDS, and descends again into a drug addiction so severe that a staffer at the Betty Ford Center calls her the "female version of Elvis"
Michelle Pfeiffer—*Married to the Mob, Tequila Sunrise,* and *Dangerous Liaisons* prove that this actress is more than just a pretty face
Jesse Jackson—He may not have clinched the nomination, but Jesse Jackson's presidential campaign shows Democrats that he is a political force to be reckoned with
Phantom of the Opera—Rising from his lonely catacomb, this anguished spirit of the night beguiles us once again with a vision of the tragic depths of love
Merv Griffin—At sixty-three, the former talk show host becomes a billionaire and takes over ownership of Trump's Resorts International, beating the Donald at his own game
Anne Tyler—With her new novel *Breathing Lessons* and a film adaptation of her 1985 bestseller, *The Accidental Tourist,* a reclusive novelist is faced by an adoring public
Orel Hershiser—Squeaky clean or tough and mean? Off the diamond he may be an angel, but this World Series MVP is uncompromising when he pitches.
Jodie Foster—No longer haunted by would-be Reagan assassin John Hinckley, she makes an acclaimed comeback as a rape victim who fights back in *The Accused*
Shi Peipu—Posing as a woman throughout his twenty-year relationship with French diplomat Bernard Boursicot, a one-time singer with the Peking opera inspires David Hwang's Tony-award-winning play, *M. Butterfly*
Kevin Costner—*Bull Durham*'s down-to-earth romantic lead sends hearts aflutter and critics abuzz
Florence Griffith Joyner—She may have won four medals as a sprinter at the Seoul Olympics, but she's still got two feet firmly on the ground
David Hockney—Twenty-five years after making the move from England to sunny California, artist David Hockney and his bright canvases are the talk of the art scene
Jessica Rabbit—The hottest woman on celluloid isn't a woman at all, according to fans of this sultry 'toon
Stephen Hawking—Plagued by Lou Gehrig's disease, a Cambridge University mathematics professor works to unwind the mysteries of the universe—and writes a bestselling book
Tom Hanks—A familiar face hits the *Big* time with his portrayal of a thirteen-year-old trapped in a thirty-five-year-old's body
Fergie—The Duchess of York's first year with the Windsors is not the fairy tale it had been cut out to be
Tracy Chapman—A serious black folk musician sings about a revolution and becomes one of the most successful recording artists of the year
Sage Volkman—Thanks to a strong will and the miracles of modern surgery, a six-year-old burn survivor gets back her smile

1989

George and Barbara Bush—In their first joint Oval Office interview, the First Couple talk politics, family, and pocket change
Jack Nicholson—As *Batman*'s Joker, he romps in a role that fits him as closely as his white grease paint
Arsenio Hall—This hippest night-owl of them all hops to the top of the talk-show totem pole
Robert Fulghum—His unlikely bestseller, *All I Really Need To Know I Learned in Kindergarten*, goes to the head of the class
Julio Berumen—The San Francisco Bay Area earthquake's pluckiest survivor takes his first steps with a new leg

Princess Anne—Once Britain's least-liked royal, she becomes an object of desire
Mikhail Gorbachev—He shrugs when the Eastern bloc cracks and proves he's serious about perestroika
John Goodman—The TV Barr-tender and newly minted movie star is an extra-large hit in any medium
Gaia—The Greek earth goddess lends her name to James Lovelock's daring theory that the planet itself is alive
Manuel Noriega—The Panamanian dictator gives American leaders fits, but he may be nearing his last hurrah
Michael Milken—A junk bond entrepreneur makes $1.1 billion financing corporate takeovers—but his indictment brings an era to an end
Billy Crystal—Learning that an orgasm can be faked, he becomes a genuine sex symbol in *When Harry Met Sally* . . .
Paula Abdul—No longer just Janet Jackson's footwork coach, she steps out as a song-and-dance sensation
Spike Lee—The director raises a ruckus—and important questions—with his film *Do The Right Thing*
Ellen Barkin—She's tough, vulnerable, smart, very sexy, and doesn't quite add up; which may be why she's so riveting onscreen
Madonna—In another typical year, she irks some Christians, splits from Sean, dallies with Warren, and gets canned by Pepsi
Deborah Gore Dean—As the HUD scandal unravels, it's clear that she saw government as a game show and helped her friends win valuable prizes
Pete Rose—Charlie Hustle battles bad press, baseball commissioner A. Bartlett Giamatti, and his own demons, and takes a called strike three
Pablo Escobar—A Colombian drug lord markets death by the kilo while evading an outraged citizenry
Salman Rushdie—For publishing the controversial *The Satanic Verses* he now lives with the threat he'll perish
Michelle Pfeiffer—In *The Fabulous Baker Boys* she adds a dash of hot pepper to a delicious dish
Elizabeth Morgan—Jailed for shielding her daughter from alleged sexual abuse, she is freed at last
Robert Mapplethorpe—The photographer rattles the art world and Jesse Helms with a shocking retrospective
Captain Al Haynes—In crash-landing a crippled DC-10 in Sioux City, Iowa, he saves lives with grit and cool
Donna Karan—Her DKNY collection secures the designer's position as high fashions's newest mogul

1990

George Bush—His place in history insecure, he faces a sea of troubles—and his most daunting crisis lies before him in the treacherous Middle East
Julia Roberts—After becoming the first big new female star of the '90s in *Pretty Woman* she's, well, sitting pretty
Ken Burns—The producer of the eleven-hour epic *The Civil War* makes a big bang in an unlikely place—public television
Patrick Swayze—More mesomorphic than ectoplasmic in *Ghost*, he's every woman's dream of a heavenly body
Francis Ford Coppola—The acclaimed director stages the movies' most ambitious mob scene with his sequel *The Godfather, Part III*
Delta Burke—She has unkind words for her *Designing Women* producers; the next thing she loses may not be pounds
Saddam Hussein—His invasion of Kuwait—bloody politics as usual for him—brings the world to the brink of war
Michael Ovitz—The man everyone in Hollywood would like to know spins gold out of tinsel
Nancy Cruzan—Finally off life support after eight years in a coma, she dramatizes the need for living wills
Colin Powell—America's top man in uniforms raises the world's shield in the desert against Saddam Hussein
Fidel Castro—Cuba's leader stands alone and defiant after watching the lights go out all over the Communist world
Effi Barry—She's a model of wifely decorum as husband Marion, Washington's mayor, goes up in a puff of smoke
Dr. Anthony Fauci—He's used to taking the heat: He's America's point man in the fight against AIDS
M.C. Hammer—He brings showbiz flash and footwork to rap—and cashes in with the year's hottest LP

Bart Simpson—TV's intemperate urchin suits his audience to a T(shirt)—while authority figures have a cow
Nancy Ziegenmeyer—A housewife and rape victim goes public to fight a once-unmentionable crime
Sinead O'Connor—Her haunting rebel voice is heard in an age of flashing legs and lip sync
Nelson Mandela—He steps from the dim recesses of a South African jail into the harsh reality of freedom
Neil Bush—His questionable involvement with a Denver S&L puts a First Family face on the $500-billion S&L scandal
Keenan Ivory Wayans—His *In Living Color* brings howls of laughter and out-Foxes the network establishment
Claudia Schiffer—No guesswork about this supermodel's genes—they come from Germany, via Bardot
William Styron—His *Visible Darkness*, an account of his bleak depression, helps fellow suffers see the light
Laura Palmer—Wasn't washed up when she was washed up—she's the Girl Most Likely To Pique on Twin Peaks
Bo Jackson—He can hit, run, rattle, and roll—and sell well enough to score on Madison Avenue
Princess Caroline—Eight years after her mother's death Monaco's First Lady is coping once more with tragedy, her happiness shattered by her husband's violent death

1991

George and Barbara Bush—The first couple reflect on war, peace, their kids, and even Palm Beach
Magic Johnson—He copes with testing HIV-positive by mounting a full-court press against AIDS
Luke Perry—This hunk steals not only the *Beverly Hills, 90210* spotlight but also the hearts of girls in all zip codes
Jodie Foster—As a first-time director she's known as BLT (bossy little thing) because she isn't silent as a lamb
Anita Hill—Her testimony doesn't stop Clarence Thomas,

THE SEXIEST MAN ALIVE

PEOPLE has honored someone with this title beginning in 1985. Here is a look at the magazine's hunks of the year.

1985
Mel Gibson
1986
Mark Harmon
1987
Harry Hamlin
1988
John F. Kennedy Jr.
1989
Sean Connery
1990
Tom Cruise
1991
Patrick Swayze
1992
Nick Nolte
1993
Richard Gere and Cindy Crawford (The Sexiest Couple Alive)

John F. Kennedy won the title in 1988, but as this recent picture shows, he's a contender any year.

but it starts a national debate on sexual harassment
Garth Brooks—His country album *Ropin' the Wind* crosses over to lasso the attention of all America
Princess Diana—Surviving digs at her marriage and her AIDS activism, she turns a very regal thirty
William Kennedy Smith—He beats a charge of rape, but his famous family may never be the same again
Terry Anderson—Unbowed after nearly seven years as a Beirut hostage, he emerges eager to catch up
Julia Roberts—With a busted engagement and a box-office bust, she ends the year flying off to Neverland
Boris Yeltsin—By elbowing aside both Gorby and the Kremlin hard-liners, he becomes Russia's new voice
Kenneth Branagh—Taking a break from the Bard, he goes Hollywood with the hit *noir* thriller *Dead Again*
Anjelica Huston—Recovered from the loss of a father and a lover, she emerges as Morticia, the *Addam*'s coolest ghoul
Jeffrey Dahmer—His confession could not explain why his grisly serial killings went so long undetected
Elizabeth Taylor—She must be the world's most incurable romantic; will altar trip No. 8 be her last?
Robert Bly—He says there's a bit of "hairy primate" in us all, and *Iron John*'s (mostly male) readers go ape
John Singleton—His *Boyz 'n the Hood* opens middle-class eyes to inner-city life—not bad for a twenty-three-year-old
Naomi Campbell—With her drop-dead looks and her diva's temperament, she reigns over high-fashion runways
Axl Rose—Lowering the sonic boom onstage and off befits the rock monster who is Guns N' Roses' lead pistol
The 4,600-Year-Old Man—Freed from an Alpine deep freeze, he becomes the modern world's unlikeliest souvenir
Mariah Carey—She becomes pop's queen by sharing her musical *Emotions*, not by truth-or-baring her life
Derek Humphry—His best-selling suicide manual, *Final Exit,* ignites a passionate public debate about the right to die
Pee-Wee Herman—Loses his image at an X-rated theater—but not his public, nor the support of Hollywood
Norman Schwarzkopf—A hero after the Gulf, he now faces the challenges of a new post-army career
Jimmy Connors—Written off as a tennis has-been, he defiantly returns to the present tense at the U.S. Open

1992

Bill Clinton—The president reflects on his family, his grueling year, and his beliefs
Hillary Clinton—She adds her thoughts on Chelsea, being First Lady, and her upbringing
Cindy Crawford—She shows the brains behind the beauty, becoming a video celebrity
Ross Perot—Trying to crash the two major parties, he goes from can-do to quitter and back
Denzel Washington—As a mesmerizing *Malcolm X* he catapults to super stardom
Princess Diana—She dumps her hubby but gets to keep the kids, the perks, and the palace
Woody Allen—His breakup with Mia Farrow is like *Annie Hall Goes Ballistic*
Barney—The purple dino fossilizes the Ninja Turtles and gives kid-vid a Jurassic spark
Billy Ray Cyrus—All pecs and no talent, said critics, but he's raising Nashville's pulse
Larry King—*Larry King Live* is the whistle-stop that White House contenders have to visit this year
Terry McMillan—She can breathe easy now that her novel *Waiting to Exhale* is a surprise smash
Gregory K.—He changes his name and sets legal precedents by divorcing his mother
Desiree Washington—She scores a knockout in court over heavyweight champ Mike Tyson
Diane English—The producer makes *Murphy Brown* a single mom and herself a lightning rod
Madonna—She bares her bod, blankets the media, and leaves fans asking, "Yikes! What's next?"
George Smoot—He finds the missing ripples that confirm the universe began with a Big Bang
Katie Couric—With political know-how and a chipper personality, she boosts the *Today* show
Fabio—Once a fantasy figure on romance-novel covers, he actually moves and speaks
Arthur Ashe—He brings eloquence, guts, and grace to his instructive fight against AIDS

Dana Carvey—Whether he's doing Bush, Perot, or *Wayne*'s Garth, he's always hilariously on target
Bernadine Healy—The first woman to head the National Institute of Health is brash and brainy, and gives women's health research a shot in the arm
Carol Moseley Braun—The first black woman to be a U.S. senator defies naysayers to win a place in the history books
Henri Matisse—Sybarite and family man, this glorious painter had crowds standing in line to see his work
Sharon Stone—She shows a *Basic Instinct* for sensuality and stardom—and doesn't sit like a lady
Whoopi Goldberg—The actor is suddenly a Hollywood force more prolific than some studios

1993

Bill Clinton—The President discusses crime, jobs, his bad back, and Chelsea
Hilary Rodham Clinton— Joining the conversation, she reflects on family life and the value of prayer
Princess Diana—She may be out of power in the palace, but she still has a place in Britons' hearts
Michael Jackson—The pop star can moonwalk but he can't hide from career-threatening allegations of child abuse
Yasir Arafat—With a handshake seen around the world, the PLO leader makes peace with his sworn enemy
Oprah Winfrey—This talk-show host becomes the world's highest-paid entertainer, sheds sixty pounds, and stays single
Shannen Doherty—Unlike *Beverly Hills, 90210*'s Brenda, the feisty actress runs amok in several zip codes
David Letterman—Once an after-hour prankster, now he's the leader of the late-night pack
Janet Reno—She wows Washington with her guts and candor, though you can't please everyone
Howard Stern—Radio's raffish raconteur exposes his *Private Parts,* and everybody wants a peek
Baby Jessica—She focuses our eyes and hearts on the tangled arguments over parental rights
Lyle Lovett—Country's wry specialist in heartache and rue wins the hand of winsome Julia Roberts
Ol' Man River—The Mississippi inspires words of awe and rage, from days gone by to last summer's rampaging floods
Jerry Seinfeld—He's got TV's most buzzed-about sitcom, a hot book—and an eighteen-year-old girlfriend
Katherine Ann Power—In facing her bloody past she prompts a rethinking of '60s ideals
Eddie Vedder—His hell-bound vocals make Pearl Jam jell. Now he's got just one problem—he's a star
Vincent Foster—His suicide brings sadness and self-examination to Washington's inner circle
Sheik Omar Abdel Rahman—A blind cleric is accused of inciting his U.S. followers to bomb and kill
Michael Jordan—His surprise retirement shows that even the highest fliers need to be well grounded
Rush Limbaugh—He bashes liberals for fun, profit, and the devotion of a fanatic following on air and in print
Andrew Wiles—A shy Princeton prof you've never heard of awes the great minds of math
Tommy Lee Jones—He's not the man you want on your tail, but you sure want to see him on the big screen
Susan Powter—Her hot *Stop The Insanity!* suggests anger might be the best weight-loss prescription
Lorena Bobbitt—She provokes the national imagination with an act few could view with detachment
Tom Hanks—Seen this year in three diverse and challenging roles, this movie star doesn't get caught up in the glitz of Hollywood

PEOPLE'S BEST AND WORST DRESSED

Who are the biggest fashion victors and victims? The following celebrities found themselves on PEOPLE's Best Dressed and Worst Dressed lists most often.

ALL-TIME WINNERS

3 Times
Princess Caroline
Princess Diana
Kevin Costner
Jackie Onassis

2 Times
Corbin Bernsen
Delta Burke
Cher
Tom Cruise
Mel Gibson
Don Johnson
Angela Lansbury
Cyndi Lauper
Donna Mills
Julia Roberts
Liz Taylor
Prince William
Bruce Willis

ALL-TIME SINNERS

5 Times
Sarah Ferguson
Madonna

4 Times
Arsenio Hall
Daryl Hannah

3 Times
Roseanne Arnold
Rosanna Arquette
Kim Basinger
Prince

2 Times
Paula Abdul
Cher
Geena Davis
Princess Diana
Andrea Evans
Goldie Hawn
Elton John
Demi Moore
Princess Stephanie
Liz Taylor
Ivana Trump
Raquel Welch

1994'S BEST AND WORST

10 Best Dressed:
Lloyd Bentsen
Boyz II Men
Daisy Fuentes
Hugh Grant
Tom Hanks
Heather Locklear
Sarah Jessica Parker
Barbra Streisand
Tracey Ullman
Barbara Walters

10 Worst Dressed:
Christina Applegate
The Arquettes (Patricia, Rosanna, Alexis, and David)
Hillary Rodham Clinton
Brett Butler
Sarah Ferguson
Kim Fields
Ethan Hawke
Susan Lucci
Prince
Howard Stern

THE PEOPLE REGISTER

THE PEOPLE REGISTER

Unce upon a time Mrs. Astor took it upon herself to select the 400 who mattered. Here is a slightly more egalitarian analog for our times—a quirky but thorough compilation of 400 compelling contemporaries. One Tori is in (Amos), while another Tori (Spelling) is not, but that Tori's more accomplished old man (Aaron) is here. And Spelling the younger can be found in the Register of Thousands that begins on page 426.

BRYAN ADAMS

Birthplace: Kingston, Canada
Birthdate: 11/5/59
Occupation: Singer, songwriter, guitarist
Education: High school dropout
Debut: (Song) "Let Me Take You Dancing," 1981
Signature: "(Everything I Do) I Do it for You"
Facts: In 1994, became the first rock musician to play in Vietnam since the U.S. withdrawal.

When he was 18, Adams's songs were performed by bands such as Kiss and Loverboy.
Major Awards: Grammy, Best Song Written Specifically for a Movie, "(Everything I Do) I Do It for You," 1991

ANDRÉ AGASSI

Birthplace: Las Vegas, NV
Birthdate: 4/29/70
Occupation: Tennis player
Education: Nick Bollettieri Tennis Academy
Facts: His father was so determined that André would grow up to be a tennis star that he hung a ball and racquet over the infant's crib and, as soon as his son could sit up, gave him a Ping-Pong paddle and a balloon.

Celebrated his fourth birthday by hitting balls for fifteen minutes with tennis great Jimmy Connors.
Infamy: Admitted to using beer and marijuana as a young teen player.
Famous Relative: Mike Agassi, former Iranian Olympic boxer, father
Major Titles: U.S. Open, 1994; Wimbledon, 1992; semi-finalist, French Open, 1988; semi-finalist, U.S. Open, 1988

TROY KENNETH AIKMAN

Birthplace: Cerritos, CA
Birthdate: 11/21/66
Occupation: Football player
Education: Attended University of Oklahoma, UCLA
Signature: Quarterback for the Dallas Cowboys
Facts: Number one pick in the NFL's 1989 draft.

By age 27, he had won two Super Bowls, the youngest of only five quarterbacks in history to do so.

The Cowboys gave him the largest rookie contract in NFL history: six years for $11,037,000.

In the 1990 season, he was hit so often that he was dubbed "Troy Ache-man."
Infamy: In 1993 Aikman became the first player in football history to leave the NFL Pro Bowl early (he had a charity meeting early the next day). Paul Tagliabue fined him $10,000 for leaving after the third quarter.
Original Job: Baseball player
Relationship: Janine Turner
Major Award: Named MVP of the 1993 Super Bowl

JASON ALEXANDER

Real Name: Jay Scott Greenspan
Birthplace: Newark, NJ
Birthdate: 9/23/59
Occupation: Actor
Education: Boston University
Debut: (Film) *The Burning,* 1981; (TV) *Senior Trip!,* 1981
Signature: *Seinfeld*
Facts: *Seinfeld* creator Larry David modeled the George character after himself.
Marriage: Daena E. Title
Child: Gabriel
Major Awards: Tony, Best Actor, *Jerome Robbins' Broadway,* 1989; Grammy, Best Cast Show Album, *Jerome Robbins' Broadway* (with others), 1989
Quote: "I started losing my hair when I was a wee kid of 16."

TIM ALLEN

Birthplace: Denver, CO
Birthdate: 6/13/53
Occupation: Comedian, actor
Education: Western Michigan University
Debut: (TV) *Showtime Comedy Club All-Stars II*
Signature: *Home Improvement*
Facts: Has nine brothers and sisters.

His personal staff did not submit his name to the Academy of Television Arts and Sciences by the 1994 deadline, and so he could not be considered for an Emmy (actors are responsible for submitting their own names).

Appeared in Mr. Goodwrench commercials.
Infamy: He served 28 months in jail for the attempted dealing of cocaine in 1978.
Original Job: Creative director for an advertising agency

WOODY ALLEN

Real Name: Allen Stewart Konigsberg; legal name Heywood Allen
Birthplace: Brooklyn, NY
Birthdate: 12/1/35
Occupation: Actor, director, writer
Education: Attended NYU, CCNY
Debut: (Film) *What's New Pussycat?,* 1965
Signature: *Annie Hall,* 1977
Facts: Plays clarinet every Monday night at Michael's Pub in Manhattan. Missed the Academy Awards ceremony for *Annie Hall* because it was on a Monday night.

Among his many neuroses: takes his temperature every two hours during the day, won't take showers if the drain is in the middle.

Was suspended from New York University for inattention to his work.
Infamy: After details became known of his affair with Soon-Yi, Mia Farrow's oldest adopted daughter, Farrow accused him of sexual abuse of her younger children. In 1993, he was denied custody but retained visitation rights of their adopted children, Dylan and Moses, and biological son, Satchel.
Original Job: During high school, he supplied comic snippets to newspaper columnists Walter Winchell and Earl Wilson. He later became a hired gag-writer on a retainer of $25 a week.
Marriage: Louise Lasser (divorced)
Major Awards: Oscar, Best Director, *Annie Hall,* 1977; Oscar, Best Original Screenplay, *Annie Hall,* 1977; Oscar, Best Original Screenplay, *Hannah and Her Sisters,* 1986; Golden Globe, Best Screenplay, *The Purple Rose of Cairo,* 1986

TORI AMOS

Birthdate: 1964
Occupation: Singer, songwriter
Education: High school
Debut: (Album) *Y Kant Tori Read?,* 1988
Signature: "Crucify"
Facts: She started playing the piano by age three. At age five she won a scholarship to study piano in a conservatory in Baltimore but was kicked out by age 11 for refusing to practice.

Father was an evangelical preacher, a fact that figures heavily into her sex-laden lyrics in songs like "Leather" and "God."
Original Job: Piano player in Los Angeles lounges
Relationship: Eric Rose
Quote: "I have vivid memories

of being a prostitute in another life."

MAYA MARGUERITA ANGELOU

Real Name: Margueritte Annie Johnson
Birthplace: St. Louis, MO
Birthdate: 4/4/28
Occupation: Writer, actor, singer, dancer
Education: California Labor School
Debut: (Film) *Calypso Heatwave,* 1957
Signature: *I Know Why the Caged Bird Sings*
Facts: Nicknamed "Maya" by her brother, who called her "My" or "Mine."

At age seven, she was raped by her mother's boyfriend. Several days after her testimony at the trial, her assailant was found dead—killed by her uncles. She blamed herself for the death and did not speak for the next five years.

Tried to join the army in the late '40s, but was turned down after a security check revealed that the California Labor School was listed as subversive.

Infamy: In the late 1950s, she worked as a madam, managing two prostitutes in San Diego. Her guilty conscience caused her to quit after only a short stint.
Original Job: The first black—and the first female—streetcar conductor in San Francisco at age 16.
Marriages: Tosh Angelos (divorced), Vusumzi Make
Major Award: Grammy, Best Spoken Word Recording, *On the Pulse of Morning,* 1993

GIORGIO ARMANI

Birthplace: Piacenza, Italy
Birthdate: 7/11/34
Occupation: Fashion designer
Facts: Entered medical school but after two years decided to join the military.

Designed uniforms for the Italian Air Force (1980).

Original Job: Medical Assistant for Italian military, window dresser in a Milan department store
Major Awards: Neiman-Marcus Award, Distinguished Service in the Field of Fashion, 1979; Cutty Sark Award, Outstanding International Designer, 1981

TOM ARNOLD

Birthplace: Ottumwa, IA
Birthdate: 3/6/59
Occupation: Actor
Education: Attended Indian Hills Community College in Ottumwa, Iowa
Debut: (TV) *Roseanne*
Signature: Husband of Roseanne
Facts: The 26,000 square foot, 30-room house that the Arnolds shared is the largest residence in Iowa.

Converted to Judaism when he married Roseanne.

Infamy: He was once arrested for urinating in public on a McDonald's restaurant.

He was a cocaine addict when Roseanne recruited him to work on her show.

Original Job: Ham packer at a Hormel plant, box stacker, bartender, bouncer
Marriage: Roseanne Barr (separated)

DAN AYKROYD

Birthplace: Ottawa, Canada
Birthdate: 7/1/52
Occupation: Actor, writer
Education: Attended Carleton University
Debut: (TV) *Saturday Night Live,* 1975; (Film) *1941,* 1979
Signature: *Ghostbusters*
Facts: His grandfather was a Royal Canadian Mountie.

Was expelled for delinquency from St. Pius X Preparatory Seminary.

Had a cameo role in *Indiana Jones and the Temple of Doom,* 1984.

A police buff, he rides an Ontario provincial police motorcycle, collects police badges, sometimes rides shotgun with detectives in squad cars, and owns, in partnership with several Toronto police officers, a Toronto bar called Crooks.

He is very interested in the supernatural and has an extensive collection of books on the subject. He admits, "I've never seen a full apparition, but I once saw what could be termed ectoplasmic light, and that scared the hell out of me."

Original Job: Stand-up comedian.
Marriage: Maureen Lewis (divorced), Donna Dixon
Children: Oscar, Mark, Lloyd
Major Award: Emmy, Best Writing in a Comedy, Variety, or Music Series, *Saturday Night Live,* 1977

KATHY BAKER

Birthplace: Midland, TX
Birthdate: 6/8/50
Occupation: Actor
Education: University of California at Berkeley
Debut: (Film) *The Right Stuff,* 1983
Facts: Raised in a Quaker household.

Left acting at one point because did not feel happy doing violent '70s theater.

Original Job: Trained in Paris as a Cordon Bleu cook, dubbed French films for the American market
Major Awards: Emmy, Best Actress in a Drama Series, *Picket Fences,* 1993; Golden Globe, Best Actress in a Drama Series, *Picket Fences,* 1994

SCOTT BAKULA

Birthplace: St. Louis, MO
Birthdate: 10/9/55
Occupation: Actor
Education: Attended University of Kansas
Debut: (TV) *Gung Ho,* 1986; (Film) *Sibling Rivalry,* 1990 ; (Stage) *Marilyn: An American Fable,* 1983
Signature: *Quantum Leap*
Facts: The *Quantum Leap* album on Crescendo Records features songs that Bakula performed during the five-year run of the TV series.

Was nominated for a Tony award in 1988 for the Broadway musical *Romance/Romance.*

Marriage: Krista
Child: Chelsy
Major Award: Golden Globe, Best Actor in a Drama Series, *Quantum Leap,* 1992

ALEC BALDWIN

Real Name: Alexander Rae Baldwin III
Birthplace: Massapequa, NY
Birthdate: 4/3/58
Occupation: Actor
Education: NYU, attended Lee Strasberg Theatre Institute
Debut: (TV) *The Doctors,* early '80s
Signature: *The Hunt for Red October*
Facts: He is not naturally tall, dark, and handsome—he dyes his fair hair black.

Originally wanted to be a lawyer.

Was engaged to Janine Turner (*Northern Exposure*); she had the wedding dress ready and the invitations were sent out when they broke up.

Original Job: Waiter and doorman at Studio 54
Marriage: Kim Basinger
Famous Relatives: William Baldwin, actor, brother; Stephen Baldwin, actor, brother; Daniel Baldwin, actor, brother

STEPHEN BALDWIN

Birthplace: Massapequa, NY
Birthdate: 1966
Occupation: Actor
Debut: (TV) *The Prodigious Hickey,* 1987; (Film) *Homeboy,* 1988
Signature: *Threesome*
Facts: Worked as a Calvin Klein model before he started acting.

He played the teenage "Buffalo Bill" Cody on the TV series *The Young Riders,* 1989–92.

Older sister Elizabeth is the head of his fan club.

Original Job: Worked in a Manhattan pizza parlor when he was discovered by an agent
Marriage: Kennya
Child: Alaia
Famous Relatives: Alec Baldwin, actor, brother; William Baldwin, actor, brother; Daniel Baldwin, actor, brother

WILLIAM BALDWIN

Birthplace: Massapequa, NY
Birthdate: 1963
Occupation: Actor
Education: State University of New York at Binghamton
Debut: (Film) *Born on the Fourth of July,* 1989
Signature: *Backdraft*
Facts: Original ambition was to play professional baseball with the New York Yankees.

In one day he went from an

acting agent to a modeling agent and then to a photographer and did a modeling shoot for Calvin Klein Jeans. Claims he lived for a year on the money he made on that one shoot.
Original Job: Worked for a year on Capitol Hill as an aide to Rep. Thomas Downey (D., N.Y.)
Relationship: Chynna Phillips
Famous Relatives: Alec Baldwin, actor, brother; Stephen Baldwin, actor, brother; Daniel Baldwin, actor, brother
Quote: "I can honestly say that if Alec had never gone into the business, I wouldn't be an actor."

ANTONIO BANDERAS

Birthplace: Málaga, Spain
Birthdate: 1960
Occupation: Actor
Education: School of Dramatic Art, Málaga, Spain
Debut: (Stage) *Los Tarantos,* 1981; (Film) *Labyrinth of Passion,* 1982
Signature: *Philadelphia*
Facts: Modeled for Ralph Lauren and Gucci.

Would love to play the Hunchback of Notre Dame, but thinks he won't be able to because of his good looks.
Original Job: Model, waiter
Marriage: Ana Leza
Quote: "I thought to myself, 'Oh my God. How disgusting.' Then I went to the first rehearsal and it was . . . so easy. I didn't lose my fingers, my ear didn't fall down. Nothing happens if you're sure of who you are." (On his first kiss in a role as a homosexual, in the 1988 Almodóvar movie *Law of Desire.*)

CLIVE BARKER

Birthplace: Liverpool, England
Birthdate: 1952
Occupation: Author
Education: University of Liverpool
Signature: *The Inhuman Condition*
Facts: As a child in Liverpool, heard tales of hook-handed escaped lunatic.

Believes in ghosts, banshees, and fairies.

Attended autopsies to see what it felt like to hold a human brain.
Original Job: Illustrator, painter, actor

ELLEN BARKIN

Birthplace: Bronx, NY
Birthdate: 4/16/54
Occupation: Actor
Education: High School of the Performing Arts, Hunter College
Debut: (Film) *Diner,* 1982
Signature: *Sea of Love*
Facts: At New York's High School of the Performing Arts, she was often passed over for roles because she wasn't considered pretty enough.
Original Job: Waitress
Marriage: Gabriel Byrne (separated)
Child: Romy Marion

CHARLES BARKLEY

Birthplace: Leeds, AL
Birthdate: 2/20/63
Occupation: Basketball player
Education: Attended Auburn University
Facts: He is the shortest player (6' 6") ever to lead the NBA in rebounding.

At birth, he was anemic and weighed only six pounds, twelve ounces. Doctors administered blood transfusions to keep him alive.

During his college years, he battled a weight problem, at one point exceeding 300 pounds. Schoolmates nicknamed him "Boy Gorge," "The Round Mound of Rebound," and "The Leaning Tower of Pizza."

Turned down offers of over $500,000 from trade shows because he believes that fans should not have to pay for autographs.
Infamy: During the 1989–90 season, he racked up nearly $36,000 in fines, setting an NBA record. His misconduct included spitting on a referee, making a bet with another player, and fighting.

In March 1991 Barkley spit at a fan yelling racial epithets at him, but missed and hit an eight-year-old girl instead.
Marriage: Maureen

DREW BARRYMORE

Real Name: Andrew Barrymore
Birthplace: Los Angeles, CA
Birthdate: 2/22/75
Occupation: Actor
Education: High school dropout
Debut: (Film) *Altered States,* 1980
Signature: *E.T,. the Extra-Terrestrial*
Facts: Starred in a TV commercial for Gainsburgers when she was 11 months old.

After drug rehabilitation, she starred in *Fifteen and Getting Straight* (1989), a TV movie about drug abuse, and wrote her own autobiography, *Little Lost Girl,* at age 14 to clear the air. Credits musician David Crosby for helping her get over drugs.
Infamy: Began drinking at age nine and started taking drugs at 10.

In 1992 posed nude for *Interview* magazine.
Marriage: Jeremy Thomas (divorced)
Famous Relatives: John Barrymore Jr., actor and director, father; Lionel Barrymore, actor, great-uncle; John Barrymore Sr., actor, grandfather

KIM BASINGER

Birthplace: Athens, GA
Birthdate: 12/8/53
Occupation: Actor
Education: Attended University of Georgia
Debut: (Film) *Hard Country,* 1981
Signature: *9 1/2 Weeks*
Facts: Filed for bankruptcy in May 1993 after a $8.1 million verdict was rendered against her in favor of Main Line Pictures, after she dropped out of the movie *Boxing Helena.* Had to limit her monthly living expenses to $10,000 under bankruptcy plan.

Developed agoraphobia while a model. Threw her modeling portfolio off the Brooklyn Bridge.

Was involved with Prince before marrying Alec Baldwin.

Bought Braselton, a town in Georgia, for $20 million in 1989, with plans to develop it into a tourist attraction.
Infamy: In 1983, she appeared in an eight-page *Playboy* spread.
Original Job: Breck shampoo model, as her mother had been, then a Ford model. Pursued a singing career under the nom-de-chant Chelsea.
Marriages: Ron Britton (divorced), Alec Baldwin

ANGELA BASSETT

Birthplace: New York, NY
Birthdate: 8/16/58
Occupation: Actor
Education: Yale University
Debut: (Film) *FX,* 1986
Signature: *What's Love Got To Do With It?*
Facts: Helped integrate her high school, where she was on the honor roll and the cheerleading squad. Went to college on a scholarship.
Original Job: Hair stylist, photo researcher at *US News and World Report*
Major Award: Golden Globe, Best Actress in a Comedy or Musical, *What's Love Got to Do With It,* 1994

KATHY BATES

Real Name: Kathleen Doyle
Birthplace: Memphis, TN
Birthdate: 6/28/48
Occupation: Actor
Education: Southern Methodist University
Debut: (Film) *Taking Off,* 1971; (TV) *The Love Boat,* 1977; (Stage) *Casserole,* 1975
Signature: *Misery*
Facts: She lost the screen roles of characters she originated on the stage (Frankie in *Frankie and Johnny in the Claire de Lune* and Lenny McGrath in *Crimes of the Heart*) to Michelle Pfeiffer and Diane Keaton.

Terrence McNally created the character Frankie (in *Frankie and Johnny in the Claire de Lune*) with her in mind.
Original Job: Singing waitress in the Catskills, cashier in the gift shop of Museum of Modern Art in New York
Marriage: Tony Campisi (engaged)
Major Award: Oscar, Best Actress, *Misery,* 1990; Golden Globe, Best Actress in a Drama, *Misery,* 1990

WARREN BEATTY

Real Name: Henry Warren Beaty
Birthplace: Richmond, VA

Birthdate: 3/30/37
Occupation: Actor, producer, director, screenwriter
Education: Attended Northwestern University
Debut: (Film) *Splendor in the Grass,* 1961
Signature: *Shampoo*
Facts: Turned down football scholarships to go to drama school.

Is famed for his reluctance to do interviews and his tendency to pause for a minute or more before giving a yes or no answer.

Original Job: Bricklayer, dishwasher, construction worker, piano player
Marriage: Annette Bening
Children: Kathlyn, son (not named at press time)
Famous Relative: Shirley MacLaine, actor, sister
Major Awards: Golden Globe, Most Promising Newcomer—Male, 1962; Golden Globe, Best Actor in a Comedy, *Heaven Can Wait,* 1979; Oscar, Best Director, *Reds,* 1981; Golden Globe, Best Director, *Reds,* 1982
Quote: "For me, the highest level of sexual excitement is in a monogamous relationship."

BECK

Real Name: Beck Hansen
Birthplace: Los Angeles, CA
Birthdate: 1971
Occupation: Singer, songwriter
Education: High school dropout
Debut: (Album) *Mellow Gold,* 1993
Signature: "Loser"
Facts: Although he claims to have never watched the channel, he's written a song called "MTV Makes Me Want To Smoke Crack."

In 1993 he was living in a rat-infested shed behind a house, earning four dollars an hour.

Described *Mellow Gold* as "a satanic K-Tel record that's been found in a trash dumpster."

Original Job: Odd jobs, including painting signs, moving refrigerators and furniture, blowing leaves, taking ID photos at a New York YMCA, checking jackets at a Greenwich Village bookstore, selling hot dogs at children's birthday parties, and clerking in a video store.
Famous Relatives: Bibbe Hansen, guitarist, mother; Al Hansen, artist, grandfather

SHARI BELAFONTE

Birthplace: New York, NY
Birthdate: 9/22/54
Occupation: Actor
Education: Carnegie-Mellon University
Debut: (Film) *If You Could See What I Hear,* 1982
Signature: *Hotel*
Facts: As a model, appeared on more than 200 magazine covers and in numerous TV commercials.

Made guest appearances on *Love Boat, Hart to Hart, Matt Houston, Code Red,* and numerous other TV shows.

Original Job: Publicist's assistant at Hanna Barbera Productions, model
Marriages: Robert Harper (divorced), Sam Behrens
Famous Relative: Harry Belafonte, singer and actor, father

ANNETTE BENING

Birthplace: Topeka, KS
Birthdate: 5/29/58
Occupation: Actor
Education: Mesa College, San Francisco State University; American Conservatory Theater, San Francisco
Debut: (Stage) *Coastal Disturbances,* 1986; (Film) *The Great Outdoors,* 1988
Signature: *The Grifters*
Fact: Originally cast as Catwoman in *Batman Returns,* she got pregnant and lost the role to Michelle Pfeiffer.
Original Job: Cook on a charter boat for a year, to pay for college
Marriages: Steve White (divorced), Warren Beatty
Children: Kathlyn, son (not named at press time)

TONY BENNETT

Real Name: Anthony Dominick Benedetto
Birthplace: Astoria, NY
Birthdate: 8/3/26
Occupation: Singer
Education: Attended Manhattan's School of Industrial Art
Debut: (Album) *The Boulevard of Broken Dreams,* 1950
Signature: "I Left My Heart in San Francisco"
Facts: Marched with Martin Luther King Jr. in Selma in 1965 at the urging of Harry Belafonte.

Sang under the name Joe Bari until Bob Hope, who invited him to sing at his Paramount Theater show in 1950, introduced him as Tony Bennett.

Served two years as an infantryman in Europe during World War II.

Original Job: Singing waiter
Marriages: Patricia Beech (divorced), Sandra Grant (divorced)
Children: Danny, Daegal, Joanna, Antonia
Major Awards: Grammy, Best Pop Vocal—Male, "I Left My Heart in San Francisco," 1962; Grammy, Record of the Year, "I Left My Heart in San Francisco," 1962

CANDICE BERGEN

Birthplace: Beverly Hills, CA
Birthdate: 5/9/46
Occupation: Actor, photojournalist
Education: Attended University of Pennsylvania
Debut: (Film) *The Group,* 1966
Signature: *Murphy Brown*
Facts: As a child, her father's puppet, Charlie McCarthy, had a bigger bedroom and more clothes than she did.

As a photojournalist, was published in *Life* and *Playboy.*

Wrote a play, *The Freezer,* which is included in *Best Short Plays of 1968.*

Original Job: Model
Marriage: Louis Malle
Child: Chloe
Famous Relative: Edgar Bergen, ventriloquist, father
Major Awards: Emmy, Best Actress in a Comedy Series, *Murphy Brown,* 1989, 1990, 1992; Golden Globe, Best Actress in a Comedy Series, *Murphy Brown,* 1989, 1992

HALLE BERRY

Birthplace: Cleveland, OH
Birthdate: 8/14/68
Occupation: Actor
Debut: (TV) *Living Dolls,* 1989
Signature: *Boomerang*
Facts: Elected prom queen her senior year in high school, she was accused of stuffing the ballot box. Was forced to share the title with a "white, blond, blue-eyed, all-American girl."

Lost eighty percent of the hearing in her left ear from an injury sustained from a physically abusive lover. (She rarely wears her hearing aid.)

Her husband's name is tattooed on her rear end.

Learned she was a diabetic when she collapsed in a coma while filming the TV series *Living Dolls.*

She was first runner-up in the 1986 Miss USA pageant.

Played crackhead in Spike Lee's *Jungle Fever* (1991) and did not bathe for days to prepare for the role.

Infamy: Sued by a Chicago dentist (and former boyfriend) who claims she never repaid the $80,000 she borrowed from him.
Original Job: Model
Marriage: David Justice

MAYIM BIALIK

Birthdate: 12/12/75
Occupation: Actor
Debut: (Film) *Pumpkinhead,* 1988
Signature: *Blossom*
Facts: Started ballet at age four, piano at age six, started going on auditions by age 11, and by age 13 she was in her first major movie, *Beaches.*

Accepted into both Harvard and Yale, she deferred her admission to work on *Blossom.*

Once played the conch shell on stage with the Violent Femmes.

JOSIE BISSETT

Birthplace: Seattle, WA
Birthdate: 10/5/69
Occupation: Actor
Debut: (Film) *Desire,* 1989
Signature: *Melrose Place*
Facts: Appeared in the TV miniseries based on Danielle Steel's book *Secrets.*

Played recurring role of Cara on *The Hogan Family,* 1990–91.

Infamy: As an unknown, starred in *Desire,* an Italian exploitation film about an American pianist who seeks

enrollment in a prestigious music school in Venice. Bissett appears extensively in the nude and in simulated sex scenes.
Original Job: Model
Marriage: Rob Estes

CLINT BLACK

Birthplace: Long Branch, NJ
Birthdate: 2/4/62
Occupation: Singer, songwriter
Education: High school
Debut: (Album) *Killin' Time*, 1989
Signature: "Killin' Time"
Facts: He was the first country artist since Freddy Fender to reach Billboard #1 with his first charted single.

Recorded a R&B record with the Pointer sisters, who were surprised at his ability to sing in this genre.

Appeared in the 1994 movie *Maverick*.
Infamy: In 1992 Black fired his manager of five years, Bill Ham, and hired his wife's mother as his personal assistant. Ham filed a breach of contract suit in Los Angeles Superior Court, and Black filed a $2 million countersuit.
Original Job: Construction worker
Marriage: Lisa Hartman

STEVEN BOCHCO

Birthplace: New York, NY
Birthdate: 12/16/43
Occupation: Producer, screenwriter
Education: Carnegie Institute of Technology
Debut: (TV) *A Fade To Black*, 1967
Signature: *NYPD Blue*
Facts: *Hill Street Blues* won twenty-six Emmys.

His father, Rudolph Bochco, was a child prodigy violinist who later played with orchestras in Broadway shows and with leading artists at Carnegie Hall.

Wrote material for *Ironside* and was the story editor for *Columbo*.

Turned down the presidency of CBS Entertainment in 1987.
Infamy: *L.A. Law* co-creator Terry Louise Fisher filed a $50 million dollar breach of contract suit against him and Fox in 1978, after she was removed from the show at his request. The case was settled out of court.
Original Job: Assistant to the head of the story department at Universal Studios
Marriage: Barbara Bosson
Children: Jeffrie, Melissa
Famous Relative: Alan Rachins, actor, brother-in-law
Major Awards: Emmy, Outstanding Drama Series, *Hill Street Blues*, 1981, 1982, 1983, 1984; Emmy, Outstanding Drama Series, *L.A. Law*, 1987, 1989, 1990, 1991; George Foster Peabody Award; Edgar Allen Poe Award

MICHAEL BOLTON

Real Name: Michael Bolotin
Birthplace: New Haven, CT
Birthdate: 2/26/53
Occupation: Singer, songwriter
Education: High school dropout
Debut: Album (with his band, Blackjack): *Blackjack*, 1979
Album (solo): *Michael Bolton*, 1983
Facts: Wrote ballads and love songs for other artists, including Laura Branigan, Cher, The Pointer Sisters, Barbra Streisand.

After the breakup of his band, Blackjack, he began recording solo in 1983.

In the mid 1980s, he was a regular opening act for metal acts such as Ozzy Osbourne and Krokus.

A research library in the New York Medical College was dedicated to him in 1993 for his work as honorary chairman of This Close for Cancer Research.
Infamy: After a two-week trial (1994), a jury ruled that Bolton's "Love Is a Wonderful Thing" is remarkably similar to the Isley Brothers song "Love Is a Wonderful Thing."
Marriages: Maureen McGuire (divorced), Nicollette Sheridan (relationship)
Children: Isa, Holly, Taryn
Major Awards: Grammy, Best Pop Vocal—Male, "How Am I Supposed to Live Without You," 1989; Grammy, Best Pop Vocal—Male, "When a Man Loves a Woman," 1991; American Music Awards, Favorite Male Vocalist, 1992; American Music Awards, Favorite Pop/Rock Album, 1992

JON BON JOVI

Real Name: John Bongiovi
Birthplace: Sayreville, NJ
Birthdate: 5/2/62
Occupation: Singer, songwriter
Education: High school
Debut: (Album) *Bon Jovi*, 1984
Signature: Bon Jovi
Facts: Polygram executives gave the band a contract with the following conditions: John Bongiovi would become Jon Bon Jovi, and only he would be given a contract. The other four members of the band would become Jon Bon Jovi's employees.

His first solo album, *Blaze of Glory* (1990), was "written for and inspired by" the film *Young Guns II*, in which he had a cameo role.

Title of Bon Jovi's first album, *7800° Fahrenheit*, refers to the temperature of an exploding volcano.
Infamy: Had a legal dispute with cousin Tony Bongiovi, who owned the Record Plant, a New York City recording studio, over the extent to which Tony had aided his cousin's career. In 1984, Tony brought a lawsuit against Bon Jovi, the outcome of which gave him a producer's credit, a fee, royalties from Bon Jovi's first album, a cash award, and a one percent royalty from the group's next two albums.
Original Job: Floor sweeper at the Record Plant
Marriage: Dorothea Hurley
Major Awards: Golden Globe, Best Song, "Blaze of Glory," 1991; American Music Awards, Best Pop/Rock Single, "Blaze of Glory," 1991

BONO

Real Name: Paul Hewson
Birthplace: Dublin, Ireland
Birthdate: 5/10/60
Occupation: Singer, songwriter
Education: High school
Debut: EP (with U2): *U2:3*, 1979
Signature: U2
Facts: Got his nickname from a billboard advertising Bono Vox, a hearing aid retailer.

In November 1987, they opened for themselves at the L.A. Coliseum as the country-rock group The Dalton Brothers.
Infamy: Was the first winner in Grammy history to say "f—" during its live telecast (1994).
Marriage: Alisa
Children: Eve, Jordan
Major Awards: Grammy, Album of the Year, *The Joshua Tree*, 1987; Grammy, Best Rock Performance—Duo or Group, *The Joshua Tree*, 1987; Grammy, Best Video—Long Form, *Where the Streets Have No Name*, 1988; Grammy, Best Rock Performance—Duo or Group, "Desire," 1988; Grammy, Best Rock Performance—Duo or Group, *Achtung Baby*, 1992; Grammy, Best Alternative Performance, *Zooropa*, 1993

KENNETH BRANAGH

Birthplace: Belfast, Northern Ireland
Birthdate: 12/10/60
Occupation: Actor, director
Education: Attended the Royal Academy of Dramatic Arts
Debut: (Stage) *Another Country*, 1982
Signature: *Henry V*
Facts: The first installment of Branagh's autobiography, *Beginning*, is already in a paperback.

Grew up in poverty in the shadow of a tobacco factory in Belfast.

Co-founded England's Renaissance Theater Company.

Was nominated for a Best Actor Academy Award for *Henry V* but lost to Daniel Day-Lewis for his role in *My Left Foot*.
Marriage: Emma Thompson

MARLON BRANDO

Birthplace: Omaha, NE
Birthdate: 4/3/24
Occupation: Actor
Education: Expelled from Shattuck Military Academy, attended New School for Social Research
Debut: (Stage) *I Remember Mama*, 1944; (Film) *The Men*, 1950

Signature: *The Godfather*
Fact: Exiled himself on his private island, Tetiaroa, near Tahiti, which he bought after filming *Mutiny on the Bounty* there in 1960.
Infamy: Son Christian killed daughter Cheyenne's boyfriend and is serving time for manslaughter (1990).
Original Job: Tile fitter, elevator operator
Marriages: Anna Kashfi (divorced), Movita Castenada (annulled), Tarita Teripia
Children: Christian Devi, Miko, Rebecca, Simon Tehotu, Cheyenne, Ninna Priscilla
Major Awards: Oscar, Best Actor, *On the Waterfront,* 1955; Golden Globe, Best Actor, *On the Waterfront,* 1955; Oscar, Best Actor, *The Godfather,* 1972; Golden Globe, Best Actor, *The Godfather,* 1973; Emmy, Best Supporting Actor in a Limited Series, *Roots,* 1979; Golden Globe, World Film Favorite—Male, 1956, 1973, 1974

TONI BRAXTON

Birthplace: Severn, MD
Birthdate: 1968
Occupation: Singer
Education: Attended Bowie State University
Fact: Learned to sing in a church choir. Her three sisters sing backup vocals on her albums. She and her sisters were only allowed to listen to gospel music, but she would "sneak into empty rooms to watch Soul Train."
Major Awards: Grammy, Best New Artist, 1993; Grammy, Best R&B Vocal—Female, "Another Sad Love Song," 1993

BEAU BRIDGES

Real Name: Lloyd Vernet Bridges III
Birthplace: Los Angeles, CA
Birthdate: 12/9/41
Occupation: Actor, director
Education: Attended UCLA; University of Hawaii
Debut: (Film) *Force of Evil,* 1948; (TV) *Sea Hunt,* 1957; (Stage) *Where's Daddy,* 1966
Signature: *The Fabulous Baker Boys*
Facts: Nicknamed after Ashley Wilkes's son in the classic film *Gone with the Wind.*

Although only 5'9" played basketball as a freshman at UCLA.
Marriages: Juli Bridges (divorced), Wendy Pierce
Children: Jordan, Emily, Dylan, Casey (adopted)
Famous Relatives: Lloyd Bridges, actor, father; Jeff Bridges, actor, brother.
Major Awards: Emmy, Best Actor in a Made-for-TV Movie, *Without Warning—The James Brady Story,* 1992; Golden Globe, Best Actor in a Made-for-TV Movie, *Without Warning—The James Brady Story,* 1992; Emmy, Best Supporting Actor in a Miniseries, *The Positively True Adventures of the Alleged Texas Cheerleader–Murdering Mom,* 1993; Golden Globe, Best Supporting Actor in a Miniseries, *The Positively True Adventures of the Alleged Texas Cheerleader–Murdering Mom,* 1993

JEFF BRIDGES

Birthplace: Los Angeles, CA
Birthdate: 12/4/49
Occupation: Actor
Education: High school, Herbert Berghof Studio
Debut: (TV) *Sea Hunt,* 1957; (Film) *The Company She Keeps,* 1950
Signature: *The Fabulous Baker Boys*
Facts: Joined the Coast Guard Reserves in 1968 to avoid the draft.

At age 16, he wrote a song included on the soundtrack of the 1969 film *John and Mary,* which starred Dustin Hoffman and Mia Farrow, and sold two compositions to Quincy Jones. To date, he has written over 200 songs.
Infamy: In high school, developed a dependency on marijuana. He joined DAWN (Developing Adolescents Without Narcotics) and kicked the habit.
Marriage: Susan Gaston, photographer
Children: Isabelle, Jessica, Hayley
Famous Relatives: Lloyd Bridges, actor, father; Beau Bridges, actor, brother

CHRISTIE BRINKLEY

Birthplace: Malibu, CA
Birthdate: 2/2/54
Occupation: Supermodel
Education: Attended UCLA
Debut: (Film) *National Lampoon's Vacation,* 1983
Signature: Cover Girl Cosmetics model
Facts: An avid Francophile, Brinkley transferred from her local high school to the Lycée Français in Los Angeles. She later dropped out of college and worked at odd jobs selling ice cream, clothes, and plants to earn money for a ticket to Paris.

Designed the cover for Billy Joel's *River of Dreams* album.
Original Job: Painter
Marriages: Jean Francois Allaux (divorced), Billy Joel (divorced)
Famous Relative: Don Brinkley, scriptwriter, producer, father
Child: Alexa Ray

MATTHEW BRODERICK

Birthplace: New York, NY
Birthdate: 3/21/62
Occupation: Actor
Debut: (Stage) *Torch Song Trilogy,* 1982; (Film) *Max Dugan Returns,* 1983
Signature: *Ferris Bueller's Day Off*
Fact: Was heavily influenced by father James Broderick, who played the father in the TV series *Family* and died of cancer in 1982.
Infamy: While on vacation in Northern Ireland in 1987 with his then-girlfriend, actress Jennifer Grey, Broderick suffered a broken leg when the car he was driving collided with another automobile, killing its two occupants. Broderick was acquitted of one count of manslaughter and reckless driving.
Relationship: Sarah Jessica Parker
Famous Relative: James Broderick, character actor, father
Major Award: Tony, Best Supporting Actor, *Brighton Beach Memoirs,* 1983

GARTH BROOKS

Real Name: Troyal Garth Brooks
Birthplace: Tulsa, OK
Birthdate: 2/7/62
Occupation: Singer, songwriter
Education: Oklahoma State University
Debut: (Album) *Garth Brooks,* 1989
Signature: *Ropin' the Wind*
Facts: At age 28, Garth became the youngest member of Nashville's Grand Ole Opry in 1990.

Brooks met his future wife while working as a bouncer. (He threw her out for fighting.)

In 1991, *Ropin' the Wind* became the first country album ever to reach No. 1 on the *Billboard* pop chart.

The video for "The Thunder Rolls," about a cheating husband shot by his battered wife after coming home drunk, was banned Country Music Television and the Nashville Network. Thousands of shelters for battered women in America used the video in group counseling sessions.

Brooks half-sister is his bassist, his brother handles the books, and a college roommate is one of his guitarists.
Original Job: Bouncer in a nightclub
Marriage: Sandy Mahr
Child: Taylor Mayne Pearl
Famous Relative: Colleen Carroll, singer, mother
Major Award: Grammy, Best Country Vocal—Male, *Ropin' the Wind,* 1991

JAMES L. BROOKS

Birthplace: North Bergen, NJ
Birthdate: 5/9/40
Occupation: Producer, director, actor, screenwriter
Education: Attended New York University
Debut: (TV) *Room 222,* 1969; (Film) *Starting Over,* 1979
Signature: Creator of *The Mary Tyler Moore Show* and others
Facts: Founded Gracie Films, which produces *The Simpsons,* in 1984.

With fellow writer Allan Burns, created *The Mary Tyler Moore Show* in 1970.

Original Job: Copyboy for CBS News
Marriages: Marianne Catherine Morrissey (divorced), Holly Beth Holmberg
Children: Amy Lorraine, Chloe, Cooper
Major Awards: Emmy, Best Writing in a Comedy Series, *The Mary Tyler Moore Show,* 1971, 1977; Emmy, Best Comedy Series, *The Mary Tyler Moore Show,* 1975, 1976, 1977; Emmy, Best Comedy Series, *Taxi,* 1979, 1980, 1981; Emmy, Outstanding Variety, Music, or Comedy Program, *The Tracey Ullman Show,* 1989; Emmy, Outstanding Animated Program, *The Simpsons,* 1990, 1991; Oscar, Best Director, *Terms of Endearment,* 1983; Oscar, Best Adapted Screenplay, *Terms of Endearment,* 1984; Golden Globe, Best Adapted Screenplay, *Terms of Endearment,* 1984

MEL BROOKS

Real Name: Melvin Kaminski
Birthplace: Brooklyn, NY
Birthdate: 6/28/26
Occupation: Actor, writer, director, producer
Education: Attended Boston College
Debut: (Stage) *Broadway Revue,* 1949; (TV) *Your Show of Shows,* 1950
Signature: *Blazing Saddles*
Facts: Fought in Battle of the Bulge during World War II.

Co-creator of the TV series *Get Smart.*

Original Job: Drummer
Marriages: Florence Baum (divorced), Anne Bancroft
Children: Nicholas, Edward, Maximillian
Major Awards: Emmy, Writing in a Variety or Music Program, *Howard Morris Special,* 1967; Oscar, Best Original Screenplay, *The Producers,* 1968

PIERCE BROSNAN

Birthplace: Navan, County Meath, Ireland
Birthdate: 5/16/52
Occupation: Actor
Debut: (Film) *The Mirror Crack'd,* 1980; (TV) *Remington Steel,* 1982; (Stage) *Wait Until Dark,* 1976
Signature: *Remington Steele*
Facts: Wife, Cassandra (best known for playing Countess Lisl in *For Your Eyes Only,* 1981), introduced Brosnan to Albert Broccoli, producer of the 007 series. Brosnan almost replaced Roger Moore as James Bond, but couldn't get out of his contract with NBC's *Remington Steele.*

Ran away with the circus as a fire eater in his teens.

Original Job: Commercial artist
Marriage: Cassandra Harris (deceased)
Children: Charlotte, Christoper, Sean

BOBBY BROWN

Birthplace: Boston, MA
Birthdate: 2/5/69
Occupation: Singer, dancer
Debut: Album (solo): *King of Stage,* 1987; (Film) *Ghostbusters II,* 1989
Signature: "My Prerogative"
Facts: In 1989, became the first teenager since Stevie Wonder to have an album (*Don't Be Cruel)* at the top of the *Billboard* charts.

Turned away from life on the street in 1980, after he witnessed the fatal stabbing of his best friend by another youth.

Made his unofficial debut at age three, when his mother put him up on stage during a James Brown concert.

His wedding reception cost $1 million and was attended by 800 guests.

Infamy: Fined $580 for lewdness on stage at a concert in Augusta, Georgia, 1993.

Brown was arrested at a 1989 Columbus, Georgia, concert for dancing suggestively with a woman he pulled from the audience, which violated a local ordinance "prohibiting the simulation of sexual intercourse" onstage.

Marriage: Whitney Houston
Children: Bobbi Kristina Brown and three children from previous relationships
Major Award: Grammy, Best R&B Vocal—Male, "Every Little Step," 1989

JACKSON BROWNE

Birthplace: Heidelberg, Germany
Birthdate: 10/9/48
Occupation: Singer, songwriter
Education: High school
Debut: (Album) *Jackson Browne,* 1972
Signature: "Tender is the Night"
Facts: Wanted to play the piano as a child, but his father was a Dixieland jazz fan and insisted that Jackson learn to play the trumpet.

Recorded with Tim Buckley and Nico in 1967 in New York City and was a member of Andy Warhol's entourage.

Co-wrote "Take It Easy" with Glenn Frey of the Eagles, which was their first hit single. Produced Warren Zevon's first album.

Albums reflect difficult phases in his life: his fourth record, *The Pretender* (1976), is associated with his first wife's suicide. The title song of *I'm Alive* seems to allude to his breakup with actress Daryl Hannah in 1992, after a rocky ten-year relationship.

Infamy: Accused of beating former long-time girlfriend Darryl Hannah.
Marriages: Phyllis Major (deceased), Lynne Sweeney (divorced)
Children: Ryan Daniel, Ethan Zane

PEABO BRYSON

Real Name: Robert Peabo Bryson
Birthplace: Greenville, SC
Birthdate: 4/13/51
Occupation: Singer
Debut: (Album) *Reaching for the Sky,* 1978
Signature: "Beauty and the Beast"
Facts: In February 1992, became the first artist to have three separate records ("A Whole New World," "We Kiss in a Shadow," "By the Time This Night Is Over") at the top of four different charts (Hot 100, Hot Adult Contemporary, Classical Crossover, Contemporary Jazz).

Brought up on a farm, Peabo was the oldest of four children. "I was taught to work hard—man, I could slop hogs and pick cotton with the best of them."

Original Job: Backup singer for Al Freeman and the Upsetters
Major Awards: Oscar, Best Song, "Beauty and the Beast," 1992; Grammy, Best Pop Performance—Duo or Group, "Beauty and the Beast," 1992; Grammy, Best Song Written Specifically for a Movie, "Beauty and the Beast," 1992; Oscar, Best Song, "A Whole New World" (with Regina Belle), 1993; Grammy, Best Pop Performance—Duo or Group, "A Whole New World" (with Regina Belle), 1993; Grammy, Song of the Year, "A Whole New World" (with Regina Belle), 1993

JIMMY BUFFETT

Birthplace: Pascagoula, MS
Birthdate: 12/25/46
Occupation: Singer, songwriter
Education: University of Southern Mississippi
Debut: (Album) *Down to Earth,* 1970
Signature: "Margaritaville"
Facts: Has chaired Florida's Save the Manatee Club since its inception in 1981. In 1992, sued the parent Florida Audubon Society for independent control of the club, arguing that the society was "too cozy" with many of the businesses he felt were polluters.

Wrote a children's book, *The Jolly Man,* with his eight-year-old daughter in 1987. Also wrote a novel, *Tales from Margaritaville* (1989).

In 1991, four Cuban exiles seeking political asylum swam to Buffett's Florida house. He handed them over to the authorities after offering them refreshments.

Original Job: Reviewer for *Billboard* magazine and freelance writer for *Inside Sports* and *Outside* magazines
Marriage: Jane Slagsvol

TIMOTHY BUSFIELD

Birthplace: Lansing, MI
Birthdate: 6/12/57
Occupation: Actor
Education: East Tennessee State University; Actor's Theatre of Louisville
Debut: (Stage) Richard III at Circle Rep.'s Young Playwrights Festival

Signature: *thirtysomething*
Facts: Busfield played Michael J. Fox's college buddy on *Family Ties* before joining the cast of *thirtysomething*.
Infamy: In March of 1993 a 17-year-old actress filed a civil suit against Busfield, accusing him of sexual assault. He denied the charges that he fondled the actress on the Minnesota set of his film, *Little Big League*.
Marriages: Radha Delmarter (divorced), Jennifer Meriwen
Children: Willy, Daisy, Samuel Clark
Major Award: Emmy, Best Supporting Actor in a Drama Series, *thirtysomething*, 1991

BRETT BUTLER

Birthplace: Montgomery, AL
Birthdate: 1/30/58
Occupation: Actor
Debut: (TV) *Dolly*, 1988
Signature: *Grace Under Fire*
Facts: Writes short stories and poetry in her spare time.

Was named after Lady Brett Ashley in Ernest Hemingway *The Sun Also Rises*.

Butler was discovered while working at the Lone Star Cafe Steak House in Georgia. A wealthy club owner asked her to figure a tip, and she responded "I can't believe you've got ten million dollars and your IQ matches your inseam." She was hired on the spot.
Original Job: Cocktail waitress
Marriages: Charles Wilson (divorced), Ken Ziegler

JOEY BUTTAFUOCO

Birthplace: Massapequa, NY
Birthdate: 1956
Occupation: Mechanic
Signature: Had an affair with Amy Fisher
Facts: On his first date with Mary Jo Buttafuoco in 1972, Joey took her to see *Deliverance*.

Owns a boat aptly named "Double Trouble," which he allegedly used for love trysts with Fisher.

In1988, entered a drug rehab program for cocaine abuse.
Infamy: In 1993, Joey was indicted for the statutory rape of Amy Fisher, sentenced to six months in prison, a $5,000 fine, and five years' probation.
Original Job: Mechanic at Complete Auto Body
Marriage: Mary Jo Buttafuoco
Children: Paul, Jessica

DAVID BYRNE

Birthplace: Dumbarton, Scotland
Birthdate: 5/14/52
Occupation: Singer, songwriter, director
Education: Attended Rhode Island School of Design
Debut: (Song) "Love Goes to Building on Fire," 1976
Signature: Talking Heads
Facts: Talking Heads' debut single was produced by Tony Bongiovi, uncle to Jon Bon Jovi.

In its first gig, the band opened for The Ramones.
Marriage: Adelle Lutz
Child: Malu.
Major Awards: Grammy, Best Album Package, *Speaking in Tongues* (with Talking Heads), 1983; Oscar, Best Original Film Score, *The Last Emperor* (with Ryuichi Sakamoto and Gong Su), 1988; Grammy, Best Original Film Score, *The Last Emperor* (with Ryuichi Sakamoto and Gong Su), 1988

NICOLAS CAGE

Real Name: Nicolas Coppola
Birthplace: Long Beach, CA
Birthdate: 1/7/64
Occupation: Actor
Education: High school dropout
Debut: (TV) *The Best of Times*, 1980; (Film) *Valley Girl*, 1983
Signature: *Raising Arizona*
Facts: Was expelled from elementary school.

Changed his last name to have an identity independent of his famous uncle. He assumed the name Cage in admiration of the avant-garde composer John Cage and comic-book character Luke Cage.

His method acting techniques have involved having wisdom teeth removed without Novocaine for his role as a wounded war veteran in *Birdy*, slashing his arm with a knife in *Racing with the Moon*, and eating a live cockroach for *Vampire's Kiss*.
Child: Weston (by ex-girlfriend Christina Fulton).
Famous Relatives: Francis Ford Coppola, director, uncle; Talia Shire, actor, aunt

DEAN CAIN

Birthplace: Mt. Clemens, MI
Birthdate: 7/31/66
Occupation: Actor
Education: Princeton University
Debut: (TV) *The ABC Saturday Mystery*, 1990; (Film) *The Stone Boy*, 1983
Signature: *Lois & Clark: The New Adventures of Superman*
Facts: Passed up seventeen college football scholarships. He was a star defensive back (set an NCAA Division 1-AA record for interceptions in a season) and dated fellow student Brooke Shields for two years.

Was signed by the Buffalo Bills after his graduation in 1988, but injured his knee three days before his first preseason NFL game.

Had a recurring role in *Beverly Hills 90210*, in 1992
Original Job: Professional football player

MICHAEL CAINE

Real Name: Maurice Joseph Micklewhite
Birthplace: London, England
Birthdate: 3/14/33
Occupation: Actor
Debut: (Film) *A Hill in Korea*, 1956.
Signature: *Alfie*
Facts: Fell in love with wife when he saw her on TV in a commercial for Maxwell House Coffee (1971).

Caine's brother David's existence in a mental hospital was kept secret from him for over forty years, although his mother visited David regularly until she died in 1989.

Changed his last name to Caine after seeing the marquee for *The Caine Mutiny*, 1954.
Original Job: Cement mixer, dishwasher, driller, production office assistant
Marriages: Patricia Haines (divorced), Shakira Baksh
Children: Dominique, Natasha
Major Awards: Oscar, Best Supporting Actor, *Hannah and Her Sisters*, 1986; Golden Globe, Best Actor in a Comedy, *Educating Rita*, 1984; Golden Globe, Best Actor in a Miniseries, *Jack the Ripper*, 1989

JANE CAMPION

Birthplace: Wellington, New Zealand
Birthdate: 1955
Occupation: Director, screenwriter
Education: Sydney College of the Arts; Australian Film, Television, and Radio School
Debut: (Film) *Peel*, 1982; (TV) *Two Friends*, 1986
Signature: *The Piano*
Facts: Became the first woman to receive Cannes Film Festival's top award, in 1994.

Son died ten days after his birth in 1993.

Her father was the second unit director for *The Piano*, 1993.
Original Job: Assistant to a London producer of films and documentaries
Marriage: Colin Englert
Child: Jasper (deceased)
Famous Relatives: Richard Campion, opera and theater director, father; Edith Campion, actor and writer, mother
Major Award: Cannes Palme d'Or, Best Short Film, *Peel*, 1982; Cannes Palme d'Or, Best Film, *The Piano;* Oscar, Best Original Screenplay, *The Piano*, 1993

JENNIFER CAPRIATI

Birthplace: Long Island, NY
Birthdate: 3/29/76
Occupation: Tennis player
Education: High school
Facts: Capriati was the youngest player (13) ever to turn pro, the youngest Grand Slam semi-finalist (age 14 in 1990 French Open), the youngest Grand Slam semi-finalist ever (age 14 in 1990 French Open) and the youngest to win at Wimbledon (1990).

Began swimming at one month and was competing with five-year-olds at local swim events by fifteen months. At nine months, before she could walk, Capriati was climbing on the

jungle gym and swinging from monkey bars.
Infamy: Police gave her a citation for allegedly shoplifting jewelry in December 1993.
Arrested in March 1994 for possession of marijuana in her hotel room. Went into a detox clinic for 30 days.
Major Titles: Wimbledon, 1990; semi-finalist, French Open, 1990; Olympics, Gold Medal, 1992

MARIAH CAREY

Birthplace: New York, NY
Birthdate: 3/27/70
Occupation: Singer
Education: High school
Debut: (Album) *Mariah Carey,* 1990
Signature: "Vision of Love"
Facts: Her vocal range spans five octaves.
Her wedding cost half a million dollars. She watched tapes of the 1981 wedding of Charles and Diana in preparation.
Infamy: Sued by her stepfather in 1992 for failing to share profits from her 1990 album.
Original Job: Waitress, hat checker, restaurant hostess
Marriage: Tommy Mottola
Major Awards: Grammy, Best Pop Vocal—Female, "Vision of Love," 1990; Grammy, Best New Artist, 1990

KEITH CARRADINE

Birthplace: San Mateo, CA
Birthdate: 8/8/51
Occupation: Actor
Education: Attended Colorado State
Debut: (Stage) *Hair,* 1969; (Film) *McCabe and Mrs. Miller,* 1971
Signature: *The Will Rogers Follies*
Facts: An accomplished singer and songwriter, he has recorded two albums, *I'm Easy* (1976) and *Lost and Found* (1978).
Did not meet his first daughter, Martha (child of Sheley Plimpton, whom he met on set of *Hair,* 1969), until she was four years old.
Marriage: Sandra Will
Children: Martha Plimpton, Caleb, Sorel
Famous Relatives: John Carradine, actor, father; David Carradine, actor, brother; Robert Carradine, actor, brother
Major Award: Oscar, Best Song, "It's Easy," 1976

JIM CARREY

Birthplace: Jacksons Point, Canada
Birthdate: 1/17/62
Occupation: Actor
Debut: (TV) *The Duck Factory,* 1984; (Film) *Finders Keepers,* 1984
Signature: *Ace Ventura: Pet Detective*
Fact: A coalition of fire prevention groups demanded that his Fire Marshall Bill sketches on *In Living Color* be taken off the air because of the negative effect it was having on children.
Marriage: Melissa Womer (divorced), Lauren Holly (relationship)
Child: Jane

JOHNNY CARSON

Birthplace: Corning, IA
Birthdate: 10/23/25
Occupation: Talk-show host
Education: University of Nebraska
Debut: (TV) *Carson's Cellar,* 1951
Signature: *The Tonight Show*
Facts: Declined role to play lead in the series that became *The Dick Van Dyke Show.*
As a twelve-year-old, performed at local parties as "The Great Carsoni."
His son Richard was killed when his car plunged off a road (1991).
Third wife Joanna Holland received $20 million in cash and property in divorce settlement, 1983.
Served with the U.S. Naval Reserve during World War II.
Original Job: Radio announcer, ventriloquist, magician
Marriages: Joan Wolcott (divorced), Joanne Copeland (divorced), Joanna Holland (divorced), Alexis Mass
Children: Christopher, Richard, Cory
Major Awards: Elected to the Emmy Hall of Fame in 1987; Kennedy Center honoree, 1993

DAVID CARUSO

Birthplace: Queens, NY
Birthdate: 1/17/56
Occupation: Actor
Debut: (Film) *An Officer and a Gentleman,* 1982
Signature: *NYPD Blue*
Facts: Caruso used to stand in police lineups in New York's 112th Precinct for $25, the same precinct in which *NYPD Blue* is set.
Producer Steven Bochco originally worked with Caruso in 1981, when he played a tough Irish gang leader in the first three episodes of *Hill Street Blues.*
Made his acting debut as a stock boy who assists Margaret Hamilton in a Maxwell House ad.
Original Job: Loading dock worker, waiter
Marriages: Sherry Maugans (divorced), Rachel Ticotin (divorced)
Child: Greta
Major Award: Golden Globe, Best Actor in a Drama Series, *NYPD Blue,* 1994

DANA CARVEY

Birthplace: Missoula, MT
Birthdate: 4/2/55
Occupation: Actor
Edcation: San Francisco State University
Debut: (Film) *This is Spinal Tap,* 1981; (TV) *One of the Boys,* 1981
Signature: *Wayne's World*
Facts: Church Lady (character on *Saturday Night Live*) was a composite of several women at Carvey's Lutheran church who expressed indignation at his family's irregular attendance and less-than-complete commitment to the church.
His version of Garth is based on his real-life brother, Brad.
Original Job: Stand-up comedian
Marriage: Paula
Children: Dex, Thomas
Major Award: Emmy, Best Individual Performance in a Variety or Music Program, *The Saturday Night Live Presidential Bash,* 1993
Quote: "No dates . . . No proms. No football games. No driver's license. Basically, I was a fetus with shoes." (On his life in high school.)

JOHNNY CASH

Real Name: J. R. Cash
Birthplace: Kingsland, AR
Birthdate: 2/26/32
Occupation: Singer, songwriter
Debut: (Song) "Hey Porter," 1955
Signature: "I Walk The Line"
Facts: Cash is one-fourth Cherokee Indian.
He cannot read music.
Created seventy-five cuts for his 1994 album, produced by Rick Rubin (of Beastie Boys fame), which included songs written for him by Red Hot Chili Pepper Flea and Glenn Danzig.
Known as "the Man in Black," which is the title of his 1975 autobiography. Cash adopted this persona while working in a trio that only wore matching black outfits.
Wrote a novel, *Man in White,* in 1986.
He chose John as a first name when the military wouldn't accept initials.
Infamy: Cash was addicted to Dexadrine in the '60s.
Original Job: Door-to-door appliance salesman, factory worker
Marriages: Vivian Liberto (divorced), June Carter
Children: Rosanne, Kathleen, Cindy, Tara, John Carter, stepchildren Rebecca Carlene, Rozanna Lea
Major Awards: Grammy, Best Country Performance—Duo or Group, "Jackson" (with June Carter), 1967; Grammy, Best Country Vocal—Male, "Folsom Prison Blues," 1968; Grammy, Best Country Vocal—Male, "A Boy Named Sue," 1969; Grammy, Best Country Performance—Duo or Group, "If I Were a Carpenter" (with June Carter), 1970; Grammy, Best Spoken Word Recording, Interviews from the Class of '55 (with others), 1986; Grammy, Legend Award, 1991; elected to Country Music Hall of Fame, 1980; elected to the Rock and Roll Hall of Fame, 1992

ROSANNE CASH

Birthplace: Memphis, TN
Birthdate: 5/24/55
Occupation: Singer, songwriter
Education: State Community College; attended Vanderbilt University and Lee Strasberg Theatre Institute
Debut: "Blue Moon with Heartache," 1979
Signature: "I Don't Know Why You Don't Want Me"
Fact: Never intended to become a musician. Her original ambition was to become a serious fiction writer.
Infamy: In 1982, entered a drug rehabilitation program for a cocaine dependency she had developed in 1979.
Original Job: Worked in wardrobe department during her father's tour. One day the tour managers asked her to come on stage and sing harmony.
Marriage: Rodney Crowell (divorced)
Children: Caitlin Rivers, Chelsea Jane, Carrie Kathleen
Famous Relatives: Johnny Cash, country singer, father; June Carter Cash, country singer, stepmother; Carlene Carter, country singer, stepsister
Major Award: Grammy, Best Country Vocal—Female, "I Don't Know Why You Don't Want Me," 1985

DAVID CASSIDY

Birthplace: New York, NY
Birthdate: 4/12/50
Occupation: Actor
Debut: (Stage) *The Fig Leaves Are Falling,* 1968; (Film) *Instant Karma,* 1990
Signature: *The Partridge Family*
Facts: In 1993, starred with half-brother Shaun in the Broadway musical *Blood Brothers,* about English twins separated at birth.

Shirley Jones was David's stepmother, and he dated TV sister Susan Dey.
Infamy: As a teenager, Cassidy got kicked out of three high schools.
Original Job: Worked in the mailroom of a textile company
Marriages: Kay Lenz (divorced), Meryl Tanz (divorced), Sue Shifrin
Child: Beau
Famous Relatives: Shaun Cassidy, actor, half-brother; Jack Cassidy, father, actor; Shirley Jones, actor, stepmother

STOCKARD CHANNING

Real Name: Susan Williams Antonia Stockard Channing Schmidt
Birthplace: New York, NY
Birthdate: 2/13/44
Occupation: Actor
Education: Radcliffe College
Debut: (Film) *The Comforts of Home,* 1970; (Stage) *Two Gentlemen of Verona,* 1971
Signature: *Grease*
Facts: Channing's father died when she was six years old, leaving her with a generous trust fund. She spent her formative years riding around in a chauffeured limousine with her two white poodles.
Original Job: Production assistant at public television station WGBH in Boston
Marriages: Walter Channing (divorced), Paul Schmidt (divorced), David Debin (divorced), David Rawley (dissolved)
Major Award: Tony, Best Actress, *Joe Egg,* 1985

CHEVY CHASE

Real Name: Cornelius Crane Chase
Birthplace: New York, NY
Birthdate: 10/8/43
Occupation: Actor
Education: Bard College
Debut: (Film) *The Groove Tube,* 1974
Signature: *National Lampoon* movies
Facts: Worked as a writer for *Mad Magazine* (1969).

In 1968 signed as a recording artist with MGM Records.

While still at school, teamed up with friends to write an underground TV show that later became an off-off broadway show and movie, *The Groove Tube* (1974).
Infamy: Entered the Betty Ford rehabilitation center in 1986 due to an addiction to pain killers and alcohol.
Original Job: Magazine writer, tennis pro, bartender
Marriages: Jacqueline Carlin (divorced), Jayni Chase
Children: Cydney Cathalene, Caley, Emily
Major Awards: Emmy, Best Supporting Actor in a Variety or Music Program, *Saturday Night Live,* 1976; Emmy, Best Writing in a Comedy, Variety, or Music Series, *Saturday Night Live,* 1976; Emmy, Best Writing in a Comedy, Variety, or Music Special, *The Paul Simon Special,* 1978

DEEPAK CHOPRA

Birthplace: India
Birthdate: 1949
Occupation: Author
Education: All-India Institute of Medicine
Facts: Dr. Chopra practices a form of ayurvedic medicine called Maharishi Ayur-Veda, named after the Indian spiritual leader who taught transcendental meditation to the Beatles. The system is based on a 5,000-year-old Indian holistic health system involving herbal remedies, massage, yoga, and transcendental meditation. (Ayur-Veda is derived from the Sanskrit roots for "life" and "knowledge.")

CONNIE CHUNG

Real Name: Constance Yu-Hwa Chung
Birthplace: Washington, D.C.
Birthdate: 8/20/46
Occupation: TV journalist
Education: University of Maryland
Facts: First joined CBS as a general assignment reporter in 1971, covering McGovern's presidential campaign and Watergate.

Tenth child; five of the Chungs' first nine children died in their native China during World War II, when medical care was often unavailable for civilians. Her father was a diplomat in Chiang Kai-shek's government and moved to Washington, D.C., in 1944.
Original Job: Copy clerk with a television station.
Marriage: Maury Povich
Major Awards: Emmy, "Shot in Hollywood," 1987; Emmy, "Interview with Marlon Brando," 1989

TOM CLANCY

Birthplace: Baltimore, MD
Birthdate: 1947
Occupation: Author
Debut: (Book) *The Hunt for Red October,* 1984
Signature: Espionage thriller novels
Facts: First short story was rejected by *Analog* science fiction magazine. Had just one article (on the MX missile system) to his credit when *Hunt for Red October* was published.

Served in the U.S. Army Reserve Officers' Training Corps, but his extremely poor eyesight kept him from serving in the Vietnam War.

Part-owner of the Baltimore Orioles, he also led the effort to bring an NFL expansion team to Baltimore for the 1994 season.

Clear and Present Danger was the best-selling book of the '80s.
Original Job: Insurance agent
Marriage: Wanda Thomas
Children: Michelle, Christine, Kathleen, Tom

ERIC CLAPTON

Real Name: Eric Clapp
Birthplace: Ripley, England
Birthdate: 3/30/45
Occupation: Singer, guitarist, songwriter
Education: Attended Kingston Art School
Debut: (Album) *The Yardbirds,* 1963
Signature: "Layla"
Facts: At the Ealing Club in London, occasionally substituted for lead singer Mick Jagger in Blues, Incorporated.

Earned the nickname "Slowhand" because his powerful playing regularly broke his guitar strings, which he then changed onstage to the accompaniment of a slow handclap from listeners.

The song "Layla" was reportedly inspired by an affair that Clapton had at the time with George Harrison's wife Patti, and was dedicated "to the wife of my best friend."

Tragedy struck in 1991, when his four-and-a-half-year-old son died in a fall from Clapton's ex-girlfriend's apartment. The song "Tears in Heaven" is a tribute to him.

Infamy: After release of *Layla and Other Assorted Love Songs* (1970), dropped out of sight for two and a half years because of a heroin addiction. He was brought out of seclusion by Pete Townshend of The Who.
Original Job: Construction worker
Marriage: Patricia Anne Boyd-Harrison (divorced)
Child: Conor (deceased)
Major Awards: Grammy, Record of the Year, Song of the Year, and Best Pop Vocal—Male, "Tears in Heaven," 1992; Grammy, Album of the Year, *The Concert for Bangladesh* (with George Harrison and Friends), 1972; Grammy, Album of the Year, *Unplugged,* 1992; Grammy, Best Rock Vocal—Male, "Bad Love," 1990; Grammy, Best Rock Vocal—Male, "Tears in Heaven," 1992; Grammy, Best Rock Vocal—Male, "Layla," 1992

GLENN CLOSE

Birthplace: Greenwich, CT
Birthdate: 3/19/47
Occupation: Actor
Education: William and Mary College
Debut: (Stage) *Love for Love,* 1974; (TV) *Too Far to Go,* 1979; (Film) *The World According to Garp,* 1982
Signature: *Fatal Attraction*
Facts: When she was 13, her father opened a clinic in the Belgian Congo (now Zaire) and ran it for sixteen years. During most of that time, the Close children lived alternately in Africa and at boarding schools in Switzerland.

Owns a store in Bozeman, Montana, and recently announced that it will no longer sell porn magazines.

Chosen by Andrew Lloyd Webber to replace Patti LuPone in *Sunset Boulevard,* 1994.
Original Job: Toured Europe and the U.S. as a member of Up With People.
Marriages: Cabot Wade (divorced), James Marlas (divorced)
Children: Annie Maude Starke (from relationship with John Starke)
Major Awards: Tony, Best Actress, *The Real Thing,* 1984; Tony, Best Actress, *Death and the Maiden,* 1992

NATALIE COLE

Real Name: Stephanie Natalie Maria Cole
Birthplace: Los Angeles, CA
Birthdate: 2/6/49
Occupation: Singer
Education: University of Massachusetts at Amherst
Debut: (Album) *Inseparable,* 1975
Signature: "Unforgettable"
Facts: In the late '70s, was nicknamed Natalie "Queen" Cole by the media. Aretha "Queen of Soul" Franklin took offense at the comparison, and a feud developed between the two singers.

Often asked father to bring home latest Beatles records, which he did despite his dislike for the music. He would slip in records of Ella Fitzgerald.
Infamy: Was ruled incapable of handling her own affairs due to drug and alcohol dependency and, in 1983 her mother was named conservator of her estate. Cole entered drug treatment program at Hazelden Clinic in Minnesota and remained there for almost a year.
Original Job: Receptionist
Marriages: Marvin Yancy (divorced), Andre Fischer (divorced)
Child: Robert.
Famous Relatives: Nat "King" Cole, singer, father; Maria Hawkings Cole, singer, mother
Major Awards: Grammy, Best New Artist, 1975; Grammy, Best R&B Vocal—Female, "This Will Be," 1975; Grammy, Best R&B Vocal—Female, "Sophisticated Lady (She's a Different Lady)," 1976; Grammy, Record of the Year, "Unforgettable" (with Nat King Cole), 1991; Grammy, Album of the Year, *Unforgettable,* 1991; Grammy, Best Jazz Vocal, "Take a Look," 1993

SEAN CONNERY

Real Name: Thomas Connery
Birthplace: Edinburgh, Scotland
Birthdate: 8/25/30
Occupation: Actor
Debut: (Stage) *South Pacific,* 1951
Signature: James Bond
Facts: Connery grew up in a poor, industrial district of Scotland during the depression. At seven years old he took a job delivering milk before school, and by age 13 he quit school.

Served in the British Navy from 1947 to 1950. Was discharged due to ulcers.

In 1950, represented Scotland in London's Mr. Universe competition.
Original Job: Lifeguard, milkman, bricklayer, plasterer, coffin polisher, and usher
Marriages: Diane Cilento (divorced), Micheline Roquebrune
Child: Jason.
Major Awards: Golden Globe, World Film Favorite, 1972 (with Charles Bronson); Oscar, Best Supporting Actor, *The Untouchables,* 1988; Golden Globe, Best Supporting Actor, *The Untouchables,* 1988

HARRY CONNICK JR.

Birthplace: New Orleans, LA
Birthdate: 9/11/67
Occupation: Singer
Education: Attended Loyola University, Hunter College, Manhattan School of Music
Debut: (Album) *Harry Connick, Jr.,* 1987
Signature: (Song) "It Had To Be You"
Facts: Performed annually at the New Orleans Jazz & Heritage Festival from the time he was eight.

He also recorded two albums of Dixieland music on little-known labels—the first when he was nine and the second when he was ten.

Learned jazz music from Ellis Marsalis, the patriarch of the Marsalis family at the New Orleans Center for the Creative Arts.
Infamy: Arrested for having a gun in his luggage at New York's JFK airport.
Marriage: Jill Goodacre
Major Awards: Grammy, Best Jazz Vocal—Male, *When Harry Met Sally,* 1989; Grammy, Best Jazz Vocal—Male, "We Are in Love," 1990

DAVID COPPERFIELD

Birthplace: Metuchen, NJ
Birthdate: 9/16/56
Occupation: Magician
Education: Attended Fordham University
Debut: (TV) *The Magic of ABC,* 1977
Facts: Has levitated a Ferrari, walked through the Great Wall of China, and made the Statue of Liberty disappear. He has also extricated himself from a safe in a building about to be demolished by explosives and a steel box on a raft heading for the Niagara Falls.

By age twelve, had performed at local birthday parties for a fee of five dollars, under the name "Davino, the Boy Magician."

In 1982 developed Project Magic, a program designed to help people with physical and mental disabilities by teaching them magic.
Marriage: Claudia Schiffer (engaged)

FRANCIS FORD COPPOLA

Birthplace: Detroit, MI
Birthdate: 4/7/39
Occupation: Director and writer
Education: Hofstra University, UCLA Film School
Debut: (Film) *Dementia 13,* 1963
Signature: *The Godfather*
Facts: First dreamed of becoming a filmmaker and owning his own production company at age ten, while bedridden with polio. He put on shows for himself using puppets, a tape recorder, a film projector, and a television set.

Coppola's interest in producing a film about the automaker Preston Tucker—*Tucker: The Man and His Dream,* (1988)—began when his father invested and lost $5,000 in the automaker's company.

Directed Michael Jackson in the 15-minute Epcot Center feature *Captain EO.*

First son, Gian Carlo, was killed in a boating accident in 1986.

Owns a vineyard in California's Napa Valley. Also owns a restaurant in San Francisco and property in Belize; he hopes to make that country the hub for a huge telecommunications center.
Original Job: Worked for famous B-movie producer/director Roger Corman as dialogue director, sound man, and associate producer
Marriage: Eleanor Neil
Children: Gian Carlo (deceased), Roman, Sofia
Famous Relatives: Talia Shire, actor, sister; Nicholas Cage, actor, nephew
Major Awards: Oscar, Best Original Screenplay, *Patton* (with Edmund H. North), 1970; Oscar, Best Adapted Screenplay, *The Godfather* (with Mario Puzo), 1972; Golden Globe, Best Director, *The Godfather,* 1972; Golden Globe, Best Screenplay, *The Godfather* (with Mario Puzo), 1972; Oscar, Best Director, *The Godfather Part II,* 1974; Oscar, Best Adapted Screenplay, *The Godfather Part II* (with Mario Puzo), 1974; Golden Globe, Best Director, *Apocalypse Now,* 1980; Golden Globe, Best Score, *Apocalypse Now* (with Carmine Coppola), 1980

BILLY CORGAN

Birthplace: Chicago, IL
Birthdate: 1968
Occupation: Singer, songwriter, guitarist
Education: High school
Debut: (Album) *Gish,* 1991 (with Smashing Pumpkins)
Signature: Smashing Pumpkins
Facts: Favorite recordings include blues, '70s pop, and bebop jazz.

Lived in five different homes by the time he was five years old. When his father and stepmother split, Billy continued to live with her, even though both of his biological parents were within an hour's drive.

Met Smashing Pumpkins bassisst D'Arcy in an argument outside a Chicago nightclub. His first words to her were: "You're full of s—!"
Infamy: The neuroses he is known for—like refusing to get up before mid-afternoon and making lists for everything—point to the mental illness that drove him to the brink of suicide, almost breaking up the band.
Marriage: Chris Fabian

BILL COSBY

Birthplace: Philadelphia, PA
Birthdate: 7/12/37
Occupation: Actor, comedian, producer, author
Education: Attended Temple University; Doctor of Education from University of Massachusetts at Amherst
Debut: (TV) *I, Spy,* 1965; (Film) *Hickey and Boggs,* 1971
Signature: *The Cosby Show*
Facts: Grew up in a housing project in Philadelphia.

A gifted athlete, he was noticed by a scout for the Green Bay Packers.

Has played the drums since he was eleven. A jazz aficionado, is president of the Rhythm and Blues Hall of Fame.
Original Job: Shined shoes, delivered groceries
Marriage: Camille Hanks
Children: Erika Ranee, Erinn Charlene, Ennis William, Ensa Camille, Evin Harrah
Major Awards: Emmy, Best Actor in a Drama Series, *I Spy,* 1966, 1967, 1968; Emmy, *Bill Cosby Special,* 1969; Emmy, *The New Fat Albert Show,* 1981; NAACP Image Award, 1976; Emmy, Best Comedy Series, *The Cosby Show,* 1985; Golden Globe, Best Actor in a Comedy Series, *The Cosby Show,* 1985, 1986; elected to the Emmy Hall of Fame, 1991; Grammy, Best Comedy Recording, *I Started Out as a Child,* 1964; *Why Is There Air,* 1965; *Wonderfulness,* 1966; *Revenge,* 1967; *To Russell, My Brother, Whom I Slept With,* 1968; *Bill Cosby,* 1969; *Those of You with or without Children, You'll Understand,* 1986; Grammy, Best Recording for Children, *Bill Cosby Talks to Kids About Drugs,* 1971; Grammy, Best Recording for Children, *The Electric Company* (with Lee Chamberlin and Rita Moreno), 1972

ELVIS COSTELLO

Real Name: Declan McManus
Birthplace: London, England
Birthdate: 8/25/55
Occupation: Singer, songwriter
Education: High school dropout
Debut: (Album) *My Aim Is True,* 1977
Signature: *Elvis Costello & The Attractions*
Fact: Got his first contract with CBS Records by performing on the sidewalk in front of the hotel where the label's sales conference was in progress. Was arrested for disturbing the peace, but achieved his purpose.
Infamy: In a drunken argument in 1979, used racial epithets in referring to Ray Charles and James Brown. American disk jockeys took his records off their playlists, and he received numerous death threats.
Original Job: Computer operator at an Elizabeth Arden cosmetics factory
Marriages: Mary (divorced), Caitlin O'Riordan
Child: Matthew
Famous Relative: Ross McManus, singer, father

KEVIN COSTNER

Birthplace: Lynwood, CA
Birthdate: 1/18/55
Occupation: Actor, director, producer
Education: California State University at Fullerton
Debut: (Film) *Sizzle Beach,* 1979
Signature: *Dances with Wolves*
Facts: At 18, built a canoe and paddled down the same rivers that Lewis and Clark had navigated on their way to the Pacific.

As a teenager, he sang in the church choir.

Turned down the leading role in *War Games* (played by Matthew Broderick) to play Alex, the character who commits suicide, in *The Big Chill.* Only two weeks before the film's release, Alex's part was cut. But director Lawrence Kasdan promised Costner that he would write a part for him in another film, and tailored the role of Jake in *Silverado* (1985) for Costner.
Original Job: Worked in marketing, stage managed Raleigh Studios in L.A
Marriage: Cindy Silva
Children: Annie, Lily, Joe
Major Awards: Oscar, Best Director, *Dances with Wolves,* 1991; Oscar, Best Picture, *Dances with Wolves* (produced with Jim Wilson), 1991; Golden Globe, Best Director, *Dances with Wolves,* 1991

KATIE COURIC

Birthplace: Arlington, VA
Birthdate: 1/7/57
Occupation: Broadcast journalist
Education: University of Virginia
Signature: *Today*
Fact: After hearing Couric read a report on the air, the president of CNN banned the young assignment editor from further television appearances, complaining about her high pitched, squeaky voice. Keeping her spirits, Couric began working with a voice coach.
Original Job: Desk assistant at ABC News in Washington, DC
Marriage: Jay Monahan
Child: Elinor Tully

CINDY CRAWFORD

Birthplace: De Kalb, IL
Birthdate: 2/20/66
Occupation: Supermodel
Education: Attended Northwestern University
Signature: *House of Style*
Facts: Crawford was the valedictorian of her high school class, and received a full scholarship to study chemical engineering in college. There, a professor accused Crawford of cheating after she received a perfect score on a calculus midterm exam.

Supports P-FLAG (Parents and Friends of Lesbians and Gays) and leukemia research (her brother died of the disease at age three).
Infamy: Posed for the cover of *Vanity Fair* shaving lesbian singer k.d. lang, prompting a renewal of international rumors she and husband

Richard Gere are each homosexual and maintain the marriage for appearances only. In May 1994, the couple took out a $30,000 ad in the *Times* of London denying the rumors.
Original Job: Spent summers during high school detassling corn in fields
Marriage: Richard Gere

MICHAEL CRICHTON

Real Name: John Michael Crichton
Birthplace: Chicago, IL
Birthdate: 10/28/42
Occupation: Writer, director
Education: Harvard; Harvard Medical School
Debut: (Book) *Odds On* (under the pseudonym John Lange), 1966; (Film) *Westworld,* 1973
Signature: *Jurassic Park*
Facts: Published a travel article in the *New York Times* when he was 14.

Developed FilmTrak, a computer program for film production and is creator of the computer game Amazon.
Infamy: In 1974 was fired as screenwriter of the film adaptation of *The Terminal Man* when his screenplay deviated too much from the book.
Original Job: Anthropology professor
Marriages: Joan Radam (divorced), Kathy St. Johns (divorced), Anne Marie Martin
Child: Taylor

TOM CRUISE

Real Name: Thomas Cruise Mapother IV
Birthplace: Syracuse, NY
Birthdate: 7/3/62
Occupation: Actor
Education: High school dropout
Debut: (Film) *Endless Love,* 1981
Signature: *Top Gun*
Facts: Dyslexia put him in remedial reading courses in school, but Cruise proved himself in sports.

At age 14, enrolled in a seminary to become a priest. Dropped out after one year.

Took up acting after losing his place on a high school wrestling team due to a knee injury.

Member of the Church of Scientology.
Original Job: Busboy
Marriages: Mimi Rogers (divorced), Nicole Kidman
Child: Adopted daughter Isabella Jane
Major Award: Golden Globe, Best Actor, *Born on the Fourth of July,* 1990

BILLY CRYSTAL

Birthplace: New York, NY
Birthdate: 3/14/47
Occupation: Comedian, actor
Education: Attended Marshall University, Nassau Community College; New York University
Debut: (TV) *Soap,* 1977; (Film) *Rabbit Test,* 1978
Signature: *When Harry Met Sally*
Facts: Went to college on a baseball scholarship and hosted a campus radio talk show.

First theater job as a house manager for *You're a Good Man Charlie Brown,* 1968.

Studied directing under Martin Scorsese at New York University.
Infamy: Walked off the set of his first *Saturday Night Live* appearance after his seven-minute monologue was cut from the show.
Original Job: Substitute teacher, writer
Marriage: Janice Goldfinger
Children: Jennifer, Lindsay
Famous Relative: Milt Gabler, founded Commodore Records and later headed Decca Records, uncle
Major Awards: Emmy, Best Individual Performance in a Variety or Music Program, *The 63rd Annual Oscars,* 1991; Emmy, Best Writing in a Variety or Music Program, *Midnight Train to Moscow,* 1990; Emmy, Best Writing in a Variety or Music Program, *The 63rd Annual Oscars,* 1991; Emmy, Best Writing in a Variety or Music Program, *The 64th Annual Oscars,* 1992
Quote: "My father used to bring home jazz musicians at Passover. We had swinging seders."

MACAULAY CULKIN

Birthplace: New York, NY
Birthdate: 8/26/80
Occupation: Actor
Education: Attends the Professional Children's School
Debut: (Stage) *Bach Babies,* 1984
Signature: *Home Alone*
Facts: His allowance is $5 a day.

Didn't enjoy his first screen kiss (in *My Girl*) because it required fifteen takes.

Studied one year of pre-ballet at the 92nd street Y on a Harkness Scholarship in dance and the George Ballanchine School of American Ballet, and in 1987 appeared with the New York City Ballet at Licnoln Center in *The Nutcraker.*

Culkin's footage was edited out of the film *Born on the Fourth of July* (1989).
Famous Relatives: Christopher Culkin, stage actor, father; Bonnie Bedelia, actor, aunt; Shane Culkin, actor, brother; Kiernan Culkin, actor, brother

JAMIE LEE CURTIS

Birthplace: Los Angeles, CA
Birthdate: 11/22/58
Occupation: Actor
Education: Choate; attended the University of the Pacific
Debut: (TV) *Operation Petticoat,* 1977; (Film) *Halloween,* 1978
Signature: *Anything But Love*
Facts: Very athletic, Curtis was trained as a dancer and appeared on *Circus of the Stars* as an acrobat.

Curtis became interested in her husband Chris Guest when she saw his picture in *Rolling Stone.* She gave him her home number through an agent.
Infamy: Admitted to using cocaine, even with her father, although not abusing it. She quit completely in 1983.
Marriage: Christopher Guest
Child: Annie
Famous Relatives: Tony Curtis, actor, father; Janet Leigh, actor, mother
Major Award: Golden Globe, Best Actress in a Comedy Series, *Anything But Love,* 1990

BILLY RAY CYRUS

Birthplace: Flatwoods, KY
Birthdate: 8/25/61
Occupation: Singer
Education: Attended Kentucky's Georgetown College
Debut: (Song) "Achy-Breaky Heart," 1992
Signature: "Achy-Breaky Heart"
Facts: "Where Am I Gonna Live?" was written right after his wife threw him out of the house. He gave her half the royalties.

After a concert, one woman told Cyrus how her seven-year-old autistic boy spoke for the first time after hearing his song, and the first words out of his mouth were "achy-breaky heart."

Claims that a "psychic vibe" in his family convinced him to give up playing baseball and become a musician; he didn't start playing until he was 20.
Infamy: Songwriter Danny Mote filed a copyright infringement suit against Cyrus in 1993, claiming that Cyrus's song "She's Not Crying Anymore" was copied from Mote's song "Crying Eyes."
Original Job: Car salesman
Marriage: Cindy (divorced)
Famous Relative: Ronald Ray Cyrus, one of Kentucky's most popular politicians, father

ROSIE DALEY

Birthplace: South Seaville, NJ
Birthdate: 1961
Occupation: Chef, cookbook author
Debut: Head Chef at the Cal-a-Vie spa in San Diego
Signature: Oprah Winfrey's personal chef
Facts: Daley helped Winfrey lose seventy-two pounds in eight months. Before accepting the job as Oprah's personal chef, Daley refused similar offers from celebrities like Paula Abdul.

In the Kitchen with Rosie: Oprah's Favorite Recipes is the fastest-selling hardcover in history.
Original Job: Dishwasher in a roadside diner; worked in health food restaurants after high school while pursuing a career in art

TYNE DALY

Real Name: Ellen Tyne Daly
Birthplace: Madison, WI
Birthdate: 2/21/46

Occupation: Actor
Education: Attended Brandeis University; studied at the American Music and Dramatic Academy
Debut: (TV) *The Virginian,* 1962; (Film) *John and Mary,* 1969; (Stage) *The Butter and Egg Man,* 1966
Signature: *Cagney & Lacey*
Fact: In 1983, 1984, and 1985 Tyne Daly and *Cagney & Lacey* costar Sharon Gless were up against each other for the Emmy for Best Actress in Dramatic Series. Daly won all three times.
Marriage: Georg Stanford Brown (divorced)
Children: Alisabeth, Kathryne, Alyxandra
Famous Relatives: James Daly, actor, father; Hope Newell, actor, mother; Timothy Daly, actor, brother
Major Awards: Emmy, Best Actress in a Drama Series, *Cagney & Lacey,* 1983, 1984, 1985, 1988; Tony, Best Actress (Musical), *Gypsy,* 1990

JEFF DANIELS

Birthplace: Georgia
Birthdate: 2/19/55
Occupation: Actor
Education: Attended University of Central Michigan; apprentice at New York's Circle Rep
Debut: (Stage) *The Farm,* 1976, (Film) *Ragtime,* 1981
Signature: *The Purple Rose of Cairo*
Facts: In 1989, played guitar on Don Johnson's album, *Let It Roll.*
Original Job: Lumberyard worker
Marriage: Kathleen Treado
Child: Ben

TED DANSON

Real Name: Edward Bridge Danson III
Birthplace: San Diego, CA
Birthdate: 12/29/47
Occupation: Actor
Education: Attended Stanford University; Carnegie-Mellon University
Debut: (TV) *Somerset;* 1975; (Film) *The Onion Field,* 1979
Signature: *Cheers*
Facts: Father was the director of a local Native American museum.

In 1981, was the Ramis man on TV ads for cologne and men's toiletry products.

While at Stanford, followed a good-looking waitress to an audition "just to be near her" and ended up winning a part.

Tap dances.

Infamy: Appeared at companion Whoopi Goldberg's 1993 Friars Club roast in blackface.
Marriages: Randall Lee Gosch (divorced), Casey Coates (divorced), Mary Steenburgen (relationship)
Children: Kate, Alexis
Major Awards: Emmy, Best Actor in a Comedy Series, *Cheers,* 1990, 1993; Golden Globe, Best Actor in a Comedy Series, *Cheers,* 1990, 1991; Golden Globe, Best Actor in a Made-for-TV Movie, *Something About Amelia,* 1985

LOLITA DAVIDOVICH

Birthplace: Ontario, Canada
Birthdate: 1961
Occupation: Actor
Debut: (Film) *Class,* 1983
Signature: *Blaze*
Facts: The daughter of Yugoslavian parents, grew up speaking Serbo-Croatian. Denies any similarity to the heroine of Nabokov's novel and makes her friend call her Lolly. When she first started acting, was billed as Lolita David. "I don't know if my mother realizes to this day what she got me into by naming me Lolita."
Quote: "I've never been in a movie that's made any money. Maybe some of them broke even."

JAYE DAVIDSON

Birthplace: Riverside, CA
Birthdate: 1967
Occupation: Actor, model
Education: High school
Debut: (Film) *The Crying Game,* 1992
Signature: *The Crying Game*
Facts: Studied ballet as a child but gave it up because it seemed too demanding.

Worked for the Walt Disney corporation in London.

Original Job: Hairdresser, sales clerk

GEENA DAVIS

Real Name: Virginia Davis
Birthplace: Wareham, MA
Birthdate: 1/21/57
Occupation: Actor
Education: Boston University
Debut: (Film) *Tootsie,* 1982; (TV) *Buffalo Bill,* 1983
Signature: *Thelma and Louise*
Facts: Six-foot Davis, two inches taller than the cutoff established by professional modeling agencies, worked as a waitress to pay her bills. Finally she lied about her height and was accepted by the Zoli agency.

While working as a saleswoman at Anne Taylor, Davis got a job as a human mannequin in the store window.

Marriages: Richard Emmolo (divorced), Jeff Goldblum (divorced), Renny Harlin
Major Award: Oscar, Best Supporting Actress, *The Accidental Tourist,* 1989

DANIEL DAY-LEWIS

Birthplace: London, England
Birthdate: 4/29/57
Occupation: Actor
Education: Old Vic Theatre School
Debut: (Film) *Sunday, Bloody Sunday,* 1971
Signature: *My Left Foot*
Fact: At 16, accidentally overdosed on migraine medicine and suffered from two weeks of hallucinations. Because of this, he was mistakenly diagnosed as a heroin addict and placed in a mental hospital. To escape, he had to put on his "greatest performance of sanity."
Original Job: Loaded trucks
Famous Relatives: C. Day-Lewis, former poet laureate of Britain, father; Sir Michael Balcon, producer, grandfather; Jane Balcon, actress, mother
Major Award: Oscar, Best Actor, *My Left Foot,* 1989

ROBERT DE NIRO

Birthplace: New York, NY
Birthdate: 8/17/43
Occupation: Actor
Education: Attended the High School of Music and Art and dropped out; studied at the Dramatic Workshop, the Luther James Studio, the Stella Adler Studio, and the Actor's Studio
Debut: (Film) *Greetings,* 1969
Signature: *Taxi Driver*
Facts: Although commonly regarded as Italian-American, De Niro is more Irish in ancestry.

First acting experience was playing the Cowardly Lion in a Public School 41 production of *The Wizard of Oz.*

Co-owns Rubicon, a San Francisco restaurant with Francis Ford Coppola.

The pop group Bananarama recorded a song (1984) called "Robert De Niro's Waiting." They originally wanted to use Al Pacino's name, but Pacino refused to let them.

De Niro grew up in New York City's Little Italy, just a few blocks away from his future friend, Martin Scorsese.

Marriage: Diahnne Abbott (divorced)
Child: Raphael.
Major Awards: Oscar, Best Supporting Actor, *The Godfather Part II,* 1974; Oscar, Best Actor, *Raging Bull,* 1981; Golden Globe, Best Actor, *Raging Bull,* 1981

CALVERT DEFOREST

Birthplace: Brooklyn NY
Birthdate: 1923
Occupation: Actor
Debut: *Late Night with David Letterman*
Signature: Larry "Bud" Melman
Facts: For the first thirty-six years of his life, Calvert obeyed the wish of his mother that he not go into show business.

Admits that his longest conversation with Letterman lasted less than five minutes.

Original Job: Receptionist at a drug rehab facility

ELLEN DEGENERES

Birthdate: 1958
Occupation: Actor
Signature: *Ellen*
Facts: Considered becoming a professional golfer.

In the 1980s the Showtime cable network, looking to name someone Funniest Person in America, found DeGeneres at a comedy club in New Orleans. She was given the title, and toured the country in a Winnebago with a big nose above the front bumper. It earned her the scorn of other comics, who thought she received the title undeservedly.

Was the first female comic ever to be invited to sit on Carson's couch in her first appearance on *The Tonight Show.*

Original Job: Saleswoman, waitress

DANA DELANY

Birthplace: New York, NY
Birthdate: 3/11/56
Occupation: Actor
Education: Phillips Andover Academy; attended Wesleyan University
Debut: (Film) *The Fan,* 1981; (TV) *Love of Life,* 1979; (Stage) *A Life*
Signature: *China Beach*
Facts: Delany's first real love affair was a three-year relationship with actor Treat Williams.

While struggling to become an actress, Delany spent her nights working at an after-hours club where Bruce Willis tended bar.

Original Job: Cocktail waitress
Major Award: Emmy, Best Actress in a Drama Series, *China Beach,* 1988

JOHNNY DEPP

Birthplace: Owensboro, KY
Birthdate: 6/9/63
Occupation: Actor
Education: High school dropout
Debut: (Film) *Nightmare on Elm Street,* 1984
Signature: *21 Jump Street*
Facts: Dropped out of school at age 16 and joined a series of garage bands, one of which (The Kids) opened for Iggy Pop. Moved to L.A., where his ex-wife introduced him to actor Nicholas Cage, who spawned Depp's career.

Once owned a painting of a clown by executed serial killer John Wayne Gacy; now Depp has a pathological fear of clowns.

Tattoos: "Betty Sue" and "Wino Forever."

Co-owns The Viper Room, the '30s-style nightclub in which River Phoenix died (1994).

Original Job: Rock guitarist, sold pens over the phone
Marriages: Lori Anne Allison (divorced), Sherilyn Fenn (engaged, never married), Jennifer Grey (engaged, never married), Winona Ryder (engaged, never married), Kate Moss (relationship)

DANNY DEVITO

Birthplace: Neptune, NJ
Birthdate: 11/17/44
Occupation: Actor, director, producer
Education: American Academy of Dramatic Arts
Debut: (Stage) *The Man With a Flower in His Mouth,* 1969
Signature: *Taxi*
Facts: After high school he worked in his sister's hair salon and was known as "Mr. Danny." Got his part in *One Flew Over the Cuckoo's Nest* (1975) through producer Michael Douglas, whom DeVito had met in summer stock a few years before. Kirk Douglas had directed DeVito in *Scalawag* in 1973.

Original Job: Hairdresser, theatrical makeup artist, valet
Marriage: Rhea Perlman
Children: Lucie, Chet, Gracie, Jake
Major Awards: Emmy, Best Supporting Actor in a Comedy Series, *Taxi,* 1981; Golden Globe, Best Supporting Actor in a Comedy Series, *Taxi,* 1979

LEONARDO DICAPRIO

Birthdate: 1975
Occupation: Actor
Debut: (Film) *Parenthood,* 1990
Signature: *This Boy's Life*
Facts: Rejected by a talent agent when he was ten years old for having a bad haircut.

First memory is of wearing red-and-yellow tap shoes and being lifted onto a stage by his father to entertain people waiting for a concert.

First acting experience was in a Matchbox car commercial.

CELINE DION

Birthplace: Charlemagne, Canada
Birthdate: 3/30/68
Occupation: Singer
Education: High school dropout
Fact: Celine had nine best-selling French albums behind her before she recorded *Unison* in 1990.
Infamy: In 1990 Celine refused to accept a Quebec music award as Anglophone artist of the year, declaring she was "proud to be Quebeçoise." The Anglophone press criticized her harshly for exploiting the incident for its publicity value.
Marriage: Rene Angelil (engaged)
Major Awards: Grammy, Best Pop Performance—Duo or Group, "Beauty and the Beast" (with Peabo Bryson), 1992; Grammy, Best Song Written Specifically for a Movie, "Beauty and the Beast" (with Peabo Bryson), 1992

SHANNEN DOHERTY

Birthplace: Memphis, TN
Birthdate: 4/12/71
Occupation: Actor
Debut: (Film) *Night Shift,* 1982
Signature: *Beverly Hills, 90210*
Facts: Before her role on *90210,* Doherty starred in *Little House on the Prairie* with Melissa Gilbert and *Our House* with Wilfred Brimley.

Led the Pledge of Allegiance at the Republican National Convention in 1992.

Subject of *I Hate Brenda* newsletter.

Infamy: Notorious for her antics off the set, including an alleged brawl with another woman at a nightclub.

Admits to abusing drugs and alcohol.

Marriage: Ashley Hamilton (divorced)

PHIL DONAHUE

Birthplace: Cleveland, OH
Birthdate: 12/21/35
Occupation: Talk show host
Education: Notre Dame University
Debut: (TV) KYW-AM-TV, Cleveland, 1957
Signature: *Donahue*
Facts: With *The Phil Donahue Show* in 1967, he pioneered the concept of audience participation. He says, "Two or three shows in, I realized the audience was asking some very good questions during the commercials. Then, on some given day which I don't even remember, I jumped out of the chair and went into the audience. A woman stood up and asked the guest a question. And that, that was nirvana."

First met Marlo Thomas when she was a guest on his show.

Original Job: Salesman
Marriages: Marge Cooney (divorced), Marlo Thomas
Children: Michael, Kevin, Daniel, Kim, Maryrose
Major Awards: Emmy, Best Host of a Talk Show, *Donahue,* 1977, 1979, 1980, 1982, 1983, 1985, 1986, 1988; elected to the Emmy Hall of Fame, 1992

MICHAEL DOUGLAS

Birthplace: New Brunswick, NJ
Birthdate: 9/25/44
Occupation: Actor, producer, director
Education: University of California, Santa Barbara
Debut: (TV) *The Experiment,* 1969; (Film) *Hail, Hero!,* 1969
Signature: *Fatal Attraction*
Facts: His film company, Big Stick Productions, produced *One Flew Over the Cuckoo's Nest* (1975) and *The China Syndrome* (1979), in which he starred.

Directed two episodes of TV show *The Streets of San Francisco,* in which he costarred.

Flunked out of college during his freshman year.

Marriage: Diandra Luker
Child: Cameron.
Famous Relatives: Kirk Douglas, actor, father; Diana Dill, actress, mother
Major Awards: Oscar, Best Actor, *Wall Street,* 1988; Golden Globe, Best Actor, *Wall Street,* 1988

ROBERT DOWNEY JR.

Birthplace: New York, NY
Birthdate: 4/4/65
Occupation: Actor
Education: High school dropout
Debut: (Film) *Pound,* 1970
Signature: *Chaplin*
Facts: Was the live-in companion of actress Sarah Jes-

sica Parker for seven years.

Is working on a musical career and has written over thirty original songs. His version of *Chaplin*'s theme song, "Smile," is on the soundtrack album.

In *Pound,* he was five years old and played a puppy.

Infamy: Claims he once resembled the fast-living cocaine addict he played in *Less Than Zero.* Drugs were condoned in his family, and he started abusing at an early age. "I was pulling 360s in the Universal parking lot and disappearing for three days for things one needs blood transfusions to recuperate from."
Original Job: Waiter
Marriage: Deborah Falconer
Famous Relative: Robert Downey, underground filmmaker, father

DR. DRE

Real Name: Andre Young
Occupation: Rap artist, record producer
Debut: Album (solo): *The Chronic,* 1993
Album (with N.W.A.): *Boys-n-the-Hood,* 1986
Signature: *The Chronic*
Facts: Dre's signature "hopping" car is a black 1964 Chevrolet Impala.

Founding member of N.W.A., a group labeled "the Sex Pistols of rap," in his late 20s. *Efil4zaggin* (with N.W.A.) was the first hardcore rap album to make it to No.1 on the *Billboard* pop charts.

Dre launched the rap career of his brother, Warren G, and his brother's friend, Snoop Doggy Dogg; his label, Death Row Records, released Snoop's debut album.

Infamy: On parole for three violent incidents since 1991, he wears an electronic tracking bracelet and is under court orders to be in his $1 million house by 9p.m. every night.

TV Show host Dee Barnes filed a multimillion-dollar law suit against Dre after he pushed her against the wall of a Hollywood nightclub in the early '90s.

Arrested in a New Orleans hotel lobby after a scuffle ended in the battery of an officer.

Former colleague Eazy-E sued Dre under federal racketeering laws.

Convicted of a misdemeanor assault for breaking the jaw of an aspiring record producer.
Major Award: Grammy, Best Rap Performance—Solo, *Let Me Ride,* 1993

RICHARD DREYFUSS

Birthplace: Brooklyn, NY
Birthdate: 10/29/47
Occupation: Actor
Education: Attended San Fernando Valley State College
Debut: (Stage) *In Mama's House,* 1968; (Film) *Valley of the Dolls,* 1967
Signature: *Close Encounters of the Third Kind*
Facts: In 1978, at age 29, became the youngest man to win an Academy Award for Best Actor (for *The Goodbye Girl*).

Wife was diagnosed with Lupus (a disease that causes the body's immune system to attack its own tissue) and in 1986 newborn son Ben was diagnosed with Peter's Anomaly (a rare defect in which the cornea of the eye is fused to the iris). Dreyfuss and his wife donated $300,000 to a Lupus research lab at UCLA and have raised funds for an international eye-research facility at the University of California in San Diego.

As a conscientious objector during the Vietnam War, he worked two years in L.A. County General Hospital (1969-71).

Infamy: In 1982, got into an accident with his Mercedes and was arrested for illegal possession of cocaine and Percodan. The court ordered rehabilitation in lieu of a trial.
Marriage: Jeramie Rain
Children: Emily, Benjamin, Harry
Major Awards: Golden Globe, Best Actor in a Comedy, *The Goodbye Girl,* 1978; Oscar, Best Actor, *The Goodbye Girl,* 1977

DAVID DUCHOVNY

Birthplace: New York, NY
Birthdate: 1961
Occupation: Actor
Education: Princeton, master's degree from Yale
Debut: (Film) *Julia Has Two Lovers,* 1991
Signature: *The X-Files*
Facts: Duchovny was working on his Ph.D. dissertation "Magic and Technology in Contemporary Fiction" when he got his first acting job in a Lowenbrau beer commercial.

Played Denise the transvestite detective on *Twin Peaks,* 1990–91.

Original Job: Teaching assistant at Yale

BOB DYLAN

Real Name: Robert Zimmerman
Birthplace: Duluth, MN
Birthdate: 5/24/41
Occupation: Singer, songwriter
Education: Attended University of Minnesota
Debut: (Album) *Bob Dylan,* 1961
Signature: "Blowin' in the Wind"
Facts: Took stage name from Dylan Thomas.

His backup band, The Hawks, later evolved into The Band.

Motorcycle crash in July 1966 led to a brief retirement.

Became a born-again Christian in 1979.

Original Job: Performed with a Texas carnival
Marriage: Sarah Lowndes (divorced)
Children: Jesse, Maria, Jakob, Samuel, and Anna
Major Awards: Grammy, Best Album Cover—Photography, *Bob Dylan's Greatest Hits,* 1967; Grammy, Album of the Year, *The Concert for Bangladesh* (with George Harrison and Friends), 1972; Grammy, Best Rock Vocal—Male, *Gotta Serve Somebody,* 1979; Grammy Lifetime Achievement Award, 1991

CLINT EASTWOOD

Birthplace: San Francisco, CA
Birthdate: 5/31/30
Occupation: Actor, director
Education: Los Angeles City College
Debut: (Film) *Revenge of the Creature,* 1955
Signature: *Dirty Harry*
Facts: He was drafted in 1951 but en route to Korea his plane crashed. He swam miles to shore and was made swimming instructor at a boot camp, where he met actors Martin Milner and David Janssen, who sparked his acting career.

Elected mayor of Carmel, CA, in 1986; reelected in 1988.

Jazz musician and self-taught piano player, he plays three songs in the movie *In the Line of Fire.* Also composed two Cajun-inspired instrumentals for *A Perfect World.*

Original Job: Lumberjack, forest fire fighter, steelworker
Marriages: Maggie Johnson (divorced), Frances Fisher (relationship)
Children: Kyle, Alison
Major Awards: Golden Globe, Best Director, *Unforgiven,* 1993; Golden Globe, Cecil B. DeMille Award, 1988; Oscar, Best Picture, *Unforgiven,* 1992

ROGER EBERT

Birthplace: Urbana, IL
Birthdate: 6/18/42
Occupation: Film critic, writer
Education: University of Illinois; attended University of Cape Town, South Africa; University of Chicago
Debut: Film critic for the *Chicago Sun-Times* (1967)
Signature: *Siskel & Ebert*
Facts: While at the University of Illinois, Ebert was editor of the *Daily Illini* and president of the U.S. Student Press Association, 1963–64.

Ebert wrote the screenplay for the movie version of *Beyond the Valley of the Dolls,* 1970. He also wrote a novel, *Behind the Phantom's Mask,* which was released in 1993.

He is a member of the Studebaker Drivers' Club.

Major Award: Pulitzer Prize, 1975; Emmy, 1979
Marriage: Chaz Hammelsmith

NORA EPHRON

Birthplace: New York, NY
Birthdate: 5/19/41
Occupation: Journalist, screenwriter
Education: Wellesley College
Debut: (Book) *Wallflower at the Orgy,* 1970; (TV) *Perfect Gentleman,* 1978
Signature: *Heartburn*
Facts: While in college she was the subject of the play *Take Her, She's Mine,* written by her parents.

Her book *Heartburn* was adapted into a 1986 movie starring Jack Nicholson and Meryl Streep. Wrote screenplays for *Silkwood* and *When Harry Met Sally.*
Marriages: Dan Greenburg (divorced), Carl Bernstein (divorced), Nicholas Pileggi
Famous Relatives: Henry Ephron, screenwriter, father; Phoebe Ephron, screenwriter, mother; Delia Ephron, writer, sister

LINDA EVANGELISTA

Birthplace: Canada
Birthdate: 6/10/65
Occupation: Supermodel
Facts: Earns approximately $6,000 per show, $750 an hour for doing fashion advertisement shoots, and could top $500,000 for personal product endorsements.
Marriages: Gerald Marie (divorced), Kyle MacLachlan (relationship)

FABIO

Real Name: Fabio Lanzoni
Birthplace: Milan, Italy
Birthdate: 3/15/61
Occupation: Model
Debut: (TV) *Acapulco H.E.A.T.*
Facts: Posed for more than 100 bodice-ripping romance novel covers in 1992 and earned up to $3,000 per book cover.

Broke his left leg at age 16, and rehabilitation started him on the road to body building. He shaves his forty-eight-inch chest twice a week.

Has expanded his career to writing and developing exercise equipment and fitness techniques.

In 1993, wrote his own book, *Pirate.*

DONALD FAGEN

Birthplace: Passaic, NJ
Birthdate: 1/10/48
Occupation: Singer, keyboardist
Education: Bard College
Debut: (Song) "Can't Buy a Thrill," 1973
Signature: Steely Dan
Facts: *Kamakiriad,* released in 1993, was his first album in ten years.

The name Steely Dan was taken from William Burrough-s's novel *Naked Lunch,* in which it referred to a steam-powered dildo.

After the breakup of Steely Dan, Fagen worked as music editor for *Premiere* magazine.

CHRIS FARLEY

Birthplace: Madison, WI
Birthdate: 1960
Occupation: Actor
Education: Attended Marquette University
Signature: *Saturday Night Live*
Fact: His childhood heroes were John Belushi, Dan Aykroyd, and Bill Murray, and just like them he started out doing standup at Second City in Chicago.
Original Job: Worked at an oil company

LOUIS FARRAKHAN

Real Name: Louis Eugene Walcott
Birthplace: New York, NY
Birthdate: 5/11/33
Occupation: Muslim minister and African-American leader
Education: Winston-Salem Teachers College
Facts: In 1985, he launched POWER, a door-to-door beauty products company with money borrowed from Muammar Kaddafi.

Formerly called himself Louis X. He was given the name Farrakhan in 1965 by Muslim leader Elijah Muhammed.
Original Job: Calypso singer
Marriage: Betsy
Children: Nine children

MIA FARROW

Birthplace: Los Angeles, CA
Birthdate: 2/9/45
Occupation: Actor
Education: Attended Marymount in Los Angeles and Cygnet House in London
Debut: (Stage) *The Importance of Being Earnest,* 1963
Signature: *Rosemary's Baby*
Facts: Mother—biological or adoptive—of twelve kids.

Was on first cover of PEOPLE, March 4, 1974.
Infamy: Was awarded custody of the two children she and Woody Allen adopted, as well as the couple's biological son, after a highly publicized case involving allegations of molestation by Allen.
Marriages: Frank Sinatra (divorced), Andre Previn (divorced)
Children: Soon-Yi, Keili, Tam, Lark, Daisy, Moses, Isaiah Justus, Fletcher, Matthew, Sascha, Satchel (Seamus), Dylan (Eliza)
Famous Relatives: Maureen O'Sullivan, actress, mother; John Farrow, director, father

SHERILYN FENN

Birthplace: Detroit, MI
Birthdate: 2/1/65
Occupation: Actor
Debut: (Film) *The Wild Life,* 1984
Signature: *Twin Peaks*
Facts: After high school, tried to become a Playboy bunny, but flunked out of bunny school. In 1990 (after her success on the TV series *Twin Peaks*) she was invited to pose for a centerfold in the magazine.

Appeared in ads for Calvin Klein perfumes.
Marriage: Johnny Depp (engaged, never married) Toulouse Holiday (engaged)

SALLY FIELD

Birthplace: Pasadena, CA
Birthdate: 11/6/46
Occupation: Actor
Education: Columbia Pictures Workshop, Actor's Studio, 1973–75
Debut: (TV) *Gidget,* 1965
Signature: *The Flying Nun*
Facts: Was a cheerleader in high school.

Won the lead role in *Gidget* from among 150 other finalists.

Though entertaining, *The Flying Nun* discouraged people from thinking of her as a serious actress; the producers of the movie *True Grit* refused even to give her an audition. She was paid $4,000 a week for the television show.
Marriages: Steve Craig (divorced), Alan Greisman (divorced)
Children: Peter, Eli, Samuel
Famous Relatives: Mary Field Mahoney, actress, mother; Jock Mahoney, actor, stepfather
Major Awards: Emmy, *Sybil,* 1977; Oscar, Best Actress, *Norma Rae,* 1979; Golden Globe, Best Actress, *Norma Rae,* 1979; Oscar, Best Actress, *Places in the Heart,* 1984

RALPH FIENNES

Birthplace: Suffolk, England
Birthdate: 12/22/62
Education: London's Royal Academy of Dramatic Art
Debut: (Stage) British Royal Shakespeare Company; (Film) *Wuthering Heights,* 1992
Signature: *Schindler's List*
Facts: Fiennes gained 28 pounds to play Amon Goeth in *Schindler's List,* 1993. He was chosen by director Steven Spielberg for the role after Spielberg saw Fiennes's performance in the British TV movie *A Dangerous Man: Lawrence After Arabia.*
Marriage: Alex Kingston

ZLATA FILIPOVIC

Birthplace: Sarajevo, Bosnia-Herzegovina
Birthdate: 1980
Occupation: Author
Debut: (Book) *Zlata's Diary,* 1993
Signature: *Zlata's Diary*
Facts: Hailed as "Bosnia's Anne Frank," Zlata became famous for her diary describing her family's struggle to survive during the siege of Sarajevo from 1991 to 1993.

A portion of her royalties goes toward helping Bosnian children.

The diary has been optioned by Universal Pictures.
Infamy: Critics have questioned the political and commercial motives behind hav-

ing her diary published. The *New York Times Book Review, The New Republic,* and *The Globe and Mail* all gave it negative reviews, some complaining that the book appears to be heavily revised by its editors.

CARRIE FISHER

Birthplace: Burbank, CA
Birthdate: 10/21/56
Occupation: Actor, novelist, screenwriter
Education: Dropped out of Beverly Hills High School; attended Sarah Lawrence College and Central School of Speech and Drama, London
Debut: (Stage) *Irene,* 1972
Signature: *Star Wars*
Facts: Sang in her mother's Las Vegas nightclub act.

Her first public appearance was in a *Life* magazine photograph with her mother shortly after her father had run off to marry Elizabeth Taylor.
Infamy: Was a user of LSD and Percodan; almost overdosed, 1985.
Marriage: Paul Simon (divorced)
Child: Billie
Famous Relatives: Debbie Reynolds, actress, mother; Eddie Fisher, singer, father
Quote: "You find me a kid that thinks he got enough affection and attention as a child and I'll show you Dan Quayle."

BRIDGET FONDA

Birthplace: Los Angeles, CA
Birthdate: 1/27/64
Occupation: Actor
Education: attended New York University; studied at the Lee Strasberg Institute and with Harold Guskin
Debut: (TV) *21 Jump Street,* 1989; (Film) *Aria,* 1987
Signature: *Point of No Return*
Facts: Named after Bridget Hayward, a woman her father had loved who had committed suicide.

Her movie debut was in *Aria,* in which she stripped naked, had sex, then committed suicide during her eight minutes on screen with no dialogue.
Relationship: Eric Stoltz
Famous Relatives: Peter Fonda, actor, father; Susan Brewer, actor, mother; Henry Fonda, actor, grandfather; Jane Fonda, actor, aunt

JANE FONDA

Birthplace: New York, NY
Birthdate: 12/21/37
Occupation: Actor, political activist, fitness instructor
Education: Attended Vassar College; studied method acting in Lee Strasberg's Actors Studio
Debut: (Film) *Tall Story,* 1960
Signature: *Barbarella*
Facts: Mother committed suicide in a sanitarium in 1953.

Jane Fonda's Workout is the bestselling video in history.
Infamy: Spent much of the '70s speaking for the Black Panthers and against the Vietnam War and was almost arrested for treason, earning her the nickname "Hanoi Jane." **Marriages:** Roger Vadim (divorced), Tom Hayden (divorced), Ted Turner
Famous Relatives: Henry Fonda, actor, father; Peter Fonda, actor, brother; Bridget Fonda, actor, niece
Major Awards: Oscar, Best Actress, *Klute,* 1971; Oscar, Best Actress, *Coming Home,* 1978. Golden Globe, World Film Favorite—Female, 1973, 1979, 1980

HARRISON FORD

Birthplace: Chicago, IL
Birthdate: 7/13/42
Occupation: Actor, director
Education: Ripon College
Debut: (Film) *Dead Heat on a Merry-Go-Round,* 1966
Signature: *Indiana Jones*
Fact: Scar beneath his lower lip was the result of a motorcycle accident.
Original Job: Carpentry
Marriages: Mary Ford (divorced), Melissa Mathison
Children: Willard, Benjamin, Malcolm, Georgia.

JODIE FOSTER

Real Name: Alicia Christian Foster
Birthplace: Los Angeles, CA
Birthdate: 11/19/62
Occupation: Actor, director
Education: Yale
Debut: (TV) *Mayberry RFD,* 1969; (Film) *Napoleon and Samantha,* 1972
Signature: *Silence of the Lambs*
Facts: Started at three years old as the bare-bottomed Coppertone child in the then-ubiquitous advertisement. She got the job when, too young to wait in the car, she was noticed at her brother's casting call. By age eight, she had appeared in over 40 commercials.

At 13, played a hooker in *Taxi Driver.* Because she was so young, the film's producers hired her sister Constance to double for her in a nude scene. Before she got the role, she had to pass psychological tests. "I spent four hours with a shrink to prove I was normal enough to play a hooker. Does that make sense?"

As valedictorian in high school, she gave her graduation speech in French.
Infamy: Object of would-be presidential assassin John Hinckley's obsession.
Famous Relative: Buddy Foster, actor, brother
Major Awards: Oscar, Best Actress, *The Accused,* 1988; Oscar, Best Actress, *The Silence of the Lambs,* 1991

MICHAEL J. FOX

Birthplace: Edmonton, Canada
Birthdate: 6/9/61
Occupation: Actor
Education: High school dropout
Debut: (TV) *Palmerstown, U.S.A ,* 1980; (Film) *Midnight Madness,* 1980
Signature: *Family Ties*
Facts: When he got the audition for *Family Ties,* he was $35,000 in debt, living on macaroni and cheese, and had been forced to sell off a sectional couch piece by piece to raise money.

Eric Stoltz was first cast in *Back to the Future,* but when he proved to be "too intense for the comedy," Fox got the role. For seven weeks he played Alex on *Family Ties* by day, then transformed himself into Marty McFly for the film.

Heavy smoker, but asks not to be photographed smoking to avoid becoming a negative role model for his younger fans.
Marriage: Tracy Pollan
Child: Sam Michael
Major Awards: Golden Globe, Best Actor in a Comedy Series, *Family Ties,* 1989; Emmy, Best Actor in a Comedy Series, *Family Ties,* 1985, 1986, 1987, 1988

ARETHA FRANKLIN

Birthplace: Memphis, TN
Birthdate: 3/25/42
Occupation: Singer
Education: High school dropout
Debut: (Song) "Rock-A-Bye Your Baby with a Dixie Melody," 1961
Signature: "Respect"
Facts: Started out as a gospel singer in her father's Baptist church in Detroit in the '50s. Her father was minister of the New Bethel Baptist Church, one of the largest pastorates in the U.S., until 1979, when he went into a coma after being shot in his home by a burglar.
Infamy: Was sued for breach of contract in 1984 when she was unable to open in the Broadway musical *Sing, Mahalia, Sing* , mainly because of her fear of flying.
Marriages: Ted White (divorced), Glynn Thurman (divorced)
Children: Clarence, Edward, Teddy, Kecalf
Major Awards: Inducted into the Rock and Roll Hall of Fame, 1987; Grammy, Best Rhythm and Blues Song, "Respect," 1967; Grammy, Best R&B Vocal—Female, "Respect," 1967; Grammy, Best R&B Vocal—Female, "Chain of Fools," 1968; Grammy, Best R&B Vocal—Female, "Share Your Love with Me," 1969; Grammy, Best R&B Vocal—Female, "Don't Play That Song," 1970; Grammy, Best R&B Vocal—Female, *Bridge Over Troubled Water,* 1971; Grammy, Best R&B Vocal—Female, *Young, Gifted, & Black,* 1972; Grammy, Best R&B Vocal—Female, "Master of Eyes," 1973; Grammy, Best Female R&B Vocal—Female, "Ain't Nothing Like the Real Thing," 1974; Grammy, Best

R&B Vocal—Female, "Hold On I'm Comin'," 1981; Grammy, Best R&B Vocal—Female, "Freeway of Love," 1985; Grammy, Best R&B Vocal—Female, *Aretha*, 1987; Grammy, Best R&B Duo or Group, "I Knew You Were Waiting (For Me)" (with George Michael), 1987; Grammy Legend Award, 1991; NARAS Lifetime Achievement Award, 1994

DENNIS FRANZ

Birthplace: Chicago, IL
Birthdate: 10/28/44
Occupation: Actor
Debut: (TV) *The Chicago Story*, 1981
Signature: *NYPD Blue*
Facts: Claims he was the "worst postman in the history of the post office" before becoming an actor. "I used to start my route at daybreak, and I would finish long after dark. I'd stop for donuts, I'd play with animals, I'd go home with my bag of mail and just lay around the house a bit."

Served eleven months in Vietnam with an elite Airborne division.
Relationship: Joanie Zeck

ZSA ZSA GABOR

Real Name: Sari Gabor
Birthplace: Budapest, Hungary
Birthdate: 2/6/18
Occupation: Actor
Debut: (Film) *Lovely To Look At*, 1952
Signature: *Moulin Rouge*
Facts: Her compendium of humorous advice on relationships, *Complete Guide to Men (How To Catch a Man, How To Marry a Man, How To Get Rid of a Man)* was published by Doubleday in 1970.

Actor George Sanders had been married to her older sister Magda before marrying Zsa Zsa in 1949.

While appearing in *Forty Carats* at a Philadelphia dinner theater in 1983, she walked off the stage, complaining that handicapped patrons were making too much noise.
Infamy: Involved in many highly publicized controversies, including disputes over unpaid hotel bills and unpaid parking tickets.

George Sanders once hired private detectives to obtain evidence for use in a divorce hearing. When the detectives broke in on her and caught her with South American playboy Porfirio Rubirosa, she served them champagne.

In 1989, found guilty of slapping a Beverly Hills cop who pulled over her Rolls Royce.
Marriages: Burhan Belge (divorced), Conrad Hilton (divorced), George Sanders (divorced), Herbert Hunter (divorced), Joshua Kosden, Jr. (divorced), Jack Ryan (divorced), Michael O'Hara (divorced), Felipe Alba (ceremony declared invalid), Prince Frederick von Anhalt, Duke of Saxony, 1986
Child: Francesca
Famous Relative: Eva Gabor, actor, sister
Major Award: Golden Globe, Most Glamorous Actress, 1958

PETER GABRIEL

Birthplace: Cobham, England
Birthdate: 5/13/50
Occupation: Singer, songwriter
Education: High school
Debut: (Song) "The Silent Sun" (with Genesis), 1968
Signature: Genesis
Facts: Father developed an early version of cable TV.

Founding member of Genesis, which he started in 1967 with equally unhappy friends from Charterhouse, one of England's oldest and most privileged schools. Quit the band in 1975, just when it was on the verge of mass recognition.
Marriage: Jill (divorced)
Children: Anna, Melanie
Major Awards: Grammy, Best New Age Recording, *Passion—Music for the Last Temptation of Christ*, 1989; Grammy, Best Music Video, Short Form, *Digging in the Dirt*, 1992

ANDY GARCIA

Birthplace: Havana, Cuba
Birthdate: 4/12/56
Occupation: Actor
Education: Attended Florida International University in Miami
Debut: (TV) *Hill Street Blues* (pilot), 1981; (Film) *Blue Skies Again*, 1983
Signature: *The Godfather Part III*
Facts: Family fled from Castro's Cuba to Florida when he was a boy.

The 1990 movie *Internal Affairs* was written with Garcia in mind.

Married his high school sweetheart.
Original Job: Standup comic, waiter
Marriage: Maria Victoria
Children: Dominik, Daniela

JERRY GARCIA

Real Name: Jerome John Garcia
Birthplace: San Francisco, CA
Birthdate: 8/1/42
Occupation: Guitarist, singer
Education: High school dropout
Debut: (Album) *Grateful Dead*, 1967
Facts: Prior to The Dead, Garcia played banjo in Mother McCree's Uptown Jug Champions.

Garcia formed New Riders of the Purple Sage.

The Dead's mammoth performance in front of the Egyptian pyramids in September 1978 was capped off with a total eclipse of the moon.
Original Job: Salesman and teacher at music store
Marriages: Sarah Katz (divorced), Carolyn Adams (divorced), Deborah Koons
Children: Heather, Annabelle, Trixie

JAMES GARNER

Real Name: James Baumgarner
Birthplace: Norman, OK
Birthdate: 4/7/28
Occupation: Actor and producer
Education: Attended University of Oklahoma
Debut: (Film) *Toward the Unknown*, 1956
Signature: *The Rockford Files*
Facts: Part Cherokee Indian.

Received two Purple Hearts during the Korean War.
Original Job: Merchant marine, gas station attendant, traveling salesman, truck cleaner, carpet layer, hod carrier, maintenance man, swimsuit model
Marriage: Lois Clarke
Children: Kimberley, Gretta, Scott
Major Awards: Emmy, Best Actor in a Drama Series, *The Rockford Files*, 1977; elected to the Emmy Hall of Fame, 1990
Quote: "If you have any pride in your work, you don't go on TV."

JANEANE GAROFALO

Birthplace: New Jersey
Birthdate: 9/28/64
Occupation: Actor, stand-up comic
Education: Providence College
Debut: (Film) *Reality Bites*, 1994; (TV) *MTV's Half-Hour Comedy Hour*, 1994
Fact: Has "Think" tatooed on her arm.
Original Job: Bike messenger, receptionist
Quote: "If I've learned one thing in life, it's that I can always count on pinkeye at the most inappropriate moment."

ANTHONY GEARY

Birthplace: Coalville, UT
Birthdate: 5/29/47
Occupation: Actor
Education: Attended University of Utah
Debut: (TV) *Bright Promise*, 1969; (Film) *Blood Sabbath*, 1969
Signature: *General Hospital*
Facts: Geary quit *General Hospital* in 1984 because he hated the heart-throb status. The character was originally designed to appear for only 13 weeks. He returned in 1990 as Luke Spencer's cousin Bill Eckert, a German-Italian machinist. Luke reemerged on October 29, 1993.

Geary has appeared on the stage at the Los Angeles Theater Center in productions of Ibsen and Tennessee Williams, and in a national stage tour of *Jesus Christ, Superstar*.

During time off from Luke, had a bawdy nightclub act with dancers called The Smut Queens.
Major Award: Emmy, Best Actor in a Daytime Drama, *General Hospital*, 1982

CYNTHIA GEARY

Birthplace: Jackson, MS
Birthdate: 3/21/66
Occupation: Actor
Education: Attended University of Mississippi, UCLA
Debut: (Film) *8 Seconds,* 1993
Signature: *Northern Exposure*
Facts: Won Jackson, MS, Junior Miss title in 1983.
Original Job: Waitress
Quote: "There's a voice inside of me that says 'Get real, Cynthia. You may be a leading lady, but you're no supermodel.'"

RICHARD GERE

Birthplace: Philadelphia, PA
Birthdate: 8/31/48
Occupation: Actor
Education: Attended University of Massachusetts
Debut: (Film) *Report to the Commissioner,* 1975
Signature: *An Officer and a Gentleman*
Facts: Won a gymnastics scholarship to the University of Massachusetts.

In 1973, first studied the "middle way" of Siddhartha Gotama Buddha as preached by a Japanese sect. In 1982, switched faith to the Tibetan school of Buddhism. In 1986, became a student of the exiled Dalai Lama.

First three big film roles (*Days of Heaven,* 1978, *American Gigolo,* 1980, and *An Officer and a Gentleman,* 1982) were roles turned down by John Travolta.
Infamy: Took out a $30,000 ad wtih wife Cindy Crawford in the *Times* of London in May 1994 denying rumors of their homosexuality.
Original Job: Rock musician
Marriage: Cindy Crawford

BALTHAZAR GETTY

Birthdate: 1/22/75
Occupation: Actor
Debut: (Film) *Lord of the Flies,* 1990
Signature: *Where the Day Takes You*
Facts: At age 14, Getty was plucked from his classroom at the Bel Air Prep school and given the lead role in *Lord of the Flies,* his first acting experience.

Moved out of his mother's house and into an apartment with his girlfriend (actress Lala Sloatman) at age 15.

Has a tattoo of the Maiden of Ireland on his shoulder and a shamrock on his back.

Belongs to a rap group, 13th Floor, with fellow actor David Arquette.
Famous Relative: J. Paul Getty, billionaire oil tycoon, grandfather

MEL GIBSON

Birthplace: Peekskill, NY
Birthdate: 1/3/56
Occupation: Actor
Education: University of New South Wales
Debut: (Film) *Summer City,* 1977
Signature: *The Road Warrior*
Facts: Father moved the family from New York to Australia in the '60s so his sons wouldn't be drafted.

The night before his audition for *Mad Max,* he got into a barroom fight in which his face was badly beaten, an accident that won him the role.

Took up acting only because his sister submitted an application to the National Institute of Dramatic Art behind his back.
Marriage: Robyn Moore
Children: Hannah, Edward, Christian, Will, Lucian
Famous Relative: Eva Mylott, opera singer, grandmother

KATHIE LEE GIFFORD

Real Name: Kathie Epstein
Birthplace: Paris, France
Birthdate: 8/16/53
Occupation: Talk-show host, singer
Education: Attended Oral Roberts University
Debut: (TV) *$100,000 Name That Tune,* 1976
Signature: *Live! With Regis and Kathie Lee*
Facts: Despite having a Jewish father, became a born-again Christian at age 11.

Organized a folk singing group while at Oral Roberts University.
Original Job: Gospel singer
Marriages: Paul Johnson (divorced), Frank Gifford
Children: Cody Newton, Cassidy Erin

MELISSA GILBERT

Birthplace: Los Angeles, CA
Birthdate: 5/8/64
Occupation: Actor
Education: Attended the University of Southern California
Debut: (TV) *Little House on the Prairie,* 1974
Signature: *Little House on the Prairie*
Facts: Was involved with Rob Lowe for six years and broke up with him due to his infidelities.

There is a sign on the front lawn of Gilbert's house in California that says "Little House on the Valley."
Marriage: Bo Brinkman (divorced), Bruce Boxleitner (relationship)
Child: Cody
Famous Relatives: Sara Gilbert, actor, sister; Jonathan Gilbert, actor, brother; Robert Crane, creator of *The Honeymooners,* grandfather; Paul Gilbert, actor, father; Barbara Crane, dancer and actor, mother

WHOOPI GOLDBERG

Real Name: Caryn Johnson
Birthplace: New York, NY
Birthdate: 11/13/49
Occupation: Actor
Education: School for the Performing Arts, New York
Debut: (Film) *The Color Purple,* 1985
Signature: *Ghost*
Facts: Kicked a heroin addiction in the '70s.

Began performing at age eight with the Helena Rubenstein Children's Theater and later enrolled in the Hudson Guild children's arts program.

Co-owns the West Hollywood restaurant Eclipse with Steven Seagal and Joe Pesci.
Infamy: Was roasted by black-faced companion Ted Danson at a Friars Club event, 1993.
Original Job: Bricklayer, hairdresser, bank teller, and make-up artist for a funeral parlor
Marriage: One prior marriage, David Claessen (divorced), Lyle Trachtenberg
Child: Alexandrea Martin
Major Awards: Grammy, Best Comedy Recording, *Whoopi Goldberg,* 1985; Golden Globe, Best Actress, *The Color Purple,* 1986; Oscar, Best Supporting Actress, *Ghost,* 1990; Golden Globe, Best Supporting Actress, *Ghost,* 1991

JEFF GOLDBLUM

Birthplace: Pittsburgh, PA
Birthdate: 10/22/52
Occupation: Actor
Education: Trained at Sanford Meisner's Neighborhood Playhouse in New York City
Debut: (Stage) *Two Gentlemen of Verona,* 1971
Signature: *The Big Chill*
Facts: Brother Rick died at twenty-three from a rare virus picked up on a North African trip.

Starred as a stockbroker turned P.I. with Ben Vereen in the TV series, *Tenspeed and Brownshoe,* 1980.
Marriages: Patricia Gaul (divorced), Geena Davis (divorced)

JOHN GOODMAN

Birthplace: Afton, MO
Birthdate: 6/20/52
Occupation: Actor
Education: Southwest Missouri State University
Debut: (Film) *Eddie Macon's Run,* 1983
Signature: *Roseanne*
Facts: Made a living doing dinner and children's theater before Broadway debut in 1979 in *Loose Ends.*

Acted in college with Kathleen Turner and Tess Harper.

Appeared in commercials for Coors beer, Crest toothpaste, and 7-Up.
Original Job: Bouncer
Marriage: Annabeth Hartzog
Child: Molly
Major Award: Golden Globe, Best Actor in a Comedy Series, *Roseanne,* 1993

KELSEY GRAMMER

Birthplace: St. Thomas, Virgin Islands
Birthdate: 2/20/55
Occupation: Actor
Education: Attended Julliard School
Debut: (TV) *Another World,* 1983
Signature: *Frasier*
Facts: Father and sister were murdered; his two half-brothers died in a scuba accident.
Infamy: Arrested for driving

under the influence of drugs (1987); failed to show up for two arraignments for a cocaine arrest (1988); sentenced to community service and 30 days in prison (1990).
Original Job: Theatrical painter
Marriages: Doreen Alderman (divorced), Barrie Buckner (divorced), Cerlette Lamme (divorced), Leigh-Anne Cauhany (divorced), Tammi Alexander (engaged)
Children: Greer, Spencer

AMY GRANT

Birthplace: Augusta, GA
Birthdate: 11/25/60
Occupation: Singer
Education: Attended Vanderbilt University
Debut: (Album) *Amy Grant,* 1976
Facts: "Baby, Baby" (Grant's first hit single) was written for her infant daughter, Millie.

Recorded her first album at age 16 and recorded eight more before her first truly big album, *Age to Age,* came out in 1980.
Infamy: When Grant moved from gospel to pop music, some Christian radio stations refused to play her albums and condemned her for selling out her Christian values.
Marriage: Gary Chapman
Children: Matt, Millie, Sarah Cannon
Major Awards: Grammy, Best Gospel Performance—Contemporary, *Age to Age,* 1982; Grammy, Best Gospel Vocal—Female, "Ageless Medley Myrrh," 1983; Grammy, Best Gospel Vocal—Female, "Angels," 1984; Grammy, Best Gospel Vocal—Female, *Unguarded,* 1985; Grammy, Best Gospel Vocal, "Lead Me On," 1988

HUGH GRANT

Birthplace: London, England
Birthdate: 9/9/60
Occupation: Actor
Education: Attended New College, Oxford University
Debut: (Film) *Privileged,* 1982
Signature: *Four Weddings and a Funeral*
Facts: Grant opted not to do a nude scene with Andie MacDowell in *Four Weddings and a Funeral* when a makeup artist asked if he wanted definition painted on his body.

While at Oxford, formed a revue group, The Jockeys of Norfolk.

Grant is very popular in Japan, and there are two books on him published there, *Hugh Grant Vol. 1* and *Hugh Grant Vol. 2.*
Relationship: Elizabeth Hurley

LINDA GRAY

Birthplace: Santa Monica, CA
Birthdate: 9/12/40
Occupation: Actor
Education: Studied with Charles Conrad
Debut: (TV) *Marcus Welby, M.D.,* 1974
Signature: *Dallas*
Fact: Before landing any big acting roles, was a model and appeared in over 400 TV commercials.
Original Job: Model
Marriage: Ed Thrasher (divorced)

WAYNE GRETZKY

Birthplace: Brantford, Canada
Birthdate: 1/26/61
Occupation: Hockey player
Education: High school dropout
Facts: Began skating at age two, entered the Branford Novice All-Star Team at age six, and was playing against fourteen-year-olds by age eight.

In the 1979–80 season Gretzky became the youngest player ever to score 50 or more goals and 100 or more points in a season, and the youngest player to be voted Most Valuable Player.
Marriage: Janet Jones
Child: Paulina
Major Awards/Titles: NHL MVP, 1980, 1981, 1982, 1983, 1984, 1985, 1986 1987, 1989; NHL Sportsmanship Award, 1980, 1991, 1992; NHL leading scorer, 1980, 1981, 1982, 1983, 1984, 1985, 1986, 1987, 1990, 1991

MELANIE GRIFFITH

Birthplace: New York, NY
Birthdate: 8/9/57
Occupation: Actor
Education: Attended Pierce College
Debut: (Film) *Night Moves,* 1975
Signature: *Working Girl*
Facts: Alfred Hitchcock, who was in love with Griffith's mother, gave Melanie a tiny wooden coffin containing a wax replica of her mother, outfitted in the same clothes she had worn in *The Birds,* on her sixth birthday

At 14, left home to move in with Don Johnson, who was then 22. She married him at 18 and was divorced a year later. In 1988, on her way to the Hazelden Clinic for rehab, she called Don from the plane and renewed their love.

Was clawed in the face by a lioness in the filming of *Roar* (1981).
Infamy: Was addicted to drugs and alcohol in the late '70s and early '80s, and studio executives refused to speak with her. In 1980, she was hit by a car while crossing Sunset Boulevard. She suffered a broken leg and arm, but her doctor said that if she hadn't been so drunk she probably would have been killed.
Original Job: Model
Marriages: Don Johnson (divorced), Steven Bauer (divorced), Don Johnson (separated)
Children: Alexander, Dakota
Famous Relative: Tippi Hedren, actor, mother
Major Award: Golden Globe, Best Actress in a Comedy, *Working Girl,* 1989

NANCI GRIFFITH

Birthplace: Austin, TX
Birthdate: 1954
Occupation: Singer, songwriter
Education: University of Texas
Debut: (Album) *There's a Light Beyond These Woods,* 1978
Signature: "From a Distance"
Facts: Began writing songs while in grade school.

Songs she wrote were recorded by Emmylou Harris, Suzy Bogguss, and Kathy Mattea, among others.

Although her name has been connected to Ireland, she has no Irish blood (her mother's family came from Scotland).
Original Job: Elementary school teacher
Marriage: Eric Taylor (divorced)
Major Award: Grammy, Best Contemporary Folk Recording, *Other Voices/Other Rooms,* 1993

JOHN GRISHAM

Birthplace: Arkansas
Birthdate: 1955
Occupation: Author
Education: Mississippi State, University of Mississippi Law School
Debut: (Book) *A Time to Kill,* 1989
Signature: *The Firm*
Facts: Little League baseball coach.

Wife edits his books as he writes them.

Was inspired to write *A Time to Kill* by testimony he heard at the De Soto County courthouse from a ten-year-old girl who was testifying against a man who had raped her and left her for dead.

Served as a Democrat in the Mississippi State Legislature for seven years (1983–90).

Shaves only once a week, before church on Sunday.

In 1989 formed comic book company Bongo Comics Group.
Original Job: Attorney
Marriage: Renee
Children: Ty, Shea, Abe, Homer

CHARLES GRODIN

Birthplace: Pittsburgh, PA
Birthdate: 4/21/35
Occupation: Actor, writer
Education: University of Miami, Pittsburgh Playhouse School, studied with Lee Strasberg and Uta Hagen
Debut: (Stage) *Tchin-Tchin,* 1962
Signature: *Midnight Run*
Facts: Grodin was almost cast in the lead role in *The Graduate* but lost it due to an argument with the producers over salary.

Only leases white or gray Cadillac DeVille sedans because he doesn't like to attract attention.
Marriages: Julia (divorced), Elissa (divorced)
Children: Marion, Nicky
Quote: On a *Tonight Show*

appearance, Grodin told Johnny Carson, "It's hard for me to answer a question from someone who really doesn't care about the answer." Carson banned Grodin from the show.

MATT GROENING

Birthplace: Portland, OR
Birthdate: 2/15/54
Occupation: Cartoonist
Education: Evergreen College
Debut: (Comic Strip) *Life in Hell* (in the *Los Angeles Reader*), April 1980
Signature: *The Simpsons*
Facts: Elected student-body president in high school. Once elected, tried to rewrite the student government constitution to arrogate absolute power to himself.

In Los Angeles, ghostwrote the autobiography of an elderly film director who also employed him as a chauffeur, and worked as a landscaper for a sewage treatment plant.

The members of the Simpson family bear the same names as members of Groening's family (although *Bart* is an anagram for *brat*).

Groening's home in Venice, CA, is near a canal so he can canoe without leaving the front yard.
Original Job: Writer
Marriage: Deborah Caplan
Child: Homer
Major Award: Emmy, Outstanding Animated Program, *The Simpsons,* 1990, 1991

GENE HACKMAN

Real Name: Eugene Alden Hackman
Birthplace: San Bernardino, CA
Birthdate: 1/30/30
Occupation: Actor
Education: Pasadena Playhouse; attended University of Illinois, School of Radio Technique in NY
Debut: (Stage) *Any Wednesday,* 1964
Signature: *The French Connection*
Facts: Did his own driving in the car-chase scenes in *The French Connection,* 1971.

At the Pasadena Playhouse, he and classmate Dustin Hoffman were voted the two least likely to succeed.
Original Job: Doorman, truck driver, shoe salesman, soda jerk, furniture mover
Marriages: Faye Maltese (divorced), Betsy Arakawa
Children: Elizabeth, Leslie, Christopher
Major Awards: Oscar, Best Actor, *The French Connection,* 1971; Golden Globe, Best Actor, *The French Connection,* 1972; Oscar, Best Supporting Actor, *Unforgiven,* 1992; Golden Globe, Best Supporting Actor, *Unforgiven,* 1993

ARSENIO HALL

Birthplace: Cleveland, OH
Birthdate: 2/12/59
Occupation: Talk-show host
Education: Attended Ohio University; Kent State University
Debut: (TV) *The ABC 1/2 Hour Comedy Hour,* 1983
Signature: *The Arsenio Hall Show*
Facts: Appeared in the cult film *Amazon Women on the Moon,* 1987.

Became interested in magic at age 7, and later performed at birthday parties and bar mitzvahs, eventually leading to an appearance on a local TV special, *The Magic of Christmas.*

His interest in talk shows began early. While a young boy, he used to arrange the living room chairs for a make-believe show he pretended to host.

Has dated Emma Samms, Paula Abdul, and Sinéad O'Connor.
Original Job: Advertising

HAMMER

Real Name: Stanley Kirk Burrell
Birthplace: Oakland, CA
Birthdate: 3/29/63
Occupation: Rap artist, dancer
Education: High school
Debut: (Song) "Ring 'Em," 1987; (TV) *Amen,* 1991
Facts: While doing impressions of James Brown on the Oakland Coliseum parking lot, was noticed by Charlie Finley, owner of the A's, who made him a batboy and later executive vice president.

Joined Navy for three years and began intensive Bible studies.

Started Bust It Records with money from two Oakland ballplayers, selling singles from the trunk of his car.

Owns a race horse, Dance Floor, that came in third in 1992 Kentucky Derby.
Infamy: Was sued by two Oakland ballplayers for reneging on their 1987 loan.
Marriage: Stephanie
Major Awards: Grammy, Best Rap Performance—Solo and Best Rhythm and Blues Song, "U Can't Touch This" (as M.C. Hammer), 1990; Grammy, Best Music Video—Long Form, *Please Hammer Don't Hurt 'Em: The Movie* (as M.C. Hammer), 1990

TOM HANKS

Birthplace: Concord, CA
Birthdate: 7/9/56
Occupation: Actor
Education: Attended Chabot College, California State University–Sacramento
Debut: (Film) *He Knows You're Alone,* 1980
Signature: *Big*
Facts: Attended at least five different elementary schools.

After a one-shot guest spot on *Happy Days,* producer Ron Howard asked him to read for a secondary part in *Splash,* but he got the lead instead.

Played Michael J. Fox's alcoholic uncle on the sitcom *Family Ties.*
Marriages: Samantha Lewes (divorced), Rita Wilson
Children: Colin, Elizabeth, Chester
Major Awards: Golden Globe, Best Actor in a Comedy, *Big,* 1989; Oscar, Best Actor, *Philadelphia,* 1994; Golden Globe, Best Actor, *Philadelphia,* 1994

DARYL HANNAH

Birthplace: Chicago, IL
Birthdate: 1960
Occupation: Actor
Education: Studied ballet with Maria Tallchief; studied at Chicago's Goodman Theater; attended UCLA
Debut: (Film) *The Fury,* 1976
Signature: *Splash*
Facts: When alone at home, sometimes wears Fred Astaire's shoes, which she bought at an auction.

Her childhood interest in movies grew out of a lifelong battle with insomnia. Was diagnosed as "semiautistic" by psychiatrists.

In high school, was the only female member of the soccer team.

Played keyboard in some of ex-boyfriend Jackson Browne's videos. Sang back-up vocals in his hit, "You're a Friend of Mine" (1975).
Famous Relatives: Page Hannah, actress, sister; Haskell Wexler, cinematographer, uncle

TONYA HARDING

Birthplace: Portland, OR
Birthdate: 1971
Occupation: Figure skater
Education: High school
Facts: Father bought her a .22 rifle when she was five, and she killed her first deer at age 14.

After the 1994 Olympics, an offer was made to Tanya from All Japan Women's Professional Wrestling Association.

Hobbies include drag racing, hunting, and pool.

Suffers from asthma; her breathing capacity during programs is only about twenty percent that of a normal skater.
Infamy: On January 27, 1994, admitted to lying about having no knowledge of the assault on rival skater Nancy Kerrigan. Pled guilty to hindering prosecution and so avoided possible jail time. Was forced to resign from U.S. Figure Skating Association, pay a $100,000 fine, perform community service, and pay legal fees.
Marriage: Jeff Gillooly (divorced)

WOODY HARRELSON

Birthplace: Midland, TX
Birthdate: 7/23/61
Occupation: Actor
Education: Hanover College
Debut: (Film) *Wildcats,* 1986
Signature: *Cheers*
Facts: A hyperactive child, sometimes prone to violence, was placed in a school for problem students. "Violence

was almost an aphrodisiac for me." Took Ritalin.

His absent father was convicted of murdering a federal judge and sentenced to life in prison when Woody was a freshman in college.

Is lead singer and composer for a ten-piece "blues-a-billy" band, Manly Moondog and the Three Kool Kats.

Dated Brooke Shields, Carol Kane, Glenn Close, and Moon Unit Zappa.

Infamy: Admits to having been a sex addict.
Original Job: Claims he had over seventeen different jobs in one year, including waiting tables and short-order cooking, and was fired from almost all of them
Marriages: Nancy Simon (divorced), Laura Louie (relationship)
Child: Denni Montana
Major Award: Emmy, Best Supporting Actor in a Comedy Series, *Cheers,* 1989

MICKEY HART

Real Name: Michael Hart
Birthplace: New York, NY
Birthdate: 9/11/44
Occupation: Drummer, songwriter
Debut: Became drummer for the Grateful Dead in February 1968 after becoming friendly with drummer Bill Kreutzmann
Signature: Grateful Dead
Facts: In the early '90s, was assigned to digitally remaster collections of music from around the world by the Smithsonian Institution and the Library of Congress, including some century-old recordings.

While in the U.S. Air Force, Hart won in his weight class at the United States military European judo championship.

His 1989 solo album, *Music to Be Born,* used his son Taro's heartbeat, recorded from the womb.

Infamy: In the late '60s the Grateful Dead hired Hart's father (Lenny Hart) as their business manager. By 1970 it was discovered he was embezzling money from the band, and he was arrested and imprisoned. The Dead did not blame Hart for his father's actions but he felt obligated to leave the group for a while.

Along with Bob Weir and manager Danny Rifkin, arrested in 1980 for suspicion of inciting a riot when they intervened in an attempted drug bust during a Dead concert.

Marriages: Mary Holloway (divorced), Carol Orbach
Children: Taro, Creek, Reya.
Major Award: Grammy, Best World Music Performance, *Planet Drum,* 1991

PHIL HARTMAN

Birthplace: Ontario, Canada
Birthdate: 9/24/48
Occupation: Actor, writer
Debut: (TV) *Our Time,* 1985
Signature: *Saturday Night Live*
Facts: When Hartman left *Saturday Night Live* in 1994, he had set a record for the longest run (eight seasons, 153 shows) by a regular cast member.

Hartman co-wrote the film *Pee Wee's Big Adventure* with Paul Reubens, and starred as Kap'n Karl on the TV show *Pee-Wee's Playhouse.*

Original Job: Graphic designer (designed the Crosby, Stills, and Nash logo)
Marriage: Brynn Omdahl
Children: Sean, Birgen
Major Award: Emmy, Best Writing in a Variety or Music Program, *Murderers Among Us,* 1989

DAVID HASSELHOFF

Birthplace: Baltimore, MD
Birthdate: 7/17/52
Occupation: Actor
Debut: (TV) *The Young and the Restless,* 1975–82
Signature: *Knight Rider*
Facts: Hasselhoff is a successful recording star in Europe, and has toured Germany and Austria. He performed a concert in front of 500,000 people at the Berlin Wall.

Baywatch was the first American show to appear in mainland China. It is the most watched show on the planet, seen by almost a billion people every day.

Marriage: Catherine Hickland (divorced), Pamela Bach

TERI HATCHER

Birthplace: Sunnyvale, CA
Birthdate: 12/8/64
Occupation: Actor
Education: Attended DeAnza Junior College
Debut: (TV) *The Love Boat,* 1985; (Film) *Tango & Cash,* 1989
Signature: *Lois & Clark: The New Adventures of Superman*
Facts: Played Penny Parker on *MacGyver* in 1985, a role that later became a recurring character.
Infamy: Before *Lois and Clark,* she made an independent film, *Cool Surface,* with nudity and simulated sex scenes.
Original Job: Dancer in San Francisco
Marriage: Jon Tenney (engaged)
Quote: "Despite the fact that I have a good-size pair of breasts . . . in *Lois & Clark* I have the opportunity to show the world they're not my only attribute."

ETHAN HAWKE

Birthplace: Austin, TX
Birthdate: 11/6/70
Occupation: Actor
Education: Attended New York University; studied acting at the McCarter Theatre in Princeton, the British Theatre Association, and Carnegie-Mellon University
Debut: (Film) *Explorers,* 1985; (Stage) *The Seagull,* 1992
Signature: *Dead Poets Society*
Facts: Hawke was seen out drinking and dancing with the married Julia Roberts in April 1994.

Starred in *Explorers* when he was 14 with River Phoenix.

His own singing was featured in the *Reality Bites* soundtrack.

GOLDIE HAWN

Birthplace: Takoma Park, MD
Birthdate: 11/21/45
Occupation: Actor
Education: American University
Debut: (Film) *The One and Only Genuine Family Band,* 1968
Signature: *Private Benjamin*
Facts: Discovered while dancing in the chorus of an Andy Griffith TV special in 1967. Became a regular on *Laugh-In.*

Father performed as a musician at the White House.

Original Job: Go-go dancer in New York and Las Vegas
Marriages: Gus Trikonis (divorced), Bill Hudson (divorced), Kurt Russell (relationship)
Children: Katie, Oliver, Wyatt
Major Awards: Oscar, Best Supporting Actress, *Cactus Flower,* 1970; Golden Globe, Best Supporting Actress, *Cactus Flower,* 1970

DON HENLEY

Birthplace: Linden, TX
Birthdate: 7/22/47
Occupation: Singer, songwriter, drummer, guitarist
Signature: The Eagles
Fact: Played in Linda Ronstadt's backup band, out of which the Eagles emerged.
Major Awards: Co-recipient (with other members of the Eagles) of Grammy Awards for best pop vocal performance by a group, 1975, for "Lyin' Eyes,"; record of the year, 1977, *Hotel California;* best arrangement for voices, 1977, "New Kid In Town;" best rock vocal performance by a group, 1979, "Heartache Tonight;" solo Grammy Awards for best rock vocal performance by a male, 1985 and 1989; Grammy Award, "The Boys of Summer," 1985; Grammy Award, "The End of the Innocence," 1990

KATHARINE HEPBURN

Birthplace: Hartford, CT
Birthdate: 11/8/07
Occupation: Actor
Education: Bryn Mawr College
Debut: (Stage) *The Czarina,* 1928; (Film) *A Bill of Divorcement,* 1932
Signature: *The African Queen*
Facts: In her strict New England home, where her father was a surgeon and her mother a militant suffragette, Hepburn and her siblings took cold showers every morning.

Since she was considered too much of a tomboy, she was educated by home tutors.

Decided to take up acting once she realized there was

little opportunity for a woman to become a doctor.
Original Job: Sold balloons
Marriages: Ludlow Ogden Smith (divorced), Spencer Tracy (relationship)
Major Awards: Oscar, Best Actress, *Morning Glory,* 1933; Oscar, Best Actress, *Guess Who's Coming to Dinner,* 1967; Oscar, Best Actress, *The Lion in Winter,* 1968; Emmy, Best Actress in a Drama Special, *Love Among the Ruins,* 1975; Oscar, Best Actress, *On Golden Pond,* 1981; Kennedy Center Honor for Lifetime Achievement, 1990
Quote: "I am revered rather like an old building."

BARBARA HERSHEY

Real Name: Barbara Herzstein
Birthplace: Hollywood, CA
Birthdate: 2/5/48
Occupation: Actor
Education: High school
Debut: (TV) *Gidget,* 1965; (Film) *With Six You Get Eggroll,* 1968
Signature: *Hannah and Her Sisters*
Facts: In 1972, changed her name to Barbara Seagull, but changed it back to Hershey in 1975.

Was a pom-pom girl and member of the drill team in high school. She graduated in only two and a half years.

Her son Free changed his name to Tom when he was nine.
Infamy: Admits to using peyote in the '70s.
Marriage: Stephen Douglas (divorced)
Child: Tom (with David Carradine)
Major Awards: Emmy, Best Actress in a Miniseries, *A Killing in a Small Town,* 1990; Golden Globe, Best Actress in a Miniseries, *A Killing in a Small Town,* 1991

DUSTIN HOFFMAN

Birthplace: Los Angeles, CA
Birthdate: 8/8/37
Occupation: Actor
Education: Attended Los Angeles Conservatory of Music, Santa Monica City College; studied at the Pasadena Playhouse and the Actor's Studio
Debut: (Stage) *Yes Is for a Very Young Man,* 1960
Signature: *The Graduate*
Facts: Played Tiny Tim in junior high school.

Slept on Gene Hackman's kitchen floor while looking for work.

Achieved Ratso's distinctive walk in *Midnight Cowboy* by putting pebbles in his shoe.

When taking the screen test for *The Graduate,* Hoffman said, "I don't think I'm right for the role. He's a kind of Anglo-Saxon, tall, slender, good-looking chap. I'm short and Jewish." During the screen test he forgot his lines and was nervous and clumsy.

Hoffman originally wanted to be a concert pianist. Also studied to be a doctor.
Original Job: Washing dishes, checking coats, waiting tables, cleaning a dance studio, selling toys at Macy's, attendant in a psychiatric institution
Marriages: Anne Byrne (divorced), Lisa Gottsegen
Children: Karina, Jenna, Jacob, Rebecca, Max, Alexandra
Major Awards: Emmy, Best Actor in a Made-for-TV Movie, *Death of a Salesman,* 1986; Oscar, Best Actor, *Kramer vs. Kramer,* 1980; Oscar, Best Actor, *Rain Man,* 1989

ANTHONY HOPKINS

Birthplace: Port Talbot, South Wales
Birthdate: 12/31/37
Occupation: Actor
Education: Welsh College of Music and Drama; Royal Academy of Dramatic Art, London
Debut: (Stage) *Julius Caesar,* 1964; (Film) *The Lion in Winter,* 1968
Signature: *The Silence of the Lambs*
Facts: Debuted as conductor with the New Symphony Orchestra at Royal Albert Hall, 1982.

In 1993 was knighted.

Understudied for Laurence Olivier in *Dance Of Death,* 1966.
Original Job: Steelworker
Marriages: Petronella Barker (divorced), Jennifer Ann Lynton
Child: Abigail
Major Awards: Emmy, Best Actor in a Drama or Comedy Special, *The Lindbergh Kidnapping Case,* 1976; Emmy, Best Actor in a Miniseries, *The Bunker,* 1981; Oscar, Best Actor, *Silence of the Lambs,* 1991

WHITNEY HOUSTON

Birthplace: Newark, NJ
Birthdate: 8/9/63
Occupation: Singer
Education: High school
Debut: (Album) *Whitney Houston,* 1985
Facts: Got her start at age eight singing in the New Hope Baptist Junior Choir.

Sang backup for Chaka Khan, Lou Rawls, Dionne Warwick.

As a model, appeared on the cover of *Seventeen.*

Was an actress in her early days, appearing on *Silver Spoons* and *Gimme a Break.*
Original Job: Model
Marriage: Bobby Brown
Child: Bobbi Kristina
Famous Relatives: Cissy Houston, singer, mother; Thelma Houston, singer, aunt; Dionne Warwick, singer, cousin
Major Awards: Grammy, Best Pop Vocal—Female, "Saving All My Love for You," 1985; Grammy, Best Pop Vocal—Female, "I Wanna Dance with Somebody," 1987; Grammy, Best Pop Vocal—Female, "I Will Always Love You," 1993; Grammy, Record of the Year, "I Will Always Love You," 1993; Grammy, Album of the Year, *The Bodyguard Soundtrack,* 1993; Emmy, Best Individual Performance in a Variety or Music Program, *The 28th Annual Grammy Awards,* 1986

HELEN HUNT

Birthplace: Los Angeles, CA
Birthdate: 6/15/63
Occupation: Actor
Education: Attended UCLA
Debut: (TV) *Pioneer Woman,* 1973; (Film) *Rollercoaster,* 1977
Signature: *Mad About You*
Facts: Hunt studied acting, got an agent, and got a part in the TV movie *Pioneer Woman* by age nine.

Began a two-year romance with actor Matthew Broderick while working on *Project X* (1986).
Famous Relatives: Gordon Hunt, director, father; Peter Hunt, director, uncle
Major Award: Golden Globe, Best Actress in a Comedy Series, *Mad About You,* 1994

HOLLY HUNTER

Birthplace: Conyers, GA
Birthdate: 3/20/58
Occupation: Actor
Education: Carnegie Mellon University
Debut: (Film) *The Burning,* 1981; (Stage) *Crimes of the Heart,* 1981
Signature: *Broadcast News*
Facts: Director Jane Campion was originally looking for a tall, statuesque Sigourney Weaver–type for the lead in *The Piano.*

Youngest of seven children, grew up on a cattle and hay farm in Georgia, where she drove a tractor.

Appeared in pilot for television series *Fame* (1982).
Major Awards: Emmy, Best Actress in a Miniseries, *Roe vs. Wade,* 1989; Oscar, Best Actress, *The Piano,* 1993; Golden Globe, Best Actress, *The Piano,* 1993; Emmy, Best Actress in a Miniseries, *The Positively True Adventures of the Alleged Texas Cheerleader-Murdering Mom,* 1993

CHRISSIE HYNDE

Birthplace: Akron, OH
Birthdate: 9/7/51
Occupation: Singer
Education: Attended Kent State University
Debut: (Album) *The Pretenders,* 1980
Signature: Leader of rock band The Pretenders
Fact: Born in Ohio, she has lived in London since the late '70s.
Original Job: Waitress, handbag saleswoman, messenger
Marriage: Jim Kerr (divorced)
Children: Two daughters, an 11-year-old fathered by Kinks' singer Ray Davies and a nine-year-old by her ex-husband, rock singer Jim Kerr.

ICE CUBE

Real Name: Oshea Jackson
Birthplace: Los Angeles, CA
Birthdate: 1969
Occupation: Rap artist, actor
Education: Phoenix Institute of Technology
Debut: Album (with N.W.A.): *Boyz N the Hood,* 1986. Album (solo): *Amerikka's Most Wanted,* 1990
Signature: *Boyz N the Hood*
Facts: Former lyricist of the rap group N.W.A. His 1991 album, *Death Certificate,* stirred controversy because it contained racist attacks on Koreans and called for the murder of a Jewish man.

Began writing rap lyrics at age 14.
Quote: "Rap is the network newscast black people never had."

ICE-T

Real Name: Tracy Morrow
Birthplace: Newark, NJ
Occupation: Rap artist, actor
Debut: (Film) *Breakin',* 1984; (Single) "The Coldest Rap," 1982
Signature: *New Jack City*
Facts: Born in the late 1950s, he is very tight-lipped about his past, and jokes that he'll only give his real age in court.

Appeared in the films *Breakin'* and *Breakin' II,* among others.

Spent four years running with gangs in South Central Los Angeles.

Served four years as a ranger in the U.S. Army.

Was raised by an aunt in Los Angeles after both of his parents died by the time he was in seventh grade.
Relationship: Darlene
Children: Latisha, Little Ice
Major Award: Grammy, Best Rap Performance—Duo or Group, "Back on the Block" (with others), 1990

KATHY IRELAND

Birthplace: Santa Barbara, CA
Birthdate: 3/8/63
Occupation: Model
Debut: Joined Elite Agency in 1980
Signature: *Sports Illustrated* swimsuit cover girl
Facts: First job was delivering newspapers at age 11 in Santa Barbara.

Joined the cast of *Melrose Place* in 1994.
Original Job: Newspaper carrier
Marriage: Greg Olsen
Famous Relatives: Mary Ireland, actor, sister; Cynthia Ireland, actor, sister

JEREMY IRONS

Birthplace: Cowes, Isle of Wight, England
Birthdate: 9/19/48
Occupation: Actor
Education: Bristol Old Vic Theatre School
Debut: (Stage) *Godspell,* 1972
Signature: *The French Lieutenant's Woman*
Facts: At school, excelled at rugby, the fiddle, and clarinet and headed the cadet corps.

Made his mark with the BBC series *Brideshead Revisited,* 1981.

Played a dual role as twin brothers in *Dead Ringers,* a 1988 movie he considers his best work.
Original Job: Housecleaner, gardener, assistant stage manager, busker (singing and playing guitar outside movie theaters)
Marriage: Sinéad Moira Cusack
Children: Samuel James, Maximilian Paul
Major Awards: Tony, Best Actor, *The Real Thing,* 1984; Oscar, Best Actor, *Reversal of Fortune,* 1991; Golden Globe, Best Actor, *Reversal of Fortune,* 1991

JOHN IRVING

Birthplace: Exeter, NH
Birthdate: 3/2/42
Occupation: Author
Education: University of New Hampshire, University of Iowa
Debut: (Book) *Setting Free the Bears,* 1969
Signature: *The World According to Garp*
Fact: His support for the freedom to create pornography, described in an article entitled "Pornography and the New Puritans" (*New York Times Book Review,* March 29, 1992) drew an angry letter from Andrea Dworkin in the *New York Times Book Review* (May 3, 1992).
Marriages: Shyla Leary (divorced), Janet Turnbull
Children: Colin, Brendan

CHRIS ISAAK

Birthplace: Stockton, CA
Birthdate: 6/26/56
Occupation: Singer, songwriter, actor
Education: University of the Pacific
Debut: (Album) *Silvertone* (with Silvertone), 1985
Signature: "Wicked Game"
Facts: In 1987, performed "Blue Hotel" on TV show *The Last Resort,* which flopped in the U.S. but was a hit in France.

His acting debut was 1988's *Married to the Mob.*

Appeared in many movies, including *Married to the Mob* (1988), *Silence of the Lambs* (1991), and *Little Buddha* (1993).
Original Job: Amateur boxer, tour guide for a film studio

ALAN JACKSON

Birthplace: Newnan, GA
Birthdate: 10/17/58
Occupation: Singer, songwriter
Education: Attended South Georgia College
Debut: (Album) *Here in the Real World,* 1989
Signature: "Neon Rainbow"
Facts: In 1985, his wife got Jackson his big break. A flight attendant, she cornered Glen Campbell in the Atlanta airport and asked him to listen to her husband's tape.

Started wearing his trademark white Stetson to hide scars above his left eyebrow (a result of a childhood accident with a coffee table).
Original Job: Forklift operator, car salesman, home builder
Marriage: Denise
Child: Mattie

BO JACKSON

Birthplace: Bessemer, AL
Birthdate: 11/30/62
Occupation: Football player, baseball player
Education: Auburn University
Facts: Was the first person to play both pro football and pro baseball in the same year, starting for both the Kansas City Royals and the L.A. Raiders in 1988 and 1989.

As a third grader, Bo was told he wasn't eligible to join his grammar school's track team. After outrunning all the other kids in fourth, fifth, and sixth grades, Jackson made the team.
Major Awards: Heisman Trophy, 1985; MVP, Major League Baseball All-Star game, 1989

JANET JACKSON

Birthplace: Gary, IN
Birthdate: 5/16/66
Occupation: Singer, actor
Debut: (TV) *Good Times,* 1977
Facts: With 1986 song "When I Think of You," she and brother Michael become the first siblings in the rock era to have number one songs as soloists.

Paula Abdul was Janet's choreographer before starting her own career.

Played Charlene DuPrey on the TV series *Diff'rent Strokes.*
Marriages: James DeBarge (annulled), Rene Elizondo
Famous Relatives: Michael, singer, brother; La Toya, singer, sister; Tito, singer, brother; Randy, singer, brother; Marlon, singer, brother; Jermaine, singer, brother; Jackie, singer, brother
Major Awards: Grammy, Best R&B Song, "That's the Way Love Goes," 1993; Grammy, Best Music Video—Long Form, *Rhythm Nation 1814,* 1989

JESSE JACKSON

Birthplace: Greenville, SC
Birthdate: 10/8/41
Occupation: Civil rights leader, politician
Education: North Carolina AT&T; Chicago Theological Seminary
Signature: Founded the Rainbow Coalition
Facts: Quarterback at all-black Sterling High School, received football scholarship to University of Illinois but says he was denied the position because he was black.
Original Job: Minister
Marriage: Jacqueline Lavinia Brown
Major Award: Grammy, Best Spoken Word Recording,

"Speech by Rev. Jesse Jackson, July 27" (from Aretha Franklin's *One Lord, One Faith, One Baptism*), 1988

MICHAEL JACKSON

Birthplace: Gary, IN
Birthdate: 8/29/58
Occupation: Singer, songwriter, actor
Debut: (Stage) Mr. Lucky's, Gary, IN (with Jackson 5), 1966
Signature: *Thriller*
Facts: Built amusement park on property and maintains a menagerie of animals including Bubbles, the Chimp.

Gave Elizabeth Taylor away at her marriage to Larry Fortensky in 1991.

Surgery includes four nose jobs, two nose adjustments, and cleft put in his chin. Carol Publishing's unauthorized biography claims that Michael had the surgery to avoid resembling his abusive father as much as possible.

Infamy: Settled out of court a civil lawsuit alleging child molestation; criminal investigation continues.
Famous Relatives: Janet, singer, sister; LaToya, singer, sister; Tito, singer, brother; Randy, singer, brother; Marlon, singer, brother; Jermaine, singer, brother; Jackie, singer, brother
Marriage: Lisa Marie Presley
Major Awards: Grammy, Best R&B Vocal—Male, "Don't Stop 'Till You Get Enough," 1979; Grammy, Album of the Year, *Thriller,* 1983; Grammy, Best Pop Vocal—Male, *Thriller,* 1983; Grammy, Best R&B Song, "Billie Jean," 1983; Grammy, Best R&B Vocal—Male, "Billie Jean," 1983; Grammy, Best Recording for Children, *E.T. The Extraterrestrial,* 1983; Grammy, Record of the Year, "Beat It," 1984; Grammy, Best Pop Vocal—Male, "Beat It," 1984; Grammy, Song of the Year, "We Are the World" (with Lionel Richie), 1985; Grammy, Best Music Video, Short Form, *Leave Me Alone,* 1989; Grammy, Legend Award, 1993

MICK JAGGER

Birthplace: Dartford, England
Birthdate: 7/26/43
Occupation: Singer, songwriter
Education: Attended London School of Economics
Debut: (Song) "Come On" (cover of Chuck Berry original), 1963
Signature: Rolling Stones
Facts: Went to elementary school with guitarist Keith Richards but lost touch with him until they met again on a London train in 1960.

Sang backup on Carly Simon's 1973 hit, "You're So Vain."

Co-owned the Philadelphia Furies with Peter Frampton, Rick Wakeman, and Paul Simon.

Marriages: Bianca Peres Morena de Macias (divorced), Jerry Hall
Children: Karis, Jade, Elizabeth Scarlett, James Leroy Augustine, Georgia May
Major Awards: Grammy, Best Album Package, *Tattoo You* (with the Rolling Stones), 1981; Grammy, NARAS Lifetime Achievement Award, 1986; inducted into the Rock and Roll Hall of Fame (with the Rolling Stones), 1989

PETER JENNINGS

Birthplace: Toronto, Canada
Birthdate: 7/29/38
Occupation: Broadcast journalist
Education: Attended Carleton University and Rider College
Debut: At age nine, hosted *Peter's People,* a CBC radio show for children
Signature: *ABC's World News Tonight*
Facts: At 26, was the youngest network anchor ever. ABC removed him after three years. Took over as permanent anchor in 1983.
Original Job: Bank teller and late-night radio host
Marriage: First marriage ended in divorce, Valerie Godsoe (divorced), Kati Marton (divorced)
Children: Elizabeth, Christopher
Famous Relative: Charles Jennings, vice president of programming at CBC, father

BILLY JOEL

Birthplace: Bronx, NY
Birthdate: 5/9/49
Occupation: Singer, songwriter, piano player
Education: High school
Debut: (Song) "You Got Me Hummin'" (cover of Sam and Dave original, with The Hassles), 1965
Signature: "Piano Man"
Facts: Had a suicidal period when he was in his early twenties; after taking pills and swallowing furniture polish, he spent three weeks in Meadowbrook Hospital.

As a Long Island teenager, was a local welterweight boxing champion.

Wrote "New York State of Mind" within twenty minutes of returning home from California in 1975.

Original Job: Rock critic for *Changes* magazine
Marriages: Elizabeth Weber (divorced), Christie Brinkley (divorced)
Child: Alexa Ray
Major Awards: Grammy, Record of the Year, "Just the Way You Are," 1978; Grammy, Song of the Year, "Just the Way You Are," 1978; Grammy, Album of the Year, *Billy Joel,* 1979; Grammy, Best Pop Vocal—Male, "52nd Street," 1979; Grammy, Best Rock Vocal—Male, "Glass Houses," 1980; Grammy, Best Recording for Children, *In Harmony 2* (with others), 1982; Grammy, Legend Award, 1991

ELTON JOHN

Real Name: Reginald Kenneth Dwight
Birthplace: Pinner, England
Birthdate: 3/25/47
Occupation: Singer, songwriter, piano player
Education: Attended Royal Academy of Music, London
Debut: (Album) *Come Back Baby* (with Bluesology), 1965
Signature: "Rocket Man"
Facts: Took his name from first names of Bluesology members Elton Deal and John Baldry.

Wrote "Philadelphia Freedom" in 1975 for Billie Jean King.

Is godfather to Sean Lennon.

Along with Tim Rice (of *Little Shop of Horrors* fame), scored the 1994 Disney movie *The Lion King.*

Attended London's Royal Academy of Music but quit three weeks before final exams.

Original Job: Worked at Mills Music Publishers
Marriage: Renate Blauer (divorced)
Major Award: Grammy, Best Pop Performance—Duo or Group, "That's What Friends Are For" (with Dionne & Friends), 1986

BEVERLY JOHNSON

Birthplace: Buffalo, NY
Birthdate: 10/13/52
Occupation: Model, actor
Education: Attended Northeastern University
Facts: Father was a Blackfoot Indian and her mother a Louisiana Creole.

Almost qualified for the 1968 Olympics in the 100-yard freestyle swimming competition.

Received a full academic scholarship to Northeastern.

First black woman to appear on the covers of *Elle* and *Vogue* magazines.

After many years of voice lessons, recorded an album called *Don't Lose the Feeling* (1977) with rock singer Phil Anatasia.

Child: Anansa

DON JOHNSON

Birthplace: Flat Creek, MO
Birthdate: 12/15/49
Occupation: Actor
Education: Attended University of Kansas; studied at the American Conservatory Theater in San Francisco
Debut: (Stage) *Fortunes and Men's Eyes,* 1969; (Film) *The Magic Garden of Stanley Sweetheart,* 1970
Signature: *Miami Vice*
Facts: At age 12, seduced his babysitter. When he was 16, moved out of his dad's place and moved in with a 26-year-old cocktail waitress. At the University of Kansas, he became romantically involved with a drama professor.
Infamy: When he was 12, was caught stealing a car and sent to a juvenile detention home.

Admits to having been addicted to alcohol and cocaine.
Original Job: Worked in a meat-packing plant
Marriages: Melanie Griffith (divorced, remarried, separated)
Child: Jesse (with Patti D'Arbanville), Dakota
Major Award: Golden Globe, Best Actor in a Drama Series, *Miami Vice,* 1986

MAGIC JOHNSON

Real Name: Earvin Johnson
Birthplace: Lansing, MI
Birthdate: 8/14/59
Occupation: Basketball player (retired)
Education: Attended Michigan State University
Facts: On November 7, 1991, announced that he was retiring from basketball after being diagnosed HIV positive. Was diagnosed only months after marrying longtime friend Earletha "Cookie" Kelly, who was in the early stages of pregnancy.

Given his nickname in high school by a local sportswriter after a game in which he scored thirty-six points and had eighteen rebounds.
Infamy: In 1992, admitted he caught the AIDS virus from "messing around with too many women."
Marriage: Earletha "Cookie" Kelly
Children: Andre, Earvin III
Major Awards: Grammy, Best Spoken Word Album, *What You Can Do to Avoid AIDS* (with Robert O'Keefe), 1992; MVP, National Collegiate Athletic Association Final Four playoff tournament, 1979; MVP, NBA Championship Series, 1980, 1982, 1987; All-NBA First Team, 1983, 1984, 1985, 1986, 1987, 1988; MVP, NBA (regular season), 1987

QUINCY JONES

Birthplace: Chicago, IL
Birthdate: 3/14/33
Occupation: Composer, producer
Education: Attended Seattle University; Berklee College of Music; Boston Conservatory
Debut: Trumpeter, arranger, for Lionel Hampton Orchestra, 1950–53
Signature: Produced *Off the Wall, Thriller,* and *Bad*
Facts: Established his own label, Qwest, in 1981 and founded *Vibe* magazine.

Scored the TV series *Roots* in 1977.

Has worked with many prominent pop and jazz artists, including Ray Charles, Miles Davis, Ella Fitzgerald, Dizzy Gillespie, Ice-T, Chaka Khan, and Sarah Vaughan.

Middle name is Delight.
Marriages: Jeri Caldwell (divorced), Ulla Anderson (divorced), Peggy Lipton (divorced), Nastassja Kinski (relationship)
Children: Jolie, Martina-Lisa, Quincy III, Kidada, Rashida

TOMMY LEE JONES

Birthplace: San Saba, TX
Birthdate: 9/15/46
Occupation: Actor
Education: Harvard University
Debut: (Stage) *A Patriot for Me,* 1969; (Film) *Love Story,* 1970
Signature: *The Executioner's Song*
Facts: Roomed with Vice President Al Gore while attending Harvard.

Is a champion polo player.

Is an 18th generation Texan.
Original Job: Worked in oil fields
Marriages: Katherine Lardner (divorced), Kimberlea Gayle Cloughley
Major Awards: Emmy, Best Actor in a Minseries, *The Executioner's Song,* 1983; Oscar, Best Supporting Actor, *The Fugitive,* 1994; Golden Globe, Best Supporting Actor, *The Fugitive,* 1994

MICHAEL JORDAN

Birthplace: Brooklyn, NY
Birthdate: 2/17/63
Occupation: Basketball player (retired); baseball player
Education: Attended the University of North Carolina
Signature: Chicago Bulls star
Facts: In retirement, Jordan plays minor league baseball. Also continues to play golf and hopes to take a shot at the PGA tour.

He was cut from the varsity basketball team in high school.
Marriage: Juanita Vanoy
Children: Jeffrey, Marcus, Jasmine
Major Awards/Titles: College Player of the Year, 1984; Olympic Gold Medal, 1984, 1992; NBA scoring leader, 1987, 1988, 1989, 1990, 1991, 1992, 1993; NBA All-Star team (7 seasons); NBA MVP, regular season, 1988, 1991, 1992; NBA MVP, finals, 1991, 1992, 1993

DONNA KARAN

Real Name: Donna Faske
Birthplace: Forest Hills, NY
Birthdate: 10/2/48
Occupation: Fashion designer
Education: Parson's School of Design
Signature: DKNY clothes
Facts: While in college, worked for designers Chuck Howard and Liz Claiborne.

After serving a long apprenticeship with the Anne Klein collection, at age 26 was given full creative control by the principal owner of the firm after Anne Klein died of cancer in 1974.

Close personal friend to many stars including Barbra Streisand.
Original Job: Sales clerk at a Long Island dress shop
Marriages: Mark Karan (divorced), Stephen Weiss
Child: Gabrielle
Major Awards: Coty Award, 1977, 1981; named to Coty Hall of Fame, 1984

HARVEY KEITEL

Birthplace: Brooklyn, NY
Birthdate: 5/13/39
Occupation: Actor, producer
Education: Studied with Lee Strasberg at the Actor's Studio and Stella Adler
Debut: (Film) *Who's That Knocking at My Door?,* 1968
Signature: *The Piano*
Facts: Joined the U.S. Marine Corps at age 16 and served in Lebanon.

Answered a newspaper ad placed by Martin Scorsese, then an NYU student director, seeking actors for his first film in 1965, which started off their professional relationship.

Was cast as the lead in *Apocalypse Now,* but had a falling out with director Francis Ford Coppola and was fired on location in the Philippines. He was replaced by Martin Sheen.

As a child, Keitel had a severe stutter.

Unusual among Hollywood actors for his willingness to show frontal nudity in his films *(The Piano, Bad Lieutenant).*
Infamy: Was asked to leave the Alexander Hamilton Vocational School in Brooklyn because of truancy.
Original Job: Shoe salesman
Marriage: Lorraine Bracco (divorced)
Child: Stella

JOHN F. KENNEDY JR.

Birthplace: Washington, DC
Birthdate: 11/25/60
Occupation: Publisher of political magazine (in development)
Education: Brown University; attended University of Delhi, India; New York University Law School
Facts: First baby in the White House since 1893.

Worked in the Peace Corps in Guatemala following a devastating earthquake.

Failed the bar exam twice.
Famous Relatives: John F. Kennedy, president, father; Jacqueline Onassis, first lady, mother; Ted Kennedy, senator, uncle

NANCY KERRIGAN

Birthdate: 1970
Occupation: Figure skater
Facts: Mother Brenda is legally blind from a rare virus she suffered from when Nancy was just a toddler; she watches her daughter skate via TV monitor.

Began skating at age six.
Major Titles: Gold Medal at 1990 U.S. Olympic Festival; Bronze Medal at 1991 world championships and U.S. championships; Bronze Medal at 1992 Olympics; Silver Medal at 1994 Olympics.

NICOLE KIDMAN

Birthplace: Hawaii
Birthdate: 1966

Occupation: Actor
Education: St. Martin's Youth Theatre, Melbourne, Australia
Debut: (Film) *Bush Christmas,* 1983
Facts: Became an overnight star in Australia with her performance in the miniseries *Vietnam,* 1988.
Marriage: Tom Cruise
Child: Adopted daughter Isabella Jane

ANTHONY KIEDIS

Birthplace: Grand Rapids, MI
Occupation: Singer
Education: Attended UCLA
Debut: (Album) *Red Hot Chili Peppers,* 1984
Signature: Red Hot Chili Peppers
Facts: He and fellow Chili Pepper Michael "Flea" Balzary were classmates at Hollywood's Fairfax High School.

Played Sylvester Stallone's son in the 1978 film *F.I.S.T.*

The group was originally called Tony Flow and the Miraculously Majestic Masters of Mayhem.

Quit taking drugs, drinking, and eating meat after guitarist Hillel Slovak died of a heroin overdose in 1988. The RHCP songs "Under the Bridge," "Knock Me Down," and "My Lovely Man" all relate to Slovak's death.
Infamy: Kiedis appeared in U.S. Health Department ads advocating the use of condoms to stop AIDS, but the ads never ran—government officials yanked them when they learned that Kiedis had once been charged with lewdness for exposing himself to a female University of Virginia student backstage after a concert.
Original Job: Actor
Famous Relative: Blackie Dammett, actor, father

LARRY KING

Real Name: Lawrence Harvey Zeiger
Birthplace: Brooklyn, NY
Birthdate: 11/19/33
Occupation: Talk show host
Facts: In February of 1992, Ross Perot announced his bid for the presidency on *Larry King Live.*

Father died of a heart attack when Larry was ten, and he grew up on public assistance.

As a teenager, ran away to get married. Had the ceremony annulled shortly thereafter.

Graduated from high school just one point above passing.
Infamy: In December of 1971, he was arrested for stealing money a financier had given him for the New Orleans D.A.'s investigation into the death of John F. Kennedy. King had used the money to pay taxes after he had blown his own money on Cadillacs, expensive restaurants, and gambling debts.
Original Job: Janitor at a local AM station in Florida
Marriages: Alene Akins (divorced, remarried, divorced), Mickey Sutphin (divorced), Sharon Leporte (divorced), Julie Alexander (divorced)
Child: Chaia

STEPHEN KING

Birthplace: Portland, ME
Birthdate: 9/21/47
Occupation: Author
Education: University of Maine
Debut: (Book) *Carrie,* 1974
Signature: Horror novels
Facts: Family was deserted by father, who went out for pack of cigarettes and never returned.

Wrote first short story at age seven.

Had his first story published in a comic book fan magazine, *Comics Review,* in 1965.

Was working as a high school English teacher at Hampden Academy, in Maine, when his first book was published.

Used the pseudonym Richard Bachman for five novels, including *The Running Man* (made into an Arnold Schwarzenegger film, 1987).
Original Job: Laborer in an industrial laundry
Marriage: Tabitha Spruce
Children: Joe, Owen, Naomi

GREG KINNEAR

Birthplace: Logansport, IN
Birthdate: 1964
Occupation: Talk-show host
Education: University of Arizona
Debut: (TV) *Movietime,* 1987
Signature: *Talk Soup*
Facts: Lived in Beirut, Lebanon, with family and then evacuated to Athens, Greece when the Lebanese civil war broke out.

Worked on the advertising campaigns for such films as *Space Sluts in the Slammer, The Imp,* and the *Ghoulies* series.

Hosted syndicated action game show, *College Mad House.*

CALVIN KLEIN

Real Name: Richard Klein
Birthplace: New York, NY
Birthdate: 11/19/42
Occupation: Fashion designer
Education: Fashion Institute of Technology
Facts: Rescued his daughter from kidnappers in 1978.

As a boy in the Bronx, grew up around the corner from Ralph Lifshitz (now Ralph Lauren).

Former junk bond czar Michael Milken issued $80 million in high-interest Klein bonds in the '80s.
Infamy: Was addicted to valium and alcohol in the '80s, and checked into a Minnesota rehabilitation center for 31 days in 1988.
Marriages: Jayne Centre (divorced), Kelly Rector
Child: Marci
Major Awards: Coty Award, 1973, 1974,1975; elected to American Fashion Critics Circle Hall of Fame, 1975
Quote: "Anything I've ever wanted to do, I've done. Anyone I've wanted to be with, I've had."

TED KOPPEL

Birthplace: Lancashire, England
Birthdate: 2/8/40
Occupation: Broadcast journalist
Education: Syracuse University; Stanford University
Debut: (Radio) WMCA radio
Signature: *Nightline*
Facts: Author, *Adlai Stevenson: In the National Interest.*

When he joined ABC in 1963, he was the youngest news reporter ever to join a network.

Emigrated to the U.S. from England in 1953.
Marriage: Grace Anne Dorney
Major Award: Elected to the Emmy Hall of Fame, 1991

KARL LAGERFELD

Birthplace: Hamburg, Germany
Birthdate: 9/10/38
Occupation: Fashion designer
Education: Lycée Montaigne
Debut: First prize, women's coat design, International Wool Secretariat contest, 1954
Facts: Drew illustrations for books as a child. Apprenticed to Pierre Balmain, designing clothes for Sophia Loren, Rita Hayworth, and Gina Lollobrigida.

Led the pret-à-porter wave of designers in the '60s in Paris, working at various times for Fendi furs and Charles Jourdan shoes.

Initiated art deco revival in early '70s.

Created the perfume Chloé for Elizabeth Arden (1975).
Under the pen name Minouflet de Vermenou, he reviews books for French *Vogue.*

RICKI LAKE

Birthplace: New York, NY
Birthdate: 9/21/68
Occupation: Actor, talk show host
Education: Attended Ithaca College
Debut: (Film) *Hairspray,* 1988
Signature: *The Ricki Lake Show*
Facts: Lost 115 pounds over a two-and-a-half-year period.

Lake plays the flute, piccolo, clarinet, and piano.
Original Job: Cabaret singer, appeared off-Broadway in 1983
Marriage: Rob Sussman

K.D. LANG

Real Name: Katherine Dawn Lang
Birthplace: Consort, Canada
Birthdate: 9/2/61
Occupation: Singer, songwriter
Education: Attended college in Red Deer, Alberta, Canada
Debut: (Album) *A Truly Western Experience,* 1984
Facts: Acted in the movie

Salmonberries, 1991.

Duetted with Roy Orbison on a remake of his song "Crying" in 1988, shortly before he died.
Infamy: Her recordings have been boycotted in the conservative areas of the South and cattle ranching areas of central Canada because she is a lesbian and an animal rights activist.
Original Job: Performance artist
Major Awards: Grammy, Best Pop Vocal—Female, "Constant Craving," 1992; Grammy, Best Country Vocal—Female, "Absolute Torch and Twang," 1989; Grammy, Best Country Vocal—Collaboration, "Crying" (with Roy Orbison), 1988
Quote: "I have a little bit of penis envy. They're ridiculous, but they're cool."

ANGELA LANSBURY

Birthplace: London, England
Birthdate: 10/16/25
Occupation: Actor
Education: Attended Webber-Douglas School of Singing and Dramatic Arts; attended Feagin School of Drama and Radio
Debut: (Film) *Gaslight,* 1944
Signature: *Murder, She Wrote*
Facts: Escaped with her family to the U.S. when the Germans began to bomb London in World War II.

In 1943, went to MGM to audition for *The Picture of Dorian Gray* and was told the studio was looking for someone to play the role of the maid in *Gaslight.* She auditioned and got it.

In the seven years she was under contract to MGM, she appeared in seventy films.
Original Job: Ticket taker in the theater in which her mother worked; clerk in department store
Marriages: Richard Cromwell (divorced), Peter Pullen Shaw
Children: Anthony Peter, Deidre Angela
Famous Relative: Moyna McGill, actor, mother
Major Awards: Golden Globe, Best Supporting Actress, *The Picture of Dorian Gray,* 1946; Golden Globe, Best Supporting Actress, *The Manchurian Candidate,* 1963; Golden Globe, Best Actress in a TV Series—Drama, *Murder, She Wrote,* 1985, 1987, 1990, 1992; Tony, Best Actress (Musical), *Mame,* 1966; Tony, Best Actress (Musical), *Dear World,* 1969; Tony, Best Actress (Musical), *Gypsy,* 1975; Tony, Best Actress (Musical), *Sweeney Todd,* 1979

JOHN LARROQUETTE

Birthplace: New Orleans, LA
Birthdate: 11/25/47
Occupation: Actor
Debut: (TV) *Doctor's Hospital,* 1976–8
Signature: *Night Court*
Facts: Narrator of *The Texas Chainsaw Massacre.*

Played squadron member Robert Anderson in the TV series *Baa Baa Black Sheep,* 1976–78.

Larroquette is an alcoholic who sobered up without the help of Alcoholics Anonymous.
Original Job: Disc jockey
Marriage: Elizabeth
Children: Lisa, Jonathan, Benjamin
Major Award: Emmy, Best Supporting Actor in a Comedy Series, *Night Court,* 1985, 1986, 1987, 1988

QUEEN LATIFAH

Real Name: Dana Owens
Birthplace: East Orange, NJ
Birthdate: 1970
Occupation: Rap artist, actor
Education: High school
Debut: (Album) *All Hail the Queen,* 1989; (TV) *The Fresh Prince of Bel-Air,* 1991; (Film) *Jungle Fever,* 1991
Facts: Was a power forward on two state championship basketball teams in high school.

Trained in karate and use of firearms by her policeman father.

CEO of Flavor Unit, a management and production company whose clients include Naughty By Nature and FU-Schnickens.
Original Job: Worked at a Burger King, cashier at the Wiz

RALPH LAUREN

Real Name: Ralph Lifshitz
Birthplace: Bronx, NY
Birthdate: 10/14/39
Occupation: Fashion designer
Education: Attended City College of New York
Facts: Never attended design school.

As a boy in the Bronx, grew up around the corner from Calvin Klein.

First break was designing a neckwear line for Beau Brummell, 1967.

Outfitted Robert Redford for his role in *The Great Gatsby,* 1974.
Original Job: Salesman at Brooks Brothers, stock boy at Alexander's department store
Marriage: Ricky Low Beer
Children: Andrew, David, Dylan
Major Awards: American Fashion Critics Coty Award, 1970, 1973, 1974, 1976, 1977, 1981, 1984; elected to Coty Hall of Fame, 1971; Council of Fashion Designers of America Award, 1981

MARTIN LAWRENCE

Birthplace: Frankfurt, Germany
Birthdate: 1965
Occupation: Actor
Education: High school
Debut: (TV) *What's Happening Now,* 1987; (Film) *Do the Right Thing,* 1989
Signature: *Martin*
Facts: He was a *Star Search* winner, a street performer in Washington Square Park, and a stand-up comic at the Improv's open mike night.

Worked at Sears in Queens with Salt-N-Pepa and Kid 'N Play.
Infamy: After a February 1994 appearance on *Saturday Night Live* in which he told women to "put a Tic-Tac in your ass" to remain clean, Lawrence was banned from all NBC productions.
Original Job: Gas station attendant, store clerk

SPIKE LEE

Real Name: Shelton Lee
Birthplace: Atlanta, GA
Birthdate: 3/20/57
Occupation: Filmmaker, director
Education: Morehouse College; New York University
Debut: (Film) *She's Gotta Have It,* 1986
Signature: *Do the Right Thing*
Facts: Lee is known as the unofficial New York Knick, sitting courtside and shouting out to players on both teams. During the 1994 Eastern Conference Championships, some fans felt that his harassment of an Indiana Pacer caused the player to score the most points in the game and defeat the Knicks.

Taught at Harvard as a visiting professor in 1992.

A film he made at NYU, *Joe's Barbershop: We Cut Heads,* was the first student work ever selected for Lincoln Center's "New Directors, New Films" showcase and won a student award from the Academy of Motion Pictures Arts and Sciences.
Original Job: Advertising copywriter
Marriage: Tonya Linette Lewis

JENNIFER JASON LEIGH

Real Name: Jennifer Morrow
Birthplace: Los Angeles, CA
Birthdate: 2/5/62
Occupation: Actor
Education: Lee Strasberg Institute
Debut: (Film) *Death of a Stranger,* 1971
Signature: *The Best Little Girl in the World*
Facts: In order to prepare for roles, she writes a complete imaginary diary for the character.

Dieted down to 86 pounds for her role as an anorexic in the TV movie *The Best Little Girl in the World,* 1981.
Famous Relatives: Vic Morrow, actor, father; Barbara Turner, screenwriter, mother
Major Award: Golden Globe, Special Achievement, *Short Cuts,* 1994

LAURA LEIGHTON

Birthplace: Iowa City, IA
Birthdate: 3/14/69
Education: High school
Signature: *Melrose Place*
Facts: In 1987, toured with the traveling singing troupe Young Americans.
Original Job: TV commercial actress
Relationship: Grant Show
Quote: "I didn't even have a television when I was growing up."

JAY LENO

Real Name: James Leno
Birthplace: New Rochelle, NY
Birthdate: 4/28/50
Occupation: Talk show host, comedian
Education: Emerson College
Debut: (Film) *Silver Bears,* 1978; (TV) *The Marilyn McCoo & Billy Davis Jr. Show,* 1977
Signature: *The Tonight Show*
Facts: Collects antique cars and motorcycles.

Made first appearance on *The Tonight Show* in 1977.

While in grade school, Leno executed such pranks as flushing tennis balls down the toilet and hiding a dog in his locker. His fifth grade teacher wrote on his report card, "If Jay spent as much time studying as he does trying to be a comedian, he'd be a big star."
Original Job: Rolls Royce mechanic, deliveryman
Marriage: Mavis Nicholson

DAVID LETTERMAN

Birthplace: Indianapolis, IN
Birthdate: 4/12/47
Occupation: Talk show host
Education: Ball State University
Debut: (TV) *The Starland Vocal Band Show,* 1977
Signature: *Late Show with David Letterman*
Facts: While working as a weather announcer at a local TV station, he congratulated a tropical storm on being upgraded to a hurricane.

Was the announcer for the late-night movie program *Freeze Dried Movies.* On the program, he blew up a model of the television station at which he was working.
Infamy: Margaret Ray has continually stalked him at his New Canaan, CT, home. She was caught at or in his home eight times from 1988-1993.
Original Job: TV announcer, weatherman
Marriage: Michelle Cook (divorced)
Major Awards: Emmy, Writing in a Variety or Music Show, *Late Night with David Letterman,* 1984, 1985, 1986, 1987; Emmy, Best Host of a Daytime Variety Series, *The David Letterman Show,* 1981

JULIETTE LEWIS

Birthplace: San Fernando Valley, CA
Birthdate: 6/21/73
Occupation: Actor
Debut: (TV) *I Married Dora,* 1987; (Film) *My Stepmother Is an Alien,* 1988
Signature: *Cape Fear*
Facts: Went to court to become legally "emancipated" so that she would be exempt from laws that limit child actors to five hours of work on school days, in 1987.

Dated Brad Pitt. She met him on the set of the TV movie *Too Young to Die* in 1989.
Famous Relative: Geoffrey Lewis, actor, father

RUSH LIMBAUGH

Birthplace: Cape Girardeau, MO
Birthdate: 12/12/51
Occupation: Talk-show host
Education: Attended Southeastern Missouri State University
Debut: (Radio) *The Rush Limbaugh Show*
Facts: Claims he does not own a pair of blue jeans.

More than 300 "Rush rooms" have opened in restaurants nationwide for the purpose of broadcasting Rush Limbaugh's programs to patrons.

Met his current wife, Marta Fitzgerald, via electronic mail on CompuServe Information Service. They were married by Supreme Court Justice Clarence Thomas.
Infamy: A controversy occurred when the Florida Citrus Commission advertised orange juice on Rush's show in April 1994. The ads generated 7,500 calls and provoked a call from the National Organization for Women, as well as various gay and lesbian groups, to boycott Florida orange juice. Meanwhile, about 30 Rush supporters bought out the entire supply of orange juice at an Orlando, Florida store in a counter-protest.
Original Job: Disc jockey, PR man for the Kansas City Royals
Marriages: Roxy Maxine McNeely (divorced), Michelle Sixta (divorced), Marta Fitzgerald

HEATHER LOCKLEAR

Birthplace: Los Angeles, CA
Birthdate: 9/25/61
Occupation: Actor
Education: Attended UCLA
Debut: (TV) *Dynasty,* 1981
Signature: *Dynasty*
Facts: Served over six years as the spokesperson for the Health and Tennis Corporation of America.

Played officer Stacy Sheridan on the crime drama series *TJ Hooker* with William Shatner, 1982–87.
Marriage: Tommy Lee (divorced)
Relationship: Richie Sambora

JULIA LOUIS-DREYFUS

Birthplace: New York, NY
Birthdate: 1/13/61
Occupation: Actor
Education: Northwestern University
Debut: (TV) *Saturday Night Live,* 1982
Facts: Parents were divorced when she was only one year old.

Met husband in college and worked with him on *Saturday Night Live.*
Original Job: Member of the Second City comedy troupe
Marriage: Brad Hall
Child: Henry

COURTNEY LOVE

Birthplace: Eugene, OR
Birthdate: 1966
Occupation: Singer, songwriter
Education: High school dropout
Debut: (Album) *Pretty on the Inside,* 1991
Signature: Hole
Facts: Ran away to Europe at 15; her grandfather's death left her a millionaire.

Mother was the psychologist who examined Katherine Anne Power (60s radical and fugitive who recently confessed to being an accessory to bank robbery).

Appeared in the film *Straight to Hell,* 1987.

Before founding Hole, Love was lead vocalist for the San Diego rock band Faith No More in the early '80s "for about a week" (before they found Chuck Mosely). She also played with Kat Bjelland of the Minneapolis all-girl band Babes in Toyland and future L7 member Jennifer Finch in Sugar Baby Doll.

Named their daughter Frances after the '30s actress Frances Farmer, who is the subject of Nirvana song "Frances Farmer Will Have Her Revenge on Seattle."
Infamy: In her early teens, was sent to a juvenile detention center after stealing a Kiss T-shirt from a department store.
Original Job: Danced in strip joints in L.A. and Alaska
Marriage: Kurt Cobain (deceased)
Child: Frances Bean
Famous Relatives: Linda Carroll, psychologist, mother; Hank Harrison, author, father

LYLE LOVETT

Birthplace: Klein, TX
Birthdate: 11/1/57
Occupation: Singer, songwriter
Education: Texas A&M
Debut: (Album) *Lyle Lovett,* 1986
Facts: Played guitar in coffee shops while in college.

Lives in a clapboard house built by his grandparents.

Is afraid of cows.
Marriage: Julia Roberts
Major Awards: Grammy, *Lyle Lovett and His Large Band,* 1989

JON LOVITZ

Birthplace: Tarzana, CA
Birthdate: 7/21/57
Occupation: Actor
Education: Attended University of California–Irvine
Debut: (TV) *The Tonight Show,* 1985
Signature: *Saturday Night Live*
Facts: Provides the voice for the animated sitcom *The Critic.* Has also provided voices for *The Simpsons* and the film *An American Tail 2: Fievel goes West,* 1991.

Had his own special, *The Please Watch the Jon Lovitz Special,* which aired in 1992.

Original Job: Waiter, orderly, messenger
Quote: "Anybody who tells you he doesn't want to be famous is full of crap."

ROB LOWE

Birthplace: Charlottesville, VA
Birthdate: 3/17/64
Occupation: Actor
Education: High school
Debut: (TV) *A New Kind of Family,* 1978
Signature: *St. Elmo's Fire*
Facts: As a child, he memorized all the lines to *The Wizard of Oz* and liked to dress up as Batman.

Played in the celebrity all-star game at Dodger Stadium while in high school, where his classmates included Emilio Estevez and Sean Penn.

Lowe is deaf in his right ear.
Infamy: Lowe admitted to having sex with a teenage girl and recording the act, and was sued by her mother. He performed 20 hours of community service.
Marriage: Sheryl Berkoff
Child: Edward Matthew
Famous Relative: Chad Lowe, actor, brother

SUSAN LUCCI

Birthplace: Scarsdale, NY
Birthdate: 12/23/48
Occupation: Actor
Education: Marymount College
Debut: (TV) *All My Children,* 1969
Signature: *All My Children*
Facts: Lucci was nominated 14 times for the best actress in a daytime series, and lost every time.

Made the semifinals in New York State Miss Universe pageant, 1968. Dropped out of the competition to finish her college exams.

As Erica Kane, Lucci has impersonated a nun, been kidnapped, rescued a lover from prison using a helicopter, and stared down a grizzly bear.
Original Job: "Color girl" for CBS, sitting for cameras as a new lighting system for color TV was being developed
Marriage: Helmut Huber
Children: Liza Victoria, Andreas Martin

LORETTA LYNN

Real Name: Loretta Webb
Birthplace: Butcher Hollow, KY
Birthdate: 4/14/35
Occupation: Singer, songwriter
Debut: (Single) "Honky Tonk Girl," 1960
Signature: "Coal Miner's Daughter"
Facts: First woman to earn a certified gold country album.

Her first number one single "Don't Come Home A-Drinkin' (With Lovin' on Your Mind)" was banned from several stations. Many of her songs have been banned, including "Rated X" and "The Pill."

Married when she was 13. "By the time I was 17, I had four kids, and I had never been anywhere." She was a grandmother at 31 one year after her twins (her last children) were born.
Marriage: Oliver Vanetta Lynn Jr.
Children: Betty Sue Lynn Markworth, Jack Benny (deceased), Clara Lynn Lyell, Ernest Ray, Peggy, Patsy
Major Awards: Grammy, Best Country Performance—Duo or Group, "After the Fire Is Gone" (with Conway Twitty), 1971; Grammy, Best Recording for Children, *Sesame Country* (with others), 1981; inducted into the Country Music Hall of Fame, 1988

ANDIE MACDOWELL

Real Name: Rose Anderson MacDowell
Birthplace: Gaffney, SC
Birthdate: 4/21/58
Occupation: Actor
Education: Attended Winthrop College
Debut: (Film) *Greystoke: The Legend of Tarzan, Lord of the Apes,* 1984
Signature: *Green Card*
Facts: After *Greystoke* was filmed, MacDowell's part was overdubbed with a British accent provided by Glenn Close.

Played Jimi Hendrix's "Angel" at her wedding.
Original Job: Elite model
Marriage: Paul Qualley
Children: Justin, Rainey
Major Award: Golden Globe, Special Achievement, *Short Cuts,* 1994

KYLE MACLACHLAN

Birthplace: Yakima, WA
Birthdate: 2/22/59
Occupation: Actor
Education: University of Washington, Seattle
Debut: (Film) *Dune,* 1984
Signature: *Twin Peaks*
Fact: Read the Hardy Boys and imagined himself as one of the investigators.
Relationship: Linda Evangelista
Major Award: Golden Globe, Best Actor in a Drama Series, *Twin Peaks,* 1991

SHIRLEY MACLAINE

Real Name: Shirley MacLaine Beaty
Birthplace: Richmond, VA
Birthdate: 4/24/34
Occupation: Actor
Education: Washington School of Ballet
Debut: (Stage) *Oklahoma!,* 1950
Signature: *Terms of Endearment*
Facts: Starred in her own TV series, *Shirley's World* (1971–72).

Was performing with the Washington School of Ballet by the time she was 12, but soon grew too tall to be a ballerina.

Following a show biz cliché, she got the lead in the 1954 Broadway show *The Pajama Game* when the lead hurt her ankle.

As a young girl, often had to come to the aid of her bookish and picked-on younger brother with fists blazing.
Infamy: Ridiculed for her oft-expressed beliefs in reincarnation. Satirized herself in the "Pavilion of Former Lives" in the film *Defending Your Life* (1991).
Original Job: Dancer
Marriage: Steve Parker (divorced)
Child: Stephanie Sachiko
Famous Relative: Warren Beatty, actor, brother
Major Award: Oscar, Best Actress, *Terms of Endearment,* 1983

ELLE MACPHERSON

Real Name: Eleanor Gow
Birthplace: Sydney, Australia
Birthdate: 1965
Occupation: Supermodel, actor
Debut *Sports Illustrated* swimsuit model
Facts: Appeared in every issue of *Elle* magazine from 1982 to 1988.

Made her acting debut as the nymph like muse Sheila in the 1994 film *Sirens.*

Launched a designer lingerie line in Australia and New Zealand in 1991.
Marriage: Gilles Bensimon (divorced)

JOHN MADDEN

Birthplace: Austin, MN
Birthdate: 4/10/36
Occupation: Sportscaster
Education: California Polytechnic University
Debut: Assistant coach, Santa Maria, CA
Signature: CBS football analyst
Fact: Coached the Oakland Raiders for ten years and had a record of 103-32-7.
Marriage: Virginia Madden
Major Awards: American Football League Coach of the Year, 1969; American Sportscaster Association, Sports Personality of the Year, 1985; Emmy, Best Sports Personality—Analyst, 1982, 1983, 1987, 1988

MADONNA

Real Name: Madonna Louise Veronica Ciccone
Birthplace: Bay City, MI
Birthdate: 8/16/58
Occupation: Singer
Education: Attended University of Michigan
Debut: Dancer, Alvin Ailey Dance Company, 1979
Signature: *Material Girl*
Facts: She starred in an exploitation film called *A Certain Sacrifice* in 1980.

Early in her career, posed nude for a New York photographer. Those photos later appeared in *Playboy.*

She appears in a nightclub scene from the 1983 movie *Vision Quest,* singing "Crazy for You" in the background.
Infamy: Madonna swore fourteen times while on *The Late Show with David Letterman,* in

order to get revenge for his many jokes at her expense. She also handed Letterman a pair of her panties and told him to smell them.

Her video for "Justify My Love" (1990) was banned from MTV.

Her book *Sex* (1992) was originally banned in Japan, where it is against the law to show pubic hair. Officials eventually relented since the book was being distributed anyway.

Original Job: Modeled, worked in a doughnut shop
Marriage: Sean Penn (divorced)
Major Awards: Grammy, Best Music Video—Long Form, *Madonna—Blonde Ambition World Tour Live,* 1991

JOHN MALKOVICH

Birthplace: Christopher, IL
Birthdate: 12/9/53
Occupation: Actor
Education: Attended Eastern Illinois University, Illinois State University.
Debut: (Stage) *True West,* 1982
Signature: *Dangerous Liaisons*
Facts: Played football and tuba in high school.

Took up acting in college when he fell for a female drama student.

Co-founded the Steppenwolf Theatre in Chicago, in 1976.

Original Job: Enrolled in Eastern Illinois University with plans of becoming an environmentalist
Marriages: Glenne Headly (divorced), Nicoletta Peyran
Children: Amandine, Lowey
Major Award: Emmy, Best Supporting Actor in a Made-for-TV Movie, *Death of a Salesman,* 1986

DAVID MAMET

Birthplace: Chicago, IL
Birthdate: 11/30/47
Occupation: Writer, director
Education: Goddard College; studied at the Neighborhood Playhouse in New York
Debut: (Play) *The Duck Variations,* 1971
Signature: *Glengarry Glen Ross*
Facts: Wrote a children's book, *Warm and Cold,* in 1985.

Has worked as a busboy, driven a cab, worked at *Oui* magazine, and waited tables. Was an assistant office manager for a real estate business in Chicago and taught drama at Yale, New York University, and the University of Chicago.

Wrote the screenplays for *The Postman Always Rings Twice* (1981), *The Verdict* (1982), and *The Untouchables* (1987).

Original Job: Worked backstage at the Hull House Theatre in Chicago
Marriages: Lindsay Crouse (divorced); Rebecca Pidgeon
Children: Willa, Zoisa
Major Award: Pulitzer Prize, *Glengarry Glen Ross,* 1984

NELSON MANDELA

Birthplace: Umtata, South Africa
Birthdate: 7/18/18
Occupation: President, South Africa
Education: Attended University College of Fort Hare and Witwatersrand University, University of South Africa
Signature: President of South Africa
Facts: Helped found the Congress Youth League, a division of the African National Congress, in 1944.

Sentenced to five years in prison for inciting African strikes and for leaving the country without a valid passport in 1962. Sentenced to life imprisonment for sabotage and treason in 1964 and was released in February of 1990.

Before his arrest, Mandela lived in the underground and was known as "the Black Pimpernel."

Original Job: Worked at the Mandela and Tambo law firm in the 1950s
Marriages: Edith Ntoko (divorced); Nomzamo Winnie Madikileza (divorced)
Children: Makaziwe Phumla, Zenani, Zinziswa
Famous Relative: Henry Mandela, Tembu tribe chief, father
Major Awards: Nobel Peace Prize (with Willem de Klerk), 1993; Simón Bolívar International Prize from UNESCO, 1983

BARRY MANILOW

Real Name: Barry Alan Pincus
Birthplace: Brooklyn, NY
Birthdate: 6/17/46
Occupation: Singer, songwriter
Education: Attended New York College of Music, Julliard
Debut: (Album) *Barry Manlow I,* 1975
Signature: "I Write the Songs"
Facts: Arranged music for Bette Midler's band.

Wrote and sang jingles for Dr. Pepper, Pepsi, and McDonald's ("You Deserve a Break Today").

Father deserted family when he was two years old, and he was left to be raised by his mother and grandparents.

Original Job: Worked in mail room at CBS
Major Award: Grammy, Best Pop Vocal—Male, "Copacabana (At the Copa)," 1978

WYNTON MARSALIS

Birthplace: New Orleans, LA
Birthdate: 10/18/61
Occupation: Trumpeter
Education: Attended Julliard School of Music on a full scholarship
Debut: (Band) Art Blakey's Jazz Messengers, 1980
Facts: His first trumpet was a hand-me-down from bandleader Al Hirt.

Played with New Orleans Philharmonic at age 14.

Released his first classical album, *Trumpet Concertos,* in 1983. Was first artist ever to receive—or even be nominated for—awards in both jazz and classical categories in a single year.

Child: Tracy
Famous Relatives: Ellis Marsalis, musician, father; Branford Marsalis, musician, brother
Major Awards: Grammy, Best Jazz Performance—Soloist, "Think of One," 1983; Grammy, Best Jazz Performance—Soloist, "Hot House Flowers," 1984; Grammy, Best Jazz Performance—Soloist, "Black Codes from the Underground," 1985; Grammy, Best Jazz Performance—Group, "Black Codes from the Underground," 1985; Grammy, Best Jazz Performance—Group, "J Mood," 1986; Grammy, Best Jazz Performance—Group, *Marsalis Standard Time Volume I,* 1987

PENNY MARSHALL

Real Name: Carole Penny Marshall
Birthplace: New York NY
Birthdate: 10/15/42
Occupation: Actor, director
Education: Attended University of New Mexico
Debut: (TV) *The Danny Thomas Hour,* 1967
Signature: *Laverne and Shirley*
Facts: Even though the family was Congregationalist, Marshall's mother was convinced that Jewish men make the best husbands, so she sent Penny to a Jewish summer camp each year.

Lost the part of Sally on TV's *All in the Family* to Sally Struthers.

Was first woman director to have a film take in more than $100 million at the box office *(Big).*

Original Job: Dance instructor, secretary
Marriages: Michael Henry (divorced), Rob Reiner (divorced)
Child: Tracy Lee
Famous Relatives: Garry Marshall, director, producer, brother; Tony Maschiarelli, producer, father

STEVE MARTIN

Birthplace: Waco, TX
Birthdate: 8/14/45
Occupation: Actor, writer
Education: Attended Long Beach State College, UCLA
Debut: (TV) *The Smothers Brothers Comedy Hour,* 1967
Signature: *Comedy Is Not Pretty*
Facts: Lived behind Disneyland and got his start there performing magic tricks and playing the banjo.

Is a dedicated art collector.

Original Job: Sold guidebooks at Disneyland
Marriage: Victoria Tennant (divorced)
Major Awards: Grammy, Best Comedy Recording, *Let's Get Small,* 1977; Grammy, Best Comedy Recording, *A Wild and*

Crazy Guy, 1978; Emmy, Best Writing in a Comedy, Variety, or Music Program, *The Smothers Brothers Comedy Hour,* 1969

MARLEE MATLIN

Birthplace: Morton Grove, IL
Birthdate: 8/24/65
Occupation: Actor
Education: William Rainey Harper College
Debut: (Film) *Children of a Lesser God*
Signature: *Children of a Lesser God*
Facts: Became deaf through a case of roseola infantum at the age of 18 months.

A devout baseball fan, she takes her own glove to games.

At age 21, youngest to win an Oscar for Best Actress (for *Children of a Lesser God*).

Original Job: Policewoman, studying criminal justice in college
Marriage: Kevin Grandalski
Major Awards: Oscar and Golden Globe, Best Actress, *Children of a Lesser God,* 1987

PAUL MCCARTNEY

Real Name: James Paul McCartney
Birthplace: Liverpool, England
Birthdate: 6/18/42
Occupation: Singer, songwriter, bassist
Education: High school
Debut: Formed the Quarry Men, Moondogs, and the Silver Beatles with John Lennon and George Harrison, 1956–1962
Signature: *The Beatles*
Facts: When he wanted to use "Yesterday" in his 1984 film *Give My Regards to Broad Street,* he had to apply to the publishers for its use; he no longer owned the copyright of the most recorded song in history (over 2,500 cover versions exist).

Was the first Beatle to quit in 1970, releasing his solo album *McCartney* almost simultaneously with the band's release of *Let It Be.*

His version of "Mary Had a Little Lamb" hit number nine on the British charts in June 1972.

In the Paul McCartney Kindergarten in Krakow, Poland, children are taught English through McCartney's songs.

Infamy: Admitted to taking LSD and was arrested numerous times with Linda for possession of marijuana and for growing it at their Scotland farmhouse. Because of this, his application for a U.S. passport was refused many times.
Marriage: Linda Eastman
Children: James, Mary, Stella
Major Awards: Grammy, Best New Artist (with the Beatles), 1964; Grammy, Best Pop Vocal—Duo or Group, *A Hard Day's Night* (with the Beatles), 1964; Grammy, Song of the Year, "Michelle" (with John Lennon), 1966; Grammy, Best Rock Vocal, "Eleanor Rigby," 1966; Grammy, Album of the Year, *Sgt. Pepper's Lonely Hearts Club Band* (with the Beatles), 1967; Grammy, Best Score, *Let It Be* (with the Beatles), 1970; Oscar, Best Score, *Let It Be* (with the Beatles), 1970; Grammy, Best Pop Performance—Duo or Group, *Band on the Run* (with Wings), 1974; Grammy, Hall of Fame Winner, *Sgt. Pepper's Lonely Hearts Club Band* (with the Beatles), 1992; NARAS Lifetime Achievement Award, 1990; inducted into the Rock and Roll Hall of Fame (with Beatles), 1988

REBA MCENTIRE

Birthplace: McAlester, OK
Birthdate: 3/28/55
Occupation: Singer, songwriter
Education: Southeastern State University
Debut: (Song) "I Don't Want to Be a One-Night Stand," 1976
Signature: "Is There Life Out There?"
Facts: As a teenager, performed with her brother and sister in the Singing McEntires. Their first single was a tribute to her grandfather, rodeo rider John McEntire.

Appeared in the 1990 movie *Tremors.*

Marriages: Charlie Battles (divorced), Narvel Blackstock
Child: Shelby Stephen
Major Awards: Grammy, Best Country Female Vocalist, 1987; Grammy, Best Country Vocal—Female, "Whoever's in New England," 1986; Grammy, Best Country Vocal—Collaboration, "Does He Love You" (with Linda Davis), 1993

MEAT LOAF

Real Name: Marvin Lee Aday
Birthplace: Dallas, TX
Birthdate: 9/27/47
Occupation: Singer
Education: High school
Debut: (Album) *Bat out of Hell,* 1977
Signature: *Bat out of Hell*
Facts: Weighed 240 pounds in seventh grade.

Nicknamed by his high school football coach.

Bat out of Hell, the third best-selling album ever, still sells 15,000 copies a week, sixteen years after its release.

Twenty-two lawsuits with his manager, publisher, and other associates led to $85 million in losses.

Acted in off-broadway production of *The Rocky Horror Picture Show,* 1974.

Original Job: Baseball coach

NATALIE MERCHANT

Birthplace: Jamestown, NY
Occupation: Singer, songwriter
Education: Attended Jamestown Community College
Debut: (Album) *Human Conflict No. 5,* 1982
Signature: 10,000 Maniacs
Facts: The band mistakenly took its name from the B-movie *2000 Maniacs.*

Split from the group in the summer of 1993, citing the desire to work solo.

Between touring for *Blind Man's Zoo* and recording *Our Time in Eden,* volunteered at a Harlem daycare center for homeless kids.

LORNE MICHAELS

Real Name: Lorne Lipowitz
Birthplace: Toronto, Canada
Birthdate: 11/17/44
Occupation: Producer, writer
Education: University of Toronto
Debut: TV (writer): *Rowan and Martin's Laugh-In,* 1968
Signature: *Saturday Night Live*
Facts: In addition to *Saturday Night Live,* Michaels produces *The Kids in the Hall* and *Late Night with Conan O'Brien.* He has also produced the films *Three Amigos* (1986), *Wayne's World* (1992), *Wayne's World 2* (1993), *The Coneheads* (1993), and *Lassie* (1994).
Marriages: Rosie Shuster (divorced), Susan Forristal (divorced), Alice Barry
Child: Henry Abraham
Major Awards: Writers Guild of America Awards (4); Emmy, Best Writing in a Comedy, Variety, or Music Special, *Lily,* 1974, 1976; Emmy, Best Writing in a Comedy, Variety, or Music Series, *Saturday Night Live,* 1976, 1977; Emmy, Best Writing in a Comedy, Variety or Music Series, *The Paul Simon Special,* 1978; Emmy, Best Writing in a Variety or Music Program, *Murderers Among Us,* 1989

DEMI MOORE

Real Name: Demetria Guynes
Birthplace: Roswell, NM
Birthdate: 11/11/62
Occupation: Actor
Education: Left high school to model in Europe, studied with Zina Provendie
Debut: (Film) *Choices,* 1981
Signature: *Ghost*
Facts: Was cross-eyed as a child and had an operation to correct it, wearing a patch over one eye.

Decided to become an actress in high school when she lived in the same building as Nastassja Kinski.

In order to play coke addict Jules in the 1985 movie *St. Elmo's Fire,* she had to sign a contract stipulating that she would stop her own alcohol and drug abuse, an agreement that caused her to turn her life around.

She and Bruce Willis were married on November 21, 1987, by singer Little Richard.

Infamy: Posed nude and pregnant on the cover of *Vanity Fair.*
Original Job: Model
Marriages: Freddy Moore (divorced), Bruce Willis
Children: Rumer Glenn, Scout Larue, Tallulah Belle

VAN MORRISON

Real Name: George Ivan Morrison
Birthplace: Belfast, Northern Ireland.
Birthdate: 8/31/45
Occupation: Singer, songwriter
Education: High school dropout
Debut: (Song) "Don't Start Crying" (with Them), 1964
Signature: "Brown Eyed Girl"
Facts: Was lead singer of Them from 1964 to 1967 and has worked solo ever since.

In 1965, wrote "Gloria," which achieved moderate success but didn't hit the U.S. top ten until it was covered by The Shadows of Knight in 1966.
Marriage: Janet Planet (divorced)

ROB MORROW

Birthplace: New Rochelle, NY
Birthdate: 7/21/62
Occupation: Actor
Debut: (TV) *Tattingers,* 1988
Signature: *Northern Exposure*
Facts: In 1990, turned down a role in the proposed CBS series *The Antagonists* to appear in the play *The Substance of Fire,* in a part written for him. After refusing the TV role, his manager told him that he would never work again, and his agent wanted to dump him. Both forgave him very quickly after he landed the lead role in *Northern Exposure,* 1990.

In 1991, worked at Vassar College as director on a twenty-minute film he wrote about a child reacting to his divorced mother's new relationship.
Original Job: Waiter, balloon messenger

KATE MOSS

Birthplace: London, England
Birthdate: 1/16/74
Occupation: Supermodel
Education: High school dropout (?)
Debut: Storm modeling agency, 1988
Signature: Calvin Klein ads
Facts: Parents divorced when Moss was 13; she lived with mother and brother lived with father.

Appeared topless in *Face* at age 15.

Attended a rough public high school. Was one of the most popular girls. Smoked, drank, dated older boys.
Infamy: Has been accused of being anorexic, which she denies. Has also been accused of encouraging anorexia in others.
Relationship: Johnny Depp
Quote: "I'm not anorexic, I'm not a heroin addict, I'm not pregnant—all the shit they fucking say about me is not true. It's a load of lies the media made."

EDDIE MURPHY

Birthplace: Brooklyn, NY
Birthdate: 4/3/61
Occupation: Actor
Education: Attended Nassau Community College
Debut: (TV) *Saturday Night Live,* 1980–83
Signature: *Beverly Hills Cop*
Facts: Father was a policeman who died when Eddie was five.

Was voted most popular at Roosevelt Jr.-Sr. High School in NY.

Created and produced the TV series *The Royal Family,* which was cut short upon the sudden death of the star Redd Foxx.

Co-owns the L.A. restaurant Georgia with Denzel Washington.
Original Job: Shoe store clerk
Marriage: Nicole Mitchell
Children: Bria, Miles Mitchell
Major Award: Grammy, Best Comedy Recording, *Eddie Murphy—Comedian,* 1983

BILL MURRAY

Birthplace: Wilmette, IL
Birthdate: 9/21/50
Occupation: Actor, writer
Education: Loyola Academy; attended Regis College; attended Second City Workshop in Chicago
Debut: (TV) *Saturday Night Live,* 1977–80
Signature: *Ghostbusters*
Facts: Was a pre-med student at St. Regis College.

Provided the voice of Johnny Storm, the Human Torch, on Marvel Comics' radio show, *The Fantastic Four.* This is where he was heard by the producers of *Saturday Night Live.*

Bill's son, Homer Banks, is named after the legendary Chicago Cub, Ernie Banks.

In 1981, performed the song "The Best Thing (Love Song)" for John Waters's *Polyester.*
Original Job: Pizza maker.
Marriage: Margaret Kelly
Famous Relative: Brian Doyle-Murray, actor, brother
Major Award: Emmy, Best Writing in a Comedy Series, *Saturday Night Live,* 1977

MIKE MYERS

Birthplace: Scarborough, Canada
Birthdate: 1964
Occupation: Actor, writer
Education: High school
Debut: (TV) *Mullarkey & Myers,* 1984–86
Signature: *Wayne's World*
Facts: His TV debut came at age eight when he appeared in a TV commercial with Gilda Radner.

Met his wife at a hockey game.

Had been doing the Wayne character since high school. "I did him in kitchens at parties to make girls laugh."
Marriage: Robin Ruzan
Major Awards: Emmy Award, Outstanding Writing in a Comedy Series, *Saturday Night Live,* 1989; Emmy, Best Writing in a Variety or Music Program, *Murderers Among Us,* 1989

MARTINA NAVRATILOVA

Birthplace: Prague, Czechoslovakia
Birthdate: 10/18/56
Occupation: Tennis player
Education:
Facts: Holds the most singles titles of any tennis player in history, male or female (167).

Holds the record for most Wimbledon singles titles (nine).

Played her last major tournament at Wimbledon in 1994, at age 37. Lost in the finals to Conchita Martinez, a 22-year-old.

Defected from Czechoslovakia during the 1975 U.S. Open, at age 18.

Dated Rita Mae Brown and Nancy Leiberman.

Has written a novel, *The Total Zone,* with mystery writer Liz Nickles.

With Pam Shriver, won 109 consecutive doubles matches from 1983 to 1985.
Infamy: In 1991, former lover Judy Nelson filed a palimony suit against Navratilova, which led to a much-publicized case.

During an interview in Germany in 1994, Navratilova said she might adopt a child someday. This announcement caused an uproar both in Germany and internationally.
Major Titles: Wimbledon singles titles 1978-79, 1982-87, 1990; U.S. Open singles titles 1983-84, 1986-87; French Open singles titles 1982, 1984; Australian Open singles titles 1981, 1983, 1985; non-calendar year Grand Slam 1984-85; doubles Grand Slam 1984 (with Pam Shriver); 36 Grand Slam doubles titles

LIAM NEESON

Birthplace: Ballymena, Northern Ireland
Birthdate: 6/7/52
Occupation: Actor
Debut: (Stage) *In the Risen,* 1976; (Film) *Excalibur,* 1981
Signature: *Schindler's List*
Facts: At age nine, joined a boxing team run by a priest. Nose was broken during an early match, and had it set on sight by his manager. Quit boxing at age 17.

First starring role was the disfigured hero of the film *Darkman,* 1990.
Original Job: Forklift operator, architect's assistant, amateur boxer
Marriage: Natasha Richardson

WILLIE NELSON

Birthplace: Abbott, TX
Birthdate: 4/30/33
Occupation: Singer, songwriter, guitarist, actor
Education: Attended Baylor University in Texas
Debut: (Album) *... And Then I Wrote,* 1962; (Film) *The Electric Horseman,* 1979
Signature: "Mamas, Don't Let Your Babies Grow Up to Be Cowboys"

Facts: Nelson taught at Baptist Sunday school until officials objected to him playing in seedy bars.

Sold his first song "Family Bible" for $50 to feed his family; it became a huge hit performed by more than 70 country artists.

Organized Farm-Aid concerts to help midwestern farmers stricken by drought and threatened with foreclosure.

Began writing songs at age seven.

Infamy: In 1991, after a seven-year dispute with the IRS over $16.7 million in back taxes, the government seized most of Nelson's possessions (country club, recording studio, forty-four acre ranch, twenty other properties in four states, instruments, recordings, and memorabilia).

Arrested in 1994 for possession of marijuana.

Original Job: Janitor, door-to-door salesman (Bibles, encyclopedias, vacuum cleaners, sewing machines), hosted country music shows on Texas radio stations
Marriages: Martha Matthews (divorced), Shirley Collie (divorced), Connie (divorced), Annie D'Angelo
Children: Lana, Paula Carlene, Amy, Susie, Lukas Autry, Jacob Micah, Billy
Major Awards: Grammy, Best Country Vocal—Male, "Blue Eyes Cryin' in the Rain," 1975; Grammy, Best Country Vocal—Male, "Georgia on My Mind," 1978; Grammy, Best Country Vocal—Male, "Always on My Mind," 1982; Grammy, Legend Award, 1990; Grammy, Best Country Song, "On the Road Again," 1980; Grammy, Best Country Performance—Duo or Group, "Mamas Don't Let Your Babies Grow Up to Be Cowboys" (with Waylon Jennings), 1978; Grammy, Best Country Song, "Always on My Mind," 1982; inducted into the Country Music Hall of Fame in 1993

AARON NEVILLE

Birthplace: New Orleans, LA
Birthdate: 1/24/41
Occupation: Singer
Debut: (Single) "Over You," 1960
Signature: Singer with the Neville Brothers
Facts: Worked as a longshoreman on the docks in New Orleans to pay the record company for the studio time he used to record songs like "Over You" and "Tell It Like It Is."

A staunch Catholic, he credits his success to his faith in God. To this day he still offers novenas to St. Jude. "There's always something impossible to pray for."

Infamy: Spent six months in jail for auto theft in 1959.
Marriage: Joel
Children: Ernestine, Ivan, Jason, Aaron Jr.
Famous Relatives: Art, Charles, and Cyril Neville (all brothers, all singers)
Major awards: Grammy, Best Pop Vocal—Duo or Group with Vocal, "Don't Know Much" (with Linda Ronstadt), 1989; Grammy, Best Pop Vocal—Duo or Group with Vocal, "All My Life" (with Linda Ronstadt), 1990; Down Beat Blues, Soul, R&B Award, 1990

WAYNE NEWTON

Birthplace: Norfolk, VA
Birthdate: 4/3/42
Occupation: Entertainer
Education: High school dropout
Debut: (TV) *Jackie Gleason and His American Scene Magazine,* 1962; (Film) *80 Steps to Jonah,* 1969
Facts: Protege of Jackie Gleason.

Partly Native American.

Earns $250,000 a week for his Las Vegas performances.

Infamy: In 1992, declared bankruptcy, listing debts of more than $20 million.
Marriages: Elaine Okamura (divorced), Kathleen McCrone
Child: Erin

JACK NICHOLSON

Birthplace: Neptune, NJ
Birthdate: 4/22/37
Occupation: Actor, director, producer, screenwriter
Education: Studied with The Players Ring acting group
Debut: (Stage) *Tea and Sympathy,* 1957; (Film) *Cry-Baby Killer,* 1958
Signature: *The Shining*
Facts: Recorded *The Elephant's Child,* a children's record, with Bobby McFerrin (1987).
Infamy: Known for being a ladies' man, Nicholson had a 17-year relationship with actress Anjelica Huston that ended in 1990 when Nicholson revealed that actress Rebecca Broussard, his daughter's best friend, was carrying his child.
Original Job: Office boy in MGM's cartoon department
Marriages: Sandra Knight (divorced), Rebecca Broussard (relationship)
Children: Jennifer, Lorraine, Raymond
Major Awards: Golden Globe, Best Actor, *Chinatown,* 1975; Oscar, Best Actor, *One Flew Over the Cuckoo's Nest,* 1975; Golden Globe, Best Actor, *One Flew Over the Cuckoo's Nest,* 1976; Golden Globe, Best Actor in a Comedy, *Prizzi's Honor,* 1986; Oscar, Best Supporting Actor, *Terms of Endearment,* 1984; Golden Globe, Best Supporting Actor, *Terms of Endearment,* 1984; Grammy, Best Recording for Children, *The Elephant's Child,* 1987

LESLIE NIELSEN

Birthplace: Regina, Canada
Birthdate: 2/11/26
Occupation: Actor, writer
Education: Attended Lorne Greene's Academy of Radio Arts, Toronto
Debut: (TV) *Actor's Studio,* 1950; (Film) *Forbidden Planet,* 1956
Signature: *Naked Gun*
Facts: Grew up in a log cabin 200 miles south of the Arctic Circle.

Suffered a childhood case of rickets. Legally deaf.

Served in the Canadian Air Force during World War II.

Original Job: Radio announcer, disc jockey
Marriages: Monica Boyer (divorced), Sandy Ullman (divorced), Barbaree Earl (divorced)
Children: Thea, Maura
Famous Relative: Eric Nielsen, member of Canadian Parliament, brother

CONAN O'BRIEN

Birthplace: Brookline, MA
Birthdate: 4/18/63
Occupation: Talk-show host, writer
Education: Harvard University
Debut: (TV) *Not Necessarily the News,* 1985
Signature: *NBC's Late Night with Conan O'Brien*
Facts: Has written for *Saturday Night Live* and *The Simpsons.*

While at Harvard served as president of *The Harvard Lampoon* for two years, the first person to do so since Robert Benchley in 1912.

First TV producing attempt was *Lookwell* (1991), a sitcom pilot starring Adam West as a former TV detective who begins to fight crime in reality.

Major Award: Emmy, Best Writing in a Variety or Music Program, *Murderers Among Us,* 1989

ROSIE O'DONNELL

Birthplace: Commack, NY
Birthdate: 1962
Occupation: Actor, comedian
Debut: (TV) *Gimme a Break,* 1986
Signature: *The Flintstones*
Fact: Won the *Star Search* comedy competition five times.

SHAQUILLE O'NEAL

Birthplace: Newark, NJ
Birthdate: 3/6/72
Occupation: Basketball player
Education: Attended Louisiana State University
Facts: His rap album, *Shaq Diesel,* sold more than one million copies. Got his rap start by singing on "What's Up Doc," a song put out in 1993 by his favorite rap group, FU-Schnickens.

He stands seven feet one inch, weighs 303 pounds, and wears size twenty-one triple-E shoes.

His first name translates ironically as "little one."

Spent most of his adolescence in Germany, where his stepfather was an army sergeant.

LENA OLIN

Birthplace: Stockholm, Sweden
Birthdate: 3/22/55
Occupation: Actor

Debut: (Film) *Fanny and Alexander,* 1983
Signature: *Havana*
Facts: Hired as an extra by Ingmar Bergman at the age of 17.

While starring in *The Dream Play,* a Swedish drama about an actress who becomes pregnant, she became pregnant.
Child: August
Famous Relative: Stij Olin, radio personality, father

ASHLEY OLSEN

Birthdate: 1987
Occupation: Actor
Debut: (TV) *Full House,* 1987
Facts: Three minutes older than fraternal twin sister Mary-Kate and has a freckle under her nose.

Their mother says, "When they need someone to be more active or emotional, they let Ashley do it."

How is she different from her twin? "My voice is deeper."
Famous Relative: Jamie Olsen, former dancer with the Los Angeles Ballet, mother

MARY-KATE OLSEN

Birthdate: 1987
Occupation: Actor
Debut: (TV) *Full House,* 1987
Facts: Wants to be a candymaker or a cowgirl when she grows up.

Both twins earn income not only from the show but also through sale of the talking Michelle doll.

"Mary-Kate is more serious, so she gets the serious lines to do," says her mother.
Famous Relative: Jamie Olsen, former dancer with the Los Angeles Ballet, mother

OZZY OSBOURNE

Real Name: John Michael Osbourne
Birthplace: Aston, England
Birthdate: 12/3/48
Occupation: Singer
Debut: (Album) *Black Sabbath,* 1970
Signature: Black Sabbath
Facts: In 1984, splintered glass from a broken mirror in the video for "So Tired" lodged in Osbourne's throat, but no permanent injury occurred.

Was sued, unsuccessfully, in 1987 by the parents of California teenager John McCollum. McCollum's parents claimed that Osbourne's song "Suicide Solution" influenced the youth to kill himself. Osbourne said, "If I wrote music for people who shot themselves after listening to my music, I wouldn't have much of a following."
Infamy: Was a burglar until he spent two months in Winston Green Prison.

Osbourne bit the head off a dove during a meeting of Los Angeles record executives. Later he tried it at a concert with a bat and the bat bit him.
Original Job: Slaughterhouse worker, burglar
Marriages: Thelma Osbourne (divorced), Sharon Arden

MICHAEL OVITZ

Birthplace: Encino, CA
Birthdate: 12/14/46
Occupation: Superagent
Education: UCLA
Facts: Began as a mailroom clerk in the William Morris Agency.

Was pre-med student at UCLA.

Practices aikido, a Japanese form of martial arts. He discovered Steven Seagal, who was training him in martial arts.
Original Job: Tour guide at Universal Studios
Marriage: Judy Reich

AL PACINO

Real Name: Alfredo James Pacino
Birthplace: New York, NY
Birthdate: 4/25/39
Occupation: Actor
Education: High School of the Performing Arts, Actor's Studio
Debut: (Stage) *The Peace Creeps,* 1966; (Film) *Me, Natalie,* 1969
Signature: *The Godfather*
Fact: Has been involved with actresses Jill Clayburgh, Marthe Keller, and Diane Keaton.
Original Job: Mail deliverer at *Commentary* magazine, messenger, movie theater usher, building superintendent
Major Awards: Tony, Best Supporting Actor (Dramatic), *Does a Tiger Wear a Necktie?,* 1969; Tony, Best Actor, *The Basic Training of Pavlo Hummel,* 1977; Golden Globe, Best Actor, *Serpico,* 1974; Oscar, Best Actor, *Scent of a Woman,* 1992; Golden Globe, Best Actor, *Scent of a Woman,* 1993

ANNA PAQUIN

Birthplace: Wellington, New Zealand
Birthdate: 1982
Occupation: Actor
Debut: (Film) *The Piano,* 1993
Signature: *The Piano*
Facts: First acting experience was as a skunk in a school play.

Had appeared only in a TV commercial before her role in *The Piano,* for which she was selected from 5,000 other girls auditioning for the part. She was nine years old during the filming.
Major Award: Academy Award for Best Supporting Actress, *The Piano,* 1994

SARAH JESSICA PARKER

Birthplace: Nelsonville, OH
Birthdate: 3/25/65
Occupation: Actor
Education: American Ballet Theater, Professional Children's School in New York
Debut: (TV) *The Little Match Girl,* 1973
Facts: Sang in Metropolitan Opera productions of *Hansel and Gretel, Cavalleria Rusticana, Pagliacci,* and *Parade.*

Starred as nerdy Patty Green on the CBS TV sitcom *Square Pegs,* 1982–83.

Played Annie in the Broadway musical, 1979–80.
Original Job: Dancer with Cincinnati Ballet and the American Ballet Theatre
Relationship: Matthew Broderick

DOLLY PARTON

Birthplace: Sevierville, TN
Birthdate: 1/19/46
Occupation: Singer, songwriter
Education: High school
Debut: (Song) "Puppy Love," 1956
Signature: "9 to 5"
Facts: Met her husband in the Wishy Washy laundromat.

Has her own theme park, Dollywood, located in Gatlinburg at the edge of the Smoky Mountains. In her hometown of Sevierville, Tennessee, there is a statue of her on the Sevier County Courthouse lawn.
Marriage: Carl Dean
Major Awards: Grammy, Best Country Vocal—Female, "Here You Come Again," 1978; Grammy, Best Country Vocal—Female, "9 to 5," 1981; Grammy, Best Country Performance—Duo or Group, *Trio* (with Linda Rondstadt and Emmylou Harris), 1987
Quote: "Left to my own, I'd rather look like trash. I love tacky clothes. My look came from a very serious honest place, and that was a country girl's idea of what glamour was."

LUCIANO PAVAROTTI

Birthplace: Modena, Italy
Birthdate: 10/12/35
Occupation: Singer
Education: Istituto Magistrale Carlo Sigonio
Debut: (Stage) *La Bohème,* 1961
Facts: Established Opera Company of Philadelphia/Luciano Pavarotti Vocal Company, 1980.

Makes at least $100,000 per concert. His fortune is estimated to be between $25 and $50 million.

Dreads the anticipation of singing more than singing itself. "The ten minutes before the performance you wouldn't wish on your worst enemies."

Half a billion people saw the televised "Three Tenors" concert (with Placido Domingo and José Carreras) in 1990.

In 1990, the only musicians who sold more recordings than Pavarotti were Madonna and Elton John.
Infamy: He was sued by the BBC when it found out that a 1992 Pavarotti concert it had bought for broadcast had really been lip-synched.
Original Job: Elementary school teacher, salesman
Marriage: Adua Veroni

Children: Lorenza, Cristina, Giuliana
Major Awards: Grammy, Best Classical Vocal Performance, *Luciano Pavarotti—Hits from London Center,* 1978; Grammy, Best Classical Vocal Performance, *O Sole Mio (Favorite Neapolitan Songs),* 1979; Grammy, Best Classical Vocal Performance, *Live from Lincoln Center—Sutherland—Horne—Pavarotti* (with Joan Sutherland and Marilyn Horne), 1981; Grammy, Best Classical Vocal Performance, *Luciano Pavarotti in Concert,* 1988; Grammy, Best Classical Vocal Performance, *Carreras, Domingo, Pavarotti in Concert* (with José Carreras and Placido Domingo), 1990

PEPA

Real Name: Sandra Denton
Birthplace: Queens, NY
Birthdate: 9/9/69
Occupation: Rap artist
Education: Queensborough Community College
Debut: (Album) *Hot, Cool & Vicious,* 1986
Signature: Salt-N-Pepa
Facts: Pepa and Salt both worked at Sears with Martin Lawrence and Kid 'N Play.

Received Grammy Award nomination in 1989 in the newly created rap category, but boycotted the show when the awards program did not televise the presentation of the award.
Original Job: Telephone customer service representative
Relationship: Chuck D

ROSIE PEREZ

Occupation: Actress, choreographer
Education: Los Angeles City College
Debut: (TV) *Soul Train*
Signature: *Do the Right Thing*
Facts: Was discovered as a dancer at the L.A. club Funky Reggae by Spike Lee, who offered her a role in *Do the Right Thing.*

Choreographer for the TV comedy/variety show *In Living Color.* Has choreographed numbers for Bobby Brown and Diana Ross.
Original Job: Dancer

ROSS PEROT

Real Name: Henry Ross Perot
Birthplace: Texarkana, TX
Birthdate: 6/27/30
Occupation: Businessman
Education: Attended Texarkana Junior College; United States Naval Academy, 1953
Facts: Led a rescue attempt to free two of his employees from Iranian terrorists and developed a plan to aid Vietnam prisoners.

While working as a horse breaker he broke his own nose twice.

Once met his annual sales quota at IBM by January 19th of the year.

Although he had never seen the ocean or a naval vessel, he badgered his senator into appointing him to the U.S. Naval Academy in Annapolis. While there, he was class president, chairman of the honor committee, and battalion commander.
Original Job: Sold Christmas cards, horse equipment, magazines, and garden seeds; worked as a horse breaker, bought and sold livestock, and delivered newspapers
Marriage: Margot Birmingham
Children: Ross Jr., Nancy, Suzanne, Carolyn, Katherine

JOE PESCI

Birthplace: Newark, NJ
Birthdate: 2/9/43
Occupation: Actor
Education: High school dropout
Debut: (Radio) *Star Kids,* 1947; (Film) *Hey, Let's Twist!,* 1961
Signature: *My Cousin Vinny*
Facts: Played guitar for Joey Dee and the Starliters.

At age five appeared in Broadway musicals and Eddie Dowling plays. At age ten became a regular on TV's *Star Time Kids* doing impersonations and singing.

Was managing a restaurant in the Bronx when called by Robert De Niro and Martin Scorsese to play Jake LaMotta's brother in *Raging Bull,* 1978.

He appears in some of his films under the psuedonym Joe Ritchie.
Original Job: Has worked as a nightclub singer, stand-up comic, barber, postal worker, delivery boy, produce manager, answering service worker, and restaurant manager
Marriages: Two prior marriages, Martha Haro
Child: Tiffany
Major Award: Oscar, Best Supporting Actor, *Goodfellas,* 1991

MICHELLE PFEIFFER

Birthplace: Santa Ana, CA
Birthdate: 4/29/57
Occupation: Actor
Education: Golden West Junior College; attended Golden West College
Debut: (Film) *The Hollywood Knights,* 1980; (TV) *Delta House,* 1979
Signature: *The Fabulous Baker Boys*
Facts: Had one line on TV show *Fantasy Island.*

Got her first break by winning the Miss Orange County Beauty Pageant.

In 1993, she decided to be a single mother and adopted a baby girl, Claudia Rose, who was given the last name Kelley after Pfeiffer's marriage.

Had the leading role in *Grease 2,* 1982.
Original Job: Supermarket cashier, court reporter, model
Marriages: Peter Horton (divorced), David E. Kelley
Child: Claudia Rose, John Henry
Major Award: Golden Globe, Best Actress, *The Fabulous Baker Boys,* 1990

DAVID HYDE PIERCE

Birthplace: Albany, NY
Birthdate: 4/3/59
Occupation: Actor
Education: Yale
Debut: (Stage) *Beyond Therapy,* 1982; (TV) *Powers That Be,* 1991
Signature: *Frasier*
Facts: Realized he had a strong resemblance to his TV brother Frasier (Kelsey Grammer) after being mistaken for Grammer many times before he even accepted the role. In the orginal storyline for *Frasier,* Pierce's character (Niles) didn't exist but was added after producers, who saw Pierce in *The Powers That Be,* noticed the resemblance.
Original Job: Clothing salesman, church organist

DAVE PIRNER

Birthdate: 1965
Occupation: Singer, songwriter, guitarist
Debut: (Album) *Say What You Will,* 1984
Signature: Soul Asylum
Facts: Played drums at age 17 with group The Shitz. Joined Dan Murphy and Karl Mueller to form Loud Fast Rules and, later, Soul Asylum.

Likes trains, doesn't own a television or CD player.

The Minneapolis group had been together ten years and was on the verge of breaking up when their sixth album, 1992's *Grave Dancers Union,* hit the *Billboard* top ten.
Relationship: Winona Ryder (engaged)

BRAD PITT

Birthplace: Shawnee, OK
Birthdate: 12/18/63
Occupation: Actor
Education: Attended University of Missouri at Columbia; studied acting with Roy London
Debut: (TV) *Dallas*; (Film) *Cutting Class,* 1989
Signature: *A River Runs Through It*
Facts: Got his big break when he was seen in a sexy Levi's TV ad in 1989.

Is perhaps best known for his portrayal of the hitchhiker in the 1991 movie *Thelma and Louise.* He was cast only after William Baldwin turned down the role, choosing to star in *Backdraft* instead.
Original Job: Chauffeur for Strip-O-Gram women, dressed up as the El Pollo Loco restaurant chicken

PAULA POUNDSTONE

Birthplace: Alabama
Birthdate: 1959
Occupation: Comedian, actor
Education: High school dropout
Facts: Spends an average of forty-two weeks a year on the road.

Performs annually at the high school from which she dropped out.

Owns five cats.

Major Award: American Comedy Award, Best Female Stand-Up, 1989
Quote: "Life revolves around cat food."

SUSAN POWTER

Birthplace: Sydney, Australia
Birthdate: 1958
Occupation: Weight-loss expert
Education: High school dropout
Debut: (Book) *Stop the Insanity,* 1993
Facts: Attended a Dominican convent in Australia until she was ten, when her family moved to Pelham Manor, NY.

Dropped out of school in the ninth grade.

Her idol is Jean Harris, the murderer of the Scarsdale diet doctor.

Her residence in Dallas consists of a duplex: her husband and two sons live upstairs, and her ex-husband lives downstairs.

Original Job: Nurse's aide, secretary, topless dancer
Marriages: Nick (divorced), Lincoln Apeland

LISA MARIE PRESLEY-JACKSON

Birthplace: Memphis,TN
Birthdate: 2/1/68
Signature: Daughter of Elvis and Priscilla Presley
Facts: Will probably inherit $150 million on her thirtieth birthday.

When Lisa Marie once said she had never seen snow, Elvis flew her to Utah.

Marriages: Danny Keogh (divorced), Michael Jackson
Children: Danielle, Benjamin

PRISCILLA PRESLEY

Birthplace: Brooklyn, NY
Birthdate: 5/24/45
Occupation: Actor
Education: Studied with Milton Katselas; attended Steven Peck Theatre Art School, Chuck Norris Karate School
Debut: (TV) *Those Amazing Animals,* 1980
Signature: *Dallas*
Fact: Began dating Elvis in Germany when he was in the Army and she was the fourteen-year-old daughter of an Air Force officer. Formed Bis and Beau boutique with dress designer Olivia, and marketed their exclusive designs to Barbra Streisand, Cher, Julie Christie, and others.
Original Job: Wella Balsam model
Marriages: Elvis Presley (divorced), Marco Garibaldi
Children: Lisa Marie, Navarone Anthony

PRINCE

Real Name: Prince Rogers Nelson
Birthplace: Minneapolis, MN
Birthdate: 6/7/58
Occupation: Singer, songwriter, actor
Education: High school dropout
Debut: (Album) *For You,* 1978
Signature: Pop star and sex symbol
Facts: Named after the Prince Roger Trio, a jazz group led by his father.

Can play over two dozen instruments.

Now known as a symbol, or referred to as "the artist formerly known as Prince."

Major Awards: Grammy, Best Rock Performance—Duo or Group, *Purple Rain* (with The Revolution), 1984; Grammy, Best Rhythm and Blues Song, "I Feel for You," 1984; Grammy, Best Soundtrack Album, *Purple Rain* (with The Revolution, John L. Nelson, Lisa & Wendy), 1984; Grammy, Best R&B Duo or Group, "Kiss "(with The Revolution), 1986

DENNIS QUAID

Birthplace: Houston, TX
Birthdate: 4/9/54
Occupation: Actor
Education: Attended the University of Houston
Debut: (Film) *September 30, 1955,* 1978
Fact: Wrote songs for three of his films: *The Night the Lights Went Out in Georgia* in 1981, *Tough Enough* in 1983, and *The Big Easy* in 1987.
Marriages: Pamela Jayne Soles (divorced), Meg Ryan
Child: Jack
Famous Relative: Randy Quaid, actor, brother

BONNIE RAITT

Birthplace: Burbank, CA
Birthdate: 9/8/49
Occupation: Singer, songwriter
Education: Attended Radcliffe College
Debut: (Album) *Bonnie Raitt,* 1971
Facts: Grew up in a Quaker family in L.A.

Got her first guitar for Christmas when she was eight.

Marriage: Michael O'Keefe
Famous Relative: John Raitt, actor, father
Major Awards: Grammy, Album of the Year and Best Rock Vocal—Female, *In The Nick of Time,* 1989; Grammy, Best Rock Performance—Duo or Group, "Good Man, Good Woman" (with Delbert McClinton), 1991

ROBERT REDFORD

Real Name: Charles Robert Redford Jr.
Birthplace: Santa Monica, CA
Birthdate: 8/18/37
Occupation: Actor, director, producer
Education: University of Colorado, Pratt Institute of Design, the American Academy of Dramatic Arts
Debut: (Stage) *Tall Story,* 1959; (Film) *War Hunt,* 1962
Signature: *Butch Cassidy and the Sundance Kid*
Facts: Went to college on a baseball scholarship but lost it due to alcohol abuse. Left school in 1957 to go to Europe; lived in Paris and Florence as a painter.

Founded the nonprofit Sundance Institute in Park City, Utah, in 1981, which sponsors an annual film festival and provides support for independent film production.

Infamy: As a teenager, Redford stole and resold hubcaps.
Original Job: Carpenter, shop assistant, oil field worker
Marriage: Lola Van Wangeman (divorced)
Children: Shauna, Amy Hart, David James
Major Award: Golden Globe, New Male Film Star, *Daisy Clover,* 1966; Golden Globe, Male World Film Favorite, 1975, 1977, 1978; Oscar, Best Director, *Ordinary People,* 1981

KEANU REEVES

Birthplace: Beirut, Lebanon
Birthdate: 9/2/64
Occupation: Actor
Education: High school dropout
Debut: (Film) *The River's Edge,* 1986
Signature: *Bill and Ted's Excellent Adventure*
Facts: His father is Chinese-Hawaiian and his mother is English.

His first name means "cool breeze over the mountains" in Hawaiian.

Had traveled around the world by the time he was two years old.

Was the MVP on his high school hockey team in Toronto. A skilled goalie, Reeves earned the name "The Wall."

PAUL REISER

Birthplace: New York, NY
Birthdate: 3/30/57
Occupation: Actor, comedian
Education: SUNY-Binghamton
Debut: (Film) *Diner,* 1982
Signature: *Mad About You*
Facts: Has appeared in several hit films, including *Beverly Hills Cop* (1984), *Aliens* (1986), and *Beverly Hills Cop II* (1987).

Dubbed by reporters as part of the Four Funniest Men in the World Club, which includes Jerry Seinfeld, Larry Miller, and Mark Schiff. The members meet every New Year's Day for lunch (once they even met in London when Reiser was there filming *Aliens).*

Original Job: Health food distributor
Marriage: Paula

BURT REYNOLDS

Birthplace: Waycross, GA
Birthdate: 2/11/36
Occupation: Actor
Education: Attended Florida State University; Palm Beach Junior College; Hyde Park Playhouse
Debut: (Stage) *Mister Roberts,* 1956

Signature: *Smokey and the Bandit*
Facts: Reynolds was signed to play football with the Colts but a car accident pushed him into acting.

He is part Cherokee and part Italian.

His father was the chief of police in Palm Beach, Florida.
Infamy: Appeared nude in centerfold of the April 1972 issue of *Cosmopolitan.*

In the late '80s, unfounded AIDS rumors circulated when Reynolds was suffering from temporomandibular joint disorder.
Original Job: Bouncer, dishwasher, stunt man
Marriages: Judy Carne (divorced), Loni Anderson (divorced)
Major Awards: Emmy, Best Actor in a Comedy Series, *Evening Shade,* 1991; Golden Globe, Best Actor in a Comedy Series, *Evening Shade,* 1992

ANNE RICE

Real Name: Howard Allen O'Brien
Birthdate: 10/4/41
Occupation: Writer
Education: North Texas State University, San Francisco State College
Debut: (Book) *Interview with a Vampire,* 1976
Facts: Is the author of a series of hardcore pornographic novels under the name A. N. Roquelaure (which means "cloak").

Is afraid of the dark.

Was originally named after her father and mother's maiden name; changed name to Anne by the time she was in first grade.

In 1972, her six-year-old daughter died of leukemia.
Marriage: Stan Rice
Children: Michelle (deceased), Christopher

MICHAEL RICHARDS

Birthplace: Culver City, CA
Birthdate: 7/14/50
Occupation: Actor
Education: Los Angeles Valley College, California Insitute of the Arts
Debut: (TV) *Fridays,* 1980
Signature: *Seinfeld*
Facts: Has appeared in guest spots on *Hill Street Blues* and *Miami Vice.*

Starred with Weird Al Yankovic in the film *UHF,* 1989.

He was drafted at the height of the Vietnam War in 1970: "When the drill sergeant yelled at me on the first day, I tried to explain the duffel bag was too heavy."
Original Job: Postal worker, school bus driver
Marriages: Cathleen (divorced), Ann Talman (relationship)
Child: Sophia
Major Award: Emmy, Best Supporting Actor in a Comedy Series, *Seinfeld,* 1993

NATASHA RICHARDSON

Birthplace: London, England
Birthdate: 5/11/63
Occupation: Actor
Education: Central School for Speech and Drama
Debut: (Stage) *On the Razzle,* 1983
Signature: *The Handmaid's Tale*
Facts: At age four appeared as a bridesmaid of Vanessa Redgrave in *The Charge of the Light Brigade*

Was named after the heroine in Tolstoy's *War and Peace.*
Marriages: Robert Fox (divorced), Liam Neeson
Famous Relatives: Vanessa Redgrave, actor, mother; Tony Richardson, director, father; Joely Richardson, actor, sister; Lynn Redgrave, actor, aunt

PAT RILEY

Birthplace: Rome, NY
Birthdate: 3/20/45
Occupation: Basketball coach
Education: University of Kentucky
Signature: Coach of the New York Knicks
Facts: Played basketball in high school, and played for the Wildcats at the University of Kentucky.

Was drafted by the San Diego Rockets in 1967 and was traded to the Los Angeles Lakers after three seasons.

Is a member of the Screen Actor's Guild.
Infamy: Riley was expelled from a Roman Catholic boarding school at age eight, and in junior high he broke forty or fifty windows in his school and broke into the cafeteria and ate all the ice cream.
Original Job: Professional basketball player
Marriage: Chris Rodstrom
Children: James Patrick, Elisabeth

JOAN RIVERS

Real Name: Joan Alexandra Molinsky
Birthplace: Brooklyn, NY
Birthdate: 6/8/37
Occupation: Talk show host
Education: Connecticut College for Women, Barnard College
Debut: (TV) *The Tonight Show,* 1965
Facts: Wrote for *Candid Camera* and *The Ed Sullivan Show.*
Original Job: Publicist at Lord & Taylor, fashion coordinator for Bond Clothing Stores, office temporary secretary, syndicated columnist.
Marriage: Edgar Rosenberg (deceased), Orin Lehman (relationship)
Child: Melissa
Major Awards: Clio Award, 1976, 1982; Emmy, Best Host of a Talk Show, *The Joan Rivers Show,* 1990

TIM ROBBINS

Birthplace: West Covina, CA
Birthdate: 10/16/58
Occupation: Writer, director, actor
Education: Attended New York University, SUNY-Plattsburgh and UCLA
Debut: (Film) *No Small Affair,* 1984
Signature: *The Player*
Facts: Was kicked off the hockey team in high school for fighting.

Founded Los Angeles theater group Actors' Gang.

Has been an outspoken political activist and peace advocate.
Original Job: Factory worker
Relationship: Susan Sarandon
Children: Jack Henry, Miles
Major Awards: Golden Globe, Best Actor in a Comedy, *The Player,* 1993; Golden Globe, Special Achievement, *Short Cuts,* 1994

JULIA ROBERTS

Birthplace: Smyrna, GA
Birthdate: 10/28/67
Occupation: Actor
Education: High school
Debut: (TV) *Crime Story*
Signature: *Pretty Woman*
Facts: Middle name is Fiona.

Originally wanted to be a veterinarian.

In 1986, she played opposite her brother (actor Eric Roberts) in the film *Blood Red.*
Original Job: Worked in a shoe store and an ice cream shop
Marriage: Lyle Lovett
Famous Relatives: Eric Roberts, actor, brother; Lisa Roberts, actress, sister
Major Awards: Golden Globe, Best Supporting Actress, *Steel Magnolias,* 1990; Golden Globe, Best Actress in a Comedy, *Pretty Woman,* 1991

AXL ROSE

Real Name: William Bailey
Birthplace: Lafayette, IN
Birthdate: 1962
Occupation: Singer
Education: High school dropout
Debut: (EP) *Live ?!*@ Like a Suicide,* 1986 (with Guns N' Roses)
Facts: 1987 debut album, *Appetite for Destruction,* has sold more than 18 million copies.

In the middle of a 1991 St. Louis concert, Rose jumped into the crowd to remove a camera from a fan. The band left the stage, and the crowd rioted. Sixty fans ended up in the hospital, the brand-new concert hall suffered $500,000 in damages, and all of the band's equipment was destroyed.

Discovered when he was 17 that his real surname was Rose (his biological father had left when Axl was a baby, and his mother remarried). He took his stage name from a band he used to play with in Indiana. Had his name officially changed to W. Axl Rose in 1986.
Infamy: By the time he was 20, he had been jailed on numerous occasions for battery, contributing to the delinquency of a minor, public

intoxication, criminal trespass, and mischief.

In 1990, he was arrested for allegedly hitting a neighbor over the head with a bottle after she complained about loud music.

Ex-wife Erin Everly and ex-fiancée Stephanie Seymour have filed separate suits against Rose charging that he subjected them to physical abuse.

Marriages: Erin Invicta Everly (divorced)

ROSEANNE

Birthplace: Salt Lake City, UT
Birthdate: 11/3/52
Occupation: Actor
Education: High school dropout
Debut: (Film) *She-Devil,* 1989
Signature: *Roseanne*
Facts: Dropped out of high school to hitchhike across country, landing in a Colorado artists' colony at age 18.

Had cosmetic surgery and weight reduction in 1993. Breasts were reduced from 40DD to 38C.

Has a tattoo on her upper right thigh that reads: "Property of Tom Arnold."

Physically and sexually abused as a child. Suppressed memory of the abuse until an adult.

Gave up baby girl for adoption at age 18.

Born to Jewish parents but raised as a Mormon in Salt Lake City. Her dad sold crucifixes door to door.

Infamy: Grabbed her crotch, spit, and screeched while singing the national anthem at a San Diego baseball game in 1990.
Original Job: Window dresser, cocktail waitress
Marriages: Bill Petland (divorced), Tom Arnold (separated)
Children: Brandi, Jessica, Jennifer, Jake
Major Awards: Golden Globe, Best Actress in a Comedy Series, *Roseanne,* 1993; Emmy, Best Actress in a Comedy Series, *Roseanne,* 1993

RITA RUDNER

Birthplace: Miami, FL
Birthdate: 1956
Occupation: Actor, comedian
Education: High school
Debut: (Film) *The Wrong Guys,* 1988; (TV) *Funny People,* 1988; (Book) *Naked Beneath My Clothes,* 1992
Facts: Writes movies with her husband, Martin Bergman.

First time on stage she slipped and fell.

Appeared in about sixty TV commercials before turning to comedy.

Original Job: Dancer
Marriage: Martin Bergman, theatrical producer

MEG RYAN

Birthplace: Fairfield, CT
Birthdate: 11/19/61
Occupation: Actor
Education: Attended New York University
Debut: (TV) *As the World Turns*
Signature: *When Harry Met Sally*
Fact: Became high school homecoming queen when the original queen was suspended.
Marriage: Dennis Quaid
Child: Jack Henry

WINONA RYDER

Real Name: Winona Laura Horowitz
Birthplace: Winona, MN
Birthdate: 10/29/71
Occupation: Actor
Debut: (Film) *Lucas,* 1985
Signature: *Beetlejuice*
Facts: Her childhood home in Elk, CA, had no electricity.

In junior high school, was attacked and beaten by fellow students during her first week at a new school, apparently because they mistook her for a boy.

Has read *The Catcher in the Rye* countless times, and travels with a copy.

Relationship: Johnny Depp (engaged but never married), David Pirner (engaged)
Famous Relative: Timothy Leary, psychologist, countercultural philosopher, godfather
Major Award: Golden Globe, Best Supporting Actress, *The Age of Innocence,* 1994

SALT

Real Name: Cheryl James
Birthplace: Queens, NY
Birthdate: 3/28/69
Occupation: Rap artist
Education: Queensborough Community College
Debut: (Album) *Hot, Cool & Vicious,* 1986
Facts: Salt teamed with Pepa to create first female rap group to crossover to the *Billboard* Pop Chart with the gold single "Push It."

Both Salt and Pepa worked at Sears with Martin Lawrence and Kid 'N Play.

Original Job: Telephone customer service representative

SUSAN SARANDON

Real Name: Susan Abigail Tomaling
Birthplace: New York, NY
Birthdate: 10/4/46
Occupation: Actor
Education: Catholic University of America
Debut: (Film) *Joe,* 1970
Signature: *Thelma and Louise*
Facts: Her background is Welsh-Italian. Was one of nine children, and attended Catholic school.
Original Job: While in college, worked in the drama department, modeled, and cleaned apartments
Marriages: Chris Sarandon (divorced), Tim Robbins (relationship)
Children: Eva Maria Livia, Jack Henry, Miles

DIANE SAWYER

Birthplace: Glasgow, KY
Birthdate: 12/22/45
Occupation: Broadcast journalist
Education: Wellesley College
Debut: (TV) WLKY-TV, Louisville, 1967
Signature: *Primetime Live*
Facts: Was national Junior Miss, largely on the strength of her interview and essays.

As a weathercaster in Louisville, KY, she spruced up forecasts with quotes from her favorite poems.

Served as staff assistant to former President Nixon and helped him research his memoirs.

Marriage: Mike Nichols
Major Awards: Emmy, "PanAm Flight 103," 1990; Emmy, "Murder in Beverly Hills," 1991

CLAUDIA SCHIFFER

Birthplace: Germany
Birthdate: 8/24/71
Occupation: Supermodel
Education: High school
Facts: Tripped during her runway modeling debut in 1990.

Earns as much as $15,000 a day.

Marriage: David Copperfield (engaged)

ARNOLD SCHWARZENEGGER

Birthplace: Graz, Austria
Birthdate: 7/30/47
Occupation: Actor, director, bodybuilder
Education: University of Wisconsin
Debut: (Film) *Hercules in New York,* 1969
Signature: *The Terminator*
Facts: After coming to the U.S. in the '60s, founded a bricklaying business, Pumping Bricks, to finance his bodybuilding career.

Won the Austrian Junior Olympic weightlifting championship as well as Junior Mr. Europe and several curling titles.

In 1974, acted in *Happy Anniversary and Goodbye,* an unsold CBS sitcom pilot starring Lucille Ball and Art Carney.

Has killed over 275 people on screen.

Original Job: Managed a Munich health club
Marriage: Maria Owings Shriver
Children: Katherine Eunice, Christina Maria Aurelia, Patrick
Quote: "Everything I have ever done in my life has always stayed. I've just added to it . . . But I will not change. Because when you are successful and you change, you are an idiot."

MARTIN SCORSESE

Birthplace: New York, NY
Birthdate: 11/17/42
Occupation: Director
Education: New York University
Debut: (Film) *Boxcar Bertha,* 1972
Signature: *Taxi Driver*
Facts: Collaborated on the

production of Michael Jackson's *Bad* video in 1987.

Was originally enrolled as an English major before switching to film.

Original Job: Faculty assistant and instructor in film department at NYU
Marriages: Larraine Marie Brennan (divorced), Julia Cameron (divorced), Isabella Rosellini (divorced), Barbara DeFina
Children: Catherine Terese, Domenica Elizabeth

STEVEN SEAGAL

Birthplace: Lansing, MI
Birthdate: 4/10/51
Occupation: Actor, producer
Education: Attended Orange Coast College, Fullerton College
Debut: (Film) *Above the Law,* 1988
Signature: *Hard to Kill*
Facts: Founder, Aikido Ten Shin Dojo, Los Angeles.

First non-Asian to open a martial arts academy in Japan.

In 1968, moved to Japan, where he taught English and wrote articles for Japanese magazines and newspapers.

Organized security for the departure of the Shah's family from Iran.

Commands the title of Shihan (Master of Masters).

Original Job: Martial arts instructor, bodyguard
Marriages: Miyako Fujitani (divorced), Kelly LeBrock
Children: Justice, Annaliza, Arrisa, Dominic San Rocco

JERRY SEINFELD

Birthplace: Brooklyn, NY
Birthdate: 4/29/55
Occupation: Actor
Education: Queens College
Debut: (Stand-up) Catch a Rising Star, Manhattan, 1976
Signature: *Seinfeld*
Facts: The first time he appeared on stage, he was so nervous he forgot his routine and only mumbled the words "The beach. Driving. Shopping. Parents," and walked off.

Owns several dozen pairs of sneakers, including a custom pair of "Air Seinfelds."

Has practiced yoga for twenty years and is a strict vegetarian.

Infamy: Seinfeld created a stir when he began dating 18-year-old Shoshanna Lonstein.
Original Job: Sought the worst jobs possible, including selling light bulbs over the phone and costume jewelry on the streets of New York, to force himself to succeed at comedy
Relationship: Shoshanna Lonstein
Major Awards: American Comedy Award, Funniest Male Stand-up, 1988; Emmy, Best Comedy Series, *Seinfeld,* 1993; Golden Globe, Best Actor in a Comedy Series, *Seinfeld,* 1994

JANE SEYMOUR

Real Name: Joyce Frankenberg
Birthplace: Hillingdon, Middlesex, England
Birthdate: 2/15/51
Occupation: Actor
Education: Attended Arts Educational School, London
Debut: (Film) *Oh, What a Lovely War,* 1968
Signature: *Dr. Quinn, Medicine Woman*
Facts: Danced with the London Festival Ballet at 13.

Named Honorary Citizen of Illinois by Governor Thompson in 1977.

Original Job: Ballet dancer
Marriages: David Flynn (divorced), James Keach
Children: Jennifer, Katie, Sean
Major Awards: Emmy, Best Supporting Actress in a Miniseries, *Onassis,* 1988; Golden Globe, Best Actress in a Miniseries, *East of Eden,* 1982

PAUL SHAFFER

Birthplace: Thunder Bay, Ontario, Canada
Birthdate: 11/28/49
Occupation: Musician, bandleader
Education: University of Toronto
Debut: (TV) *Saturday Night Live,* 1975
Signature: *Late Show with David Letterman*
Facts: Appeared in the movie *This Is Spinal Tap,* 1984.

Stared in sitcom *A Year at the Top,* which was canceled after only six episodes.

Still lives in the same hotel room he rented on his first trip to New York.

Marriage: Cathy Vasapoli
Daughter: Victoria Lily

TUPAC SHAKUR

Birthplace: New York, NY
Occupation: Rap artist
Education: Baltimore School for the Arts
Debut: (Film) *Juice,* 1992
Album (solo): *2Pacalypse Now,* 1992
Facts: Made his acting debut at age 13 in a production of *A Raisin in the Sun.*

Nickname: "Rebel of the Underground."

Member of the rap group Digital Underground.

Grandfather Elmer Pratt, a member of the Black Panthers, is currently serving a life sentence for murder in California. His mother, an activist herself, testifed at the trial of the Chicago Seven, and Tupac was almost born in jail.

Infamy: Convicted of attacking a former employee on a music video set. Served fifteen days in jail, forty-five days of community service, fined $2,000.

In 1993, arrested in Atlanta for allegedly shooting two off-duty police officers.

Famous Relative: Elmer Pratt, political activist, grandfather

GARRY SHANDLING

Birthplace: Chicago, IL
Birthdate: 11/29/49
Occupation: Actor, writer, comedian
Education: University of Arizona
Debut: (TV) *Sanford & Son,* 1976
Signature: *Larry Sanders*
Fact: Wrote for *Sanford & Son, Welcome Back Kotter,* and *Three's Company.*
Relationship: Linda Doucett

WILLIAM SHATNER

Birthplace: Montreal, Canada
Birthdate: 3/22/31
Occupation: Actor, author, producer, director
Education: McGill University
Debut: (TV) *Goodyear TV Playhouse,* 1956
Signature: *Star Trek*
Facts: Has written a series of books, beginning with *TekWar,* which were turned into movies in which he stars.

Most celebrated pre-*Trek* experience was as a guest on one of the most famous *Twilight Zone* episodes, "Nightmare at 20,000 Feet," in 1963.

One of his leisure activities is breeding horses.

Original Job: Novelist
Marriages: Gloria Rand (divorced), Marcy Lafferty
Children: Three daughters with Gloria Rand

CHARLIE SHEEN

Real Name: Carlos Irwin Estevez
Birthplace: New York, NY
Birthdate: 9/3/65
Occupation: Actor
Education: High school dropout
Debut: (TV) *The Execution of Private Slovik,* 1975
Signature: *Platoon*
Facts: Pitched on the Santa Monica High School baseball team. Was kicked off the team for skipping school.

A Peace of My Mind, a collection of his poetry, was published in 1991.

As a teenager produced and directed over 200 Super-8 and video short films, some starring futures stars such as Sean and Chris Penn, Rob and Chad Lowe, and his brother Emilio Estevez.

Child: Cassandra (with Ginger Lynn Allen)
Famous Relatives: Martin Sheen, actor, father; Emilio Estevez, actor, brother

GRANT SHOW

Birthplace: Detroit, MI
Birthdate: 4/27/63
Occupation: Actor
Education: UCLA, London Academy of Music and Dramatic Arts
Signature: *Melrose Place*
Facts: Started out as friend of Luke Perry on *Beverly Hills, 90210* before moving to the spin-off series *Melrose Place.*

Played police officer Rick Hyde on *Ryan's Hope,* but left the role to study acting in London.

Relationship: Laura Leighton

ANDREW SHUE

Birthplace: South Orange, NJ
Birthdate: 2/20/67
Occupation: Actor
Education: Dartmouth
Signature: *Melrose Place*
Facts: Played professional soccer for the Bulawayo Highlanders after graduating from Dartmouth.

Taught math in Zimbabwe.

Original Job: Professional soccer player, math instructor
Famous Relative: Elisabeth Shue, actor, sister

NEIL SIMON

Birthplace: Bronx, NY
Birthdate: 7/4/27
Occupation: Playwright, screenwriter, producer
Education: New York University
Debut: (Play) *Adverntures of Marco Polo: A Musical Fantasy,* 1959; (Screenplay) *After the Fox,* 1966
Signature: *The Odd Couple*
Facts: Flew in the U.S. Air Force, 1945–46.

Met his third wife in 1985 when she was handing out perfume samples at the Beverly Hills Neiman Marcus store.

Owns Eugene O'Neill Theatre in New York.

Original Job: Mail room clerk
Marriages: Joan Baim (deceased), Marsha Mason (divorced), Diane Lander (divorced, remarried, divorced)
Children: Two daughters
Major Awards: Tony, Best Author (Dramatic), *The Odd Couple,* 1965; Golden Globe, Best Screenplay, *The Goodbye Girl,* 1978; Tony, Best Play, *Biloxi Blues,* 1985; Tony, Best Play, *Lost in Yonkers,* 1991; Pulitzer Prize, Best Play, *Lost in Yonkers,* 1991

PAUL SIMON

Birthplace: Newark, NJ
Birthdate: 10/13/41
Occupation: Singer, songwriter
Education: Queens College; attended Brooklyn Law School
Debut: (Song) "Hey Schoolgirl" (with Art Garfunkel, under the name Tom and Jerry), 1957
Signature: "Graceland"
Facts: Met Garfunkel in high school; in sixth grade, he played the White Rabbit to Garfunkel's Cheshire Cat in *Alice in Wonderland.*

Co-owned the Philadelphia Furies, a soccer team, with Mick Jagger, Peter Frampton, and Rick Wakeman.

Marriages: Peggy Harper (divorced), Carrie Fisher (divorced), Edie Brickell
Children: Harper, Adrian Edward
Famous Relative: Louis Simon, bassist, father
Major Awards: Grammy, Record of the Year, "Mrs. Robinson" (with Simon & Garfunkel), 1968; Grammy, Best Pop Performance—Duo or Group, "Mrs. Robinson" (with Simon & Garfunkel), 1968; Grammy, Best Soundtrack Album, *The Graduate* (with Dave Grusin), 1968; Grammy, Record of the Year, "Bridge Over Troubled Water" (with Simon & Garfunkel), 1970; Grammy, Album of the Year, *Bridge Over Troubled Water* (with Simon & Garfunkel), 1970; Grammy, Song of the Year, "Bridge Over Troubled Water," 1970; Grammy, Best Rock/Contemporary Song, "Bridge Over Troubled Water," 1970; Grammy, Album of the Year, *Still Crazy After All These Years,* 1975; Grammy, Best Pop Vocal—Male, "Still Crazy After All These Years," 1975; Grammy, Album of the Year, *Graceland,* 1986; Emmy, Best Writing in a Comedy, Variety or Music Special, *The Paul Simon Special,* 1978; inducted into the Rock and Roll Hall of Fame (with Art Garfunkel), 1990

O.J. SIMPSON

Real Name: Orenthal James Simpson
Birthplace: San Francisco, CA
Birthdate: 7/9/47
Occupation: Football player (retired), actor
Education: Attended City College of San Francisco; University of Southern California
Debut: Halfback, Buffalo Bills, 1969
Facts: Had rickets as a child, wore braces on his legs.

In 1979, his son drowned in the family swimming pool.

Films include *The Towering Inferno* and *The Naked Gun.*

Infamy: In 1994, was indicted for the murder of ex-wife Nicole and her friend Ronald Goldman.
Major Titles: Heisman Trophy, 1968; set many NFL rushing records including first to gain 2,000 yeards in season, 1973; Pro Football Hall of Fame, 1985
Marriages: Marquerite L. Whitley (divorced), Nicole (divorced)
Children: Arnelle, Jason, Aaren (deceased) (with Marguerite Whitley), Sydney, Justin

FRANK SINATRA

Birthplace: Hoboken, NJ
Birthdate: 12/12/15
Occupation: Singer, actor
Education: Attended Drake Institute
Debut: (Radio) *Lucky Strike Hit Parade*
Signature: "My Way"
Facts: Provided a voice for the 1988 film *Who Framed Roger Rabbit.*

Weighed over thirteen pounds at birth and was mistaken for stillborn until his grandmother held him under a cold water faucet.

Begged executives at Columbia to let him play the key role of Maggio in *From Here to Eternity,* and agreed to play the part for only $8,000.

Original Job: Worked on the news truck of the *Jersey Observer;* later was a copy boy and covered college sports
Marriages: Nancy Barbato (divorced), Ava Gardner (divorced), Mia Farrow (divorced), Barbara Marx
Children: Nancy, Christine, Frank Jr.
Major Awards: Special Academy Award, 1945; Academy Award, Supporting Actor, *From Here to Eternity,* 1953; Grammy, Best Album, *Come Dance with Me,* 1959; Grammy, Best Album, *September of My Years,* 1965; Grammy, Best Album, *Moonlight,* 1966; Grammy, Record of the Year "Moonlight," 1966; Grammy, Best Male Vocalist, 1959, 1965, 1966; Emmy, Outstanding Musical Special, *Frank Sinatra: A Man and His Music,* 1965; Presidential Medal of Freedom, 1985

SINBAD

Real Name: David Adkins
Birthplace: Benton Harbor, MI
Birthdate: 11/10/56
Occupation: Actor, comedian
Education: Attended University of Denver
Debut: (TV) *Comedy Tonight,* 1985; (Film) *That's Adequate,* 1989
Signature: *A Different World*
Facts: Finalist in the comedy competition on *Star Search* in 1984.

Intended to play pro basketball.

Infamy: While in the Air Force, impersonated officers and went AWOL.
Marriage: Meredith
Children: Paige, Royce

TOM SKERRITT

Birthplace: Detroit, MI
Birthdate: 8/25/33
Occupation: Actor
Education: Attended Wayne State University and UCLA
Debut: (Film) *War Hunt,* 1962
Signature: *Picket Fences*
Facts: Had a recurring role as Evan Drake on *Cheers,* 1982–93.

In 1991, appeared in a series of Guess? jeans ads.

Appeared as doctor Duke Forest in the film *M*A*S*H* (1970) and as Captain Dallas in *Alien* (1979).

Met Robert Redford during production of *War Hunt.* Both were unknowns, and were reunited after thirty years on *A River Runs Through It* (1992).

Marriage: One prior marriage, Sue Aran
Child: Matthew, Colin, Erin, Andrew
Major Award: Emmy, Best Actor in a Drama Series, *Picket Fences,* 1993

SLASH

Real Name: Saul Hudson
Birthplace: Stoke-on-Trent, England
Birthdate: 1965
Occupation: Guitarist
Debut: (EP) *Live ?!*@ Like a Suicide* (with Guns N' Roses), 1986
Facts: His mother, Ola, was a costume designer for the Pointer Sisters and David Bowie. His father Anthony

designed album covers.

Grew up in California's Laurel Canyon. His next-door neighbor was Joni Mitchell.

At Guns N' Roses' first official Los Angeles show, two people showed up.

When they toured with Aerosmith in 1987, their contract stipulated that consumption of chemical substances would be confined to their dressing room so as not to tempt Aerosmith members.

Infamy: The song "Coma" was based on his numerous heroin overdoses.

Marriage: Renee

CHRISTIAN SLATER

Real Name: Christian Hawkins
Birthplace: New York, NY
Birthdate: 8/18/69
Occupation: Actor
Education: Dalton School, Professional Children's School
Debut: (TV) *One Life to Live,* 1976
Signature: *Heathers*
Facts: Began his career in the stage revival of *The Music Man,* at the age of nine.

Dated Winona Ryder and Samantha Mathis.

Infamy: Arrested twice for drunk driving, sentenced to ten days in jail in 1990.
Famous Relatives: Mary Jo Slater, casting director, mother; Michael Hawkins, stage actor, father

WILL SMITH

Birthplace: Philadelphia, PA
Birthdate: 9/25/68
Occupation: Actor, rap artist
Education: High school
Debut: Rapper as part of DJ Jazzy Jeff & the Fresh Prince
Signature: *The Fresh Prince of Bel Air*
Facts: Turned down a scholarship to MIT to pursue music.

By 1989 had made and lost his first million dollars, the latter due to excessive spending.

Earned his nickname, the Prince, from a teacher in Overbrook High School because of his regal attitude and ability to talk his way out of difficult situations.

Original Job: Rap artist
Marriage: Sheree Zampino
Child: Will III
Major Awards: Grammy, Best Rap Performance—Solo, "Parents Just Don't Understand" (with D.J. Jazzy Jeff & the Fresh Prince), 1988; Grammy, Best Rap Performance—Duo or Group, "Summertime" (with D.J. Jazzy Jeff & the Fresh Prince), 1991

WESLEY SNIPES

Birthplace: Orlando, FL
Birthdate: 7/31/63
Occupation: Actor
Education: Attended New York City's High School of the Performing Arts, SUNY-Purchase
Debut: (Film) *Wildcats,* 1985
Signature: *New Jack City*
Facts: Has studied martial arts, including the African/Brazilian version Capoeira, since his youth.

Appeared in commercials for Levi's 501 Jeans and Coca-Cola Classic.

Snipes came to director Spike Lee's attention when he played a young punk who threatens Michael Jackson in the Martin Scorsese directed video *Bad,* 1987.

Original Job: Street and Puppet Theater in his troupe, Struttin' Street Stuff; installed telephones
Marriage: One marriage (divorced)
Child: Jelani
Major Award: ACE Award, *Vietnam War Story,* 1989

SNOOP DOGGY DOGG

Real Name: Calvin Braudus
Birthplace: Long Beach, CA
Birthdate: 1971
Occupation: Rap artist
Education: High school
Debut: (Album) *Doggystyle,* 1993
Facts: Nickname "Snoop" was given to him by his mother; "Doggy Dogg" came from a cousin who used to call himself Tate Doggy Dog.

Says his musical heroes are Al Green, Curtis Mayfield, and L. J. Reynolds of the Dramatics.

Infamy: One month after graduating from Long Beach Polytechnic High School, was arrested and incarcerated on a drug charge.

In 1993 went on trial for murder of Phil Woldermariam, having been arrested while driving the Jeep from which two fatal gunshots were fired by his bodyguard. It was reported that the victim was seen arguing with the rapper and his friend and brandishing a weapon prior to the shooting. Snoop's attorney claimed that Woldermariam (on probation after serving a one-year jail term for firing a firearm on public property) had previously assaulted the rapper with a gun, holding it to his head and threatening his life during the filming of a video.

Original Job: Sold candy, delivered newspapers, bagged groceries

TOM SNYDER

Birthplace: Milwaukee, WI
Birthdate: 5/12/36
Occupation: Talk show host
Education: Marquette University
Debut: (Radio) WRIT-AM, Milwaukee
(TV) KNBC-TV News, Los Angeles, 1970
Signature: *Tomorrow*
Facts: David Letterman, who's company is producing Snyder's new late-night talk show, *Late Late Show with Tom Snyder,* is the one who took over Snyder's time slot when NBC dropped *Tomorrow* in 1982.
Major Award: Emmy, Best Host, *Tomorrow,* 1974

STEPHEN SONDHEIM

Birthplace: New York, NY
Birthdate: 3/22/30
Occupation: Composer, lyricist
Education: Williams College
Debut: (Stage) *Girls of Summer,* 1956
Signature: Wrote lyrics for *West Side Story*
Facts: In May 1992, turned down the NEA's Medal of Arts Award, claiming the agency is "a symbol of censorship and repression rather than encouragement and support."

When Sondheim left home at age 15, he was taken in by Oscar Hammerstein II (lyricist of *Oklahoma!*), who taught him how to structure songs.

Original Job: Wrote for Topper TV series, 1953; crossword puzzle writer
Major Awards: Pulitzer Prize, Best Play, *Sunday in the Park with George,* 1985; Grammy, Song of the Year, "Send in the Clowns," 1975; Grammy, Best Cast Show Album, *Company,* 1970; Grammy, Best Cast Show Album, *A Little Night Music,* 1973; Grammy, Best Cast Show Album, *Sweeney Todd,* 1979; Grammy, Best Cast Show Album, *Sunday in the Park with George,* 1984; Grammy, Best Cast Show Album, *West Side Story,* 1985; Grammy, Best Cast Show Album *Follies in Concert,* 1986; Grammy, Best Cast Show Album, *Into the Woods,* 1988; Oscar, Best Song, "Sooner or Later (I Always Get My Man)," 1990; Tony, Best Score, *Company,* 1971; Tony, Best Score; *Follies,* 1972; Tony. Best Score, *A Little Night Music,* 1973; Tony, Best Score, *Sweeney Todd,* 1979; Tony, Best Score, *Into the Woods,* 1988
Quote: "I like neurotic people. I like troubled people. Not that I don't like squared away people, but I prefer neurotic people. . . . Songs can't develop uncomplicated characters or unconflicted people. You can't just tell the sunny side and have a story with any richness to it."

AARON SPELLING

Birthplace: Dallas, TX
Birthdate: 4/22/28
Occupation: Producer, writer
Education: Attended the Sorbonne. Southern Methodist University
Signature: *Beverly Hills, 90210*
Facts: Served in U.S. Army Air Force, 1942–45; awarded the Bronze Star and Purple Heart with Oak Leaf Cluster.

In 1969, founded Thomas-Spelling Productions with actor Danny Thomas.

Has produced network hit series such as *The Mod Squad, Starsky and Hutch, S.W.A.T., Charlie's Angels, Family, Dynasty, Beverly Hills, 90210,* and *Melrose Place.*

Original Job: Actor
Marriage: Carole Gene Marer
Children: Victoria Davey, Randall Gene, Tori

Major Award: Emmy, Outstanding Drama/Comedy Special, *Day One,* 1989
Quote: "I just got tired of the critics saying that I was the master of schlock. It didn't bother me until my kids began growing up and reading it. Well, I'm proud of those entertainment shows they call schlock."

STEVEN SPIELBERG

Birthplace: Cincinnati, OH
Birthdate: 12/18/47
Occupation: Director, producer
Education: California State College at Long Beach
Debut: (TV) *Night Gallery,* 1969
Signature: *E.T., the Extra-Terrestrial*
Facts: Made the film *Firelight* at age 16, about the reflecting telescope he made himself, and persuaded a Phoenix, AZ, movie house to show it.

Became a TV director at Universal Pictures at age 20 after finding an empty office and pretending he belonged there.

Was not accepted by the University of Southern California's film department.

Co-owns the LA restaurant Dive!

Marriages: Amy Irving (divorced), Kate Capshaw
Children: Max, Sasha, Sawyer, stepdaughter Jessica, adopted son Theo
Major Awards: Oscar, Irving G. Thalberg Memorial Award, 1986; Oscar, Best Director, *Schindler's List,* 1994; Golden Globe, Best Director, *Schindler's List,* 1994

BRUCE SPRINGSTEEN

Birthplace: Freehold, NJ
Birthdate: 9/23/49
Occupation: Singer, songwriter
Education: Attended Ocean City Community College
Debut: (Album) *Greetings from Asbury Park,* 1973
Signature: *Born in the USA*
Facts: E Street Band, formed in 1973, was named after the road in Belmar, NJ, where keyboardist David Sancious's mother lives.

After a 1976 Memphis concert, was caught climbing over the wall to Graceland.

Gave the song "Because the Night" to Patti Smith's producer, who was working in the adjacent recording studio.

In 1986, he rejected a $12 million offer from Lee Iococca to use "Born in the U.S.A." for Chrysler commercials.

Marriages: Julianne Phillips (divorced), Patti Scialfa
Children: Evan, Jessica
Major Awards: Grammy, Best Recording for Children, *In Harmony 2* (with others), 1982; Grammy, Best Rock Vocal, "Dancing in the Dark," 1984; Grammy, Best Rock Vocal, "Tunnel of Love," 1987; Oscar, Best Song, "Streets of Philadelphia," 1994; Golden Globe, Best Song, "Streets of Philadelphia," 1994

SYLVESTER STALLONE

Birthplace: Hell's Kitchen, New York
Birthdate: 4/6/46
Occupation: Actor, writer, director
Education: American School of Switzerland; attended University of Miami
Debut: (Film) *Lords of Flatbush,* 1973
Signature: *Rocky*
Facts: When he was born, the forceps severed a nerve in his face and partially paralyzed his lip, chin, and half of his tongue.

Had rickets as a child.

In high school he played football, fenced, and threw discus.

His paintings have been featured in galleries.

In *Bananas* (1971), played a goon who was thrown off a subway by Woody Allen.

Infamy: As a boy was kicked out of fourteen schools in eleven years.

In 1971 appeared in a soft-core porn film, *A Party at Kitty & Stud's.*

Original Job: Usher, fish salesman, zoo attendant, bookstore detective, teacher at American School of Switzerland.
Marriages: Sasha Czack (divorced), Brigitte Nielsen (divorced)
Children: Sage, Seth (with Sasha Czack)
Famous Relative: Frank Stallone, musician, brother

DANIELLE STEEL

Real Name: Danielle Schuelein-Steel
Birthplace: New York, NY
Birthdate: 8/14/47
Occupation: Writer
Education: Lycée Français; attended Parsons School of Design; New York University
Debut: (Book) *Going Home,* 1973
Facts: Wrote over thirty best-selling novels in twenty years, including *The Ring* (1980), *Secrets* (1985), and *Daddy* (1989).
Infamy: After marrying Claude Eric Lazard in 1972, Steel married three convicts in a row, the second while he was still in prison, and the third while eight months pregnant with his child.
Original Job: Vice president of public relations and new business for Supergirls, Ltd., a PR and ad agency
Marriages: Claude Eric Lazard (divorced), Danny Zugelder (divorced), Bill Toth (divorced), John Traina
Children: Beatrix, Nicholas, Samantha, Victoria, Vanessa, Max, Zara

HOWARD STERN

Birthplace: New York, NY
Birthdate: 1/12/54
Occupation: Radio DJ
Education: Boston University
Signature: *The Howard Stern Show*
Facts: 1994 Libertarian gubernatorial candidate in New York but dropped out of race before the elections.

Once fired for referring to station management as "scumbags" on the air during a salary dispute.

Practices transcendental meditation each morning in the limo ride to work.

Infamy: After angry listeners provided the FCC with transcripts of Stern's show about masturbating to Aunt Jemima and having rough sex with actress Michelle Pfeiffer, the commission fined Infinity Broadcasting, which owns WNBC-New York, $600,000.
Marriage: Allison Pullman

PATRICK STEWART

Birthplace: Mirfield, England
Birthdate: 7/13/40
Occupation: Actor, writer
Education: Attended Bristol Old Vic Theatre School
Debut: (Stage) *Treasure Island,* 1959
Signature: *Star Trek: The Next Generation*
Facts: Was so sure that he was going to be fired from the initial season of *Star Trek: The Next Generation* that he didn't unpack his bags for six weeks.
Original Job: Journalist
Marriage: Sheila (divorced)
Children: Sofie, Daniel
Quote: "I was brought up in a very poor and very violent household. I spent much of my childhood being afraid."

BEN STILLER

Birthplace: New York, NY
Birthdate: 1966
Occupation: Actor
Education: Attended UCLA
Debut: (Film) *Reality Bites,* 1994
Signature: *A Different World*
Facts: Began making Super-8 movies about getting revenge on bullies in his neighborhood when he was 10.

His short film parody of *The Color of Money* landed him a job at *Saturday Night Live* and his own show on MTV.

Marriage: Jeanne Tripplehorn (engaged)
Famous Relatives: Jerry Stiller, comedian, father; Anne Meara, comedian, mother

STING

Real Name: Gordon Sumner
Birthplace: Wallsend, Tyne and Wear, England
Birthdate: 10/2/51
Occupation: Singer, songwriter, actor
Education: Attended Warwick University
Debut: (Song) "Fall Out" (with the Police), 1977
Signature: *The Police*
Facts: In 1978, rejected the part of the villain in James Bond film *For Your Eyes Only.*

He gained his nickname by wearing a black-and-yellow striped shirt, like a bee.

Received a seaman's card and worked as a bass player

with the Ronnie Pierson trio on Princess Cruise Lines at age 17.

Claimed in a 1993 *Rolling Stone* interview that by practicing meditation, he can make love for more than five hours at a time.
Original Job: Teacher, construction worker, clerk for Inland Revenue
Marriages: Frances Eleanor Tomelty (divorced), Trudie Styler
Children: Joseph, Katherine, Mickey, Jake
Major Awards: Grammy, Best Rock Performance—Duo or Group, "Don't Stand So Close to Me" (with the Police), 1981; Grammy, Song of the Year, "Every Breath You Take," 1983; Grammy, Best Pop Performance—Duo or Group, "Every Breath You Take" (with the Police), 1983; Grammy, Best Pop Vocal—Male, "Bring on the Night," 1987; Grammy, Best Rock Song/Vocal Performance, "Soul Cages," 1991; Grammy, Best Pop Vocal—Male, "If I Ever Lose My Faith in You," 1993; Grammy, Best Music Video—Long Form, *Ten Summoner's Tales,* 1993

OLIVER STONE

Birthplace: New York, NY
Birthdate: 9/15/46
Occupation: Director, writer, producer
Education: Attended Yale University; New York University film school
Debut: (Film) *Seizure,* 1974
Signature: *Platoon*
Facts: Served in the U.S. Merchant Marines, 1966; in the Army in Vietnam, 1967–68. Awarded Bronze Star and Purple Heart with Oak Leaf Cluster.

Made acting debut as a bum in *The Hand* (1981), which he wrote and directed.
Original Job: Taxi driver in New York City, teacher at Free Pacific Institute in South Vietnam
Marriages: Majwa Sarkis (divorced), Elizabeth Burkit Cox (divorced)
Children: Sean, Michael
Major Awards: Oscar, Best Adapted Screenplay, *Midnight Express,* 1978; Oscar, Best Director, *Platoon,* 1986; Golden Globe, Best Director, *Platoon,* 1987; Oscar, Best Director, *Born on the Fourth of July,* 1991; Golden Globe, Best Director, *Born on the Fourth of July,* 1990; Golden Globe, Best Screenplay, *Born on the Fourth of July* (with Ron Kovic), 1990; Golden Globe, Best Director, *JFK,* 1992

SHARON STONE

Birthplace: Meadville, PA
Birthdate: 3/10/58
Occupation: Actor
Education: Attended Edinboro State University
Debut: (Film) *Stardust Memories,* 1981
Signature: *Basic Instinct*
Facts: She has an I.Q. of 154.

Between 1977 and 1980, became one of the top ten models at the Ford Agency.
Infamy: Posed nude for *Playboy* just days after finishing *Total Recall,* 1990.
Original Job: Model
Marriages: George Englund (divorced), Michael Greenburg (divorced)
Quote: "If I was just intelligent, I'd be OK. But I am fiercely intelligent, which most people find threatening. . . . I have a strong point of view based on my experience. It may or may not be the correct one, but it is an informed one, and I'm willing to fight for it. If I were a petite, brunette, ethnic lawyer then my behavior would be totally acceptable. But we Barbie Dolls are not supposed to behave the way I do."

MADELEINE STOWE

Birthplace: Los Angeles, CA
Birthdate: 8/18/58
Occupation: Actor
Education: Attended USC
Signature: *The Last of the Mohicans*
Facts: Starred in first film, *Tropical Snow,* in 1986, but the film was not released until 1989. *Stakeout* was her first released film in 1987.
Marriage: Brian Benben
Major Award: Golden Globe, Special Achievement, *Short Cuts,* 1994

MERYL STREEP

Real Name: Mary Louise Streep
Birthplace: Summit, NJ
Birthdate: 6/22/49
Occupation: Actor
Education: Vassar College; MFA, Yale University
Debut: (Stage) *Trelawny of the Wells,* N.Y. Shakespeare Festival, 1975
Signature: *Sophie's Choice*
Facts: When she was 12, began studying with vocal coach Estelle Liebling, who had also taught diva Beverly Sills.

In high school, was a cheerleader and homecoming queen.

Formed a child support group with Annette Bening, Carrie Fisher, and Tracey Ullman, in which they watch each other's children.
Original Job: Waitress
Marriage: Don Gummer
Children: Henry, Mary Willa, Grace Jane, Louisa Jacobson
Major Awards: Emmy, Best Actress in a Miniseries, *Holocaust,* 1978; Oscar, Best Supporting Actress, *Kramer vs. Kramer,* 1980; Golden Globe, Best Supporting Actress, *Kramer vs. Kramer;* 1980; Golden Globe, Best Actress, *The French Lieutenant's Woman,* 1982; Oscar, Best Actress, *Sophie's Choice,* 1982; Golden Globe, Best Actress, *Sophie's Choice,* 1983

BARBRA STREISAND

Real Name: Barbara Streisand
Birthplace: Brooklyn, NY
Birthdate: 4/24/42
Occupation: Singer
Education: Attended Yeshiva University
Debut: (Stage) *Another Evening with Harry Stoones,* 1961

(Film) *Funny Girl,* 1968
Facts: Her father died when she was 15 months old.

She graduated from high school two years early.

Although she had never sung before an audience before, she won a talent contest in a Greenwich Village bar and won a singing job at another bar.

Her Oscar for *Funny Girl* (1968) tied with Katharine Hepburn for *A Lion in Winter,* the only tie for a Best Actress Academy Award.
Infamy: Theater usher, switchboard operator, waitress
Original Job: Singer, actress
Marriage: Elliot Gould (divorced)
Child: Jason Emanuel
Major Awards: Emmy for Outstanding Program Achievements in Entertainment, *My Name is Barbra,* 1965; Academy Award and Golden Globe for Best Actress, *Funny Girl,* 1968; co-recipient Academy Award for Best Song, "Evergreen," 1976; Georgie Award AGVA 1977; Grammy Awards for Best Female Pop Vocalist 1963–65, 1977, 1986; Grammy Award for Best Songwriter (with Paul Williams), 1977; Tony special award, 1970

ELIZABETH TAYLOR

Birthplace: London, England
Birthdate: 2/27/32
Occupation: Actor
Education: Byron House, Hawthorne School, Metro-Goldwyn-Mayer School
Debut: (Film) *There's One Born Every Minute,* 1942
Facts: After friend Rock Hudson died from AIDS, became the founding chair of the American Foundation for AIDS Research (AMFAR) in 1985.

Almost died from pnuemonia and had an emergency tracheotomy in 1961.

When she was three years old she danced before Queen Elizabeth and Princess Margaret. She met construction worker Larry Fortensky, whom she married in 1992, at the Betty Ford Clinic.
Infamy: Checked herself into the Betty Ford Clinic to overcome alcohol dependency, 1983. Returned in 1988 to overcome painkiller depencency.
Marriages: Nicholas Conrad Hilton Jr. (divorced), Michael Wilding (divorced), Mike Todd (deceased), Eddie Fisher (divorced), Richard Burton (divorced, remarried, divorced), John Warner (divorced), Larry Fortensky
Children: Michael, Christo-

pher, Elizabeth, adopted German orphan Maria Carson
Major Awards: French Legion of Honor, 1987; Academy Award for Best Actress: *Butterfield 8,* 1960; Academy Award, Best Actress, *Who's Afraid of Virginia Woolf,* 1966

EMMA THOMPSON

Birthplace: London, England
Birthdate: 4/15/59
Occupation: Actor
Education: Cambridge University
Debut: (Film) *Henry V,* 1989
Signature: *Howard's End*
Facts: Wrote screenplay adaptation of *Sense and Sensibilities* by Jane Austen, whose novels she began reading at age nine.

When first met her husband, Kenneth Branagh, she "thought he had strange hair."

Lives on the street on which she was raised, opposite her mother and down the street from her younger sister, Sophie.
Marriage: Kenneth Branagh
Famous Relatives: Eric Thompson, producer, father; Phyllida Law, actor, mother; Sophie Thompson, actor, sister
Major Award: Academy Award for Best Actress, Howard's End, 1993

MARISA TOMEI

Birthplace: Brooklyn, NY
Birthdate: 12/4/64
Occupation: Actor
Education: Attended Boston University
Debut: (Film) *The Flamingo Kid,* 1984
Signature: *My Cousin Vinny*
Facts: Attended Boston University for one year, until she got a role on *As the World Turns.*

Played Lisa Bonet's roommate during the first season of *A Different World* (1987–88).
Major Award: Oscar, Best Supporting Actress, *My Cousin Vinny,* 1993

JEANNE TRIPPLEHORN

Birthplace: Tulsa, OK
Birthdate: 1963
Occupation: Actor
Education: Attended Tulsa University, Juilliard
Debut: (TV) *The Perfect Tribute*
Signature: *Basic Instinct*
Quote: On a rough sex scene with Michael Douglas in *Basic Instinct*: "My head kept hitting the wall. That's what I call a hard day's work."
Original Job: Radio and television personality in Tulsa, OK
Marriage: Ben Stiller (engaged)

CHRISTY TURLINGTON

Birthplace: Walnut Creek, CA
Birthdate: 1/2/69
Occupation: Supermodel
Education: Attended UCLA
Facts: Her face was used on mannequins at the Metropolitan Museum of Art's costume galleries.

JANINE TURNER

Real Name: Janine Gauntt
Birthplace: Lincoln, NE
Birthdate: 12/6/63
Occupation: Actor
Education: Attended Professional Children's School
Debut: (TV) *Dallas*
Signature: *Northern Exposure*
Facts: Was engaged to Alec Baldwin. Her wedding dress was ready and invitations had been sent out when they broke up.

Took her acting surname from her father Turner Gauntt, a pilot for Braniff.

Died her hair blond for role as kleptomaniac spy Laura Templeton on *General Hospital* (1982).
Original Job: Model
Relationship: Troy Aikman

KATHLEEN TURNER

Real Name: Mary Kathleen Turner
Birthplace: Springfield, MO
Birthdate: 6/19/54
Occupation: Actor
Education: Studied at London's Central School of Speech and Drama; attended Southwest Missouri State University; University of Maryland
Debut: (Stage) *Gemini,* 1978
Signature: *Peggy Sue Got Married*
Facts: Places pencil erasers at the back of her mouth to practice her sultry voice.

Daughter of a U.S. foreign service officer, she grew up in Canada, Cuba, Washington, DC, and Venezuela before settling in London.
Infamy: Husband was the leaseholder of a building in New York City where eighty-seven people were killed by a fire caused by arson. He pled guilty in 1992 to building code violations, paying $60,000 to be used by a Bronx community service center and performing fifty hours of community service.
Original Job: Waitress
Marriage: Jay Weiss
Child: Rachel Ann
Major Awards: Golden Globe, Best Actress in a Comedy, *Romancing the Stone,* 1985; Golden Globe, Best Actress in a Comedy, *Prizzi's Honor,* 1986

TED TURNER

Real Name: Robert Edward Turner
Birthplace: Cincinnati, OH
Birthdate: 11/19/38
Occupation: Media executive, owner of Atlanta Braves and Hawks
Education: Attended Brown University
Debut: In 1970, bought failing Atlanta TV station, which he turned into WTBS
Signature: *CNN*
Facts: Won the America's Cup in his yacht, *Courageous,* in 1977.
Infamy: Was "asked to leave" Brown University in 1967 for having a girl in his room after hours; was subsequently awarded an honorary degree.
Original Job: Selling space on billboards in family business
Marriages: Judy Nye (divorced), Jane Shirley Smith (divorced), Jane Fonda
Children: Laura Lee, Robert Edward IV, Rhett, Beau, Jennie
Major Award: Elected to the Emmy Hall of Fame, 1991

TINA TURNER

Real Name: Anna Mae Bullock
Birthplace: Nutbush, TN
Birthdate: 11/25/40
Occupation: Singer, actor
Debut: (Song) "Fool in Love," 1960
Facts: "River Deep, Mountain High" (1966) was number one in Britain and earned the Ike and Tina Turner Revue the chance to open for the Rolling Stones in 1969.
Marriage: Ike Turner (divorced)
Major Awards: Grammy, Best R&B Duo or Group, "Proud Mary" (with Ike Turner), 1972; Grammy, Record of the Year and Best Pop Vocal—Female, "What's Love Got to Do With It?," 1984; inducted into Rock and Roll Hall of Fame, 1991; Grammy, Best Rock Vocal of the Year, "Better Be Good to Me," 1985; Grammy, Best Rock Vocal of the Year, "One of the Living," 1986; Grammy, Best Rock Vocal of the Year, "Back Where You Started," 1986; Grammy, Best Rock Vocal of the Year, *Tina Live in Europe,* 1988

SCOTT TUROW

Birthplace: Chicago, IL
Birthdate: 4/12/49
Occupation: Author, attorney
Education: Amherst College; Stanford University; Harvard Law School
Debut: (Book) *Presumed Innocent,* 1987
Facts: Has said that, although it's difficult to juggle two careers, he has no intention of giving up his law practice.

Writes mornings in his study, works until the phone starts to ring at about 10 a.m. At noon, takes the train into Chicago to meet with law clients.
Marriage: Annette
Children: Three children

RICHARD TYLER

Birthplace: Australia
Birthdate: 1949
Occupation: Designer
Facts: Celebrity customers include Julia Roberts, Kim Basinger, Janet Jackson, Nichole Kidman, Sigourney Weaver, and Anjelica Huston.

His women's jackets are supposed to make women look taller, thinner, and sexier.

Designed flamboyant stage outfits for Elton John, Rod Stewart, and Diana Ross, among others.
Original Job: Cutter in shirt factory
Marriage: Lisa Trafficante
Child: Sheridan

STEVEN TYLER

Real Name: Steven Tallarico
Birthplace: Boston, MA
Birthdate: 3/26/48
Education: High school dropout
Debut: (Album) *Aerosmith,* 1973
Signature: Aerosmith
Facts: Met future Aerosmith members Joe Perry and Tom Hamilton at Lake Sunapee, NH, where their families had vacation houses.

Seriously injured in a motorcycle accident in 1981, capping a long period of discord and debauchery among band members. "I lay there in the hospital crying and flipping out, knowing some other group was going to step into our space. Through the stupor of my medication, I pictured a spotlight. We walked out of it."

When the band reformed in 1984, they got a contract with Geffen but had to audition first.

Aerosmith co-owns the West Hollywood restaurant House of Blues with Dan Aykroyd and Jim Belushi.
Infamy: Alcohol and drug use
Children: Mia (with Cyrinda Tallarico), Liv, actress (with Bebe Buell)
Major Awards: Best Rock Performance by a Duo or Group with Vocal, "Janie's Got a Gun"

BLAIR UNDERWOOD

Birthplace: Tacoma, WA
Birthdate: 8/25/64
Occupation: Actor
Education: Attended Carnegie-Mellon University
Debut: (TV) *The Cosby Show,* 1985
Signature: *L.A. Law*
Facts: Underwood says he was stopped for speeding and a gun was put to his head when he reached for his driver's license. He said he is conscious of subtle racism: "You think twice about offering to help an elderly lady cross the street because she's going to scream 'rape' or think you're stealing."
Marriage: Desirée Da Costa

JOHN UPDIKE

Birthplace: Shillington, PA
Birthdate: 3/18/32
Occupation: Writer
Education: Harvard College; Oxford University
Debut: (Book) *The Carpentered Hen and Other Tame Creatures,* 1958
Signature: *Rabbit, Run*
Facts: Collected Walt Disney comic books.
Marriages: Mary Entwhistle Pennington (divorced), Martha R. Bernhard
Major Awards: Pulitzer Prize, *Rabbit Is Rich,* 1982; American Book Award, *Rabbit Is Rich,* 1982

JEAN-CLAUDE VAN DAMME

Real Name: Jean-Claude Van Vorenberg
Birthplace: Brussels, Belgium
Birthdate: 1961
Occupation: Actor, martial arts expert
Debut: (Film) *Rue Barbare (Barbarous Street),* 1983
Signature: *Kickboxer*
Facts: A middleweight champion in the Professional European Karate Association, he began studying karate at 11 years old.

Van Damme's fight scenes are so intense that he won't film them in the United States for fear of being sued.

Changed his name to Frank Cujo in 1983; however, changed it again after the release of the Stephen King film *Cujo.*
Infamy: In 1989, sued for "willfully" gouging the eye of an extra in a sword fight while filming *Cyborg.*
Original Job: Ran the California Gym in Brussels before coming to the U.S. in 1981; worked as a limo and taxi driver, bouncer, carpet installer, and pizza deliveryman
Marriage: Gladys Portugues (divorced)
Children: Kristopher, Bianca

EDDIE VAN HALEN

Birthplace: Nijmegen, Holland
Birthdate: 1/26/57
Occupation: Singer, guitarist
Education: Attended Pasadena City College
Debut: (album) *Van Halen,* 1978
Facts: When Van Halen wanted to propose to Valerie Bertinelli, he first asked her father for her hand.

Did guitar work on Michael Jackson's "Beat It," free of charge, as a favor.

Formed the group Broken Combs with brother Alex, later changed the name to Mammoth. Formed Van Halen in 1974.

Album and recording studio that Eddie owns, 5150, is named after the New York police code for the criminally insane.
Marriage: Valerie Bertinelli
Child: Wolfgang
Major Award: Grammy, Best Hard Rock Performance, *For Unlawful Carnal Knowledge* (with Van Halen), 1991

LUTHER VANDROSS

Birthplace: New York, NY
Birthdate: 4/20/51
Occupation: Singer, songwriter
Education: Attended Western Michigan University
Debut: (Song) "Everybody Rejoice (A Brand New Day)" from *The Wiz,* 1978
Signature: "Here and Now"
Facts: Started playing the piano at age three.

Sister was a member of the '50s group The Crests.

His first group, Listen My Brother, formed while he was a high school student, played at the Apollo, and appeared on the first episode of *Sesame Street.*
Original Job: S&H Green Stamp defective-merchandise clerk
Major Awards: Grammy, Best R&B Vocal—Male, "Here and Now," 1990; Grammy, Best R&B Song, "Power of Love/Love Power," 1991; Grammy, Best R&B Vocal—Male, *Power of Love,* 1991

EDDIE VEDDER

Real Name: Eddie Mueller
Birthplace: Chicago, IL
Occupation: Singer, songwriter
Education: High school
Debut: (Album) *Ten,* 1992
Signature: Leader of Pearl Jam
Facts: Vedder, a Red Hot Chili Peppers roadie, was introduced to future Pearl Jam members by Jack Irons.

"Vedder" is his mother's maiden name.
Original Job: Worked at service station, waited tables
Marriage: Beth Liebling
Quote: "I think celebrities suck."

VENDELA

Real Name: Vendela Kirsebom
Birthplace: Sweden
Birthdate: 1/12/67
Occupation: Supermodel
Education: Attended UCLA film school
Signature: *Sports Illustrated* swimsuit model
Facts: Parents were printing and graphics professionals and part-time potato farmers.

Speaks Swedish, Italian, German, and English fluently.

GIANNI VERSACE

Birthplace: Reggio di Calabria, Italy
Birthdate: 12/2/46
Occupation: Fashion designer
Facts: Has designed costumes for operas and ballets in Milan, Leningrad, Brussels, and other cities. Versace collaboration with the French choreographer Maurice Bejart was the subject of a 1989 film by Sergio Salerni entitled *La Fortuna dell' Amicizia* (*The Good Fortune of Friendship*).

Versace's mother was a boutique owner and dress maker.

Studied architectural design in Italy and earned a degree allowing him to work as an architect or building contractor's assistant.
Original Job: Part-time fashion buyer for his mother
Major Awards: The Cutty Sark American Award for Excellence in Men's Fashion, 1983, 1988; Italy's Occhio d'Oro (Golden Eye) Award, 1982, 1984, 1990, 1991; Council of Fashion Designers of America, International Award, 1993

ROBERT JAMES WALLER

Birthplace: Rockford, Iowa
Birthdate: 8/1/39
Occupation: Author, professor of business management
Education: University of Northern Iowa, Indiana University
Debut: (Book) *The Bridges of Madison County,* 1991
Facts: The books on his desk reportedly range from *A History of Mathematics* to issues of *Guns & Ammo.*

Won college basketball scholarship.

Wrote his second book, *Slow Waltz in Cedar Bend,* in ten days.

Used an old door lain across a wooden sawhorse for a table until he replaced it with a new $700 table he named "Steve."
Original Job: Taught management and economics; dean of business school
Marriage: Georgia Ann Wiedemeier
Child: Rachael

BARBARA WALTERS

Birthplace: Boston, MA
Birthdate: 9/25/31
Occupation: Broadcast journalist
Education: Sarah Lawrence College
Debut: (TV) *The Today Show,* 1974
Signature: *20/20*
Facts: In 1957, Don Hewitt, now executive producer of *60 Minutes,* told Walters: "You're marvelous, but stay out of television."

Walters was the only woman reporter in the press group that accompanied President Nixon on his historic trip to China in 1972.
Original Job: Intent on becoming a teacher, went for her master's in education while working as a secretary
Marriages: Robert Henry Katz (annulled), Merv Adelman (divorced), Sen. John Warner (relationship)
Child: Jacqueline Dena
Major Awards: Emmy, Best Host on a Talk Show, *Today,* 1975; Emmy, Best Interviewer, *The Barbara Walters Show,* 1982; elected to the Television Hall of Fame, 1990

VERA WANG

Birthplace: New York, NY
Birthdate: 1949
Occupation: Designer
Education: Sarah Lawrence College
Debut: Former *Vogue* fashion editor and Ralph Lauren design director
Signature: Owner, Vera Wang Bridal House Ltd.
Facts: Placed fifth in pairs at the 1969 United States Figure Skating Championships with her partner, James Stuart.

Designed Nancy Kerrigan's skating outfits for the 1994 Winter Olympics in Lillehammer, Norway.

Wang became a bridal gown designer after being disappointed with the selection for her own 1989 wedding. She settled on one that cost $10,000.
Original Job: Figure skater
Marriage: Arthur Becker
Child: Cecelia

DENZEL WASHINGTON

Birthplace: Mt. Vernon, NY
Birthdate: 12/8/54
Occupation: Actor
Education: Fordham University; studied acting at the American Conservatory Theatre, San Francisco
Debut: (Film) *Carbon Copy,* 1980
Signature: *Malcolm X*
Facts: Played Malcolm X in *When the Chickens Come Home to Roost* on Broadway, as well as in the 1992 Spike Lee movie.

In college, played football and basketball and wrote poetry before deciding to try acting.
Original Job: Drama instructor
Marriage: Paulette Pearson
Children: John David, Katia
Major Awards: Oscar, Best Supporting Actor, *Glory,* 1989; Golden Globe, Best Supporting Actor, *Glory,* 1989

WENDY WASSERSTEIN

Birthplace: Brooklyn, NY
Birthdate: 10/18/50
Occupation: Playwright
Education: Mount Holyoke College, City College of New York, Yale University School of Drama
Debut: (Stage) *Any Woman Can't,* 1973
Signature: *The Heidi Chronicles*
Facts: Almost enrolled in business school rather than pursuing drama.

Brother sent her a note prior to a premiere: "Can't come to play tonight. Am buying Nabisco."
Famous Relative: Bruce Wasserstein, investment banking star, brother
Major Awards: Pulitzer Prize, *The Heidi Chronicles,* 1988; Tony Award, *The Heidi Chronicles,* 1988

SIGOURNEY WEAVER

Real Name: Susan Weaver
Birthplace: New York, NY
Birthdate: 10/8/49
Occupation: Actor
Education: Stanford University; MFA, Yale University
Debut: (Stage) *The Constant Wife* (with Ingrid Bergman), 1974
Signature: *Alien*
Facts: Took her name from a character in *The Great Gatsby.*

As a senior at Stanford, she dressed as an elf and lived in a treehouse with her boyfriend.

Accepted at Yale Drama School as "Mr." Sigourney Weaver.
Marriage: Jim Simpson
Child: Charlotte
Famous Relatives: Sylvester "Pat" Weaver, president of NBC, co-founder of cable television, father; Elizabeth Inglis, actor, mother
Major Awards: Golden Globe, Best Actress, *Gorillas in the Mist,* 1989; Golden Globe, Best Supporting Actress, *Working Girl,* 1989

ANDREW LLOYD WEBBER

Birthplace: London, England
Birthdate: 3/22/48
Occupation: Composer, producer
Education: Attended Magdelen College of Oxford University; Royal Academy of Music; Oxford, Guildhall School of Music, Royal College of Music
Debut: (Stage) *Joseph and the Amazing Technicolor Dreamcoat,* 1968
Signature: *Phantom of the Opera*
Fact: In 1969, was commissioned by RCA to write an opera based on a single, "Jesus Christ Superstar."
Marriages: Sarah Jane Tudor Hugill (divorced), Sarah Brightman (divorced), Madeleine Astrid Gurdon
Children: Nicholas, Imogen, Alastair
Famous Relative: William Webber, London College of Music Director, father
Major Awards: Grammy, Best Cast Show Album, *Evita* (with Tim Rice), 1980; Grammy, Best Cast Show Album, *Cats,* 1983; Grammy, Legend Award, 1990; New York Drama Critics Award, *Evita,* 1980; Tony, Best Score, *Evita* (music; Tim Rice, lyrics), 1980; Tony, Best Score, *Cats* (music; T. S. Eliot, lyrics), 1983; Tony Award, Best Musical, *Phantom of the Opera*

ROBIN WILLIAMS

Birthplace: Chicago, IL
Birthdate: 7/21/52
Occupation: Actor
Education: Claremont Men's College, College of Marin, Juilliard School
Debut: (TV) *Laugh-In,* 1977
Signature: *Mork and Mindy*
Facts: Grew up on a thirty-room estate in Bloomfield Hills, MI.

Spent most of childhood playing with his 2,000 toy soldiers.

Second wife was a former nanny of Robin's children and his personal assistant. She served as a producer for *Mrs. Doubtfire,* 1994.
Infamy: Sued for $6.2 milion in 1986 by former companion Michelle Tish Carter, who claimed that he gave her herpes during their two-year relationship. Williams countersued for extortion.

Shared cocaine with John Belushi only a few hours before Belushi's death.
Original Job: Street mime
Marriages: Valeri Velardi (divorced), Marsha Garces
Children: Zachary, Zelda, Cody Alan

Major Awards: Golden Globe, Best Actor in a Comedy Series, *Mork and Mindy,* 1979; Emmy, Best Individual Performance in a Variety or Music Program, *A Carol Burnett Special,* 1987; Emmy, Best Individual Performance in a Variety or Music Program, *ABC Presents a Royal Gala,* 1988; Golden Globe, Best Actor in a Comedy, *Good Morning, Vietnam,* 1988; Golden Globe, Best Actor in a Comedy, *The Fisher King,* 1992; Golden Globe, Special Achievement, *Aladdin,* 1993; Golden Globe, Best Actor in a Comedy, *Mrs. Doubtfire,* 1994; Grammy, Best Comedy Recording, *Reality . . . What a Concept,* 1979; Grammy, Best Comedy Recording, *A Night at the Met,* 1987; Grammy, Best Comedy Recording, *Good Morning, Vietnam,* 1978; Grammy, Best Recording for Children, *Pecos Bill,* 1988

BRUCE WILLIS

Birthplace: Idar-Oberstein, Germany
Birthdate: 3/19/55
Occupation: Actor
Education: Attended Montclair State College.
Debut: (Stage) *Heaven and Earth,* 1977
Signature: *Moonlighting*
Facts: Was student council president in high school.

The stammer he'd had since childhood disappeared whenever he performed.

Willis and Demi Moore were married on November 21, 1987, by singer Little Richard.

Has his own band, Bruno.

Infamy: During his senior year in high school, was expelled after a racial disturbance and was only permitted to graduate because his father hired an attorney to get him reinstated.
Original Job: DuPont plant worker, bartender, commercial actor for Levi's 501 jeans
Marriage: Demi Moore
Children: Rumer Glenn, Scout Larue, Tallulah Belle
Major Awards: Emmy, Best Actor in a Drama Series, *Moonlighting,* 1987; Golden Globe, Best Actor in a Comedy Series, *Moonlighting,* 1987

AUGUST WILSON

Birthplace: Pittsburgh, PA
Birthdate: 4/27/45
Occupation: Playwright
Debut: (Play) *Ma Rainey's Black Bottom,* 1981
Signature: *The Piano Lesson*
Fact: Founded the black activist theater company Black Horizon on the Hill in the 1960s.
Marriage: Judy Oliver
Major Awards: Pulitzer Prize, Best Play, *Fences,* 1987, Best Play, *The Piano Lesson,* 1990, Best Play, *Two Trains Running,* 1992; Tony, Best Play, *Fences,* 1987

CASSANDRA WILSON

Birthplace: Jackson, MS
Birthdate: 1955
Occupation: Singer
Education: Attended Milsap College
Debut: (Album) *Point of View,* 1986
Signature: Jazz singer
Facts: Wilson's father, jazz guitarist Herman B. Fowlkes, thought blues were "too common," but Wilson says, "I think you just get the blues automatically in Mississippi. You don't really have to have it in the house. You walk outside and it's in the air."

Parents told her that when she sang in kindergarten she had the loudest voice of any of the children.

Played Dorothy in high school production of *The Wizard of Oz.*

Original Job: Worked in a TV station
Famous Relative: Herman B. Fowlkes, jazz guitarist, father

OPRAH WINFREY

Birthplace: Kosciusko, MS
Birthdate: 1/29/54
Occupation: Talk-show host
Education: Tennesee State University
Debut: (Radio Reporter) WVOL, Nashville, 1971–72
Signature: *The Oprah Winfrey Show*
Facts: Delivered Easter sermon to congregation when she was two years old.

Once approached Aretha Franklin as she was stepping out of a limo and convinced Franklin that she had been abandoned. Aretha gave her $100, which Oprah used to stay in a hotel.

As a college sophomore, was the first African-American news co-anchor on a local TV station.

In college, won the title of Miss Tennessee and competed in the Miss Black America contest.

After being sexually abused at age nine by an older cousin and later by a family friend, she ran away from home at age 13.

Original Job: News reporter, WVOL radio, WTVF television, Nashville, TN
Marriage: Stedman Graham (engaged)
Major Awards: Emmy, Best Host of a Talk Show, *The Oprah Winfrey Show,* 1987, 1991, 1992

DEBRA WINGER

Birthplace: Cleveland, OH
Birthdate: 5/17/55
Occupation: Actor
Education: Attended California State University at Northridge
Debut: (TV) *Wonder Woman,* 1976–77
Signature: *An Officer and a Gentleman*
Facts: In 1972, moved to Israel and served in the army for three months.

At 18 was in a coma after an accident at an amusement park where she was working in a troll costume.

Played Wonder Woman's younger sister, Drusilla the Wonder Girl, in the 1976–77 TV show.

Provided the voice (mixed with that of an elderly woman) for the title character of *E.T.: The Extra-Terrestrial,* 1982.

Original Job: Amusement park troll
Marriage: Timothy Hutton (divorced)
Child: Emmanuel Noah

ALFRE WOODARD

Birthplace: Tulsa, OK
Birthdate: 11/8/53
Occupation: Actor
Education: Boston University
Debut: (Stage) *Horatio,* 1974
Signature: *Cross Creek*
Facts: Played Dr. Roxanne Turner on the series *St. Elsewhere,* 1985–87.

Nominated for an Oscar for *Cross Creek.*

Marriage: Roderick Spenser
Children: Adopted two children
Major Awards: Emmy, Best Supporting Actress in a Drama Series, *Hill Street Blues,* 1984; Emmy, Best Guest Performer, *L.A. Law,* 1987

WYNONNA

Real Name: Cristina Judd
Birthplace: Ashland, KY
Birthdate: 5/3/64
Occupation: Singer
Education: High school
Debut: (Song) "Had a Dream" (with The Judds), 1984
Signature: *Wynonna*
Facts: Drives a 1957 Chevy and a turquoise Harley Davidson.

Had asthma as a child.

Adopted her name after the town of Wynona, OK, mentioned in the song "Route 66."

The Judds got their first recording contract when mother Naomi, a nurse, gave a tape to patient Diana Maher, daughter of record producer Brent Maher.

Famous Relatives: Naomi Judd, country singer, mother; Ashley Judd, actress, sister
Major Awards: Grammy: Best Country Song, "Love Can Build a Bridge," 1991; Best Country Performance by a Group or Duo, "Mama He's Crazy," 1984; "Why Not Me," 1985; "Grandpa (Tell Me 'Bout the Good Old Days)," 1986; "Give a Little Love," 1988; "Love Can Build a Bridge," 1991

YANNI

Real Name: Chrysomallis Yanni
Birthplace: Kalamata, Greece
Birthdate: 11/4/54
Occupation: Musician, pianist
Education: University of Minnesota

Debut: (Album) *Optimystique,* 1986
Facts: Former member of the Greek National Swimming Team.
Toured with the cult rock band Chameleon.
His music is used on broadcasts of numerous sporting events, including the Tour de France, the Olympic Games, and the World Series.
Relationship: Linda Evans

DAPHNE ZUNIGA

Birthplace: Berkeley, CA
Birthdate: 1962
Occupation: Actor
Education: Attended UCLA
Debut: (Film) *Pranks,* 1982
Signature: *Melrose Place*
Facts: Played John Cusack's reluctant traveling companion in Rob Reiner's college romance film, *The Sure Thing,* 1985.
Said that therapy helped her to find a steady boyfriend.

THE REGISTER OF THOUSANDS

Here's a celebrity data base covering the multitudes of shakers and shapers, the near-great and notorious, those who grace the screen and the tube, the page and the stage—a resource to discover the real names, birthdates, birthplaces, occupations, and claims to fame of a large slice of pop culture. Those who are coy about their birthdates or are too new on the scene to be sufficiently well documented have been passed over for this year's list—but stay tuned.

AAMES, WILLIE (Willie Upton). Los Angeles, CA, 7/15/60. Actor. *Eight Is Enough.*
ABBOTT, JIM. Flint, MI, 9/19/67. One-handed baseball pitcher.
ABDUL, PAULA. Los Angeles, CA, 6/19/63. Singer, dancer, choreographer, recently filed for divorce from Emilio Estevez. "Straight Up."
ABRAHAM, F. MURRAY. Pittsburgh, PA, 10/24/39. Actor. *Amadeus.*
ABRAHAMS, JIM. Milwaukee, WI, 5/10/44. Producer, writer, director. *Airplane!; The Naked Gun.*
ABRAHAMS, MICK. Luton, England, 4/7/43. Guitarist. Jethro Tull.
ACE, JOHNNY (Johnny Alexander). Memphis, TN, 6/9/29. Singer, keyboardist. "Pledging My Love."
AD-ROCK, KING (Adam Horovitz). New York, NY, 10/31/66. Rap artist. The Beastie Boys.
ADAMS, BROOKE. New York, NY, 2/8/49. Actor. *Invasion of the Body Snatchers.*
ADAMS, DON. New York, NY, 4/13/26. Actor. Maxwell Smart on *Get Smart.*
ADAMS, DOUGLAS. Cambridge, England, 3/11/52. Novelist. *The Hitchhiker's Guide to the Galaxy.*
ADAMS, EDIE (Elizabeth Edith Enke). Kingston, PA, 4/16/27. Actor. *The Ernie Kovacs Show.*
ADAMS, MAUD (Maud Wikstrom). Lulea, Sweden, 2/12/45. Actor. *Octopussy.*
ADAMSON, STUART (William Adamson). Manchester, England, 4/11/58. Guitarist, singer. Big Country.
ADJANI, ISABELLE. Paris, France, 6/27/55. Actor. *Camille Claudel.*
AGAR, JOHN. Chicago, IL, 1/31/21. Actor. The *Sands of Iwo Jima.*
AGNEW, PETE. Scotland, 9/14/46. Bassist, singer. Nazareth.
AGNEW, SPIRO. Baltimore, MD, 11/9/18. Politician. Resigned as vice president.
AGUTTER, JENNY. Taunton, England, 12/20/52. Actor. *Logan's Run.*
AIELLO, DANNY. New York, NY, 6/20/33. Actor, writer. *Moonstruck.*
AIMEE, ANOUK (Françoise Soyra Dreyfus). Paris, France, 4/27/34. Actor. *A Man and a Woman.*
AKERS, KAREN. New York, NY, 10/13/45. Cabaret singer.
ALBERT, EDDIE (Eddie Albert Heimberger). Rock Island, IL, 4/22/08. Actor, father of Edward. Oliver Wendell Douglas on *Green Acres.*
ALBERT, EDWARD. Los Angeles, CA, 2/20/51. Actor, son of Eddie. *Midway.*
ALBRECHT, BERNIE (Bernard Dicken). Salford, England, 1/4/56. Guitarist. Joy Division; New Order.
ALDA, ALAN (Alan D'Abruzzo). New York, NY, 1/28/36. Actor, writer, director, son of Robert Alda. Benjamin Franklin "Hawkeye" Pierce on *M*A*S*H.*
ALDRIN, BUZZ (Edwin Eugene Aldrin Jr.). Montclair, NJ, 1/20/30. Astronaut, businessman.
ALEXANDER, GARY. Chattanooga, TN, 9/25/43. Singer, guitarist. The Association.
ALEXANDER, JANE (Jane Quigley). Boston, MA, 10/28/39. Actor. *All the President's Men.* Head of the National Endowment for the Arts.
ALI, MUHAMMAD (Cassius Clay). Louisville, KY, 1/17/42. Boxing great.
ALLEN, DEBBIE. Houston, TX, 1/16/50. Choreographer, actor, sister of Phylicia Rashad. *Fame.*
ALLEN, DUANE. Taylortown, TX, 4/29/43. Singer. The Oak Ridge Boys.
ALLEN, JOAN. Rochelle, IL, 8/20/56. Actor. *Compromising Positions.*
ALLEN, KAREN. Carrollton, IL, 10/5/51. Actor. *Raiders of the Lost Ark.*
ALLEN, NANCY. New York, NY, 6/24/50. Actor. *Robocop.*
ALLEN, PAPA DEE (Thomas Allen). Wilmington, DE, 7/18/31. Keyboardist, singer. War.
ALLEN, RICK. Sheffield, England, 11/1/63. One-armed drummer. Def Leppard.
ALLEN, ROD (Rod Bainbridge). Leicester, England, 3/31/44. Bassist, singer. The Fortunes.
ALLEN, STEVE. New York, NY, 12/26/21. Writer, performer, variety show host, husband of Jayne Meadows. *The Steve Allen Show.*
ALLEN, VERDEN. Hereford, England, 5/26/44. Keyboardist. Mott The Hoople.
ALLEY, KIRSTIE. Wichita, KS, 1/12/55. Actor, married to Parker Stevenson. Rebecca Howe on *Cheers.*
ALLISON, JERRY. Hillsboro, TX, 8/31/39. Drummer. Buddy Holly & The Crickets.
ALLMAN, GREGG. Nashville, TN, 12/8/47. Keyboardist, guitarist, singer, formerly married to Cher. The Allman Brothers Band.
ALLSUP, MIKE. Modesto, CA, 3/8/47. Guitarist. Three Dog Night.
ALLYSON, JUNE (Ella Geisman). Westchester, NY, 10/7/17. Actor. *The Dupont Show Starring June Allyson; Lassie.*
ALMOND, MARC (Peter Almond). Southport, England, 7/9/59. Singer. Soft Cell.
ALONSO, MARIA CONCHITA. Cuba, 1957. Actor. *The Running Man.*
ALPERT, HERB. San Francisco, CA, 3/31/35. Trumpeter, band leader, cofounder of A&M Records. The Tijuana Brass.
ALSTON, BARBARA. Brooklyn, NY, 1945. Singer. The Crystals.
ALSTON, SHIRLEY (Shirley Owens). Passaic, NJ, 6/10/41. Singer. The Shirelles.
ALT, CAROL. Queens, NY, 12/1/60. Supermodel.
ALTMAN, ROBERT. Kansas City, MO, 2/20/25. Director, writer, producer. *The Player.*
ALVARADO, TRINI. New York, NY, 1967. Actor. *Rich Kids.*
AMIN, IDI. Koboko, Uganda, 1/1/25. Political leader, former president of Uganda.
AMIS, SUZY. Oklahoma City, OK, 1/5/62. Actor. *Blown Away.*
AMOS, JOHN. Newark, NJ, 12/27/41. Actor. James Evans on *Good Times.*
AMOS, WALLY JR. Tallahassee, FL, 7/1/36. Business executive. Famous Amos chocolate chip cookies.
ANDERSON, ALFA. 9/7/46. Singer. Chic.
ANDERSON, HARRY. Newport, RI, 10/14/52. Actor. Judge Harry Stone on *Night Court.*
ANDERSON, IAN. Edinburgh, Scotland, 8/10/47. Singer, flautist. Jethro Tull.
ANDERSON, JON. Lancashire, England, 10/25/44. Singer, drummer. Yes.
ANDERSON, KEVIN. Illinois, 1/13/60. Actor. *Sleeping with the Enemy.*
ANDERSON, LAURIE. Chicago IL, 6/5/47. Singer, performance artist.
ANDERSON, LONI. St. Paul, MN, 8/5/46. Actor. Receptionist Jennifer Marlowe on *WKRP in Cincinnati.*
ANDERSON, MELISSA SUE. Berkeley, CA, 9/26/62. Actor. Mary Ingalls Kendall on *Little House on the Prairie.*
ANDERSON, MELODY. Edmonton, Canada, 1/3/55. Actor. Dale Arden in *Flash Gordon.*
ANDERSON, RICHARD. Long Branch, NJ, 8/8/26. Actor. Oscar Goldman on *The Six Million Dollar Man* and *The Bionic Woman.*
ANDERSON, RICHARD DEAN. Minneapolis, MN, 1/23/50. Actor. *MacGyver.*
ANDERSON, RICK. St. Paul, MN, 8/1/47. Bassist. The Tubes.
ANDERSON, TERRY. 10/27/47. Journalist, former hostage.
ANDERSSON, BENNY (Goran Andersson). Stockholm, Sweden, 12/16/46. Keyboards, singer. Abba.
ANDERSSON, BIBI. Stockholm, Sweden, 11/11/35. Actor. *The Seventh Seal.*
ANDES, MARK. Philadelphia, PA, 2/19/48. Bassist. Spirit.
ANDRESS, URSULA. Berne, Switzerland, 3/19/36. Actor. *Dr. No.*

ANDRETTI, MARIO. Montona Trieste, Italy, 2/28/40. Auto racer.
ANDREW, PRINCE. London, England, 2/19/60. British royalty, son of Queen Elizabeth II.
ANDREWS, ANTHONY. London, England, 1/12/48. Actor. *Brideshead Revisited.*
ANDREWS, BARRY. England, 9/12/56. Keyboardist. XTC.
ANDREWS, JULIE (Julia Wells). Walton-on-Thames, England, 10/1/35. Actor, singer. *The Sound of Music.*
ANKA, PAUL. Ottawa, Canada, 7/30/41. Singer, songwriter. "Diana."
ANN-MARGRET (Ann-Margret Olsson). Valsjobyn, Sweden, 4/28/41. Actor, singer. *Viva Las Vegas.*
ANNAUD, JEAN-JACQUES. Draveil, France, 10/1/43. Writer, director. *Quest for Fire; The Lover.*
ANNE, PRINCESS. London, England, 2/19/60. British royalty, daughter of Queen Elizabeth II.
ANSPACH, SUSAN. New York, NY, 11/23/45. Actor. *Five Easy Pieces.*
ANT, ADAM (Stewart Goddard). London, England, 11/3/54. Singer. Adam & The Ants.
ANTHONY, MICHAEL. Chicago, IL, 6/20/55. Bassist. Van Halen.
ANTON, SUSAN. Oak Glen, CA, 10/12/50. Actor, singer. *Goldengirl.*
ANWAR, GABRIELLE. Laleham, England, 1970. Actor. Tangoed with Al Pacino in *Scent of a Woman.*
APPICE, CARMINE. New York, NY, 12/15/46. Drummer. Vanilla Fudge.
APPLEGATE, CHRISTINA. Hollywood, CA, 11/25/72. Actor. Kelly Bundy on *Married . . . with Children.*
AQUINO, CORAZON. Tarlac, Philippines, 1/25/33. Political leader. Former president of the Philippines.
ARAFAT, YASIR. Cairo, Egypt, 8/24/29. Political leader. Head of the PLO.
ARCHER, ANNE. Los Angeles, CA, 8/25/47. Actor. Wife of Michael Douglas in *Fatal Attraction.*
ARENHOLZ, STEPHEN. The Bronx, NY, 4/29/69. Actor. Guy in a bear suit.
ARGENT, ROD. St. Albans, England, 6/14/45. Keyboardist. The Zombies.
ARKIN, ALAN. New York, NY, 3/26/34. Actor, director, writer, folk singer, and member of Second City. *The In-Laws.*
ARMATRADING, JOAN. Basseterre, West Indies, 12/9/50. Singer, songwriter. "Me, Myself, I."
ARMSTRONG, BESS. Baltimore, MD, 12/11/53. Actor. Julia Peters on *On Our Own.*
ARMSTRONG, NEIL. Wapakoneta, OH, 8/5/30. Astronaut.
ARNAZ, DESI JR. Los Angeles, CA, 1/19/53. Actor, singer, son of Lucille Ball and Desi Arnaz. *Here's Lucy.*
ARNAZ, LUCIE. Los Angeles, CA, 7/17/51. Actor, daughter of Lucille Ball and Desi Arnaz, married to Laurence Luckinbill. *Here's Lucy.*
ARNESS, JAMES (James Aurness). Minneapolis, MN, 5/26/23. Actor, brother of Peter Graves. *Gunsmoke.*
ARQUETTE, PATRICIA. New York, NY, 4/8/68. Actor, granddaughter of Cliff Arquette, sister of Rosanna. *True Romance.*
ARQUETTE, ROSANNA. New York, NY, 8/10/59. Actor, granddaughter of Cliff Arquette, sister of Patricia, and inspiration for Toto song "Rosanna." *Desperately Seeking Susan.*
ARTHUR, BEATRICE (Bernice Frankel). New York, NY, 5/13/26. Actor. *Maude.*
ASH, DANIEL. 7/31/57. Guitarist, singer. Bauhaus; Love and Rockets.
ASHER, PETER. London, England, 6/22/44. Singer. Peter and Gordon.
ASHFORD, NICKOLAS. Fairfield, SC, 5/4/42. Singer. Ashford and Simpson.
ASHFORD, ROSALIND. Detroit, MI, 9/2/43. Singer. Martha & The Vandellas.
ASHLEY, ELIZABETH (Elizabeth Ann Cole). Ocala, FL, 8/30/39. Actor. *Evening Shade.*
ASNER, EDWARD. Kansas City, KS, 11/15/29. Actor. *Lou Grant.*
ASSANTE, ARMAND. New York, NY, 10/4/49. Actor. *The Doctors.*
ASTBURY, IAN. Heswall, England, 5/14/62. Singer. The Cult.
ASTIN, JOHN. Baltimore, MD, 3/30/30. Actor, formerly married to Patty Duke, father of Sean Astin. Gomez Addams on *The Addams Family.*
ASTIN, SEAN. Santa Monica, CA, 2/25/71. Actor, son of John Astin and Patty Duke. *Encino Man.*
ASTLEY, RICK. Warrington, England, 2/6/66. Singer, songwriter. "Never Gonna Give You Up."
ASTON, JAY. London, England, 5/4/61. Singer. Bucks Fizz.
ASTON, JOHN. England, 11/30/57. Guitarist. Psychedelic Furs.
ATKINS, CHET. Luttrell, TN, 6/20/24. Virtuoso guitarist.
ATKINS, CHRISTOPHER. Rye, NY, 2/21/61. Actor. *The Blue Lagoon.*
ATKINSON, PAUL. Cuffley, England, 3/19/46. Guitarist. The Zombies.
ATTENBOROUGH, RICHARD. Cambridge, England, 8/29/23. Actor, producer, director. *Gandhi.*
ATWOOD, MARGARET. Ottawa, Canada, 11/18/39. Author, poet. *The Handmaid's Tale.*
AUBERJONOIS, RENE. New York, NY, 6/1/40. Actor. Security Chief Odo on *Deep Space Nine.*
AUTRY, ALAN. Shreveport, LA. Actor. Bubba Skinner on *In the Heat of the Night.*
AUTRY, GENE. Tioga, TX, 9/29/07. Screen's first singing cowboy. *The Gene Autry Show.*
AVALON, FRANKIE (Francis Thomas Avallone). Philadelphia, PA, 9/18/40. Singer, actor. *Beach Blanket Bingo.*
AVORY, MICK. London, England, 2/15/44. Drummer. The Kinks.
AXTON, HOYT. Duncan, OK, 3/25/38. Singer, songwriter, actor. *Gremlins.*
AZNAVOUR, CHARLES (Shahnour Varenagh Aznourian). Paris, France, 5/22/24. Singer, songwriter, actor. *The Tin Drum.*
BACALL, LAUREN (Betty Perske). New York, NY, 9/16/24. Actor, formerly married to Humphrey Bogart, married to Jason Robards. *Key Largo.*
BACH, BARBARA. Queens, NY, 8/27/47. Actor, married to Ringo Starr. *The Spy Who Loved Me.*
BACHMAN, RANDY. Winnipeg, Canada, 9/27/43. Guitarist, singer. Bachman-Turner Overdrive; The Guess Who.
BACHMAN, ROBBIE. Winnipeg, Canada, 2/18/53. Drummer. Bachman-Turner Overdrive.
BACON, KEVIN. Philadelphia, PA, 7/8/58. Actor. *Footloose.*
BADANJEK, JOHN. 1948. Drummer. Mitch Ryder & The Detroit Wheels.
BAEZ, JOAN. Staten Island, NY, 1/9/41. Folk singer and songwriter, peace and civil rights activist.
BAILEY, PHILIP. Denver, CO, 5/8/51. Singer, conga player, percussionist. Earth, Wind & Fire.
BAILEY, TOM. Halifax, England, 6/18/57. Singer, keyboardist. Thompson Twins.
BAIN, BARBARA. Chicago, IL, 9/13/34. Actor. *Mission: Impossible.*
BAIO, SCOTT. Brooklyn, NY, 9/22/61. Actor. Charles "Chachi" Arcola on *Happy Days.*
BAKER, ANITA. Detroit, MI, 12/20/57. R&B singer.
BAKER, CARROLL. Johnstown, PA, 5/28/31. Actor. *Kindergarten Cop.*
BAKER, CHERYL (Rita Crudgington). London, England, 3/8/54. Singer. Bucks Fizz.
BAKER, GINGER (Peter Baker). Lewisham, England, 8/19/39. Drummer. Cream; Blind Faith.
BAKER, JOE DON. Groesbeck, TX, 2/12/36. Actor. *Walking Tall.*
BAKER, MICKEY (McHouston Baker). Louisville, KY, 10/15/25. Singer. Mickey & Sylvia.
BAKKER, JIM. Muskegon, MI, 1/2/40. TV evangelist, participant in the PTL scandal.
BAKKER, TAMMY FAYE. International Falls, MN, 3/7/42. TV evangelist. Former wife of PTL founder Jim Bakker.
BAKSHI, RALPH. Haifa, Palestine, 10/29/38. Animator, writer, director. *Fritz the Cat.*
BALABAN, BOB. Chicago, IL, 8/16/45. Actor. Roles in *Midnight Cowboy, Little Man Tate.*
BALDWIN, ADAM. Chicago, IL, 2/27/62. Actor. *My Bodyguard.*
BALIN, MARTY. Cincinnati, OH, 1/30/42. Singer. Jefferson Airplane/Starship.
BALL, DAVID. Blackpool, England, 5/3/59. Keyboardist. Soft Cell.
BALL, ROGER. Dundee, Scotland, 6/4/44. Alto and baritone saxophonist. Average White Band.
BALLARD, FLORENCE. Detroit, MI, 6/30/43. Singer. The Supremes.
BALLARD, HANK. Detroit, MI, 11/18/36. Singer/songwriter. "Work with Me Annie."

BALLARD, KAYE (Catherine Gloria Balotta). Cleveland, OH, 11/20/26. Actor, singer.
BALSAM, MARTIN. New York, NY, 11/4/19. Actor. *On the Waterfront.*
BALSLEY, PHILIP. 8/8/39. Singer. Kingsmen; Statler Brothers.
BAMBAATAA, AFRIKA. The Bronx, NY, 1958. Rap/hip-hop DJ.
BANALI, FRANKIE. 11/14/55. Musician. Quiet Riot.
BANANA (Lowell Levinger). Cambridge, MA, 1946. Keyboardist, guitarist. The Youngbloods.
BANCROFT, ANNE (Anna Maria Italiano). The Bronx, NY, 9/17/31. Actor. Mrs. Robinson in *The Graduate.*
BANKS, TONY. East Heathly, England, 3/27/51. Keyboardist. Genesis.
BANKS, TYRA. Los Angeles, CA, 12/4/73. Actor, model. *Martin.*
BARBATA, JOHN. 4/1/45. Drummer. The Turtles; Jefferson Starship.
BARBEAU, ADRIENNE. Sacramento, CA, 6/11/45. Actor. Carol on *Maude.*
BARBIERI, RICHARD. 11/30/57. Keyboardist. Japan.
BARDOT, BRIGITTE. Paris, France, 9/28/34. Sex goddess. *And God Created Woman.*
BARGERON, DAVE. Massachusetts, 9/6/42. Trombonist. Blood, Sweat and Tears.
BARKER, BOB. Darrington, WA, 12/12/23. Game show host. *The Price Is Right.*
BARNES, LEO. 10/5/55. Musician. Hothouse Flowers.
BARRE, MARTIN. 11/17/46. Guitarist. Jethro Tull.
BARRERE, PAUL. Burbank, CA, 7/3/48. Lead guitarist. Little Feat.
BARRETT, ASTON. Kingston, Jamaica, 11/22/46. Bassist. Bob Marley & The Wailers.
BARRETT, CARLTON. Kingston, Jamaica, 12/17/50. Drummer. Bob Marley & The Wailers.
BARRETT, MARCIA. St. Catherine's, Jamaica, 10/14/48. Singer. Boney M.
BARRETT, RONA. New York, NY, 10/8/36. News correspondent, columnist.
BARRETT, SYD (Roger Barrett). Cambridge, England, 1/6/46. Singer, guitarist. Pink Floyd.
BARRY, MARION. Itta Bena, MS, 3/6/36. Former mayor of Washington, served six-month prison term for cocaine possession.
BARRYMORE, JOHN DREW. Beverly Hills, CA, 6/4/32. Actor, father of Drew Barrymore.
BARSON, MIKE. England, 5/21/58. Keyboardist. Madness.
BARTEL, PAUL. New York, NY, 8/6/38. Director, writer, actor. *Eating Raoul.*
BARTHOL, BRUCE. Berkeley, CA, 1947. Bassist. Country Joe & The Fish.
BARYSHNIKOV, MIKHAIL. Riga, Latvia, 1/27/48. Dancer, actor. *White Nights.*
BATEMAN, JASON. Rye, NY, 1/14/69. Actor, brother of Justine. David on *The Hogan Family.*
BATEMAN, JUSTINE. Rye, NY, 2/19/66. Actor, sister of Jason. Mallory Keaton on *Family Ties.*
BATES, ALAN. Allestree, England, 2/17/34. Actor. *An Unmarried Woman.*
BATTLE, KATHLEEN. Portsmouth, OH, 8/13/48. Opera singer.
BAUER, JOE. Memphis, TN, 9/26/41. Drummer. The Youngbloods.
BAUER, STEVEN (Steven Echevarria). Havana, Cuba, 12/2/56. Actor, formerly married to Melanie Griffith. *Wiseguy.*
BAUMGARTNER, STEVE. Philadelphia, PA, 10/28/67. Writer, actor. *My Best Friend's Girl.*
BAXTER, JEFF "SKUNK." Washington, DC, 12/13/48. Lead Guitarist. Steely Dan; The Doobie Brothers.
BAXTER, KEITH. Monmouthshire, Wales, 4/29/33. Actor.
BAXTER, MEREDITH. Los Angeles, CA, 6/21/47. Actor, formerly married to David Birney. Elyse Keaton on *Family Ties.*
BEACHAM, STEPHANIE. Hertfordshire, England, 2/28/47. Actor. Sable Scott Colby on *The Colbys.*
BEAKY (John Dymond). Salisbury, England, 7/10/44. Guitarist. Dave Dee, Dozy, Beaky, Mick and Tich.
BEALS, JENNIFER. Chicago, IL, 12/19/63. Actor. *Flashdance.*
BEARD, FRANK. Dallas, TX, 1949. Drummer. ZZ Top.
BEASLEY, ALLYCE. Brooklyn, NY, 7/6/54. Actor. Agnes Dipesto on *Moonlighting.*
BEATRICE, PRINCESS. London, England, 2/19/60. British royalty, daughter of Prince Andrew and the Duchess of York.
BEATTY, NED. Lexington, KY, 7/6/37. Actor. *Deliverance.*
BECK, JEFF. Wallington, England, 6/24/44. Guitarist. The Yardbirds; The Jeff Beck Group; The Jan Hammer Group.
BECK, JOHN. Chicago, IL, 1/28/43. Actor. Mark Graison on *Dallas.*
BECK, MICHAEL. Memphis, TN, 2/4/49. Actor. *Xanadu.*
BECKER, BORIS. Liemen, Germany, 11/22/67. Tennis player.
BECKER, WALTER. New York, NY, 2/20/50. Bassist. Steely Dan.
BECKLEY, GERRY. Texas, 9/12/52. Singer, guitarist. America.
BEDELIA, BONNIE. New York, NY, 3/25/46. Actor. *Presumed Innocent.*
BEDFORD, MARK. London, England, 8/24/61. Bassist. Madness.
BEEFHEART, CAPTAIN (Van Vliet). Glendale, CA, 1/15/41. Singer, high school friend of Frank Zappa. Captain Beefheart & The Magic Band.
BEERS, GARY. 6/22/57. Bassist, singer. INXS
BEGLEY, ED JR. Los Angeles, CA, 9/16/49. Actor. Dr. Victor Ehrlich on *St. Elsewhere.*
BEL GEDDES, BARBARA (Barbara Geddes Lewis). New York, NY, 10/31/22. Actor. *Vertigo.*
BELAFONTE, HARRY. New York, NY, 3/1/27. Actor, singer, father of Shari. "The Banana Boat Song."
BELL, ANDY. Peterborough, England, 4/25/64. Singer. Erasure.
BELL, RICKY. Boston, MA, 9/18/67. Singer. New Edition.
BELL, ROBERT. Youngstown, OH, 10/8/50. Bassist. Kool & The Gang.
BELL, RONALD. Youngstown, OH, 11/1/51. Saxophonist. Kool & The Gang.
BELLADONNA, JOEY. Oswego, NY. Singer. Anthrax.
BELLAMY, GEORGE. Sunderland, England, 10/8/41. Guitarist. The Tornados.
BELLAMY, TONY. Los Angeles, CA, 9/12/40. Singer, guitarist. Redbone.
BELLO, FRANK. 7/9/65. Bassist. Anthrax.
BELMONDO, JEAN-PAUL. Paris, France, 4/9/33. Actor. *Breathless.*
BELUSHI, JIM. Chicago, IL, 6/15/54. Actor, brother of late John Belushi. *K-9.*
BENATAR, PAT (Pat Andrzejewski). Brooklyn, NY, 1/10/53. Singer. "Heartbreaker."
BENEDICT, DIRK (Dirk Niewoehner). Helena, MT, 3/1/45. Actor. Lt. Templeton Peck on *The A-Team.*
BENJAMIN, RICHARD. New York, NY, 5/22/38. Actor, director. *Love at First Bite; Goodbye, Columbus.*
BENNETT, BRIAN. London, England, 2/9/40. Drummer. The Shadows.
BENNETT, ESTELLE. New York, NY, 7/22/44. Singer. The Ronettes.
BENNETT, PATRICIA. New York, NY, 4/7/47. Singer. The Chiffons.
BENNETT, VERONICA. New York, NY, 8/10/43. Lead singer. The Ronettes.
BENSON, GEORGE. Pittsburgh, PA, 3/22/43. Singer, guitarist. "Give Me the Night."
BENSON, RENALDO. Detroit, MI, 1947. Singer. The Four Tops.
BENSON, ROBBY (Robby Segal). Dallas, TX, 1/21/56. Actor, writer, director. *Ice Castles.*
BERADINO, JOHN. Los Angeles, CA, 5/1/17. Actor, baseball player. Dr. Hardy on *General Hospital.*
BERENGER, TOM. Chicago, IL, 5/31/50. Actor. *Platoon.*
BERENSON, MARISA. New York, NY, 2/15/47. Actor. *Barry Lyndon.*
BERGEN, POLLY (Nellie Burgin). Knoxville, TN, 7/14/30. Singer, actor. *The Winds of War.*
BERGER, ALAN. 11/8/49. Bassist. Southside Johnny & The Asbury Jukes.
BERGMAN, INGMAR. Uppsala, Sweden, 7/14/18. Writer, director. *The Silence.*
BERKOWITZ, DAVID. New York, NY, 6/1/53. Serial killer. Son of Sam.
BERLE, MILTON (Milton Berlinger). New York, NY, 7/12/08. Actor. *The Milton Berle Show.*
BERNHARD, SANDRA. Flint, MI, 6/6/55. Actor, singer. *Roseanne.*
BERNSEN, CORBIN. Los Angeles, CA, 9/7/54. Actor, married to Amanda Pays. Arnie Becker on *L.A. Law.*
BERRI, CLAUDE (Claude Langmann). Paris, France, 7/1/34. Actor, director, producer of films.
BERRY, BILL. Hibbing, MN, 7/31/58. Drummer. R.E.M.

BERRY, CHUCK. San Jose, CA, 10/18/26. Rock and Roll legend, singer and guitarist. "Johnny B. Goode."
BERRY, JAN. Los Angeles, CA, 4/3/41. Singer. Jan & Dean.
BERTINELLI, VALERIE. Wilmington, DE, 4/23/60. Actor, married to Eddie Van Halen. Barbara Cooper Royer on *One Day at a Time.*
BETTS, DICKEY. West Palm Beach, FL, 12/12/43. Guitarist, singer. The Allman Brothers Band.
BIEHN, MICHAEL. Anniston, AL, 7/29/56. Actor. *The Terminator.*
BIG FIGURE, THE (John Martin). 1947. Drummer. Dr. Feelgood.
BILLINGSLEY, BARBARA. Los Angeles, CA, 12/22/22. Actor. June Cleaver on *Leave It to Beaver.*
BILLINGSLEY, PETER. New York, NY, 1972. Child actor. *A Christmas Story.*
BILLINGSLEY, RAY. Wake Forest, NC, 7/25/57. Cartoonist. *Curtis.*
BIRD, LARRY. West Baden, IN, 12/7/56. Basketball great. Boston Celtics.
BIRNEY, DAVID. Washington, DC, 4/23/39. Actor, formerly married to Meredith Baxter. *St. Elsewhere.*
BIRRELL, PETE. Manchester, England, 5/9/41. Bassist. Freddie & The Dreamers.
BIRTLES, BEEB (Gerard Birtlekamp). Amsterdam, the Netherlands, 11/28/48. Guitarist. The Little River Band.
BISHOP, JOEY (Joey Gottlieb). The Bronx, NY, 2/3/18. Actor. *The Joey Bishop Show.*
BISSET, JACQUELINE. Waybridge, England, 9/13/44. Actor. *The Deep.*
BIVINS, MICHAEL. 8/10/68. Singer. New Edition, Bell Biv DeVoe.
BLACK, CILLA (Cilla White). Liverpool, England, 5/27/43. Singer, TV personality.
BLACK, JET (Brian Duffy). England, 8/26/58. Drummer. The Stranglers.
BLACK, KAREN (Karen Ziegler). Park Ridge, IL, 7/1/42. Actor. *Easy Rider.*
BLACKMON, LARRY. New York, 5/29/56. Singer, drummer. Cameo.
BLACKMORE, RITCHIE. Weston-Super-Mare, England, 4/14/45. Guitarist. Deep Purple; Rainbow.
BLADD, STEPHEN JO. Boston, MA, 7/13/42. Drummer, singer. The J. Geils Band.
BLADES, RUBEN. Panama City, Panama, 7/16/48. Actor, singer. *The Milagro Beanfield War.*
BLAIR, BONNIE. Cornwall, NY, 3/18/64. Speed skater.
BLAIR, LINDA. Westport, CT, 1/22/59. Actor. *The Exorcist.*
BLAKE, ROBERT (Michael Gubitosi). Nutley, NJ, 9/18/33. Actor. *Baretta.*
BLAKELY, SUSAN. Frankfurt, Germany, 9/7/50. Actor. *Rich Man, Poor Man.*
BLAKLEY, ALAN. Bromley, England, 4/1/42. Guitarist. Brian Poole & The Tremeloes.
BLAND, BOBBY. Rosemark, TN, 1/27/30. Singer.
BLASS, BILL. Ft. Wayne, IN, 6/22/22. Fashion designer.
BLEDSOE, TEMPESTT. Chicago, IL, 8/1/73. Actor. Vanessa Huxtable on *The Cosby Show.*
BLOOM, CLAIRE. London, England, 2/15/31. Actor. *Richard III.*
BLOOM, ERIC. Long Island, NY, 12/1/44. Lead guitarist, keyboardist. Blue Öyster Cult.
BLOW, KURTIS (Kurtis Walker). New York, NY, 8/9/59. DJ, rapper.
BLUECHEL, TED JR. San Pedro, CA, 12/2/42. Singer, drummer. The Association.
BLUME, JUDY. Elizabeth, NJ, 2/12/38. Novelist. *Are You There God? It's Me Margaret.*
BLUNSTONE, COLIN. Hatfield, England, 6/24/45. Singer. The Zombies.
BOBBY G. (Bobby Gubby). London, England, 8/23/53. Singer. Bucks Fizz.
BOGARDE, DIRK. Hampstead, England, 3/28/21. Actor. *Death in Venice.*
BOGERT, TIM. Richfield, NJ, 8/27/44. Bassist. Vanilla Fudge.
BOGLE, BOB. Portland, OR, 1/16/37. Guitarist, bassist. The Ventures.
BOGOSIAN, ERIC. Woburn, MA, 4/24/53. Actor, writer. *Talk Radio.*
BOLAN, MARC (Mark Feld). Hackney, England, 9/30/47. Singer, guitarist. T. Rex.
BOLDER, TREVOR. 6/9/50. Bassist. Spiders from Mars; Uriah Heep.
BOLOGNA, JOSEPH. Brooklyn, NY, 12/30/38. Actor. *Chapter Two.*
BONADUCE, DANNY. 8/13/59. Actor, radio personality. Danny on *The Partridge Family.*
BOND, RONNIE (Ronnie Bullis). Andover, England, 5/4/43. Drummer. The Troggs.
BONDS, GARY (Gary Anderson). Jacksonville, FL, 6/6/39. Singer.
BONET, LISA. San Francisco, CA, 11/16/67. Actor. Denise Huxtable on *The Cosby Show.*
BONHAM-CARTER, HELENA. London, England, 5/26/66. Actor. *A Room with a View.*
BONNER, FRANK. Little Rock, AR, 2/28/42. Actor. Herb Tarlek on *WKRP in Cincinnati.*
BONO, CHASTITY. Los Angeles, CA, 3/4/69. Daughter of Sonny and Cher.
BONO, SONNY (Salvatore Bono). Detroit, MI, 2/16/35. Singer, actor, director, mayor of Palm Springs, formerly married to Cher, father of Chastity. *The Sonny and Cher Comedy Hour.*
BONSALL, BRIAN. 12/3/82. Child actor. *Family Ties.*
BONSALL, JOE. Philadelphia, PA, 5/18/44. Singer. The Oak Ridge Boys.
BOONE, PAT. Jacksonville, FL, 6/1/34. Singer, actor. *The Pat Boone Show.*
BOONE, STEVE. North Carolina, 9/23/43. Bassist, singer. The Lovin' Spoonful.
BOOTHE, POWERS. Snyder, TX, 6/1/49. Actor. *Guyana Tragedy: The Story of Jim Jones.*
BORGNINE, ERNEST (Ernest Borgnino). Hamden, CT, 1/24/17. Actor. *McHale's Navy.*
BOSSON, BARBARA. Charleroi, PA, 11/1/39. Actor, married to producer Steven Bochco. Fay Furillo on *Hill Street Blues.*
BOSTWICK, BARRY. San Mateo, CA, 2/24/45. Actor. *The Rocky Horror Picture Show.*
BOTTOMS, JOSEPH. Santa Barbara, CA, 4/22/54. Actor. *The Black Hole.*
BOTTOMS, SAM. Santa Barbara, CA, 10/17/55. Actor. *Apocalypse Now.*
BOTTOMS, TIMOTHY. Santa Barbara, CA, 8/30/51. Actor. *Johnny Got His Gun.*
BOTTUM, RODDY. Los Angeles, CA, 7/1/63. Keyboardist. Faith No More.
BOUCHARD, JOE. Long Island, NY, 11/9/48. Bassist, singer. Blue Öyster Cult.
BOWE, RIDDICK. New York, NY, 8/10/67. Boxer, former heavyweight champion of the world.
BOWERS, TONY. 10/31/56. Bassist. Simply Red.
BOWIE, DAVID (David Jones). Brixton, England, 1/8/47. Singer, actor, married to Iman. *Ziggy Stardust and the Spiders from Mars.*
BOX, MICK. London, England, 6/8/47. Guitarist, songwriter. Uriah Heep.
BOXLEITNER, BRUCE. Elgin, IL, 5/12/50. Actor. *Scarecrow and Mrs. King.*
BOY GEORGE (George O'Dowd). Eltham, England, 6/14/61. Singer. Culture Club.
BOYLE, LARA FLYNN. Davenport, IA, 3/24/70. Actor. *Twin Peaks.*
BOYLE, PETER. Philadelphia, PA, 10/18/33. Actor. *Young Frankenstein.*
BRACCO, LORRAINE. Brooklyn, NY, 1955. Actor. *GoodFellas.*
BRADBURY, RAY. Waukegan, IL, 8/22/20. Novelist. *The Martian Chronicles.*
BRAGG, BILLY (Steven Bragg). Barking, England, 12/20/57. Punk/R&B singer, songwriter.
BRAID, LES (William Braid). Liverpool, England, 9/15/41. Bassist. The Swinging Blue Jeans.
BRAMLETT, BONNIE. Acton, IL, 11/8/44. Singer. Delaney & Bonnie.
BRAMLETT, DELANEY. Pontotoc County, MS, 7/1/39. Guitarist, singer. Delaney & Bonnie.
BRANDAUER, KLAUS MARIA. Altaussee, Austria, 6/22/44. Actor. *Out of Africa.*
BRATTON, CREED. Sacramento, CA, 2/8/43. Guitarist. The Grass Roots.
BRAUNN, ERIK. Boston, MA, 8/11/50. Guitarist, singer. Iron Butterfly.
BREATHED, BERKE. Encino, CA, 6/21/57. Cartoonist. *Bloom County.*
BRENNAN, EILEEN. Los Angeles, CA, 9/3/35. Actor. *Private Benjamin.*
BRENNEMAN, AMY. New London, CT, 6/22/64. Actor. *NYPD Blue.*
BRENNER, DAVID. Philadelphia, PA, 2/4/45. Stand-up comedian. *Nightlife.*
BREWER, DONALD. Flint, MI, 9/3/48. Drummer. Grand Funk Railroad.
BRICKELL, EDIE. Oak Cliff, TX, 1966. Singer, songwriter, married to Paul Simon. Edie Brickell and New Bohemians.
BRIDGES, LLOYD. San Leandro, CA, 1/15/13. Actor, father of Beau and Jeff. *Sea Hunt.*
BRIDGES, TODD. San Francisco, CA, 5/27/66. Actor. Willis Jackson on *Diff'rent Strokes.*
BRIGATI, EDDIE. Garfield, NJ, 10/22/46. Singer, percussionist. The (Young) Rascals.

BRIGGS, DAVID. Melbourne, Australia, 1/26/51. Guitarist. The Little River Band.
BRILEY, ALEX. 4/12/56. Singer. The Village People.
BRIMLEY, WILFORD. Salt Lake City, UT, 9/27/34. Actor. *Cocoon.*
BRINKLEY, DAVID. Wilmington, NC, 7/10/20. Pioneer news journalist and anchor. *This Week with David Brinkley.*
BRIQUETTE, PETE (Patrick Cusack). Ireland, 7/2/54. Bassist, singer. The Boomtown Rats.
BRITTANY, MORGAN (Suzanne Cupito). Los Angeles, CA, 12/5/51. Actor. Katherine Wentworth on *Dallas.*
BRITTON, CHRIS. Watford, England, 6/21/45. Guitarist. The Troggs.
BROKAW, TOM. Yankton, SD, 2/6/40. News journalist and anchor. *NBC Nightly News.*
BROLIN, JAMES (James Bruderlin). Los Angeles, CA, 7/18/40. Actor, father of Josh. Dr. Steven Kiley on *Marcus Welby, M.D.*
BRONSON, CHARLES (Charles Buchinsky). Ehrenfield, PA, 11/3/21. Actor, widower of Jill Ireland. *Death Wish.*
BROOKER, GARY. Southend, England, 5/29/45. Singer, keyboardist. Procol Harum.
BROOKS, ALBERT (Albert Einstein). Los Angeles, CA, 7/22/47. Actor, writer, director. *Defending Your Life.*
BROOKS, LALA. Brooklyn, NY, 1946. Singer. The Crystals.
BROTHERS, JOYCE (Joyce Bauer). New York, NY, 10/20/28. Psychologist.
BROWN, BLAIR. Washington, DC, 1948. Actor. *The Days and Nights of Molly Dodd.*
BROWN, BRYAN. Panania, Australia, 6/23/47. Actor, married to Rachel Ward. *FX.*
BROWN, DAVID. Houston, TX, 2/15/47. Bassist. Santana.
BROWN, ERROL. Kingston, Jamaica, 11/12/48. Singer. Hot Chocolate.
BROWN, GEORG STANFORD. Havana, Cuba, 6/24/43. Actor. *Colossus: The Forbin Project.*
BROWN, GEORGE. Jersey City, NJ, 1/5/49. Drummer. Kool and The Gang.
BROWN, HAROLD. Long Beach, CA, 3/17/46. Drummer. War.
BROWN, IAN. Sale, England, 2/20/63. Singer. Stone Roses.
BROWN, JAMES. Augusta, GA, 5/3/33. The Godfather of Soul.
BROWN, JIM. St. Simons Island, GA, 2/17/36. Football player, actor. *The Dirty Dozen.*
BROWN, JIMMY. Birmingham, England, 11/20/57. Drummer. UB40.
BROWN, MICHAEL (Michael Lookofsky). New York, NY, 4/25/49. Keyboardist. The Left Banke.
BRUCE, JACK. Glasgow, Scotland, 5/14/43. Singer, bassist. Cream.
BRUCE, MICHAEL. 3/16/48. Guitarist, keyboardist. Alice Cooper.
BRUFORD, BILL. London, England, 5/17/48. Drummer. Yes.
BRYAN, DAVID (David Rashbaum). New Jersey, 2/7/62. Keyboardist. Bon Jovi.
BRYON, DENNIS. Cardiff, Wales, 4/14/49. Drummer. Amen Corner.
BRZEZICKI, MARK. Slough, England, 6/21/57. Drummer. Big Country.
BUCHANAN, PAUL. Scotland. Singer, synthesizer player. Blue Nile.
BUCHHOLZ, FRANCIS. 2/19/50. Guitarist. Scorpions.
BUCK, PETER. Athens, GA, 12/6/56. Guitarist. R.E.M.
BUCK, ROBERT. Guitarist. 10,000 Maniacs.
BUCKINGHAM, LINDSEY. Palo Alto, CA, 10/3/47. Guitarist, singer. Fleetwood Mac.
BUCKLER, RICK (Paul Buckler). 12/6/56. Drummer, singer. The Jam.
BUCKLEY, BETTY. Big Spring, TX, 7/3/47. Actor. *Eight Is Enough.*
BUJOLD, GENEVIEVE. Montreal, Canada, 7/1/42. Actor. *Dead Ringers.*
BUNKER, CLIVE. 12/12/46. Drummer. Jethro Tull.
BUNNELL, DEWEY. Yorkshire, England, 1/19/51. Singer, guitarist. America.
BURCHILL, CHARLIE. Glasgow, Scotland, 11/27/59. Guitarist. Simple Minds.
BURDEN, IAN. 12/24/57. Synthesizer player. Human League.
BURDON, ERIC. Walker-on-Tyne, England, 5/11/41. Singer, songwriter. The Animals; War.
BURGHOFF, GARY. Bristol, CT, 5/24/43. Actor. Radar O'Reilly on *M*A*S*H.*
BURKE, DELTA. Orlando, FL, 7/30/56. Actor, married to Gerald McRaney. *Designing Women.*
BURKE, SOLOMON. Philadelphia, PA, 1936. Country-gospel-R&B singer, songwriter.
BURNEL, JEAN-JACQUES. London, England, 2/21/52. Bassist. The Stranglers.
BURNETT, CAROL. San Antonio, TX, 4/26/33. Actor. *The Carol Burnett Show.*
BURNETTE, DORSEY. Memphis, TN, 12/28/32. Bassist. Dorsey and Johnny Burnette.
BURNETTE, JOHNNY. Memphis, TN, 3/25/34. Guitarist. Dorsey and Johnny Burnette.
BURNS, BOB. Drummer. Lynyrd Skynyrd.
BURNS, GEORGE (Nathan Birnbaum). New York, NY, 1/20/1896. Actor and comedian. *The George Burns and Gracie Allen Show.*
BURR, CLIVE. 3/8/57. Drummer. Iron Maiden.
BURRELL, BOZ (Raymond Burrell). Lincoln, England, 1946. Bassist. Bad Company.
BURROWS, DARREN E. Winfield, KS, 9/12/66. Actor. Ed Chigliak on *Northern Exposure.*
BURSTYN, ELLEN (Edna Rae Gillhooley). Detroit, MI, 12/7/32. Actor. *Alice Doesn't Live Here Anymore.*
BURT, HEINZ. Hargin, Germany, 7/24/42. Bassist. The Tornados.
BURTON, LEVAR. Landstuhl, Germany, 2/16/57. Actor. Geordi LaForge on *Star Trek: The Next Generation.*
BURTON, TREVOR. Aston, England, 3/9/44. Lead guitarist. The Move.
BUSEY, GARY. Goose Creek, TX, 6/29/44. Actor. *The Buddy Holly Story.*
BUSH, BARBARA. Rye, NY, 6/8/25. Former First Lady, married to George Bush.
BUSH, GEORGE. Milton, MA, 6/12/24. Political leader, husband of Barbara. Forty-first president of the U.S.
BUSH, KATE. Bexleyheath, England, 7/30/58. Singer, songwriter.
BUSHY, RONALD. Washington, DC, 9/23/45. Drummer. Iron Butterfly.
BUTKUS, DICK. Chicago, IL, 12/9/42. Football player, actor. *My Two Dads.*
BUTLER, GEEZER (Terry Butler). Birmingham, England, 7/17/49. Bassist. Black Sabbath.
BUTLER, JERRY. Sunflower, MS, 12/8/39. Singer. The Impressions.
BUTLER, JOE. Glen Cove, NY, 9/16/43. Drummer, singer. The Lovin' Spoonful.
BUTLER, RICHARD. England, 6/5/56. Singer, lyricist. Psychedelic Furs.
BUTLER, TONY. Ealing, England, 2/13/57. Bassist. Big Country.
BUTTONS, RED (Aaron Chwatt). New York, NY, 2/5/19. Performer. *The Red Buttons Show.*
BUXTON, GLEN. Akron, OH, 11/10/47. Guitarist. Alice Cooper.
BUZZI, RUTH. Westerly, RI, 7/24/36. Actor. *Laugh-In.*
BYRNE, GABRIEL. Dublin, Ireland, 1950. Actor, married to Ellen Barkin. *Miller's Crossing.*
BYRON, DAVID. Essex, England, 1/29/47. Singer. Uriah Heep.
CAAN, JAMES. The Bronx, NY, 3/26/39. Actor. *The Godfather.*
CADDY, ALAN. London, England, 2/2/40. Guitarist. The Tornados; Johnny Kidd & The Pirates.
CAESAR, SID. Yonkers, NY, 9/8/22. Performer. *Your Show of Shows.*
CAFFEY, CHARLOTTE. Santa Monica, CA, 10/21/53. Singer. The Go-Gos.
CAGE, JOHN. New York, NY, 9/5/12. Composer, author. Composed scores for choreography by Merce Cunningham.
CAIN, JONATHAN. Chicago, IL, 2/26/50. Keyboardist. Journey.
CALABRO, THOMAS. 2/29/59. Actor. Michael Mancini on *Melrose Place.*
CALE, JOHN. Garnant, Wales, 12/4/40. Bassist, keyboardist, violist, singer. The Velvet Underground.
CALIFORNIA, RANDY (Randy Wolfe). Los Angeles, CA, 2/20/51. Guitarist, singer. Spirit.
CALLOW, SIMON. London, England, 6/15/49. Actor. *A Room with a View.*
CALVERT, BERNIE. Burnley, England, 9/16/43. Bassist. The Hollies.
CAMERON, KIRK. Canoga Park, CA, 10/12/70. Actor, brother of Candace. Mike Seaver on *Growing Pains.*
CAMP, COLLEEN. San Francisco, CA, 1953. Actor. Kristin Shepard on *Dallas.*
CAMPBELL, ALI (Alastair Campbell). Birmingham, England, 2/15/59. Lead singer, guitarist. UB40.
CAMPBELL, BILL. Chicago, IL, 1960. Actor. *The Rocketeer.*

CAMPBELL, BRUCE. Royal Oak, MI, 6/22/58. Actor, producer, screenwriter. *The Adventures of Briscoe County Jr.*
CAMPBELL, GLEN. Delight, AR, 4/22/35. Actor, singer. *The Glen Campbell Goodtime Hour.*
CAMPBELL, MIKE. Panama City, FL, 2/1/54. Guitarist. Tom Petty & The Heartbreakers.
CAMPBELL, NAOMI. London, England, 5/22/70. Supermodel.
CAMPBELL, ROBIN. Birmingham, England, 12/25/54. Lead guitarist, singer. UB40.
CAMPBELL, TISHA. Oklahoma City, OK, 10/13/70. Actor. *Martin.*
CANN, WARREN. Victoria, Canada, 5/20/52. Drummer. Ultravox.
CANNON, DYAN (Samille Diane Friesen). Tacoma, WA, 1/4/37. Actor. *Bob & Carol & Ted & Alice.*
CAPALDI, JIM. Evesham, England, 8/24/44. Drummer, singer. Traffic.
CAPSHAW, KATE (Kathleen Sue Nail). Ft. Worth, TX, 1953. Actor, married to Steven Spielberg. *Indiana Jones and the Temple of Doom.*
CARA, IRENE. New York, NY, 3/18/59. Actor, singer. *Fame.*
CARDIN, PIERRE. Venice, Italy, 7/7/22. Fashion designer.
CARDINALE, CLAUDIA. Tunis, Tunisia, 4/15/39. Actor. *The Pink Panther.*
CAREY, HARRY JR. Saugus, CA, 5/16/21. Announcer for the Chicago Cubs.
CAREY, TONY. 10/16/53. Keyboardist. Rainbow.
CARLIN, GEORGE. New York, NY, 5/12/37. Actor. "Seven Dirty Words."
CARLISLE, BELINDA. Hollywood, CA, 8/16/58. Singer, songwriter.
CARLOS, BUN (Brad Carlson). Rockford, IL, 6/12/51. Drummer. Cheap Trick.
CARMEN, ERIC. Cleveland, OH, 8/11/49. Singer. The Raspberries.
CARNE, JUDY (Joyce Botterill). Northampton, England, 3/27/39. Actor. *Laugh-In.*
CARNEY, ART. Mt. Vernon, NY, 11/4/18. Actor and comedian. Ed Norton on *The Honeymooners.*
CAROLINE, PRINCESS. Monte Carlo, Monaco, 1/23/57. Daughter of Princess Grace of Monaco.
CARON, LESLIE. Paris, France, 7/1/31. Actor. *Lili.*
CARPENTER, JOHN. Carthage, NY, 1/16/48. Director, writer. *Halloween.*
CARPENTER, RICHARD. New Haven, CT, 10/15/46. Keyboardist, singer. The Carpenters.
CARR, DAVID. Leyton, England, 8/4/43. Keyboardist. The Fortunes.
CARRACK, PAUL. Sheffield, England, 4/21/51. Singer, songwriter. Squeeze; Ace; Mike and the Mechanics.
CARRADINE, DAVID. Hollywood, CA, 12/8/36. Actor, son of John Carradine, brother of Keith and Robert. *Kung Fu.*
CARRADINE, ROBERT. Hollywood, CA, 3/24/54. Actor, son of John, brother of David and Keith. *Revenge of the Nerds.*
CARRERA, BARBARA. Managua, Nicaragua, 12/31/51. Model, actor. *Dallas.*
CARROLL, DIAHANN (Diahann Johnson). New York, NY, 7/17/35. Actor, singer, married to Vic Damone. *I Know Why the Caged Bird Sings.*
CARRY, JULIUS. Actor. Mitchell Baldwin on *Murphy Brown.*
CARTER, DIXIE. McLemoresville, TN, 5/25/39. Actor. Julia Sugarbaker on *Designing Women.*
CARTER, JIMMY. Plains, GA, 10/1/24. Political leader. Thirty-ninth president of the U.S.
CARTER, LYNDA. Phoenix, AZ, 7/24/51. Actor. *Wonder Woman.*
CARTER, NELL. Birmingham, AL, 9/13/48. Actor, singer. *Gimme a Break.*
CARTERIS, GABRIELLE. 1/2/61. Actor. Andrea Zuckerman on *Beverly Hills 90210.*
CARTWRIGHT, VERONICA. Bristol, England, 1950. Actor. *Alien.*
CASADY, JACK. Washington, DC, 4/13/44. Bass guitarist. Jefferson Airplane/Starship.
CASEY, HARRY WAYNE (Harold Casey). Hialeah, FL, 1/31/51. Singer, keyboardist. KC & The Sunshine Band.
CASH, ROSEANNE. Memphis, TN, 5/24/55. Actor, singer, daughter of Johnny Cash.
CASS, PEGGY (Mary Margaret Cass). Boston, MA, 5/21/24. Actor. Panelist on *To Tell The Truth.*
CASSIDY, ED. Chicago, IL, 5/4/31. Drummer. Spirit.
CASSIDY, JOANNA. Camden, NJ, 8/2/44. Actor. Jo Jo White on *Buffalo Bill.*
CASTRO, FIDEL (Fidel Ruz). Mayari, Cuba, 8/13/26. Political leader. President of Cuba.
CATES, PHOEBE. New York, NY, 7/16/63. Actor, married to Kevin Kline. *Fast Times at Ridgemont High.*
CATHERALL, JOANNE. Sheffield, England, 9/18/62. Singer. Human League.
CATTINI, CLEM. 8/28/39. Drummer. Johnny Kidd & The Pirates; Tornados.
CATTRALL, KIM. Liverpool, England, 8/21/56. Actor. *The Bonfire of the Vanities.*
CAVALIERE, FELIX. Pelham, NY, 11/29/44. Singer, keyboardist. The (Young) Rascals.
CAVETT, DICK. Gibbon, NE, 11/19/36. Actor, talk show host. *The Dick Cavett Show.*
CEASE, JEFF. Nashville, TN, 6/24/67. Guitarist. The Black Crowes.
CETERA, PETER. Chicago, IL, 9/13/44. Singer, songwriter. Chicago.
CHADWICK, LES (John Chadwick). Liverpool, England, 5/11/43. Bassist. Gerry & The Pacemakers.
CHAMBERLAIN, RICHARD (George Chamberlain). Los Angeles, CA, 3/31/35. Actor. *Dr. Kildare.*
CHAMBERLAIN, WILT (Wilton Norman Chamberlain). West Philadelphia, PA, 8/21/36. Basketball great.
CHAMBERS, GEORGE. Flora, MS, 9/26/31. Bassist, singer. The Chambers Brothers.
CHAMBERS, JOE. Scott County, MS, 8/24/42. Guitarist, singer. The Chambers Brothers.
CHAMBERS, LESTER. Flora, MS, 4/13/40. Harmonicist, singer. The Chambers Brothers.
CHAMBERS, MARTIN. Hereford, England, 9/4/51. Drummer. The Pretenders.
CHAMBERS, TERRY. England, 7/18/55. Drummer. XTC.
CHAMBERS, WILLIE. Flora, MS, 3/3/38. Guitarist, singer. The Chambers Brothers.
CHANDLER, CHAS (Bryan Chandler). Heaton, England, 12/18/38. Bassist. The Animals.
CHANDLER, GENE (Gene Dixon). Chicago, IL, 7/6/37. Singer, songwriter.
CHANNING, CAROL. Seattle, WA, 1/31/21. Actor. *Hello, Dolly!*
CHAO, ROSALIND. Los Angeles, CA. Actor. Soon-Lee on *M*A*S*H.*
CHAPLIN, GERALDINE. Santa Monica, CA, 7/31/44. Actor. *Dr. Zhivago.*
CHAPMAN, ROGER. Leicester, England, 4/8/44. Singer. Family.
CHAPMAN, TRACY. Cleveland, OH, 3/30/64. Folk singer, songwriter.
CHAQUICO, CRAIG. 9/26/54. Singer, guitarist. Jefferson Starship.
CHARISSE, CYD (Tula Ellice Finklea). Amarillo, TX, 3/8/22. Actor. *Brigadoon.*
CHARLES, RAY (Ray Robinson). Albany, GA, 9/23/30. Singer, songwriter. "Georgia on My Mind."
CHARLTON, MANUEL. 7/25/41. Guitarist, singer, songwriter. Nazareth.
CHARO. Murcia, Spain, 1/15/51. Actor, singer. *The Love Boat.*
CHECKER, CHUBBY (Ernest Evans). Spring Gulley, SC, 10/3/41. Singer, songwriter. Popularized the Twist and Limbo.
CHER (Cherilyn Sarkisian La Piere). El Centro, CA, 5/20/46. Singer, actor, formerly married to Sonny Bono and Gregg Allman. *Moonstruck.*
CHERRY, NENEH. Stockholm, Sweden, 10/10/64. Rap/pop singer, songwriter.
CHILD, JULIA. Pasadena, CA, 8/15/12. TV chef, author. *Mastering the Art of French Cooking.*
CHILES, LOIS. Alice, TX, 1950. Model, actor. *The Way We Were.*
CHILTON, ALEX. Memphis, TN, 12/28/50. Guitarist, singer. The Box Tops; Big Star.
CHONG, RAE DAWN. Vancouver, Canada, 1962. Actor, daughter of Thomas Chong. *The Color Purple.*
CHONG, THOMAS. Edmonton, Canada, 5/24/38. Singer, actor, writer, director, former partner of Cheech Marin, father of Rae Dawn Chong. *Up in Smoke.*
CHRISTIAN, GARRY. 2/27/55. Singer. The Christians.
CHRISTIAN, ROGER. 2/13/50. Singer. The Christians.
CHRISTIAN, RUSSELL. 6/8/56. Singer. The Christians.
CHRISTIE, JULIE. Chukua, India, 4/14/41. Actor. *Dr. Zhivago.*
CHRISTIE, LOU (Lugee Sacco). Glenwillard, PA, 2/19/43. Singer, songwriter. "Lightnin' Strikes."
CHRISTO (Christo Javacheff). Gabrovo, Bulgaria, 6/13/35. Artist. The Umbrellas.
CHRISTOPHER, WILLIAM. Evanston, IL, 10/27/32. Actor. Father Francis Mulcahy on *M*A*S*H.*

CHUCK D. (Charles Ridenhour). 1960. Rap artist. Public Enemy.
CHURCHILL, CHICK. Mold, Wales, 1/2/49. Keyboardist. Ten Years After.
CIPOLLINA, JOHN. Berkeley, CA, 8/24/43. Guitarist. Quicksilver Messenger Service.
CLAIBORNE, LIZ (Elisabeth Claiborne). Brussels, Belgium, 3/31/29. Fashion designer.
CLARK, ALAN. Durham, NC, 3/5/52. Keyboardist. Dire Straits.
CLARK, DAVE. Tottenham, England, 12/15/42. Drummer. The Dave Clark Five.
CLARK, DICK. Mt. Vernon, NY, 11/30/29. Producer, music/game show host. *The Picture of Dorian Gray; American Bandstand.*
CLARK, GENE (Harold Clark). Tipton, MO, 11/17/41. Singer, percussionist. The Byrds.
CLARK, GRAEME. Glasgow, Scotland, 4/15/66. Bassist. Wet Wet Wet.
CLARK, NEIL. 7/3/55. Guitarist. Lloyd Cole & The Commotions.
CLARK, PETULA. Ewell, England, 11/15/32. Actor, singer. *Downtown.*
CLARK, ROY. Meherrin, VA, 4/15/33. Country singer, songwriter. *Hee Haw.*
CLARK, STEVE. Hillsborough, England, 4/23/60. Guitarist. Def Leppard.
CLARKE, ALLAN (Harold Clarke). Salford, England, 4/5/42. Singer. The Hollies.
CLARKE, EDDIE. 10/5/50. Guitarist. Motörhead.
CLARKE, MICHAEL. New York, NY, 6/3/44. Drummer. The Byrds.
CLARKE, VINCE. Basildon, England, 7/3/61. Keyboardist. Erasure.
CLAY, ANDREW DICE. Brooklyn, NY, 1958. Actor. *The Adventures of Ford Fairlaine.*
CLAYBURGH, JILL. New York, NY, 4/30/44. Actor. *An Unmarried Woman.*
CLAYTON, ADAM. Ireland, 3/13/60. Bassist. U2.
CLAYTON-THOMAS, DAVID (David Thomsett). Surrey, England, 9/13/41. Lead singer. Blood, Sweat & Tears.
CLEESE, JOHN. Weston-Super-Mare, England, 10/27/39. Actor. *Monty Python's Flying Circus.*
CLIFF, JIMMY (Jimmy Chambers). Somerton, Jamaica, 1949. Reggae singer, songwriter.
CLIFFORD, DOUG. Palo Alto, CA, 4/24/45. Drummer. Creedence Clearwater Revival.
CLINTON, BILL. Hope, AK, 8/9/46. Husband of Hillary Rodham, father of Chelsea. President of the United States.
CLINTON, CHELSEA. Arkansas, 2/27/80. Daughter of Bill and Hillary.
CLINTON, GEORGE. Kannapolis, NC, 7/22/40. Funk pioneer, singer. Parliament; Funkadelic.
CLINTON, HILLARY RODHAM. Park Ridge, IL, 10/26/47. Wife of Bill, mother of Chelsea. First Lady.
CLOONEY, ROSEMARY. Maysville, KY, 5/23/28. Actor, singer.
CLYDE, JEREMY. England, 3/22/44. Singer, guitarist. Chad & Jeremy.
COBURN, JAMES. Laurel, NE, 8/31/28. Actor. *The Magnificent Seven.*
COCA, IMOGENE. Philadelphia, PA, 11/18/08. Actor. *Your Show of Shows.*
COCHRANE, TOM. 5/14/53. Singer, guitarist. Red Rider.
COCKER, JOE (John Cocker). Sheffield, England, 5/20/44. Singer.
COEN, ETHAN. St. Louis Park, MN, 1958. Director, writer. Brother of Joel. *Raising Arizona.*
COEN, JOEL. St. Louis Park, MN, 1955. Director, writer. Brother of Ethan. *Raising Arizona.*
COGHLAN, JOHN. Dulwich, England, 9/19/46. Drummer. Status Quo.
COHEN, DAVID. Brooklyn, NY, 1942. Keyboardist. Country Joe & The Fish.
COHEN, LEONARD. Montreal, Canada, 9/21/34. Singer, songwriter, poet.
COLBERT, CLAUDETTE (Lily Chauchoin). Paris, France, 9/13/05. Actor. *It Happened One Night.*
COLE, BRIAN. Tacoma, WA, 9/8/42. Singer, bassist. The Association.
COLE, LLOYD. Scotland, 1/31/61. Singer, guitarist. Lloyd Cole & The Commotions.
COLEMAN, DABNEY. Austin, TX, 1/3/32. Actor. *Buffalo Bill.*
COLEMAN, GARY. Zion, IL, 2/8/68. Actor. Arnold Jackson on *Diff'rent Strokes.*
COLEY, DORIS. Passaic, NJ, 8/2/41. Singer. The Shirelles.
COLLA, JOHNNY. California, 7/2/52. Saxophonist, guitarist. Huey Lewis & The News.
COLLEN, PHIL. 12/8/57. Guitarist. Def Leppard.
COLLINS, ALLEN. Jacksonville, FL, 7/19/52. Guitarist. Lynyrd Skynyrd.
COLLINS, GARY. Boston, MA, 4/30/38. Actor, talk show host. *Home.*
COLLINS, JOAN. London, England, 5/23/33. Actor. Alexis Carrington Colby on *Dynasty.*
COLLINS, JUDY. Seattle, WA, 5/1/39. Folk/rock guitarist, singer, songwriter. "Send in the Clowns."
COLLINS, PHIL. Chiswick, England, 1/30/51. Singer, drummer. Genesis.
COLLINS, STEPHEN. Des Moines, IA, 10/1/47. Actor. *Tales of the Gold Monkey.*
COLOMBY, BOBBY. New York, NY, 12/20/44. Drummer, singer. Blood, Sweat & Tears.
COLT, JOHNNY. Cherry Point, NC, 5/1/66. Bassist. The Black Crowes.
COLUMBUS, CHRIS. Spangler, PA, 9/10/58. Director. *Home Alone.*
CONAWAY, JEFF. New York, NY, 10/5/50. Actor. Bobby Wheeler on *Taxi.*
CONNELLY, JENNIFER. New York, NY, 12/12/70. Actor. *The Rocketeer.*
CONNOLLY, BRIAN. Hamilton, Scotland, 10/5/49. Singer. Sweet.
CONNORS, JIMMY. Belleville, IL, 9/2/52. Tennis player.
CONNORS, MIKE (Krekor Ohanian). Fresno, CA, 8/15/25. Actor. *Mannix.*
CONRAD, WILLIAM. Louisville, KY, 9/27/20. Actor. *Nero Wolfe.*
CONROY, KEVIN. Westport, CT, 11/30/55. Actor. Voice of Batman in *Batman: The Animated Series.*
CONSTANTINE, MICHAEL. Reading, PA, 5/22/27. Actor. *Room 222.*
CONTI, TOM. Paisley, Scotland, 11/22/41. Actor. *Reuben Reuben.*
CONWAY, KEVIN. New York, NY, 5/29/42. Actor. *Slaughterhouse Five.*
CONWAY, TIM (Thomas Daniel Conway). Willoughby, OH, 12/15/33. Actor. *The Carol Burnett Show.*
COODER, RY (Ryland Cooder). Los Angeles, CA, 3/15/47. Folk blues guitarist, composer.
COOK, ELISHA JR. San Francisco, CA, 12/26/03. Actor. *The Maltese Falcon.*
COOK, JEFF. Fort Payne, AL, 8/27/49. Singer, fiddler, guitarist, keyboardist. Alabama.
COOK, NORMAN (Quentin Cook). 7/31/63. Singer. The Housemartins.
COOK, PAUL. London, England, 7/20/56. Drummer. The Sex Pistols.
COOK, PETER. Torquay, England, 11/17/37. Actor. *Bedazzled.*
COOK, STU. Oakland, CA, 4/25/45. Bassist. Creedence Clearwater Revival.
COOKE, SAM. Chicago, IL, 1/22/31. Gospel-R&B singer. "Twistin' the Night Away."
COONCE, RICKY. Los Angeles, CA, 8/1/47. Drummer. The Grass Roots.
COOPER, ALICE (Vincent Furnier). Detroit, MI, 2/4/48. Singer, songwriter. Alice Cooper.
COOPER, JACKIE (John Cooper Jr.). Los Angeles, CA, 9/15/22. Actor, director. *Superman.*
COPE, JULIAN. Bargoed, Wales, 10/21/57. Singer, bassist. The Teardrop Explodes.
COPELAND, STEWART. Alexandria, Egypt, 7/16/52. Drummer, singer. The Police.
CORBIN, BARRY. Dawson County, TX, 10/16/41. Actor. Maurice Minnifield on *Northern Exposure.*
CORLEY, PAT. Dallas, TX, 6/1/30. Actor. Phil the bartender on *Murphy Brown.*
CORNICK, GLENN. Barrow-in-Furness, Scotland, 4/24/47. Bassist. Jethro Tull.
CORNISH, GENE. Rochester, NY, 5/14/45. Guitarist. The (Young) Rascals.
CORNWELL, HUGH. London, England, 8/28/49. Singer, guitarist. The Stranglers.
CORT, BUD (Walter Edward Cox). New Rochelle, NY, 3/29/50. Actor. *Harold and Maude.*
COSTELL, DAVID. Pittsburgh, PA, 3/15/44. Bassist. Gary Lewis and the Playboys.
COULIER, DAVID. Detroit, MI. Actor. Joey Gladstone on *Full House.*
COVERDALE, DAVID. Saltburn-by-the-Sea, England, 9/22/49. Singer. Whitesnake.
COWSILL, BARRY. Newport, RI, 9/14/54. Bassist, singer. The Cowsills.
COWSILL, BILL. Newport, RI, 1/9/48. Guitarist, singer. The Cowsills.
COWSILL, BOB. Newport, RI, 8/26/49. Guitarist, singer. The Cowsills.
COWSILL, JOHN. Newport, RI, 3/2/56. Drummer. The Cowsills.

COWSILL, PAUL. Newport, RI, 11/11/52. Keyboardist, singer. The Cowsills.
COWSILL, SUE. Newport, RI, 5/20/60. Singer. The Cowsills.
COX, ANDY. Birmingham, England, 1/25/60. Guitarist. Fine Young Cannibals.
COX, COURTENEY. Birmingham, AL, 6/15/64. Actor. *Ace Ventura: Pet Detective.*
COX, RONNY. Cloudcroft, NM, 8/23/38. Actor. *Beverly Hills Cop.*
COYOTE, PETER (Peter Cohon). New York, NY, 1942. Actor. *Jagged Edge.*
CRAIG, MIKEY. Hammersmith, England, 2/15/60. Bassist. Culture Club.
CRAVEN, WES. Cleveland, OH, 8/2/39. Director, novelist. *A Nightmare on Elm Street.*
CRAWFORD, JOHN. 1/17/60. Bassist, singer. Berlin.
CRAWFORD, MICHAEL (Michael Dumble-Smith). Salisbury, England, 1/19/42. Actor, singer. *The Phantom of the Opera.*
CRAWFORD, RANDY (Veronica Crawford). Macon, GA, 2/18/52. Rock-R&B singer, songwriter.
CRAY, ROBERT. Columbus, GA, 8/1/53. Contemporary blues singer, songwriter. "Smoking Gun."
CREGAN, JIM. 3/9/46. Guitarist. Steve Harley & Cockney Rebel.
CREME, LOL. Manchester, England, 9/19/47. Singer, guitarist. 10cc; Godley & Creme.
CRENNA, RICHARD. Los Angeles, CA, 11/30/27. Actor. *Rambo: First Blood Part II.*
CREWSDON, ROY. Manchester, England, 5/29/41. Guitarist. Freddie & The Dreamers.
CRISS, PETER (Peter Crisscoula). Brooklyn, NY, 12/27/47. Drummer, singer. Kiss.
CROFTS, DASH. Cisco, TX, 8/14/40. Singer, guitarist, mandolinist. Seals & Crofts.
CRONIN, KEVIN. Evanston, IL, 10/6/51. Singer. REO Speedwagon.
CRONKITE, WALTER. St. Joseph, MO, 11/4/16. News journalist and anchor. *CBS Evening News.*
CRONYN, HUME (Hume Blake). London, Canada, 7/18/11. Actor, writer, director. *The Postman Always Rings Twice.*
CROPPER, STEVE. Willow Springs, MO, 10/21/41. Guitarist. Booker T. & The MG's.
CROSBY, CATHY LEE. Los Angeles, CA, 12/2/49. Actor. *That's Incredible!*
CROSBY, DAVID (David Van Cortland). Los Angeles, CA, 8/14/41. Singer, guitarist. The Byrds; Crosby, Stills, Nash & Young.
CROSBY, DENISE. Hollywood, CA, 1958. Actor, granddaughter of Bing Crosby. *Star Trek: The Next Generation.*
CROSBY, HARRY. Los Angeles, CA, 8/8/58. Actor, singer.
CROSS, BEN. London, England, 12/16/48. Actor. *Chariots of Fire.*
CROSS, CHRIS (Chris St. John). London, England, 7/14/52. Bassist, synthesizer player. Ultravox.
CROSS, CHRISTOPHER (Christopher Geppert). San Antonio, TX, 5/3/51. Guitarist, singer, songwriter. "Ride Like the Wind."
CROUSE, LINDSAY. New York, NY, 5/12/48. Actor. *The Verdict.*
CRYER, JON. New York, NY, 4/16/65. Actor. *The Famous Teddy Z.*
CULLIMORE, STAN. 4/6/62. Bassist. The Housemartins.
CULLUM, JOHN. Knoxville, TN, 3/2/30. Actor. Holling Vincoeur on *Northern Exposure.*
CULP, ROBERT. Berkeley, CA, 8/16/30. Actor. *I Spy.*
CUMMINGS, BURTON. Winnipeg, Canada, 12/31/47. Singer, keyboardist. The Guess Who.
CUMMINGS, GEORGE. Meridian, MS, 7/28/38. Lead guitarist. Dr. Hook.
CUNNINGHAM, BILL. Memphis, TN, 1/23/50. Bassist, pianist. The Box Tops; Big Star.
CUNNINGHAM, TOM. Glasgow, Scotland, 6/22/65. Drummer. Wet Wet Wet.
CUOMO, MARIO. Queens, NY, 6/15/32. Political leader. Governor of New York.
CURRIE, ALANNAH. Auckland, New Zealand, 9/20/59. Singer, saxophonist, percussionist. Thompson Twins.
CURRIE, BILLY. Huddersfield, England, 4/1/52. Synthesizer player, keyboardist. Ultravox.
CURRIE, CHERRIE. Los Angeles, CA, 1960. Singer, married to Robert Hays. The Runaways.
CURRY, TIM. Cheshire, England, 4/19/46. Actor. *The Rocky Horror Picture Show.*
CURTIN, JANE. Cambridge, MA, 9/6/47. Actor. *Kate & Allie.*
CURTIS, CHRIS (Chris Crummy). Oldham, England, 8/26/41. Singer, drummer. The Searchers.
CURTIS, SONNY. Meadow, TX, 5/9/37. Guitarist. Buddy Holly & The Crickets.
CURTIS, TONY (Bernard Schwartz). New York, NY, 6/3/24. Actor, father of Jamie Lee Curtis, formerly married to Janet Leigh. *Some Like It Hot.*
CUSACK, CYRIL. Durban, South Africa, 11/26/10. Actor. *Fahrenheit 451.*
CUSACK, JOAN. Evanston, IL, 10/11/62. Actor. *Working Girl.*
CUSACK, JOHN. Chicago, IL, 6/28/66. Actor. *The Grifters.*
CUSACK, SINEAD. Ireland, 2/18/48. Actor, married to Jeremy Irons.
D'ALEO, ANGELO. The Bronx, NY, 2/3/41. Singer. Dion & The Belmonts.
D'ANGELO, BEVERLY. Columbus, OH, 11/15/54. Actor. *Hair.*
D'ARBY, TERENCE TRENT. New York, NY, 5/15/62. R&B singer, songwriter. "Wishing Well."
DAFOE, WILLEM. Appleton, WI, 7/22/55. Actor. *Mississippi Burning.*
DAHMER, JEFFREY. Milwaukee, WI, 1960. Serial killer.
DALE, GLEN (Richard Garforth). Deal, England, 4/2/43. Guitarist, singer. The Fortunes.
DALLIN, SARAH. Bristol, England, 12/17/61. Singer. Bananarama.
DALTON, TIMOTHY. Colwyn Bay, Wales, 3/21/44. Actor. James Bond in *The Living Daylights.*
DALTREY, ROGER. London, England, 3/1/44. Lead singer. The Who.
DALY, GARY. Merseyside, England, 5/5/62. Singer. China Crisis.
DALY, TIMOTHY. New York, NY, 3/1/56. Actor. *Wings.*
DAMMERS, JERRY (Jerry Dankin). 5/22/54. Keyboardist. The Specials.
DAMONE, VIC (Vito Farinola). Brooklyn, NY, 6/12/28. Actor, married to Diahann Caroll. *The Vic Damone Show.*
DANCE, CHARLES. Worcestershire, England, 10/10/46. Actor. *The Jewel in the Crown.*
DANELLI, DINO. New York, NY, 7/23/45. Drummer. The (Young) Rascals.
DANGERFIELD, RODNEY (Jacob Cohen). Babylon, NY, 11/22/21. Actor. *Back to School.*
DANIEL, JEFFREY. Los Angeles, CA, 8/24/55. Singer. Shalamar.
DANIELS, WILLIAM. Brooklyn, NY, 3/31/27. Actor. *St. Elsewhere.*
DANKO, RICK. Simcoe, Canada, 12/9/43. Bassist, singer. The Band.
DANNER, BLYTHE. Philadelphia, PA, 2/3/43. Actor. *The Prince of Tides.*
DANTE, MICHAEL (Ralph Vitti). Stamford, CT, 1935. Actor. Crazy Horse in *Custer.*
DANZA, TONY. Brooklyn, NY, 4/21/51. Actor. Tony Micelli on *Who's the Boss?*
DARIN, BOBBY (Walden Cassotto). The Bronx, NY, 5/14/36. Pop singer, songwriter.
DAVIDSON, JOHN. Pittsburgh, PA, 12/13/41. Game show host. *Hollywood Squares.*
DAVIDSON, LENNY. Enfield, England, 5/30/44. Guitarist. The Dave Clark Five.
DAVIES, DAVE. Muswell Hill, England, 2/3/47. Singer, guitarist. The Kinks.
DAVIES, IVA. Australia, 5/22/55. Guitarist, singer. Icehouse.
DAVIES, RAY. Muswell Hill, England, 6/21/44. Singer, guitarist. The Kinks.
DAVIES, RICHARD. England, 7/22/44. Singer, keyboardist. Supertramp.
DAVIS, BILLY JR. St. Louis, MO, 6/26/40. Singer. The 5th Dimension.
DAVIS, CLIFTON. Chicago, IL, 10/4/45. Actor, singer, composer. *Never Can Say Goodbye.*
DAVIS, JIM (James Robert Davis). Marion, IN, 7/28/45. Cartoonist. *Garfield.*
DAVIS, MAC. Lubbock, TX, 1/21/42. Singer, songwriter, actor. *The Mac Davis Show.*
DAVIS, MARTHA. Berkeley, CA, 1/15/51. Singer. The Motels.
DAVIS, OSSIE. Cogdell, GA, 12/18/17. Actor, writer. *Evening Shade.*
DAVIS, PAUL. Manchester, England, 3/7/66. Keyboardist. Happy Mondays.
DAVIS, ROB. Carshalton, England, 10/1/47. Lead guitarist, singer. Mud.
DAVIS, SPENCER. Swansea, Wales, 7/17/42. Guitarist. The Spencer Davis Group.
DAVIS, WILLIE. 1940. Drummer. Joey Dee and the Starliters.
DAY, DORIS (Doris Kappelhoff). Cincinnati, OH, 4/3/24. Actor, performer. *The Doris Day Show.*
DAY, MARK. Manchester, England, 12/29/61. Guitarist. Happy Mondays.

DE BURGH, CHRIS (Chris Davidson). Argentina, 10/15/48. Singer, songwriter. "Lady in Red."
DE FREITAS, PETE. Port of Spain, West Indies, 8/2/61. Drummer. Echo & The Bunnymen.
DE HAVILLAND, OLIVIA. Tokyo, Japan, 7/1/16. Actor. *Gone with the Wind.*
DE LAURENTIS, DINO. Torre Annunziata, Italy, 8/8/19. Producer. *King Kong; Conan the Barbarian.*
DEACON, JOHN. Leicester, England, 8/19/51. Bassist. Queen.
DEAN, JIMMY. Plainview, TX, 8/10/28. Performer. *The Jimmy Dean Show.*
DEBARGE, EL (Eldra DeBarge). Grand Rapids, MI, 6/4/61. Singer, keyboardist, record producer.
DEE, DAVE (Dave Harman). Salisbury, England, 12/17/43. Lead singer, tambourinist. Dave Dee, Dozy, Beaky, Mick and Tich.
DEE, JOEY (Joey DiNicola). Passaic, NJ, 6/11/40. Singer. Joey Dee and the Starliters.
DEE, KIKI. Bradford, England, 3/6/47. Pop singer.
DEE, RUBY. Cleveland, OH, 10/27/24. Actor. *Do the Right Thing.*
DEE, SANDRA (Alexandra Zuck). Bayonne, NJ, 4/23/42. Actor. *Gidget.*
DEKKER, DESMOND (Desmond Dacris). Kingston, Jamaica, 7/16/42. Reggae singer, songwriter.
DELON, ALAIN. Sceaux, France, 11/8/35. Actor. *Is Paris Burning?*
DELP, BRAD. Boston, MA, 6/12/51. Guitarist, singer. Boston.
DELUISE, DOM. Brooklyn, NY, 8/1/33. Actor. *The Dom DeLuise Show.*
DELUISE, PETER. Hollywood, CA, 1967. Actor. Doug Penhall on *21 Jump Street.*
DEMME, JONATHAN. Rockville Centre, MD, 2/22/44. Director, producer, writer. *The Silence of the Lambs; Swimming to Cambodia.*
DEMORNAY, REBECCA. Santa Rosa, CA, 8/29/62. Actor. *The Hand That Rocks the Cradle.*
DEMPSEY, PATRICK. Lewiston, ME, 1/13/66. Actor. *Loverboy.*
DENEUVE, CATHERINE. Paris, France, 10/22/43. Actor. *The Last Metro.*
DENNEHY, BRIAN. Bridgeport, CT, 7/9/39. Actor. *Cocoon.*
DENSMORE, JOHN. Los Angeles, CA, 12/1/45. Drummer. The Doors.
DENVER, BOB. New Rochelle, NY, 1/9/35. Actor. Gilligan on *Gilligan's Island.*
DENVER, JOHN (Henry Deutschendorf). Roswell, NM, 12/31/43. Country singer, songwriter, actor. "Country Roads."
DEPARDIEU, GERARD. Chateauroux, France, 12/27/48. Actor. *Green Card.*
DEREK, BO (Mary Cathleen Collins). Long Beach, CA, 11/20/56. Actor, married to John Derek. *10.*
DEREK, JOHN. Hollywood, CA, 8/12/26. Actor, director, married to Bo Derek. *The Ten Commandments.*
DERN, BRUCE. Chicago, IL, 6/4/36. Actor, father of Laura. *Coming Home.*
DERN, LAURA. Los Angeles, CA, 2/10/67. Actor, daughter of Bruce Dern and Diane Ladd. *Jurassic Park.*
DERRINGER, RICK. Galena, OH, 8/5/47. Singer, songwriter, producer. The McCoys.
DESTRI, JIMMY. 4/13/54. Keyboardist. Blondie.
DEVANE, WILLIAM. Albany, NY, 9/5/37. Actor. Greg Sumner in *Knots Landing.*
DEVITO, TOMMY. Montclair, NJ, 6/19/36. Singer, guitarist. The Four Seasons.
DEVOE, RONALD. 11/17/67. Singer. New Edition; Bell Biv DeVoe.
DEY, SUSAN. Pekin, IL, 12/10/52. Actor. *L.A. Law.*
DEYOUNG, CLIFF. Inglewood, CA, 2/12/45. Actor. *The Hunger.*
DEYOUNG, DENNIS. Chicago, IL, 2/18/47. Singer, keyboardist. Styx.
DIAMOND, NEIL (Noah Kaminsky). New York, NY, 1/24/41. Singer, songwriter. *The Jazz Singer.*
DIAMONDE, DICK (Dingeman Van Der Sluys). Hilversum, Holland, 12/28/47. Bassist. The Easybeats.
DIANA, PRINCESS (Diana Frances Spencer). Sandringham, England, 7/1/61. Princess of Wales. British royalty, married to (and separated from) Prince Charles.
DICKEN (Jeff Pain). 4/4/50. Singer. Mr. Big.
DICKERSON, B. B. (Morris Dickerson). Torrance, CA, 8/3/49. Bassist, singer. War.
DICKINSON, ANGIE (Angie Brown). Kulm, ND, 9/30/32. Actor. *Police Woman.*
DICKINSON, BRUCE (Paul Dickinson). Worksop, England, 8/7/58. Singer. Iron Maiden.
DIDDLEY, BO (Otha Bates). McComb, MS, 12/28/28. Legendary blues guitarist, singer, songwriter.
DIFFORD, CHRIS. London, England, 11/4/54. Singer, guitarist. Squeeze.
DILLER, PHYLLIS (Phyllis Driver). Lima, OH, 7/17/17. Actor. *The Phyllis Diller Show.*
DILLON, KEVIN. Mamaroneck, NY, 8/19/65. Actor. *The Doors.*
DILLON, MATT. New Rochelle, NY, 2/18/64. Actor. *The Outsiders.*
DIMAGGIO, JOE. Martinez, CA, 11/25/14. Baseball great. New York Yankees. Once married to Marilyn Monroe.
DIMUCCI, DION. The Bronx, NY, 7/18/39. Lead singer. Dion & The Belmonts.
DIO, RONNIE JAMES. Cortland, NY, 7/10/48. Singer. Rainbow; Black Sabbath.
DITKA, MIKE. Carnegie, PA, 10/18/39. NFL football player, coach.
DIXON, DONNA. Alexandria, VA, 7/20/57. Actor, married to Dan Aykroyd. *Bosom Buddies.*
DIXON, JEANE. Medford, WI, 1/5/18. Astrologer, author.
DOBSON, KEVIN. New York, NY, 3/18/43. Actor. *Knots Landing.*
DOHERTY, DENNY. Halifax, Canada, 11/29/41. Singer. The Mamas and the Papas.
DOLENZ, MICKEY (George Dolenz). Los Angeles, CA, 3/8/45. Singer, drummer. The Monkees.
DOMINO, FATS (Antoine Domino). New Orleans, LA, 2/26/28. Legendary singer, songwriter.
DONAHUE, TROY (Merle Johnson). New York, NY, 1/27/36. Actor. *Hawaiian Eye.*
DONALDSON, SAM. El Paso, TX, 3/11/34. News reporter and anchor. *Prime Time Live.*
DONEGAN, LAWRENCE. 7/13/61. Bassist. Lloyd Cole & The Commotions.
DONEGAN, LONNIE (Anthony Donegan). Glasgow, Scotland, 4/29/31. Folk/blues guitarist, banjoist, and singer.
DONOVAN (Donovan Leitch). Glasgow, Scotland, 2/10/46. Folk/psychedelic singer, songwriter, father of Ione Skye and Donovan Leitch. "Mellow Yellow."
DONOVAN, JASON. Malvern, Australia, 6/1/68. Singer, actor.
DORMAN, LEE. St. Louis, MO, 9/19/45. Bassist. Iron Butterfly.
DOUGHTY, NEAL. Evanston, IL, 7/29/46. Keyboardist. REO Speedwagon.
DOUGLAS, BUSTER (James Douglas). Columbus, OH, 4/7/60. Boxer. Defeated Mike Tyson.
DOUGLAS, DONNA (Dorothy Bourgeois). Baywood, LA, 9/26/35. Actor. Elly May Clampett on *The Beverly Hillbillies.*
DOUGLAS, KIRK (Issur Danielovitch). Amsterdam, NY, 12/9/16. Actor, producer, father of Michael. *Spartacus.*
DOW, TONY. Hollywood, CA, 4/13/45. Actor. Wally Cleaver on *Leave It to Beaver.*
DOWN, LESLEY-ANN. London, England, 3/17/54. Actor. *Dallas.*
DOWNEY, BRIAN. Dublin, Ireland, 1/27/51. Drummer. Thin Lizzy.
DOWNEY, MORTON JR., 12/9/33. Controversial talk show host, actor.
DOWNS, HUGH. Akron, OH, 2/14/21. Host, actor, commentator. *20/20.*
DOYLE, DAVID. Omaha, NE, 12/1/25. Actor. John Bosley on *Charlie's Angels.*
DOZY (Trevor Davies). Enford, England, 11/27/44. Bassist. Dave Dee, Dozy, Beaky, Mick and Tich.
DRAGON, DARYL. Los Angeles, CA, 8/27/42. Keyboardist. The Captain & Tennille.
DREJA, CHRIS. Surbiton, England, 11/11/45. Guitarist. The Yardbirds.
DRYDEN, SPENCER. New York, NY, 4/7/38. Drummer. Jefferson Airplane/Starship.
DUBROW, KEVIN. 10/29/55. Lead singer. Quiet Riot.
DUDIKOFF, MICHAEL. Redondo Beach, CA, 10/8/54. Actor. *American Ninja.*
DUFFY, BILLY. 5/12/61. Lead guitarist. The Cult.
DUFFY, JULIA. Minneapolis, MN, 6/27/50. Actor. *Newhart.*
DUFFY, PATRICK. Townsend, MT, 3/17/49. Actor. Bobby Ewing on *Dallas.*
DUKAKIS, MICHAEL. Brookline, MA, 11/3/33. Politician. Presidential candidate.
DUKAKIS, OLYMPIA. Lowell, MA, 6/20/31. Actor. *Moonstruck.*
DUKE, DAVID. Tulsa, OK, 1951. White supremacist, politician.

DUKE, PATTY (Anna Marie Duke). New York, NY, 12/14/46. Actor, formerly married to John Astin, mother of Sean Astin. *The Patty Duke Show.*

DUKES, DAVID. San Francisco, CA, 6/6/45. Actor. *Sisters.*

DULLEA, KEIR. Cleveland, OH, 5/30/36. Actor. *2001: A Space Odyssey.*

DUNAWAY, DENNIS. Cottage Grove, OR, 12/9/48. Bassist. Alice Cooper.

DUNAWAY, FAYE. Bascom, FL, 1/14/41. Actor. *Mommie Dearest.*

DUNCAN, GARY (Gary Grubb). San Diego, CA, 9/4/46. Guitarist. Quicksilver Messenger Service.

DUNCAN, SANDY. Henderson, TX, 2/20/46. Actor. *Funny Face.*

DUNN, DONALD. Memphis, TN, 11/24/41. Bassist. Booker T. & The MG's.

DUNN, LARRY. Colorado, 6/19/53. Keyboardist. Earth, Wind & Fire.

DUNNE, GRIFFIN. New York, NY, 6/8/55. Actor. *After Hours.*

DURBIN, DEANNA (Edna Durbin). Winnipeg, Canada, 12/4/21. Actor. *One Hundred Men and a Girl.*

DURNING, CHARLES. Highland Falls, NY, 2/28/33. Actor. *Evening Shade.*

DURY, IAN. Upminster, England, 5/12/42. Singer. Ian Dury & The Blockheads.

DUTTON, CHARLES. Baltimore, MD, 1/30/51. Actor. *Roc.*

DUVALL, ROBERT. San Diego, CA, 1/5/31. Actor. *Tender Mercies.*

DUVALL, SHELLEY. Houston, TX, 7/7/49. Actor, producer. *The Shining.*

DYSART, RICHARD. Brighton, MA, 3/30/29. Actor. Leland McKenzie on *L.A. Law.*

EARLE, STEVE. Fort Monroe, VA, 1/17/55. Country/rock singer, songwriter. Guitar Town.

EASTON, ELLIOT (Elliot Shapiro). Brooklyn, NY, 12/18/53. Guitarist. The Cars.

EASTON, SHEENA (Sheena Orr). Bellshill, Scotland, 4/27/59. Rock/R&B singer.

EBSEN, BUDDY (Christian Ebsen Jr.). Belleville, IL, 4/2/08. Actor. Jed Clampett on *The Beverly Hillbillies.*

ECHOLS, JOHN. Memphis, TN, 1945. Lead guitarist. Love.

EDDY, DUANE. Corning, NY, 4/28/38. Legendary rock guitarist.

EDEN, BARBARA (Barbara Huffman). Tucson, AZ, 8/23/34. Actor. Jeannie in *I Dream of Jeannie.*

EDGE, GRAEME. Rochester, England, 3/30/42. Drummer. The Moody Blues.

EDGE, THE (David Evans). Wales, 8/8/61. Guitarist. U2.

EDMONTON, JERRY. Canada, 10/24/46. Drummer. Steppenwolf.

EDWARD, PRINCE. London, England, 2/19/60. British royalty, son of Queen Elizabeth II.

EDWARDS, BERNARD. Greenville, NC, 10/31/52. Bassist. Chic.

EDWARDS, BLAKE (William Blake McEdwards). Tulsa, OK, 7/26/22. Writer, director. The *Pink Panther* series.

EDWARDS, NOKIE. Washington, DC, 5/9/39. Lead guitarist. The Ventures.

EGGAR, SAMANTHA. London, England, 3/5/39. Actor. *The Collector.*

EIKENBERRY, JILL. New Haven, CT, 1/21/47. Actor. Ann Kelsey on *L.A. Law.*

EKBERG, ANITA. Malmo, Sweden, 9/29/31. Actor. *La Dolce Vita.*

EKLAND, BRITT. Stockholm, Sweden, 9/29/31. Actor. *After the Fox.*

ELIZONDO, HECTOR. New York, NY, 12/22/36. Actor. *Freebie and the Bean.*

ELLERBEE, LINDA. Bryan, TX, 8/15/44. News commentator. *Our World.*

ELLIOTT, BOBBY. Burnley, England, 12/8/42. Drummer. The Hollies.

ELLIOTT, CHRIS. New York, NY, 1960. Comedy writer, actor. *Get a Life.*

ELLIOTT, DENNIS. London, England, 8/18/50. Drummer. Foreigner.

ELLIOTT, JOE. Sheffield, England, 8/1/59. Singer. Def Leppard.

ELLIOTT, SAM. Sacramento, CA, 8/9/44. Actor. *Tombstone.*

ELLIS, RALPH. Liverpool, England, 3/8/42. Guitarist, singer. The Swinging Blue Jeans.

ELMORE, GREG. San Diego, CA, 9/4/46. Drummer. Quicksilver Messenger Service.

ELSWIT, RIK. New York, NY, 7/6/45. Guitarist, singer. Dr. Hook.

ELVIRA (Cassandra Peterson). Manhattan, KS, 9/17/51. Horror film hostess.

ELWES, CARY. London, England, 10/26/62. Actor. *The Princess Bride.*

EMERSON, KEITH. Todmorden, England, 11/1/44. Keyboardist. Emerson, Lake & Palmer.

ENGEL, SCOTT (Noel Engel). Hamilton, OH, 1/9/44. Singer. The Walker Brothers.

ENGLUND, ROBERT. Hollywood, CA, 6/6/49. Actor. Freddie Krueger in *Nightmare on Elm Street* series.

ENNIS, RAY. Liverpool, England, 5/26/42. Lead guitarist, singer. The Swinging Blue Jeans.

ENO, BRIAN. Woodbridge, England, 5/15/48. Synthesizer player, producer. Cofounder of Roxy Music.

ENTNER, WARREN. Boston, MA, 7/7/44. Singer, guitarist. The Grass Roots.

ENTWISTLE, JOHN. Chiswick, England, 10/9/44. Bassist. The Who.

ENYA (Eithne Ni Bhraona). Gweedore, Ireland, 1962. Singer, composer.

ERRICO, GREG. San Francisco, CA, 9/1/46. Drummer. Sly & The Family Stone.

ERVING, JULIUS. Roosevelt, NY, 2/22/50. Basketball great. Philadelphia 76ers.

ESIASON, BOOMER (Norman Julius Esiason Jr.). West Islip, NY, 4/17/61. NFL football player.

ESPOSITO, GIANCARLO. Copenhagen, Denmark, 4/26/58. Actor. *Do the Right Thing.*

ESSEX, DAVID (David Cook). Plaistow, England, 7/23/47. Drummer, singer, songwriter, actor. *Stardust.*

ESTEFAN, GLORIA (Gloria Fajardo). Havana, Cuba, 9/1/57. Latin pop singer. The Miami Sound Machine.

ESTEVEZ, EMILIO. New York, NY, 5/12/62. Actor, writer, recently filed for divorce from Paula Abdul, son of Martin Sheen. *Repo Man.*

ESTRADA, ERIK. New York, NY, 3/16/49. Actor. Frank "Ponch" Poncherello on *CHiPS.*

EUGENIE, PRINCESS. London, England, 2/19/60. British royalty, daughter of Prince Andrew and the Duchess of York.

EVANS, DALE (Francis Smith). Uvalde, TX, 10/31/12. Actor. *The Yellow Rose of Texas.*

EVANS, LINDA (Linda Evanstad). Hartford, CT, 11/18/42. Actor. *Dynasty.*

EVANS, MARK. Melbourne, Australia, 3/2/56. Bassist. AC/DC.

EVANS, MIKE (Michael Jonas Evans). Salisbury, NC, 11/3/49. Actor. Lionel on *The Jeffersons.*

EVANS, TOM. Liverpool, England, 6/5/47. Bassist, singer. Badfinger.

EVERETT, CHAD (Raymond Lee Cramton). South Bend, IN, 6/11/36. Actor. *Medical Center.*

EVERLY, DON (Isaac Everly). Brownie, KY, 2/1/37. Singer, guitarist. The Everly Brothers.

EVERLY, PHIL. Chicago, IL, 1/19/39. Singer, guitarist. The Everly Brothers.

EVERT, CHRIS (Christine Marie Evert). Ft. Lauderdale, FL, 12/21/54. Tennis player.

EVIGAN, GREG. South Amboy, NJ, 10/14/53. Actor. *B.J. and the Bear.*

FABARES, SHELLEY (Michelle Marie Fabares). Santa Monica, CA, 1/19/44. Actor, married to Mike Farrell, niece of Nanette Fabray. Christine Armstrong on *Coach.*

FABIAN (Fabian Forte). Philadelphia, PA, 2/6/43. Singer, actor. *American Bandstand.*

FABRAY, NANETTE (Ruby Nanette Fabares). San Diego, CA, 10/27/20. Actor, aunt of Shelley Fabares. *One Day at a Time.*

FAHEY, SIOBHAN. 9/10/60. Singer. Bananarama.

FAIRBANKS, DOUGLAS JR. New York, NY, 12/9/09. Actor. *Gunga Din.*

FAIRCHILD, MORGAN (Patsy McClenny). Dallas, TX, 2/3/50. Actor. *Falcon Crest.*

FAIRWEATHER-LOW, ANDY. Ystrad Mynach, Wales, 8/8/50. Singer, guitarist. Amen Corner.

FAITH, ADAM (Terence Nelhams). Acton, England, 6/23/40. Singer, actor, financial adviser.

FAITHFULL, MARIANNE. Hampstead, England, 12/29/46. Folk/rock singer.

FAKIR, ABDUL. Detroit, MI, 12/26/35. Singer. The Four Tops.

FALANA, LOLA (Loletha Elaine Falana). Philadelphia, PA, 9/11/43. Singer.

FALCO (Johann Hoelcel). 2/19/57. Singer, songwriter. "Rock Me Amadeus."

FALCONER, EARL. Birmingham, England, 1/23/59. Bassist. UB40.

FALK, PETER. New York, NY, 9/16/27. Actor. *Columbo.*

FALTSKOG, AGNETHA. Jonkoping, Sweden, 4/5/50. Singer. Abba.

FAMBROUGH, HENRY. 5/10/38. Singer. The (Detroit) Spinners.

FAME, GEORGIE (Clive Powell). Leigh, England, 9/26/43. Singer, keyboardist. Georgie Fame & The Blue Flames.
FARENTINO, JAMES. Brooklyn, NY, 2/24/38. Actor. *Dynasty.*
FARINA, DENNIS. Chicago, IL, 2/29/44. Actor. *Crime Story.*
FARNER, MARK. Flint, MI, 9/29/48. Singer, guitarist. Grand Funk Railroad.
FARR, JAMIE (Jameel Joseph Farah). Toledo, OH, 7/1/34. Actor. Maxwell Klinger on *M*A*S*H.*
FARRELL, BOBBY. Aruba, West Indies, 10/6/49. Singer. Boney M.
FARRELL, MIKE. St. Paul, MN, 2/6/39. Actor, writer, director, married to Shelley Fabares. B. J. Hunnicutt on *M*A*S*H.*
FARRIS, STEVE. 5/1/57. Guitarist. Mr. Mister.
FARRISS, ANDREW. Perth, Australia, 3/27/59. Keyboardist. INXS.
FARRISS, JON. Perth, Australia, 8/10/61. Drummer, singer. INXS.
FAULKNER, ERIC. Edinburgh, Scotland, 10/21/55. Guitarist. The Bay City Rollers.
FAWCETT, FARRAH. Corpus Christi, TX, 2/2/47. Actor. Married to Ryan O'Neal. Jill Munroe on *Charlie's Angels.*
FELDMAN, COREY. Reseda, CA, 7/16/71. Actor. *Stand By Me.*
FELDON, BARBARA (Barbara Hall). Pittsburgh, PA, 3/12/41. Actor. Agent 99 on *Get Smart.*
FELDSHUH, TOVAH. New York, NY, 12/27/53. Actor. *The Idolmaker.*
FELICIANO, JOSE. Lares, Puerto Rico, 9/10/45. Singer, guitarist. *Chico and the Man.*
FELL, NORMAN. Philadelphia, PA, 3/24/24. Actor. Stanley Roper on *Three's Company.*
FERGUSON, JAY (John Ferguson). Burbank, CA, 5/10/47. Singer. Spirit.
FERGUSON, LARRY. Nassau, Bahamas, 4/14/48. Keyboardist. Hot Chocolate.
FERGUSON, SARAH. London, England, 10/15/59. Duchess of York. Married to (and separated from) Prince Andrew.
FERRARO, GERALDINE. Newburgh, NY, 8/26/35. Politician, first woman vice-presidential candidate.
FERRER, MEL (Melchor Gaston Ferrer). Elberon, NJ, 8/25/12. Producer, director, actor, widower of Audrey Hepburn. *Falcon Crest.*
FERRER, MIGUEL. Santa Monica, CA, 2/7/54. Actor, son of Jose Ferrer and Rosemary Clooney. *Twin Peaks.*
FERRIGNO, LOU. Brooklyn, NY, 11/9/52. Actor, bodybuilder. *The Incredible Hulk.*
FERRIS, BARBARA. London, England, 10/3/40. Actor. *The Strauss Family.*
FERRY, BRYAN. Durham, England, 9/26/45. Singer, songwriter. Roxy Music.
FIEGER, DOUG. Detroit, MI, 8/20/52. Singer, guitarist. The Knack.
FIELDER, JIM. Denton, TX, 10/4/47. Bassist. Blood, Sweat & Tears.
FIELDS, KIM. Los Angeles, CA, 5/12/69. Actor. Dorothy "Tootie" Ramsey on *The Facts of Life.*
FIERSTEIN, HARVEY. Brooklyn, NY, 6/6/54. Actor, writer. *Mrs. Doubtfire.*
FINCH, RICHARD. Indianapolis, IN, 1/25/54. Bassist. KC & The Sunshine Band.
FINER, JEM. Ireland. Banjoist. The Pogues.
FINGERS, JOHNNIE (Johnnie Moylett). Ireland, 9/10/56. Keyboardist, singer. The Boomtown Rats.
FINN, TIM. 6/25/52. Singer, keyboardist. Split Enz.
FINNEY, ALBERT. Salford, England, 5/9/36. Actor. *Shoot the Moon.*
FIRTH, COLIN. Grayshott, England, 9/10/60. Actor. *Another Country.*
FISH (Derek Dick). Dalkeith, Scotland, 4/25/58. Singer. Marillion.
FISHBURNE, LARRY. Augusta, GA, 7/30/61. Actor. *Deep Cover.*
FISHER, AMY. New York, NY, 1974. The "Long Island Lolita."
FISHER, EDDIE. Philadelphia, PA, 8/10/28. Singer, married to Debbie Reynolds, father of Carrie Fisher. *The Eddie Fisher Show.*
FISHER, MATTHEW. Croydon, England, 3/7/46. Keyboardist. Procol Harum.
FISHER, ROGER. Seattle, WA, 2/14/50. Guitarist. Heart.
FITZGERALD, GERALDINE. Dublin, Ireland, 11/24/14. Actor. *Wuthering Heights.*
FLACK, ROBERTA. Black Mountain, NC, 2/10/39. Pop singer. "The First Time Ever I Saw Your Face."
FLEA (Michael Balzary). Melbourne, Australia. Singer, bassist. The Red Hot Chili Peppers.
FLEETWOOD, MICK. London, England, 6/24/42. Drummer. Fleetwood Mac.
FLEMING, PEGGY. San Jose, CA, 7/27/48. Ice skater. Olympic gold medalist.
FLETCHER, ANDY. Basildon, England, 7/8/60. Keyboardist. Depeche Mode.
FLETCHER, LOUISE. Birmingham, AL, 7/22/34. Actor. *One Flew over the Cuckoo's Nest.*
FLOYD, EDDIE. Montgomery, AL, 6/25/35. R&B singer, songwriter.
FOGELBERG, DAN. Peoria, IL, 8/13/51. Guitarist, singer, songwriter.
FOGERTY, JOHN. Berkeley, CA, 5/28/45. Singer, guitarist. Creedence Clearwater Revival.
FOGERTY, TOM. Berkeley, CA, 11/9/41. Guitarist. Creedence Clearwater Revival.
FOLLOWS, MEGAN. Toronto, Canada, 3/14/68. Actor. *Anne of Green Gables.*
FONDA, PETER. New York, NY, 2/23/39. Actor, son of Henry Fonda, brother of Jane, father of Bridget. *Easy Rider.*
FONTAINE, JOAN (Joan de Havilland). Tokyo, Japan, 10/22/17. Actor, sister of Olivia de Havilland. *Suspicion.*
FONTANA, WAYNE (Glyn Ellis). Manchester, England, 10/28/40. Singer. Wayne Fontana & The Mindbenders.
FORD, FAITH. Alexandria, LA, 9/14/64. Actor. Corky Sherwood Forrest on *Murphy Brown.*
FORD, FRANKIE (Frankie Guzzo). Gretna, LA, 8/4/40. Singer.
FORD, LITA. London, England, 9/23/59. Lead guitarist. The Runaways.
FOREMAN, CHRIS. England, 8/8/58. Guitarist. Madness.
FOREMAN, GEORGE. Marshall, TX, 1/10/49. Boxer, actor. *George.*
FORSSI, KEN. Cleveland, OH, 1943. Bassist. Love.
FORSTER, ROBERT. Rochester, NY, 7/13/41. Actor. *Banyon.*
FORSYTHE, JOHN (John Freund). Penns Grove, NJ, 1/29/18. Actor. Blake Carrington on *Dynasty.*
FORTUNE, NICK (Nick Fortuna). Chicago, IL, 5/1/46. Bassist. The Buckinghams.
FOSTER, MEG. Reading, PA, 5/14/48. Actor. *Cagney and Lacey.*
FOX, JACKIE. California, 1960. Bassist. The Runaways.
FOX, JAMES. London, England, 5/19/39. Actor. *The Loneliness of the Long Distance Runner.*
FOX, SAMANTHA. England, 1966. Singer. "Naughty Girls (Need Love Too)."
FOX, TERRY (Terrance Stanley Fox). Winnipeg, Canada, 7/28/58. Track athlete, fund-raiser.
FOXTON, BRUCE. 9/1/55. Guitarist. The Jam.
FOXWORTH, ROBERT. Houston, TX, 11/1/41. Actor. Chase Gioberti on *Falcon Crest.*
FRAKES, JONATHAN. Bethlehem, PA, 1952. Actor. Commander William Riker on *Star Trek: The Next Generation.*
FRAME, RODDY. East Kilbride, Scotland, 1/29/64. Singer, guitarist. Aztec Camera.
FRAMPTON, PETER KENNETH. Beckenham, England, 4/22/50. Guitarist, singer, songwriter.
FRANCIOSA, ANTHONY (Anthony Papaleo). New York, NY, 10/25/28. Actor. *The Long Hot Summer.*
FRANCIS, ANNE. Ossining, NY, 9/16/32. Actor, former child model.
FRANCIS, BILL. Mobile, AL, 1/16/42. Keyboardist, singer. Dr. Hook.
FRANCIS, CONNIE (Connie Franconero). Newark, NJ, 12/12/38. Singer. "Where the Boys Are."
FRANKLIN, MELVIN (David English). Montgomery, AL, 10/12/42. Singer. The Temptations.
FRANTZ, CHRIS (Charlton Frantz). Fort Campbell, KY, 5/8/51. Drummer. Talking Heads.
FRASER, ANDY. London, England, 8/7/52. Bassist. Free.
FRASER, BRENDAN. Indianapolis, IN, 1967. Actor. *Encino Man.*
FRAZIER, JOE. Beaufort, SC, 1/17/44. Boxer, former heavyweight champ.
FREDRIKSSON, MARIE. Sweden, 5/30/58. Singer. Roxette.
FREEMAN, BOBBY. San Francisco, CA, 6/13/40. Singer, songwriter.
FREEMAN, MORGAN. Memphis, TN, 6/1/37. Actor, director. *Driving Miss Daisy.*
FREHLEY, ACE (Paul Frehley). The Bronx, NY, 4/22/51. Guitarist, singer. Kiss.
FREIBERG, DAVID. Boston, MA, 8/24/38. Bassist. Quicksilver Messenger Service.
FREWER, MATT. Washington, DC, 1/4/58. Actor. *Max Headroom.*
FREY, GLENN. Detroit, MI, 11/6/48. Singer, songwriter. The Eagles.

FRICKER, BRENDA. Dublin, Ireland, 2/17/45. Actor. *My Left Foot.*
FRIPP, ROBERT. Wimborne Minster, England, 1946. Guitarist. King Crimson.
FROST, CRAIG. Flint, MI, 4/20/48. Keyboardist. Grand Funk Railroad.
FRY, MARTIN. Manchester, England, 3/9/58. Singer. ABC.
FULLER, BOBBY. Goose Creek, TX, 10/22/42. Singer, guitarist. The Bobby Fuller Four.
FUNICELLO, ANNETTE. Utica, NY, 10/22/42. Actor, Mouseketeer. *Beach Blanket Bingo.*
FUNT, ALLEN. New York, NY, 9/16/14. Producer. *Candid Camera.*
FURAY, RICHIE. Yellow Springs, OH, 5/9/44. Singer, guitarist. Buffalo Springfield; Poco.
FURUHOLMEN, MAGS. Oslo, Norway, 11/1/62. Keyboardist, singer. a-ha.
GABLE, JOHN CLARK. Los Angeles, CA, 3/20/61. Actor. Son of Clark Gable.
GABOR, EVA. Budapest, Hungary, 2/11/20. Actor. Lisa Douglas on *Green Acres.*
GAHAN, DAVE. Epping, England, 5/9/62. Singer. Depeche Mode.
GAIL, MAXWELL. Derfoil, MI, 4/5/43. Actor. Sergeant Stanley Wojohowicz on *Barney Miller.*
GALLAGHER, PETER. Armonk, NY, 8/19/55. Actor. *sex, lies and videotape.*
GARDNER, CARL. Tyler, TX, 4/29/27. Lead singer. The Coasters.
GARFAT, JANCE. California, 3/3/44. Bassist, singer. Dr. Hook.
GARFUNKEL, ART. New York, NY, 11/5/42. Singer, actor, former partner of Paul Simon. *Carnal Knowledge.*
GARLAND, BEVERLY. Santa Cruz, CA, 10/17/30. Actor. *My Three Sons.*
GARNES, SHERMAN. New York, NY, 6/8/40. Singer. Frankie Lymon & The Teenagers.
GARR, TERI. Lakewood, OH, 12/11/49. Actor. *Tootsie.*
GARRETT, BETTY. St. Joseph, MO, 5/23/19. Actor. *All in the Family.*
GARRITY, FREDDIE. Manchester, England, 11/14/40. Singer. Freddie & The Dreamers.
GARSON, GREER. County Down, Northern Ireland, 9/29/08. Actor. *Mrs. Miniver.*
GARTH, JENNIE. Champaign, IL, 4/3/72. Actor. Kelly Taylor on *Beverly Hills 90210.*
GARTSIDE, GREEN (Green Strohmeyer-Gartside). Cardiff, Wales, 6/22/56. Singer. Scritti Politti.
GARY, BRUCE. Burbank, CA, 4/7/52. Drummer. The Knack.
GATES, DAVID. Tulsa, OK, 12/11/40. Keyboardist, singer. Bread.
GATLIN, RUDY. 8/20/52. Singer. The Gatlin Brothers.
GATLIN, STEVE. 4/4/51. Singer. The Gatlin Brothers.
GAUDIO, BOB. The Bronx, NY, 11/17/42. Singer, organist. The Four Seasons.
GAYLE, CRYSTAL (Brenda Webb). Baintsville, KY, 1/9/51. Country singer.
GAYLORD, MITCH. Van Nuys, CA, 1961. Gymnast.
GAYNOR, MITZI (Francesca Marlene Von Gerber). Chicago, IL, 9/4/31. Actor. *Anything Goes.*
GAZZARA, BEN (Biago Gazzara). New York, NY, 8/28/30. Actor. *Inchon.*
GEILS, J. (Jerome Geils). New York, NY, 2/20/46. Guitarist. The J. Geils Band.
GELDOF, BOB. Dublin, Ireland, 10/5/54. Singer. The Boomtown Rats.
GERARD, GIL. Little Rock, AR, 1/23/43. Actor. *Buck Rogers in the 25th Century.*
GERARDO. Ecuador, 1965. Rap artist. "Rico Suave."
GERTZ, JAMI. Chicago, IL, 10/28/65. Actor. *Less Than Zero.*
GESSLE, PER. 1/12/59. Guitarist, singer. Roxette.
GETTY, ESTELLE. New York, NY, 7/25/23. Actor. Sophia Petrillo on *The Golden Girls.*
GHOSTLEY, ALICE. Eve, MO, 8/14/26. Actor. *Bewitched.*
GIAMMARESE, CARL. Chicago, IL, 8/21/47. Guitarist. The Buckinghams.
GIANNINI, GIANCARLO. Spezia, Italy, 8/1/42. Actor. *Seven Beauties.*
GIBB, BARRY. Manchester, England, 9/1/47. Singer, guitarist. The Bee Gees.
GIBB, CYNTHIA. Bennington, VT, 12/14/63. Actor. *Madman of the People.*
GIBB, MAURICE. Manchester, England, 12/22/49. Singer, bassist. The Bee Gees.
GIBB, ROBIN. Manchester, England, 12/22/49. Singer. The Bee Gees.
GIBBINS, MIKE. Swansea, Wales, 3/12/49. Drummer. Badfinger.
GIBBONS, BILLY. Houston, TX, 12/16/49. Guitarist, singer. ZZ Top.
GIBBONS, LEEZA. 3/26/57. TV personality. *Entertainment Tonight.*
GIBBS, MARLA. Chicago, IL, 6/14/46. Actor. Florence Johnston on *The Jeffersons.*
GIBSON, DEBBIE. Long Island, NY, 8/31/70. Singer, songwriter.
GIBSON, HENRY. Germantown, PA, 9/21/35. Actor. Poet from *Laugh-In.*
GIFFORD, FRANK. Santa Monica, CA, 8/16/30. Football player turned sports commentator, married to Kathie Lee Gifford. *Monday Night Football.*
GIFT, ROLAND. Birmingham, England, 5/28/62. Singer. Fine Young Cannibals.
GIGUERE, RUSS. Portsmouth, NH, 10/18/43. Singer, guitarist. The Association.
GILBERT, GILLIAN. Manchester, England, 1/27/61. Keyboardist. New Order.
GILBERT, SARA (Rebecca Sara MacMahon). Santa Monica, CA, 1/29/75. Actor, sister of Melissa and Jonathan Gilbert. Darlene Conner on *Roseanne.*
GILES, MIKE. Bournemouth, England, 1942. Drummer. King Crimson.
GILL, PETER. Liverpool, England, 3/8/64. Drummer. Frankie Goes to Hollywood.
GILLAN, IAN. Hounslow, England, 8/19/45. Singer. Deep Purple.
GILLIAM, TERRY. Minneapolis, MN, 11/22/40. Writer, director, actor. *Monty Python and the Holy Grail.*
GILMORE, JIMMIE DALE. Tulia, TX, 1945. Country singer. "Dallas."
GILMOUR, DAVID. Cambridge, England, 3/6/47. Singer, guitarist. Pink Floyd.
GINTY, ROBERT. New York, NY, 11/14/48. Actor. *Baa Baa Black Sheep.*
GIVENS, ROBIN. New York, NY, 11/27/64. Actor, formerly married to Mike Tyson. *Head of the Class.*
GLASER, PAUL MICHAEL. Cambridge, MA, 3/25/43. Actor, director. Det. Dave Starsky on *Starsky and Hutch.*
GLASS, RON. Evansville, IN, 7/10/45. Actor. *Barney Miller.*
GLEASON, JOANNA. Winnipeg, Canada, 6/2/50. Actor. *Into the Woods.*
GLENN, SCOTT. Pittsburgh, PA, 1/26/42. Actor. *The Right Stuff.*
GLESS, SHARON. Los Angeles, CA, 5/31/43. Actor. Chris Cagney on *Cagney and Lacey.*
GLITTER, GARY (Paul Gadd). Banbury, England, 5/8/40. Singer, songwriter.
GLOVER, CRISPIN. New York, NY, 1964. Actor. George McFly in *Back to the Future.*
GLOVER, DANNY. San Francisco, CA, 7/22/47. Actor. *Lethal Weapon.*
GLOVER, JOHN. Kingston, NY, 8/7/44. Actor. *Shamus.*
GLOVER, ROGER. Brecon, Wales, 11/30/45. Bassist. Deep Purple.
GOBLE, GRAHAM. Adelaide, Australia, 5/15/47. Guitarist. Little River Band.
GODLEY, KEVIN. Manchester, England, 10/7/45. Singer, drummer. 10cc; Godley & Creme.
GODUNOV, ALEXANDER (Aleksandr Godunov). Ujno-Sakhalin, Russia, 11/28/49. Dancer, actor. *Witness.*
GOLD, TRACEY. New York, NY, 5/16/69. Actor. *Growing Pains.*
GOLDEN, WILLIAM LEE. Brewton, AL, 1/12/39. Singer. The Oak Ridge Boys.
GOLDING, LYNVAL. 7/24/51. Guitarist. The Specials.
GOLDTHWAIT, BOBCAT. Syracuse, NY, 5/1/62. Actor. *Police Academy* series.
GOLDWYN, TONY. Los Angeles, CA, 5/20/60. Actor. *Ghost.*
GOLINO, VALERIA. Naples, Italy, 10/22/66. Actor. *Rain Man.*
GOODALL, JANE. London, England, 4/3/34. Anthropologist, author. *In the Shadow of Man.*
GOODEN, DWIGHT. Tampa, FL, 11/16/64. Baseball pitcher. New York Mets.
GOODEN, SAM. Chattanooga, TN, 9/2/39. Singer. The Impressions.
GOODING, CUBA JR. The Bronx, NY, 1968. Actor. *Boyz N the Hood.*
GORBACHEV, MIKHAIL. Privolnoye, Russia, 3/2/31. Former leader of the USSR.
GORE, ALBERT JR. Washington, DC, 3/31/48. Vice president of the United States.
GORE, LESLEY. New York, NY, 5/2/46. Singer.
GORE, MARTIN. Basildon, England, 7/23/61. Keyboardist. Depeche Mode.
GORHAM, SCOTT. Santa Monica, CA, 3/17/51. Guitarist. Thin Lizzy.
GORMAN, STEVE. Hopkinsville, KY, 8/17/65. Drummer. The Black Crowes.
GORME, EYDIE. New York, NY, 8/16/32. Singer. Steve and Eydie.

GORRIE, ALAN. Perth, Scotland, 7/19/46. Singer, bassist. Average White Band.
GORSHIN, FRANK. Pittsburgh, PA, 4/5/33. Actor. The Riddler on *Batman*.
GOSSETT, LOUIS JR. Brooklyn, NY, 5/27/36. Actor. *An Officer and a Gentleman*.
GOTTI, JOHN. New York, NY, 10/27/40. Reputed mob leader.
GOUDREAU, BARRY. Boston, MA, 11/29/51. Guitarist. Boston.
GOULD, BILLY. Los Angeles, CA, 4/24/63. Bassist. Faith No More.
GOULD, BOON. 3/14/55. Guitarist. Level 42.
GOULD, ELLIOTT (Elliott Goldstein). Brooklyn, NY, 8/29/38. Actor. Formerly married to Barbra Streisand. *Bob & Carol & Ted & Alice*.
GOULD, PHIL. 2/28/57. Drummer. Level 42.
GOULDMAN, GRAHAM. Manchester, England, 5/10/45. Singer, guitarist. 10cc.
GOULET, ROBERT. Lawrence, MA, 11/26/33. Singer, actor. *Blue Light*.
GRAF, STEFFI. Bruhl, Germany, 6/14/69. Tennis player, youngest woman to win French Open.
GRAHAM, BILLY. Charlotte, NC, 11/7/18. Evangelist. *Billy Graham Crusades*.
GRAHAM, LARRY. Beaumont, TX, 8/14/46. Bass guitarist. Sly & The Family Stone.
GRAMM, LOU. Rochester, NY, 5/2/50. Singer. Foreigner.
GRANDMASTER FLASH (Joseph Saddler). New York, NY, 1958. Rap artist. Grandmaster Flash; Melle Mel & The Furious Five.
GRANDY, FRED. Sioux City, IA, 6/29/48. Actor, politician. Burl "Gopher" Smith on *The Love Boat*.
GRANGER, FARLEY. San Jose, CA, 7/1/25. Actor. *Strangers on a Train*.
GRANT, EDDY (Edmond Grant). Plaisance, Guyana, 3/5/48. Reggae singer, songwriter.
GRANT, LEE (Lyova Rosenthal). New York, NY, 10/31/27. Actor. *Peyton Place*.
GRANTHAM, GEORGE. Cordell, OK, 11/20/47. Drummer, singer. Poco.
GRATZER, ALAN. Syracuse, NY, 11/9/48. Drummer. REO Speedwagon.
GRAVES, PETER (Peter Aurness). Minneapolis, MN, 3/18/26. Actor, brother of James Arness. Jim Phelps on *Mission: Impossible*.
GRAY, EDDIE. 2/27/48. Guitarist. Tommy James & The Shondells.
GRAY, LES. Carshalton, England, 4/9/46. Singer. Mud.
GRAY, SPALDING. Barrington, RI, 6/5/41. Actor, writer, performance artist. *The Killing Fields*.
GREBB, MARTY. Chicago, IL, 9/2/46. Keyboardist. The Buckinghams.
GRECH, RICK. Bordeaux, France, 11/1/46. Bassist. Blind Faith.
GREEN, AL (Al Greene). Forrest City, AR, 4/13/46. R&B singer, songwriter.
GREEN, KARL. Salford, England, 7/31/47. Bassist. Herman's Hermits.
GREENAWAY, PETER. Newport, Wales, 4/5/42. Director, writer. *The Cook, the Thief, His Wife and Her Lover*.
GREENFIELD, DAVE. Keyboardist. The Stranglers.
GREENSPOON, JIMMY. Los Angeles, CA, 2/7/48. Organist. Three Dog Night.
GREENWOOD, ALAN. New York, NY, 10/20/51. Keyboardist. Foreigner.
GREGG, BRIAN. Bassist. Johnny Kidd & The Pirates.
GREGORY, GLENN. Sheffield, England, 5/16/58. Singer. Heaven 17.
GREY, JENNIFER. New York, NY, 3/26/60. Actor. *Dirty Dancing*.
GREY, JOEL (Joel Katz). Cleveland, OH, 4/11/32. Musical comedy performer. *Cabaret*.
GRIER, DAVID ALAN. Detroit, MI, 6/30/55. Actor. *In Living Color*.
GRIER, ROSEY (Roosevelt Grier). Cuthbert, GA, 7/14/32. Football player, actor.
GRIFFITH, ANDY. Mt. Airy, NC, 6/1/26. Actor, writer, producer. *The Andy Griffith Show*.
GRILL, ROB. Los Angeles, CA, 11/30/44. Bassist, singer. The Grass Roots.
GROSS, MARY. Chicago, IL, 3/25/53. Actor. *Saturday Night Live*.
GROSS, MICHAEL. Chicago, IL, 6/21/47. Actor. Steven Keaton on *Family Ties*.
GRUNDY, HUGH. Winchester, England, 3/6/45. Drummer. The Zombies.
GUCCIONE, BOB. New York, NY, 12/17/30. Publisher, founder of *Penthouse*.
GUEST, CHRISTOPHER. New York, NY, 2/5/48. Actor, writer. *This Is Spinal Tap*.
GUEST, LANCE. Saratoga, CA, 7/21/60. Actor. *Knots Landing*.
GUEST, WILLIAM. Atlanta, GA, 6/2/41. Singer. Gladys Knight & The Pips.
GUILLAUME, ROBERT (Robert Williams). St. Louis, MO, 11/30/37. Actor. Benson DuBois on *Soap*.
GUINNESS, ALEC. London, England, 4/2/14. Actor. *The Bridge on the River Kwai*.
GULAGER, CLU. Holdenville, OK, 11/16/28. Actor. *The Last Picture Show*.
GUMBEL, BRYANT. New Orleans, LA, 9/29/48. News show host and sportscaster. *Today*.
GUSTAFSON, KARIN. Miami, FL, 6/23/59. Actor. *Taps*.
GUSTAFSON, STEVEN. Bassist. 10,000 Maniacs.
GUTHRIE, ARLO. New York, NY, 7/10/47. Folk singer, songwriter. "Alice's Restaurant."
GUTTENBERG, STEVE. Brooklyn, NY, 8/24/58. Actor. *Three Men and a Baby*.
GUY, BILLY. Attasca, TX, 6/20/36. Baritone. The Coasters.
GUY, BUDDY. Lettsworth, LA, 7/30/36. Blues guitarist.
GUY, JASMINE. Boston, MA, 3/10/64. Actor. Whitley Gilbert on *A Different World*.
HAAS, LUKAS. West Hollywood, CA, 4/16/76. Actor. *Witness*.
HACK, SHELLEY. Greenwich, CT, 7/6/52. Actor. *Charlie's Angels*.
HACKETT, BUDDY (Leonard Hacker). Brooklyn, NY, 8/31/24. Actor. *It's a Mad Mad Mad Mad World; The Love Bug*.
HADLEY, TONY. Islington, England, 6/2/59. Singer. Spandau Ballet.
HAGAR, SAMMY. Monterey, CA, 10/13/49. Singer, guitarist. Van Halen.
HAGERTY, JULIE. Cincinnati, OH, 6/15/55. Actor. *Airplane!*
HAGMAN, LARRY (Larry Hageman). Fort Worth, TX, 9/21/31. Actor, son of Mary Martin. J. R. Ewing on *Dallas*.
HAHN, JESSICA. Massapequa, NY, 7/7/59. *Playboy* model, involved in PTL Jim Bakker scandal.
HAID, CHARLES. San Francisco, CA, 6/2/43. Actor, director, producer. Andrew Renko on *Hill Street Blues*.
HAIM, COREY. Toronto, Canada, 12/23/72. Actor. *The Lost Boys*.
HALE, BARBARA. DeKalb, IL, 4/18/22. Actor, mother of William Katt. Della Street on *Perry Mason*.
HALEY, BILL. Highland Park, MI, 7/6/25. Singer, guitarist. Bill Haley & His Comets.
HALFORD, ROB. Birmingham, England, 8/25/51. Singer. Judas Priest.
HALL, ANTHONY MICHAEL. Boston, MA, 4/14/68. Actor. *Sixteen Candles*.
HALL, BRUCE. Champaign, IL, 5/3/53. Bassist. REO Speedwagon.
HALL, DARYL (Daryl Hohl). Pottstown, PA, 10/11/49. Singer, guitarist. Hall & Oates.
HALL, DEIDRE. 10/31/47. Actor. Marlena Evans on *Days of Our Lives*.
HALL, FAWN. Annandale, VA, 1959. Secretary for Oliver North. Iran-Contra scandal.
HALL, MONTY. Winnipeg, Canada, 8/25/24. TV personality. *Let's Make a Deal*.
HALL, TERRY. England, 3/19/59. Singer. The Specials.
HAM, GREG. Australia, 9/27/53. Saxophonist, keyboardist, flautist. Men at Work.
HAM, PETE. Swansea, Wales, 4/27/47. Guitarist, pianist, singer. Badfinger.
HAMEL, VERONICA. Philadelphia, PA, 11/20/43. Actor. Joyce Davenport on *Hill Street Blues*.
HAMILL, DOROTHY. Chicago, IL, 7/26/56. Ice skater. Olympic gold medalist.
HAMILL, MARK. Oakland, CA, 9/25/52. Actor. Luke Skywalker in *Star Wars* trilogy.
HAMILTON, GEORGE. Memphis, TN, 8/12/39. Actor. *Love at First Bite*.
HAMILTON, LINDA. Salisbury, MD, 9/26/56. Actor. Sarah Connor in *The Terminator*.
HAMILTON, SCOTT. Haverford, PA, 8/28/58. Ice skater.
HAMILTON, TOM. Colorado Springs, CO, 12/31/51. Bassist. Aerosmith.
HAMLIN, HARRY. Pasadena, CA, 10/30/51. Actor. *L.A. Law*.
HAMLISCH, MARVIN. New York, NY, 6/2/44. Composer. *The Way We Were; The Sting*.
HAMMETT, KIRK. 11/18/62. Guitarist. Metallica.
HAMPSHIRE, SUSAN. London, England, 5/12/41. Actor. *The Forsythe Saga*.
HANCOCK, HERBIE (Herbert Jeffrey Hancock). Chicago, IL, 4/12/40. Jazz pianist, composer. "Rockit."
HARDISON, KADEEM. Brooklyn, NY, 7/24/66. Actor. Dwayne Wayne on *A Different World*.

HAREWOOD, DORIAN. Dayton, OH, 8/6/50. Actor. *Roots—The Next Generation.*
HARKET, MORTEN. Konigsberg, Norway, 9/14/59. Lead singer. a-ha.
HARLEY, STEVE (Steve Nice). London, England, 2/27/51. Singer. Steve Harley & Cockney Rebel.
HARMON, MARK. Los Angeles, CA, 9/2/51. Actor. *St. Elsewhere.*
HARPER, JESSICA. Chicago, IL, 10/10/49. Actor.
HARPER, TESS. Mammoth Spring, AR, 8/15/50. Actor. *Crimes of the Heart.*
HARPER, VALERIE. Suffern, NY, 8/22/40. Actor. Rhoda Morgenstern on *The Mary Tyler Moore Show.*
HARRINGTON, PAT. New York, NY, 8/13/29. Actor. Dwayne Schneider on *One Day at a Time.*
HARRIS, ADDI. Passaic, NJ, 1/22/40. Singer. The Shirelles.
HARRIS, BARBARA (Sandra Markowitz). Evanston, IL, 7/25/35. Actor. *Family Plot.*
HARRIS, ED. Tenafly, NJ, 11/28/50. Actor. *The Right Stuff.*
HARRIS, JULIE. Grosse Point, MI, 12/2/25. Actor. *Knots Landing.*
HARRIS, MEL (Mary Ellen Harris). Bethlehem, PA, 7/12/57. Actor. Hope Murdoch Steadman on *thirtysomething.*
HARRIS, RICHARD. Limerick, Ireland, 10/1/30. Actor. *A Man Called Horse.*
HARRISON, BILLY. Belfast, Ireland, 10/14/42. Lead guitarist. Them.
HARRISON, GEORGE. Liverpool, England, 2/25/43. Singer, lead guitarist. The Beatles.
HARRISON, GREGORY. Catalina Island, CA, 5/31/50. Actor. *Trapper John, MD.*
HARRISON, JENILEE. Northridge, CA, 6/12/59. Actor. Jamie Ewing Barnes on *Dallas.*
HARRISON, JERRY. Milwaukee, WI, 2/21/49. Keyboardist. Talking Heads.
HARRISON, NOEL. London, England, 1/29/36. Singer, actor. *The Girl from U.N.C.L.E.*
HARRY, DEBORAH. Miami, FL, 7/1/45. Singer. Blondie.
HART, MARY. Sioux Falls, SD, 11/8/50. TV hostess. *Entertainment Tonight.*
HARTLEY, MARIETTE. New York, NY, 6/21/40. Actor. *Peyton Place.*
HARTMAN, DAVID. Pawtucket, RI, 5/19/35. Actor, talk show host. *Good Morning America.*

HARTMAN, JOHN. Falls Church, VA, 3/18/50. Drummer. The Doobie Brothers.
HASSAN, NORMAN. Birmingham, England, 11/26/57. Percussionist. UB40.
HATFIELD, BOBBY. Beaver Dam, WI, 8/10/40. Singer. The Righteous Brothers.
HATHAWAY, DONNY. Chicago, IL, 10/1/45. R&B keyboardist, singer, songwriter.
HATTON, BILLY. Liverpool, England, 6/9/41. Bassist. The Fourmost.
HAUER, RUTGER. Breukelen, Netherlands, 1/23/44. Actor. *Blade Runner.*
HAVENS, RICHIE. Brooklyn, NY, 1/21/41. Folk/blues guitarist, singer, songwriter.
HAWKING, STEPHEN. Oxford, England, 1/8/42. Theoretical physicist, author of *A Brief History of Time.*
HAY, COLIN. Scotland, 6/29/53. Singer. Men at Work.
HAY, ROY. Southend, England, 8/12/61. Guitarist, keyboardist. Culture Club.
HAYDOCK, ERIC. Stockport, England, 2/3/42. Bassist. The Hollies.
HAYES, CHRIS. California, 11/24/57. Lead guitarist. Huey Lewis & The News.
HAYES, ISAAC. Covington, TN, 8/20/42. R&B/rock saxophonist, keyboardist, singer, songwriter.
HAYS, ROBERT. Bethesda, MD, 7/24/47. Actor, married to Cherie Currie. *Airplane!*
HAYWARD, JUSTIN. England, 10/14/46. Singer, songwriter. The Moody Blues.
HEADLY, GLENNE. New London, CT, 3/13/55. Actor. *Dirty Rotten Scoundrels.*
HEADON, NICKY. Bromley, England, 5/30/55. Drummer. The Clash.
HEALEY, JEFF. Toronto, Canada, 1966. Singer, songwriter, guitarist.
HEARD, JOHN. Washington, DC, 3/7/46. Actor. Father in *Home Alone.*
HEATON, PAUL. Birkenhead, England, 5/9/62. Singer, guitarist. The Housemartins.
HEDREN, TIPPI (Natalie Kay Hedren). New Ulm, MN, 1/19/35. Actor. Mother of Melanie Griffith. *The Birds.*
HEFNER, HUGH. Chicago, IL, 4/9/26. Publisher, founder of *Playboy.*

HELL, RICHARD (Richard Myers). Lexington, KY, 10/2/49. Bassist. Television.
HELLER, JOSEPH. New York, NY, 5/1/23. Author, dramatist. *Catch-22.*
HELLIWELL, JOHN. England, 2/15/45. Saxophonist. Supertramp.
HELM, LEVON. Marvell, AR, 5/26/42. Drummer, singer. The Band.
HELMSLEY, HARRY. New York, NY, 3/4/09. Businessman, married to Leona Helmsley.
HELMSLEY, LEONA. New York, NY, 7/4/20. Hotel executive, married to Harry Helmsley. Convicted of tax evasion.
HEMINGWAY, MARGAUX. Portland, OR, 2/1/55. Actor, model, granddaughter of Ernest Hemingway, sister of Mariel. *Lipstick.*
HEMINGWAY, MARIEL. Ketchum, ID, 11/22/61. Actor, granddaughter of Ernest Hemingway, sister of Margaux. *Manhattan.*
HEMSLEY, SHERMAN. Philadelphia, PA, 2/1/38. Actor. George on *The Jeffersons.*
HENDERSON, ALAN. Belfast, Ireland, 11/26/44. Bassist. Them.
HENDERSON, BILLY. 8/9/39. Singer. The (Detroit) Spinners.
HENDERSON, FLORENCE. Dale, IN, 2/14/34. Actor. Carol Brady on *The Brady Bunch.*
HENLEY, DON. Gilmer, TX, 7/22/47. Singer, songwriter, drummer. The Eagles.
HENNER, MARILU. Chicago, IL, 4/6/52. Actor. Elaine Nardo on *Taxi.*
HENNING, DOUG (Douglas James Henning). Fort Gary, Canada, 5/3/47. Magician. *The Magic Show.*
HENRIKSEN, LANCE. New York, NY, 1940. Actor. *Aliens.*
HENRY, BUCK (Buck Zuckerman). New York, NY, 12/9/30. Actor, writer. *Get Smart; That Was the Week That Was.*
HENRY, CLARENCE. Algiers, LA, 3/19/37. Singer. "Ain't Got No Home."
HENRY, JUSTIN. Rye, NY, 5/25/71. Actor. *Kramer vs. Kramer.*
HENRY, PRINCE. London, England, 2/19/60. British royalty, son of Prince Charles and Princess Diana.

HENSLEY, KEN. England, 8/24/45. Keyboardist, guitarist, singer, percussionist. Uriah Heep.
HENSLEY, PAMELA. Los Angeles, CA, 10/3/50. Actor. C. J. Parsons on *Matt Houston.*
HERMAN, PEE-WEE (Paul Reubenfeld). Peekskill, NY, 8/27/52. Children's performer. *Pee-Wee's Playhouse.*
HERRMANN, EDWARD. Washington, DC, 7/21/43. Actor. *The Paper Chase.*
HERVEY, JASON. Los Angeles, CA, 4/6/72. Actor. Wayne Arnold on *The Wonder Years.*
HESSEMAN, HOWARD. Salem, OR, 2/27/40. Actor. Dr. Johnny Fever on *WKRP in Cincinnati.*
HESTON, CHARLTON (Charles Carter). Evanston, IL, 10/4/24. Actor. *The Ten Commandments.*
HETFIELD, JAMES. 8/3/63. Singer, guitarist. Metallica.
HEWETT, HOWARD. Akron, OH, 10/1/55. Singer. Shalamar.
HEYWARD, NICK. 5/20/61. Guitarist, singer. Haircut 100.
HICKS, CATHERINE. New York, NY, 8/6/51. Actor. *Peggy Sue Got Married.*
HICKS, TONY. Nelson, England, 12/16/43. Guitarist. The Hollies.
HILL, ANITA. Tulsa, OK, 7/30/56. Lawyer, law professor. Accused Supreme Court nominee Clarence Thomas of sexual harrassment.
HILL, ARTHUR. Saskatchewan, Canada, 8/1/22. Actor. *Owen Marshall, Counsellor at Law.*
HILL, DAVE. Fleet Castle, England, 4/4/52. Guitarist. Slade.
HILL, DUSTY. Dallas, TX, 5/19/49. Bassist, singer. ZZ Top.
HILL, STEVEN. Seattle, WA, 2/24/22. Actor. *Law and Order.*
HILLERMAN, JOHN. Denison, TX, 12/20/32. Actor. Jonathan Quayle Higgins III on *Magnum P.I.*
HILLERMAN, TONY. Sacred Heart, OK, 5/27/25. Novelist.
HILLMAN, CHRIS. Los Angeles, CA, 12/4/44. Singer, bassist. The Byrds.
HINES, GREGORY. New York, NY, 2/14/46. Actor, dancer. *The Cotton Club.*
HINGLE, PAT. Denver, CO, 7/19/23. Actor. *Gunsmoke.*
HINSLEY, HARVEY. Northampton, England, 1/19/48. Guitarist. Hot Chocolate.
HIRSCH, GARY "CHICKEN." England, 1940. Drummer. Country Joe & The Fish.

HIRSCH, JUDD. New York, NY, 3/15/35. Actor. Alex Rieger on *Taxi*.
HITCHCOCK, RUSSELL. 6/15/49. Singer. Air Supply.
HO, DON. Kakaako, HI, 8/13/30. Singer. "Tiny Bubbles."
HOBBS, RANDY. 3/22/48. Bassist. The McCoys.
HODGE, PATRICIA. Lincolnshire, England, 9/29/46. Actor. *The Elephant Man.*
HODGSON, ROGER. Portsmouth, England, 3/21/50. Guitarist. Supertramp.
HODO, DAVID. 7/7/50. Singer. The Village People.
HOFFS, SUSANNA. Newport Beach, CA, 1/17/57. Guitarist, singer. The Bangles.
HOGAN, HULK (Terry Gene Bollea). Augusta, GA, 8/11/53. Wrestler, former World Federation heavyweight champion.
HOGAN, PAUL. Lightning Ridge, Australia, 10/8/39. Actor. *Crocodile Dundee.*
HOLBROOK, HAL. Cleveland, OH, 2/17/25. Actor. *All the President's Men.*
HOLDER, NODDY (Neville Holder). Walsall, England, 6/15/50. Guitarist, singer. Slade.
HOLLAND, JOOLS (Julian Holland). 1/24/58. Keyboardist. Squeeze.
HOLLIMAN, EARL. Delhi, LA, 9/11/28. Actor. *Police Woman.*
HOLLIS, MARK. Tottenham, England, 1955. Singer, guitarist, keyboardist. Talk Talk.
HOLM, CELESTE. New York, NY, 4/29/19. Actor. *All About Eve.*
HOLMES, LARRY. Cuthbert, GA, 11/3/49. Boxer. Heavyweight champ.
HOOK, PETER. Salford, England, 2/13/56. Bassist. Joy Division; New Order.
HOOKER, JOHN LEE. Clarksdale, MS, 8/22/17. Legendary blues guitarist, singer, songwriter.
HOOKS, JAN. 4/23/57. Actor. Carlene Frazier Dobber on *Designing Women.*
HOPE, BOB (Leslie Hope). Eltham, England, 5/29/03. Actor, performer for overseas troops. *The Road* movies with Bing Crosby.
HOPE, DAVE. Kansas, 10/7/49. Bassist. Kansas.
HOPKIN, MARY. Pontardawe, Wales, 5/3/50. Singer, discovered by the Beatles. "Those Were the Days."
HOPKINS, TELMA. Louisville, KY, 10/28/48. Singer, actor, former member of Tony Orlando & Dawn. *Family Matters.*
HOPPER, DENNIS. Dodge City, KS, 5/17/36. Actor, director. *Easy Rider.*
HOPPER, SEAN. California, 3/31/53. Keyboardist. Huey Lewis & The News.
HOPWOOD, KEITH. Manchester, England, 10/26/46. Guitarist. Herman's Hermits.
HORNE, LENA. Brooklyn, NY, 6/30/17. Singer, actor.
HORNSBY, BRUCE. Williamsburg, VA, 11/23/54. Singer, keyboardist, accordionist. Bruce Hornsby & The Range.
HOSKINS, BOB. Bury St. Edmunds, England, 10/26/42. Actor. *Who Framed Roger Rabbit.*
HOWARD, ALAN. Dagenham, England, 10/17/41. Bassist. Brian Poole & The Tremeloes.
HOWARD, ARLISS. Independence, MO, 1955. Actor. *Full Metal Jacket.*
HOWARD, KEN. El Centro, CA, 3/28/44. Actor. *The White Shadow.*
HOWARD, RON. Duncan, OK, 3/1/54. Actor, director. Richie Cunningham on *Happy Days.*
HOWE, STEVE. London, England, 4/8/47. Guitarist, singer. Yes; Asia.
HUCKNALL, MICK "RED." Manchester, England, 6/8/60. Singer. Simply Red.
HUDLIN, REGINALD. Centerville, IL, 12/15/61. Director, writer, producer. Brother of Warrington. *House Party.*
HUDLIN, WARRINGTON. East St. Louis, IL, 1952. Producer, director. Brother of Reginald. *House Party.*
HUDSON, GARTH. London, Canada, 8/2/37. Organist. The Band.
HUGG, MIKE. Andover, England, 8/11/42. Drummer. Manfred Mann.
HUGHES, GLENN. 7/18/50. Singer. The Village People.
HULCE, TOM. White Water, WI, 12/6/53. Actor. *Amadeus.*
HUMAN BEATBOX (Darren Robinson). 6/10/67. Rap artist. Fat Boys.
HUMPERDINCK, ENGELBERT (Arnold Dorsey). Madras, India, 5/2/36. Pop singer. *The Engelbert Humperdinck Show.*
HUMPHREYS, PAUL. London, England, 2/27/60. Keyboardist. Orchestral Manoeuvres in the Dark (OMD).
HUNT, BILL. 5/23/47. Keyboardist. Electric Light Orchestra (ELO).
HUNT, LINDA. Morristown, NJ, 4/2/45. Actor. *The Year of Living Dangerously.*
HUNTER, IAN. Shrewsbury, England, 6/3/46. Singer, guitarist. Mott The Hoople.
HUNTER, TAB (Arthur Gelien). New York, NY, 7/11/31. Actor. *Damn Yankees.*
HUPPERT, ISABELLE. Paris, France, 3/16/55. Actor. *Entre Nous.*
HURT, JOHN. Shirebrook, England, 1/22/40. Actor. *The Elephant Man.*
HURT, MARY BETH (Mary Beth Supinger). Marshalltown, IA, 9/26/48. Actor, formerly married to William Hurt. *The World According to Garp.*
HURT, WILLIAM. Washington, DC, 3/20/50. Actor, formerly married to Mary Beth Hurt. *Children of a Lesser God.*
HUSSEIN, SADDAM. Tikrit, Iraq, 4/28/37. Leader of Iraq.
HUSSEY, WAYNE. 5/26/59. Guitarist, singer. The Mission.
HUSTON, ANJELICA. Santa Monica, CA, 7/8/51. Actor, daughter of John Huston. *Prizzi's Honor.*
HUTCHENCE, MICHAEL. Sydney, Australia, 1/22/60. Singer. INXS.
HUTTER, RALF. Krefeld, Germany, 1946. Keyboardist, drummer, singer. Kraftwerk.
HUTTON, DANNY. Buncrana, Ireland, 9/10/46. Singer. Three Dog Night.
HUTTON, LAUREN (Mary Hutton). Charleston, SC, 11/17/43. Actor, model. *American Gigolo.*
HUTTON, TIMOTHY. Malibu, CA, 8/16/60. Actor, director. *Ordinary People.*
HUXLEY, RICK. Dartford, England, 8/5/42. Guitarist. The Dave Clark Five.
IACOCCA, LEE (Lido Anthony Iacocca). Allentown, PA, 10/15/24. Auto executive, author. *Iacocca.*
IAN, JANIS (Janis Fink). New York, NY, 4/7/51. Folk/rock singer, songwriter.
IDLE, ERIC. Durham, England, 3/29/43. Actor. *Monty Python's Flying Circus.*
IDOL, BILLY (Billy Broad). Stanmore, England, 11/30/55. Singer, songwriter.
IGLESIAS, JULIO. Madrid, Spain, 9/23/43. Pop singer, songwriter.
ILLSLEY, JOHN. Leicester, England, 6/24/49. Bassist. Dire Straits.
IMAN. Mogadishu, Somalia, 7/25/55. Model, married to David Bowie.
INGELS, MARTY. Brooklyn, NY, 3/9/36. Actor, agent, married to Shirley Jones. *The Pruitts of Southampton.*
INGLE, DOUG. Omaha, NE, 9/9/46. Singer, keyboardist. Iron Butterfly.
INGRAM, JAMES. Akron, OH, 2/16/56. R&B singer, songwriter.
INNES, NEIL. Essex, England, 12/9/44. Singer, keyboardist. The Bonzo Dog Doo-Dah Band.
INNIS, ROY. Saint Croix, Virgin Islands, 6/6/34. Civil rights leader.
IOMMI, TONY. Birmingham, England, 2/19/48. Guitarist. Black Sabbath.
IRELAND, PATRICIA. Oak Park, IL, 10/19/45. Political activist. President of NOW.
IRVING, AMY. Palo Alto, CA, 9/10/53. Actor. *Yentl.*
IRWIN, BILL. Santa Monica, CA, 4/11/50. Actor. *Eight Men Out.*
ISLEY, O'KELLY. Cincinnati, OH, 12/25/37. Singer. The Isley Brothers.
ISLEY, RONALD. Cincinnati, OH, 5/21/41. Lead singer. The Isley Brothers.
ISLEY, RUDOLPH. Cincinnati, OH, 4/1/39. Singer. The Isley Brothers.
IVEY, JUDITH. El Paso, TX, 9/4/51. Actor. *Designing Women.*
IVORY, JAMES. Berkeley, CA, 6/7/28. Director, producer. *Howard's End.*
JABS, MATTHIAS. 10/25/56. Guitarist. Scorpions.
JACKEE (JACKEE HARRY). Winston-Salem, NC, 8/14/56. Actor. *227.*
JACKSON, EDDIE. 1/29/61. Bassist, singer. Queensryche.
JACKSON, FREDDIE. New York, NY, 10/2/56. R&B singer, songwriter.
JACKSON, GLENDA. Birkenhead, England, 5/9/36. Actor. *Women in Love.*
JACKSON, JACKIE (Sigmund Jackson). Gary, IN, 5/4/51. Singer, brother of Michael and Janet Jackson. The Jacksons.
JACKSON, JERMAINE. Gary, IN, 12/11/54. Singer, brother of Michael and Janet. The Jacksons.
JACKSON, JOE. Burton-on-Trent, England, 8/11/55. Singer, songwriter.

JACKSON, KATE. Birmingham, AL, 10/29/48. Actor. Sabrina Duncan on *Charlie's Angels*.
JACKSON, MARLON. Gary, IN, 3/12/57. Singer, brother of Michael and Janet. The Jacksons.
JACKSON, PERVIS. 5/17/38. Singer. The (Detroit) Spinners.
JACKSON, TITO (Toriano Jackson). Gary, IN, 10/15/53. Singer, brother of Michael and Janet. The Jacksons.
JACKSON, TONY. Liverpool, England, 7/16/40. Singer, bassist. The Searchers.
JACKSON, VICTORIA. Miami, FL, 8/2/58. Actor. *Saturday Night Live*.
JACOBI, DEREK. London, England, 10/22/38. Actor. *The Day of the Jackal*.
JACOBI, LOU. Toronto, Canada, 12/28/13. Actor. *Irma La Douce*.
JAGGER, BIANCA. Managua, Nicaragua, 5/2/45. Socialite, actor. Divorced from Mick Jagger.
JAM MASTER JAY (Jason Mizell). New York, NY, 1965. DJ. Run-D.M.C.
JAMES, CLIFTON. Portland, OR, 5/29/25. Actor. *Cool Hand Luke*.
JAMES, ETTA. Los Angeles, CA, 1938. Singer. Bridged R&B and rock.
JAMES, RICK (James Johnson). Buffalo, NY, 2/1/52. Funk singer, songwriter. "Super Freak."
JAMES, TOMMY (Tommy Jackson). Dayton, OH, 4/29/47. Singer. Tommy James & The Shondells.
JANIS, CONRAD. New York, NY, 2/11/28. Actor, musician. Frederick McConnell on *Mork and Mindy*.
JARDINE, AL. Lima, OH, 9/3/42. Guitarist, singer. The Beach Boys.
JARREAU, AL. Milwaukee, WI, 3/12/40. Jazz singer, sang theme song to *Moonlighting*.
JAZZIE B. (Beresford Romeo). England, 1/26/63. Rap artist. Soul II Soul.
JEFFRIES, LIONEL. London, England, 6/10/26. Actor, director. *The Water Babies*.
JENNER, BRUCE. Mount Kisco, NY, 10/28/49. Track athlete, sportscaster. Olympic gold medalist.
JENNINGS, WAYLON. Littlefield, TX, 6/15/37. Country singer, songwriter. *The Dukes of Hazzard* theme song.
JETER, MICHAEL. Lawrenceburg, TN, 8/26/52. Actor. *Evening Shade*.
JETT, JOAN. Philadelphia, PA, 9/22/60. Singer, guitarist. "I Love Rock 'n' Roll."
JILLIAN, ANNE (Anne Nauseda). Cambridge, MA, 1/29/51. Actor. *It's a Living*.
JOHANSEN, DAVID. Staten Island, NY, 1/9/50. Actor, singer, a.k.a. Buster Poindexter. *Scrooged*.
JOHN, DR. (Malcolm Rebennack). New Orleans, LA, 11/21/40. Rock/cajun/ blues singer, songwriter. "Right Place Wrong Time."
JOHN PAUL II, POPE. Wadowice, Poland, 5/18/20. First non-Italian pope since the Renaissance.
JOHNS, GLYNIS. Durban, South Africa, 10/5/23. Actor. *Glynis*.
JOHNSON, ARTE. Benton Harbor, MI, 1/20/34. Actor. *Laugh-In*.
JOHNSON, BEN. Pawhuska, OK, 6/13/18. Actor. *The Last Picture Show*.
JOHNSON, HOLLY (William Johnson). Khartoum, Sudan, 2/19/60. Singer. Frankie Goes to Hollywood.
JOHNSON, HOWIE. Washington, DC, 1938. Drummer. The Ventures.
JOHNSON, LADY BIRD. Karnack, TX, 12/22/12. Former First Lady, wife of Lyndon.
JOHNSON, MATT. 8/15/61. Singer, guitarist. The The.
JOHNSON, VAN. Newport, RI, 8/25/16. Actor. *The Caine Mutiny*.
JOHNSON, WILKO (John Wilkinson). 1947. Guitarist. Dr. Feelgood.
JON, JOHN. 2/26/61. Musician. Bronski Beat.
JONES, ALAN. Swansea, Wales, 2/6/47. Baritone saxophonist. Amen Corner.
JONES, BOOKER T. Memphis, TN, 12/11/44. Keyboardist. Booker T. & The MG's.
JONES, DAVY. Manchester, England, 12/30/45. Singer, actor. The Monkees.
JONES, DEAN. Decatur, AL, 1/25/31. Actor. *The Shaggy D.A.*
JONES, GRACE. Spanishtown, Jamaica, 5/19/52. Singer, actor. *A View to a Kill*.
JONES, GRAHAM. 7/8/61. Guitarist. Haircut 100.
JONES, HOWARD. Southampton, England, 2/23/55. Singer, songwriter.
JONES, JAMES EARL. Arkabutla, MS, 1/17/31. Actor, voice of Darth Vader. *The Great White Hope*.
JONES, JEFFREY. Buffalo, NY, 9/28/47. Actor. Principal Ed Rooney in *Ferris Bueller's Day Off*.
JONES, JENNIFER (Phyllis Isley). Tulsa, OK, 3/2/19. Actor. *The Song of Bernadette*.
JONES, JOHN PAUL (John Paul Baldwin). Sidcup, England, 6/3/46. Bassist. Led Zeppelin.
JONES, KENNY. London, England, 9/16/48. Drummer. The Small Faces.
JONES, MICK. Brixton, England, 6/26/55. Guitarist, singer. The Clash; Big Audio Dynamite.
JONES, MICK. London, England, 12/27/44. Guitarist. Foreigner.
JONES, NEIL. Llanbradach, Wales, 3/25/49. Guitarist. Amen Corner.
JONES, PAUL (Paul Pond). Portsmouth, England, 2/24/42. Singer, harmonicist. Manfred Mann.
JONES, RANDY. 9/13/52. Singer. The Village People.
JONES, RAY. Oldham, England, 10/22/39. Bassist. Billy J. Kramer & The Dakotas.
JONES, RICKIE LEE. Chicago, IL, 11/8/54. Rock/jazz singer songwriter.
JONES, SAM J. Chicago, IL, 8/12/54. Actor. *Flash Gordon*.
JONES, SHIRLEY. Smithton, PA, 3/31/34. Actor, married to Marty Ingels. *The Partridge Family*.
JONES, STEVE. London, England, 9/3/55. Guitarist. The Sex Pistols.
JONES, TERRY. Colwyn Bay, Wales, 2/1/42. Actor, director, writer. *Monty Python's Life of Brian*.
JONES, TOM (Tom Woodward). Pontypridd, Wales, 6/7/40. Pop singer.
JORDAN, LONNIE (Leroy Jordan). San Diego, CA, 11/21/48. Keyboardist, singer. War.
JOURARD, JEFF. 1955. Guitarist. The Motels.
JOURDAN, LOUIS (Louis Gendre). Marseilles, France, 6/19/20. Actor. *Gigi*.
JOYCE, MIKE. Manchester, England, 6/1/63. Drummer. The Smiths.
JOYNER-KERSEE, JACKIE. St. Louis, IL, 3/3/62. Track athlete. Olympic gold medalist.
JUDD, NAOMI (Diana Judd). Ashland, KY, 1/11/46. Country singer, mother of Wynonna and Ashley. The Judds.
JULIA, RAUL. San Juan, PR, 3/9/40. Actor. *The Addams Family*.
JUMP, GORDON. Dayton, OH, 4/1/27. Actor. Arthur Carlson on *WKRP in Cincinnati*.
JUSTMAN, SETH. Washington, DC, 1/27/51. Keyboardist, singer. The J. Geils Band.
KAHN, MADELINE. Boston, MA, 9/29/42. Actor. *Blazing Saddles*.
KALE, JIM. 8/11/43. Bassist. The Guess Who.
KANE, BIG DADDY. New York, NY, 9/10/68. Rap artist, songwriter. "Long Live the Kane."
KANE, CAROL. Cleveland, OH, 6/18/52. Actor. Simka Graves on *Taxi*.
KANTNER, PAUL. San Francisco, CA, 3/12/42. Guitarist. Jefferson Airplane; Starship.
KAPRISKY, VALERIE. Paris, France, 1963. Actor. *Breathless*.
KARPOV, ANATOLY. Zlatoust, Russia, 5/23/51. Chess player. International grandmaster, world champion.
KARRAS, ALEX. Gary, IN, 7/15/35. Former football player, actor. *Webster*.
KASPAROV, GARRY. Baku, Russia, 4/13/63. Chess player. International grandmaster, world champion.
KATH, TERRY. Chicago, IL, 1/31/46. Guitarist. Chicago.
KATT, WILLIAM. Los Angeles, CA, 2/16/55. Actor, son of Barbara Hale. *The Greatest American Hero*.
KATZ, STEVE. New York, NY, 5/9/45. Guitarist, harmonicist, singer. Blood, Sweat & Tears.
KAUKONEN, JORMA. Washington, DC, 12/23/40. Guitarist. Jefferson Airplane; Hot Tuna.
KAVNER, JULIE. Los Angeles, CA, 9/7/51. Actor. Voice of Marge Simpson on *The Simpsons; Rhoda*.
KAY, JOHN (Joachim Krauledat). Tilsit, Germany, 4/12/44. Guitarist, singer. Steppenwolf.
KAYE, STUBBY. New York, NY, 11/11/18. Actor. *Guys and Dolls*.
KAYLAN, HOWARD (Howard Kaplan). New York, NY, 6/22/47. Singer, saxophonist. The Turtles.
KAZURINSKY, TIM. Johnstown, PA, 3/3/50. Actor. *Saturday Night Live*.
KEACH, STACY (William Keach Jr.). Savannah, GA, 6/2/41. Actor. *Mickey Spillane's Mike Hammer*.
KEANE, BIL. Philadelphia, PA, 10/5/22. Cartoonist. *The Family Circus*.
KEATON, DIANE (Diane Hall). Los Angeles, CA, 1/5/46. Actor. *Annie Hall*.

KEATON, MICHAEL (Michael Douglas). Coraopolis, PA, 9/9/51. Actor. *Batman.*
KEEBLE, JON. London, England, 7/6/59. Drummer. Spandau Ballet.
KEEL, HOWARD (Harold Leek). Gillespie, IL, 4/13/19. Actor. Clayton Farlow on *Dallas.*
KEENAN, BRIAN. New York, NY, 1/28/44. Drummer. The Chambers Brothers; Manfred Mann.
KEESHAN, BOB (Robert James Keeshan). Lynbrook, NY, 6/27/27. TV personality, author. *Captain Kangaroo.*
KEFFORD, ACE (Christopher Kefford). Mosely, England, 12/10/46. Bassist. The Move.
KEITH, BRIAN. Bayonne, NJ, 11/14/21. Actor. Bill Davis on *Family Affair.*
KEITH, DAVID LEMUEL. Knoxville, TN, 5/8/54. Actor. *An Officer and a Gentleman.*
KELLER, MARTHE. Basel, Switzerland, 1/28/45. Actor. *Marathon Man.*
KELLERMAN, SALLY. Long Beach, CA, 6/2/37. Actor. Hot Lips in the movie *M*A*S*H.*
KELLEY, DEFOREST. Atlanta, GA, 1/20/20. Actor. Dr. Leonard "Bones" McCoy on *Star Trek.*
KELLEY, KITTY. Spokane, WA, 4/4/42. Unauthorized biographer.
KELLING, GRAEME. Paisley, Scotland, 4/4/57. Guitarist. Deacon Blue.
KELLY, GENE. Pittsburgh, PA, 8/23/12. Actor, dancer, director. *Singin' in the Rain.*
KELLY, MARK. Dublin, Ireland, 4/9/61. Keyboardist. Marillion.
KELLY, MOIRA. 1968. Actor. *The Cutting Edge.*
KEMP, GARY. Islington, England, 10/16/60. Guitarist, brother of Martin. Spandau Ballet.
KEMP, MARTIN. London, England, 10/10/61. Bassist, brother of Gary. Spandau Ballet.
KENDRICKS, EDDIE. Birmingham, AL, 12/17/39. Singer. The Temptations.
KENNEDY, GEORGE. New York, NY, 2/18/25. Actor. *Cool Hand Luke.*
KENNEDY, TED. Brookline, MA, 2/22/32. Politician, brother of John and Robert.
KENNIBREW, DEE DEE (Dolores Henry). Brooklyn, NY, 1945. Singer. The Crystals.
KENNY G. 6/5/56. Jazz saxophone player.
KENSIT, PATSY. London, England, 3/4/68. Actor. *Lethal Weapon 2.*
KERNS, JOANNA (Joanna De Varona). San Francisco, CA, 2/12/53. Actor. Maggie Seaver on *Growing Pains.*
KERR, DEBORAH. Helensburg, Scotland, 9/30/21. Actor. *The King and I.*
KERR, JIM. Glasgow, Scotland, 7/9/59. Singer. Simple Minds.
KHAN, CHAKA (Yvette Marie Stevens). Great Lakes, IL, 3/23/53. Singer. Rufus.
KIDD, JOHNNY (Frederick Heath). London, England, 12/23/39. Singer. Johnny Kidd & The Pirates.
KIDDER, MARGOT. Yellow Knife, Canada, 10/17/48. Actor. Lois Lane in *Superman.*
KIEL, RICHARD. Detroit, MI, 9/13/39. Actor. Jaws in *The Spy Who Loved Me.*
KILMER, VAL. Los Angeles, CA, 12/31/59. Actor, married to Joanne Whalley-Kilmer. Jim Morrison in *The Doors.*
KILPATRICK, JAMES JR. Oklahoma City, OK, 11/1/20. Journalist. *60 Minutes.*
KIMBALL, BOBBY (Bobby Toteaux). Vinton, LA, 3/29/94. Lead singer. Toto.
KING, ALAN (Irwin Kniberg). Brooklyn, NY, 12/26/27. Producer. *The Andersen Tapes.*
KING, B. B. (Riley King). Itta Bena, MS, 9/16/25. Legendary blues guitarist, singer, songwriter.
KING, BEN E. (Ben E. Nelson). Henderson, NC, 9/23/38. Singer. The Drifters.
KING, BILLIE JEAN. Long Beach, CA, 11/22/43. Tennis player.
KING, CAROLE (Carole Klein). Brooklyn, NY, 2/9/40. Singer, songwriter.
KING, CORETTA SCOTT. Marion, AL, 4/27/27. Author, lecturer, widow of Martin Luther King Jr.
KING, DON. Cleveland, OH, 8/20/31. Boxing promoter.
KING, MARK. Isle of Wight, England, 10/20/58. Singer, bassist. Level 42.
KING, PERRY. Alliance, OH, 4/30/48. Actor. Cody Allen on *Riptide.*
KING, WILLIAM. Alabama, 1/30/49. Trumpeter, keyboardist. The Commodores.
KINGSLEY, BEN (Krishna Bhanji). Snaiton, England, 12/31/43. Actor. *Gandhi.*
KINSKI, NASTASSJA (Nastassja Naksszynski). Berlin, Germany, 1/24/60. Actor. *Cat People.*
KIRBY, BRUNO (Bruce Kirby Jr.). New York, NY, 4/28/49. Actor. *City Slickers.*
KIRKE, SIMON. Wales, 7/28/49. Drummer. Bad Company; Free.
KIRKLAND, SALLY. New York, NY, 10/31/44. Actor. *Anna.*
KIRKMAN, TERRY. Salina, KS, 12/12/41. Singer, keyboardist. The Association.
KIRKPATRICK, JEANE. Duncan, OK, 11/19/26. Diplomat. Former U.S. representative to the U.N.
KISSINGER, HENRY. Fuerth, Germany, 5/27/23. Richard Nixon's secretary of state.
KITT, EARTHA. North, SC, 1/26/28. Actor, singer. *The Mark of the Hawk.*
KLEIN, DANNY. New York, NY, 5/13/46. Bassist. The J. Geils Band.
KLEIN, ROBERT. New York, NY, 2/8/42. Actor. *Comedy Tonight.*
KLEMPERER, WERNER. Cologne, Germany, 3/22/20. Actor. Colonel Wilhelm Klink on *Hogan's Heroes.*
KLINE, KEVIN. St. Louis, MO, 10/24/47. Actor, married to Phoebe Cates. *The Big Chill.*
KLUGMAN, JACK. Philadelphia, PA, 4/27/22. Actor. Oscar Madison on *The Odd Couple.*
KNIGHT, GLADYS. Atlanta, GA, 5/28/44. Singer. Gladys Knight & The Pips.
KNIGHT, JONATHAN. Boston, MA, 11/29/69. Singer. New Kids on the Block.
KNIGHT, JORDAN. Boston, MA, 5/17/71. Singer. New Kids on the Block.
KNIGHT, MERALD. Atlanta, GA, 9/4/42. Singer. Gladys Knight & The Pips.
KNIGHT, MICHAEL E. Princeton, NJ, 5/7/59. Actor. Tad Martin on *All My Children.*
KNIGHT, SHIRLEY. Goessell, KS, 7/5/36. Actor. *The Dark at the Top of the Stairs.*
KNIGHTS, DAVE. Islington, England, 6/28/45. Bassist. Procol Harum.
KNOPFLER, DAVID. Glasgow, Scotland, 12/27/52. Guitarist. Dire Straits.
KNOPFLER, MARK. Glasgow, Scotland, 8/12/49. Singer, guitarist. Dire Straits.
KNOTTS, DON. Morgantown, WV, 7/21/24. Actor. Barney Fife on *The Andy Griffith Show.*
KNOWLES, PATRIC (Reginald Lawrence Knowles). Horsforth, England, 11/11/11. Actor. *How Green Was My Valley.*
KNOX, ALEXANDER. Strathroy, Canada, 1/16/07. Actor. *Gorky Park.*
KNOX, BUDDY (Wayne Knox). Happy, TX, 4/14/33. Rock/country singer, songwriter.
KNUDSEN, KEITH. Ames, IA, 10/18/52. Drummer, singer. The Doobie Brothers.
KOCH, ED. New York, NY, 12/12/24. Former mayor of New York.
KOENIG, WALTER. Chicago, IL, 9/14/36. Actor, writer, director, producer. Pavel Chekov on *Star Trek.*
KOOL ROCK. (Damon Wimbley). 11/4/66. Rap artist. Fat Boys.
KOPELL, BERNIE. New York, NY, 6/21/33. Actor. Dr. Adam Bricker on *The Love Boat.*
KORMAN, HARVEY. Chicago, IL, 2/15/27. Actor. *The Carol Burnett Show.*
KOSSOFF, PAUL. London, England, 9/14/50. Guitarist. Free.
KOTTO, YAPHET. New York, NY, 11/15/37. Actor. *Live and Let Die.*
KRABBE, JEROEN. Amsterdam, The Netherlands, 12/5/44. Actor. *The Fugitive.*
KRAMER, BILLY J. (Billy J. Ashton). Bootle, England, 8/19/43. Singer. Billy J. Kramer & The Dakotas.
KRAMER, JOEY. New York, NY, 6/21/50. Drummer. Aerosmith.
KRANTZ, JUDITH. New York, NY, 1/9/28. Novelist. *Scruples.*
KRAVITZ, LENNY. New York, NY, 1964. Singer, songwriter. "Are You Gonna Go My Way?"
KREUTZMANN, BILL JR. Palo Alto, CA, 5/7/46. Drummer. Grateful Dead.
KRIEGER, ROBBIE. Los Angeles, CA, 1/8/46. Guitarist. The Doors.
KRIGE, ALICE. Upington, South Africa, 6/28/55. Actor. *Chariots of Fire.*
KRISTOFFERSON, KRIS. Brownsville, TX, 6/22/36. Singer, songwriter, actor. *Amerika.*
KUBRICK, STANLEY. The Bronx, NY, 7/26/28. Director, producer, writer. *2001: A Space Odyssey.*
KUHLKE, NORMAN. Liverpool, England, 6/17/42. Drummer. The Swinging Blue Jeans.

KURALT, CHARLES. Wilmington, NC, 9/10/34. News reporter, commentator. *On the Road with Charles Kuralt.*
KURTZ, SWOOSIE. Omaha, NE, 9/6/44. Actor. *Sisters.*
KWAN, NANCY. Hong Kong, 5/19/39. Actor. *The World of Suzie Wong.*
LABELLE, PATTI (Patricia Holt). Philadelphia, PA, 5/24/44. Pop/soul singer.
LADD, CHERYL (Cheryl Stoppelmoor). Huron, SD, 7/12/51. Actor. Kris Munroe on *Charlie's Angels.*
LADD, DIANE (Diane Ladner). Meridian, MS, 11/29/32. Actor, mother of Laura Dern. *Alice Doesn't Live Here Anymore.*
LAHTI, CHRISTINE. Birmingham, MI, 4/4/50. Actor. *Swing Shift.*
LAINE, DENNY (Brian Hines). England, 10/29/44. Singer, guitarist. The Moody Blues.
LAKE, GREG. Bournemouth, England, 11/10/48. Bassist, singer. Emerson, Lake & Palmer; King Crimson.
LAMARR, HEDY (Hedwig Kiesler). Vienna, Austria, 9/11/15. Actor. *Ecstasy.*
LAMAS, LORENZO. Los Angeles, CA, 1/20/58. Actor. Lance Cumson on *Falcon Crest.*
LAMBERT, CHRISTOPHER. New York, NY, 3/29/57. Actor. *Greystoke: The Legend of Tarzan, Lord of the Apes.*
LAMM, ROBERT. New York, NY, 10/13/44. Singer, keyboardist. Chicago.
LAMOUR, DOROTHY (Mary Dorothy Slaton). New Orleans, LA, 12/10/14. Actor. *Road to Singapore.*
LANCASTER, ALAN. London, England, 2/7/49. Bassist. Status Quo.
LANCASTER, BURT. New York, NY, 11/2/13. Actor. *From Here to Eternity.*
LANDAU, MARTIN. Brooklyn, NY, 6/20/31. Actor. *Mission: Impossible.*
LANDERS, AUDREY. Philadelphia, PA, 7/18/59. Actor. Afton Cooper on *Dallas.*
LANDESBERG, STEVE. The Bronx, NY, 11/3/45. Actor. Detective Arthur Dietrich on *Barney Miller.*
LANDIS, JOHN. Chicago, IL, 8/3/50. Director. *Twilight Zone—The Movie.*
LANE, ABBE. Brooklyn, NY, 12/14/35. Actor, formerly married to Xavier Cugat. *Xavier Cugat Show.*
LANE, CHARLES. New York, NY, 12/5/53. Director. *Sidewalk Stories.*
LANE, DIANE. New York, NY, 1/22/65. Actor. *Rumble Fish.*
LANE, RONNIE. Plaistow, England, 4/1/46. Bassist. The Small Faces.
LANG, BOB. Manchester, England, 1/10/46. Bassist. Wayne Fontana & The Mindbenders.
LANGE, HOPE. Redding Ridge, CT, 11/28/31. Actor. *The Ghost and Mrs. Muir.*
LANGE, JESSICA. Cloquet, MN, 4/20/49. Actor, cohabitant of Sam Shepard. *Tootsie.*
LANGE, TED. Oakland, CA, 1/5/47. Actor. Isaac Washington on *The Love Boat.*
LANGELLA, FRANK. Bayonne, NJ, 1/1/40. Actor. *Dracula.*
LANIER, ALLEN. 6/25/46. Guitarist, keyboardist. Blue Öyster Cult.
LANSING, ROBERT (Robert Brown). San Diego, CA, 6/5/29. Actor. *The Man Who Never Was.*
LAPREAD, RONALD. Alabama, 9/4/50. Bassist, trumpeter. The Commodores.
LARDIE, MICHAEL. 9/8/58. Musician. Great White.
LARUE, FLORENCE. Pennsylvania, 2/4/44. Singer. The 5th Dimension.
LASSER, LOUISE. New York, NY, 4/11/39. Actor, formerly married to Woody Allen. *Bananas.*
LAUDER, ESTEE. New York, NY, 7/1/08. Fashion designer.
LAUPER, CYNDI. New York, NY, 6/20/53. Singer, actor, professional wrestling promoter. *She's So Unusual.*
LAURENT, YVES SAINT. Oran, Algeria, 8/1/36. Fashion designer.
LAURIE, PIPER (Rosetta Jacobs). Detroit, MI, 1/22/32. Actor. Mother in *Carrie.*
LAVERN, ROGER (Roger Jackson). Kidderminster, England, 11/11/38. Keyboardist. The Tornados.
LAVIN, LINDA. Portland, ME, 10/15/39. Actor, singer. *Alice.*
LAWRENCE, CAROL (Carol Laraia). Melrose Park, IL, 9/5/35. Actor, singer. *West Side Story.*
LAWRENCE, JOEY. Montgomery, PA, 4/20/76. Actor, singer. *Blossom.*
LAWRENCE, VICKI. Inglewood, CA, 3/26/49. Actor. *Mama's Family.*
LAWSON, LEIGH. Atherston, England, 7/21/45. Actor. *Tess.*
LAWTON, JOHN. 6/11/46. Singer. Uriah Heep.
LEA, JIMMY. Melbourne Arms, England, 6/14/52. Bassist, keyboardist, violinist. Slade.
LEACH, ROBIN. London, England, 8/29/41. TV host. *Lifestyles of the Rich and Famous.*
LEACHMAN, CLORIS. Des Moines, IA, 4/30/30. Actor. Phyllis Lyndstrom on *The Mary Tyler Moore Show.*
LEADON, BERNIE. Minneapolis, MN, 7/19/47. Guitarist, singer. The Eagles.
LEAR, FRANCES. Hudson, NY, 7/14/23. Magazine editor, formerly married to Norman. Founder of *Lear's.*
LEAR, NORMAN. New Haven, CT, 7/27/22. Producer, director, formerly married to Frances. *All in the Family.*
LEARNED, MICHAEL. Washington, DC, 4/9/29. Actor. Olivia on *The Waltons.*
LEBON, SIMON. Bushey, England, 10/27/58. Lead singer. Duran Duran.
LECKENBY, DEREK. Leeds, England, 5/14/46. Lead guitarist. Herman's Hermits.
LEE, ALVIN. Nottingham, England, 12/19/44. Guitarist, singer. Ten Years After.
LEE, ARTHUR. Memphis, TN, 1945. Guitarist, singer. Love.
LEE, BARBARA. New York, NY, 5/16/47. Singer. The Chiffons.
LEE, BEVERLY. Passaic, NJ, 8/3/41. Singer. The Shirelles.
LEE, BRENDA (Brenda Tarpley). Lithonia, GA, 12/11/44. Singer.
LEE, GEDDY. Willowdale, Canada, 7/29/53. Singer, bassist. Rush.
LEE, JASON SCOTT. Los Angeles, CA, 1966. Actor. *Dragon: The Bruce Lee Story.*
LEE, JOHNNY. Texas City, TX, 7/3/46. Singer. "Lookin' for Love."
LEE, MICHELE (Michele Dusiak). Los Angeles, CA, 6/24/42. Actor. Karen Fairgate MacKenzie on *Knots Landing.*
LEE, PEGGY (Norma Delores Egstrom). Jamestown, ND, 5/26/20. Actor, singer. *The Jazz Singer.*
LEE, RIC. Cannock, England, 10/20/45. Drummer. Ten Years After.
LEE, STAN. New York, NY, 12/28/22. Artist, writer, Marvel Comics legend.
LEE, TOMMY (Tommy Bass). Athens, Greece, 10/3/62. Drummer. Mötley Crüe.
LEEDS, GARY. Glendale, CA, 9/3/44. Drummer. The Walker Brothers.
LEESE, HOWARD. Los Angeles, CA, 6/13/51. Keyboardist, guitarist. Heart.
LEEVES, JANE. East Grinstead, England, 1963. Actor. Daphne Moon on *Frasier.*
LEEWAY, JOE. London, England, 1957. Percussionist. Thompson Twins.
LEGUIZAMO, JOHN. Bogota, Columbia, 7/22/65. Actor. *Carlito's Way.*
LEIBMAN, RON. New York, NY, 10/11/37. Actor. *Kaz.*
LEIGH, JANET (Jeannette Helen Morrison). Merced, CA, 7/6/27. Actor, mother of Jamie Lee Curtis. *Psycho.*
LEITCH, DONOVAN. 8/16/68. Actor, son of folk singer Donovan, brother of Ione Skye.
LEMAT, PAUL. Rahway, NJ, 9/22/52. Actor. *American Graffiti.*
LEMIEUX, MARIO. Montreal, Canada, 10/5/65. NHL hockey player. Pittsburgh Penguins.
LEMMON, CHRIS. Los Angeles, CA, 1/22/54. Actor, son of Jack Lemmon. *Swing Shift.*
LEMMON, JACK. Boston, MA, 2/8/25. Actor, father of Chris Lemmon. *Some Like It Hot.*
LEMMY (Ian Kilmister). Stoke-on-Trent, England, 12/24/45. Bassist, singer. Motorhead.
LEMON, MEADOWLARK. Wilmington, NC, 4/25/32. Basketball player. Harlem Globetrotters.
LENNON, JULIAN. Liverpool, England, 4/8/63. Singer, songwriter, son of John Lennon.
LENNOX, ANNIE. Aberdeen, Scotland, 12/25/54. Singer, songwriter. Eurythmics.
LEONARD, ROBERT SEAN. Westwood, NJ, 2/28/69. Actor. *Dead Poets Society.*
LEONARD, SHELDON (Sheldon Bershad). New York, NY, 2/22/07. Actor. *It's a Wonderful Life.*
LEONARD, SUGAR RAY. Wilmington, NC, 5/17/56. Boxer.
LERNER, MICHAEL. Brooklyn, NY, 6/22/41. Actor. *Barton Fink.*
LESH, PHIL (Phil Chapman). Berkeley, CA, 3/15/40. Bassist. Grateful Dead.
LESTER, ROBERT "SQUIRREL." 1/13/30. Singer. The Chi-Lites.
LEVERT, EDDIE. Canton, OH, 6/16/42. Singer. The O'Jays.

LEVIN, DRAKE. Guitarist. Paul Revere & The Raiders.
LEVY, EUGENE. Hamilton, Canada, 12/17/46. Actor, writer. *SCTV.*
LEWIS, AL (Alexander Meister). New York, NY, 4/30/23. Actor. *The Munsters.*
LEWIS, CARL (Carl Frederick Carlton). Birmingham, AL, 7/1/61. Track athlete. Olympic gold medalist.
LEWIS, EMMANUEL. New York, NY, 3/9/71. Actor. Webster Long on *Webster.*
LEWIS, GARY (Gary Levitch). New York, NY, 7/31/46. Singer, drummer, son of Jerry Lewis. Gary Lewis & The Playboys.
LEWIS, HUEY (Hugh Cregg III). New York, NY, 7/5/50. Singer. Huey Lewis & The News.
LEWIS, JERRY (Joseph Levitch). Newark, NJ, 3/16/26. Actor, father of Gary Lewis. *The Nutty Professor.*
LEWIS, JERRY LEE. Ferriday, LA, 9/29/35. Legendary rock keyboardist, singer, songwriter.
LEWIS, PETER. Los Angeles, CA, 7/15/45. Guitarist, singer. Moby Grape.
LIDDY, G. GORDON. New York, NY, 11/30/30. Watergate participant, talk show host. *The G. Gordon Liddy Show.*
LIFESON, ALEX. Fernie, Canada, 8/27/53. Guitarist. Rush.
LIGHT, JUDITH. Trenton, NJ, 2/9/49. Actor. Angela on *Who's the Boss?*
LIGHTFOOT, GORDON. Orillia, Canada, 11/17/38. Folk guitarist, singer, songwriter.
LINCOLN, ABBEY (Anna Marie Woolridge). Chicago, IL, 8/6/30. Singer, actor. *For Love of Ivy.*
LINDEN, HAL (Hal Lipschitz). The Bronx, NY, 3/20/31. Actor. *Barney Miller.*
LINDES, HAL. Monterey, CA, 6/30/53. Guitarist. Dire Straits.
LINDSEY, MARK. Eugene, OR, 3/9/42. Singer, saxophonist. Paul Revere & The Raiders.
LINDUP, MIKE. 3/17/59. Keyboardist, singer. Level 42.
LINKLETTER, ART. Moose Jaw, Canada, 7/17/12. TV personality. *People Are Funny.*
LINN-BAKER, MARK. St. Louis, MO, 6/17/54. Actor. Cousin Larry Appleton on *Perfect Strangers.*
LINVILLE, LARRY. Ojai, CA, 9/29/39. Actor. Frank Burns on *M*A*S*H.*
LIOTTA, RAY. Newark, NJ, 12/18/55. Actor. *GoodFellas.*
LITHGOW, JOHN. Rochester, NY, 10/19/45. Actor. *The World According to Garp.*
LITTLE EVA. Bellhaven, NC, 6/29/45. Singer. "The Loco-Motion."
LITTLE RICHARD (Richard Penniman). Macon, GA, 12/5/35. Legendary singer, songwriter.
LIVGREN, KERRY. Kansas, 9/18/49. Guitarist. Kansas.
L.L. COOL J (James Todd Smith). New York, NY, 1/14/68. Rap artist.
LLOYD, CHRISTOPHER. Stamford, CT, 10/22/38. Actor. "Reverend Jim" Ignatowski on *Taxi.*
LLOYD, EMILY. London, England, 9/29/70. Actor. *Wish You Were Here.*
LLOYD WEBBER, ANDREW. London, England, 3/22/48. Composer, producer. *Cats.*
LOCKE, JOHN. Los Angeles, CA, 9/25/43. Keyboardist. Spirit.
LOCKE, SONDRA. Shelbyville, TN, 5/28/47. Actor. *The Gauntlet.*
LOCKHART, JUNE. New York, NY, 6/25/25. Actor. *Lost in Space.*
LOCKWOOD, GARY. Van Nuys, CA, 2/21/37. Actor. *2001: A Space Odyssey.*
LOCORRIERE, DENNIS. Union City, NJ, 6/13/49. Lead singer. Dr. Hook.
LODGE, JOHN. England, 7/20/45. Bassist. The Moody Blues.
LOFGREN, NILS. Chicago, IL, 6/21/51. Guitarist, keyboardist, singer, songwriter.
LOGGIA, ROBERT. Staten Island, NY, 1/3/30. Actor. *Mancuso, FBI.*
LOGGINS, KENNY. Everett, WA, 1/7/48. Singer, songwriter.
LOLLOBRIGIDA, GINA. Subiaco, Italy, 7/4/27. Actor. *Circus.*
LOM, HERBERT. Prague, Czechoslovakia, 1/9/17. Actor. *Spartacus.*
LONG, SHELLEY. Ft. Wayne, IN, 8/23/49. Actor. Diane Chambers on *Cheers.*
LONGMUIR, ALAN. Edinburgh, Scotland, 6/20/53. Bassist. The Bay City Rollers.
LONGMUIR, DEREK. Edinburgh, Scotland, 3/19/55. Drummer. The Bay City Rollers.
LORD, JACK (Jack Ryan). New York, NY, 12/30/30. Actor. *Hawaii Five-O.*
LORD, JON. Leicester, England, 6/9/41. Keyboardist. Deep Purple.
LOREN, SOPHIA (Sophia Scicolone). Rome, Italy, 9/20/34. Actor. *Two Women.*
LOUGANIS, GREG. El Cajon, CA, 1/29/60. Diver. Olympic gold medalist.
LOUGHNANE, LEE. Chicago, IL, 10/21/46. Trumpeter. Chicago.
LOUISE, TINA (Tina Blacker). New York, NY, 2/11/34. Actor. Ginger Grant on *Gilligan's Island.*
LOVE, MIKE. Baldwin Hills, CA, 3/15/41. Singer. The Beach Boys.
LOVELADY, DAVE. Liverpool, England, 10/16/42. Drummer. The Fourmost.
LOWE, CHAD. Dayton, OH, 1/15/68. Actor, brother of Rob Lowe. *Life Goes On.*
LOWE, CHRIS. Blackpool, England, 10/4/59. Keyboardist. Pet Shop Boys.
LUCIA, PETER. 2/2/47. Drummer. Tommy James & The Shondells.
LUCKINBILL, LAURENCE. Fort Smith, AR, 11/21/34. Actor, married to Lucie Arnaz. *The Boys in the Band.*
LUDLUM, ROBERT. New York, NY, 5/25/27. Novelist, actor, producer. *The Gemini Contenders.*
LUFT, LORNA. Los Angeles, CA, 11/21/52. Actor, half-sister of Liza Minnelli. *Where the Boys Are.*
LUKATHER, STEVE. Los Angeles, CA, 10/21/57. Lead guitarist. Toto.
LULU (Marie Lawrie). Glasgow, Scotland, 11/3/48. Singer, actor. *To Sir with Love.*
LUNDEN, JOAN. Fair Oaks, CA, 9/19/50. Broadcast journalist. *Good Morning America.*
LUNDGREN, DOLPH. Stockholm, Sweden, 11/3/59. Actor. *Rocky IV.*
LUPONE, PATTI. Northport, NY, 4/21/49. Actor. *Life Goes On.*
LUPUS, PETER. Indianapolis, IN, 6/17/37. Actor. Willie Armitage on *Mission: Impossible.*
LWIN, ANNABELLA (Myant Aye). Rangoon, Burma, 10/31/65. Singer. Bow Wow Wow.
LYDON, JOHN. London, England, 1/31/56. Singer, a.k.a. Johnny Rotten. The Sex Pistols; Public Image Ltd.
LYMON, FRANKIE. New York, NY, 9/30/42. Lead singer. Frankie Lymon & The Teenagers.
LYNCH, STAN. Gainesville, FL, 5/21/55. Drummer. Tom Petty & The Heartbreakers.
LYNGSTAD, FRIDA (Anni-Frid Lyngstad). Narvik, Sweden, 11/15/45. Singer. Abba.
LYNNE, JEFF. Birmingham, England, 12/30/47. Singer, guitarist. Electric Light Orchestra (ELO).
LYNOTT, PHIL. Dublin, Ireland, 8/20/51. Singer, bassist. Thin Lizzy.
LYONS, LEO. Standbridge, England, 11/30/43. Bassist. Ten Years After.
LYTE, MC. New York, NY, 1971. Rap artist.
MA, YO-YO. Paris, France, 10/7/55. Cello virtuoso.
MACARTHUR, JAMES. Los Angeles, CA, 12/8/37. Actor, son of Helen Hayes. Danny Williams on *Hawaii Five-O.*
MACCHIO, RALPH. Long Island, NY, 11/4/62. Actor. *The Karate Kid.*
MACCORKINDALE, SIMON. Cambridge, England, 2/12/53. Actor. *Falcon Crest.*
MACDONALD, EDDIE. St. Asaph, Wales, 11/1/59. Bassist. The Alarm.
MACDONALD, ROBIN. Nairn, Scotland, 7/18/43. Guitarist. Billy J. Kramer & The Dakotas.
MACGOWAN, SHANE. Kent, England, 12/25/57. Guitarist, singer. The Pogues.
MACGRAW, ALI. Pound Ridge, NY, 4/1/39. Actor. *Love Story.*
MACKAY, ANDY. London, England, 7/23/46. Saxophonist, woodwindist. Roxy Music.
MACKAY, DUNCAN. 7/26/50. Keyboardist. Steve Harley & Cockney Rebel.
MACLEAN, BRYAN. Los Angeles, CA, 1947. Guitarist, singer. Love.
MACLEOD, GAVIN. Mt. Kisco, NY, 2/28/31. Actor. Captain Stubing of *The Love Boat.*
MACNAUGHTON, ROBERT. New York, NY, 12/19/66. Actor. *E.T., the Extra-Terrestrial.*
MACNEE, PATRICK. London, England, 2/6/22. Actor. *The Avengers.*
MACNEIL, ROBERT. Montreal, Canada, 1/19/31. Broadcast journalist. *MacNeil/Lehrer Report.*
MACNELLY, JEFF (Jeffrey Kenneth MacNelly). New York, NY, 9/17/47. Cartoonist. *Shoe.*
MACNICOL, PETER. Dallas, TX, 4/10/54. Actor. *Sophie's Choice.*
MADIGAN, AMY. Chicago, IL, 9/11/51. Actor. *Places in the Heart.*
MADSEN, MICHAEL. Chicago, IL, 1959. Actor, brother of Virginia. *Reservoir Dogs.*

MADSEN, VIRGINIA. Winnetka, IL, 9/11/63. Actor, sister of Michael. *Electric Dreams.*
MAGNUSON, ANN. Charleston, WV, 1/4/56. Actor. Catherine Hughes on *Anything but Love.*
MAGUIRE, LES. Wallasey, England, 12/27/41. Keyboardist, saxophonist. Gerry & The Pacemakers.
MAHONEY, JOHN. Manchester, England, 6/20/40. Actor. Father of Dr. Crane on *Cheers* and *Frasier.*
MAJORS, LEE (Lee Yeary). Wyandotte, MI, 4/23/39. Actor. Formerly married to Farrah Fawcett. *The Six Million Dollar Man.*
MAKEPEACE, CHRIS. Montreal, Canada, 4/22/64. Actor. *My Bodyguard.*
MAKO (Makoto Iwamatsu). Kobe, Japan, 12/10/33. Actor. *The Sand Pebbles.*
MALDEN, KARL (Mladen Sekulovich). Gary, IN, 3/22/14. Actor, American Express spokesperson. *The Streets of San Francisco.*
MALONE, DOROTHY. Chicago, IL, 1/30/25. Actor. *Written on the Wind.*
MALTIN, LEONARD. New York, NY, 12/18/50. Film critic. *Entertainment Tonight.*
MANDEL, HOWIE. Toronto, Canada, 11/29/55. Actor. Dr. Wayne Fiscus on *St. Elsewhere.*
MANDELA, WINNIE. Transkei, South Africa, 9/26/34. Political activist, formerly married to Nelson Mandela.
MANDRELL, BARBARA. Houston, TX, 12/25/48. Country singer. Barbara Mandrell & The Mandrell Sisters.
MANETTI, LARRY. Chicago, IL, 7/23/47. Actor. Rick on *Magnum, P. I.*
MANN, MANFRED (Michael Lubowitz). Johannesburg, South Africa, 10/21/40. Keyboardist. Manfred Mann.
MANN, TERRENCE. Kentucky, 1945. Actor. *Les Misérables.*
MANOFF, DINAH. New York, NY, 1/25/58. Actor. Carol Weston on *Empty Nest.*
MANSON, CHARLES. Cincinnati, OH, 11/11/34. Murderer, cult leader.
MANTEGNA, JOE. Chicago, IL, 11/13/47. Actor. *The Godfather, Part III.*
MANZANERA, PHIL. London, England, 1/31/51. Guitarist. Roxy Music.
MANZAREK, RAY. Chicago, IL, 2/12/35. Keyboardist. The Doors.
MARCEAU, MARCEL. Strasbourg, France, 3/22/23. Actor, pantomimist. *Bip.*
MARCHAND, NANCY. Buffalo, NY, 6/19/28. Actor. *Lou Grant.*
MARCOS, IMELDA. Talcoban, the Philippines, 7/2/31. Wife of late Ferdinand Marcos.
MARCOVICCI, ANDREA. New York, NY, 11/18/48. Actor, singer. *Trapper John, MD.*
MARGO, MITCH. Brooklyn, NY, 5/25/47. Tenor singer. The Tokens.
MARGO, PHIL. Brooklyn, NY, 4/1/42. Bass singer. The Tokens.
MARIN, CHEECH (Richard Marin). Los Angeles, CA, 7/13/46. Actor, writer, former partner of Tommy Chong. *Up in Smoke.*
MARINARO, ED. New York, NY, 3/31/50. Actor, football player. *Hill Street Blues.*
MARK, MARKY (Mark Wahlberg). Dorchester, MA, 6/5/71. Rap artist, Calvin Klein underwear model, brother of Donny Wahlberg.
MARLEY, ZIGGY (David Marley). Jamaica, 1968. Singer, songwriter, son of Bob Marley. Ziggy Marley & The Melody Makers.
MARR, JOHNNY. 10/31/63. Guitarist. The Smiths.
MARRIOTT, STEVE. Bow, England, 1/30/47. Singer, guitarist. The Small Faces.
MARS, MICK (Bob Deal). Terre Haute, IN, 4/4/55. Guitarist. Mötley Crüe.
MARSALIS, BRANFORD. Breaux Bridge, LA, 8/26/60. Jazz musician, bandleader, saxophonist. Brother of Wynton Marsalis. Musical director of *The Tonight Show.*
MARSDEN, FREDDIE. Liverpool, England, 10/23/40. Drummer. Gerry & The Pacemakers.
MARSDEN, GERRY. Liverpool, England, 9/24/42. Singer, lead guitarist. Gerry & The Pacemakers.
MARSH, IAN. Sheffield, England, 11/11/56. Keyboardist. The Human League; Heaven 17.
MARSHALL, E. G. (Everett Marshall). Owatonna, MN, 6/18/10. Actor. *Twelve Angry Men.*
MARSHALL, PETER. Huntington, WV, 3/30/30. TV personality. Host of *The Hollywood Squares.*
MARTELL, VINCE. New York, NY, 11/11/45. Guitarist. Vanilla Fudge.
MARTIN, ANDREA. Portland, ME, 1/15/47. Writer, actor. *SCTV.*
MARTIN, DEAN (Dino Crocetti). Steubenville, OH, 6/17/17. Actor, singer. Ex-partner of Jerry Lewis.
MARTIN, DEWEY. Chesterville, Canada, 9/30/42. Singer, drummer. Buffalo Springfield.
MARTIN, DICK. Battle Creek, MI, 1/30/23. Actor. Cohost of *Laugh-In.*
MARTIN, JIM. Oakland, CA, 7/21/61. Guitarist. Faith No More.
MARTIN, PAMELA SUE. Westport, CT, 1/15/53. Actor. *Dynasty.*
MARTINDALE, WINK (Winston Conrad Martindale). Bells, TN, 12/4/34. TV personality. Host of *Tic Tac Dough.*
MARTINI, JERRY. Colorado, 10/1/43. Saxophonist. Sly & The Family Stone.
MARVIN, HANK (Brian Rankin). Newcastle, England, 10/28/41. Lead guitarist. The Shadows.
MARX, RICHARD. Chicago, IL, 9/16/63. Singer, songwriter.
MASON, DAVE. Worcester, England, 5/10/47. Singer, guitarist. Traffic.
MASON, JACKIE. Sheboygan, WI, 6/9/34. Actor. *Chicken Soup.*
MASON, MARSHA. St. Louis, MO, 4/3/42. Actor. *The Goodbye Girl.*
MASON, NICK. Birmingham, England, 1/27/45. Drummer. Pink Floyd.
MASSI, NICK (Nick Macioci). Newark, NJ, 9/19/35. Singer, bassist. The Four Seasons.
MASTELOTTO, PAT. 9/10/55. Drummer. Mr. Mister.
MASTERSON, MARY STUART. Los Angeles, CA, 6/28/66. Actor. *Fried Green Tomatoes.*
MASTERSON, PETER. Houston, TX, 6/1/34. Actor, writer, director. *The Exorcist.*
MASTRANGELO, CARLO. The Bronx, NY, 10/5/39. Bass singer. Dion & The Belmonts.
MASTRANTONIO, MARY ELIZABETH. Oak Park, IL, 11/17/58. Actor. *The Color of Money.*
MASTROIANNI, MARCELLO. Fontana Liri, Italy, 9/28/24. Actor. *La Dolce Vita.*
MASUR, RICHARD. New York, NY, 11/20/48. Actor. *One Day at a Time.*
MATHERS, JERRY. Sioux City, IA, 6/2/48. Actor. Theodore "Beaver" Cleaver on *Leave It to Beaver.*
MATHESON, TIM. Glendale, CA, 12/31/47. Actor. *National Lampoon's Animal House.*
MATHIS, JOHNNY. San Francisco, CA, 9/30/35. Pop singer.
MATLOCK, GLENN. 8/27/56. Bassist. The Sex Pistols.
MATTHAU, WALTER (Walter Matuschanskayasky). New York, NY, 10/1/20. Actor. *The Odd Couple.*
MATTHEWS, IAN (Ian McDonald). Lincolnshire, England, 6/16/45. Singer, guitarist. Matthew's Southern Comfort.
MATURE, VICTOR. Louisville, KY, 1/29/15. Actor. *Samson and Delilah.*
MAUS, JOHN. New York, NY, 11/12/43. Singer. The Walker Brothers.
MAXFIELD, MIKE. Manchester, England, 2/23/44. Lead guitarist. Billy J. Kramer & The Dakotas.
MAY, BRIAN. Twickenham, England, 7/19/47. Guitarist. Queen.
MAY, ELAINE (Elaine Berlin). Philadelphia, PA, 4/21/32. Actor, director, writer. *Ishtar.*
MAY, PHIL. Dartford, England, 11/9/44. Singer. The Pretty Things.
MAYALL, JOHN. Macclesfield, England, 11/29/33. Singer, keyboardist, harmonicist. The Bluesbreakers.
MAYFIELD, CURTIS. Chicago, IL, 6/3/42. Singer, songwriter, record producer, paralyzed in an accident during a concert. "Superfly."
MAYS, WILLIE. Fairfield, AL, 5/6/31. Baseball player. San Francisco Giants.
MAZAR, DEBI. Queens, NY, 1964. Actor. *Civil Wars; L.A. Law.*
MAZURSKY, PAUL. Brooklyn, NY, 4/25/30. Producer, director, writer, actor. *Down and Out in Beverly Hills.*
M.C. ERIC. 8/19/70. Rap artist. Technotronic.
MCA (Adam Yauch). Brooklyn, NY, 8/15/67. Rap artist. The Beastie Boys.
MCCALLUM, DAVID. Glasgow, Scotland, 9/19/33. Actor. *The Great Escape.*
MCCARTHY, ANDREW. Westfield, NJ, 11/29/62. Actor. *Less Than Zero.*
MCCARTHY, KEVIN. Seattle, WA, 2/15/14. Actor. *Invasion of the Body Snatchers.*

MCCARTNEY, LINDA (Louise Eastman). New York, NY, 9/24/42. Pianist, singer, percussionist, photographer, married to Paul McCartney.
MCCARTY, JIM. Liverpool, England, 7/25/43. Drummer. The Yardbirds; Mitch Ryder & The Detroit Wheels.
MCCAULEY, JACKIE. Coleraine, Ireland, 12/14/46. Keyboardist. Them.
MCCAULEY, PATRICK. Northern Ireland, 3/17/44. Drummer. Them.
MCCLANAHAN, RUE. Healdton, OK, 2/21/34. Actor. Blanche Devereaux on *The Golden Girls.*
MCCLARY, THOMAS. 10/6/50. Lead guitarist. The Commodores.
MCCLINTON, DELBERT. 11/4/40. Singer, songwriter.
MCCLURE, DOUG. Glendale, CA, 5/11/35. Actor. *The Virginian.*
MCCLURG, EDIE. Kansas City, MO, 7/23/50. Actor. *The Hogan Family.*
MCCLUSKEY, ANDY. Wirral, England, 6/24/59. Singer. Orchestral Manoeuvres in the Dark (OMD).
MCCOO, MARILYN. Jersey City, NJ, 9/30/43. Singer, cohost of *Solid Gold.* The 5th Dimension.
MCCREADY, MIKE. 4/5/66. Guitarist. Pearl Jam.
MCCULLOCH, IAN. Liverpool, England, 5/5/59. Singer. Echo & The Bunnymen.
MCDANIELS, DARRYL D. New York, NY, 1964. Rap artist. Run-D.M.C.
MCDONALD, COUNTRY JOE. El Monte, CA, 1/1/42. Guitarist, singer. Country Joe & The Fish.
MCDONALD, IAN. London, England, 6/25/46. Saxophonist. King Crimson.
MCDONALD, MICHAEL. St. Louis, MO, 12/2/52. Singer, songwriter, keyboardist. The Doobie Brothers.
MCDONALD, PAT. 8/6/52. Musician. Timbuk 3.
MCDONNELL, MARY. Ithaca, NY, 1952. Actor. *Dances with Wolves.*
MCDORMAND, FRANCES. Illinois, 1958. Actor. *Mississippi Burning.*
MCDOWALL, RODDY. London, England, 9/17/28. Actor. *Planet of the Apes.*
MCDOWELL, MALCOLM. Leeds, England, 6/19/43. Actor. *A Clockwork Orange.*
MCENROE, JOHN JR. Wiesbaden, Germany, 2/16/59. Tennis player. Formerly married to Tatum O'Neal.
MCFERRIN, BOBBY. New York, NY, 3/11/50. Singer. "Don't Worry, Be Happy."
MCGAVIN, DARREN. Spokane, WA, 5/7/22. Actor. *The Night Stalker.*
MCGEOCH, JOHN. Guitarist. Siouxsie & The Banshees.
MCGILLIS, KELLY. Newport Beach, CA, 7/9/57. Actor. *Witness.*
MCGOVERN, ELIZABETH. Evanston, IL, 7/18/61. Actor. *Ragtime.*
MCGOVERN, MAUREEN. Youngstown, OH, 7/27/49. Singer, actor. "The Morning After."
MCGUINN, ROGER "JIM." Chicago, IL, 7/13/42. Singer, guitarist. The Byrds.
MCGUINNESS, TOM. Wimbledon, England, 12/2/41. Bassist. Manfred Mann.
MCINTOSH, LORRAINE. Glasgow, Scotland, 5/13/64. Singer. Deacon Blue.
MCINTYRE, FRITZ. 9/2/58. Keyboardist. Simply Red.
MCINTYRE, JOE. Needham, MA, 12/31/73. Singer. New Kids on the Block.
MCINTYRE, ONNIE. Lennox Town, Scotland, 9/25/45. Guitarist. Average White Band.
MCJOHN, GOLDY. 5/2/45. Organist. Steppenwolf.
MCKAGAN, DUFF ROSE (Michael McKagan). Bassist. Guns N' Roses.
MCKEAN, MICHAEL. New York, NY, 10/17/47. Actor, writer. Lenny Kosnowski on *Laverne & Shirley.*
MCKELLAR, DANICA. La Jolla, CA. Actor. Winnie Cooper on *The Wonder Years.*
MCKELLEN, IAN. Burnley, England, 5/25/39. Shakespearian actor.
MCKEON, NANCY. Westbury, NY, 4/4/66. Actor. Jo Polniaczek on *The Facts of Life.*
MCKEOWN, LESLIE. 11/12/55. Singer. The Bay City Rollers.
MCKUEN, ROD. Oakland, CA, 4/29/33. Poet. *Laugh-In.*
MCLAGAN, IAN. England, 5/12/46. Keyboardist. The Faces.
MCLEAN, DON. New Rochelle, NY, 10/2/45. Singer, songwriter.
MCLEMORE, LAMONTE. St. Louis, MO, 9/17/39. Singer. The 5th Dimension.
MCMAHON, ED. Detroit, MI, 3/6/23. Announcer and host. *The Tonight Show; Star Search.*
MCNALLY, JOHN. Liverpool, England, 8/30/41. Singer, guitarist. The Searchers.
MCNEIL, MIKE. Scotland, 7/20/58. Keyboardist. Simple Minds.
MCNICHOL, KRISTY. Los Angeles, CA, 9/9/62. Actor. Barbara Weston on *Empty Nest.*
MCPHATTER, CLYDE. Durham, NC, 11/13/33. Lead singer. The Drifters.
MCPHERSON, GRAHAM. Hastings, England, 1/13/61. Singer. Madness.
MCQUEEN, BUTTERFLY. Tampa, FL, 1/8/11. Actor. Prissy in *Gone with the Wind.*
MCRANEY, GERALD. Collins, MS, 8/19/48. Actor, married to Delta Burke. John D. "Mac" MacGillis on *Major Dad.*
MCVIE, CHRISTINE (Christine Perfect). England, 7/12/44. Keyboardist, singer. Fleetwood Mac.
MCVIE, JOHN. London, England, 11/26/45. Bassist. Fleetwood Mac.
MEADOWS, AUDREY. Wu Chang, China, 2/8/26. Actor. Alice Kramden on *The Honeymooners.*
MEADOWS, JAYNE (Jayne Cotter). Wu Chang, China, 9/27/20. Actor, quiz show regular. Married to Steve Allen, sister of Audrey.
MEANEY, COLM. Dublin, Ireland, 1953. Actor. Miles O'Brien on *Star Trek: The Next Generation.*
MEARA, ANNE. Brooklyn, NY, 9/20/29. Actor, partner/married to Jerry Stiller, mother of Ben Stiller. *The Out-of-Towners.*
MEAT LOAF (Marvin Lee Aday). Dallas, TX, 9/27/47. Singer, actor. *The Rocky Horror Picture Show.*
MEDLEY, BILL. Santa Ana, CA, 9/19/40. Singer. The Righteous Brothers.
MEDRESS, HANK. Brooklyn, NY, 11/19/38. Tenor singer. The Tokens.
MEHTA, ZUBIN. Bombay, India, 4/29/36. Conductor.
MEINE, KLAUS. 5/25/48. Singer. Scorpions.
MEISNER, RANDY. Scottsbluff, NE, 3/8/47. Bassist, singer. The Eagles; Poco.
MELLENCAMP, JOHN. Seymour, IN, 10/7/51. Guitarist, singer, songwriter.
MENDOZA, MARK. Long Island, NY, 6/13/54. Bassist. Twisted Sister.
MENKEN, ALAN. New Rochelle, NY, 1949. Composer. *Beauty and the Beast.*
MERCHANT, JIMMY. New York, NY, 2/10/40. Singer. Frankie Lymon & The Teenagers.
MEREDITH, BURGESS. Cleveland, OH, 11/16/07. Actor. The Penguin on *Batman.*
MESSINA, JIM. Maywood, CA, 12/5/47. Guitarist, singer. Poco.
METCALF, LAURIE. Edwardsville, IL, 6/16/55. Actor. Jackie Conner Harris on *Roseanne.*
METHENY, PAT. Lee's Summit, MO, 8/12/54. Jazz guitarist. "Offramp."
MEYERS, ARI. New York, NY, 1970. Actor. Emma McArdle on *Kate & Allie.*
MEYERS, AUGIE. San Antonio, TX, 5/31/40. Keyboardist. Texas Tornados.
MIALL, TERRY LEE. England, 11/8/58. Drummer. Adam & The Ants.
MICHAEL, GEORGE (Georgios Kyriacou Panayiotou). London, England, 6/25/63. Singer, songwriter. Wham!
MICK (Michael Wilson). Amesbury, England, 3/4/44. Drummer. Dave Dee, Dozy, Beaky, Mick and Tich.
MIDLER, BETTE. Honolulu, HI, 12/1/45. Actor, singer. "The Rose."
MIDORI. Osaka, Japan, 10/25/71. Violinist.
MIFUNE, TOSHIRO. Tsingtao, China, 4/1/20. Actor. *Throne of Blood.*
MIKE D. (Mike Diamond). New York, NY, 11/20/65. Rap artist. The Beastie Boys.
MILANO, ALYSSA. New York, NY, 12/19/72. Actor. Samantha Micelli on *Who's the Boss?*
MILANO, FRED. The Bronx, NY, 8/26/40. Tenor singer. Dion & The Belmonts.
MILES, SARAH. Ingatestone, England, 12/31/41. Actor. *Ryan's Daughter.*
MILES, SYLVIA. New York, NY, 9/9/34. Actor. *Midnight Cowboy.*
MILES, VERA (Vera Ralston). Boise City, OK, 8/23/29. Actor. *Psycho.*
MILKEN, MICHAEL. Van Nuys, CA, 1946. Financier. Convicted of securities violations.
MILLER, ANN (Lucille Ann Collier). Chireno, TX, 4/12/23. Actor. *On the Town.*
MILLER, CHARLES. Olathe, KS, 6/2/39. Saxophonist, clarinetist. War.
MILLER, DENNIS. Pittsburgh, PA, 11/3/53. TV personality. *Saturday Night Live.*

MILLER, JERRY. Tacoma, WA, 7/10/43. Guitarist. Moby Grape.
MILLER, PENELOPE ANN. Santa Monica, CA, 1/13/64. Actor. *Carlito's Way.*
MILLER, ROGER. Fort Worth, TX, 1/2/36. Rock/country singer, songwriter.
MILLER, STEVE. Milwaukee, WI, 10/5/43. Singer, guitarist. The Steve Miller Band.
MILLS, HAYLEY. London, England, 4/18/46. Actor, daughter of John Mills, sister of Juliet Mills. *The Parent Trap.*
MILLS, JOHN. Suffolk, England, 2/22/08. Actor, father of Hayley and Juliet Mills. *Ryan's Daughter.*
MILLS, JULIET. London, England, 11/21/41. Actor, daughter of John Mills, sister of Hayley Mills. *Nanny and the Professor.*
MILLS, MIKE. 12/17/58. Bassist. R.E.M.
MILLS, STEPHANIE. New York, NY, 3/22/57. Actor, singer. *The Wiz.*
MILLWARD, MIKE. Bromborough, England, 5/9/42. Guitarist, singer. The Fourmost.
MIMIEUX, YVETTE. Los Angeles, CA, 1/8/39. Actor. *The Black Hole.*
MINNELLI, LIZA. Los Angeles, CA, 3/12/46. Singer, actor, daughter of Vincente Minnelli and Judy Garland, half-sister of Lorna Luft. *Cabaret; The Sterile Cuckoo.*
MINNESOTA FATS. New York, NY, 1913. Billiards player. Portrayed by Jackie Gleason in *The Hustler.*
MINOGUE, KYLIE. Melbourne, Australia, 5/28/68. Actor, singer.
MIOU-MIOU (Sylvette Hery). Paris, France, 2/22/50. Actor. *Going Places.*
MIRABELLA, GRACE. Maplewood, NJ, 6/10/30. Fashion editor, publishing executive. *Mirabella.*
MITCHELL, JONI (Roberta Anderson). Fort McLeod, Canada, 11/7/43. Folk singer, songwriter.
MITCHELL, LIZ. Clarendon, Jamaica, 7/12/52. Singer. Boney M.
MITCHELL, MITCH. London, England, 7/9/46. Drummer. The Jimi Hendrix Experience.
MITCHELL, NEIL. Helensborough, Scotland, 6/8/67. Keyboardist. Wet Wet Wet.
MITCHUM, JAMES. Los Angeles, CA, 5/8/41. Actor, son of Robert. *Thunder Road.*
MITCHUM, ROBERT. Bridgeport, CT, 8/6/17. Actor, father of James. *Cape Fear; The Night of the Hunter.*
MODINE, MATTHEW. Loma Linda, CA, 3/22/59. Actor. *Vision Quest.*
MOFFAT, DONALD. Plymouth, England, 12/26/30. Actor. *Clear and Present Danger; Tales of the City.*
MOLL, RICHARD. Pasadena, CA, 1/13/43. Actor, stands 6' 8". Bailiff Nostradamus "Bull" Shannon on *Night Court.*
MOLLAND, JOEY. Liverpool, England, 6/21/48. Guitarist, keyboardist, singer. Badfinger.
MONARCH, MICHAEL. Los Angeles, CA, 7/5/50. Guitarist. Steppenwolf.
MONDALE, WALTER "FRITZ." Ceylon, MN, 1/5/28. Politician. Presidential candidate.
MONEY, EDDIE (Eddie Mahoney). Brooklyn, NY, 3/2/49. Singer.
MONTALBAN, RICARDO. Mexico City, Mexico, 11/25/20. Actor. *Fantasy Island.*
MONTANA, JOE. New Eagle, PA, 6/11/56. Football great.
MONTGOMERY, ELIZABETH. Los Angeles, CA, 4/15/33. Actor. Samantha Stephens on *Bewitched.*
MONTGOMERY, GEORGE (George Letz). Brady, MT, 8/29/16. Actor. *The Texas Rangers.*
MONTGOMERY, JOHN MICHAEL. Lexington, KY, 1/20/65. Country singer.
MOODY, MICKY. 8/30/50. Guitarist. Whitesnake.
MOONEY, KEVIN. England, 5/5/62. Bassist. Adam & The Ants.
MOORE, DUDLEY. Dagenham, England, 4/19/35. Actor. *Arthur.*
MOORE, MARY TYLER. Brooklyn, NY, 12/29/36. Actor. *The Mary Tyler Moore Show.*
MOORE, MELBA. New York, NY, 10/29/45. R&B singer, actor. *Purlie.*
MOORE, ROGER. London, England, 10/14/27. Actor, replaced Sean Connery as James Bond. *Live and Let Die.*
MOORE, SAM. Miami, FL, 10/12/35. Singer. Sam & Dave.
MORAN, ERIN. Burbank, CA, 10/18/61. Actor. Joanie Cunningham on *Happy Days.*
MORANIS, RICK. Toronto, Canada, 4/18/54. Actor, writer. *Honey, I Shrunk the Kids.*
MOREAU, JEANNE. Paris, France, 1/23/28. Actor. *Jules et Jim.*
MORENO, RITA (Rosita Dolores Alverio). Humacao, PR, 12/11/31. Actor. *West Side Story.*
MORGAN, HARRY (Henry Bratsburg). Detroit, MI, 4/10/15. Actor. *M*A*S*H.*
MORIARTY, CATHY. The Bronx, NY, 11/29/60. Actor. *Raging Bull.*
MORIARTY, MICHAEL. Detroit, MI, 4/5/41. Actor. *Law and Order.*
MORITA, NORIYUKI "PAT." Isleton, CA, 6/28/32. Actor. *The Karate Kid.*
MORRIS, GREG. Cleveland, OH, 9/27/34. Actor. *Mission: Impossible.*
MORRIS, STEPHEN. Macclesfield, England, 10/28/57. Drummer. New Order.
MORRISON, STERLING. East Meadow, NY, 8/29/42. Singer, bassist, guitarist. The Velvet Underground.
MORRISSEY (Stephen Morrissey). Manchester, England, 5/22/59. Singer. The Smiths.
MORSE, DAVID. Hamilton, MA, 10/11/53. Actor. *St. Elsewhere.*
MORTON, JOE. New York, NY, 10/18/47. Actor. *Terminator 2: Judgment Day.*
MORVAN, FABRICE. Guadeloupe, 5/14/66. "Singer." Milli Vanilli.
MOSLEY, BOB. Paradise Valley, CA, 12/4/42. Bassist. Moby Grape.
MOSS, JON. Wandsworth, England, 9/11/57. Drummer. Culture Club.
MOSS, KATE. London, England, 1/16/74. Supermodel.
MOST, DONNY. New York, NY, 8/8/53. Actor. Ralph Malph on *Happy Days.*
MOSTEL, JOSH. New York, NY, 12/21/46. Actor. *City Slickers.*
MOULDING, COLIN. Swindon, England, 8/17/55. Bassist, singer. XTC.
MOUNT, DAVE. Carshalton, England, 3/3/47. Drummer, singer. Mud.
MOYERS, BILL. Hugo, OK, 6/5/34. Journalist, commentator. *Bill Moyers' Journal.*
MOYET, ALISON (Genevieve Moyet). Basildon, England, 6/18/61. Singer. Yazoo.
MUDD, ROGER. Washington, DC, 2/9/28. Broadcast journalist, newscaster.
MULDAUR, DIANA. New York, NY, 8/19/38. Actor. *L.A. Law; Star Trek: The Next Generation.*
MULGREW, KATE. Dubuque, IA, 4/29/55. Actor. *Ryan's Hope.*
MULHARE, EDWARD. County Cork, Ireland, 4/8/23. Actor. *Knight Rider.*
MULHERN, MATT. Philadelphia, PA, 7/21/60. Actor. 2nd Lt. Gene Holowachuk on *Major Dad.*
MULL, MARTIN. Chicago, IL, 8/18/43. Actor. *Mary Hartman, Mary Hartman.*
MULLEN, LARRY JR. Dublin, Ireland, 10/31/61. Drummer. U2.
MULLIGAN, RICHARD. New York, NY, 11/13/32. Actor. Dr. Harry Weston on *Empty Nest.*
MUMY, BILLY. El Centro, CA, 2/1/54. Actor. *Lost in Space.*
MURPHY, MICHAEL. Los Angeles, CA, 5/5/38. Actor. *Manhattan.*
MURPHY, PETER. 7/11/57. Singer. Bauhaus.
MURRAY, DAVE. London, England, 12/23/58. Lead guitarist. Iron Maiden.
MUSIC, LORENZO. Brooklyn, NY, 5/2/37. Actor, writer. Carlton the Doorman on *Rhoda.*
NABORS, JIM. Sylacauga, GA, 6/12/32. Actor. Gomer Pyle on *The Andy Griffith Show.*
NADER, RALPH. Winsted, CT, 2/27/34. Political activist, author. *Unsafe at Any Speed.*
NAMATH, JOE. Beaver Falls, PA, 5/31/43. Football great, endorser.
NASH, BRIAN. Liverpool, England, 5/20/63. Guitarist. Frankie Goes to Hollywood.
NASH, GRAHAM. Blackpool, England, 2/2/42. Guitarist. The Hollies; Crosby, Stills, Nash & Young.
NAUGHTON, DAVID. West Hartford, CT, 2/13/51. Actor. *An American Werewolf in London.*
NAUGHTON, JAMES. Middletown, CT, 12/6/45. Actor. *The Good Mother.*
NAVRATILOVA, MARTINA. Prague, Czechoslovakia, 10/10/56. Tennis player.
NEAL, PATRICIA. Packard, KY, 1/20/26. Actor. *Hud.*
NEGRON, CHUCK. The Bronx, NY, 6/8/42. Singer. Three Dog Night.
NEIL, VINCE (Vince Wharton). Hollywood, CA, 2/8/61. Singer. Mötley Crüe.
NEILL, SAM. Ireland, 9/14/47. Actor. *Jurassic Park.*
NELLIGAN, KATE. London, Canada, 3/16/51. Actor. *The Prince of Tides.*
NELSON, CRAIG T. Spokane, WA, 4/4/46. Actor, writer. Hayden Fox on *Coach.*
NELSON, DAVID. New York, NY, 10/24/36. Actor, son of Ozzie and Harriet, brother of Ricky. David Nelson on *The Adventures of Ozzie and Harriet.*

NELSON, JUDD. Portland, ME, 11/28/59. Actor. *The Breakfast Club.*
NELSON, SANDY. Santa Monica, CA, 12/1/38. Rock/jazz drummer.
NELSON, TRACY. Santa Monica, CA, 10/25/63. Actor, daughter of Rick Nelson. *Father Dowling Mysteries.*
NEMES, LES. England, 12/5/60. Bassist. Haircut 100.
NESMITH, MIKE (Robert Nesmith). Dallas, TX, 12/30/42. Singer, guitarist, actor. The Monkees.
NEVILLE, ART. New Orleans, LA, 12/17/37. Singer, keyboardist. The Neville Brothers.
NEVILLE, CHARLES. 12/28/38. Saxophonist. The Neville Brothers.
NEVILLE, CYRIL. 1/10/48. Singer, percussionist. The Neville Brothers.
NEWHART, BOB (George Newhart). Chicago, IL, 9/5/29. Actor, comedian. *The Bob Newhart Show.*
NEWLEY, ANTHONY. Hackney, England, 9/24/31. Actor, composer. "The Candy Man."
NEWMAN, PAUL. Cleveland, OH, 1/26/25. Actor, writer, producer, director, chef/philanthropist, married to Joanne Woodward. *Cool Hand Luke.*
NEWMAN, RANDY. New Orleans, LA, 11/28/43. Singer, songwriter.
NEWTON, JUICE. Virginia Beach, VA, 2/18/52. Country singer. "Angel of the Morning."
NEWTON-JOHN, OLIVIA. Cambridge, England, 9/26/48. Singer, actor. *Grease.*
NGUYEN, DUSTIN. Saigon, Vietnam, 1962. Actor. *21 Jump Street.*
NICHOL, AL. Winston-Salem, NC, 3/31/46. Guitarist, keyboardist, singer. The Turtles.
NICKS, STEVIE. Phoenix, AZ, 5/26/48. Singer. Fleetwood Mac.
NIELSEN, RICK. Rockford, IL, 12/22/46. Singer, guitarist. Cheap Trick.
NIELSON, BRIGITTE. Denmark, 7/15/63. Actor, formerly married to Sylvester Stallone. *Red Sonja.*
NILSSON (Harry Nelson). Brooklyn, NY, 6/15/41. Singer, songwriter.
NIMOY, LEONARD. Boston, MA, 3/26/31. Actor, director. Mr. Spock on *Star Trek.*
NOIRET, PHILIPPE. Lille, France, 10/1/30. Actor. *Cinema Paradiso.*
NOLAN, MIKE. Dublin, Ireland, 12/7/54. Singer. Bucks Fizz.
NOLTE, NICK. Omaha, NE, 2/8/40. Actor. *48 Hrs.*
NOONAN, PEGGY. New York, NY, 9/7/50. Author, presidential speechwriter. Responsible for phrase "a kinder, gentler nation."
NOONE, PETER. Davyhulme, England, 11/5/47. Singer. Herman's Hermits.
NORRIS, CHUCK (Carlos Ray). Ryan, OK, 3/10/40. Karate champion, actor. *Good Guys Wear Black.*
NORTH, OLIVER. San Antonio, TX, 10/7/43. Presidential aide, senatorial candidate. Iran-Contra.
NORTON, KEN. Jacksonville, IL, 8/9/45. Boxer, actor. *The Gong Show.*
NOURI, MICHAEL. Washington, DC, 12/9/45. Actor. *Flashdance.*
NOVAK, KIM (Marilyn Novak). Chicago, IL, 2/13/33. Actor. *Vertigo.*
NOVELLO, DON. Ashtabula, OH, 1/1/43. Actor. Father Guido Sarducci.
NUGENT, TED. Detroit, MI, 12/13/48. Hard rock guitarist, actor.
NUMAN, GARY (Gary Webb). Hammersmith, England, 3/8/58. Singer. "Cars."
O'CONNOR, CARROLL. New York, NY, 8/2/24. Actor. Archie Bunker on *All in the Family.*
O'CONNOR, DONALD. Chicago, IL, 8/28/25. Actor. *Singin' in the Rain.*
O'CONNOR, SANDRA DAY. El Paso, TX, 3/26/30. Supreme Court Justice.
O'CONNOR, SINEAD. Dublin, Ireland, 12/8/66. Cleanshaven singer.
O'DONNELL, CHRIS. Winnetka, IL, 1970. Actor. *Scent of a Woman.*
O'HARA, BRIAN. Liverpool, England, 3/12/42. Guitarist, singer. The Fourmost.
O'HARA, CATHERINE. Toronto, Canada, 3/4/54. Actor. Mother in *Home Alone.*
O'HARA, MAUREEN (Maureen Fitz-Simons). Dublin, Ireland, 8/17/21. Actor. *How Green Was My Valley.*
O'NEAL, ALEXANDER. 11/14/53. Songwriter.
O'NEAL, RYAN (Patrick Ryan O'Neal). Los Angeles, CA, 4/20/41. Actor, father of Tatum O'Neal, married to Farrah Fawcett. *Love Story.*
O'NEAL, TATUM. Los Angeles, CA, 11/5/63. Actor, daughter of Ryan, formerly married to John McEnroe. *Paper Moon.*
O'NEILL, ED. Youngstown, OH, 4/12/46. Actor. Al Bundy on *Married . . . with Children.*
O'NEILL, JENNIFER. Rio de Janeiro, Brazil, 2/20/49. Actor, former model. *Summer of '42.*
O'NEILL, JOHN. 8/26/57. Guitarist. The Undertones.
O'SHEA, MILO. Dublin, Ireland, 6/2/26. Actor. *The Verdict.*
O'SULLIVAN, GILBERT (Raymond O'Sullivan). Waterford, Ireland, 12/1/46. Singer, songwriter.
O'SULLIVAN, MAUREEN. Byle, Ireland, 5/17/11. Actor. *Hannah and Her Sisters.*
O'TOOLE, ANNETTE (Annette Toole). Houston, TX, 4/1/53. Actor. *Superman III.*
O'TOOLE, MARK. Liverpool, England, 1/6/64. Bassist. Frankie Goes to Hollywood.
O'TOOLE, PETER. Connemara, Ireland, 8/2/32. Actor. *Lawrence of Arabia.*
OAKEY, PHILIP. Sheffield, England, 10/2/55. Singer. The Human League.
OAKLEY, BERRY. Chicago, IL, 4/4/48. Bassist. The Allman Brothers Band.
OATES, JOHN. New York, NY, 4/7/49. Singer, guitarist. Hall & Oates.
OCASEK, RIC (Ric Otcasek). Baltimore, MD, 3/23/49. Singer, guitarist. The Cars.
OCEAN, BILLY (Leslie Charles). Fyzabad, Trinidad, 1/21/50. Rock/R&B singer, songwriter.
OLDFIELD, MIKE. Reading, England, 5/15/53. Bassist, composer. "Tubular Bells."
OLDMAN, GARY. New Cross, England, 3/21/58. Actor, formerly married to Uma Thurman. *Bram Stoker's Dracula.*
OLIN, KEN. Chicago, IL, 7/30/54. Actor, director. Michael Steadman on *thirtysomething.*
OLMOS, EDWARD JAMES. East Los Angeles, CA, 2/24/47. Actor. Martin Castillo on *Miami Vice.*
ONTKEAN, MICHAEL. Vancouver, Canada, 1/24/46. Actor. *Twin Peaks.*
OPPENHEIMER, ALAN. New York, NY, 4/23/30. Actor. Gene Kinsella on *Murphy Brown.*
ORANGE, WALTER. Florida, 12/10/47. Singer, drummer. The Commodores.
ORBACH, JERRY. The Bronx, NY, 10/20/35. Actor. *Law and Order.*
ORLANDO, TONY (Michael Cassivitis). New York, NY, 4/3/44. Singer. Tony Orlando & Dawn.
ORR, BENJAMIN (Benjamin Orzechowski). Cleveland, OH, 8/9/55. Singer, bass guitarist. The Cars.
ORZABAL, ROLAND (Roland Orzabal de la Quintana). Portsmouth, England, 8/22/61. Guitarist, keyboardist. Tears for Fears.
OSBORNE, JEFFREY. Providence, RI, 3/9/48. Singer, songwriter, drummer. L.T.D.
OSGOOD, CHARLES. New York, NY, 1/8/33. Broadcast journalist, author.
OSKAR, LEE (Oskar Hansen). Copenhagen, Denmark, 3/24/46. Harmonicist. War.
OSMOND, ALAN. Ogden, UT, 6/22/49. Singer, member of the Osmond family. The Osmonds.
OSMOND, DONNY. Ogden, UT, 12/9/57. Singer, member of the Osmond family. *The Donny & Marie Show.*
OSMOND, JAY. Ogden, UT, 3/2/55. Singer, member of the Osmond family. The Osmonds.
OSMOND, MARIE (Olive Marive Osmond). Ogden, UT, 10/13/59. Singer, member of the Osmond family. *The Donny & Marie Show.*
OSMOND, MERRILL. Ogden, UT, 4/30/53. Singer, member of the Osmond family. The Osmonds.
OSMOND, WAYNE. Ogden, UT, 8/28/51. Singer, member of the Osmond family. The Osmonds.
OTIS, JOHNNY (John Veliotes). Vallejo, CA, 12/28/21. R&B drummer, pianist, and songwriter.
OWEN, RANDY. Fort Payne, AL, 12/13/49. Singer, guitarist. Alabama.
OWENS, SHIRLEY. Passaic, NJ, 6/10/41. Lead singer. The Shirelles.
OXENBERG, CATHERINE. New York, NY, 9/21/61. Actor. Amanda Carrington on *Dynasty.*
OZ, FRANK. Hereford, England, 5/25/44. Puppeteer, film director. *The Muppet Show.*
PACULA, JOANNA. Tamaszow Lubelski, Poland, 1/2/57. Actor. *Gorky Park.*

PAGE, JIMMY. Heston, England, 1/9/44. Guitarist. Led Zeppelin.
PAICE, IAN. Nottingham, England, 6/29/48. Drummer. Deep Purple.
PAICH, DAVID. Los Angeles, CA, 6/25/54. Keyboardist, singer. Toto.
PALANCE, JACK (Walter Palanuik). Lattimer, PA, 2/18/20. Actor. *City Slickers.*
PALIN, MICHAEL. Sheffield, England, 5/5/43. Actor, writer. *Monty Python's Flying Circus.*
PALMER, BETSY. East Chicago, IN, 11/1/26. Actor. Panelist on *I've Got a Secret.*
PALMER, CARL. Birmingham, England, 3/20/51. Drummer. Emerson, Lake & Palmer; Asia.
PALMER, JOHN. 5/25/43. Keyboardist. Family.
PALMER, ROBERT (Alan Palmer). Batley, England, 1/19/49. Singer, songwriter. "Addicted to Love."
PANKOW, JAMES. Chicago, IL, 8/20/47. Trombonist. Chicago.
PANOZZO, CHUCK. Chicago, IL, 9/20/47. Bassist. Styx.
PANOZZO, JOHN. Chicago, IL, 9/20/47. Drummer. Styx.
PARAZAIDER, WALTER. Chicago, IL, 3/14/45. Saxophonist. Chicago.
PARE, MICHAEL. Brooklyn, NY, 10/9/59. Actor. *Eddie and the Cruisers.*
PARFITT, RICK (Richard Harrison). Redhill, England, 10/25/43. Guitarist, singer. Status Quo.
PARILLAUD, ANNE. France, 1961. Actor. *La Femme Nikita.*
PARKER, FESS. Fort Worth, TX, 8/16/25. Actor. *Daniel Boone.*
PARKER, GRAHAM. Deepcut, England, 11/18/50. Singer. Graham Parker & The Rumour.
PARKER, JAMESON. Baltimore, MD, 11/18/47. Actor. *Simon and Simon.*
PARKER, MARY-LOUISE. Ft. Jackson, SC, 8/2/64. Actor. *Fried Green Tomatoes.*
PARKER, RAY JR. Detroit, MI, 5/1/54. Singer, songwriter. "Ghostbusters."
PARSONS, ESTELLE. Lynn, MA, 11/2/27. Actor. *Roseanne.*
PARTRIDGE, ANDY. Malta, 11/11/53. Guitarist, singer. XTC.
PATERSON, GERRY. Winnepeg, Canada, 5/26/45. Drummer. The Guess Who.
PATINKIN, MANDY (Mandel Patinkin). Chicago, IL, 11/30/52. Actor. *Yentl.*
PATRIC, JASON. Queens, NY, 1966. Actor. *Rush.*
PATRICK, ROBERT. Marietta, GA, 1959. Actor. Evil T-1000 in *Terminator 2: Judgment Day.*
PATTEN, EDWARD. Atlanta, GA, 8/2/39. Singer. Gladys Knight & The Pips.
PATTERSON, LORNA. Whittier, CA, 6/1/57. Actor. *Private Benjamin.*
PATTERSON, MELODY. Los Angeles, CA, 1947. Actor. Wrangler Jane on *F Troop.*
PATTINSON, LES. Ormskirk, England, 4/18/58. Bassist. Echo & The Bunnymen.
PATTON, MIKE. Eureka, CA, 1/27/68. Lead singer. Faith No More.
PATTON, WILL. Charleston, SC, 6/14/54. Actor. *No Way Out.*
PAULEY, JANE. Indianapolis, IN, 10/31/50. News show hostess, commentator. *Real Life with Jane Pauley.*
PAYCHECK, JOHNNY. Greenfield, OH, 5/31/41. Singer. "Take This Job and Shove It."
PAYNE, BILL. Waco, TX, 3/12/49. Keyboardist. Little Feat.
PAYS, AMANDA. Berkshire, England, 6/6/59. Actor, married to Corbin Bernsen. *The Flash.*
PAYTON, DENIS. Walthamstow, England, 8/11/43. Saxophonist. The Dave Clark Five.
PAYTON, LAWRENCE. Detroit, MI. Singer. The Four Tops.
PAYTON, WALTER. Columbia, MS, 6/25/54. Football player.
PEARL, MINNIE (Sarah Cannon). Centerville, TN, 10/25/12. Actor. *Hee Haw.*
PEARSON, DELROY. Romford, England, 4/11/70. Singer. Five Star.
PEARSON, DENIECE. Romford, England, 6/13/68. Lead singer. Five Star.
PEARSON, DORIS. Romford, England, 6/8/66. Singer. Five Star.
PEARSON, LORRAINE. Romford, England, 8/10/67. Singer. Five Star.
PEARSON, STEDMAN. Romford, England, 6/29/64. Singer. Five Star.
PEART, NEIL. Hamilton, Canada, 9/12/52. Drummer. Rush.
PECK, GREGORY (Eldred Peck). La Jolla, CA, 4/5/16. Actor, producer. *To Kill a Mockingbird.*
PEEK, DAN. Panama City, FL, 11/1/50. Singer, guitarist. America.
PELE, PEROLA NEGRA (Edson Arantes do Nascimento). Tres Coracoes, Brazil, 10/23/40. Soccer legend.
PELLOW, MARTI (Mark McLoughlin). Clydebank, Scotland, 3/23/66. Singer. Wet Wet Wet.
PENA, ELIZABETH. Elizabeth, NJ, 9/23/61. Actor. *La Bamba.*
PENDER, MIKE (Michael Prendergast). Liverpool, England, 3/3/42. Singer, lead guitarist. The Searchers.
PENDERGRASS, TEDDY. Philadelphia, PA, 3/26/50. R&B singer, songwriter, drummer.
PENDLETON, AUSTIN. Warren, OH, 3/27/40. Actor. *What's Up Doc?*
PENDLETON, BRIAN. Wolverhampton, England, 4/13/44. Guitarist. The Pretty Things.
PENGILLY, KIRK. 7/4/58. Guitarist, saxophonist, singer. INXS.
PENN, SEAN. Burbank, CA, 8/17/60. Actor, director, formerly married to Madonna. *Fast Times at Ridgemont High.*
PENNY, JOE. London, England, 9/14/56. Actor. Jake Styles on *Jake and the Fatman.*
PERKINS, CARL (Carl Lee Perkings). Ridgely, TN, 4/9/32. Legendary singer, songwriter. "Blue Suede Shoes."
PERKINS, ELIZABETH. Queens, NY, 11/18/61. Actor. *Big.*
PERLMAN, RHEA. Brooklyn, NY, 3/31/48. Actor, married to Danny DeVito. Carla Tortelli LeBec on *Cheers.*
PERLMAN, RON. New York, NY, 4/13/50. Actor. The Beast in *Beauty and the Beast.*
PEROT, HENRY ROSS. Texarkana, TX, 6/27/30. Self-made billionaire businessman, former presidential candidate.
PERRINE, VALERIE. Galveston, TX, 9/3/43. Actor. *Lenny.*
PERRY, JOE. Boston, MA, 9/10/50. Guitarist. Aerosmith.
PERRY, LUKE (Perry Coy III). Fredericktown, OH, 10/11/66. Actor. *Beverly Hills 90210.*
PERRY, STEVE. Hanford, CA, 1/22/53. Singer. Journey.
PERRY, WILLIAM "THE REFRIGERATOR." Aiken, SC, 12/16/62. Very large football player. Chicago Bears.
PESCOW, DONNA. Brooklyn, NY, 3/24/54. Actor. *Saturday Night Fever.*
PETERS, BERNADETTE (Bernadette Lazzara). New York, NY, 2/28/48. Actor, performer. *Pennies from Heaven.*
PETERS, BROCK. New York, NY, 7/27/27. Actor, singer. *To Kill a Mockingbird.*
PETERS, MIKE. Prestatyn, Wales, 2/25/59. Guitarist, singer. The Alarm.
PETERSEN, WILLIAM. Chicago, IL, 1953. Actor. *To Live and Die in L.A.*
PETERSON, DEBBI. Los Angeles, CA, 8/22/61. Drummer, singer. The Bangles.
PETERSON, SYLVIA. New York, NY, 9/30/46. Singer. The Chiffons.
PETERSON, VICKI. Los Angeles, CA, 1/11/58. Guitarist, singer. The Bangles.
PETERSSON, TOM. Rockford, IL, 5/9/50. Singer, bassist. Cheap Trick.
PETTY, LORI. Chattanooga, TN. Actor. *A League of Their Own.*
PETTY, TOM. Gainesville, FL, 10/20/53. Singer, guitarist. Tom Petty & The Heartbreakers.
PFISTERER, ALBAN. Switzerland, 1947. Drummer, keyboardist. Love.
PHANTOM, SLIM JIM (Jim McDonnell). 3/20/61. Drummer. The Stray Cats.
PHILBIN, REGIS. New York, NY, 8/25/34. Talk show host. *Live with Regis and Kathie Lee.*
PHILIP, PRINCE (Philip Mountbatten). Corfu, Greece, 6/10/21. Husband of Queen Elizabeth II, Duke of Edinburgh.
PHILLIPS, CHYNNA. Los Angeles, CA, 4/29/68. Singer, half-sister of Mackenzie, daughter of John and Michelle. Wilson Phillips.
PHILLIPS, JOHN. Parris Island, SC, 8/30/35. Singer, formerly married to Michelle, father of Mackenzie and Chynna. The Mamas & the Papas.
PHILLIPS, LOU DIAMOND. Philippines, 2/17/62. Actor. *La Bamba.*
PHILLIPS, MACKENZIE. Alexandria, VA, 11/10/59. Actor, daughter of John Phillips, half-sister of Chynna. Julie Cooper Horvath on *One Day at a Time.*
PHILLIPS, MICHELLE (Holly Gilliam). Santa Ana, CA, 6/4/44. Actor, formerly married to John, mother of Chynna. Anne Matheson on *Knots Landing.*
PHILTHY ANIMAL (Philip Taylor). Chesterfield, England, 9/21/54. Drummer. Motorhead.
PICKETT, WILSON. Prattville, AL, 3/18/41. Singer, songwriter. "In the Midnight Hour."
PIERSON, KATE. Weehawken, NJ, 4/27/48. Organist, singer. The B-52's.
PILATUS, ROBERT. New York, NY, 6/8/65. "Singer." Milli Vanilli.

PINCHOT, BRONSON. New York, NY, 5/20/59. Actor. Balki Bartokomous on *Perfect Strangers*.
PINDER, MIKE. Birmingham, England, 12/27/41. Keyboardist. The Moody Blues.
PINKNEY, BILL. Sumter, NC, 8/15/25. Bassist. The Drifters.
PIRRONI, MARCO. England, 4/27/59. Guitarist. Adam & The Ants.
PISCOPO, JOE. Passaic, NJ, 6/17/51. Actor. *Saturday Night Live*.
PITNEY, GENE. Hartford, CT, 2/17/41. Singer, songwriter.
PLACE, MARY KAY. Tulsa, OK, 9/23/47. Actor. *The Big Chill*.
PLANT, ROBERT. Bromwich, England, 8/20/48. Singer. Led Zeppelin.
PLEASENCE, DONALD. Worksop, England, 10/5/19. Actor. *You Only Live Twice*.
PLESHETTE, JOHN. New York, NY, 7/27/42. Actor. Richard Avery on *Knots Landing*.
PLESHETTE, SUZANNE. New York, NY, 1/31/37. Actor. Emily Hartley on *The Bob Newhart Show*.
PLOWRIGHT, JOAN. Brigg, England, 10/28/29. Actor. *Enchanted April*.
PLUMB, EVE. Burbank, CA, 4/29/58. Actor. Jan Brady on *The Brady Bunch*.
PLUMMER, AMANDA. New York, NY, 3/23/57. Actor. *The Fisher King*.
PLUMMER, CHRISTOPHER. Toronto, Canada, 12/13/27. Actor. Baron von Trapp in *The Sound of Music*.
POINTER, ANITA. East Oakland, CA, 1/23/48. Singer. Pointer Sisters.
POINTER, BONNIE. East Oakland, CA, 6/11/51. Singer. Pointer Sisters.
POINTER, JUNE. East Oakland, CA, 11/30/54. Singer. Pointer Sisters.
POINTER, RUTH. East Oakland, CA, 3/19/46. Singer. Pointer Sisters.
POITIER, SIDNEY. Miami, FL, 2/20/27. Actor. *Guess Who's Coming to Dinner*.
POLANSKI, ROMAN. Paris, France, 8/18/33. Director, writer. *Rosemary's Baby*.
POLLACK, SYDNEY. South Bend, Indiana, 7/1/34. Director, producer, actor. *The Way We Were*.
POLLAN, TRACY. New York, NY, 6/22/60. Actor, married to Michael J. Fox. *Family Ties*.
POOLE, BRIAN. Barking, England, 11/2/41. Singer. Brian Poole & The Tremeloes.
POP, IGGY (James Osterburg). Ann Arbor, MI, 4/21/47. Singer, songwriter.
POPCORN, FAITH. New York, NY, 5/11/43. Trend analyst, consultant.
PORCARO, STEVE. Los Angeles, CA, 9/2/57. Keyboardist, singer. Toto.
PORTZ, CHUCK. Santa Monica, CA, 3/28/45. Bassist. The Turtles.
POST, MARKIE. Palo Alto, CA, 11/4/50. Actor. Christine Sullivan on *Night Court*.
POTTER, CAROL. Tenafly, NJ, 5/21/48. Actor. *Beverly Hills 90210*.
POTTS, ANNIE. Nashville, TN, 10/28/52. Actor. Mary Jo Shively on *Designing Women*.
POVICH, MAURY. Washington, DC, 1/7/39. Talk show host, married to Connie Chung. *A Current Affair*.
POWELL, BILLY. Florida, 6/3/52. Keyboardist. Lynyrd Skynyrd.
POWELL, COLIN. New York, NY, 5/5/37. Military leader, Gulf War hero.
POWELL, DON. 9/10/50. Drummer. Slade.
POWERS, STEPHANIE (Stefania Federkiewicz). Hollywood, CA, 11/12/42. Actor. Jennifer on *Hart to Hart*.
PRATER, DAVE. Ocilla, GA, 5/9/37. Singer. Sam and Dave.
PRENTISS, PAULA (Paula Ragusa). San Antonio, TX, 3/4/39. Actor. *What's New Pussycat?*
PRESLEY, REG (Reginald Ball). Andover, England, 6/12/43. Singer. The Troggs.
PRESTON, KELLY. Honolulu, HI, 10/13/62. Actor. *52 Pick-Up*.
PRICE, ALAN. Fairfield, Durham, 4/19/41. Keyboardist. The Animals.
PRICE, LLOYD. Kenner, LA, 5/9/33. Singer, songwriter.
PRICE, RICK. 6/10/44. Bassist. Wizzard.
PRIDE, CHARLEY. Sledge, MS, 3/18/38. Country singer, songwriter.
PRIEST, STEVE. London, England, 2/23/50. Bassist. Sweet.
PRIESTLEY, JASON. Vancouver, Canada, 8/28/69. Actor. Brandon Walsh on *Beverly Hills 90210*.
PRIESTMAN, HENRY. 7/21/58. Singer. The Christians.
PRIME, JAMES. Kilmarnock, Scotland, 11/3/60. Keyboardist. Deacon Blue.
PRINCE MARK D. 2/19/60. Rap artist. Fat Boys.
PRINCIPAL, VICTORIA. Fukuoka, Japan, 1/3/45. Actor. Pam Ewing on *Dallas*.
PRITCHARD, BARRY. Birmingham, England, 4/3/44. Guitarist, singer. The Fortunes.
PROBY, P. J. (James Smith). Houston, TX, 11/6/38. Singer, actor.
PROWSE, JULIET. Bombay, India, 9/25/36. Actor, dancer.
PRYCE, JONATHAN. North Wales, 6/1/47. Actor. *Brazil*.
PRYOR, NICHOLAS. Baltimore, MD, 1/28/35. Actor. *Risky Business*.
PRYOR, RICHARD. Peoria, IL, 12/1/40. Actor. *Stir Crazy*.
PUERTA, JOE. 7/2/51. Bassist, singer. Bruce Hornsby & The Range.
PULLMAN, BILL. Hornell, NY, 1954. Actor. *Ruthless People*; *Malice*.
PURCELL, SARAH. Richmond, IN, 10/8/48. TV personality. Cohost on *Real People*.
QADDAFI, MUAMMAR. Sirta, Libya, 1942. Political leader. Libyan head of state.
QUAID, RANDY. Houston, TX, 10/1/50. Actor, brother of Dennis. *The Last Picture Show*.
QUAIFE, PETE. Tavistock, England, 12/31/43. Bassist. The Kinks.
QUATRO, SUZI (Suzi Quatrocchio). Detroit, MI, 6/3/50. Singer, songwriter, actor.
QUAYLE, DAN. Indianapolis, IN, 2/4/47. Vice president under George Bush.
QUAYLE, MARILYN. Indianapolis, IN, 7/29/49. Lawyer, author, married to Dan. *Embrace the Serpent*.
QUINLAN, KATHLEEN. Mill Valley, CA, 11/19/54. Actor. *Clara's Heart*.
QUINN, AIDAN. Chicago, IL, 3/8/59. Actor. *The Playboys*.
QUINN, ANTHONY. Chihuahua, Mexico, 4/21/15. Actor. *Zorba the Greek*.
QUINN, DEREK. Manchester, England, 5/24/42. Lead guitarist. Freddie & The Dreamers.
RABBITT, EDDIE. New York, NY, 11/27/41. Singer, songwriter. "I Love a Rainy Night."
RAFFERTY, GERRY. Paisley, Scotland, 4/16/47. Singer, songwriter. "Baker Street."
RAFFI. Cairo, Egypt, 7/8/48. Singer, songwriter, children's performer. *Everything Grows*.
RAFFIN, DEBORAH. Los Angeles, CA, 3/13/53. Actor. *Once Is Not Enough*.
RALPH, SHERYL LEE. Waterbury, CT, 12/30/56. Actor. *The Distinguished Gentleman*.
RALPHS, MICK. Hereford, England, 3/31/44. Guitarist. Mott The Hoople; Bad Company.
RAMIS, HAROLD. Chicago, IL, 11/21/44. Writer, director, actor. Egon Spengler in *Ghostbusters*.
RAMONE, DEE DEE (Douglas Colvin). Fort Lee, VA, 9/18/52. Bassist. The Ramones.
RAMONE, JOEY (Jeffrey Hyman). Forest Hills, NY, 5/19/52. Singer. The Ramones.
RAMONE, JOHNNY (John Cummings). Long Island, NY, 10/8/48. Guitarist. The Ramones.
RAMONE, TOMMY (Thomas Erdelyi). Budapest, Hungary, 1/29/49. Drummer. The Ramones.
RAMOS, LARRY JR. (Hilario Ramos Jr.). Kauai, HI, 4/19/42. Singer, guitarist. The Association.
RAMPLING, CHARLOTTE. Surmer, England, 2/5/46. Actor. *The Verdict*.
RAMSEY, AL. New Jersey, 7/27/43. Guitarist. Gary Lewis & The Playboys.
RANDALL, TONY (Leonard Rosenberg). Tulsa, OK, 2/26/20. Actor. Felix Unger on *The Odd Couple*.
RAPHAEL, SALLY JESSY. Easton, PA, 2/25/43. talk show hostess. *Sally Jessy Raphäel*.
RAPP, DANNY. Philadelphia, PA, 5/10/41. Lead singer. Danny & The Juniors.
RAREBELL, HERMAN. 11/18/49. Drummer. Scorpions.
RASCHE, DAVID. St. Louis, MO, 8/7/44. Actor. *Sledge Hammer*.
RASHAD, AHMAD. Portland, OR, 11/19/49. Football player, sportscaster, husband of Phylicia.
RASHAD, PHYLICIA. Houston, TX, 6/19/48. Actor, sister of Debbie Allen, wife of Ahmad. Clair Huxtable on *The Cosby Show*.
RATHER, DAN. Wharton, TX, 10/31/31. News reporter, anchor. *The CBS Evening News*.
RATZENBERGER, JOHN. Bridgeport, CT, 4/6/47. Actor. Cliff Claven on *Cheers*.

RAWLS, LOU. Chicago, IL, 12/1/36. R&B singer. "Lady Love."
RAY, JAMES EARL. Alton, IL, 3/10/28. Assassin. Killed Martin Luther King Jr.
RAYE, MARTHA (Margie Yvonne Reed). Butte, MT, 8/27/16. Actor. *The Martha Raye Show.*
REA, CHRIS. Middlesbrough, England, 3/4/51. Singer, songwriter, guitarist.
REAGAN, NANCY. New York, NY, 7/6/21. Former First Lady, married to president Ronald Reagan.
REAGAN, RONALD. Tampico, IL, 2/6/11. Politician, actor, father of Ron Jr., husband of Nancy. Fortieth U.S. president. *Bedtime for Bonzo.*
REAGAN, RONALD JR. Los Angeles, CA, 5/20/58. Performer, son of former president Ronald Reagan.
REASON, REX. Berlin, Germany, 11/30/28. Actor. *This Island Earth.*
RECORD, EUGENE. 12/23/40. Lead singer. The Chi-Lites.
REDDING, NOEL. Folkestone, England, 12/25/45. Bassist, The Jimi Hendrix Experience.
REDDY, HELEN. Melbourne, Australia, 10/25/42. Pop singer. *The Helen Reddy Show.*
REDGRAVE, CORIN. London, England, 6/16/39. Actor. *A Man for All Seasons.*
REDGRAVE, LYNN. London, England, 3/8/43. Actor, sister of Vanessa. *House Calls.*
REDGRAVE, VANESSA. London, England, 1/30/37. Actor, sister of Lynn. *Playing for Time.*
REED, LOU (Louis Firbank). Long Island, NY, 3/2/43. Singer, songwriter. The Velvet Underground.
REED, OLIVER. Wimbledon, England, 2/13/38. Actor. *The Three Musketeers.*
REED, PAMELA. Tacoma, WA, 4/2/53. Actor. *The Right Stuff.*
REEMS, HARRY (Herbert Streicher). The Bronx, NY, 8/27/47. Actor. *Deep Throat.*
REEVE, CHRISTOPHER. New York, NY, 9/25/52. Actor. *Superman.*
REEVES, KEANU. Beirut, Lebanon, 9/2/64. Actor. Ted in *Bill and Ted's Excellent Adventure.*
REEVES, MARTHA. Alabama, 7/18/41. Lead singer. Martha & The Vandellas.
REEVES, STEVE. Glasgow, MT, 1/21/26. Actor. *Hercules.*
REGALBUTO, JOE. Brooklyn, NY. Actor. Frank Fontana on *Murphy Brown.*
REID, JIM. East Kilbride, Scotland, 1961. Guitarist, singer. The Jesus & Mary Chain.
REID, TIM. Norfolk, VA, 12/19/44. Actor, producer. Gordon "Venus Flytrap" Sims on *WKRP in Cincinnati.*
REID, WILLIAM. East Kilbride, Scotland, 1958. Guitarist, singer. The Jesus & Mary Chain.
REINER, CARL. New York, NY, 3/20/22. Actor, writer, and director. *The Dick Van Dyke Show.*
REINER, ROB. New York, NY, 3/6/45. Actor, writer, producer, director, son of Carl, formerly married to Penny Marshall. Mike Stivic on *All in the Family.*
REINHOLD, JUDGE (Edward Ernest Reinhold Jr.). Wilmington, DE, 5/21/57. Actor. Rosewood in *Beverly Hills Cop.*
REINKING, ANN. Seattle, WA, 11/10/49. Actor, dancer. *Annie.*
REITMAN, IVAN. Komarno, Czechoslovakia, 10/26/46. Director, producer. *Ghostbusters.*
RELF, KEITH. Richmond, England, 3/22/43. Singer, harmonicist. The Yardbirds.
RETTIG, TOMMY. Jackson Heights, NY, 12/10/41. Actor. *Lassie.*
REVERE, PAUL. Harvard, NE, 1/7/38. Keyboardist. Paul Revere & The Raiders.
REYNOLDS, DEBBIE (Mary Frances Reynolds). El Paso, TX, 4/1/32. Actor, married to Eddie Fisher, mother of Carrie Fisher. *Singin' in the Rain.*
REYNOLDS, MARJORIE. Buhl, ID, 8/12/21. Actor. *The Life of Riley.*
RHODES, NICK (Nicholas Bates). Mosely, England, 6/8/62. Keyboardist. Duran Duran.
RIBEIRO, ALFONSO. New York, NY, 9/21/71. Actor, dancer. *Fresh Prince of Bel Air.*
RICH, ADAM. New York, NY, 10/12/68. Actor. Nicholas Bradford on *Eight Is Enough.*
RICH, CHARLIE. Forrest City, AR, 12/14/32. Country singer, pianist. "Behind Closed Doors."
RICHARD, CLIFF (Harry Webb). Lucknow, India, 10/14/40. Singer, drummer. The Shadows.
RICHARDS, KEITH. Dartford, England, 12/18/43. Guitarist. The Rolling Stones.
RICHARDSON, MIRANDA. Southport, England, 1958. Actor. *The Crying Game.*
RICHARDSON, SUSAN. Coatesville, PA, 3/11/52. Actor. Susan Bradford on *Eight Is Enough.*
RICHIE, LIONEL. Tuskegee, AL, 6/20/49. Singer, songwriter. The Commodores.
RICHRATH, GARY. Peoria, IL, 10/18/49. Guitarist. REO Speedwagon.
RICKLES, DON. New York, NY, 5/8/26. Actor. *The Don Rickles Show.*
RICKMAN, ALAN. Hammersmith, England, 1946. Actor. *Die Hard.*
RIDGELEY, ANDREW. Windlesham, England, 1/26/63. Guitarist. Wham!
RIEGERT, PETER. New York, NY, 4/11/47. Actor. *Crossing Delancey.*
RIGBY, CATHY. Long Beach, CA, 12/12/52. Gymnast.
RIGG, DIANA. Doncaster, England, 7/20/38. Actor. Emma Peel on *The Avengers.*
RIGGS, BOBBY. Los Angeles, CA, 2/25/18. Tennis player, defeated by Billie Jean King.
RINGWALD, MOLLY. Sacramento, CA, 2/18/68. Actor. *Sixteen Candles.*
RITTER, JOHN. Burbank, CA, 9/17/48. Actor, producer. Jack Tripper on *Three's Company.*
RIVERA, CHITA. Washington, DC, 1/23/33. Singer.
RIVERA, GERALDO. New York, NY, 7/4/43. Talk show host and reporter. *Geraldo.*
RIVERS, JOHNNY (John Ramistella). New York, NY, 11/7/42. Soul/rock singer, songwriter.
RIZZUTO, PHIL. New York, NY, 9/25/18. Baseball great, sports announcer.
ROBARDS, JASON. Chicago, IL, 7/26/22. Actor, married to Lauren Bacall. *Inherit the Wind.*
ROBERTS, ERIC. Biloxi, MS, 4/18/56. Actor, brother of Julia. *The Pope of Greenwich Village.*
ROBERTS, ORAL. Ada, OK, 1/24/18. Evangelist. Oral Roberts University.
ROBERTS, TANYA (Tanya Leigh). The Bronx, NY, 10/15/55. Actor. *Charlie's Angels.*
ROBERTS, TONY. New York, NY, 10/22/39. Actor. *Play It Again, Sam.*
ROBERTS, XAVIER. Cleveland, GA, 10/31/55. Businessman. Creator of Cabbage Patch Kids.
ROBERTSON, BRIAN. Glasgow, Scotland, 9/12/56. Guitarist. Thin Lizzy.
ROBERTSON, CLIFF. La Jolla, CA, 9/9/25. Actor. *Charly.*
ROBERTSON, PAT (Marion Gordon Robertson). Lexington, VA, 3/22/30. Evangelist, TV personality. Founder of Christian Broadcasting Network.
ROBERTSON, ROBBIE (Jaime Robertson). Toronto, Canada, 7/5/44. Guitarist, singer. The Band.
ROBINSON, CHRIS. Atlanta, GA, 12/20/66. Singer. The Black Crowes.
ROBINSON, CYNTHIA. Sacramento, CA, 1/12/46. Trumpeter. Sly & The Family Stone.
ROBINSON, JAY. New York, NY, 4/14/30. Actor. *The Robe.*
ROBINSON, RICH. Atlanta, GA, 5/24/69. Guitarist. The Black Crowes.
ROBINSON, SMOKEY (William Robinson). Detroit, MI, 2/19/40. Motown singer, songwriter. Smokey Robinson & The Miracles.
ROCK, CHRIS. New York, NY, 1967. Actor. *Saturday Night Live.*
ROCKER, LEE (Leon Drucher). 1961. Double bassist. The Stray Cats.
ROCKWELL. Detroit, MI, 3/15/64. Singer, son of Berry Gordy. "Somebody's Watching Me."
RODGERS, NILE. New York, NY, 9/19/52. Guitarist. Chic.
RODGERS, PAUL. Middlesbrough, England, 12/17/49. Singer. Free; Bad Company.
ROE, TOMMY. Atlanta, GA, 5/9/43. Singer, songwriter.
ROGERS, GINGER (Virginia Katherine McMath). Independence, MO, 7/16/11. Actor, dancing partner of Fred Astaire. *Top Hat.*
ROGERS, KENNY. Houston, TX, 8/21/38. Country singer, actor. "The Gambler."
ROGERS, MIMI. Coral Gables, FL, 1/27/56. Actor. Formerly married to Tom Cruise. *Someone To Watch Over Me.*
ROGERS, MISTER (Fred Rogers). Latrobe, PA, 3/20/28. Children's host, producer. *Mr. Rogers' Neighborhood.*
ROGERS, ROY (Leonard Slye). Cincinnati, OH, 11/5/12. TV cowboy, singer. *Happy Trails with Roy and Dale.*
ROGERS, WAYNE. Birmingham, AL, 4/7/33. Actor. Trapper John on *M*A*S*H.*
ROGERS, WILL JR. New York, NY, 10/12/12. Actor, lecturer. *The Story of Will Rogers.*

ROKER, ROXIE. Miami, FL, 8/28/29. Actor. Helen Willis on *The Jeffersons.*
ROLLE, ESTHER. Pompano Beach, FL, 11/8/22. Actor. *Driving Miss Daisy.*
ROLLINS, HOWARD JR. Baltimore, MD, 10/17/50. Actor. *In the Heat of the Night.*
ROMAN, RUTH. Boston, MA, 12/23/24. Actor. *The Long Hot Summer.*
RONSTADT, LINDA. Tucson, AZ, 7/15/46. Singer, actor. *The Pirates of Penzance.*
ROONEY, ANDY. Albany, NY, 1/14/20. News commentator. *60 Minutes.*
ROONEY, MICKEY (Joe Yule Jr.). Brooklyn, NY, 9/23/20. Actor. *National Velvet.*
ROSE, PETE. Cincinnati, OH, 4/14/41. Baseball player and manager. Cincinnati Reds.
ROSS, DIANA. Detroit, MI, 3/26/44. Singer, actor, former member of the Supremes. *Lady Sings the Blues.*
ROSS, KATHARINE. Hollywood, CA, 1/29/43. Actor. *The Graduate.*
ROSS, MARION. Albert Lea, MN, 10/25/28. Actor. Marion Cunningham on *Happy Days.*
ROSS, RICKY. Dundee, Scotland, 12/22/57. Singer. Deacon Blue.
ROSSELLINI, ISABELLA. Rome, Italy, 6/18/52. Actor. *Blue Velvet.*
ROSSI, FRANCIS. Forest Hill, England, 4/29/49. Guitarist, singer. Status Quo.
ROSSINGTON, GARY. Jacksonville, FL, 12/4/51. Guitarist. Lynyrd Skynyrd.
ROTH, DAVID LEE. Bloomingtom, IN, 10/10/55. Singer. Van Halen.
ROTH, TIM. London, England, 1961. Actor. *Reservoir Dogs.*
ROTHERY, STEVE. Brampton, England, 11/25/59. Guitarist. Marillion.
ROTHWELL, RIC. Stockport, England, 3/11/44. Drummer. Wayne Fontana & The Mindbenders.
ROUNDTREE, RICHARD. New Rochelle, NY, 9/7/42. Actor. *Shaft.*
ROURKE, MICKEY. Schenectady, NY, 1956. Actor. *9 1/2 Weeks.*
ROWLAND, KEVIN. Wolverhampton, England, 8/17/53. Singer, guitarist. Dexy's Midnight Runners.
ROWLANDS, GENA. Cambria, WI, 6/19/34. Actor. *Gloria.*
RUDD, PHILIP. Australia, 5/19/46. Drummer. AC/DC.
RUEHL, MERCEDES. Queens, NY. Actor. *Lost in Yonkers.*
RUFFIN, DAVID. Meridian, MS, 1/18/41. Singer. The Temptations.
RUNDGREN, TODD. Philadelphia, PA, 6/22/48. Singer, songwriter.
RUSHDIE, SALMAN. Bombay, India, 6/19/47. Author. *The Satanic Verses.*
RUSSELL, GRAHAM. 6/1/50. Singer. Air Supply.
RUSSELL, JACK. 12/5/60. Singer. Great White.
RUSSELL, JANE. Bemidji, MN, 6/21/21. Actor, pinup girl. *The Outlaw.*
RUSSELL, KURT. Springfield, MA, 3/17/51. Actor, cohabitant of Goldie Hawn. *Tombstone.*
RUSSELL, LEON (Hank Wilson). Lawton, OK, 4/2/41. Country/blues singer, songwriter.
RUSSELL, NIPSEY. Atlanta, GA, 10/13/24. Actor. *Car 54, Where Are You?*
RUSSELL, THERESA (Theresa Paup). San Diego, CA, 3/20/57. Actor. *Black Widow.*
RUTHERFORD, MIKE. Guildford, England, 10/2/50. Guitarist. Genesis; Mike & The Mechanics.
RUTHERFORD, PAUL. Liverpool, England, 12/8/59. Singer. Frankie Goes to Hollywood.
RUTTAN, SUSAN. 9/16/48. Actor. Roxanne on *L.A. Law.*
RYAN, TOM. Anderson, IN, 6/6/26. Cartoonist. *Tumbleweeds.*
RYDER, MITCH (William Levise Jr.). Detroit, MI, 2/26/45. Singer. Mitch Ryder & The Detroit Wheels.
RYDER, PAUL. Manchester, England, 4/24/64. Bassist. Happy Mondays.
RYDER, SHAUN. Little Hulton, England, 8/23/62. Singer. Happy Mondays.
SABATINI, GABRIELA. Buenos Aires, Argentina, 5/16/70. Tennis player.
SADE (Helen Folasade Adu). Ibadan, Nigeria, 1/16/59. Singer.
SAGAL, KATEY. Los Angeles, CA, 1956. Actor. Peg on *Married . . . with Children.*
SAGAN, CARL. New York, NY, 11/9/34. Astronomer. *Cosmos.*
SAGET, BOB. Philadelphia, PA, 5/17/56. Actor. *Full House.*
SAHM, DOUG. San Antonio, TX, 11/6/41. Singer, guitarist. Sir Douglas Quintet.
SAINT, EVA MARIE. Newark, NJ, 7/4/24. Actor. *On the Waterfront.*
SAINT JAMES, SUSAN (Susan Miller). Los Angeles, CA, 8/14/46. Actor. Kate on *Kate & Allie.*
SAJAK, PAT. Chicago, IL, 10/26/46. Game show host. *Wheel of Fortune.*
SALAZAR, ALBERTO. Havana, Cuba, 8/7/58. Track athlete, won New York City Marathon.
SALES, SOUPY. Wake Forest, NC, 1/8/30. TV personality. *The Soupy Sales Show.*
SALINGER, J. D. (Jerome David Salinger). New York, NY, 1/1/19. Author. *The Catcher in the Rye.*
SALT, JENNIFER. Los Angeles, CA, 9/4/44. Actor. *Midnight Cowboy.*
SAMBORA, RICHIE. 7/11/59. Guitarist. Bon Jovi.
SAMMS, EMMA. London, England, 8/28/60. Actor. Fallon Carrington Colby on *Dynasty* and *The Colbys.*
SAMPRAS, PETE. Washington, DC, 8/12/71. Tennis player.
SAMWELL-SMITH, PAUL. Richmond, England, 5/8/43. Bassist. The Yardbirds.
SAN GIACOMO, LAURA. New Jersey, 1962. Actor. *sex, lies and videotape.*
SANDERS, RICHARD. Harrisburg, PA, 8/23/40. Actor. Les Nessman on *WKRP in Cincinnati.*
SANDS, JULIAN. Yorkshire, England, 1958. Actor. *A Room with a View.*
SANDY, GARY. Dayton, OH, 11/3/46. Actor. Andy Travis on *WKRP in Cincinnati.*
SANFORD, ISABEL. New York, NY, 8/29/33. Actor. Louise on *The Jeffersons.*
SANTANA, CARLOS. Autlan de Navarro, Mexico, 7/20/47. Guitarist, singer. Santana.
SANTIAGO, HERMAN. New York, NY 2/18/41. Singer. Frankie Lymon & The Teenagers.
SARANDON, CHRIS. Beckley, WV, 7/24/42. Actor, former husband of Susan. Leon in *Dog Day Afternoon.*
SASSOON, VIDAL. London, England, 1/17/28. Hairstylist.
SAVAGE, FRED. Highland Park, IL, 7/9/76. Actor. Brother of Ben. Kevin Arnold on *The Wonder Years.*
SAVAGE, JOHN (John Youngs). Long Island, NY, 8/25/49. Actor. *The Deer Hunter.*
SAVAGE, RICK. Sheffield, England, 12/2/60. Bassist. Def Leppard.
SAVANT, DOUG. 6/21/64. Actor. *Melrose Place.*
SAWYER, RAY. Chickasaw, AL, 2/1/37. Lead singer. Dr. Hook.
SAYER, LEO (Gerard Sayer). Shoreham-by-Sea, England, 5/21/48. Singer, songwriter. "You Make Me Feel Like Dancing."
SCABIES, RAT (Chris Miller). Kingston-upon-Thames, England, 7/30/57. Drummer. The Damned.
SCACCHI, GRETA. Milan, Italy, 2/18/60. Actor. *Presumed Innocent.*
SCAGGS, BOZ (William Scaggs). Ohio, 6/8/44. Guitarist, singer, songwriter. "Lowdown."
SCALIA, JACK. Brooklyn, NY, 11/10/51. Actor. *Wolf.*
SCARPELLI, GLENN. Staten Island, NY, 7/6/68. Actor. Alex Handris on *One Day at a Time.*
SCHACHER, MEL. Flint, MI, 4/3/51. Bassist. Grand Funk Railroad.
SCHEIDER, ROY. Orange, NJ, 11/10/32. Actor. Chief Brody in *Jaws.*
SCHELL, MAXIMILIAN. Vienna, Austria, 12/8/30. Actor. *Judgment at Nuremberg.*
SCHENKER, RUDOLPH. 8/31/48. Guitarist. Scorpions.
SCHERMIE, JOE. Madison, WI, 2/12/45. Bassist. Three Dog Night.
SCHNEIDER, FRED. Newark, GA, 7/1/51. Keyboardist, singer. The B-52's.
SCHNEIDER, MARIA. Paris, France, 3/27/52. Actor. *Last Tango in Paris.*
SCHNEIDER-ESLEBEN, FLORIAN. Dusseldorf, Germany, 1947. Keyboardist, drummer, singer, woodwindist. Kraftwerk.
SCHOLZ, TOM. Toledo, OH, 3/10/47. Guitarist, keyboardist. Boston.
SCHON, NEAL. San Mateo, CA, 2/27/54. Guitarist. Journey.
SCHORR, DANIEL. New York, NY, 8/31/16. Broadcast journalist. *CBS News.*
SCHRODER, RICK. Staten Island, NY, 4/13/70. Actor. *Lonesome Dove.*
SCHULTZ, DWIGHT. Baltimore, MD, 11/24/47. Actor. H. M. "Howling Mad" Murdock on *The A-Team.*
SCHULZ, CHARLES. Minneapolis, MN, 11/26/22. Cartoonist. *Peanuts.*
SCHWARZKOPF, NORMAN. Trenton, NJ, 8/22/34. Retired army general, Gulf War hero.

SCHYGULLA, HANNA. Katlowitz, Germany, 12/25/43. Actor. *Dead Again.*
SCIORRA, ANNABELLA. New York, NY, 1964. Actor. *The Hand That Rocks the Cradle.*
SCOLARI, PETER. New Rochelle, NY, 9/12/55. Actor. *Bosom Buddies.*
SCOTT, ANDY. Wrexham, Wales, 6/30/51. Guitarist. Sweet.
SCOTT, BON (Ronald Scott). Kirriemuir, Scotland, 7/9/46. Singer. AC/DC.
SCOTT, GEORGE C. Wise, VA, 10/18/27. Actor, married to Trish Van Devere. *Patton.*
SCOTT, GORDON (Gordon Werschkul). Portland, OR, 8/3/27. Actor. *Tarzan's Hidden Jungle.*
SCOTT, HOWARD. San Pedro, CA, 3/15/46. Guitarist, singer. War.
SCOTT, MIKE. Edinburgh, Scotland, 12/14/58. Singer, guitarist. The Waterboys.
SCOTT, RIDLEY. South Shields, England, 11/30/37. Director, brother of director Tony. *Thelma and Louise.*
SCOTT, WILLARD. Alexandria, VA, 3/7/34. Weatherman. *Today.*
SEAL, ELIZABETH. Genoa, Italy, 8/28/33. Actor. *Irma La Douce.*
SEALE, BOBBY. Dallas, TX, 10/20/36. Political activist, author. Cofounder of the Black Panthers.
SEALS, JIM. Sidney, TX, 10/17/41. Singer, guitarist, saxophonist, violinist. Seals & Crofts.
SEAVER, TOM. Fresno, CA, 11/17/44. Baseball pitcher. New York Mets.
SEBASTIAN, JOHN. New York, NY, 3/17/44. Singer, guitarist, harmonicist, autoharpist. "The Lovin' Spoonful."
SEDAKA, NEIL. Brooklyn, NY, 3/13/39. Pop singer, songwriter. "Laughter in the Rain."
SEEGER, PETE. New York, NY, 5/3/19. Folk singer, songwriter, guitarist, social activist. Founded The Weavers.
SEGAL, GEORGE. New York, NY, 2/13/34. Actor. *Look Who's Talking.*
SEGER, BOB. Dearborn, MI, 5/6/45. Singer, songwriter. The Silver Bullet Band.
SELLECCA, CONNIE. The Bronx, NY, 5/25/55. Actor, married to John Tesh. *Hotel.*
SELLECK, TOM. Detroit, MI, 1/29/45. Actor. *Magnum, P.I.*
SENDAK, MAURICE. New York, NY, 1/10/28. Author, illustrator. *Where the Wild Things Are.*
SENSIBLE, CAPTAIN (Ray Burns). England, 4/23/55. Bassist. The Damned.
SERAPHINE, DANNY. Chicago, IL, 8/28/48. Drummer. Chicago.
SERGEANT, WILL. Liverpool, England, 4/12/58. Guitarist. Echo & The Bunnymen.
SETZER, BRIAN. 4/10/60. Guitarist, singer. The Stray Cats.
SEVERIN, STEVE. 9/25/55. Bassist. Siouxsie & The Banshees.
SEYMOUR, STEPHANIE. San Diego, CA, 7/23/68. Supermodel.
SHALIT, GENE. New York, NY, 1932. Critic. *Today.*
SHANDLING, GARY. Chicago, IL, 11/29/49. Actor. *The Larry Sanders Show.*
SHANNON, DEL (Charles Westover). Coopersville, MI, 12/30/34. Singer, songwriter. "Runaway."
SHAPIRO, HELEN. Bethnal Green, England, 9/28/46. Singer, actor. Cabaret Performer.
SHARIF, OMAR (Michel Shalhoub). Alexandria, Egypt, 4/10/32. Actor. *Dr. Zhivago.*
SHARKEY, FEARGAL. 8/13/58. Singer. The Undertones.
SHARP, DAVE. Salford, England, 1/28/59. Guitarist. The Alarm.
SHARPTON, AL. Brooklyn, NY, 1954. Politician, activist, clergyman.
SHAVER, HELEN. St. Thomas, Canada, 2/24/51. Actor. *The Amityville Horror.*
SHAW, SANDIE (Sandra Goodrich). Dagenham, England, 2/26/47. Pop singer.
SHAW, TOMMY. Montgomery, AL, 9/11/52. Lead guitarist. Styx.
SHAWN, WALLACE. New York, NY, 11/12/43. Playwright, actor. *My Dinner with Andre.*
SHEA, JOHN. North Conway, NH, 4/14/49. Actor. *Lois & Clark.*
SHEARER, HARRY. Los Angeles, CA, 12/23/43. Actor. *This Is Spinal Tap.*
SHEEDY, ALLY. New York, NY, 6/13/62. Actor. *WarGames.*
SHEEHAN, FRAN. Boston, MA, 3/26/49. Bassist. Boston.
SHEEN, MARTIN (Ramon Estevez). Dayton, OH, 8/3/40. Actor, father of Charlie Sheen and Emilio Estevez. *Apocalypse Now.*
SHEILA E. (Sheila Escovedo). Oakland, CA, 12/12/59. Drummer, singer.
SHELDON, SIDNEY. Chicago, IL, 2/11/17. Novelist, producer. *The Other Side of Midnight.*
SHELLEY, CAROLE. London, England, 8/16/39. Actor. *The Elephant Man.*
SHELLEY, PETE. 4/17/55. Guitarist, singer. The Buzzcocks.
SHEPARD, SAM (Sam Rogers). Ft. Sheridan, IL, 11/5/43. Playwright, actor. *True West; The Right Stuff.*
SHEPHERD, CYBILL. Memphis, TN, 2/18/50. Actor. Maddie Hayes on *Moonlighting.*
SHERIDAN, JIM. Dublin, Ireland, 1949. Director, writer. *My Left Foot.*
SHERIDAN, NICOLLETTE. Worthington, England, 11/21/63. Actor, model. *The Sure Thing.*
SHIELDS, BROOKE. New York, NY, 5/31/65. Model, actor. *The Blue Lagoon.*
SHIRE, TALIA. Lake Success, NY, 4/25/46. Actor, sister of Francis Ford Coppola. *Rocky I–V.*
SHORROCK, GLENN. Rochester, England, 6/30/44. Singer. The Little River Band.
SHORT, MARTIN. Toronto, Canada, 3/26/50. Actor. Ed Grimley on *Saturday Night Live.*
SHOWALTER, MAX (Casey Adams). Caldwell, KS, 6/2/17. Actor. First Ward Cleaver in the *Leave It to Beaver* pilot, "It's a Small World."
SHRIVER, MARIA. Chicago, IL, 11/6/55. Broadcast journalist, married to Arnold Schwarzenegger. *First Person with Maria Shriver.*
SIEGEL, JAY. Brooklyn, NY, 10/20/39. Baritone singer. The Tokens.
SIEGEL, JERRY. Cleveland, OH, 10/17/14. Cartoonist. *Superman.*
SIKKING, JAMES B. Los Angeles, CA, 3/5/34. Actor. Lt. Howard Hunter on *Hill Street Blues.*
SILLS, BEVERLY. New York, NY, 5/25/29. Opera singer.
SILVER, RON. New York, NY, 7/2/46. Actor, director. *Reversal of Fortune.*
SILVERMAN, JONATHAN. Los Angeles, CA, 8/5/66. Actor. *Brighton Beach Memoirs.*
SIMMONS, GENE (Chaim Witz). Haifa, Israel, 8/25/50. Long-tongued bassist, singer. Kiss.
SIMMONS, JEAN. London, England, 1/31/29. Actor. *The Thorn Birds.*
SIMMONS, JOSEPH. Queens, NY, 1964. Rap artist. Run-D.M.C.
SIMMONS, PATRICK. San Jose, CA, 1/23/50. Guitarist, singer. The Doobie Brothers.
SIMMONS, RICHARD. New Orleans, LA, 7/12/48. Health guru. *Sweatin' to the Oldies.*
SIMON, CARLY. New York, NY, 6/25/45. Singer, songwriter, childrens' book author.
SIMONE, NINA. Tryon, NC, 2/21/33. Singer. Soundtrack for *The Crying Game.*
SIMONON, PAUL. Brixton, England, 12/15/55. Bassist. The Clash.
SIMPSON, O. J. (Orenthal James Simpson). San Francisco, CA, 7/9/47. Actor, sportscaster, football great. Alleged murderer of his ex-wife and her friend. *The Naked Gun.*
SINCLAIR, MADGE. Kingston, Jamaica, 4/28/38. Actor. *Trapper John, MD.*
SINGER, LORI. Corpus Christi, TX, 5/6/62. Actor. *Fame.*
SINGLETON, JOHN. Los Angeles, CA, 1/6/68. Director, writer. *Boyz N the Hood.*
SINGLETON, STEPHEN Sheffield, England, 4/17/59. Saxophonist. ABC.
SIOUX, SIOUXSIE (Susan Dallon). Chiselhurst, England, 5/27/57. Singer. Siouxsie & The Banshees.
SISKEL, GENE. Chicago, IL, 1/26/46. Critic. *Siskel & Ebert & The Movies.*
SIXX, NIKKI (Frank Ferrano). Seattle, WA, 12/11/58 Bassist. Mötley Crüe.
SKELTON, RED (Richard Skelton). Vincennes, IN, 7/18/13. Actor. *The Red Skelton Show*
SKYE, IONE (Ione Leitch). London, England, 9/4/71. Actor, daughter of folk singer Donovan, brother of Donovan Leitch. *Say Anything.*
SLATER, HELEN. New York, NY, 12/15/65. Actor. *Supergirl.*
SLATER, RODNEY. Lincolnshire, England, 11/8/44. Saxophonist, trumpeter. The Bonzo Dog Doo-Dah Band.
SLEDGE, DEBBIE. Philadelphia, PA, 7/9/54. Singer. Sister Sledge.
SLEDGE, JONI. Philadelphia, PA, 9/13/56. Singer. Sister Sledge.
SLEDGE, KATHY. Philadelphia, PA, 1/6/59. Singer. Sister Sledge.
SLEDGE, KIM. Philadelphia, PA, 8/21/57. Singer. Sister Sledge.
SLEDGE, PERCY. Leighton, AL, 11/25/40. Singer. "When a Man Loves a Woman."

SLICK, GRACE (Grace Wing). Chicago, IL, 10/30/39. Singer. Jefferson Airplane/Starship.
SLIWA, CURTIS. New York, NY, 3/26/54. Founder of the Guardian Angels.
SMIRNOFF, YAKOV (Yakov Pokhis). Odessa, Russia, 1/24/51. Actor. *What a Country!*
SMITH, ADRIAN. Huckney, England, 2/27/57. Guitarist. Iron Maiden.
SMITH, BOB. Buffalo, NY, 11/27/17. Entertainer. *Howdy Doody.*
SMITH, BOBBIE. 4/10/36. Singer. The (Detroit) Spinners.
SMITH, CHARLES MARTIN. Los Angeles, CA, 10/30/53. Actor. *American Graffiti.*
SMITH, CLAYDES. Jersey City, NJ, 9/6/48. Guitarist. Kool & The Gang.
SMITH, CURT. Bath, England, 6/24/61. Singer, bassist. Tears for Fears.
SMITH, MAGGIE. Ilford, England, 12/28/34. Actor. *Sister Act.*
SMITH, JACLYN. Houston, TX, 10/26/47. Actor. Kelly Garrett on *Charlie's Angels.*
SMITH, JEFF. Seattle, WA, 1/22/39. TV personality, chef, author. *The Frugal Gourmet.*
SMITH, JEROME. Miami, FL, 6/18/53. Guitarist. KC & The Sunshine Band.
SMITH, LARRY. Oxford, England, 1/18/44. Drummer. The Bonzo Dog Doo-Dah Band.
SMITH, LIZ. Fort Worth, TX, 2/2/23. Gossip columnist.
SMITH, MIKE. Neath, Wales, 11/4/47. Tenor saxophonist. Amen Corner.
SMITH, MIKE. Edmonton, England, 12/12/43. Singer, keyboardist. The Dave Clark Five.
SMITH, PATTI. Chicago, IL, 12/30/46. Singer, songwriter.
SMITH, PHIL. 5/1/59. Saxophonist. Haircut 100.
SMITH, ROBERT. Crawley, England, 4/21/59. Guitarist, singer. The Cure.
SMITS, JIMMY. New York, NY, 7/9/55. Actor. Victor Sifuentes on *L.A. Law.*
SMOTHERS, DICK. New York, NY, 2/20/39. Actor, singer, brother of Tom. *The Smothers Brothers Comedy Hour.*
SMOTHERS, TOM. New York, NY, 2/2/37. Actor, singer, brother of Dick. *The Smothers Brothers Comedy Hour.*
SNEED, FLOYD. Calgary, Canada, 11/22/43. Drummer. Three Dog Night.
SNODGRESS, CARRIE. Chicago, IL, 10/27/46. Actor. *Diary of a Mad Housewife.*
SNYDER, TOM. Milwaukee, WI, 5/12/36. Newscaster, interviewer. *Tomorrow.*
SOMERS, SUZANNE (Suzanne Mahoney). San Bruno, CA, 10/16/46. Actor. *Three's Company.*
SOMERVILLE, JIMMY. Glasgow, Scotland, 6/22/61. Dance/rock singer, keyboardist.
SOMMER, ELKE (Elke Schletz). Berlin, Germany, 11/5/40. Actor. *A Shot in the Dark.*
SORVINO, PAUL. New York, NY, 1939. Actor. *GoodFellas.*
SOTHERN, ANN (Harriet Lake). Valley City, ND, 1/22/09. Actor. *The Ann Sothern Show.*
SOUL, DAVID (David Solberg). Chicago, IL, 8/28/43. Actor. Kevin "Hutch" Hutchinson on *Starsky and Hutch.*
SOUTH, JOE. Atlanta, GA, 2/28/40. Rock/country guitarist, singer, songwriter.
SOUTHSIDE JOHNNY (Johnny Lyon). Neptune Park, NJ, 12/4/48. Singer. Southside Johnny & The Asbury Jukes.
SPACEK, SISSY (Mary Elizabeth Spacek). Quitman, TX, 12/25/49. Actor. *Coal Miner's Daughter.*
SPADER, JAMES. Boston, MA, 2/7/60. Actor. *sex, lies, and videotape.*
SPANO, JOE. San Francisco, CA, 7/7/46. Actor. Henry Goldblume on *Hill Street Blues.*
SPANO, VINCENT. New York, NY, 10/18/62. Actor. *Rumble Fish.*
SPEAR, ROGER. London, England, 6/29/43. Saxophonist, kazooist. The Bonzo Dog Doo-Dah Band.
SPECTOR, PHIL. New York, NY, 12/26/40. Music producer. Wall of sound.
SPELLING, TORI. Los Angeles, CA, 5/16/73. Actor. *Beverly Hills, 90210.*
SPENCE, ALEXANDER. Windsor, Canada, 4/18/46. Guitarist, lead singer. Moby Grape.
SPENCER, JEREMY. West Hartlepoole, England, 7/4/48. Guitarist. Fleetwood Mac.
SPILLANE, MICKEY (Frank Morrison). New York, NY, 3/9/18. Author. Mike Hammer detective stories.
SPINKS, LEON. St. Louis, MO, 7/11/53. Boxer, former heavyweight champion, brother of Michael.
SPINKS, MICHAEL. St. Louis, MO, 7/29/56. Boxer. Olympic gold medalist, brother of Leon.
SPOCK, BENJAMIN. New Haven, CT, 5/2/03. Physician, author. *Common Sense Book of Baby Care.*
SPOONER, BILL. Phoenix, AZ, 4/16/49. Guitarist. The Tubes.
SPRINGFIELD, DUSTY (Mary O'Brien). Hampstead, England, 4/16/39. Folk/pop singer.
SPRINGFIELD, RICK (Richard Spring Thorpe). Sydney, Australia, 8/23/49. Singer, actor. *General Hospital.*
SQUIER, BILLY. Wellesley, MA, 5/12/50. Singer. "Everybody Wants You."
SQUIRE, CHRIS. London, England, 3/4/48. Bassist. Yes.
SQUIRE, JOHN. Sale, England, 11/24/62. Lead guitarist. The Stone Roses.
ST. JOHN, JILL (Jill Oppenheim). Los Angeles, CA, 8/19/40. Actor. *Diamonds are Forever.*
STACK, ROBERT. Los Angeles, CA, 1/13/19. Actor. Eliot Ness on *The Untouchables.*
STAFFORD, JIM. Eloise, FL, 1/16/44. Singer, songwriter. "Spiders and Snakes."
STAMOS, JOHN. Cypress, CA, 8/19/63. Actor. *Full House.*
STAMP, TERENCE. London, England, 7/23/39. Actor. *Superman II.*
STANLEY, PAUL (Paul Eisen). Queens, NY, 1/20/50. Guitarist, singer. Kiss.
STANSFIELD, LISA. Rochdale, England, 4/11/66. Singer, songwriter. "All Around the World."
STANSHALL, VIVIAN. Shillingford, England, 3/21/43. Singer, trumpeter. The Bonzo Dog Doo-Dah Band.
STANTON, HARRY DEAN. West Irvine, KY, 7/14/26. Actor. *Paris, Texas.*
STAPLES, NEVILLE. 4/11/56. Singer, percussionist. The Specials.
STAPLES, PETE. Andover, England, 5/3/44. Bassist. The Troggs.
STAPLETON, JEAN (Jeanne Murray). New York, NY, 1/19/23. Actor. Edith Bunker on *All in the Family.*
STAPLETON, MAUREEN. Troy, NY, 6/21/25. Actor. *Airport.*
STARR, RINGO (Richard Starkey). Liverpool, England, 7/7/40. Drummer, singer, actor, married to Barbara Bach. The Beatles.
STAUBACH, ROGER. Cincinnati, OH, 2/5/42. NFL football player. Dallas Cowboys.
STAX, JOHN (John Fullegar). London, England, 4/6/44. Bassist. The Pretty Things.
STEEL, JOHN. Gateshead, England, 2/4/41. Drummer. The Animals.
STEELE, DAVID. Birmingham, England, 9/8/60. Keyboardist, bassist. Fine Young Cannibals.
STEELE, MICHAEL. 6/2/54. Bassist, singer. The Bangles; The Runaways.
STEELE, TOMMY (Thomas Hicks). Bermondsey, England, 12/17/36. Guitarist, singer, actor.
STEENBURGEN, MARY. Newport, AR, 2/8/53. Actor. *Parenthood.*
STEIGER, ROD. Westhampton, NY, 4/14/25. Actor. *In the Heat of the Night.*
STEIN, CHRIS. Brooklyn, NY, 1/5/50. Guitarist. Blondie.
STEIN, MARK. Bayonne, NJ, 3/11/47. Singer, organist. Vanilla Fudge.
STEINBERG, DAVID. Winnipeg, Canada, 8/9/42. Actor, director. *Paternity.*
STEINEM, GLORIA. Toledo, OH, 3/25/34. Women's rights activist.
STERBAN, RICHARD. Camden, NJ, 4/24/44. Singer, bassist. The Oak Ridge Boys.
STERN, DANIEL. Bethesda, MD, 8/28/57. Actor, narrator of *The Wonder Years. City Slickers.*
STERN, ISAAC. Kreminiecz, Russia, 7/21/20. Violinist.
STERNHAGEN, FRANCES. Washington, DC, 1/13/30. Actor. *Driving Miss Daisy.*
STEVENS, ANDREW. Memphis, TN, 6/10/55. Actor. *Dallas.*
STEVENS, CAT (Steven Georgiou). Soho, England, 7/21/47. Folk singer, songwriter—left recording upon conversion to Islam.
STEVENS, CONNIE (Concetta Ann Ingolia). Brooklyn, NY, 8/8/38. Actor. *Hawaiian Eye.*
STEVENS, FISHER. Chicago, IL, 11/27/63. Actor. *Short Circuit.*
STEVENS, RAY. Clarksdale, GA, 1/24/39. Singer. *Andy Williams Presents Ray Stevens.*
STEVENS, SHAKIN' (Michael Barratt). Ely, Wales, 3/4/48. Singer, actor.
STEVENS, STELLA (Estelle Eggleston). Hot Coffee, MS, 10/1/36. Actor. *Santa Barbara.*
STEVENSON, DON. Seattle, WA, 10/15/42. Drummer. Moby Grape.

STEVENSON, MCLEAN. Bloomington, IL, 11/14/29. Actor. Lt. Colonel Henry Blake on *M*A*S*H.*
STEVENSON, PARKER. Philadelphia, PA, 6/4/52. Actor, married to Kirstie Alley. *Falcon Crest.*
STEWART, AL. Glasgow, Scotland, 9/5/45. Guitarist, singer, songwriter.
STEWART, DAVE. Sunderland, England, 9/9/52. Keyboardist, guitarist. Eurythmics.
STEWART, ERIC. Manchester, England, 1/20/45. Singer, guitarist. 10cc.
STEWART, JIMMY. Indiana, PA, 5/20/08. Actor. *It's a Wonderful Life.*
STEWART, MARTHA (Martha Haworth). Bardwell, KY, 10/7/22. Actor. *Holocaust.*
STEWART, ROD. Highgate, England, 1/10/45. Singer, songwriter.
STIERS, DAVID OGDEN. Peoria, IL, 10/31/42. Actor. Dr. Charles Emerson Winchester on *M*A*S*H.*
STILES, RAY. Carshalton, England, 11/20/46. Bassist, singer. Mud.
STILLER, JERRY. New York, NY, 6/8/31. Actor, partner/married to Anne Meara, father of Ben Stiller.
STILLS, STEPHEN. Dallas, TX, 1/3/45. Singer, guitarist. Buffalo Springfield; Crosby, Stills, Nash & Young.
STIPE, MICHAEL. Decatur, GA, 1/4/60. Singer, songwriter. R.E.M.
STOCKDALE, JAMES. Abington, IL, 12/23/23. Vietnam POW, running mate of presidential candidate Ross Perot.
STOCKWELL, DEAN. Hollywood, CA, 3/5/35. Actor. Al Calavicci on *Quantum Leap.*
STOCKWELL, JOHN (John Samuels). Galveston, TX, 3/25/61. Actor. *My Science Project.*
STOLTZ, ERIC. American Samoa, 9/30/61. Actor. *Mask.*
STONE, DEE WALLACE (Deanna Bowers). Kansas City, MO, 12/14/48. Actor. Mother in *E.T., the Extra-Terrestrial.*
STONE, FREDDIE. Dallas, TX, 6/5/46. Guitarist. Sly & The Family Stone.
STONE, ROSIE. Vallejo, CA, 3/21/45. Singer, keyboardist. Sly & The Family Stone.
STONE, SLY (Sylvester Stewart). Dallas, TX, 3/15/44. Singer, keyboardist, guitarist. Sly & The Family Stone.
STORCH, LARRY. New York, NY, 1/8/23. Actor. *F Troop.*
STORM, GALE (Josephine Cottle). Bloomington, TX, 4/5/22. Actor. *My Little Margie.*
STRASSMAN, MARCIA. New York, NY, 4/28/48. Actor. Julie Kotter on *Welcome Back Kotter.*
STRATHAIRN, DAVID. San Francisco, CA, 1949. Actor. *Matewan.*
STRATTON, DENNIS. London, England, 11/9/54. Guitarist. Iron Maiden.
STRAUSS, PETER. Croton-on-Hudson, NY, 2/20/47. Actor. *The Jericho Mile.*
STRICKLAND, KEITH. Athens, GA, 10/26/53. Drummer. The B-52's.
STRITCH, ELAINE. Detroit, MI, 2/2/25. Actor. *September.*
STRODE, WOODY. Los Angeles, CA, 7/25/14. Actor. *The Cotton Club.*
STRUMMER, JOE (John Mellors). Ankara, Turkey, 8/21/52. Singer, guitarist. The Clash.
STRUTHERS, SALLY. Portland, OR, 7/28/48. Actor. Gloria Bunker Stivic on *All in the Family.*
STRYKERT, RON. Australia, 8/18/57. Guitarist. Men at Work.
STUART, CHAD. England, 12/10/43. Singer, guitarist. Chad & Jeremy.
STUART, HAMISH. Glasgow, Scotland, 10/8/49. Singer, guitarist. Average White Band.
STUBBS, LEVI (Levi Stubbles). Detroit, MI, 6/6/36. Lead singer. The Four Tops.
SUCH, ALEC. 11/14/56. Bassist. Bon Jovi.
SULLIVAN, SUSAN. New York, NY, 11/18/44. Actor. Maggie Gioberti Channing on *Falcon Crest.*
SULLIVAN, TOM. Boston, MA, 3/27/47. Singer, actor, composer. "If You Could See What I Hear."
SUMMER, DONNA (LaDonna Gaines). Boston, MA, 12/31/48. Disco/pop singer. "Love To Love You Baby."
SUMMERS, ANDY (Andrew Somers). Poulton le Fylde, France, 12/31/42. Guitarist, singer. The Police.
SUMNER, BARNEY (Bernard Dicken). Salford, England, 1/4/56. Guitarist, singer. New Order.
SUTHERLAND, DONALD. St. John, Canada, 7/17/35. Actor, father of Kiefer. *Ordinary People.*
SUTHERLAND, KIEFER. Los Angeles, CA, 12/18/66. Actor, son of Donald. *Flatliners.*
SUTTON, JOHN. Rawalpindi, India, 10/22/08. Actor. *Of Human Bondage.*
SUZMAN, JANET. Johannesburg, South Africa, 2/9/39. Actor. *Nicholas and Alexandra.*
SVENSON, BO. Goreborg, Sweden, 2/13/41. Actor. *Walking Tall.*
SWAGGART, JIMMY. Ferriday, LA, 3/15/35. Evangelist.
SWANN, LYNN. Alcoa, TN, 3/7/52. NFL football player.
SWAYZE, PATRICK. Houston, TX, 8/18/52. Actor, dancer. *Dirty Dancing.*
SWEENEY, D. B. Shoreham, NY, 1961. Actor. *The Cutting Edge.*
SWEET, DERRELL. 5/16/47. Drummer, percussionist, singer. Nazareth.
SWEET, MATTHEW. Lincoln, NE, 10/6/64. Singer, songwriter, guitarist. "Girlfriend."
SWENSON, INGA. Omaha, NE, 12/29/32. Actor. Gretchen Kraus on *Benson.*
SWIT, LORETTA. Passaic, NJ, 11/4/37. Actor. Margaret "Hot Lips" Houlihan on *M*A*S*H.*
SYLVIAN, DAVID (David Batt). Lewisham, England, 2/23/58. Singer, guitarist. Japan.
T, MR. (Lawrence Tero). Chicago, IL, 5/21/52. Actor and wrestler. Bosco "B.A." Baracus on *The A-Team.*
TAJ MAHAL. New York, NY, 5/17/42. Singer, songwriter, composer. "Sounder."
TAKEI, GEORGE. Los Angeles, CA, 4/20/39. Mr. Sulu on *Star Trek.*
TALBOT, MICK. London, England, 9/11/58. Keyboardist. The Style Council.
TALLEY, GARY. Memphis, TN, 8/17/47. Guitarist. The Box Tops/Big Star.
TALLEY, NEDRA. New York, NY, 1/27/46. Singer. The Ronettes.
TAMBLYN, RUSS. Los Angeles, CA, 12/30/35. Actor. *West Side Story.*
TAMBOR, JEFFREY. San Francisco, CA, 7/8/44. Actor. *Hill Street Blues.*
TANDY, RICHARD. Birmingham, England, 3/26/48. Bassist. Electric Light Orchestra (ELO).
TARKENTON, FRAN. Richmond, VA, 2/3/40. Football player, sportscaster. *Monday Night Football.*
TAUPIN, BERNIE. Sleaford, England, 5/22/50. Lyricist. Wrote for Elton John.
TAYLOR, ANDY. Tynemouth, England, 2/16/61. Guitarist. Duran Duran.
TAYLOR, CLIVE. Cardiff, Wales, 4/27/49. Bassist. Amen Corner.
TAYLOR, DICK. Dartford, England, 1/28/43. Lead guitarist. The Pretty Things.
TAYLOR, JAMES. South Carolina, 8/16/53. Lead singer. Kool & The Gang.
TAYLOR, JAMES. Boston, MA, 3/12/48. Folk-oriented singer, songwriter.
TAYLOR, JOHN. Birmingham, AL, 6/20/60. Bassist. Duran Duran.
TAYLOR, LARRY. Brooklyn, NY, 6/26/42. Bassist. Canned Heat.
TAYLOR, LILI. Chicago, IL, 1967. Actor. *Mystic Pizza.*
TAYLOR, ROD. Sydney, Australia, 1/11/30. Actor. *The Time Machine.*
TAYLOR, ROGER. King's Lynn, England, 7/26/49. Drummer. Queen.
TENCH, BENMONT. Gainesville, FL, 9/7/54. Keyboardist. Tom Petty & The Heartbreakers.
TENNANT, NEIL. Gosforth, England, 7/10/54. Singer. Pet Shop Boys.
TENNANT, VICTORIA. London, England, 9/30/53. Actor, formerly married to Steve Martin. *L.A. Story.*
TENNILLE, TONI. Montgomery, AL, 5/8/43. Singer. The Captain & Tennille.
TERRANOVA, JOE. 1/30/41. Baritone. Danny & The Juniors.
TERRELL, TAMMI. Philadelphia, PA, 1946. Singer. "Your Precious Love."
TESH, JOHN. Garden City, NY, 7/9/52. Host and composer, married to Connie Sellecca. *Entertainment Tonight.*
THICKE, ALAN. Canada, 3/1/47. Actor. *Growing Pains.*
THISTLETHWAITE, ANTHONY. Leicester, England, 8/31/55. Saxophonist. The Waterboys.
THOMAS, B. J. (Billy Joe Thomas). Houston, TX, 8/7/42. Pop singer. "Raindrops Keep Fallin' on My Head."
THOMAS, BETTY. Saint Louis, MO, 7/27/48. Actor. Lucy Bates on *Hill Street Blues.*

THOMAS, DAVE. Saint Catharines, Canada, 6/20/49. Actor. Doug MacKenzie on *SCTV.*
THOMAS, HENRY. San Antonio, TX, 9/8/72. Actor. Elliot in *E.T., the Extra-Terrestrial.*
THOMAS, JAY. New Orleans, LA, 7/12/48. Actor, radio personality. *Murphy Brown.*
THOMAS, MARLO (Margaret Thomas). Detroit, MI, 11/21/38. Actor, married to Phil Donahue, daughter of Danny Thomas. *That Girl.*
THOMAS, MARY. Brooklyn, NY, 1946. Singer. The Crystals.
THOMAS, PHILIP MICHAEL. Columbus, OH, 5/26/49. Actor. Ricardo Tubbs on *Miami Vice.*
THOMAS, RAY. Stourport-on-Severn, England, 12/29/42. Flautist, harmonicist, singer. The Moody Blues.
THOMAS, RICHARD. New York, NY, 6/13/51. Actor. John Boy on *The Waltons.*
THOMPKINS, RUSSELL JR. Philadelphia, PA, 3/21/51. Lead singer. The Stylistics.
THOMPSON, LEA. Rochester, MN, 5/31/61. Actor. *Back to the Future.*
THOMPSON, PAUL. Jarrow, England, 5/13/51. Drummer. Roxy Music.
THOMPSON, SADA. Des Moines, IA, 9/27/29. Actor. *Family.*
THOMPSON, TONY. 11/15/54. Drummer. Chic.
THOMSON, DOUGIE. Scotland, 1951. Bassist. Supertramp.
THORN, TRACEY. 9/26/62. Singer. Everything but the Girl.
THORNE-SMITH, COURTNEY. 11/8/68. Actor. *Melrose Place.*
THORNTON, BLAIR. Vancouver, Canada, 7/23/50. Guitarist. Bachman-Turner Overdrive.
THOROGOOD, GEORGE. Wilmington, DE, 1951. Singer, guitarist. George Thorogood and the Delaware Destroyers.
THURMAN, UMA. Boston, MA, 4/29/70. Actor, formerly married to Gary Oldman. *Dangerous Liaisons.*
TICH (Ian Amey). Salisbury, England, 5/15/44. Lead guitarist. Dave Dee, Dozy, Beaky, Mick and Tich.
TIEGS, CHERYL. Alhambra, CA, 9/25/47. Model, author. *The Way to Natural Beauty.*
TIFFANY (Tiffany Renee Darwish). Norwalk, CA, 10/2/71. Singer.
TILBROOK, GLENN. London, England, 8/31/57. Singer, lead guitarist. Squeeze.
TILLIS, MEL. Pahokee, FL, 8/8/32. Singer, songwriter.
TILLY, MEG. Texada, Canada, 1960. Actor, sister of Jennifer. *The Big Chill.*
TILTON, CHARLENE. San Diego, CA, 12/1/58. Actor. Lucy Ewing Cooper on *Dallas.*
TIM, TINY. New York, NY, 4/12/22. Entertainer. "Tiptoe Through the Tulips."
TIPTON, GLENN. Birmingham, England, 10/25/48. Guitarist. Judas Priest.
TOLHURST, LOL (Laurence Tolhurst). 2/3/59. Keyboardist. The Cure.
TOLKAN, JAMES. Calumet, MI, 6/20/31. Actor. Principal in *Back to the Future.*
TOMLIN, LILY (Mary Jean Tomlin). Detroit, MI, 9/1/39. Actor. *Rowan & Martin's Laugh-In.*
TONE-LOC. Los Angeles, CA, 3/3/66. Rap artist. "Wild Thing."
TOPHAM, ANTHONY "TOP." England, 1947. Guitarist. The Yardbirds.
TORK, PETER (Peter Halsten Thorkelson). Washington, DC, 2/13/44. Keyboardist, bassist, actor. The Monkees.
TORME, MEL. Chicago, IL, 9/13/25. Singer.
TORN, RIP. Temple, TX, 2/6/31. Actor. *Blind Ambition.*
TORRENCE, DEAN. Los Angeles, CA, 3/10/40. Singer. Jan & Dean.
TOWNSEND, ROBERT. Chicago, IL, 2/6/57. Actor. *Hollywood Shuffle.*
TOWNSHEND, PETE. Chiswick, England, 5/19/45. Guitarist. The Who.
TOWNSON, RON. St. Louis, MO, 1/20/33. Singer. The 5th Dimension.
TRAVANTI, DANIEL J. Kenosha, WI, 3/7/40. Actor. Captain Frank Furillo on *Hill Street Blues.*
TRAVERS, BILL. Newcastle-upon-Tyne, England, 1/3/22. Actor, producer, director. *Born Free.*
TRAVERS, BRIAN. Birmingham, England, 2/7/59. Saxophonist. UB40.
TRAVIS, RANDY (Randy Traywick). Marshville, NC, 5/4/59. Country singer, songwriter.
TRAVOLTA, JOHN. Englewood, NJ, 2/18/54. Actor. *Saturday Night Fever.*
TREBEK, ALEX. Sudbury, Canada, 7/22/40. Game show host. *Jeopardy!*
TRESVANT, RALPH. Boston, MA, 5/16/68. Singer. New Edition.
TREVOR, CLAIRE. New York, NY, 3/8/09. Actor. *Key Largo.*
TREWAVAS, PETER. Middlesborough, England, 1/15/59. Keyboardist. Marillion.
TRITT, TRAVIS. Marietta, GA, 2/9/63. Country singer, songwriter.
TROWER, ROBIN. Southend, England, 3/9/45. Guitarist. Procol Harum.
TRUDEAU, GARRY (Garretson Beckman Trudeau). New York, NY, 1948. Cartoonist. *Doonesbury.*
TRUGOY THE DOVE (David Jolicoeur). 9/21/68. Musician. De La Soul.
TRUMP, DONALD. New York, NY, 6/14/46. Real estate developer, author. Married to Marla Maples, formerly married to Ivana Winkelmayr Trump.
TRUMP, MARLA MAPLES. 10/27/63. Actor. Married to Donald Trump. *The Will Rogers Follies.*
TSONGAS, PAUL. Lowell, MA, 2/14/41. Politician. Presidential candidate.
TUCKER, JIM. Los Angeles, CA, 10/17/46. Guitarist. The Turtles.
TUCKER, MICHAEL. Baltimore, MD, 2/6/44. Actor. *L.A. Law.*
TUCKER, MICK. Harlesden, England, 7/17/49. Drummer. Sweet.
TUCKER, TANYA (Denise Tucker). Seminole, TX, 10/10/58. Pop singer. "Delta Dawn."
TUFANO, DENNIS. Chicago, IL, 9/11/46. Guitarist, lead singer. The Buckinghams.
TUNE, TOMMY. Wichita Falls, TX, 2/28/39. Actor, director, choreographer, dancer.
TURBO B. 4/30/67. Rap artist. Snap.
TURNER, C. F. Winnipeg, Canada, 10/16/43. Bassist, singer. Bachman-Turner Overdrive.
TURNER, IKE. Clarksdale, MS, 11/5/31. Singer, songwriter, formerly married to Tina Turner. Ike & Tina Turner.
TURNER, LANA (Julia Jean Mildred Frances Turner). Wallace, ID, 2/8/81. Actor. *Imitation of Life.*
TURNER, LONNIE. Berkeley, CA, 2/24/47. Bassist, singer. The Steve Miller Band.
TUROW, SCOTT. Chicago, IL, 4/12/49. Author. *The Burden of Proof.*
TURTURRO, JOHN. Brooklyn, NY, 2/28/57. Actor. *Barton Fink.*
TWIGGY (Lesley Hornby). London, England, 9/19/49. Model, actor. *The Boy Friend.*
TWIST, NIGEL. Manchester, England, 7/18/58. Drummer. The Alarm.
TYLER, BONNIE. Swansea, Wales, 6/8/53. Singer. "Total Eclipse of the Heart."
TYSON, CICELY. New York, NY, 12/19/33. Actor. *The Autobiography of Miss Jane Pittman.*
TYSON, MIKE. New York, NY, 7/1/66. Boxing champ, convicted rapist, formerly married to Robin Givens.
UECKER, BOB. Milwaukee, WI, 1/26/35. Actor. *Mr. Belvedere.*
UGGAMS, LESLIE. New York, NY, 5/25/43. Singer, actor. Kizzy in *Roots.*
ULLMAN, TRACEY. Hackbridge, England, 12/29/59. Actor. *The Tracey Ullman Show.*
ULLMANN, LIV. Tokyo, Japan, 12/16/39. Actor. *Persona.*
ULVAEUS, BJORN. Gothenburg, Sweden, 4/25/45. Guitarist, singer. Abba.
URICH, ROBERT. Toronto, Canada, 12/19/46. Actor. *Spenser: For Hire.*
VACCARO, BRENDA. Brooklyn, NY, 11/18/39. Actor. *Midnight Cowboy.*
VADIM, ROGER. Paris, France, 1/26/28. Movie director.
VALE, JERRY. New York, NY, 7/8/32. Pop singer. "Innamorata."
VALE, MIKE. 7/17/49. Bassist. Tommy James & The Shondells.
VALENTINE, HILTON. North Shields, England, 5/21/43. Guitarist. The Animals.
VALENTINE, SCOTT. Saratoga Springs, NY, 6/3/58. Actor. Nick Moore on *Family Ties.*
VALLI, FRANKIE (Frank Castelluccio). Newark, NJ, 5/3/37. Lead singer. The Four Seasons.
VALLONE, RAF (Raffaele Vallone). Tropea, Italy, 2/17/18. Actor. *Obsession.*
VALORY, ROSS. San Francisco, CA, 2/2/49. Bassist. Journey.
VAN ARK, JOAN. New York, NY, 6/16/43. Actor. Val Ewing *Knots Landing.*
VAN DEVERE, TRISH (Patricia Dressel). Englewood Cliffs, NJ, 3/9/45. Actor, married to George C. Scott. *The Day of the Dolphin.*
VAN DOREN, MAMIE (Joan Lucile Olander). Rowena, SD, 2/6/33. Actor. *Ain't Misbehavin'.*

VAN DYKE, DICK. West Plains, MO, 12/13/25. Actor and performer, brother of Jerry. *The Dick Van Dyke Show.*
VAN DYKE, JERRY. Danville, IL, 7/27/31. Actor, brother of Dick. *Coach.*
VAN HALEN, ALEX. Nijmegen, Holland, 5/8/55. Drummer. Van Halen.
VAN PATTEN, DICK. New York, NY, 12/9/28. Actor. *Eight Is Enough.*
VAN PEEBLES, MARIO. New York, NY, 1/15/57. Actor, director, writer, son of Melvin. *Posse.*
VAN PEEBLES, MELVIN. Chicago, IL, 8/21/32. Actor, writer, composer, father of Mario. *Sweet Sweetback's Badasssss Song.*
VAN ZANDT, DONNIE. Florida, 6/11/52. Singer, guitarist. .38 Special.
VAN ZANDT, STEVIE. 11/22/50. Bassist. E Street Band.
VANDA, HARRY (Harry Vandenberg). The Hague, The Netherlands, 3/22/47. Guitarist. The Easybeats.
VANDERBILT, GLORIA. New York, NY, 2/20/24. Fashion designer. Gloria Vanderbilt Jeans.
VANIAN, DAVE (David Letts). 10/12/56. Singer. The Damned.
VANITY (Denise Mathews). Niagara, Canada, 1/3/63. Former singer and actor (a.k.a. D. D. Winters), now Christian Evangelist, bible student. *The Last Dragon.*
VANNELLI, GINO. Montreal, Canada, 6/16/52. Singer, songwriter. "Living Inside Myself."
VARNEY, JIM. Lexington, KY, 6/15/49. Actor. *Ernest Goes to Camp.*
VAUGHAN, SARAH. 3/27/24. Blues singer.
VAUGHN, ROBERT. New York, NY, 11/22/32. Actor. *The Man from U.N.C.L.E.*
VEE, BOBBY (Robert Velline). Fargo, ND, 4/30/43. Singer, songwriter.
VEGA, SUZANNE. New York, NY, 8/12/59. Folk-oriented guitarist, singer, songwriter. "Luka."
VELEZ, EDDIE (Edwin Velez). New York, NY, 6/4/58. Actor. *Extremities.*
VELJOHNSON, REGINALD. Queens, NY, 8/16/52. Actor. *Family Matters.*
VERDON, GWEN. Culver City, CA, 1/13/25. Actor, dancer, choreographer. *The Cotton Club.*
VEREEN, BEN. Miami, FL, 10/10/46. Actor, performer. Chicken George Moore on *Roots.*
VERLAINE, TOM (Thomas Miller). Mt. Morris, NJ, 12/13/49. Singer, lead guitarist. Television.
VERUSCHKA. 1943. Model, actor. *Blow Up.*
VESTINE, HENRY. Washington, DC, 12/25/44. Guitarist. Canned Heat.
VICKERS, MIKE. Southampton, England, 4/18/41. Guitarist. Manfred Mann.
VIDAL, GORE (Eugene Luther Vidal). West Point, NY, 10/3/25. Author, dramatist. *Lincoln: A Novel.*
VINCENT, JAN-MICHAEL. Denver, CO, 7/15/44. Actor. *The Mechanic.*
VINTON, BOBBY. Canonsburg, PA, 4/16/35. Singer, songwriter.
VIRTUE, MICKEY. Birmingham, England, 1/19/57. Keyboardist. UB40.
VOIGHT, JON. Yonkers, NY, 12/29/38. Actor. *Midnight Cowboy.*
VOLMAN, MARK. Los Angeles, CA, 4/19/47. Singer, saxophonist. The Turtles.
VON BULOW, CLAUS. Copenhagen, Denmark, 8/11/26. Businessman. Subject of the motion picture *Reversal of Fortune.*
VON SYDOW, MAX. Lund, Sweden, 7/10/29. Actor. *The Greatest Story Ever Told.*
VONNEGUT, KURT JR. Indianapolis, IN, 11/11/22. Author. Married to Jill Krementz. *Slaughterhouse Five.*
WAAKTAAR, PAUL. Oslo, Norway, 9/6/61. Guitarist, singer. a-ha.
WAGGONER, LYLE. Kansas City, KS, 4/13/35. Actor. *Wonder Woman.*
WAGNER, JACK. Washington, MO, 10/3/59. Actor, singer. Frisco Jones on *General Hospital.*
WAGNER, LINDSAY. Los Angeles, CA, 6/22/49. Actor. *The Bionic Woman.*
WAGNER, ROBERT. Detroit, MI, 2/10/30. Actor, widower of Natalie Wood. Jonathan Hart on *Hart to Hart.*
WAHL, KEN. Chicago, IL, 2/14/53. Actor. Vinnie Terranova on *Wiseguy.*
WAHLBERG, DONNIE. Dorchester, MA, 8/17/70. Singer, brother of Marky Mark. New Kids on the Block.
WAILER, BUNNY (Neville O'Riley). Kingston, Jamaica, 4/10/47. Singer, percussionist. Bob Marley & The Wailers.
WAITE, JOHN. Lancaster, England, 7/4/54. Singer, songwriter.
WAITS, TOM. Pomona, CA, 12/7/49. Singer, actor, composer. *Short Cuts.*
WALDHEIM, KURT. Woerdern, Austria, 12/21/18. Political leader. President of Austria.
WALKEN, CHRISTOPHER. Astoria, NY, 3/31/43. Actor. *The Deer Hunter.*
WALKER, ALICE. Eatonton, GA, 2/9/44. Author. *The Color Purple.*
WALKER, CLINT. Hartford, IL, 5/30/27. Actor. *Cheyenne.*
WALKER, DAVID. Montgomeryville, AL, 5/12/43. Keyboardist. Gary Lewis & The Playboys.
WALKER, JIMMIE. New York, NY, 6/25/48. Actor. J. J. Evans on *Good Times.*
WALKER, JUNIOR (Autry DeWalt II). Blytheville, AR, 1942. Saxophonist, singer. Junior Walker & The All-Stars.
WALKER, MORT. El Dorado, KS, 9/3/23. Cartoonist. *Beetle Bailey.*
WALLACE, MIKE (Myron Leon Wallace). Brookline, MA, 5/9/18. News reporter and interviewer, anchor. *60 Minutes.*
WALLACH, ELI. Brooklyn, NY, 12/7/15. Actor. *The Good, the Bad and the Ugly.*
WALLER, GORDON. Braemar, Scotland, 6/4/45. Singer. Peter and Gordon.
WALLINGER, KARL. Prestatyn, Wales, 10/19/57. Keyboardist, guitarist. World Party.
WALSH, JOE. Cleveland, OH, 11/20/47. Guitarist, singer. The Eagles; The James Gang.
WALSH, M. EMMET. Ogdensburg, NY, 3/22/35. Actor. *Blood Simple.*
WALSTON, RAY. New Orleans, LA, 11/22/18. Actor. Uncle Martin on *My Favorite Martian.*
WALTER, JESSICA. Brooklyn, NY, 1/31/44. Actor. *Play Misty for Me.*
WALTER, TRACEY. Jersey City, NJ. Actor. Bob the Goon in *Batman.*
WARD, BILL. Birmingham, England, 5/5/48. Drummer. Black Sabbath.
WARD, BURT. Los Angeles, CA, 7/6/46. Actor. *Batman.*
WARD, FRED. San Diego, CA, 1943. Actor. *Henry and June.*
WARD, RACHEL. London, England, 1957. Actor. *Against All Odds.*
WARD, SELA. Meridian, MS, 7/11/56. Actor. *Sisters.*
WARDEN, JACK (Jack Warden Lebzelter). Newark, NJ, 9/18/20. Actor. Harry Fox on *Crazy Like a Fox.*
WARE, MARTYN. Sheffield, England, 5/19/56. Synthesizer player. The Human League; Heaven 17.
WARFIELD, MARSHA. Chicago, IL, 3/5/55. Actor. Roz Russell on *Night Court.*
WARNER, DAVID. Manchester, England, 7/29/41. Actor. *The Omen.*
WARNER, JULIE. New York, NY, 1965. Actor. *Doc Hollywood.*
WARNER, MALCOLM-JAMAL. Jersey City, NJ, 8/18/70. Actor. Theo Huxtable on *The Cosby Show.*
WARNES, JENNIFER. Orange County, CA, 1947. Pop singer.
WARREN, LESLEY ANN. New York, NY, 8/16/46. Actor. *Mission: Impossible.*
WARRICK, RUTH. St. Joseph, MO, 6/29/15. Actor. Phoebe Wallingford on *All My Children.*
WARWICK, CLINT (Clinton Eccles). Birmingham, England, 6/25/40. Bassist. The Moody Blues.
WARWICK, DIONNE (Marie Warrick). East Orange, NJ, 12/12/40. Gospel/pop singer.
WATERS, JOHN. Baltimore, MD, 4/22/46. Director, writer, actor. *Hairspray; Pink Flamingos; Serial Mom.*
WATERS, ROGER. Great Bookham, England, 9/9/44. Singer, bassist. Pink Floyd.
WATERSTON, SAM. Cambridge, MA, 11/15/40. Actor. *The Killing Fields.*
WATLEY, JODY. Chicago, IL, 1/30/59. Singer. Shalamar.
WATSON, BRUCE. Ontario, Canada, 3/11/61. Guitarist. Big Country.
WATT, BEN. 12/6/62. Guitarist, keyboardist, singer. Everything but the Girl.
WATTS, CHARLIE. Islington, England, 6/2/41. Drummer. The Rolling Stones.
WATTS, OVEREND (Peter Watts). Birmingham, England, 5/13/49. Bassist. Mott The Hoople.
WAXMAN, AL. Toronto, Canada, 3/2/34. Actor. Bert Samuels on *Cagney and Lacey.*
WAYANS, KEENEN IVORY. New York, NY, 6/8/58. Actor, director, writer. *In Living Color.*

WAYBILL, FEE (John Waldo). Omaha, NE, 9/17/50. Singer. The Tubes.
WAYNE, CARL. Mosely, England, 8/18/44. Singer. The Move.
WAYNE, PATRICK. Los Angeles, CA, 7/15/39. Actor. *McClintock!*
WEATHERS, CARL. New Orleans, LA, 1/14/48. Actor. Apollo Creed in *Rocky*.
WEAVER, BLUE (Derek Weaver). Cardiff, Wales, 3/3/49. Organist. Amen Corner.
WEAVER, DENNIS. Joplin, MO, 6/4/25. Actor. *McCloud*.
WEAVER, FRITZ. Pittsburgh, PA, 1/19/26. Actor. *Marathon Man*.
WEBB, PAUL. 1/16/62. Bassist. Talk Talk.
WEIDER, JOHN. England, 4/21/47. Bassist. Family.
WEIR, BOB. San Francisco, CA, 10/6/47. Guitarist. Grateful Dead.
WEITZ, BRUCE. Norwalk, CT, 5/27/43. Actor. Mick Belker on *Hill Street Blues*.
WELCH, BRUCE (Bruce Cripps). Bognor Regis, England, 11/2/41. Guitarist. The Shadows.
WELCH, RAQUEL (Raquel Tejada). Chicago, IL, 9/5/40. Actor. *One Million Years B.C.*
WELD, TUESDAY (Susan Weld). New York, NY, 8/27/43. Actor. *Looking for Mr. Goodbar*.
WELLER, PAUL. Woking, England, 5/25/58. Singer, guitarist. The Style Council.
WELLER, PETER. Stevens Point, WI, 6/24/47. Actor. *Robocop*.
WELLS, CORY. Buffalo, NY, 2/5/44. Singer. Three Dog Night.
WELLS, KITTY. Nashville, TN, 8/30/19. Country singer.
WELNICK, VINCE. Phoeix, AZ, 2/21/51. Keyboardist. The Tubes.
WELTER, PAUL. 5/25/58. Singer, bassist. The Jam.
WENDT, GEORGE. Chicago, IL, 10/17/48. Actor. Norm Peterson on *Cheers*.
WEST, ADAM (William Anderson). Walla Walla, WA, 9/19/29. Actor. *Batman*.
WEST, JOHN. Uhrichsville, OH, 7/31/39. Guitarist. Gary Lewis & The Playboys.
WEST, RICK. Dagenham, England, 5/7/43. Lead guitarist. Brian Poole & The Tremeloes.
WESTHEIMER, RUTH (Karola Ruth Siegel). Frankfurt, Germany, 6/4/28. Sex therapist. *Ask Dr. Ruth*.
WETTON, JOHN. Derbyshire, England, 7/12/49. Lead singer, bassist. Asia.
WEYMOUTH, TINA. Coronado, CA, 11/22/50. Bassist. Talking Heads.
WHALEY, FRANK. Syracuse, NY, 1963. Actor. *The Doors*.
WHALLEY-KILMER, JOANNE. Manchester, England, 8/25/64. Actor, married to Val Kilmer. *Willow*.
WHELCHEL, LISA. Fort Worth, TX, 5/29/63. Actor. Blair Warner on *The Facts of Life*.
WHITAKER, FOREST. Longview, TX, 7/15/61. Actor. *The Crying Game*.
WHITAKER, JOHNNY. Van Nuys, CA, 12/13/59. Actor. Jody on *Family Affair*.
WHITE, BARRY. Galveston, TX, 9/12/44. R&B singer, songwriter.
WHITE, BETTY. Oak Park, IL, 1/17/24. Actor. Rose Nylund on *The Golden Girls*.
WHITE, CHRIS. Barnet, England, 3/7/43. Bassist. The Zombies.
WHITE, DAVE (David Tricker). Philadelphia, PA, 9/1/40. Singer. Danny & The Juniors.
WHITE, JALEEL. Los Angeles, CA, 11/27/76. Actor. Steve Urkel on *Family Matters*.
WHITE, MARK. Sheffield, England, 4/1/61. Guitarist. ABC.
WHITE, MAURICE. Memphis, TN, 12/19/44. Singer, drummer, kalimba player. Earth, Wind & Fire.
WHITE, VANNA. North Myrtle Beach, SC, 2/18/57. Letter turner extraordinaire. *Wheel of Fortune*.
WHITE, VERDINE. Illinois, 7/25/51. Singer, bassist. Earth, Wind & Fire.
WHITELAW, BILLIE. Coventry, England, 6/6/32. Actor. *Charlie Bubbles*.
WHITFORD, BRAD. Winchester, MA, 2/23/52. Guitarist. Aerosmith.
WHITMORE, JAMES. White Plains, NY, 10/1/21. Actor. *Will Rogers, USA*.
WHITNEY, CHARLIE. England, 6/4/44. Guitarist. Family.
WIEST, DIANNE. Kansas City, MO, 3/28/48. Actor. *Hannah and Her Sisters*.
WILCOX, LARRY. San Diego, CA, 8/8/47. Actor. Officer Jon Baker on *CHiPS*.
WILDE, KIM (Kim Smith). London, England, 11/18/60. Singer, songwriter.
WILDER, ALAN. 6/1/59. Singer, synthesizer player. Depeche Mode.
WILDER, GENE (Jerome Silberman). Milwaukee, WI, 6/11/35. Actor, director, writer, widower of Gilda Radner. *Young Frankenstein*.
WILLIAM, PRINCE. London, England, 2/19/60. British royalty, son of Prince Charles and Princess Diana.
WILLIAMS, ANDY. Wall Lake, IA, 12/3/30. Pop singer. "Where Do I Begin?"
WILLIAMS, BARRY. Santa Monica, CA, 9/30/54. Actor. Greg on *The Brady Bunch*.
WILLIAMS, BILLY DEE. New York, NY, 4/6/37. Actor. *Lady Sings the Blues*.
WILLIAMS, CINDY. Van Nuys, CA, 8/22/47. Actor. Shirley Feeney on *Laverne & Shirley*.
WILLIAMS, CLARENCE III. New York, NY, 8/21/39. Actor. Lincoln Hayes on *The Mod Squad*.
WILLIAMS, CLIFF. Rumford, England, 12/14/29. Bass guitarist. AC/DC.
WILLIAMS, DENIECE (Deniece Chandler). Gary, IN, 6/3/51. Gospel/pop singer.
WILLIAMS, ESTHER. Los Angeles, CA, 8/8/23. Actor, swimmer. *Bathing Beauty*.
WILLIAMS, HANK JR. Shreveport, LA, 5/26/49. Country singer, songwriter. "Texas Women."
WILLIAMS, JOBETH. Houston, TX, 1953. Actor. *The Big Chill*.
WILLIAMS, JOHN TOWNER. Queens, NY, 2/8/32. Composer, conductor. *Jaws; Star Wars*.
WILLIAMS, MAISIE. Montserrat, West Indies, 3/25/51. Singer. Boney M.
WILLIAMS, MILAN. Mississippi, 3/28/48. Keyboardist, trombonist, guitarist, drummer. The Commodores.
WILLIAMS, MONTEL. Baltimore, MD, 7/3/56. Talk show host. *The Montel Williams Show*.
WILLIAMS, OTIS (Otis Miles). Texarkana, TX, 10/30/49. Singer. The Temptations.
WILLIAMS, PAUL. Birmingham, AL, 7/2/39. Singer. The Temptations.
WILLIAMS, TONY. Elizabeth, NJ, 4/5/28. Lead singer. The Platters.
WILLIAMS, TREAT (Richard Williams). Rowayton, CT, 12/1/51. Actor. *Prince of the City*.
WILLIAMS, VANESSA. New York, NY, 3/18/63. Model, pop singer, first black Miss America (lost crown for violating moral codes).
WILLIAMS, WALTER. 8/25/42. Singer. The O'Jays.
WILLIAMS, WENDY O. (Wendy Orlean Williams). Rochester, NY, 1946. Entertainer, singer.
WILLIAMSON, NICOL. Hamilton, Scotland, 9/14/38. Actor. *Excalibur*.
WILLIG, GEORGE. New York, NY, 6/11/49. Actor, stuntman. Climbed World Trade Center.
WILSON, AL "BLIND OWL." Boston, MA, 7/4/43. Guitarist, singer, harmonicist. Canned Heat.
WILSON, ANN. San Diego, CA, 6/19/51. Lead singer. Heart.
WILSON, BARRY J. London, England, 3/18/47. Drummer. Procol Harum.
WILSON, BRIAN. Inglewood, CA, 6/20/42. Bassist, keyboardist, singer, father of Wendy and Carnie. The Beach Boys.
WILSON, CARL. Hawthorne, CA, 12/21/46. Guitarist, singer. The Beach Boys.
WILSON, CARNIE. Los Angeles, CA, 4/29/68. Singer, daughter of Brian, sister of Wendy. Wilson Phillips.
WILSON, CINDY. Athens, GA, 2/28/57. Guitarist, singer. The B-52's.
WILSON, DEMOND. Valdosta, GA, 10/13/46. Actor. *Sanford and Son*.
WILSON, DON. Tacoma, WA, 2/10/37. Guitarist. The Ventures.
WILSON, FLIP (Clerow Wilson). Jersey City, NJ, 12/8/33. Actor. *The Flip Wilson Show*.
WILSON, JOYCE. Detroit, MI, 12/14/46. Singer. Tony Orlando & Dawn.
WILSON, MARY. Greenville, MS, 3/6/44. Singer. The Supremes.
WILSON, NANCY. Chillicothe, OH, 2/20/37. R&B singer.
WILSON, NANCY. San Francisco, CA, 3/16/54. Guitarist, singer. Heart.
WILSON, TOM. Grant Town, WV, 8/1/31. Cartoonist. *Ziggy*.
WILSON, TONY. Trinidad, 10/8/47. Bassist, singer. Hot Chocolate.
WILSON, WENDY. Los Angeles, CA, 10/16/69. Singer, sister of Carnie, daughter of Brian. Wilson Phillips.
WINCHELL, PAUL. New York, NY, 12/21/22. Ventriloquist, actor. *The Paul Winchell-Jerry Mahoney Show*.
WINDOM, WILLIAM. New York, NY, 9/28/23. Actor. *Murder She Wrote*.
WINFIELD, DAVE. Saint Paul, MN, 10/3/51. Baseball player.

WINFIELD, PAUL. Los Angeles, CA, 5/22/40. Actor. *Sounder.*
WINKLER, HENRY. New York, NY, 10/30/45. Actor, producer, director. Arthur "The Fonz" Fonzarelli on *Happy Days.*
WINNINGHAM, MARE. Phoenix, AZ, 5/6/59. Actor. *St. Elmo's Fire.*
WINSTON, JIMMY (James Langwith). London, England, 4/20/45. Organist. The Small Faces.
WINTER, EDGAR. Beaumont, TX, 12/28/46. Blues/rock keyboardist, brother of Johnny.
WINTER, JOHNNY. Beaumont, TX, 2/23/44. Blues/rock guitarist, brother of Edgar.
WINTERS, JONATHAN. Dayton, OH, 11/11/25. Actor. *The Jonathan Winters Show.*
WINTERS, SHELLEY (Shirley Schrift). St. Louis, MO, 8/18/22. Actor. *The Poseidon Adventure.*
WINWOOD, MUFF (Mervyn Winwood). Birmingham, England, 6/14/43. Singer, songwriter, bassist. The Spencer Davis Group.
WINWOOD, STEVE. Birmingham, England, 5/12/48. Singer, songwriter. The Spencer Davis Group; Traffic; Blind Faith.
WITHERS, BILL. Slab Fork, WV, 7/4/38. Pop singer, songwriter, guitarist.
WITHERS, JANE. Atlanta, GA, 4/12/26. Actor. Josephine the Plumber on TV commercials.
WOLF, PETER (Peter Blankfield). New York, NY, 3/7/46. Singer. The J. Geils Band.
WOLTERS, JOHN. 4/28/45. Drummer, singer. Dr. Hook.
WOMACK, BOBBY. Cleveland, OH, 3/4/44. Gospel/R&B singer, songwriter, guitarist.
WONDER, STEVIE (Steveland Judkins). Saginaw, MI, 5/13/50. Singer, songwriter, formerly married to Syreeta Wright.
WONG, B. D. San Francisco, CA, 10/24/62. Actor. *M. Butterfly.*
WOOD, DANNY. Boston, MA, 5/14/71. Singer. New Kids on the Block.
WOOD, RON. England, 6/1/47. Guitarist. The Rolling Stones.
WOOD, ROY (Ulysses Adrian Wood). Birmingham, England, 11/8/46. Singer, guitarist, cellist. Electric Light Orchestra (ELO); Wizzard; The Move.
WOOD, STUART. Edinburgh, Scotland, 2/25/57. Guitarist. The Bay City Rollers.
WOODS, JAMES. Vernal, UT, 4/18/47. Actor. *Salvador.*
WOODWARD, EDWARD. Croydon, England, 6/1/30. Actor. *The Equalizer.*
WOODWARD, JOANNE. Thomasville, GA, 2/27/30. Actor, married to Paul Newman. *The Three Faces of Eve.*
WOODWARD, KEREN. Bristol, England, 4/2/61. Singer. Bananarama.
WORLEY, JO ANNE. Lowell, IN, 9/6/37. Actor, singer. *Laugh-In.*
WRAY, FAY. Alberta, Canada, 9/10/07. Actor. *King Kong.*
WRIGHT, ADRIAN. Sheffield, England, 6/30/56. Projector operator for on-stage slides and films. The Human League.
WRIGHT, LITTLE STEVIE. Leeds, England, 12/20/48. Singer. The Easybeats.
WRIGHT, MAX. Detroit, MI, 8/2/43. Actor. Willie Tanner on *ALF.*
WRIGHT, PAT. Brooklyn, NY, 1945. Singer. The Crystals.
WRIGHT, RICK. London, England, 7/28/45. Keyboardist. Pink Floyd.
WRIGHT, STEVEN. New York, NY, 12/6/55. Comedian.
WRIGHT, SYREETA. Pittsburgh, PA, 1946. Singer, songwriter, formerly married to Stevie Wonder.
WUHL, ROBERT. Union City, NJ, 10/9/51. Actor, writer. *Bull Durham.*
WYATT, JANE. New York, NY, 8/13/12. Actor. *Father Knows Best.*
WYMAN, BILL (William Perks). London, England, 10/24/36. Bassist. The Rolling Stones.
WYMAN, JANE (Sarah Jane Fulks). St. Joseph, MO, 1/4/14. Actor, formerly married to Ronald Reagan. Angela Channing on *Falcon Crest.*
WYNETTE, TAMMY. Red Bay, MS, 5/5/42. Country singer. "Stand by Your Man."
YAMAGUCHI, KRISTI. Hayward, CA, 7/12/71. Skater, Olympic gold medalist.
YANKOVIC, WEIRD AL (Alfred Matthew Yankovic). Los Angeles, CA, 10/23/59. Singer, spoof artist. "Like a Surgeon."
YANOVSKY, ZAL. Toronto, Canada, 12/19/44. Guitarist, singer. The Lovin' Spoonful.
YARROW, PETER. New York, NY, 5/31/38. Composer, author, singer. Peter, Paul and Mary.
YELTSIN, BORIS. Burka, Russia, 2/1/31. Russian political leader.
YESTER, JIM. Birmingham, AL, 11/24/39. Singer, guitarist. The Association.
YOAKAM, DWIGHT. Pikesville, KY, 10/23/56. Country singer. "Honky Tonk Man."
YORK, MICHAEL. Fulmer, England, 3/27/42. Actor. *Logan's Run.*
YORK, PETE. Redcar, England, 8/15/42. Drummer. The Spencer Davis Group.
YOUNG, ANGUS. Glasgow, Scotland, 3/31/59. Guitarist. AC/DC.
YOUNG, GEORGE. Glasgow, Scotland, 11/6/47. Guitarist. The Easybeats.
YOUNG, JAMES. Chicago, IL, 11/14/48. Guitarist. Styx.
YOUNG, JESSE COLIN (Perry Miller). New York, NY, 11/11/44. Guitarist, bassist, singer. The Youngbloods.
YOUNG, LORETTA (Gretchen Young). Salt Lake City, UT, 1/6/13. Actor. *The Farmer's Daughter.*
YOUNG, MALCOLM. Glasgow, Scotland, 1/6/53. Guitarist. AC/DC.
YOUNG, NEIL. Toronto, Canada, 11/12/45. Singer, songwriter, guitarist. Buffalo Springfield; Crosby, Stills, Nash & Young.
YOUNG, PAUL. Luton, England, 1/17/56. Singer, songwriter.
YOUNG, ROBERT. Chicago, IL, 2/22/07. Actor. *Marcus Welby, M.D.*
YOUNG, RUSTY. Long Beach, CA, 2/23/46. Pedal steel guitarist. Poco.
YOUNG, SEAN. Louisville, KY, 11/20/59. Actor. *No Way Out.*
YOUNG MC (Marvin Young). London, England, 1968. Rap artist.
YOUNGMAN, HENNY (Henry Youngman). Liverpool, England, 1/12/06. Actor. "Take my wife... please!"
ZADORA, PIA. New York, NY, 5/4/56. Actor. *Naked Gun 33 1/3.*
ZAHN, PAULA. Naperville, IL, 2/24/56. Broadcast journalist. *CBS This Morning.*
ZAL, ROXANA. Los Angeles, CA, 11/8/69. Actor. *Something About Amelia.*
ZANDER, ROBIN. Rockford, IL, 1/23/53. Singer, guitarist. Cheap Trick.
ZAPPA, DWEEZIL. Los Angeles, CA, 9/5/69. Guitarist, son of Frank, brother of Moon Unit. MTV.
ZAPPA, MOON UNIT. Hollywood, CA, 9/28/68. Singer, daughter of Frank, sister of Dweezil. "Valley Girl."
ZEHRINGER, RICK. Fort Recovery, OH, 5/8/47. Lead guitarist, singer. The McCoys.
ZEMECKIS, ROBERT. Chicago, IL, 1952. Director. *Back to the Future.*
ZEVON, WARREN. Chicago, IL, 1/24/47. Singer, songwriter. "Werewolves of London."
ZIERING, IAN. 4/30/64. Actor. *Beverly Hills 90210.*
ZIMBALIST, STEPHANIE. Encino, CA, 10/8/56. Actor, daughter of Efrem. Laura Holt on *Remington Steele.*
ZMED, ADRIAN. Chicago, IL, 3/4/54. Actor. Vince Romano on *T. J. Hooker.*

HAPPY BIRTHDAY! THE GREATS' NATAL DATES

January 1
Idi Amin
Frank Langella
Don Novello
J.D. Salinger

January 2
Jim Bakker
Gabrielle Carteris
Chick Churchill
Roger Miller
Joanna Pacula

January 3
Melody Anderson
Dabney Coleman
Mel Gibson
Robert Loggia
Victoria Principal
Stephen Stills
Bill Travers
Vanity

January 4
Bernie Albrecht
Dyan Cannon
Matt Frewer
Ann Magnuson
Michael Stipe
Barney Sumner
Jane Wyman

January 5
Suzy Amis
George Brown
Jeane Dixon
Robert Duvall
Diane Keaton
Ted Lange
Walter Mondale
Chris Stein

January 6
Syd Barrett
Mark O'Toole
John Singleton
Kathy Sledge
Loretta Young
Malcolm Young

January 7
Nicolas Cage
Katie Couric
Kenny Loggins
Maury Povich
Paul Revere

January 8
David Bowie
Stephen Hawking
Robbie Krieger
Butterfly McQueen
Yvette Mimieux
Charles Osgood
Soupy Sales
Larry Storch

January 9
Joan Baez
Bill Cowsill
Bob Denver
Scott Engel
Crystal Gayle
David Johansen
Judith Krantz
Herbert Lom
Jimmy Page

January 10
Pat Benatar
Donald Fagen
George Foreman
Bob Lang
Cyril Neville
Maurice Sendak
Rod Stewart

January 11
Naomi Judd
Vicki Peterson
Rod Taylor

January 12
Kirstie Alley
Anthony Andrews
Per Gessle
William Lee Golden
Cynthia Robinson
Vendela
Henny Youngman

January 13
Kevin Anderson
Patrick Dempsey
Robert "Squirrel" Lester
Julia Louis-Dreyfus
Graham McPherson
Penelope Ann Miller
Richard Moll
Robert Stack
Frances Sternhagen
Gwen Verdon

January 14
Jason Bateman
Faye Dunaway
L.L. Cool J
Andy Rooney
Carl Weathers

January 15
Captain Beefheart
Lloyd Bridges
Charo
Martha Davis
Chad Lowe
Andrea Martin
Pamela Sue Martin
Peter Trewavas
Mario Van Peebles

January 16
Debbie Allen
Bob Bogle
John Carpenter
Bill Francis
Alexander Knox
Kate Moss
Sade
Jim Stafford
Paul Webb

January 17
Muhammad Ali
Jim Carrey
David Caruso
John Crawford
Steve Earle
Joe Frazier
Susanna Hoffs
James Earl Jones
Vidal Sassoon
Betty White
Paul Young

January 18
Kevin Costner
David Ruffin
Larry Smith

January 19
Desi Arnaz Jr.
Dewey Bunnell
Michael Crawford
Phil Everly
Shelley Fabares
Tippi Hedren
Harvey Hinsley
Robert MacNeil
Robert Palmer
Dolly Parton
Jean Stapleton
Mickey Virtue
Fritz Weaver

January 20
Buzz Aldrin
George Burns
Arte Johnson
DeForest Kelley
Lorenzo Lamas
David Lynch
John Michael Montgomery
Patricia Neal
Paul Stanley
Eric Stewart
Ron Townson

January 21
Robby Benson
Geena Davis
Mac Davis
Jill Eikenberry
Richie Havens
Billy Ocean
Steve Reeves

January 22
Linda Blair
Sam Cooke
Balthazar Getty
Addi Harris
John Hurt
Michael Hutchence
Diane Lane
Piper Laurie
Chris Lemmon
Steve Perry
Jeff Smith
Ann Sothern

January 23
Richard Dean Anderson
Princess Caroline
Bill Cunningham
Earl Falconer
Gil Gerard
Rutger Hauer
Jeanne Moreau
Anita Pointer
Chita Rivera
Patrick Simmons
Robin Zander

January 24
Ernest Borgnine
Neil Diamond
Jools Holland
Nastassja Kinski
Michael Ontkean
Oral Roberts
Yakov Smirnoff
Ray Stevens
Warren Zevon

January 25
Corazon Aquino
Andy Cox
Richard Finch
Dean Jones
Dinah Manoff

January 26
Jazzie B
David Briggs
Scott Glenn
Wayne Gretsky
Eartha Kitt
Paul Newman
Andrew Ridgeley
Gene Siskel
Bob Uecker
Roger Vadim
Eddie Van Halen

January 27
Mikhail Baryshnikov
Bobby Bland
Troy Donahue
Brian Downey
Bridget Fonda
Gillian Gilbert
Seth Justman
Nick Mason
Mike Patton
Mimi Rogers
Nedra Talley

January 28
Alan Alda
John Beck
Brian Keenan
Marthe Keller
Nicholas Pryor
Dave Sharp
Dick Taylor

January 29
David Byron
John Forsythe
Roddy Frame
Sara Gilbert
Noel Harrison
Eddie Jackson
Anne Jillian
Greg Louganis
Victor Mature
Tommy Ramone
Katharine Ross
Tom Selleck
Oprah Winfrey

January 30
Marty Balin
Phil Collins
Charles Dutton
Gene Hackman
William King
Dorothy Malone
Steve Marriott
Dick Martin
Vanessa Redgrave
Joe Terranova
Jody Watley

January 31
John Agar
Harry Wayne Casey
Carol Channing
Lloyd Cole
Terry Kath
John Lydon
Phil Manzanera
Suzanne Pleshette
Jean Simmons
Jessica Walter

February 1
Mike Campbell
Don Everly
Dennis Farina
Sherilynn Fenn
Margaux Hemingway
Sherman Hemsley
Rick James
Terry Jones
Billy Mumy
Lisa Marie Presley-Jackson
Ray Sawyer
Boris Yeltsin

February 2
Christie Brinkley
Garth Brooks
Alan Caddy
Farrah Fawcett
Gale Gordon
Peter Lucia
Graham Nash
Liz Smith
Tom Smothers
Elaine Stritch
Ross Valory

February 3
Joey Bishop
Angelo D'Aleo
Blythe Danner
Dave Davies
Morgan Fairchild
Eric Haydock
Fran Tarkenton
Lol Tolhurst

February 4
Michael Beck
Clint Black
David Brenner
Alice Cooper
Florence LaRue
Dan Quayle
John Steel

February 5
Bobby Brown
Red Buttons
Christopher Guest
Barbara Hershey
Jennifer Jason Leigh
Charlotte Rampling
Roger Staubach
Cory Wells

February 6
Rick Astley
Tom Brokaw
Natalie Cole
Fabian
Mike Farrell

Zsa Zsa Gabor
Alan Jones
Patrick Macnee
Ronald Reagan
Rip Torn
Robert Townsend
Michael Tucker
Mamie Van Doren

February 7
David Bryan
Miguel Ferrer
Jimmy Greenspoon
Alan Lancaster
James Spader
Brian Travers

February 8
Brooke Adams
Brian Bennett
Creed Bratton
Gary Coleman
John Grisham
Robert Klein
Ted Koppel
Jack Lemmon
Audrey Meadows
Vince Neil
Nick Nolte
Mary Steenburgen
Lana Turner
John Williams

February 9
Mia Farrow
Carole King
Judith Light
Roger Mudd
Joe Pesci
Janet Suzman
Travis Tritt
Alice Walker

February 10
Laura Dern
Donovan
Roberta Flack
Jimmy Merchant
Mark Spitz
Robert Wagner
Don Wilson

February 11
Eva Gabor
Conrad Janis
Tina Louise
Leslie Nielsen
Burt Reynolds
Sidney Sheldon

February 12
Maud Adams
Joe Don Baker
Judy Blume
Cliff DeYoung
Arsenio Hall
Joanna Kerns
Simon MacCorkindale
Ray Manzarek
Joe Schermie

February 13
Tony Butler
Stockard Channing
Roger Christian
Peter Hook
David Naughton
Kim Novak
Oliver Reed
George Segal
Bo Svenson
Peter Tork

February 14
Hugh Downs
Roger Fisher
Florence Henderson
Gregory Hines
Paul Tsongas
Ken Wahl

February 15
Mick Avory
Marisa Berenson
Claire Bloom
David Brown
Ali Campbell
Mikey Craig
Matt Groening
John Helliwell
Harvey Korman
Kevin McCarthy
Jane Seymour

February 16
Sonny Bono
LeVar Burton
James Ingram
William Katt
John McEnroe Jr.
Andy Taylor

February 17
Alan Bates
Jim Brown
Brenda Fricker
Hal Holbrook
Michael Jordan
Lou Diamond Phillips
Gene Pitney
Raf Vallone

February 18
Robbie Bachman
Randy Crawford
Sinead Cusack
Dennis DeYoung
Matt Dillon
George Kennedy
Juice Newton
Jack Palance
Molly Ringwald
Herman Santiago
Greta Scacchi
Cybill Shepherd
John Travolta
Vanna White

February 19
Mark Andes
Justine Bateman
Francis Buchholz
Lou Christie
Jeff Daniels
Falco
Tony Iommi
Holly Johnson
Smokey Robinson

February 20
Edward Albert
Robert Altman
Charles Barkley
Walter Becker
Ian Brown
Randy California
Cindy Crawford
Sandy Duncan
J. Geils
Kelsey Grammer
Jennifer O'Neill
Sidney Poitier
Andrew Shue
Dick Smothers
Peter Strauss
Gloria Vanderbilt
Nancy Wilson

February 21
Christopher Atkins
Jean-Jacques Burnel
Tyne Daly
Jerry Harrison
Gary Lockwood
Rue McClanahan
Nina Simone
Vince Welnick

February 22
Drew Barrymore
Jonathan Demme
Julius Erving
Ted Kennedy
Sheldon Leonard
Kyle MacLachlan
John Mills
Miou-Miou
Robert Young

February 23
Peter Fonda
Howard Jones
Mike Maxfield
Steve Priest
David Sylvian
Brad Whitford
Johnny Winter
Rusty Young

February 24
Barry Bostwick
James Farentino
Steven Hill
Paul Jones
Edward James Olmos
Helen Shaver
Lonnie Turner
Paula Zahn

February 25
Sean Astin
George Harrison
Mike Peters
Sally Jessy Raphael
Bobby Riggs
Stuart Wood

February 26
Michael Bolton
Jonathan Cain
Johnny Cash
Fats Domino
John Jon
Tony Randall
Mitch Ryder
Sandie Shaw

February 27
Adam Baldwin
Garry Christian
Chelsea Clinton
Eddie Gray
Steve Harley
Howard Hesseman
Paul Humphreys
Ralph Nader
Neal Schon
Grant Show
Adrian Smith
Elizabeth Taylor
Joanne Woodward

February 28
Mario Andretti
Stephanie Beacham
Frank Bonner
Charles Durning
Phil Gould
Robert Sean Leonard
Gavin MacLeod
Bernadette Peters
Bubba Smith
Joe South
Tommy Tune
John Turturro
Cindy Wilson

March 1
Harry Belafonte
Dirk Benedict
Roger Daltrey
Timothy Daly
Ron Howard
Alan Thicke

March 2
John Cowsill
John Cullum
Mark Evans
John Irving
Jennifer Jones
Eddie Money
Jay Osmond
Lou Reed
Al Waxman

March 3
Willie Chambers
Jance Garfat
Jackie Joyner-Kersee
Tim Kazurinsky
Dave Mount
Mike Pender
Tone-Loc
Blue Weaver

March 4
Chastity Bono
Harry Helmsley
Patsy Kensit
Catherine O'Hara
Paula Prentiss
Chris Rea
Chris Squire
Shakin' Stevens
Bobby Womack
Adrian Zmed

March 5
Alan Clark
Samantha Eggar
Eddy Grant
James B. Sikking
Dean Stockwell
Marsha Warfield

March 6
Tom Arnold
Marion Barry
Kiki Dee
David Gilmour
Hugh Grundy
Ed McMahon
Shaquille O'Neal
Rob Reiner
Mary Wilson

March 7
Tammy Faye Bakker
Paul Davis
Matthew Fisher
John Heard
Willard Scott
Lynn Swann
Daniel J. Travanti
Chris White
Peter Wolf

March 8
Mike Allsup
Cheryl Baker
Clive Burr
Cyd Charisse
Mickey Dolenz
Ralph Ellis
Peter Gill
Randy Meisner
Gary Numan
Aidan Quinn
Lynn Redgrave
Claire Trevor

March 9
Trevor Burton
Jim Cregan
Martin Fry
Marty Ingels
Raul Julia
Emmanuel Lewis
Mark Lindsey
Jeffrey Osborne
Mickey Spillane
Robin Trower
Trish Van Devere

March 10
Prince Edward
Jasmine Guy
Chuck Norris
James Earl Ray
Tom Scholz
Sharon Stone
Dean Torrence

March 11
Douglas Adams
Sam Donaldson
Bobby McFerrin
Susan Richardson
Ric Rothwell
Mark Stein
Bruce Watson

March 12
Barbara Feldon
Mike Gibbins
Marlon Jackson
Al Jarreau
Paul Kantner
Liza Minnelli
Brian O'Hara
Bill Payne
James Taylor

March 13
Adam Clayton
Dana Delany
Glenne Headly
Deborah Raffin
Neil Sedaka

March 14
Michael Caine
Billy Crystal
Megan Follows
Boon Gould
Quincy Jones
Walter Parazaider

March 15
Ry Cooder
David Costell
Fabio
Judd Hirsch
Phil Lesh

Mike Love
Bret Michaels
Rockwell
Howard Scott
Sly Stone
Jimmy Lee Swaggart

March 16
Michael Bruce
Erik Estrada
Isabelle Huppert
Jerry Lewis
Kate Nelligan
Nancy Wilson

March 17
Harold Brown
Lesley-Anne Down
Patrick Duffy
Scott Gorham
Mike Lindup
Rob Lowe
Patrick McCauley
Kurt Russell
John Sebastian

March 18
Bonnie Blair
Irene Cara
Kevin Dobson
Peter Graves
John Hartman
Wilson Pickett
Charley Pride
John Updike
Vanessa Williams
Barry J. Wilson

March 19
Ursula Andress
Paul Atkinson
Glenn Close
Terry Hall
Clarence Henry
Derek Longmuir
Ruth Pointer
Bruce Willis

March 20
John Clark Gable
Holly Hunter
William Hurt
Spike Lee
Hal Linden
Carl Palmer
Slim Jim Phantom
Carl Reiner
Mr. Rogers
Theresa Russell

March 21
Matthew Broderick
Timothy Dalton
Cynthia Geary
Roger Hodgson
Gary Oldman
Vivian Stanshall
Rosie Stone
Russell Thompkins Jr.

March 22
George Benson
Jeremy Clyde
Randy Hobbs
Werner Klemperer
Andrew Lloyd Webber
Karl Malden
Marcel Marceau
Stephanie Mills
Matthew Modine
Lena Olin
Keith Relf
Pat Robertson
William Shatner
Harry Vanda
M. Emmet Walsh

March 23
Princess Eugenie
Chaka Khan
Ric Ocasek
Marti Pellow
Amanda Plummer

March 24
Lara Flynn Boyle
Robert Carradine
Norman Fell
Lee Oskar
Donna Pescow

March 25
Hoyt Axton
Bonnie Bedelia
Johnny Burnette
Aretha Franklin
Paul Michael Glaser
Mary Gross
Elton John
Neil Jones
Sarah Jessica Parker
Gloria Steinem
John Stockwell
Maisie Williams

March 26
Alan Arkin
James Caan
Leeza Gibbons
Jennifer Grey
Vicki Lawrence
Leonard Nimoy
Teddy Pendergrass
Diana Ross
Fran Sheehan
Martin Short
Curtis Sliwa
Richard Tandy
Steven Tyler

March 27
Tony Banks
Mariah Carey
Judy Carne
Andrew Farriss
Austin Pendleton
Maria Schneider
Tom Sullivan
Sarah Vaughan
Michael York

March 28
Dirk Bogarde
Ken Howard
Reba McEntire
Chuck Portz
Salt
Dianne Wiest
Milan Williams

March 29
Jennifer Capriati
Bud Cort
Hammer
Eric Idle
Bobby Kimball
Christopher Lambert

March 30
John Astin
Warren Beatty
Tracy Chapman
Eric Clapton
Richard Dysart
Graeme Edge
Peter Marshall
Paul Reiser

March 31
Rod Allen
Herb Alpert
Richard Chamberlain
Liz Claiborne
William Daniels
Albert Gore
Sean Hopper
Shirley Jones
Ed Marinaro
Al Nichol
Rhea Perlman
Mick Ralphs
Christopher Walken
Angus Young

April 1
John Barbata
Alan Blakley
Billy Currie
Rudolph Isley
Gordon Jump
Ronnie Lane
Ali MacGraw
Phil Margo
Toshiro Mifune
Annette O'Toole
Debbie Reynolds
Mark White

April 2
Dana Carvey
Glen Dale
Buddy Ebsen
Mikhail Gorbachev
Alec Guinness
Linda Hunt
Pamela Reed
Leon Russell
Keren Woodward

April 3
Alec Baldwin
Jan Berry
Marlon Brando
Doris Day
Jennie Garth
Jane Goodall
Marsha Mason
Eddie Murphy
Wayne Newton
Tony Orlando
Barry Pritchard
Mel Schacher

April 4
Maya Angelou
Robert Downey Jr.
Steve Gatlin
Dave Hill
Kitty Kelley
Graeme Kelling
Christine Lahti
Mick Mars
Nancy McKeon
Craig T. Nelson
Berry Oakley

April 5
Allan Clarke
Agnetha Faltskog
Maxwell Gail
Frank Gorshin
Peter Greenaway
Mike McCready
Michael Moriarty
Gregory Peck
Gale Storm
Tony Williams

April 6
Stan Cullimore
Marilu Henner
Jason Hervey
John Ratzenberger
John Stax
Billy Dee Williams

April 7
Mick Abrahams
Patricia Bennett
Francis Ford Coppola
Buster Douglas
Spencer Dryden
James Garner
Bruce Gary
Janis Ian
Elaine Miles
John Oates
Wayne Rogers

April 8
Patricia Arquette
Roger Chapman
Steve Howe
Julian Lennon
Edward Mulhare

April 9
Jean-Paul Belmondo
Les Gray
Hugh Hefner
Mark Kelly
Michael Learned
Carl Perkins
Dennis Quaid

April 10
Peter MacNicol
John Madden
Harry Morgan
Steven Seagal
Brian Setzer
Omar Sharif
Bobbie Smith
Bunny Wailer

April 11
Stuart Adamson
Joel Grey
Bill Irwin
Louise Lasser
Delroy Pearson
Peter Riegert
Richie Sambora
Lisa Stansfield
Neville Staples

April 12
Alex Briley
David Cassidy
Shannen Doherty
Andy Garcia
Herbie Hancock
John Kay
David Letterman
Ann Miller
Ed O'Neill
Will Sergeant
Tiny Tim
Scott Turow
Jane Withers

April 13
Don Adams
Peabo Bryson
Jack Casady
Lester Chambers
Jimmy Destri
Tony Dow
Al Green
Garry Kasparov
Howard Keel
Brian Pendleton
Ron Perlman
Rick Schroder
Lyle Waggoner

April 14
Ritchie Blackmore
Dennis Bryon
Julie Christie
Larry Ferguson
Anthony Michael Hall
Buddy Knox
Jay Robinson
Pete Rose
John Shea
Rod Steiger

April 15
Claudia Cardinale
Graeme Clark
Roy Clark
Elizabeth Montgomery
Emma Thompson

April 16
Edie Adams
Ellen Barkin
Jon Cryer
Lukas Haas
Gerry Rafferty
Bill Spooner
Dusty Springfield
Bobby Vinton

April 17
Boomer Esiason
Pete Shelley
Stephen Singleton

April 18
Barbara Hale
Hayley Mills
Rick Moranis
Conan O'Brien
Les Pattinson
Eric Roberts
Alexander Spence
Mike Vickers
James Woods

April 19
Tim Curry
Dudley Moore
Alan Price
Larry Ramos Jr.
Mark Volman

April 20
Craig Frost
Jessica Lange
Joey Lawrence
Ryan O'Neal
George Takei
Luther Vandross
Jimmy Winston

April 21
Paul Carrack
Tony Danza
Queen Elizabeth II
Charles Grodin
Patti LuPone

Andie MacDowell
Elaine May
Iggy Pop
Anthony Quinn
Robert Smith
John Weider

April 22
Eddie Albert
Joseph Bottoms
Glen Campbell
Peter Kenneth Frampton
Ace Frehley
Chris Makepeace
Jack Nicholson
Aaron Spelling
John Waters

April 23
Valerie Bertinelli
David Birney
Steve Clark
Sandra Dee
Jan Hooks
Lee Majors
Alan Oppenheimer
Captain Sensible

April 24
Eric Bogosian
Doug Clifford
Glenn Cornick
Billy Gould
Shirley MacLaine
Paul Ryder
Richard Sterban
Barbra Streisand

April 25
Andy Bell
Michael Brown
Stu Cook
Meadowlark Lemon
Paul Mazursky
Al Pacino
Talia Shire
Bjorn Ulvaeus

April 26
Carol Burnett
Giancarlo Esposito

April 27
Anouk Aimee
Sheena Easton
Pete Ham
Coretta Scott King
Jack Klugman
Kate Pierson
Marco Pirroni
Clive Taylor

April 28
Ann-Margret
Duane Eddy
Saddam Hussein
Bruno Kirby
Jay Leno
Madge Sinclair
Marcia Strassman
John Wolters

April 29
Andre Agassi
Duane Allen
Stephen Arenholz
Keith Baxter
Daniel Day-Lewis
Lonnie Donegan
Carl Gardner
Celeste Holm
Tommy James
Rod McKuen
Zubin Mehta
Kate Mulgrew
Michelle Pfeiffer
Chynna Phillips
Eve Plumb
Francis Rossi
Jerry Seinfeld
Uma Thurman
Carnie Wilson

April 30
Turbo B
Jill Clayburgh
Gary Collins
Perry King
Cloris Leachman
Al Lewis
Willie Nelson
Merrill Osmond
Bobby Vee
Ian Ziering

May 1
John Beradino
Judy Collins
Johnny Colt
Steve Farris
Nick Fortune
Bobcat Goldthwait
Joseph Heller
Ray Parker Jr.
Phil Smith

May 2
Jon Bon Jovi
Lesley Gore
Lou Gramm
Engelbert Humperdinck
Bianca Jagger
Goldy McJohn
Lorenzo Music
Benjamin Spock

May 3
David Ball
James Brown
Christopher Cross
Bruce Hall
Doug Henning
Mary Hopkin
Pete Seeger
Pete Staples
Frankie Valli
Wynonna

May 4
Nickolas Ashford
Jay Aston
Ronnie Bond
Ed Cassidy
Jackie Jackson
Randy Travis
Pia Zadora

May 5
Gary Daly
Ian McCulloch
Kevin Mooney
Cathy Moriarty
Michael Murphy
Michael Palin
Colin Powell
Bill Ward
Tammy Wynette

May 6
Willie Mays
Bob Seger
Lori Singer
Mare Winningham

May 7
Michael Knight
Bill Kreutzmann Jr.
Darren McGavin
Rick West

May 8
Philip Bailey
Chris Frantz
Melissa Gilbert
Gary Glitter
David Lemuel Keith
James Mitchum
Don Rickles
Paul Samwell-Smith
Toni Tennille
Alex Van Halen
Rick Zehringer

May 9
Candice Bergen
Pete Birrell
James L. Brooks
Sonny Curtis
Nokie Edwards
Albert Finney
Richie Furay
Dave Gahan
Paul Heaton
Glenda Jackson
Billy Joel
Steve Katz
Mike Millward
Tom Petersson
Dave Prater
Lloyd Price
Tommy Roe
Mike Wallace

May 10
Jim Abrahams
Bono
Henry Fambrough
Jay Ferguson
Graham Gouldman
Dave Mason
Danny Rapp

May 11
Eric Burdon
Les Chadwick
Louis Farrakhan
Doug McClure
Faith Popcorn
Natasha Richardson

May 12
Stephen Baldwin
Bruce Boxleitner
George Carlin
Lindsay Crouse
Billy Duffy
Ian Dury
Emilio Estevez
Kim Fields
Susan Hampshire
Katharine Hepburn
Ian McLagan
Tom Snyder
Billy Squier
David Walker
Steve Winwood

May 13
Beatrice Arthur
Peter Gabriel
Harvey Keitel
Danny Klein
Lorraine McIntosh
Paul Thompson
Overend Watts
Stevie Wonder

May 14
Ian Astbury
Jack Bruce
David Byrne
Tom Cochrane
Gene Cornish
Bobby Darin
Meg Foster
Derek Leckenby
Fabrice Morvan
Danny Wood

May 15
Terence Trent D'Arby
Brian Eno
Graham Goble
Mike Oldfield

May 16
Pierce Brosnan
Harry Carey Jr.
Tracey Gold
Glenn Gregory
Janet Jackson
Barbara Lee
Gabriela Sabatini
Derrell Sweet
Ralph Tresvant

May 17
Bill Bruford
Dennis Hopper
Pervis Jackson
Jordan Knight
Sugar Ray Leonard
Maureen O'Sullivan
Bob Saget
Taj Mahal
Debra Winger

May 18
Joe Bonsall
Pope John Paul II

May 19
Nora Ephron
James Fox
David Hartman
Dusty Hill
Grace Jones
Nancy Kwan
Joey Ramone
Philip Rudd
Pete Townshend
Martyn Ware

May 20
Warren Cann
Cher
Joe Cocker
Sue Cowsill
Tony Goldwyn
Nick Heyward
Brian Nash
Bronson Pinchot
Ronald Reagan Jr.
Jimmy Stewart

May 21
Mike Barson
Peggy Cass
Ronald Isley
Stan Lynch
Carol Potter
Judge Reinhold
Leo Sayer
Mr. T
Hilton Valentine

May 22
Charles Aznavour
Richard Benjamin
Naomi Campbell
Michael Constantine
Jerry Dammers
Iva Davies
Morrissey
Bernie Taupin
Paul Winfield

May 23
Rosemary Clooney
Joan Collins
Betty Garrett
Bill Hunt
Anatoly Karpov

May 24
Gary Burghoff
Roseanne Cash
Thomas Chong
Bob Dylan
Patti LaBelle
Priscilla Presley
Derek Quinn
Rich Robinson

May 25
Dixie Carter
Justin Henry
Robert Ludlum
Mitch Margo
Ian McKellen
Klaus Meine
Frank Oz
John Palmer
Connie Sellecca
Beverly Sills
Leslie Uggams
Paul Weller

May 26
Verden Allen
James Arness
Helena Bonham-Carter
Ray Ennis
Levon Helm
Wayne Hussey
Peggy Lee
Stevie Nicks
Gerry Paterson
Philip Michael Thomas
Hank Williams Jr.

May 27
Cilla Black
Todd Bridges
Louis Gossett Jr.
Tony Hillerman
Henry Kissinger
Siouxsie Sioux
Bruce Weitz

May 28
Carroll Baker
John Fogerty
Roland Gift
Gladys Knight
Sondra Locke
Kylie Minogue

May 29
Annette Bening
Larry Blackmon
Gary Brooker
Kevin Conway
Roy Crewsdon

Anthony Geary
Bob Hope
Clifton James
Lisa Whelchel

May 30
Lenny Davidson
Keir Dullea
Marie Fredriksson
Nicky Headon
Ted McGinley
Clint Walker

May 31
Tom Berenger
Clint Eastwood
Sharon Gless
Gregory Harrison
Augie Meyers
Joe Namath
Johnny Paycheck
Brooke Shields
Lea Thompson
Peter Yarrow

June 1
Rene Auberjonois
David Berkowitz
Pat Boone
Powers Boothe
Pat Corley
Jason Donovan
Morgan Freeman
Andy Griffith
Mike Joyce
Peter Masterson
Lorna Patterson
Jonathan Pryce
Graham Russell
Alan Wilder
Ron Wood
Edward Woodward

June 2
Joanna Gleason
William Guest
Tony Hadley
Charles Haid
Marvin Hamlisch
Stacy Keach
Sally Kellerman
Jerry Mathers
Charles Miller
Milo O'Shea
Max Showalter
Michael Steele
Charlie Watts

June 3
Michael Clarke
Tony Curtis
Ian Hunter
John Paul Jones
Curtis Mayfield
Billy Powell
Suzi Quatro
Scott Valentine
Deniece Williams

June 4
Roger Ball
John Drew Barrymore
El DeBarge
Bruce Dern
Michelle Phillips
Parker Stevenson
Eddie Velez
Gordon Waller
Dennis Weaver
Ruth Westheimer
Charlie Whitney

June 5
Laurie Anderson
Richard Butler
Tom Evans
Spalding Gray
Kenny G.
Robert Lansing
Marky Mark
Bill Moyers
Freddie Stone

June 6
Sandra Bernhard
Gary Bonds
David Dukes
Robert Englund
Harvey Fierstein
Roy Innis
Amanda Pays
Tom Ryan
Levi Stubbs
Billie Whitelaw

June 7
James Ivory
Tom Jones
Liam Neeson
Prince

June 8
Kathy Baker
Mick Box
Barbara Bush
Russell Christian
Griffin Dunne
Sherman Garnes
Mick "Red" Hucknall
Neil Mitchell
Chuck Negron
Doris Pearson
Robert Pilatus
Nick Rhodes
Joan Rivers
Boz Scaggs
Jerry Stiller
Bonnie Tyler
Keenen Ivory Wayans

June 9
Johnny Ace
Trevor Bolder
Johnny Depp
Michael J. Fox
Billy Hatton
Jon Lord
Jackie Mason

June 10
Shirley Alston
Human Beatbox
Linda Evangelista
Lionel Jeffries
Grace Mirabella
Shirley Owens
Prince Philip
Rick Price
Andrew Stevens

June 11
Adrienne Barbeau
Joey Dee
Chad Everett
John Lawton
Joe Montana
Bonnie Pointer
Donnie Van Zandt
Gene Wilder
George Willig

June 12
Timothy Busfield
George Bush
Bun Carlos
Vic Damone
Brad Delp
Jenilee Harrison
Jim Nabors
Reg Presley

June 13
Tim Allen
Christo
Bobby Freeman
Ben Johnson
Howard Leese
Dennis Locorriere
Mark Mendoza
Deniece Pearson
Ally Sheedy
Richard Thomas

June 14
Rod Argent
Boy George
Marla Gibbs
Steffi Graf
Jimmy Lea
Will Patton
Donald Trump
Muff Winwood

June 15
Jim Belushi
Simon Callow
Courteney Cox
Mario Cuomo
Julie Hagerty
Russell Hitchcock
Noddy Holder
Helen Hunt
Waylon Jennings
Nilsson
Jim Varney

June 16
Eddie Levert
Ian Matthews
Laurie Metcalf
Corin Redgrave
Joan Van Ark
Gino Vannelli

June 17
Norman Kuhlke
Mark Linn-Baker
Peter Lupus
Barry Manilow
Dean Martin
Joe Piscopo

June 18
Tom Bailey
Roger Ebert
Carol Kane
E.G. Marshall
Paul McCartney
Alison Moyet
Isabella Rossellini
Jerome Smith

June 19
Paula Abdul
Tommy DeVito
Larry Dunn
Louis Jourdan
Nancy Marchand
Malcolm McDowell
Phylicia Rashad
Gena Rowlands
Salman Rushdie
Kathleen Turner
Ann Wilson

June 20
Danny Aiello
Michael Anthony
Chet Atkins
Olympia Dukakis
John Goodman
Billy Guy
Martin Landau
Cyndi Lauper
Alan Longmuir
John Mahoney
Lionel Richie
John Taylor
Dave Thomas
James Tolkan
Brian Wilson

June 21
Meredith Baxter
Berke Breathed
Chris Britton
Mark Brzezicki
Ray Davies
Michael Gross
Mariette Hartley
Bernie Kopell
Joey Kramer
Juliette Lewis
Nils Lofgren
Joey Molland
Jane Russell
Doug Savant
Maureen Stapleton
Prince William

June 22
Peter Asher
Gary Beers
Bill Blass
Klaus Maria Brandauer
Amy Brenneman
Bruce Campbell
Tom Cunningham
Green Gartside
Howard Kaylan
Kris Kristofferson
Michael Lerner
Alan Osmond
Tracy Pollan
Todd Rundgren
Jimmy Somerville
Meryl Streep
Lindsay Wagner

June 23
Bryan Brown
Adam Faith
Karin Gustafson

June 24
Nancy Allen
Jeff Beck
Colin Blunstone
Georg Stanford Brown
Jeff Cease
Mick Fleetwood
John Illsley
Michele Lee
Andy McCluskey
Curt Smith
Peter Weller

June 25
Tim Finn
Eddie Floyd
Allen Lanier
June Lockhart
Ian McDonald
George Michael
David Paich
Walter Payton
Carly Simon
Jimmie Walker
Clint Warwick

June 26
Billy Davis Jr.
Chris Isaak
Mick Jones
Larry Taylor

June 27
Isabelle Adjani
Julia Duffy
Bob Keeshan
Henry Ross Perot

June 28
Kathy Bates
Mel Brooks
John Cusack
Dave Knights
Alice Krige
Mary Stuart Masterson
Noriyuki "Pat" Morita

June 29
Gary Busey
Fred Grandy
Colin Hay
Little Eva
Ian Paice
Stedman Pearson
Roger Spear
Ruth Warrick

June 30
Florence Ballard
David Alan Grier
Lena Horne
Hal Lindes
Andy Scott
Glenn Shorrock
Adrian Wright

July 1
Wally Amos Jr.
Dan Aykroyd
Claude Berri
Karen Black
Roddy Bottum
Delaney Bramlett
Genevieve Bujold
Leslie Caron
Olivia De Havilland
Princess Diana
Jamie Farr
Farley Granger
Deborah Harry
Estee Lauder
Carl Lewis
Sydney Pollack
Fred Schneider
Mike Tyson

July 2
Pete Briquette
Johnny Colla
Imelda Marcos
Joe Puerta
Ron Silver
Paul Williams

July 3
Paul Barrere
Betty Buckley
Neil Clark
Vince Clarke

Tom Cruise
Johnny Lee
Montel Williams

July 4
Leona Helmsley
Gina Lollobrigida
Kirk Pengilly
Geraldo Rivera
Eva Marie Saint
Neil Simon
Jeremy Spencer
John Waite
Al "Blind Owl" Wilson
Bill Withers

July 5
Shirley Knight
Huey Lewis
Michael Monarch
Robbie Robertson

July 6
Allyce Beasley
Ned Beatty
Gene Chandler
Rik Elswit
Nanci Griffith
Shelley Hack
Bill Haley
Jon Keeble
Janet Leigh
Nancy Reagan
Glenn Scarpelli
Sylvester Stallone
Burt Ward

July 7
Pierre Cardin
Shelley Duvall
Warren Entner
Jessica Hahn
David Hodo
Joe Spano
Ringo Starr

July 8
Kevin Bacon
Andy Fletcher
Anjelica Huston
Graham Jones
Raffi
Jeffrey Tambor
Jerry Valy

July 9
Marc Almond
Frank Bello
Brian Dennehy
Tom Hanks
Jim Kerr
Kelly McGillis
Mitch Mitchell
Fred Savage
Bon Scott
O.J. Simpson
Debbie Sledge
Jimmy Smits
John Tesh

July 10
David Brinkley
Ronnie James Dio
Ron Glass
Arlo Guthrie
Jerry Miller
Neil Tennant
Max Von Sydow

July 11
Giorgio Armani
Tab Hunter
Peter Murphy
Leon Spinks
Sela Ward

July 12
Milton Berle
Bill Cosby
Mel Harris
Cheryl Ladd
Christine McVie
Liz Mitchell
Richard Simmons
Jay Thomas
John Wetton
Kristi Yamaguchi

July 13
Stephen Jo Bladd
Lawrence Donegan
Harrison Ford
Robert Forster
Cheech Marin
Roger "Jim" McGuinn
Patrick Stewart
Spud Webb

July 14
Polly Bergen
Ingmar Bergman
Chris Cross
Rosey Grier
Frances Lear
Harry Dean Stanton

July 15
Willie Aames
Alex Karras
Peter Lewis
Brigitte Nielsen
Linda Ronstadt
Jan-Michael Vincent
Patrick Wayne
Forest Whitaker

July 16
Ruben Blades
Phoebe Cates
Stewart Copeland
Desmond Dekker
Corey Feldman
Tony Jackson
Ginger Rogers

July 17
Lucie Arnaz
Geezer Butler
Diahann Carroll
Spencer Davis
Phyllis Diller
David Hasselhoff
Art Linkletter
Donald Sutherland
Mick Tucker
Mike Vale

July 18
Papa Dee Allen
James Brolin
Terry Chambers
Hume Cronyn
Dion DiMucci
Glenn Hughes
Audrey Landers
Robin MacDonald
Nelson Mandela
Elizabeth McGovern
Martha Reeves
Red Skelton
Nigel Twist

July 19
Allen Collins
Alan Gorrie
Pat Hingle
Bernie Leadon
Brian May

July 20
Paul Cook
Donna Dixon
John Lodge
Mike McNeil
Diana Rigg
Carlos Santana

July 21
Lance Guest
Edward Herrmann
Don Knotts
Leigh Lawson
Jon Lovitz
Jim Martin
Matt Mulhern
Henry Priestman
Isaac Stern
Cat Stevens
Robin Williams

July 22
Estelle Bennett
Albert Brooks
George Clinton
Willem Dafoe
Richard Davies
Louise Fletcher
Danny Glover
Don Henley
John Leguizamo
Alex Trebek

July 23
Dino Danelli
David Essex
Martin Gore
Woody Harrelson
Andy Mackay
Larry Manetti
Edie McClurg
Stephanie Seymour
Terence Stamp
Blair Thornton

July 24
Heinz Burt
Ruth Buzzi
Lynda Carter
Lynval Golding
Kadeem Hardison
Robert Hays
Laura Leighton
Michael Richards
Chris Sarandon

July 25
Ray Billingsley
Manuel Charlton
Estelle Getty
Barbara Harris
Iman
Jim McCarty
Woody Strode
Verdine White

July 26
Blake Edwards
Dorothy Hamill
Mick Jagger
Stanley Kubrick
Duncan Mackay
Jason Robards
Roger Taylor

July 27
Peggy Fleming
Norman Lear
Maureen McGovern
Brock Peters
John Pleshette
Al Ramsey
Betty Thomas
Jerry Van Dyke

July 28
George Cummings
Jim Davis
Terry Fox
Simon Kirke
Sally Struthers
Rick Wright

July 29
Michael Biehn
Neal Doughty
Peter Jennings
Geddy Lee
Marilyn Quayle
Michael Spinks
David Warner

July 30
Paul Anka
Delta Burke
Kate Bush
Larry Fishburne
Buddy Guy
Anita Hill
Ken Olin
Rat Scabies
Arnold Schwarz-enegger

July 31
Daniel Ash
Bill Berry
Dean Cain
Geraldine Chaplin
Norman Cook
Karl Green
Gary Lewis
Wesley Snipes
John West

August 1
Rick Anderson
Tempestt Bledsoe
Ricky Coonce
Robert Cray
Dom DeLuise
Joe Elliott
Jerry Garcia
Giancarlo Giannini
Arthur Hill
Yves Saint Laurent
Robert James Waller
Tom Wilson

August 2
Joanna Cassidy
Doris Coley
Wes Craven
Pete de Freitas
Garth Hudson
Victoria Jackson
Carroll O'Connor
Peter O'Toole
Mary-Louise Parker
Edward Patten
Max Wright

August 3
Tony Bennett
B.B. Dickerson
James Hetfield
John Landis
Beverly Lee
Gordon Scott
Martin Sheen

August 4
David Carr
Frankie Ford

August 5
Loni Anderson
Neil Armstrong
Rick Derringer
Rick Huxley
Jonathan Silverman

August 6
Paul Bartel
Dorian Harewood
Catherine Hicks
Abbey Lincoln
Pat McDonald

August 7
Bruce Dickinson
Andy Fraser
John Glover
David Rasche
Alberto Salazar
B. J. Thomas

August 8
Richard Anderson
Philip Balsley
Princess Beatrice
Keith Carradine
Harry Crosby
Dino De Laurentiis
The Edge
Andy Fairweather-Low
Chris Foreman
Dustin Hoffman
Donny Most
Connie Stevens
Mel Tillis
Larry Dee Wilcox
Esther Williams

August 9
Kurtis Blow
Sam Elliott
Melanie Griffith
Billy Henderson
Whitney Houston
Ken Norton
Benjamin Orr
David Steinberg

August 10
Ian Anderson
Rosanna Arquette
Antonio Banderas
Veronica Bennett
Michael Bivins
Riddick Bowe
Jimmy Dean
Jon Farriss
Eddie Fisher
Bobby Hatfield
Lorraine Pearson

August 11
Erik Braunn
Eric Carmen
Hulk Hogan
Mike Hugg
Joe Jackson
Jim Kale
Denis Payton
Claus Von Bulow

August 12
John Derek
George Hamilton
Roy Hay
Sam J. Jones
Mark Knopfler
Pat Metheny
Marjorie Reynolds
Pete Sampras
Suzanne Vega

August 13
Kathleen Battle
Danny Bonaduce
Fidel Castro
Dan Fogelberg
Pat Harrington
Don Ho
Feargal Sharkey
Jane Wyatt

August 14
Halle Berry
Dash Crofts
David Crosby
Alice Ghostley
Larry Graham
Jackee
Magic Johnson
Steve Martin
Susan Saint James
Danielle Steel

August 15
Princess Anne
Julia Child
Mike Connors
Linda Ellerbee
Tess Harper
Matt Johnson
MCA
Bill Pinkney
Rose-Marie
Pete York

August 16
Bob Balaban
Angela Bassett
Belinda Carlisle
Robert Culp
Frank Gifford
Kathie Lee Gifford
Eydie Gorme
Timothy Hutton
Madonna
Fess Parker
Carole Shelley
James Taylor
Reginald Veljohnson
Lesley Ann Warren

August 17
Robert De Niro
Steve Gorman
Colin Moulding
Maureen O'Hara
Sean Penn
Kevin Rowland
Gary Talley
Donnie Wahlberg

August 18
Dennis Elliott
Martin Mull
Roman Polanski
Robert Redford
Christian Slater
Madeleine Stowe
Ron Strykert
Patrick Swayze
Malcolm-Jamal Warner
Carl Wayne
Shelley Winters

August 19
Ginger Baker
Bill Clinton
John Deacon
Kevin Dillon
Peter Gallagher
Ian Gillan
Billy J. Kramer
M.C. Eric
Gerald McRaney
Diana Muldaur
Jill St. John
John Stamos

August 20
Joan Allen
Connie Chung
Doug Fieger
Rudy Gatlin
Isaac Hayes
Don King
Phil Lynott
James Pankow
Robert Plant

August 21
Kim Cattrall
Wilt Chamberlain
Carl Giammarese
Kenny Rogers
Kim Sledge
Joe Strummer
Melvin Van Peebles
Clarence Williams III

August 22
Ray Bradbury
Valerie Harper
John Lee Hooker
Roland Orzabal
Debbi Peterson
Norman Schwarzkopf
Cindy Williams

August 23
Ronny Cox
Barbara Eden
Bobby G.
Gene Kelly
Shelley Long
Vera Miles
Shaun Ryder
Richard Sanders
Rick Springfield

August 24
Yasir Arafat
Mark Bedford
Jim Capaldi
Joe Chambers
John Cipollina
Jeffrey Daniel
David Freiberg
Steve Guttenberg
Ken Hensley
Marlee Matlin
Claudia Schiffer

August 25
Anne Archer
Sean Connery
Elvis Costello
Billy Ray Cyrus
Mel Ferrer
Rob Halford
Monty Hall
Van Johnson
Regis Philbin
John Savage
Gene Simmons
Tom Skerritt
Blair Underwood
Joanne Whalley-Kilmer
Walter Williams

August 26
Jet Black
Bob Cowsill
Macaulay Culkin
Chris Curtis
Geraldine Ferraro
Michael Jeter
Branford Marsalis
Fred Milano
John O'Neill

August 27
Barbara Bach
Tim Bogert
Jeff Cook
Daryl Dragon
Pee-Wee Herman
Alex Lifeson
Glenn Matlock
Martha Raye
Harry Reems
Tuesday Weld

August 28
Clem Cattini
Hugh Cornwell
Ben Gazzara
Scott Hamilton
Donald O'Connor
Wayne Osmond
Jason Priestley
Roxie Roker
Emma Samms
Elizabeth Seal
Danny Seraphine
David Soul
Daniel Stern

August 29
Richard Attenborough
Rebecca DeMornay
Richard Gere
Elliott Gould
Michael Jackson
Robin Leach
George Montgomery
Sterling Morrison
Isabel Sanford

August 30
Elizabeth Ashley
Timothy Bottoms
John McNally
Micky Moody
John Phillips
Kitty Wells

August 31
Jerry Allison
James Coburn
Debbie Gibson
Buddy Hackett
Van Morrison
Rudolph Schenker
Daniel Schorr
Anthony Thistlethwaite
Glenn Tilbrook

September 1
Greg Errico
Gloria Estefan
Bruce Foxton
Barry Gibb
Lily Tomlin
Dave White

September 2
Rosalind Ashford
Jimmy Connors
Sam Gooden
Marty Grebb
Mark Harmon
Fritz McIntyre
Steve Porcaro
Keanu Reeves

September 3
Eileen Brennan
Donald Brewer
Al Jardine
Steve Jones
Gary Leeds
Valerie Perrine
Charlie Sheen
Mort Walker

September 4
Martin Chambers
Gary Duncan
Greg Elmore
Mitzi Gaynor
Judith Ivey
Merald Knight
Ronald LaPread
Jennifer Salt
Ione Skye

September 5
John Cage
William Devane
Carol Lawrence
Bob Newhart
Al Stewart
Raquel Welch
Dweezil Zappa

September 6
Dave Bargeron
Jane Curtin
Swoosie Kurtz
Claydes Smith
Paul Waaktaar
Jo Anne Worley

September 7
Alfa Anderson
Corbin Bernsen
Susan Blakely
Chrissie Hynde
Julie Kavner
Peggy Noonan
Richard Roundtree
Benmont Tench

September 8
Sid Caesar
Brian Cole
Michael Lardie
David Steele
Henry Thomas

September 9
Doug Ingle
Michael Keaton
Kristy McNichol
Sylvia Miles
Cliff Robertson
Dave Stewart
Roger Waters

September 10
Chris Columbus
Siobhan Fahey
Jose Feliciano
Johnnie Fingers
Colin Firth
Danny Hutton
Amy Irving
Big Daddy Kane
Charles Kuralt
Pat Mastelotto
Joe Perry
Don Powell
Fay Wray

September 11
Harry Connick Jr.
Lola Falana
Mickey Hart
Earl Holliman
Hedy Lamarr
Amy Madigan
Virginia Madsen
Jon Moss
Tommy Shaw
Mick Talbot
Dennis Tufano

September 12
Barry Andrews
Gerry Beckley
Tony Bellamy
Darren E. Burrows
Linda Gray
Neil Peart
Brian Robertson
Peter Scolari
Barry White

September 13
Barbara Bain
Jacqueline Bisset
Nell Carter
Peter Cetera
David Clayton-Thomas
Claudette Colbert
Randy Jones
Richard Kiel
Joni Sledge
Mel Torme

September 14
Pete Agnew
Barry Cowsill
Faith Ford
Morten Harket
Walter Koenig
Paul Kossoff
Sam Neill
Joe Penny
Nicol Williamson

September 15
Les Braid
Jackie Cooper
Prince Henry
Tommy Lee Jones
Oliver Stone

September 16
Lauren Bacall
Ed Begley Jr.
Joe Butler
Bernie Calvert
David Copperfield
Peter Falk
Anne Francis
Allen Funt
Kenny Jones
B.B. King
Richard Marx
Susan Ruttan

September 17
Anne Bancroft
Elvira

Jeff MacNelly
Roddy McDowall
Lamonte McLemore
John Ritter
Fee Waybill

September 18
Frankie Avalon
Ricky Bell
Robert Blake
Joanne Catherall
Kerry Livgren
Dee Dee Ramone
Jack Warden

September 19
Jim Abbott
John Coghlan
Lol Creme
Lee Dorman
Jeremy Irons
Joan Lunden
Nick Massi
David McCallum
Bill Medley
Nile Rodgers
Twiggy
Adam West

September 20
Alannah Currie
Sophia Loren
Anne Meara
Chuck Panozzo
John Panozzo

September 21
Leonard Cohen
Henry Gibson
Larry Hagman
Stephen King
Ricki Lake
Rob Morrow
Bill Murray
Catherine Oxenberg
Philthy Animal
Alfonso Ribeiro
Trugoy the Dove

September 22
Scott Baio
Shari Belafonte
David Coverdale
Joan Jett
Paul LeMat

September 23
Jason Alexander
Steve Boone
Ronald Bushy
Ray Charles
Lita Ford
Julio Iglesias
Ben E. King
Elizabeth Pena
Mary Kay Place
Mickey Rooney
Bruce Springsteen

September 24
Phil Hartman
Gerry Marsden
Linda McCartney
Anthony Newley

September 25
Gary Alexander
Michael Douglas
Mark Hamill
John Locke
Heather Locklear
Onnie McIntyre
Juliet Prowse
Christopher Reeve
Phil Rizzuto
Steve Severin
Will Smith
Cheryl Tiegs
Barbara Walters

September 26
Melissa Sue Anderson
Joe Bauer
George Chambers
Craig Chaquico
Donna Douglas
Georgie Fame
Bryan Ferry
Linda Hamilton
Mary Beth Hurt
Winnie Mandela
Olivia Newton-John
Tracey Thorn

September 27
Randy Bachman
Wilford Brimley
William Conrad
Greg Ham
Jayne Meadows
Meat Loaf
Greg Morris
Sada Thompson

September 28
Brigitte Bardot
Jeffrey Jones
Marcello Mastroianni
Helen Shapiro
William Windom
Moon Unit Zappa

September 29
Gene Autry
Anita Ekberg
Britt Ekland
Mark Farner
Bryant Gumbel
Patricia Hodge
Madeline Kahn
Jerry Lee Lewis
Larry Linville
Emily Lloyd

September 30
Marc Bolan
Angie Dickinson
Deborah Kerr
Frankie Lymon
Dewey Martin
Johnny Mathis
Marilyn McCoo
Sylvia Peterson
Victoria Tennant
Barry Williams

October 1
Julie Andrews
Jean-Jacques Annaud
Jimmy Carter
Stephen Collins
Rob Davis
Richard Harris
Donny Hathaway
Howard Hewett
Jerry Martini
Walter Matthau
Philippe Noiret
Randy Quaid
Stella Stevens
James Whitmore

October 2
Richard Hell
Freddie Jackson
Donna Karan
Don McLean
Philip Oakey
Mike Rutherford
Sting
Tiffany

October 3
Lindsey Buckingham
Chubby Checker
Barbara Ferris
Pamela Hensley
Tommy Lee
Gore Vidal
Jack Wagner
Dave Winfield

October 4
Armand Assante
Clifton Davis
Jim Fielder
Charlton Heston
Chris Lowe
Anne Rice
Susan Sarandon

October 5
Karen Allen
Clive Barker
Leo Barnes
Josie Bissett
Eddie Clarke
Jeff Conaway
Brian Connolly
Bob Geldof
Glynis Johns
Bil Keane
Mario Lemieux
Carlo Mastrangelo
Steve Miller
Donald Pleasence

October 6
Kevin Cronin
Bobby Farrell
Thomas McClary
Matthew Sweet
Bob Weir

October 7
June Allyson
Toni Braxton
Kevin Godley
Dave Hope
Yo-Yo Ma
John Mellencamp
Oliver North
Martha Stewart

October 8
Rona Barrett
Robert Bell
George Bellamy
Chevy Chase
Michael Dudikoff
Paul Hogan
Jesse Jackson
Sarah Purcell
Johnny Ramone
Hamish Stuart
Sigourney Weaver
Tony Wilson
Stephanie Zimbalist

October 9
Scott Bakula
Jackson Browne
John Entwistle
Michael Pare
Robert Wuhl

October 10
Neneh Cherry
Charles Dance
Jessica Harper
Martin Kemp
Martina Navratilova
Alan Rachins
David Lee Roth
Tanya Tucker
Ben Vereen

October 11
Joan Cusack
Daryl Hall
Ron Leibman
David Morse
Luke Perry
Grant Shaud

October 12
Susan Anton
Kirk Cameron
Melvin Franklin
Sam Moore
Luciano Pavarotti
Adam Rich
Will Rogers Jr.
Dave Vanian

October 13
Karen Akers
Tisha Campbell
Sammy Hagar
Beverly Johnson
Nancy Kerrigan
Robert Lamm
Marie Osmond
Kelly Preston
Nipsey Russell
Demond Wilson

October 14
Harry Anderson
Marcia Barrett
Greg Evigan
Billy Harrison
Justin Hayward
Ralph Lauren
Roger Moore
Cliff Richard

October 15
Mickey Baker
Richard Carpenter
Chris De Burgh
Sarah Ferguson
Lee Iacocca
Tito Jackson
Linda Lavin
Penny Marshall
Tanya Roberts
Don Stevenson

October 16
Tony Carey
Barry Corbin
Gary Kemp
Angela Lansbury
Dave Lovelady
Tim Robbins
Suzanne Somers
C.F. Turner
Wendy Wilson

October 17
Sam Bottoms
Beverly Garland
Alan Howard
Margot Kidder
Michael McKean
Howard Rollins Jr.
Jim Seals
Jerry Siegel
Jim Tucker
George Wendt

October 18
Chuck Berry
Peter Boyle
Mike Ditka
Russ Giguere
Keith Knudsen
Melina Mercouri
Erin Moran
Joe Morton
Gary Richrath
George C. Scott
Vincent Spano

October 19
Richard Dreyfuss
Patricia Ireland
John Lithgow
Karl Wallinger

October 20
Joyce Brothers
Alan Greenwood
Mark King
Ric Lee
Jerry Orbach
Tom Petty
Bobby Seale
Jay Siegel

October 21
Charlotte Caffey
Julian Cops
Steve Cropper
Eric Faulkner
Lee Loughnane
Steve Lukather
Manfred Mann

October 22
Eddie Brigati
Catherine Deneuve
Joan Fontaine
Bobby Fuller
Annette Funicello
Jeff Goldblum
Valeria Golino
Derek Jacobi
Ray Jones
Christopher Lloyd
Tony Roberts
John Sutton

October 23
Johnny Carson
Freddie Marsden
Perola Negra Pele
Weird Al Yankovic
Dwight Yoakam

October 24
F. Murray Abraham
Jerry Edmonton
Kevin Kline
David Nelson
B.D. Wong
Bill Wyman

October 25
Jon Anderson
Anthony Franciosa
Matthias Jabs
Midori
Tracy Nelson
Rick Parfitt
Minnie Pearl
Helen Reddy
Marion Ross
Glenn Tipton

October 26
Hillary Rodham Clinton
Cary Elwes
Keith Hopwood
Bob Hoskins
Ivan Reitman
Pat Sajak
Jaclyn Smith
Keith Strickland

October 27
Terry Anderson
William Christopher
John Cleese
Ruby Dee
Nanette Fabray
John Gotti
Simon LeBon
Marla Maples
Carrie Snodgress

October 28
Jane Alexander
Steve Baumgartner
Michael Crichton
Wayne Fontana
Dennis Franz
Jami Gertz
Telma Hopkins
Bruce Jenner
Hank Marvin
Stephen Morris
Joan Plowright
Annie Potts
Julia Roberts

October 29
Ralph Bakshi
Kevin Dubrow
Kate Jackson
Denny Laine
Melba Moore
Winona Ryder

October 30
Harry Hamlin
Grace Slick
Charles Martin Smith
Otis Williams
Henry Winkler

October 31
King Ad-Rock
Barbara Bel Geddes
Tony Bowers
Bernard Edwards
Dale Evans
Lee Grant
Deidre Hall
Sally Kirkland
Annabella Lwin
Johnny Marr
Larry Mullen Jr.
Jane Pauley
Dan Rather
Xavier Roberts
David Ogden Stiers

November 1
Rick Allen
Ronald Bell
Barbara Bosson
Keith Emerson
Robert Foxworth
Mags Furuholmen
Rick Grech
James Kilpatrick Jr.
Lyle Lovett
Eddie MacDonald
Betsy Palmer
Dan Peek

November 2
Burt Lancaster
k.d. lang
Estelle Parsons
Brian Poole
Bruce Welch
Alfre Woodard

November 3
Adam Ant
Roseanne Arnold
Charles Bronson
Michael Dukakis
Mike Evans
Larry Holmes
Steve Landesberg
Lulu
Dolph Lundgren
Dennis Miller
James Prime
Gary Sandy

November 4
Martin Balsam
Art Carney
Walter Cronkite
Chris Difford
Ralph Macchio
Delbert McClinton
Markie Post
Kool Rock
Mike Smith
Loretta Swit

November 5
Bryan Adams
Art Garfunkel
Peter Noone
Tatum O'Neal
Roy Rogers
Sam Shepard
Paul Simon
Elke Sommer
Ike Turner

November 6
Sally Field
Glenn Frey
Ethan Hawke
P.J. Proby
Doug Sahm
Maria Shriver
George Young

November 7
Billy Graham
Joni Mitchell
Johnny Rivers

November 8
Alan Berger
Bonnie Bramlett
Alain Delon
Mary Hart
Rickie Lee Jones
Terry Lee Miall
Bonnie Raitt
Esther Rolle
Rodney Slater
Courtney Thorne-Smith
Roy Wood
Roxana Zal

November 9
Spiro Agnew
Joe Bouchard
Lou Ferrigno
Tom Fogerty
Alan Gratzer
Phil May
Pepa
Carl Sagan
Dennis Stratton

November 10
Glen Buxton
Greg Lake
MacKenzie Phillips
Ann Reinking
Jack Scalia
Roy Scheider

November 11
Bibi Andersson
Paul Cowsill
Chris Dreja
Stubby Kaye
Patric Knowles
Roger Lavern
Charles Manson
Ian Marsh
Vince Martell
Demi Moore
Andy Partridge
Kurt Vonnegut Jr.
Jonathan Winters
Jesse Colin Young

November 12
Errol Brown
Tonya Harding
John Maus
Leslie McKeown
Stephanie Powers
Wallace Shawn
Neil Young

November 13
Whoopi Goldberg
Joe Mantegna
Clyde McPhatter
Richard Mulligan

November 14
Frankie Banali
Prince Charles
Freddie Garrity
Robert Ginty
Brian Keith
Alexander O'Neal
McLean Stevenson
Alec Such
Yanni
James Young

November 15
Edward Asner
Petula Clark
Beverly D'Angelo
Yaphet Kotto
Frida Lyngstad
Tony Thompson
Sam Waterston

November 16
Lisa Bonet
Dwight Gooden
Clu Gulager
Burgess Meredith

November 17
Martin Barre
Gene Clark
Peter Cook
Danny DeVito
Ronald DeVoe
Bob Gaudio
Lauren Hutton
Gordon Lightfoot
Mary Elizabeth Mastrantonio
Lorne Michaels
Martin Scorsese
Tom Seaver

November 18
Margaret Atwood
Hank Ballard
Imogene Coca
Linda Evans
Kirk Hammett
Andrea Marcovicci
Graham Parker
Jameson Parker
Elizabeth Perkins
Herman Rarebell
Susan Sullivan
Brenda Vaccaro
Kim Wilde

November 19
Dick Cavett
Jodie Foster
Larry King
Jeane Kirkpatrick
Calvin Klein
Hank Medress
Kathleen Quinlan
Ahmad Rashad
Meg Ryan
Ted Turner

November 20
Kaye Ballard
Jimmy Brown
Mike D
Bo Derek
George Grantham
Veronica Hamel
Richard Masur
Ray Stiles
Joe Walsh
Sean Young

November 21
Goldie Hawn
Dr. John
Lonnie Jordan
Laurence Luckinbill
Lorna Luft
Juliet Mills
Harold Ramis
Nicollette Sheridan
Marlo Thomas

November 22
Aston Barrett
Boris Becker
Tom Conti
Jamie Lee Curtis
Rodney Dangerfield
Terry Gilliam
Mariel Hemingway
Billie Jean King
Floyd Sneed
Stevie "Little Steven" Van Zandt
Robert Vaughn
Ray Walston
Tina Weymouth

November 23
Susan Anspach
Bruce Hornsby

November 24
Donald Dunn
Geraldine Fitzgerald
Chris Hayes
Dwight Schultz
John Squire
Jim Yester

November 25
Christina Applegate
Joe DiMaggio
Amy Grant
John F. Kennedy Jr.
John Larroquette
Ricardo Montalban
Steve Rothery
Percy Sledge

November 26
Cyril Cusack
Robert Goulet
Norman Hassan
Alan Henderson
John McVie
Charles Schulz
Tina Turner

November 27
Charlie Burchill
Dozy
Robin Givens
Eddie Rabbitt
Bob Smith
Fisher Stevens
Jaleel White

November 28
Beeb Birtles
Alexander Godunov
Ed Harris
Hope Lange
Judd Nelson
Randy Newman

November 29
Felix Cavaliere
Denny Doherty
Barry Goudreau
Jonathan Knight
Diane Ladd
Howie Mandel
John Mayall
Andrew McCarthy
Garry Shandling

November 30
John Aston
Richard Barbieri
Dick Clark
Kevin Conroy
Richard Crenna
Roger Glover
Rob Grill
Robert Guillaume
Billy Idol
Bo Jackson
G. Gordon Liddy
Leo Lyons
Mandy Patinkin
June Pointer

Rex Reason
Ridley Scott

December 1
Woody Allen
Carol Alt
Eric Bloom
John Densmore
David Doyle
Bette Midler
Sandy Nelson
Gilbert O'Sullivan
Richard Pryor
Lou Rawls
Charlene Tilton
Treat Williams

December 2
Steven Bauer
Ted Bluechel Jr.
Cathy Lee Crosby
Julie Harris
Michael McDonald
Tom McGuinness
Rick Savage
Howard Stern

December 3
Brian Bonsall
Ozzy Osbourne
Andy Williams

December 4
Tyra Banks
Jeff Bridges
John Cale
Deanna Durbin
Chris Hillman
Wink Martindale
Bob Mosley
Gary Rossington
Southside Johnny
Marisa Tomei

December 5
Morgan Brittany
Jeroen Krabbe
Charles Lane
Little Richard
Jim Messina
Les Nemes
Jack Russell

December 6
Peter Buck
Rick Buckler
Tom Hulce
James Naughton
Janine Turner
Ben Watt
Steven Wright

December 7
Larry Bird
Ellen Burstyn
Mike Nolan
Tom Waits
Eli Wallach

December 8
Gregg Allman
Kim Basinger
Jerry Butler
David Carradine
Phil Collen
Bobby Elliott
Teri Hatcher
James MacArthur
Sinead O'Connor
Paul Rutherford
Maximilian Schell
Flip Wilson

December 9
Joan Armatrading
Beau Bridges
Dick Butkus
Rick Danko
Kirk Douglas
Morton Downey Jr.
Dennis Dunaway
Douglas Fairbanks Jr.
Buck Henry
Neil Innes
John Malkovich
Michael Nouri
Donny Osmond
Dick Van Patten

December 10
Kenneth Branagh
Susan Dey
Ace Kefford
Dorothy Lamour
Mako
Walter Orange
Tommy Rettig
Chad Stuart

December 11
Bess Armstrong
Teri Garr
David Gates
Jermaine Jackson
Booker T. Jones
Brenda Lee
Rita Moreno
Nikki Sixx

December 12
Bob Barker
Dickey Betts
Mayim Bialik
Clive Bunker
Jennifer Connelly
Sheila E.
Connie Francis
Terry Kirkman
Ed Koch
Rush Limbaugh
Cathy Rigby
Frank Sinatra
Mike Smith
Dionne Warwick

December 13
Jeff "Skunk" Baxter
John Davidson
Ted Nugent
Randy Owen
Christopher Plummer
Dick Van Dyke
Tom Verlaine
Johnny Whitaker

December 14
Patty Duke
Cynthia Gibb
Abbe Lane
Jackie McCauley
Charlie Rich
Mike Scott
Dee Wallace Stone
Cliff Williams
Joyce Wilson

December 15
Carmine Appice
Dave Clark
Tim Conway
Reginald Hudlin
Don Johnson
Paul Simonon
Helen Slater

December 16
Benny Andersson
Steven Bochco
Ben Cross
Billy Gibbons
Tony Hicks
William Perry
Liv Ullmann

December 17
Carlton Barrett
Sarah Dallin
Dave Dee
Bob Guccione
Eddie Kendricks
Eugene Levy
Mike Mills
Art Neville
Paul Rodgers
Tommy Steele

December 18
Chas Chandler
Ossie Davis
Elliot Easton
Ray Liotta
Leonard Maltin
Brad Pitt
Keith Richards
Steven Spielberg
Kiefer Sutherland

December 19
Jennifer Beals
Alvin Lee
Robert MacNaughton
Alyssa Milano
Tim Reid
Cicely Tyson
Robert Urich
Maurice White
Zal Yanovsky

December 20
Jenny Agutter
Anita Baker
Billy Bragg
Bobby Colomby
John Hillerman
Chris Robinson
Little Stevie Wright

December 21
Phil Donahue
Chris Evert
Jane Fonda
Josh Mostel
Kurt Waldheim
Carl Wilson
Paul Winchell

December 22
Barbara Billingsley
Hector Elizondo
Maurice Gibb
Robin Gibb
Lady Bird Johnson
Rick Nielsen
Ricky Ross
Diane Sawyer

December 23
Corey Haim
Jorma Kaukonen
Johnny Kidd
Susan Lucci
Dave Murray
Eugene Record
Ruth Roman
Harry Shearer
James Stockdale
Eddie Vedder

December 24
Ian Burden
Lemmy

December 25
Jimmy Buffett
Robin Campbell
O'Kelly Isley
Annie Lennox
Shane MacGowan
Barbara Mandrell
Noel Redding
Hanna Schygulla
Sissy Spacek
Henry Vestine

December 26
Steve Allen
Elisha Cook Jr.
Abdul Fakir
Alan King
Donald Moffat
Phil Spector

December 27
John Amos
Peter Criss
Gerard Depardieu
Tovah Feldshuh
Mick Jones
David Knopfler
Les Maguire
Mike Pinder

December 28
Dorsey Burnette
Alex Chilton
Dick Diamonde
Bo Diddley
Lou Jacobi
Stan Lee
Charles Neville
Johnny Otis
Maggie Smith
Denzel Washington
Edgar Winter

December 29
Ted Danson
Mark Day
Marianne Faithfull
Mary Tyler Moore
Paula Poundstone
Inga Swenson
Ray Thomas
Tracey Ullman
Jon Voight

December 30
Joseph Bologna
Davy Jones
Jack Lord
Jeff Lynne
Mike Nesmith
Sheryl Lee Ralph
Del Shannon
Patti Smith
Russ Tamblyn

December 31
Barbara Carrera
Rosalind Cash
Burton Cummings
John Denver
Tom Hamilton
Anthony Hopkins
Val Kilmer
Ben Kingsley
Tim Matheson
Joe McIntyre
Sarah Miles
Pete Quaife
Donna Summer
Andy Summers

1995'S WATERSHED BIRTHDAYS

The following folks will have reason to celebrate (or toast themselves) a little harder this year as they reach birthday milestones.

Turning 90
Claudette Colbert

Turning 80
Hedy Lamarr
Victor Mature
Harry Morgan
Anthony Quinn
Frank Sinatra
Eli Wallach
Ruth Warrick

Turning 75
Ray Bradbury
David Brinkley
William Conrad
Nanette Fabray
Eva Gabor
Leona Helmsley
Louis Jourdan
DeForest Kelley
James Kilpatrick Jr.
Werner Klemperer
Peggy Lee
Walter Matthau
Jayne Meadows
Toshiro Mifune
Ricardo Montalban
Jack Palance
Pope John Paul II
Tony Randall
Andy Rooney
Mickey Rooney
Isaac Stern
Jack Warden

Turning 70
Robert Altman
Mickey Baker
Barbara Bush
Johnny Carson
Mike Connors
David Doyle
Farley Granger
Bill Haley
Julie Harris
Tony Hillerman
Hal Holbrook
Clifton James
George Kennedy
B.B. King
Angela Lansbury
Jack Lemmon
June Lockhart
Dorothy Malone
Paul Newman
Donald O'Connor
Fess Parker
Bill Pinkney
Rose-Marie
Cliff Robertson
Maureen Stapleton
Rod Steiger
Elaine Stritch
Mel Torme
Dick Van Dyke
Gwen Verdon
Gore Vidal
Dennis Weaver
Jonathan Winters

Turning 65
Buzz Aldrin
Neil Armstrong
John Astin
Polly Bergen
Bobby Bland
Ray Charles
Sean Connery
Pat Corley
John Cullum
Robert Culp
Beverly Garland
Ben Gazzara
Frank Gifford
Bob Guccione
Gene Hackman
Richard Harris
Buck Henry
Don Ho
Cloris Leachman
Robert Lester
G. Gordon Liddy
Abbey Lincoln
Robert Loggia
Jack Lord
Peter Marshall
Paul Mazursky
Grace Mirabella
Donald Moffat
Philippe Noiret
Alan Oppenheimer
Henry Ross Perot
Pat Robertson
Jay Robinson
Soupy Sales
Maximilian Schell
Stephen Sondheim
Frances Sternhagen
Rod Taylor
Robert Wagner
Andy Williams
Joanne Woodward
Edward Woodward

Turning 60
Woody Allen
Herb Alpert
Bibi Andersson
Julie Andrews
Sonny Bono
Eileen Brennan
Glen Campbell
Diahann Carroll
Richard Chamberlain
Christo
Michael Dante
Alain Delon
Bob Denver
Phil Donahue
Donna Douglas
Abdul Fakir
Geraldine Ferraro
Eddie Floyd
Henry Gibson
Charles Grodin
Barbara Harris
David Hartman
Tippi Hedren
Judd Hirsch
Alex Karras
Abbe Lane
Carol Lawrence
Jerry Lee Lewis
Loretta Lynn
Ray Manzarek
Nick Massi
Johnny Mathis
Doug McClure
Dudley Moore
Sam Moore
Jerry Orbach
Luciano Pavarotti
John Phillips
Nicholas Pryor
Little Richard
Dean Stockwell
Donald Sutherland
Jimmy Lee Swaggart
Russ Tamblyn
Bob Uecker
Bobby Vinton
Lyle Waggoner
M. Emmet Walsh
Gene Wilder

Turning 50
Maud Adams
Karen Akers
Barbara Alston
Susan Anspach
Rod Argent
Bob Balaban
John Barbata
Adrienne Barbeau
Dirk Benedict
Ritchie Blackmore
Colin Blunstone
Barry Bostwick
David Brenner
Chris Britton
Gary Brooker
Ronald Bushy
Eric Clapton
Doug Clifford
Stu Cook
Gene Cornish
Dino Danelli
Jim Davis
Clifton Davis
John Densmore
Cliff DeYoung
Mickey Dolenz
Lee Dorman
Tony Dow
Chris Dreja
David Dukes
John Echols
Rik Elswit
Little Eva
Mia Farrow
Jose Feliciano
Bryan Ferry
John Fogerty
Brenda Fricker
Ian Gillan
Michelle Gilliam
Jimmie Dale Gilmore
Ron Glass
Roger Glover
Kevin Godley
Graham Gouldman
Hugh Grundy
Deborah Harry
Donny Hathaway
Goldie Hawn
John Helliwell
Ken Hensley
Linda Hunt
Patricia Ireland
Bianca Jagger
Davy Jones
Steve Katz
Marthe Keller
Dee Dee Kennibrew
Dave Knights
Steve Landesberg
Leigh Lawson
Arthur Lee
Ric Lee
Lemmy
Peter Lewis
John Lithgow
John Lodge
Frida Lyngstad
Terrence Mann
Vince Martell
Steve Martin
Nick Mason
Ian Matthews
Onnie McIntyre
Goldy McJohn
Don McLean
John McVie
Bette Midler
Melba Moore
Rushton Moreve
Van Morrison
James Naughton
Ken Norton
Michael Nouri
Walter Parazaider
Gerry Paterson
Chuck Portz
Priscilla Presley
Victoria Principal
Noel Redding
Rob Reiner
Pat Riley
Mitch Ryder
Diane Sawyer
Joe Schermie
Bob Seger
Tom Selleck
Carly Simon
Bubba Smith
Rod Stewart
Eric Stewart
Al Stewart
Stephen Stills
Rosie Stone
Pete Townshend
Robin Trower
Bjorn Ulvaeus
Trish Van Devere
Gordon Waller
August Wilson
Henry Winkler
Jimmy Winston
John Wolters
Rick Wright
Neil Young

Turning 40
Isabelle Adjani
Kirstie Alley
Melody Anderson
Michael Anthony
Scott Bakula
Frankie Banali
Leo Barnes
Sandra Bernhard
Sam Bottoms
Lorraine Bracco
Dana Carvey
Roseanne Cash
Terry Chambers
Garry Christian
Neil Clark
Kevin Conroy
Elvis Costello
Kevin Costner
Willem Dafoe
Jeffrey Daniel
Jeff Daniels
Iva Davies
Kevin Dubrow
Griffin Dunne
Steve Earle
Eric Faulkner
Bruce Foxton
Peter Gallagher
Boon Gould
Kelsey Grammer
David Grier
John Grisham
Julie Hagerty
Glenne Headly
Nicky Headon
Margaux Hemingway
Howard Hewett
Mark Hollis
Arliss Howard
Isabelle Huppert
Billy Idol
Iman
Joe Jackson
Howard Jones
Mick Jones
Steve Jones
Jeff Jourard
William Katt
Alice Krige
David Lee Roth
Ray Liotta
Derek Longmuir
Stan Lynch
Yo-Yo Ma
Howie Mandel
Mick Mars
Pat Mastelotto
Reba McEntire
Leslie McKeown
Laurie Metcalf
Colin Moulding
Kate Mulgrew
Philip Oakey
Lena Olin
Benjamin Orr
Jay Osmond
Tanya Roberts
Xavier Roberts
Peter Scolari
Connie Sellecca
Captain Sensible
Steve Severin
Pete Shelley

Maria Shriver
Paul Simonon
Jimmy Smits
Andrew Stevens
Anthony Thistlethwaite
Alex Van Halen
Marsha Warfield
Bruce Willis
Debra Winger
Steven Wright

Turning 30
Frank Bello
Jon Cryer
Tom Cunningham
Mike D
Kevin Dillon
Robert Downey Jr.
Linda Evangelista
Sherilynn Fenn
Gerardo
Jami Gertz
Steve Gorman
Jam Master Jay
Diane Lane
John Leguizamo
Mario Lemieux
Annabella Lwin
Elle Macpherson
Marlee Matlin
John Michael Montgomery
Sarah Jessica Parker
Robert Pilatus
Charlie Sheen
Brooke Shields
Helen Slater
Eddie Vedder
Julie Warner

Turning 21
Drew Barrymore
Mayim Bialik
Balthazar Getty
Sara Gilbert

Turning 20
Jennifer Capriati
Lukas Haas
Joey Lawrence
Fred Savage
Jaleel White

HOMETOWNS OF THE STARS

ALABAMA

Anniston
Michael Biehn
Bessemer
Bo Jackson
Brewton
William Lee Golden
Birmingham
Nell Carter
Courteney Cox
Louise Fletcher
Kate Jackson
Eddie Kendricks
Carl Lewis
Wayne Rogers
John Taylor
Paul Williams
Jim Yester
Chickasaw
Ray Sawyer
Decatur
Dean Jones
Fairfield
Willie Mays
Fort Payne
Jeff Cook
Randy Owen
Leeds
Charles Barkley
Leighton
Percy Sledge
Marion
Coretta Scott King
Mobile
Jimmy Buffett
Bill Francis
Montgomery
Brett Butler
Eddie Floyd
Melvin Franklin
Tommy Shaw
Toni Tennille
Montgomeryville
David Walker
Prattville
Wilson Pickett
Tuskegee
Lionel Richie
Wetumpka
Andrew Thrasher
Gerhard Thrasher

ARIZONA

Phoenix
Lynda Carter
Stevie Nicks
Bill Spooner
Vince Welnick
Mare Winningham
Tucson
Barbara Eden
Linda Ronstadt

ARKANSAS

Blythesville
Junior Walker
Delight
Glen Campbell
Hope
Bill Clinton
Fort Smith
Laurence Luckinbill
Forrest City
Al Green
Charlie Rich
Jonesboro
John Grisham
Kingsland
Johnny Cash
Little Rock
Frank Bonner
Mammoth Spring
Tess Harper
Marvell
Levon Helm
Newport
Mary Steenburgen

CALIFORNIA

Alhambra
Cheryl Tiegs
Burbank
Paul Barrere
Jay Ferguson
Bruce Gary
Erin Moran
Sean Penn
Eve Plumb
Bonnie Raitt
John Ritter
Baldwin Hills
Mike Love
Berkeley
Melissa Sue Anderson
Bruce Barthol
John Cipollina
Robert Culp
Martha Davis
John Fogerty
Tom Fogerty
James Ivory
Phil Lesh
Lonnie Turner
Daphne Zuniga
Beverly Hills
John Drew Barrymore
Candice Bergen
Canoga Park
Kirk Cameron
Catalina Island
Gregory Harrison
Cerritos
Troy Kenneth Aikman
Concord
Tom Hanks
Coronado
Tina Weymouth
Culver City
Gwen Verdon
Cypress
John Stamos
East Los Angeles
Edward James Olmos
East Oakland
Anita Pointer
Bonnie Pointer
June Pointer
Ruth Pointer
El Cajon
Greg Louganis
El Centro
Cher
Ken Howard
Billy Mumy
El Monte
Country Joe McDonald
Encino
Berke Breathed
Stephanie Zimbalist
Eureka
Mike Patton
Fair Oaks
Joan Lunden
Fresno
Mike Connors
Tom Seaver
Glendale
Captain Beefheart
Gary Leeds
A Martinez
Tim Matheson
Doug McClure
Hanford
Steve Perry
Hawthorne
Carl Wilson
Hayward
Kristi Yamaguchi
Hollywood
Christina Applegate
Belinda Carlisle
David Carradine
Robert Carradine
Denise Crosby
Peter DeLuise
John Derek
Tony Dow
Robert Englund
Barbara Hershey
Vince Neil
Stephanie Powers
Katharine Ross
Dean Stockwell
Moon Unit Zappa
Inglewood
Cliff DeYoung
Vicki Lawrence
Brian Wilson
Isleton
Noriyuki "Pat" Morita
La Jolla
Danica McKellar
Gregory Peck
Cliff Robertson
Loma Linda
Matthew Modine
Long Beach
Harold Brown
Nicolas Cage
Bo Derek
Sally Kellerman
Billie Jean King
Cathy Rigby
Snoop Doggy Dogg
Rusty Young
Los Angeles
Willie Aames
Paula Abdul
Edward Albert
Anne Archer
Desi Arnaz Jr.
Lucie Arnaz
Tyra Banks
Drew Barrymore
Meredith Baxter
Ed Begley Jr.
Tony Bellamy
John Beradino
Corbin Bernsen
Jan Berry
Barbara Billingsley
Chastity Bono
Roddy Bottum
Eileen Brennan
Beau Bridges
Jeff Bridges
Morgan Brittany
James Brolin
Albert Brooks
Randy California
Richard Chamberlain
Rosalind Chao
Natalie Cole
Ry Cooder
Ricky Coonce
Jackie Cooper
Richard Crenna
Cathy Lee Crosby
David Crosby
Harry Crosby
Cherrie Currie
Jamie Lee Curtis
Jeffrey Daniel
John Densmore
Laura Dern
Mickey Dolenz
Daryl Dragon
Mia Farrow
Kim Fields
Carrie Frances Fisher
Bridget Fonda
Jodie Foster
John Clark Gable
Melissa Gilbert
Sharon Gless
Tony Goldwyn
Billy Gould
Jimmy Greenspoon
Rob Grill
Mark Harmon
Pamela Hensley
Jason Hervey
Chris Hillman
Dustin Hoffman
David Hungate
Helen Hunt
Ice Cube
Etta James
William Katt
Julie Kavner
Diane Keaton
Val Kilmer
Robbie Krieger
Lorenzo Lamas
Jason Scott Lee
Michele Lee
Howard Leese
Jennifer Jason Leigh
Chris Lemmon
Juliette Lewis
Peter Lewis
John Locke
Heather Locklear
Lorna Luft
Steve Lukather
James MacArthur
Bryan MacLean
Cheech Marin
Mary Stuart Masterson
Kristy McNichol
Yvette Mimieux
Liza Minnelli
James Mitchum
Michael Monarch
Elizabeth Montgomery
Rushton Moreve
Michael Murphy
Ryan O'Neal
Tatum O'Neal
David Paich
Melody Patterson
Debbi Peterson
Vicki Peterson
Chynna Phillips
Steve Porcaro
Deborah Raffin
Ronald Reagan Jr.
Michael Richards
Bobby Riggs
Katey Sagal
Susan Saint James
Jennifer Salt
Harry Shearer
James B. Sikking
Jonathan Silverman
John Singleton
Charles Martin Smith
Jill St. John
Robert Stack
Madeleine Stowe
Woody Strode
Kiefer Sutherland
George Takei
Russ Tamblyn
Tone-Loc
Dean Torrence
Jim Tucker
Mark Volman
Lindsay Wagner
Burt Ward
Patrick Wayne
Jaleel White
Esther Williams
Carnie Wilson
Wendy Wilson
Paul Winfield
Weird Al Yankovic
Roxana Zal
Dweezil Zappa
Lynwood
Kevin Costner
Malibu
Christie Brinkley
Timothy Hutton
Martinez
Joe DiMaggio
Maywood
Jim Messina
Merced
Janet Leigh
Mill Valley
Kathleen Quinlan
Modesto
Mike Allsup
Mark Spitz
Monterey
Sammy Hagar
Hal Lindes
Newport Beach
Susanna Hoffs

Kelly McGillis
Ted McGinley
Northridge
Jenilee Harrison
Norwalk
Tiffany
Oak Glen
Susan Anton
Oakland
Stu Cook
Sheila E.
Mark Hamill
Hammer
Ted Lange
Jim Martin
Rod McKuen
Palo Alto
Lindsey Buckingham
Doug Clifford
Amy Irving
Bill Kreutzmann Jr.
Markie Post
Ojai
Larry Linville
Paradise Valley
Bob Mosley
Pasadena
Julia Child
Sally Field
Harry Hamlin
Richard Moll
Pomona
Tom Waits
Redondo Beach
Michael Dudikoff
Reseda
Corey Feldman
Riverside
Jaye Davidson
Sacramento
Adrienne Barbeau
Creed Bratton
Sam Elliott
Molly Ringwald
Cynthia Robinson
San Bernardino
Gene Hackman
San Bruno
Ron McKernan
Suzanne Somers
San Diego
Mayim Bialik
Ted Danson
Gary Duncan
Robert Duvall
Greg Elmore
Nanette Fabray
Lonnie Jordan
Robert Lansing
Theresa Russell
Stephanie Seymour
Charlene Tilton
Fred Ward
Larry Dee Wilcox
Ann Wilson

San Francisco
Herb Alpert
Lisa Bonet
Todd Bridges
Colleen Camp
Elisha Cook Jr.
David Dukes
Clint Eastwood
Greg Errico
Bobby Freeman
Jerry Garcia
Danny Glover
Charles Haid
Paul Kantner
Joanna Kerns
Johnny Mathis
O.J. Simpson
Joe Spano
David Strathairn
Jeffrey Tambor
Ross Valory
Bob Weir
Nancy Wilson
B.D. Wong
San Jose
Chuck Berry
Peggy Fleming
Farley Granger
Patrick Simmons
San Leandro
Lloyd Bridges
San Mateo
Barry Bostwick
Keith Carradine
Neal Schon
San Pedro
Ted Bluechel Jr.
Howard Scott
Santa Ana
Bill Medley
Michelle Pfeiffer
Michelle Phillips
Santa Barbara
Joseph Bottoms
Sam Bottoms
Timothy Bottoms
Santa Cruz
Beverly Garland
Santa Monica
Sean Astin
Charlotte Caffey
Geraldine Chaplin
Shelley Fabares
Miguel Ferrer
Frank Gifford
Sara Gilbert
Scott Gorham
Linda Gray
Anjelica Huston
Bill Irwin
Penelope Ann Miller
Sandy Nelson
Tracy Nelson
Chuck Portz
Robert Redford
Charlie Sheen

Barry Williams
Santa Rosa
Rebecca DeMornay
Saratoga
Lance Guest
Saugus
Harry Carey Jr.
Sherman Oaks
Ashley Fuller Olsen
Mary Kate Olsen
Stockton
Chris Isaak
Sunnyvale
Teri Hatcher
Tarzana
Jon Lovitz
Torrance
B.B. Dickerson
Vallejo
Johnny Otis
Rosie Stone
Van Nuys
Mitch Gaylord
Gary Lockwood
Michael Milken
Johnny Whitaker
Cindy Williams
West Corvina
Tim Robbins
West Hollywood
Lukas Haas
Whittier
Lorna Patterson

COLORADO

Colorado Springs
Tom Hamilton
Denver
Tim Allen
Philip Bailey
Pat Hingle
Jan-Michael Vincent

CONNECTICUT

Bridgeport
Brian Dennehy
John Ratzenberger
Bristol
Gary Burghoff
Fairfield
Meg Ryan
Greenwich
Glenn Close
Shelley Hack
Hamden
Ernest Borgnine
Hartford
Linda Evans
Katharine Hepburn
David Naughton
Gene Pitney
Middletown
James Naughton
New Haven
Michael Bolton
Richard Carpenter

Jill Eikenberry
Norman Lear
Benjamin Spock
New London
Amy Brenneman
Glenne Headly
Norwalk
Bruce Weitz
Redding Ridge
Hope Lange
Rowayton
Treat Williams
Stamford
Michael Dante
Christopher Lloyd
Waterbury
Sheryl Lee Ralph
Westport
Linda Blair
Kevin Conroy
Pamela Sue Martin
Winsted
Ralph Nader

DELAWARE

Wilmington
Papa Dee Allen
Valerie Bertinelli
Judge Reinhold
George Thorogood

DISTRICT OF COLUMBIA

Jeff "Skunk" Baxter
David Birney
Blair Brown
Ronald Bushy
Jack Casady
Connie Chung
Matt Frewer
Albert Gore
Goldie Hawn
John Heard
Edward Herrmann
William Hurt
Howie Johnson
Seth Justman
Jorma Kaukonen
John F. Kennedy Jr.
Michael Learned
Roger Mudd
Michael Nouri
Maury Povich
Chita Rivera
Pete Sampras
Frances Sternhagen
Peter Tork
Henry Vestine

FLORIDA

Bascom
Faye Dunaway
Coral Gables
Mimi Rogers
Eloise
Jim Stafford

Ft. Lauderdale
Chris Evert
Gainesville
Stan Lynch
Tom Petty
Benmont Tench
Hialeah
Harry Wayne Casey
Jacksonville
Gary Bonds
Pat Boone
Allen Collins
Gary Rossington
Miami
Karin Gustafson
Deborah Harry
Victoria Jackson
Robert Johnson
Sam Moore
Sidney Poitier
Roxie Roker
Rita Rudner
Jerome Smith
Ben Vereen
Ocala
Elizabeth Ashley
Orlando
Delta Burke
Pahokee
Mel Tillis
Panama City
Mike Campbell
Dan Peek
Pompano Beach
Esther Rolle
Tallahassee
Wally Amos Jr.
Tampa
Dwight Gooden
Butterfly McQueen
West Palm Beach
Dickey Betts

GEORGIA

Albany
Ray Charles
Athens
Kim Basinger
Peter Buck
Keith Strickland
Cindy Wilson
Atlanta
William Guest
DeForest Kelley
Gladys Knight
Merald Knight
Spike Lee
Edward Patten
Chris Robinson
Rich Robinson
Tommy Roe
Nipsey Russell
Joe South
Jane Withers
Augusta
James Brown
Larry Fishburne

Amy Grant
Hulk Hogan
Clarksdale
Ray Stevens
Cleveland
Xavier Roberts
Cogdell
Ossie Davis
Columbus
Robert Cray
Conyers
Holly Hunter
Cuthbert
Rosey Grier
Larry Holmes
Decatur
Michael Stipe
Eatonton
Alice Walker
Lithonia
Brenda Lee
Macon
Randy Crawford
Little Richard
Marietta
Robert Patrick
Travis Tritt
Newark
Fred Schneider
Newman
Alan Jackson
Ocilla
Dave Prater
Plains
Jimmy Carter
Savannah
Stacy Keach
Smyrna
Julia Roberts
St. Simons Island
Jim Brown
Sylacauga
Jim Nabors
Thomasville
Joanne Woodward
Valdosta
Demond Wilson
Waycross
Burt Reynolds
Pernell Roberts

HAWAII

Honolulu
Bette Midler
Kelly Preston
Kakaako
Don Ho
Kauai
Larry Ramos Jr.

IDAHO

Buhl
Marjorie Reynolds
Ketchum
Mariel Hemingway
Wallace
Lana Turner

ILLINOIS
Abington
James Stockdale
Acton
Bonnie Bramlett
Alton
James Earl Ray
Belleville
Jimmy Connors
Buddy Ebsen
Bloomington
McLean Stevenson
Carrollton
Karen Allen
Centerville
Reginald Hudlin
Champaign
Jennie Garth
Bruce Hall
Chicago
John Agar
Laurie Anderson
Michael Anthony
Barbara Bain
Bob Balaban
Adam Baldwin
Jennifer Beals
John Beck
Jim Belushi
Tom Berenger
Tempestt Bledsoe
Dick Butkus
Jonathan Cain
Bill Campbell
Ed Cassidy
Peter Cetera
Gene Chandler
Sam Cooke
Michael Crichton
John Cusack
Clifton Davis
Bruce Dern
Dennis DeYoung
Phil Everly
Dennis Farina
Harrison Ford
Nick Fortune
Dennis Franz
Mitzi Gaynor
Jami Gertz
Carl Giammarese
Marla Gibbs
Marty Grebb
Mary Gross
Michael Gross
Dorothy Hamill
Herbie Hancock
Daryl Hannah
Jessica Harper
Donny Hathaway
Hugh Hefner
Marilu Henner
Quincy Jones
Rickie Lee Jones
Sam J. Jones
Terry Kath
Walter Koenig
Harvey Korman
John Landis
Abbey Lincoln
Nils Lofgren
Lee Loughnane
Amy Madigan
Michael Madsen
Dorothy Malone
David Mamet
Larry Manetti
Joe Mantegna
Ray Manzarek
Richard Marx
Curtis Mayfield
Roger "Jim" McGuinn
Martin Mull
Bob Newhart
Kim Novak
Donald O'Connor
Berry Oakley
Ken Olin
James Pankow
Chuck Panozzo
John Panozzo
Walter Parazaider
Mandy Patinkin
William Petersen
Aidan Quinn
Harold Ramis
Lou Rawls
Jason Robards
Pat Sajak
Danny Seraphine
Gary Shandling
Sidney Sheldon
Maria Shriver
Gene Siskel
Grace Slick
Patti Smith
Carrie Snodgress
David Soul
Fisher Stevens
Mr. T
Lili Taylor
Mel Torme
Robert Townsend
Dennis Tufano
Scott Turow
Melvin Van Peebles
Ken Wahl
Marsha Warfield
Jody Watley
Raquel Welch
George Wendt
Robin Williams
James Young
Robert Young
Robert Zemeckis
Warren Zevon
Adrian Zmed
Christopher
John Malkovich
Danville
Jerry Van Dyke
De Kalb
Cindy Crawford
DeKalb
Barbara Hale
East St. Louis
Warrington Hudlin
Edwardsville
Laurie Metcalf
Elgin
Bruce Boxleitner
Evanston
William Christopher
Kevin Cronin
Joan Cusack
Neal Doughty
Barbara Harris
Charlton Heston
Elizabeth McGovern
Grant Shaud
Eddie Vedder
Ft. Sheridan
Sam Shepard
Gillespie
Howard Keel
Great Lakes
Chaka Khan
Hartford
Clint Walker
Highland Park
Fred Savage
Jacksonville
Ken Norton
Melrose Park
Carol Lawrence
Morton Grove
Marlee Matlin
Naperville
Paula Zahn
Oak Park
Patricia Ireland
Mary Elizabeth Mastrantonio
Betty White
Park Ridge
Karen Black
Hillary Rodham Clinton
Pekin
Susan Dey
Peoria
Dan Fogelberg
Richard Pryor
Gary Richrath
David Ogden Stiers
Rochelle
Joan Allen
Rock Island
Eddie Albert
Rockford
Bun Carlos
Rick Nielsen
Tom Petersson
Robin Zander
Saint Louis
Jackie Joyner-Kersee
Tampico
Ronald Reagan
Urbana
Roger Ebert
Waukegan
Ray Bradbury
Wilmette
Bill Murray
Winnetka
Virginia Madsen
Chris O'Donnell
Zion
Gary Coleman

INDIANA
Anderson
Tom Ryan
Bloomington
David Lee Roth
Dale
Florence Henderson
East Chicago
Betsy Palmer
Evansville
Ron Glass
Ft. Wayne
Bill Blass
Shelley Long
Gary
Jackie Jackson
Janet Jackson
Jermaine Jackson
Marlon Jackson
Michael Jackson
Tito Jackson
Alex Karras
Karl Malden
Deniece Williams
Indianapolis
Richard Finch
Brendan Fraser
David Letterman
Peter Lupus
Jane Pauley
Dan Quayle
Marilyn Quayle
Kurt Vonnegut Jr.
Lafayette
Axl Rose
Lowell
Jo Anne Worley
Marion
Jim Davis
Richmond
Sarah Purcell
Seymour
John Mellencamp
South Bend
Chad Everett
Sydney Pollack
Terre Haute
Mick Mars
West Baden
Larry Bird
Vincennes
Red Skelton

IOWA
Ames
Richie Hayward
Keith Knudsen
Charles City
Robert James Waller
Corning
Johnny Carson
Davenport
Lara Flynn Boyle
Des Moines
Stephen Collins
Cloris Leachman
Sada Thompson
Dubuque
Kate Mulgrew
Marshalltown
Mary Beth Hurt
Ottumwa
Tom Arnold
Sioux City
Fred Grandy
Jerry Mathers
Wall Lake
Andy Williams

KANSAS
Caldwell
Max Showalter
Dodge City
Dennis Hopper
El Dorado
Mort Walker
Goessell
Shirley Knight
Kansas City
Edward Asner
Lyle Waggoner
Leavenworth
Melissa Etheridge
Manhattan
Elvira
Olathe
Charles Miller
Salina
Terry Kirkman
Topeka
Annette Bening
Wichita
Kirstie Alley
Winfield
Darren E. Burrows

KENTUCKY
Ashland
Naomi Judd
Wynonna
Baintsville
Crystal Gayle
Bardwell
Martha Stewart
Brownie
Don Everly
Butcher Hollow
Loretta Lynn
Flatwoods
Billy Ray Cyrus
Fort Campbell
Chris Frantz
Glasgow
Diane Sawyer
Hopkinsville
Steve Gorman
Lexington
Ned Beatty
Richard Hell
John Michael Montgomery
Jim Varney
Louisville
Muhammad Ali
Mickey Baker
William Conrad
Telma Hopkins
Victor Mature
Sean Young
Maysville
Rosemary Clooney
Owensboro
Johnny Depp
Packard
Patricia Neal
Pikesville
Dwight Yoakam
West Irvine
Harry Dean Stanton

LOUISIANA
Alexandria
Faith Ford
Algiers
Clarence Henry
Baywood
Donna Douglas
Breaux Bridge
Branford Marsalis
Delhi
Earl Holliman
Ferriday
Jerry Lee Lewis
Jimmy Lee Swaggart
Gretna
Frankie Ford
Kenner
Lloyd Price
Lettsworth
Buddy Guy
New Orleans
Sam Clayton
Harry Connick Jr.
Fats Domino
Kenny Gradney
Bryant Gumbel
Dr. John
Dorothy Lamour
John Larroquette
Wynton Marsalis
Aaron Neville
Art Neville
Randy Newman

Anne Rice
Richard Simmons
Jay Thomas
Ray Walston
Carl Weathers
Shreveport
Alan Autry
Hank Williams Jr.
Vinton
Bobby Kimball

MAINE
Lewiston
Patrick Dempsey
Portland
Stephen King
Linda Lavin
Andrea Martin
Judd Nelson

MARYLAND
Baltimore
Spiro Agnew
Bess Armstrong
John Astin
Tom Clancy
Charles Dutton
David Hasselhoff
Ric Ocasek
Jameson Parker
Nicholas Pryor
Howard Rollins Jr.
Dwight Schultz
Michael Tucker
John Waters
Montel Williams
Bethesda
Robert Hays
Daniel Stern
Rockville Centre
Jonathan Demme
Salisbury
Linda Hamilton

MASSACHUSETTS
Boston
Jane Alexander
Ricky Bell
Stephen Jo Bladd
Erik Braunn
Peggy Cass
Gary Collins
Brad Delp
Warren Entner
David Freiberg
Barry Goudreau
Jasmine Guy
Anthony Michael Hall
Madeline Kahn
Jonathan Knight
Jordan Knight
Jack Lemmon
Leonard Nimoy
Joe Perry
Ruth Roman
Fran Sheehan
James Spader
Tom Sullivan
Donna Summer
James Taylor
Uma Thurman
Ralph Tresvant
Barbara Walters
Al "Blind Owl" Wilson
Danny Wood
Brighton
Richard Dysart
Brookline
Michael Dukakis
Ted Kennedy
Conan O'Brien
Mike Wallace
Cambridge
Banana
Jane Curtin
Paul Michael Glaser
Anne Jillian
Alan Rachins
Sam Waterston
Dorchester
Marky Mark
Donnie Wahlberg
Hamilton
David Morse
Lawrence
Robert Goulet
Lowell
Olympia Dukakis
Paul Tsongas
Lynn
Estelle Parsons
Milton
George Bush
Needham
Joe McIntyre
Roxbury
Bobby Brown
Springfield
Kurt Russell
Wareham
Geena Davis
Wellesley
Billy Squier
Winchester
Brad Whitford
Woburn
Eric Bogosian
Nancy Kerrigan

MICHIGAN
Ann Arbor
Iggy Pop
Battle Creek
Dick Martin
Bay City
Madonna
Benton Harbor
Arte Johnson
Sinbad
Birmingham
Christine Lahti
Calumet
James Tolkan
Coopersville
Del Shannon
Dearborn
Bob Seger
Derfoil
Maxwell Gail
Detroit
Rosalind Ashford
Anita Baker
Florence Ballard
Hank Ballard
Renaldo Benson
Sonny Bono
Ellen Burstyn
Alice Cooper
Francis Ford Coppola
David Coulier
Abdul Fakir
Sherilynn Fenn
Doug Fieger
Glenn Frey
David Grier
Casey Kasem
Richard Kiel
Piper Laurie
Ed McMahon
Harry Morgan
Michael Moriarty
Ted Nugent
Ray Parker Jr.
Lawrence Payton
Suzi Quatro
Smokey Robinson
Rockwell
Diana Ross
Mitch Ryder
Tom Selleck
Tom Skerritt
Elaine Stritch
Levi Stubbs
Marlo Thomas
Lily Tomlin
Robert Wagner
Joyce Wilson
Max Wright
Flint
Jim Abbott
Sandra Bernhard
Donald Brewer
Mark Farner
Craig Frost
Mel Schacher
Grand Rapids
El DeBarge
Anthony Kiedis
Grosse Point
Julie Harris
Highland Park
Bill Haley
Lansing
Timothy Busfield
Magic Johnson
Steven Seagal
Mt. Clemens
Dean Cain
Muskegon
Jim Bakker
Royal Oak
Bruce Campbell
Saginaw
Stevie Wonder
Wyandotte
Lee Majors

MINNESOTA
Albert Lea
Marion Ross
Bemidji
Jane Russell
Ceylon
Walter Mondale
Cloquet
Jessica Lange
Duluth
Bob Dylan
Hibbing
Bill Berry
International Falls
Tammy Faye Bakker
Minneapolis
Richard Dean Anderson
James Arness
Julia Duffy
Terry Gilliam
Peter Graves
Bernie Leadon
Prince
Charles Schulz
New Ulm
Tippi Hedren
Owatonna
E.G. Marshall
Rochester
Lea Thompson
Saint Paul
Dave Winfield
St. Louis Park
Ethan Coen
Joel Coen
St. Paul
Loni Anderson
Rick Anderson
Mike Farrell
Winona
Winona Ryder

MISSISSIPPI
Arkabutla
James Earl Jones
Biloxi
Eric Roberts
Clarksdale
John Lee Hooker
Ike Turner
Collins
Gerald McRaney
Columbia
Walter Payton
Flora
George Chambers
Lester Chambers
Willie Chambers
Greenville
Mary Wilson
Hot Coffee
Stella Stevens
Itta Bena
Marion Barry
B.B. King
Jackson
Cynthia Geary
Kosciusko
Oprah Winfrey
Leland
Johnny Winter
McComb
Bo Diddley
Meridian
George Cummings
Diane Ladd
David Ruffin
Sela Ward
Pontotoc County
Delaney Bramlett
Red Bay
Tammy Wynette
Scott County
Joe Chambers
Sledge
Charley Pride
Sunflower
Jerry Butler

MISSOURI
Afton
John Goodman
Cape Girardeau
Rush Limbaugh
Eve
Alice Ghostley
Flat Creek
Don Johnson
Independence
Arliss Howard
Ginger Rogers
Joplin
Dennis Weaver
Kansas City
Robert Altman
Edie McClurg
Herb Reed
Dee Wallace Stone
Dianne Wiest
Lee's Summit
Pat Metheny
Springfield
Kathleen Turner
St. Joseph
Walter Cronkite
Betty Garrett
Ruth Warrick
Jane Wyman
St. Louis
Maya Angelou
Scott Bakula
Billy Davis Jr.
Lee Dorman
Robert Guillaume
Kevin Kline
Mark Linn-Baker
Marsha Mason
Michael McDonald
Lamonte McLemore
David Rasche
Leon Spinks
Michael Spinks
Betty Thomas
Ron Townson
Shelley Winters
Tipton
Gene Clark
Washington
Jack Wagner
West Plains
Dick Van Dyke
Willow Springs
Steve Cropper

MONTANA
Brady
George Montgomery
Butte
Martha Raye
Glasgow
Steve Reeves
Helena
Dirk Benedict
Missoula
Dana Carvey
David Lynch
Townsend
Patrick Duffy

NEBRASKA
Gibbon
Dick Cavett
Harvard
Paul Revere
Laurel
James Coburn
Lincoln
Matthew Sweet
Janine Turner
Omaha
Marlon Brando
David Doyle
Doug Ingle
Swoosie Kurtz
Nick Nolte
Inga Swenson
Fee Waybill
Scottsbluff
Randy Meisner

NEVADA
Las Vegas
Andre Agassi

NEW HAMPSHIRE
Exeter
John Irving

North Conway
John Shea
Portsmouth
Russ Giguere

NEW JERSEY

Asbury Park
Danny DeVito
Atlantic City
Rosalind Cash
Bayonne
Sandra Dee
Brian Keith
Frank Langella
Mark Stein
Camden
Joanna Cassidy
Richard Sterban
East Orange
Dionne Warwick
Elberon
Mel Ferrer.
Elizabeth
Judy Blume
Elizabeth Pena
Tony Williams
Englewood
John Travolta
Englewood Cliffs
Trish Van Devere
Freehold
Bruce Springsteen
Garfield
Eddie Brigati
Hoboken
Frank Sinatra
Jersey City
George Brown
Marilyn McCoo
Claydes Smith
Tracey Walter
Malcolm-Jamal Warner
Flip Wilson
Long Branch
Richard Anderson
Clint Black
Maplewood
Grace Mirabella
Metuchen
David Copperfield
Montclair
Buzz Aldrin
Tommy DeVito
Morristown
Linda Hunt
Mt. Morris
Tom Verlaine
Neptune
Jack Nicholson
Neptune Park
Southside Johnny
New Brunswick
Michael Douglas
Newark
Jason Alexander
John Amos
Connie Francis
Whitney Houston
Ice-T
Jerry Lewis
Ray Liotta
Nick Massi
Shaquille O'Neal
Joe Pesci
Eva Marie Saint
Paul Simon
Frankie Valli
Jack Warden
Nutley
Robert Blake
Orange
Roy Scheider
Passaic
Shirley Alston
Doris Coley
Joey Dee
Donald Fagen
Addi Harris
Beverly Lee
Shirley Owens
Joe Piscopo
Loretta Swit
Penns Grove
John Forsythe
Bruce Willis
Princeton
Michael Knight
Rahway
Paul LeMat
Richfield
Tim Bogert
Sayreville
Jon Bon Jovi
South Amboy
Greg Evigan
South Seaville
Rosie Daley
Summit
Meryl Streep
Tenafly
Ed Harris
Carol Potter
Trenton
Judith Light
Norman Schwarzkopf
Union City
Dennis Locorriere
Robert Wuhl
Weehawken
Kate Pierson
Westfield
Andrew McCarthy
Westwood
Robert Sean Leonard

NEW MEXICO

Austin
John Madden
Cloudcroft
Ronny Cox
Roswell
John Denver
Demi Moore

NEW YORK

Albany
William Devane
Andy Rooney
Amsterdam
Kirk Douglas
Armonk
Peter Gallagher
Astoria
Christopher Walken
Babylon
Rodney Dangerfield
The Bronx
Stephen Arenholz
Anne Bancroft
Ellen Barkin
Joey Bishop
James Caan
Angelo D'Aleo
Bobby Darin
Dion DiMucci
Ace Frehley
Bob Gaudio
Billy Joel
Stanley Kubrick
Steve Landesberg
Hal Linden
Penny Marshall
Carlo Mastrangelo
Fred Milano
Cathy Moriarty
Chuck Negron
Jerry Orbach
Harry Reems
Tanya Roberts
Connie Sellecca
Neil Simon
Brooklyn
Woody Allen
Barbara Alston
Scott Baio
Allyce Beasley
Pat Benatar
Joseph Bologna
Lorraine Bracco
Lala Brooks
Mel Brooks
Andrew Dice Clay
David Cohen
Peter Criss
Vic Damone
William Daniels
Tony Danza
Calvert Deforest
Dom DeLuise
Richard Dreyfuss
Elliot Easton
James Farentino
Lou Ferrigno
Harvey Fierstein
Louis Gossett Jr.
Elliott Gould
Steve Guttenberg
Buddy Hackett
Kadeem Hardison
Richie Havens
Lena Horne
Marty Ingels
Michael Jordan
Harvey Keitel
Dee Dee Kennibrew
Alan King
Carole King
Larry King
Martin Landau
Abbe Lane
Michael Lerner
Mitch Margo
Phil Margo
Paul Mazursky
MCA
Anne Meara
Hank Medress
Eddie Money
Mary Tyler Moore
Eddie Murphy
Lorenzo Music
Nilsson
Michael Pare
Rosie Perez
Rhea Perlman
Donna Pescow
Priscilla Presley
Joe Regalbuto
Joan Rivers
Mickey Rooney
Jack Scalia
Neil Sedaka
Jerry Seinfeld
Al Sharpton
Jay Siegel
Chris Stein
Connie Stevens
Larry Taylor
Mary Thomas
Marisa Tomei
John Turturro
Brenda Vaccaro
Eli Wallach
Wendy Wasserstein
Jessica Walter
Pat Wright
Buffalo
Rick James
Beverly Johnson
Jeffrey Jones
Nancy Marchand
Bob Smith
Cory Wells
Carthage
John Carpenter
Commack
Rosie O'Donnell
Corning
Duane Eddy
Cornwall
Bonnie Blair
Cortland
Ronnie Dio
Croton-on-Hudson
Peter Strauss
East Meadow
Sterling Morrison
Forest Hills
Donna Karan
Joey Ramone
Garden City
John Tesh
Glen Cove
Joe Butler
Harlem
Freddie Jackson
Highland Falls
Charles Durning
Hornell
Bill Pullman
Hudson
Frances Lear
Ithaca
Mary McDonnell
Jackson Heights
Tommy Rettig
Kingston
John Glover
Lake Success
Talia Shire
Long Island
Eric Bloom
Joe Bouchard
Jennifer Capriati
Billy Crystal
Debbie Gibson
Ralph Macchio
Mark Mendoza
Johnny Ramone
Lou Reed
John Savage
Lynbrook
Bob Keeshan
Mamaroneck
Kevin Dillon
Massapequa
Alec Baldwin
Stephen Baldwin
William Baldwin
Joey Buttafuoco
Jessica Hahn
Mt. Kisco
Bruce Jenner
Gavin MacLeod
Mt. Vernon
Art Carney
Dick Clark
Denzel Washington
New Rochelle
Bud Cort
Bob Denver
Matt Dillon
Jay Leno
Don McLean
Alan Menken
Rob Morrow
Richard Roundtree
Peter Scolari
New York
King Ad-Rock
Brooke Adams
Don Adams
Danny Aiello
Karen Akers
Alan Alda
Nancy Allen
Steve Allen
Trini Alvarado
Susan Anspach
Carmine Appice
Alan Arkin
Patricia Arquette
Rosanna Arquette
Beatrice Arthur
Armand Assante
Rene Auberjonois
Lauren Bacall
Martin Balsam
Rona Barrett
Paul Bartel
Angela Bassett
Walter Becker
Bonnie Bedelia
Barbara Bel Geddes
Harry Belafonte
Shari Belafonte
Richard Benjamin
Estelle Bennett
Patricia Bennett
Veronica Bennett
Marisa Berenson
David Berkowitz
Milton Berle
Peter Billingsley
Kurtis Blow
Steven Bochco
Riddick Bowe
Matthew Broderick
James L. Brooks
Joyce Brothers
Michael Brown
George Burns
Red Buttons
John Cage Jr.
Irene Cara
Mariah Carey
George Carlin
Diahann Carroll
David Cassidy
Phoebe Cates
Stockard Channing
Chevy Chase
Michael Clarke
Jill Clayburgh
Bobby Colomby
Jeff Conaway
Jennifer Connelly
Kevin Conway
Peter Coyote
Lindsay Crouse
Jon Cryer
Macaulay Culkin
Tony Curtis
Mike D
Terence Trent D'Arby

Timothy Daly
Dino Danelli
Robert De Niro
Dana Delany
Neil Diamond
Kevin Dobson
Troy Donahue
Robert Downey Jr.
Spencer Dryden
Patty Duke
Griffin Dunne
Hector Elizondo
Chris Elliott
Rik Elswit
Nora Ephron
Emilio Estevez
Erik Estrada
Douglas Fairbanks Jr.
Peter Falk
Louis Farrakhan
Tovah Feldshuh
Amy Fisher
Jane Fonda
Peter Fonda
Anthony Franciosa
Allen Funt
Art Garfunkel
Sherman Garnes
Ben Gazzara
J. Geils
Estelle Getty
Robert Ginty
Robin Givens
Crispin Glover
Tracey Gold
Whoopi Goldberg
Gale Gordon
Lesley Gore
Eydie Gorme
John Gotti
Grandmaster Flash
Lee Grant
Alan Greenwood
Jennifer Grey
Melanie Griffith
Bob Guccione
Christopher Guest
Arlo Guthrie
Marvin Hamlisch
Pat Harrington
Mickey Hart
Mariette Hartley
Joseph Heller
Harry Helmsley
Leona Helmsley
Lance Henriksen
Buck Henry
Catherine Hicks
Gregory Hines
Judd Hirsch
Celeste Holm
Tab Hunter
Janis Ian
Jam Master Jay
Conrad Janis
Big Daddy Kane
Steve Katz
Stubby Kaye
Howard Kaylan
Brian Keenan
George Kennedy
Bruno Kirby
Sally Kirkland
Calvin Klein
Danny Klein
Robert Klein
Ed Koch
Bernie Kopell
Yaphet Kotto
Joey Kramer
Judith Krantz
Lenny Kravitz
Ricki Lake
Christopher Lambert
Robert Lamm
Burt Lancaster
Charles Lane
Diane Lane
Louise Lasser
Estee Lauder
Cyndi Lauper
Ralph Lauren
Barbara Lee
Stan Lee
Ron Leibman
Sheldon Leonard
Al Lewis
Emmanuel Lewis
Gary Lewis
Huey Lewis
G. Gordon Liddy
L.L. Cool J
June Lockhart
Jack Lord
Julia Louis-Dreyfus
Tina Louise
Robert Ludlum
Frankie Lymon
MC Lyte
Robert MacNaughton
Jeff MacNelly
Leonard Maltin
Barry Manilow
Dinah Manoff
Andrea Marcovicci
Ed Marinaro
Vince Martell
Richard Masur
Walter Matthau
John Maus
Linda McCartney
Darryl D. McDaniels
Bobby McFerrin
Michael McKean
Jimmy Merchant
Ari Meyers
Alyssa Milano
Sylvia Miles
Stephanie Mills
Minnesota Fats
Melba Moore
Joe Morton
Donny Most
Josh Mostel
Diana Muldaur
Richard Mulligan
David Nelson
Peggy Noonan
Carroll O'Connor
John Oates
Tony Orlando
Charles Osgood
Catherine Oxenberg
Al Pacino
Ron Perlman
Bernadette Peters
Brock Peters
Sylvia Peterson
Regis Philbin
Robert Pilatus
Bronson Pinchot
John Pleshette
Suzanne Pleshette
Amanda Plummer
Tracy Pollan
Faith Popcorn
Colin Powell
Eddie Rabbitt
Nancy Reagan
Christopher Reeve
Carl Reiner
Rob Reiner
Paul Reiser
Alfonso Ribeiro
Adam Rich
Don Rickles
Peter Riegert
Geraldo Rivera
Johnny Rivers
Phil Rizzuto
Tony Roberts
Jay Robinson
Chris Rock
Nile Rodgers
Will Rogers Jr.
Rose-Marie
Carl Sagan
J. D. Salinger
Isabel Sanford
Herman Santiago
Susan Sarandon
Daniel Schorr
Annabella Sciorra
Martin Scorsese
John Sebastian
Pete Seeger
George Segal
Maurice Sendak
Gene Shalit
Wallace Shawn
Ally Sheedy
Brooke Shields
Beverly Sills
Ron Silver
Carly Simon
Christian Slater
Helen Slater
Curtis Sliwa
Jimmy Smits
Dick Smothers
Tom Smothers
Wesley Snipes
Stephen Sondheim
Paul Sorvino
Vincent Spano
Phil Spector
Mickey Spillane
Sylvester Stallone
Jean Stapleton
Danielle Steel
Howard Stern
Jerry Stiller
Oliver Stone
Larry Storch
Marcia Strassman
Barbra Streisand
Susan Sullivan
Taj Mahal
Nedra Talley
Richard Thomas
Tiny Tim
Claire Trevor
Garry Trudeau
Donald Trump
Steven Tyler
Cicely Tyson
Mike Tyson
Leslie Uggams
Jerry Valy
Joan Van Ark
Dick Van Patten
Mario Van Peebles
Gloria Vanderbilt
Luther Vandross
Robert Vaughn
Suzanne Vega
Eddie Velez
Jimmie Walker
Julie Warner
Lesley Ann Warren
Keenen Ivory Wayans
Sigourney Weaver
Tuesday Weld
Billy Dee Williams
Vanessa Williams
Clarence Williams III
George Willig
Paul Winchell
William Windom
Henry Winkler
Peter Wolf
Steven Wright
Jane Wyatt
Peter Yarrow
Jesse Colin Young
Pia Zadora

Newburgh
Geraldine Ferraro

Northport
Patti LuPone

Ogdensburg
M. Emmet Walsh

Ossining
Anne Francis

Oswego
Joey Belladonna

Peekskill
Mel Gibson
Pee-Wee Herman

Pelham
Felix Cavaliere

Pound Ridge
Ali MacGraw

Queens
Carol Alt
Barbara Bach
Tony Bennett
David Caruso
Mario Cuomo
Debi Mazar
Jason Patric
Elizabeth Perkins
Mercedes Ruehl
Joseph Simmons
Paul Stanley
Reginald Veljohnson
John Williams

Rochester
Gene Cornish
Robert Forster
Lou Gramm
John Lithgow
Wendy O. Williams

Rome
Pat Riley

Roosevelt
Julius Erving

Rye
Christopher Atkins
Jason Bateman
Justine Bateman
Barbara Bush
Justin Henry

Saratoga Springs
Scott Valentine

Schenectady
Mickey Rourke

Shoreham
D.B. Sweeney

South Bronx
Afrika Bambaataa
Cuba Gooding Jr.

Staten Island
Joan Baez
David Johansen
Robert Loggia
Glenn Scarpelli
Rick Schroder

Suffern
Valerie Harper

Syracuse
Tom Cruise
Bobcat Goldthwait
Alan Gratzer
Frank Whaley

Troy
Maureen Stapleton

Utica
Annette Funicello

West Islip
Boomer Esiason

West Point
Gore Vidal

Westbury
Nancy McKeon

Westchester
June Allyson
Susan Lucci

Westhampton
Rod Steiger

White Plains
James Whitmore

Yonkers
Sid Caesar
Jon Voight

NORTH CAROLINA

Bellhaven
Little Eva

Black Mountain
Roberta Flack

Charlotte
Billy Graham

Cherry Point
Johnny Colt

Durham
Alan Clark
Clyde McPhatter

Greenville
Bernard Edwards

Henderson
Ben E. King

Kannapolis
George Clinton

Marshville
Randy Travis

Mt. Airy
Andy Griffith

Salisbury
Mike Evans

Sumter
Bill Pinkney

Tryon
Nina Simone

Wake Forest
Ray Billingsley
Soupy Sales

Wilmington
David Brinkley
Charles Kuralt
Meadowlark Lemon
Sugar Ray Leonard

Winston–Salem
Jackee
Al Nichol

NORTH DAKOTA

Fargo
Bobby Vee

Jamestown
Peggy Lee

Kulm
Angie Dickinson

Valley City
Ann Sothern

OHIO

Akron
Glen Buxton
Hugh Downs
Howard Hewett
Chrissie Hynde
James Ingram
Alliance
Perry King
Ashtabula
Don Novello
Canton
Eddie Levert
Chillicothe
Nancy Wilson
Cincinnati
Marty Balin
Doris Day
Julie Hagerty
O'Kelly Isley
Ronald Isley
Rudolph Isley
Charles Manson
Roy Rogers
Pete Rose
Steven Spielberg
Roger Staubach
Ted Turner
Cleveland
Kaye Ballard
Halle Berry
Eric Carmen
Tracy Chapman
Wes Craven
Ruby Dee
Phil Donahue
Keir Dullea
Ken Forssi
Joel Grey
Arsenio Hall
Hal Holbrook
Carol Kane
Don King
Burgess Meredith
Greg Morris
Paul Newman
Benjamin Orr
Jerry Siegel
Joe Walsh
Debra Winger
Bobby Womack
Columbus
Beverly D'Angelo
Buster Douglas
Philip Michael Thomas
Dayton
Dorian Harewood
Tommy James
Gordon Jump
Chad Lowe
Gary Sandy
Martin Sheen
Jonathan Winters
Fort Recovery
Rick Zehringer
Fredericktown
Luke Perry
Galena
Rick Derringer
Greenfield
Johnny Paycheck
Hamilton
Scott Engel
Lakewood
Teri Garr
Lima
Phyllis Diller
Al Jardine
Nelsonville
Sarah Jessica Parker
Portsmouth
Kathleen Battle
Steubenville
Dean Martin
Toledo
Jamie Farr
Tom Scholz
Gloria Steinem
Uhrichsville
John West
Wapakoneta
Neil Armstrong
Warren
Austin Pendleton
Willoughby
Tim Conway
Yellow Springs
Richie Furay
Youngstown
Robert Bell
Ronald Bell
Maureen McGovern
Ed O'Neill

OKLAHOMA

Ada
Oral Roberts
Boise City
Vera Miles
Cordell
George Grantham
Duncan
Hoyt Axton
Ron Howard
Jeane Kirkpatrick
Healdton
Rue McClanahan
Holdenville
Clu Gulager
Hugo
Bill Moyers
Lawton
Leon Russell
McAlester
Reba McEntire
Norman
James Garner
Oklahoma City
Suzy Amis
Tisha Campbell
James Kilpatrick Jr.
Pawhuska
Ben Johnson
Ryan
Chuck Norris
Sacred Heart
Tony Hillerman
Shawnee
Brad Pitt
Tulsa
Garth Brooks
David Duke
Blake Edwards
David Gates
Anita Hill
Jennifer Jones
Mary Kay Place
Tony Randall
Alfre Woodard

OREGON

Cottage Grove
Dennis Dunaway
Eugene
Mark Lindsey
Pendleton
Elaine Miles
Portland
Bob Bogle
Matt Groening
Tonya Harding
Margaux Hemingway
Clifton James
Ahmad Rashad
Gordon Scott
Sally Struthers
Salem
Howard Hesseman

PENNSYLVANIA

Allentown
Lee Iacocca
Beaver Falls
Joe Namath
Bethlehem
Jonathan Frakes
Mel Harris
Canonsburg
Bobby Vinton
Carnegie
Mike Ditka
Charleroi
Barbara Bosson
Coatesville
Susan Richardson
Coraopolis
Michael Keaton
Easton
Sally Jessy Raphael
Ehrenfield
Charles Bronson
Germantown
Henry Gibson
Glenwillard
Lou Christie
Harrisburg
Richard Sanders
Haverford
Scott Hamilton
Johnstown
Carroll Baker
Tim Kazurinsky
Kingston
Edie Adams
Latrobe
Mister Rogers
Lattimer
Jack Palance
Meadville
Sharon Stone
Montgomery
Joey Lawrence
New Eagle
Joe Montana
Philadelphia
F. Murray Abraham
Mark Andes
Frankie Avalon
Kevin Bacon
Steve Baumgartner
George Benson
Joe Bonsall
Peter Boyle
David Brenner
Solomon Burke
Imogene Coca
Bill Cosby
David Costell
Blythe Danner
John Davidson
Fabian
Lola Falana
Barbara Feldon
Norman Fell
Eddie Fisher
Richard Gere
Scott Glenn
Jeff Goldblum
Frank Gorshin
Charles Grodin
Veronica Hamel
Sherman Hemsley
Joan Jett
Bil Keane
Gene Kelly
Jack Klugman
Audrey Landers
Patti LaBelle
Elaine May
Bret Michaels
Dennis Miller
Matt Mulhern
Teddy Pendergrass
Danny Rapp
Todd Rundgren
Bob Saget
Debbie Sledge
Joni Sledge
Kathy Sledge
Kim Sledge
Parker Stevenson
Russell Thompkins Jr.
Tammi Terrell
Fritz Weaver
Dave White
Syreeta Wright
Pittsburgh
August Wilson
Pottstown
Daryl Hall
Reading
Michael Constantine
Meg Foster
Shillington
John Updike
Smithton
Shirley Jones
Spangler
Chris Columbus
West Philadelphia
Wilt Chamberlain

RHODE ISLAND

Barrington
Spalding Gray
Newport
Harry Anderson
Barry Cowsill
Bill Cowsill
Bob Cowsill
John Cowsill
Paul Cowsill
Sue Cowsill
Van Johnson
Pawtucket
David Hartman
Providence
Jeffrey Osborne
Westerly
Ruth Buzzi

SOUTH CAROLINA

Aiken
William Perry
Beaufort
Joe Frazier
Charleston
Lauren Hutton
Will Patton
Columbia
Alex English
Fairfield
Nickolas Ashford
Ft. Jackson
Mary-Louise Parker
Gaffney
Andie MacDowell
Greenville
Peabo Bryson
Jesse Jackson
North Myrtle Beach
Vanna White
North
Eartha Kitt
Parris Island
John Phillips
Spring Gulley
Chubby Checker

SOUTH DAKOTA

Huron
Cheryl Ladd
Rowena
Mamie Van Doren
Sioux Falls
Mary Hart
Yankton
Tom Brokaw

TENNESSEE

Alcoa
Lynn Swann
Bells
Wink Martindale
Centerville
Minnie Pearl
Chattanooga
Gary Alexander
Sam Gooden
Lori Petty
Covington
Isaac Hayes
Knoxville
Polly Bergen
John Cullum
David Lemuel Keith
Lawrenceburg
Michael Jeter
Luttrell
Chet Atkins
McLemoresville
Dixie Carter
Memphis
Johnny Ace
Kathy Bates
Joe Bauer
Michael Beck
Dorsey Burnette
Johnny Burnette
Roseanne Cash
Alex Chilton
Bill Cunningham
Shannen Doherty
Donald Dunn
John Echols
Aretha Franklin
Morgan Freeman
George Hamilton
Booker T. Jones
Arthur Lee
Lisa Presley
Cybill Shepherd
Andrew Stevens
Gary Talley
Maurice White
Nashville
Gregg Allman
Jeff Cease

Annie Potts
Kitty Wells
Nutbush
Tina Turner
Ridgely
Carl Perkins
Rosemark
Bobby Bland
Sevierville
Dolly Parton
Shelbyville
Sondra Locke

TEXAS

Abbott
Willie Nelson
Alice
Lois Chiles
Amarillo
Cyd Charisse
Attasca
Billy Guy
Austin
Dabney Coleman
Nanci Griffith
Ethan Hawke
Beaumont
Larry Graham
Edgar Winter
Big Spring
Betty Buckley
Bloomington
Gale Storm
Brownsville
Kris Kristofferson
Bryan
Linda Ellerbee
Chireno
Ann Miller
Cisco
Dash Crofts
Corpus Christi
Farrah Fawcett
Lori Singer
Dallas
Frank Beard
Robby Benson
Pat Corley
Morgan Fairchild
Dusty Hill
Peter MacNicol
Meat Loaf
Mike Nesmith
Bobby Seale
Aaron Spelling
Stephen Stills
Freddie Stone
Sly Stone
Spud Webb
Dawson County
Barry Corbin
Denison
John Hillerman
Denton
Jim Fielder
El Paso
Sam Donaldson
Judith Ivey
Sandra Day O'Connor
Debbie Reynolds
Fort Worth
Kate Capshaw
Larry Hagman
Roger Miller
Fess Parker
Liz Smith
Lisa Whelchel
Galveston
Valerie Perrine
John Stockwell
Barry White
Gilmer
Don Henley
Goose Creek
Gary Busey
Bobby Fuller
Groesbeck
Joe Don Baker
Happy
Buddy Knox
Henderson
Sandy Duncan
Hillsboro
Jerry Allison
Houston
Debbie Allen
David Brown
Shelley Duvall
Robert Foxworth
Billy Gibbons
Barbara Mandrell
Peter Masterson
Annette O'Toole
P.J. Proby
Dennis Quaid
Randy Quaid
Phylicia Rashad
Kenny Rogers
Jaclyn Smith
Patrick Swayze
B. J. Thomas
Jobeth Williams
Karnack
Lady Bird Johnson
Klein
Lyle Lovett
Littlefield
Waylon Jennings
Longview
Forest Whitaker
Lubbock
Mac Davis
Marshall
George Foreman
Meadow
Sonny Curtis
Midland
Kathy Baker
Woody Harrelson
Carolyn McCormick
Oak Cliff
Edie Brickell
Orange
Bubba Smith
Plainview
Jimmy Dean
Quitman
Sissy Spacek
San Antonio
Carol Burnett
Christopher Cross
Augie Meyers
Ollie North
Paula Prentiss
Doug Sahm
Henry Thomas
San Saba
Tommy Lee Jones
Seminole
Tanya Tucker
Sidney
Jim Seals
Snyder
Powers Boothe
Taylortown
Duane Allen
Temple
Rip Torn
Texarkana
Henry Ross Perot
Otis Williams
Texas City
Johnny Lee
Tioga
Gene Autry
Tulia
Jimmie Dale Gilmore
Tyler
Carl Gardner
Uvalde
Dale Evans
Waco
Steve Martin
Bill Payne
Wharton
Dan Rather
Wichita Falls
Tommy Tune

UTAH

Coalville
Anthony Geary
Ogden
Alan Osmond
Donny Osmond
Jay Osmond
Marie Osmond
Merrill Osmond
Wayne Osmond
Salt Lake City
Roseanne Arnold
Wilford Brimley
Loretta Young
Vernal
James Woods

VERMONT

Bennington
Cynthia Gibb

VIRGINIA

Alexandria
Donna Dixon
MacKenzie Phillips
Willard Scott
Annandale
Fawn Hall
Arlington
Katie Couric
Charlottesville
Rob Lowe
Falls Church
John Hartman
Fort Lee
Dee Dee Ramone
Fort Monroe
Steve Earle
Lexington
Pat Robertson
Meherrin
Roy Clark
Norfolk
Wayne Newton
Tim Reid
Richmond
Warren Beatty
Shirley MacLaine
Fran Tarkenton
Virginia Beach
Juice Newton
Williamsburg
Bruce Hornsby
Wise
George C. Scott

WASHINGTON

Darrington
Bob Barker
Everett
Kenny Loggins
Seattle
Josie Bissett
Carol Channing
Judy Collins
Roger Fisher
Steven Hill
Kevin McCarthy
Ann Reinking
Nikki Sixx
Jeff Smith
Don Stevenson
Jean Smart
Spokane
Kitty Kelley
Darren McGavin
Craig T. Nelson
Tacoma
Dyan Cannon
Brian Cole
Jerry Miller
Pamela Reed
Blair Underwood
Don Wilson
Walla Walla
Adam West
Yakima
Kyle MacLachlan

WEST VIRGINIA

Beckley
Chris Sarandon
Charleston
Ann Magnuson
Grant Town
Tom Wilson
Huntington
Peter Marshall
Morgantown
Don Knotts
Slab Fork
Bill Withers
Wheeling
John Corbett

WISCONSIN

Appleton
Willem Dafoe
Beaver Dam
Bobby Hatfield
Cambria
Gena Rowlands
Kenosha
Daniel J. Travanti
Madison
Tyne Daly
Joe Schermie
Medford
Jeane Dixon
Milwaukee
Jim Abrahams
Jeffrey Dahmer
Jerry Harrison
Al Jarreau
Steve Miller
Tom Snyder
Bob Uecker
Gene Wilder
Sheboygan
Jackie Mason
Stevens Point
Peter Weller
White Water
Tom Hulce

AMERICAN SAMOA

Eric Stoltz

ALGERIA

Yves Saint Laurent

ARGENTINA

Chris De Burgh
Gabriela Sabatini

AUSTRALIA

Bryan Brown
Iva Davies
Jason Donovan
Graham Goble
Greg Ham
Paul Hogan
Jerry Speiser
Ron Strykert
John Rees
Melbourne
David Briggs
Mark Evans
Andrew Farriss
Jon Farriss
Kylie Minogue
Helen Reddy
Sydney
Michael Hutchence
Elle Macpherson
Rick Springfield
Rod Taylor

AUSTRIA

Klaus Maria Brandauer
Arnold Schwarzenegger
Kurt Waldheim
Vienna
Hedy Lamarr
Maximilian Schell

BAHAMAS

Larry Ferguson

BELGIUM

Brussels
Liz Claiborne
Jean Claude Van Damme

BRAZIL

Jennifer O'Neill
Perola Negra Pele

BULGARIA

Christo

BURMA

Annabella Lwin

CANADA

Bryan Adams
Paul Anka
Margaret Atwood
Dan Aykroyd
Warren Cann
Hume Cronyn
Rick Danko
Celine Dion
Denny Doherty
Jerry Edmonton
Graham Greene
Wayne Gretsky
Doug Henning
Arthur Hill
Garth Hudson
Alexander Knox
k.d. lang
Geddy Lee
Eugene Levy
Alex Lifeson
Gordon Lightfoot
Art Linkletter

Dewey Martin
Joni Mitchell
Mike Myers
Kate Nelligan
Leslie Nielsen
Neil Peart
Helen Shaver
Floyd Sneed
Alexander Spence
Donald Sutherland
Alan Thicke
Dave Thomas
Meg Tilly
Alex Trebek
Vanity
Jim Walker
Fay Wray
Edmonton
Melody Anderson
Thomas Chong
Michael J. Fox
Montreal
Genevieve Bujold
Leonard Cohen
Mario Lemieux
Robert MacNeil
Chris Makepeace
William Shatner
Gino Vannelli
Ontario
Lolita Davidovich
Phil Hartman
Bruce Watson
Toronto
Jim Carrey
Megan Follows
Corey Haim
Jeff Healey
Lou Jacobi
Peter Jennings
Howie Mandel
Lorne Michaels
Rick Moranis
Catherine O'Hara
Christopher Plummer
Robbie Robertson
Martin Short
Robert Urich
Al Waxman
Zal Yanovsky
Neil Young
Vancouver
Rae Dawn Chong
Michael Ontkean
Jason Priestley
Marc Singer
Blair Thornton
Winnipeg
Randy Bachman
Robbie Bachman
Burton Cummings
Deanna Durbin
Terry Fox
Joanna Gleason
Margot Kidder
Gerry Paterson
David Steinberg
C.F. Turner

CHINA

Joan Chen
Audrey Meadows
Jayne Meadows
Toshiro Mifune

COLOMBIA

John Leguizamo

CUBA

Fidel Castro
Maria Conchita Alonso
Havana
Steven Bauer
Georg Stanford Brown
Gloria Estefan
Andy Garcia
Alberto Salazar

CZECHOSLOVAKIA

Herbert Lom
Martina Navratilova
Ivan Reitman

DENMARK

Giancarlo Esposito
Brigitte Nielson
Lee Oskar
Claus Von Bulow

ECUADOR

Gerardo

EGYPT

Stewart Copeland
Omar Sharif
Yasir Arafat
Raffi

ENGLAND

Mick Abrahams
Jenny Agutter
Marc Almond
Jon Anderson
Julie Andrews
Gabrielle Anwar
Rod Argent
Ian Astbury
Rick Astley
Paul Atkinson
Tom Bailey
Ginger Baker
Tony Banks
Alan Bates
Stephanie Beacham
Jeff Beck
Andy Bell
George Bellamy
Jacqueline Bisset
Ritchie Blackmore
Alan Blakley
Colin Blunstone
Sir Dirk Bogarde
Marc Bolan
Ronnie Bond
David Bowie
Billy Bragg
Chris Britton
Gary Brooker
Ian Brown
Mark Brzezicki
Dewey Bunnell
Eric Burdon
Boz Burrell
Trevor Burton
Kate Bush
Tony Butler
David Byron
Bernie Calvert
Jim Capaldi
Judy Carne
David Carr
Veronica Cartwright
Chas Chandler
Eric Clapton
Dave Clark
Petula Clark
Steve Clark
Vince Clarke
David Clayton-Thomas
John Cleese
John Coghlan
Phil Collins
Peter Cook
David Coverdale
Mikey Craig
Michael Crawford
Billy Currie
Tim Curry
Chris Curtis
Glen Dale
Sarah Dallin
Charles Dance
Lenny Davidson
Dave Davies
Ray Davies
Rob Davis
Dave Dee
Kiki Dee
Princess Diana
Bruce Dickinson
Chris Dreja
Ian Dury
Graeme Edge
Bobby Elliott
Keith Emerson
Brian Eno
John Entwistle
David Essex
Adam Faith
Marianne Faithfull
Georgie Fame
Bryan Ferry
Ralph Fiennes
Colin Firth
Matthew Fisher
Andy Fletcher
Peter Kenneth Frampton
Jon Foxx
Robert Fripp
Peter Gabriel
Dave Gahan
Boy George
Mike Giles
Ian Gillan
Gary Glitter
Martin Gore
Les Gray
Hugh Grundy
Stephen Hawking
Roy Hay
Eric Haydock
Nicky Headon
Paul Heaton
Tony Hicks
Dave Hill
Harvey Hinsley
Patricia Hodge
Roger Hodgson
Noddy Holder
Mark Hollis
Bob Hope
Bob Hoskins
Alan Howard
Mike Hugg
Ian Hunter
Gordon Huntley
John Hurt
Rick Huxley
Eric Idle
Billy Idol
Neil Innes
Jeremy Irons
Glenda Jackson
Joe Jackson
Mick Jagger
Elton John
Howard Jones
John Paul Jones
Mick Jones
Paul Jones
Ray Jones
Ace Kefford
Mark King
Ben Kingsley
Patric Knowles
Ted Koppel
Billy J. Kramer
Greg Lake
Ronnie Lane
Roger Lavern
Leigh Lawson
Jimmy Lea
Simon LeBon
Derek Leckenby
Alvin Lee
Ric Lee
Jane Leeves
Chris Lowe
John Lydon
Leo Lyons
Shane MacGowan
Les Maguire
Steve Marriott
Hank Marvin
Dave Mason
Ian Matthews
Brian May
Phil May
John Mayall
Patrick McCauley
Andy McCluskey
Malcolm McDowell
Tom McGuinness
Ian McKellen
Graham McPherson
Sarah Miles
Sir John Mills
Mike Millward
Donald Moffat
Dudley Moore
Stephen Morris
Jon Moss
Colin Moulding
Dave Mount
Alison Moyet
Graham Nash
Anthony Newley
Peter Noone
Gary Numan
Mike Oldfield
Gary Oldman
Roland Orzabal
Ozzy Osbourne
Jimmy Page
Ian Paice
Robert Palmer
Rick Parfitt
Graham Parker
Les Pattinson
Amanda Pays
Denis Payton
Delroy Pearson
Deniece Pearson
Doris Pearson
Lorraine Pearson
Stedman Pearson
Brian Pendleton
Philthy Animal
Robert Plant
Donald Pleasence
Joan Plowright
Brian Poole
Reg Presley
Jonathan Pryce
Pete Quaife
Charlotte Rampling
Chris Rea
Noel Redding
Oliver Reed
Keith Relf
Nick Rhodes
Keith Richards
Miranda Richardson
Alan Rickman
Andrew Ridgeley
Diana Rigg
Paul Rodgers
Francis Rossi
Steve Rothery
Ric Rothwell
Kevin Rowland
Mike Rutherford
Shaun Ryder
Paul Samwell-Smith
Julian Sands
Leo Sayer
Ridley Scott
Jane Seymour
Helen Shapiro
Sandie Shaw
Nicollette Sheridan
Glenn Shorrock
Paul Simonon
Siouxsie Sioux
Slash
Rodney Slater
Adrian Smith
Curt Smith
Maggie Smith
Larry Smith
Mike Smith
Robert Smith
Diane Spencer
Jeremy Spencer
Dusty Springfield
John Squire
Lisa Stansfield
Vivian Stanshall
Pete Staples
John Steel
Tommy Steele
Cat Stevens
Dave Stewart
Patrick Stewart
Rod Stewart
Ray Stiles
Sting
David Sylvian
Bernie Taupin
Andy Taylor
Dick Taylor
Roger Taylor
Neil Tennant
Ray Thomas
Paul Thompson
Pete Townshend
Bill Travers
Peter Trewavas
Robin Trower
Mick Tucker
Tracey Ullman
Hilton Valentine
Mike Vickers
John Waite
Roger Waters
Carl Wayne
Bruce Welch
Paul Weller
Rick West
John Wetton
Chris White
Billie Whitelaw
Cliff Williams
Milan Williams

Edward Woodward
Keren Woodward
Little Stevie Wright
Michael York
Pete York
Paul Young
Birmingham
David Ball
Jimmy Brown
Geezer Butler
Ali Campbell
Robin Campbell
Andy Cox
Earl Falconer
Roland Gift
Rob Halford
Norman Hassan
Tony Iommi
Jeff Lynne
Nick Mason
Carl Palmer
Mike Pinder
Barry Pritchard
David Steele
Richard Tandy
Glenn Tipton
Brian Travers
Mickey Virtue
Bill Ward
Clint Warwick
Overend Watts
Muff Winwood
Steve Winwood
Roy Wood
Cambridge
Douglas Adams
Richard Attenborough
David Gilmour
Simon MacCorkindale
Olivia Newton-John
Enford
Barry Andrews
John Aston
Jazzie B
Mike Barson
Jet Black
Richard Butler
Terry Chambers
Jeremy Clyde
Richard Davies
Chris Foreman
Samantha Fox
Justin Hayward
John Helliwell
Ken Hensley
Gary "Chicken" Hirsch
Denny Laine
John Lodge
Ian McLagan
Christine McVie
Terry Lee Miall
Kevin Mooney
Les Nemes
Marco Pirroni
Captain Sensible
Chad Stuart
Anthony "Top" Topham
John Weider
Charlie Whitney
Ron Wood
Hereford
Verden Allen
Martin Chambers
Frank Oz
Mick Ralphs
Islington
Tony Hadley
Gary Kemp
Dave Knights
Charlie Watts
Leicester
Rod Allen
Roger Chapman
John Deacon
John Illsley
Jon Lord
Anthony Thistlethwaite
Liverpool
Clive Barker
Cilla Black
Les Braid
Kim Cattrall
Les Chadwick
Ralph Ellis
Ray Ennis
Tom Evans
Peter Gill
George Harrison
Billy Hatton
Tony Jackson
Norman Kuhlke
Julian Lennon
Dave Lovelady
Freddie Marsden
Gerry Marsden
Paul McCartney
Jim McCarty
Ian McCulloch
John McNally
Joey Molland
Brian Nash
Brian O'Hara
Mark O'Toole
Mike Pender
Paul Rutherford
Will Sergeant
Ringo Starr
Henny Youngman
London
Prince Andrew
Anthony Andrews
Princess Anne
Adam Ant
Peter Asher
Jay Aston
Mick Avory
Cheryl Baker
Princess Beatrice
Mark Bedford
Brian Bennett
Claire Bloom
Helena Bonham-Carter
Mick Box
Bill Bruford
Jean-Jacques Burnel
Alan Caddy
Michael Caine
Simon Callow
Naomi Campbell
Prince Charles
Joan Collins
Paul Cook
Hugh Cornwell
Elvis Costello
Ben Cross
Chris Cross
Roger Daltrey
Daniel Day-Lewis
Chris Difford
Lesley-Anne Down
Prince Edward
Samantha Eggar
Queen Elizabeth II
Dennis Elliott
Cary Elwes
Princess Eugenie
Sarah Ferguson
Barbara Ferris
Mick Fleetwood
Lita Ford
James Fox
Andy Fraser
Bobby G
Jane Goodall
Alec Guinness
Susan Hampshire
Steve Harley
Noel Harrison
Prince Henry
Steve Howe
Paul Humphreys
Derek Jacobi
Lionel Jeffries
Kenny Jones
Mick Jones
Steve Jones
Jon Keeble
Martin Kemp
Patsy Kensit
Johnny Kidd
Paul Kossoff
Alan Lancaster
Angela Lansbury
Robin Leach
Joe Leeway
Emily Lloyd
Andrew Lloyd Webber
Ida Lupino
Andy Mackay
Patrick Macnee
Phil Manzanera
Ian McDonald
Roddy McDowall
John McVie
Hayley Mills
Juliet Mills
Mitch Mitchell
Roger Moore
Kate Moss
Dave Murray
Joe Penny
Steve Priest
Corin Redgrave
Lynn Redgrave
Vanessa Redgrave
Vernon Reid
Natasha Richardson
Tim Roth
Emma Samms
Vidal Sassoon
Carole Shelley
Jean Simmons
Ione Skye
Roger Spear
Chris Squire
Terence Stamp
John Stax
Dennis Stratton
Mick Talbot
Elizabeth Taylor
Victoria Tennant
Emma Thompson
Glenn Tilbrook
Twiggy
Rachel Ward
Kim Wilde
Prince William
Barry J. Wilson
Jimmy Winston
Rick Wright
Bill Wyman
Young MC
Manchester
Stuart Adamson
Pete Birrell
Lol Creme
Roy Crewsdon
Paul Davis
Mark Day
Wayne Fontana
Martin Fry
Freddie Garrity
Barry Gibb
Maurice Gibb
Robin Gibb
Gillian Gilbert
Kevin Godley
Graham Gouldman
Keith Hopwood
Mick "Red" Hucknall
Davy Jones
Mike Joyce
Bob Lang
John Mahoney
Mike Maxfield
Morrissey
Derek Quinn
Paul Ryder
Eric Stewart
Nigel Twist
David Warner
Joanne Whalley-Kilmer
Merseyside
Gary Daly
Salford
Bernie Albrecht
Allan Clarke
Albert Finney
Karl Green
Peter Hook
Dave Sharp
Barney Sumner
Sheffield
Rick Allen
Paul Carrack
Joanne Catherall
Joe Cocker
Joe Elliott
Glenn Gregory
Ian Marsh
Philip Oakey
Michael Palin
Rick Savage
Stephen Singleton
Martyn Ware
Mark White
Adrian Wright

FRANCE

Jean-Jacques Annaud
Alain Delon
Gerard Depardieu
Rick Grech
Louis Jourdan
Marcel Marceau
Philippe Noiret
Anne Parillaud
Andy Summers
Paris
Isabelle Adjani
Anouk Aimee
Charles Aznavour
Brigitte Bardot
Jean-Paul Belmondo
Claude Berri
Leslie Caron
Claudette Colbert
Catherine Deneuve
Kathie Lee Gifford
Isabelle Huppert
Valerie Kaprisky
Yo-Yo Ma
Miou-Miou
Jeanne Moreau
Roman Polanski
Maria Schneider
Roger Vadim

GERMANY

Boris Becker
Susan Blakely
Jackson Browne
Heinz Burt
LeVar Burton
Steffi Graf
Ralf Hutter
John Kay
Henry Kissinger
Werner Klemperer
Martin Lawrence
Karl Lagerfeld
John McEnroe Jr.
Florian Schneider-Esleben
Hanna Schygulla
Ruth Westheimer
Berlin
Nastassja Kinski
Rex Reason
Elke Sommer

GREECE

Tommy Lee
Prince Philip
Yanni

GUADELOUPE

Fabrice Morvan

GUYANA

Eddy Grant

HOLLAND

Dick Diamonde
Harry Vanda
Alex Van Halen
Eddie Van Halen

HONG KONG

Nancy Kwan

HUNGARY

Eva Gabor
Zsa Zsa Gabor
Tommy Ramone

INDIA

Deepak Chopra
Julie Christie
Engelbert Humperdinck
Cliff Richard
John Sutton
Bombay
Zubin Mehta
Juliet Prowse
Salman Rushdie

IRAQ

Saddam Hussein

IRELAND

Ciaran Braonain
Pete Briquette
Pierce Brosnan
Adam Clayton
Sinead Cusack
Enya
Jem Finer
Johnnie Fingers
Richard Harris

Danny Hutton
Jackie McCauley
Edward Mulhare
Liam Neeson
Sam Neill
Maire Ni Braonain
Maureen O'Sullivan
Gilbert O'Sullivan
Peter O'Toole
Pol O. Braonain
Noel O. Dugain
Padraig O. Dugain
Belfast
Kenneth Branagh
Billy Harrison
Alan Henderson
Van Morrison
Dublin
Bono
Gabriel Byrne
Brian Downey
Geraldine Fitzgerald
Brenda Fricker
Bob Geldof
Mark Kelly
Phil Lynott
Colm Meaney
Larry Mullen Jr.
Mike Nolan
Sinead O'Connor
Maureen O'Hara
Milo O'Shea
Jim Sheridan

ISRAEL
Gene Simmons

ITALY
Mario Andretti
Giorgio Armani
Pierre Cardin
Dino De Laurentiis
Giancarlo Giannini
Valeria Golino
Gina Lollobrigida
Marcello Mastroianni
Luciano Pavarotti
Elizabeth Seal
Raf Vallone
Gianni Versace
Milan
Fabio
Greta Scacchi
Rome
Sophia Loren
Isabella Rossellini

JAMAICA
Marcia Barrett
Jimmy Cliff
Grace Jones
Ziggy Marley
Liz Mitchell
Kingston
Aston Barrett
Carlton Barrett
Errol Brown
Desmond Dekker
Madge Sinclair
Bunny Wailer

JAPAN
Victoria Principal
Mako
Midori
Tokyo
Olivia De Havilland
Joan Fontaine
Liv Ullmann

LEBANON
Keanu Reeves

LIBYA
Muammar Qaddafi

MEXICO
Anthony Quinn
Ricardo Montalban
Carlos Santana

MONACO
Princess Caroline

NETHERLANDS
Beeb Birtles
Rutger Hauer
Jeroen Krabbe

NEW ZEALAND
Jane Campion
Alannah Currie
Anna Paquin

NICARAGUA
Barbara Carrera
Bianca Jagger

NIGERIA
Sade

NORWAY
Morten Harket
Oslo
Mags Furuholmen
Paul Waaktaar

PALESTINE
Ralph Bakshi

PANAMA
Ruben Blades

PHILLIPPINES
Imelda Marcos
Corazon Aquino
Lou Diamond Phillips

POLAND
Joanna Pacula
Pope John Paul II

PUERTO RICO
Jose Feliciano
Raul Julia
Rita Moreno

RUSSIA
Alexander Godunov
Mikhail Gorbachev
Anatoly Karpov
Garry Kasparov
Yakov Smirnoff
Isaac Stern
Boris Yeltsin

SCOTLAND
Roger Ball
David Byrne
Brian Connolly
Tom Conti
Glenn Cornick
Sheena Easton
Roddy Frame
Alan Gorrie
Graeme Kelling
Deborah Kerr
Annie Lennox
Robin MacDonald
Onnie McIntyre
Neil Mitchell
Marti Pellow
James Prime
Gerry Rafferty
Jim Reid
William Reid
Ricky Ross
Bon Scott
Gordon Waller
Nicol Williamson
Edinburgh
Ian Anderson
Sean Connery
Eric Faulkner
Alan Longmuir
Derek Longmuir
Mike Scott
Stuart Wood
Glasgow
Jack Bruce
Charlie Burchill
Graeme Clark
Tom Cunningham
Lonnie Donegan
Donovan
Jim Kerr
David Knopfler
Mark Knopfler
Lulu
Lorraine McIntosh
Brian Robertson
Jimmy Somerville
Al Stewart
Hamish Stuart
Angus Young
George Young
Malcolm Young

SOMALIA
Iman

SOUTH AFRICA
Cyril Cusack
Glynis Johns
Alice Krige
Nelson Mandela
Winnie Mandela
Manfred Mann
Janet Suzman

SPAIN
Antonio Banderas
Charo
Julio Iglesias

SWEDEN
Maud Adams
Ann-Margret
Ingmar Bergman
Anita Ekberg
Agnetha Faltskog
Frida Lyngstad
Andy Partridge
Bo Svenson
Bjorn Ulvaeus
Max Von Sydow
Stockholm
Benny Andersson
Bibi Andersson
Neneh Cherry
Britt Ekland
Dolph Lundgren
Lena Olin

SUDAN
Holly Johnson

SWITZERLAND
Ursula Andress
Marthe Keller
Alban Pfisterer

TRINIDAD
Billy Ocean

TUNISIA
Claudia Cardinale

TURKEY
Joe Strummer

UGANDA
Idi Amin

VIETNAM
Dustin Nguyen

VIRGIN ISLANDS
Roy Innis
Kelsey Grammer

WALES
Keith Baxter
John Cale
Chick Churchill
Julian Cops
Timothy Dalton
The Edge
Andy Fairweather-Low
Roger Glover
Peter Greenaway
Mary Hopkin
Anthony Hopkins
Terry Jones
Neil Jones
Tom Jones
Simon Kirke
Eddie MacDonald
Mike Peters
Andy Scott
Mike Smith
Shakin' Stevens
Karl Wallinger
Cardiff
Dennis Bryon
Green Gartside
Clive Taylor
Blue Weaver
Swansea
Spencer Davis
Mike Gibbins
Pete Ham
Alan Jones
Bonnie Tyler

WEST INDIES
Joan Armatrading
Bobby Farrell
Pete de Freitas
Maisie Williams